MACROECONOMICS

National income and related statistics for selected years, 1929–1973

National income statistics in rows 1–17 are in billions of current dollars. Details may not add to totals because of rounding.

			1929	1933	1939	1940	1942	1944	1946	1948	1950	1952
THE SUM OF	1	Personal consumption expenditures	77.5	45.9	67.2	71.2	88.9	108.5	144.3	175.4	192.7	219.7
	2	Gross private domestic investment	16.7	1.7	9.3	13.6	10.5	7.8	31.3	48.1	54.2	54.0
	3	Government purchases	9.3	8.6	14.6	15.0	62.7	105.6	39.9	40.8	47.1	83.8
	4	Net exports	0.4	0.1	0.8	2.4	−0.3	−2.2	7.1	5.4	0.7	1.0
EQUALS	5	Gross domestic product	103.8	56.2	91.9	101.2	161.6	219.7	222.6	269.7	294.6	358.6
LESS	6	Consumption of fixed capital	9.6	7.4	9.1	9.5	13.6	19.4	23.8	28.3	29.9	36.2
EQUALS	7	Net domestic product	94.2	48.9	82.8	91.7	148.1	200.3	198.8	241.4	264.7	322.3
LESS	8	Net foreign factor income earned in the U.S.	−0.7	−0.3	−0.4	−0.4	−0.5	−0.5	−0.7	−1.5	−1.5	−2.1
LESS	9	Indirect business taxes	8.4	8.0	10.4	11.0	11.1	16.6	17.3	19.3	24.5	30.1
EQUALS	10	National income	86.5	41.2	72.8	81.1	137.5	184.2	182.2	223.6	241.7	294.3
LESS	11	Social security contributions	0.3	0.3	2.2	2.4	3.5	5.2	7.7	6.0	7.4	9.3
	12	Corporate income taxes	1.4	0.5	1.4	2.8	11.4	12.9	9.1	12.4	17.9	19.4
	13	Undistributed corporate profits	3.4	−0.8	2.4	3.6	6.4	6.9	10.2	16.4	16.4	12.2
PLUS	14	Transfer payments*	3.8	5.6	6.0	6.0	7.1	6.5	23.8	21.9	29.7	22.6
EQUALS	15	Personal income	85.2	46.8	72.8	78.3	123.3	165.7	179.0	210.7	229.7	276.0
LESS	16	Personal taxes	2.3	1.2	2.2	2.3	5.7	18.6	18.4	20.6	20.1	33.5
EQUALS	17	Disposable income	82.9	45.6	70.6	76.0	117.7	147.0	160.7	190.1	209.6	242.5

RELATED STATISTICS			1929	1933	1939	1940	1942	1944	1946	1948	1950	1952
	18	Real gross domestic product (in billions of 1992 dollars)	790.9	577.3	866.5	941.2	1,308.9	1,644.7	1,447.7	1,491.0	1,611.3	1,798.7
	19	Percent change in real GDP	—	−1.2	8.1	8.6	18.8	8.0	−11.0	4.2	8.9	3.7
	20	Real disposable income per capita (in 1992 dollars)	5,213	3,831	5,250	5,558	7,065	7,452	7,150	6,994	7,415	7,613
	21	Consumer price index (1982–84 = 100)	17.0	13.0	13.9	14.0	16.3	17.6	19.5	24.1	24.1	26.5
	22	Rate of inflation (%)	0.0	−5.1	−1.4	0.7	10.9	1.7	8.3	8.1	1.3	1.9
	23	Index of industrial production (1992 = 100)	—	—	—	—	—	—	—	22.6	24.7	27.8
	24	Supply of money, M1 (in billions of dollars)	26.6	19.9	34.2	39.7	55.4	85.3	106.5	112.3	114.1	125.2
	25	Prime interest rate (%)	5.50	1.50	1.50	1.50	1.50	1.50	1.50	1.75	2.07	3.0
	26	Population (in millions)	121.8	125.6	131.0	132.1	134.9	138.4	141.4	146.6	152.3	157.6
	27	Civilian labor force (in millions)	49.2	51.6	55.2	55.6	56.4	54.6	57.5	60.6	62.2	62.1
	28	Unemployment (in millions)	1.6	12.8	9.5	8.1	2.7	0.7	2.3	2.3	3.3	1.9
	29	Unemployment rate as % of civilian labor force	3.2	24.9	17.2	14.6	4.7	1.2	3.9	3.8	5.3	3.0
	30	Index of productivity (1992 = 100)	—	—	—	—	—	—	—	35.2	39.1	41.4
	31	Annual change in productivity (%)	—	—	—	—	—	—	—	4.4	8.7	2.8
	32	Trade balance on current account (in billions of dollars)	—	—	—	—	—	—	4.9	2.4	−1.8	0.6
	33	Public debt (in billions of dollars)	16.9	22.5	48.2	50.7	79.2	204.1	271.0	252.0	256.9	259.1

* Includes a statistical discrepancy.

	1954	1956	1958	1960	1962	1964	1965	1966	1967	1968	1969	1970	1971	1972	1973
	240.7	271.9	296.3	332.2	363.4	411.4	444.3	481.9	509.5	559.8	604.7	648.1	702.5	770.7	851.6
	53.8	72.2	64.5	78.8	87.9	101.7	118.0	130.4	128.0	139.9	155.0	150.2	176.0	205.6	242.9
	86.4	91.6	106.1	113.2	131.4	144.4	153.0	173.6	194.6	212.1	223.8	236.1	249.9	268.9	287.6
	0.3	2.3	0.4	2.4	2.4	5.5	3.9	1.9	1.4	−1.3	−1.2	1.2	−3.0	−8.0	0.6
	381.3	438.0	467.3	526.6	585.2	663.0	719.1	787.8	833.6	910.6	982.2	1,035.6	1,125.4	1,237.3	1,382.6
	40.5	47.1	52.5	56.6	60.4	66.0	70.2	75.9	82.3	89.8	98.3	107.0	116.5	127.6	140.0
	340.8	390.9	414.8	470.0	524.8	597.0	648.9	711.9	751.3	820.8	883.9	928.6	1,008.9	1,109.7	1,242.6
	−2.2	−2.5	−2.7	−3.2	−4.3	−5.0	−5.4	−5.2	−5.5	−6.2	−6.1	−6.4	−7.7	−8.7	−12.7
	33.2	32.8	38.0	43.7	50.1	57.9	62.3	68.2	71.3	79.7	84.6	94.4	108.0	113.1	123.0
	309.8	360.6	379.5	429.8	479.0	544.1	592.0	648.9	685.5	747.3	805.4	840.6	908.6	1,005.3	1,132.3
	10.6	13.5	15.9	21.9	25.4	30.1	31.6	40.6	45.5	50.4	57.8	62.0	69.6	79.5	97.9
	17.6	22.0	19.0	22.7	24.0	28.0	30.9	33.7	32.7	39.4	39.7	34.4	37.7	41.9	49.3
	12.3	16.9	12.1	15.0	17.4	22.0	27.8	30.5	27.1	26.6	24.1	20.3	28.6	36.9	53.5
	26.4	32.3	37.8	42.3	44.8	50.5	55.0	61.6	70.5	83.6	95.5	113.2	127.5	141.8	175.9
	295.7	340.5	370.3	412.5	457.0	514.5	556.7	605.7	650.7	714.5	779.3	837.1	900.2	988.8	1,107.5
	31.8	38.7	40.9	48.7	54.8	56.0	61.9	71.0	77.9	92.1	109.9	109.0	108.7	132.0	140.6
	263.9	301.8	329.4	363.8	402.2	458.5	494.8	534.7	572.9	622.5	669.4	728.1	791.5	856.8	967.0
	1954	1956	1958	1960	1962	1964	1965	1966	1967	1968	1969	1970	1971	1972	1973
	1,868.2	2,040.2	2,057.5	2,262.9	2,454.8	2,708.4	2,881.1	3,069.2	3,147.2	3,293.9	3,393.6	3,397.6	3,510.0	3,702.3	3,916.3
	−0.7	2.0	−1.0	2.4	6.1	5.8	6.4	6.5	2.5	4.7	3.0	0.1	3.3	5.5	5.8
	7,822	8,432	8,421	8,681	9,098	9,825	10,311	10,735	11,081	11,468	11,726	12,039	12,366	12,794	13,566
	26.9	27.2	28.9	29.6	30.2	31.0	31.5	32.4	33.4	34.8	36.7	38.8	40.5	41.8	44.4
	0.7	1.5	2.8	1.7	1.0	1.3	1.6	2.9	3.1	4.2	5.5	5.7	4.4	3.2	6.2
	28.6	33.6	31.9	36.5	39.8	45.0	49.5	53.8	55.0	58.1	60.7	58.7	59.5	65.3	70.6
	130.3	136.0	138.4	140.7	147.8	160.3	167.8	172.0	183.3	197.4	203.9	214.4	228.3	249.2	262.8
	3.05	3.77	3.83	4.82	4.50	4.50	4.54	5.63	5.61	6.30	7.96	7.91	5.72	5.25	8.03
	163.0	168.9	174.9	180.7	186.5	191.9	194.3	196.6	198.7	200.7	202.7	205.1	207.7	209.9	211.9
	62.3	66.6	67.6	69.6	70.6	73.1	74.5	75.8	77.3	78.7	80.7	82.8	84.4	87.0	89.4
	3.5	2.8	4.6	3.9	3.9	3.8	3.4	2.9	3.0	2.8	2.8	4.1	5.0	4.9	4.4
	5.5	4.1	6.8	5.5	5.5	5.2	4.5	3.8	3.8	3.6	3.5	4.9	5.9	5.6	4.9
	43.9	45.8	50.5	51.4	55.7	60.5	62.7	65.2	66.6	68.9	69.2	70.5	73.6	76.0	78.4
	2.2	0.1	2.8	1.7	4.7	4.6	3.5	4.0	2.2	3.4	0.4	2.0	4.3	3.3	3.2
	0.2	2.7	0.8	2.8	3.4	6.8	5.4	3.0	2.6	0.6	0.4	2.3	−1.4	−5.8	7.1
	270.8	272.7	279.7	290.5	302.9	316.1	322.3	328.5	340.4	368.7	365.8	380.9	408.2	435.9	466.3

(Continued)

MACROECONOMICS

Principles, Problems, and Policies

Fourteenth Edition

CAMPBELL R. McCONNELL
PROFESSOR OF ECONOMICS, EMERITUS
UNIVERSITY OF NEBRASKA

STANLEY L. BRUE
PROFESSOR OF ECONOMICS
PACIFIC LUTHERAN UNIVERSITY

Boston   Burr Ridge, IL   Dubuque, IA   Madison, WI   New York   San Francisco   St. Louis
Bangkok   Bogotá   Caracas   Lisbon   London   Madrid
Mexico City   Milan   New Delhi   Seoul   Singapore   Sydney   Taipei   Toronto

. . . .

**To Mem
and to Terri and
Craig**

. . . .

Irwin/McGraw-Hill

A Division of The **McGraw·Hill** Companies

Macroeconomics
Principles, Problems, and Policies

5 6 7 8 9 0   VNH   VNH   9 4 3 2 1 0

ISBN 0-07-289841-0
ISBN 0-07-366217-8 (*Wall Street Journal* edition)

Editorial director: Michael Junior
Publisher: Gary Burke
Sponsoring editor: Lucille Sutton
Developmental editor: Marilea Fried
Marketing manager: Nelson Black
Project manager: Eva Marie Strock
Production supervisors: Diane Renda and Pam Augspurger

Supplements coordinator: Louis Swaim
Designer: Amanda Kavenagh
Cover designer: Francis Owens
Editorial assistant: Lee Hertel
Compositor: York Graphic Services, Inc.
Typeface: Janson Text
Printer: Von Hoffmann Press, Inc.

Last Word illustrations and back cover illustration by Jacques Cournoyer

Library of Congress Cataloging-in-Publication Data
McConnell, Campbell R.
   Macroeconomics: principles, problems, and policies / Campbell R.
McConnell, Stanley L. Brue. — 14th ed.
     p.   cm.
   Includes bibliographical references and index.
   ISBN 0-07-289841-0
   1. Macroeconomics.   I. Brue, Stanley L., 1945– . II. Title.
HB172.5.M3743   1998
339—DC21   98–19045
                               CIP

http://www.mhhe.com

Campbell R. McConnell earned his Ph.D. from the University of Iowa after receiving degrees from Cornell College and the University of Illinois. He taught at the University of Nebraska–Lincoln from 1953 until his retirement in 1990. He is also coauthor of *Contemporary Labor Economics*, 5th ed. (McGraw-Hill) and has edited readers for the principles and labor economics courses. He is a recipient of both the University of Nebraska Distinguished Teaching Award and the James A. Lake Academic Freedom Award and is past president of the Midwest Economics Association. Professor McConnell was awarded an honorary Doctor of Laws degree from Cornell College in 1973 and received its Distinguished Achievement Award in 1994. His primary areas of interest are labor economics and economic education. He has an extensive collection of jazz recordings and enjoys reading jazz history.

Stanley L. Brue did his undergraduate work at Augustana College (SD) and received his Ph.D. from the University of Nebraska–Lincoln. He teaches at Pacific Lutheran University, where he has been honored as recipient of the Burlington Northern Faculty Achievement Award. He has also received the national Leavey Award for excellence in economic education. Professor Brue is past president and a current member of the International Executive Board of Omicron Delta Epsilon International Economics Honorary. He is coauthor of *Economic Scenes*, 5th ed. (Prentice-Hall) and *Contemporary Labor Economics*, 5th ed. (McGraw-Hill) and author of *The Evolution of Economic Thought*, 5th ed. (HB/Dryden). For relaxation, he enjoys boating on Puget Sound and skiing trips with his family.

CONTENTS IN BRIEF

List of Key Graphs   xv
Preface   xvi
Contributors   xxiii

PART 1

AN INTRODUCTION TO ECONOMICS AND THE ECONOMY

To the Student   2
1   The Nature and Method of Economics   3
2   The Economizing Problem   22
3   Understanding Individual Markets: Demand and Supply   42
4   Pure Capitalism and the Market System   61
5   The Mixed Economy: Private and Public Sectors   77
6   The United States in the Global Economy   100

PART 2

NATIONAL INCOME, EMPLOYMENT, AND FISCAL POLICY

7   Measuring Domestic Output, National Income, and the Price Level   124
8   Macroeconomic Instability: Unemployment and Inflation   148
9   Building the Aggregate Expenditures Model   172
10   Aggregate Expenditures: The Multiplier, Net Exports, and Government   199
11   Aggregate Demand and Aggregate Supply   221
12   Fiscal Policy   243

PART 3

MONEY, BANKING, AND MONETARY POLICY

13   Money and Banking   264
14   How Banks Create Money   287
15   Monetary Policy   305

PART 4

PROBLEMS AND CONTROVERSIES IN MACROECONOMICS

16   Extending the Analysis of Aggregate Supply   330
17   Disputes in Macro Theory and Policy   350
18   Economic Growth   368
19   Budget Deficits and the Public Debt   386

PART 5

INTERNATIONAL ECONOMICS AND THE WORLD ECONOMY

20   International Trade   404
21   Exchange Rates, The Balance of Payments, and Trade Deficits   429
22   The Economics of Developing Countries   452
23   Transition Economies: Russia and China   474

Glossary   G-1
Index   I-1

CONTENTS

List of Key Graphs   xv
Preface   xvi
Contributors   xxii

PART 1

AN INTRODUCTION TO ECONOMICS AND THE ECONOMY

To the Student   2

1 THE NATURE AND METHOD OF ECONOMICS   3

The Economic Perspective
Scarcity and choice • Rational behavior •
Marginalism: Benefits and costs

Why Study Economics?
Economics for citizenship • Professional and
personal applications

Economic Methodology
Theoretical economics • Policy economics

Macroeconomics and Microeconomics
Macroeconomics • Microeconomics • Positive and
normative economics

Pitfalls to Objective Thinking
Biases • Loaded terminology • Definitions •
Fallacy of composition • Causation fallacies

A Look Ahead

LAST WORD Fast-Food Lines: An Economic
Perspective

Appendix to Chapter 1: Graphs and Their Meaning
Construction of a graph • Direct and inverse
relationships • Dependent and independent
variables • Other things equal • Slope of a line •
Vertical intercept • Equation of a linear relationship
• Slope of a nonlinear curve

2 THE ECONOMIZING PROBLEM   22

The Foundation of Economics
Unlimited wants • Scarce resources

Economics: Employment and Efficiency
Full employment: Using available resources • Full
production: Using resources efficiently • Production
possibilities table • Production possibilities curve •

Law of increasing opportunity cost • Allocative
efficiency revisited

Unemployment, Growth and the Future
Unemployment and productive inefficiency •
A growing economy • A qualification: International
trade • Applications

Economic Systems
Pure capitalism • The command economy • Mixed
systems • The traditional economy

The Circular Flow Model
Resource and product markets • Limitations

LAST WORD Women and Expanded Production
Possibilities

3 UNDERSTANDING INDIVIDUAL MARKETS: DEMAND AND SUPPLY   42

Markets

Demand
Law of demand • The demand curve • Individual
and market demand • Determinants of demand •
Change in demand • Changes in quantity demanded

Supply
Law of supply • The supply curve • Determinants
of supply • Changes in supply • Changes in
quantity supplied

Supply and Demand: Market Equilibrium
Surpluses • Shortages • Equilibrium price and
quantity • Rationing function of prices • Changes
in supply, demand, and equilibrium • A reminder:
"Other things equal" • Application: Pink salmon

LAST WORD Ticket Scalping: A Bum Rap?

4 PURE CAPITALISM AND THE MARKET SYSTEM   61

Capitalist Ideology
Private property • Freedom of enterprise and choice
• Self-interest • Competition • Markets and prices
• Limited government

Other Characteristics
Extensive use of technology and capital goods •
Specialization • Use of money

The Competitive Market System

The Market System at Work
Determining what is to be produced • Organizing production • Distributing total output • Accommodating change

Competition and the "Invisible Hand"
LAST WORD   Pink Flamingos and "Dollar Votes"

5 THE MIXED ECONOMY: PRIVATE AND PUBLIC SECTORS   77

Households as Income Receivers
The functional distribution of income • The personal distribution of income

Households as Spenders
Personal taxes • Personal saving • Personal consumption expenditures

The Business Population

Legal Forms of Businesses
Sole proprietorship • Partnership • Corporation • Large corporations

Economic Functions of Government

Legal and Social Framework

Maintaining Competition

Redistribution of Income

Reallocation of Resources
Spillovers or externalities • Public goods and services • Quasipublic goods • Allocation of resources to public and quasipublic goods

Stabilization

The Circular Flow Revisited

Government Finance

Government Growth: Purchases and Transfers

Federal Finance
Federal expenditures • Federal tax revenues

State and Local Finance
Fiscal federalism • Lotteries
LAST WORD   The Financing of Corporate Activity

6 THE UNITED STATES IN THE GLOBAL ECONOMY   100

World Trade
Volume and pattern • Rapid trade growth • Participants

Back to the Circular Flow

Specialization and Comparative Advantage
Basic principle • Comparative costs • Terms of trade • Gains from specialization and trade

Foreign Exchange Market
Dollar-yen market • Changing rates: Depreciation and appreciation

Government and Trade
Trade impediments and subsidies • Why government trade interventions? • Costs to society

Multilateral Trade Agreements and Free-Trade Zones
Reciprocal Trade Agreements Act and GATT • European Union • North American Free Trade Agreement • Hostile trade blocs or further integration?

American Firms in the World Economy
LAST WORD   Buy American: The Global Refrigerator

PART 2

NATIONAL INCOME, EMPLOYMENT, AND FISCAL POLICY

7 MEASURING DOMESTIC OUTPUT, NATIONAL INCOME, AND THE PRICE LEVEL   124

Macroeconomic Measurement

Gross Domestic Product
Avoidance of multiple counting • Exclusion of nonproduction transactions • Two sides to GDP: Spending and income

Expenditures Approach
Personal consumption expenditures (C) • Gross private domestic investment (I_g) • Government purchases (G) • Net exports (X_n) • The GDP equation: $C + I_g + G + X_n$

Income Approach
Compensation of employees • Rents • Interest • Proprietors' income • Corporate profits • Three adjustments

Other National Accounts
Net domestic product (NDP) • National income (NI) • Personal income (PI) • Disposable income (DI) • The circular flow revisited

Nominal versus Real GDP
Adjustment process in a one-good economy • Real-world considerations and data

The Consumer Price Index

GDP and Economic Well-Being
Nonmarket transactions • Leisure • Improved
product quality • Composition and distribution of
output • Per capita output • GDP and the
environment • The underground economy

LAST WORD   Does the CPI Overstate Inflation?

**8   MACROECONOMIC INSTABILITY:
UNEMPLOYMENT AND INFLATION   148**

The Business Cycle
Phases of the cycle • Causation: A first glance •
Noncyclical fluctuations • Cyclical impact: Durables
and nondurables

Unemployment
Types of unemployment • Definition of "full
employment" • Measurement of unemployment •
Economic cost of unemployment • Noneconomic
costs • International comparisons

Inflation Defined and Measured
Meaning of inflation • Measurement of inflation •
Facts of inflation • Causes: Theories of inflation •
Complexities

Redistribution Effects of Inflation
Fixed-nominal-income receivers • Savers • Debtors
and creditors • Anticipated inflation • Addenda

Output Effects of Inflation
Stimulus of demand-pull inflation • Cost-push
inflation and unemployment • Hyperinflation and
breakdown

LAST WORD   The Stock Market and
Macroeconomic Instability

**9   BUILDING THE AGGREGATE
EXPENDITURES MODEL   172**

Historical Backdrop
Classical economics and Say's law • The Great
Depression and Keynes

Simplifications

Tools of the Aggregate Expenditures Model

Consumption and Saving
Income-consumption and income-saving
relationships • The consumption schedule • The
saving schedule • Average and marginal propensities
• Nonincome determinants of consumption and
saving • Shifts and stability

Investment
Expected rate of return • The real interest rate •
Investment demand curve • Shifts in the investment
demand curve • Investment schedule • Instability of
investment

**Equilibrium GDP: Expenditures-Output
Approach**
Tabular analysis • Graphical analysis

**Equilibrium GDP: Leakages-Injections
Approach**
Tabular analysis • Graphical analysis

Planned versus Actual Investment
Disequilibrium and inventories • Attainment of
equilibrium

LAST WORD   John Maynard Keynes (1883–1946)

**10   AGGREGATE EXPENDITURES: THE MULTIPLIER,
NET EXPORTS, AND GOVERNMENT   199**

Changes in Equilibrium GDP and the Multiplier
The multiplier effect

International Trade and Equilibrium Output
Net exports and aggregate expenditures • The net
export schedule • Net exports and equilibrium
GDP • International economic linkages

Adding the Public Sector
Simplifying assumptions • Government purchases
and equilibrium GDP • Taxation and equilibrium
GDP • Balanced-budget multiplier

Equilibrium versus Full-Employment GDP
Recessionary gap • Inflationary gap

Historical Applications
The Great Depression • Vietnam War inflation

Critique and Preview
LAST WORD   Squaring the Economic Circle

**11   AGGREGATE DEMAND AND
AGGREGATE SUPPLY   221**

Aggregate Demand
Aggregate demand curve • Derivation of the
aggregate demand curve from the aggregate
expenditures model • Determinants of aggregate
demand • Aggregate demand shifts and the
aggregate expenditures model

Aggregate Supply
Aggregate supply curve • Determinants of aggregate
supply

Equilibrium: Real Output and the Price Level

Changes in Equilibrium
Shifting of aggregate demand • Multiplier with price-level changes • A ratchet effect? • Shifting of aggregate supply

LAST WORD   Why Is Unemployment in Europe So High?

12 FISCAL POLICY   243

Legislative Mandates

Discretionary Fiscal Policy
Expansionary fiscal policy • Contractionary fiscal policy • Financing of deficits and disposing of surpluses • Policy options: G or T

Nondiscretionary Fiscal Policy: Built-In Stabilizers
Automatic or built-in stabilizers • Actual versus full-employment budget • Proposed balanced-budget requirement

Problems, Criticisms, and Complications
Problems of timing • Political problems • Crowding-out effect • Fiscal policy, aggregate supply, and inflation • Fiscal policy in the open economy • Supply-side fiscal policy

LAST WORD   The Leading Indicators

PART 3

MONEY, BANKING, AND MONETARY POLICY

13 MONEY AND BANKING   264

The Functions of Money

The Supply of Money
Money Definition $M1$ • Money Definition $M2$ • Money Definition $M3$ • Near monies: Implications • Credit cards

What "Backs" the Money Supply?
Money as Debt • Value of money • Money and prices • Stabilization of money's value

The Demand for Money
Transactions demand, D_t • Asset demand, D_a • Total money demand, D_m

The Money Market
Responses to a shortage of money • Responses to a surplus of money

The Federal Reserve and the Banking System
Historical background • Board of governors • Assistance and advice • The 12 Federal Reserve banks • Commercial banks and thrifts • Fed functions and the money supply • Federal reserve independence

Recent Developments in Money and Banking
The relative decline of banks and thrifts • Globalization of financial markets • Electronic money

LAST WORD   The Global Greenback

14 HOW BANKS CREATE MONEY   287

The Balance Sheet of a Commercial Bank

Prologue: The Goldsmiths

A Single Commercial Bank
Formation of a commercial bank • Money-creating transactions of a commercial bank • Profits, liquidity, and the Federal funds market

The Banking System: Multiple-Deposit Expansion
The banking system's lending potential • The monetary multiplier • Some modifications • Need for monetary control

LAST WORD   The Bank Panics of 1930–1933

15 MONETARY POLICY   305

The Goal of Monetary Policy

Consolidated Balance Sheet of the Federal Reserve Banks
Assets • Liabilities

Tools of Monetary Policy
Open-market operations • The reserve ratio • The discount rate • Easy money and tight money • Relative importance

Monetary Policy, Real GDP, and the Price Level
Cause-effect chain • Effects of an easy money policy • Effects of a tight money policy • Refinements and feedback • Monetary policy and aggregate supply

Effectiveness of Monetary Policy
Strengths of monetary policy • Shortcomings and problems • Recent focus: The federal funds rate • Monetary policy and the international economy

The "Big Picture"

LAST WORD   For the Fed, Life Is a Metaphor

PART 4

PROBLEMS AND CONTROVERSIES IN MACROECONOMICS

16 EXTENDING THE ANALYSIS OF AGGREGATE SUPPLY   330

Short-Run and Long-Run Aggregate Supply
Definitions: Short run and long run • Short-run aggregate supply • Long-run aggregate supply • Equilibrium in the extended AD-AS model

Applying the Extended AD-AS Model
Demand-pull inflation in the extended AD-AS model • Cost-push inflation in the extended AD-AS model • Recession and the extended AD-AS model

The Phillips Curve
The basic idea • Tradeoffs • Stagflation: A shifting Phillips Curve? • Adverse aggregate supply shocks • Stagflation's demise

Natural-Rate Hypothesis
Adaptive expectations theory • Rational expectations theory • Changing interpretations

Supply-Side Economics
Tax-transfers disincentives • Laffer Curve • Criticisms of the Laffer Curve • Overregulation • Reaganomics

LAST WORD   Price and Wage Controls

17 DISPUTES IN MACRO THEORY AND POLICY   350

Some History: Classics and Keynes
Classical view • Keynesian view

What Causes Macro Instability?
Mainstream view • Monetarist view • Real-business-cycle view • Coordination failures

Does the Economy "Self-Correct"?
New classical view of self-correction • Mainstream view of self-correction

Rules or Discretion?
In support of policy rules • In defense of discretionary stabilization policy • Increased macro stability

Summary of Alternative Views
LAST WORD   Profit Sharing: Making Wages Flexible

18 ECONOMIC GROWTH   368

Growth Economics
Two definitions • Growth as a goal • Arithmetic of growth

Ingredients of Growth
Supply factors • Demand factor • Efficiency factor

Graphical Analysis
Growth and production possibilities • Extended AD-AS model

Growth in the United States

Accounting for Growth
Input versus productivity • Quantity of labor • Technological advance • Quantity of capital • Education and training • Resource allocation and scale economies • Detriments to growth • Other contributing factors • Macroeconomic instability and growth

The Productivity Slowdown
Significance • Causes of the slowdown

A "New Economy"?

Growth Policies
Demand-side policies • Supply-side policies
LAST WORD   Is Growth Desirable?

19 BUDGET DEFICITS AND THE PUBLIC DEBT   386

Deficits and Debt: Definitions

Budget Philosophies
Annually balanced budget • Cyclically balanced budget • Functional finance

The Public Debt: Facts and Figures
Causes • Quantitative aspects

Economic Implications: False Issues
Going bankrupt? • Shifting burdens

Implications and Issues
Income distribution • Incentives • External debt • Curb on fiscal policy • Crowding out and the stock of capital

Recent Federal Deficits
Large size

Budget Deficits and Trade Deficits
Higher interest rates • Dollar appreciation • Trade deficits • Related effects • Policy responses • Positive role of debt

LAST WORD   "The Entitlements Problem"

PART 5

INTERNATIONAL ECONOMICS AND THE WORLD ECONOMY

20 INTERNATIONAL TRADE   404

Facts of International Trade

The Economic Basis for Trade

Comparative Advantage: Graphical Analysis
Two isolated nations • Specializing according to comparative advantage • Terms of trade • Gains from trade • Trade with increasing costs • The case for free trade

Supply and Demand Analysis of Exports and Imports
Supply and demand in the United States • Supply and demand in Canada • Equilibrium world price, exports, and imports

Trade Barriers
Economic impact of tariffs • Economic impact of quotas

The Case for Protection: A Critical Review
Military self-sufficiency argument • Increased domestic employment argument • Diversification for stability argument • Infant industry argument • Protection against dumping argument • Cheap foreign labor argument • A summing up

Costs of Protection
Cost to society • Impact on income distribution

U.S. International Trade Policy
Generalized trade liberalization • Aggressive export promotion • Bilateral negotiations

LAST WORD   Petition of the Candlemakers, 1845

21 EXCHANGE RATES, THE BALANCE OF PAYMENTS, AND TRADE DEFICITS   429

Financing International Trade
U.S. export transaction • U.S. import transaction

The Balance of Payments
Current account • Capital account • Official reserves account • Payments deficits and surpluses

Flexible Exchange Rates
Depreciation and appreciation • Determinants of exchange rates • Flexible rates and the balance of payments • Disadvantages of flexible exchange rates

Fixed Exchange Rates
Use of reserves • Trade policies • Exchange controls and rationing • Domestic macroeconomic adjustments

International Exchange-Rate Systems
The gold standard: Fixed exchange rates • The Bretton Woods system • The current system: The managed float

Recent U.S. Trade Deficits
Causes of the trade deficit • Implications of U.S. trade deficits

LAST WORD   Speculation in Currency Markets

22 THE ECONOMICS OF DEVELOPING COUNTRIES   452

The Rich and the Poor
Growth, decline, and income gaps • Implications

Obstacles to Economic Development
Natural resources • Human resources • Capital accumulation • Technological advance • Sociocultural and institutional factors

The Vicious Circle

Role of Government
A positive role • Public sector problems • A mixed bag

Role of Advanced Nations
Expanding trade • Foreign aid: Public loans and grants • Private capital flows

Where From Here?
DVC policies for promoting growth • IAC policies for fostering DVC Growth

LAST WORD   Famine in Africa

23 TRANSITION ECONOMIES: RUSSIA AND CHINA   474

Ideology and Institutions

State Ownership and Central Planning
Planning goals and techniques

Problems with Central Planning
The coordination problem • The incentive problem

Collapse of the Soviet Economy
Declining growth • Poor product quality • Lack of consumer goods • Large military burden • Agricultural drag

The Russian Transition to a Market System

Privatization • Price reform • Promotion of competition • Joining the world economy • Price-level stabilization • Major problems • Future prospects

Market Reforms in China

Agricultural and rural reform • Reform of urban industries • Special economic zones • Development of supporting institutions • Transformation of the SOEs

Outcomes and Prospects

Positive outcomes of reform • Problems

Conclusion

LAST WORD   I Think Everything Will Be Okay.

Glossary   **G-1**

Index   **I-1**

LIST OF KEY GRAPHS

2–1 Production Possibilities Curve   27

2–6 Circular Flow of Output and Income   37

3–5 Supply and Demand Model   54

9–2 Consumption and Saving Schedules   177

9–5 Investment Demand Curve   183

9–9 Aggregate Expenditures—Domestic
         Output Model   191

10–8 Recessionary and Inflationary Gaps   214

11–7 Aggregate Demand and Aggregate
         Supply Model   233

13–2 Money Demand and Money Supply
         Model   273

15–2 Monetary Policy and Equilibrium   314

15–4 Mainstream Theory of Employment and
         Stabilization Policies   326

20–2 Specialization and the Gains from
         International Trade   409

21–3 Market for Foreign Exchange   435

Welcome to the fourteenth edition of *Macroeconomics* (and its companion editions of *Economics* and *Microeconomics*), the nation's best-selling economics texts. About 4.5 million U.S. students have used this book. It has been adapted into Canadian, Australian, Italian, and Russian editions and translated into French, Spanish, and several other languages.

The resurging U.S. economy, changes in the focus of monetary policy, economic turmoil in Southeast Asia, swings in exchange rates, capitalism in Russia—what an interesting time to teach and learn economics! Clearly, those who understand economic principles will have a distinct advantage in making sense of the economy and successfully participating in it.

WHAT'S NEW?

We thoroughly revised, polished, and updated this edition. (Using a software analogy, this is version 14.0, not 13.1 or 13.2.) The comments of over 100 reviewers motivated many of the changes and helped us create a text full of energy and innovation.

Highly Revised Chapters

Three chapters in this edition are quite revised.
* *Chapter 16: Extending the Analysis of Aggregate Supply.* In this greatly revised chapter we introduce the distinction between short-run and long-run aggregate supply and then use that distinction to develop an "extended aggregate demand and aggregate supply model." We then use that model to analyze demand-pull inflation, cost-push inflation, and recession. In the remainder of the chapter we look at other aggregate supply topics such as the Phillips Curve and supply-side economics.
* *Chapter 17: Disputes in Macro Theory and Policy.* In this nearly new chapter we broaden the ideas developed in Chapter 16 to discuss modern disputes in macro theory and policy. We now use the classic Keynesian discussion of previous editions as a

historical backdrop to an examination of modern debates on (1) the sources of macro instability, (2) the extent of "self-correction" in the economy, and (3) the debate over "rules" versus "discretion." This chapter systematically examines new classical economics and introduces ideas such as misperceptions theory, coordination failures, efficiency wages, and insider-outsider relationships.
* *Chapter 23: Transition Economies: Russia and China.* We added a discussion of China to the previous edition's chapter on Russia. We look briefly at Marxian ideology, and the institutions, goals, and major problems of central planning, and then turn to the collapse of the Soviet economy, the elements of the Russian reform, and contemporary outcomes. Finally, we discuss the main features of market reform in China, including rapid economic growth and remaining difficulties.

New Pedagogy

* *Quick Quizzes.* We added 4 multiple-choice questions as Quick Quizzes to each of the 13 Key Graphs. Each quiz relates to the content of the specific Key Graph and is written in the same style and at the same level of difficulty as the test bank questions. The correct answers are provided upside down so students can instantly measure their understanding of key concepts.
* *Internet Questions.* Each chapter contains two Web-Based Questions which require students to access specified Internet addresses. These questions help students apply specific economic concepts and introduce them to relevant *Macroeconomic* Internet sites.

A Building-Block Approach to Macro

With the changes in this edition, we created a fully integrated building-block approach to macro theory, policy, and issues. Specifically, we
* Build the aggregate expenditures model (AE model)

- Derive aggregate demand from the AE model and develop the aggregate-demand-aggregate supply model (AD-AS model)
- Use the AD-AS model to discuss fiscal policy
- Introduce monetary considerations into the AD-AS model
- Use the AD-AS model to discuss monetary policy
- Extend the AD-AS model by distinguishing between short-run and long-run aggregate supply
- Apply the "extended AD-AS model" to macroeconomic instability, modern macroeconomic disputes, and economic growth

Greater Emphasis on the Economic Perspective

Newly organized Chapter 1 now begins with a discussion of scarcity and choice, rational behavior, and marginal analysis. In Chapter 2 we use the ideas of marginal benefits and marginal costs to determine the optimal position on the production possibilities curve. We continue to reinforce the economic perspective in the remainder of the book in a number of discussions, including those on investment decisions and international trade theory.

Added Directness, Reduced Formalism, Extra Human Interest Material

Our line-by-line editing adds directness and reduces formalism, but we were careful to *not* reduce the thoroughness of our explanations. Where needed, the "extra sentence of explanation" remains a distinguishing characteristic of *Macroeconomics*. Students will especially enjoy our new Last Words in Chapter 4, Pink Flamingos and "Dollar Votes;" and Chapter 23, I Think Everything Will be OK. All 23 Last Words present interesting applications with attractive modern art.

Other New Topics and Revised Discussions

Along with the changes just discussed, there are many other revisions. Here are just a few examples.
- **Part 1.** *Chapter 1*: Figure 1-1 and its discussion revised; new, livelier examples. *Chapter 2*: Improved discussion of the economic rationale for increasing costs; new applications (land-use controversies, devas-

tation from war, and emerging technologies); consolidated discussion of economic systems. *Chapter 3*: New examples: increased demand for sports-utility vehicles; improved fuel efficiency of aircraft engines; increased demand for salsa; buyout of haddock fishing boats; the decline in the price of pink salmon. *Chapter 4*: Improved discussion of consumer sovereignty; improvements to Table 4-4 on least-cost production; new Global Perspective on the Index of Economic Freedom. *Chapter 5*: New explicit definitions of stocks and bonds; new discussion of the principal-agent problem; new Global Perspective on government employment as a percentage of total employment for various countries. *Chapter 6*: Improved explanation of the most-favored nation clause.
- **Part 2.** *Chapter* 7: Changed terminology relating to Figure 7-2 (from "expanding, static, and declining economy" to "expanding, static, and declining production capacity"); simplification of the explanation of the GDP price index (new Tables 7-5 and 7-6); fuller discussion of the CPI. *Chapter 8*: Improved discussion of structural unemployment; revision of the discussion of Okun's law; addition to Table 8-2 of unemployment rates by education. *Chapter 9*: Figure 9-5 (investment demand) is now a Key Graph; new Figure 9-6 shows shifts in the investment-demand curve; new Figure 9-7 links the real interest rate, the investment-demand curve, and the economy's investment schedule. *Chapter 10*: Figure 10-8 on recessionary and inflationary gaps is now a Key Graph. *Chapter 11*: Improved discussion of possible causes of downward price and wage inflexibility. *Chapter 12*: New discussion of the proposed balanced-budget requirement; clarified discussion of the crowding-out effect of fiscal policy, including criticisms of the idea.
- **Part 3.** *Chapter 13*: "Unit of account" replaces the term "measure of value;" new section on recent developments in money and banking (relative decline of banks and thrifts, globalization of financial markets, and electronic money and smart cards). *Chapter 15:* Expanded discussion of the Fed's targeting of the Federal funds rate; new Global Perspective 15-1 lists the names (including nicknames) of the central banks of selected nations.
- **Part 4.** *Chapter 16*: "New" chapter extends the analysis of aggregate supply. *Chapter 17*: "New" chapter contrasts contemporary views on macro theory

and policy. *Chapter 18*: Covers economic growth (Chapter 19 in the thirteenth edition); discusses the weak productivity gains in services; discusses the controversial idea of a "new economy." *Chapter 19*: Updated section on the policy responses to budget deficits, including the deficit reduction legislation of 1992 and the line-item veto.

• *Part 5*. *Chapter 20*: Chapter on international trade tightened. *Chapter 21*: Improved explanation of the balance of payments; major consolidation of the discussion of past exchange-rate systems and the section on U.S. trade deficits. *Chapter 22*: New world map indicating industrially advanced nations, middle-income developing nations, and low-income developing nations (Global Perspective 22-1); revised discussion of international debt difficulties, including mention of the recent IMF bailouts of the Southeast Asian economies; entirely new policy section on development. *Chapter 23*: Extensively revised chapter now includes discussion of the transition to markets in China as well as in Russia.

New Last Words

Several Last Words are new; others have been revised and updated. All 23 Last Words are accompanied by new art. We continue to place these boxes at the ends of chapters, where they are least likely to interrupt readers' concentration.

The new Last Word topics are women and production possibilities (Chapter 2); consumer sovereignty, dollar votes, and plastic pink flamingos (Chapter 4); the demise of wage and price controls (Chapter 16); enterprise transition to capitalism in Russia (Chapter 23).

FUNDAMENTAL GOALS

Although the fourteenth edition only modestly resembles the first, our intention remains the same: to introduce the beginning economics students to principles essential to understanding the basic economizing problem, specific economic issues, and the policy alternatives available for dealing with them. Two fortunate by-products of this objective are an ability to reason accurately and dispassionately about economic matters and a lasting interest in economics. As always,

we present the principles and problems of economics in a straightforward, logical fashion. *We continue to stress clarity of presentation, step-by-step organization, and consistency of level of analysis.*

DISTINGUISHING FEATURES

• *Comprehensive Explanations at an Appropriate Level.* *Macroeconomics* is comprehensive, analytical, and challenging yet accessible to a wide range of students. Its thoroughness and accessibility enable instructors to select topics for special classroom emphasis with confidence that students can read and comprehend independently other assigned material in the book.

• *Comprehensive Definition of Economics.* Because students must first understand the fundamentals, we devoted nearly all of Chapter 2 to a careful statement and development of the economizing problem and an exploration of its implications. This foundation will help put into proper perspective essential economic concepts.

• *Fundamentals of the Market System.* Economies throughout the world are making difficult transitions from planning to markets. Our detailed description of the institutions and operation of the *market system* in Chapter 4 is now more relevant than before. We pay particular attention to property rights, freedom of enterprise and choice, competition, and the role of profits because these concepts are poorly understood by beginning students.

• *Early Integration of International Economics.* We give the principles and institutions of the global economy early treatment. Chapter 6 examines the growth of world trade, the major participants in world trade, specialization and comparative advantage, the foreign exchange market, tariffs and subsidies, and various trade agreements. This strong introduction to international economics permits "globalization" of later macroeconomics and microeconomics discussions.

• *Early and Extensive Treatment of Government.* Government is an integral component of modern capitalism. This book introduces the economic functions of government early and treats them systematically in Chapter 5. The controversy over the proper role of government in stabilizing the economy is central to the macroeconomic policy chapters.

- *Emphasis on Economic Growth.* This edition continues to emphasize economic growth. Chapter 2 uses the production possibilities curve to show the basic ingredients of growth. Chapter 18 discusses the rate and causes of growth, in addition to some of the controversies surrounding it. Chapter 22 focuses on the developing countries and the growth obstacles they confront. Chapter 23 looks at growth in the transition economies of the Soviet Union and China.

ORGANIZATION AND CONTENT

Macroeconomics reflects the challenge specific topics and concepts will likely pose for average students. For instance, the theory of macro output and price-level determination are carefully treated. Here, simplicity is correlated with comprehensiveness, not brevity.

Our experience suggests that in treating each basic topic—aggregate demand and aggregate supply, money and banking, and international economics—it is desirable to couple analysis with policy. Generally, we use a three-step development of analytical tools: (1) verbal descriptions and illustrations, (2) numerical examples, and (3) graphical presentation based on these numerical illustrations.

All these considerations caused us to organize the book into five parts: Part 1: An Introduction to Economics and the Economy; Part 2: National Income, Employment, and Fiscal Policy; Part 3: Money, Banking, and Monetary Policy; Part 4: Problems and Controversies in Macroeconomics; Part 5: International Economics and the World Economy.

ORGANIZATIONAL ALTERNATIVES

Although instructors generally agree on the content of the principles of macroeconomics course, they often differ as how to arrange the material; *Macroeconomics* provides considerable organizational flexibility. Previous users tell us they often substantially rearrange chapters with little sacrifice of continuity.

The AD-AS model is preceded by two chapters on aggregate expenditures analysis. Those who want to rely exclusively on AD-AS can omit these two chapters, supplementing the AD discussion with discussion of investment demand and the multiplier implicit within shifts of the AD curve.

PEDAGOGICAL AIDS

Macroeconomics has always been student-oriented. The To the Student statement at the beginning of Part 1 details the many pedagogical aids. The fourteenth edition is also accompanied by a variety of high-quality supplements.

The Supplements

- *Study Guide.* William Walstad—one of the world's foremost experts on economic education—prepared the fourteenth edition of the *Study Guide*, which many students find indispensable. Each chapter has an introductory statement, a checklist of behavioral objectives, an outline, a list of important terms, fill-in questions, problems and projects, objective questions, and discussion questions. Answers to *Macroeconomics'* end-of-chapter Key Questions appear at the end of the *Study Guide*, along with the text's Glossary.

The *Study Guide*, which is available in a separate macro edition, is a superb "portable tutor" for the principles student.

- *Instructor's Resource Manual.* Professor Arienne Turner of Fullerton College revised and updated the *Instructor's Resource Manual*. It comprises chapter summaries, listings of "what's new" in each chapter, new teaching tips and suggestions, learning objectives, chapter outlines, data and visual aid sources with suggestions for classroom use, and questions and problems. Answers to the text's end-of-chapter Key Questions are also included.

The *Manual* is again available for use with IBM-PC compatibles and MacIntosh computers. The PC version is also available in CD-ROM format. Users can print out portions of the *Manual's* contents, complete with their own additions and alterations, for use as student handouts or in whatever ways they might wish.

- *Three Test Banks.* Two test banks of objective, predominately multiple-choice questions and a third test bank of short-answer essay questions and problems supplement this edition of *Macroeconomics*.

- Test Bank I. This test bank now includes more than 5200 questions, most all written by the text authors.

- Test Bank II. Written by William Walstad, this test bank contains more than 5000 questions. All Test Bank II questions are now organized according to level of difficulty: easy, moderate, or difficult.
- Test Bank III. Also prepared by William Walstad, Test Bank III contains "constructive response" testing to evaluate student understanding in a manner different from conventional multiple-choice and true-false questions. Suggested answers to the essay and problem questions are included.

For all test items in Test Banks I and II, the nature of each question is identified (for example, G = graphical; C = complex analysis; etc.), as are the numbers of the text pages that are the basis for each question. Also, each chapter in Test Banks I and II includes an outline or table of contents that groups questions by topics. In all, more than 10,000 questions of equality give instructors maximum testing flexibility while assuring the fullest possible text correlation.

Additional Supplements

- **Computerized Testing.** Test Banks I, II, and III are available in computerized versions, both for IBM-PC and compatibles and MacIntosh computers. These systems generate multiple tests, scrambled tests, and high-quality graphs. Developed by the Brownstone Research group, this software meets the needs of the widest spectrum of computer users.
- **Color Transparencies (Figures and Tables).** We offer over 150 full-color transparencies for overhead projectors. They include most figures and tables in *Macroeconomics* and are available on request to adopters.
- **PowerPoint Presentation.** Norman Hollingsworth of DeKalb College once again created our PowerPoint Presentation slides, which consist of over 1000 audio-enhanced images.
- **Student Software.** *DiscoverEcon* is available for *Macroeconomics*. This menu-driven software, which was developed by Gerald Nelson at the University of Illinois, gives students a complete tutorial linked to the text. Each chapter features two essay questions and a multiple-choice test. Whenever relevant, interactive graphing problems let students observe how the economic picture is altered when they select different data. Links to the Glossary and text references clarify key concepts.

Two additional interactive tutorials are available with this edition: *Macroeconomics Interactive CD-ROM* and *WinEcon*.

Developed by Charles Link and Jeffrey Miller at the University of Delaware, the *Macroeconomics Interactive CD-ROM* gives students a rich, easy-to-use menu covering core topics in introductory economics with an audio component that makes it an excellent tool for reviewing basic concepts. The tutorial has a real-world focus: Newspaper and magazine articles highlight economic concepts, and interactive videos allow students to "interview" business leaders.

WinEcon is an interactive software package offering over 75 hours of tutorial material. It includes self-assessment questions and exams, economic databases, and an economic glossary and references to leading economic texts. It is the first computer-based learning package to cover the entire first-year economics syllabus. *WinEcon* combines two products in one: teaching software and student tools, and *WinEcon* Lecturer with tests, exams, course management, and customization program. It was developed at the University of Bristol with the help of the Teaching and Learning Technology Programme Economics Consortium (TLTP), a group of eight United Kingdom university economics departments.

- **Website for Students and Instructors.** Our dynamic text Website can be found at http://www.mhhe.com/economics/mcconnell. At the Website, students can find learning support, including answers to the text's Key Questions.
- **MHLA.** McGraw-Hill Learning Architecture is our on-line student tutorial and course-management program, which includes materials directly linked to McConnell and Brue, *Macroeconomics*, fourteenth edition.

ACKNOWLEDGMENTS

We give special thanks to James Reese of the University of South Carolina at Spartansburg, who wrote the 46 end-of-chapter Internet Exercises.

Our colleagues at the University of Nebraska–Lincoln and Pacific Lutheran University generously shared knowledge of their specialties with us and provided encouragement.

As indicated, the fourteenth edition benefited from a number of perceptive reviews. In both quantity and quality, the reviewers were a rich source of suggestions for this revision. These contributors are listed at the end of this Preface.

Professor Thomas Barbiero of Ryerson Polytechnical Institute provided helpful ideas in his role as coauthor of the Canadian edition of *Macroeconomics*. Also, we greatly appreciate the suggestions for improvement provided by Professor Walstad, the author of the *Study Guide*. Thanks also to Robert Jensen, who proofread the entire manuscript (twice), and William Harris of the University of Delaware, who supplied a number of new questions for Test Bank I.

We are greatly indebted to the many professionals at McGraw-Hill—in particular, Gary Burke, Lucille Sutton, Marilea Fried, Lee Hertel, Nelson Black, Marty Quinn, Miller Murray, Eve Strock, Francis Owens, Diane Renda, and Pam Augspurger—for their publishing expertise.

We thank Ed Millman and Susan Gottfried for their thorough and sensitive editing, Amanda Kavanagh for her creative design, and Jacques Cournoyer for his vivid Last Word illustrations.

We also strongly acknowledge the newly integrated Irwin/McGraw-Hill sales staff, who greeted this edition with wholehearted enthusiasm.

Campbell R. McConnell
Stanley L. Brue

CONTRIBUTORS

REVIEWERS

David Allen, University of Alabama–Huntsville
Kevin Baird, Montgomery County Community College
Joe A. Bell, Southwest Missouri State University
Dixie Blackley, LeMoyne College
John Boffoe-Bonnie, Pennsylvania State University–Media
Carol Condon, Kean College of New Jersey
Betsy Crowell, University of Michigan–Dearborn
Norman Cure, Macomb Community College
Chris Duelfer, Cedar Crest College
Robert Eggleston, Shippensburg University
Ron Elkins, Central Washington University
Arthur Friedberg, Mohawk Valley Community College
Jeff D. Gibbs, Abraham Baldwin College
Sadie Gregory, Virginia State University
Medhi Haririan, Bloomsburg University of Pennsylvania
Paul Harris, Camden County College
Gus Herring, Brookhaven College
Calvin Hoerneman, Delta College
John Hill, Northeastern State University
Katherine M. Huger, Charleston Southern University
Mashid Jalilvand, University of Wisconsin–Stout
Zeinholm Kabis, St. Ambrose University
James Kahiga, DeKalb College
Demetri Kantarelis, Assumption College
Mehmet Karaaslan, Alfred University
Elizabeth Kelly, University of Wisconsin–Madison
Vani Kotcherlokota, University of Nebraska–Kearny
Ross LaRoe, Denison University
Mark S. LeClair, Fairfield University
Judy Lee, Leeward Community College
Jon G. Lindgren, North Dakota State University
Patrick Litzinger, Robert Morris College
Elizabeth J. Lott, Pace University
William C. O'Connor, Western Montana College
Martha L. Olney, University of California–Berkeley

Lucjan Orlowski, Sacred Heart University
Joseph Prinzinger, Lynchburg College
Janet M. Rives, University of Northern Iowa
Henry Ryder, Gloucester County Community College
John Saussey, Harrisburg Area Community College
Charlene Schick, Cypress College
Teresa Sherrouse, Augusta College
Dorothy Siden, Salem State College
Victor Ukpolo, Austin Peay State University
Janet West, University of Nebraska–Omaha
Fred E. Williams, Montreat College
Study Guide Student Reviewers from Anne Arundel Community College, Arnold, Maryland:
Erica Beisler
John Botwright
Pam Newman
Chris Rzepkowski
Laureen Thomas
Kathy Van Liew
and their instructor, Professor Raymond F. Turner

FOCUS GROUP PARTICIPANTS

Vinod Agarwal, Old Dominion University
Hamid Azari, Alabama State University
Dan Berkowitz, University of Pittsburgh
Larry Biacci, Pennsylvania State University–Hazelton
Michael Brandl, West Texas A & M University
Christopher Brown, Arkansas State University–Mountain Home
Lindsey Calkins, John Carroll University
James Cobbe, Florida State University
David Connell, University of Nebraska at Omaha
Arifeen M. Daneshyan, Kutztown University
Allen Dickes, Washburn University
Michael Gootzeit, University of Memphis
Linda Harris Dobkins, Emory and Henry College
Robert Ebert, Baldwin-Wallace College
Jill Herndon, Hamline University
Julie Hotchkiss, Georgia State University

Christopher Lingle, Case Western Reserve University
Darryl Lowry, Roanoke College
Larry Mack, North Highland Community College
Bart Macomber, Highland Community College
Richard McGrath, College of William and Mary
Dennis O'Toole, Virginia Commonwealth University
Walter Park, The American University
C. S. Pyun, University of Memphis
Charles Roberts, Western Kentucky University
Steve Rockland, San Diego State University
Julie Ryan, Beaver College
Ken Scalet, York College
Chuck Slusher, University of North Carolina–Chapel Hill
Gerald Stollman, Oakland Community College
Robert Tansky, St. Clair Community College
Roy Townsend, Greenville Technical College
Arienne Turner, Fullerton College
David Vernon, Lubbock Christian University
Eugene Williams, McMurry University
Hamid Zangeneh, Widener University

QUESTIONNAIRE RESPONDENTS

Emmanuel Asigbee, Kirkwood Community College
Jan E. Christopher, Delaware State University
Betty Chu, San Jose State University
John Connelly, Corning Community College
Larry DeBrock, University of Illinois
Floyd Allen DeCook, Broward Community College

John W. Dorsey, University of Maryland at College Park
Rodney D. Green, Howard University
Barnali Gupta, Miami University
Ruby Hargrove, St. Augustine's College
Michael N. Hayes, Radford University
Mark L. Huston, San Diego Mesa College
Patti J. Impink, Macon College
Mark Karscig, Central Missouri State University
Erwin L. Kelly, Jr., California State University–Sacramento
Philip J. Lane, Fairfield University
John R. Moroney, Texas A&M University
Dennis L. Nelson, University of Minnesota–Duluth
Mehdi Pousti, Kansas State University
David L. Priddy, Piedmont Virginia Community College
Michael Reclam, Virginia Military Institute
David Roe, Furman University
Richard Rosenberg, Pennsylvania State University
Nancy Short, Chandler-Gilbert Community College
Mary Huff Stevenson, University of Massachusetts–Boston
Robert Vowels, Tennessee State University
Robert B. Wagner, Houston Community College
Mike M. Williams, Bethune Cookman/Daytona Beach Community College
Edgar W. Wood, University of Mississippi
Wendy V. Wysocki, Monroe County Community College
Janice Yee, Wartburg College
Armand Zottola, Central Connecticut State University

1

An
Introduction to
Economics and
the Economy

TO THE STUDENT

Economics is largely concerned with efficiency—accomplishing goals using the best methods. Several features of this book and its ancillaries are designed to improve your efficiency in learning economics (and therefore your course grade):

- *Appendix on graphs* Being comfortable with graphical analysis and a few quantitative concepts is a big advantage in understanding principles of economics. The appendix to Chapter 1 reviews graphing, line slopes, and linear equations. Be sure to not skip it.

- *Introductions* The introductory paragraphs of each chapter place the chapter in the proper context, state its main objectives, and tell you how it is organized. These introductions lead you into the economic analysis.

- *Terminology* A significant portion of any introductory course is terminology. Key terms are set in **boldface type,** listed at the end of each chapter, and defined in the glossary at the end of the book.

- *Reviews* Important things should be said more than once. Each chapter contains a summary and two or three Quick Reviews. These reviews will help you focus on essential ideas and study for exams. If any review statement seems unclear, you should reread the corresponding section of the text.

- *Key Graphs* Graphs that have special relevance are labeled Key Graphs, and each includes a multiple-choice Quick Quiz. Your instructor may or may not emphasize all these figures, but you should pay special attention to those that are discussed in class; you can be certain that there will be exam questions on them.

- *Figure legends* The legends accompanying the figures in this book are self-contained analyses of the figures. Study these legends carefully—they are quick synopses of important ideas.

- *Globalization* The economics of individual nations are becoming part of an overall global economy. To gain appreciation of this wider economic environment, be sure to take a look at the Global Perspectives, which compare the United States to other selected nations.

- *Last Words* Each chapter concludes with a Last Word minireading. While it is tempting to ignore these sections, don't. Some of them are revealing applications of economic concepts; others are short case studies. A few present views which contrast with mainstream thinking; and most are fun to read. All will broaden your grasp of economics.

- *Questions* A comprehensive list of questions is located at the end of each chapter. The old cliché that you "learn by doing" is very relevant to economics. Answering these questions will enhance your understanding. Several of the questions are designated as Key Questions and are answered in the *Study Guide* and the *Instructor's Resource Manual,* and they can also be found at our Website, http://www.mhhe.com/economics/mcconnell. You can turn to these particular questions when they are cited in each chapter, or later, after you have read the full chapter.

- *Study Guide* We enthusiastically recommend the *Study Guide* accompanying this text. This "portable tutor" contains not only a broad sampling of various kinds of questions but a host of useful learning aids.

You will find in Chapter 1 that economics involves a special way of thinking—a unique approach to analyzing problems. The overriding goal of this book is to help you acquire that skill. If our cooperative efforts—yours, ours, and your instructor's—are successful, you will be able to comprehend a whole range of economic, social, and political problems that otherwise would have remained murky and elusive.

CHAPTER ONE

The Nature and Method of Economics

Human beings, those unfortunate creatures, are plagued with wants. We want, among other things, love, social recognition, and the material necessities and comforts of life. Our efforts to meet our material wants, that is, to improve our well-being or "make a living," are the concern of economics.

Biologically, we need only air, water, food, clothing, and shelter. But, in contemporary society, we also seek the many goods and services associated with a comfortable or affluent standard of living. Fortunately, society is blessed with productive resources—labor and managerial talent, tools and machinery, land and mineral deposits—which are used to produce goods and services. This production satisfies many of our material wants and occurs through the organizational mechanism called the *economic system* or, more simply, *the economy*.

The blunt reality, however, is that the total of all our material wants is many times greater than the productive capacity of our limited resources. Thus, the complete satisfaction of material wants is impossible. This unyielding reality provides our definition of **economics:** *the social science concerned with the efficient use of limited or scarce resources to achieve maximum satisfaction of human material wants.*

Although it may not be evident, most of the headline-grabbing issues of our time—inflation, unemployment, health care, social security, budget deficits, discrimination, tax reform, poverty and inequality, pollution, and government regulation and deregulation of business—are rooted in the one challenge of using scarce resources efficiently.

In this first chapter, however, we will not plunge into problems and issues; instead, we will discuss some important preliminaries. Specifically, we first look at the economic perspective—how economists think about problems. Next, we state some of the benefits of studying economics. Then we consider the specific methods economists use to examine economic behavior and the economy, distinguishing between macroeconomics and microeconomics. Finally, we examine the problems, limitations, and pitfalls that hinder sound economic reasoning.

THE ECONOMIC PERSPECTIVE

Economists view things through a unique perspective. This **economic perspective** or *economic way of thinking* has several critical and closely interrelated features.

Scarcity and Choice

From our definition of economics, it is easy to see why economists view the world through the lens of scarcity. Since human and property resources are scarce (limited), it follows that the goods and services we produce must also be scarce. Scarcity limits our options and necessitates that we make choices. Because we "can't have it all," we must decide what we will have.

At the core of economics is the idea that "there is no free lunch." You may get treated to lunch, making it "free" to you, but there is a cost to someone—ultimately to society. Scarce inputs of land, equipment, farm labor, the labor of cooks and waiters, and managerial talent are required. Because these resources could be used in alternative production activities, they and the other goods and services they could have produced are sacrificed in making the "free" lunch available. Economists call these sacrifices *opportunity costs*.

Rational Behavior

Economics is grounded on the assumption of "rational self-interest." That is, individuals make rational decisions to achieve the greatest satisfaction or the maximum fulfillment of their goals. For instance, they spend their incomes to get the greatest benefit from the goods and services they can afford.

Rational behavior means that different people will make different choices because their preferences, circumstances, and available information differ. You may have decided that it is in your best interest to attend college before entering the full-time labor force, while a high school classmate has chosen to forgo additional schooling and go to work. Why the different choices? Your academic abilities, along with your family's income, may be greater than your classmate's. You may also know that college-educated workers have better job opportunities and lower unemployment rates than less educated workers. Hence, you opted for college, while your former classmate—the one with less academic ability, less money, and less information—chose a job. Both choices reflect the pursuit of self-interest and are rational, but they are based on differing circumstances and information.

Of course, rational decisions may change as circumstances change. Suppose the Federal government decides it is in the national interest to increase the supply of college-educated workers. It might offer 2 years of "free" community college to all low-income students. Under these new conditions, your high school classmate might now opt for college rather than a job.

It is important to remember that rational self-interest is not the same as selfishness. People make personal sacrifices to help family members or friends, and they contribute to charities because they derive pleasure from doing so. Parents help pay for their children's education for the same reason. These self-interested, but unselfish, acts help maximize the givers' satisfaction as much as any personal purchase of goods or services.

Marginalism: Benefits and Costs

The economic perspective focuses largely on **marginal analysis**—comparisons of marginal benefits and marginal costs. (Used this way, "marginal" means "extra," "additional," or "a change in.") Most choices or decisions involve changes in the status quo. Should you go to school for another year or not? Should you spend more or less money on compact discs each month? Similarly, businesses regularly must decide whether to employ more or fewer workers or to produce more or less output.

Each option involves marginal benefits and, because of scarcity, marginal costs. In making choices rationally, the decision maker must compare these two amounts. Example: Your time is scarce. What will you do with 2 "free" hours on a Saturday afternoon? You could watch Gigantic State University's Fighting Aardvarks play basketball on television. The *marginal benefit* to you would be the pleasure of seeing the game. The *marginal cost* would be the benefit from the other things you have to sacrifice to watch the game, including perhaps studying, jogging, or taking a nap. If the marginal benefit exceeds the marginal cost, then it is rational to watch the game. But if you determine that the marginal cost of watching the game is greater than the marginal benefit, then you should select one of the other options.

On the national level, government regularly makes decisions involving marginal benefits and marginal costs. More spending on health care may mean less spending on libraries, aid to the poor, or military security. In a world of scarcity, the decision to obtain the marginal benefit associated with some specific option always includes the marginal cost of forgoing something else. Again, there is no free lunch.

One somewhat surprising implication of decisions based on marginal analysis is that there *can* be too much of a good thing. Although certain goods and services seem inherently desirable—education, health care, a clean environment—we can in fact have too much of them. "Too much" occurs when we keep producing them beyond the point where their marginal cost (the value of the forgone options) equals their marginal benefit.

If we choose to produce so much health care that its marginal cost to society exceeds its marginal benefit, we are providing "too much" of it even though we all agree that health care is a good thing. When the marginal costs of health care exceed the marginal benefits, we are sacrificing alternative products (for example, education and pollution reduction) which are more valuable than health care *at the margin*—the place where we consider the very last units of each. **(Key Question 1)**

This chapter's Last Word provides an everyday application of the economic perspective.

WHY STUDY ECONOMICS?

Is studying economics worth your time and effort? More than half a century ago John Maynard Keynes (1883–1946), one of the most influential economists of this century, said:

> The ideas of economists and political philosophers, both when they are right and when they are wrong, are more powerful than is commonly understood. Indeed the world is ruled by little else. Practical men, who believe themselves to be quite exempt from any intellectual influences, are usually the slaves of some defunct economist.

Most of the ideologies of the modern world have been shaped by prominent economists of the past—Adam Smith, David Ricardo, John Stuart Mill, Karl Marx, and John Maynard Keynes. And current world leaders routinely solicit the advice and policy suggestions of today's economists.

For example, the President of the United States benefits from the recommendations of his Council of Economic Advisers. The broad range of economic issues facing political leaders is suggested by the contents of the annual *Economic Report of the President.*

Areas covered typically include unemployment, inflation, economic growth, taxation, poverty, international trade, health care, pollution, discrimination, immigration, regulation, and education, among others.

Economics for Citizenship

A basic understanding of economics is essential if we are to be well-informed citizens. Most of today's political problems have important economic aspects: How important is it that we balance the Federal budget? How can we make the social security retirement program financially secure? Why do we continue to have large international trade deficits? How can we best reduce pollution? What must we do to keep inflation in check? What can be done to boost U.S. productivity and economic growth? Are existing welfare programs effective and justifiable? Do we need to reform our tax system? How should we respond to growing market dominance by a few firms in some high-technology sectors of the economy?

As voters, we can influence the decisions of our elected officials in responding to such questions. But intelligence at the polls requires a basic working knowledge of economics. And a sound grasp of economics is even more helpful to the politicians themselves.

A survey by the National Center for Research in Economic Education suggests that economic illiteracy is widespread in the United States. The public, high school seniors, and college seniors show a broad lack of knowledge of the basic economics needed to understand economic events and changes in the national economy. When asked questions about fundamental economics, only 39 percent of the general public, 35 percent of high school seniors, and 51 percent of college seniors gave correct answers.

Professional and Personal Applications

Economics lays great stress on precise, systematic analysis. Thus, studying economics invariably helps students improve their analytical skills, which are in great demand in the workplace. Also, the study of economics helps us make sense of the everyday activity we observe around us. How is it that so many different people, in so many different places, doing so many different things, produce exactly the goods and services we want to buy? Economics provides an answer.

Economics is also vital to business. An understanding of the basics of economic decision making and the operation of the economic system enables business managers and executives to increase profit. The executive who understands when to use new technology, when to merge with another firm, when to expand employment, and so on, will outperform the executive who is less deft at such decision making. The manager who understands the causes and consequences of recessions (downturns in the overall economy) can make more intelligent business decisions during these periods.

Economics helps consumers and workers make better buying and employment decisions. How can you spend your limited money income to maximize your satisfaction? How can you hedge against the reduction in the dollar's purchasing power that accompanies inflation? Is it more economical to buy or lease a car? Should you use a credit card or pay cash? Which occupations pay well; which are most immune to unemployment?

Similarly, an understanding of economics makes for better financial decisions. Someone who understands the relationship between budget deficits and interest rates, between foreign exchange rates and exports, between interest rates and bond prices, is in a better position to successfully allocate personal savings. So, too, is someone who understands the business implications of emerging new technologies.

In spite of these practical benefits, however, you should know that economics is *mainly* an academic, not a vocational, subject. Unlike accounting, advertising, corporate finance, and marketing, economics is not primarily a how-to-make-money area of study. Knowledge of economics and mastery of the economic perspective will help you run a business or manage your personal finances, but that is not its primary objective. Instead, economics ultimately examines problems and decisions from the *social*, rather than the *personal*, point of view. The production, exchange, and consumption of goods and services are discussed from the viewpoint of society's best interest, not strictly from the standpoint of one's own pocketbook.

QUICK REVIEW 1-1

■ Economics is concerned with obtaining maximum satisfaction through the efficient use of scarce resources.

■ The economic perspective stresses **(a)** resource scarcity and the necessity of making choices, **(b)** the assumption of rational behavior, and **(c)** comparisons of marginal benefit and marginal cost.

■ Your study of economics will help you as a voting citizen as well as benefit you professionally and personally.

ECONOMIC METHODOLOGY

The tasks and procedures involved in economics are summarized in Figure 1-1.

Theoretical Economics

All sciences are based on observable and verifiable behavior, realities, or facts. As a social science, economics examines the observable and verifiable behavior of individuals (consumers, workers) and institutions (business, government) engaged in the production, exchange, and consumption of goods and services.

Fact gathering about economic activity and economic outcomes can be a complex process. Because

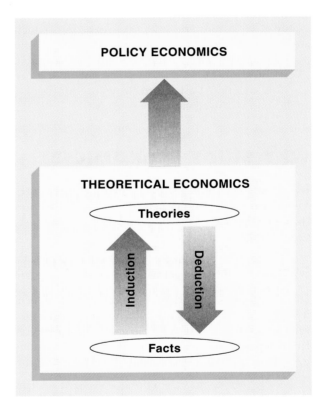

FIGURE 1-1 The relationship between facts, principles, and policies in economics In analyzing problems or aspects of the economy, economists may use the inductive method, through which they gather, systematically arrange, and generalize from facts. Alternatively, they may use the deductive method, in which they develop hypotheses which are then tested against facts. Generalizations derived from either method are useful not only in explaining economic behavior but also as a basis for formulating economic policies.

the world of reality is cluttered with innumerable interrelated facts, economists, like all scientists, must be highly selective in gathering information. They must determine which facts are relevant to the problem under consideration. But even when this sorting process is complete, the relevant information may at first seem random and unrelated.

The economist thus seeks *principles*—generalizations about the way individuals and institutions behave. The process of deriving principles is called **theoretical economics** or *economic analysis* (see the lower box in Figure 1-1). *The role of economic theorizing or economic analysis is to systematically arrange facts, interpret them, and generalize from them.* Principles and theories, the end result of economic analysis, bring order and meaning to facts by putting them in correct relationship to one another. As economist Kenneth Boulding states, "Theories without facts may be barren, but facts without theories are meaningless."[1]

As seen in Figure 1-1, economists are as likely to move from theories to facts in studying economic behavior as they are to move from facts to theories. That is, economists use both deductive and inductive methods. **Induction** moves from facts to theory, from the particular to the general. In this approach, an accumulation of facts is arranged systematically and analyzed to derive the underlying principle. The left, upward arrow from "facts" to "theories" in the figure suggests the inductive method.

Usually, economists create generalizations through **deduction.** They draw on casual observation, insight, logic, or intuition to frame a tentative, untested principle called a *hypothesis.* For example, they may conjecture, based on "armchair logic," that consumers will buy more of a product when its price falls. To test this hypothesis, economists must subject it to systematic and repeated comparison with relevant facts. Do real-world data confirm an inverse relationship between price and the amount purchased? This testing process, sometimes called *empirical economics*, is implied by the right, downward arrow from "theories" to "facts" in Figure 1-1.

Deduction and induction are complementary, rather than opposing, techniques of investigation. A hypothesis formed by deduction provides guidelines for the economist in gathering and organizing factual data. Conversely, some understanding of factual, real-world evidence is required to formulate meaningful hypotheses.

Economic **principles** and theories are *meaningful statements about economic behavior or the economy.* They are drawn from facts, while facts themselves help prove the validity of principles already established. Good theories are supported by facts concerning how individuals and institutions actually behave in producing, exchanging, and consuming goods and services. Since these facts may change in time, economists must continually check principles and theories against the shifting economic environment.

Several other points relating to economic principles are important to know.

Terminology   Economists speak of *laws, principles, theories,* and *models.* These terms are sometimes confusing to students, but they all mean essentially the same thing: They are generalizations about the economic behavior of individuals and institutions. The terms "economic laws" and "principles" are useful, but they are somewhat misleading because they imply a high degree of exactness, universal application, and even moral rightness that is rare in social science. The word "theory" is often used in economics even though many people incorrectly believe theories have nothing to do with real-world applications. Economists often use the term "model," which refers to a simplified picture of reality, an abstract generalization of how relevant facts actually relate to one another.

In this book we use these four terms synonymously. Custom or convenience will govern each particular choice. Thus, the relationship between the price of a product and the amount of the product consumers purchase will be called the *law of demand,* rather than the theory or principle of demand, simply because this is the custom.

Generalizations   As we have already mentioned, economic principles are **generalizations** relating to economic behavior or to the economy itself. They are imprecise because economic facts are usually diverse; no two individuals or institutions act in exactly the same way. *Economic principles are expressed as the tendencies of typical, or average consumers, workers, or business firms.* For example, when economists say that consumer spending rises when personal income increases, they are well aware that some households may save *all* of an increase in their incomes. But, on average, and for the full economy, spending goes up when income increases. Similarly, economists say that consumers buy more of a particular product when its price falls. Some consumers may increase their purchases by a large amount, others by a small amount,

---

[1]Kenneth E. Boulding, *Economic Analysis: Microeconomics,* 4th ed. (New York: Harper & Row, 1966), p. 5.

and a few not at all. This "price-quantity" principle, however, holds for the typical consumer and for consumers as a group.

"Other-Things-Equal" Assumption

Like other scientists, economists use the *ceteris paribus* or **other-things-equal assumption** to construct their generalizations. They assume that all other variables except those under immediate consideration are held constant for a particular analysis. For example, consider the relationship between the price of Pepsi and the amount purchased. It helps to assume that, of all the factors which might influence the amount of Pepsi purchased (for example, the price of Pepsi, the price of Coca-Cola, and consumer incomes and preferences), only the price of Pepsi varies. The economist can then focus on the "price of Pepsi–purchases of Pepsi" relationship without being confused by changes in other variables.

Natural scientists such as chemists or physicists can usually conduct controlled experiments where "all other things" are in fact held constant (or virtually so). They can test with great precision the assumed relationship between two variables. For example, they might examine the height from which an object is dropped and the length of time it takes to hit the ground. But economics is not a laboratory science. Economists test their theories using real-world data, which are generated by the actual operation of the economy. In this rather bewildering environment, "other things" *do* change. Despite the development of complex statistical techniques designed to hold other things equal, controls are less than perfect. As a result, economic principles are less certain and less precise than those of laboratory sciences.

Abstractions

Economic principles, or theories, are *abstractions*—simplifications which omit irrelevant facts and circumstances. These models do *not* mirror the full complexity of the real world. The very process of sorting out and analyzing facts involves simplification and removal of clutter. Unfortunately, this "abstraction" leads some people to consider economic theory impractical and unrealistic. This is nonsense! Economic theories are practical precisely because they *are* abstractions. The full scope of economic reality itself is too complex and bewildering to be understood as a whole. Economists abstract, that is, build models, to give meaning to an otherwise overwhelming and confusing maze of facts. Theorizing for this purpose is highly practical.

Graphical Expression

Many of the economic models in this book are expressed graphically; the most important are labeled Key Graphs. We strongly urge you to read the appendix to this chapter as a review of graphs.

Policy Economics

Applied economics or **policy economics** recognizes the principles and data which can be used to formulate policies, as shown in the upper part of Figure 1-1. Economic theories are the foundation of economic policy—a course of action based on economic principles and intended to resolve a specific problem or further a nation's economic goals. Economic policy normally is applied to problems after they arise. However, if economic analysis can predict some undesirable event such as unemployment, inflation, or an increase in poverty, then it may be possible to avoid or moderate that event through economic policy.

Economic Policy

The creation of policies to achieve specific goals is no simple matter. Here are the basic steps in policymaking:

1. *State the goal.* The first step is to make a clear statement of the economic goal. If we say that we want "full employment," do we mean that everyone between, say, 16 and 65 years of age should have a job? Or do we mean that everyone who wants to work should have a job? Should we allow for some unemployment caused by inevitable changes in the structure of industry and workers voluntarily changing jobs? The goal must be specific.

2. *Determine the policy options.* The next step is to formulate alternative policies designed to achieve the goal, and determine the possible effects of each policy. This requires a detailed assessment of the economic impact, benefits, costs, and political feasibility of the alternative policies. For example, to achieve full employment, should government use fiscal policy (which involves changing government spending and taxes), monetary policy (which entails altering the supply of money), an education and training policy which enhances worker employability, or a policy of wage subsidies to firms that hire disadvantaged workers?

3. *Implement and evaluate the policy which was selected.* After implementing the policy, we need to evaluate how well it worked. Only through unbiased evaluation can we improve on economic policy. Did a specific change in taxes or the money supply alter the level of employment to the extent predicted? Did deregulation of a particular industry (for example, the airlines) yield the predicted beneficial results? If not, why not? **(Key Question 5)**

Economic Goals   If economic policies are designed to achieve certain economic goals, then we need to recognize a number of goals which are widely accepted in the United States and many other countries. They include:

1. *Economic growth*   Produce more and better goods and services, or, more simply, develop a higher standard of living.
2. *Full employment*   Provide suitable jobs for all citizens who are willing and able to work.
3. *Economic efficiency*   Achieve the maximum fulfillment of wants using the available productive resources.
4. *Price-level stability*   Avoid large upswings and downswings in the general price level; that is, avoid inflation and deflation.
5. *Economic freedom*   Guarantee that businesses, workers, and consumers have a high degree of freedom in their economic activities.
6. *Equitable distribution of income*   Ensure that no group of citizens faces stark poverty while others enjoy extreme luxury.
7. *Economic security*   Provide for those who are chronically ill, disabled, handicapped, laid off, aged, or otherwise unable to earn minimal levels of income.
8. *Balance of trade*   Seek a reasonable overall balance with the rest of the world in international trade and financial transactions.

Although most of us might accept these goals as generally stated, we might also disagree substantially on their specific meanings. What are "large" changes in the price level? What is a "high degree" of economic freedom? What is an "equitable" distribution of income? How can we measure precisely such abstract goals as "economic freedom"? These objectives are often the subject of spirited public debate.

Also, some of these goals are complementary; when one is achieved, some other one will also be realized. For example, achieving full employment means eliminating unemployment, which is a basic cause of inequitable income distribution. But other goals may conflict or even be mutually exclusive. They may en-

tail **tradeoffs,** meaning that to achieve one we must sacrifice another. For example, efforts to equalize the distribution of income may weaken incentives to work, invest, innovate, and take business risks, all of which promote economic growth. Taxing high-income people heavily and transferring the tax revenues to low-income people is one way to equalize the distribution of income. But then the incentives to high-income individuals may diminish because higher taxes reduce their rewards for working. Similarly, low-income individuals may be less motivated to work when government stands ready to subsidize them.

When goals conflict, society must develop a system of priorities for the objectives it seeks. If more economic freedom is accompanied by less economic security and more economic security allows less economic freedom, society must assess the tradeoffs and decide on the optimal (best) balance between them.

QUICK REVIEW 1-2

■ Economic theories (laws, principles, or models) are generalizations relating to the economic behavior of individuals and institutions; good theories are supported by facts.

■ Induction observes facts and generalizes from them; deduction uses logic to create hypotheses and then tests them with factual data.

■ Policymaking requires a clear statement of goals, a thorough assessment of options, and an unbiased evaluation of results.

■ Some of society's economic goals are complementary, while others conflict; where conflicts exist, tradeoffs arise.

MACROECONOMICS AND MICROECONOMICS

Economists derive and apply principles about economic behavior at two levels.

Macroeconomics

Macroeconomics examines either the economy as a whole or its basic subdivisions or aggregates such as the government, household, and business sectors. An **aggregate** is a collection of specific economic units treated as if they were one unit. Therefore, we might lump together the millions of consumers in the U.S. economy and treat them as if they were one huge unit called "consumers."

In using aggregates, macroeconomics seeks to obtain an overview, or general outline, of the structure of the economy and the relationships of its major aggregates. Macroeconomics speaks of such economic measures as *total* output, *total* employment, *total* income, *aggregate* expenditures, and the *general* level of prices in analyzing various economic problems. No or very little attention is given to specific units making up the various aggregates. Macroeconomics examines the forest, not the trees.

Microeconomics

Microeconomics looks at specific economic units. At this level of analysis, the economist observes the details of an economic unit, or very small segment of the economy, under the figurative microscope. In microeconomics we talk of an individual industry, firm, or household. We measure the price of a *specific* product, the number of workers employed by a *single* firm, the revenue or income of a *particular* firm or household, or the expenditures of a *specific* firm, government entity, or family. In microeconomics, we examine the trees, not the forest.

The macro-micro distinction does not mean that economics is so highly compartmentalized that every topic can be readily labeled as either macro or micro; many topics and subdivisions of economics are rooted in both. Example: While the problem of unemployment is usually treated as a macroeconomic topic (because unemployment relates to *aggregate* spending), economists recognize that the decisions made by *individual* workers in searching for jobs and the way *specific* product and labor markets operate are also critical in determining the unemployment rate. **(Key Question 7)**

Positive and Normative Economics

Both macroeconomics and microeconomics involve facts, theories, and policies. Each contains elements of *positive* economics and *normative* economics. **Positive economics** focuses on facts (once removed at the level of theory) and avoids value judgments. It tries to establish scientific statements about economic behavior. Positive economics deals with what the economy is actually like. Such factually based analysis is critical to good policy analysis.

In contrast, **normative economics** involves value judgments about what the economy should be like or what particular policy actions should be recommended to get it to be that way. Normative economics looks at the desirability of certain aspects of the economy. It underlies expressions of support for particular economic policies.

Positive economics concerns *what is*, while normative economics embodies subjective feelings about *what ought to be*. Examples: Positive statement: "The unemployment rate in several European nations is higher than that in the United States." Normative statement: "European nations ought to undertake policies to reduce their unemployment rates." A second positive statement: "Other things equal, if tuition is increased, enrollment at Gigantic State University will fall." Normative statement: "Tuition should be lowered at GSU so that more students can obtain an education." Whenever words such as "ought" or "should" appear in a sentence, there is a strong chance you are encountering a normative statement.

As you can imagine, most of the disagreement among economists involves normative, value-based policy questions. Of course, there is often some disagreement about which theories or models best represent the economy and its parts. But most economic controversy reflects differing opinions or value judgments about what society itself should be like. **(Key Question 8)**

QUICK REVIEW 1-3

■ Macroeconomics examines the economy as a whole; microeconomics focuses on specific units of the economy.

■ Positive economics deals with factual statements ("what is"); normative economics involves value judgments ("what ought to be").

PITFALLS TO OBJECTIVE THINKING

Because they affect us so personally, we often have difficulty thinking objectively about economic issues. Here are some common pitfalls to avoid in successfully applying the economic perspective.

Biases

Most people bring a bundle of biases and preconceptions to the field of economics. For example, you might think that corporate profits are excessive or that lending money is always superior to borrowing money. Perhaps you believe that government is necessarily less efficient than businesses or that more government regulation is always better than less. Biases cloud thinking and interfere with objective analysis. The beginning economics student must be willing to shed biases and preconceptions which are not supported by facts.

Loaded Terminology

The economic terminology used in newspapers and popular magazines is sometimes emotionally biased, or loaded. The writer or the interest group he or she represents may have a cause to promote or an ax to grind and may slant an article accordingly. High profits may be labeled "obscene," low wages may be called "exploitive," or self-interested behavior may be "greed." Government workers may be referred to as "mindless bureaucrats," and those favoring stronger government regulations may be called "socialists." To objectively analyze economic issues, you must be prepared to reject or discount such terminology.

Definitions

Some of the terms used in economics have precise technical definitions which are quite different from those implied by their common usage. This is generally not a problem if everyone understands these definitions and uses them consistently. For example, "investment" to the average citizen means the purchase of stocks and bonds in security markets, as when someone "invests" in Microsoft stock or government bonds. But to the economist, "investment" means the purchase of real capital assets such as machinery and equipment or the construction of a new factory building. It does not mean the purely financial transaction of swapping cash for securities.

Fallacy of Composition

Another pitfall in economic thinking is the assumption that what is true for one individual or part of a whole is necessarily true for a group of individuals or the whole. This is a logical fallacy called the **fallacy of composition;** the assumption is *not* correct. A statement which is valid for an individual or part is *not* necessarily valid for the larger group or whole.

Consider the following example from outside of economics. You are at a football game and the home team makes an outstanding play. In the excitement, you leap to your feet to get a better view. A valid statement: "If you, *an individual*, stand, your view of the game is improved." But is this also true for the

group—for everyone watching the play? Not necessarily. If *everyone* stands to watch the play, everyone—including you—will probably have a worse view than when all remain seated.

A second example comes from economics: An *individual* farmer who reaps a particularly large crop is likely to realize a sharp gain in income. But this statement cannot be generalized to farmers as a *group*. The individual farmer's large or "bumper" crop will not influence (reduce) crop prices because each farmer produces a negligible fraction of the total farm output. But for *all* farmers as a group, prices decline when total output increases. Thus, if all farmers reap bumper crops, the total output of farm products will rise, depressing crop prices. If the price declines are relatively large, total farm income might actually *fall*.

Recall our earlier distinction between macroeconomics and microeconomics: *The fallacy of composition reminds us that generalizations valid at one of these levels of analysis may or may not be valid at the other.*

Causation Fallacies

Causation is sometimes difficult to identify in economics. Two important fallacies often interfere with economic thinking.

Post Hoc Fallacy You must think very carefully before concluding that because event A precedes event B, A is the cause of B. This kind of faulty reasoning is known as the *post hoc, ergo propter hoc*, or **"after this, therefore because of this" fallacy.**

Example: Suppose that early each spring the medicine man of a tribe performs a special dance. A week or so later the trees and grass turn green. Can we safely conclude that event A, the medicine man's dance, has caused event B, the landscape's turning green? Obviously not. The rooster crows before dawn, but this does not mean the rooster is responsible for the sunrise!

Gigantic State University hires a new basketball coach and the team's record improves. Is the new coach the cause? Maybe. But perhaps the presence of more experienced players or an easier schedule is the true cause.

Correlation versus Causation Do not confuse correlation, or connection, with causation. Correlation between two events or two sets of data indicates they are associated in some systematic and dependable way. For example, we may find that when variable X increases, Y also increases. But this corre-

Fast-Food Lines: An Economic Perspective

How can the economic perspective help us understand the behavior of fast-food consumers?

You enter a fast-food restaurant. Do you immediately look to see which line is the shortest? What do you do when you are in the middle of a long line and a new station opens? Have you ever gone to a fast-food restaurant, seen very long lines, and then left? Have you ever become annoyed when someone in front of you in line placed an order that took a long time to fill?

The economic perspective is useful in analyzing the behavior of fast-food customers. These customers are at the restaurant because they expect the marginal benefit from the food they buy to match or exceed its marginal cost. When customers enter the restaurant, they scurry to the *shortest* line, believing that the shortest line will reduce their time cost of obtaining their food. They are acting purposefully; time is limited and people prefer using it in some way other than standing in line.

If one fast-food line is temporarily shorter than other lines, some people will move toward that line. These movers apparently view the time saving associated with the shorter line to exceed the cost of moving from their present line. The line changing tends to equalize line lengths. No further movement of customers between lines occurs once all lines are about equal.

Fast-food customers face another cost-benefit decision when a clerk opens a new station at the counter. Should they move to the new station or stay put? Those who shift to the new line decide that the time saving from the move exceeds the extra cost of physically moving. In so deciding, customers must also consider just how quickly they can get to the new station compared with others who may

be contemplating the same move. (Those who hesitate in this situation are lost!)

Customers at the fast-food establishment select lines without having perfect information. For example, they do not first survey those in the lines to determine what they are ordering before deciding which line to enter. There are two reasons for this. First, most customers would tell them "It's none of your business," and therefore no information would be forthcoming. Second, even if they could obtain the information, the amount of time necessary to get it (a cost) would most certainly exceed any time saving associated with finding the best line (the benefit). Because information is costly to obtain, fast-food patrons select lines without perfect information. Thus, not all decisions turn out as expected. For example, you might enter a short line and find that the person in front of you is ordering hamburgers and fries for 40 people in the Greyhound bus parked out back! Nevertheless, at the time you made your decision, you thought it was optimal.

Imperfect information also explains why some people who arrive at a fast-food restaurant and observe long lines decide to leave. These people conclude that the marginal cost (monetary plus time costs) of obtaining the fast food is too large relative to the marginal benefit. They would not have come to the restaurant in the first place had they known the lines would be so long. But getting that information by, say, employing an advance scout with a cellular phone would cost more than the perceived benefit.

Finally, customers must decide what to order when they arrive at the counter. In making their choices they again compare marginal costs and marginal benefits in attempting to obtain the greatest personal satisfaction or well-being for their expenditure.

Economists believe that what is true for the behavior of customers at fast-food restaurants is true for economic behavior in general. Faced with an array of choices, consumers, workers, and businesses rationally compare marginal costs and marginal benefits in making decisions.

lation does not necessarily mean that there is causation—that an increase in X is the cause of an increase in Y. The relationship could be purely coincidental or dependent on some other factor, Z, not included in the analysis.

Here is an economic example: Economists have found a positive correlation between education and income. In general, people with more education earn higher incomes than people with less education. Common sense suggests education is the cause and higher incomes are the effect; more education implies a more knowledgeable and productive worker, and such workers receive larger salaries.

But causation could also partly run the other way. People with higher incomes could buy more education, just as they buy more furniture and steaks. Or is part of the relationship explainable in still other ways? Are education and income correlated because the characteristics—ability, motivation, personal habit—required to succeed in education are the same ones required to be a productive and highly paid worker? If so, then people with those traits will probably obtain more education *and* earn higher incomes. But greater education will not be the sole cause of the higher income. **(Key Question 9)**

A LOOK AHEAD

The ideas in this chapter will come into much sharper focus as you advance through Part 1, where we develop specific economic principles and models. Specifically, in Chapter 2 we build a model of the production choices facing an economy. In Chapter 3 we develop a model that will help you understand how prices and quantities of goods and services are established in individual markets. In Chapter 4 we combine all markets in the economy to see how the so-called *market system* works. Finally, in Chapters 5 and 6 we examine important sectors (components) of the economy, specifically, the private sector, the government sector, and the international sector.

CHAPTER SUMMARY

1. Economics is the study of the efficient use of scarce resources in the production of goods and services to satisfy as many wants as possible.

2. The economic perspective includes three elements: scarcity and choice, rational behavior, and marginalism. It sees individuals and institutions making rational decisions based on comparisons of marginal costs and marginal benefits.

3. A knowledge of economics contributes to effective citizenship and provides useful insights for politicians, consumers, and workers.

4. The tasks of empirical economics are **(a)** gathering economic facts relevant to a particular problem or specific segment of the economy, and **(b)** testing hypotheses against the facts to validate theories.

5. Generalizations stated by economists are called principles, theories, laws, or models. The derivation of these principles is the object of theoretical economics.

6. Induction distills theories from facts; deduction uses logic to derive hypotheses that are then tested against facts.

7. Economic principles are valuable predictors. They are the bases for economic policy, which is designed to identify and solve problems and control undesirable events.

8. Our society accepts certain shared economic goals, including economic growth, full employment, economic efficiency, price-level stability, economic freedom, equity in the distribution of income, economic security, and a reasonable balance in our international trade and finance. Some of these goals are complementary; others entail tradeoffs.

9. Macroeconomics looks at the economy as a whole or its major aggregates; microeconomics examines specific economic units or institutions.

10. Positive statements state facts ("what is"); normative statements express value judgments ("what ought to be").

11. In studying economics we encounter such pitfalls as biases and preconceptions, unfamiliar or confusing terminology, the fallacy of composition, and the difficulty of establishing clear cause-effect relationships.

TERMS AND CONCEPTS

economics	induction	policy economics	positive economics
economic perspective	deduction	tradeoffs	normative economics
marginal analysis	generalizations	macroeconomics	fallacy of composition
theoretical economics	"other-things-equal"	aggregate	"after this, therefore
principles	assumption	microeconomics	because of this" fallacy

STUDY QUESTIONS

1. KEY QUESTION Use the economic perspective to explain why someone who is normally a light eater at a standard restaurant may become somewhat of a glutton at a buffet-style restaurant which charges a single price for all you can eat.

2. Distinguish between the inductive and deductive methods for establishing economic principles. Why must both methods ultimately involve gathering facts?

3. Why is it significant that economics is not a laboratory science? What problems may be involved in deriving and applying economic principles?

4. Explain the following statements:
   a. Good economic policy requires good economic theory.
   b. Generalization and abstraction are nearly synonymous.
   c. Facts serve to sort out good and bad theories.
   d. The *other things equal assumption* helps isolate key economic relationships.

5. KEY QUESTION Explain in detail the interrelationships between economic facts, theory, and policy. Critically evaluate this statement: "The trouble with economic theory is that it is not practical. It is detached from the real world."

6. To what extent do you accept the eight economic goals stated and described in this chapter? What priorities do you assign to them?

7. KEY QUESTION Indicate whether each of the following statements applies to microeconomics or macroeconomics:
   a. The unemployment rate in the United States was 4.9 percent in August 1997.
   b. The Alpo dogfood plant in Bowser, Iowa, laid off 15 workers last month.
   c. An unexpected freeze in central Florida reduced the citrus crop and caused the price of oranges to rise.
   d. Our national output, adjusted for inflation, grew by 2 percent in 1995.
   e. Last week Wells Fargo Bank lowered its interest rate on business loans by one-half of 1 percentage point.
   f. The consumer price index rose by 2.3 percent in 1997.

8. KEY QUESTION Identify each of the following as either a positive or a normative statement:
   a. The high temperature today was 89 degrees.
   b. It was too hot today.
   c. The general price level rose by 4.4 percent last year.
   d. Inflation eroded living standards last year and should be reduced by government policies.

9. KEY QUESTION Explain and give an example of (a) the fallacy of composition, and (b) the "after this, therefore because of this" fallacy. Why are cause-and-effect relationships difficult to isolate in economics?

10. Suppose studies show that students who study more hours receive higher grades. Does this relationship guarantee that any particular student who studies longer will get higher grades?

11. Studies indicate that married men on average earn more income than unmarried men of the same age. Why must we be cautious in concluding that marriage is the *cause* and higher income is the *effect*?

12. (Last Word) Use the economic perspective to explain the behavior of the *workers* (rather than the customers) observed at a fast-food restaurant. Why are these workers there, rather than, say, cruising around in their cars? Why do they work so diligently? Why do so many of them quit these jobs once they have graduated from high school?

13. WEB-BASED QUESTION Economic Goals— **Are They Being Achieved?** The three primary economic goals are economic growth, full employment, and price-level stability. The White House http://www.whitehouse.gov/fsbr/esbr.html provides links to economic information produced by a number of federal agencies. Visit their links for Output, Income, Expenditures, and Wealth, and Employment, Unemployment, and Earnings.

14. WEB-BASED QUESTION Normative Economics—**Republicans versus Democrats** Many economic policy statements made by both the Republicans http://www.rnc.org/ and the Democrats http://www.democrats.org/ are normative rather than positive economic statements. Visit both the Republican and Democratic Web sites and compare and contrast their views on how to achieve economic goals. How much of the rhetoric is based on positive statements compared with normative statements?

Graphs and Their Meaning

If you glance quickly through this text, you will find many graphs. Some seem simple, while others seem more formidable. All are important. They are included to help you visualize and understand economic relationships. Physicists and chemists sometimes illustrate their theories by building arrangements of multicolored wooden balls, representing protons, neutrons, and electrons, which are held in proper relation to one another by wires or sticks. Economists most often use graphs to illustrate their models. By understanding these "pictures," you can more readily comprehend economic relationships. Most of our principles or models explain relationships between just two sets of economic facts, which can be conveniently represented with two-dimensional graphs.

Construction of a Graph

A graph is a visual representation of the relationship between two variables. Table 1 is a hypothetical illustration showing the relationship between income and consumption for the economy as a whole. Without even studying economics, we would expect intuitively that people would buy more goods and services when their incomes go up. Thus we are not surprised to find in Table 1 that total consumption in the economy increases as total income rises.

The information in Table 1 is expressed graphically in Figure 1. Here is how it is done: We want to show visually or graphically how consumption changes as income changes. Since income is the determining factor, we represent it on the **horizontal axis** of the graph, as is customary. And because consumption depends on income, we represent it on the **vertical axis** of the graph, as is also customary. Actually, what we are doing is representing the *independent variable* on the horizontal axis and the *dependent variable* on the vertical axis.

Now we arrange the vertical and horizontal scales of the graph to reflect the ranges of values of consumption and income, and we mark the scales in convenient increments. As you can see, the values marked on the scales cover all the values in Table 1. The increments on both scales are $100 for approximately each $\frac{1}{2}$ inch.

Because the graph has two dimensions, each point within it represents an income value and its associated consumption value. To find a point that represents one of the five income-consumption combinations in Table 1, we draw perpendiculars from the appropriate values on the vertical and horizontal axes. For example, to plot point *c* (the $200 income–$150 consumption point), perpendiculars are drawn up from the horizontal (income) axis at $200 and across from the vertical (consumption) axis at $150. These perpendiculars intersect at point *c*, which represents this particular income-consumption combination. You should verify that the other income-consumption combinations shown in Table 1 are properly located in Figure 1. Finally, by assuming that the same general relationship between income and consumption prevails for all other incomes, we draw a line or smooth curve to connect these points. That line or curve represents the income-consumption relationship.

If the graph is a straight line, as in Figure 1, we say the relationship is *linear*.

Direct and Inverse Relationships

The line in Figure 1 slopes upward to the right, so it depicts a direct relationship between income and con-

TABLE 1 The relationship between income and consumption

Income per week	Consumption per week	Point
$ 0	$ 50	a
100	100	b
200	150	c
300	200	d
400	250	e

TABLE 2 The relationship between ticket prices and attendance

Ticket price	Attendance, thousands	Point
$25	0	a
20	4	b
15	8	c
10	12	d
5	16	e
0	20	f

sumption. By a **direct relationship** (or positive relationship) we mean that two variables—in this case, consumption and income—change in the *same* direction. An increase in consumption is associated with an increase in income; a decrease in consumption accompanies a decrease in income. When two sets of data are positively or directly related, they always graph as an *upsloping* line, as in Figure 1.

In contrast, two sets of data may be inversely related. Consider Table 2, which shows the relationship between the price of basketball tickets and game attendance at Gigantic State University. Here we have a negative or **inverse relationship** because the two variables change in *opposite* directions. When ticket prices decrease, attendance increases. When ticket prices increase, attendance decreases. The six data points in Table 2 are plotted in Figure 2. Observe that an inverse relationship always graphs as a *downsloping* line.

Dependent and Independent Variables

Although it is not always easy, economists seek to determine which variable is the "cause" and which is the "effect." Or, more formally, they seek the independent variable and the dependent variable. The **independent variable** is the cause or source; it is the variable that changes first. The **dependent variable** is the effect or outcome; it is the variable which changes because of the change in the independent variable. As noted in our income-consumption example, income generally is the independent variable and consumption the dependent variable. Income causes consumption to be what it is rather than the other way around. Similarly, ticket

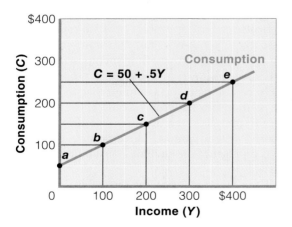

FIGURE 1 **Graphing the direct relationship between consumption and income** Two sets of data which are positively or directly related, such as consumption and income, graph as an upsloping line.

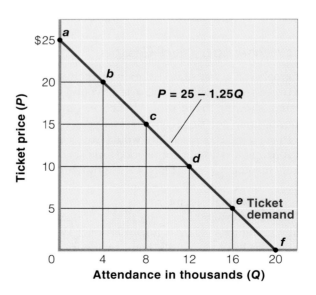

FIGURE 2 **Graphing the inverse relationship between ticket prices and game attendance** Two sets of data which are negatively or inversely related, such as ticket price and the attendance at basketball games, graph as a downsloping line.

prices determine attendance at GSU basketball games; attendance does not determine ticket prices. Ticket price is the independent variable, and the quantity of tickets purchased is the dependent variable.

You may recall from your high school courses that mathematicians always put the independent variable (cause) on the horizontal axis and the dependent variable (effect) on the vertical axis. Economists are less tidy; their graphing of independent and dependent variables is more arbitrary. Their conventional graphing of the income-consumption relationship is consistent with mathematical presentation, but economists put price and cost data on the vertical axis. Hence, economists' graphing of GSU's ticket price–attendance data conflicts with normal mathematical procedure.

Other Things Equal

Our simple two-variable graphs purposely ignore many other factors which might affect the amount of consumption occurring at each income level or the number of people who attend GSU basketball games at each possible ticket price. When economists plot the relationship between any two variables, they invoke the *ceteris paribus* (other things equal) assumption. Thus, in Figure 1 all factors other than income which might affect the amount of consumption are presumed to be constant or unchanged. Similarly, in Figure 2 all factors other than ticket price which might influence attendance at GSU basketball games are assumed constant. In reality, "other things" are not equal; they often change, and when they do, the relationship represented in our two tables and graphs will change. Specifically, the lines we have plotted would shift to new locations.

Consider a stock market "crash." The dramatic drop in the value of stocks might cause people to feel less wealthy and therefore less willing to consume at each level of income. The result might be a downward shift of the consumption line. To see this, you should plot a new consumption line in Figure 1, assuming that consumption is, say, $20 less at each income level. Note that the relationship remains direct; the line merely shifts downward to reflect less consumption spending at each income level.

Similarly, factors other than ticket prices might affect GSU game attendance. If a professional basketball team locates in the same city as GSU, attendance at GSU games might be less at each ticket price. To see this, redraw Figure 2, assuming that 2000 fewer students attend GSU games at each ticket price. **(Key Appendix Question 2)**

Slope of a Line

Lines can be described in terms of their slopes. The **slope of a straight line** is the ratio of the vertical change (the rise or drop) to the horizontal change (the run) between any two points of the line.

Positive Slope   Between point *b* and point *c* in Figure 1 the rise or vertical change (the change in consumption) is +$50 and the run or horizontal change (the change in income) is +$100. Therefore:

$$\text{Slope} = \frac{\text{vertical change}}{\text{horizontal change}} = \frac{+50}{+100} = \frac{1}{2} = .5$$

Note that our slope of $\frac{1}{2}$ or .5 is positive because consumption and income change in the same direction; that is, consumption and income are directly or positively related.

The slope of .5 tells us there will be a $1 increase in consumption for every $2 increase in income. Similarly, it indicates that for every $2 decrease in income there will be a $1 decrease in consumption.

Negative Slope   Between any two of the identified points in Figure 2, say, point *c* and point *d*, the vertical change is −5 (the drop) and the horizontal change is +4 (the run). Therefore:

$$\text{Slope} = \frac{\text{vertical change}}{\text{horizontal change}} = \frac{-5}{+4} = -1\frac{1}{4} = -1.25$$

This slope is negative because ticket price and attendance have an inverse relationship.

Note that on the horizontal axis attendance is stated in thousands of people. So the slope of −5/+4 or −1.25 means that lowering the price by $5 will increase attendance by 4000 people. This is the same as saying that a $1.25 price reduction will increase attendance by 1000 persons.

Slopes and Measurement Units   The slope of a line will be affected by the choice of units for either variable. If, in our ticket price illustration, we had chosen to measure attendance in individual people, our horizontal change would have been 4000 and the slope would have been

$$\text{Slope} = \frac{-5}{+4000} = \frac{-1}{+800} = -.00125$$

The slope depends on the way the relevant variables are measured.

Slopes and Marginal Analysis   Recall that economics is largely concerned with changes from the status quo. The concept of slope is important in economics because it reflects marginal changes—those involving 1 more (or 1 less) unit. For example, in Figure 1 the .5 slope shows that $.50 of extra or marginal consumption is associated with each $1 increase in income. In this example, people collectively will consume $.50 of any $1 increase in their incomes and reduce their consumption by $.50 for each $1 decline in income.

Infinite and Zero Slopes   Many variables are unrelated or independent of one another. For example, the quantity of wristwatches purchased is not related to the price of bananas. In Figure 3a we represent the price of bananas on the vertical axis and the quantity of watches demanded on the horizontal axis. The graph of their relationship is the line parallel to the vertical axis, indicating that the same quantity of watches is purchased no matter what the price of bananas. The slope of such a line is *infinite*.

Similarly, aggregate consumption is completely unrelated to the nation's divorce rate. In Figure 3b we put consumption on the vertical axis and the divorce rate on the horizontal axis. The line parallel to the horizontal axis represents this lack of relatedness. This line has a slope of *zero*.

Vertical Intercept

A line can be located on a graph (without plotting points) if we know its slope and its vertical intercept. The **vertical intercept** of a line is the point where the line meets the vertical axis. In Figure 1 the intercept is $50. This intercept means that if current income were zero, consumers would still spend $50. They might do this through borrowing or by selling off some of their assets. Similarly, the vertical intercept in Figure 2 shows that at a $25 ticket price, GSU's basketball team would be playing in an empty arena.

Equation of a Linear Relationship

If we know the vertical intercept and slope, we can describe a line succinctly in equation form. In its general form, the equation of a line is

$$y = a + bx$$

where y = dependent variable
  a = vertical intercept
  b = slope of line
  x = independent variable

For our income-consumption example, if C represents consumption (the dependent variable) and Y represents income (the independent variable), we can write $C = a + bY$. By substituting the known values of the intercept and the slope, we get

$$C = 50 + .5Y$$

This equation also allows us to determine the amount of consumption C at any specific level of income. You should use it to confirm that at the $250 income level, consumption is $175.

When economists reverse mathematical convention by putting the independent variable on the vertical axis and the dependent variable on the horizontal axis, then y stands for the independent variable, rather than the dependent variable in the general form. We noted previously that this case is relevant for our GSU ticket price–attendance data. If P represents the ticket price (independent variable) and Q represents attendance (dependent variable), their relationship is given by

$$P = 25 - 1.25Q$$

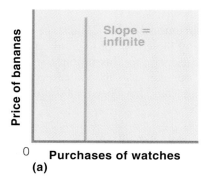

(a)

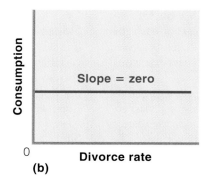

(b)

FIGURE 3 **Infinite and zero slopes** (a) A line parallel to the vertical axis has an infinite slope. Here, purchases of watches remain the same no matter what happens to the price of bananas. (b) A line parallel to the horizontal axis has a slope of zero. Here, consumption remains the same no matter what happens to the divorce rate. In both (a) and (b), the two variables are totally unrelated to one another.

where the vertical intercept is 25 and the negative slope is $-1\frac{1}{4}$ or -1.25. Knowing the value of P lets us solve for Q, our dependent variable. You should use this equation to predict GSU ticket sales when the ticket price is $7.50. **(Key Appendix Question 3)**

Slope of a Nonlinear Curve

We now move from the simple world of linear relationships (straight lines) to the more complex world of nonlinear relationships. The slope of a straight line is the same at all its points. The slope of a line representing a nonlinear relationship changes from one point to another. Such lines are referred to as *curves*. (It is also permissible to refer to a straight line as a "curve.")

Consider the downsloping curve in Figure 4. Its slope is negative throughout, but the curve flattens as we move down along it. Thus, its slope constantly changes; the curve has a different slope at each point.

To measure the slope at a specific point, we draw a straight line tangent to the curve at that point. A line is *tangent* at a point if it touches, but does not intersect, the curve at that point. Thus line *aa* is tangent to the curve in Figure 4 at point *A*. The slope of the curve at that point is equal to the slope of the tangent line. Specifically, the total vertical change (drop) in the tangent line *aa* is -20 and the total horizontal change (run) is $+5$. Because the slope of the tangent

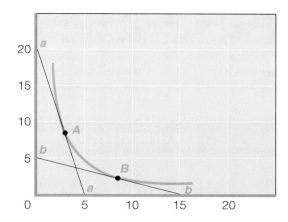

FIGURE 4 **Determining the slopes of curves** The slope of a nonlinear curve changes from point to point on the curve. The slope at any point (say, *B*) can be determined by drawing a straight line tangent to that point (line *bb*) and calculating the slope of that line.

line *aa* is $-20/+5$, or -4, the slope of the curve at point *A* is also -4.

Line *bb* in Figure 4 is tangent to the curve at point *B*. Following the same procedure, we find the slope at *B* to be $-5/+15$, or $-\frac{1}{3}$. Thus, in this flatter part of the curve, the slope is less negative. **(Key Appendix Question 6)**

APPENDIX SUMMARY

1. Graphs are a convenient and revealing way to represent economic relationships.

2. Two variables are positively or directly related when their values change in the same direction. The line (curve) representing two directly related variables slopes upward.

3. Two variables are negatively or inversely related when their values change in opposite directions. The curve representing two inversely related variables slopes downward.

4. The value of the dependent variable (the "effect") is determined by the value of the independent variable (the "cause").

5. When the "other factors" which might affect a two-variable relationship are allowed to change, the graph of the relationship will likely shift to a new location.

6. The slope of a straight line is the ratio of the vertical change to the horizontal change between any two points. The slope of an upsloping line is positive; the slope of a downsloping line is negative.

7. The slope of a line or curve depends on the units used in measuring the variables. It is especially relevant for economics because it measures marginal changes.

8. The slope of a horizontal line is zero; the slope of a vertical line is infinite.

9. The vertical intercept and slope of a line determine its location; they are used in expressing the line—and the relationship between the two variables—as an equation.

10. The slope of a curve at any point is determined by calculating the slope of a straight line tangent to the curve at that point.

APPENDIX TERMS AND CONCEPTS - - - - - - - - - - - - - - - - - -

horizontal axis   direct relationship   independent variable   slope of a straight line
vertical axis   inverse relationship   dependent variable   vertical intercept

APPENDIX STUDY QUESTIONS -

1. Briefly explain the use of graphs as a way to represent economic relationships. What is an inverse relationship? How does it graph? What is a direct relationship? How does it graph? Graph and explain the relationships you would expect to find between **(a)** the number of inches of rainfall per month and the sale of umbrellas, **(b)** the amount of tuition and the level of enrollment at a university, and **(c)** the size of a university's athletic scholarships and the number of games won by its football team.

In each case cite and explain how variables other than those specifically mentioned might upset the expected relationship. Is your graph in part b, above, consistent with the fact that, historically, enrollments and tuition have both increased? If not, explain any difference.

2. KEY APPENDIX QUESTION Indicate how each of the following might affect the data shown in Table 2 and Figure 2 of this appendix:
   a. GSU's athletic director schedules higher-quality opponents.
   b. GSU's Fighting Aardvarks experience three losing seasons.
   c. GSU contracts to have all its home games televised.

3. KEY APPENDIX QUESTION The following table contains data on the relationship between saving and income. Rearrange these data into a meaningful order and graph them on the accompanying grid. What is the slope of the line? The vertical intercept? Interpret the meaning of both the slope and the intercept. Write the equation which represents this line. What would you predict saving to be at the $12,500 level of income?

Income (per year)	Saving (per year)
$15,000	$1,000
0	−500
10,000	500
5,000	0
20,000	1,500

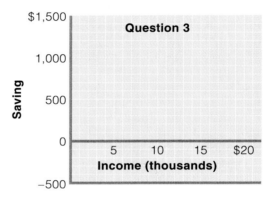

4. Construct a table from the data shown on the graph below. Which is the dependent variable and which the independent variable? Summarize the data in equation form.

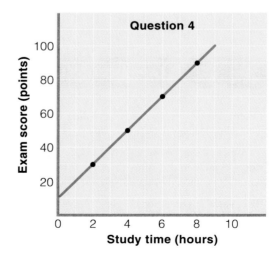

5. Suppose that when the interest rate which must be paid to borrow funds is 16 percent, businesses find it unprofitable to invest in machinery and equipment. However, when the interest rate is 14 percent, $5 billion worth of investment is profitable. At 12 percent interest, a total of $10 billion of investment is profitable. Similarly, total investment increases by $5 billion for each successive 2-percentage-point decline in the interest rate. Describe the relevant relationship between the interest rate and investment in words, in a table, graphically, and as an equation. Put the interest rate on the vertical axis and investment on the horizontal axis. In your equation use the form $i = a + bI$, where i is the interest rate, a is the vertical intercept, b is the slope of the line (which is negative), and I is the level of investment. Comment on the advantages and disadvantages of the verbal, tabular, graphical, and equation forms of description.

6. KEY APPENDIX QUESTION The accompanying graph shows curve XX' and tangents at points A, B, and C. Calculate the slope of the curve at these three points.

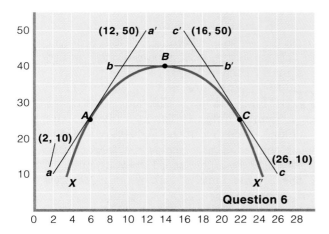

Question 6

7. In the accompanying graph, is the slope of curve AA' positive or negative? Does the slope increase or decrease as we move along the curve from A to A'? Answer the same two questions for curve BB'.

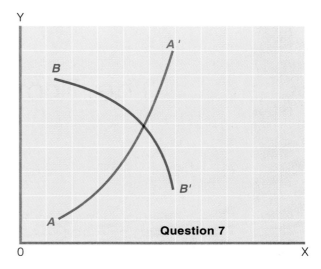

Question 7

2

The Economizing Problem

You make decisions every day that capture the essence of economics. Suppose you have $40 and are deciding how to spend it. Should you buy a pair of new jeans? Two or three compact discs? A ticket for a music concert?

Similarly, what should you do with your time between 3 and 6 o'clock on, say, a Thursday afternoon? Should you work extra hours at your part-time job? Do research on a term project? Prepare for an economics quiz? Watch TV? Take a nap?

Money and time are both scarce, and making decisions in the context of scarcity always means there are costs. If you choose the jeans, the cost is the forgone CDs or concert. If you nap or watch TV, the cost might be a low score on your quiz.

Scarcity, choices, and costs—these are the key elements of this chapter. Here we introduce and explore the fundamentals of economic science. We first illustrate, extend, and modify our definition of economics and explore the so-called *economizing problem* by means of a model. Next, we briefly survey the ways diverse economies respond to the economizing problem. Finally, we develop an overview of the market system in the form of the circular flow model.

THE FOUNDATION OF ECONOMICS

Two fundamental facts together constitute the **economizing problem** and provide a foundation for the field of economics:

1. *Society's material wants, that is, the material wants of its citizens and institutions, are virtually unlimited and insatiable.*

2. *Economic resources—the means of producing goods and services—are limited or scarce.*

You must fully understand these two facts because all that follows depends directly on them.

Unlimited Wants

In stating the first fact, what do we mean by "material wants?" We mean, first, the desires of consumers to obtain and use various goods and services that provide **utility,** meaning pleasure or satisfaction.[1] An amazingly wide range of products accomplishes this, from houses and automobiles to toothpaste, pizzas, sweaters, and hamburgers. Innumerable prod-

---

[1]This definition leaves a variety of wants—recognition, status, love, and so forth—for the other social sciences to examine and study.

ucts sometimes classified as *necessities* (food, shelter, and clothing) and *luxuries* (perfumes, yachts, racecars) can satisfy human wants. Of course, what is a luxury to Smith may be a necessity to Jones, and what is a necessity today may have been a luxury a few years ago.

Services satisfy our wants as much as products do. Repair work on a car, the removal of an inflamed appendix, legal and accounting advice, and haircuts and hairstyling all satisfy human wants. Actually, we buy many goods, such as automobiles and washing machines, for the services they render. Thus, the differences between goods and services are often smaller than they would appear to be.

"Wants" also include the desires of businesses and units of government to satisfy material goals. Businesses want factory buildings, machinery, trucks, warehouses, communication systems, and other things that help them achieve their production goals. Government, reflecting the collective wants of its citizenry or goals of its own, seeks highways, mass transit systems, schools, and military equipment.

We say that, as a group, these wants are *insatiable*, or *unlimited*, meaning that our desires for goods and services cannot be completely satisfied. Our desires for a *particular* good or service can be satisfied; over a short period of time we can surely get enough toothpaste or pasta. And one appendicitis operation is plenty.

But goods *in general* are another story. We do not, and presumably cannot, get enough. A simple mental experiment can help verify this: Suppose all members of society were asked to list the goods and services they would buy if they had unlimited income. Do you imagine that their list would ever end?

Furthermore, over time, wants multiply. As we fill some of the wants on the list, new ones pop up. Material wants have a high reproduction rate. The rapid introduction of new products whets our appetites, and extensive advertising persuades us that we need items we might not otherwise have desired. Not long ago, we did not want personal computers, Internet service, video recorders, fax machines, and compact discs because they did not exist. Also, we often cannot stop with simple satisfaction: The acquisition of an Escort or Geo has been known to whet the appetite for a Porsche or Mercedes.

At any specific time the individuals and institutions constituting society have innumerable unfulfilled material wants. Some wants—food, clothing, shelter—have biological roots. But some are also influenced by the conventions and customs of society. The specific kinds of food, clothing, and shelter we seek are frequently determined by the general social and cultural environment in which we live. Over time, wants change and multiply, fueled by the development of new products and extensive promotion.

The overall objective of all economic activity is to satisfy these diverse material wants.

Scarce Resources

In stating the second fundamental fact—*economic resources are limited or scarce*—what do we mean by **economic resources?** In general, we mean all natural, human, and manufactured resources which go into the production of goods and services. This covers a lot of ground: all the factory and farm buildings and all the equipment, tools, and machinery used to produce manufactured goods and agricultural products; all transportation and communication facilities; the innumerable types of labor; and land and mineral resources of all kinds. Economists broadly classify these as either *property* resources—land or raw materials and capital—or *human* resources—labor and entrepreneurial ability.

Resource Categories   Let's examine four specific categories of resources.

Land   Land means much more to the economist than to most people. Land is all natural resources—all "gifts of nature"—usable in the production process. Such resources as arable land, forests, mineral and oil deposits, and water resources come under this classification.

Capital   Capital (or *capital goods* or *investment goods*) includes all manufactured aids to production, that is, all tools, machinery, equipment, and factory, storage, transportation, and distribution facilities used in producing goods and services and getting them to the ultimate consumer. The process of producing and purchasing capital goods is known as **investment.**

Two other points are pertinent. First, *capital goods* differ from *consumer goods* since the latter satisfy wants directly, while the former do so indirectly by aiding production of consumer goods. Second, the term "capital" as here defined does *not* refer to money. True, business executives and economists often talk of "money capital," meaning money available to purchase machinery, equipment, and other productive facilities. But money, as such, produces nothing, so it is not an economic resource. *Real capital*—tools, machinery, and other productive equipment—is an economic resource; *money* or *financial capital* is not.

Labor Labor is a broad term for all the physical and mental talents of individuals available and usable in producing goods and services. (This *excludes* a special set of talents—entrepreneurial ability—which, because of its special significance in a capitalistic economy, we consider separately.) The services of a logger, retail clerk, machinist, teacher, professional football player, and nuclear physicist all fall under the general heading "labor."

Entrepreneurial Ability Finally, there is the special human resource we label **entrepreneurial ability** or, simply, *enterprise*. The entrepreneur performs four related functions:

1. The entrepreneur *takes the initiative* in combining the resources of land, capital, and labor to produce a good or service. Both a sparkplug and a catalyst, the entrepreneur is the driving force behind production and the agent who combines the other resources in what is hoped will be a successful business venture.

2. The entrepreneur *makes basic business-policy decisions*, that is, those nonroutine decisions which set the course of a business enterprise.

3. The entrepreneur *is an innovator*—the one who attempts to introduce on a commercial basis new products, new productive techniques, or even new forms of business organization.

4. The entrepreneur *is a risk bearer.* This is apparent from a close examination of the other three entrepreneurial functions. The entrepreneur in a capitalistic system has no guarantee of profit. The reward for his or her time, efforts, and abilities may be profits *or* losses and eventual bankruptcy. The entrepreneur risks not only time, effort, and business reputation but his or her invested funds and those of associates or stockholders.

Since these four resources—land, labor, capital, and entrepreneurial ability—are combined to *produce* goods and services, they are called the **factors of production.**

Resource Payments The income received from supplying raw materials and capital equipment (the property resources) is called *rental income* and *interest*

income, respectively. The income accruing to those who supply labor is called *wages*, which includes salaries and all wage and salary supplements such as bonuses, commissions, and royalties. Entrepreneurial income is called *profits*, which may be negative—that is, losses.

Relative Scarcity The four types of economic resources, or factors of production, or *inputs*, have one fundamental characteristic in common: *They are scarce or limited in supply.* Our "spaceship earth" contains only limited amounts of resources to use in producing goods and services. Quantities of arable land, mineral deposits, capital equipment, and labor (time) are all limited; they are available only in finite amounts. Because of the scarcity of productive resources and the constraint that this scarcity puts on productive activity, output itself is limited. Society is not able to produce and consume all the goods and services it wants. Thus, in the United States, one of the most affluent nations, output per person was limited to $28,500 in 1996. In the poorest nations, annual output per person is as low as $200 or $300!

ECONOMICS: EMPLOYMENT AND EFFICIENCY

The economizing problem is thus at the heart of the definition of economics, first stated in Chapter 1: *Economics is the social science concerned with the problem of using scarce resources to attain the maximum fulfillment of society's unlimited wants.* Economics is concerned with "doing the best with what we have." Because our resources are scarce, we cannot satisfy all our unlimited wants. The next best thing is to achieve the greatest possible satisfaction of those wants.

Economics is thus a science of efficiency—the best use of scarce resources. Society wants to use its limited resources efficiently; it desires to produce as many goods and services as possible from its available resources, so that it maximizes total satisfaction. To realize this outcome, it must achieve both full employment and full production.

Full Employment: Using Available Resources

By **full employment** we mean the use of all available resources. No workers should be involuntarily out of work; the economy should provide employment for all who are willing and able to work. Nor should capital equipment or arable land sit idle. But note that we say all *available* resources should be employed. Each society has certain customs and practices which determine what particular resources are available for employment. For example, in most countries legislation and custom provide that children and the very aged should not be employed. Similarly, to maintain productivity, it is desirable to allow farmland to lie fallow periodically. And it is desirable to "conserve" some resources for use by future generations.

Full Production: Using Resources Efficiently

The employment of all available resources is not enough to achieve efficiency. Full production must also be realized. By **full production** we mean that all employed resources should be used so that they provide the maximum possible satisfaction of our material wants. If we fail to realize full production, economists say our resources are *underemployed*.

Full production implies two kinds of efficiency—productive and allocative efficiency:

1. **Productive efficiency** is the production of *any particular mix of goods and services in the least costly way*. When we produce, say, compact discs at the lowest achievable unit cost, we are expending the smallest amount of resources to produce CDs and therefore making available the largest amount of resources to produce other desired products. Suppose society has only $100 of resources available. If we can produce a CD for only $5 of resources, then $95 of resources will be available to produce other goods. This is clearly better than producing the CD for $10 and having only $90 of resources for alternative uses.

   In real-world terms, productive efficiency requires that Ford pickups and Dodge vans be produced with computerized and roboticized assembly techniques. It would be wasteful of scarce resources—that is, inefficient—to use the primitive assembly lines of the 1920s. Similarly, it would be inefficient to have farmers harvesting wheat with scythes or picking corn by hand since mechanical harvesting equipment is available to do the job at a much lower cost per unit.

2. **Allocative efficiency** is the production of *that particular mix of goods and services most wanted by society*. For example, society wants resources allocated to compact discs and cassettes, not to 45 rpm records. We want personal computers (PCs), not manual typewriters. Furthermore, we do not want to devote *all* our resources to producing CDs and PCs; we want to assign some of them to producing automobiles and office buildings. Allocative efficiency requires that the "right" mix of goods and services be produced—each item at least unit cost. It means apportioning limited resources among firms and industries in such a way that society obtains the combination of goods and services which it wants the most. **(Key Question 5)**

Production Possibilities Table

Because resources are scarce, a full-employment, full-production economy cannot have an unlimited output of goods and services. Therefore, people must choose which goods and services to produce and which to forgo. The necessity and consequences of these choices can best be understood through a production possibilities model. Let's examine the model first as a table, then as a graph.

Assumptions We begin our discussion with four simplifying assumptions:

1. *Full employment and productive efficiency* The economy is employing all its available resources (full employment) and producing goods and services at least cost (productive efficiency). We will consider allocative efficiency later.

2. *Fixed resources* The available supplies of the factors of production are fixed in both quantity and quality. Nevertheless, they can be reallocated, within limits, among different uses; for example, land can be used for factory sites or for food production.

3. *Fixed technology*   The state of technology—the methods used to produce output—does not change during our analysis. This assumption and the previous one imply that we are looking at an economy at one specific time or over a very short period of time. Later in the analysis, we will examine the situation over a longer period.

4. *Two goods*   The economy is producing only two goods: pizzas and industrial robots. Pizza symbolizes **consumer goods,** products which satisfy our wants *directly*; industrial robots symbolize **capital goods,** products which satisfy our wants *indirectly* by enabling more efficient production of consumer goods.

The Need for Choice   From our assumptions, we see that society must choose among alternatives. Limited resources mean limited outputs of pizza and robots. And since all available resources are fully employed, to increase the production of robots we must shift resources away from the production of pizza. The reverse is also true: To increase the production of pizza, we must take resources from the production of robots. There is no such thing as a free pizza. This, recall, is the essence of the economizing problem.

A **production possibilities table** lists the different combinations of two products which can be produced with a specific set of resources (and with full employment *and* productive efficiency). Table 2-1 is such a table for a pizza-robot economy; the data are, of course, hypothetical. At alternative A, this economy would be devoting all its available resources to the production of robots (capital goods); at alternative E, all resources would go to pizza production (consumer goods). Those alternatives are unrealistic extremes; an economy typically produces both capital and consumer goods, as in B, C, and D. As we move

from alternative A to E, we increase the production of pizza at the expense of robot production.

Because consumer goods satisfy our wants directly, any movement toward E looks tempting. In producing more pizzas, society increases the current satisfaction of its wants. But there is a cost: fewer robots. This shift of resources to consumer goods catches up with society over time as the stock of capital goods dwindles—or at least ceases to expand at the current rate—with the result that some potential for greater production is lost. By moving toward alternative E, society chooses "more now" at the expense of "much more later."

By moving toward A, society chooses to forgo current consumption. The sacrifice of current consumption frees resources which can be used to increase the production of capital goods. By building up its stock of capital this way, society will have greater future production and, therefore, greater future consumption. By moving toward A, society is choosing "more later" at the cost of "less now."

Generalization: *At any point in time, an economy achieving full employment and productive efficiency must sacrifice some of one good to obtain more of another good. Scarce resources prohibit such an economy from having more of both goods.*

Production Possibilities Curve

The data and ideas of a production possibilities table can also be shown graphically. We use a simple two-dimensional graph, arbitrarily representing the output of capital goods (here, robots) on the vertical axis and the output of consumer goods (here, pizza) on the horizontal axis, as shown in **Figure 2-1 (Key Graph).** Following the procedure given in the appendix to Chapter 1, we graph a **production possibilities curve.**

Each point on the production possibilities curve represents some maximum output of the two products. The curve is a production *frontier* because it shows the limit of attainable outputs. To obtain the various combinations of pizza and robots that fall *on* the production possibilities curve, society must achieve both full employment and productive efficiency. Points lying *inside* (to the left of) the curve are also attainable but not as desirable as points on the curve. Points inside the curve imply that the economy could have more of both robots and pizza if it achieved full employment and productive efficiency. Points lying *outside* (to the right of) the production possibilities

TABLE 2-1   Production possibilities of pizza and robots with full employment and productive efficiency

Type of product	Production alternatives				
	A	B	C	D	E
Pizza (in hundred thousands)	0	1	2	3	4
Robots (in thousands)	10	9	7	4	0

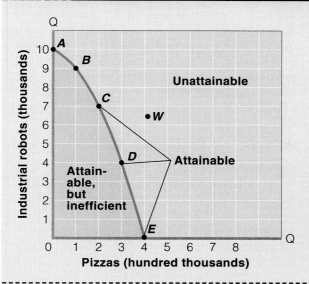

FIGURE 2-1 The production possibilities curve Each point on the production possibilities curve represents some maximum combination of two products which can be produced if full employment and full production are achieved. When operating on the curve, more robots means less pizza, and vice versa. Limited resources and a fixed technology make any combination of robots and pizza lying outside the curve (such as at *W*) unattainable. Points inside the curve are attainable, but they indicate that full employment and productive efficiency are not being realized.

QUICK QUIZ 2-1

1. **Production possibilities curve *ABCDE* is concave because:**
   a. the marginal benefit of pizza declines as more pizza is consumed.
   b. the curve gets steeper as we move from *E* to *A*.
   c. it reflects the law of increasing opportunity costs.
   d. resources are scarce.

2. **The *marginal* opportunity cost of the second unit of pizza is:**
   a. 2 units of robots.
   b. 3 units of robots.
   c. 7 units of robots.
   d. 9 units of robots.

3. **The *total* opportunity cost of 7 units of robots is:**
   a. 1 unit of pizza.
   b. 2 units of pizza.
   c. 3 units of pizza.
   d. 4 units of pizza.

4. **All points on this production possibilities curve necessarily represent:**
   a. allocative efficiency.
   b. less than full use of resources.
   c. unattainable levels of output.
   d. productive efficiency.

Answers: 1. c; 2. a; 3. b; 4. d

---

curve, like point *W*, would represent a greater output than that at any point on the curve, but such points are unattainable with the current supplies of resources and technology.

Law of Increasing Opportunity Cost

Because resources are scarce relative to the virtually unlimited wants which they can be used to satisfy, people must choose among alternatives. More of pizza means less of robots. The amount of other products which must be forgone or sacrificed to obtain 1 unit of a specific good is called the **opportunity cost** of

that good. In our case, the amount of robots which must be given up to get another unit of pizza is the *opportunity cost*, or simply the *cost*, of that unit of pizza.

In moving from alternative A to B in Table 2-1, we find that the cost of 1 additional unit of pizza is 1 less unit of robots. But as we now pursue the concept of cost through the additional production possibilities—B to C, C to D, and D to E—an important economic principle is revealed: The opportunity cost of each additional unit of pizza is greater than that of the previous one. When we move from A to B, just 1 unit of robots is sacrificed for 1 more unit of pizza; but going from B to C sacrifices 2 additional units of robots for 1 more unit of pizza; then 3 more of robots for 1 more of pizza; and finally 4 for 1. Conversely, you should confirm that as we move from E to A, the cost of an additional robot is $\frac{1}{4}$, $\frac{1}{3}$, $\frac{1}{2}$, and 1 unit of pizza, respectively, for the four successive moves.

Note two points about these opportunity costs:

1. Our costs are measured in *real* terms, that is, in actual goods rather than money. We will shift to monetary comparisons in a moment.

2. We are discussing *marginal* (meaning "extra") opportunity costs, rather than cumulative or total opportunity costs. For example, the marginal opportunity cost of the third unit of pizza in Table 2-1 is 3 units of robots (= 7 − 4). But the *total* opportunity cost of 3 units of pizza is 6 units of robots (= 1 unit of robots for the first unit of pizza *plus* 2 units of robots for the second unit of pizza *plus* 3 units of robots for the third unit of pizza).

The **law of increasing opportunity costs** generalizes our example: The more of a product which is produced, the greater is its opportunity cost ("marginal" being implied).

Concavity The law of increasing opportunity costs is reflected in the shape of the production possibilities curve: The curve is *concave*, or bowed out, from the origin. In Figure 2-1, you can see that when the economy moves from A to E, it must give up successively larger amounts of robots (1, 2, 3, and 4) to acquire equal increments of pizza (1, 1, 1, and 1). This reality is evidenced in the slope of the production possibilities curve, which becomes steeper as we move from A to E. A curve that gets steeper as you move down along it is always concave as viewed from the origin.

Economic Rationale What is the economic rationale for the law of increasing opportunity costs? Why does the sacrifice of robots increase as we produce more pizza? The answer is that *economic resources are not completely adaptable to alternative uses.* Many resources are better at producing one good than at producing others. Fertile farmland is highly conducive to producing the ingredients needed to make pizza, while land containing rich mineral deposits is highly suited to producing the materials needed to make robots. As we step up pizza production, resources that are less and less adaptable to making pizza must be "pushed" into pizza production. If we start at A and move to B, we can shift the resources whose productivity of pizza is greatest in relation to their productivity of robots. But as we move from B to C, C to D, and so on, resources highly productive of pizza become increas-

ingly scarce. To get more pizza, resources whose productivity in robots is great in relation to their productivity in pizza will be needed. It will take more and more of such resources, and hence a greater sacrifice of robots, to achieve each increase of 1 unit in the production of pizza. This lack of perfect flexibility, or interchangeability, on the part of resources is the cause of increasing opportunity costs. **(Key Question 6)**

Allocative Efficiency Revisited

Our analysis has assumed full employment and productive efficiency, both of which are necessary to produce at *any point* on an economy's production possibilities curve. We now turn to allocative efficiency, which requires that the economy produce at the most valued, or *optimal*, point on the production possibilities curve. Of all the attainable combinations of pizza and robots on the curve in Figure 2-1, which is best? That is, what specific quantities of resources should be allocated to pizza and what specific quantities to robots?

Our discussion of the *economic perspective* in Chapter 1 puts us on the right track. Recall that economic decisions center on comparisons of marginal benefits and marginal costs. Any economic activity—for example, production or consumption—should be expanded as long as marginal benefits exceed marginal costs and should be reduced if marginal costs are greater than marginal benefits. The optimal amount of the activity occurs where MB = MC.

Consider pizza. We already know from the law of increasing opportunity costs that the marginal cost (MC) of additional units of pizza will rise as more units are produced. This can be shown with an upsloping MC curve, as in Figure 2-2. We are also aware that we obtain extra or marginal benefits (MB) from additional units of pizza. However, although material wants in the aggregate are insatiable, the second unit of a particular product yields less additional utility or benefit to you than the first. And a third will provide even less MB than the second. So it is for society as a whole. Therefore, we can portray the marginal benefits from pizza with a downsloping MB curve, as in Figure 2-2.

The optimal quantity of pizza production is indicated by the intersection of the MB and MC curves: 200,000 units in Figure 2-2. Why is this the optimal quantity? If only 100,000 pizzas were produced, the marginal benefit of pizza would exceed its marginal cost. In money terms, MB might be $15, while MC

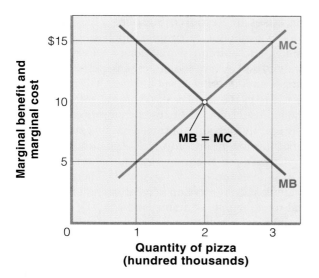

FIGURE 2-2 Allocative efficiency: MB = MC Resources are being allocated efficiently to a product when its output quantity is such that its marginal benefit (MB) equals its marginal cost (MC). Here, the optimal quantity of pizza is 200,000.

----

is only $5. This suggests that society would be *underallocating* resources to pizza production; more of it should be produced.

How do we know? Because society values an additional pizza as being worth $15, while the alternative products which the required resources could produce are worth only $5. Society benefits—it is better off in the sense of having a higher-valued output to enjoy—whenever it can gain something worth $15 by forgoing something worth only $5. A reallocating of resources from other products to pizza would mean society is using its resources more efficiently. Each additional pizza up to 200,000 would provide such a gain, indicating that allocative efficiency would be improved by this production. But when MB = MC, the benefits of producing pizza or alternative products with the available resources are equal. Allocative efficiency is achieved where MB = MC.

The production of 300,000 pizzas would represent an *overallocation* of resources to their production. Here the MC of pizza is $15 and its MB is only $5. This means 1 unit of pizza is worth only $5 to society, while the alternative products which the required resources could otherwise produce are valued at $15. By producing 1 less unit, society loses a pizza worth $5. But by reallocating the freed resources, it gains other products worth $15. When society gains some-

thing worth $15 by forgoing something worth only $5, it is better off. In Figure 2-2, such net gains can be realized until pizza production has been reduced to 200,000.

Generalization: *Resources are being efficiently allocated to any product when its output is such that its marginal benefit equals its marginal cost (MB = MC).* Suppose that by applying the above analysis to robots, we find their optimal (MB = MC) output is 7000. This would mean that alternative *C* on our production possibilities curve—200,000 pizzas and 7000 robots—would result in allocative efficiency for our hypothetical economy. **(Key Question 9)**

QUICK REVIEW 2-2

■ The production possibilities curve illustrates four concepts: **(a)** *scarcity* of resources is implied by the area of unattainable combinations of output lying outside the production possibilities curve; **(b)** *choice* among outputs is reflected in the variety of attainable combinations of goods lying along the curve; **(c)** *opportunity cost* is illustrated by the downward slope of the curve; **(d)** the law of *increasing opportunity costs* is implied by the concavity of the curve.

■ Full employment and productive efficiency must be realized for the economy to operate on its production possibilities curve.

■ A comparison of marginal benefits and marginal costs is needed to determine allocative efficiency—the best or optimal output mix on the curve.

UNEMPLOYMENT, GROWTH, AND THE FUTURE

Let's now release the first three assumptions underlying the production possibilities curve to see what happens.

Unemployment and Productive Inefficiency

The first assumption was that our economy was achieving full employment and productive efficiency. Our analysis and conclusions change if some resources are idle (unemployment) or if least-cost production is not realized. The five alternatives in Table 2-1 represent maximum outputs; they illustrate the combinations of robots and pizzas which can be produced when the economy is operating at full capacity—with full employment and productive efficiency. With un-employment or inefficient production, the economy would produce less than each alternative shown in the table.

Graphically, situations of unemployment or productive inefficiency are represented by points *inside* the original production possibilities curve (reproduced in Figure 2-3). Point *U* is one such point. Here the economy is falling short of the various maximum combinations of pizza and robots reflected by the points *on* the production possibilities curve. The arrows in Figure 2-3 indicate three possible paths back to full employment and least-cost production. A move toward full employment and productive efficiency would yield a greater output of one or both products.

A Growing Economy

When we drop the assumptions that the quantity and quality of resources and technology are fixed, the production possibilities curve shifts positions; that is, the potential maximum output of the economy changes.

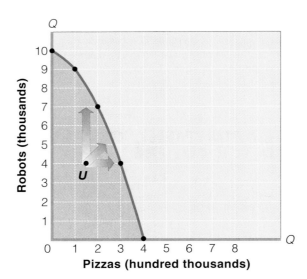

FIGURE 2-3 Unemployment, productive inefficiency, and the production possibilities curve   Any point inside the production possibilities curve, such as *U*, represents unemployment or a failure to achieve productive efficiency. The arrows indicate that, by realizing full employment and productive efficiency, the economy could operate on the curve. This means it could produce more of one or both products than it is producing at point *U*.

- -

Increases in Resource Supplies   Let's first abandon the assumption that total supplies of land, labor, capital, and entrepreneurial ability are fixed in both quantity and quality. Common sense tells us that over time a nation's growing population will bring about increases in the supplies of labor and entrepreneurial ability. Also, labor quality usually improves over time. Historically, our stock of capital has increased at a significant, though unsteady, rate. And although we are depleting some of our energy and mineral resources, new sources are being discovered. The drainage of swamps and the development of irrigation programs add to our supply of arable land.

The net result of these increased supplies of the factors of production is the ability to produce more of both pizza and robots. Thus 20 years from now, the production possibilities in Table 2-1 may be superseded by those shown in Table 2-2. The greater abundance of resources would result in a greater potential output of one or both products at each alternative. Economic growth in the sense of an expanded potential output will have occurred.

But such a favorable change in the production possibilities data does not *guarantee* that the economy will actually operate at a point on its new production possibilities curve. Some 130 million jobs will give the United States full employment now, but 10 or 20 years from now its labor force will be larger, and 130 million jobs will not be sufficient for full employment. The production possibilities curve may shift, but at the future date the economy may fail to produce at a point on that new curve.

Advances in Technology   Our second assumption is that we have constant or unchanging technology. Actually, though, technology has progressed greatly over time. An advancing technology involves both

TABLE 2-2   Production possibilities of pizza and robots with full employment and productive efficiency

Type of product	Production alternatives				
	A′	B′	C′	D′	E′
Pizza (in hundred thousands)	0	2	4	6	8
Robots (in thousands)	14	12	9	5	0

new and better goods *and* improved ways of producing them. For now, let's think of technological advances as being only improvements in capital facilities—more efficient machinery and equipment. Such technological advances alter our previous discussion of the economizing problem by improving productive efficiency, allowing society to produce more goods with fixed resources. As with increases in resource supplies, technological advances enable the production of more robots *and* more pizza.

Thus, when either supplies of resources increase or an improvement in technology occurs, the production possibilities curve in Figure 2-3 shifts outward and to the right, as illustrated by curve *A'*, *B'*, *C'*, *D'*, *E'* in Figure 2-4. Such an outward shift of the production possibilities curve represents growth of economic capacity or, simply, **economic growth:** *the ability to produce a larger total output.* This growth is the result of (1) increases in supplies of resources, (2) improvements in resource quality, and (3) technological advance.

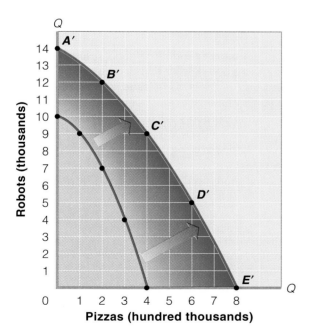

FIGURE 2-4 Economic growth and the production possibilities curve The expanding resource supplies, improved resource quality, and technological advances which occur in a dynamic economy move the production possibilities outward and to the right, allowing the economy to have larger quantities of both types of goods.

The consequence of growth is that our full-employment economy can enjoy a greater output of both robots and pizza. *While a static, no-growth economy must sacrifice some of one product to get more of another, a dynamic, growing economy can have larger quantities of both products.*

Economic growth does *not* typically mean proportionate increases in a nation's capacity to produce all its products. Note in Figure 2-4 that at the maximums, the economy can produce twice as much pizza as before but only 40 percent more robots. You should sketch in two new production possibilities curves: one showing the situation where a better technique for producing robots has been developed while the technology for producing pizza is unchanged, and the other illustrating an improved technology for pizza while the technology for producing robots remains constant.

Present Choices and Future Possibilities An

economy's current choice of positions on its production possibilities curve is a basic determinant of the future location of that curve. Let's designate the two axes of the production possibilities curve as *goods for the future* and *goods for the present*, as in Figure 2-5. Goods for the future are such things as capital goods, research and education, and preventive medicine. They increase the quantity and quality of property resources, enlarge the stock of technological information, and improve the quality of human resources. As we have already seen, goods for the future, like industrial robots, are the ingredients of economic growth. Goods for the present are pure consumer goods such as pizza, clothing, soft drinks, and boom boxes.

Now suppose there are two economies, Alta and Zorn, which are initially identical in every respect except one: Alta's current choice of positions on its production possibilities curve strongly favors present goods rather than future goods. Point *A* in Figure 2-5a indicates this choice. It is located quite far down the curve to the right, indicating a high priority for goods for the present, at the expense of fewer goods for the future. Zorn, in contrast, makes a current choice that stresses larger amounts of future goods and lesser amounts of present goods, as shown by point *Z* in Figure 2-5b.

Now, other things equal, we can expect the future production possibilities curve of Zorn to be farther to the right than Alta's curve. By currently choosing an output more favorable to technological advance and to increases in the quantity and quality of resources,

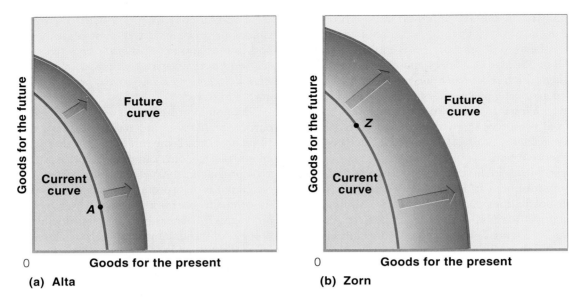

FIGURE 2-5 **An economy's present choice of positions on its production possibilities curve helps determine the curve's future location** A nation's current choice favoring "present goods," as made by Alta in (a), will cause a modest outward shift of the curve in the future. A nation's current choice favoring "future goods," as made by Zorn in (b), will result in a greater outward shift in the curve in the future.

Zorn will achieve greater economic growth than Alta. In terms of capital goods, Zorn is choosing to make larger current additions to its "national factory"—to invest more of its current output—than Alta. The payoff from this choice for Zorn is more rapid growth—greater future production capacity. The opportunity cost is fewer consumer goods in the present for Zorn to enjoy. **(Key Questions 10 and 11)**

A Qualification: International Trade

The message of the production possibilities curve is that an individual nation is limited to the combinations of output indicated by its production possibilities curve. *But this message must be modified when international specialization and trade exist.*

You will see in later chapters that a nation can avoid the output limits imposed by its domestic production possibilities curve through international specialization and trade. *International specialization* means directing domestic resources to output which a nation is highly efficient at producing. *International trade* involves the exchange of these goods for goods produced abroad. Specialization and trade enable a na-

tion to get more of a desired good at less sacrifice of some other good. Rather than sacrifice 3 robots to get a third unit of pizza, as in Table 2-1, a nation might be able to obtain the third unit of pizza by trading only 2 units of robots for it. Specialization and trade have the same effect as having more and better resources or discovering improved production techniques; both increase the quantities of capital and consumer goods available to society. The output gains

QUICK REVIEW 2-3

■ Unemployment and the failure to achieve productive efficiency cause the economy to operate at a point inside its production possibilities curve.

■ Increases in resource supplies, improvements in resource quality, and technological advance cause economic growth, depicted as an outward shift of the production possibilities curve.

■ An economy's present choice of capital and consumer goods helps determine the future location of its production possibilities curve. (See Global Perspective 2-1.)

■ International specialization and trade enable a nation to obtain more goods than indicated by its production possibilities curve.

from greater international specialization and trade are the equivalent of economic growth.

Applications

There are many possible applications of production possibilities analysis. Here are a few examples.

1. Wartime Production At the beginning of World War II (1939–1945), the United States had considerable unemployment. By quickly employing its idle resources, the U.S. economy was able to produce an almost unbelievably large quantity of war goods and at the same time increase the output of consumer goods (as shown in Figure 2-3). The Soviet Union, in contrast, entered World War II at almost capacity production; it was operating close to full employment. Its military preparations required considerable shifting of resources from the production of civilian goods, and its standard of living dropped substantially.

The U.S. position during the Vietnam conflict was similar to that of the Soviet Union during World War II. The U.S. economy was fully employed in the mid-1960s, and the government accelerated military spending for Vietnam while simultaneously increasing expenditures on domestic "war on poverty" programs. This attempt to achieve both more pizza and more robots, or more guns and more butter, at the same time in a full-employment economy was doomed to failure. The attempt to spend beyond our capacity to produce—to realize a point like W in Figure 2-1—contributed to the high inflation of the 1970s.

2. Discrimination Discrimination based on race, gender, age, sexual orientation, or ethnic background impedes the efficient employment of human resources, keeping the economy operating at some point inside its production possibilities curve. Discrimination prevents blacks, women, and others from obtaining jobs in which society can use their skills and talents efficiently. Elimination of discrimination would help move the economy from some point inside the production possibilities curve toward a point on the curve.

3. Land-Use Controversies The tradeoffs portrayed in the production possibilities curve are part of many controversies relating to alternative uses of publicly owned land. One example is the conflict between the logging industry in the Pacific Northwest

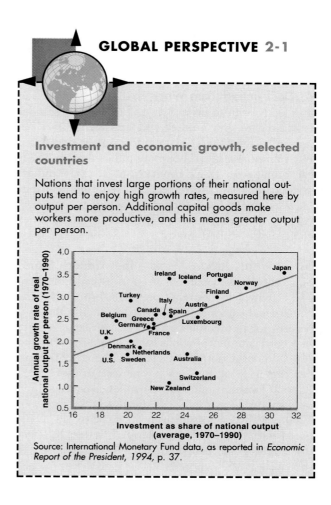

GLOBAL PERSPECTIVE 2-1

Investment and economic growth, selected countries

Nations that invest large portions of their national outputs tend to enjoy high growth rates, measured here by output per person. Additional capital goods make workers more productive, and this means greater output per person.

Source: International Monetary Fund data, as reported in *Economic Report of the President*, 1994, p. 37.

and environmentalists trying to save that area's spotted owls. Envision a production possibilities curve with "lumber production" on one axis and "spotted owls" on the other. It so happens that the spotted owl depends on the mature trees in national forests for nests and survival. Increasing the output of lumber limits the owl's habitat, destroys the species, and thus reduces environmental quality. Maintaining the mature forests preserves the owl but destroys thousands of jobs in the logging and lumber industry.

A second land-use example is the continuing debate on whether more Federal land in Alaska and the southwest should be included in the nation's system of national parks and monuments. Some of the land under question contains sizable oil, natural gas, and mineral deposits, but usually no drilling or mining is allowed in national parks and monuments. Here, the relevant production possibilities curve has "national parks and monuments" on one axis and "minerals" on the other. The concepts of resource scarcity, opportunity costs, and the necessity of choice again become quite apparent.

4. Destruction from War In the early 1990s, Iraq invaded Kuwait to bring Kuwait's oil resources under Iraqi control. But a quick and decisive military response by the United States and its allies devastated Iraq's economy. Allied bombing inflicted great physical damage on Iraq's production facilities and its system of roads, bridges, and communications. Devastation of Iraq's human resources was also severe. Consequently, Iraq's production possibilities curve swiftly shifted inward.

5. Growth: Japan versus the United States Since the 1950s, Japan has been investing more than 25 percent of its domestic output in productive machinery and equipment, compared with only about 10 percent for the United States. The consequences are in accord with our previous discussion. From 1960 to 1990, domestic output expanded at about 6.4 percent per year in Japan but only 3.2 percent in the United States. (Japan's production possibilities curve shifted outward twice as rapidly as did the U.S. curve.) In 1980 output per person in Japan was $16,711, compared with $17,643 in the United States; by 1995 these figures had changed to $39,640 and $26,980, respectively.

6. Famine in Africa Modern industrial societies take economic growth—rightward shifts of the production possibilities curve—for granted. But periodic catastrophic famines in sub-Saharan nations of Africa show that in some circumstances the production possibilities curve may shift leftward. In addition to drought, a cause of African famines is ecological degradation—poor land-use practices. Land has been deforested, overfarmed, and overgrazed, causing the production possibilities of these highly agriculturally oriented countries to diminish. In fact, the per capita domestic outputs of most of these nations declined in the past decade or so.

7. Emerging Technologies The world economies are experiencing a spurt of new technologies relating to computers, communications, and biotechnology. Technological advances have dropped the prices of computers and greatly enhanced their speed. Cellular phones, the Internet, and fax ma-

chines have increased communication capability, enhancing production and improving the efficiency of markets. Advances in biotechnology, specifically genetic engineering, have resulted in important agricultural and medical discoveries. Some observers believe that these new technologies are of such significance that they will ultimately contribute to faster economic growth than has occurred in the recent past (faster rightward shifts in nations' production possibilities curves).

ECONOMIC SYSTEMS

A society needs to select an **economic system**—*a particular set of institutional arrangements and a coordinating mechanism*—to respond to the economizing problem. Economic systems can differ as to (1) who owns the factors of production and (2) the method used to coordinate and direct economic activity.

Pure Capitalism

The private ownership of resources and the use of a system of markets and prices to coordinate and direct economic activity characterize *laissez-faire capitalism,* or **pure capitalism.** In such **market systems** each participant acts in his or her own self-interest; each individual or business seeks to maximize its satisfaction or profit through its own decisions regarding consumption or production. The system allows for the private ownership of capital, communicates through prices, and coordinates economic activity through *markets*—places where buyers and sellers come together. Goods and services are produced and resources are supplied by whomever is willing and able to do so. The result is competition among many small, independently acting buyers and sellers of each product and resource. Thus, economic power is widely dispersed.

Advocates of pure capitalism argue that such an economy promotes efficiency in the use of resources, stability of output and employment, and rapid economic growth. Hence, there is little or no need for government planning, control, or intervention. The term "laissez-faire" means "let it be," that is, keep government from interfering with the economy. The idea is that such interference will disturb the efficient working of the market system. Government's role is therefore limited to protecting private property and establishing an environment appropriate to the operation of the market system.

The Command Economy

The polar alternative to pure capitalism is the **command economy** or *communism*, characterized by public (government) ownership of virtually all property resources and economic decision making through central economic planning. All major decisions concerning the level of resource use, the composition and distribution of output, and the organization of production are determined by a central planning board appointed by government. Business firms are governmentally owned and produce according to government directives. The planning board determines production goals for each enterprise, and the plan specifies the amounts of resources to be allocated to each enterprise so that it can reach its production goals. The division of output between capital and consumer goods is centrally decided, and capital goods are allocated among industries on the basis of the central planning board's long-term priorities.

Mixed Systems

Pure capitalism and the command economy are extremes; real-world economies fall between the two. The U.S. economy leans toward pure capitalism, but with important differences. Government actively participates in the economy by promoting economic stability and growth, providing certain goods and services which would be underproduced or not produced at all by the market system, and modifying the distribution of income. In contrast to wide dispersion of economic power among many small units, as implied by pure capitalism, U.S. capitalism has spawned a number of very powerful economic organizations in the form of large corporations and labor unions. The ability of these power blocs to manipulate some markets to their advantage is a further reason for government involvement in the economy.

While the former Soviet Union historically approximated the command economy, it relied to some extent on market-determined prices and had some private ownership. Recent reforms in the former Soviet Union, China, and most of the eastern European nations have moved these economies toward more capitalistic, market-oriented systems.

North Korea and Cuba are the best remaining examples of centrally planned economies.

But private ownership and reliance on the market system do not always go together, nor do state ownership and central planning. For example, the fascism of Hitler's Nazi Germany has been dubbed *authoritarian capitalism* because the economy had a high degree of governmental control and direction but property was privately owned. In contrast, the present economic system of China might be called *market socialism*. It is characterized by extensive government ownership of natural resources and capital coupled with considerable reliance on free markets to organize and coordinate some parts of economic activity. The Swedish economy is also a hybrid system. Although more than 90 percent of Sweden's business activity is in private hands, government is deeply involved in redistributing income. Similarly, the capitalistic Japanese economy involves much planning and coordination between government and the business sector.

The Traditional Economy

Some developing countries have customary or **traditional economies,** in which production methods, exchange of goods, and distribution of income are all sanctioned by custom. Heredity and caste dictate the economic roles of individuals, and changes in socioeconomic status are rare. Technological change may also be constrained because it clashes with tradition and threatens the social fabric. Economic activity is often secondary to religious and cultural values and society's desire to perpetuate the status quo.

The main point here is that there is no unique or universally accepted way to respond to the economizing problem. Various societies, having different cultural and historical backgrounds, different mores and customs, and contrasting ideological frameworks—not to mention a great diversity of resources—use different institutions to deal with the reality of scarcity. The best method for responding to this reality in one society may or may not be appropriate in another society.

THE CIRCULAR FLOW MODEL

Because market systems now dominate the world economy, our focus in the remainder of this chapter, and the two following, is on how nations use markets to respond to the economizing problem. Our goal in this last section is modest: We want to identify the major groups of decision makers and the major markets in the market system. Our tool is the circular flow diagram.

Resource and Product Markets

Figure 2-6 (Key Graph) shows two groups of decision makers: households and businesses. (Government will be added as a third decision maker in Chapter 5.) The coordinating mechanism which aligns the decisions of households and businesses is the market system, in particular resource and product markets.

The upper half of the diagram portrays the **resource market,** *the place where resources or the services of resource suppliers are bought and sold.* Households (that is, people) either own all economic resources directly or own them indirectly through their ownership of business corporations. These households *supply* their resources to businesses. Businesses *demand* resources because resources are necessary for producing goods and services. The interaction of the demand for and supply of the immense variety of human and property resources establishes the price of each resource. The payments which businesses make to obtain resources are costs to businesses, but those payments simultaneously are flows of wage, rent, interest, and profit income to the households supplying the resources. Thus resources flow from households to businesses, and money flows from businesses to households.

Now consider the **product market,** *the place where goods and services of businesses are bought and sold,* depicted in the bottom half of the diagram. The money income received by households from the sale of resources does not, as such, have real value. Consumers cannot eat or wear coins and paper money. But they can spend their money for goods and services. And by their willingness to spend money income, households express their *demand* for a vast variety of goods and services. Simultaneously, businesses combine the resources they have obtained to produce and *supply* these goods and services. The interaction of consumer demand and business supply decisions determines product prices. The flow of consumer expenditures for goods and services constitutes sales revenues for businesses.

This **circular flow model** suggests a complex, interrelated web of decision making and economic activity. Note that households and businesses participate in both basic markets, but on different sides of each. Businesses are on the buying or demand side of resource markets, and households (as resource owners and suppliers) are on the selling or supply side. In the product market, these positions are reversed; households are on the buying or demand side, and businesses on the selling or supply side. Each group of economic units both buys and sells.

Moreover, the specter of scarcity haunts these transactions. Because households have only limited amounts of resources to supply to businesses, consumers' money incomes are limited, which means that each consumer's income will go only so far. A limited amount of money income clearly will not permit the purchase of all the goods and services the consumer might like to buy. Similarly, because resources are scarce, the output of finished goods and services is also necessarily limited.

To summarize: In a monetary economy, households, as resource owners, sell their resources to businesses and, as consumers, spend the resource income by buying goods and services. Businesses must buy resources to produce goods and services; their finished products are then sold to households in exchange for consumption expenditures or, as business sees it, revenues. These revenues are used to purchase additional resources to maintain the circular flow. The net result is, in Figure 2-6, a counterclockwise *real flow* of economic resources and finished goods and services, and a clockwise *money flow* of income and consumption expenditures. These flows are simultaneous and repetitive.

Limitations

Our model simplifies in many ways. Transactions between households and between businesses are concealed. Government and the "rest of the world" are ignored as decision makers. The model implies constant flows of output and income, while in fact these flows vary over time. Nor is the circular flow a perpetual-motion machine; production exhausts human energies and absorbs physical resources, the latter creating potential problems of environmental pollution. Finally, our model does not explain how product and resource prices are actually determined. We turn to this last topic in Chapter 3.

KEY GRAPH

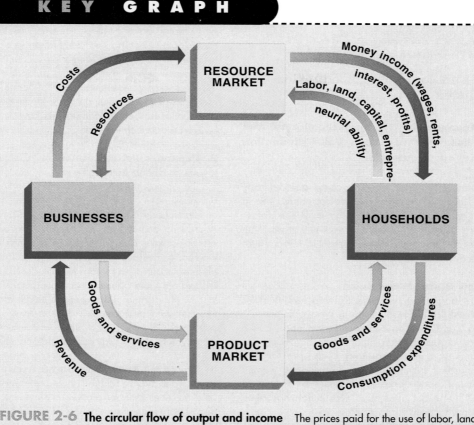

FIGURE 2-6 The circular flow of output and income   The prices paid for the use of labor, land, capital, and entrepreneurial ability are determined in the resource market shown in the upper loop. Businesses are on the demand side and households are on the supply side of this market. The prices of finished goods and services are determined in the product market shown in the lower loop. Households are on the demand side and businesses are on the supply side of this market.

QUICK QUIZ 2-6

1. The resource market is where:
   a. households sell products and businesses buy products.
   b. businesses sell resources and households sell products.
   c. households sell resources and businesses buy resources (or the services of resources).
   d. businesses sell resources and households buy resources (or the services of resources).

2. Which of the following would be determined in the product market?
   a. a manager's salary.
   b. the price of equipment used in a bottling plant.
   c. the price of 80 acres of farmland.
   d. the price of a new pair of athletic shoes.

3. In this circular flow diagram:
   a. money flows counterclockwise.
   b. resources flow counterclockwise.
   c. goods and services flow clockwise.
   d. households are on the supply side of the product market.

4. In this circular flow diagram:
   a. households spend income in the product market.
   b. firms supply resources to households.
   c. households receive income through the product market.
   d. households produce goods.

Answers: 1. c; 2. d; 3. b; 4. a

Women and Expanded Production Possibilities

A large increase in the number of employed women has shifted the U.S. production possibilities curve outward.

One of the more remarkable trends of the past half-century in the United States has been the substantial rise in the number of women working in the paid workforce. Today, nearly 60 percent of women work full- or part-time in paid jobs, compared to only 40 percent in 1965. There are many reasons for this increase.

1. Women's Rising Wage Rates Women have acquired more education and skill training, which have greatly increased their productivity in the workplace. As a result, the wages women can earn in the labor market have increased rapidly over time. These higher wages have boosted women's opportunity costs—the forgone wage earnings—of staying at home. In response, women have substituted labor market employment for now more "expensive" home activities. This substitution has been particularly pronounced for married women.

Higher wages for women have produced other reallocations of time and purchasing patterns to facilitate labor market work. Day care services have partly replaced personal childcare. Restaurant meals, fast food, prepared take-home meals, and pizza delivery now substitute for elaborate homemade family meals. Convenience stores and catalog sales have proliferated, as have lawn-care and in-home cleaning services. Shorter family vacations by airplane have replaced longer cross-country trips by car. Microwave ovens, dishwashers, automatic washers and dryers, and other household "capital goods" are now commonly used to enhance productivity in the home. These and similar household adjustments have helped make labor force participation more attractive for women.

2. Expanded Job Accessibility Greater accessibility to jobs, as distinct from higher pay, is a second factor boosting the employment of women. Service industries which traditionally have employed mainly women have expanded both absolutely and relatively in the past several decades. A growing demand for teachers, nurses, secretarial workers, salesclerks, and other service jobs has attracted many women to the labor market. Also, population has shifted from farms and rural regions to urban areas, where jobs for women are more abundant and geographically accessible. Finally, the decline in the average length of the workweek, together with an increased availability of part-time jobs, have made it easier for women to combine labor market employment with child-rearing and household activities.

3. Changing Preferences and Attitudes Women as a group have changed their preferences from household activities to labor market employment. An increasing number of women have found personal fulfillment in jobs, careers, and earnings. More broadly, most industrial societies now widely accept and encourage labor force participation by married women, including women with preschool children. Today about 60 percent of American mothers with preschool children participate in the labor force, compared to only 30 percent in 1970. More than

---

CHAPTER SUMMARY

1. Economics is grounded on two basic facts: **(a)** human material wants are virtually unlimited; **(b)** economic resources are scarce.

2. Economic resources may be classified as property resources—raw materials and capital—or as human resources—labor and entrepreneurial ability. These resources (land, capital, labor, and entrepreneurial ability) are the factors of production.

3. Economics is concerned with the problem of using or managing scarce resources to produce goods and services which fulfill the material wants of society. Both full employment and efficient use of available resources are essential to maximize want satisfaction.

4. Efficient use of resources consists of productive efficiency (producing all output combinations in the least costly way) and allocative efficiency (producing the specific output mix most desired by society).

5. An economy which is achieving full employment and productive efficiency—that is, operating on its production possibilities curve—must sacrifice the output of some types of goods and services to achieve increased production of others. Because resources are not equally produc-

half of today's employed mothers return to work before their youngest child is 2 years old.

4. Declining Birthrates There were 3.8 lifetime births per woman in 1957 at the peak of the baby boom, but that number is less than 2 today. This marked decline in the typical family size has freed up time for greater labor force participation since child rearing and associated homemaking activities are time-consuming. Not only do women now have fewer children, but these children are also spaced closer together in age. Thus, women who leave their jobs during their children's early years can return to the labor force sooner.

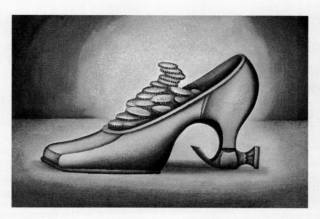

The decline in birthrates has resulted from the widespread availability and use of birth control methods, coupled with changing lifestyles. But higher wage rates have also been at work. Women with relatively high wage earnings, on average, have fewer children than women with lower earnings. The opportunity cost of children—the income sacrificed by not being employed—rises as wage earnings rise. In the language of economics, the higher "price" associated with children has reduced the "quantity of children demanded."

5. Rising Divorce Rates Marital instability, as evidenced by high divorce rates in the 1970s and 1980s, may have motivated many women to establish and maintain labor market ties. The economic impact of divorce on nonworking women is often disastrous because alimony and child support are not always forthcoming. Most previously nonworking women enter the labor force following divorce. And married women—perhaps even women contemplating marriage—increasingly may have participated in the labor force to protect themselves against the financial difficulties of potential divorce.

6. Stagnating Male Earnings A final factor explaining the rise in the women's labor force participation rate is that men's real earnings have risen very slowly in the past two decades, particularly for men without college degrees. This stagnation has motivated many wives to enter the labor force to maintain family living standards. If wives had not entered the labor force in record numbers in the past two decades, many households would have suffered absolute or relative declines in their real incomes.

Together, these factors have produced a rapid rise in the availability of women workers in the United States. This increase in the *quantity of resources* has helped push the U.S. production possibilities curve outward. That is, it has greatly contributed to U.S. economic growth.

---

tive in all possible uses, shifting resources from one use to another brings the law of increasing opportunity costs into play. The production of additional units of a product entails the sacrifice of *increasing* amounts of the other product.

6. Allocative efficiency means operating at the optimal point on the production possibilities curve. That point represents the highest-valued mix of goods and is determined by expanding the production of each good until its marginal benefit (MB) equals its marginal cost (MC).

7. Over time, technological advance and increases in the quantity and quality of resources allow the economy to produce more of all goods and services—to experience economic growth. Society's choice as to the mix of con-

sumer goods and capital goods in current output is a major determinant of the future location of the production possibilities curve and thus of economic growth.

8. The various economic systems of the world differ in their ideologies and also in their responses to the economizing problem. Basic differences center on **(a)** whether most resources are owned by government or held privately and **(b)** whether economic activity is coordinated mainly by a market system or by central planning.

9. The circular flow model provides an overview of the operation of the capitalist system. This simple model locates the product and resource markets and shows the major income-expenditure flows and resource-output flows that constitute the lifeblood of the capitalistic economy.

TERMS AND CONCEPTS

economizing problem
utility
economic resources
land
capital
investment
labor
entrepreneurial ability

factors of
   production
full employment
full production
productive efficiency
allocative efficiency
consumer goods
capital goods

production possibilities
   table
production possibilities
   curve
opportunity cost
law of increasing
   opportunity costs
economic growth

economic system
pure capitalism
market systems
command economy
traditional economies
resource market
product market
circular flow model

STUDY QUESTIONS

1. Explain this statement: "If resources were unlimited and freely available, there would be no subject called *economics.*"

2. Comment on the following statement from a newspaper article: "Our junior high school serves a splendid hot meal for $1 without costing the taxpayers anything, thanks in part to a government subsidy."

3. Critically analyze: "Wants aren't insatiable. I can prove it. I get all the coffee I want to drink every morning at breakfast." Explain: "Goods and services are scarce because resources are scarce." Analyze: "It is the nature of all economic problems that absolute solutions are denied to us."

4. What are economic resources? What are the major functions of the entrepreneur?

5. **KEY QUESTION** Why is the problem of unemployment part of the subject matter of economics? Distinguish between productive efficiency and allocative efficiency. Give an illustration of achieving productive, but not allocative, efficiency.

6. **KEY QUESTION** Here is a production possibilities table for war goods and civilian goods:

Type of production	Production alternatives				
	A	B	C	D	E
Automobiles	0	2	4	6	8
Rockets	30	27	21	12	0

   a. Show these data graphically. Upon what specific assumptions is this production possibilities curve based?

   b. If the economy is at point C, what is the cost of one more automobile? One more rocket? Explain how the production possibilities curve reflects the law of increasing opportunity costs.

   c. What must the economy do to operate at some point on the production possibilities curve?

7. What is the opportunity cost of attending college?

8. Suppose you arrive at a store expecting to pay $100 for an item but learn that a store 2 miles away is charging $50 for it. Would you drive there and buy it? How does your decision benefit you? What is the opportunity cost of your decision? Now suppose that you arrive at a store expecting to pay $6000 for an item but learn that it costs $5950 at the other store. Do you make the same decision as before? Perhaps surprisingly, you should! Explain why.

9. **KEY QUESTION** Specify and explain the shapes of the marginal-benefit and marginal-cost curves. How are these curves used to determine the optimal allocation of resources to a particular product? If current output is such that marginal cost exceeds marginal benefit, should more or fewer resources be allocated to this product? Explain.

10. **KEY QUESTION** Label point G inside the production possibilities curve you drew in question 6. What does it indicate? Label point H outside the curve. What does that point represent? What must occur before the economy can attain the level of production shown by point H?

11. **KEY QUESTION** Referring again to question 6, suppose improvement occurs in the technology of producing rockets but not in the production of automobiles. Draw the new production possibilities curve. Now assume that a technological advance occurs in producing automobiles but not in producing rockets. Draw the new production possibilities curve. Now draw a production possibilities curve which reflects technological improvement in the production of both products.

12. Explain how, if at all, each of the following affects the location of the production possibilities curve:
   a. Standardized examination scores of high school and college students decline.
   b. The unemployment rate falls from 9 to 6 percent of the labor force.
   c. Defense spending is reduced to allow government to spend more on health care.
   d. Society decides it wants compact discs rather than long-playing records.
   e. A new technique improves the efficiency of extracting copper from ore.
   f. A new baby boom increases the size of the nation's workforce.

13. Explain: "Affluence tomorrow requires sacrifice today."

14. Suppose that, based on a nation's production possibilities curve, an economy must sacrifice 10,000 pizzas domestically to get the 1 additional industrial robot it desires but that it can get the robot from another country in exchange for 9000 pizzas. Relate this information to the following statement: "Through international specialization and trade, a nation can reduce its opportunity cost of obtaining goods and thus 'get outside its production possibilities curve.'"

15. Contrast how pure capitalism and a command economy try to cope with economic scarcity.

16. Explain this statement: "Although the United States has a capitalist economy, *not* a traditional economy,

traditions (for example, weddings, Christmas, and Halloween) play an important role in determining what goods get produced."

17. Portray the major features of the circular flow model. In what way are businesses and households both *suppliers* and *demanders* in this model? Explain how scarcity enters the model.

18. **(Last Word)** Which *two* of the six reasons listed in the Last Word do you think are the *most important* in explaining the rise in participation of women in the workplace? Explain your reasoning.

19. **WEB-BASED QUESTION** **Different Geographical Areas and Outputs—Japan and the United States** Compared to the United States, Japan has 4 percent of the geographical area (slightly smaller than California) and 47 percent of the population (1996 estimates). Other things equal, Japan should have far less than 47 percent of the U.S. output. Visit the OECD (Organization for Economic Cooperation and Development) http://www.oecd.org/std/gdp.htm and calculate the ratio of Japan's gross domestic product (a measure of national output) to the gross domestic product of the United States. Is the ratio above or below 47 percent? What might explain this difference?

20. **WEB-BASED QUESTION** **Increasing Productivity in Hong Kong** The Hong Kong Productivity Council http://hkpcms.hkpc.org/ was established in 1967 to promote increased productivity. Its mission is "to achieve a more effective utilization of available resources and to enhance the value-added content of products and services. The aim is to increase efficiency and competitiveness, thereby contributing to raising the standard of living of people in Hong Kong." How does the Council define productivity, and how does it try to increase it?

CHAPTER THREE

Understanding Individual Markets: Demand and Supply

According to an old joke, if you teach a parrot to say "Demand and supply," you have an economist. There is an element of truth in this quip. The tools of demand and supply can take us far in understanding not only specific economic issues but also how the entire economy works.

Our circular flow model in Chapter 2 identified the participants in the product and resource markets. There, we asserted that prices were determined by the "interaction" between demand and supply in these markets. In this chapter we examine that interaction in detail, explaining how prices and output quantities are determined.

MARKETS

Recall from Chapter 2 that a **market** is *an institution or mechanism which brings together buyers ("demanders") and sellers ("suppliers") of particular goods, services, or resources.* Markets exist in many forms. The corner gas station, the fast-food outlet, the local music store, a farmer's roadside stand—all are familiar markets. The New York Stock Exchange and the Chicago Board of Trade are markets where buyers and sellers of stocks and bonds and farm commodities from all over the world communicate with one another and buy and sell. Auctioneers bring together potential buyers and sellers of art, livestock, used farm equipment, and, sometimes, real estate. The all-American quarterback and his agent bargain with the owner of an NFL team. A graduating finance major interviews with Citicorp or Wells Fargo at the university placement office.

All these situations which link potential buyers with potential sellers are markets. As our examples imply, some markets are local, while others are national or international. Some are highly personal, involving face-to-face contact between demander and supplier; others are impersonal, with buyer and seller never seeing or knowing each other.

To keep things simple, this chapter focuses on markets consisting of large numbers of independently acting buyers and sellers exchanging a standardized product. These are the highly competitive markets such as a central grain exchange, a stock market, or a market for foreign currencies in which the equilibrium price is "discovered" by the interacting decisions of buyers and sellers. They are *not* the markets in which one or a handful of producers "set" prices, such as the markets for commercial airplanes or greeting cards.

DEMAND

Demand is *a schedule or a curve showing the various amounts of a product consumers are willing and able to purchase at each of a series of possible prices during a specified period of time.*[1] Demand, therefore, shows the quantities of a product which will be purchased at various possible prices, *other things equal.* Demand can easily be shown in table form. Table 3-1 is a hypothetical **demand schedule** for a single consumer purchasing bushels of corn.

The portrayal of demand in Table 3-1 reflects the relationship between the possible prices of corn and the quantity of corn the consumer would be willing and able to purchase at each of these prices. We say willing and *able* because willingness alone is not effective in the market. You may be willing to buy a Porsche, but if this willingness is not backed by the necessary dollars, it will not be effective and, therefore, not be reflected in the market. In Table 3-1, if the price of corn were $5 per bushel, our consumer would be willing and able to buy 10 bushels per week; if it were $4, the consumer would be willing and able to buy 20 bushels per week; and so forth.

The table showing demand does not tell us which of the five possible prices will actually exist in the corn market. This depends on demand *and supply.* Demand is simply a statement of a buyer's plans, or intentions, with respect to the purchase of a product.

To be meaningful, the quantities demanded at each price must relate to a specific period—a day, a week, a month. Saying "A consumer will buy 10 bushels of corn at $5 per bushel" is meaningless. Saying "A consumer will buy 10 bushels of corn *per week* at $5 per bushel" is clear and meaningful. Without a specific time period we would not know whether demand for a product was large or small.

Law of Demand

A fundamental characteristic of demand is this: *All else equal, as price falls, the quantity demanded rises, and as price rises, the corresponding quantity demanded falls.* In short, there is a negative or *inverse* relationship between price and quantity demanded. Economists call this inverse relationship the **law of demand.**

---

[1]This definition obviously is worded to apply to product markets. To adjust it to apply to resource markets, substitute the word "resource" for "product" and the word "businesses" for "consumers."

TABLE 3-1   An individual buyer's demand for corn

Price per bushel	Quantity demanded per week
$5	10
4	20
3	35
2	55
1	80

The "other things equal" assumption is critical here. Many factors other than the price of the product being considered affect the amount purchased. The quantity of Nikes purchased will depend not only on the price of Nikes but also on the prices of such substitutes as Reeboks, Adidas, and Filas. The law of demand in this case says that fewer Nikes will be purchased if the price of Nikes rises *and the prices of Reeboks, Adidas, and Filas all remain constant.* In short, if the *relative price* of Nikes increases, fewer Nikes will be bought. However, if the price of Nikes and all other competing shoes increase by some amount—say, $5—consumers might buy more, less, or the same amount of Nikes.

What is the foundation for the law of demand? There are several levels of analysis on which to argue the case. Let's look at three of them:

1. Common sense and simple observation are consistent with the law of demand. People ordinarily *do* buy more of a product at a low price than at a high price. Price is an obstacle which deters consumers from buying. The higher this obstacle, the less of a product they will buy; the lower the price obstacle, the more they will buy. The fact that businesses have "sales" is evidence of their belief in the law of demand. Businesses reduce their inventories by lowering prices, not by raising them.

2. In any specific time period, each buyer of a product will derive less satisfaction (or benefit or utility) from each successive unit of the good consumed. The second Big Mac will yield less satisfaction to the consumer than the first, and the third still less satisfaction than the second. That is, consumption is subject to **diminishing marginal utility.** And because successive units of a particular product yield less and less marginal utility, consumers will buy additional units only if the price of those units is reduced.

3. The law of demand can also be explained in terms of income and substitution effects. The **income effect** indicates that a lower price increases the purchasing power of a buyer's money income, enabling the buyer to purchase more of the product than she or he could buy before. A higher price has the opposite effect.

The **substitution effect** suggests that at a lower price, buyers have the incentive to substitute the now cheaper good for similar goods which are now relatively more expensive. Consumers tend to substitute cheap products for dear products.

For example, a decline in the price of beef will increase the purchasing power of consumer incomes, enabling them to buy more beef (the income effect). At a lower price, beef is relatively more attractive and is substituted for pork, mutton, chicken, and fish (the substitution effect). The income and substitution effects combine to make consumers able and willing to buy more of a product at a low price than at a high price.

The Demand Curve

The inverse relationship between price and quantity demanded for any product can be represented on a simple graph, in which, by convention, we measure *quantity demanded* on the horizontal axis and *price* on the vertical axis. In Figure 3-1 we have plotted the five price-quantity data points in Table 3-1 and con-

nected them with a smooth curve, labeled *D*. Such a curve is called a **demand curve.** It slopes downward and to the right because the relationship it portrays between price and quantity demanded is inverse. The law of demand—people buy more at a low price than at a high price—is reflected in the downward slope of the demand curve.

Table 3-1 and Figure 3-1 contain exactly the same data and reflect the same relationship between price and quantity demanded. But the advantage of a graph is that it shows the relationship more simply and clearly than a table or a description in words. Moreover, graphs allow us to very easily show the effects of *changes* in variables. Graphs are thus valuable tools in economic analysis.

Individual and Market Demand

Until now we have concentrated on just one consumer. But competition requires that many buyers are in each market. We can get from *individual* demand to *market* demand by adding the quantities demanded by all consumers at each of the various possible prices. If there are just three buyers in the market, as represented in Table 3-2, it is relatively easy to determine the total quantity demanded at each price. Figure 3-2 shows the graphical summing procedure: At each price we add the individual quantities demanded to obtain the total quantity demanded for that price; we then plot the price and total quantity as one point of the market demand curve.

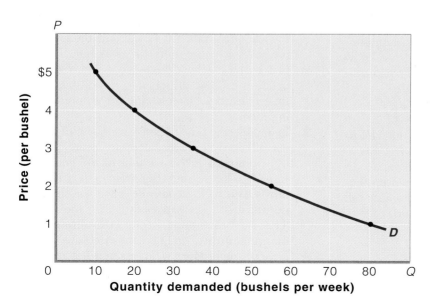

Quantity demanded (bushels per week)

FIGURE 3-1 An individual buyer's demand for corn An individual's demand schedule graphs as a downsloping curve such as *D* because price and quantity demanded are inversely related. Specifically, the law of demand generalizes that, other things equal, consumers will buy more of a product as its price declines. Here and in later figures, *P* stands for price, and *Q* stands for quantity (either demanded or supplied.)

TABLE 3-2 Market demand for corn, three buyers

Price per bushel	Quantity demanded							Total quantity demanded per week
	First buyer		Second buyer		Third buyer			
$5	10	+	12	+	8	=		30
4	20	+	23	+	17	=		60
3	35	+	39	+	26	=		100
2	55	+	60	+	39	=		154
1	80	+	87	+	54	=		221

Competition, of course, entails many more than three buyers of a product. To avoid hundreds or thousands or millions of additions, we suppose that all the buyers in a market are willing and able to buy the same amounts at each of the possible prices. Then we just multiply those amounts by the number of buyers to obtain the market demand. Curve D_1 in Figure 3-3 was obtained this way, for a market with 200 corn buyers whose demand is that in Table 3-1. Table 3-3 shows the calculations.

Determinants of Demand

An economist constructing a demand curve such as D_1 in Figure 3-3 assumes that price is the most important influence on the amount of any product purchased. But the economist knows that other factors can and do affect purchases. These factors are called **determinants of demand,** and they are assumed to be constant when a demand curve like D_1 is drawn. They are the "other things equal" in the relationship

between price and quantity demanded. When any of these determinants changes, the location of the demand curve will shift to the right or left. For this reason, determinants of demand are sometimes referred to as *demand shifters.*

The basic determinants of demand are (1) consumers' tastes and preferences, (2) the number of consumers in the market, (3) consumers' money incomes, (4) the prices of related goods, and (5) consumer expectations about future prices and incomes.

Change in Demand

A change in one or more of the determinants of demand will change the demand data (the demand schedule) in Table 3-3 and therefore the location of the demand curve in Figure 3-3. A change in the demand schedule or, graphically, a shift in the location of the demand curve is called a *change in demand.*

If consumers become willing and able to buy more corn at each possible price than is reflected in column 4 in Table 3-3, this *increase in demand* means a shift of the demand curve to the *right*, say, from D_1 to D_2. Conversely, a *decrease in demand* occurs when consumers buy less corn at each possible price than is indicated in column 4, Table 3-3. Graphically, a decrease in demand is shown as a shift of the demand curve to the *left*, say, from D_1 to D_3 in Figure 3-3.

Let's now examine how changes in each determinant affect demand.

Tastes A favorable change in consumer tastes or preferences for a product—one which makes the product more desirable—means that more of it will be demanded at each price. Demand will increase; the

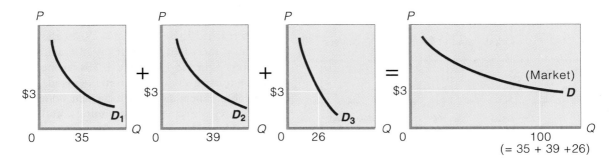

FIGURE 3-2 Market demand for corn, three buyers The market demand curve D is found by adding horizontally the individual demand curves (D_1, D_2, and D_3) of all consumers in the market. At the price of $3, for example, the three individual curves yield a total quantity demanded of 100 bushels.

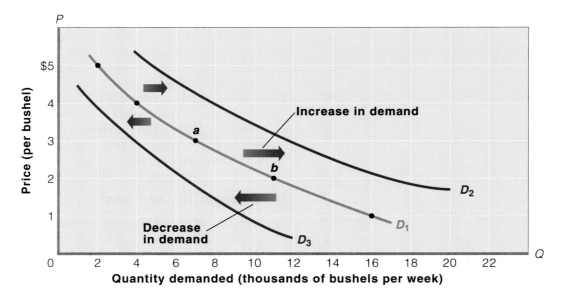

FIGURE 3-3 Changes in the demand for corn A change in one or more of the determinants of demand causes a change in demand. An increase in demand is shown as a shift of the demand curve to the right, as from D_1 to D_2. A decrease in demand is shown as a shift of the demand curve to the left, as from D_1 to D_3. These changes in demand are distinguished from a change in quantity demanded, which is caused by a change in the price of the product, as shown by a movement from, say, point a to point b on fixed demand curve D_1.

----

demand curve will shift rightward. An unfavorable change in consumer preferences will decrease demand, shifting the demand curve to the left.

New products can affect consumer tastes; for example, the introduction of compact discs has greatly decreased the demand for cassette tapes. Consumers concern about the health hazards of cholesterol and obesity have increased the demands for broccoli, low-calorie sweeteners, and fresh fruit while decreasing the demands for beef, veal, eggs, and whole milk. Over the past several years, the demands for light

TABLE 3-3   Market demand for corn, 200 buyers

(1) Price per bushel	(2) Quantity demanded per week, single buyer		(3) Number of buyers in the market		(4) Total quantity demanded per week
$5	10	×	200	=	2,000
4	20	×	200	=	4,000
3	35	×	200	=	7,000
2	55	×	200	=	11,000
1	80	×	200	=	16,000

trucks and sports utility vehicles have greatly increased, driven by a change in tastes. So, too, has the demand for bagels.

Number of Buyers An increase in the number of consumers in a market increases demand. A decrease in the number of consumers decreases demand. For example, improvements in communications have given financial markets international range, increasing demand for stocks and bonds. And the baby boom after World War II increased demand for diapers, baby lotion, and the services of obstetricians. When the baby boomers reached their 20s in the 1970s, the demand for housing increased. Conversely, the aging of the baby boomers in the 1980s and 1990s has been a factor in the relative slump in housing demand. Also, increasing life expectancy has increased demands for medical care, retirement communities, and nursing homes. And international trade agreements such as the North American Free Trade Agreement (NAFTA) and the General Agreement on Tariffs and Trade (GATT) have reduced foreign trade barriers to American farm products, increasing the demands for those products.

Income How changes in money income affect demand is more complex. For most commodities, a rise in income causes an increase in demand. Consumers typically buy more steaks, sunscreen, and stereos as their incomes increase. Conversely, the demands for such products decline as incomes fall. Commodities whose demand varies *directly* with money income are called *superior*, or **normal, goods.**

Although most products are normal goods, there are a few exceptions. As incomes increase beyond some point, the amount of bread or lard or cabbages purchased at each price may diminish because higher incomes allow consumers to buy more high-protein foods, such as dairy products and meat. Rising incomes may also decrease the demands for used clothing and third-hand automobiles. Similarly, rising incomes may cause demands for hamburger and charcoal grilles to decline as wealthier consumers switch to T-bones and gas grilles. Goods whose demand varies *inversely* with money income are called **inferior goods.**

Prices of Related Goods A change in the price of a related good may increase or decrease the demand for a product, depending on whether the related good is a substitute or a complement. A **substitute good** is one that can be used in place of another good. A **complementary good** is one used together with another good.

Substitutes Beef and chicken are examples of substitute goods. When the price of beef rises, consumers buy less beef, increasing the demand for chicken. Conversely, as the price of beef falls, consumers buy more beef, decreasing the demand for chicken. *When two products are substitutes, the price of one and the demand for the other move in the same direction.* So it is with Nikes and Reeboks, sweaters and jackets, Toyotas and Hondas, and Coke and Pepsi.

Complements Complementary goods are used together and are usually demanded together. If the price of gasoline falls and, as a result, you drive your car more, this extra driving increases your demand for motor oil. Thus, gas and oil are jointly demanded; they are complements. So it is with ham and eggs, tuition and textbooks, movies and popcorn, cameras and film. *When two products are complements, the price of one good and the demand for the other good move in opposite directions.*

Unrelated Goods Many goods are not related to one another; they are *independent goods.* Examples are such pairs of goods as butter and golf balls, potatoes and automobiles, bananas and wristwatches. A change

in the price of one has little or no impact on the demand for the other.

Expectations Consumer expectations about future product prices, product availability, and future income can shift demand. Consumer expectations of higher future prices may prompt them to buy now to "beat" anticipated price rises, thus increasing today's demand. Similarly, the expectations of rising incomes may induce consumers to be freer in current spending. In contrast, the expectation of falling prices or falling income will decrease current demand for products.

First example: If freezing weather destroys much of Florida's citrus crop, consumers may reason that the price of orange juice will rise. They may stock up on orange juice by purchasing large quantities now.

Second example: In late 1993 there was a substantial increase in the demand for guns. Reason? The expectation that Congress would pass more stringent gun control laws.

Third example: A first-round NFL draft choice might splurge for a new Mercedes in anticipation of a lucrative professional football contract.

In summary, an *increase* in demand—the decision by consumers to buy larger quantities of a product at each possible price—can be caused by:
1. A favorable change in consumer tastes
2. An increase in the number of buyers
3. Rising incomes if the product is a normal good
4. Falling incomes if the product is an inferior good
5. An increase in the price of a substitute good
6. A decrease in the price of a complementary good
7. Consumer expectations of higher future prices and incomes

Be sure you can "reverse" these generalizations to explain a *decrease* in demand. Table 3-4 provides additional illustrations to reinforce your understanding of the determinants of demand. **(Key Question 2)**

Changes in Quantity Demanded

A *change in demand* must not be confused with a *change in quantity demanded.* A **change in demand** is a shift of the entire curve to the right (an increase in demand) or to the left (a decrease in demand). It occurs because the consumer's state of mind about purchasing the product has been altered. The cause is a change in one or more of the determinants of demand. Recall that "demand" is a schedule or curve; therefore, a "change in demand" means a change in the entire schedule and a shift of the entire curve.

TABLE 3-4   **Determinants of demand: factors which shift the demand curve**

Determinant	Examples
Change in buyer tastes	Physical fitness increases in popularity, increasing the demand for jogging shoes and bicycles.
Change in number of buyers	Japan reduces import quotas on U.S. telecommunications equipment, increasing the demand for it; a birthrate decline reduces the demand for education.
Change in income	An increase in incomes increases the demand for such normal goods as butter, lobster, and filet mignon while reducing the demand for such inferior goods as cabbage, turnips, retreaded tires, and used clothing.
Change in the prices of related goods	A reduction in airfares reduces the demand for bus transportation (substitute goods); a decline in the price of compact disc players increases the demand for compact discs (complementary goods).
Change in expectations	Inclement weather in South America causes the expectation of higher future coffee prices, thereby increasing the current demand for coffee.

In contrast, a **change in quantity demanded** designates the movement from one point to another point—from one price-quantity combination to another—on a fixed demand schedule or demand curve. The cause of such a change is an increase or decrease in the price of the product being considered. In Table 3-3, for example, a decline in the price from $5 to $4 will increase the quantity of corn demanded from 2000 to 4000 bushels.

In Figure 3-3 the shift of the demand curve D_1 to either D_2 or D_3 is a change in demand. But the movement from point a to point b on curve D_1 represents a change in quantity demanded: demand has not changed; it is the entire curve, and it remains fixed in place.

QUICK REVIEW 3-1

■ A market is any arrangement which facilitates the purchase and sale of goods, services, and resources.

■ Demand is a schedule or a curve showing the amount of a product buyers are willing and able to purchase at each potential price in a series of prices.

■ The law of demand states that, other things equal, the quantity of a good purchased varies inversely with its price.

■ The demand curve shifts because of changes in (a) consumer tastes, (b) the number of buyers in the market, (c) incomes, (d) the prices of substitute or complementary goods, and (e) expectations.

■ A change in demand is a shift of the entire demand curve; a change in quantity demanded is a movement from one point to another on a firm's stable demand curve.

SUPPLY

Supply is *a schedule or curve showing the amounts of a product a producer is willing and able to produce and make available for sale at each of a series of possible prices during a specific period.*[2] Table 3-5 is a hypothetical **supply schedule** for a single producer of corn. It shows the quantities of corn which will be supplied at various prices, other things equal.

---
[2]This definition is worded to apply to product markets. To adjust it to apply to resource markets, substitute "resource" for "product" and change "owner" to "producer."

TABLE 3-5 An individual producer's supply of corn

Price per bushel	Quantity supplied per week
$5	60
4	50
3	35
2	20
1	5

Law of Supply

Table 3-5 shows a positive or direct relationship between price and quantity supplied. *As price rises, the corresponding quantity supplied rises; as price falls, the quantity supplied falls.* This particular relationship is called the **law of supply.** A supply schedule tells us that firms will produce and offer for sale more of their product at a high price than at a low price. This, again, is basically common sense.

Price is an obstacle from the standpoint of the consumer, who is on the paying end. The higher the price, the less the consumer will buy. But the supplier is on the receiving end of the product's price. To a supplier, price represents *revenue* and thus is an incentive to produce and sell a product. The higher the price, the greater this incentive and the greater the quantity supplied.

Consider a farmer who can shift resources among alternative products. As price moves up in Table 3-5, the farmer finds it profitable to take land out of wheat, oats, and soybean production and put it into corn. And the higher corn prices allow the farmer to cover the increased costs associated with more intensive cultivation and the use of more seed, fertilizer, and pesticides. The overall result is more corn.

Now consider a manufacturer. Beyond some production quantity, manufacturers usually encounter increasing costs per added unit of output. Certain productive resources—in particular, the firm's plant and machinery—cannot be expanded quickly. So the firm uses more of the other resources, such as labor, to produce more output. But at some point the existing plant becomes increasingly crowded and congested, meaning that each added worker produces less added output. As a result, the cost of successive units of output rises. The firm will not produce these more costly units unless it receives a higher price for them. Again, price and quantity supplied are directly related.

The Supply Curve

As with demand, it is convenient to represent supply graphically. In Figure 3-4, curve S_1 is a graph of the market supply data in Table 3-6. Those data assume there are 200 suppliers in the market, each willing and able to supply corn according to Table 3-5. That is, we obtain the market **supply curve** by horizontally adding the supply curves of the individual producers. Note that the axes in Figure 3-4 are the same as those used in our graph of market demand, except for the change from "quantity demanded" to "quantity supplied" on the horizontal axis.

Determinants of Supply

In constructing a supply curve, the economist assumes that price is the most significant influence on the quantity supplied of any product. But other factors (the "other things equal") can and do affect supply. The supply curve is drawn assuming that these other things are fixed and do not change. If any of them does change, a *change in supply* will occur—the entire supply curve will shift.

The basic **determinants of supply** are (1) resource prices, (2) the technique of production, (3) taxes and subsidies, (4) prices of other goods, (5) price expectations, and (6) the number of sellers in the market. A change in any one or more of these determinants of supply, or *supply shifters*, will move the supply curve for a product either to the right or to the left. A shift to the *right*, as from S_1 to S_2 in Figure 3-4, designates an *increase* in supply: Producers supply larger quantities of the product at each possible price. A shift to the *left*, as from S_1 to S_3, indicates a *decrease* in supply: Suppliers offer less output at each price.

Changes in Supply

Let's consider how changes in each of the determinants affect supply. As our discussion proceeds, remember that costs are a major factor underlying supply curves; anything that affects costs (other than changes in output itself) usually shifts the supply curve.

Resource Prices The prices of the resources used in the production process help determine the costs of production incurred by firms. Higher *resource* prices raise production costs and, assuming a particular *product* price, squeeze profits. This reduction in profits reduces the incentive for firms to supply output at each product price. In contrast, lower resource prices

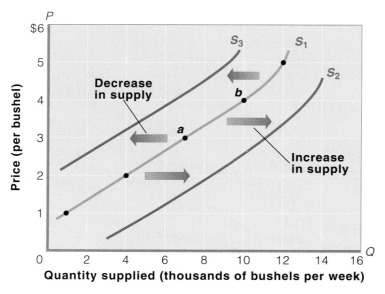

FIGURE 3-4 Changes in the supply of corn A change in one or more of the determinants of supply causes a change in supply. An increase in supply is shown as a rightward shift of the supply curve, as from S_1 to S_2. A decrease in supply is depicted as a leftward shift of the curve, as from S_1 to S_3. In contrast, a change in the quantity supplied is caused by a change in the product's price and is shown by a movement from one point to another, as from a to b, on a fixed supply curve.

induce firms to supply more output at each product price since production costs fall and profits expand.

It follows that a decrease in resource prices will increase supply, shifting the supply curve to the right. If prices of seed and fertilizer decrease, we can expect the supply of corn to increase. Conversely, an increase in resource prices will raise production costs and reduce supply, shifting the supply curve to the left. Increases in the prices of iron ore and coke will increase the cost of producing steel and reduce its supply.

Technology Improvements in technology enable firms to produce units of output with fewer resources. Because resources are costly, using fewer of them lowers production costs and increases supply. Example: Recent improvements in the fuel efficiency of aircraft engines have reduced the cost of providing passenger

air service. Thus, airlines now offer more air service than previously at each ticket price; the supply of air service has increased.

Taxes and Subsidies Businesses treat most taxes as costs. An increase in sales or property taxes will increase production costs and reduce supply. In contrast, subsidies are "taxes in reverse." If government subsidizes the production of a good, it in effect lowers production costs and increases supply.

Prices of Other Goods Firms producing a particular product, say, soccer balls, can sometimes use their plant and equipment to produce alternative goods, say, basketballs and volleyballs. Higher prices of these "other goods" may entice soccer ball producers to switch production to them in order to increase profits. This *substitution in production* results in a decline in the supply of soccer balls. Alternatively, lower prices of basketballs and volleyballs may entice producers of these goods to produce more soccer balls, increasing their supply.

Expectations Expectations about the future price of a product can affect the producer's current willingness to supply that product. It is difficult, however, to generalize about how the expectation of higher prices affects the present supply of a product. Farmers anticipating a higher corn price in the future might withhold some of their current corn harvest from the market, which would cause a decrease in the current supply of corn. Similarly, if the price of Intel stock is expected to rise significantly in the near future, the supply offered for sale today might decrease. In contrast, in many types of manufacturing industries, ex-

TABLE 3-6   Market supply of corn, 200 producers

(1) Price per bushel	(2) Quantity supplied per week, single producer		(3) Number of sellers in the market		(4) Total quantity supplied per week
$5	60	×	200	=	12,000
4	50	×	200	=	10,000
3	35	×	200	=	7,000
2	20	×	200	=	4,000
1	5	×	200	=	1,000

pected price increases may induce firms to add another shift of workers or expand their production facilities, causing current supply to increase.

Number of Sellers Other things equal, the larger the number of suppliers, the greater the market supply. As more firms enter an industry, the supply curve shifts to the right. Conversely, the smaller the number of firms in the industry, the less the market supply. This means that as firms leave an industry, the supply curve shifts to the left. Example: The United States and Canada have imposed restrictions on haddock fishing to replenish dwindling stocks. As part of that policy, the Federal government has bought the boats of some of the haddock fishermen as a way of putting them out of business and decreasing the catch. The result has been a decline in the market supply of haddock.

Table 3-7 is a checklist of the determinants of supply, along with further illustrations. **(Key Question 5)**

Changes in Quantity Supplied

The distinction between a *change in supply* and a *change in quantity supplied* parallels that between a change in demand and a change in quantity demanded. Because supply is a schedule or curve, a **change in supply** means a change in the entire schedule and a shift of the entire curve. An increase in supply shifts the curve to the right; a decrease in supply shifts it to the left. The cause of a change in supply is a change in one or more of the determinants of supply.

In contrast, a **change in quantity supplied** is a movement from one point to another on a fixed supply curve. The cause of such a movement is a change in the price of the specific product being considered. In Table 3-6, a decline in the price of corn from $5 to $4 decreases the quantity of corn supplied from 12,000 to 10,000 bushels. This is a change in quantity supplied, not a change in supply. Supply is the full schedule of prices and quantities shown, and this schedule does not change when price changes.

QUICK REVIEW 3-2

■ A supply schedule or curve shows that, other things equal, the quantity of a good supplied varies directly with its price.

■ The supply curve shifts because of changes in **(a)** resources prices, **(b)** technology, **(c)** taxes or subsidies, **(d)** prices of other goods, **(e)** expectations of future prices, and **(f)** the number of suppliers.

■ A change in supply is a shift of the supply curve; a change in quantity supplied is a movement from one point to another on a fixed supply curve.

TABLE 3-7   **Determinants of supply: factors which shift the supply curve**

Determinant	Examples
Change in resource prices	A decline in the price of fertilizer increases the supply of wheat; an increase in the price of irrigation equipment reduces the supply of corn.
Change in technology	The development of a more effective insecticide for corn rootworm increases the supply of corn.
Changes in taxes and subsidies	An increase in the excise tax on cigarettes reduces the supply of cigarettes; a decline in subsidies to state universities reduces the supply of higher education.
Change in prices of other goods	A decline in the prices of mutton and pork increases the supply of beef.
Change in expectations	Expectations of substantial declines in future oil prices cause oil companies to increase current supply.
Change in number of suppliers	An increase in the number of firms producing personal computers increases the supply of personal computers; formation of women's professional basketball leagues increases the supply of women's professional basketball games.

SUPPLY AND DEMAND: MARKET EQUILIBRIUM

We can now bring together supply and demand to see how the buying decisions of households and the selling decisions of businesses interact to determine the price of a product and the quantity actually bought and sold. In Table 3-8, columns 1 and 2 repeat the market supply of corn (from Table 3-6), and columns 2 and 3 repeat the market demand for corn (from Table 3-3). Note that column 2 lists a common set of prices. We assume competition—a large number of buyers and sellers.

Surpluses

We have limited our examples to only five possible prices. Of these, which will actually prevail as the market price for corn? We can find an answer through trial and error; for no particular reason, let's start with $5. We immediately see that this cannot be the prevailing market price. At the $5 price, producers are willing to produce and offer for sale 12,000 bushels of corn, but buyers are willing to buy only 2000 bushels. The $5 price encourages farmers to produce lots of corn but discourages most consumers from buying it. The result is a 10,000-bushel **surplus** or *excess supply* of corn. This surplus, shown in column 4 in Table 3-8, is the excess of quantity supplied over quantity demanded at $5. Corn farmers would find themselves with 10,000 unsold bushels of output.

A price of $5—even if it existed temporarily in the corn market—could not persist over a period of time. The very large surplus of corn would prompt com-

peting sellers to lower the price to encourage buyers to take the surplus off their hands.

Suppose the price goes down to $4. The lower price encourages consumers to buy more corn and, at the same time, induces farmers to offer less of it for sale. The surplus diminishes to 6000 bushels. Nevertheless, since there is still a surplus, competition among sellers will once again reduce the price. Clearly, then, the prices of $5 and $4 are unstable—they will not survive—because they are "too high." The market price of corn must be less than $4.

Shortages

Let's jump now to $1 as the possible market price of corn. Observe in column 4 in Table 3-8 that at this price, quantity demanded exceeds quantity supplied by 15,000 units. The $1 price discourages farmers from devoting resources to corn production and encourages consumers to attempt to buy more than is available. The result is a 15,000-bushel **shortage** of, or *excess demand* for, corn. The $1 price cannot persist as the market price. Many consumers who are willing and able to buy at this price will not get corn. They will express a willingness to pay more than $1 to get some of the available output. Competition among these buyers will drive up the price to something greater than $1.

Suppose the competition among buyers boosts the price to $2. This higher price reduces, but does not eliminate, the shortage of corn. For $2, farmers devote more resources to corn production, and some buyers who were willing to pay $1 per bushel choose not to buy corn at $2. But a shortage of 7000 bushels still exists at $2. This shortage will push the market price above $2.

Equilibrium Price and Quantity

By trial and error we have eliminated every price but $3. At $3, *and only at this price*, the quantity of corn that farmers are willing to produce and supply is identical with the quantity consumers are willing and able to buy. There is neither a shortage nor a surplus of corn at that price.

With no shortage or surplus at $3, there is no reason for the price of corn to change. Economists call this price the *market-clearing* or **equilibrium price**, equilibrium meaning "in balance" or "at rest." At $3, quantity supplied and quantity demanded are in balance at the **equilibrium quantity** of 7000 bushels. So

TABLE 3-8   Market supply of and demand for corn

(1) Total quantity supplied per week	(2) Price per bushel	(3) Total quantity demanded per week	(4) Surplus (+) or shortage (−)
12,000	$5	2,000	+10,000↓
10,000	4	4,000	+6,000↓
7,000	3	7,000	0
4,000	2	11,000	−7,000↑
1,000	1	16,000	−15,000↑

Arrows indicate effect on price.

$3 is the only stable price of corn under the supply and demand conditions shown in Table 3-8.

The price of corn—or of any other product bought and sold in competitive markets—will be established where the supply decisions of producers and the demand decisions of buyers are mutually consistent. Such decisions are consistent only at the equilibrium price (here, $3) and equilibrium quantity (here, 7000 bushels). At a higher price, suppliers want to sell more than consumers want to buy and a surplus results; at any lower price, consumers want to buy more than producers make available for sale and a shortage results. Such discrepancies between the supply and demand intentions of sellers and buyers then prompt price changes that bring the two sets of intentions into accord.

A graphical analysis of supply and demand should yield these same conclusions. **Figure 3-5 (Key Graph)** shows the market supply and demand curves for corn on the same graph. (The horizontal axis now measures both quantity demanded and quantity supplied.)

Graphically, the intersection of the supply curve and demand curve for a product indicates the market equilibrium. Here, equilibrium price and quantity are $3 per bushel and 7000 bushels. At any above-equilibrium price, quantity supplied exceeds quantity demanded This surplus of corn causes price reductions by sellers who are eager to rid themselves of their surplus. The falling price causes less corn to be offered and simultaneously encourages consumers to buy more. The market moves to its equilibrium.

Any price below the equilibrium price creates a shortage; quantity demanded now exceeds quantity supplied. Buyers try to obtain the product by offering to pay more for it; this drives the price upward toward its equilibrium level. The rising price simultaneously causes producers to increase the quantity supplied and many buyers to leave the market, eliminating the shortage. Again the market moves to its equilibrium.

Rationing Function of Prices

The ability of the competitive forces of supply and demand to establish a price at which selling and buying decisions are consistent is called the **rationing function of prices.** In our case, the equilibrium price of $3 clears the market, leaving no burdensome surplus for sellers and no inconvenient shortage for potential buyers. And it is the combination of freely made individual decisions that sets this market-clearing price. In effect, the market mechanism of supply and demand says that any buyer willing and able to pay $3 for a bushel of corn will be able to acquire one; buyers who are not, will not. Similarly, any seller willing and able to produce bushels of corn and offer them for sale at $3 will be able to do so; sellers who are not, will not. **(Key Question 7)**

Changes in Supply, Demand, and Equilibrium

We know that demand might change because of fluctuations in consumer tastes or incomes, changes in consumer expectations, or variations in the prices of related goods. Supply might change in response to changes in resource prices, technology, or taxes. What effects will such changes in supply and demand have on equilibrium price and quantity?

Changes in Demand Suppose that supply is constant and demand increases, as shown in Figure 3-6a. As a result, the new intersection of the supply and demand curves is at higher values on both the price and quantity axes. Clearly, an increase in demand raises both equilibrium price and equilibrium quantity. Conversely, a decrease in demand, such as that shown in Figure 3-6b, reduces both equilibrium price and equilibrium quantity. (The value of graphical analysis is now apparent: We need not fumble with columns of figures to determine the outcomes, but only compare the new and the old points of intersection on the graph.)

Changes in Supply Let's now suppose demand is constant but supply increases, as in Figure 3-6c. The new intersection of supply and demand is located at a lower equilibrium price but at a higher equilibrium quantity. An increase in supply reduces equilibrium price but increases equilibrium quantity. In contrast, if supply decreases, as in Figure 3-6d, the equilibrium price rises while the equilibrium quantity declines.

Complex Cases When both supply and demand change, the effect is a combination of the individual effects.

1. Supply Increase; Demand Decrease What effect will a supply increase and a demand decrease have on equilibrium price? Both changes decrease price, so the net result is a price drop greater than that resulting from either change alone.

What about equilibrium quantity? Here the effects of the changes in supply and demand are op-

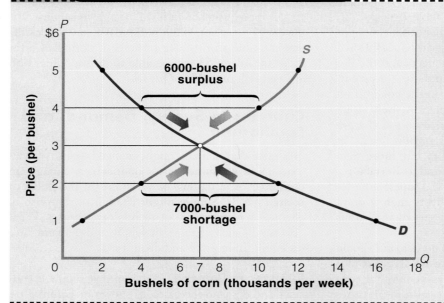

FIGURE 3-5 Equilibrium price and quantity The intersection of the downsloping demand curve *D* and the upsloping supply curve *S* indicates the equilibrium price and quantity, here $3 and 7000 bushels of corn. The shortages of corn at below-equilibrium prices, for example, 7000 bushels at $2, drive up price. These higher prices increase the quantity supplied and reduce the quantity demanded until equilibrium is achieved. The surpluses caused by above-equilibrium prices, for example, 6000 bushels at $4, push price down. As price drops, the quantity demanded rises and the quantity supplied falls until equilibrium is established. At the equilibrium price and quantity, there are neither shortages nor surpluses of corn.

QUICK QUIZ 3-5

1. Demand curve *D* is downsloping because:
  a. producers offer less of a product for sale as the price of the product falls.
  b. lower prices of a product create income and substitution effects which lead consumers to purchase more of it.
  c. the larger the number of buyers in a market, the lower the product price.
  d. price and quantity demanded are directly (positively) related.

2. Supply curve *S*:
  a. reflects an inverse (negative) relationship between price and quantity supplied.
  b. reflects a direct (positive) relationship between price and quantity supplied.
  c. depicts the collective behavior of buyers in this market.

  d. shows that producers will offer more of a product for sale at a low product price than at a high product price.

3. At the $3 price:
  a. quantity supplied exceeds quantity demanded.
  b. quantity demanded exceeds quantity supplied.
  c. the product is abundant and a surplus exists.
  d. there is no pressure on price to rise or fall.

4. At price $5 in this market:
  a. there will be a shortage of 10,000 units.
  b. there will be a surplus of 10,000 units.
  c. quantity demanded will be 12,000 units.
  d. quantity demanded will equal quantity supplied.

Answers: 1. b; 2. b; 3. d; 4. b

---

posed: The increase in supply increases equilibrium quantity, but the decrease in demand reduces it. The direction of the change in quantity depends on the relative sizes of the changes in supply and demand. If the increase in supply is larger than the decrease in demand, the equilibrium quantity will increase. But if the decrease in demand is greater than the increase in supply, the equilibrium quantity will decrease.

2. *Supply Decrease; Demand Increase* A decrease in supply and an increase in demand both increase price. Their combined effect is an increase in equilibrium price greater than that caused by either change separately. But their effect on equilibrium quantity is again indeterminate, depending on the relative sizes of the changes in supply and demand. If the decrease in supply is larger than the increase in de-

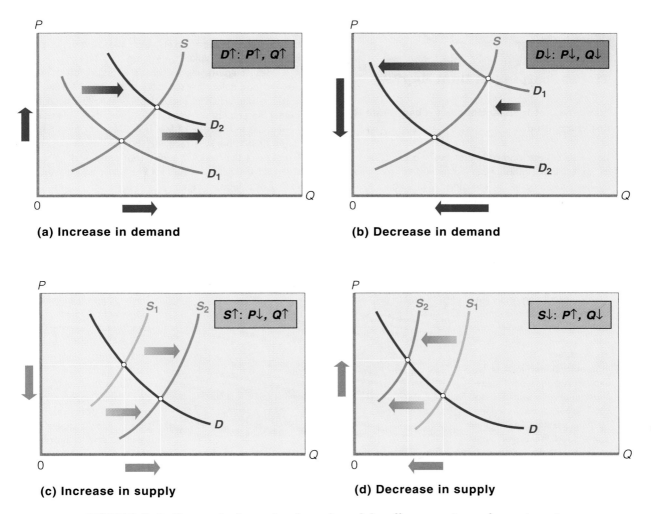

FIGURE 3-6 Changes in demand and supply and the effects on price and quantity   The increase in demand from D_1 to D_2 in (a) increases both equilibrium price and quantity. The decrease in demand from D_1 to D_2 in (b) decreases both equilibrium price and quantity. The increase in supply from S_1 to S_2 in (c) decreases equilibrium price and increases equilibrium quantity. The decline in supply from S_1 to S_2 in (d) increases equilibrium price and reduces equilibrium quantity. The boxes in the top right corners summarize the respective changes and outcomes. The upward arrows in the boxes signify increases in demand (*D*), supply (*S*), equilibrium price (*P*), and equilibrium quantity (*Q*); the downward arrows signify decreases in these items.

mand, the equilibrium quantity will decrease. In contrast, if the increase in demand is greater than the decrease in supply, the equilibrium quantity will increase.

3. Supply Increase; Demand Increase   What if supply and demand both increase? A supply increase drops equilibrium price, while a demand increase boosts it. If the increase in supply is greater than the increase in demand, the equilibrium price will fall. If the opposite holds, the equilibrium price will rise.

   The effect on equilibrium quantity is certain: The increases in supply and in demand each raise equilibrium quantity. Therefore, the equilibrium quantity will increase by an amount greater than that caused by either change alone.

Ticket Scalping: A Bum Rap?

Some market transactions get a bad name that is not warranted.

Tickets to athletic and artistic events are sometimes resold at higher-than-original prices—a market transaction known by the unsavory term "scalping." For example, a $40 ticket to a college bowl game may be resold by the original buyer for $200, $250, or more. The media often denounce scalpers for "ripping off" buyers by charging "exorbitant" prices. Scalping and extortion are synonymous in some people's minds.

But is scalping really sinful? We must first recognize that such ticket resales are voluntary—not coerced— transactions. This implies that both buyer and seller expect to gain from the exchange or it would not occur. The seller must value the $200 more than seeing the game, and the buyer must value seeing the game more than the $200. So there are no losers or victims here: Both buyer and seller benefit from the transaction. The "scalping" market simply redis-

tributes assets (game tickets) from those who value them less to those who value them more.

Does scalping impose losses or injury on other parties—in particular, the sponsors of the event? If the sponsors are injured, it is because they initially priced tickets below the equilibrium level. In so doing they suffer an economic loss in the form of less revenue and profit than they might have otherwise received. But the loss is self-inflicted because of their pricing error. That mistake is quite separate and distinct from the fact that some tickets were later resold at a higher price.

What about spectators? Does scalping somehow impose losses by deteriorating the quality of the game's audience? No! People who most want to see the game—generally those with the greatest interest in and understanding of the game—will pay the scalper's high prices. Ticket scalping also benefits the athletic teams and performing artists—they will appear before more dedicated and perhaps more appreciative audiences.

So, is ticket scalping undesirable? Not on economic grounds. Both seller and buyer of a "scalped" ticket benefit, and a more interested and appreciative audience results. Game sponsors may sacrifice revenue and profits, but that stems from their own misjudgment of the equilibrium price.

4. Supply Decrease; Demand Decrease What of decreases in both supply and demand? If the decrease in supply is greater than the decrease in demand, equilibrium price will rise. If the reverse is true, equilibrium price will fall. Because decreases in supply and in demand each reduce equilibrium quantity, we can be sure that equilibrium quantity will fall.

Table 3-9 summarizes these four cases. To understand them fully you should draw supply and demand diagrams for each case to confirm the effects listed in the table.

Special cases might arise where a decrease in demand and a decrease in supply, or an increase in demand and an increase in supply, exactly cancel out. In both cases, the net effect on equilibrium price will be zero; price will not change. **(Key Question 8)**

TABLE 3-9   Effects of changes in both supply and demand

Change in supply	Change in demand	Effect on equilibrium price	Effect on equilibrium quantity
1 Increase	Decrease	Decrease	Indeterminate
2 Decrease	Increase	Increase	Indeterminate
3 Increase	Increase	Indeterminate	Increase
4 Decrease	Decrease	Indeterminate	Decrease

A Reminder: "Other Things Equal"

We must stress once again that specific demand and supply curves (such as those in Figure 3-6) show relationships between prices and quantities demanded and supplied, *other things equal*. The downsloping demand curves tell us that price and quantity demanded are inversely related, other things equal. The upsloping supply curves imply that price and quantity supplied are directly related, other things equal.

If you forget the other-things-equal assumption, you can encounter situations which *seem* to be in conflict with these basic principles. For example, suppose salsa manufacturers sell 1 million bottles of salsa at $4 a bottle in 1 year; 2 million bottles at $5 in the next year; and 3 million at $6 in the year thereafter. Price and quantity purchased vary directly, and these data seem to be at odds with the law of demand. But there is no conflict here; these data do *not* refute the law of demand. The catch is that the law of demand's other-things-equal assumption has been violated over the 3 years in the example. Specifically, because of changing tastes and growing incomes, the demand for salsa has increased sharply, as in Figure 3-6a. The result is higher prices *and* larger quantities purchased.

As another example, the price of coffee occasionally has shot upward at the same time that the quantity of coffee produced has declined. These events seemingly contradict the direct relationship between price and quantity denoted by supply. The catch again is that the other-things-equal assumption underlying the upsloping supply curve was violated. Poor coffee harvests decreased supply, as in Figure 3-6d, increasing the equilibrium price of coffee and reducing the equilibrium quantity.

These examples also emphasize the importance of our earlier distinction between a change in quantity demanded (or supplied) and a change in demand (supply). In Figure 3-6a a change in demand caused a change in the quantity supplied. In Figure 3-6d a change in supply caused a change in quantity demanded.

Application: Pink Salmon

To reinforce the concepts we just discussed, let's briefly examine the real-world market for pink salmon—a market in which price has dramatically changed.

In the early 1970s, fishermen earned today's equivalent of $.60 for each pound of pink salmon delivered

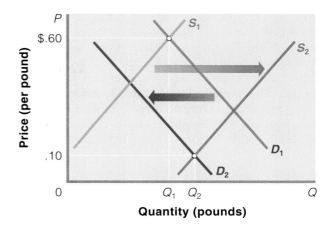

FIGURE 3-7 The market for pink salmon Since the early 1970s, the supply of pink salmon has increased and the demand for pink salmon has decreased. As a result, the price of pink salmon has declined, here from $.60 to $.10 a pound. Since supply has increased more than demand has declined, the equilibrium quantity of pink salmon has increased, here from Q_1 to Q_2.

to the docks. This equilibrium price is shown in Figure 3-7 at the intersection of supply curve S_1 and demand curve D_1. The corresponding equilibrium quantity of pink salmon—the type most often used for canning—was Q_1 pounds. (The actual "quantity numbers" are unimportant to our analysis.)

Between the early 1970s and late 1990s, changes in supply and demand occurred in the market for pink salmon. On the supply side, improved technology in the form of larger, more efficient fishing boats greatly increased the catch and lowered the cost of obtaining the fish. Also, the then-high profits at the $.60 price encouraged many new fishermen to enter the industry. As a result of these changes, the supply of pink salmon greatly increased and the supply curve shifted to the right, as from S_1 to S_2 in Figure 3-7.

Over the same years, the demand for pink salmon declined, as represented by the shift from demand curve D_1 to D_2 in Figure 3-7. The decline in demand resulted mainly from changes in consumer tastes, together with increases in consumer income: Buyers shifted their preferences away from canned fish and toward higher-quality fresh or frozen fish, including higher-quality species of salmon such as Chinook and Coho.

These supply and demand changes had a sizable effect on the price of pink salmon, as shown in Figure

3-7. By 1997 the equilibrium price had fallen to just $.10 per pound—83 percent below the price in the early 1970s. Both the increase in supply and the decrease in demand helped reduce the equilibrium price. However, the equilibrium *quantity* of pink salmon increased, as represented by the increase from Q_1 to Q_2. This change in quantity occurred because the increase in the supply of pink salmon exceeded the decline in demand.

QUICK REVIEW 3-3

■ In competitive markets, prices adjust to the equilibrium level at which quantity demanded equals quantity supplied.

■ The equilibrium price and quantity are those indicated by the intersection of the supply and demand curves for any product or resource.

■ An increase in demand increases equilibrium price and quantity; a decrease in demand decreases equilibrium price and quantity.

■ An increase in supply reduces equilibrium price but increases equilibrium quantity; a decrease in supply increases equilibrium price but reduces equilibrium quantity.

■ Over time, equilibrium price and quantity may change in directions which seem at odds with the laws of demand and supply because the other-things-equal assumption is violated.

CHAPTER SUMMARY

1. A market is any institution or arrangement which brings together buyers and sellers of a product, service, or resource.

2. Demand is a schedule or curve representing the willingness of buyers in a specific period to purchase a particular product at each of various prices. The law of demand implies that consumers will buy more of a product at a low price than at a high price. Therefore, other things equal, the relationship between price and quantity demanded is negative or inverse and is graphed as a downsloping curve. Market demand curves are found by adding horizontally the demand curves of the many individual consumers in the market.

3. Changes in one or more of the determinants of demand—consumer tastes, the number of buyers in the market, the money incomes of consumers, the prices of related goods, and consumer expectations—shift the market demand curve. A shift to the right is an increase in demand; a shift to the left is a decrease in demand. A change in demand is different from a change in the quantity demanded, the latter being a movement from one point to another point on a fixed demand curve because of a change in the product's price.

4. Supply is a schedule or curve showing the amounts of a product which producers are willing to offer in the market at each possible price during a specific period. The law of supply states that, other things equal, producers will offer more of a product at a high price than at a low price. Thus, the relationship between price and quantity supplied is positive or direct, and supply is graphed as an upsloping curve. The market supply curve is the horizontal summation of the supply curves of individual producers of the product.

5. Changes in one or more of the determinants of supply—resource prices, production techniques, taxes or subsidies, the prices of other goods, price expectations, or the number of sellers in the market—shift the supply curve of a product. A shift to the right is an increase in supply; a shift to the left is a decrease in supply. In contrast, a change in the price of the product being considered causes a change in the quantity supplied, which is shown as a movement from one point to another point on a fixed supply curve.

6. The equilibrium price and quantity are those indicated by the intersection of the supply and demand curves. The interaction of market demand and market supply adjusts the price to the point at which quantity demanded and quantity supplied are equal. This is the equilibrium price. The corresponding quantity is the equilibrium quantity.

7. The ability of market forces to synchronize selling and buying decisions to eliminate potential surpluses and shortages is known as the rationing function of prices.

8. A change in either demand or supply changes the equilibrium price and quantity. Increases in demand raise both equilibrium price and equilibrium quantity; decreases in demand reduce both equilibrium price and equilibrium quantity. Increases in supply reduce equilibrium price and increase equilibrium quantity; decreases in supply raise equilibrium price and reduce equilibrium quantity.

9. Simultaneous changes in demand and supply affect equilibrium price and quantity in various ways, depending on their direction and relative magnitudes.

TERMS AND CONCEPTS

market
demand
demand schedule
law of demand
diminishing marginal
  utility
income effect
substitution effect
demand curve

determinants of demand
normal good
inferior good
substitute good
complementary good
change in demand
change in quantity
  demanded
supply

supply schedule
law of supply
supply curve
determinants of supply
change in supply
change in quantity
  supplied
surplus
shortage

equilibrium price
equilibrium quantity
rationing function of
  prices

STUDY QUESTIONS

1. Explain the law of demand. Why does a demand curve slope downward? What are the determinants of demand? What happens to the demand curve when each of these determinants changes? Distinguish between a change in demand and a change in the quantity demanded, noting the cause(s) of each.

2. KEY QUESTION What effect will each of the following have on the demand for product B?
  a. Product B becomes more fashionable.
  b. The price of substitute product C falls.
  c. Income declines and B is an inferior good.
  d. Consumers anticipate the price of B will be lower in the near future.
  e. The price of complementary product D falls.
  f. Foreign tariff barriers on B are eliminated.

3. Explain the following news dispatch from Hull, England: "The fish market here slumped today to what local commentators called 'a disastrous level'— all because of a shortage of potatoes. The potatoes are one of the main ingredients in a dish that figures on almost every café-menu—fish and chips."

4. Explain the law of supply. Why does the supply curve slope upward? What are the determinants of supply? What happens to the supply curve when each of these determinants changes? Distinguish between a change in supply and a change in the quantity supplied, noting the cause(s) of each.

5. KEY QUESTION What effect will each of the following have on the supply of product B?
  a. A technological advance in the methods of producing B.
  b. A decline in the number of firms in industry B.
  c. An increase in the prices of resources required in the production of B.

  d. The expectation that the equilibrium price of B will be lower in the future than it is currently.
  e. A decline in the price of product A, a good whose production requires substantially the same techniques and resources as does the production of B.
  f. The levying of a specific sales tax on B.
  g. The granting of a 50-cent per-unit subsidy for each unit of B produced.

6. "In the corn market, demand often exceeds supply and supply sometimes exceeds demand." "The price of corn rises and falls in response to changes in supply and demand." In which of these two statements are the terms "supply" and "demand" used correctly? Explain.

7. KEY QUESTION Suppose the total demand for wheat and the total supply of wheat per month in the Kansas City grain market are as follows:

Thousands of bushels demanded	Price per bushel	Thousands of bushels supplied	Surplus (+) or shortage (−)
85	$3.40	72	_____
80	3.70	73	_____
75	4.00	75	_____
70	4.30	77	_____
65	4.60	79	_____
60	4.90	81	_____

  a. What is the equilibrium price? What is the equilibrium quantity? Fill in the surplus-shortage column and use it to explain why your answers are correct.
  b. Graph the demand for wheat and the supply of wheat. Be sure to label the axes of your graph correctly. Label equilibrium price *P* and equilibrium quantity *Q*.

c. Why will $3.40 not be the equilibrium price in this market? Why not $4.90? "Surpluses drive prices up; shortages drive them down." Do you agree?

d. Now suppose that the government establishes a ceiling (maximum legal) price of, say, $3.70 for wheat. Explain carefully the effects of this ceiling price. Demonstrate your answer graphically. What might prompt government to establish a ceiling price?

8. **KEY QUESTION** How will each of the following changes in demand and/or supply affect equilibrium price and equilibrium quantity in a competitive market; that is, do price and quantity rise, fall, or remain unchanged, or are the answers indeterminate because they depend on the magnitudes of the shifts? You should use supply and demand diagrams to verify the answers.

a. Supply decreases and demand is constant.
b. Demand decreases and supply is constant.
c. Supply increases and demand is constant.
d. Demand increases and supply increases.
e. Demand increases and supply is constant.
f. Supply increases and demand decreases.
g. Demand increases and supply decreases.
h. Demand decreases and supply decreases.

9. "Prices are the automatic regulator which tends to keep production and consumption in line with each other." Explain.

10. Explain: "Even though parking meters may yield little or no net revenue, they should nevertheless be retained because of the rationing function they perform."

11. Use two market diagrams to explain how an increase in state subsidies to public colleges might affect tuition and enrollments in both public and private colleges.

12. Critically evaluate: "In comparing the two equilibrium positions in Figure 3-6a, I note that a larger amount is actually purchased at a higher price. This refutes the law of demand."

13. Suppose you go to a recycling center and are paid $.25 per pound for your aluminum cans. However, the recycler charges you $.20 per bundle to accept your old newspapers. Use demand and supply diagrams to portray both markets. Explain how different government policies with respect to the recycling of aluminum and paper might account for these different market outcomes.

14. **Advanced analysis:** Assume that demand for a commodity is represented by the equation $P = 10 - .2Q_d$ and supply by the equation $P = 2 + .2Q_s$, where Q_d and Q_s are quantity demanded and quantity supplied, respectively, and P is price. Using the equilibrium condition $Q_s = Q_d$, solve the equations to determine equilibrium price. Now determine equilibrium quantity. Graph the two equations to substantiate your answers.

15. **(Last Word)** Discuss the economic aspects of ticket scalping, specifying gainers and losers.

16. **WEB-BASED QUESTION** Changes in Supply—USDA's Weekly Weather and Crop Bulletin The USDA (United States Department of Agriculture) http://www.usda.gov/nass/ publishes a weekly weather and crop bulletin, found under Today's Reports at their home page. Select a crop to analyze (corn, soybeans, cotton, rice, sorghum, or winter wheat), and then predict whether there will be an increase or a decrease in the supply of that crop based on the report. Assuming that demand remains unchanged, do you expect prices to increase or decrease within the next month? To check your price forecast, visit USDA's Market News http:/www.ams.usda.gov/marketnews.htm during the next month.

17. **WEB-BASED QUESTION** Changes in Demand—Baby Diapers and Retirement Villages Other things equal, an increase in the number of buyers for a product or service will increase demand. Baby diapers and retirement villages are two products designed for different population groups. The U.S. Census http://www.census.gov/ipc/www/idbpyr.html provides population pyramids (graphs which show the distribution of population by age and sex) for countries for the current year, 2025, and 2050. View the population pyramids for Mexico, Japan, and the United States. Which country would you expect to have the greatest percentage increase in demand for baby diapers in the year 2050? For retirement villages? Which country would you expect to have the greatest absolute increase in demand for baby diapers? For retirement villages?

CHAPTER FOUR

Pure Capitalism and the Market System

In Chapter 3 we saw how equilibrium prices and quantities are established in individual product and resource markets. We now widen our focus to take in all product and resource markets—the *competitive market system,* also known as the *private enterprise system* or, simply, *capitalism.* The press and television regularly report on the progress of Russia, the eastern European nations, and China in their transitions from command economies to capitalism. Precisely what are the features of capitalism these nations are trying to emulate?

In this chapter, we describe the capitalist ideology and explain how pure, or laissez-faire, capitalism would operate. Although it has never actually existed, pure capitalism provides a useful approximation to the economies of the United States and many other industrially advanced nations. We will modify this approximation in later chapters to correspond more closely to the reality of modern capitalism.

In examining pure capitalism, we first discuss its basic assumptions and institutions—the significant practices, relationships, and organizations. We then consider certain other institutions common to all advanced industrial economies. Finally, we explain how a market system coordinates economic activity and contributes to the efficient use of scarce resources. In achieving this third goal, we rely heavily on Chapter 3's explanation of supply and demand in individual markets.

CAPITALIST IDEOLOGY

Let's begin by examining in some detail the basic tenets that define capitalism: (1) private property, (2) freedom of enterprise and choice, (3) self-interest as the dominant motive, (4) competition, (5) reliance on the market system, and (6) a limited role for government.

Private Property

In a capitalist system, property resources (land, capital) are usually owned by private individuals and firms, not by government. In fact, the private ownership of capital is what gives capitalism its name. This right of **private property,** coupled with the freedom to negotiate binding legal contracts, allows private persons or businesses to obtain, control, employ, and dispose of property resources as they see fit. The right to bequeath—the right of a property owner to designate who receives his or her property at the time of death—sustains the institution of private property.

Property rights are significant because they encourage investment, innovation, exchange, and economic growth. Why would anyone stock a store, construct a factory, or clear land for farming if someone else, including government, could take that property for his or her own benefit?

Property rights also apply to intellectual property via patents and copyrights. These long-term protections encourage people to write books, music, and computer programs and to invent new products and production processes without fear that others will steal them and the rewards they may bring.

Another important role of property rights is that they facilitate exchange. A title to an automobile or deed to a cattle ranch assures the buyer that the seller is the legitimate owner. Finally, with property rights, people can spend their time, energy, and resources producing more goods and services, rather than using them to protect and retain the property they have already produced and acquired.

There are broad legal limits to this right of private ownership. For example, the use of private property to produce illegal drugs is prohibited. And even in pure capitalism, government ownership of certain property resources may be essential to produce "public goods": national defense, basic education, and courtrooms and prisons, for instance.

Freedom of Enterprise and Choice

Closely related to private ownership of property is freedom of enterprise and choice. Capitalism requires that various economic units make certain choices, which are expressed and implemented through the free markets of the economy.

Freedom of enterprise means that private businesses are free to obtain economic resources, to organize those resources in the production of goods and services of the firm's own choosing, and to sell them in the markets of their choice. In pure capitalism no artificial obstacles or restrictions imposed by government or other producers block an entrepreneur's decision to enter or leave a particular industry.

Freedom of choice means that owners can employ or dispose of their property and money as they see fit. It also means that workers are free to enter any lines of work for which they are qualified. Finally, it means that consumers are at liberty, within the limits of their incomes, to buy that collection of goods and services which best satisfies their wants.

Freedom of *consumer* choice in a capitalist economy is perhaps the most profound of these freedoms. The consumer is in a particularly strategic position;

in a sense, the consumer is sovereign. Consumers ultimately decide via their choices what the capitalist economy should produce. Businesses and resource suppliers then make their free choices within these constraints. They are not really "free" to produce goods and services consumers do not desire because producing such items would be unprofitable.

Again, all these choices are free only within broad legal limitations. Illegal choices are punished through fines and imprisonment. (The degree of economic freedom varies greatly from nation to nation, as indicated in Global Perspective 4-1.)

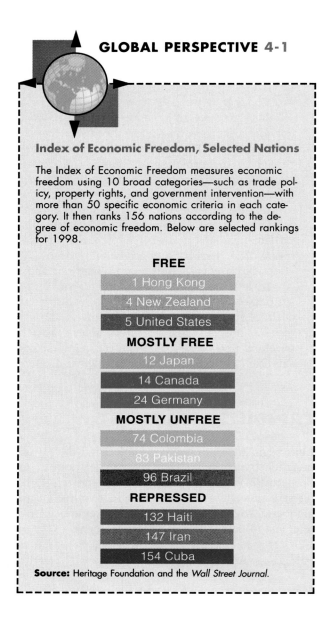

GLOBAL PERSPECTIVE 4-1

Index of Economic Freedom, Selected Nations

The Index of Economic Freedom measures economic freedom using 10 broad categories—such as trade policy, property rights, and government intervention—with more than 50 specific economic criteria in each category. It then ranks 156 nations according to the degree of economic freedom. Below are selected rankings for 1998.

FREE
1 Hong Kong
4 New Zealand
5 United States

MOSTLY FREE
12 Japan
14 Canada
24 Germany

MOSTLY UNFREE
74 Colombia
83 Pakistan
96 Brazil

REPRESSED
132 Haiti
147 Iran
154 Cuba

Source: Heritage Foundation and the *Wall Street Journal.*

Self-Interest

The primary driving force of capitalism is **self-interest.** Each economic unit attempts to do what is best for itself. Entrepreneurs aim to maximize their firm's profit or, in adverse circumstances, minimize losses. Property owners attempt to get the highest price for the sale or rent of their resources. Workers attempt to maximize their utility (satisfaction) by finding jobs which offer the best combination of wages, fringe benefits, and working conditions. Consumers, in purchasing a specific product, seek to obtain it at the lowest possible price. Consumers also apportion their expenditures to maximize their utility. In brief, capitalism presumes self-interest as the *modus operandi* for the various economic units as they express their free choices. The motive of self-interest gives direction and consistency to what might otherwise be an extremely chaotic economy.

Pursuit of self-interest should not be confused with selfishness. A stockholder may invest to receive the best available corporate dividends but then donate much of it to the United Way or give it to grandchildren. A worker may take a second job to help pay college tuition for her or his children. An entrepreneur may make a fortune and donate much of it to a charitable foundation.

Competition

Freedom of choice exercised in promotion of one's own monetary returns is the basis for competition. In its pure form, **competition** requires:

1. Large numbers of independently acting buyers and sellers operating in the market for any particular product or resource

2. Freedom of buyers and sellers to enter or leave any particular market, based on their economic self-interest

Large Numbers   The essence of competition is the widespread diffusion of economic power within the two major aggregates—businesses and households—that comprise the economy. When many buyers and many sellers are in a particular market, no one buyer or seller is able to demand or supply a quantity of the product sufficiently large to affect its price. Let's examine this statement in terms of the supply side of the product market.

We know that when a product becomes unusually scarce, its price rises. An unseasonable frost in Florida may seriously reduce the supply of citrus crops and sharply increase the price of oranges. Similarly, if a single producer or a small group of producers acting together can somehow restrict the total output of a product, then it can raise the price to the seller's advantage. By controlling supply, a firm can "rig the market" on its own behalf. In its purest form, competition means there are so many independently acting firms that each has virtually no influence over the market supply or, therefore, over price *because it is contributing an almost negligible fraction of the total output.*

Suppose there are 10,000 farmers, each producing and selling 100 bushels of corn in the Kansas City grain market when the price of corn is $4 per bushel. Could a single farmer who feels dissatisfied with that price cause an artificial scarcity of corn to boost the price above $4? The answer is "no." Even if Farmer Jones withheld his output completely, he would reduce the total amount supplied only from 1,000,000 to 999,900 bushels. This is not much of a shortage! Supply would be virtually unchanged, and the $4 price would persist.

Competition means that each seller is providing a minuscule amount of the market supply. Individual sellers can make no noticeable impact on total output; thus a seller cannot as an individual producer manipulate product price, which is why economists say that an individual competitive seller is "at the mercy of the market."

The same reasoning applies to the demand side of the market. Buyers are plentiful and act independently. Thus single buyers cannot manipulate the market to their advantage by refusing to buy at the market price.

The widespread diffusion of economic power underlying competition controls the use and limits the potential abuse of that power. A producer charging more than the equilibrium price will lose sales to other producers. An employer paying less than the equilibrium wage rate will lose workers to other employers. Competition is the basic regulatory force in pure capitalism.

Easy Entry and Exit   Competition also implies that it is simple for producers to enter or leave an industry; there are no artificial barriers to the expansion or contraction of specific industries. This freedom of an industry to expand or contract provides a competitive economy with the flexibility needed to remain efficient over time. Freedom of entry and exit allows the economy to adjust to changes in consumer tastes, technology, and resource availability.

Markets and Prices

The basic coordinating mechanism of a capitalist economy is the market system. Without a market economy, there is no capitalism. Decisions made by buyers and sellers of products and resources become effective through a system of markets. We know from Chapters 2 and 3 that a market is a mechanism or arrangement which brings buyers (demanders) and sellers (suppliers) into contact with one another. The preferences of sellers and buyers are registered on the supply and demand sides of various markets, and the outcome of these choices is a set of product and resource prices. These prices are guideposts on which resource owners, entrepreneurs, and consumers make and revise their free choices as they pursue their self-interests.

Just as competition is the controlling mechanism, so a system of markets and prices is the basic organizing force. The market system is an elaborate communication system through which innumerable individual free choices are recorded, summarized, and balanced against one another. Those who obey the dictates of the market system are rewarded; those who ignore them are penalized by the system. Through this communication system, society decides what the economy should produce, how production can be efficiently organized, and how the fruits of productive effort are distributed among the individual economic units which make up capitalism.

Not only is the market system the mechanism through which society decides how it allocates its resources and distributes the resulting output, but it is through the market system that these decisions are carried out. All this will be detailed in the final sections of this chapter.

Limited Government

A pure capitalist economy promotes a high degree of efficiency in the use of its resources. There is little need for governmental intervention in the operation of such an economy beyond its role of imposing broad legal limits on the exercise of individual choices and the use of private property. The concept of pure capitalism as a self-regulating and self-adjusting economy precludes any extensive economic role for government. However, as you will find in Chapter 5, a number of limitations and potentially undesirable outcomes associated with capitalism and the market system have resulted in active government participation in the economy.

OTHER CHARACTERISTICS

Private property, freedom of enterprise and choice, self-interest as a motivating force, competition, and reliance on a market system are more or less exclusively associated with pure capitalism.

In addition, certain institutions and practices are characteristic of all modern economies, including those with much central command: (1) the use of advanced technology and large amounts of capital goods, (2) specialization, and (3) the use of money. Advanced technology and specialization are prerequisites to efficient employment of an economy's resources. The use of money helps society specialize and use advanced technology.

Extensive Use of Technology and Capital Goods

All advanced industrial economies are based on state-of-the-art technology and the extensive use of capital goods. In pure capitalism, the opportunity and motivation for technological advance are created by competition, freedom of choice, self-interest, and the fact that monetary rewards for new products or production techniques accrue directly to the innovator. Pure capitalism therefore encourages extensive use and rapid development of complex capital goods: tools, machinery, large-scale factories, and facilities for storage, communication, transportation, and marketing. In the command economy, in contrast, the motivation for technological advance is weak; it must come through the directive of the central plan.

Why are advanced technology and capital goods important? Because the most direct method of producing a product is usually the least efficient. The inefficiencies of direct production can be avoided through **roundabout production**—the construction and use of capital to aid in the production of consumer goods. It would be ridiculous for a farmer to go at production with bare hands. There are huge benefits—in the form of more efficient production and, therefore, a more abundant output—from creating tools of production (capital equipment) and using them in the production process. The farmer's output will increase with the use of a plow, a tractor, storage bins, and so on. There is a better way for the farmer to get water out of a well than to dive in after it!

But there is a hitch. Recall the main message of the production possibilities curve: For an economy operating on its production possibilities curve, resources used to produce capital goods must be diverted from the production of consumer goods. Society must sacrifice some consumer goods today to produce the capital goods which will give it more consumer goods tomorrow. Greater abundance tomorrow requires sacrifices today. **(Key Question 2)**

Specialization

The extent to which society relies on **specialization** is astounding. The majority of consumers produce virtually none of the goods and services they consume, and they consume little or nothing of what they produce. The worker who spends most of a lifetime machining parts for marine engines may never "consume" an ocean cruise. The worker who devotes 8 hours a day to installing windows in Fords may own a Honda. Few households seriously consider producing their own food, shelter, and clothing. Many farmers sell their milk to the local dairy and then buy margarine at the local general store. Society learned long ago that self-sufficiency breeds inefficiency. The jack-of-all-trades may be a very colorful individual but is certainly not efficient.

Division of Labor In what ways does human specialization—called the **division of labor**—enhance a society's output?

1. *Makes use of ability differences* Specialization enables individuals to take advantage of existing differences in their abilities and skills. If caveman A is strong, swift, and accurate with a spear, and caveman B is weak and slow but patient, their distribution of talents can be most efficiently used if A hunts and B fishes.

2. *Allows learning by doing* Even if the abilities of A and B are identical, specialization may be ad-

vantageous. By devoting all your time to a single task, you are more likely to develop the appropriate skills and to discover improved techniques than by apportioning your time among a number of diverse tasks. You learn to be a good hunter by hunting!

3. *Saves time* Specialization—devoting all one's time to, say, a single task—avoids the loss of time involved in shifting from one job to another.

For all these reasons the division of labor results in greater total output from society's limited human resources.

Geographic Specialization Specialization also works on a regional and international basis. Oranges could be grown in Nebraska, but because of the unsuitability of the land, rainfall, and temperature, the costs would be very high. Florida could achieve some success in the production of wheat, but for similar reasons such production would be costly. That is why Nebraskans produce those products—wheat in particular—for which their resources are best adapted, and Floridians do the same, producing oranges and other citrus fruits. In specializing, both produce more than is needed locally. Then, very sensibly, Nebraskans and Floridians swap some of their surpluses—wheat for oranges. Specialization thus enables each area to make the goods it can most efficiently produce, and it permits both to enjoy a larger amount of all goods than would otherwise be available.

Similarly, on an international basis the United States specializes in such items as commercial aircraft and computers, which it sells abroad in exchange for video recorders from Japan, bananas from Honduras, and woven baskets from Thailand. Both human specialization and geographical specialization are essential in achieving efficiency in the use of resources.

Use of Money

Virtually all economies, advanced or primitive, use money. Money performs several functions, but first and foremost it is a **medium of exchange**; it makes trade easier.

In our example, Nebraskans must exchange wheat for Florida's oranges if both states are to share in the benefits of specialization. If trade were highly inconvenient or prohibited for some reason, the gains from their specialization would be lost. Nebraska and Florida would then be forced to be more self-sufficient—to produce both wheat and oranges and whatever else their consumers desire. *A convenient means of exchanging goods is a prerequisite of specialization.*

Exchange can, and sometimes does, occur on the basis of **barter,** that is, swapping goods for goods, say, wheat for oranges. But barter can pose serious problems for the economy because it requires a *coincidence of wants* between the two transactors. In our example, we assumed that Nebraskans had excess wheat to trade and wanted oranges. And we assumed Floridians had excess oranges to swap and wanted wheat. So exchange occurred. But if this coincidence of wants does not exist, trade is stymied.

Suppose Nebraska does not want any of Florida's oranges but is interested in buying potatoes from Idaho. Ironically, Idaho wants Florida's oranges but not Nebraska's wheat. And, to complicate matters, suppose that Florida wants some of Nebraska's wheat but none of Idaho's potatoes. The situation is summarized in Figure 4-1.

In no case do we find a coincidence of wants. Trade by barter clearly would be difficult. To overcome such a stalemate, economies use **money,** which is simply a convenient social invention to facilitate exchanges of goods and services. Historically, cattle, cigarettes, shells, stones, pieces of metal, and many other commodities have been used, with varying degrees of success, as a medium for facilitating exchange. But to be money, an item needs to pass only one test: *It must be generally acceptable to sellers in exchange for goods and services.* Money is socially defined; whatever society accepts as a medium of exchange *is* money.

Most economies use pieces of paper as money. This is true with the Nebraska-Florida-Idaho economy; the three states use paper dollars as money. The use of dollars as a medium of exchange allows them to overcome their trade stalemate, as demonstrated in Table 4-1.

Specifically:

1. Floridians exchange money for some of Nebraska's wheat.
2. Nebraskans exchange the money earned from the sale of wheat for some of Idaho's potatoes.
3. Idahoans exchange the money received from the sale of potatoes for some of Florida's surplus oranges.

The willingness to accept paper money (or any other kind of money) as a medium of exchange has permitted a three-way trade which allows each state to specialize in one product and obtain the other product(s) its residents desire, despite the absence of a coincidence of wants between any two of the parties. Barter, resting as it does on a coincidence of wants, would not have permitted this exchange and so would not have allowed the three states to specialize. The efficiencies of specialization would then have been lost to those states.

On a global basis the fact that different nations have different currencies complicates international

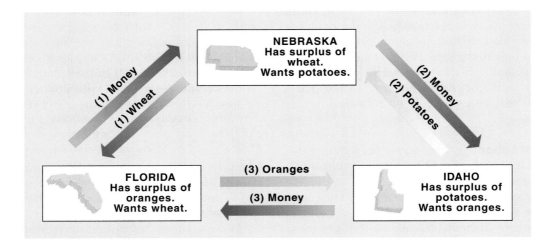

FIGURE 4-1 Money facilitates trade where wants do not coincide By the use of money as a medium of exchange, trade can be accomplished despite a noncoincidence of wants. (1) Nebraska trades the wheat that Florida wants for money from Floridians; (2) Nebraska trades the money for the potatoes it wants from Idaho; (3) Idaho trades the money to Florida for the oranges it wants.

specialization and exchange. However, foreign exchange markets permit U.S. residents, Japanese, Germans, Britons, and Mexicans to exchange dollars, yen, marks, pounds, and pesos for one another to complete international exchanges of goods and services.

A final example: Imagine a Detroit laborer producing crankshafts for Oldsmobiles. At the end of the week, instead of receiving a piece of paper endorsed by the company comptroller, or a few pieces of paper engraved in green and black, the worker receives from the company paymaster four Oldsmobile crankshafts. With no desire to hoard crankshafts, the worker ventures into the Detroit business district to spend this income on a bag of groceries, a pair of jeans, and a movie. Obviously, the worker is faced with some inconvenient and time-consuming trading, and may not be able to negotiate any exchanges at all. Finding a clothier with jeans who happens to be in the market for an Oldsmobile crankshaft can be a formidable task. And if the jeans do not trade evenly for crankshafts, how do the transactors "make change"? It is fair to say that money is one of the great social inventions of civilization.

QUICK REVIEW 4-2

■ Advanced economies achieve greater efficiency in production through the use of large quantities of technologically advanced capital goods.

■ Specialization enhances efficiency by allowing individuals, regions, and nations to produce those goods and services for which their resources are best suited.

■ The use of money facilitates the exchange of goods and services which specialization requires.

THE COMPETITIVE MARKET SYSTEM

We noted earlier that a fundamental feature of capitalism is its reliance on a market system. We have also stressed that a capitalistic system is characterized by competition, freedom of enterprise, and choice. Consumers are free to buy what they choose; businesses, to produce and sell what they choose; and resource suppliers, to make their property and human resources available in whatever occupations they choose. We may wonder why such an economy does not collapse in chaos. If consumers want breakfast cereal, businesses choose to produce aerobic shoes, and resource suppliers want to offer their services in man-

ufacturing computer software, production would seem to be deadlocked because of the apparent inconsistency of these free choices.

In reality, the millions of decisions made by households and businesses are highly consistent. Firms *do* produce those particular goods and services which consumers want. Households *do* provide the kinds of labor which businesses want to hire. In the next two sections you will see how a competitive market system constitutes a coordinating mechanism which overcomes the potential chaos suggested by freedom of enterprise and choice. The competitive market system is a mechanism both for communicating decisions of consumers, producers, and resource suppliers to one another and for synchronizing those decisions toward consistent production objectives.

The Five Fundamental Questions

To understand the operation of a market economy, we must first recognize that every economy must respond to these Five Fundamental Questions:

1. *How much of a society's resources should be used?* What proportion of available resources should be used in producing goods and services?

2. *What is to be produced?* What collection of goods and services will best satisfy society's material wants?

3. *How is that output to be produced?* How should production be organized? What firms should do the producing, and what production techniques should they use?

4. *Who is to receive the output?* How should households share the output of the economy?

5. *Can the system adapt to change?* Can it adjust to changes in consumer wants, resource supplies, and technology?

The **Five Fundamental Questions** are merely an elaboration of the economic choices underlying Chapter 2's production possibilities curve. These questions would be irrelevant were it not for the economizing problem: scarce resources in a world of unlimited wants.

THE MARKET SYSTEM AT WORK

We will defer the "how much" question until we discuss macroeconomics, which deals in detail with the complex question of levels of resource usage. Chapter

2's circular flow diagram (Figure 2-6) provides the setting for our discussion of the remaining questions. In examining how the market system answers these questions, we must draw upon our understanding of supply and demand (Chapter 3).

Determining What Is to Be Produced

With product and resource prices in place—established by competing buyers and sellers in both the product and resource markets—how would a purely capitalist economy decide on the specific types and quantities of goods to be produced? Knowing that businesses seek profits and want to avoid losses, we can generalize that those goods and services which can be produced at a profit will be produced and those whose production entail a loss will not. Two things determine profits and losses:

1. The total revenue a firm receives when it sells its product

2. The total cost of producing the product

Both total revenue and total cost are price-times-quantity figures. Total revenue is found by multiplying product price by the quantity of the product sold. Total cost is found by multiplying the price of each resource used by the amount employed and summing the results.

Economic Costs and Profits   To say that those products which can be produced profitably *will* be produced and those which cannot *will not* is an accurate generalization only if the meaning of **economic costs** is clearly understood.

Let's again think of businesses as simply organizational charts, that is, businesses "on paper," distinct from the capital, raw materials, labor, and entrepreneurial ability which make them going concerns. To become actual producing firms, these "on paper" businesses must secure all four types of resources. *Economic costs are the payments which must be made to secure and retain the needed amounts of these resources.* The per-unit size of these costs—that is, the resource prices—will be determined by supply and demand in the resource market. Like land, labor, and capital, entrepreneurial ability is a scarce resource and has a price tag on it. Costs therefore must include not only wage and salary payments to labor and interest and rental payments for capital and land but also payments to the entrepreneur for the functions he or she performs in organizing and combining the other resources to produce

a commodity. The payment for these contributions of the entrepreneur is called **normal profit.**

A product will be produced only when total revenue is large enough to pay wages, interest, rent, and a normal profit to the entrepreneur. However, if the total revenue from the sale of a product exceeds all these economic costs, the remainder will go to the entrepreneur as an added reward. This return above all economic costs is called *pure profit* or **economic profit.** Economic profit is *not* an economic cost because it need not be realized for the business to acquire and retain the entrepreneurial resource. But economic profit *is* the profit which lures other producers to a particular industry.

Profits and Expanding Industries   An example will explain how the market system determines what goods will be produced. With current technology, suppose the most favorable relationship between total revenue and total cost in producing product X occurs when the firm's output is 15 units. Assume, too, that the least-cost combination of resources in producing 15 units of X is 2 units of labor, 3 units of land, 1 of capital, and 1 of entrepreneurial ability, selling at prices of $2, $1, $3, and $3, respectively. Finally, suppose that the 15 units of X which these resources produce can be sold for $1 per unit, or $15 total. Will firms produce X? Yes, because each firm will be able to pay wage, rent, interest, and normal profit costs of $13 [= (2 × $2) + (3 × $1) + (1 × $3) + (1 × $3)]. The difference between total revenue of $15 and total cost of $13 is an economic profit of $2.

This economic profit is evidence that industry X is prosperous. It will become an **expanding industry** as new firms, attracted by these above-normal profits, are formed or shift from less profitable industries.

But the entry of new firms will be self-limiting. As new firms enter industry X, the market supply of product X will increase relative to the market demand. This will lower the market price of X (as in Figure 3-6c), and economic profit will in time diminish and then disappear. The market supply and demand conditions prevailing when economic profit becomes zero will determine the total amount of X produced. At this point the industry will be at its "equilibrium size," at least until a further change in market demand or supply upsets that equilibrium.

Losses and Declining Industries   But what if the initial market situation for product X were less favorable? Suppose conditions in the product market were

such that the firm could sell the 15 units of X at a price of just $.75 per unit. Total revenue would then be $11.25 (= 15 × $0.75). After paying wage, rental, and interest costs of $10, the firm would obtain a below-normal profit of $1.25. In other words, *losses* of $1.75 (= $11.25 − $13) would be incurred.

Certainly, firms would not be attracted to this unprosperous **declining industry.** On the contrary, if these losses persisted, some of the firms in industry X would go out of business or migrate to more prosperous industries where normal or even economic profits prevailed. However, as this happened, the market supply of X would fall relative to the market demand. Product price would rise (as in Figure 3-6d), and the losses would eventually disappear. Industry X would then stop shrinking. The supply and demand situation which prevailed when economic profit became zero would determine the total output of product X. Again, the industry would for the moment have reached its equilibrium size.

Consumer Sovereignty and "Dollar Votes"

In the market system, consumers are sovereign; they have the ultimate authority in determining the types and quantities of goods produced. **Consumer sovereignty** works through consumer demand. Consumer demand is crucial in determining the types and quantities of goods produced. Consumers, unrestrained by government and with money incomes from the sale of their resources, spend their dollars on those goods they are most willing and able to buy. These expenditures are **dollar votes** through which consumers register their wants via the demand side of the product market. If the dollar votes for a certain product are great enough to provide a normal profit, businesses will produce that product. If there is an increase in consumer demand, so that enough dollar votes are cast to provide an economic profit, that profit will cause an expansion of the industry and an increase in the output of the product.

Conversely, a decrease in consumer demand, that is, fewer dollar votes cast for the product, will result in losses and, in time, contraction of the industry. As firms leave the industry, the output of the product will decline. Indeed, the industry may cease to exist. Again, the consumers are sovereign; they collectively direct resources away from industries which are not meeting their wants.

The dollar votes of consumers determine not only which industries continue to exist but also which individual products survive or fail. Example: In 1991,

responding to doctors and nutritionists, McDonald's introduced its low-fat McLean burger. Good idea? Not really. Most consumers found the new product "too dry" and "not tasty," so sales were meager. In 1996 McDonald's quietly dropped the McLean burger from its menu at the same time that it introduced its higher-fat Arch Deluxe burger. In effect, consumers had collectively "voted out" the McLean burger.

Market Restraints on Freedom From the viewpoint of businesses, we now see that firms are not really free to produce what they wish. Consumers' buying decisions make the production of some products profitable and others not, thus restricting the choice of businesses in deciding what to produce. Businesses must match their production choices with consumer choices or face losses and eventual bankruptcy.

It is the same for resource suppliers. The demand for resources is a **derived demand**—derived, that is, from the demand for the goods and services which the resources help produce. There is a demand for autoworkers because there is a demand for automobiles. There is no demand for buggy-whip braiders because there is no demand for buggy whips. Resource suppliers are not free to allocate their resources to the production of goods which consumers do not value highly. Firms do not produce such products because consumer demand is not sufficient to make them profitable.

In brief: Consumers register their preferences on the demand side of the product market; producers and resource suppliers respond appropriately in seeking to further their own self-interests. The market system communicates the wants of consumers to businesses and resource suppliers and elicits appropriate responses.

Organizing Production

How is production to be organized in a market economy? This Fundamental Question is composed of three subquestions:

1. How should resources be allocated among specific industries?
2. What specific firms should do the producing in each industry?
3. What combinations of resources—what technology—should each firm employ?

The preceding section answered the first two subquestions. The market system steers resources to those industries whose products consumers want—simply because those industries survive, are profitable, and pay for resources. It simultaneously deprives unwanted industries of profits and hence of scarce resources.

The second and third subquestions are closely intertwined. In a competitive market economy, the firms which survive to do the producing are the ones willing and able to employ the most economically efficient technique of production. And the most efficient technique depends on:

1. The available technology, that is, the alternative combinations of resources which will produce the desired results
2. The prices of the needed resources

The combination of resources which is most efficient economically depends not only on the state of available technology but on the relative worth of the required resources as measured by their market prices. A technique which requires just a few physical inputs of resources to produce a specific output may be highly *in*efficient economically *if* the required resources are valued very highly in the market. *Economic efficiency means obtaining a particular output of product with the least input of scarce resources, when both output and resource inputs are measured in dollars and cents.* That combination of resources which will produce, say, $15 worth of product X at the lowest possible money cost is the most efficient.

Suppose there are three possible techniques for producing the desired $15 worth of product X. Suppose also that the quantity of each resource required by each production technique and the prices of the required resources are as shown in Table 4-1. By multiplying the required quantities of each resource by its price in each of the three techniques, the total cost of producing $15 worth of X by each technique is determined.

Technique 2 is economically the most efficient because it is the least costly. It permits society to obtain $15 worth of output by using a smaller amount of resources—$13 worth—than the $15 worth required by the two other techniques.

But will firms actually use technique 2? The answer is "yes." Firms will want to use the most efficient technique because it yields the greatest profit.

A change in either technology *or* resource prices, however, may cause the firm to shift from the technology it is using. If the price of labor falls to $.50, technique 1 becomes superior to technique 2. Businesses will find they can lower their costs by shifting to a technology which uses more of the resource whose price has fallen. Exercise: Would a new technique involving 1 unit of labor, 4 of land, 1 of capital, and 1 of entrepreneurial ability be preferable to the techniques listed in Table 4-1, assuming the resource prices shown there? **(Key Question 8)**

Distributing Total Output

The market system enters the picture in two ways in solving the problem of distributing total output. Generally, any specific product will be distributed to consumers on the basis of their ability and willingness to pay the existing market price for it. If the price of some product, say, a pocket calculator, is $15, then those buyers who are able and willing to pay that price will get a pocket calculator; those who are not, will not. This is the rationing function of equilibrium prices.

The sizes of consumers' money incomes determines their ability to pay the equilibrium prices for pocket calculators and other products. And con-

TABLE 4-1   Three techniques for producing $15 worth of product X

Resource	Price per unit of resource	Technique 1 Units	Technique 1 Cost	Technique 2 Units	Technique 2 Cost	Technique 3 Units	Technique 3 Cost
Labor	$2	4	$ 8	2	$ 4	1	$ 2
Land	1	1	1	3	3	4	4
Capital	3	1	3	1	3	2	6
Entrepreneurial ability	3	1	3	1	3	1	3
Total cost of $15 worth of X			$15		$13		$15

sumers' money incomes depend on the quantities of the various property and human resources they supply and on the prices in the resource market. Resource prices are key in determining the size of each household's claim against the total output of society. Within the limits of a consumer's money income, however, it is a person's willingness to pay the equilibrium price for a pocket calculator which determines whether or not a unit of this product is distributed to her or him. And this willingness to buy the calculator depends on that consumer's preference for it compared with other available products and their relative prices. Thus, product price is not only key in determining how output is distributed, it also is central in determining the spending patterns of consumers.

There is nothing particularly ethical about the market system as a mechanism for distributing output. Households which accumulate large amounts of property resources by inheritance, through hard work and frugality, through business acumen, or by illegal activities will receive large incomes and thus command large shares of the economy's total output. Others, offering unskilled and relatively unproductive labor resources which elicit low wages, will receive meager money incomes and small portions of total output.

Accommodating Change

Industrial societies are dynamic: Consumer preferences, technology, and supplies of resources all change. This means that the particular allocation of resources which is *now* the most efficient for a *specific* pattern of consumer tastes, for a *specific* range of technological alternatives, and for *specific* supplies of resources will become obsolete and inefficient as consumer preferences change, new techniques of production are discovered, and resource supplies change over time. Can the market economy adjust to these changes so that resources are still used efficiently?

Guiding Function of Prices Suppose consumer tastes change. Specifically, assume that, because of greater health consciousness, consumers decide they want more exercise bikes and fewer cigarettes than the economy currently provides. This change in consumer tastes will be communicated to producers through an increase in demand for bikes and a decline in demand for cigarettes. Bike prices will rise and cigarette prices will fall. Now, assuming firms in both industries were enjoying precisely normal profits before

these changes in consumer demand, higher exercise bike prices mean economic profit for the bike industry, and lower cigarette prices mean losses for the cigarette industry. Self-interest induces new competitors to enter the prosperous bike industry. Losses in time force firms to leave the depressed cigarette industry.

These adjustments in the business sector are appropriate for the assumed changes in consumer tastes. Society—meaning consumers—wants more exercise bikes and fewer cigarettes, and that is precisely what it is getting as the bike industry expands and the cigarette industry contracts. This is consumer sovereignty at work.

But will resource *suppliers* be agreeable to these adjustments? Will the market system prompt resource suppliers to shift their human and property resources from the cigarette to the bike industry, permitting the output of bikes to expand at the expense of cigarette production? The answer is "yes."

The economic profit which initially follows the increase in demand for bikes not only will induce that industry to expand but also will give it the revenue needed to obtain the resources essential to its growth. Higher bike prices will permit firms in that industry to pay higher prices for resources, increasing resource demand and drawing resources from less urgent alternative employments.

The reverse occurs in the adversely affected cigarette industry. The losses following the decline in consumer demand will cause a decline in the demand for resources in that industry. Workers and other resources will be released from the shrinking cigarette industry but will find employment in the expanding bike industry. Furthermore, the increased demand for resources in the bike industry will mean higher resource prices in that industry than those being paid in the cigarette industry, where declines in resource demand have lowered resource prices. The resulting differential in resource prices will provide the incentive for resource owners to further their self-interests by shifting their resources from the cigarette to the bike industry. And this is the precise shift needed to permit the bike industry to expand and the cigarette industry to contract.

The ability of the market system to communicate changes in such basic data as consumer tastes and to elicit appropriate responses from businesses and resource suppliers is called the *directing* or **guiding function of prices.** By affecting product prices and profits, changes in consumer tastes direct the expansion of some industries and the contraction of others. These

Pink Flamingos and "Dollar Votes"

After 40 years, consumer sovereignty and "dollar votes" still support continued production of plastic pink flamingos. Lovers of the icon say that critics do not have a leg to stand on.

LEOMINSTER, Mass.—One of the icons of the American landscape–not the bald eagle or the bison, but the plastic pink flamingo–is approaching 40. And it's still not getting any respect.

Despite its enduring appeal (15 million to 20 million have been sold), the lawn ornament can't seem to escape the T-word, a fate that ruffles the feathers of flamingo fans.

"People say they're tacky, but all great art began as tacky," said Don Featherstone, the Union Products vice president and artist whose signature is molded in every flamingo body. "Art Deco in New York was torn down. But now, they're putting it back up."

Featherstone himself is a bit of a strange bird. A sculptor with a classical art background, he and his wife of 20 years dress alike every day. He attends many flamingo-themed social events sponsored by groups such as the Society for the Preservation of the Plastic Lawn Flamingo.

His plastic company's catalog pictures page after page of adornments suited for any gardener's fancy: a

22-inch black-and-white penguin, a blue-headed pheasant, a green-chested rooster.

All nice, but just not the same thing.

"I tried to put some ducks out there because this is duck country," said Mary-Elizabeth Buckham, who has a flock of pink plastic birds on the lawn of her Victorian home in Centreville, Md. "But nobody wanted to see what they were doing."

Buckham dresses her 34 birds—curving pink necks, spindly wire legs and hollow bodies with molding feather detail—in homemade clothes and rearranges them every week for an adoring public.

At Christmas there was a nativity scene with flamingo wise men and a flamingo baby Jesus. At Thanksgiving there was a "flurkey flock," and at Halloween, flamingo ghosts. Even lawn jockeys aren't that versatile.

The first pink flamingo ornaments, in 1952, were flat, made of plywood. They were made of foam a few years later, but dogs tended to eat them. They've been made of plastic since 1957.

Some versions just didn't fly. A movable-leg model some years back was a flop.

Half a million of the birds move off store shelves in America, Mexico and South America every year, at $9.95 a pair. With numbers like that, Featherstone says he'll suffer the sarcasm.

"As long as they keep buying them, I really don't care," he said with a smile.

Source: Carolyn Thompson, "Flamingo Sales still In the Pink," Associated Press, May 28, 1996. Printed by permission of the Associated Press.

---

adjustments carry through to the resource market as expanding industries demand more resources and contracting industries demand fewer; the resulting changes in resource prices guide resources from the contracting to the expanding industries. Without a market system, some administrative agency, presumably a government planning board, would have to direct businesses and resources into appropriate industries.

Similar analyses show that the system can and does adjust to other fundamental changes—for example, to changes in technology and in the available supplies of various resources.

Role in Promoting Progress Adjusting to changes is one thing; initiating desirable changes is another. Does the competitive market system promote technological improvements and capital accumulation—the two changes that lead to greater productivity and a higher level of material well-being for society?

Technological Progress The market system provides a strong incentive for technological advance. This advance may occur as improved production methods or as new products. A firm developing a new cost-cutting technique has a temporary advantage over its rivals. By passing part of its cost reduction to the consumer through a lower product price, the firm can increase sales and obtain economic profit at the expense of rival firms. Similarly, a firm which successfully introduces a popular new product gains revenue and enhances economic profit at the expense of rival firms. Moreover, the market system is conducive to the rapid spread of technological advance throughout the industry. Rival firms must follow the lead of the most progressive firm or suffer immediate losses and eventual failure.

The lower product price or improved product which a technological advance permits will cause the innovating industry to expand. The expansion may result when existing firms increase their output or when new firms enter the industry, lured by economic profit created by the technological advance. As the industry expands, resources are shifted from less progressive industries to more progressive industries. And so it should be. Efficiency in the use of scarce resources demands that resources be continually reallocated from less efficient industries to those which become relatively more efficient in fulfilling society's wants.

Capital Accumulation A technological advance typically requires additional capital goods. The market system provides the resources necessary to produce those capital goods by adjusting the product market and resource market through increased dollar votes for capital goods. That is, the market system acknowledges dollar voting for capital goods as well as for consumer goods.

But who will register votes for capital goods? First, the entrepreneur, as a receiver of profit income, can be expected to apportion part of that income to the purchase of capital goods. Doing so will yield an even greater profit income in the future if the innovation is successful. Moreover, by paying interest, the entrepreneur can borrow portions of the incomes of households and use the borrowed funds to cast dollar votes for the production of more capital goods. **(Key Question 10)**

COMPETITION AND THE "INVISIBLE HAND"

In capitalism the market system is the organizational mechanism and competition is the mechanism of control. Supply and demand communicate the wants of

consumers (society) to businesses and, through businesses, to resource suppliers. It is competition, however, which forces businesses and resource suppliers to make appropriate responses.

But competition does more than guarantee responses appropriate to the wishes of society. It also forces firms to adopt the most efficient production techniques, keeping costs and prices at their lowest levels. In a competitive market, more efficient firms will eventually eliminate a firm which fails to use the least-costly production technique. And we have seen that competition provides an environment conducive to such technological advance.

In 1776 Adam Smith, in his book *The Wealth of Nations*, first noted that the operation of a competitive market system creates a curious and important unity between private and social interests. Firms and resource suppliers, seeking to further their own self-interests and operating within the framework of a highly competitive market system, will simultaneously, as though guided by an **"invisible hand,"** promote the public or social interest. For example, we have seen that in a competitive environment, businesses use the least-costly combination of resources to produce a specific output because it is in their private self-interests to do so. To act otherwise would be to forgo profit or even to risk business failure. But, at the same time, it is clearly also in the social interest to use scarce resources in the least-costly (most efficient) way.

In our more-bikes–fewer-cigarettes illustration, it is self-interest, awakened and guided by the competitive market system, which induces responses appropriate to the change in society's wants. Businesses seeking to make higher profits and to avoid losses, and resource suppliers pursuing greater monetary awards, negotiate changes in the allocation of resources and end up with the output that society demands. The force of competition controls or guides self-interest in such a way that it automatically, and quite unintentionally, furthers the best interests of society. The "invisible hand" tells us that when firms maximize their profits, society's domestic output is also maximized.

The virtues of the market system are thus implicit in our discussion. Three merit emphasis:

1. *Efficiency* The basic economic argument for the market system is that it promotes the efficient use of resources. The competitive market system guides resources into the production of those goods and services most wanted by society. It forces the use of the most efficient techniques in organizing resources for production, and it leads to the development and adoption of new and more efficient production techniques.

2. *Incentives* The market system provides incentives for improvement and innovation. Greater work effort means higher money incomes, which can be translated into a higher standard of living. Similarly, the assuming of risks by entrepreneurs can result in substantial profit incomes. Successful innovations may also generate economic rewards.

3. *Freedom* The major noneconomic argument for the market system is its great emphasis on personal freedom. In contrast to central planning, the market system can coordinate economic activity without coercion. The market system permits—indeed, it thrives on—freedom of enterprise and choice. Entrepreneurs and workers are not herded from industry to industry by government directives to meet production targets established by some governmental agency. On the con-

trary, they are free to further their own self-interests, subject to the rewards and penalties imposed by the market system itself.

QUICK REVIEW 4-3

■ The output mix of the market system is determined by profits, which in turn depend heavily on consumer preferences. Profits cause preferred, efficient industries to expand; losses cause inefficient industries to contract.

■ Competition forces industries to use the least-costly (most efficient) production methods.

■ Consumer incomes and product prices determine the distribution of output among households in a market economy.

■ Competitive markets reallocate resources in response to changes in consumer tastes, technological advances, and changes in supplies of resources.

■ The "invisible hand" of the market system channels the pursuit of self-interest to the good of society.

CHAPTER SUMMARY

1. The capitalist system is characterized by private ownership of resources, including capital, and the freedom of individuals to engage in economic activities of their choice to advance their own material well-being. Self-interest is the driving force of such an economy, and competition functions as a regulatory or control mechanism.

2. In the capitalist system, markets and prices organize and make effective the many millions of individual decisions which determine what is produced, the methods of production, and the sharing of output. The capitalist ideology envisions government playing a minor and relatively passive economic role.

3. Specialization and an advanced technology based on the extensive use of capital goods are common to all advanced industrial economies.

4. Functioning as a medium of exchange, money circumvents problems of bartering and thus permits easy trade and greater specialization, both domestically and internationally.

5. Every economy faces Five Fundamental Questions: **(a)** How much of available resources should be employed to produce goods? **(b)** What goods and services are to be produced? **(c)** How should they be produced? **(d)** To whom

should the output be distributed? **(e)** Can the system adapt to changes in consumer tastes, resource supplies, and technology?

6. In a market economy those products whose production and sale yield total revenue sufficient to cover all costs, including a normal profit, are produced. Those whose production does not yield a normal profit, or more, are not produced.

7. Economic profit designates an industry as prosperous and promotes its expansion. Losses mean an industry is unprosperous and result in contraction of that industry.

8. Consumer sovereignty means that both businesses and resource suppliers channel their efforts in accordance with the wants of consumers.

9. Competition forces firms to use the least-costly, and therefore the most economically efficient, production techniques.

10. The prices commanded by the resources owned and supplied by each household will determine that household's claim on the economy's output. Within the limit of each household's money income, consumer preferences and the relative prices of products determine the distribution of total output.

11. The competitive market system can communicate changes in consumer tastes to resource suppliers and entrepreneurs, prompting appropriate adjustments in the allocation of the economy's resources. The competitive market system also provides an environment conducive to technological advance and capital accumulation.

12. Competition, the primary mechanism of control in the market economy, promotes a unity of private and social interests; as though directed by an "invisible hand," competition harnesses the self-interest motives of businesses and resource suppliers to simultaneously further the social interest in using scarce resources efficiently.

TERMS AND CONCEPTS

private property
freedom of enterprise
freedom of choice
self-interest
competition
roundabout production
specialization

division of labor
medium of exchange
barter
money
Five Fundamental
  Questions
economic costs

normal profit
economic profit
expanding industry
declining industry
consumer sovereignty
dollar votes
derived demand

guiding function of
  prices
"invisible hand"

STUDY QUESTIONS

1. Explain each of these statements:
  a. Capitalism not only *accepts* self-interest as a fact of human existence; it *relies* on self-interest to achieve society's material goals.
  b. Where there is private property, property rights, and economic freedom, there will be capitalism; unlike the command economy, capitalism emerges spontaneously.

2. **KEY QUESTION** What advantages result from "roundabout" production? What problem is involved in increasing a full-employment economy's stock of capital goods? Illustrate this problem using the production possibilities curve. Does an economy with unemployed resources face the same problem?

3. What are the advantages of specialization in the use of human and material resources? Explain: "Exchange is the necessary consequence of specialization."

4. What problems does barter entail? Indicate the economic significance of money as a medium of exchange. "Money is the only commodity that is good for nothing but to be gotten rid of. It will not feed you, clothe you, shelter you, or amuse you unless you spend or invest it. It imparts value only in parting."[1] Explain this statement.

5. Briefly describe how the market system answers the Fundamental Questions. Why must economic choices be made?

6. Evaluate and explain the following statements:
  a. The capitalistic system is a profit and loss economy.
  b. Competition is the indispensable disciplinarian of the market economy.
  c. Production methods which are inferior in the engineering sense may be the most efficient methods in the economic sense.

7. Explain the meaning and implications of the following quotation.

> The beautiful consequence of the market is that it is its own guardian. If output prices or certain kinds of remuneration stray away from their socially ordained levels, forces are set into motion to bring them back to the fold. It is a curious paradox which thus ensues: the market, which is the acme of individual economic freedom, is the strictest taskmaster of all. One may appeal the ruling of a planning board or win the dispensation of a minister; but there is no appeal, no dispensation, from the anonymous pressures of the market mechanism. Economic freedom is thus more illusory than at first appears. One can do as one pleases in the market. But

[1]Federal Reserve Bank of Philadelphia, "Creeping Inflation," *Business Review*, August 1957, p. 3.

if one pleases to do what the market disapproves, the price of individual freedom is economic ruination.[2]

8. **KEY QUESTION** Assume that a business firm finds its profit will be at a maximum when it produces $40 worth of product A. Suppose also that each of the three techniques shown in the following table will produce the desired output.

Resource	Price per unit of resource	Resource units required		
		Technique 1	Technique 2	Technique 3
Labor	$3	5	2	3
Land	4	2	4	2
Capital	2	2	4	5
Entrepreneurial ability	2	4	2	4

a. With the resource prices shown, which technique will the firm choose? Why? Will production entail profit or losses? Will the industry expand or contract? When will a new equilibrium output be achieved?

b. Assume now that a new technique, technique 4, is developed. It combines 2 units of labor, 2 of land, 6 of capital, and 3 of entrepreneurial ability. In view of the resource prices in the table, will the firm adopt the new technique? Explain your answer.

c. Suppose now that an increase in the labor supply causes the price of labor to fall to $1.50 per unit, all other resource prices being unchanged. Which technique will the producer now choose? Explain.

d. "The market system causes the economy to conserve most in the use of those resources which are particularly scarce in supply. Resources which are scarcest relative to the demand for them have the highest prices. As a result, producers use these resources as sparingly as is possible." Evaluate this statement. Does your answer to question 8c bear out this contention? Explain.

9. Suppose the demand for bagels dramatically rises while the demand for breakfast cereal plummets. Explain how the competitive market economy will make the needed adjustments to reestablish an efficient allocation of society's scarce resources?

10. **KEY QUESTION** Some large hardware stores such as Home Depot boast of carrying as many as 20,000 different products in each store. What motivated the producers of these particular items—everything from screwdrivers to ladders to water heaters—to make them and offer them for sale? How did producers decide on the best combinations of resources to use? Who made these resources available, and why? Who decides whether these specific hardware products should continue to get produced and offered for sale?

11. In a single sentence, describe the meaning of the phrase "invisible hand."

12. **(Last Word)** Relate the human-interest story about the plastic pink flamingo to (a) consumer sovereignty and dollar votes, (b) freedom of enterprise, and (c) the role of profit in allocating society's scarce resources.

13. **WEB-BASED QUESTION** The United Nations' Virtual Marketplace The United Nations http://urgento.gse.rmit.edu.au/untpdc/eto has set up an Electronic Trade Opportunity (ETO), a large-scale virtual marketplace for trade offers (ETOs) from around the world. ETOs are received by millions of companies every week in one of several electronic forms. How does this new virtual marketplace improve the efficient use of resources and increase the freedom of enterprise and choice? Does it increase competition? How does it help firms in developing countries? Why would the United Nations set up such a virtual marketplace?

14. **WEB-BASED QUESTION** Barter and the IRS Bartering occurs when goods or services are exchanged without the exchange of money. For some, barter's popularity is that it enables them to avoid paying taxes to the government. How might such avoidance occur? Does the Internal Revenue Service (IRS) http://www.irs.ustreas.gov/tax_edu/teletax/tx420.html treat barter as taxable or nontaxable income? How is the value of a barter transaction determined? What are some IRS barter examples? What does the IRS require of so-called barter exchanges with regard to their members?

---

[2]Robert L. Heilbroner, *The Worldly Philosophers*, 3d ed. (New York: Simon & Schuster, 1967), p. 42.

CHAPTER FIVE

The Mixed Economy: Private and Public Sectors

Let's now move from the model of pure capitalism closer to the reality of the U.S. economy. For convenience, we divide the economy into sectors (major parts). We first describe the *private sector,* comprising the *household* sector and *business* sector, and then introduce and analyze the *public sector* (government). Because government is new to our discussion, it will get most of our attention.

Our purpose is to provide some facts and analysis about households, businesses, and governmental units since they are the primary decision makers of our mixed economy. Here, our focus is inward; we look at the domestic economy. In Chapter 6 we look outward, examining how the domestic economy relates to the rest of the world.

HOUSEHOLDS AS INCOME RECEIVERS

The household sector of the United States economy is currently composed of about 101 million households, which are the ultimate suppliers of all economic resources and, simultaneously, the major spenders in the economy.

Let's first consider households as income receivers. Two ways of looking at the income received by households are (1) according to the functions which earned it and (2) according to the households which received it.

The Functional Distribution of Income

The **functional distribution of income** indicates how total money income is divided among wages, rents, interest, and profits, that is, according to the function performed by the income receiver. Wages are paid to labor, rents and interest to owners of property resources, and profits to the owners of corporations and unincorporated businesses.

The functional distribution of total U.S. income for 1997 is shown in Figure 5-1. The largest source of income for households is the wages and salaries paid to workers by the business and government units hiring them. In our mixed economy, the bulk of total income goes to labor, not to capital. Proprietors' income—the incomes of doctors, lawyers, small-business owners, farmers, and owners of other unincorporated enterprises—is in fact a combination of wage and profit incomes. Some of this income is payment for one's own labor, and some of it is profit from one's own business.

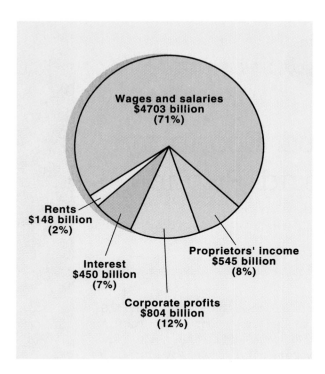

FIGURE 5-1 The functional distribution of U.S. income, 1997 Almost three-fourths of national income is received as wages and salaries. Capitalist income—corporate profit, interest, and rents—accounts for about one-fifth of total income. (*Source: Survey of Current Business,* February 1998.)

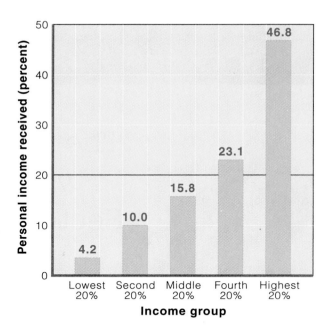

FIGURE 5-2 The distribution of income among U.S. families, 1996 Personal income is quite unequally distributed in the United States, with the top 20 percent of families receiving nearly one-half of the total income. In an equal distribution, all five vertical bars would be as high as the horizontal line drawn at 20 percent; then each 20 percent of families would get 20 percent of total income.

The other three types of earnings are self-evident: Some households own corporate stock and receive dividend incomes on their holdings. Many households also own bonds and savings accounts which yield interest income. Rental income results from households' providing buildings and natural resources (including land) to businesses.

The Personal Distribution of Income

The **personal distribution of income** indicates how total money income is divided among individual households. Figure 5-2 shows one way to present that distribution. There, households (families) are divided into five numerically equal groups or quintiles, and the heights of the bars show the percentage of total income received by each group. In 1996 the poorest 20 percent of all families received about 4 percent of

total personal income in contrast to the 20 percent they would have received if income were equally distributed. In comparison, the richest 20 percent of all families received 47 percent of personal income. On the basis of such data, most economists agree there is considerable inequality in the personal distribution of American income. **(Key Question 2)**

HOUSEHOLDS AS SPENDERS

How do households dispose of their income? Part flows to government as taxes, and the rest is divided between personal consumption expenditures and personal saving. In 1997, households disposed of their total personal income as shown in Figure 5-3.

Personal Taxes

Personal taxes, of which the Federal personal income tax is the major component, have risen in both ab-

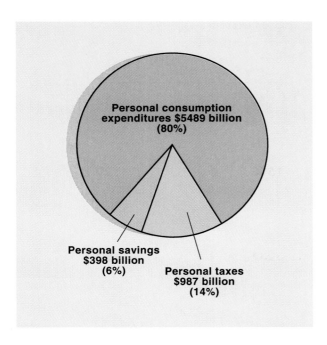

FIGURE 5-3 The disposition of household income, 1997 Household income is apportioned among taxes, saving, and consumption, with consumption being the major use of income. [*Source: Survey of Current Business,* February 1998. (The income concept in this figure differs from that used in Figure 5-1, accounting for the quantitative discrepancies between "total income" in the two figures.)]

----

solute and relative terms since World War II. In 1941, households paid $3.3 billion, or 3 percent of their $95.3 billion total income, in personal taxes, compared with $987 billion, or 14 percent of $6874 billion total income, in 1997.

Personal Saving

Economists define "saving" as that part of after-tax income which is not spent; hence, households have just two choices of what to do with their incomes after taxes—use it to consume or save it. Saving is the portion of income which is not paid in taxes or used to purchase consumers goods but which flows into bank accounts, insurance policies, bonds and stocks, mutual funds, and other financial assets.

Reasons for saving center on *security* and *speculation*. Households save to provide a nest egg for unforeseen contingencies (sickness, accident, unemploy-

ment), for retirement from the workforce, to finance the education of children, or simply for financial security. Also, people save for speculation. You might channel part of your income to purchase stocks, speculating that they will increase in value.

The desire to save is not enough. You must be *able* to save, and that depends on the size of your income. If your income is low, you may not be able to save any money. If your income is lower yet, you may *dissave*, that is, consume in excess of your after-tax income. You do this by borrowing and by digging into savings you may have accumulated in years when your income was higher.

Both saving and consumption vary directly with income; as households get more income, they save more and consume more. In fact, the top 10 percent of income receivers account for most of the personal saving in the U.S. economy.

Personal Consumption Expenditures

Figure 5-3 shows that four-fifths of total income flows from income receivers back into the business sector as personal consumption expenditures—money spent on consumer goods.

The size and composition of the economy's total output of goods and services depend on the size and composition of consumer spending. As indicated in Table 5-1, household spending is classified as expenditures on (1) durable goods, (2) nondurable goods, and (3) services.

If a product generally has an expected life of 3 years or more, it is called a **durable good;** if its life is less than 3 years, it is labeled a **nondurable good.** Automobiles, personal computers, washing machines, and most furniture are durables. Most food and clothing items are nondurables. **Services** consist of the work done for consumers by lawyers, barbers, doctors, mechanics, and so on. Observe in Table 5-1 that *the United States is a service-oriented economy in that more than one-half of consumer spending is for services.*

TABLE 5-1   The composition of personal consumption expenditures, 1997*

Types of consumption	Amount, billions	Percentage of total
Durable goods	**$ 659**	**12**
Motor vehicles and parts	$263	5
Furniture and household equipment	268	5
All others	129	2
Nondurable goods	**1593**	**29**
Food	776	14
Clothing and shoes	278	5
Gasoline and oil	125	2
Fuel oil and coal	11	0
All others	403	7
Services	**3237**	**59**
Housing	826	15
Household operations	329	6
Medical care	855	16
Transportation	236	4
Personal services, recreation, and others	991	18
Total personal consumption expenditures	**$5489**	**100**

*Excludes interest paid to businesses.

Source: Survey of Current Business, February 1998. Details may not add to totals because of rounding.

■ Wages and salaries are the major component of the functional distribution of income. The personal distribution reveals considerable inequality.

■ Eighty percent of household income is consumed; the rest is saved or paid in taxes.

■ More than half of consumer spending is for services.

THE BUSINESS POPULATION

Businesses constitute the second major part of the private sector. To avoid confusion, we must start by distinguishing among a plant, a firm, and an industry.

A **plant** is a physical establishment—a factory, farm, mine, store, or warehouse—which performs one or more functions in fabricating and distributing goods and services.

A business **firm** is a business organization which owns and operates plants. Most firms operate only one plant, but many own and operate several. Multiplant firms may own horizontal, vertical, or conglomerate combinations of plants. A **vertical combi-** nation of plants is a group of plants, with each performing a different function in the various stages of the production process. As an example, every large steel firm—USX, Bethlehem Steel, Republic Steel, and others—owns iron ore and coal mines, limestone quarries, metal refineries, rolling mills, foundries, and, in some cases, fabricating shops.

A **horizontal combination** of plants is one in which all plants perform the same function. The large chain stores in the retail field—JC Penney, Foot Locker, Toys "Я" Us, Wal-Mart—are examples.

A **conglomerate combination** is made up of plants which operate across several different markets and industries. For example, Warner-Lambert Company owns plants involved in such diverse fields as chewing gum (Trident), razors (Shick), cough drops (Halls), breath mints (Certs), and antacids (Rolaids). Firms such as these are called *conglomerates.*

An **industry** is a group of firms producing the same, or similar, products. This seems to be a simple concept, but industries are usually difficult to identify in practice. For example, how do we identify the automobile industry? The simplest answer is "all firms producing au-

THE MIXED ECONOMY: PRIVATE AND PUBLIC SECTORS

tomobiles." But how should we account for small trucks? Certainly, small pickup trucks are similar in many respects to vans and station wagons. And what about firms which make parts for cars, say, airbags? What industry are they in? Is it better to speak of the "motor vehicle industry" rather than the "automobile industry?" If so, where should we then place motorcycles?

Delineating an industry becomes even more complex because most businesses are multiproduct firms. Automobile manufacturers in the United States also make such diverse products as diesel locomotives, buses, refrigerators, guided missiles, and air conditioners. For these reasons, industry classifications are usually somewhat arbitrary.

LEGAL FORMS OF BUSINESSES

The business population is extremely diverse, ranging from giant corporations such as General Motors with 1996 sales of $168 billion and 648,000 employees to neighborhood specialty shops and "mom-and-pop" groceries with 1 or 2 employees and sales of only $200 to $300 per day. This diversity makes it necessary to classify business firms by some criterion such as legal

structure, industry or product, or size. Figure 5-4a shows how the business population is distributed among the three major legal forms: (1) the sole proprietorship, (2) the partnership, and (3) the corporation.

Sole Proprietorship

A **sole proprietorship** is a business owned and operated by one person. Usually, the proprietor (the owner) personally supervises its operation.

Advantages   This simple type of business organization has two major advantages:
1. A sole proprietorship is easy to organize; there is virtually no legal red tape or expense.
2. The proprietor is his or her own boss and has substantial freedom of action. Since the proprietor's profit income depends on the enterprise's success, there is a strong and immediate incentive to manage the business efficiently.

Disadvantages   The disadvantages of this form of business organization are several:
1. With rare exceptions, the financial resources of a sole proprietorship are insufficient to permit the firm to grow into a large enterprise. Finances are

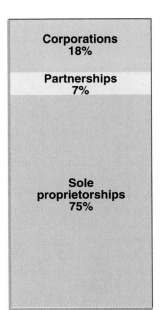

(a) Percentage of firms   (b) Percentage of sales

The business population by form of legal organization

Form	Number of firms
Sale proprietorships*	16,154,000
Partnerships	1,493,000
Corporations	3,965,000
Total	21,612,000

*Excludes farmers.

FIGURE 5-4 **The business population and shares of domestic output**   (a) Sole proprietorships dominate the business population numerically, but (b) corporations account for 90 percent of total sales (output). The table shows the population numbers.

usually limited to what the proprietor has in the bank and to what he or she can borrow. Since proprietorships often fail, commercial banks are not eager to extend them credit.

2. Being in complete control of an enterprise forces the proprietor to carry out all management functions. A proprietor must make decisions concerning buying, selling, and the hiring and training of personnel, as well as producing, advertising, and distributing the firm's product. In short, the potential benefits of specialization in business management are not available to the typical small-scale proprietorship.

3. Most important, the proprietor is subject to *unlimited liability*. Individuals in business for themselves risk not only the assets of the firm but also their personal assets. If the assets of an unsuccessful sole proprietorship are insufficient to pay the firm's bills, creditors can file claims against the proprietor's personal property.

Partnership

The **partnership** form of business organization is a natural outgrowth of the sole proprietorship. Partnerships were developed to overcome some of the shortcomings of proprietorships. In a partnership, two or more individuals (the partners) agree to own and operate a business together. Usually they pool their financial resources and business skills. Similarly, they share the risks and the profits or losses.

Advantages   What are the advantages of a partnership?

1. Like the sole proprietorship, it is easy to organize. Although a written agreement is almost invariably involved, there is not much legal red tape.

2. Greater specialization in management is possible because there are more participants.

3. Because there are several owners the odds are that the financial resources of a partnership are greater than those of a sole proprietorship. Partners can pool their financial capital and are usually somewhat better risks in the eyes of lending institutions.

Disadvantages   Partnerships may have some of the shortcomings of the proprietorship and some of their own as well:

1. Whenever several people participate in management, the division of authority can lead to

inconsistent policies or to inaction when action is required. Worse, partners may disagree on basic policy.

2. The finances of partnerships are still limited, although they are generally superior to those of a sole proprietorship. But the financial resources of three or four partners may still not be enough to ensure the growth of a successful enterprise.

3. The continuity of a partnership is precarious. Generally, when a partner dies or withdraws, the partnership must be dissolved and completely reorganized, which can disrupt its operations.

4. Unlimited liability plagues a partnership, just as it does a proprietorship. In fact, each partner is liable for all business debts incurred, not only as a result of each partner's own management decisions but also as a consequence of the actions of any other partner. A wealthy partner risks money on the prudence of less affluent partners.

Corporation

A **corporation** is a legal creation which can acquire resources, own assets, produce and sell products, incur debts, extend credit, sue and be sued, and perform the functions of any other type of enterprise. This "legal person" is distinct and separate from the individuals who own it. Hired managers operate most corporations.

Advantages   The advantages of the corporate form of business enterprise have catapulted it into a dominant position in modern U.S. capitalism. Although corporations are relatively small in number, they are frequently large in size and scale of operations. As Figure 5-4 indicates, less than 20 percent of all businesses are corporations, but they account for roughly 90 percent of all business sales.

1. The corporation is by far the most effective form of business organization for raising financial capital (money). As this chapter's Last Word reveals, the corporation features unique methods of finance—the selling of stocks and bonds—which allow the firm to pool the financial resources of extremely large numbers of people.

Financing via sales of stocks and bonds also provides advantages to the purchasers of these securities. **Stocks** are shares of ownership of a corporation. **Bonds** are promises to repay a loan, usually with a set rate of interest. Financing through stocks and bonds allows households to participate in business and share the expected monetary reward without actively engaging in management. In addition, an individual can spread any risks by buying the securities of several corporations. Finally, it is usually easy for holders of corporate securities to sell those holdings. Organized stock exchanges simplify the transfer of securities from sellers to buyers. This "ease of sale" increases the willingness of savers to make financial investments in corporate securities.

In addition, corporations have easier access to bank credit than other types of business organizations. Corporations are better risks and are more likely to become profitable clients of banks.

2. Corporations have the distinct advantage of **limited liability.** The owners (stockholders) of a corporation risk *only* what they paid for their stock. Their personal assets are not at stake if the corporation cannot pay its debts. Creditors can sue the corporation as a legal person but cannot sue the owners of the corporation as individuals. Limited liability clearly makes it easier for the corporation to sell its stock.

3. Because of their advantage in attracting financial capital, successful corporations find it easier to expand the size and scope of their operations and to realize the benefits of expansion. They can take advantage of mass-production technologies and greater specialization in the use of human resources. While the manager of a sole proprietorship may be forced to share her or his time among production, accounting, and marketing functions, a corporation can hire specialists in each of these areas and achieve greater efficiency.

4. As a legal entity, the corporation has a life independent of its owners and its officers. Sole proprietorships and partnerships are subject to sudden and unpredictable demise, but legally at least, corporations are immortal. The transfer of corporate ownership through inheritance or the sale of stock does not disrupt the continuity of the corporation. Corporations have a permanence, lacking in other forms of business organization, which is conducive to long-range planning and growth.

Disadvantages The corporation's advantages are of tremendous significance and typically override any accompanying disadvantages. Yet there are drawbacks to the corporate form:

1. Some red tape and legal expenses are involved in obtaining a corporate charter.

2. From the social point of view, the corporate form of enterprise lends itself to certain abuses. Because the corporation is a legal entity, unscrupulous business owners sometimes can avoid personal responsibility for questionable business activities by adopting the corporate form of enterprise.

3. A further disadvantage of corporations is the **double taxation** of some corporate income. Corporate profit that is shared among stockholders as *dividends* is taxed twice—once as corporate profit and again as stockholders' personal income.

4. In sole proprietorships and partnerships, the owner of the real and financial assets of the firm also directly controls those assets. In large corporations in which ownership is widely diffused over tens or hundreds of thousands of stockholders, there is *separation of ownership and control.* That is, the people who own a corporation usually do not manage it—others are hired to do so.

This reality may create a so-called **principal-agent problem.** The *principals*, in this case, are the stockholders who own the corporation. These owners hire managers as their *agents* to run the business on their behalf. But the interests of the managers (agents) and the wishes of the owners (principals) are not always in accord. The owners typically want maximum profit. Management, however, seeking the power and prestige which accompany control over a large enterprise, may favor unprofitable expansion of the firm's operations. Or a conflict of interest can develop over dividend policies, such as what portion of corporate earnings after taxes should be paid out as dividends and what portion reinvested by the firm. And corporation officials may vote themselves large salaries, pensions, and so forth out of corporate earnings which might otherwise be used for increased dividend payments.

Postscript: A number of states have passed legislation authorizing "hybrid" business structures which allow some of the advantages of corporations to firms with one or relatively few owners. Two such structures are the *limited-liability company* (LLC) and the *S corporation*.

The LLC is like an ordinary partnership for tax purposes but resembles a corporation on liability issues. Like a partnership, an LLC distributes all profit directly to owners and investors. But like a corporation, an LLC shields the personal assets of owners from liability claims. LLCs have a limited life, typically 30 or 40 years.

The S corporation is a corporation with 35 or fewer employees. The profit from the corporation passes directly through to the owners as if the firm were a sole proprietorship or partnership, so the owners avoid the double taxation on distributed profit. The owners also get the benefit of limited liability. **(Key Question 4)**

Large Corporations

A glance back at Figure 5-4 reminds us that, although relatively small in number, corporations are the major source of production in the U.S. economy. The fact that corporations constitute less than 20 percent of the business population yet produce 90 percent of total business output suggests that many corporations are very large. In 1996 some 45 corporations in the United States had annual sales over $20 billion; 143 firms realized sales over $10 billion. General Motors alone had sales of $168 billion. Remarkably, there are only 22 nations in the world whose annual domestic outputs are more than GM's sales!

But the influence of large corporations varies significantly from industry to industry. They dominate manufacturing and are strong in the transportation, communication, power utilities, and banking and financial industries. At the other extreme are some 2 million farmers whose combined sales in 1996 were less than those of the economy's two largest industrial corporations. In between are a variety of retail and service industries characterized by relatively small firms. Nevertheless, large firms do dominate the U.S. business landscape, and in terms of total output, the United States clearly is a "big business" economy.

QUICK REVIEW 5-2

■ A plant is a physical establishment which contributes to the production of goods and services; a firm is a business organization which owns and operates plants; plants may be arranged in vertical, horizontal, or conglomerate combinations.

■ The three basic legal forms of business are the sole proprietorship, the partnership, and the corporation; while sole proprietorships make up nearly three-fourths of all firms, corporations account for about nine-tenths of total sales.

■ The major advantages of corporations which have led to their popularity are a superior ability to raise financial capital, the limited liability they convey to owners, and their life beyond that of their owners and officers.

■ Very large corporations dominate many U.S. industries.

ECONOMIC FUNCTIONS OF GOVERNMENT

All economies in the real world are "mixed": Government and the market system share the responsibility of responding to the Five Fundamental Questions. The U.S. economy is predominantly a market economy, yet the economic activities of government are of great significance.

In the next several sections we discuss the major economic functions of government—the public sector. These functions are (1) providing a legal and social framework, (2) maintaining competition within markets, (3) redistributing income as necessary for equity, (4) reallocating resources, and (5) stabilizing the economy.

The first two of these economic functions strengthen and facilitate the working of the market system; the last three modify pure capitalism to achieve economic and social goals.

LEGAL AND SOCIAL FRAMEWORK

Government provides the legal framework and the services needed for a market economy to operate effectively. The legal framework sets the legal status of business enterprises, ensures the rights of private ownership, and allows the making and enforcement of contracts. Government also establishes the legal "rules of the game" governing the relationships of businesses, resource suppliers, and consumers with one another. Units of government can referee economic relationships, seek out foul play, and exercise authority in imposing appropriate penalties.

Services provided by government include police powers to maintain internal order, a system of standards for measuring the weight and quality of products, and a system of money to facilitate exchanges of goods and services.

The Pure Food and Drug Act of 1906 is an example of how government has strengthened the market system. This act sets rules of conduct governing producers in their relationships with consumers. It prohibits the sale of adulterated and misbranded foods and drugs, requires net weights and ingredients of products to be specified on their containers, establishes quality standards which must be stated on labels of packaged foods, and prohibits deceptive claims on patent-medicine labels. These measures are designed to prevent fraudulent activities by producers and to increase the public's confidence in the integrity of the market system. Similar legislation pertains to labor-management relations and relations of business firms to one another.

This type of government activity is presumed to improve resource allocation. Supplying a medium of exchange, ensuring product quality, defining ownership rights, and enforcing contracts increase the volume and safety of exchange. This widens markets and permits greater specialization in the use of property and human resources. Such specialization means a more efficient allocation of resources. However, some argue that government overregulates the interactions of businesses, consumers, and workers and say that this stifles economic incentives and impairs efficiency.

MAINTAINING COMPETITION

Competition is the basic regulatory mechanism in a capitalist economy. It is the force which subjects producers and resource suppliers to the dictates of consumer sovereignty. With competition, buyers are the boss, the market is their agent, and businesses are their servants.

It is a different story where there is only a single seller—a **monopoly**—or a small handful of sellers with *monopoly power*. Monopolists are not regulated by competition. When the number of sellers becomes so small that each seller can influence total supply, the seller or sellers have the power to set the product price. By restricting supply, these firms can charge above-competitive prices. Also, because entry to these industries is blocked, monopolists can enjoy persistent economic profits. The restricted output and the high prices and profits directly conflict with the interests of consumers. In fact, producer sovereignty supplants consumer sovereignty, and monopoly supplants competition. Where there is monopoly, the pursuit of self-interest does *not* lead to the social good. Rather, society's economic resources are *underallocated* to the monopolized product.

In the United States, government has attempted to control monopoly primarily in two ways:

1. ***Regulation and ownership*** In a few situations, industries are *natural monopolies*—industries in which technology is such that only a single seller can achieve the lowest possible costs. Government has allowed these monopolies to exist but has also created public commissions to regulate their prices and set their service standards. Some aspects of transportation, communications, electricity, and other utilities are natural monopolies which government regulates in varying degrees. Sometimes, especially at the local level of government, public ownership replaces regulation.

2. ***Antimonopoly laws*** In nearly all markets, efficient production can best be attained with a high degree of competition. The Federal government has therefore enacted a series of antitrust (antimonopoly) laws, beginning with the Sherman Act of 1890, to maintain and strengthen competition.

REDISTRIBUTION OF INCOME

The market system is impersonal. It may distribute income with more inequality than society desires. The market system yields very large incomes to those whose labor, by virtue of inherent ability and acquired education and skills, commands high wages. Similarly, those who, through hard work or easy inheritance, possess valuable capital and land receive large property incomes.

But others in society have less productive ability, have received only modest amounts of education and training, and have accumulated or inherited no property resources. Moreover, many of the aged, the physically and mentally handicapped, and female-headed families earn only very small incomes, or, like the unemployed, no incomes at all. Thus, in the market system there is considerable inequality in the distribution of income and therefore in the distribution of output among individual households. Poverty amidst overall plenty in the economy persists.

Thus, society chooses to redistribute income through a variety of government policies and programs:

1. ***Transfers*** *Transfer payments*, for example, in the form of welfare checks and food stamps, provide relief to the destitute, the dependent, the handicapped, and older citizens; unemployment compensation payments provide aid to the unemployed.

2. *Market intervention*   Government also alters the distribution of income by *market intervention*, that is, by acting to modify the prices which are or would be established by market forces. Providing farmers with above-market prices for their outputs and requiring that firms pay minimum wages are illustrations of government price fixing designed to raise incomes of specific groups.

3. *Taxation*   The personal income tax has been used historically to take a larger proportion of the incomes of the rich than of the incomes of the poor, thus narrowing the after-tax income gap between high- and low-income earners.

The *extent* to which government should redistribute income is subject to many debates. Redistribution involves both benefits and costs. The alleged benefits are greater "fairness," or "economic justice"; the alleged costs are reduced incentives to work, save, invest, and produce, and therefore less total output and income.

REALLOCATION OF RESOURCES

Market failure occurs when the competitive market system (1) produces the "wrong" amounts of certain goods and services or (2) fails to allocate any resources whatsoever to the production of certain goods and services whose output is economically justified. The first type of failure results from what economists call *spillovers*, and the second type involves *public goods*. Both kinds of market failure can be corrected by government action.

Spillovers or Externalities

When we say that competitive markets automatically bring about efficient resource use, we assume that all the benefits and costs for each product are fully reflected in the market demand and supply curves. This is not always so in real markets; certain benefits or costs may escape the buyer or seller.

A spillover occurs when some of the costs or the benefits of a good are passed on to or "spill over to" parties other than the immediate buyer or seller. Spillovers are also called *externalities* because they are benefits or costs accruing to some third party which is external to the market transaction.

Spillover Costs   Production or consumption costs inflicted on a third party without compensation are called **spillover costs.** Many spillover costs are in the form of environmental pollution. When a chemical manufacturer or meatpacking plant dumps its wastes into a lake or river, swimmers, fishermen, and boaters—and perhaps drinking-water supplies—suffer spillover costs. When a petroleum refinery pollutes the air with smoke or a paper mill creates distressing odors, the community bears spillover costs for which it is not compensated.

What are the economic effects? Recall that costs determine the position of the firm's supply curve. When a firm avoids some costs by polluting, its supply curve lies farther to the right than it does when the firm bears the full costs of production. This results in a larger output than is socially desirable—a market failure in the form of an *overallocation* of resources to the production of the good.

Correcting for Spillover Costs   Government can do two things to correct the overallocation of resources. Both solutions are designed to internalize the external costs, that is, to make the offending firm pay the costs rather than shift them to others:

1. *Legislation*   In our examples of air and water pollution, the most direct action is legislation prohibiting or limiting pollution. Such legislation forces potential polluters to pay for the proper disposal of industrial wastes—here, by installing smoke-abatement equipment or water-purification facilities. The idea is to force potential offenders, under the threat of legal action, to bear all the costs associated with production.

2. *Specific taxes*   A less direct action is based on the fact that taxes are a cost and therefore a determinant of a firm's supply curve. Government might levy a *specific tax*—a tax confined to a particular product—on each unit of the polluting firm's output. The amount of this tax would roughly equal the estimated amount of the spillover cost arising from the production of each unit of output. Through this tax, government would pass back to the offending firm a cost equivalent to the spillover cost which the firm is avoiding. This would shift the firm's supply curve to the left, reducing equilibrium output and eliminating the overallocation of resources.

Spillover Benefits   But spillovers may also appear as benefits. Production or consumption of certain goods and services may confer spillover or external benefits on third parties or on the community at large without compensating payment. Measles and polio immunization result in direct benefits to the immediate consumer of those vaccines. But immunization against contagious diseases yields widespread and substantial spillover benefits to the entire community. Discovery of an AIDS vaccine would benefit society far beyond the persons vaccinated. Unvaccinated individuals would clearly benefit by the slowing of the spread of the disease.

Education is another example of **spillover benefits.** Education benefits individual consumers: "More educated" people generally achieve higher incomes than "less educated" people. But education also provides benefits to society. The economy as a whole benefits from a more versatile and more productive labor force, on the one hand, and smaller outlays for crime prevention, law enforcement, and welfare programs, on the other. There is evidence indicating that any worker with a *specific* educational or skill level will be more productive if associated workers have more education. In other words, worker Crum becomes more productive simply because coworkers Jones and Green are more educated.

Spillover benefits mean that the market demand curve, which reflects only private benefits, understates total benefits. The demand curve for the product lies farther to the left than it would if all benefits were taken into account by the market. This means that a smaller amount of the product will be produced or, alternatively, that there will be an *underallocation* of resources to the product—again a market failure.

Correcting for Spillover Benefits How might the underallocation of resources associated with spillover benefits be corrected? The answer is to either subsidize consumers (to increase demand), subsidize producers (to increase supply), or, in the extreme, have government produce the product.

1. *Subsidize consumers* To correct the underallocation of resources to higher education, the U.S. government provides low-interest loans to students so that they can afford more education. These loans increase the demand for higher education.

Here's a more complex example: The Food Stamp Program is designed to improve the diets of low-income families. The food stamps the government gives to these families can be exchanged only for food. Stores accepting the stamps are reimbursed with money by the government. This program thus purposely increases the demand for food. Part of the rationale is that improved nutrition helps disadvantaged children perform better in school and disadvantaged adults be better employees. In helping people

become more productive, some of the benefits of the extra food consumption spill over to the society as a whole.

2. *Subsidize suppliers* In some cases government might find it more convenient and administratively simpler to correct an underallocation by subsidizing producers. This is done in higher education, where state governments provide substantial portions of the budgets of public colleges and universities. These subsidies lower the costs of producing higher education and increase its supply. Publicly subsidized immunization programs, hospitals, and medical research are other examples.

3. *Provide goods via government* A third policy option may be used where spillover benefits are extremely large: Government may finance or, in the extreme, own and operate all industries which are involved.

Public Goods and Services

Private goods, which are produced through the competitive market system, are said to be *divisible* because they are produced in units small enough to be purchased and used by individual buyers. Private goods are also subject to the **exclusion principle.** Buyers who are willing and able to pay the equilibrium price of the product obtain it, but those who are unable or unwilling to pay are *excluded* from the product and its benefits.

Certain other goods and services called **public goods** are not produced by the market system because they have the opposite characteristics. Public goods are *indivisible;* they must be produced in such large units that they cannot ordinarily be sold to individual buyers. Individuals can buy hamburgers, computers, and automobiles through the market but cannot buy aircraft carriers, highways, space telescopes, and air-traffic control.

More important, *the exclusion principle does not apply to public goods;* there is no effective way of excluding individuals from their benefits once those goods come into existence. Obtaining the benefits of private goods requires that they be *purchased;* obtaining benefits from public goods requires only that they be *available.*

The classic public goods example is a proposed lighthouse on a treacherous coast. The construction of the lighthouse would be economically justified if its benefits (fewer shipwrecks) exceeded its cost. But the benefits accruing to one user would not be great enough to justify the purchase of such an indivisible product. Moreover, once it was in operation, the warning light would be a guide to all ships; there would be no practical way to exclude any captain from using the light. Economists call this the **free-rider-problem:** people receiving benefits from a good without contributing to its cost.

Because the exclusion principle does not apply to the lighthouse, private enterprises have no economic incentive to supply it. Since the services of the lighthouse cannot be priced and sold, it would be unprofitable for a private firm to devote resources to it. So here we have a service that could yield substantial benefits but to which the market would allocate no resources. It is a public good, much like national defense, flood control, public health, satellite navigation systems, and insect-abatement programs. If society requires such goods, they must be provided by the public sector and financed by compulsory charges in the form of taxes.

Quasipublic Goods

The applicability of the exclusion principle distinguishes private from public goods, and government may provide the latter. However, many other goods and services are provided by government even though they could be made exclusive. Such goods, called **quasipublic goods,** include education, streets and highways, police and fire protection, libraries and museums, preventive medicine, and sewage disposal. These goods or services could be produced and delivered in such a way that the exclusion principle applied. All could be priced and provided by private firms through the market system. But, as noted earlier, these services have substantial spillover benefits, so they would be underproduced by the market system. Therefore, government may provide them to avoid the underallocation of resources which would otherwise occur.

Since quasipublic goods can be produced in either the private or the public sector—and because spillover benefits are difficult to measure—we can understand the continuing controversy surrounding the status of medical care and low-income housing. Are these private goods to be produced through the market system, or are they quasipublic goods to be provided by government?

Allocation of Resources to Public and Quasipublic Goods

The market system fails to allocate resources for public goods and underallocates resources for quasipublic goods. What then, is the mechanism by which such goods get produced?

Public and quasipublic goods are purchased through the government on the basis of group, or collective, choices. (Contrast this with private goods, which are purchased from private enterprises on the basis of individual choices.) The types and qualities of goods to be produced by government are determined in a democracy by political voting. That is, the members of a society vote for particular political candidates. Each candidate represents certain public policies, and those policies determine the quantities of the various public and quasipublic goods to be produced and consumed. The group choices made in the political arena supplement the choices of households and businesses in answering the Five Fundamental Questions.

How are resources reallocated from the production of private goods to the production of public and quasipublic goods? In an economy whose resources are fully employed, government must free resources from private goods production to make them available for production of public and quasipublic goods. The means of releasing resources from private uses is to reduce private demand for them. This is accomplished by levying taxes on households and businesses, taking some of their income out of the circular flow. With lower incomes and hence less purchasing power, households and businesses must curtail their consumption and investment spending. Taxes diminish the private demand for goods and services, which in turn reduces the private demand for resources. So by diverting purchasing power from private spenders to government, taxes remove resources from private uses. (Global Perspective 5-1 shows the extent to which various countries divert labor from private sector to public sector employment.)

Government expenditures of tax proceeds can then reallocate the resources to the provision of public and quasipublic goods and services. Personal and corporate income taxation releases resources from the production of consumer goods (food, clothing, television sets) and investment goods (printing presses, boxcars, warehouses). Government expenditures shift these resources to the production of public and quasipublic goods (post offices, submarines, parks). Government purposely reallocates resources to bring about significant changes in the composition of the economy's total output. **(Key Questions 9 and 10)**

STABILIZATION

Historically, the most recent function of government is that of stabilizing the economy—helping the pri-

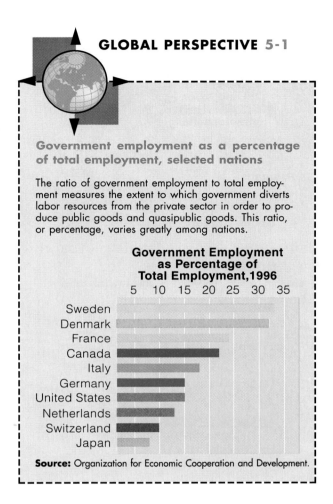

GLOBAL PERSPECTIVE 5-1

Government employment as a percentage of total employment, selected nations

The ratio of government employment to total employment measures the extent to which government diverts labor resources from the private sector in order to produce public goods and quasipublic goods. This ratio, or percentage, varies greatly among nations.

Government Employment as Percentage of Total Employment, 1996

	5	10	15	20	25	30	35
Sweden							
Denmark							
France							
Canada							
Italy							
Germany							
United States							
Netherlands							
Switzerland							
Japan							

Source: Organization for Economic Cooperation and Development.

vate economy achieve full employment of resources and stable prices. Here we will only outline (rather than fully explain) how government tries to do this; macroeconomics goes into this topic in great detail.

An economy's level of output depends directly on total or aggregate expenditure. A high level of total spending means it is profitable for industries to produce large outputs, which in turn ensures that both property and human resources will be employed at high levels. But aggregate spending may either fall short of or exceed the particular level necessary for full employment and price stability. Either of two possibilities, unemployment and inflation, may then occur:

1. *Unemployment* The level of total spending in the private sector may be too low to employ all available resources. Then government may choose to augment private spending so that total spending—private *plus* public—will be sufficient to generate full employment. Government can

do this by adjusting government spending and taxation. Specifically, it might increase its own spending on public goods and services or reduce taxes to stimulate private spending. It might also reduce interest rates to promote more private borrowing and spending.

2. *Inflation* Inflation is a rising general level of prices and is undesirable because it makes goods and services less attainable for many households. Prices of goods and services rise when the economy attempts to spend more than its capacity to produce. If aggregate spending exceeds the economy's output, prices will rise as consumers bid for available goods. That is, excessive aggregate spending is inflationary. Government's appropriate response is to eliminate the excess spending. It can do this by cutting its own expenditures, raising taxes to curtail private spending, or increasing interest rates to reduce private borrowing and spending.

QUICK REVIEW 5-3

■ Government enhances the operation of the market system by providing an appropriate legal foundation and promoting competition.

■ Transfer payments, direct market intervention, and taxation are ways government can lessen income inequality.

■ Government can correct for the overallocation of resources associated with spillover costs through legislation or specific taxes; the underallocation of resources associated with spillover benefits can be offset by government subsidies.

■ Government (rather than private firms) must provide desired public goods because such goods are indivisible and the exclusion principle does not apply to them; government also provides many quasipublic goods because of their large spillover benefits.

■ Government spending, tax revenues, and interest rates can be manipulated to stabilize the economy.

THE CIRCULAR FLOW REVISITED

Government is thoroughly integrated into the real and monetary flows that make up the economy. In Figure 5-5 we integrated government into the circular flow model of Chapter 2. In that figure flows (1) through (4) restate Figure 2-6. Flows (1) and (2) show business expenditures for the resources provided by households. These expenditures are costs to

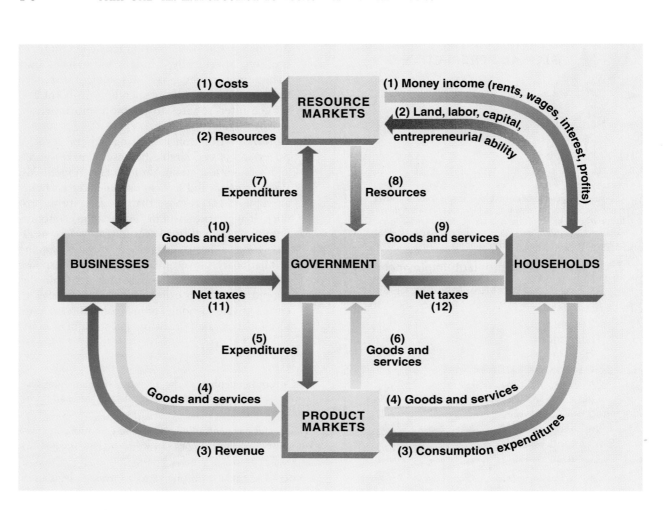

FIGURE 5-5 The circular flow and the public sector Government expenditures, taxes, and transfer payments affect the distribution of income, the allocation of resources, and the level of economic activity.

businesses but represent wage, rent, interest, and profit income to households. Flows (3) and (4) portray households' consumer expenditures for the goods and services produced by businesses.

Now consider the modifications resulting from the addition of government. Flows (5) through (8) tell us that government makes purchases in both product and resource markets. Specifically, flows (5) and (6) represent government purchases of such things as paper, computers, and military hardware from private businesses. Flows (7) and (8) reflect government purchases of resources. The Federal government employs and pays salaries to members of Congress, the armed forces, Justice Department lawyers, meat inspectors, and so on. State and local governments hire and pay teachers, bus drivers, police, and firefighters. The Federal government might also lease or purchase land to expand a military base;

a city may buy land on which to build a new elementary school.

Government then provides public goods and services to both households and businesses as shown by flows (9) and (10). Financing public goods and services requires tax payments by businesses and households as reflected in flows (11) and (12). These flows are labeled as *net* taxes to acknowledge that they also include "taxes in reverse" in the form of transfer payments to households and subsidies to businesses. Thus, flow (11) entails not merely corporate income, sales, and excise taxes flowing from businesses to government but also various subsidies to farmers, shipbuilders, and some airlines. Most business subsidies are "concealed" in the form of low-interest loans, loan guarantees, tax concessions, or public facilities provided at prices below their cost. Similarly, flow (12) includes both taxes (personal income taxes, payroll taxes) collected by government directly from households and transfer payments, for example, welfare payments and social security benefits, paid to households.

Our circular flow model shows how government can alter the distribution of income, reallocate resources, and change the level of economic activity. The structure of taxes and transfer payments can have a significant impact on income distribution. In flow (12) a tax structure which draws tax revenues primarily from well-to-do households, combined with a system of transfer payments to low-income households, will result in greater equality in the distribution of income.

Flows (6) and (8) imply an allocation of resources different from that of a purely private economy. Government buys goods and labor resources which differ from those purchased by households.

Finally, all the governmental flows suggest ways government might try to stabilize the economy. If the economy were experiencing unemployment, an increase in government spending with taxes and transfers held constant would increase total spending, output, and employment. Similarly, with the level of government expenditures constant, a decline in taxes or an increase in transfer payments would increase spendable incomes and boost private spending and employment. To fight inflation, the opposite policies would be in order: reduced government spending, increased taxes, and reduced transfers.

GOVERNMENT FINANCE

How large is the public sector? What are the main economic programs of Federal, state, and local governments? How are these programs financed? We examine these questions in the remainder of the chapter.

Government Growth: Purchases and Transfers

We can get a general impression of the size of government's economic role and how it has grown by examining government purchases of goods and services and government transfer payments. The distinction between these two kinds of outlays is significant:

1. **Government purchases** are *exhaustive;* the products purchased directly absorb (require the use of) resources and are part of the domestic output. For example, the purchase of a missile absorbs the labor of physicists and engineers along with steel, explosives, and a host of other inputs.

2. **Transfer payments** are *nonexhaustive;* they do not directly absorb resources or account for production. Social security benefits, welfare payments, veterans' benefits, and unemployment compensation are examples of transfer payments. Their key characteristic is that recipients make no current contribution to domestic output in return for these payments.

Figure 5-6 shows that government purchases of goods and services have been approximately 20 percent of domestic output over the past 35 years. Of course, domestic output has increased greatly during that time so that the *absolute* volume of government purchases has increased substantially. Government purchases were $113 billion in 1960 as compared with $1,454 billion in 1997.

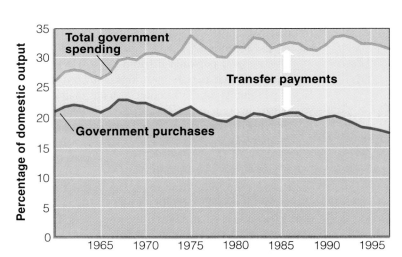

FIGURE 5-6 Government purchases, transfers, and total spending as a percentage of domestic output, 1960–1997 Government purchases have stayed close to 20 percent of domestic output since 1950. Transfer payments, however, have increased as a percentage of domestic output so that total government spending (purchases plus transfers) has grown and is now nearly one-third of domestic output.

But if we now look at transfer payments we get a different impression of government's role and growth. As Figure 5-6 reveals, transfers have grown significantly since the 1960s, rising from 5 percent of domestic output in 1960 to over 13 percent in 1997. The net result is that tax revenues required to finance total government spending—purchases plus transfers—now equal about one-third of domestic output.

In 1997 the so-called Tax Freedom Day in the United States was May 9. By this day the average worker had earned enough (from the start of the year) to pay the taxes required to finance government purchases and transfers for the year. Tax Freedom Day arrives later in several other countries, as implied in Global Perspective 5-2.

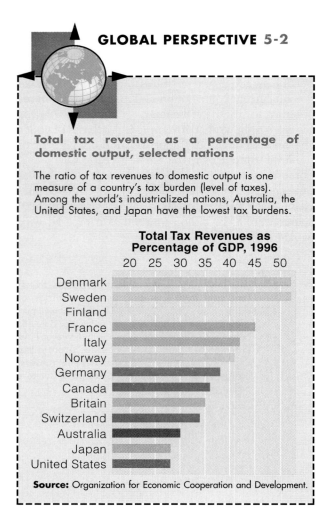

GLOBAL PERSPECTIVE 5-2

Total tax revenue as a percentage of domestic output, selected nations

The ratio of tax revenues to domestic output is one measure of a country's tax burden (level of taxes). Among the world's industrialized nations, Australia, the United States, and Japan have the lowest tax burdens.

Total Tax Revenues as Percentage of GDP, 1996

20 25 30 35 40 45 50

Denmark
Sweden
Finland
France
Italy
Norway
Germany
Canada
Britain
Switzerland
Australia
Japan
United States

Source: Organization for Economic Cooperation and Development.

FEDERAL FINANCE

Now let's look separately at the Federal, state, and local units of government to compare their expenditures and taxes. Figure 5-7 tells the story for the Federal government.

Federal Expenditures

Four important areas of Federal spending stand out: (1) pensions and income security, (2) national defense, (3) health, and (4) interest on the public debt. The *pensions and income security* category includes the many income-maintenance programs for the aged, persons with disabilities or handicaps, the unemployed, and families with no breadwinner. *National defense* constitutes about one-fifth of the Federal budget and thus underscores the high cost of military preparedness. *Health* reflects the high cost of government health programs for the retired and poor. *Interest on the public debt* is high because the public debt itself is extremely large.

Federal Tax Revenues

The revenue side of Figure 5-7 clearly shows that the personal income tax, payroll taxes, and the corporate income tax are the basic revenue getters, accounting for 45, 35, and 12 cents of each dollar collected.

Personal Income Tax The **personal income tax** is the kingpin of our national tax system and merits special comment. This tax is levied on *taxable income*, that is, on the incomes of households and unincorporated businesses after certain exemptions ($2450 for each household member) and deductions (business expenses, charitable contributions, home mortgage interest payments, certain state and local taxes) are taken into account.

The Federal personal income tax is a *progressive tax*, meaning that people with higher incomes pay a larger percentage of that income as taxes than do persons with lower incomes. The progressivity is achieved by applying higher tax rates to successive layers or brackets of income.

Columns 1 and 2 in Table 5-2 portray the mechanics of the income tax for a married couple filing a joint return in 1997. Note that a 15 percent tax rate applies to all taxable income up to $41,200, a 28 percent rate applies to additional income up to $99,600, and even greater rates apply for three more layers of additional income, the highest rate being 39.6 percent.

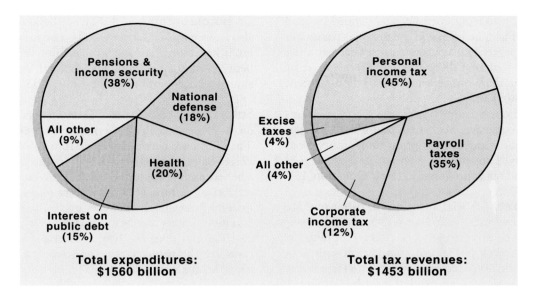

FIGURE 5-7 *Federal expenditures and tax revenues, 1996* Federal expenditures are dominated by spending for pensions and income security and spending for national defense. A full 80 percent of Federal tax revenue is derived from just two sources: the personal income tax and payroll taxes. (*Source:* U.S. Office of Management and Budget.)

The tax rates shown in column 2 in Table 5-2 are marginal tax rates. A **marginal tax rate** is the rate at which the tax is paid on each *additional* unit of taxable income. Thus, if a couple's taxable income is $50,000, they will pay the marginal tax rate of 15 percent on each dollar from $1 to $41,200 and the marginal tax rate of 28 percent on each dollar from $41,201 to $50,000. You should be able to show that their total income tax will be $8644.

The marginal tax rates in column 2 overstate the personal income tax bite because the rising rates in that column apply only to the income within each successive tax bracket. To get a better picture of the tax burden, we must consider average tax rates. The

TABLE 5-2 **Federal personal income tax rates, 1997***

(1) Total taxable income	(2) Marginal tax rate, %	(3) Total tax on highest income in bracket	(4) Average tax rate on highest income in bracket, % (3) ÷ (1)
$1 to $41,200	15.0	$ 6,180	15.0
$41,201 to $99,600	28.0	22,532	22.6
$99,601 to $151,750	31.0	38,699	25.5
$151,751 to $271,050	36.0	$81,647	30.1
Over 271,050	39.6	—	—

*Data are for a married couple filing a joint return.

average tax rate is the total tax paid divided by total taxable income. The couple in the previous paragraph is in the 28 percent tax bracket because they pay a top marginal tax rate of 28 percent on some of their income. But their average tax rate is 17.3 percent (= $8644/$50,000).

A tax whose average tax rate rises as income increases is progressive. Such a tax claims both a larger absolute amount and a larger proportion of income as income rises. Thus we can say that the Federal personal income tax is progressive. **(Key Question 15)**

Payroll Taxes Social security contributions are **payroll taxes**—taxes based on wages and salaries— used to finance two com lsory Federal programs for retired workers: social security (an income-enhancement program) and Medicare (which pays for medical services). These taxes are paid equally by employers and employees. Improvements in, and extensions of, the social security programs, plus growth of the labor force, have resulted in very significant increases in these payroll taxes in recent years. In 1998, employees and employers each paid 7.65 percent on the first $68,400 of an employee's annual earnings and 1.45 percent on all additional earnings.

Corporate Income Tax The Federal government also taxes corporate income. The **corporate income tax** is levied on a corporation's profit—the difference between its total revenue and its total expenses. For almost all corporations, the tax rate is 35 percent.

Sales and Excise Taxes Taxes on commodities or on purchases take the form of **sales and excise taxes.** The difference between the two is mainly one of coverage. Sales taxes fall on a wide range of products, whereas excises are levied individually on a small, select list of commodities. As Figure 5-7 suggests, the Federal government collects excise taxes (on such commodities as alcoholic beverages, tobacco, and gasoline) but does not levy a general sales tax; sales taxes are the primary revenue source of most state governments.

STATE AND LOCAL FINANCE

Note in Figure 5-8 that the basic sources of tax revenue for state governments are sales and excise taxes, which account for about 49 percent of all tax revenue.

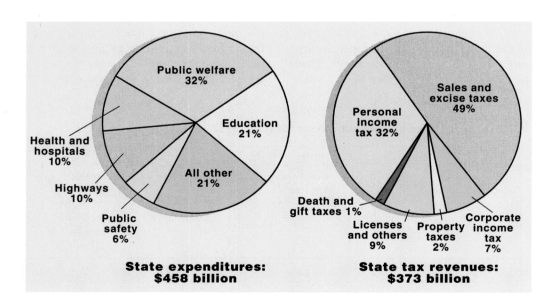

FIGURE 5-8 State expenditures and tax revenues, 1994 State governments spend mainly on public welfare and education. Their primary source of tax revenue is sales and excise taxes. (*Source:* U.S. Bureau of the Census.)

State personal income taxes, which have much more modest rates than does the Federal income tax, are the second most important source of state revenue. A tax on corporate income and license fees account for most of the remainder of state tax revenue.

The major outlays of state governments are for (1) public welfare, (2) education, (3) health and hospitals, and (4) highway maintenance and construction.

Figure 5-8 contains aggregated data, so it tells us little about the finances of individual states. And states vary significantly in the taxes levied. Thus, although personal income taxes are a major source of revenue for all state governments combined, seven states do not have a personal income tax. Also, there are great variations in the size of tax receipts and disbursements among the states.

The receipts and expenditures shown in Figure 5-9 are for all units of local government, including not only cities and towns but also counties, municipalities, townships, and school districts. One source of revenue and one use of revenue stand out: The bulk of the revenue received by local government comes from **property taxes.** And most local revenue is spent for education.

The gaping deficit found by comparing revenues and expenditures in Figure 5-9 is largely removed when nontax sources of income are taken into account: In 1994 the tax revenues of local governments were supplemented by some $242 billion in intergovernmental grants from Federal and state governments. Furthermore, local governments received an additional $93 billion as proprietary income, that is, as revenue from government-owned hospitals and utilities.

Fiscal Federalism

Historically, the tax collections of both state and local governments have fallen substantially short of their expenditures. These revenue shortfalls are largely filled by Federal transfers or grants. It is not uncommon for 15 to 20 percent of all revenue received by state and local governments to come from the Federal government. In addition to Federal grants to state and local governments, the states also make grants to local governmental units. This system of intergovernmental transfers is called **fiscal federalism.** Because the Federal budget has suffered large and persistent deficits, Federal grants in recent years have

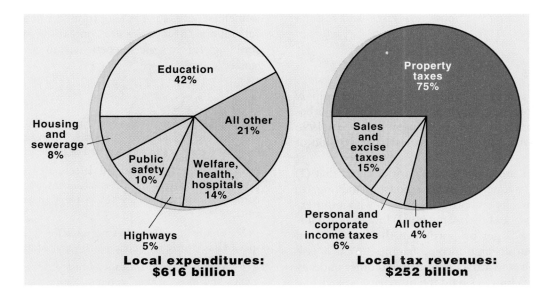

FIGURE 5-9 Local expenditures and tax revenues, 1994 The expenditures of local governments are largely for education and are financed by property taxes. (*Source:* U.S. Bureau of the Census.)

The Financing of Corporate Activity

One advantage of corporations is their ability to finance their operations through the sale of stocks and bonds. It is informative to examine the nature of corporate finance in more detail.

Generally, corporations finance their activities in three different ways. First, a very large portion of a corporation's activity is financed internally out of undistributed corporate profits. Second, as do individuals or unincorporated businesses, corporations may borrow from financial institutions. For example, a small corporation planning to build a new plant may obtain the funds from a commercial bank, a savings and loan association, or an insurance company. Third, unique to corporations, they can issue common stocks and bonds.

Stocks versus Bonds A common stock is an ownership share. The purchaser of a stock certificate has the right to vote for corporate officers and to share in dividends. If you buy 1000 of the 100,000 shares issued by Specific

Motors, Inc. (hereafter SM), then you own 1 percent of the company, are entitled to 1 percent of any dividends declared by the board of directors, and control 1 percent of the votes in the annual election of corporate officials.

In contrast, a bond is not an ownership share. A bond purchaser is simply lending money to a corporation. A bond is merely an IOU, in acknowledgment of a loan, whereby the corporation promises to pay the holder a fixed amount at some specified future date and other fixed amounts (interest payments) every year up to the bond's maturity date. For example, you might purchase a 10-year SM bond with a face value of $1000 with a 10 percent stated rate of interest. This means that, in exchange for your $1000, SM guarantees you a $100 interest payment for each of the next 10 years and then repays your $1000 principal at the end of that period.

Differences There are clearly important differences between stocks and bonds. First, as noted, the bondholder is not an owner of the company but is only a lender. Second, bonds are considered to be less risky than stocks for two reasons. On the one hand, bondholders have a "legal prior claim" upon a corporation's earnings. Dividends cannot be paid to stockholders until all interest payments that are due to bondholders have been paid. On the other hand, holders of SM stock do not know how much their

---

declined. That has caused state and local governments to increase tax rates, impose new taxes, and restrain expenditures.

Lotteries

Both state and local governments have increasingly turned to **lotteries** as a means of closing the gaps between their tax receipts and expenditures. In 1996 some 36 states had lotteries that sold $34 billion of tickets.

Lotteries are controversial. Critics argue that (1) it is morally wrong for states to sponsor gambling; (2) lotteries generate compulsive gamblers who impoverish themselves and their families; (3) low-income families spend a larger proportion of their incomes on lotteries than do high-income families; (4) as a cash business, lotteries attract criminals and other undesirables; and (5) lotteries send the message that luck and fate—rather than education, hard work, and saving and investing—are the route to wealth.

Defenders contend that (1) lotteries are preferable to taxes because they are voluntary rather than com-

pulsory; (2) they are a painless way to finance government services such as education, medical care, and welfare; and (3) lotteries are competitive with illegal gambling and thus socially beneficial in curtailing organized crime.

QUICK REVIEW 5-4

■ Government purchases account for about 20 percent of U.S. output; the addition of transfers increases government spending to almost one-third of domestic output.

■ Income security and national defense are the main areas of Federal spending; personal income, payroll, and corporate income taxes are the primary sources of revenue.

■ States rely on sales and excise taxes for revenue; their spending is largely for public welfare and education.

■ Education is the main expenditure for local governments, and most of their revenue comes from property taxes.

dividends will be or how much they might obtain for their stock if they decide to sell. If Specific Motors falls on hard times, stockholders may receive no dividends at all and the value of their stock may plummet. Provided the corporation does not go bankrupt, the holder of an SM bond is guaranteed a $100 interest payment each year and the return of his or her $1000 at the end of 10 years.

Bond Risks This is not to imply that the purchase of corporate bonds is riskless. The market value of your SM bond may vary over time in accordance with the financial health of the corporation. If SM encounters economic misfortunes which raise questions about its financial integrity, the market value of your bond may fall. Should you sell the bond prior to maturity, you may receive only $600 or $700 for it (rather than $1000) and thereby incur a capital loss.

Changes in interest rates also affect the market prices of bonds. Specifically, increases in interest rates cause bond prices to fall and vice versa. Assume you purchase a $1000 ten-year SM bond this year (1999) when the interest rate is 10 percent. This obviously means that your bond provides a $100 fixed interest payment each year. But now suppose that by next year the interest rate has jumped to 15 percent and SM must now guarantee a $150 fixed annual payment on its new (year-2000) $1000 ten-year bonds. Clearly, no sensible person will pay you $1000 for your bond, which pays only $100 of interest income per year when new bonds can be purchased for $1000 which pay the holder $150 per year. Hence, if you sell your 1999 bond before maturity, you will suffer a capital loss.

Bondholders face another element of risk due to inflation. If substantial inflation occurs over the 10-year period during which you hold an SM bond, the $1000 principal repaid to you at the end of that period will represent substantially less purchasing power than the $1000 you loaned to SM 10 years earlier. You will have lent "dear" dollars but will be repaid in "cheap" dollars.

CHAPTER SUMMARY

1. The functional distribution of income shows how society's total income is divided among wages, rents, interest, and profit; the personal distribution of income shows how total income is divided among individual households.

2. Households use their total incomes to pay personal taxes, for saving, and to buy consumer goods. Over half of their consumption expenditures are for services.

3. Sole proprietorships are firms owned and usually operated by single individuals. Partnerships are firms owned and usually operated by just a handful of individuals. Corporations are legal entities, distinct and separate from the individuals who own them. They often have thousands, or even millions, of owners—the stockholders of the firm.

4. Government enhances the operation of the market system by **(a)** providing an appropriate legal and social framework, and **(b)** acting to maintain competition.

5. Government alters the distribution of income through the tax-transfer system and by market intervention.

6. Spillovers or externalities cause the equilibrium output of certain goods to vary from the socially efficient output. Spillover costs result in an overallocation of resources, which can be corrected by legislation or specific taxes. Spillover benefits are accompanied by an underallocation of resources, which can be corrected by subsidies to consumers or producers.

7. Only government is willing to provide public goods because such goods are indivisible and entail benefits from which nonpaying consumers (free riders) cannot be excluded; private firms will not produce these goods. Quasipublic goods have some characteristics of public goods and some of private goods; they are provided by government because the private sector would underallocate resources to their production.

8. Government can reduce unemployment or inflation by altering its taxation, spending, and interest-rate policies.

9. Government purchases exhaust (use up or absorb) resources; transfer payments do not. Government purchases have been about 20 percent of domestic output since 1960. However, transfers have grown significantly, so total government spending is now nearly one-third of domestic output.

10. The main categories of Federal spending are pensions and income security, national defense, health, and interest on the public debt; revenues come primarily from personal income, payroll, and corporate income taxes.

11. The primary sources of revenue for the states are sales and excise taxes and personal income taxes; major state expenditures go to public welfare, education, health and hospitals, and highways.

12. At the local level, most revenue comes from the property tax, and education is the most important expenditure.

13. Under the U.S. system of fiscal federalism, state and local tax revenues are supplemented by sizable revenue grants from the Federal government.

TERMS AND CONCEPTS

functional distribution of income
personal distribution of income
durable good
nondurable good
services
plant
firm
vertical combination

horizontal combination
conglomerate combination
industry
sole proprietorship
partnership
corporation
stocks
bonds
limited liability

double taxation
principal-agent problem
monopoly
spillover costs
spillover benefits
exclusion principle
public goods
free-rider problem
quasipublic goods
government purchases

transfer payments
personal income tax
marginal tax rate
average tax rate
payroll taxes
corporate income tax
sales and excise taxes
property taxes
fiscal federalism
lotteries

STUDY QUESTIONS

1. Distinguish between functional and personal distributions of income.

2. KEY QUESTION Assume the five residents of Econoville receive incomes of $50, $75, $125, $250, and $500. Present the resulting personal distribution of income as a graph similar to Figure 5-2. Compare the incomes of the lowest and highest fifth of the income receivers.

3. Distinguish clearly between a plant, a firm, and an industry. Why is an "industry" often difficult to define in practice?

4. KEY QUESTION What are the major legal forms of business organization? Briefly state the advantages and disadvantages of each. How do you account for the dominant role of corporations in the U.S. economy?

5. "The legal form an enterprise assumes is dictated primarily by the financial requirements of its particular line of production." Do you agree?

6. Enumerate and briefly discuss the main economic functions of government. Which of these functions do you think is the most controversial? Explain your reasoning.

7. What divergencies arise between equilibrium and an efficient output when **(a)** spillover costs and **(b)** spillover benefits are present? How might government correct for these discrepancies? "The presence of spillover costs suggests underallocation of resources to that product and the need for governmental subsidies." Do you agree? Why or why not? Explain how zoning and seat belt laws might be used to deal with a problem of spillover costs.

8. Researchers have concluded that injuries caused by firearms cost more than $500 million a year in hospital expenses alone. Because the majority of those shot are poor and without insurance, roughly 85 percent of these hospital costs must be borne by taxpayers. Use your understanding of externalities to recommend appropriate policies.

9. KEY QUESTION What are the basic characteristics of public goods? Explain the significance of the exclusion principle. By what means does government provide public goods?

10. KEY QUESTION Draw a production possibilities curve with public goods on the vertical axis and private goods on the horizontal axis. Assuming the economy is initially operating on the curve, indicate how the production of public goods might be increased. How might the output of public goods be increased if the economy is initially operating at a point inside the curve?

11. Use your understanding of the characteristics of private and public goods to determine whether the following should be produced through the market system or provided by government: **(a)** bread; **(b)** street lighting; **(c)** bridges; **(d)** parks; **(e)** swimming pools; **(f)** medical care; **(g)** mail delivery; **(h)** housing; **(i)** air traffic control; **(j)** libraries. State why you answered as you did in each case.

12. Explain how government can manipulate its expenditures and tax revenues to reduce **(a)** unemployment and **(b)** the rate of inflation.

13. "Most government actions simultaneously affect the distribution of income, the allocation of resources, and the levels of unemployment and prices." Use the circular flow model to confirm this assertion for each of the following: **(a)** the construction of a new high school in Blackhawk County; **(b)** a 2 percent reduction in the Federal corporate income tax; **(c)** an expansion of preschool programs for disadvantaged children; **(d)** a $50 million increase in spending for space research; **(e)** the levying of a tax on air polluters; and **(f)** a $1 increase in the legally required minimum wage.

14. What is the most important source of revenue and major type of expenditure at the Federal level? At the state level? At the local level?

15. KEY QUESTION Suppose in Fiscalville there is no tax on the first $10,000 of income, but earnings between $10,000 and $20,000 are taxed at 20 percent and income between $20,000 and $30,000 at 30 percent. Any income above $30,000 is taxed at 40 percent. If your income is $50,000, how much will you pay in taxes? Determine your marginal and average tax rates. Is this a progressive tax? Explain.

16. (Last Word) Describe three ways to finance corporate activity. Make a case arguing that stocks are more risky for the financial investor than are bonds.

17. WEB-BASED QUESTION Personal Distribution of Income—What Is the Trend? Visit the U.S. Census Bureau http://www.census.gov/hhes/income/midclass/index.html. Since 1969, how has the share of aggregate household income received by the lowest and highest income quintiles (one-fifths) changed?

18. WEB-BASED QUESTION Federal Expenditures—Historical Tables and 5-Year Estimates The Office of Management and Budget provides a search page for Federal budget publications at http://www.access.gpo.gov/omb/omb003.html. Search for the current fiscal year outlays estimates by selecting Historical Tables and inserting the search words OUTLAYS BY FUNCTION AND SUBFUNCTION for the previous 25 years to 5 years in the future. Use the data provided to create pie charts for 25 years ago, the current year, and 5 years hence using the following categories: pensions and income security, national defense, health, interest on the public debt, and all other. Which categories are shrinking and which are expanding as a percentage of total expenditures?

6

The United States in the Global Economy

Backpackers in the wilderness like to think they are "leaving the world behind," but, like Atlas, they carry the world on their shoulders. Much of their backpacking equipment is imported—knives from Switzerland, rain gear from South Korea, cameras from Japan, aluminum pots made in England, miniature stoves from Sweden, sleeping bags from China, and compasses from Finland. Some backpackers wear hiking boots from Italy, sunglasses made in France, and watches from Japan. Moreover, they may drive to the trailheads in Japanese-made Toyotas or Swedish-made Volvos, sipping coffee from Brazil or snacking on bananas from Honduras.

International trade and the global economy affect all of us daily, whether we are hiking in the wilderness, driving our cars, listening to music, or working at our jobs. We cannot "leave the world behind." We are enmeshed with the rest of the world in a complex web of economic relationships—trading of goods and services, multinational corporations, cooperative ventures among the world's firms, and ties among the world's financial markets. This web is so complex that it is difficult to determine just what is—or isn't—a U.S. product. RCA television sets are made by a company based in France; a Canadian company owns Tropicana Orange Juice; and the parent company of Gerber baby food is Swiss. The Chevrolet Lumina sedan is manufactured in Canada, and a British corporation owns Burger King. Many "U.S." products are made with components from abroad, and, conversely, many "foreign" products contain numerous U.S.-produced parts. For example, international firms supply major components of the new U.S. Boeing 777 airplane (see Figure 6-1).

This chapter introduces the basic principles underlying the global economy. (A more advanced discussion of international economics is in the last part of this book.) Here, we first look at world trade today, the U.S.' role in it, and some factors which have caused it to grow. Next, we modify Chapter 5's circular flow diagram to account for international trade flows, explore the basis for world trade, and look at the system of exchange rates which facilitate it. Finally, we describe several restrictive trade practices and discuss major efforts to liberalize trade.

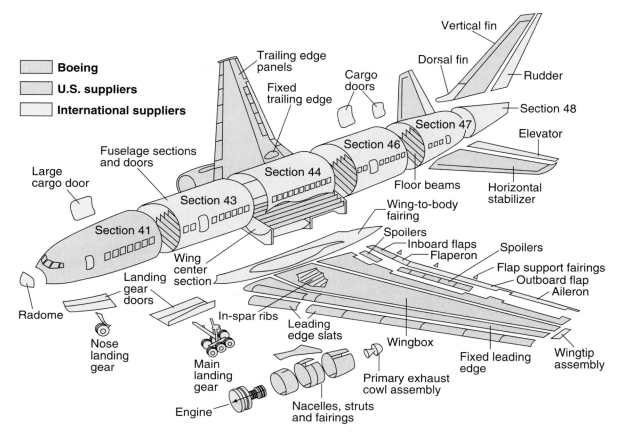

FIGURE 6-1 **The Boeing 777: who supplies the parts?** International firms supply major components of the "American" Boeing 777 aircraft. (*Source: Seattle Post Intelligencer.* Reprinted by permission.)

WORLD TRADE

The volume of world trade is so large and its characteristics are so unique that it is difficult to describe except in some general terms.

Volume and Pattern

Table 6-1 provides a rough index of the importance of world trade for several countries. Many nations with restricted resource bases and limited domestic markets cannot efficiently produce the variety of goods they want to consume. Such countries must import the goods they desire from other nations, which in turn means they must export, or sell abroad,

TABLE 6-1 **Exports of goods and services as a percentage of GDP, selected countries, 1996**

Country	Exports as percentage of GDP
Netherlands	56
Canada	38
New Zealand	30
United Kingdom	30
France	24
Italy	24
Germany	23
United States	12
Japan	10

Source: IMF, International Financial Statistics, 1997.

some of their own products. For such countries, exports may run from 25 to 35 percent or more of their domestic output. Other countries, the United States, for example, have rich and diversified resource bases and vast internal markets. They are less dependent on world trade.

Volume   For the United States and the world the volume of international trade has been increasing both absolutely and relatively. A comparison of the boxed data in Figure 6-2 reveals substantial growth in the dollar amount of U.S. exports and imports over the past several decades. The lines in the figure show the growth of exports and imports of goods and services as percentages of gross domestic product (GDP)—the dollar value of all goods and services produced within the United States. Exports and imports currently are 12 to 14 percent of GDP, more than double their percentages in 1965.

However, the United States now accounts for a diminished percentage of total world trade. In 1947 it supplied about one-third of the world's total exports, compared with about one-eighth today. World trade has increased more rapidly for other nations than it has for the United States. *But in terms of absolute volumes of imports and exports, the United States is still the world's leading trading nation.*

Dependence   There can be no question as to the United States' dependence on the world economy.

The United States is almost entirely dependent on other countries for bananas, cocoa, coffee, spices, tea, raw silk, nickel, tin, natural rubber, and diamonds. Even casual observation suggests that imported goods compete in many of our domestic markets: Japanese cameras and video recorders, French and Italian wines, Swiss and Austrian snow skis, and Japanese motorcycles and autos are a few examples. Even the "great American pastime" of baseball relies heavily on imported gloves and baseballs.

But world trade is a two-way street, and many U.S. industries benefit from foreign markets. Almost all segments of U.S. agriculture rely on sales abroad; for example, exports of rice, wheat, cotton, and tobacco vary from one-fourth to more than one-half of their total output. The U.S. computer, chemical, semiconductor, aircraft, automobile, machine tool, and coal industries, among many others, sell significant portions of their output in international markets. Table 6-2 shows some of the major commodity exports and imports of the United States.

Trade Patterns   The following facts provide an overview of the pattern of U.S. international trade:

1. The United States has a *trade deficit* in goods. In 1996 U.S. imports of goods exceeded U.S. exports of goods by $191 billion.

2. The United States has a *trade surplus* in services. In 1996 U.S. exports of services exceeded U.S. imports of services by $80 billion.

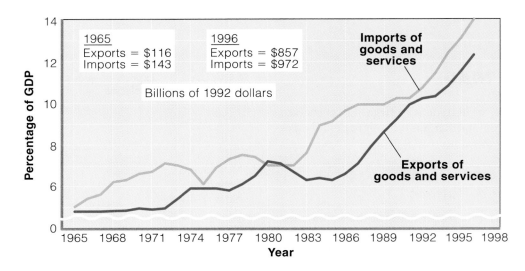

FIGURE 6-2 U.S. trade as percentage of GDP   American imports and exports have increased in volume and have more than doubled as a percentage of GDP since 1965. [*Source: Economic Report of the President, 1997.* Data from national income accounts and adjusted for inflation (1992 dollars).]

TABLE 6-2   Principal U.S. exports and imports of goods, 1996 (in billions of dollars)

Exports	Amount	Imports	Amount
Computers	$43.7	Petroleum	$72.7
Chemicals	42.5	Automobiles	65.9
Semiconductors	35.8	Computers	61.5
Consumer durables	33.2	Clothing	39.6
Aircraft	30.8	Semiconductors	36.7
Generating equipment	24.1	Household appliances	31.1
Grains	21.2	Chemicals	26.9
Telecommunications	20.3	Consumer electronics	18.4
Automobiles	17.0	Iron and steel	17.2
Nonferrous metals	15.5	Toys and sporting goods	15.4

Source: Consolidated from Department of Commerce data.

3. The United States imports some of the same categories of goods that it exports, specifically, automobiles, computers, chemicals, semiconductors, and telecommunications equipment (see Table 6-2).

4. As shown in Table 6-3, most U.S. export and import trade is with other industrially advanced nations, not with developing countries.

5. Canada is the United States' most important trading partner quantitatively. In 1996, 22 percent of U.S. exports were sold to Canadians, who in turn provided 20 percent of U.S. imports (see Table 6-3).

6. There are sizable trade deficits with Japan and China. In 1996, U.S. imports from Japan exceeded U.S. exports to Japan by $49 billion, and U.S. imports from China exceeded exports to China by $44 billion (see Table 6-3).

7. The U.S. dependence on foreign oil is reflected in the excess of imports in our trade with countries belonging to the Organization of Petroleum Exporting Countries (OPEC). In 1996, the United States imported $44 billion of goods (mainly oil) from OPEC members, while exporting $20 billion of goods to those countries (see Table 6-3).

TABLE 6-3   U.S. exports and imports of goods by area, 1996

Exports to	Value, billions of dollars		Percentage of total		Imports from	Value, billions of dollars		Percentage of total	
Industrial countries	$354		58		Industrial countries	$443		55	
Canada		$135		22	Canada		$159		20
Japan		66		11	Japan		115		14
Western Europe		137		22	Western Europe		162		20
Australia		12		2	Australia		4		1
Other		3		1	Other		3		1
Developing countries	258		42		Developing countries	360		45	
Mexico		57		9	Mexico		75		9
China		12		2	China		56		7
Eastern Europe		7		1	Eastern Europe		7		1
OPEC countries		20		3	OPEC countries		44		5
Other		162		26	Other		178		22
Total	**$612**		**100**		**Total**	**$803**		**100**	

Note: Data are on international transactions basis and exclude military shipments. Data do not add to totals because of rounding.
Source: Survey of Current Business, October 1997.

Linkages International trade requires complex financial linkages among nations. For example, how does the United States finance its $111 billion trade deficit in goods and services? How does a nation, or a person, obtain more goods from others than it provides to them? The answer is by either borrowing or by selling assets. This is how the United States finances its trade deficit. It borrows from citizens of other nations; the United States is the world's largest debtor nation. Moreover, nations with which the United States has large trade deficits, such as Japan, often "recycle their dollars" by buying U.S. assets.

Rapid Trade Growth

Several factors have propelled the rapid growth of international trade since World War II.

Transportation Technology High transportation costs are a barrier to any type of trade, particularly trade between distant places. But improvements in transportation have shrunk the globe, fostering world trade. Airplanes now transport low-weight, high-value items such as diamonds and semiconductors quickly from one nation to another. We now routinely transport oil in massive tankers, greatly reducing the cost of transportation per barrel. Grain is loaded onto oceangoing ships at modern, efficient grain silos at Great Lakes and coastal ports. Container ships transport self-contained railroad boxes directly to foreign ports, where cranes place the containers onto railroad cars for internal shipment. Natural gas flows through large-diameter pipelines from exporting to importing countries—for instance, from Russia to Germany and from Canada to the United States. Workers clean fish on large processing ships directly on the fishing grounds; refrigerated vessels then transport the fish to overseas ports.

Communications Technology World trade has also expanded because of dramatic improvements in communications technology. Telephones, fax (facsimile) machines, and computers now directly link traders around the world, allowing exporters to assess overseas markets and to complete trade deals. New communications methods enable us to move money around the world in the blink of an eye. Exchange rates, stock prices, and interest rates flash onto computer screens nearly simultaneously in Los Angeles, London, and Lisbon.

In short, exporters and importers today can as easily communicate between Sweden and Australia as between San Francisco and Oakland. A distributor in New York can get a price quote on 1000 woven baskets in Thailand as quickly as a quotation on 1000 laptop computers in New Jersey.

General Decline in Tariffs Tariffs—excise taxes (duties) on imported products—have had their ups and downs, but since 1940 they have generally fallen worldwide. A glance ahead to Figure 6-6 shows that U.S. tariffs as a percentage of imports are now about 5 percent, down from 37 percent in 1940. Many nations still have barriers to free trade, but, on average, tariffs have fallen greatly, increasing international trade.

Peace During World War II powerful industrial countries fought one another, certainly disrupting international trade. Since then, trade has not only been restored but has been bolstered by peaceful relations and by major trade agreements linking most industrial nations. In particular, Japan and Germany—two defeated World War II powers—now are major participants in world trade.

Participants

All nations of the world participate to some extent in international trade.

United States, Japan, and Western Europe As implied in Global Perspective 6-1, the top participants in world trade are the United States, Germany, and Japan. In 1996 these three nations had combined exports of $1.6 trillion. Along with Germany, other western European nations such as France, Britain, and Italy are major exporters and importers. In fact, three major "players"—the United States, Japan, and the western European nations—now dominate world trade. These three areas also form the heart of the world's financial system and headquarter most of the world's large **multinational corporations**—firms which have sizable production and distribution activities in other countries. Among the world's top 25 multinationals are Royal Dutch Shell and Unilever (Britain and the Netherlands); Ford Motor, General Motors, and IBM (United States); British Petroleum (Britain); Nestlé (Switzerland); Fiat (Italy); Siemens and Bayer Chemicals (Germany); Mitsubishi and Mitsui (Japan); and Elf Aquitaine (France).

New Players New, important participants have arrived on the world trade scene. One group of such na-

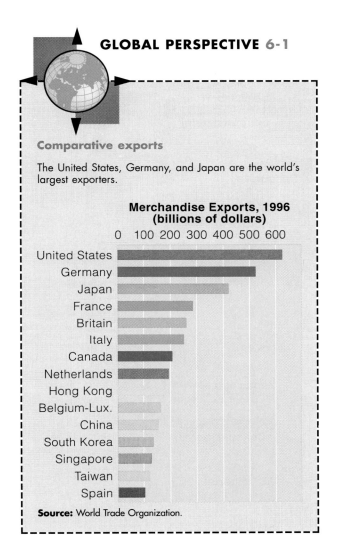

GLOBAL PERSPECTIVE 6-1

Comparative exports

The United States, Germany, and Japan are the world's largest exporters.

Merchandise Exports, 1996 (billions of dollars)

0 100 200 300 400 500 600

United States
Germany
Japan
France
Britain
Italy
Canada
Netherlands
Hong Kong
Belgium-Lux.
China
South Korea
Singapore
Taiwan
Spain

Source: World Trade Organization.

Chinese exports and imports each were about $50 billion. In 1996 they each topped $151 billion, with 33 percent of China's exports going to the United States. Also, China has been attracting much foreign investment (more than $600 billion since 1990). Experts predict China will eventually become one of the world's leading trading nations.

The collapse of communism in eastern Europe and the former Soviet Union has also altered world trade patterns. Before this collapse, the eastern European nations of Poland, Hungary, Czechoslovakia, and East Germany mainly traded with the Soviet Union and such political allies as North Korea and Cuba. Today, East Germany is reunited with West Germany, and Poland, Hungary, and the Czech Republic have established new trade relationships with western Europe and the United States.

Russia itself has initiated far-reaching market reforms, including widespread privatization of industry, and has consummated major trade deals with firms from across the globe. Although its transition to capitalism has been far from smooth, no doubt Russia can be a major trading power. Other former Soviet republics—now independent nations—such as Ukraine and Estonia also are opening their economies to international trade and finance.

BACK TO THE CIRCULAR FLOW

We can easily add "the rest of the world" to Chapter 5's circular flow model. We do so in Figure 6-3 via two adjustments:

1. Our previous "Resource Markets" and "Product Markets" now become "U.S. Resource Markets" and "U.S. Product Markets." Similarly, we add the modifier "U.S." to the "Businesses," "Government," and "Households" sectors.

2. We place the foreign sector—the "Rest of the World"—so that it interacts with "U.S. Product Markets." This sector designates all foreign nations with which the United States deals and the individuals, businesses, and governments they comprise.

Flow (13) in Figure 6-3 shows that people, businesses, and governments abroad buy U.S. products—our exports—from our product market. This goods and services flow of U.S. exports to foreign nations is accompanied by a monetary revenue flow (14) from the rest of the world to the United States. In response to these revenues from abroad, U.S. businesses demand more domestic resources [flow (2)] to produce the

tions is the newly industrializing Asian economies of Hong Kong (now part of China), Singapore, South Korea, and Taiwan. These **"Asian tigers"** have expanded their share of world exports from about 3 percent in 1972 to more than 10 percent today. Together, they export about as much as either Germany or Japan and much more than France, Britain, or Italy. Other countries in southeast Asia, particularly Malaysia and Indonesia, have also expanded their international trade.

China, with its increasing reliance on the market system, is another emerging trading power. Since initiating market reforms in 1978, its annual growth of output has averaged 9 percent (compared with 2 to 3 percent annually in the United States). At this remarkable rate, China's total output nearly doubles every 8 years! An upsurge of exports and imports has accompanied this expansion of output. In 1989

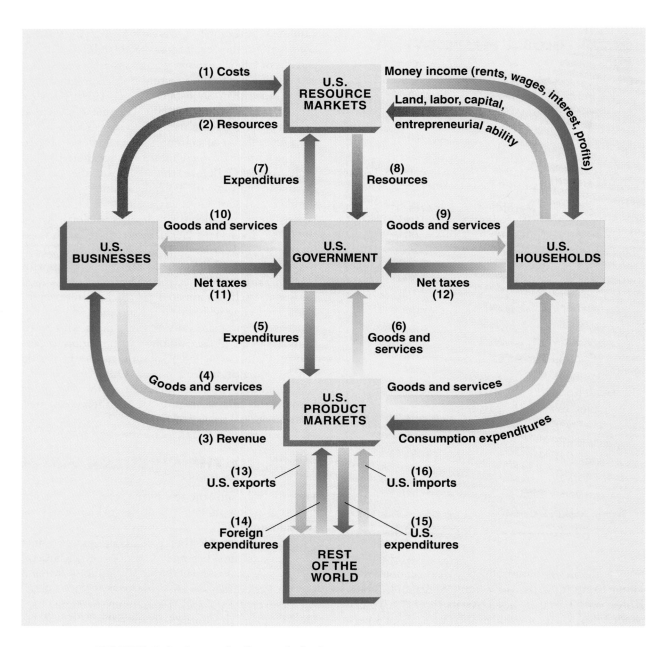

FIGURE 6-3 The circular flow with the foreign sector   Flows (13) to (16) in the lower portion of the diagram show how the U.S. economy interacts with the "Rest of the World." People abroad buy U.S. exports, contributing to U.S. business revenues and money incomes. People in the United States, in turn, spend part of their incomes to buy imports from abroad. Income from a nation's exports helps pay for its imports.

---

goods for export; they pay for these resources with revenue from abroad. Thus, the domestic flow (1) of money income (rents, wages, interest, and profits) to U.S. households rises.

But U.S. exports are only half the picture. Flow (15) shows that U.S. households, businesses, and government spend some of their income on foreign products. These products, of course, are our imports—

flow (16). Purchases of imports, say, autos and electronics, contribute to foreign output and income, which in turn enable foreign households to buy U.S. exports.

Our circular flow model is a simplification which emphasizes product market effects, but a few other U.S.–rest-of-the-world relationships also require comment. Specifically, there are linkages between the U.S. resource markets and the rest of the world.

The United States imports and exports not only products but also resources. For example, the United States imports crude oil and exports raw logs. Moreover, some U.S. firms engage in production abroad, which diverts spending on capital from our domestic resource market to resource markets in other nations. For instance, General Motors might build an auto assembly plant in Canada. Or, flowing in the other direction, Sony might construct a plant for manufacturing CD players in the United States.

There are also international flows of labor. About 1 million legal and illegal immigrants enter the United States each year, expanding the availability of labor resources in the United States and raising total output and income. On the other hand, immigration tends to increase the labor supply in certain U.S. labor markets, reducing wage rates for some types of U.S. labor.

The expanded circular flow model (Figure 6-3) also demonstrates that a nation engaged in world trade risks instability which would not affect a "closed" nation. Recessions and inflation can be highly contagious among trading nations. Suppose the nations of southeast Asia experience a severe recession. As their incomes decline, they purchase fewer U.S. exports. As a result, flows (13) and (14) in Figure 6-3 decline and inventories of unsold U.S. goods rise. U.S. firms respond by reducing their production and employment, which diminishes the flow of money income to U.S. households [flow (1)]. Recession in Asia in this case has contributed to a recession in the United States.

Figure 6-3 also helps us see that the foreign sector alters resource allocation and incomes in the U.S. economy. With a foreign sector, the United States produces more of some goods (exports) and fewer of others (imports) than it would otherwise. Thus, U.S. labor and other resources are shifted toward export industries and away from import industries. The United States uses more resources to make commercial aircraft and to grow wheat and less to make autos and clothing. So we ask: "Do these shifts of resources make economic sense? Do they enhance U.S. total

output and thus the U.S. standard of living?" We look at some answers next. **(Key Question 3)**

QUICK REVIEW 6-1

■ World trade has increased globally and nationally. In terms of volume, the United States is the world's leading international trader, with exports and imports of about 12 to 14 percent of GDP.

■ Advances in transportation and communications technology, declines in tariffs, and peaceful relations among major industrial countries all have helped expand world trade.

■ The United States, Japan, and the western European nations dominate world trade. Recent new traders are the "Asian tigers" (Hong Kong, Singapore, South Korea, and Taiwan), China, the eastern European nations, and the newly independent states formerly constituting the Soviet Union.

■ The circular flow model with foreign trade includes flows of exports from our domestic product market, imports to our domestic product market, and the corresponding flows of resources and spending.

SPECIALIZATION AND COMPARATIVE ADVANTAGE

Specialization and trade increase the productivity of a nation's resources and allow for larger total output than otherwise. This notion is not new! According to Adam Smith in 1776:

> It is the maxim of every prudent master of a family, never to attempt to make at home what it will cost him more to make than to buy. The taylor does not attempt to make his own shoes, but buys them of the shoemaker. The shoemaker does not attempt to make his own clothes, but employs a taylor. The farmer attempts to make neither the one nor the other, but employs those different artificers. . . .
>
> What is prudence in the conduct of every private family, can scarce be folly in that of a great kingdom. If a foreign country can supply us with a commodity cheaper than we can make it, better buy it of them with some part of the produce of our own industry, employed in a way in which we have some advantage.[1]

---

[1]Adam Smith, *The Wealth of Nations* (New York: Modern Library, 1937), p. 424. (Originally published in 1776.)

Nations specialize and trade for the same reasons as individuals: Specialization and exchange among individuals, regions, and nations result in greater overall output and income.

Basic Principle

In the early 1800s British economist David Ricardo expanded on Smith's idea, correctly observing that it pays for a person or a country to specialize and exchange even if that person or nation is more productive than a potential trading partner in *all* economic activities.

Consider the certified public accountant (CPA) who is also a skilled house painter. Suppose the CPA can paint her house in less time than the professional painter she is thinking of hiring. Also suppose the CPA can earn $50 per hour doing her accounting and must pay the painter $15 per hour. Let's say that it will take the accountant 30 hours to paint her house and will take the painter 40 hours.

Should the CPA take time from her accounting to paint her own house, or should she hire the painter? The CPA's opportunity cost of painting her house is $1500 (= 30 hours of sacrificed CPA time × $50 per CPA hour). The cost of hiring the painter is only $600 (= 40 hours of painting × $15 per hour of painting). Although the CPA is better at both accounting and painting, she *will get her house painted at lower cost by specializing in accounting and using some of the earnings from accounting to hire a house painter.*

Similarly, the house painter can reduce his cost of obtaining accounting services by specializing in painting and using some of his income to hire the CPA to prepare his income tax forms. Suppose that it would take the painter 10 hours to prepare his tax return, while the CPA could handle this task in 2 hours. The house painter would sacrifice $150 of income (= 10 hours of painting time × $15 per hour) to accomplish a task which he could hire the CPA to do for $100

(= 2 hours of CPA time × $50 per CPA hour). By using the CPA to prepare his tax return, the painter *lowers his cost of getting the tax return completed.*

What is true for our CPA and house painter is also true for nations. Countries can reduce their cost of obtaining desirable goods by specializing.

Comparative Costs

Our simple example clearly shows that specialization is economically desirable because it results in more efficient production. To understand the global economy, let's now put specialization in the context of trading nations, employing the familiar concept of the production possibilities table for our analysis. Suppose production possibilities for two products in Mexico and the United States are as shown in Tables 6-4 and 6-5. In these tables we assume constant costs. Each country must give up a constant amount of one product to secure a particular increment of the other product. (This assumption simplifies our discussion without impairing the validity of our conclusions.)

Specialization and trade are mutually beneficial or "profitable" to the two nations if the comparative costs of the two products within the two nations differ. What are the comparative costs of avocados and soybeans in Mexico? By comparing production alternatives *A* and *B* in Table 6-4, we see that 5 tons of soybeans (= 15 − 10) must be sacrificed to produce 20 tons of avocados (= 20 − 0). Or, more simply, in Mexico it costs 1 ton of soybeans (*S*) to produce 4 tons of avocados (*A*); that is, $1S \equiv 4A$. Because we assumed constant costs, this domestic *comparative-cost ratio* will not change as Mexico expands the output of either product. This is evident from production possibilities *B* and *C*, where we see that 4 more tons of avocados (= 24 − 20) cost 1 unit of soybeans (= 10 − 9).

Similarly, in Table 6-5, comparing U.S. production alternatives *R* and *S* reveals that in the United

TABLE 6-4   Mexico's production possibilities table (in tons)

	Production alternatives				
Product	*A*	*B*	*C*	*D*	*E*
Avocados	0	20	24	40	60
Soybeans	15	10	9	5	0

TABLE 6-5   U.S. production possibilities table (in tons)

	Production alternatives				
Product	*R*	*S*	*T*	*U*	*V*
Avocados	0	30	33	60	90
Soybeans	30	20	19	10	0

States it costs 10 tons of soybeans (= 30 − 20) to obtain 30 tons of avocados (= 30 − 0). That is, the domestic comparative-cost ratio for the two products in the United States is $1S \equiv 3A$. Comparing production alternatives S and T reinforces this: an extra 3 tons of avocados (= 33 − 30) comes at the direct sacrifice of 1 ton of soybeans (= 20 − 19).

The comparative costs of the two products within the two nations are clearly different. Economists say that the United States has a domestic comparative advantage or, simply, a **comparative advantage** over Mexico in soybeans. The United States must forgo only 3 tons of avocados to get 1 ton of soybeans, but Mexico must forgo 4 tons of avocados to get 1 ton of soybeans. In terms of domestic opportunity costs, soybeans are relatively cheaper in the United States. *A nation has a comparative advantage in some product when it can produce that product at a lower domestic opportunity cost than can a potential trading partner.* Mexico, in contrast, has a comparative advantage in avocados. While 1 ton of avocados costs $\frac{1}{3}$ ton of soybeans in the United States, it costs only $\frac{1}{4}$ ton of soybeans in Mexico. Comparatively speaking, avocados are cheaper in Mexico.

Because of these differences in domestic comparative costs, if both nations specialize, each according to its comparative advantage, each can achieve a larger total output with the same total input of resources. Together they will be using their scarce resources more efficiently.

Terms of Trade

The United States can shift production between soybeans and avocados at the rate of $1S$ for $3A$. Thus, the United States would specialize in soybeans only if it could obtain *more than* 3 tons of avocados for 1 ton of

soybeans by trading with Mexico. Similarly, Mexico can shift production at the rate of $4A$ for $1S$. So it would be advantageous to Mexico to specialize in avocados if it could get 1 ton of soybeans for *less than* 4 tons of avocados.

Suppose that through negotiation the two nations agree on an exchange rate of 1 ton of soybeans for $3\frac{1}{2}$ tons of avocados. These **terms of trade** are mutually beneficial to both countries since each can "do better" through such trade than by domestic production alone. The United States can get $3\frac{1}{2}$ tons of avocados by sending 1 ton of soybeans to Mexico, while it can get only 3 tons of avocados by shifting resources domestically from soybeans to avocados. Mexico can obtain 1 ton of soybeans at a lower cost of $3\frac{1}{2}$ tons of avocados through trade with the United States, compared to the cost of 4 tons if Mexicans produce the 1 ton of wheat themselves.

Gains from Specialization and Trade

Let's pinpoint the size of the gains in total output from specialization and trade. Suppose that, before specialization and trade, production alternative C in Table 6-4 and alternative T in 6-5 were the optimal product mixes for the two countries. These outputs are shown in column 1 in Table 6-6. That is, Mexico preferred 24 tons of avocados and 9 tons of soybeans (Table 6-4) and the United States preferred 33 tons of avocados and 19 tons of soybeans (Table 6-5) to all other alternatives available within their respective domestic economies.

Now assume both nations specialize according to comparative advantage, Mexico producing 60 tons of avocados and no soybeans (alternative E) and the United States producing no avocados and 30 tons of

TABLE 6-6 Specialization according to comparative advantage and the gains from trade (in tons)

Country	(1) Outputs before specialization	(2) Outputs after specialization	(3) Amounts traded	(4) Outputs available after trade	(5) Gains from specialization and trade (4) − (1)
Mexico	24 avocados	60 avocados	−35 avocados	25 avocados	1 avocados
	9 soybeans	0 soybeans	+10 soybeans	10 soybeans	1 soybeans
United States	33 avocados	0 avocados	+35 avocados	35 avocados	2 avocados
	19 soybeans	30 soybeans	−10 soybeans	20 soybeans	1 soybeans

soybeans (alternative R). These outputs are reflected in column 2 in Table 6-6. Using our $1S \equiv 3\frac{1}{2} A$ terms of trade, assume Mexico exchanges 35 tons of avocados for 10 tons of U.S. soybeans. Column 3 in Table 6-6 shows the quantities exchanged in this trade. As indicated in column 4, after the trade Mexico has 25 tons of avocados and 10 tons of soybeans, while the United States has 35 tons of avocados and 20 tons of soybeans. Compared with their optimum product mixes before specialization and trade (column 1), *both* nations now enjoy more avocados and more soybeans! Specifically, Mexico has gained 1 ton of avocados and 1 ton of soybeans. The United States has gained 2 tons of avocados and 1 ton of soybeans. These gains are shown in column 5, where we have subtracted the *before*-specialization outputs of column 1 from the *after*-specialization outputs in column 4.

Specialization based on comparative advantage improves global resource allocation. The same total inputs of world resources and technology results in a larger global output. If Mexico and the United States allocate all their resources to avocados and soybeans, respectively, the same total inputs of resources can produce more output between them, indicating that resources are being used or allocated more efficiently.

We noted in Chapter 2 that through specialization and international trade a nation can overcome the production constraints imposed by its domestic production possibilities table and curve. Table 6-6 and its discussion show just how this is done. The domestic production possibilities data of the two countries have not changed, meaning that neither nation's production possibilities curve has shifted. But specialization and trade mean that citizens of both countries have enjoyed increased consumption. *Thus, specialization and trade have the same effect as an increase in resources or technological progress: they make more goods available to an economy.* (**Key Question 4**)

FOREIGN EXCHANGE MARKET

People, firms, or nations which specialize in the production of specific goods or services exchange those products for money and then use the money to buy other products or to pay for the use of resources. Within the economy, prices are stated in the domestic currency and buyers use that currency to purchase domestic products. In Mexico, for example, buyers possess pesos, exactly the currency sellers want.

International markets are different. How many dollars does it take to buy a truckload of Mexican av-

ocados selling for 3000 pesos, a German automobile selling for 90,000 marks, or a Japanese motorcycle priced at 300,000 yen? Producers in Mexico, Germany, and Japan want payment in pesos, marks, and yen, respectively, so they can pay their wages, rent, interest, dividends, and taxes. A **foreign exchange market,** a market in which various national currencies are exchanged for one another, serves this need. The equilibrium prices in these markets are called **exchange rates;** an exchange rate is the rate at which the currency of one nation is exchanged for the currency of another nation. (See Global Perspective 6-2.) Two points about the foreign exchange market are particularly noteworthy:

1. *A competitive market*   Real-world foreign exchange markets conform closely to the markets discussed in Chapter 3. They are competitive markets characterized by large numbers of buyers and sellers dealing in standardized products such as the American dollar, the German mark, the British pound, the Swedish krona, and the Japanese yen.

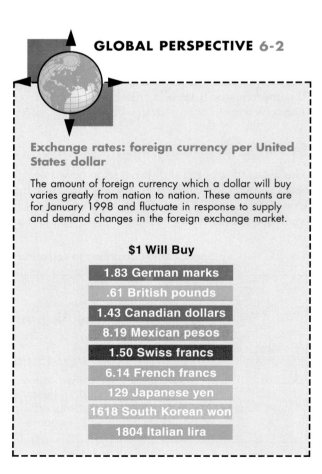

GLOBAL PERSPECTIVE 6-2

Exchange rates: foreign currency per United States dollar

The amount of foreign currency which a dollar will buy varies greatly from nation to nation. These amounts are for January 1998 and fluctuate in response to supply and demand changes in the foreign exchange market.

$1 Will Buy

1.83 German marks
.61 British pounds
1.43 Canadian dollars
8.19 Mexican pesos
1.50 Swiss francs
6.14 French francs
129 Japanese yen
1618 South Korean won
1804 Italian lira

2. *Linkages to all domestic and foreign prices*   The market price or exchange rate of a nation's currency is an unusual price; it links all domestic (say, United States) prices with all foreign (say, Japanese or German) prices. Exchange rates enable consumers in one country to translate prices of foreign goods into units of their own currency: they need only multiply the foreign product price by the exchange rate. If the dollar-yen exchange rate is $.01 (1 cent) per yen, a Sony television set priced at ¥20,000 will cost $200 (= 20,000 × $.01) in the United States. If the exchange rate is $.02 (2 cents) per yen, it will cost $400 (= 20,000 × $.02) in the United States. Similarly, all other Japanese products would double in price to U.S. buyers. As you will see, a change in exchange rates has important implications for a nation's level of domestic production and employment.

Dollar-Yen Market

How does the foreign exchange market work? Let's look briefly at the market for dollars and yen, leaving details to a later chapter. U.S. firms exporting to Japan want payment in dollars, not yen; but Japanese importers of U.S. goods possess yen, not dollars. So the Japanese importers are willing to supply their yen in exchange for dollars in the foreign exchange market. At the same time, there are U.S. importers of Japanese goods who need to pay Japanese exporters with yen, not dollars. These importers go to the foreign exchange market as demanders of yen. We then have a market in which the "price" is in dollars and the "product" is yen.

Figure 6-4 shows the supply of yen (by Japanese importers) and the demand for yen (by U.S. importers). The intersection of demand curve D_y and supply curve S_y establishes the equilibrium dollar price of yen. Here the equilibrium price of 1 yen—the dollar-yen exchange rate—is 1 cent per yen, or $.01 = ¥1. At this price, the market for yen clears; there is neither a shortage nor a surplus of yen. The equilibrium $.01 price of 1 yen means that $1 will buy 100 yen or ¥100 worth of Japanese goods. Conversely, 100 yen will buy $1 worth of U.S. goods.

Changing Rates: Depreciation and Appreciation

What might cause the exchange rate to change? The determinants of the demand for and supply of yen are similar to the determinants of demand and supply for almost any product. In the United States, several things might increase the demand for—and therefore the dollar price of—yen. Incomes might rise in the United States, enabling residents to buy not only more domestic goods but also more Sony televisions, Nikon cameras, and Nissan automobiles from Japan. So people in the United States would need more yen and the demand for yen would increase. Or a change in people's tastes might enhance their preferences for Japanese goods. When gas prices soared in the 1970s, many auto buyers in the United States shifted their demands from gas-guzzling domestic cars to gas-efficient Japanese compact cars. The result was an increased demand for yen.

The point is that an increase in the U.S. demand for Japanese goods will increase the demand for yen

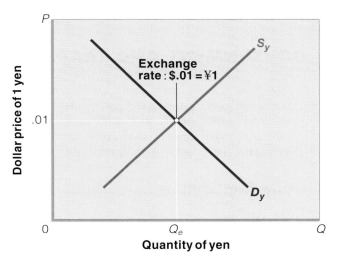

FIGURE 6-4 The market for yen   U.S. imports from Japan create a demand D_y for yen, while U.S. exports to Japan create a supply S_y of yen. The dollar price of 1 yen—the exchange rate—is determined at the intersection of the supply and demand curves. In this case the equilibrium price is $.01, meaning that 1 cent will buy 1 yen.

and raise the dollar price of yen. Suppose the dollar price of yen rises from $.01 = ¥1 to $.02 = ¥1. When the dollar price of yen increases, we say a **depreciation** of the dollar relative to the yen has occurred: It then takes more dollars (pennies in this case) to buy a single unit of the foreign currency (a yen). Alternatively stated, the *international value of the dollar* has declined. A depreciated dollar buys fewer yen and therefore fewer Japanese goods; the yen and all Japanese goods have become more expensive to U.S. buyers. Result: Consumers in the United States shift their expenditures from Japanese goods to now less expensive American goods. The Ford Taurus becomes relatively more attractive than the Honda Accord to U.S. consumers. Conversely, because each yen buys more dollars—that is, because the international value of the yen has increased—U.S. goods become cheaper to people in Japan and U.S. exports to them rise.

If the opposite event occurred—if the Japanese demanded more U.S. goods—then they would supply more yen to pay for these goods. The increase in the supply of yen relative to the demand for yen would decrease the equilibrium price of yen in the foreign exchange market. For example, the dollar price of yen might decline from $.01 = ¥1 to $.005 = ¥1. A decrease in the dollar price of yen is called an **appreciation** of the dollar relative to the yen. It means that the international value of the dollar has increased. It then takes fewer dollars (or pennies) to buy a single yen; the dollar is worth more because it can purchase more yen and therefore more Japanese goods. Each Sony Walkman becomes less expensive in terms of dollars, so people in the United States purchase more of them. In general, U.S. imports rise. Meanwhile, because it takes more yen to get a dollar, U.S. exports to Japan fall.

We summarize these currency relationships in Figure 6-5, which you should examine closely. **(Key Question 6)**

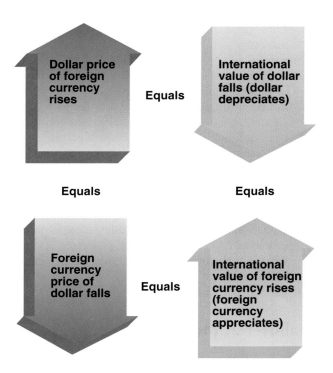

FIGURE 6-5 **Currency appreciation and depreciation** An increase in the dollar price of foreign currency is equivalent to a decline in the international value of the dollar (dollar depreciation). An increase in the dollar price of foreign currency also implies a decline in the foreign currency price of dollars. That is, the international value of foreign currency rises relative to the dollar (the foreign currency appreciates).

■ An appreciation of the dollar is an increase in the international value of the dollar relative to the currency of some other nation; a dollar now buys more units of that currency. A depreciation of the dollar is a decrease in the international value of the dollar relative to another currency; a dollar now buys fewer units of that currency.

GOVERNMENT AND TRADE

If people and nations benefit from specialization and international exchange, why do governments sometimes try to restrict the free flow of imports or to bolster exports? What kinds of world trade barriers can governments erect, and why would they do so?

Trade Impediments and Subsidies

There are four usual means by which governments might interfere with free trade:

1. **Protective tariffs** are excise taxes or duties placed on imported goods. Most are designed to shield domestic producers from foreign competition. They impede free trade by increasing the prices of imported goods, shifting demand toward domestic products. An excise tax on imported shoes, for example, would make domestically made shoes more attractive to consumers.

2. **Import quotas** are limits on the quantities or total value of specific items that may be imported. Once a quota is "filled," it chokes off imports of that product. Import quotas can be more effective than tariffs in retarding international commerce. A particular product could be imported in large quantities despite high tariffs; a low import quota completely prohibits imports once the quota is filled.

3. **Nontariff barriers** (and, implicitly, *nonquota* barriers) include licensing requirements, unreasonable standards pertaining to product quality, or simply unnecessary bureaucratic red tape in customs procedures. Some nations require that their domestic importers of foreign goods obtain licenses. By restricting the issuance of licenses, imports can be effectively impeded. Great Britain bars coal importation in this way. Also, some nations impede imports of fruit by insisting that *each* crate be inspected for worms and insects.

4. **Export subsidies** consist of governmental payments to domestic producers of export goods. The payments reduce their production costs, permitting them to charge lower prices and thus sell more exports in world markets. Two examples: Participating European governments have heavily subsidized Airbus Industries, which produces commercial aircraft. These subsidies have helped Airbus compete against Boeing, an American firm. The United States and other nations have subsidized domestic farmers, boosting domestic food supply. This has reduced the market price of food, artificially decreasing export prices on agricultural produce.

Why Government Trade Interventions?

Why would a nation want to send more of its output for consumption abroad than it gains as imported output in return? Why the impulse to impede imports or boost exports through government policy when free trade is beneficial to a nation? There are

several reasons—some legitimate, most not. We will look at two here, and examine others in a later chapter.

Misunderstanding of the Gains from Trade   It is a commonly accepted myth that the fundamental benefit of international trade is greater domestic employment in the export sector. This suggests that exports are "good" because they increase domestic employment, whereas imports are "bad" because they deprive people of jobs at home. In reality, the true benefit from international trade is the *overall* increase in output obtained through specialization and exchange. A nation can fully employ its resources, including labor, with or without international trade. International trade, however, enables society to use its resources in ways that increase its total output and therefore its overall well-being.

A nation does not need international trade to locate *on* its production possibilities curve. A closed (nontrading) national economy can have full employment without international trade. But through world trade an economy can reach a point *beyond* its domestic production possibilities curve. The gain from trade is the extra output obtained from abroad—the imports gotten for less cost than if they were produced using domestic resources. The only valid reason for exporting part of our domestic output is to obtain imports that are of greater value to us. Specialization and international exchange make this possible.

Political Considerations   While a nation as a whole gains from trade, trade may harm particular domestic industries and groups of resource suppliers. In our earlier comparative-advantage example, specialization and trade adversely affected the U.S. avocado industry and the Mexican soybean industry. Those industries might seek to preserve their economic positions by persuading their respective governments to protect them from imports—perhaps through tariffs or import quotas:

> The direct beneficiaries of import relief or export subsidy are usually few in number, but each has a large individual stake in the outcome. Thus, their incentive for vigorous political activity is strong.
> But the costs of such policies may far exceed the benefits. It may cost the public [$80,000–$120,000] a year to protect a domestic job that might otherwise pay an employee only half that amount in wages and benefits.

Furthermore, the costs of protection are widely diffused—in the United States, among 50 states and [268] million citizens. Since the cost borne by any one citizen is likely to be quite small, and may even go unnoticed, resistance at the grassroots level to protectionist measures often is considerably less than pressures for their adoption.[2]

Policymakers often see little public opposition to demands for *protectionism* because tariffs and quotas are buried in the prices of goods. Indeed, the public may be won over by the apparent plausibility ("Cut imports and prevent domestic unemployment") and patriotic ring ("Buy American!") of the protectionist arguments. The alleged benefits of tariffs are immediate and clear-cut to the public, but the adverse effects cited by economists are obscure and dispersed over the entire economy. When political deal making is added in—"You back tariffs for the apparel industry in my state, and I'll back tariffs on the auto industry in your state"—the sum can be a network of protective tariffs, import quotas, and export subsidies.

Costs to Society

Tariffs and quotas benefit domestic producers of the protected products, but they harm domestic consumers, who must pay higher than world prices for the protected goods. They also hurt those domestic firms which use the protected goods as inputs in their production processes. For example, a tariff on imported steel would boost the price of steel girders, hurting firms that construct large buildings. Also, tariffs and quotas reduce competition in the protected industries. With less competition from foreign producers, domestic firms may be slow to design and implement cost-saving production methods and introduce new and improved products.

Study after study has shown that the cost of trade protection to consumers and adversely affected input buyers exceeds the benefit to the protected firms. That is, there is a *net cost* (cost *minus* benefit) to society from trade protection. In the United States this net cost was as much as $50 billion a couple of decades ago but has dropped significantly in recent years along with declines in U.S. tariffs and quotas.

---

[2]*Economic Report of the President, 1982*, p. 177. Updated.

MULTILATERAL TRADE AGREEMENTS AND FREE-TRADE ZONES

When one nation enacts barriers against imports, the nations whose exports suffer may retaliate with trade barriers of their own. In such a *trade war*, tariffs escalate, choking off world trade and reducing everyone's economic well-being. The **Smoot-Hawley Tariff Act** of 1930 is a classic example. Although this act was meant to reduce imports and stimulate U.S. production, its high tariffs prompted affected nations to retaliate with equally high tariffs. International trade across the globe fell, lowering the output, income, and employment levels of all nations. Economic historians generally agree that the Smoot-Hawley Tariff Act was a contributing cause of the Great Depression. In view of this fact, the world's nations have worked to lower tariffs worldwide. Their pursuit of free trade has been aided by powerful domestic interest groups. Specifically, exporters of goods and services, importers of foreign components used in "domestic" products, and domestic sellers of imported products all strongly support lower tariffs worldwide.

Figure 6-6 makes clear that the United States has been a high-tariff nation over much of its history. But it also demonstrates that, in general, U.S. tariffs have declined during the past half-century.

Reciprocal Trade Agreements Act and GATT

The **Reciprocal Trade Agreements Act** of 1934 started the downward trend of tariffs. Specifically aimed at reducing tariffs, this act had two main features.

1. *Negotiating authority* It authorized the President to negotiate with foreign nations agreements reducing U.S. tariffs by up to 50 percent of the existing rates. Tariff reductions hinged on other nations' reciprocating by lowering tariffs on U.S. exports.
2. *Generalized reductions* The specific tariff reductions negotiated between the United States and any particular nation became generalized through **most-favored-nation clauses,** which often accompanied these agreements. These clauses stipulated that any subsequently reduced U.S. tariffs, resulting from negotiation with any other nation, would apply equally to the nation

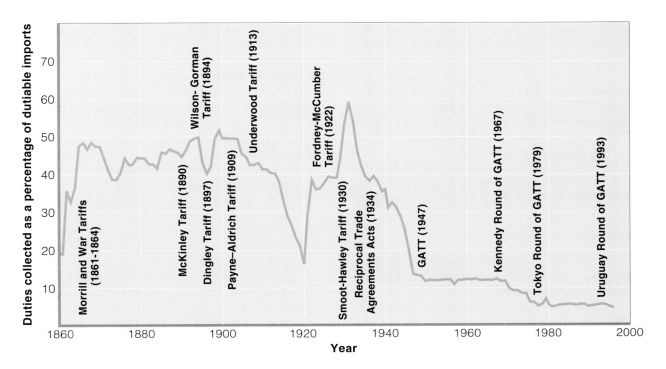

FIGURE 6-6 U.S. tariff rates, 1860–1997 U.S. tariff rates have fluctuated historically. But beginning with the Reciprocal Trade Agreements Act of 1934, the trend has been downward. (*Source:* U.S. Department of Commerce data.)

signing the original agreement. So if the United States negotiated a reduction in tariffs with, say, France, the lower U.S. tariffs on French imports would also apply to the imports of the other nations having most-favored-nation status, say, Sweden and Switzerland. This way, new reductions in U.S. tariffs automatically applied to many other nations.

But the Reciprocal Trade Agreements Act gave rise to only bilateral (between-two-nations) negotiations. Its approach was broadened in 1947 when 23 nations, including the United States, signed the **General Agreement on Tariffs and Trade (GATT).** GATT is based on three cardinal principles: (1) equal, nondiscriminatory trade treatment for all member nations; (2) the reduction of tariffs by multilateral negotiations; and (3) the elimination of import quotas.

Basically, GATT is a forum to negotiate reductions in trade barriers on a multilateral basis among nations. With 125 nations now belonging to GATT, there is little doubt that it has been a positive force in the trend toward liberalized world trade. Under its sponsorship, member nations have completed eight "rounds" of negotiations to reduce trade barriers in the post-World War II period.

GATT's Uruguay Round The eighth and most recent "round" of GATT negotiations began in Uruguay in 1986. After 7 years of wrangling, in 1993 the participant nations reached a new agreement. The agreement took effect on January 1, 1995, and its provisions will be phased in through 2005.

Under this latest GATT agreement, tariffs will be eliminated or reduced on thousands of products, with tariffs dropping overall by 33 percent. The agreement will also liberalize government rules which in the past have impeded the global market for such services as advertising, legal services, tourist services, and financial services. Quotas on imported textiles and apparel will be phased out, to be replaced with tariffs. (Tariffs are preferable to quotas, since tariffs let in an unlimited amount of imported goods; in contrast, quotas block all imports beyond a specified quantity.)

Other important provisions will reduce agricultural subsidies paid to farmers and protect intellectual property (patents, trademarks, copyrights) against piracy. Finally, the Uruguay Round of GATT created the **World Trade Organization (WTO)** as GATT's successor. The WTO has judicial powers to intermediate among members and rule on disputes involving the trade rules.

When fully implemented, the most recent GATT agreement is expected to boost the world's GDP by about $6 trillion, or 8 percent. Consumers in the United States will gain about $30 billion annually.

European Union

Countries have also sought to reduce tariffs by creating regional free-trade zones or trade blocs. The most dramatic example is the **European Union (EU),** formerly called the European Economic Community. Initiated as the Common Market in 1958, the EU now comprises 15 western European nations— France, Germany, Italy, Belgium, the Netherlands, Luxembourg, Denmark, Ireland, United Kingdom, Greece, Spain, Portugal, Austria, Finland, and Sweden.

Goals   The original Common Market called for (1) gradual abolition of tariffs and import quotas on all products traded among the participating nations; (2) establishment of a common system of tariffs applicable to all goods received from nations outside the EU; (3) free movement of capital and labor within the Common Market; and (4) creation of common policies in other economic matters of joint concern, such as agriculture, transportation, and restrictive business practices. The EU has achieved most of these goals and is now a strong **trade bloc:** a group of countries having a common identity, set of economic interests, and trade rules.

Results   The motives for creating the EU were political and economic. The main economic motive was liberalized trade for members. While it is difficult to determine how much of EU prosperity and growth has resulted from economic integration, that integration clearly has created large markets for EU industries. The resulting economies of large-scale production have enabled European industries to achieve much lower costs than they could in their small, single-nation markets.

The effects of EU success on nonmember nations, such as the United States, are mixed. A peaceful and increasingly prosperous EU makes its members better customers for U.S. exports. But U.S. and other nonmember firms encounter tariffs which make it difficult to compete against firms within the EU trade bloc. For example, before the establishment of the EU, American, German, and French automobile manufacturers all faced the same tariff selling their products in, say, Belgium. However, with the establishment of free internal trading among EU members, Belgian tariffs on German Volkswagens and French Renaults fell to zero, but an external tariff still applies to U.S. Chevrolets and Fords. This puts U.S. firms at a serious disadvantage. Similarly, EU trade restrictions hamper eastern European exports of metals, textiles, and farm products, goods which the eastern Europeans produce in abundance.

By giving preferences to countries within their free-trade zone, trade blocs such as the EU tend to reduce their trade with nonbloc members. Thus, the world loses some of the benefits of a completely open global trading system. Eliminating this disadvantage has been one of the motivations for liberalizing global trade through the World Trade Organization.

North American Free Trade Agreement

In 1993 Canada, Mexico, and the United States formed a trade bloc. The **North American Free Trade Agreement (NAFTA)** established a free-trade zone having about the same combined output of the EU but a much larger geographical area. NAFTA will eliminate tariffs and other trade barriers between Canada, Mexico, and the United States over a 15-year period.

Critics of the agreement fear that one result will be a loss of U.S. jobs as firms move to Mexico to take advantage of lower wages and weaker regulations on pollution and workplace safety. Also, there is concern that Japan and South Korea will build plants in Mexico to transport goods tariff-free to the United States, further hurting U.S. firms and workers.

Defenders of NAFTA reject these concerns. They contend that specialization according to comparative advantage will enable each nation to obtain more total output from its scarce resources. They also argue that NAFTA's free-trade zone will encourage worldwide investment in Mexico, enhancing Mexican productivity and national income. Mexican consumers will use some of that increased income to buy U.S. exports. Any loss of jobs, say defenders of NAFTA, most likely would have occurred anyway to other low-wage countries such as China.

Hostile Trade Blocs or Further Integration?

With the formation of NAFTA, it may appear that the world's nations are separating into potentially hostile trade blocs. But NAFTA is also a means for negotiating reductions in trade barriers with the EU, Japan, and other trading countries. Access to the vast North American market is as important to the EU and Japan as is access to their markets by Canada, Mexico, and the United States. NAFTA gives the United States leverage in future trade negotiations with the EU and Japan. Eventually, direct negotiations between the EU and NAFTA might link the two free-trade zones. Japan and other major trading nations, not wishing to be left out of the world's wealthiest trade markets, would be forced to eliminate their trade barriers, opening their domestic markets to additional imports. Nor do other nations and trade blocs want to be excluded from free-trade zones. Examples:

1. *APEC*   The United States and several other nations have agreed to liberalize trade and open investment over the next few decades through the Asian-Pacific Economic Cooperation (APEC) forum. APEC members are Australia, Brunei, Canada, Chile, China (Hong Kong), Indonesia, Japan, Malaysia, Mexico, New Zealand, the Philippines, Papua New Guinea, Singapore, South Korea, Taiwan, Thailand, and the United States.

2. *Chile's potential inclusion in NAFTA*   Canada, Mexico, and the United States are negotiating with Chile to become the fourth partner in NAFTA.

3. *Mercosur*   The free-trade group encompassing Brazil, Argentina, Uruguay, and Paraguay—called Mercosur—has expressed interest in eventually linking up with NAFTA.

Economists generally agree that the ideal free-trade area would encompass the entire world. **(Key Question 10)**

QUICK REVIEW 6-3

■ Governments promote exports and reduce imports through tariffs, quotas, nontariff barriers, and export subsidies.

■ The various "rounds" of the General Agreement on Tariffs and Trade (GATT) have established multinational reductions in tariffs and import quotas among the 125 member nations.

■ The Uruguay Round of GATT, which went into effect in 1995 and will be fully implemented by 2005, **(a)** reduces tariffs worldwide; **(b)** liberalizes rules impeding barriers to trade in services; **(c)** reduces agricultural subsidies; **(d)** creates new protections for intellectual property; **(e)** phases out quotas on textiles and apparel; and **(f)** sets up the World Trade Organization.

■ The European Union (EU) and the North American Free Trade Agreement (NAFTA) have reduced internal trade barriers among their members by establishing large free-trade zones.

AMERICAN FIRMS IN THE WORLD ECONOMY

Freer international trade has brought with it intense competition in the United States and the world. Not long ago three large U.S. producers dominated the U.S. automobile industry. Imported autos were an oddity, accounting for a tiny portion of auto sales. But General Motors, Ford, and Chrysler now face intense competition as they struggle for sales against Nissan, Honda, Toyota, Hyundai, BMW, and others. Similarly, imports have gained major shares of the U.S. markets for automobile tires, clothing, sporting goods, electronics, motorcycles, outboard motors, and toys.

Nevertheless, thousands of U.S. firms—large and small—have thrived and prospered in the global marketplace. Boeing, McDonald's, Dow Chemicals, Intel, Coca-Cola, 3M, Microsoft, AT&T, Monsanto, Procter & Gamble, and Hewlett-Packard are just a few of them. These and many other firms have continued to retain high market shares at home and have dramatically expanded their sales abroad. Of course, not all firms have been so successful. Some corporations simply have not been able to compete; their international competitors make better-quality products, have lower production costs, or both. Not surprisingly, the U.S. firms which have been hurt most by foreign competition are precisely those which have long enjoyed the protection of tariffs and quotas. These barriers to imports have artificially limited competition, removing the incentive to improve production methods and products. Also, trade barriers have shielded some domestic firms from the gradual changes in output and employment resulting from

Buy American: The Global Refrigerator

Humorist Art Buchwald looks at the logic of the "Buy American" campaign.

"There is only one way the country is going to get on its feet," said Baleful.

"How's that?" I asked, as we drank coffee in his office at the Baleful Refrigerator Company.

"The consumer has to start buying American," he said, slamming his fist down on the desk. "Every time an American buys a foreign refrigerator it costs one of my people his job. And every time one of my people is out of work it means he or she can't buy refrigerators."

"It's a vicious circle," I said.

Baleful's secretary came in. "Mr. Thompson, the steel broker is on the phone."

My friend grabbed the receiver. "Thompson, where is that steel shipment from Japan that was supposed to be in last weekend? . . . I don't care about weather. We're almost out of steel, and I'll have to close down the refrigerator assembly line next week. If you can't deliver when you promise, I'll find myself another broker."

"You get your steel from Japan?" I asked Baleful. "Even with shipping costs, their price is still lower than steel made in Europe. We used to get all our sheets from Belgium, but the Japanese are now giving them a run for their money."

The buzzer on the phone alerted Baleful. He listened for a few moments and then said, "Excuse me, I have a call from Taiwan. Mark Four? Look, R&D designed a new push-button door handle and we're going to send the specs to you. Tell Mr. Chow if his people send us a sample of one and can make it for us at the same price as the old handle, we'll give his company the order."

A man came in with a plastic container and said, "Mr. Baleful, you said you wanted to see one of these before we ordered them. They are the containers for the ice maker in the refrigerator."

Baleful inspected it carefully and banged it on the floor a couple of times. "What's the price on it?"

"Hong Kong can deliver it at $2 a tray, and Dong-Fu Plastics in South Korea said they can make it for $1.70."

"It's just a plastic tray. Take the South Korea bid. We'll let Hong Kong supply us with the shelves for the freezer. Any word on the motors?"

---

national shifts in comparative advantage over time. As trade protection declines under WTO and NAFTA, some U.S. firms will surely discover that they are producing goods for which the United States clearly has a comparative *dis*advantage (perhaps some types of apparel, for example).

Is the greater competition which accompanies the global economy a good thing? Although some domestic producers and their workers do not like it, foreign competition clearly benefits consumers. Imports break down the monopoly power of existing firms, reducing product prices and providing consumers with a greater variety of goods. Foreign competition also forces domestic producers to become more efficient and to improve product quality; this has already happened in several U.S. industries, including steel and autos. Evidence shows that most—but clearly not all—U.S. firms *can* and *do* compete successfully in the global economy.

What about U.S. firms which cannot successfully compete in open markets? The harsh reality is that they should go out of business, much like an unsuccessful corner boutique. Persistent economic losses mean scarce resources are not being used efficiently. Shifting these resources to alternative, profitable uses will increase total U.S. output.

CHAPTER SUMMARY

1. International trade is growing in importance globally and for the United States. World trade is significant to the United States in two respects. **(a)** The absolute volumes of American imports and exports exceed those of any other single nation. **(b)** The United States is completely dependent on trade for certain commodities and materials that cannot be obtained domestically.

2. Principal U.S. exports include chemicals, computers, consumer durables, aircraft, and grain; major U.S. imports

"There's a German company in Brazil that just came out with a new motor, and it's passed all our tests, so Johnson has ordered 50,000."

"Call Cleveland Motors and tell them we're sorry, but the price they quoted us was just too high."

"Yes, sir," the man said and departed.

The secretary came in again and said, "Harry telephoned and wanted to let you know the defroster just arrived from Finland. They're unloading the box cars now."

"Good. Any word on the wooden crates from Singapore?"

"They're at the dock in Hoboken."

"Thank heaven. Cancel the order from Boise Cascade."

"What excuse should I give them?"

"Tell them we made a mistake in our inventory, or we're switching to plastic. I don't care what you tell them."

Baleful turned to me. "Where were we?"

"You were saying that if the consumer doesn't start buying American, this country is going to be in a lot of trouble."

"Right. It's not only his patriotic duty, but his livelihood that's at stake. I'm going to Washington next week to tell the Senate Commerce Committee that if they don't get on the stick, there isn't going to be a domestic refrigerator left in this country. We're not going to stay in business for our health."

"Pour it to them," I urged him.

Baleful said, "Come out with me into the showroom." I followed him. He went to his latest model, and opened the door. "This is an American refrigerator made by the American worker, for the American consumer. What do you have to say to that?"

"It's beautiful," I said. "It puts foreign imports to shame."

Source: Art Buchwald, "Being Bullish on Buying American." Reprinted by permission. We discovered this article in *Master Curriculum Guide in Economics: Teaching Strategies for International Trade* (New York: Joint Council on Economic Education, 1988).

are petroleum, automobiles, clothing, computers, and household appliances. Quantitatively, Canada is the United States' most important trading partner.

3. Global trade has been greatly facilitated by **(a)** improvements in transportation technology, **(b)** improvements in communications technology, **(c)** general declines in tariffs, and **(d)** continuing peaceful relations among major industrial nations. The United States, Japan, and the western European nations dominate the global economy. But the total volume of trade has been increased by several new trade participants, including the "Asian tigers" (Hong Kong, Singapore, South Korea, and Taiwan), China, the eastern European countries, and the newly independent countries of the former Soviet Union.

4. The open-economy circular flow model connects the domestic U.S. economy to the rest of the world. Customers from abroad enter the U.S. product market to buy some U.S. output. These U.S. exports create business revenues and generate income in the United States. U.S. households spend some of their money incomes on products made abroad and imported to the United States.

5. Specialization based on comparative advantage enables nations to achieve higher standards of living through exchange with other countries. A trading partner should

specialize in products and services for which its domestic opportunity costs are lowest. The terms of trade must be such that both nations can get more of some output via trade than they can obtain by producing it at home.

6. The foreign exchange market sets exchange rates between nations' currencies. Foreign importers are suppliers of their currency, and domestic importers are demanders of the foreign currency. The resulting supply-demand equilibrium sets an exchange rate; such exchange rates link the price levels of all nations. Depreciation of a nation's currency reduces its imports and increases its exports; appreciation increases its imports and reduces its exports.

7. Governments shape trade flows through **(a)** protective tariffs, **(b)** quotas, **(c)** nontariff barriers, and **(d)** export subsidies. These are impediments to free trade; they result from misunderstandings about the gains to be had from trade and also result from political considerations. By increasing product prices, trade barriers cost U.S. consumers billions of dollars annually.

8. The Reciprocal Trade Agreements Act of 1934 marked the beginning of a trend toward lower U.S. tariffs. In 1947 the General Agreement on Tariffs and Trade (GATT) was formed to encourage nondiscriminatory treatment for all member trading nations, reduce tariffs, and eliminate import quotas.

9. The Uruguay Round of GATT negotiations, completed in 1993 and to be implemented through 2005, **(a)** reduces tariffs, **(b)** liberalizes trade in services, **(c)** reduces agricultural subsidies, **(d)** reduces pirating of intellectual property, **(e)** phases out import quotas on textiles and apparel, and **(f)** establishes the World Trade Organization.

10. Free-trade zones (trade blocs) may liberalize trade within regions but may also impede trade with nonbloc members. Two examples of free-trade arrangements are the European Union (EU), formerly the European Community or "Common Market," and the North American Free Trade Agreement (NAFTA), comprising Canada, Mexico, and the United States.

11. The global economy has created intense foreign competition in many U.S. product markets, but most U.S. firms can compete well both at home and in global markets.

TERMS AND CONCEPTS

multinational
   corporations
"Asian tigers"
comparative advantage
terms of trade
foreign exchange
   market
exchange rates

depreciation
appreciation
protective tariffs
import quotas
nontariff barriers
export subsidies
Smoot-Hawley Tariff
   Act

Reciprocal Trade
   Agreements Act
most-favored-nation
   clauses
General Agreement on
   Tariffs and Trade
   (GATT)

World Trade
   Organization (WTO)
European Union (EU)
trade bloc
North American Free
   Trade Agreement
   (NAFTA)

STUDY QUESTIONS

1. How important is international trade to the U.S. economy? What country is the United States' most important trading partner, quantitatively? How have persistent U.S. trade deficits been financed? "Trade deficits mean we get more merchandise from the rest of the world's nations than we provide them in return. Therefore, trade deficits are economically desirable." Do you agree? Why or why not?

2. What factors account for the rapid growth of world trade since World War II? Who are the major players in international trade today? Who are the "Asian tigers," and how important are they in world trade?

3. KEY QUESTION   Use the circular flow model (Figure 6-3) to explain how an increase in exports would affect the revenues of domestic firms, the money incomes of domestic households, and imports from abroad. Use Table 6-3 to find the exact amounts (in 1996) of U.S. exports [flow (13)] and imports [flow (16)] in the circular flow model. What do these amounts imply for flows (14) and (15)?

4. KEY QUESTION   The following are production possibilities tables for South Korea and the United States. Assume that before specialization and trade the optimal product mix for South Korea is alternative *B* and for the United States is alternative *U*.

Product	South Korea's production possibilities					
	A	*B*	*C*	*D*	*E*	*F*
Radios (in thousands)	30	24	18	12	6	0
Chemicals (in tons)	0	6	12	18	24	30

Product	U.S. production possibilities					
	R	*S*	*T*	*U*	*V*	*W*
Radios (in thousands)	10	8	6	4	2	0
Chemicals (in tons)	0	4	8	12	16	20

   a. Are comparative-cost conditions such that the two areas should specialize? If so, what product should each produce?
   b. What is the total gain in radio and chemical output which results from this specialization?
   c. What are the limits of the terms of trade? Suppose actual terms of trade are 1 unit of radios

for $1\frac{1}{2}$ units of chemicals and that 4 units of radios are exchanged for 6 units of chemicals. What are the gains from specialization and trade for each area?

   d. Can you conclude from this illustration that specialization according to comparative advantage results in more efficient use of world resources? Explain.

5. Suppose that the comparative-cost ratios of two products—baby formula and tuna fish—are as follows in the hypothetical nations of Canswicki and Tunata:

Canswicki: 1 can baby formula ≡ 2 cans tuna fish
Tunata: 1 can baby formula ≡ 4 cans tuna fish

In what product should each nation specialize? Explain why terms of trade of 1 can baby formula ≡ $2\frac{1}{2}$ cans tuna fish would be acceptable to both nations.

6. KEY QUESTION "U.S. exports create a demand for foreign currencies; foreign imports of U.S. goods generate supplies of foreign currencies." Do you agree? Would a decline in U.S. incomes or a weakening of U.S. preferences for foreign products cause the dollar to depreciate or appreciate? What would be the effects of that depreciation or appreciation on U.S. exports and imports?

7. If the French franc declines in value (depreciates) in the foreign exchange market, will it be easier or harder for the French to sell their wine in the United States? Suppose you were planning a trip to Paris. How would depreciation of the franc change the dollar cost of this trip?

8. True or False? "An increase in the American dollar price of the German mark implies that the German mark has depreciated in value." Explain.

9. What tools do governments use to promote exports and restrict imports? Who benefits and who loses from protectionist policies? What is the net outcome for society?

10. KEY QUESTION What is GATT? How does it affect nearly every person in the world? What were the major outcomes of the Uruguay Round of GATT? How is GATT related to the European Union (EU) and the North American Free Trade Agreement (NAFTA)?

11. Explain: "Free-trade zones such as the EU and NAFTA lead a double life: they can promote free trade among members, but pose serious trade obstacles for nonmembers." Do you think the net effects of these trade blocs are good or bad for world trade? Why?

12. What do you see as the competitive strengths of U.S. firms? Competitive weaknesses? Explain: "Even if Japan captured the entire worldwide auto market, that simply would mean that Japan would have to buy a whole lot of other products from abroad. Thus, the United States and other industrial nations would necessarily experience an increase in exports to Japan."

13. (Last Word) What point is Art Buchwald making in his humorous essay on the Baleful Refrigerator Company? Why might Mr. Baleful *oppose* tariffs on imported goods, even though he wants consumers to buy "American" refrigerators?

14. WEB-BASED QUESTION **Trade Balances with Partner Countries** The U.S. Census Bureau http://www.census.gov/foreign-trade/www/javabal.html ranks the top trading partners of the United States (imports and exports added together) as well as the top 10 countries with which the U.S. has a trade surplus and a trade deficit. Using the current year-to-date data, compare the top 10 deficit and surplus countries with the top 10 trading partners. Are deficit and surplus countries equally represented in the top 10 trading partners list, or is the list dominated by one group? The top 10 trade partners represent what percent of U.S. imports, and what percent of U.S. exports?

15. WEB-BASED QUESTION **Foreign Exchange Rates—The Yen for Dollars** The Federal Reserve System http://www.bog.frb.fed.us/releases/H10/hist/ provides historical foreign exchange rate data for a wide variety of currencies. The information is based on data collected by the Federal Reserve Bank of New York from a sample of market participants. Look at the data for the Japanese yen from 1990 to the present. Assume that you were in Tokyo every New Year's since January 1, 1990, to this year and bought a bento (boxed lunch) for 1000 yen. Convert this amount to dollars using the yen/dollar exchange rate for each January since 1990, and plot the dollar price of the bento over time. Has the dollar appreciated or depreciated against the yen? What was the least amount in dollars your box lunch cost? The most?

2

National
Income,
Employment,
and Fiscal
Policy

7

Measuring Domestic Output, National Income, and the Price Level

"**D**isposable Income Flat"; "Personal Consumption Surges"; "Net Investment Stagnates"; "Russia's GDP Slide Halted"; "GDP Price Index Rises Less Rapidly Than CPI."

These are typical headlines in the business and economics news. They look like gibberish—unless you know the language of macroeconomics and national income accounting. This chapter will help you learn that language and the ideas it communicates. After studying it, you will have a basic understanding of how government statisticians and accountants measure and record the levels of domestic output, national income, and prices for the economy.

In this chapter we first explain why it is important to measure the performance of an economy. Then we define the key measure of total output—gross domestic product (GDP)—and show how it is actually calculated. We also derive and explain several other important measures of output and income. Next, we turn to the measurement of the overall level of prices—the price level. We then demonstrate how GDP is adjusted for inflation or deflation so that it more accurately reflects the physical amount of a nation's production. Finally, we list and explain some limitations of the measures of domestic output and national income.

MACROECONOMIC MEASUREMENT

Our first goal is to explain the ways the overall production performance of the economy is measured. This is part of *national income accounting*, which does for the economy as a whole what private accounting does for the individual business enterprise or, for that matter, for the household.

A firm measures its flows of income and expenditures to assess its operations over some time period, usually 3 months or a year. With this information the firm can gauge its economic health. If things are going well, the accounting data can be used to explain this success. Costs might be down or output or prices up, resulting in large profit. If things are going badly, accounting measures can help discover why. And by comparing the accounts over several periods, the firm can detect the growth or decline of profit and what caused the change. All this information helps the firm's managers make intelligent business decisions.

National income accounting operates in much the same way for an economy.

1. It allows us to keep a finger on the economic pulse of a nation. A national income accounting system permits us to measure the level of production in an economy in some particular year and explain why it is at that level.

2. By comparing national accounts over a number of years, we can track the long-run course of the economy and see whether it has grown, been steady, or stagnated.

3. Information supplied by national accounts provides a basis for designing and applying public policies to improve the performance of the economy. Without national accounts, economic policy would be based on guesswork. *National income accounting allows us to assess the health of an economy and formulate policies to maintain and improve that health.*

GROSS DOMESTIC PRODUCT

There are many measures of an economy's economic performance. The best available measures, however, are based on the economy's annual total output of goods and services or, as it is sometimes called, its *aggregate output.* An economy's aggregate output is measured by its **gross domestic product** (GDP): *the total market value of all final goods and services produced within a country in 1 year.* GDP includes goods and services produced by citizen-supplied *and* foreign-supplied resources within a particular nation's geographical boundaries. Thus, U.S. GDP includes not only the value of Fords produced at a U.S.-owned factory in Michigan but also the value of Honda autos produced at a Japanese-owned factory in Ohio.

GDP measures the market value of annual output; *it is a monetary measure.* Indeed it must be if we are to compare the heterogeneous collection of goods and services produced in different years and get a meaningful idea of their relative worth.

If the economy produces three sofas and two computers in year 1 and two sofas and three computers in year 2, in which year is output greater? We cannot answer that question until price tags are attached to the various products as indicators of society's evaluation of their relative worth.

In Table 7-1, the money price of sofas is $500 and the price of computers is $2000. Year 2's output of $7000 is greater than year 1's output of $5500 because society values year 2's output more highly; society is willing to pay $1500 more for the collection of goods produced in year 2 than in year 1.

Avoidance of Multiple Counting

To measure total output accurately, all goods and services produced in any specific year must be counted once, but not more than once. Most products go through a series of production stages before reaching a market. As a result, parts of some products may be bought and sold many times. To avoid multiple counting of parts that are sold and resold, GDP includes only the market value of *final goods* and ignores transactions involving *intermediate goods.*

By **final goods** we mean goods and services being purchased for final use by the purchaser, and not for resale or further processing or manufacturing. *They are "purchases not resold."* **Intermediate goods** are goods and services that are purchased for further processing and manufacturing or for resale.

The value of final goods is included in GDP, and the value of intermediate goods is excluded. Why? Because the value of final goods already includes the value of all intermediate goods involved in producing the final goods. Counting intermediate goods separately would be **multiple counting,** which would exaggerate the value of GDP.

TABLE 7-1 **Comparing heterogeneous outputs by using money prices**

Year	Annual output	Market value
1	3 sofas and 2 computers	3 at $500 + 2 at $2000 = $5500
2	2 sofas and 3 computers	2 at $500 + 3 at $2000 = $7000

To clarify this, suppose there are five stages in manufacturing a wool suit and getting it to the consumer—the ultimate or final user. As Table 7-2 indicates, firm A, a sheep ranch, provides $120 worth of wool to firm B, a wool processor. Firm A receives $120 from B and pays it out in wages, rent, interest, and profit. Firm B processes the wool and sells it to firm C, a suit manufacturer, for $180. What does firm B do with the $180 it receives? As noted, $120 goes to firm A, and the remaining $60 is used by B to pay wages, rent, interest, and profit for the resources needed in processing the wool. The manufacturer sells the suit to firm D, a clothing wholesaler, who sells it to firm E, a retailer, and then, at last, a consumer, the final user, buys it for $350.

At each stage, the difference between what a firm has paid for the product and what it receives for selling the product is paid out as wages, rent, interest, and profit for the resources used by that firm to produce and distribute the suit.

How much of this should we include in GDP to account for the production of the suit? We should include just $350, the value of the final product. This amount includes all the intermediate transactions leading up to the product's final sale. It would be a gross distortion to include the sum of all the intermediate sales, $1140, in GDP. This would be multiple counting: counting the final product *and* the sale and resale of its various parts in the multistage production process. The production and sale of the suit have generated $350, *not* $1140, worth of output and income.

To avoid multiple counting, national income accountants are careful to calculate only the *value added* by each firm. **Value added** is the market value of a firm's output *less* the value of the inputs which it has purchased from others. For example, column 3, Table 7-2, shows that the value added by firm B is $60, the difference between the $180 value of its output and the $120 it paid for the inputs provided by firm A. By adding the values added by the five firms in Table 7-2, the total value of the suit can be accurately determined. Similarly, by calculating and summing the values added by all firms in the economy, we can determine the GDP—the market value of total output.

Exclusion of Nonproduction Transactions

GDP measures the annual production of the economy. Although many monetary transactions in the economy are for currently produced final goods and services, many other transactions are not. These nonproduction transactions must be excluded. *Nonproduction transactions* are of two major types: (1) purely financial transactions and (2) secondhand sales.

Financial Transactions Purely financial transactions are of three general kinds:

1. *Public transfer payments* These are the social security payments, welfare payments, and veterans' payments which government makes to particular households. The basic characteristic of public transfer payments is that recipients make no contribution to current production in return for them. To include them in GDP would be to overstate this year's production.

2. *Private transfer payments* These payments—for example, a university student's monthly sub-

TABLE 7-2 Value added in a five-stage production process

(1) Stage of production	(2) Sales value of materials or product	(3) Value added
	0	
Firm A, sheep ranch	$ 120	$120 (= $120 − $ 0)
Firm B, wool processor	180	60 (= 180 − 120)
Firm C, suit manufacturer	220	40 (= 220 − 180)
Firm D, clothing wholesaler	270	50 (= 270 − 220)
Firm E, retail clothier	**350**	80 (= 350 − 270)
Total sales values	$1140	
Value added (total income)		**$350**

sidy from home or an occasional gift from a wealthy relative—do not entail production but simply the transfer of funds from one private individual to another.

3. *Security transactions* Buying and selling of stocks and bonds are also excluded from GDP. Stock market transactions involve swapping paper assets. The amount spent on these assets does not directly create current production. Only the services provided by the security broker are included in GDP. However, sales of *new* issues of stocks and bonds transfer money from savers to businesses which often spend the proceeds on capital goods. Thus, these transactions may *indirectly* contribute to spending, which does account for output and hence add to GDP.

Secondhand Sales Secondhand sales are excluded from GDP because they either reflect no *current* production or involve multiple counting. Suppose you sell your 1965 Ford Mustang to a friend; this transaction should be excluded in determining this year's GDP because it does not represent any current production. Including sales of goods produced some years ago in this year's GDP would exaggerate this year's output. Similarly, if you purchased a brand new Mustang but resold it a week later to your neighbor, the sale to your neighbor would be excluded from current GDP. When you originally bought the new car, that is when its value was included in GDP. To include its resale value at a later time would be to count it twice. **(Key Question 3)**

Two Sides to GDP: Spending and Income

Let's consider how the market value of total output—or for that matter, any single unit of output—is measured. Returning to Table 7-2, how can we measure the market value of a suit?

We can determine how much a consumer, the final user, pays for it; that will tell us the value of the final product. Or we can add up all the wage, rent, interest, and profit incomes created in producing it. This second approach is the value-added technique discussed in Table 7-2.

The final-product and value-added approaches are two ways of looking at the same thing. *What is spent on a product is received as income by those who helped produce it.* Chapter 2's circular flow model demonstrated this. If $350 is spent on the suit, then $350 is the total amount of income derived from its produc-

tion. You can verify this by looking at the incomes generated by firms A, B, C, D, and E in Table 7-2—$120, $60, $40, $50, and $80—which total $350.

This equality of the expenditure for a product and the income derived from its production is guaranteed, because profit balances the two. Profit—or loss—is the income remaining after wage, rent, and interest incomes have been paid by the producer. If the wage, rent, and interest incomes the firm must pay in getting the suit produced are less than the $350 expenditure for the suit, the difference will be the firm's profit.[1] Conversely, if wage, rent, and interest incomes exceed $350, profit will be negative. That is, losses will be incurred, balancing the expenditure on the product and the income derived from its production.

It is the same for the total output of the economy. There are two ways of looking at GDP: One is to see GDP as the sum of all the expenditures in buying that total output. This is the *output*, or **expenditures, approach.** The other views GDP in terms of the income derived or created from producing it. This is the *earnings*, or *allocations*, or **income, approach.**

This year's GDP can be determined either by adding up all that is spent to buy this year's total output or by summing up all the incomes derived from the production of this year's total output. That is,

$$\left.\begin{array}{l}\text{Amount spent to}\\\text{purchase this year's}\\\text{total output}\end{array}\right\} = \left\{\begin{array}{l}\text{money income}\\\text{derived from}\\\text{producing this}\\\text{year's total output}\end{array}\right.$$

This relationship is an *identity:* an equation whose variables are defined and measured such that one side of the equation always equals the other side. Buying (spending money) and selling (receiving money income) are two aspects of the same transaction. *What is spent on a product is income to those who have contributed their human and property resources to getting that product produced and to the market.*

We can expand this identity to read as in Figure 7-1. On the output side of GDP, all final goods produced in an economy are purchased by the three domestic sectors (households, businesses, and government) and by foreign buyers. On the income side of GDP (and aside from a few complicating factors, discussed later in this chapter), the total receipts of businesses acquired from the sale of total output are allocated among resources suppliers as wage, rent, interest, and profit income.

---

[1] The term "profit" is used here in the accounting sense to include both normal profit and economic profit as defined in Chapter 4.

Expenditures, or output, approach

Income, or allocations, approach

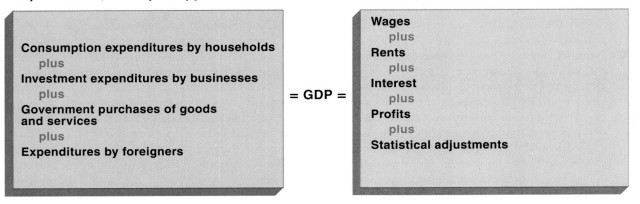

FIGURE 7-1 The expenditures and income approaches to GDP   There are two general approaches to measuring gross domestic product. We can determine GDP as the value of output by summing all expenditures on that output. Alternatively, with some modifications, we can determine GDP by adding up the components of income arising from the production of that output.

EXPENDITURES APPROACH

To determine GDP through expenditures, we add up all spending on final goods and services. But national income accountants have more precise terms for the different types of spending than those listed in the left panel in Figure 7-1.

Personal Consumption Expenditures (C)

What we have called "consumption expenditures by households" is **personal consumption expenditures** to national income accountants. It includes expenditures by households on *durable consumer goods* (automobiles, refrigerators, video recorders), *nondurable consumer goods* (bread, milk, vitamins, pencils, toothpaste), and *consumer expenditures for services* (of lawyers, doctors, mechanics, barbers). We will use the letter C to designate this part of GDP.

Gross Private Domestic Investment (I_g)

Under the heading **gross private domestic investment** (I_g), national income accountants combine:

1. All final purchases of machinery, equipment, and tools by business enterprises
2. All construction
3. Changes in inventories

This is more than we have meant by "investment" thus far. The first item simply restates our definition of investment spending as the purchase of tools, machinery, and equipment.

The second item includes such construction as building a new factory, warehouse, or store. But "all construction" also includes residential construction. Why is that investment rather than consumption? Because apartment buildings are investment goods which, like factories and stores, are income-earning assets when they are rented or leased. Other residential units which are rented or leased are, for the same reason, investment goods. And owner-occupied houses are investment goods because they *could* be rented out to yield a money-income return, even though the owners may choose not to do so. For these reasons all residential construction is considered investment.

Finally, changes in inventories are counted as investment because an increase in inventories is, in effect, "unconsumed output." And, as we know from production possibilities analysis, that is what investment is.

Inventory Changes: A Part of Investment   Let's look at inventory changes more carefully. Because GDP measures total current (this year's) output, we must include within it any products produced this year even though they are *not sold* this year. GDP must include the market value of any additions to inventories accruing during the year. A laptop computer produced in 1998 must be counted as GDP in 1998, even though it remains unsold as of February 1999. If we excluded an increase in inventories, GDP would understate the current year's total production. If businesses have more goods on their shelves and in warehouses at year's end than they had at the start, the economy has produced more than was purchased during the year. This increase in inventories must be included in GDP as part of current production, along with the value of goods which were manufactured *and sold* during the year.

What about a decline in inventories? This must be subtracted in figuring GDP. The economy can sell a total output which exceeds its production by dipping into, and thus reducing, its inventories. Then some of this year's purchases reflect not current production but a drawing down of inventories on hand at the beginning of this year. And inventories on hand at the start of any year's production represent the production of previous years. The laptop computer produced in 1998 but sold in 1999 cannot be counted as part of 1999 GDP. Because GDP is a measure of the *current* year's output, we must omit any purchases of past production, that is, any drawing down of inventories, in determining GDP. We do this by subtracting inventory decreases in determining investment expenditures.

Noninvestment Transactions We have discussed what investment is. Now we need to emphasize what it is not. Investment does *not* include the transfer of financial assets (stocks, bonds) or resale of physical assets. Economists exclude the buying of stocks and bonds from their definition of investment because such purchases merely transfer the ownership of existing assets. The same is true of the resale of existing physical assets.

Investment is the construction or manufacture of *new* capital assets. The production of these assets creates jobs and income; the transfer (sale) of claims to existing capital goods does not.

Gross versus Net Investment Our category "gross private domestic investment" includes purchases of machinery and equipment, all construction, and changes in inventories. Let's focus for a moment on the modifiers, "gross," "private," and "domestic." "Private" and "domestic" tell us that we are talking about spending by private business enterprises, not government (public) agencies, and that

investment is in the nation itself—rather than abroad.

"Gross" is not as simple. **Gross private domestic investment** includes the production of *all* investment goods—those which replace machinery, equipment, and buildings used up to produce the current year's output *and* any net additions to the economy's stock of capital. Gross investment includes both investment in replacement capital *and* investment in added capital. **Net private domestic investment,** however, refers only to investment in added capital.

To make the distinction clear: In 1997 the U.S. private sector produced and purchased $1238 billion of capital goods. But in producing that output, it used up $717 billion of machinery and equipment. Thus, it added $521 (= $1238 − $717) billion to its stock of capital. Gross private investment in 1997 was $1238 billion; net private investment was $521 billion. The difference is the value of the private capital used up in producing 1997's GDP.

Net Investment and Economic Growth The amount of a nation's capital worn out or used up in a particular year is called *depreciation*. Other things equal, the relationship between gross investment and depreciation indicates whether an economy's production capacity is expanding, static, or declining. Figure 7–2 illustrates these cases.

1. *Expanding production capacity* When gross investment exceeds depreciation (Figure 7-2a), the economy's production capacity is expanding; its stock of capital is growing. *Positive net investment expands the production capacity of the economy.* As indicated previously, this was true for the U.S. economy in 1997. It added $521 billion to the size of the "national factory" that year. This increase in capital helped shift the U.S. production possibilities curve outward.

2. *Static production capacity* When gross investment and depreciation are equal, a nation's production capacity is static (Figure 7-2b). Production capacity is standing pat; the economy produces just enough capital to replace what is consumed in producing the year's output—no more, no less. Example: In World War II, the Federal government purposely restricted private investment to free resources for the production of war goods. In 1942, gross private investment and depreciation were each about $10 billion. Thus net investment was roughly zero. At the end of 1942, our stock of capital was about the same as

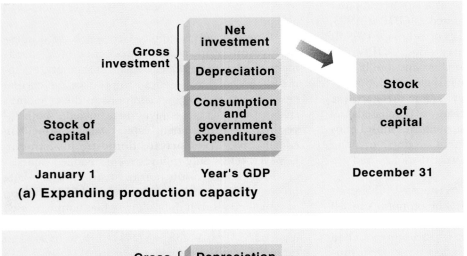

(a) Expanding production capacity

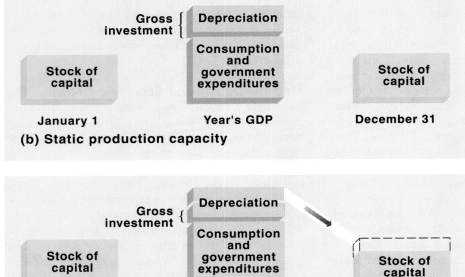

(b) Static production capacity

(c) Declining production capacity

FIGURE 7-2 Expanding, static, and declining production capacity (a) When gross investment exceeds depreciation, the economy is making a net addition to its stock of capital; all else equal, the economy's production capacity expands. (b) When gross investment precisely replaces the capital facilities depreciated in producing the year's output, the stock of capital goods remains unchanged; all else equal, the economy's production capacity is static. (c) When gross investment is insufficient to replace the capital goods depreciated in the year's production, the economy's stock of capital falls; all else equal, production capacity declines.

----

it was at the start of that year. The U.S. economy's production capacity was stationary; its production facilities did not expand.

3. ***Declining production capacity*** *When gross investment is less than depreciation, an economy's production capacity declines.* The economy uses up more capital than it produces (Figure 7-2c). When that situation occurs, net investment is negative; the economy is *disinvesting.* Depressions foster such circumstances. During bad times, when pro-

duction and employment are low, the nation has a greater production capacity than it is currently using. There is no incentive to replace depreciated capital equipment, much less add to the existing stock. Depreciation is likely to exceed gross investment, with the result that the nation's stock of capital is less at the end of each year than it was at the start.

This was the case during the Great Depression. In 1933 gross investment was about

$2 billion, while the capital consumed during that year was $8 billion. Net disinvestment was therefore $6 billion. That is, net investment was a minus $6 billion, indicating that the size of our "national factory" shrunk during that year.

We use the letter I for domestic investment spending, attaching the subscript g to mean gross investment and the subscript n to mean net investment. It is gross investment I_g that is used in determining GDP. **(Key Question 6)**

Government Purchases (G)

Government purchases (of consumption goods and capital goods) include all government spending (Federal, state, and local) on the finished products of businesses and all direct purchases of resources, including labor. It excludes all government transfer payments because such outlays reflect no current production but merely transfers of government receipts to some households. We use the letter G to indicate government purchases, the third part of GDP.

Net Exports (Xₙ)

A country's international trade transactions enter into national income accounting. Let's use the U.S. economy to show how: On the one hand, we want to include in GDP all spending that accounts for the production of goods and services in the United States. Spending by people abroad on U.S. goods accounts

for U.S. output, just as does spending by U.S. citizens in U.S. markets. Thus, we must include what the rest of the world spends on U.S. goods and services—U.S. exports—when determining GDP by the expenditures approach.

On the other hand, we know that part of the money spent for consumption, investment, and government purchases is spent on imports: goods and services produced abroad. This spending does not reflect production in the United States; it is some other nation's GDP. So we must subtract the value of imports to avoid overstating total production in the United States.

Rather than add exports and subtract imports separately, national income accountants add to GDP the difference "exports less imports." This difference, called **net exports,** is the amount by which foreign spending on a nation's goods and services exceeds that nation's spending on foreign goods and services. It is designated by X_n.

If people abroad buy $45 billion of U.S. exports, and Americans buy $35 billion of foreign imports in a year, U.S. net exports are *plus* $10 billion. If the rest of the world spends $30 billion on U.S. exports and Americans spend $40 billion on foreign imports, U.S. net exports are *minus* $10 billion.

The left side of Table 7-3 shows the computation of U.S. GDP for 1997 via the expenditures approach. Note that in 1997 Americans spent $97 billion more on foreign goods and services than the rest of the world spent on U.S. goods and services.

TABLE 7-3   Accounting statement for the U.S. economy, 1997 (in billions)

Receipts: expenditures approach		Allocations: income approach	
Personal consumption expenditures (C)	$5489	Compensation of employees	$4703
Gross private domestic investment (Iₘ)	1238	Rents	148
Government purchases (G)	1454	Interest	450
Net exports (Xₙ)	−97	Proprietors' income	545
		Corporate income taxes	319
		Dividends	336
		Undistributed corporate profits	149
		National income	$6650
		Indirect business taxes	545
		Consumption of fixed capital	868
		Net foreign factor income earned in the U.S.	21
Gross domestic product	$8084	Gross domestic product	$8084

Source: U.S. Department of Commerce data.

The GDP Equation: $C + I_g + G + X_n$

These four categories of expenditures—personal consumption expenditures *(C)*, gross private domestic investment *(I$_g$)*, government purchases *(G)*, and net exports *(X$_n$)*—include all possible types of spending. Added together, they measure the market value of the year's output or, in other words, the GDP. That is,

$$C + I_g + G + X_n = \text{GDP}$$

For the United States in 1997 (Table 7-3):

$$\$5489 + \$1238 + \$1454 - \$97 = \$8084$$

Global Perspective 7-1 compares GDPs for selected nations.

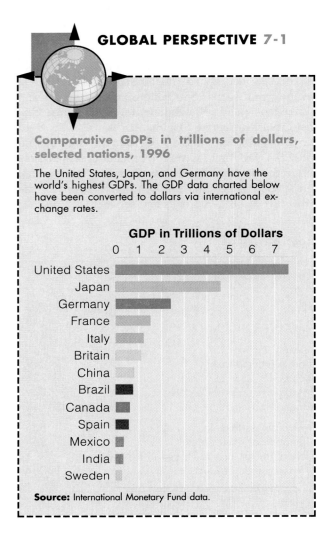

GLOBAL PERSPECTIVE 7-1

Comparative GDPs in trillions of dollars, selected nations, 1996

The United States, Japan, and Germany have the world's highest GDPs. The GDP data charted below have been converted to dollars via international exchange rates.

GDP in Trillions of Dollars

Source: International Monetary Fund data.

INCOME APPROACH[2]

The allocations side of Table 7-3 shows how 1997's $8084 of expenditure was distributed as income. It would be simple if we could say that all expenditures on the economy's annual output flowed to U.S. households as wage, rent, interest, and profit incomes. But the picture is complicated by three adjustments which are necessary to balance the expenditures and income sides of the national accounting statement. Let's first look at the various items of national income shown on the right side of Table 7-3. Then we will turn to the three complications.

Compensation of Employees

This largest income category comprises primarily the wages and salaries paid by businesses and government to suppliers of labor. It also includes wage and salary supplements, in particular, payments by employers into social insurance and into a variety of private pension, health, and welfare funds for workers. These wage and salary supplements are part of the employer's cost of obtaining labor and are treated as a component of the firm's total wage payments.

Rents

Rents consist of income payments received by households and businesses which supply property resources. Examples include the monthly payments of renters to landlords and the annual lease payments by corporate tenants for the use of office space. The number in Table 7-3 is *net* rent—gross rental income minus depreciation of rental property. It is the rental income which remains after allowable depreciation (wearing out of the property) is subtracted from gross rental revenues.

Interest

Interest comprises the money-income payments flowing from private businesses to the suppliers of money capital. It includes items such as the interest payments households receive on saving deposits, certificates of deposit (CDs), and corporate bonds.

---

[2]Some instructors may choose to omit this section because the expenditures approach is more relevant for the analysis of Chapters 9 through 12.

Proprietors' Income

What we have loosely termed "profits" until now is broken down in the national income accounts into two accounts: *proprietors' income*, or income of unincorporated businesses, and *corporate profits.* Proprietors' income is the net income of sole proprietorships and partnerships. Corporate profits cannot be described so easily because corporate earnings may be distributed in several ways.

Corporate Profits

Generally, three things can happen to corporate profits:

1. *They may be collected as corporate income taxes.* A portion will be claimed by, and therefore flow to, government as corporate income taxes.
2. *They may be distributed as dividends.* A part of the remaining corporate profits will be paid out to stockholders as dividends. Such payments flow to households, which are the ultimate owners of all corporations.
3. *They may be retained as undistributed corporate profits.* What remains of corporate profits after both corporate income taxes and dividends have been paid is called *undistributed corporate profits.* These retained corporate earnings will be invested, currently or in the future, in new plants and equipment, increasing the real assets of the businesses doing the investing.

By adding employee compensation, rents, interest, proprietors' income, and corporate profits we get U.S. **national income**—all income earned by U.S.-supplied resources, whether here or abroad. But Table 7-3 reveals that national income, shown on the right-hand side of the account, is less than the sum of expenditures, shown on the left-hand side.

Three Adjustments

We can balance both sides of the account by adding three items to national income.

Indirect Business Taxes The first adjustment is to add to national income certain taxes, called **indirect business taxes,** which firms treat as costs of production and therefore add to the prices of the products they sell. Such taxes include general sales taxes, excise taxes, business property taxes, license fees, and custom duties.

To see why we must add indirect business taxes to national income in balancing expenditures and income, assume that a firm produces a good selling at $1. Production of this item creates $1 of wage, rent, interest, and profit income. But now government imposes a 5 percent sales tax on all products sold at retail. The retailer adds this 5 percent to the price of the product, raising its price from $1 to $1.05, and thus shifts the sales tax to consumers. This $.05 is *not* earned income (is *not* part of national income), because government contributes nothing directly to the production of the good in return for the tax receipt. The value of the output is $1.05, but only $1 of this value is paid to households as wage, rent, interest, and profit income. Therefore, we must add the $.05 to the $1 of national income in calculating GDP—the total value of output. In Table 7-3 we make this adjustment for the entire economy.

Depreciation: Consumption of Fixed Capital

The second adjustment involves depreciation. The useful life of capital equipment extends far beyond the year of purchase. Capital may be purchased in 1 year and used productively for many years after that. To avoid gross understatement of profit and therefore of total income in the year of purchase, and overstatement of profit and total income in succeeding years, the total cost of such goods must be allocated over their lives. The annual charge which estimates the amount of capital equipment used up in each year's production is called *depreciation*. Depreciation is a bookkeeping entry designed to yield a more accurate statement of profit and hence total income for a firm in each year.

If profits and total income for the economy are to be stated accurately, a gigantic depreciation charge must be made against the economy's private and public stock of capital. (Public capital includes government buildings, port facilities, and so on.) This depreciation charge is called **consumption of fixed capital**—the allowance for capital goods "consumed" in producing this year's GDP. It is the portion of this year's GDP which must be set aside to replace the capital goods used up in production. That part of this charge which relates to the private sector is the difference between gross private investment, I_g, and net private investment, I_n.

For present purposes, the significance of this charge is that this part of the business sector's receipts is not available for income payments to resource suppliers. This part of receipts—this portion of the value of production—is a cost of production which reduces business profits. But, unlike other costs of production, depreciation *does not add to anyone's income*. We must therefore add consumption of fixed capital to national income in balancing an economy's expenditures and income, as in Table 7-3.

Net Foreign Factor Income   Our last step is to make a slight adjustment relating to "national" versus "domestic." National income (NI) is the total income of Americans, whether earned in the United States or abroad. But GDP measures *domestic* output—the total output produced within the boundaries of the United States, irrespective of the nationality of those providing the resources. In moving from NI to GDP, we must consider the income U.S. citizens gain from supplying resources abroad and the income foreigners gain by supplying resources in the United States. In 1997 foreign-owned resources earned $21 billion more in the United States than U.S.-supplied resources earned abroad. This difference is called *net foreign factor income*. We must *add* it to national income when computing the value of our domestic output because it derives from output produced within the borders of the United States.

Table 7-3 summarizes our discussion of the expenditures and income approaches to GDP. This table is a giant accounting statement for the U.S. economy. The left side shows what the economy produced in 1997 and the total receipts derived from that production. The right side shows how the income derived from the production of 1997's GDP was allocated.

QUICK REVIEW 7-1

■ Gross domestic product (GDP) measures the total market value of all final goods and services produced within a nation in a specific year.

■ The expenditures approach to GDP sums total spending on final goods and services: $GDP = C + I_g + G + X_n$.

■ When net investment is positive, the economy's production capacity expands; when net investment is negative, the economy's production capacity erodes.

■ The income approach to GDP sums the total income earned by a nation's resource suppliers and then adds in indirect business taxes, consumption of fixed capital (depreciation), and net foreign factor income.

OTHER NATIONAL ACCOUNTS

Our discussion has centered on GDP as the measure of an economy's annual output. But there are related national accounts of equal importance which can be derived from GDP. To obtain these other accounts, we can start with GDP and make various adjustments.

Net Domestic Product (NDP)

GDP as a measure of total output has a defect: *It fails to make allowance for replacing the capital goods used up in this year's production.* As a result, it gives an exaggerated value of the output available for consumption and for addition of new capital. For example, we observe in Table 7-3 that $868 billion of 1997's GDP consisted of depreciation (consumption of fixed capital). Thus, 1997's GDP of $8084 does not tell us what that year's production *added* to society's well-being by way of new output available for consumption and additions to the stock of capital. For this purpose it would be much more accurate to subtract from GDP the $868 billion of machinery and equipment which was consumed in producing the GDP and which had to be replaced. This subtraction gives us **net domestic product** (NDP). That is,

NDP = GDP − consumption of fixed capital

In 1997 for the United States:

	Billions
Gross domestic product	$8084
Consumption of fixed capital	− 868
Net domestic product	$7216

NDP is simply GDP adjusted for depreciation. It measures the total annual output which the entire economy—households, businesses, government, and foreigners—can consume without impairing its capacity to produce in ensuing years.

Adjusting Table 7-3 from GDP to NDP is easy on the income side: We just omit consumption of fixed capital. The other items then add up to an NDP of $7216 billion.

Things are not quite so simple on the expenditure side because consumption of fixed capital includes depreciation of both private and public capital goods. In effect, we subtract part of the $868 billion of consumption of fixed capital (specifically,

$717 billion) from gross private investment and the other part ($151 billion) from government purchases. NDP is therefore $7216 billion.

The "net" in NDP alludes to the fact that it includes *net* (not *gross*) investment in the economy. It "nets out" consumption of fixed capital from the total of private and public investment.

National Income (NI)

In analyzing some problems, it is useful to know how much a nation's resource suppliers earned for their contributions of land, labor, capital, and entrepreneurial talent. As we already noted, U.S. national income (NI) includes all income earned by U.S.-owned resources, whether located at home or abroad. To derive national income from NDP, we must make two adjustments to NDP:

1. ***Subtract net foreign factor income earned in the United States.*** We want a measure of all factor (resource) income earned by people in the United States. We thus need to exclude the factor income earned in the United States by foreigners and add the factor income earned by U.S. citizens abroad. In 1997 foreign-supplied resources earned more income in the United States than U.S.-supplied resources earned abroad. We thus accomplish our goal by subtracting from NDP the net output produced (that is, net foreign factor income earned) by foreign-owned resources in the United States.

2. ***Subtract indirect business taxes from NDP.*** Government contributes nothing directly to production in return for the indirect business tax revenues it receives; government is not an economic resource. Indirect taxes are not part of payments to resources, and thus not part of national income.

For the United States in 1997:

	Billions
Net domestic product	$7216
Net foreign factor income earned in the U.S.	−21
Indirect business taxes	−545
National income	$6650

We also know that NI can be obtained through the income approach by directly adding up employee compensation, rent, interest, proprietors' income, and corporate profits (Table 7-3).

Personal Income (PI)

Personal income (PI) includes all income *received* whether earned or unearned. It is likely to differ from national income (income *earned*) because some income earned—social security taxes (payroll taxes), corporate income taxes, and undistributed corporate profits—is not actually received by households. Conversely, some income received—transfer payments—is not currently earned. Transfer payments include such items as social security payments, unemployment compensation payments, welfare payments, disability and education payments to veterans, and private pension payments.

In moving from national income to personal income, we must subtract the three types of income which are earned but not received and add the income which is received but not currently earned. Again for the United States in 1997:

	Billions
National income (income earned)	$6650
Social security contributions	−732
Corporate income taxes	−319
Undistributed corporate profits	−149
Transfer payments	+1424
Personal income	$6874

Disposable Income (DI)

Disposable income (DI) is personal income less personal taxes. *Personal taxes* include personal income taxes, personal property taxes, and inheritance taxes, the first of the three being the greatest amount.

	Billions
Personal income (income received before personal taxes)	$6874
Personal taxes	−987
Disposable income (income received after personal taxes)	$5887

Disposable income is the amount of income which households have to dispose of as they see fit. Because economists define saving as "that part of disposable income not spent on consumer goods," it follows that households divide their disposable income between consumption *(C)* and saving *(S)*. That is,

$$DI = C + S$$

Table 7-4 summarizes the relationships between GDP, NDP, NI, PI, and DI. **(Key Question 8)**

The Circular Flow Revisited

Figure 7-3 combines the expenditures and income approaches to GDP. As a more realistic and more complex expression of the circular flow model of the economy (Chapters 2, 5, and 6), this figure deserves your careful study.

Starting at the GDP rectangle in the upper left, the expenditure side of GDP is shown by the green arrows. To the right of the GDP rectangle are the allocations of GDP and the additions and subtractions needed to derive NDP, NI, PI, and DI. Red arrows depict all allocations or income flows. Note the division of DI between consumption and saving in the household sector. For the government sector, the flows of revenue in the form of types of taxes are denoted on the right; government disbursements in the form of purchases of goods and services and transfers are shown on the left. For the business sector, we have investment expenditures on the left and the three major sources of funds for business investment on the right.

Finally, observe the role of the rest of the world in the flow diagram. Spending by people abroad on U.S. exports adds to U.S. GDP, but U.S. consumption, government, and investment expenditures buy imported products as well as domestically produced goods. The flow emanating from "Rest of the World" shows that the U.S. handles this complication by calculating *net* exports (exports minus imports). This may be a positive or a negative amount. Also, note that *net* foreign factor income earned in the United States is subtracted from NDP in deriving NI.

Figure 7-3 simultaneously portrays the expenditure and income aspects of GDP, fitting the two approaches to one another. These flows of expenditures and income are part of a continuous, repetitive process. Cause and effect are intermingled: Expenditures create income, and from this income arise expenditures, which again flow to resource owners as income.

The table inside the covers of this book contains a useful historical summary of the national accounts and related statistics.

TABLE 7-4 The relationships between GDP, NDP, NI, PI, and DI in the United States, 1997

	Billions
Gross domestic product (GDP)	$8084
Consumption of fixed capital	−868
Net domestic product (NDP)	$7216
Net foreign factor income earned in the U.S.	−21
Indirect business taxes	−545
National income (NI)	$6650
Social security contributions.....................	−732
Corporate income taxes..........................	−319
Undistributed corporate profits.................	−149
Transfer payments..................................	+1424
Personal income (PI).................................	$6874
Personal taxes.......................................	−987
Disposable income (DI)	$5887

NOMINAL VERSUS REAL GDP

Recall that GDP is the market value of all final goods and services produced in a year. So money or *nominal* values are used as a common denominator to sum a heterogeneous output into a meaningful total. But this raises a problem: The value of different years' outputs (GDPs) can be usefully compared only if the value of money itself does not change because of inflation (rising overall prices) or deflation (falling overall prices).

Inflation or deflation complicates GDP because GDP is a price-times-quantity figure. The direct data used to measure GDP are the total sales revenues of business firms, but these revenues include both output quantities and the level of prices, which means that a change in either the quantity of output or the level of prices will affect the size of the GDP. Identical changes in GDP will occur if there is, say, a 5 percent

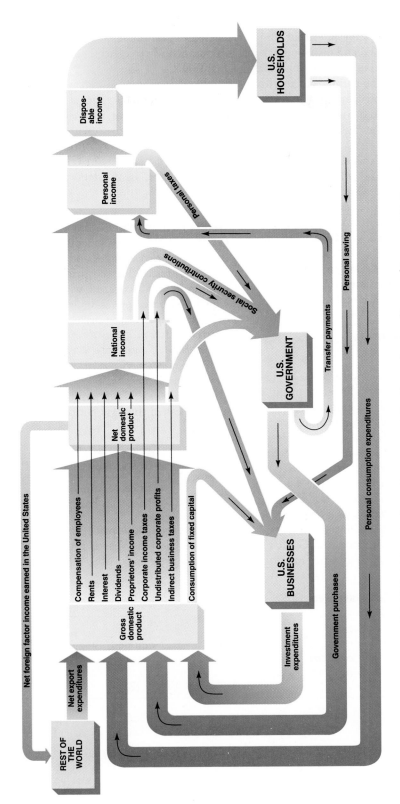

FIGURE 7-3 U.S. domestic output and the flows of expenditure and income This figure is an elaborate circular flow diagram which fits the expenditures and allocations sides of GDP to one another. The income or allocations flows are shown in red; the expenditure flows, in green. You should trace through the income and expenditure flows, relating them to the five basic national income accounting measures.

increase in output with no change in prices *or* a 5 percent increase in prices with no change in output. But it is the quantity of goods produced and distributed to households which affects their standard of living, not the price tags on these goods. The hamburger selling for $2 in 1997 yields the same satisfaction as an identical hamburger of 1970 that sold for 50 cents, *not* four times as much satisfaction, as the nominal value might imply.

Fortunately, we can resolve this difficulty by *deflating* GDP for rising prices and *inflating* it when prices are falling. These adjustments give us a picture of GDP for various years as if prices and the value of the dollar were the same as those in some reference period (or year). A GDP figure which reflects the prices prevailing when the output is produced is called unadjusted GDP, or **nominal GDP.** In contrast, a GDP figure that is deflated or inflated for price-level changes is called adjusted GDP, or **real GDP.**

Adjustment Process in a One-Good Economy

There are two ways we can adjust nominal GDP figures for price changes. Let's consider each using a simplified example. Assume an economy produces only one good, pizza, and in the amounts indicated in Table 7-5 for years 1, 2, and 3. An examination of columns 1 and 2 tells you that the nominal GDPs for years 2 and 3, as shown in column 4, greatly overstate the increases in real output occurring in those 2 years. That is, *the monetary measure of production (nominal GDP) does not accurately reflect the actual changes which have occurred in output (real GDP).* Considerable proportions of the sharp increases in nominal GDP in years 2 and 3 are due to the rather drastic inflation

shown in column 2, the remainder owing to the changes in output shown in column 1. Both increases in output and price increases are reflected in the nominal GDP.

Let's first suppose that we have directly gathered data from financial reports of businesses to derive nominal GDP in various years. In this approach, we will not know *directly* to what extent changes in price and changes in quantity of output have accounted for the observed increases in GDP. At this stage, we do not have before us the data in column 1, but only the data in column 4.

GDP Price Index   So how can we determine real GDP in our pizza-only economy? One method is to determine price changes and then adjust the nominal GDP figures. Once the price changes (as shown in column 2) are discovered, we can derive a price index which compares prices between years and estimates overall changes in the price level. Generally defined, a **price index** *measures the combined price of a particular collection of goods and services, called a "market basket," in a specific period relative to the combined price of an identical (or highly similar) group of goods and services in a reference period.* This point of reference, or benchmark, is called the base period or *base year.* More formally,

$$\text{Price index in given year} = \frac{\text{price of market basket in specific year}}{\text{price of same market basket in base year}} \times 100 \qquad (1)$$

By convention, the price ratio between the specific year and the base year is multiplied by 100. For example, a price ratio of 2/1 (= 2) is expressed as an

TABLE 7-5   **Calculating real GDP**

Year	(1) Units of output	(2) Price of pizza per unit	(3) Price index (year 1 = 100)	(4) Unadjusted, or nominal, GDP (1) × (2)	(5) Adjusted, or real, GDP
1	5	$10	100	$ 50	$50
2	7	20	200	140	70
3	8	25	250	200	80
4	10	30	____	____	____
5	11	28	____	____	____

index number of 200. Similarly, the price ratio of 1/3 (= .33) is expressed as 33.

In our simple example, our market basket consists of only one product: pizza. We see in column 2 in Table 7-5 that the price of pizza was $10 in year 1, $20 in year 2, $25 in year 3, and so on. Selecting year 1 as the base year, we can express the prices of the pizza "market basket" in, say, years 2 and 3 relative to the price of the market basket in year 1 as follows:

$$\text{Price index, year 2} = \frac{\$20}{\$10} \times 100 = 200$$

$$\text{Price index, year 3} = \frac{\$25}{\$10} \times 100 = 250$$

For year 1 the index must be 100 since the specific year and the base year are identical ($10).

These index numbers tell us that the price of pizza increased from year 1 to year 2 by 100 percent $\{=[(200 - 100)/100] \times 100\}$ and from year 1 to year 3 by 150 percent $\{=[(250 - 100)/100] \times 100\}$.

We can now use the index number in column 3 to deflate the nominal GDP figures in column 4. The simplest and most direct method of deflating is to express these index numbers as hundredths, that is, in decimal form, and divide them into the corresponding nominal GDP. This procedure yields real GDP:

$$\text{Real GDP} = \frac{\text{nominal GDP}}{\text{price index (in hundredths)}} \quad (2)$$

Column 5 shows the results. These real GDP figures measure the value of total output in years 1, 2, and 3 as if the price of pizza had been constant at $10 throughout the 3-year period. So real GDP shows the market value of each year's output measured in terms

of dollars which have the same purchasing power as in the base year.

To ensure you understand the deflating process, you should complete Table 7-5 for years 4 and 5, using equation (2). Second, you should rework the entire deflating procedure, using year 3 as the base period. You will find that in this case you must *inflate* some of the nominal GDP data, using the same procedure as used in our examples.

An Alternative Method We could more directly establish real GDP by initially gathering *separate* data on physical outputs (as in column 1) and their prices (as in column 2). Let's again consider our pizza-only economy in Table 7-5. If we first determine the physical outputs for each year, as shown in column 2, we can then see what each of those actual outputs would have sold for *if the base year price (here $10) had prevailed*. In year 2, the 7 units of pizza would be valued at $70 (= 7 units of output *times* the $10 price in the base year). As confirmed in column 5, this $70 of output *is* year 2's real GDP. Similarly, the real GDP of $80 for year 3 is found by multiplying the 8 units of output in year 3 by the $10 price in the base year.

When we determine real GDP through this method, the price index for a specific year is *implied*; it is simply the nominal GDP divided by the real GDP for that year:

$$\frac{\text{Price index}}{\text{(in hundredths)}} = \frac{\text{nominal GDP}}{\text{real GDP}} \quad (3)$$

Example: In year 2 in Table 7-5, the price index of 200, or, in hundredths, 2.00, equals the nominal GDP of $140 divided by the real GDP of $70. You should note that equation (3) is simply a rearrangement of equation (2). Table 7-6 summarizes the two methods

TABLE 7-6 **Steps for deriving real GDP from nominal GDP**

Method 1
1. Find nominal GDP for each year.
2. Compute a GDP price index.
3. Divide each year's nominal GDP by that year's price index (in hundredths) to determine real GDP.

Method 2
1. Break down nominal GDP into physical quantities of output and prices for each year.
2. Find real GDP for each year by determining the dollar amount which each year's physical output would have sold for if base-year prices had prevailed. (The GDP price index can then be found by dividing nominal GDP by real GDP.)

we have used to determine real GDP in our assumed single-good economy. **(Key Question 11)**

Real-World Considerations and Data

In the real world of many goods and services, the government's determination of real GDP and its actual price index are much more complex than in our pizza-only economy. The government accountants must assign "weights" to various categories of goods and services based on their relative proportions of total output. In the United States, accountants update these weights annually as expenditure patterns change, and they "roll" the base year continuously forward using a moving average. The actual GDP price index in the United States is called the *chain-type annual-weights price index*—a name which hints at its complexity and why we are sparing you the details.

Nevertheless, once real GDP and the GDP price index are established, the relationship between nominal GDP, real GDP, and the GDP price index is clear. Table 7-7 provides some U.S. illustrations of these relationships. Note that the point of reference for the price index is 1992, where the index value is arbitrarily set at 100. Because the long-run trend has been for the price level to rise, the pre-1992 values of real GDP (column 3) are higher than the nominal values (column 2). This upward adjustment acknowledges that prices were lower in the years before 1992. As a

result, nominal GDP understated the real output of those years and must be inflated.

The rising price level has caused nominal GDP figures for the post-1992 years to overstate real output. The government accountants therefore reduce, or deflate, these figures to gauge what GDP would have been in 1994, 1996, and so on, if 1992 prices had prevailed. So, since the 1992 reference year, real GDP has been less than nominal GDP.

By inflating the nominal pre-1992 GDP data and deflating the post-1992 data, government accountants determine annual real GDP, which can then be compared to any other year in the series. That is, the real GDP values in column 3 are directly comparable with one another in a meaningful way since they reflect changes in physical output.

Table 7-7 also reminds us that once nominal GDP and real GDP are known, the price index can be calculated, or, alternatively, if nominal GDP and the price index are known, real GDP can be calculated. Example: For 1994 nominal GDP was $6947.0 billion and real GDP was $6610.7. So the price level was 105.09 (= $6947.0/$6610.7 × 100), or 5 percent higher than in 1992. Alternatively, to find real GDP for 1994 we could express the 1994 GDP price index in hundredths (1.0509) and divide it into the nominal GDP of $6947.0.

To test your understanding of the relationships between nominal GDP, real GDP, and the price level, you should (1) determine the price-index values for

TABLE 7-7   Nominal GDP, real GDP, and GDP price index, selected years

(1) Year	(2) Nominal GDP, billions of $	(3) Real GDP, billions of $	(4) GDP price index* (1992 = 100)
1965	719.1	2881.1	24.95
1970	1035.6	3397.6	____
1975	1630.6	3873.9	42.09
1980	2784.2	____	60.34
1985	4180.7	5323.5	78.53
1990	5743.8	6136.3	93.64
1992	6244.4	6244.4	100.00
1993	6558.1	6389.6	____
1994	6947.0	6610.7	105.09
1995	7265.4	____	107.76
1996	7636.0	6928.4	110.22

*Chain-type annual-weights price index.
Source: U.S. Department of Commerce.

years 1970 and 1993, and (2) determine real GDP for years 1980 and 1995. For each of these years we have purposely left out data in Table 7-7. **(Key Question 12)**

THE CONSUMER PRICE INDEX

The GDP price index in Table 7-7 is *not* the same as the **consumer price index** (CPI), which government uses to report the rate of inflation each month. The CPI measures the prices of a market basket of some 300 consumer goods and services purchased by a typical urban consumer. The GDP index in Table 7-7 is much broader; it includes not only consumer goods and services but also capital goods, goods and services purchased by government, and goods and services entering world trade.

The present composition of the market basket used in the CPI was determined from a survey of the spending patterns of urban consumers in the 1982–1984 period. Thus the CPI in any specific year is as follows:

$$\text{CPI} = \frac{\substack{\text{price of 1982–1984 market} \\ \text{basket in specific year}}}{\substack{\text{price of same market basket} \\ \text{in base period (1982–1984)}}} \times 100$$

Unlike the GDP price index, in which the weights (relative purchases) of various goods and services are adjusted continuously, the CPI is a historical, *fixed-weight price index*. If 20 percent of consumer spending was on housing in 1982–1984, the assumption is that 20 percent of spending is still on housing in 1998. The base period is changed roughly every 10 years. The idea behind the historical, fixed-weight approach is to measure changes in the cost of a *constant* standard of living. Changes in the CPI thus allegedly measure the rate of inflation facing consumers. For example, the CPI increased from 156.9 in 1996 to 160.5 in 1997, indicating that 1996's rate of inflation was 2.3 percent [= (160.5 − 156.9)/156.9]. However, many economists believe that the CPI overstates actual inflation. We address this issue in this chapter's Last Word.

QUICK REVIEW 7-3

■ Nominal GDP is output valued at current prices; real GDP is output valued at constant prices (base-year prices).

■ The GDP price index compares the price (cost) of goods and services constituting GDP in a specific year to the price of the same market basket in a reference year.

■ A year's nominal GDP can be adjusted to real GDP by dividing the nominal GDP by the GDP price index (expressed in hundredths).

■ The consumer price index (CPI) measures changes in the prices of a fixed market basket of some 300 goods bought by the typical urban consumer.

GDP AND ECONOMIC WELL-BEING

GDP is a reasonably accurate and extremely useful measure of domestic economic performance. It is not, and was never intended to be, an index of society's overall well-being—its total satisfaction. GDP is merely a measure of the annual volume of goods and services produced. Many things could make a country better off without necessarily raising GDP, such as reduction of crime and violence, greater equality of opportunity, improved racial harmony, better understanding between parents and children, and reductions of drug and alcohol abuse.

Nevertheless, it is widely held that there should be a strong positive correlation between real GDP and economic well-being; that is, greater production should move society toward "the good life." Thus, we must understand some of the shortcomings of GDP—why it might understate or overstate real output, and why more output will not necessarily make society better off.

Nonmarket Transactions

Certain production transactions do not take place in markets. Thus, GDP as a measure of the market value of output fails to include them. Examples include the production services of a homemaker and the work of the carpenter who repairs his or her own home. Such transactions are *not* reflected in the profit and loss statements of business firms and therefore escape the national income accountants, causing GDP to be understated. However, some large nonmarket production transactions, such as the part of farmers' output which farmers consume themselves, *are* estimated by national income accountants.

Leisure

The U.S. workweek has declined significantly over the twentieth century, from about 53 hours at the turn of the century to about 36 hours now. Also, the expanded availability of paid vacations, holidays, and leave time has reduced the work year, which has given us increased leisure time and, thus, has had a positive effect on our well-being. Our system of national income accounting understates our well-being by not directly recognizing the benefits of increased leisure. Nor do national accounts reflect the satisfaction—the "psychic income"—which many people derive from their work.

Improved Product Quality

GDP is a quantitative, not a qualitative, measure. It does not accurately reflect improvements in product quality. There is a fundamental qualitative difference between a $3000 personal computer purchased today and a computer costing the same amount just a few years ago. Today's $3000 computer has far more speed and storage capacity as well as a clearer monitor and improved multimedia capabilities.

Failure to account adequately for quality improvement is a shortcoming of GDP accounting. Quality improvement clearly affects economic well-being as much as does the quantity of goods. Because product quality has improved over time, GDP understates the resulting improvement in our material well-being.

Composition and Distribution of Output

Changes in the composition of total output and its allocation among specific households may influence economic well-being. GDP, however, reflects only the size of output and tells us nothing about whether this collection of goods is "right" for society. A handgun and a set of encyclopedias, both selling for $350, are weighted equally in the GDP. Distribution is also ignored by GDP. Some economists feel that a more equal distribution of total output would increase national economic well-being. If they are correct, a future trend toward a less unequal distribution of GDP would enhance the economic well-being of society. A more unequal distribution—which appears to be occurring—would have the reverse effect.

Per Capita Output

For many purposes the most meaningful measure of economic well-being is *per capita output*, found by dividing real GDP by population. Because GDP measures the size of total output, it may conceal or misrepresent changes in the standard of living of individuals and households. GDP may rise, but if population is also growing rapidly, the per-person standard of living may be constant or even declining.

This is the plight of some developing countries. Madagascar's domestic output grew approximately 1 percent per year from 1985 to 1995. But annual population growth was 3 percent, resulting in a yearly decrease in per capita output slightly above 2 percent.

GDP and the Environment

Undesirable and much publicized "gross domestic by-products," such as dirty air and water, toxic waste, automobile junkyards, congestion, and noise, accompany production and the growth of GDP. The costs of pollution reduce our economic well-being. These spillover costs are associated with production and hence with the GDP but are not deducted from total output; thus GDP overstates our national economic well-being.

Ironically, the final physical product of economic production and consumption is garbage. A rising GDP means more garbage, and it may mean more pollution and a greater divergence between GDP and economic well-being. In fact, under existing accounting procedures, when a manufacturer pollutes a river and government spends to clean it up, the cleanup expense is added to the GDP while the pollution is not subtracted!

The Underground Economy

Economists agree there is a large underground sector in our economy. Some participants in this sector engage in illegal activities such as gambling, loan-sharking, prostitution, and the narcotics trade. These may well be "growth industries." Obviously, persons receiving income from illegal businesses choose to conceal their incomes.

However, most participants in the underground economy are in *legal* activities but do not fully report their incomes to the Internal Revenue Service (IRS).

Does the CPI Overstate Inflation?

A growing number of economists agree that the CPI overstates inflation.

They're back! Each month more than 300 price agents working for the Bureau of Labor Statistics (BLS) personally contact the same 19,000 stores, supermarkets, hospitals, bowling alleys, and other establishments to obtain the current prices of 90,000 items. The agents' task is to price the market basket of goods and services used to calculate the CPI. The prices are then sent to the BLS, where statisticians group them into seven categories: housing, food and drinks, transportation, medical care, apparel and upkeep, entertainment, and "other." The BLS then enters the numbers into its computers, cranks out the new CPI, and releases the results to the press. The next day's news tells us that the CPI rose by, say, 0.2 percent last month. This means the "inflation rate on an annual basis" is roughly 2.4 percent (= 0.2 × 12 months).

Changes in the CPI supposedly measure the rate of inflation facing consumers. But economists point to four problems with the CPI which may cause it to overstate the true rate of inflation, perhaps by as much as 1 percentage point each year.

1. Changing Spending Patterns Although the composition of the market basket remains unchanged, consumers *do* change their spending patterns. In particular, they shift their purchases in response to changes in relative prices. When the price of beef rises while the prices of fish and chicken are steady, consumers substitute fish or chicken for beef. This means that over time consumers are buying a market basket which contains more of the relatively low-priced and less of the relatively high-priced product. Because the historical, fixed-weight CPI does not account for these substitutes, it overstates the actual rate of inflation.

2. New Products Many new products such as digital answering machines, laptop computers, cellular phones, golf clubs with titanium heads, and telephone pagers are either not included or severely underweighted in the market basket used to construct the CPI. Often prices of new products drop dramatically following their introductions. The CPI,

with its historical, fixed-weight market basket, does not account for such price declines and thus overstates inflation.

3. Quality Improvements The CPI does not adequately account for quality improvements. To the extent that product quality has improved since the base period, higher prices are justified. We ought to pay more for medical care today than we did several years ago because it is generally of higher quality. The same occurs with autos, auto tires, electronics equipment, and many other items. But the CPI picks up most increases in the value of the market basket as increases in inflation, not as quality improvements. Again the CPI overstates the true rate of inflation.

4. Sale and Discount Prices In calculating the CPI, the Federal government accounts for price changes only on a same-store basis. If one of these stores raises its price on some good, then the price increase shows up in the CPI. But, in view of the higher price, many consumers may go to lower-price outlets to buy the product. Thus, all consumers do not face the price increase, as the CPI implies. As a related example, the CPI tracks full-price airfares, not discount fares. From 1978 to 1996 full-price fares increased by nearly 9 percent annually, while discount fares increased by only 2 percent annually. Failure to account fully for sale prices means the CPI overstates the true rate of inflation facing consumers.

So what if the CPI overstates inflation? The problem is that the CPI affects nearly everyone. Illustrations are numerous: Government payments to social security receivers are indexed to the CPI; when the CPI rises, social security payments automatically rise in lockstep. Millions of unionized workers have cost-of-living adjustment (COLA) clauses in their labor contracts; such adjustments are tied to increases in the CPI. Moreover, the wage expectations of nearly all workers are linked to the rate of inflation, as measured by the CPI. When the CPI rises, lenders often raise their interest rates on loans to account for inflation. Government's tax revenues may suffer from the overstatement of inflation, since personal income brackets are adjusted upward annually to reflect increases in the CPI. And the nation's economic policymakers base some of their policies on the CPI's rate of change. Finally, since the CPI is used to calculate real (inflation-adjusted) wages, an overstated rate of inflation means that real wages have grown more rapidly than the official statistics suggest.

A bell captain at a hotel or a waiter at a restaurant may underreport tips from customers. A business-person may record only a portion of sales receipts for the tax collector. A worker who wants to retain unemployment compensation benefits may obtain an "off-the-books" or "cash-only" job so there is no record of his or her work activities. A brick mason may agree to remodel a neighbor's fireplace in ex-change for the neighbor's doing off-the-books repair work on the mason's boat engine. None of these un-derground transactions, obviously, are included in GDP.

Although there is no consensus on the size of the underground economy, estimates suggest it is between 7 and 12 percent of the recorded GDP. In 1997, that meant GDP was understated by between $566 and $970 billion.

Global Perspective 7-2 indicates the relative sizes of underground economies in selected nations.

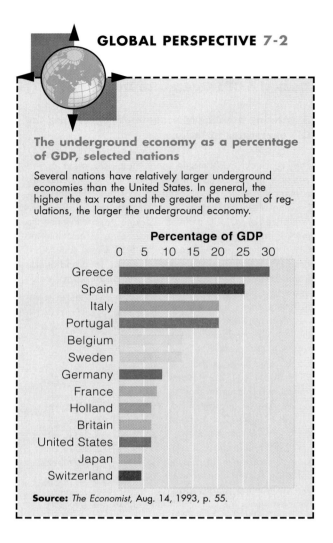

GLOBAL PERSPECTIVE 7-2

The underground economy as a percentage of GDP, selected nations

Several nations have relatively larger underground economies than the United States. In general, the higher the tax rates and the greater the number of reg-ulations, the larger the underground economy.

Percentage of GDP

Greece
Spain
Italy
Portugal
Belgium
Sweden
Germany
France
Holland
Britain
United States
Japan
Switzerland

Source: *The Economist*, Aug. 14, 1993, p. 55.

CHAPTER SUMMARY

1. Gross domestic product (GDP), a basic measure of an economy's economic performance, is the market value of all final goods and services produced within the borders of a nation in a year.

2. Intermediate goods, nonproduction transactions, and secondhand sales are purposely excluded in calculating GDP.

3. GDP may be calculated by summing total expendi-tures on all final output or by summing the income de-rived from the production of that output.

4. By the expenditures approach, GDP is determined by adding consumer purchases of goods and services, gross investment spending by businesses, government purchases, and net exports: $GDP = C + I_g + G + X_n$.

5. Gross investment is divided into **(a)** replacement in-vestment (required to maintain the nation's stock of capi-tal at its existing level), and **(b)** net investment (the net in-crease in the stock of capital). Positive net investment is associated with an expanding production capacity; nega-tive net investment, with a declining production capacity.

6. By the income or allocations approach, GDP is calculated as the sum of compensation to employees, rents, interest, proprietors' income, corporate income taxes, dividends, undistributed corporate profits, *plus* indirect business taxes, consumption of fixed capital, and net foreign factor income earned in the United States.

7. Other national accounts are derived from GDP. Net domestic product (NDP) is GDP less the consumption of fixed capital. National income (NI) is total income earned by a nation's resource suppliers; it is found by subtracting net foreign factor income earned in the United States and indirect business taxes from NDP. Personal income (PI) is the total income paid to households prior to any allowance for personal taxes. Disposable income (DI) is personal income after personal taxes have been paid. DI measures the amount of income households have available to consume or save.

8. Price indexes are computed by dividing the price of a specific collection or "market basket" of output in a particular period by the price of the same market basket in a base period and multiplying the result (the quotient) by 100. The GDP price index is used to adjust nominal GDP for inflation or deflation and thereby obtain real GDP.

9. Nominal (current-dollar) GDP measures each year's output valued in terms of the prices prevailing in that year. Real (constant-dollar) GDP measures each year's output in terms of the prices which prevailed in a selected base year. Because real GDP is adjusted for price-level changes, differences in real GDP are due only to differences in production activity.

10. The consumer price index (CPI) measures changes in the price of a market basket of some 300 goods and services purchased by urban consumers. Unlike the GDP price index, in which the weights of the goods change annually with spending patterns, the CPI is a fixed-weight price index, meaning that each year the items in the market basket remain the same as those in the base period (1982–1984).

11. National income accounting measures exclude nonmarket and illegal transactions, changes in leisure and in product quality, the composition and distribution of output, and the environmental effects of production. Nevertheless, these measures are reasonably accurate and very useful indicators of a nation's economic performance.

TERMS AND CONCEPTS

national income accounting	income approach	net exports	nominal GDP
gross domestic product	personal consumption expenditures	national income	real GDP
final goods	gross private domestic investment	indirect business taxes	price index
intermediate goods	net private domestic investment	consumption of fixed capital	consumer price index
multiple counting	government purchases	net domestic product	
value added		personal income	
expenditures approach		disposable income	

STUDY QUESTIONS

1. In what ways are national income statistics useful?

2. Explain why an economy's output, in essence, is also its income.

3. **KEY QUESTION** Why do national income accountants include only final goods in measuring GDP for a particular year? Why don't they include the value of the stocks and bonds bought and sold? Why don't they include the value of the used furniture bought and sold?

4. What is the difference between gross private domestic investment and net private domestic investment?

If you were to determine net domestic product through the expenditures approach, which of these two measures of investment spending would be appropriate? Explain.

5. Why are changes in inventories included as part of investment spending? Suppose inventories declined by $1 billion during 1999. How would this affect the size of gross private domestic investment and gross domestic product in 1999? Explain.

6. **KEY QUESTION** Use the concepts of gross and net investment to distinguish between economies in which production capacity is expanding, static, and declining. "In 1933 net private domestic investment was minus $6 billion. This means in that particular year the economy produced no capital goods at all." Do you agree? Why or why not? Explain: "Though net investment can be positive, negative, or zero, it is quite impossible for gross investment to be less than zero."

7. Define net exports. Explain how U.S. exports and imports each affect domestic production. Suppose foreigners spend $7 billion on U.S. exports in a given year and Americans spend $5 billion on imports from abroad in the same year. What is the amount of the United States' net exports? Explain how net exports might be a negative amount.

8. KEY QUESTION   Below is a list of domestic output and national income figures for a given year. All figures are in billions. The questions which follow ask you to determine the major national income measures by both the expenditures and income methods. Results you obtain with the different methods should be equal.

Personal consumption expenditures	$245
Net foreign factor income earned in the U.S.	4
Transfer payments	12
Rents	14
Consumption of fixed capital (depreciation)	27
Social security contributions	20
Interest	13
Proprietors' income	33
Net exports	11
Dividends	16
Compensation of employees	223
Indirect business taxes	18
Undistributed corporate profits	21
Personal taxes	26
Corporate income taxes	19
Corporate profits	56
Government purchases	72
Net private domestic investment	33
Personal saving	20

a. Using the above data, determine GDP by both the expenditures and income methods. Then determine NDP.
b. Now determine NI in two ways: first, by making the required additions or subtractions from NDP; and second, by adding up the types of income which make up NI.
c. Adjust NI (from part b) as required to obtain PI.
d. Adjust PI (from part c) as required to obtain DI.

9. Using the following national income accounting data, compute (a) GDP, (b) NDP, and (c) NI. All figures are in billions.

Compensation of employees	$194.2
U.S. exports of goods and services	17.8
Consumption of fixed capital	11.8
Government purchases	59.4
Indirect business taxes	14.4
Net private domestic investment	52.1
Transfer payments	13.9
U.S. imports of goods and services	16.5
Personal taxes	40.5
Net foreign factor income earned in the U.S.	2.2
Personal consumption expenditures	219.1

10. Why do national income accountants compare the market value of the total outputs in various years rather than actual physical volumes of production? What problem is posed by any comparison over time of the market values of various total outputs? How is this problem resolved?

11. KEY QUESTION   Suppose that in 1984 the total output in a single-good economy was 7000 buckets of chicken. Also suppose that in 1984 each bucket of chicken was priced at $10. Finally, assume that in 1992 the price per bucket of chicken was $16 and that 22,000 buckets were purchased. Determine the GDP price index for 1984, using 1992 as the base year. By what percentage did the price level, as measured by this index, rise between 1984 and 1992? Use the two methods listed in Table 7-6 to determine real GDP for 1984 and 1992.

12. KEY QUESTION   The following table shows nominal GDP and an appropriate price index for a group of selected years. Compute real GDP. Indicate in each calculation whether you are inflating or deflating the nominal GDP data.

Year	Nominal GDP, billions	Price index (1992 = 100)	Real GDP, billions
1959	$ 507.2	23.0	$_____
1964	663.0	24.6	$_____
1967	833.6	26.6	$_____
1973	1382.6	35.4	$_____
1988	5049.6	86.1	$_____
1995	7265.4	107.8	$_____

13. Which of the following are included in this year's GDP? Explain your answer in each case.
a. Interest on an AT&T bond
b. Social security payments received by a retired factory worker
c. The services of a painter in painting the family home
d. The income of a dentist

 e. The money received by Smith when she sells her economics textbook to a book buyer

 f. The monthly allowance which a college student receives from home

 g. Rent received on a two-bedroom apartment

 h. The money received by Mac when he resells this year's model Plymouth Prowler to Stan

 i. Interest received on corporate bonds

 j. A 2-hour decline in the length of the workweek

 k. The purchase of an AT&T bond

 l. A $2 billion increase in business inventories

 m. The purchase of 100 shares of GM common stock

 n. The purchase of an insurance policy

14. **(Last Word)** What is the CPI? What are its shortcomings in accurately measuring inflation?

15. **WEB-BASED QUESTION** **Latest Short-Term Indicators—Rank the Economies** The OECD (Organization for Economic Cooperation and Development) http://www.oecd.org/std/indksti.htm provides the latest short-term indicators of their member countries for the previous year. Of the following five countries (United States, Germany, Japan, France, and Italy), rank them from 5 to 1 for best to worse in the following categories: GDP (percentage change), CPI (percentage change), unemployment rate, and interest rate (assume lowest is best). Which economy received the greatest number of total points? Which received the lowest?

16. **WEB-BASED QUESTION** **Per Capita Gross Domestic Product** The OECD (Organization for Economic Cooperation and Development) http://www.oecd.org/std/nahome.htm provides an annual comparison of levels of GDP per capita based on both exchange rates and on purchasing power parities (PPPs). Rank the current top 10 countries using each method. How do the rankings differ, and which method is a more realistic indicator of "output per person"? What explains the difference in Japan's per capita income when calculated using exchange rates and when calculated using PPPs?

8

Macroeconomic Instability: Unemployment and Inflation

In an ideal economy, real GDP expands over time at a brisk, steady pace. Additionally, the price level remains constant or rises only slowly. The result is neither significant unemployment nor inflation. Several periods of U.S. history fit this pattern, but experience shows that steady economic growth, full employment, and a stable price level are not always achieved. Evidence: (1) The inflation rate skyrocketed to 13.5 percent in 1980. (2) During a 16-month period in the early 1980s, real output fell by 3.3 percent. (3) Three million more people were unemployed in 1982 than in 1980. (4) The annual inflation rate rose from 1.9 percent in 1986 to 4.8 percent in 1989. (5) In 1990–1991, output in the U.S. economy declined for the eighth time since 1950.

Here and in the next several chapters we explore the problem of achieving macroeconomic stability: steady economic growth, full employment, and price stability. The present chapter proceeds as follows: First, we establish an overview of the business cycle—the periodic fluctuations in output, employment, and price level characterizing market economies. Then we look in detail at unemployment: What are the various types of unemployment? How is unemployment measured? Why is unemployment undesirable? Finally, we examine inflation—a problem which plagued the United States throughout the 1970s and into the early 1980s. What are inflation's causes and consequences?

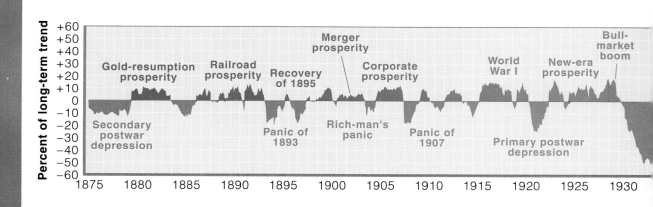

THE BUSINESS CYCLE

Nations seek economic growth, full employment, and price-level stability as their major macroeconomic goals. For the most part, the history of the industrial nations, including the United States, is one of remarkable economic growth. Technological progress, rapid increases in capital, increased skill levels of labor, and other factors have interacted to raise real GDP and real GDP per capita.

But long-run economic growth has not always been steady; it is sometimes interrupted by periods of economic instability, as revealed for the United States in Figure 8-1. In various countries at various times, rapid economic growth has been marred by inflation. At other times, growth has given way to recession and depression, that is, to declines in employment and real output. In short, both unemployment and inflation have interrupted and complicated the long-term trend of economic growth. These difficulties often are associated with *business cycles*.

Phases of the Cycle

The term **business cycle** refers to alternating increases and decreases in the level of economic activity, sometimes extending over several years. Individual business cycles (one "up" and one "down" period) vary substantially in duration and intensity. Yet all display common phases which are variously labeled by different economists. Figure 8-2 shows the four phases of a stylized business cycle.

1. *Peak* We begin our description with a **peak** at which business activity has reached a temporary maximum, such as the middle peak shown in Figure 8-2. Here the economy is at full employment and the level of real output is at or very close to its capacity. The price level is likely to rise during this phase.
2. *Recession* The peak is followed by a **recession**—a period of decline in total output, income, employment, and trade, lasting 6 months or longer. This downturn is marked by the widespread contraction of business in many sectors of the economy. But because many prices are downwardly inflexible, the price level is likely to fall only if the recession is severe and prolonged—that is, if a depression occurs.
3. *Trough* The **trough** of the recession or depression is the phase in which output and employment "bottom out" at their lowest levels. The trough phase of the cycle may be short-lived or quite long.
4. *Recovery* In the expansion or **recovery** phase, output and employment increase toward full employment. As recovery intensifies, the price level may begin to rise before there is full employment and full-capacity production.

Although they all have the same phases, business cycles vary greatly in duration and intensity. Many economists therefore prefer to talk of business *fluctuations* rather than *cycles* because cycles imply regularity while fluctuations do not. The Great Depression of the 1930s resulted in a 40 percent decline in real GDP

FIGURE 8-1 **U.S. business-cycle experience** The horizontal line at 0 represents the long-run growth trend of U.S. economic activity. The alternating periods of prosperity (green) and depressions or recessions (red) indicate deviations from this trend. (*Source:* AmeriTrust Company, Cleveland. Updated.)

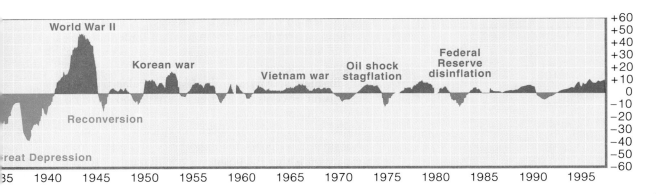

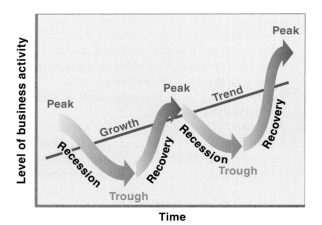

FIGURE 8-2 The business cycle Economists distinguish four phases of the business cycle, with the duration and strength of each phase being highly variable.

----

over a 3-year period in the United States and seriously impaired business activity for a decade. By comparison, more recent U.S. recessions, detailed in Table 8-1, were relatively minor in both intensity and duration.

Causation: A First Glance

Economists have suggested many theories to explain fluctuations in business activity. Some contend that major innovations, such as the railroad, the automobile, and synthetic fibers, have great impact on investment and consumption spending and therefore on

TABLE 8-1   **U.S. recessions since 1950**

Period	Duration, months	Depth (decline in real output)
1953–54	10	−3.7%
1957–58	8	−3.9
1960–61	10	−1.6
1969–70	11	−1.0
1973–75	16	−4.9
1980	6	−2.3
1981–82	16	−3.3
1990–91	8	−1.6

Source: Economic Report of the President, 1993. Updated.

output, employment, and the price level. These major innovations occur irregularly and thus contribute to the variability of economic activity.

Other economists have explained the business cycle in terms of political and random events, as suggested by some of the labeling in Figure 8-1. Wars, for example, can be economically disruptive. A virtually insatiable demand for war goods during hostilities can generate a period of overfull employment and sharp inflation, which is followed by an economic slump when peace returns and military spending plummets.

Still other economists view the business cycle as a purely monetary phenomenon. When government creates too much money, they say, an inflationary boom occurs. In contrast, too little money precipitates a decline in output and employment.

Despite these diverse opinions, most economists see changes in the level of total spending as the immediate cause of cyclical changes in the levels of real output and employment. In a market economy, businesses produce goods or services only if they can sell them profitably. If total spending sinks, many businesses find that it is no longer profitable to produce their usual volume of goods and services. Therefore, output, employment, and incomes will fall. In contrast, a higher level of spending means that more production is profitable, and output, employment, and incomes will rise. Once the economy nears full employment, further gains in real output become more difficult to achieve. Still more spending may raise the price level as consumers bid for the limited amount of available goods.

Noncyclical Fluctuations

Not all changes in business activity result from business cycles. For example, there can be **seasonal variations** in business activity. Pre-Christmas and pre-Easter buying surges cause considerable fluctuations in the tempo of business activity each year, particularly in the retail industry. Agriculture, the automobile industry, and construction are also subject to some degree of seasonality.

Business activity also displays a **secular trend**—expansion or contraction over a long period of years, say, 25, 50, or 100 years. The long-run secular trend for U.S. capitalism has been remarkable expansion. For present purposes, the importance of this long-run expansion is that the business cycle fluctuates around a long-run growth trend. Note in Figure 8-1 that cyclical fluctuations are measured as deviations from the secular growth trend. Also, the stylized cycle of Figure 8-2 is drawn against a trend of growth.

Cyclical Impact: Durables and Nondurables

The business cycle is felt in every nook and cranny of the economy. The parts of the economy are related in such a way that few, if any, escape the negative effects of depression or surging inflation. However, the business cycle affects various individuals and segments of the economy in different ways and degrees.

With regard to production and employment, service industries and industries producing nondurable consumer goods are somewhat insulated from the most severe effects of recession. And, of course, recession actually helps some firms, such as pawnbrokers and law firms specializing in bankruptcies! Who is hit hardest by recession? The firms and industries producing capital goods and consumer durables. The construction industry is particularly vulnerable. Industries and workers producing housing and commercial buildings, heavy capital goods, farm implements, automobiles, refrigerators, gas ranges, and similar products bear the brunt of bad times. Conversely, these "hard-goods" industries benefit most from expansion.

Two facts help explain the vulnerability of these industries to the business cycle.

Postponability Within limits, a purchase of hard goods can be postponed. As the economy slips into bad times, producers frequently delay the purchase of more modern production facilities and the construction of new plants. The business outlook simply does not warrant increases in the stock of capital goods. The firm's present capital facilities and buildings will likely see it through the recession. In good times, capital goods are usually replaced before they completely depreciate. When recession strikes, however, business firms patch up their outmoded equipment and make it do. As a result, investment in capital goods declines sharply. Some firms, having excess plant capacity, may not even bother to replace all the capital they are currently consuming. Net investment for them may be negative.

It is much the same for consumer durables. When recession occurs and the household must trim its budget, plans for the purchase of such durables as major appliances and automobiles feel the ax first. People

repair their old appliances and cars rather than buy new ones. Purchases of many consumer nondurables—food and clothing, for instance—are not so easily postponed; people must clothe themselves and eat. The quantity and quality of purchases of nondurables will decline to some extent, but not so much as will purchases of capital goods and consumer durables.

Monopoly Power Many industries producing capital goods and consumer durables are industries of *high concentration*, in which a small number of large firms dominate the market. These firms have monopoly power—the ability to set above-competitive prices to increase their profit. When recession hits, each of these firms is very reluctant to lower its price because doing so would upset the industry price structure. Specifically, each firm fears that its price cut would spark a *price war*—successive rounds of deeper and deeper price cuts by rivals. This reluctance to lower price means that, at least for a time, the effects of a drop in demand are primarily a decline in production and a decrease in employment.

The reverse pattern is true in nondurables, or *low-concentration* "soft-goods" industries, in which prices are established in competitive markets. Firms in such industries are unable to resist the price declines dictated by the market, so their *prices* decline more rapidly than their levels of production and employment.

Figure 8-3 provides evidence from the Great Depression on this point. It shows the percentage declines in price and quantity in 10 selected industries as the economy fell from peak prosperity in 1929 to the depth of depression in 1933. Generally, high-concentration industries make up the top half of the table and low-concentration industries the bottom half. Note the drastic production declines and relatively modest price declines of the high-concentration industries. Contrast those outcomes to the large price declines and relatively small output declines which occurred in the low-concentration industries. **(Key Question 1)**

QUICK REVIEW 8-1

■ The long-term secular trend of real domestic output has been upward in the United States.

■ The typical business cycle has four phases: peak, recession, trough, and recovery.

■ Industries producing capital goods and consumer durables normally suffer greater output and employment

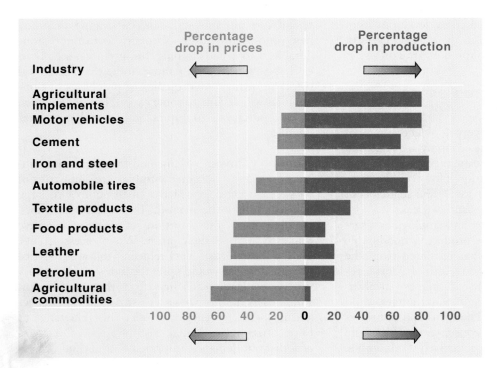

FIGURE 8-3 **Relative price and production declines in 10 industries, 1929–1933** The high-concentration (durables) industries shown in the top half had relatively small price declines and large declines in output during the early years of the Great Depression. In the low-concentration (nondurables) industries of the bottom half, price declines were relatively large, and production fell by relatively small amounts. [*Source:* Gardiner C. Means, *Industrial Prices and Their Relative Inflexibility* (U.S. Government Printing Office, 1935), p. 8.]

declines during recession than do service and nondurable consumer goods industries. The latter suffer greater price declines, however.

UNEMPLOYMENT

"Full employment" is hard to define. A person might think it means that everyone in the labor market—100 percent of the labor force—is employed. But that is not so; some unemployment is normal or warranted.

Types of Unemployment

Before defining full employment, let's first introduce three types of unemployment: frictional, structural, and cyclical.

Frictional Unemployment At any time some workers will be "between jobs." With freedom to choose occupations and jobs, some workers will be voluntarily moving from one job to another. Others will have been fired and will be seeking reemployment. Still others will be temporarily laid off from their jobs because of seasonality, for example, bad weather in the construction industry. And there will

be some particularly young workers searching for their first jobs.

As these unemployed people find jobs or are called back from temporary layoffs, other job seekers and temporarily laid-off workers will replace them in the "unemployment pool." Therefore, even though the specific individuals who are unemployed for these reasons change from month to month, this type of unemployment persists.

Economists use the term **frictional unemployment**—consisting of *search unemployment* and *wait unemployment*—for workers who are either searching for jobs or waiting to take jobs in the near future. "Frictional" correctly implies that the labor market does not operate perfectly or instantaneously—without friction—in matching workers and jobs.

Frictional unemployment is inevitable and, at least in part, desirable. Many workers who are voluntarily between jobs are moving from low-paying, low-productivity jobs to higher-paying, higher-productivity positions. This means greater income for workers and a better allocation of labor resources—and therefore a larger real output—for the economy as a whole.

Structural Unemployment Frictional unemployment blurs into a category called **structural unem-**

ployment. Here, economists use "structural" in the sense of "compositional." Changes over time in consumer demand and in technology alter the "structure" of the total demand for labor, both occupationally and geographically.

Occupationally, some skills will be less in demand or may even become obsolete; demand for other skills, including skills not existing earlier, will expand. Unemployment results because the composition of the labor force does not respond quickly or completely to the new structure of job opportunities. Some workers thus find that they have no marketable talents; their skills and experience have become obsolete or unneeded. They are structurally unemployed due to a *mismatch between their skills and the skills required by employers who are hiring workers.*

Geographically, the demand for labor also changes over time. The migration of industry and thus of employment opportunities from the Snow Belt to the Sun Belt over the past few decades is an example. Another example is the movement of jobs from inner-city factories to suburban industrial parks. These shifting job opportunities mean that some workers become structurally unemployed; there is a *mismatch between their location and the location of job openings.*

The following list presents several illustrations of structural unemployment:

1. Many years ago, highly skilled glassblowers were thrown out of work by the invention of bottle-making machines.

2. Historically, mechanization of agriculture in the south dislodged thousands of low-skilled, poorly educated blacks from their jobs. Many migrated to northern cities and suffered prolonged unemployment because of racial bias and insufficient skills.

3. Many oil field workers in U.S. "oil-patch" states found themselves structurally unemployed when the world price of oil nosedived in the 1980s. Less drilling and oil-related activity took place, resulting in widespread layoffs.

4. In the 1980s many pilots, mechanics, flight attendants, and other airline employees became structurally unemployed as a result of mergers following deregulation of the airline industry.

5. Recently, "corporate downsizing" has occurred in several major U.S. manufacturing industries. Many people losing their jobs have been corporate managers who have found it difficult to find new work.

6. Recent closures of military bases and other defense cutbacks have displaced many workers,

adding them to the roles of the structurally unemployed.

The distinction between frictional and structural unemployment is hazy. The key difference is that frictionally unemployed workers have salable skills and either are located where jobs exist or are able to move to where jobs exist. Structurally unemployed workers cannot easily be reemployed without retraining, additional education, or geographic relocation. Frictional unemployment is short-term; structural unemployment is more long-term and therefore is regarded as more serious.

Cyclical Unemployment **Cyclical unemployment** occurs in the recession phase of the business cycle. It is caused by a deficiency of total spending. As the overall demand for goods and services decreases, employment falls and unemployment rises. For this reason, cyclical unemployment is sometimes called *deficient-demand unemployment.* During the recession year 1982, for example, the unemployment rate rose to 9.7 percent. This compares with a 6.7 percent unemployment rate in the recession year 1991. Cyclical unemployment at the depth of the Great Depression in 1933 was about 25 percent of the labor force.

Definition of "Full Employment"

Full employment does *not* mean zero unemployment. Economists regard frictional and structural unemployment as essentially unavoidable in a dynamic economy. Thus, "full employment" is something less than 100 percent employment of the labor force. Specifically, the **full-employment unemployment rate** is equal to the total frictional and structural unemployment. Stated differently, the full-employment unemployment rate is achieved when cyclical unemployment is zero.

The full-employment rate of unemployment is also referred to as the **natural rate of unemployment.** The real level of domestic output associated with the natural rate of unemployment is called the economy's **potential output.** The economy's potential output is the real output produced when the economy is "fully employed."

From a slightly different vantage point the full-employment or natural rate of unemployment results when labor markets are in balance in the sense that the number of job seekers equals the number of job vacancies. The natural rate of unemployment is some positive amount because it takes time for frictionally unemployed job seekers to find open jobs they can fill. Also, it takes time for the structurally unemployed to achieve the skills and geographic relocation needed for reemployment. If the number of job seekers exceeds available vacancies, labor markets are not in balance; there is a deficiency of total spending and cyclical unemployment is present. But if total spending is excessive, a shortage of labor will arise; the number of job vacancies will exceed the number of workers seeking employment. Here, the actual rate of unemployment will be below the natural rate. Such unusually "tight" labor markets are normally associated with inflation.

The concept of the natural rate of unemployment merits elaboration in two respects:

1. **Not automatic** "Natural" does not mean the economy will always operate at the natural rate and thus realize its potential output. Our brief discussion of the business cycle demonstrated that the economy sometimes operates at an unemployment rate higher than the natural rate—due to cyclical unemployment. In contrast, the economy may on some occasions achieve an unemployment rate below the natural rate. For example, during World War II, when the natural rate was about 4 percent, the pressure of wartime production resulted in an almost unlimited demand for labor. Overtime work was common, as was "moonlighting" (working at more than one job). And the government mandated that some people working in essential industries remain in these jobs, which helped reduce frictional unemployment. As a result, the actual rate of unemployment was below 2 percent in 1943–1945, and it dropped to 1.2 percent in 1944. The economy was producing beyond its potential output, but it was building up considerable inflationary pressure in the process.

2. **Not immutable** The natural rate of unemployment is not forever fixed. It can change when demographics change or when there are changes in society's laws and customs. In the 1960s this unavoidable minimum of frictional and structural unemployment was about 4 percent of the labor force. That is, full employment meant that 96 percent of the labor force was employed. In the 1980s, economists generally agreed that the natural rate of unemployment was about 6 percent. Today, the consensus is that the rate is about 5.5 percent. Why these changes? First, the demographic makeup of the labor force has changed since the 1960s. In the

1970s and 1980s, younger workers became a larger part of the labor force. Because they traditionally have high unemployment rates, their greater relative numbers increased the natural unemployment rate. Second, laws and customs have changed. For example, the unemployment compensation program in the United States has been expanded both in the number of workers covered and in the size of benefits. By cushioning the economic impact of joblessness, unemployment compensation permits unemployed workers to engage in a more deliberate, lengthy job search, thereby increasing frictional unemployment and the natural unemployment rate.

The recent drop in the natural rate from 6 percent to about 5.5 percent has occurred mainly because the growing proportion of younger workers has reversed itself as the baby-boom generation has aged. The labor force now has a larger proportion of middle-aged workers, who traditionally have lower unemployment rates. Also, increased competition in product and labor markets has limited price and wage increases. A decade ago, a 5.5 percent rate of unemployment might have boosted the inflation rate; today, this lower unemployment rate appears to be consistent with a stable, low rate of inflation.

Measurement of Unemployment

Determining the unemployment rate means first determining who is eligible and available to work. Figure 8-4 is a helpful starting point. It shows the total U.S. population as being divided into three groups. One group is made up of people under 16 years of age and people who are institutionalized, for example, in mental hospitals or correctional institutions. These people are not considered potential members of the labor force.

A second group, labeled "Not in labor force," are adults who are potential workers but for some reason—they are homemakers, in school, or retired— are not employed and are not seeking work.

The third group is the **labor force,** which constituted about 50 percent of the total population in 1997. The labor force is all people who are able and willing to work. *Both those who are employed and those who are unemployed but actively seeking work are counted as being in the labor force.* The **unemployment rate** is the percentage of the labor force unemployed:

$$\text{Unemployment rate} = \frac{\text{unemployed}}{\text{labor force}} \times 100$$

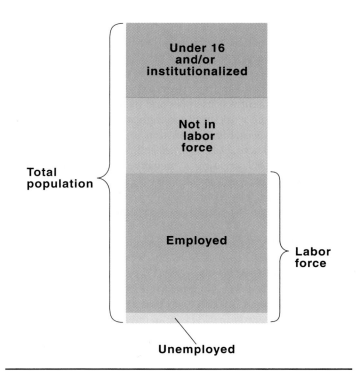

Total population 267,901,000	
Less: Under 16 and/or institutionalized . . . . –64,767,000	
Less: Not in labor force . . . . –66,837,000	
Equals: Labor force 136,297,000	
Employed 129,558,000	
Unemployed 6,739,000	

FIGURE 8-4 **The labor force, employment, and unemployment, 1997**   The labor force consists of persons 16 years of age or older who are not in institutions and who are (1) employed or (2) unemployed but seeking employment.

The statistics below Figure 8-4 show that in 1997 the unemployment rate averaged

$$\frac{6,739,000}{136,297,000} \times 100 = 4.9\%$$

Unemployment rates for select years between 1929 and 1997 are provided on the inside covers of this book.

The U.S. Bureau of Labor Statistics (BLS) determines who is employed and who is not by a nationwide random survey of some 60,000 households each month. A series of questions is asked as to which members of the household are working, unemployed and looking for work, not looking for work, and so on. From the answers, an unemployment rate is developed for the entire nation. Despite the use of scientific sampling and interviewing techniques, the data collected in this survey are subject to criticism:

1. ***Part-time employment***   The official data include all part-time workers as fully employed. In 1997 about 18.9 million people worked part-time because of personal choice. But another 2.8 million part-time workers either wanted to work full-time and could not find suitable full-time work or worked fewer hours because of a temporary slack in consumer demand. These last two groups were, in effect, partially employed and partially unemployed. By counting them as fully employed, say critics, the official BLS data understate the unemployment rate.

2. ***Discouraged workers***   You must be actively seeking work to be counted as unemployed. An unemployed individual who is not actively seeking employment is classified as "not in the labor force." The problem is that many workers, after unsuccessfully seeking employment for a time,

become discouraged and drop out of the labor force. The number of such **discouraged workers** is larger during recession than prosperity; an estimated 1.25 million people fell into this category in recession-year 1991. By not counting discouraged workers as unemployed, say critics, official data understate the unemployment rate. **(Key Question 3)**

Economic Cost of Unemployment

Unemployment above the natural rate involves great economic and social costs.

GDP Gap and Okun's Law The basic economic cost of unemployment is forgone output. *When the economy fails to create enough jobs for all who are able and willing to work, potential production of goods and services is irretrievably lost.* In terms of Chapter 2's analysis, unemployment means that society is located at some point inside its production possibilities curve. Economists measure this sacrificed output as the **GDP gap**—the amount by which *actual GDP* falls short of *potential GDP.*

Potential GDP is determined by assuming that the natural rate of unemployment exists. The growth of potential GDP is simply projected forward on the basis of the economy's "normal" growth rate of real GDP. Figure 8-5 shows the GDP gap for recent years in the United States. It also indicates the close correlation between the actual unemployment rate (Figure 8-5b) and the GDP gap (Figure 8-5a). The higher the unemployment rate, the larger the GDP gap.

Macroeconomist Arthur Okun quantified the relationship between the unemployment rate and the GDP gap. **Okun's law,** based on recent estimates, indicates that *for every 1 percentage point which the actual unemployment rate exceeds the natural rate, a GDP gap of about 2 percent occurs.* With this information, we can calculate the absolute loss of output associated with any above-natural unemployment rate. For example, in 1992 the unemployment rate was 7.4 percent, or 1.4 percentage points above the 6.0 percent natural rate of unemployment then existing. Multiplying this 1.4 percent by Okun's 2 indicates that 1992's GDP gap was 2.8 percent of potential GDP (in real terms). Then, by applying this 2.8 percent loss to 1992's potential GDP of $6300 billion, we find that the economy sacrificed $176 billion of real output because the natural rate of unemployment was not achieved. **(Key Question 5)**

As you can see in Figure 8-5, sometimes the economy's actual output will exceed its potential output. (We already noted that this happened during World War II when unemployment rates fell below 2 percent. Extra shifts of workers were employed, capital equipment was used beyond its designed capacity, and overtime work and moonlighting were common.) We observe in Figure 8-5 that an economic expansion caused actual GDP to exceed potential GDP in 1988 and 1989, creating a "negative" GDP gap. Potential GDP can occasionally be exceeded, but the excess of actual over potential GDP eventually causes inflation and cannot be sustained indefinitely.

Unequal Burdens An increase in the unemployment rate from 5.5 to, say, 9 or 10 percent might be more tolerable to society if every worker's hours of work and wage income were reduced proportionally. But this is not the case. Part of the burden of unemployment is that its cost is unequally distributed.

Table 8-2 (page 158) examines unemployment rates for various labor market groups for 2 years. The 1990–1991 recession pushed the 1992 unemployment rate to 7.4 percent. In contrast, the economy achieved full employment in 1996, with a 5.4 percent unemployment rate. By observing the large variance in unemployment rates for the different groups *within each year* and comparing the rates *between the 2 years,* we can generalize as follows:

1. *Occupation* White-collar workers enjoy lower unemployment rates than blue-collar workers. White-collar workers generally are employed in less cyclically vulnerable industries (such as services and nondurable goods) or are self-employed. Also, white-collar workers are usually less subject to unemployment during recession than blue-collar workers. Businesses want to retain their more skilled white-collar workers, in whom they have invested the expense of training. But it is not always this way. During the 1990–1991 recession, many firms "downsized" their management structures, discharging more white-collar workers than ever before. The unemployment rate of white-collar workers increased more rapidly than that of blue-collar laborers. Nevertheless, the unemployment rate of white-collar workers remained far below that of blue-collar workers.

2. *Age* Teenagers incur much higher unemployment rates than adults. Teenagers have low skill levels, more frequently quit their jobs, are more frequently discharged from jobs, and have little

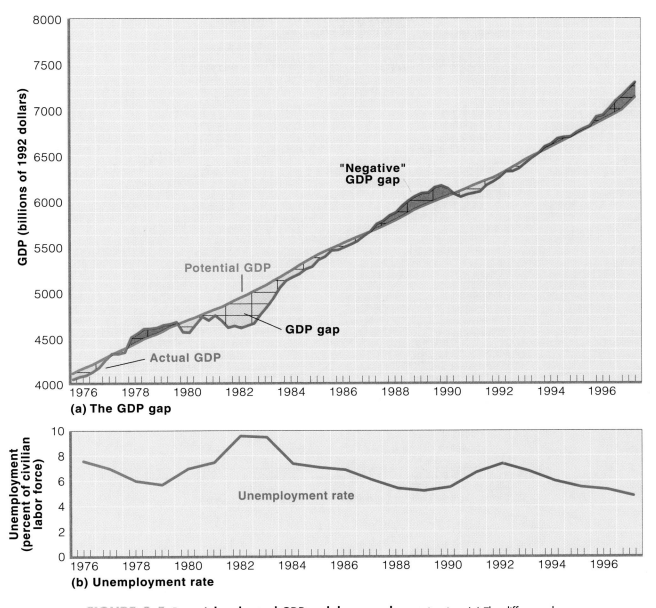

FIGURE 8-5 Potential and actual GDP and the unemployment rate (a) The difference between potential GDP and actual GDP is the GDP gap. The GDP gap measures the output the economy sacrifices because it fails to use fully its production potential. (b) A high unemployment rate means a large GDP gap, and vice versa. [*Source: Economic Report of the President* and Robert J. Gordon, *Macroeconomics*, 7th ed. (New York: Addison-Wesley, 1998). Updated.]

geographic mobility. Many unemployed teenagers are new in the labor market, searching for their first job.

3. *Race* The unemployment rate for blacks—adults and teenagers—has been roughly *twice* that of whites.

Factors explaining this discrepancy include discrimination in education and the labor market, the concentration of blacks in less skilled (blue-collar) occupations, and the geographic isolation of blacks in central-city areas where employment

TABLE 8-2   Unemployment rates by demographic group: recession (1992) and full employment (1996)*

Demographic group	Unemployment rate, 1992	Unemployment rate, 1996
Overall	7.4%	5.4%
Occupation:		
Blue-collar	9.3	7.1
White-collar	4.6	3.4
Age:		
16–19	20.2	18.1
Black, 16–19	39.8	30.6
White, 16–19	17.1	14.2
Male, 20+	7.0	4.6
Female, 20+	6.3	4.8
Race:		
Black	14.1	10.5
White	6.5	4.7
Gender:		
Female	6.9	5.4
Male	7.8	5.4
Education		
Less than high school diploma	13.5	10.9
High school degree only	7.7	5.5
College degree or more	2.9	2.2
Duration:		
15 weeks or more	2.6	1.7

*Civilian labor-force data. In 1992 the economy was suffering the lingering unemployment effects of the 1990–1991 recession.
Sources: Economic Report of the President; Employment and Earnings; Census Bureau.

opportunities for new labor market entrants are minimal.

4. Gender   Male and female unemployment rates are highly similar. The lower unemployment rate for women in 1992 occurred because there are more male than female workers in such cyclically vulnerable hard-goods industries as automobile, steel, and construction.

5. Education   Less educated workers, on average, have higher unemployment rates than workers with more education. Less education is usually associated with lower-skilled, less permanent jobs, more time in between jobs, and jobs which are more vulnerable to cyclical layoff.

6. Duration   The number of persons unemployed for long periods—15 weeks or more—as a percentage of the labor force is much less than the overall unemployment rate. But this percentage rises significantly during recessions. The "long-term" unemployed were only 1.7 percent of the labor force in 1996 compared with the overall 5.4 percent unemployment rate. A large proportion of unemployment is of relatively short duration. But also observe that the long-term unemployed were 2.6 percent of the labor force in 1992, implying more economic hardship when recessions occur.

Noneconomic Costs

Severe cyclical unemployment is more than an economic malady; it is a social catastrophe. Depression means idleness. And idleness means loss of skills, loss of self-respect, a plummeting of morale, family disintegration, and sociopolitical unrest. A job

> . . . gives hope for material and social advancement. It is a way of providing one's children a better start in life. It may mean the only honorable way of escape from the poverty of one's parents. It helps to overcome racial and other social barriers. In short . . . a job is the passport to freedom and to a better life. To deprive people of jobs is to read them out of our society.[1]

History demonstrates that severe unemployment leads to rapid and sometimes violent social and political change. The shift of U.S. political philosophy toward the left during the Depression of the 1930s is an example. The Depression-inspired New Deal was a revolution in U.S. political and economic thinking. Witness also Hitler's ascent to power against a background of unemployment. Furthermore, the high unemployment among some minorities unquestionably has been a cause of the unrest and violence which periodically plague cities in the United States and elsewhere. At the individual level, research links increases in suicide, homicide, cardiovascular mortality, and mental illness to high unemployment.

International Comparisons

Unemployment rates vary greatly among nations at any specific time. One reason for the differences is that nations have different natural rates of unemployment. Another explanation is that nations may be in different phases of their business cycles. Global Perspective 8-1 shows unemployment rates for five industrialized nations in recent years. Historically, the United States has had higher unemployment rates than most industrially advanced nations. But this pattern changed in the 1980s. The U.S. unemployment rate has been below the rates in the United Kingdom, Germany, and France in several years since 1987.

QUICK REVIEW 8-2

■ Unemployment is of three general types: frictional, structural, and cyclical.

■ The natural unemployment rate (frictional plus structural) is presently estimated to be about 5.5 percent.

■ Society loses real GDP when cyclical unemployment occurs; according to Okun's law, for each 1 percentage point of unemployment above the natural rate, the U.S.

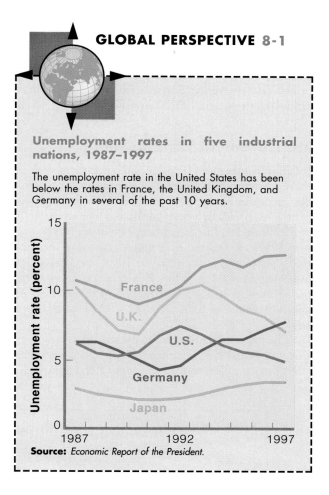

GLOBAL PERSPECTIVE 8-1

Unemployment rates in five industrial nations, 1987–1997

The unemployment rate in the United States has been below the rates in France, the United Kingdom, and Germany in several of the past 10 years.

Source: *Economic Report of the President.*

economy suffers a 2 percent decline in real GDP below potential.

■ Blue-collar workers, teenagers, blacks, and less educated workers bear a disproportionate burden of unemployment.

INFLATION DEFINED AND MEASURED

We now turn to inflation as an aspect of macroeconomic instability. The problems inflation poses are more subtle than those of unemployment.

Meaning of Inflation

Inflation is *a rising general level of prices.* This does not mean that *all* prices are rising. Even during periods of rapid inflation, some prices may be relatively constant and others falling. For example, although the United

---
[1]Henry R. Reuss, *The Critical Decade* (New York: McGraw-Hill Book Company, 1964), p. 133.

States experienced high rates of inflation in the 1970s and early 1980s, the prices of video recorders, digital watches, and personal computers declined. As you will see, one troublesome aspect of inflation is that prices rise unevenly. Some streak upward; others ascend leisurely; still others do not rise at all.

Measurement of Inflation

Inflation is measured by price-index numbers such as those introduced in Chapter 7. Recall that a price index measures the general level of prices in any year relative to prices in a base period.

To illustrate, the consumer price index (CPI) now uses 1982–1984 as the base period, meaning that period's price level is set equal to 100. The 1997 price index was about 161. Thus consumer prices were 61 percent higher in 1997 than in 1982–1984, so a set of goods which cost $100 in 1982–1984 cost $161 in 1997.

The *rate* of inflation can be calculated for any specific year (say, 1997) by subtracting the previous year's (1996) price index from that year's (1997) index, dividing by the previous year's index, and multiplying by 100 to express the result as a percentage. As an example, the CPI was 156.9 in 1996 and 160.5 in 1997, so the rate of inflation for 1997 is calculated as follows:

$$\text{Rate of inflation} = \frac{160.5 - 156.9}{156.9} \times 100 = 2.3\%$$

The so-called **rule of 70** provides a quantitative grasp of inflation's effect. If we divide the number 70 by the annual rate of inflation, the quotient is the number of years it takes for inflation to double the price level:

$$\begin{array}{l}\text{Approximate} \\ \text{number of years} \\ \text{required to double} \\ \text{price level}\end{array} = \frac{70}{\begin{array}{c}\text{annual percentage rate} \\ \text{of inflation}\end{array}}$$

Examples: A 3 percent annual rate of inflation will double the price level in about 23($= 70 \div 3$) years. Inflation of 8 percent per year will double the price level in about 9($= 70 \div 8$) years. The rule of 70 is generally applicable. You can use it, for example, to estimate how long it will take for real GDP *or* your savings account to double. **(Key Question 7)**

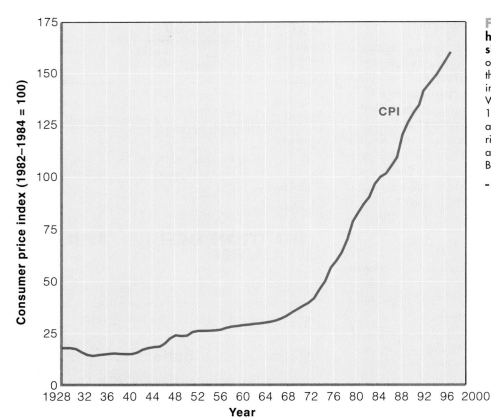

FIGURE 8-6 Price-level behavior in the United States since 1928 The price stability of the 1920s and the deflation of the early 1930s gave way to sharp inflation in the immediate post-World War II period. The 1951–1965 period saw a reasonably stable price level, but the period since 1965 has clearly been an "age of inflation." (*Source:* Bureau of Labor Statistics.)

Facts of Inflation

Figure 8-6 shows inflation in the United States since 1928. The curve represents annual values of the consumer price index relative to the base period (here, 1982–1984). That is, the CPI for the 1982–1984 period is arbitrarily set at 100.

Although the past three decades have been an "age of inflation," the U.S. economy has not always been inflation-prone. The price level was stable in the prosperous 1920s and declined—*deflation* occurred—during the early years of the Great Depression of the 1930s. Prices then rose in the immediate years after World War II (1945–1948). However, overall price stability characterized the 1951–1965 period, when the average annual increase in the price level was less than 1.5 percent. But the price increases which began in the late 1960s and surged in the 1970s introduced Americans to double-digit inflation. In 1979 and 1980 the price level rose 12 to 13 percent annually. However, by the 1990s, the inflation rate had settled back into a 2 to 4 percent annual range. Historical rates of inflation are listed on the inside covers of this textbook.

Inflation is not unique to the United States; all industrial nations have experienced this problem. Global Perspective 8-2 traces the post-1986 annual inflation rates of the United States, the United Kingdom, Japan, France, and Germany. Observe that inflation in the United States has been neither unusually high nor low relative to inflation in these other industrial countries.

Some nations have had double-digit, triple-digit, or even higher annual rates of inflation in recent years. In 1996, for example, the annual inflation rate in Turkey was 82 percent; in Venezuela, 120 percent; and in Bulgaria, 123 percent. A few nations experienced astronomical rates of inflation in 1996: Turkmenistan, 992 percent; and Angola, 4145 percent!

Causes: Theories of Inflation

Economists distinguish between two types of inflation: *demand-pull inflation* and *cost-push inflation*.

Demand-Pull Inflation   Traditionally, changes in the price level are attributed to an excess of total spending beyond the economy's capacity to produce. Because resources are fully employed, the business sector cannot respond to this excess demand by ex-

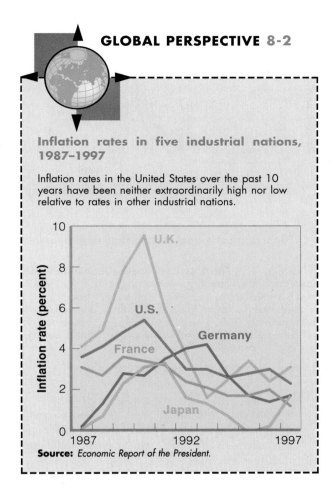

GLOBAL PERSPECTIVE 8-2

Inflation rates in five industrial nations, 1987–1997

Inflation rates in the United States over the past 10 years have been neither extraordinarily high nor low relative to rates in other industrial nations.

Source: *Economic Report of the President.*

panding output, so the excess demand bids up the prices of the limited real output, causing **demand-pull inflation.** The essence of this type of inflation is "too much spending chasing too few goods."

But the relationship between total spending, on the one hand, and output, employment, and the price level, on the other, is not so simple. Figure 8-7 will help us unravel the complications. This figure is a graph of the price level and real domestic output, with the full-employment level of output designated Q_f. The three ranges marked on the curve are ranges of price-level and real-output changes. Let's examine increases in total spending—represented by the left-to-right arrow—to see where demand-pull inflation arises:

1. *Range 1*   Toward the left in range 1, output is very low relative to the economy's full-employment output. This implies a very low level of total spending—the sum of consumption,

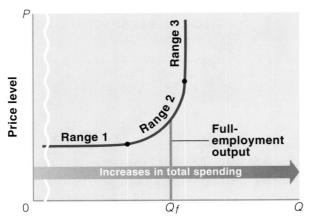

FIGURE 8-7 The price level and the level of real GDP (and thus employment) As total spending increases, the price level first stays constant as real output expands (range 1); then increases as real output approaches, reaches, and exceeds the full-employment level (range 2); and finally jumps sharply as real output nears and attains its maximum capacity (range 3). Demand-pull inflation occurs in ranges 2 and 3.

- -

investment, government, and net export spending—and a substantial GDP gap. Unemployment rates are high and businesses have much idle production capacity.

Assume now that total spending increases. As it does, real domestic output will increase, and the unemployment rate will fall. But there is little or no increase in the price level in range 1. Since firms have excess production capacity, their costs and thus their prices do not rise as they increase their output. Large amounts of idle human and property resources will be put back to work at their *existing* prices. An unemployed worker does not ask for a wage increase when called back to a job.

2. **Range 2** As output continues to expand in response to still further increases in total spending, the economy enters range 2. Here it approaches and will eventually surpass its full-employment output.

Even before full employment is achieved, the price level may begin to rise. As production expands, supplies of idle resources disappear at different rates in various sectors and industries. Bottlenecks develop in some industries, even though most still have room to expand. Some industries are able to reach their full-production

capacity before others and thus cannot respond to further increases in total spending for their products. Consequently, costs and therefore prices rise. Then, as still more labor is hired, workplaces become increasingly congested, and each added worker contributes less to output. Labor costs rise further, forcing up more product prices. As full employment is approached, many firms hire less-qualified workers, and this, too, contributes to rising costs and prices. The price-level increases which occur before Q_f is reached are sometimes called *premature inflation*; it is demand-pull inflation taking place prior to the economy's achieving its full-employment output.

As total spending in range 2 increases *beyond* output Q_f, still higher prices induce some businesses to demand, and some households to supply, resources beyond the full-employment level of output. Firms may employ additional work shifts and use overtime to achieve greater output. Households may supply additional workers such as teenagers and spouses, who previously had chosen not to enter the labor force. In this part of range 2, the part to the right of Q_f, the rate of unemployment falls below the natural rate and the actual GDP exceeds potential GDP. Here, the pace of inflation usually quickens.

3. **Range 3** As total spending increases into range 3, the economy simply cannot supply more resources. Firms cannot respond to increases in demand by increasing output. Real domestic output is at an absolute maximum, so further increases in demand do only one thing: raise the price level. The rate of inflation may be high and growing because total demand greatly exceeds society's absolute capacity to produce. The demand-pull inflation of range 2 becomes the *pure* demand-pull inflation of range 3. There is no increase in real output to absorb some of the increased spending.

Chapter 7's distinction between nominal and real GDP points up another feature of inflation. As long as the price level is constant (range 1), increases in nominal and real GDP are identical. But with inflation in range 2, nominal GDP is rising faster than real GDP, so nominal GDP must be "deflated" to measure changes in physical output. In range 3, nominal GDP is rising—perhaps rapidly due to high inflation—but real GDP is constant. In brief, the demand-pull inflation of ranges 2 and 3 breaks the equality between nominal and real GDP.

Cost-Push or Supply-Side Inflation

Inflation may also arise on the supply or cost side of the market. During several periods in our economic history the price level has risen even though aggregate demand was not excessive. These were periods when output and employment were both *declining* (evidence of a deficiency of total demand) while the general price level was *increasing*.

The theory of **cost-push inflation** explains rising prices in terms of factors which raise **per-unit production costs**. A per-unit production cost is the average cost of a particular level of output. This average cost is found by dividing the total cost of all resource inputs by the amount of output produced. That is,

$$\text{Per-unit production cost} = \frac{\text{total input cost}}{\text{units of output}}$$

Rising per-unit production costs squeeze profits and reduce the amount of output firms are willing to supply at the existing price level. As a result, the economy's supply of goods and services declines. This decline in supply drives up the price level. Under this scenario, costs are *pushing* the price level upward, rather than demand *pulling* it upward, as with demand-pull inflation.

Two potential sources of cost-push inflation are increases in nominal wages and increases in the prices of nonwage inputs such as raw materials and energy:

1. **Wage-push variant** One variation of cost-push inflation theory suggests that, under some circumstances, unions may be a source of inflation. Unions exert some control over nominal wage rates through collective bargaining. Suppose they demand and receive large increases in wages. Also suppose that these wage gains set the standard for wage increases paid to nonunion workers. If the economy's wage gains are excessive relative to such offsetting factors as an increase in output per hour worked, then producers' per-unit production costs will rise. Firms will respond by reducing the amount of goods and services they offer for sale. If there is no change in demand, this decline in supply will increase the price level. Because the culprit is an excessive increase in nominal wages, this variation of cost-push inflation is sometimes called *wage-push inflation*.

2. **Supply-shock variant** The *supply-shock* variation of cost-push inflation traces rising production costs—and therefore rising product prices—to abrupt, unanticipated increases in the costs of raw

materials or energy inputs. The rocketing prices of imported oil in 1973–1974 and again in 1979–1980 are good illustrations. As energy prices rose during these periods, the costs of producing and transporting virtually every product in the economy increased. Rapid cost-push inflation ensued.

Complexities

The real world is more complex than the distinction between demand-pull and cost-push inflation suggests. It is difficult to distinguish between demand-pull and cost-push inflation unless the original source of inflation is known. For example, suppose a major boost in total spending occurs in a fully employed economy, causing demand-pull inflation. But as the demand-pull stimulus works its way through various product and resource markets, individual firms find their wage costs, material costs, and fuel prices rising. From their perspective they must raise their prices because production costs (someone else's prices) have risen. Although this inflation is clearly demand-pull in origin, it may appear to be cost-push inflation to business firms and to government. Without proper identification of the originating source, government may mistakenly focus public policy on slowing rising costs rather than on reducing excessive total spending.

Another complexity is that cost-push inflation and demand-pull inflation differ in their sustainability. Demand-pull inflation will continue as long as there is excess total spending. Cost-push inflation automatically is self-limiting; it will die out by itself. Increased per-unit costs will lead to reduced supply, which means decreased real output and employment. These decreases will constrain further per-unit cost increases. In other words, cost-push inflation generates a recession. And in a recession, the efforts of workers and other resource suppliers are on keeping their resources employed, not on pushing up the prices of the resources they command.

QUICK REVIEW 8-3

■ Inflation is a rising general level of prices and is measured as a percentage change in a price index such as the CPI.

■ The U.S. inflation rate has been within the middle range of rates of other advanced industrial nations and far below the rates experienced by some nations.

■ Demand-pull inflation occurs when total spending exceeds the economy's ability to provide goods and services at the existing price level; total spending *pulls* the price level upward.

■ Cost-push inflation occurs when factors such as excessive wage increases and rapid increases in raw-material prices drive up per-unit production costs; higher costs *push* the price level upward.

REDISTRIBUTION EFFECTS OF INFLATION

We now turn from the causes of inflation to its effects. In this section we consider how inflation redistributes income; in the next section, we examine the possible effects of rising prices on domestic output.

The historical relationship between the price level and domestic output is ambiguous. Until recently, real output and the price level have risen and fallen together. In the past two decades, however, there have been times when real output has fallen while prices have continued to rise. We will dodge this difficulty by assuming here that real output is constant and at the full-employment level. Holding real output and income constant will allow us to isolate the effects of inflation on the distribution of that income: With a fixed national income pie, how does inflation affect the size of the slices going to different income receivers? Before we can answer, we need to discuss some terminology.

Nominal and Real Income You must first be clear about the difference between money (or nominal) income and real income. **Nominal income** is the number of dollars received as wages, rent, interest, or profits. **Real income** measures the amount of goods and services nominal income can buy.

If your nominal income increases faster than the price level, your real income will rise. If the price level increases faster than your nominal income, your real income will decline. We can determine approximately how real income changes with this formula:

Percentage change in real income ≈ percentage change in nominal income − percentage change in price level

If your nominal income rises by 10 percent and the price level rises by 6 percent in the same period, your real income will *increase* by about 4 percent. Conversely, a 6 percent increase in nominal income

accompanied by 10 percent inflation will *decrease* your real income by approximately 4 percent.[2]

The main point is this: While inflation reduces the purchasing power of the dollar—the amount of goods and services each dollar will buy—it does not necessarily decrease a person's real income. Your real income (or standard of living) drops only when your nominal income fails to keep pace with inflation.

Anticipations The redistribution effects of inflation depend on whether or not it is expected. With fully expected or **anticipated inflation,** an income receiver *may* be able to avoid or lessen the adverse effects inflation would otherwise have on real income. The generalizations which immediately follow assume **unanticipated inflation**—inflation whose full extent was *not* expected.

Fixed-Nominal-Income Receivers

Our distinction between nominal and real incomes shows that *inflation penalizes people who receive fixed nominal incomes.* Inflation redistributes real income away from fixed-income receivers and toward others in the economy. The classic case is the elderly couple living on a private pension or annuity providing a fixed amount of nominal income each month. They may have retired in, say, 1984 on what appeared to be an adequate pension. However, by 1998 they will discover that the purchasing power of that pension has been cut by one-half.

Similarly, landlords who receive lease payments of fixed dollar amounts will be hurt by inflation as they receive dollars of declining value over time. To a lesser extent some white-collar workers, some public sector employees whose incomes are dictated by fixed pay scales, and families living on fixed levels of welfare will also be victims of inflation. Note, however, that the United States has *indexed* social security benefits. This means that these payments increase when the

---

[2]A more precise calculation follows Chapter 7's process for changing nominal GDP to real GDP. Thus,

$$\text{Real income} = \frac{\text{nominal income}}{\text{price index (in hundredths)}}$$

In our first illustration, if nominal income rises by 10 percent from $100 to $110 and the price level (index) increases by 6 percent from 100 to 106, then real income has increased as follows:

$$\frac{\$110}{1.06} = \$103.77$$

The 4 percent increase in real income shown by the simple formula in the text is a reasonable approximation of the 3.77 percent yielded by our more precise formula.

consumer price index increases, preventing or lessening erosion from inflation.

Some people living on flexible incomes *may* benefit from inflation. The nominal incomes of such people may spurt ahead of the price level, with the result that their real incomes are enhanced. As an example, workers in expanding industries who are represented by strong unions may keep their nominal wages apace with, or ahead of, the rate of inflation.

Some wage earners are hurt by inflation. Those in declining industries or without strong unions may find that the price level jumps ahead of their money incomes.

Business executives and other profit receivers may benefit from inflation. If product prices rise faster than resource prices, business receipts will grow at a faster rate than costs. Thus some—but not necessarily all—profit incomes will outdistance the rising tide of inflation.

Savers

Inflation hurts savers. *As prices rise, the real value, or purchasing power, of a nest egg of savings deteriorates.* Savings accounts, insurance policies, annuities, and other fixed-value paper assets once adequate to meet rainy-day contingencies or provide for a comfortable retirement decline in real value during inflation. The simplest case is the individual who hoards money as a cash balance. A $1000 cash balance would have lost one-half its real value between 1980 and 1995. Of course, most forms of savings earn interest. But the value of savings will still decline if the rate of inflation exceeds the rate of interest.

Example: A household may save $1000 in a certificate of deposit (CD) in a commercial bank or savings and loan association at 6 percent annual interest. But if inflation is 13 percent (as in 1980), the real value or purchasing power of that $1000 will be cut to about $938 by the end of the year. The saver will receive $1060 (equal to $1000 plus $60 of interest), but deflating that $1060 for 13 percent inflation means that its real value is only about $938 (= $1060 ÷ 1.13).

Debtors and Creditors

Inflation redistributes real income between debtors and creditors. *Unanticipated inflation benefits debtors (borrowers) at the expense of creditors (lenders).* Suppose you borrow $1000 from a bank, to be repaid in 2 years. If in that time the general level of prices dou-

bles, the $1000 which you repay will have only half the purchasing power of the $1000 originally borrowed. True, if we ignore interest charges, the same number of dollars will be repaid as was borrowed. But because of inflation, each of these dollars will buy only half as much as it did when the loan was negotiated. As prices go up, the value of the dollar comes down. Thus, the borrower is loaned "dear" dollars but, because of inflation, pays back "cheap" dollars.

The inflation of the past several decades has been a windfall to those who purchased homes in earlier periods with low, fixed-interest-rate mortgages. Inflation has greatly reduced the real burden of their mortgage indebtedness. They have also benefited because the nominal value of housing has increased more rapidly then the overall price level.

The Federal government, which has amassed $5.4 trillion of public debt over the decades, has also benefited from inflation. Historically, the Federal government has regularly paid off its loans by taking out new ones. Inflation has permitted the Treasury to pay off its loans with dollars which have less purchasing power than the dollars it originally borrowed. Nominal national income and therefore tax collections rise with inflation; the amount of public debt owed does not. Thus, inflation reduces the real burden of the public debt to the Federal government. Because inflation benefits the Federal government in this way, some economists have questioned whether society can really expect government to be zealous in its efforts to halt inflation.

In fact, some nations such as Brazil once used inflation so extensively to reduce the real value of their debt that lenders forced them to borrow money in U.S. dollars or in some other relatively stable currency instead of their own currency. This prevents them from using domestic inflation as a means of subtly "defaulting" on their debt. Any inflation they generate will reduce the value of their own currencies but not the value of the dollar-denominated debt they must pay back.

Anticipated Inflation

The redistribution effects of inflation are less severe or are eliminated if people (1) anticipate inflation and (2) can adjust their nominal incomes to reflect expected price-level changes. The prolonged inflation which began in the late 1960s prompted many unions in the 1970s to insist on labor contracts with **cost-of-living adjustment** (COLA) clauses; such agreements automatically raise workers' nominal incomes when inflation occurs.

Similarly, the redistribution of income from lender to borrower might be altered if inflation is anticipated. Suppose a lender (perhaps a commercial bank or savings and loan institution) and a borrower (a household) both agree that 5 percent is a fair rate of interest on a 1-year loan *provided* the price level is stable. But assume inflation has been occurring and is expected to be 6 percent over the next year. If the bank lends the household $100 at 5 percent interest, the bank will be paid back $105 at the end of the year. But if 6 percent inflation does occur during that year, the purchasing power of the $105 will have been reduced to about $99. The *lender* will in effect have paid the *borrower* $1 to use the lender's money for a year.

The lender can avoid this subsidy by charging an **inflation premium,** that is, by increasing the interest rate by 6 percent, the amount of the anticipated inflation. By charging 11 percent, the lender will receive back $111 at the end of the year. Adjusted for the 6 percent inflation, that amount will have purchasing power of today's $105. The result then will be a mutually agreeable transfer of purchasing power from borrower to lender of $5, or 5 percent, for the use of $100 for 1 year. Financial institutions have also developed variable-interest-rate mortgages to protect themselves from the adverse effects of inflation. (Incidentally, this example points out that, rather than being a cause of inflation, high nominal interest rates are a consequence of inflation.)

Our illustration shows the difference between the real rate of interest and the money or nominal rate of interest. The **real interest rate** is *the percentage increase in purchasing power which the lender receives from the borrower.* In our example the real interest rate is 5 percent. The **nominal interest rate** is *the percentage increase in money which the lender receives.* In our example the nominal rate of interest is 11 percent. The difference in these two concepts is that the real interest rate is adjusted or deflated for the rate of inflation while the nominal interest rate is not. The nominal interest rate is the sum of the real interest rate plus the premium paid to offset the expected rate of inflation. These distinctions are illustrated in Figure 8-8.

Addenda

Three final points must be mentioned:

1. *Deflation* The effects of unanticipated deflation are substantially the reverse of those of inflation. *Assuming no change in total output,* people with fixed money incomes will find their real in-

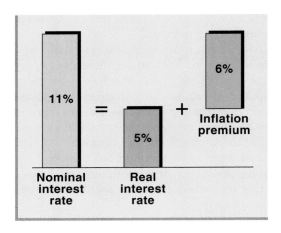

FIGURE 8-8 **The inflation premium and nominal and real interest rates** The inflation premium—the expected rate of inflation—gets built into the nominal interest rate. Here, the nominal interest rate of 11 percent comprises the real interest rate of 5 percent plus the inflation premium of 6 percent.

comes enhanced. Creditors will benefit at the expense of debtors. And savers will discover the purchasing power of their savings has grown because of the falling prices.

2. *Mixed effects* The fact that any person may be an income earner, a holder of financial assets, and an owner of real assets simultaneously will likely cushion the redistribution impact of inflation. If the individual owns fixed-value monetary assets (savings accounts, bonds, and insurance policies), inflation will lessen their real value. But that same inflation may increase the real value of any property assets (a house, land) which the person owns.

In short, many individuals are simultaneously hurt and benefitted by inflation. All these effects must be considered before we can conclude that any particular person's net position is better or worse because of inflation.

3. *Arbitrariness* The redistribution effects of inflation are *arbitrary;* they occur regardless of society's goals and values. Inflation lacks a social conscience and takes from some and gives to others, whether they be rich, poor, young, old, healthy, or infirm.

QUICK REVIEW 8-4

■ Inflation arbitrarily harms those who receive relatively fixed nominal incomes, and it helps some people who receive flexible nominal incomes.

■ Unanticipated inflation penalizes savers, and it benefits debtors at the expense of creditors.

■ The nominal interest rate exceeds the real interest rate by the expected rate of inflation.

OUTPUT EFFECTS OF INFLATION

We assumed in the last section that the economy's real output is fixed at the full-employment level. In that situation, the redistribution effects of inflation and deflation are that some groups gain real income at the expense of others. If the size of the pie is fixed and inflation causes some groups to get larger slices, other groups must get smaller slices. But, in fact, the level of domestic output—the size of the pie—may vary as the price level changes.

There is uncertainty and disagreement as to whether inflation will be accompanied by a rising or a falling real output. We will consider three scenarios, one associating inflation with an expanding output and two associating it with a declining output.

Stimulus of Demand-Pull Inflation

Some economists argue that full employment can be achieved only if some modest amount of inflation is tolerated. They base their reasoning on the ideas illustrated by Figure 8-7.

We know that the levels of real output and employment depend on total spending. If spending is low, the economy will operate in range 1. In this range the price level is stable, but real output is substantially below its potential and the unemployment rate is high. If total spending increases so that the economy moves into range 2, society must accept a higher price level—some amount of inflation—to achieve greater real output and the accompanying lower unemployment rates.

If further increases in total spending pull the economy into range 3, that spending will be purely inflationary because the full-capacity level of real output will have been reached.

It seems, then, that in range 2 there is a tradeoff between output (and thus employment) and inflation. Some moderate amount of inflation must be accepted if we are to realize high levels of output and employment. The high levels of spending which give us higher levels of output and low unemployment rates also cause some inflation. That implies there is an in-

verse relationship between the inflation rate and the unemployment rate.

This perspective has been criticized in recent years. Many economists feel that any tradeoff between the inflation rate and the unemployment rate is transitory and that there is no such tradeoff in the long run. This controversy will be explored in Chapter 16.

Cost-Push Inflation and Unemployment

There is an equally plausible set of circumstances in which inflation might reduce both output and employment. Suppose the level of total spending is initially such that the economy is enjoying full employment *and* price-level stability. If cost-push inflation occurs, the existing level of total spending will now buy less real output because of the higher price level. Thus, real output will soon fall and unemployment will rise.

Economic events of the 1970s are an example of how inflation can reduce real output. In late 1973 the Organization of Petroleum Exporting Countries (OPEC) became very effective in exerting its market power and was able to quadruple the price of oil. The cost-push inflationary effects generated rapid price-level increases in the 1973–1975 period. At the same time the U.S. unemployment rate rose from slightly less than 5 percent in 1973 to 8.5 percent in 1975. Similar outcomes occurred in 1979–1980 in response to a second OPEC oil supply shock.

Hyperinflation and Breakdown

Some economists express anxiety over our first scenario. They are fearful that the mild, "creeping" inflation which might initially accompany an economic recovery phase can snowball into severe **hyperinflation.** This is an extremely rapid inflation whose impact on real output and employment can be devastating. The economists' contention is that as prices persist in creeping upward, households and businesses will expect them to rise further. So, rather than let their idle savings and current incomes depreciate, people will "spend now" to beat anticipated price rises. Businesses will do the same by buying capital goods. Actions based on this "inflationary psychosis" will then intensify the pressure on prices, and inflation will feed on itself.

Wage-Price Inflationary Spiral Furthermore, as the price level rises, labor will demand and get higher nominal wages. Unions may seek wage increases sufficient not only to cover last year's price increases but also to compensate for inflation anticipated during the future life of their new collective bargaining agreements. Prosperity is not a good time for firms to risk strikes by resisting such demands, so they will agree, expecting to recoup their rising labor costs by boosting their prices. And for good measure, businesses may jack prices up an extra notch to be sure their profits keep up with the inflationary parade. As such price increases raise the general price level further, labor finds it once again has an excellent reason to demand and obtain substantial wage increases. But this triggers another round of price increases. And so on. The net effect is a cumulative *wage-price inflationary spiral.* Nominal wage and price rises feed on each other and transform creeping inflation into galloping inflation.

Potential Economic Collapse

Aside from its disruptive redistribution effects, hyperinflation can cause economic collapse. Severe inflation encourages speculative activity. Businesses may find it increasingly profitable to hoard both materials and finished products, anticipating further price increases. But restricting the availability of materials and products intensifies the inflationary pressure. Also, rather than invest in capital equipment, businesses and individual savers may purchase nonproductive wealth—jewels, gold and other precious metals, real estate, and so forth—as a hedge against inflation.

In the extreme, as prices shoot up sharply and unevenly, normal economic relationships are disrupted. Business owners do not know what to charge for their products. Consumers do not know what to pay. Resource suppliers want to be paid with actual output, rather than with rapidly depreciating money. Creditors avoid debtors to escape the repayment of debts with cheap money. Money eventually becomes almost worthless and ceases to do its job as a medium of exchange. The economy may be thrown into a state of barter. Production and exchange drop dramatically, and the net result is economic, social, and possibly political chaos. The hyperinflation has precipitated monetary collapse, depression, and sociopolitical disorder.

Examples

History reveals a number of examples which fit this scenario. Consider the effects of World War II on price levels in Hungary and Japan:

> The inflation in Hungary exceeded all known records of the past. In August 1946, 828 octillion (1 followed by 27 zeros) depreciated pengös equaled the value of 1 prewar pengö. The price of the American dollar reached a value of 3×10^{22} (3 followed by 22 zeros) pengös. Fishermen and farmers in 1947 Japan used scales to weigh currency and change, rather than bothering to count it. Prices rose some 116 times in Japan, 1938 to 1948.[3]

The German inflation of the 1920s was also catastrophic:

> The German Weimar Republic is an extreme example of a weak government which survived for some time through inflationary finance. On April 27, 1921, the German government was presented with a staggering bill for reparations payments to the Allies of 132 billion gold marks. This sum was far greater than what the Weimar Republic could reasonably expect to raise in taxes. Faced with huge budget deficits, the Weimar government simply ran the printing press to meet its bills.
>
> During 1922, the German price level went up 5,470 percent. In 1923, the situation worsened; the German price level rose 1,300,000,000,000 times. By October of 1923, the postage on the lightest letter sent from Germany to the United States was 200,000 marks. Butter cost 1.5 million marks per pound, meat 2 million marks, a loaf of bread 200,000 marks, and an egg 60,000 marks. Prices increased so rapidly that waiters changed the prices on the menu several times during the course of a lunch. Sometimes customers had to pay double the price listed on the menu when they ordered.[4]

A closing word of caution: Dramatic hyperinflations like these are almost invariably the consequence of imprudent expansion of the money supply by government. Such expansions result in excessive spending and thus demand-pull inflation. With appropriate public policies, however, mild inflation need not become hyperinflation.

---

[3]Theodore Morgan, *Income and Employment*, 2d ed. (Englewood Cliffs, NJ: Prentice-Hall, 1952), p. 361.

[4]Raburn M. Williams, *Inflation! Money, Jobs, and Politicians* (Arlington Heights, IL: AHM Publishing Corporation, 1980), p. 2.

CHAPTER SUMMARY

1. The United States and other industrial economies have gone through periods of fluctuations in domestic output, employment, and the price level. Although they have common phases—peak, recession, trough, recovery—business cycles vary greatly in duration and in intensity.

The Stock Market and Macroeconomic Instability

How, if at all, do changes in stock prices relate to the macroeconomy?

Financial investors daily buy and sell the stock (ownership shares) of thousands of corporations. These corporations pay dividends—a portion of their profits—to the owners of their shares. The price of a particular company's stock is determined by supply and demand. Individual stock prices generally rise and fall in concert with the collective expectations for each firm's profits. Greater profits normally result in higher dividends to the owners of the stock, and in anticipation of these higher dividends, financial investors are willing to pay more for the stock.

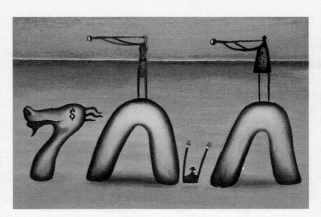

Stock market averages such as the Dow Jones Industrial Average—the weighted-average price of the stocks of 30 major U.S. industrial firms—are closely watched and reported. It is common for these price averages to change over time, or even to rise or fall sharply during a single day. On "Black Monday," October 19, 1987, the Dow Jones Industrial Average experienced a record 1-day drop of 20 percent. About $500 billion in stock market wealth evaporated in a single day. A sharp drop in stock prices also occurred in October 1997, mainly in response to rapid declines in stock prices in Hong Kong and other Southeast Asia stock markets.

The volatility of the stock market raises this question: Do changes in stock price averages *cause* macroeconomic instability? There are linkages between the stock market and the economy that might lead us to think the answer is "yes." Consider a sharp decline in stock prices. Feeling poorer, owners of stock may respond by reducing their spending on goods and services. Firms may react by cutting back on their purchases of new capital goods because that is more attractive than raising funds by issuing new shares of stock.

Studies find, however, that the consumption and investment impacts of stock price changes are relatively mild. Therefore, although stock price averages do influence total spending, the stock market is *not* a major cause of recession or inflation.

A related question emerges: Even though changes in stock prices do not *cause* significant changes in domestic output and the price level, might they *predict* such changes? That is, if stock market values are based on expected profits, wouldn't we expect rapid changes in stock price averages to forecast changes in future business conditions? Indeed, stock prices often *do* fall prior to recessions and rise prior to expansions. For this reason stock prices are among a group of 10 variables which constitute an index of leading indicators (Last Word, Chapter 12). Such an index often provides a useful clue to the future direction of the economy. But taken alone, stock market prices are not a reliable predictor of changes in GDP. Stock prices have fallen rapidly in some instances with no recession following. Black Monday itself did not produce a recession during the following 2 years. In other instances, recessions have occurred with no prior decline in stock market prices.

2. Although economists explain the business cycle in terms of such ultimate causal factors as major innovations, political events, and money creation, they generally agree that the level of total spending is the immediate determinant of real output and employment.

3. The business cycle affects all sectors of the economy, but in varying ways and degrees. The cycle has greater output and employment effects in the capital goods and durable consumer goods industries than in the services and nondurable goods industries. Over the cycle, price fluctuations are greater in competitive than in monopolistic industries.

4. Economists distinguish between frictional, structural, and cyclical unemployment. The full-employment or natural rate of unemployment, composed of frictional and structural unemployment, is currently about 5.5 percent. Part-time and discouraged workers complicate the accurate measurement of unemployment.

5. The economic cost of unemployment, as measured by the GDP gap, consists of the goods and services forgone by society when its resources are involuntarily idle. Okun's law suggests that every 1 percentage point increase in unemployment above the natural rate causes a 2 percent GDP gap.

6. Unemployment rates and inflation rates vary widely among nations. Unemployment rates differ because nations have different natural rates of unemployment and often are in different phases of their business cycles. Inflation and unemployment rates in the United States recently have been in the middle range compared with rates in other industrial nations.

7. Economists discern both demand-pull and cost-push (supply-side) inflation. Two variants of cost-push inflation are wage-push inflation and inflation caused by supply shocks.

8. Unanticipated inflation arbitrarily redistributes real income at the expense of fixed-income receivers, creditors, and savers. If inflation is anticipated, individuals and businesses may be able to take steps to lessen or eliminate adverse redistribution effects.

9. The demand-pull theory of inflation suggests that some inflation may be necessary for the economy to realize high levels of output and employment. However, the cost-push theory of inflation indicates that inflation may be accompanied by declines in real output and employment. Hyperinflation, usually associated with injudicious government policy, might undermine the monetary system and cause economic collapse.

TERMS AND CONCEPTS

business cycle	cyclical unemployment	GDP gap	anticipated inflation
peak	full-employment	Okun's law	unanticipated inflation
recession	unemployment rate	inflation	cost-of-living adjustment
trough	natural rate of	rule of 70	inflation premium
recovery	unemployment	demand-pull inflation	real interest rate
seasonal variations	potential output	cost-push inflation	nominal interest rate
secular trend	labor force	per-unit production costs	hyperinflation
frictional unemployment	unemployment rate	nominal income	
structural unemployment	discouraged workers	real income	

STUDY QUESTIONS

1. KEY QUESTION What are the four phases of the business cycle? How long do business cycles last? How do seasonal variations and secular trends complicate measurement of the business cycle? Why does the business cycle affect output and employment in capital goods industries and consumer durable goods industries more severely than in industries producing consumer nondurables?

2. What factors make it difficult to determine the unemployment rate? Why is it difficult to distinguish between frictional, structural, and cyclical unemployment? Why is unemployment an economic problem? What are the consequences of a GDP gap? What are the noneconomic effects of unemployment?

3. KEY QUESTION Use the following data to calculate **(a)** the size of the labor force and **(b)** the official unemployment rate: total population, 500; population under 16 years of age or institutionalized, 120; not in labor force, 150; unemployed, 23; part-time workers looking for full-time jobs, 10.

4. Since there is an unemployment compensation program which provides income for those out of work, why worry about unemployment?

5. KEY QUESTION Assume that in a particular year the natural rate of unemployment is 5 percent and the actual rate of unemployment is 9 percent. Use Okun's law to determine the size of the GDP gap in percentage-point terms. If the nominal GDP is $500 billion in that year, how much output is being forgone because of cyclical unemployment?

6. Explain how an *increase* in your nominal income and a *decrease* in your real income might occur simultaneously. Who loses from inflation? Who loses from unemployment? If you had to choose between **(a)** full employment with a 6 percent annual rate of inflation and **(b)** price stability with an 8 percent unemployment rate, which would you select? Why?

7. KEY QUESTION If the price index was 110 last year and is 121 this year, what is this year's rate of inflation? What is the "rule of 70"? How long would it take for the price level to double if inflation persisted at **(a)** 2, **(b)** 5, and **(c)** 10 percent per year?

8. Describe the relationship between total spending and the levels of output and employment. Explain what happens to the price level as increases in total spending move the economy from substantial unemployment to moderate unemployment, to full employment, and finally to full-capacity output.

9. Explain how hyperinflation might lead to a depression.

10. Evaluate as accurately as you can how each of the following individuals would be affected by unanticipated inflation of 10 percent per year:
   a. A pensioned railroad worker
   b. A department store clerk
   c. A UAW assembly line worker
   d. A heavily indebted farmer
   e. A retired business executive whose current income comes entirely from interest on government bonds
   f. The owner of an independent small-town department store

11. A noted television comedian once defined inflation as follows: "Inflation? That means your money today won't buy as much as it would have during the depression when you didn't have any." Is his definition accurate? Explain.

12. (Last Word) Suppose that stock prices fall by 10 percent in the stock market. All else equal, are these lower stock prices likely to *cause* a decrease in real GDP? How might these lower prices forecast a decline in real GDP?

13. WEB-BASED QUESTION **The Employment Situation—Write the News Release** Visit the U.S. Department of Labor http://stats.bls.gov/news.release/empsit.toc.htm and look at the current employment situation summary for the latest month. Then rewrite the following paragraph. See also http://stats.bls.gov/cps_faq.htm for their FAQs (frequently asked questions). Employment (rose/fell/remained unchanged), and the unemployment rate edged (up/down/stayed unchanged) to (?) percent in the latest month. The jobless rate had (risen/fallen/stayed unchanged) from (?) percent in (previous month) to (?) percent in (latest month). The number of payroll jobs (increased/decreased/ were unchanged) by (? thousand) in the latest month, with widespread gains/losses in the (?) sector of the economy. Average weekly hours (declined/increased/ unchanged), and average hourly earnings were (lower/higher/unchanged) over the month.

14. WEB-BASED QUESTION **Inflation and the "Official CPI"** Each month, BLS releases thousands of detailed CPI numbers to the press. However, the press generally focuses on the broadest, most comprehensive CPI, called the official CPI. Go to the U.S. Department of Labor http://stats.bls.gov/cpifaq.htm CPI FAQs (frequently asked questions) page. Which index is the official CPI reported in the media? Look at http://stats.bls.gov/news.release/cpi.toc.htm and find the *current* figures for the official CPI: **(a)** index level (for example, July 1992 = 140.5); **(b)** 12-month percentage change (for example, July 1991 to July 1992 = 3.2 percent); **(c)** 1-month percentage change on a seasonally adjusted basis (for example, from June 1992 to July 1992 = 0.1 percent); and **(d)** the annual percentage rate of change so far this year.

Building the Aggregate Expenditures Model

9

Two of the most critical questions in macroeconomics are: (1) What determines the level of GDP, given a nation's production capacity? (2) What factors can cause real GDP to expand in one period and fall in another? To answer these questions, we construct the *aggregate expenditures model.* Recall that to economists "aggregate" means "total" or "combined," so "aggregate expenditures" refers to the economy's total spending. The model is based on the general equality between total spending and output described in Chapter 7. One of its primary uses is in clarifying the occurrence of business fluctuations discussed in Chapter 8.

We begin this chapter with a brief review of the economic thinking and events leading to the development of the aggregate expenditures model. Next we examine the relations between income and consumption and between income and saving, both aspects of the model. Then we focus on investment—specifically how businesses choose the amounts of capital goods to buy. Finally, we combine consumption, saving, and investment into a model which can be used to determine the equilibrium level of GDP for an economy.

The model developed in this chapter applies only to a private (no government), closed (no foreign trade) economy. In the next chapter we complete the model by adding government and the foreign sector.

HISTORICAL BACKDROP

A bit of historical background will help you see how and why the aggregate expenditures model came about.

Classical Economics and Say's Law

Until the Great Depression of the 1930s, many economists of the nineteenth and early twentieth centuries—now called classical economists[1]—believed the market system would ensure full employment of the economy's resources. They acknowledged that now and then abnormal circumstances such as wars, political upheavals, droughts, speculative crises, and gold rushes would occur, deflecting the

---

[1]The most prominent classical economists were David Ricardo, John Stuart Mill, F. Y. Edgeworth, Alfred Marshall, and A. C. Pigou.

economy from full-employment status (as seen in Figure 8-1). But when these deviations did occur, automatic adjustments in prices, wages, and interest rates within the market would soon restore the economy to the full-employment level of output. A slump in output and employment would reduce prices, wages, and interest rates. Lower prices would increase consumer spending, lower wages would increase employment, and lower interest rates would boost investment spending. Any excess supply of goods and workers soon would be eliminated.

Classical macroeconomists denied the possibility of long-term underspending—a level of spending insufficient to purchase the entire full-employment output. This denial was based in part on **Say's law,** attributed to the nineteenth-century French economist J. B. Say. Say's law is the seemingly simple notion that the very act of producing goods generates an amount of income equal to the value of the goods produced. The production of any output automatically provides the income needed to take that output off the market—the income needed to buy what's produced. In other words, *supply creates its own demand.*

Say's law can best be understood in terms of a barter economy. A shoemaker, for example, produces or *supplies* shoes as a means of buying or *demanding* the shirts and stockings produced by other workers. The shoemaker's supply of shoes is his income that he will "spend" to satisfy his demand for other goods. The goods he buys (demands) will be exactly equal in value to the goods he produces (supplies). And so it allegedly is for other producers and for the entire economy. Demand must be the same as supply! The circular flow model of the economy and national income accounting both suggest something of this sort. Income generated from the production of any level of output would, when spent, be just sufficient to provide a matching total demand. Assuming the composition of output is in accord with consumer preferences, all markets would be cleared of their outputs. It would seem that what all business owners need to do to sell a full-employment output is to produce that output; Say's law guarantees there will be sufficient consumption spending to buy it all.

Say's law and classical macroeconomics are not simply a historical curiosity. A few modern economists have reformulated, revitalized, and extended the work of the nineteenth- and early twentieth-century economists to generate a "new" classical economics. (We will examine this modern reincarnation in later chapters.)

The Great Depression and Keynes

Two events weakened the theory that supply creates its own demand (Say's law) and led to the realization that underspending or overspending can occur:

The Great Depression The Depression of the 1930s was worldwide. In the United States, it cut real GDP by 40 percent and raised the unemployment rate to nearly 25 percent. Much the same occurred in other industrial nations. The negative effects of the Depression lingered for a decade. There is, obviously, a blatant inconsistency between a theory which says that unemployment is virtually impossible and the actual occurrence of a 10-year siege of very substantial unemployment.

Keynes and Keynesian Economics In 1936 British economist John Maynard Keynes (pronounced "Caines") explained why there was cyclical employment in capitalistic economies. In his *General Theory of Employment, Interest, and Money,* Keynes attacked the foundations of classical theory and touched off a major revolution in economic thinking on macroeconomic questions. Keynes disputed Say's law, pointing out that in some periods not all income will get spent on the output which is produced. When widespread underspending occurs, unsold goods will accumulate in producers' warehouses. Producers will respond to rising inventories by reducing their output and cutting their employment. A recession or depression will follow.

Because Keynes developed the ideas underlying the aggregate expenditures model, this kind of analysis is referred to as **Keynesian economics.** But the model reflects contributions of numerous other economists since Keynes. In the aggregate expenditures model, the macroeconomy is inherently unstable; it is subject to periods of recession and inflation. Keynesian economics says that capitalism is not a self-regulating system capable of uninterrupted prosperity. While capitalism is an excellent engine of long-term economic growth, we cannot always depend on it to "run itself."

Furthermore, economic fluctuations are not associated exclusively with external forces such as wars, droughts, and similar abnormalities. Rather, the Keynesian view sees the causes of unemployment and inflation as the failure of certain fundamental economic decisions—in particular, saving and investment decisions—to be completely synchronized. In addition, product prices and wages are downwardly inflexible, meaning that significant declines in prices and wages will occur only after extended and costly periods of recession or depression. Internal factors, in addition to external forces (wars and droughts), contribute to economic instability.

SIMPLIFICATIONS

Four assumptions will help us build the aggregate expenditures model:

1. Initially we will assume a "closed economy" where there are no international trade transactions. Complications arising from exports and imports in the "open economy" will be deferred to Chapter 10.
2. We will also ignore government until Chapter 10, permitting us first to demonstrate that at times laissez-faire capitalism may not achieve and maintain full employment. For now we will deal with a "private" closed economy.
3. Although both businesses and households save, we will for convenience speak as if all saving were personal saving.
4. To keep things simple, we will assume that depreciation and *net* foreign factor income earned in the United States are zero.

We should note two implications of these assumptions. First, recall from Chapter 7 that aggregate spending has four components: consumption, investment, government purchases, and net exports. Assumptions 1 and 2 mean that, for now, we are concerned only with consumption and investment.

Second, assumptions 2 through 4 permit us to treat gross domestic product (GDP), national income (NI), personal income (PI), and disposable income (DI) as being equal to each other. All the items which in practice distinguish them from one another result from depreciation, net foreign factor income earned in the United States, government (taxes and transfer payments), and business saving (see Table 7-4). Our assumptions mean that if $500 billion of goods and services is produced as GDP, exactly $500 billion of DI is received by households to use as either consumption or saving.

TOOLS OF THE AGGREGATE EXPENDITURES MODEL

The aggregate expenditures model embodies the following basic theory regarding the macroeconomy:

The amount of goods and services produced and therefore the level of employment depend directly on the level of total or aggregate expenditures. Businesses will produce a level of output they can profitably sell. Workers and machinery are idled when there are no markets for the goods and services they can produce. Total output and employment decrease when the level of aggregate expenditures decreases, and they increase when it increases.

Our strategy in this chapter is to analyze the consumption and investment components of aggregate expenditures and derive a private sector model of equilibrium GDP and employment. Chapter 10 examines changes in real GDP and adds net exports and government expenditures (along with taxes) to the model.

As we begin our discussion, be sure you understand that we are assuming the economy has substantial excess production capacity and unemployed labor (unless specified otherwise). An increase in aggregate expenditures will thus increase real output and employment but *not* the price level.

QUICK REVIEW 9-1

■ Classical macroeconomics was grounded in Say's law, which asserted that supply creates its own demand and therefore underspending leading to recessions was unlikely.

■ The Great Depression and Keynes' development of an alternative model of the macroeconomy undermined classical macroeconomics and led to the modern aggregate expenditures theory.

■ In the aggregate expenditures model, the level of total or aggregate expenditures determines the amount of output produced which in turn establishes the level of employment.

CONSUMPTION AND SAVING

In terms of absolute size, consumption is the largest component of aggregate expenditures. We therefore need to understand the determinants of consumption spending. Recall that economists define personal saving as "not spending" or "that part of disposable income (DI) not consumed." In other words, saving equals disposable income less consumption. Thus, in examining the determinants of consumption we are also exploring the determinants of saving.

Income-Consumption and Income-Saving Relationships

Many factors influence the level of consumer spending. But the most significant determinant is income—in particular, disposable income. And, since saving is that part of disposable income not consumed, DI is also the basic determinant of personal saving.

Consider some recent historical data. In Figure 9-1 each green dot represents consumption and disposable income for 1 year since 1973. The green line, fitted to these points, shows that consumption is directly related to disposable income; moreover, households clearly spend most of their incomes.

But we can say more. The black 45 degree line is added to the diagram as a reference line. Because this line bisects the 90 degree angle formed by the vertical and horizontal axes of the graph, each point on the line must be equidistant from the two axes. That is, each point on the line represents a situation in which consumption equals disposable income, or $C = DI$. We can therefore regard the vertical distance from any point on the horizontal axis to the 45 degree line as measuring either consumption *or* disposable income. If we regard it as measuring disposable income, then the vertical distance by which actual consump-

tion in any year falls short of the 45 degree line represents the amount of saving in that year. For example, in 1993 consumption was $4459 billion, and disposable income was $4829 billion; hence, saving in 1993 was $370 billion. Disposable income less consumption equals saving, or $DI - C = S$. By observing these vertical distances as we move to the left or to the right in Figure 9-1, we see that saving also varies directly with the level of disposable income: As DI increases, saving increases; as DI decreases, saving decreases.

Figure 9-1 thus suggests that (1) households consume most of their disposable incomes, and (2) both consumption and saving are directly related to the income level.

The Consumption Schedule

The dots in Figure 9-1 represent historical data—how much households *actually had as DI* and *actually did consume* (and save) over a period of years. Those data are useful for finding the relationship between DI and consumption and saving. But to build our model, we need a schedule which tells us the various amounts households would *plan* to consume at each

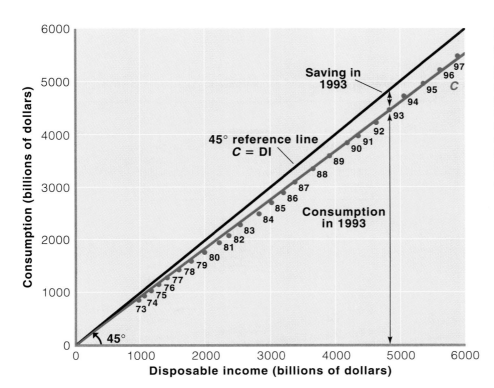

FIGURE 9-1 Consumption and disposable income, 1973–1997 Each dot in this figure shows consumption and disposable income in a specific year. The line C generalizes the relationship between consumption and disposable income. It indicates a direct relationship and shows that households consume the bulk of their incomes.

of various levels of disposable income which could prevail at *some specific time.* A hypothetical **consumption schedule** of the type we require is shown in columns 1 and 2, Table 9-1, and is plotted in **Figure 9-2a (Key Graph).** This consumption schedule reflects the direct consumption–disposable income relationship suggested by the empirical data in Figure 9-1, and it is consistent with many empirical household budget studies. Households tend to spend a *larger proportion* of a small disposable income than of a large disposable income.

The Saving Schedule

It is simple to derive a **saving schedule.** Because saving equals disposable income *less* consumption ($S = DI - C$), we need only subtract consumption (Table 9-1, column 2) from disposable income (column 1) to find the amount saved (column 3) at each DI. Thus, columns 1 and 3 in Table 9-1 are the saving schedule, plotted in Figure 9-2b. Note that there is a direct relationship between saving and DI but that saving is a smaller proportion (fraction) of a small DI than of a large DI. If households consume a smaller and smaller proportion of DI as DI increases, then they must save a larger and larger proportion.

Remembering that at each point on the 45 degree line consumption equals DI, we see that *dissaving* (consuming in excess of after-tax income) will occur at relatively low DIs like $370 billion (row 1, Table 9-1), where consumption is actually $375 billion. Households can consume more than their incomes by liquidating (selling for cash) accumulated wealth or by borrowing. Graphically, dissaving is shown as the vertical distance of the consumption schedule *above* the 45 degree line or as the vertical distance of the saving schedule *below* the horizontal axis. Dissaving at the $370 billion level of income is marked in Figure 9-2a and b. Each of the two vertical distances measures the $5 billion of dissaving occurring at the $370 billion income level.

In our example, the **break-even income** is $390 billion (row 2). This is the income level where households plan to consume their entire incomes ($C = DI$). Graphically, the consumption schedule cuts the 45 degree line, and the saving schedule cuts the horizontal axis (saving is zero) at the break-even income level.

At all higher incomes, households plan to save part of their incomes. Graphically, the vertical distance of the consumption schedule *below* the 45 degree line measures this saving, as does the vertical distance of the saving schedule *above* the horizontal axis. For example, at the $410 billion level of income (row 3), both these distances indicate $5 billion worth of saving (see Figure 9-2a and b).

TABLE 9-1   **Consumption and saving schedules (in billions) and propensities to consume and save**

(1) Level of output and income (GDP = DI)	(2) Consumption (C)	(3) Saving (S) (1) −(2)	(4) Average propensity to consume (APC) (2)/(1)	(5) Average propensity to save (APS) (3)/(1)	(6) Marginal propensity to consume (MPC) Δ(2)/Δ(1)*	(7) Marginal propensity to save (MPS) Δ(3)/Δ(1)*
(1) $370	$375	$−5	1.01	−.01	.75	.25
(2) 390	390	0	1.00	.00	.75	.25
(3) 410	405	5	.99	.01	.75	.25
(4) 430	420	10	.98	.02	.75	.25
(5) 450	435	15	.97	.03	.75	.25
(6) 470	450	20	.96	.04	.75	.25
(7) 490	465	25	.95	.05	.75	.25
(8) 510	480	30	.94	.06	.75	.25
(9) 530	495	35	.93	.07	.75	.25
(10) 550	510	40	.93	.07		

* The Greek letter Δ, delta, means "the change in."

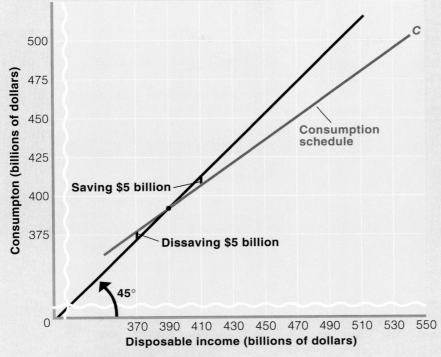

(a) Consumption schedule

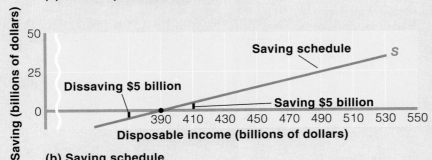

(b) Saving schedule

FIGURE 9-2 (a) Consumption and (b) saving schedules The two parts of this figure show the income-consumption and income-saving relationships in Table 9-1 graphically. The saving schedule in (b) is found by subtracting the consumption schedule in (a) vertically from the 45 degree line. Consumption equals disposable income (and saving thus equals zero) at $390 billion for these hypothetical data.

Average and Marginal Propensities

Columns 4 to 7 in Table 9-1 show additional characteristics of the consumption and saving schedules.

APC and APS   The fraction, or percentage, of any total income which is consumed is called the **average propensity to consume** (APC). The fraction of any total income which is saved is the **average propensity to save** (APS). That is,

$$APC = \frac{consumption}{income}$$

and

$$APS = \frac{saving}{income}$$

For example, at the $470 billion level of income (row 6) in Table 9-1, the APC is $\frac{450}{470} = \frac{45}{47}$, or about 96 percent, while the APS is $\frac{20}{470} = \frac{2}{47}$, or about 4 percent. Columns 4 and 5 in Table 9-1 show the APC and APS at each of the 10 levels of DI; note there that the APC falls and the APS rises as DI increases. This is another way of stating a point we just made: The fraction of total DI which is consumed declines as DI rises, and the fraction of DI which is saved rises as DI increases.

Because disposable income is either consumed or saved, the fraction of any DI consumed plus the fraction saved (not consumed) must exhaust that income. Mathematically, APC + APS = 1 at any level of disposable income. Columns 4 and 5 in Table 9-1 illustrate this.

Global Perspective 9-1 shows APCs for several countries.

MPC and MPS   The fact that households consume a certain proportion of some total income—for example, $\frac{45}{47}$ of a $470 billion disposable income—does not guarantee they will consume the same proportion of any *change* in income they might receive. The proportion, or fraction, of any change in income consumed is called the **marginal propensity to consume** (MPC), marginal meaning "extra" or "a change in." Equivalently, the MPC is the ratio of a *change* in consumption to the *change* in income which caused that change in consumption:

$$MPC = \frac{change\ in\ consumption}{change\ in\ income}$$

Similarly, the fraction of any change in income saved is the **marginal propensity to save** (MPS). The MPS

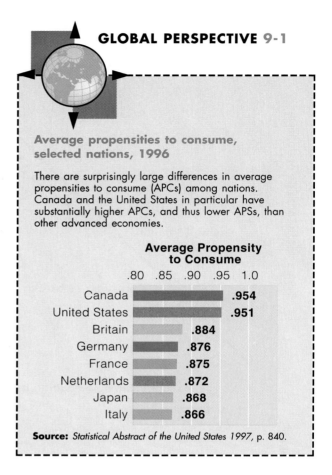

GLOBAL PERSPECTIVE 9-1

Average propensities to consume, selected nations, 1996

There are surprisingly large differences in average propensities to consume (APCs) among nations. Canada and the United States in particular have substantially higher APCs, and thus lower APSs, than other advanced economies.

Average Propensity to Consume

Canada	.954
United States	.951
Britain	.884
Germany	.876
France	.875
Netherlands	.872
Japan	.868
Italy	.866

Scale: .80 .85 .90 .95 1.0

Source: *Statistical Abstract of the United States 1997*, p. 840.

is the ratio of a *change* in saving to the *change* in income bringing it about:

$$MPS = \frac{change\ in\ saving}{change\ in\ income}$$

If disposable income is $470 billion (row 6 in Table 9-1) and household incomes rise by $20 billion to $490 billion (row 7), households will consume $\frac{15}{20}$, or $\frac{3}{4}$, and save $\frac{5}{20}$, or $\frac{1}{4}$, of that *increase in income*. In other words, the MPC is $\frac{3}{4}$ or .75, and the MPS is $\frac{1}{4}$ or .25, as shown in columns 6 and 7.

The sum of the MPC and the MPS for any change in disposable income must always be 1. Consuming and saving out of extra income is an either-or proposition; the fraction of any change in income not consumed is, by definition, saved. Therefore the fraction consumed (MPC) plus the fraction saved (MPS) must exhaust the whole change in income:

MPC + MPS = 1

In our example .75 plus .25 equals 1.

MPC and MPS as Slopes   The MPC is the numerical value of the slope of the consumption schedule, and the MPS is the numerical value of the slope of the saving schedule. We know from the appendix to Chapter 1 that the slope of any line is the ratio of the vertical change to the horizontal change involved in moving from one point to another on that line.

In Figure 9-3 we measure the slopes of the consumption and saving lines, using enlarged portions of Figures 9-2a and 9-2b. Observe that consumption changes by $15 billion (vertical change) for each $20 billion change in disposable income (horizontal change); the slope of the consumption line is thus .75 (= $15/$20)—the value of the MPC. Saving changes by $5 billion (vertical change) for every $20 billion change in disposable income (horizontal

change). The slope of the saving line therefore is .25 (= $5/$20), which is the value of the MPS. **(Key Question 6)**

Nonincome Determinants of Consumption and Saving

The level of disposable income is the basic determinant of the amounts households will consume and save, just as price is the basic determinant of the quantity demanded of a single product. Recall that changes in determinants other than price, such as consumer tastes or incomes, will shift the demand curve for a product. Similarly, certain determinants other than income might cause households to consume more or less at each possible level of income and thereby change the locations of the consumption and saving schedules. These other determinants are wealth, expectations, indebtedness, and taxation.

Wealth   Generally, the greater the wealth households have accumulated, the larger the amount of consumption and the smaller the amount of saving out of any level of current income. By "wealth" we mean both real assets (a house, automobiles, television sets, and other durables) and financial assets (cash, savings accounts, stocks, bonds, insurance policies, pensions) which households own. Households save— refrain from consumption—to accumulate wealth. The more wealth households have accumulated, the weaker the incentive to save in order to accumulate additional wealth. An increase in wealth thus shifts the saving schedule downward and the consumption schedule upward.

Examples: The dramatic stock market crash of 1929 significantly decreased the financial wealth of many families almost overnight and was a factor in the low levels of consumption in the depressed 1930s. More recently, the general decline in real estate values during 1989 and 1990 eroded household wealth and contributed to a reduction of consumer spending.

For the most part, however, the amount of wealth held by households changes only modestly from year to year and therefore does not account for large shifts in the consumption and saving schedules.

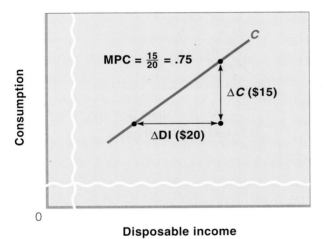

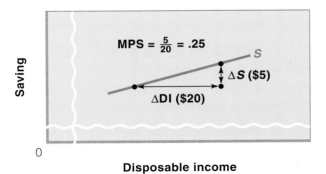

FIGURE 9-3 The marginal propensity to consume and the marginal propensity to save   The MPC is the slope (= $\Delta C/\Delta DI$) of the consumption schedule, and the MPS is the slope (= $\Delta S/\Delta DI$) of the saving schedule. The Δ means "change in."

Expectations   Household expectations about future prices, money incomes, and the availability of goods may significantly affect current spending and saving. Expectations of rising prices and product shortages tomorrow may trigger more spending and less saving today. This shifts the consumption schedule upward and the saving schedule downward.

Household Debt In drawing a particular consumption schedule, we assume that household debt as a percentage of DI is constant. When consumers as a group increase their household debt, they can increase current consumption. Increased borrowing enables consumers to increase consumption at each level of DI; it shifts the consumption schedule upward. However, when levels of household debt get abnormally high, households may elect to reduce their consumption to pay off some of their loans. At that time, the consumption schedule shifts downward.

Taxation When we add government to our analysis (Chapter 10), the convenient equality between GDP and DI breaks down. At that stage, we plot consumption and saving against GDP (not DI). You will then see that changes in taxes will shift the consumption and saving schedules. Taxes are paid partly at the expense of consumption and partly at the expense of saving. Therefore, an increase in taxes will shift both the consumption *and* saving schedules downward. Conversely, a tax reduction will be partly consumed and partly saved by households. A tax decrease will shift both the consumption *and* saving schedules upward.

Shifts and Stability

Three final points regarding the consumption and saving schedules are relevant:

1. *Terminology* The movement from one point to another on a stable consumption schedule (for example, from a to b on C_0 in Figure 9-4a) is called a *change in the amount consumed*. The sole cause of this change in consumption is a change in disposable income (or, later, GDP). On the other hand, a *change in the consumption schedule* refers to an upward or downward shift of the entire schedule—for example, a shift from C_0 to C_1 or C_2 in Figure 9-4a. A shift of the consumption schedule is caused by changes in any one or more of the four nonincome determinants just discussed. A similar distinction in terminology applies to the saving schedule in Figure 9-4b.

2. *Schedule shifts* The first three nonincome determinants of consumption (wealth, expectations, and household debt) will shift the consumption

schedule in one direction and the saving schedule in the opposite direction. If households decide to consume more at each possible level of disposable income, they want to save less, and vice versa. (Even when they spend more by borrowing, they are, in effect, reducing their current saving by the amount borrowed.) Graphically, if the consumption schedule shifts upward from C_0 to C_1 in Figure 9-4, the saving schedule will shift downward, from S_0 to S_1. Similarly, a downshift in the

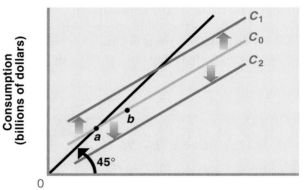

Disposable income (billions of dollars)

(a) Consumption schedule

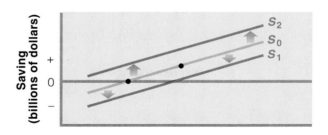

Disposable income (billions of dollars)

(b) Saving schedule

FIGURE 9-4 Shifts in the (a) consumption and (b) saving schedules Normally, if households consume more at each level of DI, they are necessarily saving less. Graphically this means that an upshift of the consumption schedule (C_0 to C_1) entails a downshift of the saving schedule (S_0 to S_1). If households consume less at each level of DI, they are saving more. A downshift of the consumption schedule (C_0 to C_2) is reflected in an upshift of the saving schedule (S_0 to S_2). (This pattern breaks down, however, when increases in consumption result from increased borrowing or when a shift in the consumption schedule results from a change in taxes.)

consumption schedule from C_0 to C_2 means an upshift in the saving schedule from S_0 to S_2.

The exception to the above generalization involves the fourth nonincome determinant: taxation. We have seen that households will consume less *and* save less when they must pay higher taxes. Thus, a tax increase will lower both the consumption *and* saving schedules, while a tax cut will shift both schedules upward.

3. **Stability** Although changes in nonincome determinants can shift the consumption and saving schedules, in practice these schedules are quite stable. Only significant increases or decreases in taxes have a major impact on the location of the schedules. Their stability may be because consumption-saving decisions are strongly influenced by *long-term* considerations such as saving to meet emergencies or saving for retirement. It may also be because changes in the nonincome determinants frequently work in opposite directions and therefore may be self-canceling.

QUICK REVIEW 9-2

■ Consumption spending and saving both rise when disposable income increases; they fall when disposable income decreases.

■ The average propensity to consume (APC) is the fraction of any specific level of disposable income which is spent on consumer goods; the average propensity to save (APS) is the fraction of any specific level of disposable income which is saved. The APC falls and the APS rises as disposable income increases.

■ The marginal propensity to consume (MPC) is the fraction of any change in disposable income which is consumed and is the slope of the consumption schedule; the marginal propensity to save (MPS) is the fraction of any change in disposable income which is saved and is the slope of the saving schedule.

■ Changes in consumer wealth, consumer expectations, household debt, and taxes can shift the consumption and saving schedules.

INVESTMENT

We now turn to investment, the second component of private spending. Recall that investment consists of expenditures on new plants, capital equipment, machinery, and so on. The investment decision is a marginal-benefit–marginal-cost decision: The mar-

ginal benefit from investment is the expected rate of return businesses hope to realize. The marginal cost is the interest rate which must be paid for borrowing funds. We will see that businesses will invest in all projects for which the expected rate of return exceeds the interest rate. Expected returns (profits) and the interest rate therefore are the two basic determinants of investment spending.

Expected Rate of Return

Investment spending is guided by the profit motive; businesses buy capital goods only when they expect such purchases to be profitable. Suppose the owner of a small cabinetmaking shop is considering investing in a new sanding machine costing $1000 and having a useful life of only 1 year. The new machine will presumably increase the firm's output and sales revenue. Suppose the *net* expected revenue from the machine (that is, after such operating costs as power, lumber, labor, and certain taxes have been subtracted) is $1100. Then, after operating costs have been accounted for, the remaining expected net revenue is sufficient to cover the $1000 cost of the machine and leave a profit of $100. Comparing this $100 profit with the $1000 cost of the machine, we find that the **expected rate of return,** r, on the machine is 10 percent (= $100/$1000).

The Real Interest Rate

One important cost associated with investing which our example has so far ignored is interest—the financial cost of borrowing the *money* capital required to purchase the *real* capital (the sanding machine).

To include the interest cost, we note that it is computed by applying the interest rate, i, to the amount borrowed—the cost of the machine. The cost of the machine is the same amount that we used to compute the rate of return, r. Thus, we can generalize as follows: If the expected rate of return (say, 10 percent) exceeds the interest rate (say, 7 percent), the investment will be profitable. But if the interest rate (say, 12 percent) exceeds the expected rate of return (10 percent), the investment will be unprofitable. The firm should undertake all profitable investment projects. That means it should invest to the point where $r = i$, since then it has undertaken all investment for which r exceeds i.

But what if the firm does *not* borrow, instead financing the investment internally out of funds saved from past profits? The role of the interest rate in investing in real capital does not change. When the firm uses money from savings to invest in the sander, it incurs an opportunity cost because it forgoes the interest income it could have earned by lending the funds to someone else.

The *real* rate of interest, rather than the nominal rate, is crucial in making investment decisions. Recall from Chapter 8 that the nominal interest rate is expressed in dollars of current value, while the real interest rate is stated in dollars of constant or inflation-adjusted value. The real interest rate is the nominal rate less the rate of inflation. In our sanding machine illustration we have implicitly assumed a constant price level so that all our data, including the interest rate, are in real terms.

But what if inflation *is* occurring? Suppose a $1000 investment is expected to yield a real (inflation-adjusted) rate of return of 10 percent and the nominal interest rate is 15 percent. At first, we would say the investment will be unprofitable. But assume there is ongoing inflation of 10 percent per year. This means the investing firm will pay back dollars with approximately 10 percent less in purchasing power. While the nominal interest rate is 15 percent, the real rate is only 5 percent (= 15 percent − 10 percent). Comparing this 5 percent real interest rate with the 10 percent expected real rate of return, we find that the investment *is* profitable and should be undertaken.

Investment Demand Curve

We now move from a single firm's investment decision to total demand for investment goods by the entire business sector. Assume every firm has estimated the expected rates of return from all investment projects and these data have been collected. The data can be *cumulated*—successively summed—by asking: How many dollars' worth of investment projects have an expected rate of return of, say, 16 percent or more? Of 14 percent or more? Of 12 percent or more? And so on.

Suppose there are no prospective investments yielding an expected return of 16 percent or more. But there are $5 billion of investment opportunities with expected rates of return between 14 and 16 percent; an *additional* $5 billion yielding between 12 and 14 percent; still an *additional* $5 billion yielding between 10 and 12 percent; and an *additional* $5 billion in each successive 2 percent range of yield down to and including the 0 to 2 percent range.

To cumulate these figures for each rate of return, *r*, we add the amounts of investment which will yield *that particular rate of return* r *or higher*. This way we obtain the data in Table 9-2, shown graphically in **Figure 9-5 (Key Graph).** In Table 9-2 the number opposite 12 percent, for example, tells us there are $10 billion of investment opportunities which yield an expected rate of return of 12 percent *or more*. The $10 billion includes the $5 billion of investment expected to yield a return of 14 percent or more *plus* the $5 billion expected to yield between 12 and 14 percent.

We know from our example of the sanding machine that an investment project will be profitable, and will be undertaken, if its expected rate of return, *r*, exceeds the real interest rate, *i*. Let's first suppose *i* is 12 percent. Businesses will undertake all investments for which *r* exceeds 12 percent. That is, they will invest until the 12 percent rate of return *equals* the 12 percent interest rate. Figure 9-5 reveals that $10 billion of investment spending will be undertaken at a 12 percent interest rate; that means $10 billion of investment projects have an expected rate of return of 12 percent or more.

Put another way: At a financial "price" of 12 percent, $10 billion of investment goods will be demanded. If the interest rate is lower, say, 8 percent, the amount of investment for which *r* equals or exceeds *i* is $20 billion. Thus, firms will demand $20 billion of investment goods at an 8 percent real interest rate. At 6 percent, they will demand $25 billion of investment goods.

TABLE 9-2   Rates of expected return and investment

Expected rate of return (r)	Cumulative amount of investment having this rate of return or higher, billions per year
16%	$ 0
14	5
12	10
10	15
8	20
6	25
4	30
2	35
0	40

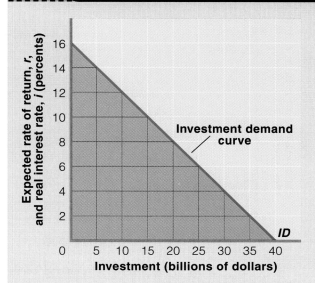

FIGURE 9-5 The investment demand curve The investment demand curve is constructed by arraying all potential investment projects in descending order of their expected rates of return. The curve is downsloping, reflecting an inverse relationship between the real interest rate (the financial "price" of each dollar of investing) and the quantity of investment demanded.

QUICK QUIZ 9-5

1. **The investment demand curve:**
   a. reflects a direct (positive) relationship between the real interest rate and investment.
   b. reflects an inverse (negative) relationship between the real interest rate and investment.
   c. shifts to the right when the real interest rate rises.
   d. shifts to the left when the real interest rate rises.

2. **In this figure:**
   a. greater cumulative amounts of investment are associated with lower expected rates of return on investment.
   b. Lesser cumulative amounts of investment are associated with lower expected rates of return on investment.
   c. higher interest rates are associated with higher expected rates of return on investment, and therefore greater amounts of investment.
   d. interest rates and investment move in the same direction.

3. **In this figure, if the real interest rate falls from 6 to 4 percent:**
   a. investment will increase from 0 to $30 billion.
   b. investment will decrease by $5 billion.
   c. the expected rate of return will rise by $5 billion.
   d. investment will increase from $25 billion to $30 billion.

4. **In this figure, investment will be:**
   a. zero if the real interest rate was zero.
   b. $40 billion if the real interest rate was 16 percent.
   c. $30 billion if the real interest rate was 4 percent.
   d. $20 billion if the real interest rate was 12 percent.

Answers: 1. b; 2. a; 3. d; 4. c

By applying the marginal-benefit–marginal-cost rule that investment projects should be undertaken up to the point where $r = i$, we see that we can add the real interest rate to the vertical axis in Figure 9-5. The curve in Figure 9-5 not only shows rates of return, it shows the quantity of investment demanded at each "price" i of investment. Various possible real interest rates are shown on the vertical axis in Figure 9-5 and the corresponding quantities of investment demanded on the horizontal axis. The inverse (downsloping) relationship between the interest rate (price) and dollar quantity of investment demanded is consistent with the *law of demand* discussed in Chapter 3. The curve labeled *ID* in Figure 9-5 is the economy's **investment demand curve.** It shows the amount of investment forthcoming at each real interest rate.

This analysis of investment allows us to anticipate an important aspect of macroeconomic policy. You will find in our discussion of monetary policy (Chapter

15) that by changing the supply of money, government can change the interest rate. It does this primarily to change the level of investment spending. At any time, firms have a variety of investment projects under consideration. If real interest rates are high, only projects with the highest expected rates of return will be undertaken. The level of investment will be low. As the real interest rate is lowered, projects whose expected rates of return are less will also become potentially profitable and investment in them will rise. To fight recession, government reduces interest rates; to fight inflation, government increases interest rates. **(Key Question 8)**

Shifts in the Investment Demand Curve

Figure 9-5 portrays the interest-rate–amount-of-investment relationship, *other things equal.* When these other things change, the investment-demand curve shifts to the right or to the left. In general, any factor which leads businesses collectively to expect greater rates of return on their investments will increase investment demand; that factor will shift the investment demand curve to the right, as from ID_0 to ID_1 in Figure 9-6. Any factor which leads businesses collectively to expect lower rates of return on their investments will shift the curve to the left, as from ID_0 to ID_2. What are these non-interest-rate determinants of investment demand?

Acquisition, Maintenance, and Operating Costs
As the sanding machine example revealed, the initial costs of capital goods, and the estimated costs of operating and maintaining those goods, affect the expected rate of return on investment. When costs fall, the expected rate of return from prospective investment projects will rise, shifting the investment demand curve to the right. Example: Lower electricity costs associated with running equipment would shift the investment demand curve to the right. Higher costs, in contrast, will shift the curve to the left.

Business Taxes
Business owners look to expected returns *after taxes* in making their investment decisions. An increase in business taxes will lower the expected profitability of investments and shift the investment demand curve to the left; a tax reduction will shift it to the right.

Technological Change
Technological progress—the development of new products, improvements in

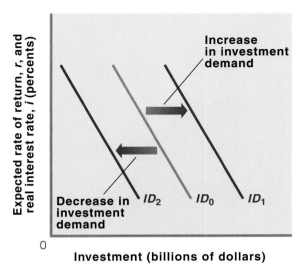

FIGURE 9-6 Shifts in the investment demand curve
Increases in investment demand are shown as rightward shifts in the investment demand curve; decreases in investment demand are shown as leftward shifts in the investment demand curve.

existing products, and the creation of new machinery and production processes—stimulates investment. The development of a more efficient machine, for example, will lower production costs or improve product quality, increasing the expected rate of return from investing in the machine. Profitable new products—mountain bikes, sports utility vehicles, high-resolution televisions, cellular phones, and so on—induce a flurry of investment as firms tool up for expanded production. A rapid rate of technological progress shifts the investment demand curve to the right.

Stock of Capital Goods on Hand
The stock of capital goods on hand, relative to output and sales, influences investment decisions by firms. When the economy is *overstocked* with production facilities and firms have excessive inventories of finished goods, the expected rate of return on new investment declines. Firms with excess production capacity have little incentive to invest in new capital. Therefore, less investment is forthcoming at each real interest rate; the investment demand curve shifts to the left.

When the economy is *understocked* with production facilities and firms are selling their output as fast as it can be produced, the expected rate of return on new investment increases. Firms add to their production facilities to meet the growing demand for their products and services. So the investment demand curve shifts to the right.

Expectations   We noted that business investment is based on *expected* returns (expected additions to profit). Capital goods are durable; they have a life expectancy of 10 or 20 years. Thus, the expected rate of return on any capital investment will depend on the firm's expectations of *future* sales, *future* operating costs, and *future* profitability of the product which the capital helps to produce. These expectations are based on forecasts of future business conditions as well as on such elusive and difficult-to-predict factors as changes in the domestic political climate, the thrust of foreign affairs, population growth, and consumer tastes. If executives become more optimistic about future sales, costs, and profits, the investment demand curve will shift to the right; a pessimistic outlook will shift it to the left.

Global Perspective 9-2 compares investment spending relative to GDP for several nations in a recent year. Domestic interest rates and investment demand determine the levels of investment relative to GDP.

QUICK REVIEW 9-3

■ A specific investment will be undertaken if the expected rate of return, *r*, equals or exceeds the real interest rate, *i*.

■ The investment demand curve shows the total monetary amounts which will be invested by an economy at various possible real interest rates.

■ The investment demand curve shifts when changes occur in **(a)** the costs of acquiring, operating, and maintaining capital goods, **(b)** business taxes, **(c)**, technology, **(d)** the stock of capital goods on hand, and **(e)** business expectations.

Investment Schedule

To add the investment decisions of businesses to the consumption plans of households, we must express investment plans in terms of the level of disposable income (DI) or gross domestic product (GDP). That is, we need to construct an **investment schedule** showing the amounts business firms collectively intend to invest at each possible level of GDP. Such a schedule represents the investment plans of businesses in the same way the consumption and saving schedules represent the consumption and saving plans of households. In developing the investment schedule, we will assume that investment is *independent* of the level of current disposable income or real output.

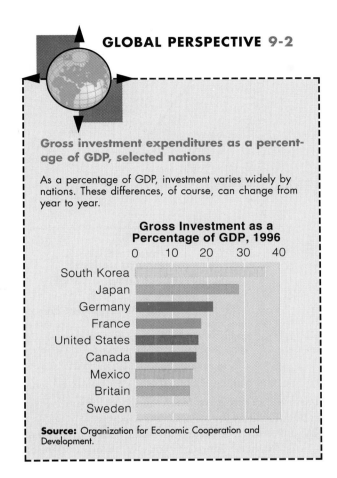

GLOBAL PERSPECTIVE 9-2

Gross investment expenditures as a percentage of GDP, selected nations

As a percentage of GDP, investment varies widely by nations. These differences, of course, can change from year to year.

Gross Investment as a Percentage of GDP, 1996

South Korea
Japan
Germany
France
United States
Canada
Mexico
Britain
Sweden

Source: Organization for Economic Cooperation and Development.

Suppose the investment demand curve is as shown in Figure 9-7a and the current real interest rate is 8 percent. This means that firms will find it profitable to spend $20 billion on investment goods. Our assumption tells us that this $20 billion of investment will occur at both low and high levels of GDP. The line I_g (*gross* investment) in Figure 9-7b shows this graphically; it is the economy's *investment schedule*. You should not confuse this investment schedule I_g with the investment demand curve *ID* in Figure 9-7a. The investment schedule shows the amount of investment forthcoming at each level of GDP. As indicated in Figure 9-7, this amount ($20 billion) is determined by the interest rate together with the location of the investment demand curve. Table 9-3 shows the investment schedule in tabular form for the GDP levels in Table 9-1.

The assumed independence of investment and income is admittedly a simplification. A higher level of

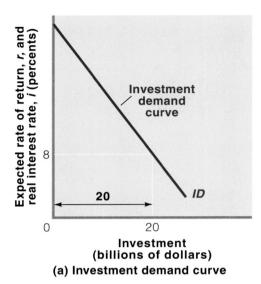

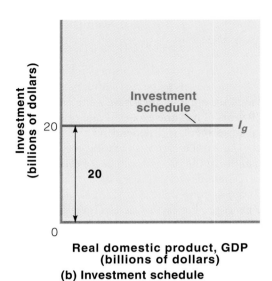

FIGURE 9-7 **(a) The investment demand curve and (b) the investment schedule**   (a) The level of investment spending (here, $20 billion) is determined by the real interest rate (here, 8 percent) together with the investment demand curve *ID*. (b) The investment schedule I_g relates the amount of investment ($20 billion) determined in (a) to the various levels of GDP.

----

business activity may *induce* additional spending on capital facilities for at least two reasons:

1. Investment is related to profit; much investment is financed internally out of business profits. Therefore, it is plausible that as GDP rises, so will business profits and therefore the level of investment.

2. At low levels of income and output, the business sector has excess production capacity; many industries have idle machinery and equipment and therefore little incentive to purchase additional capital goods. But, as the level of domestic income and output rises, this excess capacity disappears and firms are inclined to add to their stock of capital goods.

Instability of Investment

In contrast to the consumption schedule, the investment schedule is unstable; it shifts significantly upward or downward quite often. Investment, in fact, is the most volatile component of total spending. Figure 9-8 shows just how volatile investment has been. Note that its swings are much greater than are those of GDP. The figure also suggests that our simplified treatment of investment as independent of GDP (Figure 9-7b) is essentially realistic; investment does not closely follow GDP.

Factors explaining the variability of investment follow:

Durability   Because of their durability, capital goods have an indefinite useful life. Within limits, purchases of capital goods are discretionary and therefore postponable. Older equipment and buildings can be scrapped and replaced, or they can be patched up and

TABLE 9-3   **The investment schedule (in billions)**

(1) Level of real output and income	(2) Investment (I_g)
$370	$20
390	20
410	20
430	20
450	20
470	20
490	20
510	20
530	20
550	20

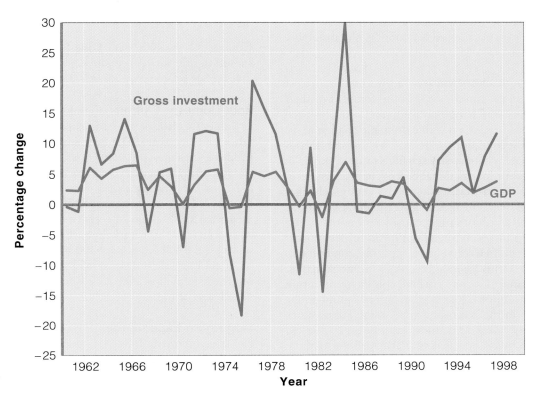

FIGURE 9-8 **The volatility of investment**   Annual percentage changes in investment spending are often several times greater than the percentage changes in GDP. (Data are in real terms.)

used for a few more years. Optimism about the future may prompt firms to replace their older facilities; modernizing their plants will call for a high level of investment. A less optimistic view, however, may lead to very small amounts of investment as older facilities are repaired and kept in use.

Irregularity of Innovation   We know that technological progress is a major determinant of investment. New products and processes stimulate investment. But history suggests that major innovations—railroads, electricity, automobiles, fiber optics, and computers—occur quite irregularly. When they do occur, they induce a vast upsurge or "wave" of investment spending which in time recedes.

A classic illustration is the widespread acceptance of the automobile in the 1920s. This event not only substantially increased investment in the automobile industry itself but also induced tremendous investment in such related industries as steel, petroleum, glass, and rubber as well as public investment in streets

and highways. But when investment in these related industries was ultimately "completed"—when enough capital facilities had been created to meet the needs of the automobile industry—total investment leveled off.

Variability of Profits   Businesses invest only when they think it will be profitable, and to a significant degree, the expectation of future profitability is influenced by the size of current profits. Current profits, however, are themselves highly variable (line 13 of the table on the inside covers provides information on undistributed corporate profits). Thus, the variability of profits contributes to the volatile nature of the incentive to invest.

The instability of profits may also cause investment fluctuations in a second way. Profits are a major source of funds for business investment. U.S. businesses often prefer this internal source of financing to increases in external debt or stock issue.

In short, expanding profits give firms both greater *incentives* and greater *means* to invest; declining profits have the reverse effects. The fact that actual profits are variable thus adds doubly to the instability of investment.

Variability of Expectations   Firms tend to project current business conditions into the future. But their expectations can change radically and quickly when some event suggests a possible dramatic change in future business conditions. Changes in the domestic political climate, changes in exchange rates, changes in the outlook for international peace, court decisions in key labor or antitrust cases, legislative actions, changes in trade barriers, changes in governmental economic policies, and a host of similar considerations may cause substantial shifts in business optimism or pessimism.

The stock market requires specific comment in this regard. Firms frequently look to the stock market as an indicator of society's overall confidence in future business conditions. Rising stock prices signify public confidence in the business future, while falling stock prices imply a lack of confidence. The stock market, however, is highly speculative. Participants who jump in and buy when stock prices begin to rise, or sell as soon as prices start to fall, can seriously magnify initially modest changes in stock prices. The volatility of this market can produce swings in optimism and pessimism, thus adding to the instability of investment spending. This stock market effect on investment, however, has proved to be relatively mild in the past several decades.

For the reasons we just discussed, changes in investment cause most fluctuations in output and employment. We can think of the volatility of investment shown in Figure 9-8 as being reflected in occasional and substantial upward and downward shifts of the investment schedule in Figure 9-7b, caused by occasional and substantial rightward and leftward shifts of the investment demand schedule in Figure 9-7a.

EQUILIBRIUM GDP: EXPENDITURES-OUTPUT APPROACH

In this and the next section, we use the consumption, saving, and investment schedules to explain the equilibrium levels of output, income, and employment. We will do so first by taking the **aggregate expenditures–domestic output** (or $C + I_g = $ GDP) **approach.**

Tabular Analysis

Columns 2 through 5 in Table 9-4 repeat the consumption and saving schedules in Table 9-1 and the investment schedule in Table 9-3.

Real Domestic Output   Let's look again at column 2, Table 9-4. It lists the various possible levels of total output—of real GDP—the business sector might produce. *Producers are willing to offer any of these 10 levels of output if they can expect to receive an identical level of income from the sale of that output.* For example, the business sector will produce $370 billion of output, incurring $370 billion of costs (wages, rents, interest, and profit) only if firms believe they can sell this output for $370 billion. Some $390 billion of output will be offered for sale if firms think they can sell this output for $390 billion. And so it is for all the other possible levels of output.

Aggregate Expenditures   In our assumed private closed economy in Table 9-4, aggregate expenditures consist of consumption (column 3) plus investment (column 5). Their sum is shown in column 6, which with column 2 makes up the **aggregate expenditures schedule** for the economy. This schedule shows the amount $(C + I_g)$ which will be spent at each possible output or income level.

At this point we are working with *planned investment*—the data in column 5, Table 9-4. These data show the amounts firms *intend* to invest, not the amounts which *actually will be invested* if there are unplanned changes in inventories.

Equilibrium GDP   Of the 10 possible levels of GDP in Table 9-4, which will be the equilibrium level? Which total output will the economy be capable of sustaining?

The equilibrium output is that output whose production will create total spending just sufficient to purchase that output. So the equilibrium level of GDP is the level where the total quantity of goods produced (GDP) equals the total quantity of goods purchased $(C + I_g)$. Look at the domestic output levels in column 2 and the aggregate expenditures levels in column 6 and you will see that this equality exists only at $470 billion of GDP (row 6) . That is the only output at which the economy is willing to spend precisely the amount necessary to take that output from the shelves. There, the annual rates of production and spending are in balance. There is no overproduction,

TABLE 9-4   Determination of the equilibrium levels of employment, output, and income: a closed private economy

(1) Possible levels of employment, millions	(2) Real domestic output (and income) (GDP = DI),* billions	(3) Consumption (C), billions	(4) Saving (S), billions	(5) Investment (I_g), billions	(6) Aggregate expenditures (C + I_g), billions	(7) Unintended investment (+) or disinvestment (−) in inventories	(8) Tendency of employment, output, and incomes
(1) 40	$370	$375	$−5	$20	$395	$−25	Increase
(2) 45	390	390	0	20	410	−20	Increase
(3) 50	410	405	5	20	425	−15	Increase
(4) 55	430	420	10	20	440	−10	Increase
(5) 60	450	435	15	20	455	−5	Increase
(6) **65**	**470**	**450**	**20**	**20**	**470**	**0**	**Equilibrium**
(7) 70	490	465	25	20	485	+5	Decrease
(8) 75	510	480	30	20	500	+10	Decrease
(9) 80	530	495	35	20	515	+15	Decrease
(10) 85	550	510	40	20	530	+20	Decrease

*If depreciation and net foreign factor income earned in the United States are zero, government is ignored, and it is assumed that all saving occurs in the household sector of the economy, GDP as a measure of domestic output is equal to NI, PI, and DI. This means that households receive a DI equal to the value of total output.

which would result in a piling up of unsold goods and therefore cutbacks in the production rate. Nor is there an excess of total spending, which would draw down inventories of goods and prompt increases in the rate of production. In short, there is no reason for businesses to alter this rate of production; $470 billion is therefore the **equilibrium GDP.**

Disequilibrium   To better understand the meaning of the equilibrium level of GDP; let's examine other levels of GDP to see why they cannot be sustained.

If businesses produced $410 billion of GDP (row 3 in Table 9-4), they would find that this output yields $405 billion in consumer spending. Supplemented by $20 billion of planned investment, total expenditures (C + I_g) would be $425 billion, as shown in column 6. The economy would provide an annual rate of spending more than sufficient to purchase the $410 billion of annual production. Because buyers would be taking goods off the shelves faster than firms could produce them, an unintended decline in business inventories of $15 billion would occur (column 7) if this situation continued. But businesses can adjust to such an imbalance between aggregate expenditures and real output by stepping up production. Greater output will increase employment and total income. In brief, if aggregate expenditures exceed the domestic

output, those expenditures will drive domestic output upward.

We can make a similar comparison of GDP (column 2) and C + I_g (column 6) at any other level of GDP *below* the $470 billion equilibrium level. In each case we will find that the economy wants to spend in excess of the level at which businesses are willing to produce. The excess of total spending at all these levels of GDP will drive GDP upward to the $470 billion equilibrium level.

The reverse is true at all levels of GDP *above* the $470 billion equilibrium level. Businesses will find that these total outputs fail to generate the spending needed to clear the shelves of goods. Being unable to recover their costs, businesses will cut back on production.

To illustrate: At the $510 billion output (row 8), business managers would find there is insufficient spending to permit the sale of all that output. Of the $510 billion of income which this output creates, $480 billion would be received back by businesses as consumption spending. Though supplemented by $20 billion of planned investment spending, total expenditures ($500 billion) would fall $10 billion short of the $510 billion quantity produced. If this imbalance persisted, $10 billion of inventories would pile up (column 7). But businesses can adjust to this unintended accumulation of unsold goods by cutting back on the rate of production. The resulting decline in output would mean fewer jobs and a decline in total income. You should verify that all other levels of GDP above the $470 billion equilibrium level would also result in insufficient spending.

The equilibrium level of GDP occurs where the total output, measured by GDP, and aggregate expenditures, $C + I_g$, are equal. Any excess of total spending over total output will drive GDP upward. Any deficiency of total spending will pull GDP downward.

Graphical Analysis

The same analysis can be shown in a graph. In **Figure 9-9 (Key Graph)** the **45 degree line** now takes on increased significance. Recall that the special property of this line is that at any point on it, the value of what is being measured on the horizontal axis (in this case GDP) is equal to the value of what is being measured on the vertical axis (here, aggregate expenditures or $C + I_g$). Having discovered in our tabular analysis that the equilibrium level of domestic output is determined where $C + I_g$ equals GDP, we can say that the 45 degree line in Figure 9-9 is a graphical statement of this equilibrium condition.

Now we must graph the aggregate expenditures schedule onto Figure 9-9. One way to do this is to duplicate the consumption schedule C in Figure 9-2a and add to it *vertically* the constant $20 billion amount of investment I_g from Figure 9-7b. This $20 billion is the amount we assumed firms plan to invest at all levels of GDP. Or, more directly, we can plot the $C + I_g$ data in column 6, Table 9-4.

Observe in Figure 9-9 that the aggregate expenditures line $C + I_g$ shows that total spending rises with income and output (GDP), but not as much as income rises, because the marginal propensity to consume—the slope of line C—is less than 1. A part of any increase in income will not be spent; it will be saved. And because the aggregate expenditures line $C + I_g$ is parallel to the consumption line C, the slope of the aggregate expenditures line also equals the MPC for the economy and is less than 1. For our particular data, aggregate expenditures rise by $15 billion for every $20 billion increase in real output and income because $5 billion of each $20 billion increment is saved. Therefore, in numerical terms the slope of the aggregate expenditures line is .75 (= $\Delta$$15/ $\Delta$$20).

The equilibrium level of GDP is the GDP which corresponds to the intersection of the aggregate expenditures schedule and the 45 degree line. This intersection locates the only point at which aggregate expenditures (on the vertical axis) are equal to GDP (on the horizontal axis). Because Figure 9-9 is based on the data in Table 9-4, we once again find that equilibrium output is $470 billion. Observe that consumption at this output is $450 billion and investment is $20 billion.

It is evident from Figure 9-9 that no levels of GDP above the equilibrium level are sustainable because at those levels $C + I_g$ falls short of GDP. Graphically, the aggregate expenditures schedule lies *below* the 45 degree line in those situations. At the $510 billion GDP level, for example, $C + I_g$ is only $500 billion. This underspending causes inventories to rise, prompting firms to readjust production downward in the direction of the $470 billion output level.

Conversely, at levels of GDP below $470 billion, the economy wants to spend in excess of what businesses are producing. Then $C + I_g$ exceeds total output. Graphically, the aggregate expenditures schedule lies *above* the 45 degree line. At the $410 billion GDP level, for example, $C + I_g$ totals $425 billion. This overspending causes inventories to decline, prompting firms to raise production toward the $470 billion GDP. Unless there is some change in the location of the aggregate expenditures line, the $470 billion level of GDP will be sustained indefinitely.

EQUILIBRIUM GDP: LEAKAGES-INJECTIONS APPROACH

The expenditures-output approach to determining GDP spotlights aggregate expenditures as the immediate determinant of the levels of output and income. Though the **leakages-injections ($S = I_g$) approach** is less direct, it does have the advantage of underscoring the *reason* $C + I_g$ and GDP are unequal at all levels of output except the equilibrium level.

The idea of the leakages-injections approach is this: Under our simplifying assumptions we know that the production of any level of real output will generate an identical amount of disposable income. But we also know a part of that income may be saved—*not* consumed—by households. Saving therefore represents a **leakage** or withdrawal of spending from the income-expenditures stream. Saving is what keeps consumption short of total output or GDP; as a result of saving, consumption by itself is insufficient to take all domestic output off the shelves, setting the stage, it would seem, for a decline in total output.

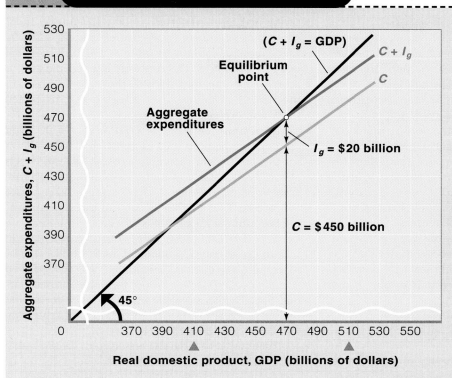

FIGURE 9-9 **The aggregate expenditures–domestic output approach to equilibrium GDP** The aggregate expenditures schedule, $C + I_g$, is determined by adding the investment schedule I_g to the upsloping consumption schedule C. Since investment is assumed to be the same at each level of GDP, the vertical distances between C and $C + I_g$ do not change. Equilibrium GDP is determined where the aggregate expenditures schedule intersects the 45 degree line, in this case at $470 billion.

QUICK QUIZ 9-9

1. **In this figure, the slope of the aggregate expenditures schedule $C + I_g$:**
   a. increases as real GDP increases.
   b. falls as real GDP increases.
   c. is constant and equals the MPC.
   d. is constant and equals the MPS.

2. **At all points on the 45 degree line:**
   a. equilibrium GDP is possible.
   b. aggregate expenditures exceed real GDP.
   c. consumption exceeds investment.
   d. aggregate expenditures are less than real GDP.

3. **The $490 billion level of real GDP is *not* at equilibrium because:**
   a. investment exceeds consumption.

   b. consumption exceeds investment.
   c. planned $C + I_g$ exceeds real GDP.
   d. planned $C + I_g$ is less than real GDP.

4. **The $430 billion level of real GDP is *not* at equilibrium because:**
   a. investment exceeds consumption.
   b. consumption exceeds investment.
   c. planned $C + I_g$ exceeds real GDP.
   d. planned $C + I_g$ is less than real GDP.

Answers: 1. c; 2. a; 3. d; 4. c

However, the business sector does not intend to sell its entire output to consumers; some domestic output will consist of capital goods sold within the business sector. Investment can therefore be thought of as an **injection** of spending into the income-expenditures stream; investment is an adjunct to consumption. Investment is thus a potential replacement for the leakage of saving.

If, at a certain level of GDP, the leakage of saving exceeds the injection of investment, then $C + I_g$ will fall short of GDP and that level of GDP is too high to be sustained. Any GDP for which saving exceeds investment is an above-equilibrium GDP. Conversely, if the injection of investment exceeds the leakage of saving, then $C + I_g$ will be greater than GDP and GDP will be driven upward. Any GDP for which investment exceeds saving is a below-equilibrium GDP.

Only where $S = I_g$—where the leakage of saving is exactly offset by the injection of investment—will aggregate expenditures equal real output. And that equality is what defines the equilibrium GDP.

In the closed private economy assumed here, there is a single leakage (saving) and a single injection (investment). In more general terms, a *leakage* is any use of income other than to purchase domestically produced output. In the expanded models that follow (in Chapter 10), we will need to incorporate the additional leakages of imports and taxes into our analysis.

Similarly, an *injection* is any supplement to consumer spending on domestic production. Again, in later models we will add injections of exports and government purchases to our discussion. But for now we need only compare the single leakage of saving with the sole injection of investment to obtain the equilibrium GDP.

Tabular Analysis

Our $C + I_g =$ GDP approach has led us to conclude that, in our example, all levels of GDP less than $470 billion are unstable. That is true because then $C + I_g$ exceeds GDP, which drives GDP upward. Now let's look at the saving schedule (columns 2 and 4) and the investment schedule (columns 2 and 5) in Table 9-4. Comparing the amounts households and firms want to save and invest at GDP levels *below* $470 billion explains the excesses of total spending. At each of these lower GDP levels, firms plan to invest more than households want to save.

For example, at a GDP of $410 billion (row 3), households will save only $5 billion but businesses will invest $20 billion. Hence, investment exceeds saving by $15 billion (= $20 − $5). Columns 6 and 2 show that aggregate expenditures exceed GDP by that same $15 billion (= $425 − $410). The small leakage of saving at this relatively low income level is more than compensated for by the larger injection of investment spending. That causes $C + I_g$ to exceed GDP and drives GDP upward.

In contrast, all levels of GDP *above* $470 billion are unstable because they exceed $C + I_g$. The reason for this insufficient spending is that at all GDP levels above $470 billion, households want to save more than firms plan to invest. The saving leakage is not compensated for by the injection of investment.

For example, households will save $30 billion at a GDP of $510 billion (row 8). Firms, however, will plan to invest only $20 billion. This $10 billion excess of saving over planned investment will reduce total spending to $10 billion below the value of total output. Specifically, aggregate expenditures will be $500 billion and real GDP is $510 billion. This spending deficiency will reduce GDP.

Again we verify that the equilibrium GDP is $470 billion. At this level of GDP the saving desires of households and the investment plans of businesses are the same ($20 billion each). When firms and households attempt to invest and save the same amounts—where leakages equal injections—aggregate expenditures will equal GDP. Here, there will be no unplanned changes in inventories.

Graphical Analysis

The leakages-injections approach to determining equilibrium GDP is demonstrated in Figure 9-10, in which we have again graphed the saving schedule in

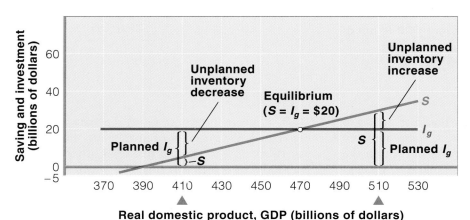

FIGURE 9-10 The leakages-injections approach to equilibrium GDP In this approach the equilibrium GDP is determined by the intersection of the saving (*S*) and planned investment (*I_g*) schedules. Only at that point will households plan to save the amount businesses want to invest. At other, nonequilibrium GDPs, overspending or underspending will result in unplanned inventory changes.

1. **The slope of the consumption schedule in this figure is .75. Thus, the**
   a. slope of the saving schedule is 1.33.
   b. marginal propensity to consume is .75.
   c. average propensity to consume is .25.
   d. slope of the saving schedule is also .75.

2. **In this figure, when consumption is a positive amount, saving**
   a. must be a negative amount.
   b. also must be a positive amount.
   c. can be either a positive or a negative amount.
   d. is zero.

3. **In this figure,**
   a. the marginal propensity to consume is constant at all levels of income.

   b. the marginal propensity to save rises as disposable income rises.
   c. consumption is inversely (negatively) related to disposable income.
   d. saving is inversely (negatively) related to disposable income.

4. **When consumption equals disposable income,**
   a. the marginal propensity to consume is zero.
   b. the average propensity to consume is zero.
   c. consumption and saving must be equal.
   d. saving must be zero.

$$APC = \frac{\text{consumption}}{\text{income}}$$

$$APS = \frac{\text{saving}}{\text{income}}$$

dustries have idle machinery and equipment and therefore little incentive to purchase additional capital goods. But, as the level of domestic income and output rises, this excess capacity disappears and firms are inclined to add to their stock of capital goods.

In contrast to the consumption schedule, the investment schedule is unstable; it shifts significantly upward or downward quite often. Investment, in fact, is the most volatile component of total spending. Figure 9-8 shows just how volatile investment has been. Note that its swings are much greater than are those of GDP. The figure also suggests that our simplified treatment of investment as independent of GDP (Figure 9-7b) is essentially realistic; investment does not closely follow GDP.

Factors explaining the variability of investment follow:

Durability Because of their durability, capital goods have an indefinite useful life. Within limits, purchases of capital goods are discretionary and therefore postponable. Older equipment and buildings can be scrapped and replaced, or they can be patched up and

Figure 9-2b and the investment schedule in 9-7b. The numerical data for these schedules are in columns 2, 4, and 5, Table 9-4. The two lines S and I_g intersect at the equilibrium GDP, $470 billion. Only here do businesses and households plan to invest and save the same amounts; only here will GDP and $C + I_g$ be the same.

At higher levels of GDP, households will save more than businesses plan to invest. Because the saving leakage will exceed the investment injection, $C + I_g$ will fall short of GDP, driving GDP downward. At the $510 billion GDP, for example, saving of $30 billion will exceed investment of $20 billion by $10 billion, with the result that $C + I_g$ will be $10 billion short of GDP.

At all levels of GDP below the $470 billion equilibrium level, businesses will plan to invest more than households save. Because the injection of investment will exceed the leakage of saving, $C + I_g$ will exceed GDP, driving GDP upward. To illustrate: At the $410 billion level of GDP the $5 billion leakage of saving is more than compensated for by the $20 billion that businesses plan to invest. The result is that $C + I_g$ will exceed GDP by $15 billion. **(Key Question 10)**

PLANNED VERSUS ACTUAL INVESTMENT

We have seen that differences between saving and investment can occur and bring about changes in the equilibrium GDP. Now we must emphasize that, in another sense, saving and investment are always equal. This apparent contradiction concerning the equality of saving and investment is resolved when we distinguish between **planned investment** and saving (which need not be equal) and **actual investment** and saving (which by definition must be equal). The catch is that *actual investment consists of planned investment and unplanned investment (unplanned changes in inventory investment). Unplanned investment acts as a balancing item which equates the actual amounts saved and invested in any period.*

Disequilibrium and Inventories

Consider, as an example, the $490 billion above-equilibrium GDP (row 7 in Table 9-4). What happens if businesses produce this output, thinking they can sell it? At this level, households save $25 billion of their $490 billion DI, so consumption is only $465

billion. *Planned* investment (column 5) is $20 billion; businesses intend to buy $20 billion worth of capital goods. This means aggregate expenditures ($C + I_g$) are $485 billion, and sales therefore fall short of production by $5 billion. This extra $5 billion of goods is retained by businesses as an *unintended* or *unplanned* increase in inventories (column 7). It is unintended because it results from the failure of total spending to take total output off the shelves. Remembering that, by definition, changes in inventories are a part of investment, we note that *actual* investment is $25 billion ($20 planned *plus* $5 unintended or unplanned). It exactly equals the saving of $25 billion, even though saving exceeds *planned* investment by $5 billion. Since firms cannot earn profits by accumulating unwanted inventories, they will cut back production.

Now look at the below-equilibrium $450 billion output (row 5, Table 9-4). Because households save only $15 billion of their $450 billion DI, consumption is $435 billion. Planned investment by firms is $20 billion, so aggregate expenditures are $455 billion. Sales exceed production by $5 billion. This is so only if an unplanned decrease in business inventories occurs. Firms must unintentionally *dis*invest $5 billion in inventories (column 7). Note again that actual investment is $15 billion ($20 planned minus $5 unplanned) and equal to saving of $15 billion, even though planned investment exceeds saving by $5 billion. The decline in inventories from the excess of sales over production will induce firms to expand production.

Once again: At all *above-equilibrium* GDPs (where saving exceeds planned investment), actual investment and saving are made equal by unintended increases in inventories which are added to planned investment. In Figure 9-9, the vertical distance of the saving schedule above the (planned) investment schedule I_g represents an unintended inventory increase.

At all *below-equilibrium* GDPs (where planned investment exceeds saving), actual investment is made equal to saving by unintended decreases in inventories, which are subtracted from planned investment. An unintended inventory decrease is shown graphically as the vertical distance of the (planned) investment schedule above the saving schedule.

Attainment of Equilibrium

These distinctions are important because they mean that it is the equality of planned investment and saving which determines the equilibrium level of GDP.

John Maynard Keynes (1883–1946)

The British economist John Maynard Keynes is the originator of the central ideas underlying the aggregate expenditures model.

In 1935 George Bernard Shaw received a letter from John Maynard Keynes in which Keynes asserted, "I believe myself to be writing a book on economic theory which will largely revolutionize . . . the way the world thinks about economic problems." And, in fact, Keynes' *General Theory of Employment, Interest, and Money* (1936) did just that: It revolutionized economic analysis and established Keynes as one of the most influential economists of all times.

Keynes was far more than an economist: He was an incredibly active, many-sided man who also played such diverse roles as principal representative of the Treasury at the World War I Paris Peace Conference, deputy for the Chancellor of the Exchequer, a director of the Bank of England, trustee of the National Gallery, chairman of the Council of the Encouragement of Music and the Arts, bursar of King's College, Cambridge, editor of the *Economic Journal*, chairman of the *Nation* and later the *New Statesman* magazines, and chairman of the National Mutual Life Assurance Society. He also ran an investment company, organized the Camargo Ballet (his wife, Lydia Lopokova, was a renowned star of the Russian Imperial Ballet), and built (profitably) the Arts Theatre at Cambridge.*

In addition, Keynes found time to amass a personal fortune by speculating in stocks, international currencies, and commodities. He was also a leading figure in the Bloomsbury group, an avant-garde group of intellectual luminaries who greatly influenced the artistic and literary standards of England.

Most importantly, Keynes was a prolific scholar. His books encompassed such widely ranging topics as probability theory, monetary economics, and the economic consequences of the World War I peace treaty. His magnum opus, however, was the *General Theory of Employment, Interest, and Money,* described by John Kenneth Galbraith as "a work of profound obscurity, badly written and prematurely published." Yet the book established the major insights discussed in the chapter: the consumption function, the investment demand curve, the investment schedule, and the equilibrium GDP.

Moreover, *General Theory* attacked the contention by the classical economists that recessions and depressions are unlikely to occur, and if they do, they will automatically correct themselves. Keynes' analysis suggested that a major decline in investment spending in a capitalist economy results in an even greater decline in total spending, total output, and total income. Further, said Keynes, the economy's slide into recession or depression was unlikely to be reversed by automatic mechanisms. The economy might therefore languish for many years in depression. Indeed, the massive unemployment of the worldwide depression of 1930s seemed to provide sufficient evidence that Keynes was right. His basic policy recommendation— government needed to play an active role in ensuring that the economy stayed fully employed—was controversial in view of the classical position that government intervention in the economy was detrimental. Keynes, a strong critic of socialism, argued that government stabilization policy was needed to ensure the continuance of the market system that classical economists, and Keynes himself, so admired.

*E. Ray Canterberry, *The Making of Economics*, 3d ed. (Belmont, CA: Wadsworth Publishing Company, 1987), p. 126.

We can think of the process by which equilibrium is achieved as follows:

1. A difference between saving and planned investment creates a difference between the production and spending plans of the economy as a whole.

2. The difference between production plans and spending plans results in unintended investment or disinvestment in inventories.

3. As long as unintended investment in inventories persists, firms will revise their production plans

downward and reduce GDP. Conversely, as long as unintended disinvestment in inventories exists, firms will revise their production plans upward and increase GDP. Both GDP movements are toward equilibrium because they bring about the equality of planned investment and saving.

4. GDP will reach equilibrium when planned investment and saving are equal. At that GDP, there is no unintended investment or disinvestment in inventories to drive GDP upward or downward. **(Key Question 11)**

QUICK REVIEW 9-4

■ In a private closed economy, equilibrium GDP occurs where aggregate expenditures equal real domestic output ($C + I_g = $ GDP).

■ Alternatively, equilibrium GDP is established where saving equals planned investment ($S = I_g$).

■ Actual investment consists of planned investment plus unplanned changes in inventories and is always equal to saving in a private closed economy.

■ At equilibrium GDP, changes in inventories are zero; no unintended investment or disinvestment occurs.

CHAPTER SUMMARY

1. Classical economists argued that because supply creates its own demand (Say's law), general underspending was improbable. Thus the economy would provide virtually continuous full employment. Even if temporary declines in total spending occurred, these declines would be compensated for by downward price and wage adjustments which would boost spending and employment, restoring the economy to its full-employment level of output.

2. The Great Depression and Keynes' *General Theory of Employment, Interest, and Money* undermined classical macroeconomics. The Great Depression challenged the classical precept that full employment was the norm in a capitalist economy. Keynes' aggregate expenditures analysis showed how periods of underspending or overspending could occur.

3. The basic tools of the aggregate expenditures model are the consumption, saving, and investment schedules, which show the various amounts households intend to consume and save and firms plan to invest at the various income and output levels, assuming a fixed price level.

4. The *average* propensities to consume and save show the fractions of any *total* income that are consumed and saved; APC + APS = 1. The *marginal* propensities to consume and save show the fractions of any *change* in total income that are consumed and saved; MPC + MPS = 1.

5. The locations of the consumption and saving schedules are determined by **(a)** the amount of wealth owned by households; **(b)** expectations of future income, future prices, and product availability; **(c)** the relative size of household debt; and **(d)** taxation. The consumption and saving schedules are relatively stable.

6. The immediate determinants of investment are **(a)** the expected rate of return and **(b)** the real rate of interest. The economy's investment demand curve can be found by

cumulating investment projects, arraying them in descending order according to their expected rates of return, graphing the result, and applying the rule that investment will be profitable up to the point at which the real interest rate, *i*, equals the expected rate of return, *r*. The investment demand curve reveals an inverse relationship between the interest rate and the level of aggregate investment.

7. Shifts in the investment demand curve can occur as the result of changes in **(a)** the acquisition, maintenance, and operating costs of capital goods; **(b)** business taxes; **(c)** technology; **(d)** the stocks of capital goods on hand; and **(e)** expectations.

8. For simplicity we assume that the level of investment determined by the current interest rate and the investment demand curve does not vary with the level of real GDP.

9. The durability of capital goods, the irregular occurrence of major innovations, profit volatility, and the variability of expectations all contribute to the instability of investment spending.

10. For a private closed economy the equilibrium level of GDP occurs when aggregate expenditures and real output are equal or, graphically, where the $C + I_g$ line intersects the 45 degree line. At any GDP greater than equilibrium GDP, real output will exceed aggregate spending, resulting in unintended investment in inventories, and eventual declines in output and income (GDP). At any below-equilibrium GDP, aggregate expenditures will exceed real output, resulting in unintended disinvestment in inventories and eventual increases in GDP.

11. The leakages-injections approach determines equilibrium GDP at the point where the amount households save and the amount businesses plan to invest are equal. This is the point where the saving and planned investment schedules intersect. Any excess of saving over planned investment will cause a shortage of total spending, forcing GDP to fall. Any excess of planned investment over saving will cause an excess of total spending, inducing GDP to rise. The change in GDP will in both cases correct the discrepancy between saving and planned investment.

12. Actual investment consists of planned investment plus unplanned changes in inventories. When planned investment diverges from saving, an unintended investment or disinvestment in inventories occurs which equates actual investment and saving. At equilibrium GDP, planned investment equals saving; inventory levels are then constant (there is no unplanned investment or disinvestment).

TERMS AND CONCEPTS

Say's law
Keynesian economics
consumption schedule
saving schedule
break-even income
average propensity to
  consume

average propensity to save
marginal propensity to
  consume
marginal propensity to
  save
expected rate of return
investment demand curve

investment schedule
aggregate expenditures–
  domestic output
  approach
aggregate expenditures
  schedule
equilibrium GDP

45 degree line
leakages-injections
  approach
leakage
injection
planned investment
actual investment

STUDY QUESTIONS

1. Relate Say's law to the view held by classical economists that the economy generally will operate at a position *on* its production possibilities curve (Chapter 2). Use production possibilities analysis to demonstrate the Keynesian view on this matter.

2. Explain what relationships are shown by **(a)** the consumption schedule, **(b)** the saving schedule, **(c)** the investment demand curve, and **(d)** the investment schedule.

3. Precisely how are the APC and the MPC different? Why must the sum of the MPC and the MPS equal 1? What are the basic determinants of the consumption and saving schedules? Of your own level of consumption?

4. Explain how each of the following will affect the consumption and saving schedules or the investment schedule:
   a. A decline in the amount of government bonds which consumers are holding
   b. The threat of limited, nonnuclear war, leading the public to expect future shortages of consumer durables
   c. A decline in the real interest rate
   d. A sharp decline in stock prices
   e. An increase in the rate of population growth

   f. The development of a cheaper method of manufacturing pig iron from ore
   g. The announcement that the social security program is to be restricted as to size of benefits
   h. The expectation that mild inflation will persist in the next decade
   i. An increase in the Federal personal income tax

5. Explain why an upshift in the consumption schedule typically involves an equal downshift in the saving schedule. What are the exceptions to this relationship?

6. KEY QUESTION   Complete the following table:

Level of output and income (GDP = DI)	Consumption	Saving	APC	APS	MPC	MPS
$240	$_____	$−4	___	___		
260	_____	0	___	___	___	___
280	_____	4	___	___	___	___
300	_____	8	___	___	___	___
320	_____	12	___	___	___	___
340	_____	16	___	___	___	___
360	_____	20	___	___	___	___
380	_____	24	___	___	___	___
400	_____	28	___	___	___	___

a. Show the consumption and saving schedules graphically.

b. Find the break-even level of income. Explain how it is possible for households to dissave at very low income levels.

c. If the proportion of total income consumed (APC) decreases and the proportion saved (APS) increases as income rises, explain both verbally and graphically how the MPC and MPS can be constant at various levels of income.

7. What are the basic determinants of investment? Explain the relationship between the real interest rate and the level of investment. Why is the investment schedule less stable than the consumption and saving schedules?

8. KEY QUESTION Assume there are no investment projects in the economy which yield an expected rate of return of 25 percent or more. But suppose there are $10 billion of investment projects yielding expected returns of between 20 and 25 percent; another $10 billion yielding between 15 and 20 percent; another $10 billion between 10 and 15 percent; and so forth. Cumulate these data and present them graphically, putting the expected rate of return on the vertical axis and the amount of investment on the horizontal axis. What will be the equilibrium level of aggregate investment if the real interest rate is **(a)** 15 percent, **(b)** 10 percent, and **(c)** 5 percent? Explain why this curve is the investment demand curve.

9. Explain graphically the determination of the equilibrium GDP by **(a)** the aggregate expenditures–domestic output approach and **(b)** the leakages–injections approach for a private closed economy. Why must these two approaches always yield the same equilibrium GDP? Explain why the intersection of the aggregate expenditures schedule and the 45 degree line determines the equilibrium GDP.

10. KEY QUESTION Assuming the level of investment is $16 billion and independent of the level of total output, complete the following table and determine the equilibrium levels of output and employment which this private closed economy would provide. What are the sizes of the MPC and MPS?

Possible levels of employment, millions	Real domestic output (GDP = DI), billions	Consumption, billions	Saving, billions
40	$240	$244	$_____
45	260	260	_____
50	280	276	_____
55	300	292	_____
60	320	308	_____
65	340	324	_____
70	360	340	_____
75	380	356	_____
80	400	372	_____

11. KEY QUESTION Using the consumption and saving data in question 10 and assuming investment is $16 billion, what are saving and planned investment at the $380 billion level of domestic output? What are saving and actual investment at that level? What are saving and planned investment at the $300 billion level of domestic output? What are the levels of saving and actual investment? Use the concept of unplanned investment to explain adjustments toward equilibrium from both the $380 and $300 billion levels of domestic output.

12. "Planned investment is equal to saving at all levels of GDP; actual investment equals saving only at the equilibrium GDP." Do you agree? Explain. Critically evaluate: "The fact that households may save more than firms want to invest is of no consequence, because events will in time force households and firms to save and invest at the same rates."

13. Advanced analysis: Linear equations for the consumption and saving schedules take the general form $C = a + bY$ and $S = -a + (1 - b)Y$, where C, S, and Y are consumption, saving, and national income, respectively. The constant a represents the vertical intercept, and b the slope of the consumption schedule.

a. Use the following data to substitute numerical values for a and b in the consumption and saving equations:

National income (Y)	Consumption (C)
$ 0	$ 80
100	140
200	200
300	260
400	320

b. What is the economic meaning of b? Of $(1 - b)$?

c. Suppose the amount of saving which occurs at each level of national income falls by $20, but that the values of b and $(1 - b)$ remain unchanged. Restate the saving and consumption equations for the new numerical values, and cite a factor which might have caused the change.

14. Advanced analysis: Suppose that the linear equation for consumption in a hypothetical economy is $C = 40 + .8Y$. Also suppose that income (Y) is $400. Determine **(a)** the marginal propensity to consume,

(b) the marginal propensity to save, **(c)** the level of consumption, **(d)** the average propensity to consume, **(e)** the level of saving, and **(f)** the average propensity to save.

15. **Advanced analysis:** Assume that the linear equation for consumption in a hypothetical private closed economy is $C = 10 + .9Y$, where Y is total real income (output). Also suppose that the equation for investment is $I_g = I_{g0} = 40$, meaning that I_g is 40 at all levels of total real income. Using the equation $Y = C + I_g$, determine the equilibrium level of Y. What are the total amounts of consumption, saving, and investment at equilibrium Y?

16. **(Last Word)** What is the significance of John Maynard Keynes book, *General Theory of Employment, Interest, and Money*, published in 1936?

17. **WEB-BASED QUESTION** **The Beige Book and Current Consumer Spending** The Beige Book http://www.bog.frb.fed.us/FOMC/BB/Current/ is a report on current economic conditions published eight times a year by the Federal Reserve System. Each Federal Reserve Bank gathers anecdotal information on current economic conditions in its district through reports from bank and branch directors and interviews with key executives, economists, market experts, and other sources. Locate the current Beige Book report. Compare consumer spending for the entire U.S. economy with consumer spending in your Federal Reserve District. What are the economic strengths and weaknesses for both? Are retailers reporting that recent sales have met their expectations? What are the expectations for the future?

18. **WEB-BASED QUESTION** Investment Instability—Changes in Real Private Nonresidential Fixed Investment Investment is the most volatile component of total spending. Real private nonresidential fixed investment is made up of two components: structures and producers' durable equipment. The Bureau of Economic Analysis provides data for real private nonresidential fixed investment in table form http://www.bea.doc.gov/briefrm/tables/ebr2.htm and graphical form http://www.bea.doc.gov/briefrm/nonresfi.htm. Has recent investment been volatile? Which is the largest component of investment, structures or producers' durable equipment? Which component has been more volatile (as measured by percentage change from preceding quarter)? Are recent quarterly percentage changes similar to previous years' changes? Looking at the investment graph, what investment forecast would you make for the forthcoming year?

CHAPTER TEN

Aggregate Expenditures: The Multiplier, Net Exports, and Government

You have seen why a particular equilibrium level of real GDP exists, specifically in a private closed economy. But recall from Chapter 8 that the GDP of U.S. capitalism is seldom stable; instead, it experiences long-run growth and is punctuated by cyclical fluctuations. We now turn our attention to why and how the equilibrium real GDP fluctuates. And since the public sector and the foreign sector *do* influence real GDP, later in this chapter we make the aggregate expenditures model more realistic by bringing these two sectors into the model.

We first analyze changes in investment spending and how they affect output, income, and employment. You will discover that a change in investment creates a multiple change in GDP. Then we "open" our simplified "closed" economy to show how exports and imports affect it. Next, we bring government—with its expenditures and taxes—into the model; the "private" economy becomes the "mixed" economy. Finally, we apply our extended model to two historical periods and consider some of the model's deficiencies.

CHANGES IN EQUILIBRIUM GDP AND THE MULTIPLIER

In the private closed economy, the equilibrium GDP will change in response to changes in the investment schedule or the saving and consumption schedules. Because the investment schedule is much less stable than the consumption and saving schedules, we will assume that the investment schedule is what changes.

Figure 10-1 shows the effect of changes in investment. Suppose the expected rate of return on investment rises (shifting the investment demand curve in Figure 9-7a to the right) or the interest rate falls (now the investment demand curve in Figure 9-7a does not shift; we instead move down the curve). As a result, investment spending increases by, say, $5 billion. This is indicated in Figure 10-1a by an upward shift of the aggregate expenditures schedule from $(C + I_g)_0$ to $(C + I_g)_1$ and in Figure 10-1b by an upward shift in the investment schedule from I_{g0} to I_{g1}. In each graph the result is a rise in the equilibrium GDP from $470 to $490 billion.

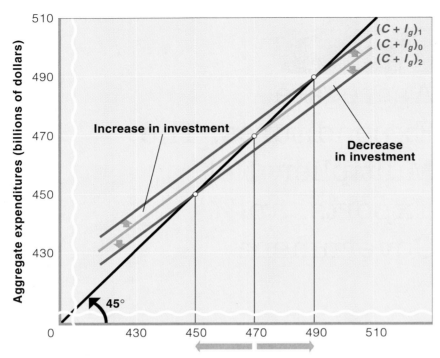

(a) Change in aggregate expenditures schedule

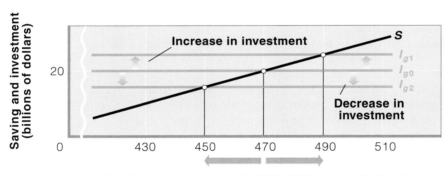

(b) Change in investment schedule

FIGURE 10-1 Changes in the equilibrium GDP caused by shifts in the aggregate expenditures schedule and the investment schedule (a) An upshift in the aggregate expenditures schedule from $(C + I_g)_0$ to $(C + I_g)_1$ will increase the equilibrium GDP. Conversely, a downshift from $(C + I_g)_0$ to $(C + I_g)_2$ will lower the equilibrium GDP. (b) An upshift in the investment schedule (I_{g0} to I_{g1}) will raise, and a downshift (I_{g0} to I_{g2}) will lower, the equilibrium GDP.

If the expected rate of return on investment decreases or the interest rate rises, the result is a decline in investment spending of, say, $5 billion. This is shown by the downward shift of the investment schedule from I_{g0} to I_{g2} in Figure 10-1b and the downward shift of the aggregate expenditures schedule from $(C + I_g)_0$ to $(C + I_g)_2$ in Figure 10-1a. In each case, the shift reduces the equilibrium GDP from the original $470 billion to $450 billion.

You should verify these conclusions in Table 9-4 by substituting first $25 billion and then $15 billion

for the $20 billion planned investment amount in column 5. If you do, you will see that $C + I_g$ becomes equal to GDP first at $490 billion (row 7) and then at $450 billion (row 5), the values indicated in Figure 10-1.

At the risk of getting ahead of ourselves, we note that the $5 billion changes in investment may be the direct result of economic policy. Looking back at Figure 9-7a, we see that the initial $20 billion of investment is associated with an 8 percent interest rate. If the economy is in recession at that investment level, monetary authorities may purposely reduce the interest rate to 6 percent (by increasing the supply of money). This will cause a $5 billion increase in investment and in aggregate expenditures to expand the economy's GDP.

Conversely, suppose the initial $20 billion of investment is "too great" and thus is causing demand-pull inflation. The monetary authorities may increase the interest rate (by reducing the money supply), causing a reduction in investment and aggregate expenditures to constrain the inflation. Monetary policy—changing the money supply to alter interest rates and aggregate expenditures—is the subject of Chapter 15.

The Multiplier Effect

You may have noticed above that a $5 billion change in investment spending led to a $20 billion change in output and income. This surprising result is called the *multiplier effect*: a change in a component of aggregate expenditures leads to a larger change in equilibrium GDP. The **multiplier** determines how much larger; it is the ratio of a change in equilibrium GDP to the change in GDP. Stated generally,

$$\text{Multiplier} = \frac{\text{change in real GDP}}{\text{initial change in spending}}$$

Here the multiplier is 4 (= $20/$5). By rearranging the above equation, we can also say that

$$\text{Change in GDP} = \text{multiplier} \times \text{initial change in spending}$$

Three points about the multiplier must be made here:
1. The "initial change in spending" is usually associated with investment spending because of its

volatility. But changes in consumption, net exports, and government purchases also lead to the multiplier effect.
2. The "initial change in spending" refers to an upshift or downshift of the aggregate expenditures schedule due to an upshift or downshift of one of its components. In Figure 10-1b we find that real GDP has increased by $20 billion because the investment schedule has shifted upward by $5 billion from I_{g0} to I_{g1}.
3. Implicit in this second point is that the multiplier works in both directions. An increase in initial spending can create a multiple increase in GDP, or a decrease in spending can be multiplied into a larger decrease in GDP.

Rationale The multiplier effect follows from two facts. First, the economy supports repetitive, continuous flows of expenditures and income through which dollars spent by Smith are received as income by Chin, then spent by Chin and received as income by Gonzales, and so on. Second, any change in income will cause both consumption and saving to vary in the same direction as, and by a fraction of, the change in income.

It follows that an initial change in the rate of spending will cause a spending chain through the economy. That chain of spending, although of diminishing importance at each successive step, will cumulate to a multiple change in GDP.

The rationale underlying the multiplier effect is illustrated numerically in Table 10-1. Suppose a $5 billion increase in investment spending occurs. This is the upshift of the aggregate expenditures schedule by $5 billion in Figure 10-1a and the upshift of the

TABLE 10-1 **The multiplier: a tabular illustration (in billions)**

	(1) Change in income	(2) Change in consumption (MPC = .75)	(3) Change in saving (MPS = .25)
Increase in investment of **$5.00**	$ 5.00	$ 3.75	$1.25
Second round	3.75	2.81	0.94
Third round	2.81	2.11	0.70
Fourth round	2.11	1.58	0.53
Fifth round	1.58	1.19	0.39
All other rounds	4.75	3.56	1.19
Total	**$20.00**	$15.00	**$5.00**

investment schedule from $20 to $25 billion in Figure 10-1b. Because we are still using the data in Table 9-1, we assume that the MPC is .75 and the MPS is .25. Also, we suppose that the economy is initially in equilibrium at $470 billion.

The initial increase in investment spending generates an equal amount of wage, rent, interest, and profit income because spending income and receiving income are two sides of the same transaction. How much consumption will be induced by this $5 billion increase in the incomes of households? The answer is found by applying the marginal propensity to consume of .75 to this change in income. Thus, the $5 billion increase in income initially raises consumption by $3.75 (= .75 × $5) billion and saving by $1.25 (= .25 × $5) billion, as shown in columns 2 and 3 in Table 10-1.

The $3.75 billion of consumption spending is received by other households as income (second round). These households consume .75 of this $3.75 billion, or $2.81 billion, and save .25 of it, or $0.94 billion. The $2.81 billion which is consumed flows to still other households as income to be spent or saved (third round). And the process continues.

Figure 10-2, derived from Table 10-1, shows the cumulative effects of this process. Each round *adds* the orange blocks to national income and GDP. The cumulation of the additional income in each round—the sum of the orange blocks—is the total change in income or GDP. Though the spending and respending effects of the increase in investment diminish with each successive round of spending, the cumulative increase in output and income will be $20 billion. The $5 billion increase in investment will therefore increase the equilibrium GDP by $20 billion, from $470 to $490 billion. Thus, the multiplier is 4 (= $20 billion ÷ $5 billion).

It is no coincidence that the multiplier effect ends at the point where exactly enough saving has been generated to offset the initial $5 billion increase in investment spending. Only then will the disequilibrium created by the investment increase be corrected. In other words, GDP and total incomes *must* rise by $20 billion to create $5 billion in additional saving to balance the $5 billion increase in investment spending. Income must increase by four times the initial excess of investment over saving, because households save one-fourth of any increase in their incomes (that is, the MPS is .25).

The Multiplier and the Marginal Propensities You may have sensed from Table 10-1 a relationship be-

tween the MPS and the multiplier. The fraction of an increase in income saved—the MPS—determines the cumulative respending effects of any initial change in spending and therefore determines the multiplier. *The MPS and the multiplier are inversely related.* The smaller the fraction of any change in income saved, the greater the respending at each round and, therefore, the greater the multiplier. If the MPS is .25, as in our example, the multiplier is 4. If the MPS were .33, the multiplier would be 3. If the MPS were .2, the multiplier would be 5. Let's see why.

Look again at Table 9-4 and Figure 10-1b. Initially the economy is in equilibrium at the $470 billion level of GDP. Now businesses increase investment by $5 billion so that planned investment of $25 billion exceeds saving of $20 billion at the $470 billion level. This means $470 billion is no longer the equilibrium GDP. By how much must output and income rise to restore equilibrium? By enough to generate $5 billion of additional saving to offset the $5 billion increase in investment. Because households save $1 out of every $4 of additional income they receive (MPS = .25),

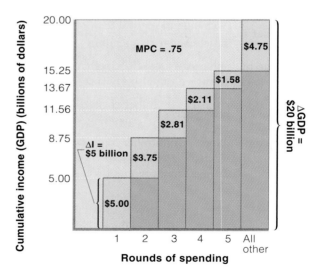

FIGURE 10-2 The multiplier process (MPC = .75) An initial change in investment spending of $5 billion creates an equal $5 billion of new income in round 1. Households spend $3.75 (= .75 × $5) billion of this new income, creating $3.75 of added income in round 2. Of this $3.75 of new income, households spend $2.81 (= .75 × $3.75) billion, and income rises by that amount in round 3. The cumulation of such income increments over the entire process eventually results in a total change of income and GDP of $20 billion. The multiplier therefore is 4 (= $20 billion ÷ $5 billion).

GDP must rise by $20 billion—four times the increase in investment—to create the $5 billion of extra saving necessary to restore equilibrium. Thus, the multiplier is 4.

If the MPS were .33, GDP would have to rise by only $15 billion (three times the increase in investment) to generate $5 billion of additional saving and restore equilibrium, and the multiplier therefore would be 3. But if the MPS were .20, GDP would have to rise by $25 billion for people to save an extra $5 billion and equilibrium to be restored; then the multiplier would be 5.

Also, recall that the MPS measures the slope of the saving schedule. In the leakages-injections ($S = I_g$) approach, this means that if the MPS is relatively large (say, .5) and the slope of the saving schedule is therefore relatively steep (.5), any upward shift in investment spending will be subject to a relatively small multiplier. A $5 billion increase in investment will entail a new point of intersection of the S and I_g schedules only $10 billion to the right of the original equilibrium GDP. The multiplier is only 2.

But if the MPS is relatively small (say, .10), the slope of the saving schedule will be relatively gentle (.10). Therefore, the same $5 billion upward shift in the investment schedule will provide a new intersection point $50 billion to the right of the original equilibrium GDP. The multiplier is 10 in this case. You should verify these two examples by drawing appropriate saving and investment diagrams.

We can summarize by saying *the multiplier is equal to the reciprocal of the MPS.* The reciprocal of any number is the quotient you obtain by dividing 1 by that number:

$$\text{Multiplier} = \frac{1}{\text{MPS}}$$

This formula is a quick way to determine the multiplier. To do so, all you need to know is the MPS.

Recall, too, from Chapter 9 that MPC + MPS = 1; it follows, then, that MPS = 1 − MPC. Therefore, we can also write the multiplier formula as

$$\text{Multiplier} = \frac{1}{1 - \text{MPC}}$$

Significance of the Multiplier The significance of the multiplier is that a small change in the investment plans of businesses or the consumption and saving plans of households can trigger a larger change in the equilibrium GDP. The multiplier magnifies the

fluctuations in business activity initiated by changes in spending.

As illustrated in Figure 10-3, the larger the MPC (the smaller the MPS), the greater the multiplier. If the MPC is .75, the multiplier is 4; a $10 billion decline in planned investment will reduce the equilibrium GDP by $40 billion. But if the MPC is only .67, the multiplier is 3; the same $10 billion drop in investment will reduce the equilibrium GDP by only $30 billion. This makes sense intuitively: A large MPC means the succeeding rounds of consumption spending shown in Figure 10-2 diminish slowly and thereby cumulate to a large change in income. Conversely, a small MPC (a large MPS) causes the increases in consumption to decline quickly so the cumulative change in income is small.

Generalizing the Multiplier The multiplier we presented above is called the *simple multiplier* because it is based on a simple model of the economy. When it is computed as 1/MPS, the simple multiplier reflects only the leakage of income into saving. In the real world successive rounds of income and spending can also be diminished by leakages into imports and taxes. As with the leakage into saving, some part of income at each round would be siphoned off as additional taxes, and another part would be used to purchase additional goods from abroad. The result of these added leakages is that the 1/MPS statement of the multiplier can be generalized. Specifically, we can

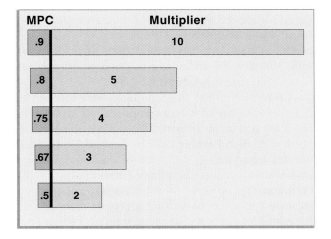

FIGURE 10-3 The MPC and the multiplier The larger the MPC (the smaller the MPS), the greater the size of the multiplier.

change the denominator to read "fraction of the change in income which is not spent on domestic output" or "fraction of the change in income which leaks, or is diverted, from the income-expenditures stream." The more realistic multiplier which results when all leakages—saving, taxes, and imports—are included is called the *complex multiplier*. The Council of Economic Advisers, which advises the President on economic matters, has estimated the complex multiplier for the United States to be about 2. **(Key Question 2)**

INTERNATIONAL TRADE AND EQUILIBRIUM OUTPUT

Our aggregate expenditures model has ignored international trade by assuming a closed economy. We now acknowledge the existence of exports and imports and note that **net exports** (exports minus imports) may be either positive or negative. Item 4 on the inside covers of this book reveals that net exports in some years have been positive (exports > imports) and in other years negative (imports > exports). In 1975, for example, net exports were a *positive* $14 billion, while in 1987 they were a *negative* $142 billion.

Net Exports and Aggregate Expenditures

Like consumption and investment, exports (X) create domestic production, income, and employment for a nation. Even though U.S. goods and services produced for export are sent abroad, foreign spending on those goods and services increases production and creates jobs and incomes in the United States. Exports must therefore be added as a component of each nation's aggregate expenditures.

Conversely, when an economy is open to international trade, part of its consumption and investment spending will be for imports (M)—goods and services produced abroad rather than in domestic industries. To avoid overstating the value of domestic production, we must reduce the sum of consumption and investment expenditures by the amount expended on imported goods. In measuring aggregate expenditures for domestic goods and services, we must subtract expenditures on imports.

In short, for a private closed economy, aggregate expenditures are $C + I_g$. But for an open economy with international trade, aggregate spending is $C + I_g + (X - M)$. Or, recalling that net exports (X_n) equal

$(X - M)$, we can say that aggregate expenditures for a private open economy are $C + I_g + X_n$.

The Net Export Schedule

Table 10-2 shows two potential net export schedules for the hypothetical economy in Tables 9-1 and 9-4. Similar to consumption and investment schedules, a net export schedule lists the amount of a particular expenditure—in this case net exports—which will occur at each level of GDP. In net export schedule X_{n1} (columns 1 and 2), exports exceed imports by $5 billion at each level of GDP. Perhaps exports are $15 billion while imports are $10 billion. In schedule X_{n2} (columns 1 and 3), imports are $5 billion higher than exports. Perhaps imports are $20 billion while exports are $15 billion. To simplify our discussion, we assume in both schedules that net exports are independent of GDP.[1]

The two net export schedules in Table 10-2 are plotted in Figure 10-4b. Schedule X_{n1} reveals that a *positive* $5 billion of net exports is associated with each level of GDP. Conversely, X_{n2} is below the horizon-

---

[1]In reality, although our *exports* depend on *foreign* incomes and are thus independent of U.S. GDP, our *imports* do vary directly with our own *domestic* national income. Just as our domestic consumption varies directly with our GDP, so do our purchases of foreign goods. As our GDP rises, U.S. households buy not only more Pontiacs and more Pepsi but also more Porsches and Perrier. However, for now we will ignore the complications of the positive relationship between imports and U.S. GDP.

TABLE 10-2 **Two net export schedules (in billions)**

(1) Level of GDP	(2) Net exports X_{n1} ($X > M$)	(3) Net exports X_{n2} ($X < M$)
$370	$+5	$−5
390	+5	−5
410	+5	−5
430	+5	−5
450	+5	−5
470	+5	−5
490	+5	−5
510	+5	−5
530	+5	−5
550	+5	−5

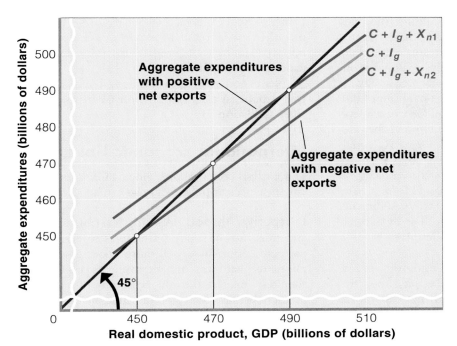

(a) Aggregate expenditures schedule

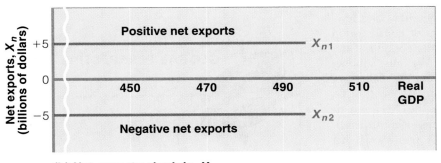

(b) Net export schedule, X_n

FIGURE 10-4 Net exports and equilibrium GDP Positive net exports such as shown by the net export schedule X_{n1} in (b) elevate the aggregate expenditures schedule in (a) from the closed-economy level of $C + I_g$ to the open-economy level of $C + I_g + X_{n1}$. Negative net exports such as depicted by the net export schedule X_{n2} in (b) lower the aggregate expenditures schedule in (a) from the closed-economy level of $C + I_g$ to the open-economy level of $C + I_g + X_{n2}$.

tal axis and thus shows net exports of *negative* $5 billion at all GDPs.

Net Exports and Equilibrium GDP

The aggregate expenditures schedule labeled $C + I_g$ in Figure 10-4a is identical to that in Table 9-4 and Figure 9-8. That is, $C + I_g$ reflects the combined consumption and gross investment expenditures occurring at each level of GDP. With no foreign sector, the equilibrium GDP will be $470 billion. This equilibrium real output is determined at the intersection of

the $C + I_g$ schedule and the 45 degree reference line. Only there will aggregate expenditures equal GDP.

But net exports can be either positive or negative. Let's see how each of the net export schedules in Figure 10-4b affects equilibrium GDP.

Positive Net Exports Suppose the net export schedule is X_{n1}. The $5 billion of additional net export expenditures by the rest of the world is accounted for by adding that $5 billion to the $C + I_g$ schedule in Figure 10-4a. Aggregate expenditures at each level of GDP are then $5 billion higher than $C + I_g$ alone.

The aggregate expenditures schedule for the open economy thus becomes $C + I_g + X_{n1}$. It shows that international trade in this case increases equilibrium GDP from $470 billion in the private closed economy to $490 billion in the private open economy.

You should verify that the new equilibrium GDP is $490 billion by adding $X_n = 5 billion to each level of aggregate expenditures in Table 9-4 and then determining the GDP for which $C + I_g + X_n$ equals GDP.

Generalization: *Positive net exports increase aggregate expenditures beyond what they would be in a closed economy and thus increase an economy's GDP.* Adding net exports of $5 billion has increased GDP by $20 billion, in this case implying a multiplier of 4.

Negative Net Exports   An extension of our reasoning enables us to determine the effect of negative net exports on equilibrium GDP. If net exports are X_{n2} in Figure 10-4b, net exports are a negative $5 billion. This means that our hypothetical economy is importing $5 billion more of goods than it is selling to people abroad. The aggregate expenditures schedule shown as $C + I_g$ in Figure 10-4a therefore overstates the expenditures on *domestic* output at each level of GDP. We must reduce the sum of consumption and investment expenditures by the $5 billion net amount spent on imported goods. We must subtract the $5 billion of *net* imports (= minus $5 billion of net exports) from $C + I_g$.

After we subtract $5 billion from the $C + I_g$ schedule in Figure 10-4a, the relevant aggregate expenditures schedule becomes $C + I_g + X_{n2}$. It shows that equilibrium GDP falls from $470 to $450. Again, a change in net exports of $5 billion has resulted in a fourfold change in GDP, reminding us that the multiplier is 4. Confirmation of the new equilibrium GDP can be obtained by subtracting $X_n = -$5$ billion from aggregate expenditures at each level of GDP in Table 9-4 and ascertaining the new equilibrium GDP for which $C + I_g + X_n$ equals GDP.

This gives a corollary to our first generalization: *Negative net exports reduce aggregate expenditures below what they would be in a closed economy and therefore decrease an economy's GDP.* Imports add to the stock of goods available in the economy but they diminish real GDP by reducing expenditures on domestically produced products.

Our generalizations of the effects of X_n on GDP mean that a decline in net exports—a decrease in exports or an increase in imports—reduces aggregate expenditures and contracts a nation's GDP.

Conversely, an increase in net exports—the result of either an increase in exports or a decrease in imports—increases aggregate expenditures and expands a nation's GDP.

Net exports vary greatly among the major industrial nations, as is shown in Global Perspective 10-1. **(Key Question 5)**

International Economic Linkages

Our analysis of net exports and real GDP reveals how circumstances or policies abroad can affect our GDP.

Prosperity Abroad   A rising level of real output and thus income among a nation's foreign trading partners permits it to sell more goods abroad, thus raising its net exports and increasing its real GDP. We should be interested in the prosperity of our trading partners because their good fortune enables them to buy more of our exports and transfer some of their prosperity to us.

Tariffs   Suppose foreign trading partners impose high tariffs on U.S. goods to reduce their imports

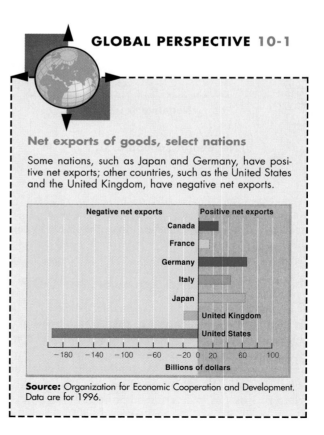

GLOBAL PERSPECTIVE 10-1

Net exports of goods, select nations

Some nations, such as Japan and Germany, have positive net exports; other countries, such as the United States and the United Kingdom, have negative net exports.

Source: Organization for Economic Cooperation and Development. Data are for 1996.

from the United States and thus to increase production in their own economies. Their imports are U.S. exports. So when they restrict their imports to stimulate *their* economies, they are reducing our (the United States) exports and depressing *our* economy. We may retaliate by imposing trade barriers on their products. If so, their exports to us will decline and their net exports may fall. It is not at all clear, then, whether tariffs increase or decrease a nation's net exports. In the Great Depression of the 1930s various nations, including the United States, imposed trade barriers as a way of reducing domestic unemployment. But rounds of retaliation simply throttled world trade, worsened the depression, and increased unemployment.

Exchange Rates Depreciation of the dollar relative to other currencies (discussed in Chapter 6) enables people abroad to obtain more dollars per unit of their own currencies. The price of U.S. goods in terms of these currencies will fall, simulating purchases of U.S. exports. Also, U.S. customers will find they need more dollars to buy foreign goods and, consequently, will reduce their spending on imports. The increased exports and decreased imports will increase U.S. net exports and thus expand the nation's GDP.

Whether depreciation of the dollar will actually raise real GDP or produce inflation depends on the initial position of the economy relative to its full-employment output. If the economy is operating below its full-employment level, depreciation of the dollar and the resulting rise in net exports will increase aggregate expenditures and thus expand real GDP. But if the economy is already fully employed, the increase in net exports and aggregate expenditures will cause demand-pull inflation. Because resources are already fully employed, the increased spending cannot expand real output; but it can and does increase the prices of the existing output.

This last example has been cast only in terms of *depreciation* of the dollar. You should now think through the impact that *appreciation* of the dollar would have on net exports and equilibrium GDP.

QUICK REVIEW 10-1

■ The multiplier effect reveals that an initial change in spending can cause magnified changes in domestic income and output. The multiplier is the factor by which the initial change is magnified: multiplier = change in real GDP/initial change in spending.

■ The higher the marginal propensity to consume (the lower the marginal propensity to save), the larger the simple multiplier: multiplier = 1/MPS.

■ Positive net exports increase aggregate expenditures on domestic output and increase equilibrium GDP; negative net exports decrease aggregate expenditures on domestic output and reduce equilibrium GDP.

ADDING THE PUBLIC SECTOR

Our final step in constructing the aggregate expenditures model is to move the analysis from that of a private (no government) open economy to a mixed economy having a public sector. This means adding government spending and taxes to the model.

Simplifying Assumptions

For clarity, the following simplifying assumptions are made:
1. We continue to use the simplified investment and net export schedules, where levels of investment and net exports are independent of the level of GDP.
2. We suppose government purchases neither depress nor stimulate private spending. They do not cause any upward or downward shifts in the consumption and investment schedules.
3. We assume government's net tax revenues—total tax revenues less "negative taxes" in the form of transfer payments—are derived entirely from personal taxes. Although DI will fall short of PI by the amount of government's tax revenues, GDP, NI, and PI will remain equal.
4. We assume that a fixed amount of taxes is collected regardless of the level of GDP.
5. We continue to suppose that, unless otherwise indicated, the price level is constant.

These assumptions will give us a simple and uncluttered view of how government spending and taxes fit within the aggregate expenditures model. Most of these assumptions will be dropped in Chapter 12 when we discuss how government uses changes in its expenditures and taxes to alter equilibrium GDP and the rate of inflation.

Government Purchases and Equilibrium GDP

Suppose government decides to purchase $20 billion of goods and services regardless of the level of GDP.

Tabular Example   Table 10-3 shows the impact of this purchase on the equilibrium GDP. Columns 1 through 4 are carried over from Table 9-4 for the private closed economy, in which the equilibrium GDP was $470 billion. The only new items are exports and imports in column 5 and government purchases in column 6. (Observe in column 5 that net exports—exports minus imports—are zero). By adding government purchases to private spending ($C + I_g + X_n$), we get a new, higher level of aggregate expenditures, as shown in column 7. Comparing columns 1 and 7, we find that aggregate expenditures and real output are equal at a higher level of GDP. Without government spending, equilibrium GDP was $470 billion (row 6); with government spending, aggregate expenditures and real output are equal at $550 billion (row 10). *Increases in public spending, like increases in private spending, shift the aggregate expenditures schedule upward and result in a higher equilibrium GDP.*

Note, too, that government spending is subject to the multiplier. A $20 billion increase in government purchases has increased equilibrium GDP by $80 billion (from $470 billion to $550 billion). The multiplier in this example is 4.

This $20 billion increase in government spending is *not* financed by increased taxes. In a moment you will find that increased taxes *reduce* equilibrium GDP.

In the leakages-injections approach, government purchases are an injection of spending. Leakages of saving and imports cause consumption of real output

to fall short of income, creating a potential spending gap. This gap may be filled by injections of investment, exports, and government purchases. In Table 10-3 the $550 billion equilibrium level of GDP (row 10) occurs where leakages equal injections, or where $S + M = I_g + X + G$. That is, when taxes are zero, $40 + 10 = 20 + 10 + 20$.

Graphical Analysis   In Figure 10-5a we add $20 billion of government purchases, G, vertically to the level of private spending, $C + I_g + X_n$. That increases the aggregate expenditures schedule (private plus public) to $C + I_g + X_n + G$, resulting in the $80 billion increase in equilibrium GDP from $470 to $550 billion.

Figure 10-5b shows the same change in equilibrium GDP via the leakages-injections approach. Like investment and exports, government spending is an injection which offsets the leakage of saving and imports. It therefore raises the "injections" schedule as shown. Assuming no taxes, the equilibrium GDP is determined by the intersection of the $S + M$ schedule and the $I_g + X + G$ schedule.

Both the aggregate expenditures and leakages-injections approaches indicate the same $550 billion equilibrium GDP. This is $80 billion more than the $470 billion equilibrium GDP of the private closed economy.

A decline in government spending G will lower the aggregate expenditures schedule in Figure 10-5a

TABLE 10-3   The impact of government purchases on equilibrium GDP

(1) Real domestic output and income (GDP = DI), billions	(2) Consumption (C), billions	(3) Saving (S), billions	(4) Investment (I_g), billions	(5) Net exports (X_n), billions Exports (X)	Imports (M)	(6) Government purchases (G), billions	(7) Aggregate expenditures ($C + I_g + X_n + G$), billions, (2) + (4) + (5) + (6)
(1) $370	$375	$-5	$20	$10	$10	$20	$415
(2) 390	390	0	20	10	10	20	430
(3) 410	405	5	20	10	10	20	445
(4) 430	420	10	20	10	10	20	460
(5) 450	435	15	20	10	10	20	475
(6) 470	450	20	20	10	10	20	490
(7) 490	465	25	20	10	10	20	505
(8) 510	480	30	20	10	10	20	520
(9) 530	495	35	20	10	10	20	535
(10) **550**	**510**	**40**	**20**	**10**	**10**	**20**	**550**

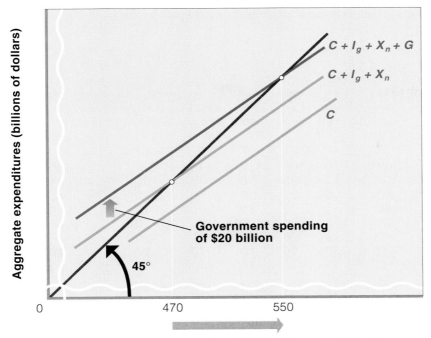

(a) Aggregate expenditures–domestic output approach

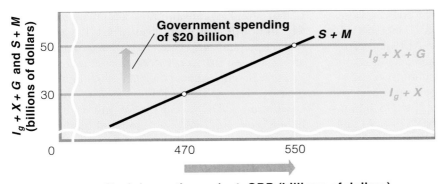

(b) Leakages–injections approach

FIGURE 10-5 Government spending and equilibrium GDP (a) *Aggregate expenditures–domestic output approach.* The addition of government expenditures of G to our analysis raises the aggregate expenditures $(C + I_g + X_n + G)$ schedule and increases the equilibrium level of GDP, as would an increase in C, I_g, or X_n. (b) *Leakages-injections approach.* Government spending is an injection which adds to private investment and export spending, raising the injection $(I_g + X + G)$ schedule and increasing the equilibrium GDP.

----

and lower the $I_g + X + G$ schedule in Figure 10-5b. In either case, the result is a multiplied decline in the equilibrium GDP. You should verify in Table 10-3 that if government spending were to decline from $20 billion to $10 billion, the equilibrium GDP would fall by $40 billion, that is, from $550 to $510 billion.

Taxation and Equilibrium GDP

Government also collects taxes. Suppose government imposes a **lump-sum tax,** which is *a tax of a constant amount or, more precisely, a tax yielding the same amount of tax revenue at each level of GDP.* Also, assume this lump-sum tax is $20 billion, so government obtains $20 billion of tax revenue at each level of GDP.

Tabular Example Table 10-4 continues our example. In it we now find taxes in column 2, and we see in column 3 that disposable (after-tax) income is lower than GDP (column 1) by the $20 billion amount of the tax. Because disposable income is used for consumer spending and saving, the tax lowers both

TABLE 10-4 Determination of the equilibrium levels of employment, output, and income: private and public sectors

(1) Real domestic output and income (GDP = NI = PI), billions	(2) Taxes (T), billions	(3) Disposable income (DI), billions, (1) − (2)	(4) Con- sump- tion (C_a), billions	(5) Saving, (S_a), billions, (3) − (4)	(6) Invest- ment (I_g), billions	(7) Net exports (X_n), billions — Exports (X)	Imports (M)	(8) Govern- ment purchases (G), billions	(9) Aggregate expenditures (C_a + I_g + X_n + G), billions, (4) + (6) + (7) + (8)
(1) $370	$20	$350	$360	$−10	$20	$10	$10	$20	$400
(2) 390	20	370	375	−5	20	10	10	20	415
(3) 410	20	390	390	0	20	10	10	20	430
(4) 430	20	410	405	5	20	10	10	20	445
(5) 450	20	430	420	10	20	10	10	20	460
(6) 470	20	450	435	15	20	10	10	20	475
(7) **490**	**20**	**470**	**450**	**20**	**20**	**10**	**10**	**20**	**490**
(8) 510	20	490	465	25	20	10	10	20	505
(9) 530	20	510	480	30	20	10	10	20	520
(10) 550	20	530	495	35	20	10	10	20	535

consumption and saving relative to what they would be in the private economy. But by how much will each decline as a result of the $20 billion in taxes? The MPC and MPS hold the answer: The MPC tells us what fraction of a decline in disposable income will come out of consumption, and the MPS indicates what fraction will come out of saving. Since the MPC is .75, if government collects $20 billion in taxes at each possible level of GDP, the amount of consumption at each level of GDP will drop by $15 billion (= .75 × $20 billion). Since the MPS is .25, the amount of saving at each level of GDP will fall by $5 billion (= .25 × $20 billion).

Columns 4 and 5 in Table 10-4 list the amounts of consumption and saving *at each level of GDP*; we see they are $15 and $5 billion smaller, respectively, than those in Table 10-3. For example, before taxes, where GDP equaled DI, consumption was $420 billion and saving $10 billion at the $430 billion level of GDP (row 4 in Table 10-3). After taxes are imposed, DI is $410 billion ($20 billion short of the $430 billion GDP), with the result that consumption is only $405 billion and saving is $5 billion (row 4, Table 10-4).

Taxes cause disposable income to fall short of GDP by the amount of the taxes. This decline in DI reduces both consumption and saving at each level of GDP. The declines in C and S are determined by the MPC and MPS.

What is the effect of taxes on equilibrium GDP? To find out, we calculate aggregate expenditures

again as shown in column 9, Table 10-4. Note there that aggregate spending is $15 billion less at each level of GDP than it was in Table 10-3. The reason is that after-tax consumption, designated by C_a, is $15 billion less at each level of GDP. Comparing real output and aggregate expenditures in columns 1 and 9, we see that the aggregate amounts produced and purchased are equal only at $490 billion of GDP (row 7). The $20 billion lump-sum tax has caused equilibrium GDP to fall by $60 billion from $550 billion (row 10, Table 10-3) to $490 billion (row 7, Table 10-4).

The leakages-injections approach confirms this result. Taxes, like saving and imports, are a leakage from the domestic income-expenditures stream. Saving, importing, and paying taxes are all uses of income which do not involve domestic consumption. Consumption will now fall short of domestic output—creating a potential spending gap—in the amount of after-tax saving and imports *plus* taxes. This gap may be filled by planned investment, exports, and government purchases. Thus, our new equilibrium condition for the leakages-injections approach is this: After-tax saving, S_a, plus imports plus taxes equals planned investment plus exports plus government purchases. Symbolically, $S_a + M + T = I_g + X + G$. You should verify in Table 10-4 that this equality of leakages and injections is fulfilled *only* at the $490 billion GDP (row 7).

Graphical Analysis   In Figure 10-6a the $20 billion *increase* in taxes shows up as a $15 (*not* $20) billion *decline* in the aggregate expenditures ($C_a + I_g + X_n + G$) schedule. Under our assumption that all taxes are personal income taxes, this decline in aggregate expenditures results solely from a decline in the consumption C component of the aggregate expenditures schedule. The equilibrium GDP changes from $550 billion to $490 billion because of this tax-caused drop in consumption. *Increases in taxes lower the aggregate expenditures schedule relative to the 45 degree line and reduce the equilibrium GDP.*

Consider now the leakages-injections approach. The analysis here is more complex because the $20 billion in taxes has a twofold effect in Figure 10-6b:

1. The taxes reduce DI by $20 billion and, with the MPS at .25, cause saving to fall by $5 billion at each level of GDP. In Figure 10-6b this is shown as a shift from $S + M$ (saving before taxes plus imports) to $S_a + M$ (saving after taxes plus imports).

2. The $20 billion in taxes is a $20 billion leakage at each GDP level which must be added to $S_a + M$ (not $S + M$), giving us $S_a + M + T$.

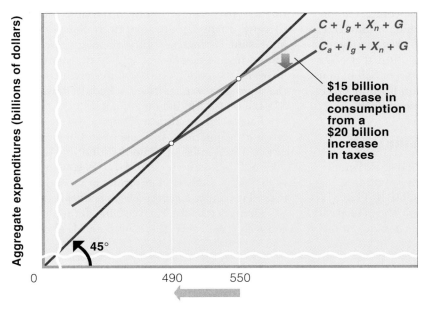

(a) Aggregate expenditures–domestic output approach

FIGURE 10-6 Taxes and equilibrium GDP   (a) *Aggregate expenditures–domestic output approach.* If the MPC is .75, the imposition of $20 billion of taxes will lower the consumption schedule by $15 billion and cause a decline in the equilibrium GDP. (b) *Leakages-injections approach.* Here taxes have a twofold effect. First, with an MPS of .25, the imposition of taxes of $20 billion will reduce disposable income by $20 billion and saving by $5 billion at each level of GDP. This is shown by the shift from S (saving before taxes) + M to S_a (saving after taxes) + M. Second the $20 billion of taxes is an additional $20 billion leakage at each GDP level, giving us $S_a + M + T$. By adding government, the equilibrium condition changes from $S + M = I_g + X$ to $S_a + M + T = I_g + X + G$.

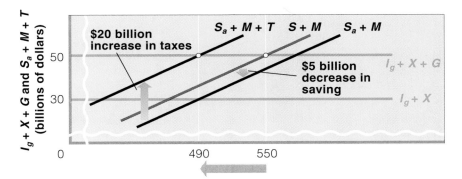

(b) Leakages-injections approach

Equilibrium now exists at the $490 billion GDP, where the total amount which households save plus imports plus the amount of taxes government intends to collect is equal to the total amount businesses plan to invest plus exports plus the amount of government purchases. The equilibrium condition for the leakages-injections approach is $S_a + M + T = I_g + X + G$. Graphically, the intersection of the $S_a + M + T$ and the $I_g + X + G$ schedules determines the equilibrium GDP.

In contrast to our previous case, a *decrease* in existing taxes will raise the aggregate expenditures schedule in Figure 10-6a as a result of an increase in consumption at all GDP levels. In Figure 10-6b a tax cut will lower the $S_a + M + T$ schedule. The result is a magnified *increase* in the equilibrium GDP. You should employ both the expenditures-output and leakages-injections approaches to confirm that a tax reduction of $10 billion (from the present $20 billion to $10 billion) will increase the equilibrium GDP from $490 to $520 billion. **(Key Question 8)**

Balanced-Budget Multiplier

There is a curious thing about our tabular and graphical illustrations. *Equal increases in government spending and taxation increase the equilibrium GDP. If G and T are each increased by a particular amount, the equilibrium level of real output will rise by the same amount.* In our

example the $20 billion increase in G and $20 billion rise in T cause the equilibrium GDP to increase by $20 billion (from $470 to $490 billion).

The rationale for this **balanced-budget multiplier** is revealed in our example. A change in government spending affects aggregate expenditures more powerfully than a tax change of the same size.

Government spending has a *direct* and unadulterated impact on aggregate expenditures. Government spending is a *direct* component of aggregate expenditures. So when government purchases increase by $20 billion, as in our example, the aggregate expenditures schedule shifts upward by the entire $20 billion.

But a change in taxes affects aggregate expenditures *indirectly* by changing disposable income and thereby changing consumption. Specifically, our lump-sum tax increase shifts the aggregate expenditures schedule downward only by the amount of the tax *times* the MPC. A $20 billion tax increase shifts the aggregate expenditures schedule downward by $15 billion (= $20 billion × .75).

The overall result is a *net* upward shift of the aggregate expenditures schedule of $5 billion that, subject to a multiplier of 4, boosts GDP by $20 billion. This $20 billion increase in GDP is equal to the size of the initial increase in government expenditures and taxes. Hence, *the balanced-budget multiplier is 1.*

The fact that the balanced-budget multiplier is 1 is clarified in Figure 10-7. With an MPC of .75, the

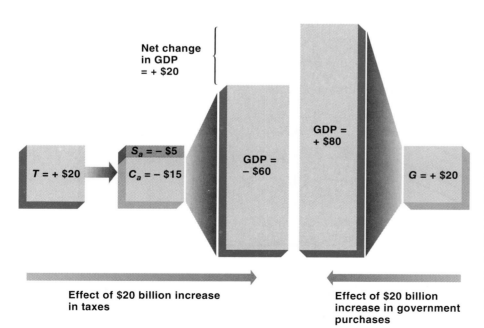

Net change in GDP = + $20

$T = + $20

$S_a = -$5
$C_a = -$15

GDP = -$60

GDP = +$80

$G = + $20

Effect of $20 billion increase in taxes

Effect of $20 billion increase in government purchases

FIGURE 10-7 The balanced-budget multiplier The balanced-budget multiplier is 1. An equal increase in taxes and government expenditures will increase GDP by an amount equal to the increase in the amount of government expenditures and taxes. Given an MPC of .75, a tax increase of $20 billion will reduce disposable income by $20 billion and lower consumption expenditures by $15 billion. Because the multiplier is 4, GDP will therefore decline by $60 billion. The $20 billion increase in government expenditures, however, will produce an increase in GDP of $80 billion. The net increase in GDP will be $20 billion, which equals the amount of the increase in government expenditures and taxes.

----

tax increase of $20 billion reduces disposable income by $20 billion and decreases consumption expenditures by $15 billion. The $15 billion decline in consumption expenditures *reduces* GDP by $60 billion (= $15 billion × the multiplier of 4). But observe in Figure 10-7 that the increase in government expenditures of $20 billion *increases* GDP by $80 billion (= $20 billion × the multiplier of 4). The equal increases of taxes and government expenditures of $20 billion thus yield a *net* increase of GDP of $20 billion (= $80 billion − $60 billion). *Equal increases in G and T expand GDP by an amount equal to those increases.*

This balanced-budget multiplier effect is not limited to situations in which the multiplier is 4. It holds no matter what the multiplier is—a fact you should verify by experimenting with different MPCs and MPSs. The balanced-budget multiplier is always 1.

EQUILIBRIUM VERSUS FULL-EMPLOYMENT GDP

Now that we have the complete aggregate expenditures model at our disposal, we can use it to evaluate the equilibrium GDP.

The $490 billion equilibrium GDP in our complete analysis (Table 10-4 and Figure 10-6) may or may not provide full employment. Indeed, our assumption thus far has been that the economy is operating at less than full employment.

Recessionary Gap

Assume in Figure 10-8a that the full-employment level of GDP is $510 billion and the aggregate expenditures schedule is $(C_a + I_g + X_n + G)_1$. This schedule intersects the 45 degree line to the left of the economy's full-employment output, so the economy's equilibrium GDP of $490 billion is $20 billion short of its full-employment output of $510 billion. According to column 1 in Table 9-4, total employment at the full-employment GDP is 75 million workers. But the economy depicted in Figure 10-8a is employing only 70 million workers; 5 million available workers are not employed. For that reason, the economy is sacrificing $20 billion of output.

The **recessionary gap** is the amount by which aggregate expenditures *at the full-employment GDP* fall short of those required to achieve the full-employment GDP. This deficiency of spending contracts or depresses the economy. Table 10-4, repre-

senting the complete economy, shows that at the full-employment level of $510 billion (column 1), the corresponding level of aggregate expenditures is only $505 billion (column 9). The recessionary gap is thus $5 billion, the amount by which the aggregate expenditures curve would have to shift upward to realize equilibrium at the full-employment GDP. Graphically, the recessionary gap is the *vertical* distance (measured at the full-employment GDP) by which the actual aggregate expenditures schedule $(C_a + I_g + X_n + G)_1$ lies below the hypothetical full-employment aggregate expenditures schedule $(C_a + I_g + X_n + G)_0$. Observe in Figure 10-8a that this recessionary gap is $5 billion. Because the multiplier is 4, we observe a $20 billion differential (the recessionary gap of $5 billion times the multiplier of 4) between the equilibrium GDP and the full-employment GDP. This $20 billion difference is the *GDP gap*—a notion we first developed when discussing Figure 8-5.

Inflationary Gap

The **inflationary gap** is the amount by which an economy's aggregate expenditures *at the full-employment GDP* exceed those just necessary to achieve the full-employment GDP. In Figure 10-8b, there is a $5 billion inflationary gap at the $510 billion full-employment GDP. This is shown by the *vertical* distance between the actual aggregate expenditures schedule $(C_a + I_g + X_n + G)_2$ and the hypothetical schedule $(C_a + I_g + X_n + G)_0$ which would be just sufficient to achieve the $510 billion full-employment GDP. Thus, the inflationary gap is the amount by which the aggregate expenditures schedule would have to shift downward to realize equilibrium at the full-employment GDP.

The effect of this inflationary gap—this excessive spending—is that it will pull up output prices. Businesses cannot respond to the $5 billion in excessive spending by expanding their real outputs, so demand-pull inflation will occur. Nominal GDP will rise because of a higher price level, but real GDP will not. Table 10-5 summarizes the steps for determining recessionary and inflationary gaps. **(Key Question 10)**

HISTORICAL APPLICATIONS

Let's see how the concepts of recessionary and inflationary gaps apply to two economic events.

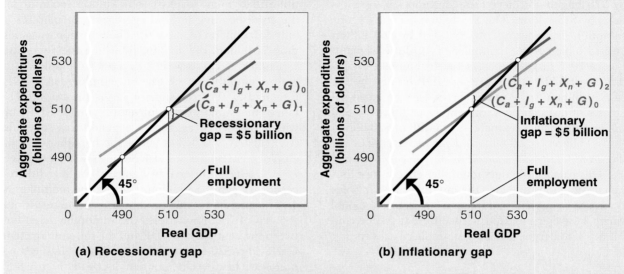

(a) Recessionary gap

(b) Inflationary gap

FIGURE 10-8 Recessionary and inflationary gaps The equilibrium and full-employment GDPs may not coincide. (a) A recessionary gap is the amount by which aggregate expenditures at the full-employment GDP fall short of those needed to achieve the full-employment GDP. Here, the $5 billion recessionary gap causes a $20 billion GDP gap. (b) An inflationary gap is the amount by which aggregate expenditures at the full-employment GDP exceed those just sufficient to achieve the full-employment GDP. Here the inflationary gap is $5 billion; this overspending produces demand-pull inflation.

QUICK QUIZ 10-8

1. **In the economy depicted:**
   a. the MPS is .50.
   b. the MPC is .75.
   c. the full-capacity level of real GDP is $530 billion.
   d. nominal GDP always equals real GDP.

2. **The inflationary gap depicted will cause:**
   a. demand-pull inflation.
   b. cost-push inflation.
   c. cyclical unemployment.
   d. frictional unemployment.

3. **The recessionary gap depicted will cause:**
   a. demand-pull inflation.
   b. cost-push inflation.

   c. cyclical unemployment.
   d. frictional unemployment.

4. **In the economy depicted, the $5 billion inflationary gap:**
   a. expands real GDP to $530 billion.
   b. leaves real GDP at $510 billion but causes inflation.
   c. could be remedied by equal $5 billion increases in taxes and government spending.
   d. implies that real GDP exceeds nominal GDP.

Answers: 1. b; 2. a; 3. c; 4. b

The Great Depression

In October 1929 the stock marked collapsed. At the same time the most severe and prolonged depression of modern times began. In the United States real GDP (in 1992 dollars) plummeted from $791 billion in 1929 to a low of $577 billion in 1933. The unemployment rate rose from 3.2 to 24.9 percent in the same period. As late as 1939, real GDP was only slightly above its level of 10 years earlier and the unemployment rate was still 17.2 percent. (As shown in Global Perspective 10-2, the Great Depression was worldwide.)

A sagging level of investment spending was the major weight which pulled U.S. capitalism into the

TABLE 10-5   Determining the recessionary and inflationary gaps

> **Steps:**
> 1. Determine the economy's full-employment GDP.
> 2. Look at the economy's current aggregate expenditures schedule, and from that schedule find the amount of expenditure which would be forthcoming at the economy's full-employment GDP.
> 3. Find the amount of expenditures just necessary to achieve the full-employment GDP.
> 4. Subtract the amount determined in step 2 from the amount determined in step 3. A negative difference identifies a recessionary gap; a positive difference reflects an inflationary gap.

economic chaos of the 1930s. In real terms, gross investment spending shrank from $92 billion in 1929 to $10 billion in 1932—an 89 percent decline. In Figure 10-8, we would depict this decline in investment as a large downward shift in the nation's aggregate expenditures schedule. The outcome in the 1930s was a severe recessionary (depressionary) gap and a historic decline in real GDP.

Several factors caused this steep decline in investment:

Overcapacity and Business Indebtedness   Flush with the prosperity of the 1920s, businesses had over-expanded their production capacity. In particular, there was tremendous expansion of the automobile industry—and the related petroleum, rubber, steel, glass, and textile industries—which ended as the market for new autos became saturated. Business indebtedness also increased rapidly during the 1920s. Furthermore, by the late 1920s much of the income of businesses was committed for the payment of interest and principal on past capital purchases and thus was not available for sustaining expenditures on new capital.

Decline in Residential Construction   The 1920s experienced a boom in residential construction in response to population growth and to housing demand which was deferred because of World War I. This investment spending began to level off as early as 1926, and by the late 1920s the construction industry had virtually collapsed.

Stock Market Crash   The most striking aspect of the Great Depression was the stock market crash of October 1929. The optimism of the prosperous 1920s had elevated stock market speculation to something of a national pastime. This speculation had bid up

stock prices to the point where they did not reflect financial reality; stock prices rose far beyond the profit-making potentials of the firms they represented. A

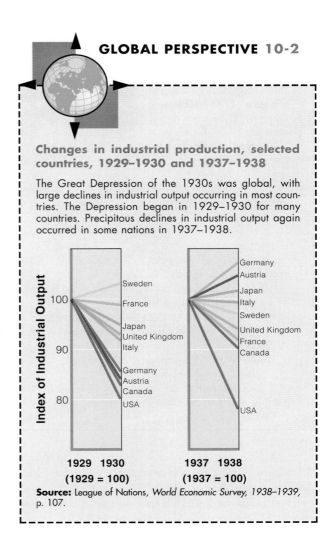

GLOBAL PERSPECTIVE 10-2

Changes in industrial production, selected countries, 1929–1930 and 1937–1938

The Great Depression of the 1930s was global, with large declines in industrial output occurring in most countries. The Depression began in 1929–1930 for many countries. Precipitous declines in industrial output again occurred in some nations in 1937–1938.

Source: League of Nations, *World Economic Survey, 1938–1939,* p. 107.

Squaring the Economic Circle

Humorist Art Buchwald examines the multiplier.

WASHINGTON—The recession hit so fast that nobody knows exactly how it happened. One day we were the land of milk and honey and the next day we were the land of sour cream and food stamps.

This is one explanation.

Hofberger, the Chevy salesman in Tomcat, Va., a suburb of Washington, called up Littleton, of Littleton Menswear & Haberdashery, and said, "Good news, the new Novas have just come in and I've put one aside for you and your wife."

Littleton said, "I can't, Hofberger, my wife and I are getting a divorce."

"I'm sorry," Littleton said, "but I can't afford a new car this year. After I settle with my wife, I'll be lucky to buy a bicycle."

Hofberger hung up. His phone rang a few minutes later.

"This is Bedcheck the painter," the voice on the other end said. "When do you want us to start painting your house?"

"I changed my mind," said Hofberger, "I'm not going to paint the house."

"But I ordered the paint," Bedcheck said. "Why did you change your mind?"

"Because Littleton is getting a divorce and he can't afford a new car."

That evening when Bedcheck came home his wife said, "The new color television set arrived from Gladstone's TV Shop."

"Take it back," Bedcheck told his wife.

"Why?" she demanded.

"Because Hofberger isn't going to have his house painted now that the Littletons are getting a divorce."

The next day Mrs. Bedcheck dragged the TV set in its carton back to Gladstone. "We don't want it."

Gladstone's face dropped. He immediately called his travel agent, Sandstorm. "You know that trip you had scheduled for me to the Virgin Islands?"

"Right, the tickets are all written up."

"Cancel it. I can't go. Bedcheck just sent back the color TV set because Hofberger didn't sell a car to Littleton because they're going to get a divorce and she wants all his money."

Sandstorm tore up the airline tickets and went over to see his banker, Gripsholm. "I can't pay back the loan this month because Gladstone isn't going to the Virgin Islands."

Gripsholm was furious. When Rudemaker came in to borrow money for a new kitchen he needed for his restaurant, Gripsholm turned him down cold. "How can I loan you money when Sandstorm hasn't repaid the money he borrowed?"

Rudemaker called up the contractor, Eagleton, and said he couldn't put in a new kitchen. Eagleton laid off eight men.

Meanwhile, General Motors announced it was giving a rebate on its new models. Hofberger called up Littleton immediately. "Good news," he said, "even if you are getting a divorce, you can afford a new car."

"I'm not getting a divorce," Littleton said. "It was all a misunderstanding and we've made up."

"That's great," Hofberger said. "Now you can buy the Nova."

"No way," said Littleton. "My business has been so lousy I don't know why I keep the doors open."

"I didn't realize that," Hofberger said.

"Do you realize I haven't seen Bedcheck, Gladstone, Sandstorm, Gripsholm, Rudemaker or Eagleton for more than a month? How can I stay in business if they don't patronize my store?"

Source: Art Buchwald, "Squaring the Economic Circle," *Cleveland Plain Dealer*, Feb. 22, 1975. Reprinted by permission.

downward adjustment was necessary, and it came suddenly and quickly in 1929.

The stock market crash had significant secondary effects. Most important were the psychological repercussions. The buoyant optimism of the 1920s gave way to a wave of crippling pessimism, and the crashing of stock prices created highly unfavorable conditions for acquiring additional money for investment.

Shrinking Money Supply The nation's money supply plummeted in the early years of the Great Depression, from $27 billion in 1929 down to $20 billion by 1933. This shrinkage resulted from forces operating both abroad and at home, including inappropriate policies of the Federal Reserve Banks. This drastic reduction of the money supply contributed heavily to a sharp decline in aggregate expenditures, including investment, which occurred in the early 1930s.

Vietnam War Inflation

The 1960s was a period of prolonged expansion of real GDP, fueled by increases in consumption spending and investment. One factor in this long expansion was the revolution in economic policy which occurred under the Kennedy and Johnson administrations. This new policy called for government to manipulate its tax collections and expenditures in such a way as to increase aggregate demand, increasing employment and real GDP. For example, in 1962 legislation was enacted which provided for a 7 percent tax credit on investment in new machinery and equipment, thus strengthening the incentives of businesses to invest. In 1964 the government cut personal and corporate income taxes, boosting consumption spending and further increasing investment spending. The unemployment rate fell from 5.2 percent in 1964 to 4.5 percent in 1965.

At this time another expansionary force came into play. The escalation of the war in Vietnam resulted in a 40 percent increase in government spending on national defense between 1965 and 1967. There was another 15 percent increase in war-related spending in 1968. Simultaneously, the draft claimed more and more young people from the ranks of the unemployed.

Remarkably, the unemployment rate fell below 4 percent during the entire 1966–1969 period. But the increased government expenditures, imposed on an already booming economy, also brought about the worst inflation in two decades. Inflation jumped from 1.6 percent in 1965 to 5.7 percent by 1970. In terms of Figure 10-8, the booming investment expenditures and the added government expenditures shifted the aggregate expenditures schedule sharply upward, creating a sizable inflationary gap.

QUICK REVIEW 10-2

■ Government purchases shift the aggregate expenditures schedule upward and raise the equilibrium GDP.

■ Taxes reduce disposable income, lower consumption spending and saving, shift the aggregate expenditures schedule downward, and reduce the equilibrium GDP.

■ The balanced-budget multiplier is 1.

■ A recessionary gap is the amount by which an economy's aggregate expenditures schedule must shift upward to achieve the full-employment GDP; the inflationary gap is the amount by which the economy's aggregate expenditures schedule must shift downward to eliminate demand-pull inflation and still achieve the full-employment GDP.

■ The Great Depression of the 1930s was a period having a large recessionary (depressionary) gap; the years of the Vietnam war (the late 1960s) were characterized by a large inflationary gap.

CRITIQUE AND PREVIEW

Our analysis and examples demonstrate the power of the aggregate expenditures model to help us understand how the economy works, how recessions or depressions can occur, and how demand-pull inflation can arise. But models are only approximations of reality—they have shortcomings. The aggregate expenditures theory has four limitations:

1. *Does not show price-level changes* The model can account for demand-pull inflation, as in Figure 10-8b, but it does not indicate how *much* the price level will rise when aggregate expenditures are excessive relative to the economy's capacity. Will the $5 billion inflationary gap of Figure 10-8b cause a 3 percent, 5 percent, 10 percent, or some other rate of inflation? By how much will the GDP price index of Chapter 7 rise for each $1 billion of the inflationary gap? The aggregate expenditures model does not include the price level; it has no way of measuring the rate of inflation.

2. *Ignores premature demand-pull inflation* In Chapter 8, specifically Figure 8-7, we noted that demand-pull inflation can occur *before* an actual economy reaches its full-employment level of output. The aggregate expenditures model does not explain why this can happen. In Figure 10-8 the economy could move from $490 billion of expenditures and real GDP to the $510 billion full-employment level of GDP without inflation occurring. In the aggregate expenditures model, inflation occurs only after the economy reaches its full-employment level of output—but that is not what often happens in reality.

3. *Bars real GDP beyond the full-employment level of output* We also know from our discussions surrounding Figures 8-5 and 8-7 that for a time an actual economy can expand beyond its full-employment real GDP. The aggregate expenditures model does not allow for this possibility. In Figure 10-8b, the economy's real output cannot expand beyond the full-employment level of $510 billion, even though the aggregate expenditures schedule is $(C_a + I_g + X_n + G)_2$. This high level of spending does *not* generate additional real output; in this model, spending simply drives up inflation.

4. *Omits cost-push inflation* We know from Chapter 8 that there are two general types of in-

flation: demand-pull inflation and cost-push inflation. The aggregate expenditures model does not address cost-push inflation.

In Chapter 11, we remedy these deficiencies while preserving the insights of the aggregate expenditures model. We use the model to derive aggregate demand—a schedule or curve relating various price levels to the amounts of real GDP which will be demanded at those price levels. When this aggregate demand curve is combined with an aggregate supply curve, we obtain an aggregate expenditures–based model which overcomes the shortcomings just discussed. The better you understand the aggregate expenditures model, the easier it will be to grasp Chapter 11's aggregate demand–aggregate supply model.

CHAPTER SUMMARY

1. A shift in the saving and consumption schedules or in the investment schedule causes the equilibrium output and income level to change by more than the amount of the initial change. This multiplier effect accompanies both increases and decreases in aggregate expenditures.

2. The multiplier is equal to the reciprocal of the marginal propensity to save: The higher the marginal propensity to save, the lower the multiplier. Also, the higher the marginal propensity to consume, the greater the multiplier.

3. The net export schedule relates net exports (exports minus imports) to levels of real GDP. In the aggregate expenditures model we assume that the level of net exports is the same at all levels of real GDP.

4. Positive net exports increase aggregate expenditures to a higher level than would be the case if the economy were a closed one, and they thereby raise equilibrium real GDP by a magnified amount; negative net exports decrease aggregate expenditures relative to those in a closed economy, decreasing equilibrium real GDP. Increases in exports or decreases in imports have an expansionary effect on real GDP, while decreases in exports or increases in imports have a contractionary effect.

5. Government purchases shift the aggregate expenditures schedule upward and raise GDP.

6. Taxation reduces disposable income, lowers both consumption spending and saving, shifts the aggregate expenditures curve downward, and reduces equilibrium GDP.

7. The equilibrium GDP and the full-employment GDP may differ. The recessionary gap is the amount by which aggregate expenditures at the full-employment GDP fall short of those needed to achieve the full-employment GDP. This gap produces a magnified GDP gap. The inflationary gap is the amount by which aggregate expenditures at the full-employment GDP exceed those just sufficient to achieve the full-employment GDP; it causes demand-pull inflation.

8. The Great Depression of the 1930s resulted from a precipitous decline in aggregate expenditures which produced a severe and long-lasting recessionary (depressionary) gap. The Vietnam war period provides a good example of an inflationary gap. An abrupt increase in aggregate demand caused by war spending led to a sizable inflationary gap, with its accompanying demand-pull inflation.

9. The aggregate expenditures model provides many insights about the macroeconomy, but it does not **(a)** show price-level changes, **(b)** account for premature demand-pull inflation, **(c)** allow for real GDP to temporarily expand beyond the full-employment output, or **(d)** account for cost-push inflation.

TERMS AND CONCEPTS

multiplier

net exports

lump-sum tax

balanced-budget
multiplier

recessionary gap

inflationary gap

STUDY QUESTIONS

1. What effect will each of the changes listed in question 4 of Chapter 9 have on the equilibrium level of GDP? Explain your answers.

2. KEY QUESTION What is the multiplier effect? What relationship does the MPC bear to the size of the multiplier? The MPS? What will the multiplier be when the MPS is 0, .4, .6, and 1? What will it be when the MPC is 1, .90, .67, .50, and 0? How much of a change in GDP will result if firms increase their level of investment by $8 billion and the MPC in the economy is .80? If the MPC is .67? Explain the difference between the simple multiplier and the complex multiplier.

3. Graphically depict the aggregate expenditures model for a private closed economy. Now show a decrease in the aggregate expenditures schedule and explain why the decline in real GDP in your diagram is greater than the initial decline in aggregate expenditures. What would be the ratio of a decline in real GDP to the initial drop in aggregate expenditures if the slope of your aggregate expenditures schedule were .8?

4. Speculate on why a planned increase in saving (an upshift of the saving schedule) by households, *not* accompanied by an increase in investment spending by firms, might result in a decline in real GDP and *no* increase in actual saving. Demonstrate this point graphically, using the leakages-injections approach to equilibrium real GDP. Now assume in your diagram that planned investment instead increases to match the initial increase in desired saving. Using your knowledge from Chapter 2, explain why these *joint* increases in planned saving and planned investment might be desirable for a society.

5. KEY QUESTION The data in columns 1 and 2 in the bottom table are for a private closed economy:
   a. Use columns 1 and 2 to determine the equilibrium GDP for this hypothetical economy.
   b. Now open this economy to international trade by including the export and import figures of columns 3 and 4. Fill in columns 5 and 6 and determine the equilibrium GDP for the open economy. Explain why this equilibrium GDP differs from that of the closed economy.
   c. Given the original $20 billion level of exports, what would be the equilibrium GDP if imports were $10 billion greater at each level of GDP? Or $10 billion less at each level of GDP? What generalization concerning the level of imports and the equilibrium GDP do these examples illustrate?
   d. What is the multiplier in these examples?

6. Assume that, without taxes, the consumption schedule of an economy is as shown:

GDP, billions	Consumption, billions
$100	$120
200	200
300	280
400	360
500	440
600	520
700	600

   a. Graph this consumption schedule and determine the MPC.
   b. Assume now that a lump-sum tax is imposed such that the government collects $10 billion in taxes at all levels of GDP. Graph the resulting con-

(1) Real domestic output (GDP = DI), billions	(2) Aggregate expenditures, private closed economy, billions	(3) Exports, billions	(4) Imports, billions	(5) Net exports, billions	(6) Aggregate expenditures, private open economy, billions
$200	$240	$20	$30	$_____	$_____
250	280	20	30	_____	_____
300	320	20	30	_____	_____
350	360	20	30	_____	_____
400	400	20	30	_____	_____
450	440	20	30	_____	_____
500	480	20	30	_____	_____
550	520	20	30	_____	_____

sumption schedule, and compare the MPC and the multiplier with that of the pretax consumption schedule.

7. Explain graphically the determination of equilibrium GDP for a private economy through the aggregate expenditures approach. Now add government spending (any amount that you choose) to your graph, showing its impact on equilibrium GDP. Finally, add taxation (any amount of lump-sum tax that you choose) to your graph and show its effect on equilibrium GDP. Looking at your graph, determine whether equilibrium GDP has increased, decreased, or stayed the same in view of the sizes of the government spending and taxes that you selected.

8. KEY QUESTION   Refer to columns 1 and 6 in the table for question 5. Incorporate government into the table by assuming that it plans to tax and spend $20 billion at each possible level of GDP. Also assume that all taxes are personal taxes and that government spending does not induce a shift in the private aggregate expenditures schedule. Compute and explain the change in equilibrium GDP caused by the addition of government.

9. What is the balanced-budget multiplier? Demonstrate the balanced-budget multiplier in terms of your answer to question 8. Explain: "Equal increases in government spending and tax revenues of n dollars will increase the equilibrium GDP by n dollars." Does this hold true regardless of the size of the MPS? Why or why not?

10. KEY QUESTION   Refer to the table below in answering the questions which follow:

(1) Possible levels of employment, millions	(2) Real domestic output, billions	(3) Aggregate expenditures $(C_a + I_g + X_n + G)$, billions
90	$500	$520
100	550	560
110	600	600
120	650	640
130	700	680

a. If full employment in this economy is 130 million, will there be an inflationary or a recessionary gap? What will be the consequence of this gap? By how much would aggregate expenditures in column 3 have to change at each level of GDP to eliminate the inflationary or recessionary gap? Explain.

b. Will there be an inflationary or recessionary gap if the full-employment level of output is $500 billion? Explain the consequences. By how much would aggregate expenditures in column 3 have

to change at each level of GDP to eliminate the inflationary or recessionary gap?

c. Assuming that investment, net exports, and government expenditures do not change with changes in real GDP, what are the sizes of the MPC, the MPS, and the multiplier?

11. Advanced analysis: Assume the consumption schedule for a private open economy is such that consumption $C = 50 + 0.8Y$. Assume further that planned investment I_g and net exports X_n are independent of the level of real GDP and constant at $I_g = 30$ and $X_n = 10$. Recall also that, in equilibrium, the real output produced (Y) is equal to aggregate expenditures: $Y = C + I_g + X_n$.

a. Calculate the equilibrium level of income or real GDP for this economy. Check your work by expressing the consumption, investment, and net export schedules in tabular form and determining the equilibrium GDP.

b. What happens to equilibrium Y if I_g changes to 10? What does this reveal about the size of the multiplier?

12. (Last Word) What is the central economic idea humorously illustrated in Art Buchwald's piece, "Squaring the Economic Circle"?

13. WEB-BASED QUESTION   The Multiplier—Calculate a Change in GDP The Bureau of Economic Analysis has current data on national income and product accounts at http://www.bea.doc.gov/briefrm/tables/ebr1.htm. Find the most current values for GDP = $C + I + G + (X - M)$. Assume a MPC of .75, and that for each of the following, the values of the initial variables are those you just discovered. What would be the new value of GDP if: **(a)** Investment increased by 5 percent? **(b)** Imports increased by 5 percent and exports increased by 5 percent? **(c)** Consumption increased by 5 percent? **(d)** Government spending increased by 5 percent? Which 5 percent increase caused GDP to change the most in absolute dollars?

14. WEB-BASED QUESTION   Net Exports—What Is the Current Economic Impact? Positive net exports have an expansionary effect on domestic GDP; negative net exports have a contractionary effect. Check the latest monthly figures at the Bureau of Economic Analysis http://www.census.gov/ftp/pub/indicator/www/ustrade.html for exports and imports of goods and services. Assume a multiplier of 4. Compared to the previous month, how much is GDP increased or decreased by a change in **(a)** net exports of goods, **(b)** net exports of services, and **(c)** net exports of goods and services? Which has the greatest impact? Should services be included or excluded from net exports?

11

Aggregate Demand and Aggregate Supply

The aggregate expenditures model developed in Chapters 9 and 10 is a *fixed-price-level model*—its focus is on changes in real GDP, not on changes in the price level. Moving closer to the real world, we now develop a *variable-price-level model* so that we can simultaneously analyze changes in real GDP *and* the price level. To do this, we need to aggregate all the individual product markets of the economy into a single market. We must combine the thousands of individual equilibrium prices—of pizzas, robots, corn, computers, crankshafts, donuts, new houses, perfume, and legal services—into an aggregate price level. Similarly, we must merge the equilibrium quantities of all the individual products and services into a real GDP. Our new graphical model measures the price level on the vertical axis and real domestic output, or real GDP or real output, on the horizontal axis.

Specifically, in this chapter we introduce the concepts of aggregate demand and aggregate supply, explaining the shapes of the aggregate demand and aggregate supply curves and the forces causing them to shift. Next, we consider the equilibrium levels of prices and real GDP. Finally, we explore the effects of shifts in the aggregate demand and aggregate supply curves on the price level and the size of real GDP.

What you learn in this chapter will help organize your thinking about equilibrium GDP, the price level, and government macroeconomic policies. The tools you acquire here will also help you in later chapters, where we contrast differing views on macroeconomic theory and policy.

AGGREGATE DEMAND

Aggregate demand *is a schedule or a curve showing the various amounts of goods and services—the amounts of real output—that domestic consumers, businesses, government, and foreign buyers collectively desire to purchase at each possible price level*. Other things equal, the lower the price level, the larger the real GDP these buyers will purchase. Conversely, the higher the price level, the smaller the real GDP they will buy. Thus, the relationship between the price level and the amount of real GDP demanded is inverse or negative.

Aggregate Demand Curve

The inverse relationship between the price level and real output is shown in Figure 11-1 where the aggregate demand curve AD slopes

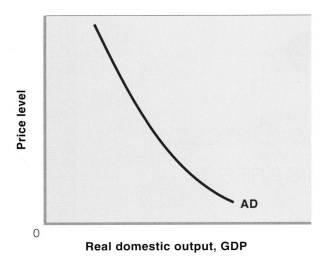

Price level

0

Real domestic output, GDP

FIGURE 11-1 The aggregate demand curve The downsloping aggregate demand curve AD indicates an inverse relationship between the price level and the amount of real domestic output purchased.

- -

downward as does the demand curve for an individual product.

Why the downward slope? The rationale is *not* the same as that for a single product. That explanation centered on income and substitution effects. When the price of an individual product falls, the consumer's (constant) nominal income will enable him or her to purchase more of the product (the income effect). And, as price falls, the consumer wants to buy more of the product because it becomes relatively less expensive than other goods (the substitution effect).

But these explanations do not work for aggregates. In Figure 11-1, when the economy moves down its aggregate demand curve, it moves to lower price levels. But our circular flow model tells us that when consumers pay lower prices for goods and services, less income is likely to flow to resource suppliers in the form of wages, rents, interest, and profits. As a result, a decrease in the price level does *not* necessarily mean an increase in the nominal income of the economy as a whole. Thus, a decline in the price level need not produce an income effect (more of a product is purchased because a decline in its price leaves buyers with more real income).

Similarly, in Figure 11-1 prices in general are falling as we move down the aggregate demand curve, so the rationale for the substitution effect (more of a

product is purchased because it becomes cheaper relative to all other products) is not applicable. There is no overall substitution effect when the price level falls.

If the substitution and income effects do not explain the downsloping aggregate demand curve, what does? The rationale rests on the following three factors.

Wealth Effect The first reason for the downsloping aggregate demand curve involves the **wealth effect**. A higher price level reduces the real value or purchasing power of the public's accumulated financial assets. In particular, the real value of assets with fixed money values, such as savings accounts or bonds, diminishes. Because of the erosion of purchasing power of such assets, the public is poorer in real terms and will reduce its spending. A household might buy a new car or a sailboat if the purchasing power of its financial asset balances is, say, $50,000. But if inflation erodes the purchasing power of the asset balances to $30,000, the family may defer its purchase.

Conversely, a decline in the price level will increase the real value or purchasing power of a household's wealth and increase consumption spending.

Interest-Rate Effect The **interest-rate effect** suggests that the aggregate demand curve is downsloping because of the impact of price-level changes on interest rates and, in turn, on consumption and investment spending. As the price level rises, so do interest rates, and rising interest rates reduce certain kinds of consumption and investment spending.

Elaboration: *The aggregate demand curve assumes the supply of money in the economy is fixed.* When the price level increases, consumers need more money for purchases and businesses similarly require more money to meet their payrolls and to buy other needed resources. In short, a higher price level increases the demand for money.

With a fixed supply of money, this increase in the demand for money drives up the price paid for its use. That price is the interest rate. Higher interest rates curtail interest-sensitive expenditures by businesses and households. A firm expecting a 10 percent return on a potential purchase of capital will find that purchase profitable when the interest rate is, say, only 7 percent. But the purchase is unprofitable and will not be made when the interest rate has risen to, say, 12 percent. Similarly, some consumers will decide *not* to purchase houses or automobiles when the interest rate rises.

Conclusion: A higher price level—by increasing the demand for money and the interest rate—reduces the amount of real output demanded.

Foreign Purchases Effect   We found in Chapter 7's discussion of national income accounting that imports and exports are components of total spending. The volumes of our imports and exports depend on, among other things, relative price levels here and abroad. If the price level rises in the United States relative to the levels in foreign countries, U.S. buyers will purchase more imports and fewer domestic goods. Similarly, the rest of the world will buy fewer U.S. goods, reducing U.S. exports. In brief, a rise in the U.S. price level will increase our imports and reduce our exports, reducing the amount of net export (export minus import) spending on U.S.-produced products.

More generally, the **foreign purchases effect** is this: A relative increase in a nation's price level reduces its net exports, resulting in a decline in the aggregate amount of domestic output demanded. Conversely, a relative decline in a nation's price level increases its net exports, thereby increasing the amount of domestic output demanded.

Derivation of the Aggregate Demand Curve from the Aggregate Expenditures Model[1]

We can derive the downsloping aggregate demand curve of Figure 11-1 directly from the aggregate expenditures model of Chapters 9 and 10. To do so, we simply need to relate the various possible price levels to corresponding equilibrium GDPs. Note first that in Figure 11-2 we have stacked the aggregate expenditures model (Figure 11-2a) and the aggregate demand curve (Figure 11-2b) vertically. We can do this because real GDP is measured on the horizontal axes of both models. Now suppose that the economy's price level is P_2 and its aggregate expenditures schedule is $(C_a + I_g + X_n + G)_2$, the middle schedule in Figure 11-2a. The equilibrium GDP is then GDP_2. So in Figure 11-2b we can plot the equilibrium real output GDP_2 and the corresponding price level P_2. This gives us one point—namely, 2′—in Figure 11-2b.

Now assume the price level drops to P_1. Other things equal, this lower price level will (1) increase

the value of wealth, boosting consumption expenditures; (2) reduce the interest rate, promoting investment expenditures; and (3) reduce imports and increase exports, increasing net export expenditures. The aggregate expenditures schedule will rise from $(C_a + I_g + X_n + G)_2$ to, say, $(C_a + I_g + X_n + G)_1$ in Figure 11-2a, giving us equilibrium at GDP_1. In Figure 11-2b we plot this new price-level–real-output combination, P_1 and GDP_1, as point 1′.

Now suppose the price level increases from the original P_2 to P_3. The real value of wealth falls, the interest rate rises, exports fall, and imports rise. Consequently, the consumption, investment, and net export schedules fall, shifting the aggregate expenditures schedule downward from $(C_a + I_g + X_n + G)_2$ to, say, $(C_a + I_g + X_n + G)_3$, which gives us equilibrium at GDP_3. This lets us locate a third point in Figure 11-2b, namely, point 3′, where the price level is P_3 and real output is GDP_3.

In summary, a decrease in the economy's price level shifts its aggregate expenditures schedule upward and increases real GDP. An increase in the price level shifts its aggregate expenditures schedule downward, reducing real GDP. The resulting price-level–real GDP combinations yield various points such as 1′, 2′, and 3′ in Figure 11-2b. Together, such points locate the downsloping aggregate demand curve for the economy.

Determinants of Aggregate Demand

Changes in the price level change the level of aggregate spending (Figure 11-2a); this, in turn, changes the amount of real GDP demanded by the economy. More specifically, an increase in the price level, *other things equal*, will decrease the quantity of real GDP demanded; a decrease in the price level will increase the amount of real GDP demanded. These changes are represented graphically as movements along a fixed aggregate demand curve. However, if one or more of those "other things" change, the entire aggregate demand curve shifts. We refer to those "other things" as **determinants of aggregate demand;** they "determine" the *location* of the aggregate demand curve.

We must then distinguish between *changes in the quantity of real output demanded* (caused by changes in the price level) and *changes in aggregate demand* (caused by changes in one or more of the determinants of aggregate demand). A similar distinction was made in

---

[1]This section presumes knowledge of the aggregate expenditures model discussed in Chapters 9 and 10 and can be skipped by readers who are not assigned those chapters.

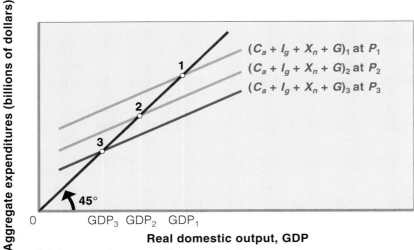

(a) Aggregate expenditures model

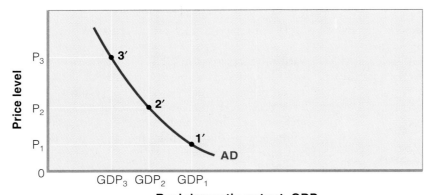

(b) Aggregate demand–aggregate supply model

FIGURE 11-2 Deriving the aggregate demand curve from the expenditures-output model Through the wealth, interest-rate, and foreign purchases effects, the consumption, investment, and net export schedules and therefore the aggregate expenditures schedule will rise when the price level declines and fall when the price level increases. If the aggregate expenditures schedule is $(C_a + I_g + X_n + G)_2$ when the price level is P_2, the equilibrium output is GDP_2; then P_2 and GDP_2 determine one point (2′) on the aggregate demand curve. A lower price level such as P_1 increases aggregate expenditures to $(C_a + I_g + X_n + G)_1$, providing point 1′ on the aggregate demand curve. Similarly, a high price level at P_3 shifts aggregate expenditures down to $(C_a + I_g + X_n + G)_3$, so P_3 and GDP_3 yield another point on the aggregate demand curve at 3′.

Chapter 3 in discussing demand curves for single products.

In Figure 11-3, an increase in aggregate demand is depicted by the rightward movement of the curve from AD_1 to AD_2. This shift indicates that, at each price level, the desired amount of real goods and services is larger than before.

A decrease in aggregate demand is shown as the leftward shift of the curve from AD_1 to AD_3, indicating that people desire to buy less real output at each price level.

To reemphasize: The changes in aggregate demand shown in Figure 11-3 occur when changes happen in any of the factors we have assumed to be constant under the phrase "other things equal." These determinants of aggregate demand, or *aggregate demand shifters*, are listed in Figure 11-3. Let's examine each of them in some detail.

Consumer Spending   Even if the price level is constant, domestic consumers collectively may alter their purchases of U.S.-produced real output. When this happens, the entire aggregate demand curve shifts. It shifts leftward, as from AD_1 to AD_3 in Figure 11-3, when consumers buy less output than before at each possible price level; it moves rightward, as from AD_1 to AD_2, when they buy more at each possible price level.

Several factors other than the price level may change consumer spending, thus shifting the aggregate demand curve. As indicated in Figure 11-3, these factors are real consumer wealth, consumer expectations, household indebtedness, and taxes.

Consumer Wealth   Consumer wealth includes all consumer assets, both financial assets such as stocks and bonds and physical assets such as houses and land.

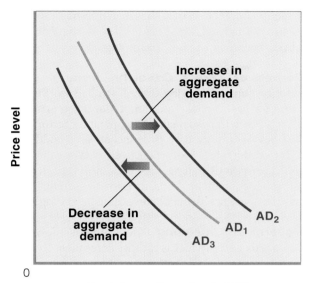

Determinants of aggregate demand: factors which shift the aggregate demand curve

1. Change in consumer spending
   a. Consumer wealth
   b. Consumer expectations
   c. Household indebtedness
   d. Taxes
2. Change in investment spending
   a. Interest rates
   b. Profit expectations on investment projects
   c. Business taxes
   d. Technology
   e. Degree of excess capacity
3. Change in government spending
4. Change in net export spending
   a. National income abroad
   b. Exchange rates

FIGURE 11-3 Changes in aggregate demand A change in one or more of the listed determinants of aggregate demand will change aggregate demand. An increase in aggregate demand is shown as a rightward shift of the AD curve, here from AD₁ to AD₂; a decrease in aggregate demand, as a leftward shift, here from AD₁ to AD₃.

A sharp decline in the real value of consumer assets encourages people to save more (buy fewer products) to restore their wealth. The resulting decline in consumer spending will decrease aggregate demand—that is, shift the aggregate demand curve leftward. In contrast, an increase in the real value of consumer wealth will increase consumption spending at each price level; the aggregate demand curve will shift rightward.

Warning: We are *not* referring here to the previously discussed "wealth effect" or "real-balances effect." That assumes a fixed aggregate demand curve and results from a change in the price level. In contrast, the change in real wealth addressed here is independent of a change in the price level; it is a *nonprice-level factor* which shifts the entire aggregate demand curve. An example would be a rocketing boost in stock prices which increases consumer wealth, even though the price level has not changed. Similarly, a sharp decline in the real value of houses and land reduces consumer wealth, independent of changes in the general price level.

Consumer Expectations Changes in expectations about the future may alter consumer spending.

When people expect their future real incomes to rise, they spend more of their current incomes. Thus present consumption spending increases (present saving falls), and the aggregate demand curve shifts rightward. An expectation that real income will decline in the future reduces present consumption spending and therefore shifts the aggregate demand curve leftward.

Similarly, a widely held expectation of surging future inflation increases aggregate demand today because consumers want to buy products before prices escalate. Conversely, expectations of lower prices in the near future may reduce present consumption. People may postpone some of their present consumption to take advantage of the future lower prices.

Household Indebtedness Households with high levels of indebtedness from past buying financed by borrowing may be forced to cut present spending to pay off their existing debt. The result is a decline in consumption spending and a leftward shift of the aggregate demand curve. When household indebtedness is low, borrowing and present consumption spending tend to increase. The aggregate demand curve shifts to the right.

Taxes A reduction in personal income tax rates raises take-home income and increases consumer purchases at each possible price level. So tax cuts shift the aggregate demand curve rightward. Tax increases reduce consumption spending and shift the aggregate demand curve to the left.

Investment Spending Investment spending—the purchase of capital goods—is a second major determinant of aggregate demand. A decline in the amount of new capital goods desired by businesses at each price level will shift the aggregate demand curve leftward. An increase in the desired amount of investment goods will increase aggregate demand. Let's consider the individual factors which can alter the level of investment spending, as listed in Figure 11-3.

Interest Rates All else equal, an increase in interest rates caused by a factor other than a change in the price level will lower investment spending and reduce aggregate demand. We are *not* referring here to the so-called "interest-rate effect" due to a change in the price level. Instead, we are identifying a change in the interest rate resulting from, say, a change in the nation's money supply. An increase in the money supply reduces the interest rate, increasing investment and aggregate demand. A decrease in the supply of money increases the interest rate, reducing investment and aggregate demand.

Expected Returns on Investment Projects Higher expected returns on investment projects will increase the demand for capital goods and shift the aggregate demand curve rightward. For example, an anticipated rise in consumer spending can improve the expected returns of possible investment projects. Alternatively, if the profit outlook on possible investment projects dims because of an expected decline in consumer spending, investment spending will decline. Consequently, aggregate demand will also decline.

Business Taxes An increase in business taxes reduces after-tax profits from corporate investment and reduces investment spending and aggregate demand. Conversely, a tax reduction increases after-tax profits from corporate investment, boosts investment spending, and pushes the aggregate demand curve rightward.

Technology New and improved technologies stimulate investment spending and increase aggregate de-

mand. Example: Recent advances in microbiology and electronics have spawned new labs and production facilities to exploit the new technologies.

Degree of Excess Capacity A rise in excess capacity—unused existing capital—will retard the demand for new capital goods and reduce aggregate demand. Other things equal, firms operating factories at well below capacity have little incentive to build new factories. But when firms collectively discover their excess capacity is dwindling, they build new factories and buy more equipment. Thus, investment spending rises and the aggregate demand curve shifts to the right.

Government Spending Government's desire to buy goods and services is a third determinant of aggregate demand. An increase in government purchases of real output at each price level will increase aggregate demand as long as tax collections and interest rates do not change as a result. An example would be a decision by government to expand the interstate highway system. In contrast, a reduction in government spending, such as a cutback in orders for military hardware, will reduce aggregate demand.

Net Export Spending The final determinant of aggregate demand is net export spending. When foreign consumers change their purchases of U.S. goods independently of changes in the U.S. price level, the nation's aggregate demand curve shifts. We specify "independently of changes in price level" to distinguish these changes from spending changes arising from the foreign purchases effect. That effect helps explain why a change in the U.S. price level moves the economy *along* its existing AD curve.

In discussing aggregate demand shifters, we instead address changes in net exports caused by factors other than changes in the price level. Increases in net exports caused by these other factors push the U.S. aggregate demand curve rightward. The logic is as follows: First, a higher level of U.S. exports constitutes an increased *foreign demand* for U.S. goods. Second, a reduction of U.S. imports implies an increased *domestic demand* for U.S.-produced products.

The non-price-level factors which alter net exports are primarily national income abroad and exchange rates.

National Income Abroad Rising national income in a foreign nation increases the foreign demand for U.S. goods, increasing aggregate demand in the United States. As income levels rise in a foreign nation, its citizens can afford to buy both more products made at home *and* more made in the United States. U.S. exports therefore rise in step with increases in the national income of U.S. trading partners. Declines in national income abroad have the opposite effect: U.S. net exports decline, shifting the U.S. aggregate demand curve leftward.

Exchange Rates A change in the exchange rate (Chapter 6) between the dollar and other currencies also affects net exports and hence aggregate demand. Suppose the dollar price of yen rises, meaning the *dollar depreciates* in terms of the yen. This is the same as saying the yen price of dollars falls—the *yen appreciates*. The new relative values of dollars and yen means consumers in Japan can obtain *more* dollars with any particular number of yen. Consumers in the United States can obtain *fewer* yen for each dollar. Japanese consumers therefore discover that U.S. goods are cheaper in terms of yen. They buy more U.S. goods. Consumers in the United States find that fewer Japanese products can be purchased with a set number of dollars. They buy fewer Japanese goods.

With respect to U.S. *exports*, a $30 pair of U.S.-made blue jeans now might be bought for 2880 yen compared to 3600 yen. And in terms of U.S. *imports*, a Japanese watch might now cost $225 rather than $180. In these circumstances U.S. exports will rise and imports will fall. This increase in net exports translates into a rightward shift of the U.S. aggregate demand curve.

You are urged to think through the opposite scenario in which the dollar appreciates (the yen depreciates).

QUICK REVIEW 11-1

■ Aggregate demand reflects an inverse relationship between the price level and the amount of real domestic output demanded.

■ Changes in the price level produce wealth, interest-rate, and foreign purchases effects which explain the downward slope of the aggregate demand curve.

■ Changes in one or more of the determinants of aggregate demand (Figure 11-3) alter the amounts of real GDP demanded at each price level; they shift the aggregate demand curve.

■ An increase in aggregate demand is shown as a rightward shift of the aggregate demand curve; a decrease, as a leftward shift of the curve.

Aggregate Demand Shifts and the Aggregate Expenditures Model[2]

The determinants of aggregate demand listed in Figure 11-3 are the components of Chapter 10's aggregate expenditures model. When one of these determinants changes, so does the location of the aggregate expenditures schedule. We can easily link shifts in the aggregate expenditures schedule to shifts of the aggregate demand curve.

Let's suppose that the price level is constant. In Figure 11-4 we begin with the aggregate expenditures schedule at $(C_a + I_g + X_n + G)_1$ in the top diagram, yielding real output of GDP_1. Assume now that more optimistic business expectations increase investment spending, so the aggregate expenditures schedule rises from $(C_a + I_g + X_n + G)_1$ to $(C_a + I_g + X_n + G)_2$. (The notation "at P_1" reminds us that the price level is assumed to be constant.) The result will be a multiplied increase in real output from GDP_1 to GDP_2.

In the lower graph the increase in investment spending is reflected in the horizontal distance between AD_1 and the broken curve to its right. The immediate effect of the increase in investment is an increase in aggregate demand by the exact amount of this new spending. But then the multiplier process magnifies the initial increase in investment into successive rounds of consumption spending and an ultimate multiplied increase in aggregate demand from AD_1 to AD_2. Equilibrium real output rises from GDP_1 to GDP_2, the same multiplied increase in real GDP as that in the top graph. *The initial increase in investment in the top graph has shifted the AD curve in the lower graph by a horizontal distance equal to the change in investment times the multiplier.* The change in real GDP is still associated with the constant price level P_1. To generalize,

$$\text{Shift of AD curve} = \text{initial change in spending} \times \text{multiplier}$$

AGGREGATE SUPPLY

Aggregate supply *is a schedule or a curve showing the level of real domestic output which will be produced at each price level.* Higher price levels create an incentive for

---

[2]This section presumes knowledge of the aggregate expenditures model (Chapters 9 and 10). It may be skipped by instructors who wish to rely exclusively on the aggregate demand–aggregate supply framework.

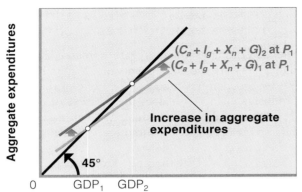

(a) Aggregate expenditures model

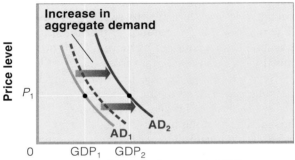

(b) Aggregate demand–aggregate supply model

FIGURE 11-4 Shifts in the aggregate expenditures schedule and in the aggregate demand curve (a) A change in some determinant of consumption, investment, or net exports (other than the price level) shifts the aggregate expenditures schedule upward from $(C_a + I_g + X_n + G)_1$ to $(C_a + I_g + X_n + G)_2$. The multiplier increases real output from GDP_1 to GDP_2. (b) The counterpart of this change is an initial rightward shift of the aggregate demand curve by the amount of initial new spending (from AD_1 to the broken curve). This leads to a multiplied rightward shift of the curve to AD_2, which is just sufficient to show the same increase in GDP as in the aggregate expenditures model.

- -

enterprises to produce and sell more output, while lower price levels reduce output. As a result, the relationship between the price level and the amount of real output businesses offer for sale is direct or positive.

Aggregate Supply Curve

For now, think of the aggregate supply curve as being made up of three distinct segments or ranges: the

(1) horizontal, (2) intermediate (upsloping), and (3) vertical ranges. Let's examine these three ranges and see what each represents. Unless specified otherwise, we assume the aggregate supply curve itself does not shift when the price level changes. You already know from our discussion of Figure 8-7 that the shape of the aggregate supply curve reflects what happens to the per-unit production cost as GDP expands or contracts. You also know from Chapter 8 that the per-unit production cost is found by dividing the total cost of all the resources used in production by the total quantity of output. That is, the per-unit production cost of a particular level of output is the average cost of that output. And the average cost of a particular output establishes the output's price level since the price level must be high enough to cover all the costs of production, including profit "costs."

Horizontal Range In Figure 11-5 the full-employment real output is designated as Q_f. Recall from Chapter 8 that the natural rate of unemployment occurs at this output. Observe in the figure that the **horizontal range** (*ab*) of aggregate supply includes only real levels of output which are substantially less than the full-employment output Q_f. Thus,

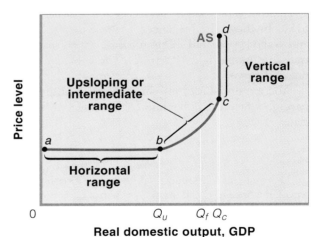

FIGURE 11-5 The aggregate supply curve The aggregate supply curve shows the level of real domestic output which will be produced at various price levels. It has three ranges: a horizontal range *ab*, where the price level remains constant as domestic output varies; a vertical range *cd*, where real domestic output is constant at the full-capacity level and only the price level can vary; and an intermediate range *bc*, where both real output and the price level are variable.

- -

the horizontal range implies that the economy is in a severe recession or depression and that large amounts of unused machinery and equipment and unemployed workers are available for production. These idle resources—both human and property—can be put back to work with little or no upward pressure on the price level. As output expands over this range from a to b, no shortages or production bottlenecks will be incurred to raise prices. Workers unemployed for 2 or 3 months will hardly expect a wage increase when recalled to their jobs. Because producers can acquire labor and other inputs at stable prices, per-unit production costs do not rise as output is expanded up to Q_u. There is no reason to raise product prices.

This horizontal range also implies that if real output falls, product and resource prices will not move downward. That means real output and employment may fall, but product prices and wages will remain rigid. Indeed, real output and employment will decline in this range *because* prices and wages are inflexible.

Vertical Range   At the other extreme, we find that the economy reaches its full-capacity real output at Q_c. Any increase in the price level in this **vertical range** (*cd*) will not produce additional real output because the economy is already operating at its full capacity. Individual firms may try to expand production by bidding resources away from other firms. But the resources and additional production which one firm gains will be lost by some other firm. This bidding will raise resource prices (costs) and ultimately product prices, but real output will remain unchanged.

Intermediate (Upsloping) Range   Finally, in the **intermediate range** (*bc*) between Q_u and Q_c, an expansion of real output is accompanied by a rising price level. The aggregate economy is made up of innumerable product and resource markets, and full employment is not reached evenly or simultaneously in the various sectors or industries. Example: As the economy expands in real-output range *bc*, the high-tech computer industry may encounter shortages of skilled workers while the automobile and steel industries still face substantial unemployment. At the same time, in certain industries raw-material shortages or other production bottlenecks may begin to appear. Expansion may also mean some firms will be forced to use older and less efficient machinery as they approach capacity production. And adding employees may create congestion in workplaces. Also, less capable workers may be hired as output expands. All these

things tend to decrease productivity, increase costs, and raise prices as production increases in range *bc*.

Once the full-employment level of GDP is reached at Q_f, for a time further price-level increases may bring forth added real output. We know from Chapter 8 that employment and real GDP can expand beyond the full-employment level of output until the economy reaches its maximum capacity. Recall from Figure 8-5 that actual GDP periodically exceeds full-employment GDP. In a prosperous economy the size of the labor force, daily working hours, and the workweek can be extended. Workers can also "moonlight"—hold more than one job. But once the economy's full capacity is reached at Q_c, the aggregate supply curve becomes vertical.

In the intermediate range of aggregate supply, per-unit production costs rise and firms must receive higher product prices for their output to be profitable. In this range rising real output is accompanied by an increasing price level.

Determinants of Aggregate Supply

Our discussion of the shape of the aggregate supply curve reveals that real output increases as the economy moves from left to right through the horizontal and intermediate ranges of aggregate supply. These changes in output result from *movements along* the aggregate supply curve and must be distinguished from *shifts* of the curve itself. An existing aggregate supply curve identifies the relationship between the price level and real output, *other things equal*. But when one or more of these other things change, the curve itself shifts.

The shift of the curve from AS_1 to AS_2 in Figure 11-6 represents an *increase* in aggregate supply. Over the intermediate and vertical ranges this shift is rightward, indicating that businesses collectively will produce more output at each price level. Over the horizontal range of the aggregate supply curve, an increase in aggregate supply can be thought of as a decline in the price level at each level of output (a downward shift of the aggregate supply curve). We will refer to an increase in aggregate supply as a "rightward" shift of the curve. The shift of the curve from AS_1 to AS_3 is a "leftward" shift, depicting a *decrease* in aggregate supply. That means businesses now will produce less output at each price level than before (or charge higher prices at each level of output).

Figure 11-6 lists the other things which shift the aggregate supply curve when they change. Called the

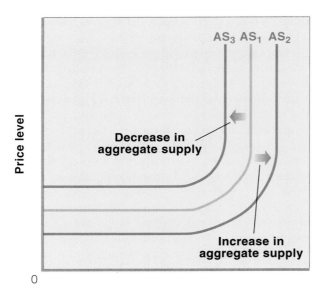

Real domestic output, GDP

**Determinants of aggregate supply:
factors which shift the aggregate supply curve**

1. Change in input prices
   a. Domestic resource availability
      a_1 Land
      a_2 Labor
      a_3 Capital
      a_4 Entrepreneurial ability
   b. Prices of imported resources
   c. Market power
2. Change in productivity
3. Change in legal-institutional environment
   a. Business taxes and subsidies
   b. Government regulations

FIGURE 11-6 Changes in aggregate supply A change in one or more of the listed determinants of aggregate supply will cause a change in aggregate supply. An increase in aggregate supply is shown as a rightward shift of the AS curve from AS_1 to AS_2; a decrease in aggregate supply, as a leftward shift from AS_1 to AS_3.

determinants of aggregate supply, they collectively determine the *location* of the aggregate supply curve. These determinants have one thing in common: When they change, per-unit production costs also change *at each price level*. This changes profits and causes producers to change their collective output *at each price level*. Hence, when one of the determinants listed in Figure 11-6 changes, the aggregate supply curve shifts. Changes which decrease per-unit production costs shift the aggregate supply curve to the right; changes which increase per-unit production costs shift it to the left. *When per-unit production costs change for reasons other than changes in real output, firms collectively alter the amount of output they produce at each price level.*

Let's examine the aggregate supply shifters in Figure 11-6 in more detail.

Input Prices Input or resource prices—to be distinguished from the output prices that make up the price level—are a major determinant of aggregate supply. All else equal, higher input prices increase per-unit production costs and reduce aggregate supply. Lower input prices do just the opposite. A number of factors influence input prices.

Domestic Resource Availability Increases in the supply of domestic resources lower resource prices and thus decrease per-unit production costs; that shifts the aggregate supply curve to the right. At any specific price level, firms collectively will then produce and offer for sale more real output than before. In contrast, declines in resource supplies increase input prices and shift the aggregate supply curve to the left.

How might changes in the availability of land, labor, capital, and entrepreneurial resources work to shift the aggregate supply curve? We can look at several examples.

1. *Land* Land resources might expand through discoveries of mineral deposits, irrigation of land, or technical innovations, permitting us to transform what were previously "nonresources" into valuable factors of production. An increase in the supply of land resources lowers the price of land inputs, lowering per-unit production costs. For example, the recent discovery that widely available materials at low temperatures can act as superconductors of electricity is expected eventually to reduce per-unit production costs by reducing electricity loss during transmission. This lower price of electricity will increase aggregate supply.

Two examples of reductions in land-resource availability may also be cited: (1) the widespread depletion of the nation's underground water reserves through irrigation, and (2) the nation's loss of topsoil through intensive farming. Eventually, these problems may increase water and land prices and shift the aggregate supply curve leftward.

2. *Labor* About 75 percent of all business costs are wages or salaries. Other things equal, changes in wages have a significant impact on per-unit production costs and on the location of the aggregate supply curve. An increase in the availability of labor resources reduces the price of labor and increases aggregate supply; a decrease has the opposite effect. Examples: The influx of women into the labor force during the past two decades placed a downward pressure on wages and expanded U.S. aggregate supply. Emigration of employable workers from abroad also has historically increased the availability of labor in the United States and reduced wages.

The great loss of life during World War II greatly diminished the postwar availability of labor in the United States, raising per-unit production costs. Currently, the AIDS epidemic has reduced the supply of labor and thus diminished the nation's aggregate supply of real output.

3. *Capital* Aggregate supply usually increases when society adds to its stock of capital. Such an addition would happen if society saved more of its income and used the savings to purchase capital goods. In much the same way, an improvement in the quality of capital reduces production costs and increases aggregate supply. For example, businesses over the years have increased aggregate supply by replacing poor-quality equipment with new, superior equipment.

On the other hand, aggregate supply declines when the quantity and quality of the nation's stock of capital diminishes. Example: In the depths of the Great Depression of the 1930s, the U.S. capital stock deteriorated because new purchases of capital were insufficient to offset the normal wearing out and obsolescence of plant and equipment. Aggregate supply declined.

4. *Entrepreneurial ability* Finally, the amount of entrepreneurial ability available to the economy may change, shifting the aggregate supply curve. Recent media focus on individuals such as Ted Turner and Bill Gates, who have amassed fortunes through entrepreneurial efforts, might conceivably increase the number of people who have entrepreneurial aspirations. If so, the aggregate supply curve might shift rightward.

Prices of Imported Resources Just as foreign demand for U.S. goods contributes to U.S. aggregate demand, resources imported from abroad add to U.S. aggregate supply. Whether domestic or imported, resources boost a nation's production capacity. Generally, a decrease in the prices of imported resources expands a nation's aggregate supply; an increase in the prices of these resources reduces a nation's aggregate supply.

Exchange-rate fluctuations are one factor that alters the price of imported resources. Suppose the dollar price of foreign currency falls—the dollar appreciates—enabling U.S. firms to obtain more foreign currency with each dollar. This means that domestic producers face a lower dollar price of imported resources. Under these conditions, U.S. firms would expand their imports of foreign resources and realize reductions in per-unit production costs at each level of output. Falling per-unit production costs of this type shift the U.S. aggregate supply curve to the right.

Also, an increase in the dollar price of foreign currency—dollar depreciation—raises the prices of imported resources. U.S. imports of these resources fall, per-unit production costs jump upward, and the U.S. aggregate supply curve moves leftward.

Market Power A change in the degree of market power or monopoly power held by sellers of resources can also affect input prices and aggregate supply. *Market power* is the ability to set a price above the price that would occur in a competitive situation. The rise and fall of market power held by the Organization of Petroleum Exporting Countries (OPEC) during the past three decades is a good illustration. The tenfold increase in the price of oil that OPEC achieved during the 1970s permeated the economy, drove up per-unit production costs, and jolted the U.S. aggregate supply curve leftward. But then a steep reduction in OPEC's market power during the mid-1980s reduced the cost of manufacturing and transporting products and, as a direct result, increased U.S. aggregate supply.

A change in the market power of labor unions also can affect the location of the aggregate supply curve. Some observers believe that unions experienced growing market power in the 1970s, resulting in union wage increases which widened the gap between union and nonunion workers. This higher pay may have increased per-unit production costs and produced leftward shifts of aggregate supply. But union market power greatly waned during the 1980s. The price of union labor fell in many industries, resulting in lower per-unit production costs. The outcome then was an increase in aggregate supply.

Productivity   Productivity relates a nation's level of real output to the quantity of input used to produce that output. In other words, **productivity** is a measure of average real output, or of real output per unit of input:

$$\text{Productivity} = \frac{\text{total output}}{\text{total inputs}}$$

An increase in productivity means the economy can obtain more real output from its limited resources—its inputs.

How does an increase in productivity affect the aggregate supply curve? We first need to see how a change in productivity alters the per-unit production cost. Suppose real output is 10 units, 5 units of input are needed to produce that quantity, and the price of each input unit is $2. Then

$$\text{Productivity} = \frac{\text{total output}}{\text{total inputs}} = \frac{10}{5} = 2$$

and

$$\frac{\text{Per-unit}}{\text{production cost}} = \frac{\text{total input cost}}{\text{total output}} = \frac{\$2 \times 5}{10} = \$1$$

Note that we obtain the total input cost by multiplying the unit input cost by the number of inputs used.

Now suppose productivity increases so that real output doubles to 20 units, while the input unit price and quantity remain constant at $2 and 5 units. You should use the above equations to confirm that productivity rises from 2 to 4 and that the per-unit production cost of the output falls from $1 to $.50. That is, the doubled productivity caused the per-unit production cost to decrease by half.

By reducing the per-unit production cost, an increase in productivity shifts the aggregate supply curve rightward; a decline in productivity increases the per-unit production cost and shifts the aggregate supply curve leftward.

You will see in Chapter 18 that productivity growth is a major factor explaining the long-term expansion of aggregate supply in the United States and the corresponding growth of real GDP. More machinery and equipment per worker, improved production technology, a better-educated and better-trained labor force, and improved forms of business enterprises have raised productivity and increased aggregate supply.

Legal-Institutional Environment   Changes in the legal-institutional setting in which businesses collectively operate may alter the per-unit costs of output and shift the aggregate supply curve. Two changes of this type are (1) changes in taxes and subsidies, and (2) changes in the extent of regulation.

Business Taxes and Subsidies   Higher business taxes, such as sales, excise, and payroll taxes, increase per-unit costs and reduce aggregate supply in much the same way as a wage increase. Example: An increase in payroll taxes paid by businesses will increase production costs and reduce aggregate supply.

Similarly, a business subsidy—a payment or tax break by government to firms—reduces production costs and increases aggregate supply. Example: During the 1970s, the government subsidized firms which produced energy from alternative sources such as wind, oil shale, and solar power. The purpose was to reduce production costs and encourage development of energy sources which might substitute for oil and natural gas. To the extent that these subsidies were successful, the aggregate supply curve moved rightward.

Government Regulation   It is usually costly for businesses to comply with government regulations. Thus, regulation increases per-unit production costs and shifts the aggregate supply curve leftward. "Supply-side" proponents of deregulation of the economy have argued forcefully that, by increasing efficiency and reducing the paperwork associated with complex regulations, deregulation will reduce per-unit costs. In this way the aggregate supply curve purportedly will shift rightward. Conversely, increases in regulation raise production costs and reduce aggregate supply.

QUICK REVIEW 11-2

■ The aggregate supply curve has three distinct ranges: a horizontal range, an upsloping intermediate range, and a vertical range.

■ In the intermediate range, per-unit production costs and therefore the price level rise as output expands toward—and beyond—its full-employment level.

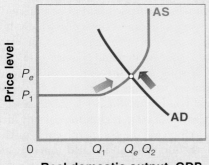

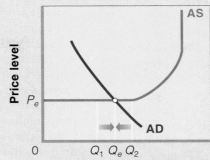

(a) Equilibrium in the intermediate range of aggregate supply

(b) Equilibrium in the horizontal range of aggregate supply

FIGURE 11-7 The equilibrium price level and equilibrium real GDP The intersection of the aggregate demand and supply curves determines the equilibrium price level and equilibrium real output. In (a), where the aggregate demand curve intersects the aggregate supply curve in its intermediate range, the price level will change to eliminate underproduction or overproduction of output; in (b), where the aggregate demand curve intersects the aggregate supply curve in its horizontal range, no change in the price level accompanies the move toward equilibrium real output.

QUICK QUIZ 11-7

1. The AD curve slopes downward because:
   a. per-unit production costs fall as real GDP increases.
   b. the income and substitution effects are at work.
   c. changes in the determinants of AD alter the amounts of real GDP demanded at each price level.
   d. decreases in the price level give rise to wealth, interest-rate, and foreign purchases effects which increase the amounts of real GDP demanded.

2. The AS curve slopes upward in the intermediate range because:
   a. per-unit production costs rise as real GDP expands toward and beyond its full-employment level.
   b. the income and substitution effects are at work.
   c. changes in the determinants of AS alter the amounts of real GDP supplied at each price level.
   d. increases in the price level give rise to wealth, interest-rate, and foreign purchases effects which increase the amounts of real GDP supplied.

3. At price level P_1 in graph (a):
   a. a GDP surplus of Q_2 minus Q_1 occurs which drives the price level up to P_e.
   b. a GDP shortage of Q_2 minus Q_1 occurs which drives the price level up to P_e.
   c. the aggregate amount of real GDP demanded is less than the aggregate amount of GDP supplied.
   d. the economy is in an "unemployment equilibrium."

4. Suppose the business sector has produced real GDP Q_2 in graph (b). We would expect:
   a. the price level to fall below P_e.
   b. the AD curve to shift to the right until it intersects AS at real GDP Q_2.
   c. the price level to rise above P_e.
   d. inventories to increase, compelling firms to reduce production to Q_e.

Answers: 1. d; 2. a; 3. b; 4. d

■ By altering the per-unit production cost independent of changes in the level of output, changes in one or more of the determinants of aggregate supply (Figure 11-6) shift the location of the aggregate supply curve.

■ An increase in aggregate supply is shown as a rightward shift of the aggregate supply curve, a decrease as a leftward shift of the curve.

EQUILIBRIUM: REAL OUTPUT AND THE PRICE LEVEL

We found in Chapter 3 that the intersection of a product's demand curve and supply curve determines its equilibrium price and quantity. Similarly, as we see in **Figure 11-7 (Key Graph)**, the intersection of the aggregate demand and aggregate supply curves determines the economy's **equilibrium price level** and **equilibrium real domestic output.**

In Figure 11-7a, where the aggregate demand curve crosses the aggregate supply curve in its intermediate range, the equilibrium price level and level of real output are P_e and Q_e, respectively. To illustrate why P_e is the equilibrium price and Q_e is the equilibrium level of output, suppose the price level were P_1 rather than P_e. We observe from the aggregate supply curve that price level P_1 would encourage businesses to produce (at most) real output Q_1. How much real output would domestic consumers, businesses, government, and foreign buyers want to purchase at P_1? The aggregate demand curve tells us the answer is Q_2. Competition among buyers to purchase the lesser available real output Q_1 will drive up the price level to P_e.

As the arrows in Figure 11-7a indicate, the rise in the price level from P_1 to P_e encourages *producers* to increase their real output from Q_1 to Q_e and simultaneously causes *buyers* to scale back their purchases from Q_2 to Q_e. When equality occurs between the amount of real output produced and the amount purchased, as it does at P_e, the economy has achieved equilibrium.

In Figure 11-7b the aggregate demand curve intersects the aggregate supply curve in the range where the aggregate supply curve is perfectly horizontal. Here, the price level does *not* play a role in bringing about the equilibrium level of real output. To understand why, first observe that the equilibrium price and real-output levels in Figure 11-7b are P_e and Q_e. If firms produce a larger output, such as Q_2, they cannot sell it all. Aggregate demand is insufficient to take all that output off the shelves. Faced with unwanted inventories of goods, businesses will reduce their production to Q_e—shown by the leftward-pointing arrow—and the market will then clear.

If firms produce only smaller output Q_1, they will find their inventory of goods quickly diminishing because the quantity of output demanded Q_e exceeds production. They will step up their production and, as shown by the rightward-pointing arrow, output will rise from Q_1 to its equilibrium level Q_e.

CHANGES IN EQUILIBRIUM

Let's now shift the aggregate demand and aggregate supply curves to see the effects on equilibrium real output and the price level.

Shifting of Aggregate Demand

Suppose households, businesses, and government decide to increase their spending—an action which shifts the aggregate demand curve to the right. Our list of determinants of aggregate demand (Figure 11-3) provides several reasons why this shift could occur. Perhaps consumers become more optimistic about future economic conditions. Such favorable expectations might stem from new technological advances which promise to increase the competitiveness of U.S. products in both domestic and world markets and therefore to increase future real income. As a result, consumers would consume more (save less) of their current incomes. Similarly, firms might anticipate enhanced future profits from current investments in new capital. They would therefore increase their investment spending on new equipment and facilities which incorporate the new technology.

As shown in Figure 11-8, the precise effects of an *increase* in aggregate demand depend on whether the economy is currently in the horizontal, intermediate, or vertical range of the aggregate supply curve.

In the horizontal range of Figure 11-8a, where there is high unemployment and much unused production capacity, an increase in aggregate demand (from AD_1 to AD_2) creates a large increase in real output (Q_1 to Q_2) and thus in employment with no increase in the price level (it remains at P_1).

In the vertical range of Figure 11-8b, where labor and capital are at their full capacities, an increase in aggregate demand (AD_5 to AD_6) affects the price level only, increasing it from P_5 to P_6. Real output remains at Q_c.

In the intermediate range of Figure 11-8c an increase in aggregate demand (AD_3 to AD_4) raises both real output (Q_3 to Q_4) *and* the price level (P_3 to P_4).

Price-level increases due to increases in aggregate demand in the vertical and intermediate ranges of the aggregate supply curve (Figure 11-8b and c) constitute *demand-pull inflation*. It results when shifts in aggregate demand *pull up* the price level. **(Key Question 4)**

Multiplier with Price-Level Changes[3]

Close inspection reveals that real GDP does not increase as much in Figure 11-8c as it does in Figure

---

[3]Instructors who do not assign Chapters 9 and 10 may want to use this section as a springboard for introducing the MPC, MPS, and multiplier concepts.

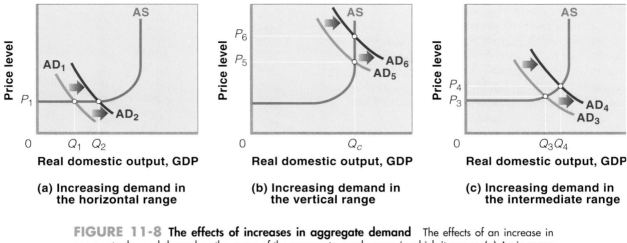

FIGURE 11-8 **The effects of increases in aggregate demand**   The effects of an increase in aggregate demand depend on the range of the aggregate supply curve in which it occurs. (a) An increase in aggregate demand in the horizontal range increases real output but leaves the price level unaffected. (b) In the vertical range, an increase in aggregate demand increases the price level, but real output cannot increase beyond the full-capacity level. (c) An increase in demand in the intermediate range increases both real output and the level of prices.

11-8a, even though the shifts in aggregate demand are of equal magnitudes. In Figure 11-9, which combines Figures 11-8a and 11-8c, we see that the shift in aggregate demand from AD_1 to AD_2 occurs in the horizontal range of the aggregate supply curve. That means the economy is in recession, with excess production capacity and a high unemployment rate. Businesses are willing to produce more output *at existing prices*. In this range, any initial change in spending and resulting multiple change in aggregate demand transmits fully into a change in real GDP and employment. The price level remains constant. In the horizontal range of aggregate supply a "full-strength" multiplier is at work.

If the economy is in either the intermediate or the vertical range of the aggregate supply curve, part or all of any initial increase in aggregate demand will be dissipated in inflation and therefore *not* be reflected in increased real output and employment. In Figure 11-9 the shift of aggregate demand from AD_2 to AD_3 is of the same magnitude as the shift from AD_1 to AD_2. But look what happens. Because we are now in the intermediate range of the aggregate supply curve, a portion of the increase in aggregate demand is absorbed as inflation as the price level rises from P_1 to P_2. Real GDP rises only to GDP'. If the aggregate supply curve had been horizontal, then the shift from AD_2 to AD_3 would have increased real output to

GDP₃. But inflation has reduced the multiplier so that the actual increase is to GDP', only about half as much as otherwise.

Our conclusion is this: *For any initial increase in aggregate demand, the resulting increase in real GDP will be*

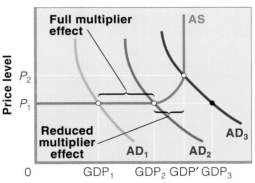

FIGURE 11-9 **Inflation and the multiplier**   The aggregate demand–aggregate supply model shows how inflation reduces the size of the multiplier. For the increase in aggregate demand from AD_1 to AD_2 the price level is constant and the multiplier is at full strength; output increases from GDP₁ to GDP₂. Although the increase in aggregate demand from AD_2 to AD_3 is of the same magnitude, the impact is partly dissipated in inflation (from P_1 to P_2), and real output increases only from GDP₂ to GDP'.

---

smaller the greater the increase in the price level. Price-level increases weaken the multiplier.

You should sketch an increase in aggregate demand equal to the shift from AD_2 to AD_3 in the vertical range of aggregate supply to confirm that this increase in spending would be entirely absorbed as inflation. The multiplier would be zero because real GDP would be unchanged.

A Ratchet Effect?

What happens when there is a *decrease* in aggregate demand? Our model predicts that in the horizontal range of aggregate supply, real GDP falls and the price level remains unchanged. In the vertical range prices fall and real output remains at the full-capacity level. In the intermediate range the model suggests that both real output and the price level diminish.

But a complicating factor raises doubts about the predicted effects of declines in aggregate demand in the vertical and intermediate ranges. The reverse movements of aggregate demand—from AD_6 to AD_5 in Figure 11-8b and from AD_4 to AD_3 in Figure 11-8c—may *not* restore the initial equilibrium positions, at least in the short term. The complication is that many prices—of both products and resources—rise quickly but are "sticky" or inflexible in a downward direction. Some economists call this the **ratchet effect** (a ratchet is a mechanism which cranks a wheel forward but not backward).

Graphical Depiction   The workings of the ratchet effect are shown in Figure 11-10. If aggregate demand increases from AD_1 to AD_2, the economy moves from the P_1Q_1 equilibrium at point *a* in the horizontal range of aggregate supply to the P_2Q_c equilibrium at *b* in the vertical range. This increase in aggregate demand has increased the price level. The higher product prices in turn result in increases in wages and other resource prices, raising per-unit production costs at each level of available GDP. Thus the aggregate supply curve shifts upward from P_1abAS to P_2cAS.

But while product prices, resource prices, and per-unit production costs easily move upward, they do not so easily come down. If aggregate demand should decrease from AD_2 to AD_1, the economy will *not* return to the original equilibrium position at *a*. Rather, the higher per-unit production costs will remain, meaning that the aggregate supply curve stays in place at P_2cAS. Thus the initial increase in demand has ratcheted up the price level from P_1 to P_2. Any subsequent decline in aggregate demand (as from AD_2 to

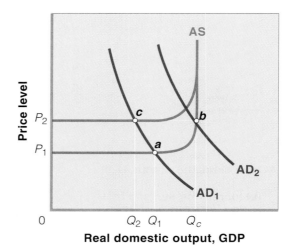

FIGURE 11-10 **The ratchet effect**   An increase in aggregate demand from AD_1 to AD_2 will move the equilibrium position from *a* to *b* with real domestic output rising from Q_1 to Q_c and the price level from P_1 to P_2. But if prices are inflexible downward, then a decline in aggregate demand from AD_2 to AD_1 will not return the economy to its original equilibrium at *a*. Rather, the new equilibrium will be at *c* with the price level remaining at P_2 and real output falling below the original level to Q_2. The ratchet effect means that the aggregate supply curve has changed from P_1abAS to P_2cAS.

AD_1) reduces real output (here, from Q_c to Q_2) but does *not* reduce the price level.

Causes of Downward Price-Level Inflexibility

The reasons for downward price inflexibility are numerous and interrelated.

1. **Wage contracts**   Wage rates often are inflexible downward, at least for a time. It is usually not profitable for firms to cut their product prices when they cannot also cut their wage rates and thus reduce their per-unit production costs. But why are wages inflexible downward? One reason is that part of the labor force works under contracts prohibiting wage cuts for the duration of the contract. (It is not uncommon for collective bargaining agreements in major industries to run for 3 years.) Similarly, wages and salaries of non-union workers are usually adjusted once a year, rather than quarterly or monthly.

2. **Morale, effort, and productivity**   Wage inflexibility downward is reinforced because employers may *not want* to reduce wage rates. Current wages may be so-called **efficiency wages**—*wages which elicit maximum work effort and thus minimize labor*

cost per unit of output. Lower wages may reduce worker morale and work effort, thereby reducing labor productivity (output per worker). While lower wage rates do reduce labor costs per hour of work, lower worker productivity means *less output* per hour of work. If the latter more than counterbalances the former, then a lower wage rate will increase, not reduce, labor costs per unit of production. In these situations, firms will resist lowering wages when faced with a decline in aggregate demand.

3. ***Training investments*** Most employers have an "investment" in the training and experience of their present workforces. If they cut wage rates and salaries when aggregate demand declines, they may lose workers more or less randomly; some highly trained and some relatively unskilled workers may quit. When highly trained workers find jobs with new firms, the old employer loses any chance of getting a return on that training investment. A better option might be to maintain wages and lay off workers on the basis of seniority. Generally, workers with less seniority who are laid off will also be less skilled workers in whom the employer's training investment is least. Equally qualified less skilled workers will be available to hire when the economy recovers.

4. ***Minimum wage*** The minimum wage imposes a legal floor under the wages of the least skilled workers. Firms cannot reduce this wage when aggregate demand declines.

5. ***Menu costs*** Firms that think a recession will be relatively short-lived may be reluctant to cut their prices. One reason is so-called **menu costs,** named after their most obvious example: the cost of printing new menus when a restaurant changes its prices. But there are other costs of changing prices. There are the costs of (1) estimating the magnitude and duration of the shift in demand to determine whether prices should be dropped, (2) repricing items held in inventory, (3) printing and mailing new catalogs, and (4) communicating new prices to customers, perhaps through advertising. When menu costs are substantial, firms may choose to avoid them by retaining current prices. That is, they will wait to see if the decline in aggregate demand is permanent.

6. ***Fear of price wars*** Some firms may be concerned that if they reduce their prices, rivals not only will match their price cuts but may retaliate by making even deeper cuts. That is, an initial price cut may touch off an unwanted *price war:* successively deeper and deeper rounds of price cuts. In this unwanted situation, all the firms end up with far less profit than if they had simply maintained their prices. For this reason, each firm may resist making the initial price cut, choosing instead to reduce production and lay off workers. A glance back at Figure 8-3 will reveal the extent of downward price inflexibility at the beginning of the Great Depression. Despite the catastrophic decline in aggregate demand which occurred between 1929 and 1933, monopolistic firms in the agricultural implements, motor vehicle, cement, iron and steel, and similar industries had a remarkable capacity to resist price cuts, accepting large declines in production and employment as an alternative.

Controversy Not all economists are persuaded that the ratchet effect is relevant today. They point to the declining power of unions in the United States and large wage cuts in several basic industries following the 1981–1982 recession as evidence of increased downward wage flexibility. They also note that growing foreign competition has undermined monopoly power and the accompanying ability of firms to resist price cuts when faced with falling demand. But defenders of the ratchet effect question whether these recent changes have altered the basic historical pattern. Since 1950 the price level has fallen in only a single year—1955. Meanwhile, in this period the economy has experienced eight recessions (listed in Table 8-1).

Shifting of Aggregate Supply

Two hypothetical situations will help illustrate the effects of a change in aggregate supply on the equilibrium price level and level of real output.

First, suppose that foreign suppliers impose steep increases on the prices of oil imported by the United States, as OPEC did in 1973–1974 and again in 1979–1980. The higher energy prices spread through the world economy, driving up the cost of producing and distributing virtually every domestically produced product and imported resource. Thus, domestic per-unit costs of production rise at each output level. The U.S. aggregate supply curve shifts leftward, say, from AS_1 to AS_2 in Figure 11-11. The price-level increase here is clearly **cost-push inflation** (Chapter 8).

The effects of a leftward shift in aggregate supply are doubly bad. When aggregate supply shifts from AS_1 to AS_2, the economy moves from point *a* to *b*. Real output declines from Q_1 to Q_2, and the price

Why is Unemployment in Europe So High?

Are the high unemployment rates in Europe the result of structural problems or deficient aggregate demand?

Several European economies have had high rates of unemployment in the past several years. For example, in 1996 France had an unemployment rate of 12.6 percent; Great Britain, 8.2 percent; Italy, 12.1 percent; and Germany, 7.2 percent.

There is little dispute that recessions in Europe in the early 1990s contributed to these high rates. Declines in aggregate demand reduced real GDP and increased unemployment. Nevertheless, a mystery remains: Why were unemployment rates in many European nations so high even *before* their recessions? In 1990 the unemployment rate in France was 9.1 percent; in Great Britain, 6.9  percent; and in Italy, 7.0 percent (compared with only 5.5 percent in the United States). And why have European unemployment rates remained far higher than those in the United States during economic recovery? There are two views on these questions.

1. High Natural Rates of Unemployment Many economists believe the high unemployment rates in Europe largely reflect high natural rates of unemployment. They envision a situation as in Figure 11-7a, where aggregate demand and aggregate supply have produced the full-employment level of real output Q_e. But high levels of frictional and structural unemployment accompany this level of output. In this view, the recent extensive unemployment in Europe has resulted from a high natural rate of unemployment, not from deficient aggregate demand. An increase in aggregate demand would push these economies beyond their full-employment levels of output, causing demand-pull inflation.

The alleged sources of the high natural rates of unemployment are government policies and union contracts which have increased the costs of hiring workers and reduced the cost of being unemployed. Examples: High minimum wages have discouraged employers from hiring low-skilled workers; generous welfare benefits have weakened incentives for people to take available jobs; restrictions against firings have discouraged firms from employing workers; 30 to 40 days per year of paid vacations and holidays have boosted the cost of hiring workers; high worker absenteeism has reduced productivity; and high employer costs of health, pension, disability, and other benefits have discouraged hiring.

2. Deficient Aggregate Demand Not all economists agree that government and union policies have pushed up Europe's natural rate of unemployment. Instead, they point to insufficient aggregate demand as the culprit. They see the European economies in terms of Figure 11-7b, where the equilibrium real output Q_e is less than it would be if aggregate demand were stronger. The argument is that the European governments have been so fearful of inflation that they have not undertaken appropriate fiscal and monetary policies (discussed later in Chapters 12 and 15) to increase aggregate demand. In this view, increases in aggregate demand would not be inflationary, since these economies have considerable excess capacity. If they are operating in the horizontal range of their aggregate supply curves, a rightward shift of their aggregate demand curves would expand output and employment without increasing inflation.

Conclusion: The debate over high unemployment in Europe reflects disagreement on where European aggregate demand curves lie relative to full-employment levels of output. If these curves are *at* the full-employment real GDP, as in Figure 11-7a, then the high levels of unemployment are "natural." Public policies should focus on lowering minimum wages, reducing vacation time, reducing welfare benefits, easing restrictions on layoffs, and so on. But if the aggregate demand curves in the European nations lie to the left of their full-employment levels of output, as in Figure 11-7b, then expansionary government policies such as reduced interest rates or tax cuts may be in order.

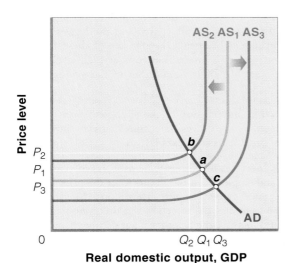

FIGURE 11-11 **The effects of changes in aggregate supply** A leftward shift of aggregate supply from AS_1 to AS_2 will cause cost-push inflation in that the price level increases from P_1 to P_2. Real output will fall from Q_1 to Q_2. A rightward shift of aggregate supply from AS_1 to AS_3 will increase real output from Q_1 to Q_3 and reduce the price level from P_1 to P_3.

----

level rises from P_1 to P_2. Employment falls and inflation occurs.

Now suppose one of the factors in Figure 11-6 changes so that aggregate supply increases. Maybe the economy experiences a sharp increase in productivity. Or perhaps a liberalization of immigration laws increases the supply of labor and pulls wage rates

down. Or maybe lower business excise tax rates reduce per-unit costs (an excise tax is a cost as viewed by a business), shifting the aggregate supply curve rightward. In Figure 11-11 the shift of aggregate supply from AS_1 to AS_3 moves the economy from a to c. Real output increases from Q_1 to Q_3, and assuming downward price and wage flexibility, the price level falls from P_1 to P_3.

The shift of the aggregate supply curve from AS_1 to AS_3 involves a change in the full-employment *and* full-capacity levels of real output. In particular, this shift signifies economic growth and indicates that the economy's potential output has increased. In terms of Chapter 2, the economy's production possibilities curve has moved outward, reflected in the rightward shift of the aggregate supply curve in Figure 11-11. **(Key Questions 5, 7, and 9)**

QUICK REVIEW 11-3

■ The equilibrium price level and amount of real output are determined at the intersection of the aggregate demand and aggregate supply curves.

■ Increases in aggregate demand in the upsloping and vertical ranges of aggregate supply cause demand-pull inflation.

■ The price level is "sticky" or inflexible in a downward direction, at least for a time.

■ Decreases in aggregate supply cause cost-push inflation.

■ Increases in aggregate supply expand real output; they result in economic growth.

CHAPTER SUMMARY

1. For purposes of analysis we consolidate—or aggregate—the outcomes from the enormous number of individual product markets into a composite market in which there are two variables—the price level and the level of real output. This is accomplished through an aggregate demand–aggregate supply model.

2. The aggregate demand curve shows the level of real output which the economy will purchase at each price level.

3. The aggregate demand curve is downsloping because of the wealth effect, the interest-rate effect, and the foreign purchases effect. The wealth or real-balances effect indicates that inflation reduces the real value or purchasing power of fixed-value financial assets held by house-

holds, causing them to cut back their consumer spending. The interest-rate effect means that, with a specific supply of money, a higher price level increases the demand for money, raising the interest rate and reducing consumption and investment purchases. The foreign purchases effect suggests that an increase in one country's price level relative to the price levels in other countries reduces the net export component of that nation's aggregate demand.

*4. A change in the price level alters the location of the aggregate expenditures schedule through the wealth,

---

*Starred summary items presume knowledge of the aggregate expenditures model presented in Chapters 9 and 10.

interest-rate, and foreign purchases effects. The aggregate demand curve is derived from the aggregate expenditures model by allowing the price level to change and observing the effect on the aggregate expenditures schedule and thus on equilibrium GDP.

5. The determinants of aggregate demand are spending by domestic consumers, businesses, government, and foreign buyers. Changes in the factors listed in Figure 11-3 cause changes in spending by these groups and shift the aggregate demand curve.

*6. With the price level held constant, increases in consumption, investment, and net export expenditures shift the aggregate expenditures schedule upward and the aggregate demand curve to the right. Decreases in these spending components produce the opposite effects.

7. The aggregate supply curve shows the levels of real output which businesses will produce at various possible price levels.

8. The shape of the aggregate supply curve depends on what happens to per-unit production costs—and therefore to the prices businesses must receive to cover costs and make a profit—as real output expands. In the horizontal range of aggregate supply, there is substantial unemployment and thus production can be increased without raising per-unit costs or prices. In the intermediate range, per-unit costs increase as production bottlenecks appear and less efficient equipment and workers are employed. Prices must therefore rise as real output is expanded. The vertical range coincides with full capacity; real output is at a maximum and cannot be increased, but the price level will rise in response to an increase in aggregate demand.

9. Figure 11-6 lists the determinants of aggregate supply: input prices, productivity, and the legal-institutional environment. A change in any one of these factors will change per-unit production costs at each level of output and therefore alter the location of the aggregate supply curve.

10. The intersection of the aggregate demand and aggregate supply curves determines an economy's equilibrium price level and real GDP.

11. Increases in aggregate demand **(a)** increase real output and employment but do not alter the price level in the horizontal range of aggregate supply, **(b)** increase both real output and the price level in the intermediate range, and **(c)** increase the price level but do not change real output in the vertical range.

12. In the intermediate and vertical ranges of the aggregate supply curve, the aggregate demand–aggregate supply model shows that the multiplier is weakened because a portion of any increase in aggregate demand is dissipated in inflation.

13. The ratchet effect is at work when prices are flexible upward but inflexible downward. An increase in aggregate demand raises the price level, but the price level does not fall when aggregate demand decreases.

14. Leftward shifts of the aggregate supply curve reflect increases in per-unit production costs and cause cost-push inflation. Rightward shifts of the aggregate supply curve result from decreases in per-unit costs and produce an expansion of real output.

TERMS AND CONCEPTS

aggregate demand
wealth effect
interest-rate effect
foreign purchases effect
determinants of
    aggregate demand
aggregate supply

horizontal range
    (of AS curve)
vertical range
    (of AS curve)
intermediate range
    (of AS curve)

determinants of
    aggregate supply
productivity
equilibrium price level
equilibrium real domestic
    output

ratchet effect
efficiency wages
menu costs

STUDY QUESTIONS

1. Why is the aggregate demand curve downsloping? Specify how your explanation differs from that for the downsloping demand curve for a single product.

2. Explain the shape of the aggregate supply curve, accounting for the horizontal, intermediate, and vertical ranges of the curve.

*3. Explain carefully: "A change in the price level shifts the aggregate expenditures curve but not the aggregate demand curve."

4. KEY QUESTION   Suppose that the aggregate demand and supply schedules for a hypothetical economy are as shown below:

Amount of real domestic output demanded, billions	Price level (price index)	Amount of real domestic output supplied, billions
$100	300	$400
200	250	400
300	200	300
400	150	200
500	150	100

a.   Use these sets of data to graph the aggregate demand and supply curves. Find the equilibrium price level and level of real output in this hypothetical economy. Is the equilibrium real output also the full-capacity real output? Explain.

b.   Why will a price level of 150 not be an equilibrium price level in this economy? Why not 250?

c.   Suppose that buyers desire to purchase $200 billion of extra real output at each price level. Sketch in the new aggregate demand curve as AD_1. What factors might cause this change in aggregate demand? What are the new equilibrium price level and level of real output? Over which range of the aggregate supply curve—horizontal, intermediate, or vertical—has equilibrium changed?

5. KEY QUESTION   Suppose that the hypothetical economy in question 4 has the following relationship between its real output and the input quantities necessary for producing that output:

Input quantity	Real domestic output
150.0	400
112.5	300
75.0	200

a.   What is productivity in this economy?

b.   What is the per-unit cost of production if the price of each input unit is $2?

c.   Assume that the input price increases from $2 to $3 with no accompanying change in productivity. What is the new per-unit cost of production? In what direction would the $1 increase in input price push the aggregate supply curve? What effect would this shift in aggregate supply have on the price level and the level of real output?

d.   Suppose that the increase in input price does not occur but, instead, that productivity increases by 100 percent. What would be the new per-unit cost of production? What effect would this change in per-unit production cost have on the aggregate supply curve? What effect would this shift of aggregate supply have on the price level and the level of real output?

6. Will an increase in the U.S. price level relative to price levels in other nations shift the U.S. aggregate demand curve? If so, in what direction? Explain. Will a decline in the dollar price of foreign currencies shift the U.S. aggregate supply curve rightward or simply move the economy along an existing aggregate supply curve? Explain.

7. KEY QUESTION   What effects would each of the following have on aggregate demand or aggregate supply? In each case use a diagram to show the expected effects on the equilibrium price level and level of real output. Assume all other things remain constant.

a.   A widespread fear of depression on the part of consumers

b.   A large purchase of wheat by Russia

c.   A $1 increase in the excise tax on cigarettes

d.   A reduction in interest rates at each price level

e.   A cut in Federal spending for health care

f.   The expectation of a rapid rise in the price level

g.   The complete disintegration of OPEC, causing oil prices to fall by one-half

h.   A 10 percent reduction in personal income tax rates

i.   An increase in labor productivity

j.   A 12 percent increase in nominal wages

k.   Depreciation in the international value of the dollar

l.   A sharp decline in the national incomes of our western European trading partners

m.   A decline in the percentage of the U.S. labor force which is unionized

8. What is the relationship between the production possibilities curve discussed in Chapter 2 and the aggregate supply curve discussed in this chapter?

9. KEY QUESTION   Other things equal, what effect will each of the following have on the equilibrium price level and level of real output?

a.   An increase in aggregate demand in the vertical range of aggregate supply

b.   An increase in aggregate supply (assume prices and wages are flexible)

---

*Questions with an asterisk presume knowledge of the aggregate expenditures model (Chapters 9 and 10).

c. Equal increases in aggregate demand and aggregate supply

d. A reduction in aggregate demand in the horizontal range of aggregate supply

e. An increase in aggregate demand and a decrease in aggregate supply

f. A decrease in aggregate demand in the intermediate range of aggregate supply (assume prices and wages are inflexible downward)

*10. Suppose that the price level is constant and investment spending increases sharply. How would you show this increase in the aggregate expenditures model? What would be the outcome? How would you show this rise in investment in the aggregate demand–aggregate supply model? What range of the aggregate supply curve is involved?

*11. Explain how an upsloping aggregate supply curve weakens the multiplier.

12. In the accompanying diagram assume that the aggregate demand curve shifts from AD₁ in year 1 to AD₂ in year 2, only to fall back to AD₁ in year 3. Locate the new year 3 equilibrium position on the assumption that prices and wages are **(a)** completely flexible and **(b)** completely rigid downward. Which of the two equilibrium positions is more desirable? Which is more realistic? Explain why the price level might be ratcheted upward when aggregate demand increases. Be sure to refer to both *efficiency wages* and *menu costs* in your answer.

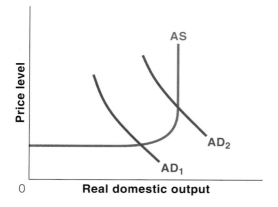

13. "Unemployment can be caused by a leftward shift of aggregate demand or a leftward shift of aggregate supply." Do you agree? Explain. In each case, specify price-level effects.

14. **(Last Word)** State the alternative views on why unemployment in Europe has recently been so high. Discuss the policy implications of each view.

15. **WEB-BASED QUESTION**   **The Interest-Rate Effect—Price Levels and Interest Rates** The interest-rate effect suggests that as the price level rises, so do interest rates, and rising interest rates reduce certain kinds of consumption and investment spending. Compare price levels http://stats.bls.gov/top20.html (initially select Consumer Price Index—All Urban Consumers) and interest rates http://www.bog.frb.fed.us/releases/h15/data.htm (initially select 1-year U.S. Treasury Bills—monthly averages) over the past decade. Do the data support the link between the price level and interest rates? Alternately, compare the producer price index and other interest-rate data. Is the relationship the same?

16. **WEB-BASED QUESTION**   **Aggregate Demand and Supply—Equilibrium Prices and GDPs** Actual data showing aggregate demand and supply curves do not exist. However, data for prices (CPI) and GDP http://www.oecd.org/std/fas.htm do exist for several countries. Look at the data for the United States, Japan, and Germany. Assume that these CPI and GDP figures represent the equilibrium price and real GDPs for their respective years. Plot the price/GDP levels for the past 3 years for each country using a graph similar to Figure 11-7. Are there any similarities across countries? What changes in aggregate demand and supply are implied by the equilibrium points?

CHAPTER TWELVE

Fiscal Policy

From time to time, national governments individually take purposeful budget actions to "stimulate their economies" or to "reign in inflation." Here are three examples:

- In the early 1980s, the United States reduced personal income tax rates by some 25 percent, without offsetting decreases in government spending. By expanding aggregate demand, this tax cut helped end the recession of 1980–1981 and promoted growth of output and employment.
- Earlier, during the Vietnam war, the United States placed a 10 percent surcharge—a tax *added* to taxes otherwise owed—on both corporate and personal income taxes. The idea was to reduce private spending and contain the demand-pull inflation it caused.
- In the mid-1990s, Japan instituted a massive government spending program to help move its economy out of recession.

What is the logic of such fiscal actions? Shouldn't government always match any increase in its spending with an increase in taxes, or match any tax cuts with cuts in government spending? Under what circumstances might government purposely change its spending and taxation—engage in so-called *fiscal policy*—to stabilize the economy? Do such policies always work?

This chapter looks briefly at the legislative mandates which give the U.S. government authority to pursue its stabilization role in the economy. It then explores the tools of government fiscal policy in terms of the aggregate demand–aggregate supply model. Next, we examine some factors which automatically adjust government expenditures and tax revenues as GDP rises and falls. Finally, problems, criticisms, and complications of government fiscal policy are addressed.

LEGISLATIVE MANDATES

The idea that government fiscal actions can exert a stabilizing influence on the economy emerged from the Depression of the 1930s. Macroeconomic theory has since played a ma-

jor role in the design of remedial fiscal (budgetary) measures.

Employment Act of 1946 In 1946, when the end of World War II re-created the specter of unemployment, the Federal government formalized its responsibility to promote economic stability. The **Employment Act of 1946** proclaims:

> The Congress hereby declares that it is the continuing policy and responsibility of the Federal Government to use all practicable means consistent with its needs and obligations and other essential considerations of national policy, with assistance and cooperation of industry, agriculture, labor and State and local governments, to coordinate and utilize all its plans, functions, and resources for the purpose of creating and maintaining, in a manner calculated to foster and promote free competitive enterprise and the general welfare, conditions under which there will be afforded useful employment opportunities, including self-employment, for those able, willing, and seeking to work and to promote maximum employment, production, and purchasing power.

The Employment Act of 1946 is a landmark in American socioeconomic legislation because it commits the Federal government to taking action through monetary and fiscal policy to maintain economic stability.

CEA and JEC   Responsibility for fulfilling the purposes of the act rests with the executive branch; the President must submit an annual economic report describing the current state of the economy and making policy recommendations to stabilize the economy. The act also established the **Council of Economic Advisers** (CEA) to assist and advise the President on economic matters, and the *Joint Economic Committee* (JEC) of Congress, which has since investigated a wide range of economic problems of national interest. In its advisory capacity as "the president's intelligence arm in the war against the business cycle," the three-member CEA and its staff gather and analyze relevant economic data and use them to make forecasts, to formulate programs and policies designed to fulfill the goals of the Employment Act, and to "educate" the president, Congress, and the general public on problems and policies relevant to the nation's economic health.

DISCRETIONARY FISCAL POLICY

Discretionary fiscal policy is the deliberate manipulation of taxes and government spending by Congress to alter real GDP and employment, control inflation, and stimulate economic growth. "Discretionary" means that the changes in taxes and government

spending are *at the option of* the Federal government. These changes do not occur automatically, independent of specific congressional action.

For clarity, we again assume government spending does not in any way affect planned private spending. Also, we assume fiscal policy affects only the aggregate demand side of the macroeconomy; it has no intended or unintended effects on aggregate supply. Both assumptions will be dropped when we examine the real-world complications and shortcomings of discretionary fiscal policy—or, more simply, *fiscal policy*.

First, we will examine fiscal policy in two situations: recession and demand-pull inflation.

Expansionary Fiscal Policy

When recession occurs, an **expansionary fiscal policy** may be in order. Consider Figure 12-1, where we suppose that a sharp decline in investment spending has shifted the economy's aggregate demand curve leftward from AD_1 to AD_2. (Disregard the arrows and the dashed line for now.) Perhaps profit expectations on investment projects have dimmed, curtailing much investment spending and reducing aggregate demand. Consequently, real GDP has fallen to $485 billion from its near full-employment level of $505 billion. Accompanying this $20 billion decline in real output is an increase in unemployment since fewer workers are needed to produce the diminished output. This economy is experiencing recession and cyclical unemployment.

What should the Federal government do to rev up the economy? It has three main fiscal policy options: (1) increase government spending, (2) reduce taxes, or (3) use some combination of the two. If the Federal budget is balanced at the outset, fiscal policy during a recession or depression should create a government **budget deficit**—government spending in excess of tax revenues.

Increased Government Spending   All else equal, an increase in government spending will shift an economy's aggregate demand curve to the right, as from AD_2 to AD_1 in Figure 12-1. To see why, suppose that the recession prompts government to initiate $5 billion of new spending on highways, satellite communications systems, and Federal prisons. We represent this new $5 billion of government spending as the horizontal distance between AD_2 and the dashed line immediately to its right. At *each* price level the amount of real output demanded is now $5 billion greater

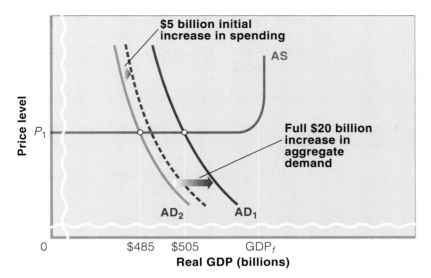

FIGURE 12-1 Expansionary fiscal policy Expansionary fiscal policy, which is represented here, uses increases in government spending or tax cuts to push the economy out of recession. In an economy with an MPC of .75, a $5 billion increase in government spending or a $6.67 billion decrease in personal taxes (producing a $5 billion initial increase in consumption) expands aggregate demand from AD_2 to the dashed curve. The multiplier then magnifies this initial increase in spending to AD_1. Hence, real GDP rises by the desired $20 billion.

than that demanded before the increase in government spending.

But the aggregate demand curve shifts rightward to AD_1; aggregate demand increases by much more than the $5 billion increase in government purchases. This occurs because the multiplier process magnifies the initial change in spending into successive rounds of new consumption spending. If the economy's MPC is .75, then the simple multiplier is 4. The aggregate demand curve thus shifts rightward by four times the distance representing the $5 billion increase in government spending. Because this particular increase in aggregate demand occurs within the horizontal range of aggregate supply, real output rises by the full extent of the multiplier. Observe that real output jumps to $505 billion, up $20 billion from its recessionary level of $485 billion. Concurrently, unemployment falls as firms call back workers laid off during the recession.

Tax Reductions Alternatively, government could reduce taxes to shift the aggregate demand curve rightward, as from AD_2 to AD_1. Suppose government cuts personal income taxes by $6.7 billion, which increases disposable income by the same amount. Consumption will rise by $5 billion (= MPC of .75 × $6.67 billion), and saving will go up by $1.67 billion (= MPS of .25 × $6.67 billion). In this case the horizontal distance between AD_2 and the dashed line in Figure 12-1 represents only the $5 billion initial increase in consumption spending. Again, we call it "initial" consumption spending because the multi-

plier process yields rounds of increased consumption spending. The aggregate demand curve eventually shifts rightward by four times the $5 billion initial increase in consumption produced by the tax cut. Real GDP rises by $20 billion, from $485 billion to $505 billion, implying a multiplier of 4. Employment also increases accordingly.

Undoubtedly you have noted that a tax cut must be somewhat larger than the proposed government spending increase to achieve the same amount of rightward shift in the aggregate demand curve. This is because part of a tax reduction boosts *saving*, not consumption. *To increase initial consumption by a specific amount, government must reduce taxes by more than that amount.* With an MPC of .75, taxes must fall by $6.67 billion for $5 billion of new consumption to be forthcoming, because $1.67 billion is saved (not consumed). If the MPC instead had been, say, .6, an $8.33 billion reduction in tax collections would have been necessary to increase initial consumption by $5 billion. The smaller the MPC, the greater the tax cut needed to accomplish a specific initial increase in consumption and a specific shift in the aggregate demand curve.

Combined Government Spending Increases and Tax Reductions Government can combine spending increases and tax cuts to produce the desired initial increase in spending and eventual increase in aggregate demand and real GDP. In the economy depicted in Figure 12-1, government might increase its spending by $1.25 billion while reducing taxes by $5 billion. You should ascertain why this combination will produce the targeted $5 billion initial increase in new spending.

If you were assigned Chapters 9 and 10, you should think through these three fiscal policy options in terms of the recessionary-gap analysis associated with the aggregate expenditures model (Figure 10-8). Recall from Chapter 11 that rightward shifts of the aggregate demand curve relate directly to upshifts of the aggregate expenditures schedule. **(Key Question 2)**

Contractionary Fiscal Policy

When demand-pull inflation occurs, a restrictive or **contractionary fiscal policy** may help control it. Figure 12-2 emphasizes the vertical range of aggregate supply. Suppose that a shift of the aggregate demand curve from AD_3 to AD_4 in the vertical range of aggregate supply has boosted the price level from P_3 to P_4. (Ignore the dashed line for now.) This increase in aggregate demand might have resulted from a sharp increase in, say, investment or net export spending. If government looks to fiscal policy to control this inflation, its options are opposite those used to combat recession. It can (1) decrease government spending, (2) raise taxes, or (3) use some combination of these two policies. When the economy faces demand-pull inflation, fiscal policy should move toward a government **budget surplus**—tax revenues in excess of government spending.

Decreased Government Spending Reduced government spending shifts the aggregate demand curve leftward to control demand-pull inflation. In Figure 12-2, the horizontal distance between AD_4 and the dashed line represents a $5 billion reduction in government spending. Once the multiplier process is complete, this spending cut will shift the aggregate demand curve leftward from AD_4 all the way to AD_3. Assuming downward price flexibility, the price level will return to P_3, where it was before demand-pull inflation occurred. Real output will remain at its full-capacity level of $515 billion of real GDP.

In the real world prices are "sticky" downward, so stopping inflation is a matter of halting the rise in the price level, not reducing it to some previous level. Demand-pull inflation usually is experienced as a continual shifting of the aggregate demand curve to the right. Fiscal policy is designed to stop such shifts, not to restore a lower previous price level. Nevertheless, Figure 12-2 displays the basic principle: Reductions in government expenditures can halt demand-pull inflation.

Increased Taxes Just as government can use tax cuts to increase consumption spending, it can use tax increases to reduce consumption spending. If the economy in Figure 12-2 has an MPC of .75, government must raise taxes by $6.67 billion to reduce consumption by $5. The $6.67 tax reduces saving by $1.67 (= the MPS of .25 × $6.67 billion) and this $1.67 billion reduction in saving, by definition, is not a spending reduction. But the $6.67 billion tax increase also reduces consumption spending by $5 billion (= the MPC of .75 × $6.67), as shown by the

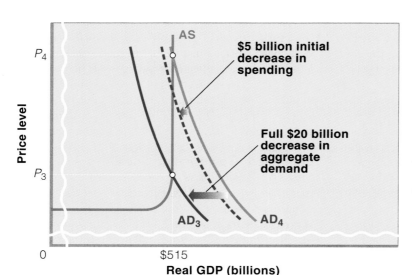

FIGURE 12-2 Contractionary fiscal policy Contractionary fiscal policy, which is represented here, uses decreases in government spending or increases in taxes to reduce demand-pull inflation. In an economy with an MPC of .75, a $5 billion decline in government spending or a $6.67 increase in taxes (producing a $5 billion initial decrease in consumption) shifts the aggregate demand curve from AD_4 to the dashed line. The multiplier effect then shifts the curve further leftward to AD_3. The overall decrease in aggregate demand halts the demand-pull inflation.

AS
P_4
$5 billion initial decrease in spending
Full $20 billion decrease in aggregate demand
Price level
P_3
AD_3
AD_4
0
$515
Real GDP (billions)

distance between AD$_4$ and the dashed line to its left in Figure 12-2. After the multiplier process, aggregate demand will have shifted leftward by $20 billion at each price level (= multiplier of 4 × $5 billion) and the price level will have fallen from P$_4$ to P$_3$. Demand-pull inflation will have been controlled.

Combined Government Spending Decreases and Tax Increases

Government can combine spending decreases and tax increases to reduce aggregate demand and check inflation. To test your understanding, you should determine why a $2 billion decline in government spending *paired* with a $4 billion increase in taxes would shift the aggregate demand curve from AD$_4$ to AD$_3$.

Also, if you were assigned Chapters 9 and 10, you should be able to explain the three fiscal policy options for fighting inflation in terms of the inflationary-gap concept developed with the aggregate expenditures model (Figure 10-8). Recall from Chapter 11 that leftward shifts of the aggregate demand curve are associated with downshifts of the aggregate expenditures schedule. **(Key Question 3)**

Financing of Deficits and Disposing of Surpluses

The expansionary effect of deficit spending on the economy depends on the method used to finance the deficit. Similarly, the anti-inflationary impact of the creation of a budget surplus depends on what is done with the surplus.

Borrowing versus New Money

There are two ways the government can finance a deficit: borrowing from (selling interest-bearing bonds to) the public and, with the help of its monetary authorities, issuing new money to its creditors. The impact of each method on aggregate demand is different:

1. *Borrowing* If the government enters the money market and borrows, it will compete with private business borrowers for funds. This added demand for funds might drive up the interest rate and crowd out some private investment spending and interest-sensitive consumer spending. Declines in private spending reduce the expansionary impact of the deficit spending.

2. *Money creation* If the government finances its deficit spending by obtaining newly created money from its monetary authorities, the crowding out of private spending can be avoided.

Federal spending can increase without any adverse effect on investment or consumption. *The creation of new money is a more expansionary (but potentially more inflationary) way of financing deficit spending than is borrowing.*

Debt Retirement versus Idle Surplus

Demand-pull inflation calls for fiscal action which will result in a budget surplus. But the anti-inflationary effect of this surplus depends on what government does with it:

1. *Debt reduction* Since the Federal government has an outstanding debt of $5.4 trillion, it is logical to think that government should use a surplus to retire outstanding debt. Using it to pay off debt, however, may reduce the anti-inflationary impact of the creation of a surplus. To retire its debt, the government buys back some of its bonds; in doing so, it transfers its surplus tax revenues back into the money market. This causes interest rates to fall and thus private borrowing and spending to rise. The increase in private spending somewhat offsets the contractionary fiscal policy which created the budget surplus.

2. *Impounding* Government can realize a greater anti-inflationary effect from its creation of a budgetary surplus by impounding the surplus funds, that is, allowing them to stand idle. When a surplus is impounded, the government is extracting and withholding purchasing power from the economy. If surplus tax revenues are not put back into the economy, no portion of that surplus can be spent. There is no chance that funds will create inflationary pressure to offset the anti-inflationary impact of the contractionary fiscal policy. We conclude that *the impounding of a budget surplus is more anti-inflationary than the use of the surplus to retire public debt.*

Policy Options: *G* or *T*?

Is it preferable to use government spending or taxes to eliminate recession and inflation? The answer depends largely on one's view as to whether the public sector is too large or too small.

"Liberal" economists, who think there are many unmet social and infrastructure needs, usually recommend that government spending be increased during recessions. In times of demand-pull inflation, they tend to recommend tax increases. Both actions either expand or preserve the absolute size of government.

"Conservative" economists, who think the public sector is too large and inefficient, usually advocate tax cuts during recessions and cuts in government spending during times of demand-pull inflation. Both actions either restrain the growth of government or reduce its absolute size.

Discretionary fiscal policy designed to stabilize the economy can be associated with either an expanding or a contracting public sector.

QUICK REVIEW 12-1

■ The Employment Act of 1946 commits the Federal government to promoting "maximum employment, production, and purchasing power."

■ Discretionary fiscal policy is the purposeful change of government expenditures and tax collections by government to promote full employment, price stability, and economic growth.

■ Government uses expansionary fiscal policy to shift the aggregate demand curve rightward—that is, to stimulate spending and expand real output. This policy involves increases in government spending, reductions in taxes, or some combination of the two.

■ Government uses contractionary fiscal policy to shift the aggregate demand curve leftward in an effort to halt demand-pull inflation. This policy entails reductions in government spending, tax increases, or some combination of the two.

■ The expansionary effect of fiscal policy is greater when the budget deficit is financed through money creation rather than via borrowing; the contractionary effect of the creation of a budget surplus is greater when the budget surplus is impounded rather than used for debt reduction.

NONDISCRETIONARY FISCAL POLICY: BUILT-IN STABILIZERS

To some degree government tax revenues change automatically, and in a countercyclical direction, over the course of the business cycle. This automatic response or *built-in stability* results from the makeup of most tax systems. We did not include this built-in stability in our discussion of fiscal policy because we implicitly assumed that the same amount of tax revenue was collected at each level of GDP. That is not actually so. In reality, our net tax system is such that *net tax revenues vary directly with GDP*. (*Net taxes* are tax revenues less transfers and subsidies. From here on, we will use the simpler "taxes" to mean "net taxes.")

Virtually any tax will yield more tax revenue as GDP rises. In particular, personal income taxes have progressive rates and thus yield more than proportionate increases in tax revenues as GDP expands. Furthermore, as GDP increases and more goods and services are purchased, revenues from corporate income taxes and sales and excise taxes also increase. And, similarly, payroll tax payments increase as economic expansion creates more jobs. Conversely, when GDP declines, tax receipts from all these sources also decline.

Transfer payments (or "negative taxes") behave in the opposite way from tax revenues. Unemployment compensation payments, welfare payments, and subsidies to farmers all *decrease* during economic expansion and *increase* during a contraction.

Automatic or Built-In Stabilizers

Figure 12-3 shows how the U.S. tax system creates built-in stability. Government expenditures G are fixed and assumed to be independent of the level of GDP; a particular level of spending is decided on by Congress. But Congress does *not* determine the *level* of tax revenues; rather, it establishes tax *rates*. Tax revenues then vary directly with the level of GDP which the economy actually realizes. The direct relationship between tax revenues and GDP is shown by the upsloping line T.

Economic Importance The economic importance of this direct relationship between tax receipts and GDP is revealed when we consider two things:
1. Taxes reduce spending and aggregate demand.
2. It is desirable from the standpoint of stability to reduce spending when the economy is moving toward inflation and to increase spending when the economy is slumping.

In other words, the tax system portrayed in Figure 12-3 builds some stability into the economy. It automatically brings about changes in tax revenues and therefore in the public budget which counter both inflation and recession. A **built-in stabilizer** is *anything which increases the government's budget deficit (or reduces its budget surplus) during a recession and increases its budget surplus (or reduces its budget deficit) during inflation without requiring explicit action by policymakers.* As Figure 12-3 reveals, this is precisely what the U.S. tax system does.

As GDP rises during prosperity, tax revenues *automatically* increase and, because they reduce spend-

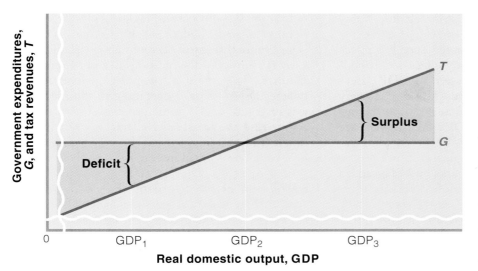

FIGURE 12-3 Built-in stability Tax revenues T vary directly with GDP, and government spending G is assumed to be independent of GDP. As GDP falls in a recession, deficits will occur automatically and will help alleviate that recession. As GDP rises during expansion, surpluses will occur automatically and will offset possible inflation.

ing, they restrain the economic expansion. That is, as the economy moves toward a higher GDP, tax revenues automatically rise and move the budget from deficit toward surplus.

Conversely, as GDP falls during recession, tax revenues *automatically* decline, increasing spending and cushioning the economic contraction. With a falling GDP, tax receipts decline and move the government's budget from surplus toward deficit. In Figure 12-3, the low level of income GDP_1 will automatically yield an expansionary budget deficit; the high and perhaps inflationary income level GDP_3 will automatically generate a contractionary budget surplus.

Tax Progressivity It is clear from Figure 12-3 that the size of the automatic budget deficits or surpluses—and therefore built-in stability—depends on how responsive tax revenues are to changes in GDP. If tax revenues change sharply as GDP changes, the slope of line T in the figure will be steep and the vertical distances between T and G—the deficits or surpluses—will be large. If tax revenues change very little when GDP changes, the slope will be gentle and built-in stability will be low.

The steepness of T in Figure 12-3 depends on the tax system itself. In a **progressive tax system,** the average tax rate (= tax revenue/GDP) rises with GDP. In a **proportional tax system,** the average tax rate remains constant as GDP rises. In a **regressive tax system,** the average tax rate falls as GDP rises. The progressive tax system has the steepest tax line T of the three. However, tax revenues will rise with GDP un-

der both the progressive and proportional tax systems, and they may rise, fall, or remain the same under a regressive tax system. But what you should realize is this: *The more progressive the tax system, the greater the economy's built-in stability.*

Changes in public policies or laws which alter the progressivity of the tax system affect the degree of built-in stability. For example, in 1993 the Clinton administration increased the highest marginal tax rate on personal income from 31 to 39.6 percent and boosted the corporate income tax 1 percentage point to 35 percent. These increases in tax rates raise the overall progressivity of the tax system, slightly bolstering the economy's built-in stability.

The built-in stability provided by our tax system has reduced the severity of business fluctuations. But built-in stabilizers can only diminish, *not* correct, major changes in equilibrium GDP. Discretionary fiscal policy—changes in tax rates and expenditures—may be needed to correct inflation or recession of any appreciable magnitude.

Actual versus Full-Employment Budget

We have built-in stability because tax revenues vary directly with GDP. But those automatic increases or decreases in tax revenues mean that the **actual budget** in any particular year does not tell us whether government's current discretionary fiscal policy is expansionary, neutral, or contractionary. Here's why: Suppose an economy is achieving full-employment output at GDP_f in Figure 12-4. But note from the government spending line G and the tax line T that there is an actual budget deficit shown by vertical distance *ab*. Now assume that investment spending plummets, swamping the expansionary effect of this budget deficit and causing a recession to GDP_r. Let's assume that government takes no new discretionary action, so lines G and T remain as shown in the figure. With the economy at GDP_r, tax revenues are lower than before, while government spending remains unaltered. The budget deficit therefore rises to *ec*, expanding from *ab* (= *ed*) by amount *dc*. The added deficit of *dc* is called a **cyclical deficit** because it relates to the business cycle. It is *not* the result of discretionary fiscal actions by government; rather, it is the by-product of the economy's slide into recession.

Note in Figure 12-4 that to find the actual deficit *ec* for year 2, we must know where lines G and T are located *and* the specific level of GDP. The same G and T lines give different deficits or surpluses with different GDPs. Thus, we cannot evaluate the government's fiscal policy—the extent to which it is expansionary, neutral, or contractionary—by looking

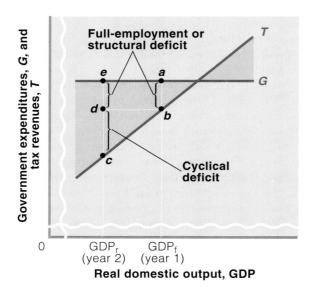

FIGURE 12-4 Full-employment (structural) deficits and cyclical deficits The actual budget deficit for any specific year is the amount by which government's expenditures exceed its tax revenues. It consists of the structural deficit (or full-employment deficit) and the cyclical deficit. At full-employment output GDP$_f$, the actual deficit is *ab*, the structural deficit is *ab*, and the cyclical deficit is zero. At recessionary output GDP$_r$, the actual budget deficit is *ec*, the structural deficit is *ed* (=*ab*), and the cyclical deficit is *dc*.

only at the size of a current budget deficit or surplus. Because an actual budget deficit or surplus is the result of more than fiscal decisions about spending and taxes (as shown by the locations of lines G and T in Figure 12-4), we must also consider the level of GDP (where the economy is operating on the horizontal axis of Figure 12-4). In the economy represented in Figure 12-4, the actual budget deficit in year 2 (GDP_r) differs from that in year 1 (GDP_f) only because GDP is lower in year 2 than in year 1.

Resolution of the Problem   Economists resolve this problem by standardizing the budget deficits and surpluses for different years in the business cycle; they do this by using the **full-employment budget.** This budget, also called the standardized budget, *measures what the Federal budget deficit or surplus would be with existing tax and government spending structures if the economy were at full employment throughout the year.* The idea is to compare actual government expenditures for each particular year with the tax revenues which would have occurred in that year if the economy had achieved full employment.

Consider Figure 12-4 once again. In full-employment year 1, the full-employment deficit is *ab*, the amount of the actual deficit. In year 2, however, the actual budget deficit of *ec* overstates the full-employment deficit. Specifically, the cyclical part of the deficit *dc* must be subtracted from the actual deficit *ec* to obtain the full-employment deficit, *ed*. We note, then, that the full-employment deficit for year 2 is the same as that for year 1 (*ed* = *ab*). By comparing these two full-employment deficits, we see that government did not change its fiscal policy between years 1 and 2.

A full-employment budget deficit is also called a **structural deficit** because it reflects the configuration of the G line and T line, *independent of any changes in GDP.* The structural deficits for years 1 and 2 in Figure 12-4 are the same (*ab* = *ed*). *Discretionary fiscal policy is reflected in deliberate changes in the full-employment deficit (structural deficit).* The actual budget deficit in any particular year is the sum of the structural and cyclical deficits. So changes in the actual budget deficit do not alone tell us whether fiscal policy has become more or less expansionary or contractionary. Changes in the structural deficit (or structural surplus) give us that information.

Historical Comparison   Figure 12-5 compares the deficits and surpluses in the U.S. full-employment budget with the deficits and surpluses in the actual

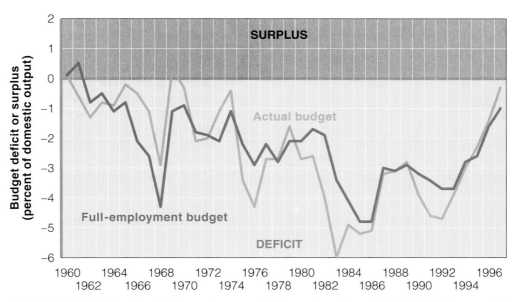

FIGURE 12-5 Actual and full-employment deficits and surpluses in the United States Full-employment (or structural) budget deficits and surpluses often differ in size from actual budget deficits and surpluses. Changes in full-employment budget deficits or surpluses are better indicators of whether government's fiscal policy is expansionary, neutral, or contractionary than are changes in actual budget deficits or surpluses. (*Source:* Congressional Budget Office.)

budget since 1960. (The deficits and surpluses are shown here as percentages of GDP.) In most years the size of the actual budget deficit or surplus differs from the size of the full-employment deficit or surplus. To reemphasize: The key to assessing discretionary fiscal policy is to disregard the actual budget deficit and instead observe the *change* in the full-employment budget (change in the structural deficit or surplus) from year to year. For example, fiscal policy was very expansionary between 1965 and 1968 and between 1981 and 1986, as reflected in the rapid increases in the full-employment deficit. In contrast, fiscal policy was contractionary in 1969, 1974, 1987, and 1996, as noted by large decreases in the full-employment deficit.

Also, observe in Figure 12-5 that structural deficits have been particularly large since 1981. A big part of the actual deficits during the 1980s and early 1990s was not cyclical (resulting from automatic decreases in tax revenues due to below-full-employment GDP). Rather, the actual deficits reflected structural imbalances between government spending and tax revenues caused by large tax cuts in the 1980s, together with increases in government spending. The year 1989 is an example. Although the economy had achieved full

employment, a sizable structural deficit remained. The same was true in 1995.

Large full-employment-budget deficits persisted through most of the 1990s. During this period the U.S. government largely abandoned discretionary fiscal policy in its attempt to reduce its large structural deficits. These budget deficits were so large that financing them increased real interest rates and undoubtedly crowded out much private investment, a scenario we will elaborate on shortly. Thus, in the 1990s the role of stabilizing the economy has fallen nearly exclusively on the nation's central bank, the Federal Reserve. This institution and its economic policies are the subject of Chapters 13 through 15. **(Key Question 7)**

Global Perspective 12-1 shows that budget deficits are not confined to the United States.

Proposed Balanced-Budget Requirement

The large annual budget deficits in the United States during the past two decades have led some congressional leaders to call for a constitutional amendment requiring that the Federal government balance its

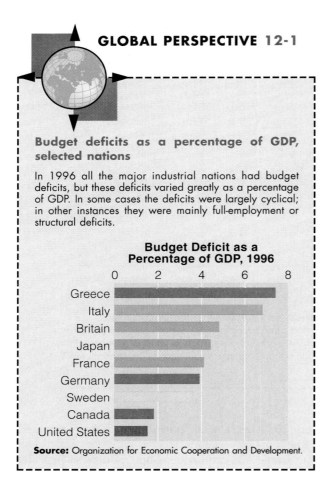

Budget deficits as a percentage of GDP, selected nations

In 1996 all the major industrial nations had budget deficits, but these deficits varied greatly as a percentage of GDP. In some cases the deficits were largely cyclical; in other instances they were mainly full-employment or structural deficits.

Budget Deficit as a Percentage of GDP, 1996

Source: Organization for Economic Cooperation and Development.

budget each year. In its strictest form (no exceptions allowed), such a mandate would virtually eliminate discretionary fiscal policy as a tool for stabilizing the economy. Specifically, government could no longer create or increase structural budget deficits as a way to halt and remedy recession.

Of even greater significance, a strict balanced-budget requirement would force government to reduce its spending or increase taxes during recession. To see why, consider Figure 12-6. Suppose that in year 1 the economy is operating at its full-employment level GDP$_f$. Note from the T_1 and G_1 lines that, in this case, the Federal government is balancing its budget: tax revenues equal government spending at GDP$_f$.

Next suppose that in year 2 the economy slides into recession, with real output declining to GDP$_r$. Tax revenues automatically decline, as shown by T_1, and a budget deficit of *ab* emerges. To comply with the balanced-budget requirement, government must

eliminate this cyclical deficit. It can do so in one of three ways:

1. Increasing taxes so that the tax line shifts upward to T_2, intersecting the G_1 line at point *a*
2. Reducing government spending so that the government spending line shifts downward to G_2, intersecting the T_1 line at point *b*
3. Increasing taxes and reducing spending in some *combination* to eliminate the budget deficit shown as distance *ab*

The problem with all three options is that they are aspects of *contractionary* fiscal policy. They all reduce aggregate demand, which *decreases* real GDP. And, as these actions further reduce real GDP, tax revenues decline once again. A new budget deficit therefore arises, requiring greater tax increases or government spending decreases to comply with the balanced-budget requirement. *Rather than stabilizing the economy, a strict balanced-budget requirement may force government to take actions which worsen recession.*

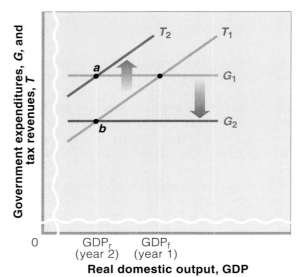

FIGURE 12-6 The effects of a requirement to balance the budget during recession A decline in real output from GDP$_f$ to GDP$_r$ will automatically create a budget deficit of *ab*. If required by law to eliminate this deficit, government will have to (1) shift the tax line upward to T_2 so that it intersects G_1 at point *a*, (2) shift the government spending line downward to G_2 so that it intersects T_1 at point *b*, or (3) enact a combination of tax increases and government spending decreases so that the new tax and government spending lines intersect at GDP$_r$. Each action is contractionary; it will cause a further decline in real GDP.

PROBLEMS, CRITICISMS, AND COMPLICATIONS

Economists recognize that governments may encounter a number of significant problems in enacting and applying fiscal policy.

Problems of Timing

Several problems of timing may arise in connection with fiscal policy:

1. *Recognition lag* The recognition lag is the time between the beginning of a recession or an inflation and the certain awareness that it is actually happening. This lag arises because of the difficulty in predicting the future course of economic activity. Although forecasting tools such as the index of leading indicators (see this chapter's Last Word) provide clues to the direction of the economy, the economy may be 4 or 6 months into a recession or inflation before that fact appears in relevant statistics and is acknowledged. Meanwhile, the economic downslide or the inflation may become more serious than it would have if the situation had been identified and acted on sooner.

2. *Administrative lag* The wheels of democratic government turn slowly. There will typically be a significant lag between the time the need for fiscal action is recognized and the time action is actually taken. The U.S. Congress has on occasion taken so much time in adjusting fiscal policy that the economic situation has changed in the interim, rendering the belated policy action inappropriate.

3. *Operational lag* There is also a lag between the time fiscal action is taken and the time that action affects output, employment, or the price level. Although changes in tax rates can be put into effect quickly, government spending on public works—the construction of dams, interstate highways, and so on—requires long planning periods and even longer periods of construction. Such spending is of questionable use in offsetting short—for example, 6- to 18-month—periods of recession. Because of such problems, discretionary fiscal policy has increasingly relied on tax changes rather than changes in spending as its main weapon.

Political Problems

Fiscal policy is created in the political arena, and this greatly complicates its use in stabilizing the economy.

Other Goals Economic stability is *not* the sole objective of government spending and taxing policies. Government is also concerned with providing public goods and services and redistributing income. A classic example of conflict of goals occurred during World War II when massive government spending for military goods caused strong and persistent inflationary pressures in the early 1940s. The defeat of Nazi Germany and Japan was simply a higher-priority goal than achieving price stability.

State and Local Finance Fiscal policies of state and local governments are frequently pro-cyclical—they worsen rather than correct recession or inflation. Unlike the Federal government, most state and local governments face constitutional or other legal requirements to balance their budgets. Like households and private businesses, state and local governments increase expenditures during prosperity and cut them during recession. During the Great Depression of the 1930s, most of the increase in Federal spending was offset by decreases in state and local spending. During the recession of 1990–1991, many state and local governments had to increase tax rates, impose new taxes, and reduce spending to offset falling tax revenues resulting from the reduced personal income and spending of their citizens.

Expansionary Bias? Rhetoric to the contrary, deficits may be politically attractive and surpluses politically painful. Fiscal policy may therefore have an expansionary-inflationary bias. Tax reductions are politically popular, and so are increases in government spending, provided the constituents of the politicians promoting them share in the benefits. But both can be inflationary. In contrast, higher taxes upset voters, while reductions in government expenditures can be politically precarious. For example, it might be political suicide for a farm-state senator to vote for tax increases and against agricultural subsidies.

A Political Business Cycle?

Some economists contend the goal of politicians is not to act in the interests of the national economy but, rather, to get reelected. A few economists have suggested the notion of a **political business cycle.** They argue that politicians might manipulate fiscal policy to maximize voter support, even though their fiscal decisions *destabilize* the economy. In this view, fiscal policy, as we have described it, may be corrupted for political purposes and actually *cause* economic fluctuations.

The populace, it is assumed, takes economic conditions into account in voting. Incumbents are penalized at the polls if the economy is depressed; they are rewarded if it is prosperous. As an election approaches, the incumbent administration (aided by an election-minded Congress) cuts taxes and increases government spending. Not only are these actions popular, they push all the critical economic indicators in positive directions. Output and real incomes rise; unemployment falls; and the price level is relatively stable. As a result, incumbents enjoy a very cordial economic environment for reelection.

But after the election, continued expansion of the economy will be reflected increasingly in a rising price level and less in growing real incomes. Growing public concern over inflation prompts politicians to enact a contractionary fiscal policy. Crudely put, a "made-in-Washington" recession is engineered by trimming government spending and increasing taxes to restrain inflation. A mild recession will not hurt an incumbent administration because the next election is still 2 or 3 years away and the critical consideration for most voters is the performance of the economy in the year or so before the election. Indeed, the recession provides a new starting point from which fiscal policy can again be used to generate another expansion in time for the next election campaign.

Such a scenario is difficult to document, and empirical tests of this theory are inconclusive. Nevertheless, there is some evidence to support the political theory of the business cycle.

Crowding-Out Effect

We now move from practical problems in implementing fiscal policy to a basic criticism of fiscal policy itself. This criticism is based on an alleged **crowding-out effect:** *An expansionary fiscal policy (deficit spending) will increase the interest rate and reduce private spending, weakening or canceling the stimulus of the fiscal policy.*

Suppose the economy is in recession and government enacts discretionary fiscal policy in the form of increased government spending. To finance its budget deficit, government borrows funds in the money market. The resulting increase in the demand for money raises the price paid for borrowing money: the interest rate. Because investment spending varies inversely with the interest rate, some investment will be choked off or crowded out. (Some interest-sensitive consumption spending—for example, purchases of automobiles on credit—may also be crowded out.)

Graphical Presentation The crowding-out effect is shown graphically in Figure 12-7. Suppose the economy has a noninflationary full-capacity level of real GDP at $515 billion, as shown in Figure 12-7a. For simplicity our aggregate supply curve here has no real-world intermediate range. Up to the $515 billion full-capacity output, the price level is constant. After the economy achieves full capacity, the vertical range of AS prevails so that any further increase in aggregate demand would be purely inflationary.

We begin in Figure 12-7a with aggregate demand at AD_1, which gives us equilibrium at real GDP of $495 billion. Assume now that government enacts an expansionary fiscal policy that shifts the aggregate demand curve rightward by $20 billion to AD_2. The economy thus achieves full-capacity output without inflation at $515 billion of GDP. Assuming an MPC of .75 and thus a simple multiplier of 4, we know that an increase in government spending of $5 billion or a decrease in taxes of $6.67 billion would create this expansionary effect. With no offsetting or complicating factors, this "pure and simple" expansionary fiscal policy moves the economy from recession to its full-capacity output.

In Figure 12-7b the complication of crowding out is shown. While fiscal policy is expansionary and designed to shift aggregate demand from AD_1 to AD_2, the borrowing needed to finance the deficit spending presumably increases the interest rate and crowds out some investment spending. The aggregate demand curve thus shifts only to AD'_2, not to AD_2.

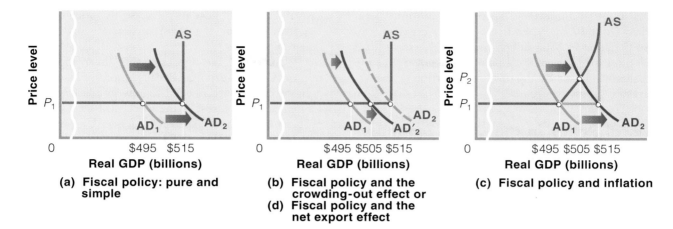

FIGURE 12-7 **Fiscal policy: the effects of crowding out, the net export effect, and inflation** With a simplified aggregate supply curve, we observe in (a) that fiscal policy is uncomplicated and works at full strength to produce full employment at a GDP of $515 billion. In (b) it is assumed that some amount of private investment is crowded out by the expansionary fiscal policy so that fiscal policy is weakened, achieving a GDP of only $505 billion. In (c) a more realistic aggregate supply curve reminds us that when the economy is in the intermediate range of the aggregate supply curve, part of the impact of an expansionary fiscal policy will be reflected in inflation (the price level rise to P_2). In (d)—the same graph as (b)—we assume that fiscal policy increases the interest rate, which attracts foreign financial capital to the United States. The dollar therefore appreciates and U.S. net exports fall, weakening the expansionary fiscal policy. GDP again rises only to $505 billion.

Equilibrium real GDP expands to $505 billion, not to the desired $515 billion. Lesson: *The crowding-out effect may weaken expansionary fiscal policy.*

Criticisms of the Crowding-Out Effect While few would question the logic of the crowding-out effect, there is disagreement as to its existence under all circumstances. Some economists argue that little crowding out will occur when there is recession. They note that the increased government spending will likely improve business profit expectations, and these improved prospects may encourage private investment. Thus, private investment need not fall, even though interest rates rise.

Also, critics of the crowding-out view point out that policymakers can counteract the crowding-out effect. Specifically, the monetary authorities could increase the supply of money by just enough to offset the deficit-caused increase in the demand for money. Then the equilibrium interest rate would not change, and the crowding-out effect would be zero. In the 1980s the monetary authorities did not increase the supply of money to "accommodate" the expansionary fiscal policy; consequently, the crowding-out effect of the large 1980s deficits may have been quite great. In comparison, in the 1960s the monetary authorities

wanted to keep interest rates stable. Hence, they increased the money supply when government borrowing threatened to push up interest rates. As a result, crowding out was less significant.

Fiscal Policy, Aggregate Supply, and Inflation

Our discussion of the complications and criticisms of fiscal policy has thus far been entirely oriented toward aggregate demand. We now consider a complication involving aggregate supply: *With an upsloping aggregate supply curve, some portion of the potential effect of an expansionary fiscal policy on real output may be dissipated in the form of inflation.* Observe in Figure 12-7c that we have switched to a more realistic aggregate supply curve which includes an intermediate range. We ignore the crowding-out effect so that the expansionary fiscal policy is successful in shifting the aggregate demand curve from AD_1 to AD_2. If the aggregate supply were shaped as in Figure 12-7a and b, full employment would now be realized at $515 billion and the price level would remain at P_1. But the upsloping intermediate range of the aggregate supply curve causes part of the increase in aggregate demand to be dissipated in higher prices. As a result, the increase in real GDP is diminished. Specifically, the price level rises from P_1 to P_2, and real GDP increases from $495 billion to $505 billion, not to $515. In the real world, expansionary fiscal policy does not escape the realities imposed by the upsloping portion of the aggregate supply curve.

Fiscal Policy in the Open Economy

Additional complications arise from the fact that each national economy is a component of the world economy.

Shocks Originating from Abroad

Events and policies abroad which affect a nation's net exports affect its own economy. Economies are open to unforeseen international *aggregate demand shocks* which can alter domestic GDP and make current domestic fiscal policy inappropriate.

Suppose the United States is in a recession and has enacted an expansionary fiscal policy to increase aggregate demand and GDP without igniting inflation (as from AD_1 to AD_2 in Figure 12-7a). Now suppose the economies of the major trading partners of the United States unexpectedly expand rapidly. Greater employment and rising incomes in those nations mean more purchases of U.S. goods. In the United States, net exports rise, and aggregate demand increases too rapidly; the nation experiences demand-pull inflation. If it had known in advance that its net exports might rise significantly, the United States would have enacted a less expansionary fiscal policy. We see, then, that participation in the world economy brings with it the complications of mutual interdependence along with the gains from specialization and trade.

Net Export Effect

The **net export effect** may also work through international trade to reduce the effectiveness of fiscal policy. We concluded in our discussion of the crowding-out effect that an expansionary fiscal policy might boost interest rates, reducing *investment* and weakening fiscal policy. Now we want to know what effect an interest-rate increase might have on a nation's *net exports* (exports minus imports).

Suppose the United States undertakes an expansionary fiscal policy which causes a higher U.S. interest rate. The higher interest rate will attract financial capital from abroad, where interest rates are unchanged. But foreign financial investors must acquire U.S. dollars to invest in U.S. securities. We know that an increase in the demand for a commodity—in this

case, dollars—will raise its price. So the price of dollars rises in terms of foreign currencies; that is, the dollar appreciates.

What will be the impact of this dollar appreciation on U.S. net exports? Because more units of foreign currencies are needed to buy goods from the United States, the rest of the world will see U.S. exports as being more expensive. Hence, U.S. exports will decline. Americans, who can now exchange their dollars for more units of foreign currencies, will buy more imports. Consequently, with U.S. exports falling and imports rising, net export expenditures in the United States will diminish; this is a contractionary change, so the U.S. expansionary fiscal policy will be partially negated.[1]

A return to our aggregate demand and supply analysis in Figure 12-7b, now labeled d, will clarify this point. An expansionary fiscal policy aimed at increasing aggregate demand from AD_1 to AD_2 may hike the domestic interest rate and ultimately reduce net exports through the process just described. The decline in the net export component of aggregate demand will partially offset the expansionary fiscal policy. The aggregate demand curve will shift rightward from AD_1 to AD'_2, *not* to AD_2, and equilibrium GDP will increase from $495 to $505, *not* to $515. Thus, the net export effect of fiscal policy joins the problems of timing, politics, crowding out, and inflation in complicating the "management" of aggregate demand.

Table 12-1 summarizes the net export effect resulting from fiscal policy. Column 1 reviews the analysis just discussed (Figure 12-7d). But note that the net export effect works in both directions. By reducing the domestic interest rate, a *contractionary* fiscal policy *increases* net exports. In this regard, you should follow through the analysis in column 2 in Table 12-1 and relate it to the aggregate demand–aggregate supply model. **(Key Question 9)**

---

[1]The appreciation of the dollar will also reduce the dollar price of foreign resources such as oil imported into the United States. As a result, aggregate supply will increase and part of the contractionary net export effect described here may be offset.

TABLE 12-1 Fiscal policy and the net export effect

(1) Expansionary fiscal policy	(2) Contractionary fiscal policy
Problem: Recession, slow growth ↓	Problem: Inflation ↓
Expansionary fiscal policy ↓	Contractionary fiscal policy ↓
Higher domestic interest rate ↓	Lower domestic interest rate ↓
Increased foreign demand for dollars ↓	Decreased foreign demand for dollars ↓
Dollar appreciates ↓	Dollar depreciates ↓
Net exports decline (aggregate demand decreases, partially offsetting the expansionary fiscal policy)	Net exports increase (aggregate demand increases, partially offsetting the contractionary fiscal policy)

■ The upsloping range of the aggregate supply curve means that part of an expansionary fiscal policy may be dissipated in inflation.

■ Fiscal policy may be weakened by the net export effect, which works through changes in (a) the interest rate, (b) the international value of the dollar, and (c) exports and imports.

Supply-Side Fiscal Policy

We have seen how movements along the aggregate supply curve can complicate the operation of fiscal policy. Let's now turn to the possibility of a more direct link between fiscal policy and aggregate supply—so-called **supply-side fiscal policy.** Economists recognize that fiscal policy—especially tax changes—*may* alter aggregate supply and affect the results of a change in fiscal policy.

Suppose in Figure 12-8 that aggregate demand and aggregate supply are AD_1 and AS_1 so that the

equilibrium level of real GDP is Q_1 and the price level is P_1. Assume further that government concludes the level of unemployment associated with Q_1 is too high and therefore enacts an expansionary fiscal policy in the form of a tax cut. The demand-side effect is an increase in aggregate demand from AD_1 to, say, AD_2. This shift increases real GDP to Q_2 but also boosts the price level to P_2.

How might tax cuts affect aggregate supply? Some economists—labeled "supply-side" economists—contend that tax reductions will shift the aggregate supply curve to the right. They give three main reasons:

1. ***Saving and investment*** Lower taxes will increase disposable incomes, increasing household saving. Similarly, tax reductions on businesses will increase the profitability of investment. In brief, lower taxes will increase saving and investment, increasing the rate of capital accumulation. The size of our "national factory"—our production capacity—will grow more rapidly.

2. ***Work incentives*** Lower personal income tax rates also increase after-tax wages from work and thus increase work incentives. Many people not already in the labor force will offer their services because after-tax wages are higher. Those already

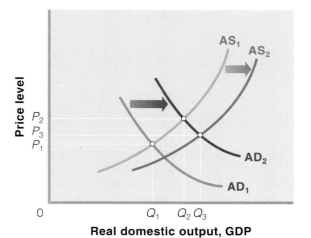

FIGURE 12-8 Supply-side effects of fiscal policy The traditional view is that tax cuts will increase aggregate demand, as from AD_1 to AD_2, increasing both real domestic output (Q_1 to Q_2) and the price level (P_1 to P_2). If the tax reductions induce favorable supply-side effects, aggregate supply will shift rightward, as from AS_1 to AS_2. This allows the economy to realize an even larger output (Q_3 compared with Q_2) and a smaller price-level increase (P_3 compared with P_2).

The Leading Indicators

One of several tools policymakers use to forecast the future direction of real GDP is a monthly index of 10 variables which in the past have together provided advance notice of changes in GDP.

"Index of Leading Indicators Falls Sharply for the Third Month—Recession Feared"; "Index of Leading Indicators Surges Again"; "Decline in Stock Market Drags Down Index of Leading Indicators." Headlines such as these appear regularly in newspapers. The focus of the articles is the Conference Board's composite index of 10 economic variables.* This "indicator" has historically reached its peak or trough in advance of the corresponding turns in the business cycle. Changes in the index of leading indicators thus provide a clue to the future direction of the economy and so may shorten the length of the "recognition lag" associated with the implementation of macroeconomic policy.

Here is how each of the 10 components of the index would change if it were predicting a *decline* in GDP. The opposite changes would forecast a *rise* in GDP.

1. Average Workweek Decreases in the length of the average workweek of production workers in manu-

facturing foretell declines in future manufacturing output and hence in GDP.

2. Initial Claims for Unemployment Insurance Higher first-time claims for unemployment insurance are associated with falling employment and subsequently sagging GDP.

3. New Orders for Consumer Goods Decreases in the number of orders received by manufacturers for consumer goods portend reduced future production—a decline in GDP.

4. Vendor Performance Somewhat ironically, better on-time delivery by sellers of inputs indicates slackening business demand and potentially falling GDP.

5. New Orders for Capital Goods A drop in orders for capital equipment and other investment goods implies reduced future aggregate demand and thus lower GDP.

6. Building Permits for Houses Decreases in the number of building permits taken out for new homes imply future declines in investment and therefore the possibility that GDP will fall.

7. Stock Prices Declines in stock prices often are reflections of expected declines in corporate sales and profits. Also, lower stock prices diminish consumer wealth, leading to possible cutbacks in consumer spending. Lower stock prices also make it less attractive for firms to issue

*The Conference Board is a private, nonprofit research and business membership group, with more than 2700 corporate and other members in 60 nations.

---

in the labor force will want to work more hours and take fewer vacations.

3. *Risk taking* Lower tax rates prod risk takers. Individuals and businesses will be more willing to risk their energies and financial capital on new production methods and new products when lower tax rates promise a larger potential after-tax reward.

Through all these avenues, lower taxes will shift aggregate supply to the right, say, from AS$_1$ to AS$_2$ in Figure 12-8, reducing inflation and further increasing real GDP.

Supply-siders also contend that lower tax *rates* need not result in lower tax *revenues*. In fact, they say that lower tax rates that cause a substantial expansion of output and income may generate *increases* in tax

revenues. This enlarged tax base may enhance total tax revenues even though tax rates are lower. (The mainstream view is that a reduction in tax rates will reduce tax revenues and increase budget deficits.)

Mainstream Skepticism Most economists are skeptical about the supply-side effects of tax cuts, particularly in view of evidence from the supply-side tax cuts of the 1980s. First, these critics feel the positive effects of a tax reduction on incentives to work, save and invest, and bear risks are not nearly as strong as supply-siders believe. Second, any rightward shifts of the aggregate supply curve will occur over an extended period of time, while the demand-side impact will be much more immediate.

new shares of stock as a way of raising funds for investment. Thus, declines in stock prices can bring forth declines in aggregate demand and GDP.

8. Money Supply Decreases in the nation's money supply are associated with falling GDP. (This component and the next will make more sense to you after you read Chapters 13 through 15.)

9. Interest-Rate Spread Increases in short-term nominal interest rates typically reflect monetary policies designed to slow the economy. Such policies have much less of an effect on long-term interest rates, which are higher than short-term rates. So a smaller difference between short-term interest rates and long-term interest rates suggests restrictive monetary policies and potentially a future decline in GDP.

10. Consumer Confidence Declines in consumer confidence about the future, measured by an index of consumer expectations, foreshadow lower consumption spending and potential future declines in GDP.

None of these factors *alone* consistently predicts the future course of the economy. It is not unusual in any month, for example, for one or two of the indicators to be decreasing while the other indicators are increasing. Rather, changes in the composite of the 10 components are what in the past have provided advance notice of a change in the direction of GDP. The rule of thumb is that three successive monthly declines or increases in the index indicate the economy will soon turn in that same direction.

Although the composite index has correctly signaled business fluctuations on numerous occasions, it has not been infallible. At times the index has provided false warnings of recessions which never happened. In other instances, recessions have so closely followed the downturn in the index that policymakers have not had sufficient time to make use of the "early" warning. Moreover, changing structural features of the economy have, on occasion, rendered the existing index obsolete and necessitated its revision.

Given these caveats, the index of leading indicators can best be thought of as a useful but not totally reliable signaling device which authorities must employ with considerable caution in formulating macroeconomic policy.

CHAPTER SUMMARY

1. Government responsibility for achieving and maintaining full employment is specified in the Employment Act of 1946. The Council of Economic Advisers (CEA) was established to advise the president on policies to fulfill the goals of the act.

2. Increases in government spending expand, and decreases contract, aggregate demand and equilibrium GDP. Increases in taxes reduce, and decreases expand, aggregate demand and equilibrium GDP. Fiscal policy therefore calls for increases in government spending and decreases in taxes—a budget deficit—to correct for recession. Decreases in government spending and increases in taxes—

a budget surplus—are appropriate fiscal policy for correcting demand-pull inflation.

3. Built-in stability arises from net tax revenues which vary directly with the level of GDP. During recession, the Federal budget automatically moves toward a stabilizing deficit; during expansion, the budget automatically moves toward an anti-inflationary surplus. Built-in stability lessens, but does not fully correct, undesired changes in the GDP.

4. An actual budget deficit consists of two elements: the structural deficit (if any) and the cyclical deficit (if any).

The structural deficit—also known as the full-employment deficit—is that part of an actual deficit which would occur even if the economy were at its full-employment output. The cyclical deficit is that part of an actual deficit which arises when real GDP is less than full-employment GDP.

5. The full-employment budget or standardized budget measures the Federal budget deficit or surplus which would occur if the economy operated at full employment throughout the year. Changes in the full-employment deficit or surplus—also called the structural deficit or surplus—provide meaningful information as to whether government's fiscal policy is expansionary, neutral, or contractionary. Changes in the actual budget deficit or surplus do not, since such deficits or surpluses depend on the state of the economy.

6. The enactment and application of appropriate fiscal policy are subject to certain problems and questions. The important ones are: **(a)** Can fiscal policy be better timed to maximize its effectiveness in heading off economic fluctuations? **(b)** Can the economy rely on Congress to enact appropriate fiscal policy? **(c)** An expansionary fiscal policy may be weakened if it crowds out some private investment spending. **(d)** Some of the effect of an expansionary fiscal policy may be dissipated in inflation. **(e)** Fiscal policy may be rendered ineffective or inappropriate by unforeseen events occurring within the borders of international trading partners. Also, fiscal policy may precipitate changes in exchange rates which weaken its effects. **(f)** Supply-side economists contend that traditional fiscal policy fails to consider the effects of tax changes on aggregate supply.

TERMS AND CONCEPTS

Employment Act of 1946
Council of Economic
  Advisers
discretionary fiscal policy
expansionary fiscal policy
budget deficit

contractionary fiscal
  policy
budget surplus
built-in stabilizer
progressive tax system
proportional tax system

regressive tax system
actual budget
cyclical deficit
full-employment budget
structural deficit
political business cycle

crowding-out effect
net export effect
supply-side fiscal policy

STUDY QUESTIONS

1. What is the central thrust of the Employment Act of 1946? What is the role of the Council of Economic Advisers (CEA) in responding to this law? Class assignment: Determine the names and educational backgrounds of the present members of the CEA.

2. KEY QUESTION   Assume that a hypothetical economy with an MPC of .8 is experiencing severe recession. By how much would government spending have to increase to shift the aggregate demand curve rightward by $25 billion? How large a tax cut would be needed to achieve this same increase in aggregate demand? Why the difference? Determine one possible combination of government spending increases and tax decreases which would accomplish this same goal.

3. KEY QUESTION   What are government's fiscal policy options for ending severe demand-pull inflation? Use the aggregate demand–aggregate supply model to show the impact of these policies on the price level. Which of these fiscal policy options do

you think a "conservative" economist might favor? A "liberal" economist?

4. (For students assigned Chapters 9 and 10) Use the aggregate expenditures model to show how government fiscal policy could eliminate either a recessionary gap or an inflationary gap (Figure 10-8). Use the concept of the balanced-budget multiplier to explain how equal increases in G and T could eliminate a recessionary gap and how equal decreases in G and T could eliminate an inflationary gap.

5. Designate each statement *true* or *false* and justify your answer:
  a. Expansionary fiscal policy during a depression will have a greater positive effect on real GDP if government borrows the money to finance the budget deficit than if it creates new money to finance the deficit.
  b. Contractionary fiscal policy during severe demand-pull inflation will be more effective if government impounds the budget surplus

rather than using the surplus to pay off some of its past debt.

6. Explain how built-in (or automatic) stabilizers work. What are the differences between proportional, progressive, and regressive tax systems as they relate to an economy's built-in stability?

7. KEY QUESTION Define the "full-employment budget," explain its significance, and state how it differs from the "actual budget." What is the difference between a structural deficit and a cyclical deficit? Suppose the economy depicted in Figure 12-4 is operating at its full-employment, noninflationary level of real output, GDP_f. What is the size of its structural deficit? Its cyclical deficit? Should government raise taxes or reduce government spending to eliminate this structural deficit? What are the risks of so doing?

8. The actual budget deficit increased significantly in 1990 and 1991, but the full-employment budget deficit remained relatively constant. Can you think of a logical explanation?

9. KEY QUESTION Briefly state and evaluate the problem of time lags in enacting and applying fiscal policy. Explain the notion of a political business cycle. What is the crowding-out effect, and why is it relevant to fiscal policy? In what respect is the net export effect similar to the crowding-out effect?

10. In view of your answers to question 9, explain the following statement: "While fiscal policy clearly is useful in combating the extremes of severe recession and demand-pull inflation, it is impossible to use fiscal policy to fine-tune the economy to the full-employment, noninflationary level of real GDP and keep the economy there indefinitely."

11. Suppose that government engages in deficit spending to push the economy away from recession and that this spending is directed toward new "public capital" such as roads, bridges, dams, harbors, office parks, and industrial sites. How might this spending increase the expected rate of return on some types of potential *private* investment projects? What are the implications for the crowding-out effect?

12. Use Figure 12-4 to explain why a deliberate increase in the structural deficit which causes the economy to expand from GDP_r to GDP_f might reduce the size of the actual deficit. In requesting a tax cut in the early 1960s, President Kennedy said, "It is a paradoxical truth that tax rates are too high today and tax revenues are too low and the soundest way to raise tax revenues in the long run is to cut tax rates now." Relate this quotation to your previous answer.

13. Discuss: "Mainstream economists tend to focus on the aggregate demand effects of tax-rate reductions; supply-side economists emphasize the aggregate supply effects." Identify three routes through which a tax cut might increase aggregate supply. If tax cuts are so good for the economy, why don't we cut taxes to zero?

14. Advanced analysis: (For students assigned Chapters 9 and 10) Assume that, without taxes, the consumption schedule for an economy is as shown below:

GDP, billions	Consumption, billions
$100	$120
200	200
300	280
400	360
500	440
600	520
700	600

a. Graph this consumption schedule and determine the size of the MPC.

b. Assume a lump-sum (regressive) tax of $10 billion is imposed at all levels of GDP. Calculate the tax rate at each level of GDP. Graph the resulting consumption schedule, and compare the MPC and the multiplier with that of the pretax consumption schedule.

c. Now suppose a proportional tax with a 10 percent tax rate is imposed instead of the regressive tax. Calculate the new consumption schedule, graph it, and note the MPC and the multiplier.

d. Finally, impose a progressive tax such that the tax rate is 0 percent when GDP is $100, 5 percent at $200, 10 percent at $300, 15 percent at $400, and so forth. Determine and graph the new consumption schedule, noting the effect of this tax system on the MPC and the multiplier.

e. Explain why proportional and progressive taxes contribute to greater economic stability, while a regressive tax does not. Demonstrate using a graph similar to Figure 12-3.

15. (Last Word) What is the composite index of leading economic indicators, and how does it relate to discretionary fiscal policy?

16. WEB-BASED QUESTION Latest Economic Indicators—How Goes the Economy? The U.S. Census Bureau http://www.census.gov/econ/www/ constantly tracks the latest economic indicators. Check last month's Economic Indicator Calendar for current indicator values. Assign a +1 to those economic indicators which point to an expansion, a −1 for those indicating contraction, or 0 if indeterminate or neutral. Sum these values for a crude forecast. How goes the economy?

17. WEB-BASED QUESTION   **The Federal Budget—What Is the Role of Fiscal Policy in the Budgetary Process?** Each year the President, through the Office of Management and Budget http://www.whitehouse.gov/WH/EOP/OMB/html/ombhome.html, sends his proposed budget to Congress. However, the House of Representatives http://www.house.gov/ budget/welcome.htm and the Senate http://www.senate.gov/~budget/ have their own opinions about what the budget should be. Using these links, trace the steps of the Federal budget process from the initial executive proposal to final presidential signature. What role does fiscal policy play in this process? What are the major policy disagreements relating to the current budget?

PART THREE

Money, Banking, and Monetary Policy

13

Money and Banking

"**M**oney bewitches people. They fret for it, and they sweat for it. They devise most ingenious ways to get it, and most ingenuous ways to get rid of it. Money is the only commodity that is good for nothing but to be gotten rid of. It will not feed you, clothe you, shelter you, or amuse you unless you spend it or invest it. It imparts value only in parting. People will do almost anything for money, and money will do almost anything for people. Money is a captivating, circulating, masquerading puzzle."[1]

Money. A fascinating aspect of the economy. And a crucial element of economics. Money is more than a tool for facilitating the economy's operation. When it is working properly, the monetary system is the lifeblood of the circular flows of income and expenditure which typify all economies. A well-operating monetary system helps achieve both full employment and efficient resource use. A malfunctioning monetary system can contribute to severe fluctuations in the economy's levels of output, employment, and prices *and* can distort the allocation of resources.

In this chapter we are concerned with the nature and functions of money and the basic institutions of the U.S. banking system. In the next chapter we examine the ways individual commercial banks and the banking system as a whole can vary the money supply. In Chapter 15 we discuss how the central banks of the economy regulate the supply of money to promote full employment and price-level stability.

We begin here with a review of the functions of money. Next, we shift to the supply of money and pose the question: What constitutes money in the United States? Third, we consider what "backs" the supply of money and what is meant by the demand for money. Then we combine the supply of money and the demand for money to portray and explain the market for money. Finally, the institutional structure of the Federal Reserve System is discussed, and recent developments relating to the banking industry are examined.

THE FUNCTIONS OF MONEY

Just what is money? There is an appropriate saying that "money *is* what money *does*."

Anything which performs the functions of money *is* money. So what are these functions?

---

[1]Federal Reserve Bank of Philadelphia, "Creeping Inflation," *Business Review*, August 1957, p. 3.

1. *Medium of exchange* First, and foremost, money is a **medium of exchange;** it is usable for buying and selling goods and services. A worker in a bakery does not want to be paid 200 bagels per week. Nor does the bakery wish to receive, say, tuna fish for its bagels. Money, however, is readily acceptable as payment. It is a social invention with which resource suppliers and producers can be paid and that can be used to buy any of the full range of items available in the marketplace. As such a medium of exchange, money allows society to escape the complications of barter. And because it provides a convenient way of exchanging goods, money allows society to gain the advantages of geographic and human specialization.

2. *Unit of account* Money is also a **unit of account.** Society uses the monetary unit as a yardstick for measuring the relative worth of a wide variety of goods, services, and resources. Just as we measure distance in miles or kilometers, we gauge the value of goods in dollars. With a money system, we need not state the price of each product in terms of all other products for which it can be exchanged; we need not specify the price of cows in terms of corn, crayons, cigars, Chevrolets, and croissants.

   This use of money as a common denominator means that the price of each product need be stated *only* in terms of the monetary unit. It permits buyers and sellers to readily compare the prices of various commodities and resources. Such comparisons aid rational decision making. In Chapter 7 we used money as a unit of account in calculating the size of the GDP. Money is also used as a unit of account for transactions involving future payments. Debt obligations of all kinds are measured in the monetary unit.

3. *Store of value* Finally, money serves as a **store of value.** Because money is the most liquid—meaning the most spendable—of all assets, it is a very convenient way to store wealth. The money you place in a safe or checking account will still be available to you months or years later when you wish to use it. Most methods of holding money do not yield monetary returns such as one gets by storing wealth in the form of real assets (property) or paper assets (stocks, bonds, and so forth). However, money does have the advantage of being *immediately* usable by a firm or a household in meeting all financial obligations.

THE SUPPLY OF MONEY

Conceptually, anything generally acceptable as a medium of exchange *is* money. Historically, whales' teeth, elephant tail bristles, circular stones, nails, slaves (yes, human beings), cattle, cigarettes, and pieces of metal have been used as media of exchange. In the United States the debts of governments and of commercial banks and other financial institutions are used as money, as you will see.

Money Definition M1

Neither economists nor public officials agree on how broadly or narrowly the economy's money supply should be defined. In the most narrow useful definition, the money supply is designated *M*1 and composed of two items:

1. Currency, that is, coins and paper money in the hands of the (nonbank) public
2. All checkable deposits, meaning deposits in commercial banks and "thrift" or savings institutions on which checks can be drawn[2]

Coins and paper money are debts of government and governmental agencies. Checking accounts represent debts of the commercial bank or savings institution. Table 13-1 shows the amount of each in the *M*1 money supply.

Currency: Coins + Paper Money From copper pennies to silver dollars, coins are the "small change" of our money supply. Coins, however, are a very small portion of the total money supply; they constitute only 2 or 3 percent of *M*1. Coins are "convenience money" which permits people to make very small purchases.

All coins in circulation in the United States are **token money.** This means the **intrinsic value**—the value of the bullion (metal) contained in the coin itself—is less than the face value of the coin. This is so to avoid the melting down of token money for profitable sale as a "commodity," in this case, bullion. If 50-cent pieces each contained 75 cents' worth of silver bullion, it would be profitable to melt them and sell the metal. Although it is illegal to do this, 50-cent

---

[2]In the ensuing discussion of the definitions of money several of the quantitatively less significant components are not explicitly discussed to sidestep a maze of details. For example, travelers' checks are included in the *M*1 money supply. Reference to the statistical appendix of any recent *Federal Reserve Bulletin* will provide you with more comprehensive definitions.

TABLE 13-1   **Alternative money definitions for the United States: M1, M2, and M3**

Money definition or concept	Absolute amount, (billions)	Percentage of concept		
		M1	M2	M3
Currency (coins and paper money)	$ 414	39%	10%	8%
plus Checkable deposits	643*	61	16	12
equals M1	**$1057**	100%		
plus Noncheckable savings deposits, including MMDAs	1314		33	25
plus Small time deposits	962*		24	18
plus Money market mutual fund balances (MMMFs)	631		16	12
equals M2	**$3964**		100%	
plus Large time deposits	1241*			24
equals M3	**$5205**			100%

*These figures include other quantitatively smaller components. Percentages may not add to 100 percent due to rounding.
Source: Federal Reserve Bulletin, December 1997, p. A12. Data are for September 1997.

pieces would disappear from circulation. This is one of the potential defects of commodity money: Its worth as a commodity may come to exceed its worth as money, ending its function as a medium of exchange.

Paper money constitutes about 37 percent of the economy's *M*1 money supply. All this $391 billion of paper currency is in the form of **Federal Reserve Notes,** issued by the Federal Reserve Banks (the U.S. central banks) with the authorization of Congress. A glance at any bill in your wallet will reveal Federal Reserve Note printed at the top of the face of the bill.

Checkable Deposits   The safety and convenience of using checks have made checking accounts the largest component of the U.S. money supply. You would not think of stuffing $4896.47 in bills and coins in an envelope and dropping it in a mailbox to pay a debt. But to write and mail a check for a large sum is commonplace. A check must be endorsed (signed on the reverse side) by the person cashing it; the writer of the check subsequently receives a record of the canceled check as a receipt attesting to the fulfillment of the obligation. Similarly, because the writing of a check requires endorsement by the person cashing it, the theft or loss of your checkbook is not nearly as calamitous as losing an identical amount of currency. Finally, it is more convenient to write a check than to transport and count out a large sum of currency. For all these reasons, *checkbook money* is the dominant form of money in the U.S. economy. About 60 percent of *M*1 is in the form of **checkable deposits,** on which checks can be drawn.

It might seem strange that checking accounts are part of the money supply. But it is clear why: Checks, which are nothing more than a way to transfer the ownership of deposits in banks and other financial institutions, are generally acceptable as a medium of exchange. True, as a stop at most gas stations will verify, checks are less generally accepted than currency for small purchases. But for major purchases sellers willingly accept checks as payment. Moreover, people can convert checkable deposits into paper money and coins on demand; checks drawn on these deposits are thus the equivalent of currency.

To summarize:

Money, *M*1 = currency + checkable deposits

Institutions Offering Checkable Deposits   In the United States, several types of financial institutions allow customers to write checks on the funds they have deposited:

1. *Commercial banks*   These banks are the primary depository institutions. They accept the deposits of households and businesses; keep the money safe until it is demanded via checks; and in the meantime use it to make available a wide variety of loans. Commercial bank loans provide short-term working capital to businesses and farmers, and they finance consumer purchases of automobiles and other durable goods.

2. *Thrift institutions*   The commercial banks are supplemented by other financial institutions—savings and loan associations (S&Ls), mutual savings banks, and credit unions—collectively designated as **thrift** or **savings institutions,** or simply "thrifts." **Savings and loan associations** and **mutual savings banks** accept the savings of households and businesses, which are then used to finance housing mortgages and provide other loans. **Credit unions** accept the deposits of their "members"—usually a group of individuals who work for the same company—and lend these funds to finance installment purchases.

The checkable deposits of banks and thrifts are known by various names—demand deposits, NOW (negotiable order of withdrawal) accounts, ATS (automatic transfer service) accounts, and share draft accounts. Nevertheless, they are all similar in that depositors can write checks on them whenever, and in whatever amount, they choose.

Qualification We must qualify our definition of money: Currency and checkable deposits owned by government (the Treasury) and by the Federal Reserve Banks, commercial banks, or other financial institutions are excluded from $M1$ and other money measures.

A paper dollar in the hands of Sally Sorenson obviously constitutes just $1 of the money supply. But if we counted dollars held by banks as part of the money supply, the same $1 would count for $2 when deposited in a bank. It would count for a $1 demand deposit owned by Sorenson and also for $1 of currency resting in the bank's till or vault. This problem of double counting is avoided by excluding currency resting in banks in determining the total money supply.

Excluding currency held by, and checkable deposits owned by, government is more arbitrary. This exclusion permits economists to better gauge the money supply and rate of spending in the private sector of the economy apart from spending initiated by government policy.

Money Definition M2

A second and broader definition of money includes $M1$ plus several near-monies. **Near-monies** are certain highly liquid financial assets which do not directly function as a medium of exchange but can be readily converted into currency or checkable deposits without risk of financial loss. There are four near-monies included along with $M1$ in the $M2$ definition of money:

1. On demand you can withdraw currency from a **noncheckable savings account** at a commercial bank or thrift institution. Or you may request that funds be transferred from a noncheckable savings account to a checkable account.

2. You can also withdraw funds quickly from a **money market deposit account** (MMDA). These are interest-bearing accounts offered by banks and thrifts which pool individual deposits to buy a variety of interest-bearing short-term securities. MMDAs have minimum balance requirements and limit how often money can be withdrawn.

3. **Time deposits** become available to a depositor only at maturity. For example, a 6-month time deposit can only be withdrawn without penalty 6 months or more after it has been deposited. In return for this withdrawal limitation, the financial institution pays a higher interest rate on such deposits than on its MMDA accounts. Although time deposits are less liquid than noncheckable savings accounts, they can be taken as currency or shifted to checkable accounts when they mature.

4. Through a telephone call, a depositor can redeem shares in a **money market mutual fund** (MMMF) offered through a mutual fund company. Such companies use the combined funds of individual shareholders to buy interest-bearing short-term credit instruments such as certificates of deposits and U.S. government securities. Thus, they in turn can offer interest on the money market accounts of their mutual fund customers (depositors).

Thus, in equation form,

$$\text{Money, } M2 = \begin{array}{l} M1 + \text{noncheckable savings} \\ \text{deposits} + \text{MMDAs} + \text{small} \\ \text{(less than \$100,000) time deposits} \\ + \text{MMMFs} \end{array}$$

That is, $M2$ includes (1) the medium-of-exchange items (currency and checkable deposits) constituting $M1$ *plus* (2) the four other items which can be quickly converted into currency and checkable deposits without financial loss. Table 13-1 shows that the addition of noncheckable savings deposits, MMDAs, small time deposits, and MMMFs yields an $M2$ money supply of $3964 billion compared to the narrower $M1$ money supply of $1057 billion.

Money Definition M3

A third money supply definition, $M3$, recognizes that large ($100,000 or more) time deposits—usually owned by businesses as certificates of deposit—are also a near-money which can be converted into checkable deposits. There is a market for these certificates, and they can be sold (liquidated) at any time, although perhaps at the risk of a loss. Adding these large time deposits to $M2$ yields the still broader $M3$ definition of money:

Money, $M3 = \dfrac{M2 + \text{large (\$100,000 or}}{\text{more) time deposits}}$

Table 13-1 reveals that the $M3$ money supply is $5205 billion.

Still other slightly less liquid assets such as certain government securities (for example, Treasury bills and U.S. savings bonds) can be easily converted into $M1$ money. Actually, there is an entire spectrum of assets which vary slightly from one another in terms of their liquidity or "moneyness." They are not, however, included in $M1$, $M2$, and $M3$.

Which definition of money shall we use? The simple $M1$ definition includes only items *directly* and *immediately* usable as a medium of exchange. For this reason it is an often-cited statistic in discussions of the money supply. However, for some purposes economists prefer the broader $M2$ definition. For example, $M2$ is used as 1 of the 10 trend variables in the index of leading indicators (Last Word, Chapter 12). And what of $M3$ and still broader definitions of money? These definitions are so inclusive that many economists question their usefulness.

We will use the narrow $M1$ definition of money in our discussion and analysis, unless stated otherwise. The important principles applying to $M1$ are also applicable to $M2$ and $M3$ because $M1$ is the base component in these broader measures.

Near-Monies: Implications

Near-monies are important for several related reasons:
1. *Spending habits*   These highly liquid assets affect people's consumption and saving habits. Usually, the greater the amount of financial wealth people hold as near-monies, the greater their willingness to spend out of their money incomes.
2. *Stability*   Conversion of near-monies into money or vice versa can affect the economy's stability. For example, during the recovery and peak phases of the business cycle, converting noncheckable financial assets into checkable deposits or currency adds to the money supply and could cause inflation. Such conversions can complicate the task of the monetary authorities in

controlling the money supply and the level of economic activity.
3. *Policy*   The specific definition of money used is important for monetary policy. For example, the money supply as measured by $M1$ might be constant, while money defined as $M2$ might be increasing. If the monetary authorities feel it is appropriate to have an expanding supply of money and if they measure the supply with the narrow $M1$ definition, they would likely call for specific actions to increase currency and checkable deposits. But if they used the broader $M2$ definitions, they would see that the desired expansion of the money supply is already taking place and that no specific policy action is needed. **(Key Question 4)**

Credit Cards

You may wonder why we have ignored credit cards—Visa, MasterCard, American Express, Discover, and so forth—in our discussion of how money is defined. After all, credit cards are a convenient way to make purchases. The answer is that a credit card is *not* really money but, rather, a means of obtaining a short-term loan from the commercial bank or other financial institution which has issued the card.

When you purchase a sweatshirt with a credit card, the issuing bank will reimburse the store. Later, you reimburse the bank. You may pay an annual fee for the services provided, and if you repay the bank in installments, you pay a sizable interest charge on the loan. Credit cards are merely a means of deferring or postponing payment for a short period.

However, credit cards and other forms of credit allow individuals and businesses to "economize" in the use of money. Credit cards permit you to have less currency and checkable deposits on hand for transactions. Credit cards help you synchronize your expenditures and your receipt of income, reducing the cash and checkable deposits you must hold.

QUICK REVIEW 13-1

■ Money serves as a medium of exchange, a unit of account, and a store of value.

■ The narrow $M1$ definition of money includes currency held by the public plus checkable deposits in commercial banks and thrift institutions.

■ Thrift institutions as well as commercial banks offer accounts on which checks can be written.

■ The *M2* definition of money includes *M1* plus noncheckable savings deposits, money market deposit accounts, small (less than $100,000) time deposits, and money market mutual fund balances; *M3* consists of *M2* plus large time deposits (more than $100,000).

WHAT "BACKS" THE MONEY SUPPLY?

This heading asks a slippery question. Our answer is at odds with most preconceptions. Essentially what backs money is the government's ability to keep the value of money relatively stable.

Money as Debt

The major components of the money supply—paper money and checkable deposits—are debts, or promises to pay. *In the United States, paper money is the circulating debt of the Federal Reserve Banks. Checkable deposits are the debts of commercial banks and thrift institutions.*

Paper currency and checkable deposits have no intrinsic value. A $5 bill is just a piece of paper. A checkable deposit is merely a bookkeeping entry. And coins, we know, have less intrinsic value than their face value. Nor will government redeem the paper money you hold for anything tangible, such as gold. In effect, the government has chosen to "manage" the nation's money supply. Its monetary authorities attempt to provide the amount of money needed for that particular volume of business activity which will promote full employment, price-level stability, and a healthy rate of economic growth.

Most economists agree that managing the money supply is more sensible than linking it to gold or any other commodity whose supply might arbitrarily and capriciously change. A large increase in the nation's gold stock as the result of a new gold discovery might increase the money supply far beyond the amount needed to transact a full-employment level of business activity. Therefore, rapid inflation might occur. Or a long-lasting decline in domestic gold production could reduce the domestic money supply to the point where economic activity is choked off and unemployment and a retarded growth rate result.

The point is that paper money cannot be converted into a fixed amount of gold or any other precious commodity; it is exchangeable only for other pieces of paper money. The government will swap one paper $5 bill for another bearing a different serial number. That is all you can get if you ask the government to redeem some of your paper money. Similarly, check money cannot be redeemed for gold but only for paper money, which, as you have just seen, will not be redeemed by the government for anything tangible.

Value of Money

If currency and checkable deposits have no intrinsic characteristics giving them value *and* if they are not backed by gold or other precious materials, then why are they money? What gives a $20 bill or a $100 checking account entry its value? The answer to these questions involves three points.

Acceptability Currency and checkable deposits are money because they are accepted as money. By virtue of long-standing business practice, currency and checkable deposits perform the basic function of money; they are acceptable as a medium of exchange. Suppose that you swap a $20 bill for a shirt or blouse at a clothing store. Why does the merchant accept this piece of paper in exchange for that product? The merchant accepts paper money because he or she is confident that others will in turn accept it in exchange for goods, services, and resources. The merchant knows that paper money can purchase the services of clerks, acquire products from wholesalers, and pay the rent on the store. We accept paper money in exchange because we are confident it will be exchangeable for real goods, services, and resources when we spend it.

Legal Tender Our confidence in the acceptability of paper money is partly a matter of law; currency has been designated as **legal tender** by government. This means paper currency *must* be accepted in payment of a debt, or else the creditor forfeits both the privilege of charging interest and the right to sue the debtor for nonpayment. Put bluntly, paper dollars are accepted as money partly because government says they are money. The paper money in our economy is **fiat money;** it is money because the government has declared it so, not because it can be redeemed for precious metal. The general acceptability of currency is also enhanced because government accepts it in payment of taxes and other obligations due the government.

Do not be overimpressed by the power of government, however. Paper currency's general acceptance in exchange is more important than government's decree that money is legal tender. The government has *not* decreed checks to be legal tender, but they successfully perform the vast bulk of the economy's exchanges of goods, services, and resources. It is true, though, that a governmental agency—the Federal Deposit Insurance Corporation (FDIC)—insures the deposits of commercial banks and S&Ls, undoubtedly contributing to the willingness of individuals and businesses to use checkable deposits as a medium of exchange.

Relative Scarcity   The value of money, like the economic value of anything else, depends on supply and demand. Money derives its value from its scarcity relative to its utility (want-satisfying power). The utility of money lies in its capacity to be exchanged for goods and services, now or in the future. The economy's demand for money thus depends on the total dollar volume of transactions in any period plus the amount of money individuals and businesses want to hold for possible future transactions. With a reasonably constant demand for money, the supply of money

will determine the value or "purchasing power" of the monetary unit (dollar, pound, peso, or whatever).

Money and Prices

The purchasing power of money is the amount of goods and services a unit of money will buy. When money rapidly loses its purchasing power, it rapidly loses its role as money.

Value of the Dollar   The amount a dollar will buy varies inversely with the price level; *a reciprocal relationship exists between the general price level and the value of the dollar.* Figure 13-1 shows this inverse relationship graphically. When the consumer price index or "cost-of-living" index goes up, the purchasing power of the dollar goes down, and vice versa. Higher prices lower the value of the dollar because more dollars will be needed to buy a particular amount of goods, services, and resources. For example, if the price level doubles, the value of the dollar declines by one-half, or 50 percent.

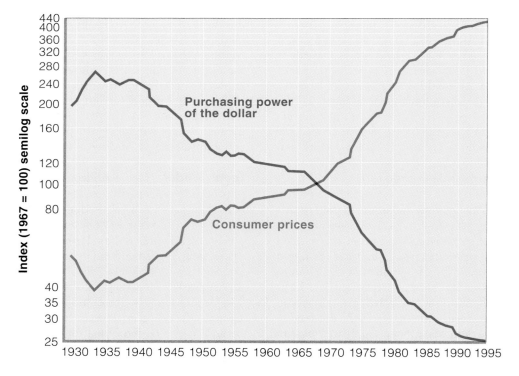

FIGURE 13-1 **The price level and the value of money**   An inverse relationship exists between the general price level and the purchasing power of the dollar. (This graph is called a "semilog chart" because equal vertical distances measure equal percentage changes rather than equal absolute changes.)

Conversely, lower prices increase the purchasing power of the dollar because fewer dollars are needed to obtain a specific quantity of goods and services. If the price level falls by, say, one-half, or 50 percent, the purchasing power of the dollar doubles.

In equation form, the relationship looks like this:

$$D = \frac{1}{P}$$

To find the value of the dollar D, divide 1 by the price level P expressed as an index number (in hundredths). If the price level is 1.0, then the value of the dollar is 1. If the price level rises to, say, 1.20, D falls to .833; a 20 percent increase in the price level reduces the value of the dollar by 16.67 percent. Check your understanding of this reciprocal relationship by determining the value of D and its percentage rise when P falls by 20 percent to 0.80. **(Key Question 6)**

Inflation and Acceptability In Chapter 8 we noted situations in which a nation's currency became worthless and unacceptable in exchange. These were circumstances in which government issued so many pieces of paper currency that the value of each of these units of money was almost totally undermined. The infamous post-World War I inflation in Germany is an example. In December 1919 there were about 50 billion marks in circulation. Four years later this figure had expanded to 496,585,345,900 billion marks! The result? The German mark in 1923 was worth an infinitesimal fraction of its 1919 value.[3]

How might inflation and the accompanying decreases in the value of a nation's currency affect the acceptability of paper currency as money? Households and businesses will accept paper currency as a medium of exchange as long as they know they can spend it without any noticeable loss in its purchasing power. But this is not the case when there is spiraling inflation. Runaway inflation, such as in Germany in the early 1920s and in several Latin-American nations in the 1980s, may significantly depreciate the value of money between the time it is received and the time it is spent. It is as if the government were constantly taxing away the purchasing power of its currency. Rapid declines in the value of a currency may cause it to cease being used as a medium of exchange. Businesses and households may refuse to accept paper

money in exchange because they do not want to bear the loss in its value which will occur while it is in their possession. (All this despite the fact that government says the paper currency is legal tender!) Without an acceptable domestic medium of exchange, the economy may try to substitute a more stable currency from another nation. Example: Many transactions in Russia and South America now occur in dollars rather than less stable rubles or pesos. At the extreme, the economy may simply revert to inefficient barter.

Similarly, people will use a particular unit of money as a store of value only as long as there is no sizable deterioration in the value of that money because of inflation. And an economy can effectively employ money as a unit of account only when its purchasing power is relatively stable. A measure of value which is subject to drastic shrinkage does not permit buyers and sellers to establish the terms of trade clearly. When the value of the dollar is declining rapidly, sellers will not know what to charge, and buyers will not know what to pay, for goods and services.

Stabilization of Money's Value

Stability of the value of money entails (1) appropriate fiscal policy, as explained in Chapter 12, and (2) intelligent management or regulation of the money supply. Businesses and households accept paper money in exchange for goods, services, and resources only when they expect it to command a roughly equivalent amount of these items when it is spent. In the United States a blending of legislation, government policy, and social practice inhibits imprudent expansion of the money supply which might seriously jeopardize money's value in exchange.

That which is true for paper currency also applies to checking account money—the debt of commercial banks and thrift institutions. Your checking account of $200 means your bank or thrift is indebted to you for that number of dollars. You can collect this debt in one of two ways. You can go to the bank or thrift and demand paper currency for your checkable deposit; this amounts to changing the debts you hold from the debts of a bank or thrift to government-issued debts. Or, and this is more likely, you can "collect" the debt which the bank or savings institution owes you by transferring this claim by check to someone else.

For example, if you buy a $200 leather coat from a store, you can pay for it by writing a check, which transfers your bank's indebtedness from you to the

---

[3]Frank G. Graham, *Exchange, Prices and Production in Hyperinflation Germany, 1920–1923* (Princeton, NJ: Princeton University Press, 1930), p. 13.

store. Your bank now owes the store the $200 it previously owed you. The store accepts this transfer of indebtedness (the check) as a medium of exchange because it can convert it into currency on demand or can transfer the debt to others in making purchases of its choice. Thus, checks, as means of transferring the debts of banks and thrifts, are acceptable as money because we know banks and thrifts will honor these claims.

The ability of banks and thrifts to honor claims against them depends on their not creating too many of these claims. You will see that a decentralized system of private, profit-seeking banks may not contain sufficient safeguards against the creation of too much check money. Thus, the U.S. banking and financial system has substantial centralization and governmental control to guard against the imprudent creation of checkable deposits.

Caution: This does not mean that in practice the monetary authorities have always judiciously controlled the supplies of currency and checkable deposits. Indeed, many economists allege that most of the inflationary woes the United States and other nations have experienced are the consequence of imprudent increases in the money supply by central banks. But that gets us ahead of our story; all you need to know for now is that a nation's monetary authorities control its supply of money. This supply is represented graphically by a vertical money supply curve, such as S_m in Figure 13-2c.

QUICK REVIEW 13-2

- In the United States, all money is essentially the debts of government, commercial banks, and thrift institutions.

- These debts efficiently perform the functions of money as long as their value, or purchasing power, is relatively stable.

- The value of money is rooted not in carefully defined quantities of precious metals but, rather, in the amount of goods, services, and resources that money will purchase.

- Government's responsibility in stabilizing the value of the monetary unit involves (1) the application of appropriate fiscal policies and (2) effective control over the supply of money.

THE DEMAND FOR MONEY

The public wants to hold some of its wealth as *money* for two basic reasons: to make purchases with it and to hold it as an asset.

Transactions Demand, D_t

People want money because it is a medium of exchange; it is convenient for purchasing goods and services. Households must have enough money on hand to buy groceries and pay mortgage and utility bills until the next paycheck. Businesses need money to pay for labor, materials, power, and other inputs. Money demanded for all such purposes is called the **transactions demand** for money.

The basic determinant of the amount of money demanded for transactions is the level of nominal GDP. The larger the total money value of all goods and services exchanged in the economy, the larger the amount of money needed to negotiate these transactions. *The transactions demand for money varies directly with nominal GDP.* We specify *nominal* GDP because households and firms will want more money for transactions if either prices rise *or* real output increases. In both instances there will be a larger dollar volume of transactions to accomplish.

In **Figure 13-2a (Key Graph)** we graph the quantity of money demanded for transactions against the interest rate. Because the amount demanded depends on the level of nominal GDP and is independent of the interest rate, the transactions demand, D_t, graphs as a vertical line. That is, we assume changes in the interest rate do not affect the amount of money demanded for transactions.

The transactions demand curve is placed at $100 billion on the assumption that each dollar held for transactions purposes is spent on the average three times per year *and* that nominal GDP is $300 billion. Thus the public needs $100 billion (= $300 billion ÷ 3) of money to purchase that GDP.

Asset Demand, D_a

The second reason for holding money derives from money's function as a store of value. People may hold their financial assets in many forms—as corporate stocks, private or government bonds, or as *M*1 money. Thus, there is an **asset demand** for money.

What determines this kind of demand for money? First, we must recognize that each of the various ways to hold financial assets has advantages and disadvantages. To simplify, let's compare holding money as an asset with holding bonds. The advantages of holding money are its liquidity and lack of risk. Money is the most liquid of all assets; it is immediately usable in making purchases. Money is an at-

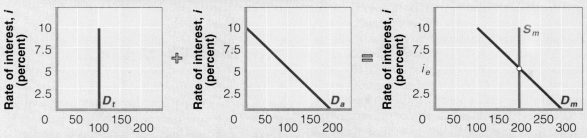

(a) Transactions demand for money, D_t

(b) Asset demand for money, D_a

(c) Total demand for money, $D_m = D_t + D_a$, and supply

FIGURE 13-2 **The demand for money and the money market** The total demand for money D_m is determined by horizontally adding the asset demand for money D_a to the transactions demand D_t. The transactions demand is vertical because it is assumed to depend on nominal GDP rather than on the interest rate. The asset demand varies inversely with the interest rate because of the opportunity cost involved in holding currency and checkable deposits which pay no interest or very low interest. Combining the money supply (stock) S_m with total money demand D_m portrays the money market and determines the equilibrium interest rate i_e.

QUICK QUIZ 13-2

1. **In this graph, at the interest rate i_e:**
   a. the amount of money demanded as an asset is $50 billion.
   b. the amount of money demanded for transactions is $200 billion.
   c. bond prices will decline.
   d. $100 billion is demanded for transactions, $100 billion is demanded as an asset, and the money supply is $200 billion.

2. **In this graph, at an interest rate of 10 percent:**
   a. no money will be demanded as an asset.
   b. total money demanded will be $200 billion.
   c. the Federal Reserve will supply $100 billion of money.
   d. there will be a $100 billion shortage of money.

3. **Curve D_a slopes downward because:**
   a. lower interest rates increase the opportunity cost of holding money.
   b. lower interest rates reduce the opportunity cost of holding money.

   c. the asset demand for money varies directly (positively) with the interest rate.
   d. the transactions-demand-for-money curve is perfectly vertical.

4. **Suppose the supply of money declined to $100 billion. The equilibrium interest rate would:**
   a. fall, the amount of money demanded for transactions would rise, and the amount of money demanded as an asset would decline.
   b. rise and the amounts of money demanded for transactions and as an asset would both fall.
   c. fall and the amounts of money demanded for transactions and as an asset would both increase.
   d. rise, the amount of money demanded for transactions would be unchanged, and the amount of money demanded as an asset would decline.

Answers: 1. d; 2. a; 3. b; 4. d

tractive asset to be holding when the prices of goods, services, and other financial assets are expected to decline. When the price of a bond falls, the bond-

holder will suffer a loss if the bond must be sold before maturity. There is no such risk with holding money.

The disadvantage of holding money as an asset is that, compared with holding bonds, it does *not* earn interest or, if it is in an interest-bearing checking account, earn as much interest income as bonds or noncheckable deposits. Idle currency, of course, earns no interest at all.

Knowing this, the problem is deciding how much of your financial assets to hold as, say, bonds and how much as money. The solution depends primarily on the rate of interest. A household or business incurs an opportunity cost when holding money; interest income is forgone or sacrificed. If a bond pays 10 percent interest, then it costs $10 per year of forgone income to hold $100 as cash or in a noninterest checkable account.

It is no surprise, then, that *the asset demand for money varies inversely with the rate of interest.* When the interest rate or opportunity cost of holding money as an asset is low, the public will choose to hold a large amount of money as assets. When the interest rate is high, it is costly to "be liquid" and the amount of assets held as money will be small. When it is expensive to hold money as an asset, people hold less of it; when money can be held cheaply, people hold more of it. This inverse relationship between the interest rate and the amount of money people want to hold as an asset is shown by D_a in Figure 13-2b.

Total Money Demand, D_m

As shown in Figure 13-2, the **total demand for money,** D_m, is found by horizontally adding the asset demand to the transactions demand. The resulting downsloping line in Figure 13-2c represents the total amount of money the public wants to hold—for transactions *and* as an asset—at each possible interest rate.

Recall that the transactions demand for money depends mainly on the nominal GDP. A change in the nominal GDP—working through the transactions demand for money—will shift the total money demand curve. Specifically, an increase in nominal GDP means the public wants to hold a larger amount of money for transactions, and this will shift the total money demand curve to the right. A decline in the nominal GDP will shift the total money demand curve to the left. As an example, suppose nominal GDP increases from $300 to $450 billion and the average dollar held for transactions is still spent three times per year. Then the transactions demand curve will shift from $100 billion (= $300 billion ÷ 3) to $150 billion (= $450 billion ÷ 3). The total money demand curve

will then lie $50 billion farther to the right at each possible interest rate.

THE MONEY MARKET

We can combine the demand for money with the supply of money to portray the **money market** and determine the equilibrium rate of interest. In Figure 13-2c the vertical line, S_m, represents the money supply. The money supply is shown as a vertical line because we assume the monetary authorities and financial institutions have provided the economy with some particular *stock* of money, such as the $M1$ total shown in Table 13-1.

Just as in a product or resource market, the intersection of demand and supply determines equilibrium price. Here, the "price" is the equilibrium interest rate (i_e), that is, the price paid for the use of money.

If disequilibrium existed in the money market, how would the money market achieve equilibrium? Consider Figure 13-3, which repeats Figure 13-2c and adds two alternative supply-of-money curves.

Responses to a Shortage of Money

Suppose the supply of money is reduced from $200 billion, S_m, to $150 billion, S_{m1}. At the previous interest rate of 5 percent, the quantity of money demanded now exceeds the quantity supplied by $50 billion. People will attempt to make up for this shortage of money by selling some of the financial assets they own (we assume for simplicity that these assets are bonds). But one person's receipt of money through the sale of a bond is another person's loss of money through the purchase of that bond. Overall, there is only $150 billion of money available. The collective attempt to get more money by selling bonds will increase the supply of bonds relative to the demand for bonds in the bond market, but it will not increase the amount of money available as a whole. The outcome is that the price of bonds will fall.

Generalization: *Lower bond prices are associated with higher interest rates.* To clarify this, suppose a bond with no expiration date pays a fixed $50 annual interest and is selling for its face value of $1000. The interest yield on this bond is 5 percent:

$$\frac{\$50}{\$1000} = 5\%$$

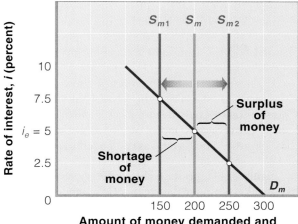

FIGURE 13-3 **Restoring equilibrium in the money market** A decrease in the supply of money creates a temporary shortage of money in the money market. People and institutions attempt to gain more money by selling bonds. The supply of bonds therefore increases, which reduces bond prices and raises interest rates. At higher interest rates, people reduce the amount of money they wish to hold. Thus, the amount of money supplied and demanded once again is equal at the higher interest rate. An increase in the supply of money creates a temporary surplus of money, resulting in an increase in the demand for bonds and higher bond prices. Interest rates fall and equilibrium is reestablished in the money market.

- -

Now suppose the price of this bond falls to $667 because of the increased supply of bonds. The $50 fixed annual interest payment will now yield $7\frac{1}{2}$ percent to whomever buys the bond:

$$\frac{\$50}{\$667} = 7\frac{1}{2}\%$$

Because all borrowers must compete by offering to pay lenders interest yields similar to those available on bonds, a higher general interest rate emerges. In Figure 13-3 the interest rate rises from 5 percent with the money supply at $200 billion to $7\frac{1}{2}$ percent when the money supply is $150 billion. This higher interest rate raises the opportunity cost of holding money and reduces the amount of money firms and households want to hold. Specifically, the amount of money demanded declines from $200 billion at the 5 percent interest rate to $150 billion at the $7\frac{1}{2}$ percent interest rate. The money market is back in equilibrium, now with the quantities of money demanded and supplied equaling $150 billion at the new $7\frac{1}{2}$ percent interest rate.

Responses to a Surplus of Money

An increase in the supply of money from $200 billion, S_m, to $250 billion, S_{m2}, results in a surplus of $50 billion at the initial 5 percent interest rate. People will now try to rid themselves of money by purchasing more bonds. But one person's expenditure of money is another person's receipt of money. The collective attempt to buy more bonds will increase the demand for bonds and pull bond prices upward.

Corollary: *Higher bond prices are associated with lower interest rates.* In our example, the $50 interest payment on a bond now priced at, say, $2000, will yield a bond buyer only $2\frac{1}{2}$ percent:

$$\frac{\$50}{\$2000} = 2\frac{1}{2}\%$$

The point is that interest rates in general will fall as people unsuccessfully attempt to reduce their money holdings below $250 billion by buying bonds. In this case, the interest rate will fall to a new equilibrium at $2\frac{1}{2}$ percent. Because the opportunity cost of holding money now is lower—being liquid is less expensive—consumers and businesses will increase the amount of currency and checkable deposits they are willing to hold from $200 billion to $250 billion. Eventually equilibrium in the money market will be restored: The quantities of money demanded and supplied will each be $250 billion at an interest rate of $2\frac{1}{2}$ percent.

In Chapter 15 you will see how monetary policy is used to change the money supply to alter the equilibrium real interest rate. A higher interest rate reduces investment and consumption spending, decreasing aggregate demand. A lower rate increases investment and consumption spending, increasing aggregate demand. Either situation ultimately affects the levels of real output, employment, and prices. **(Key Question 7)**

QUICK REVIEW 13-3

■ People hold money for transaction and asset purposes.

■ The total demand for money is the sum of the transactions and asset demands; it is graphed as an inverse relationship (downsloping line) between the interest rate and the quantity of money demanded.

■ The equilibrium interest rate is determined by money demand and supply; it occurs where people are willing to hold the exact amount of money being supplied by the monetary authorities.

■ Bond prices and interest rates are inversely related.

THE FEDERAL RESERVE AND THE BANKING SYSTEM

In the United States, the "monetary authorities" we mentioned are the members of the Board of Governors of the **Federal Reserve System** (the "Fed"). As shown in Figure 13-4, this Board directs the activities of the 12 Federal Reserve Banks, which in turn control the lending activity of the nation's banks and thrift institutions.

Historical Background

Early in the twentieth century, Congress decided that centralization and public control were essential for an efficient banking system. Decentralized, unregulated banking had fostered the inconvenience and confusion of numerous private bank notes being used as currency. It had also resulted in occasional episodes of monetary mismanagement such that the money supply was inappropriate to the needs of the economy: sometimes "too much" money precipitated rapid in-

flation; other times "too little" money stunted the economy's growth by hindering the production and exchange of goods and services. No single entity was charged with creating and implementing nationally consistent banking policies.

An unusually acute 1907 money panic motivated Congress to appoint the National Monetary Commission to study the monetary and banking problems of the economy and to outline a course of action for Congress. The result was the Federal Reserve Act of 1913.

Figure 13-4 represents the monetary system which has developed under the frequently amended Federal Reserve Act. Let's examine the nature and roles of the various parts of the Federal Reserve System and their relationships to one another.

Board of Governors

The kingpin of the U.S. money and banking system is the **Board of Governors** of the Federal Reserve System. The U.S. president, with the confirmation of

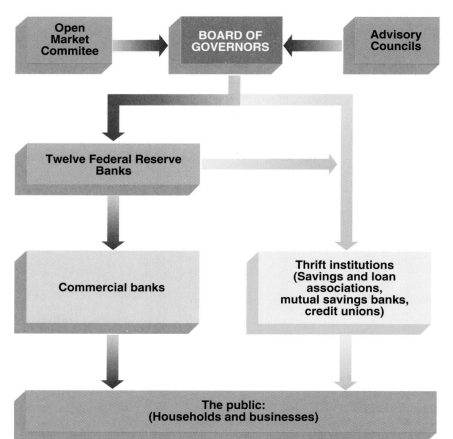

FIGURE 13-4 Framework of the Federal Reserve System and its relationship to the public With the advice of the Open Market Committee and three Advisory Councils, the Board of Governors makes the basic policy decisions providing monetary control of the U.S. money and banking systems. These decisions are made effective through the 12 Federal Reserve Banks.

----

the Senate, appoints the 7 Board members. Terms are long—14 years—and staggered so that one member is replaced every 2 years. The president selects the chairperson and vice-chairperson of the Board from among the members, and these officers serve 4-year terms. The long-term appointments provide the Board with continuity, experienced membership, and independence from political pressures which could result in inflation.

Assistance and Advice

Several entities assist the Board of Governors in determining banking and monetary policy. The first is clearly the most powerful.

The **Federal Open Market Committee** (FOMC) is made up of the 7 members of the Board of Governors plus 5 of the presidents of the Federal Reserve Banks. The FOMC sets the Fed's monetary policy and directs the purchase and sale of government securities (bills, notes, and bonds) in the open market. As you will see in Chapter 15, these aptly named *open-market operations* are the most significant technique available to the Fed for controlling the money supply.

Three **Advisory Councils** made up of private citizens meet periodically with the Board of Governors to voice their views on banking and monetary policy. The *Federal Advisory Council* is composed of 12 commercial bankers, 1 selected annually by each of the 12 Federal Reserve Banks. The *Thrift Institutions Advisory Council* consists of representatives from savings and loan associations, savings banks, and credit unions. The third advisory group, the 30-member *Consumer Advisory Council*, includes representatives of consumers of financial services and academic and legal specialists in consumer matters. As their names indicate, the councils are purely advisory. They have no policy-making powers, and the Board has no obligation to heed their advice.

The 12 Federal Reserve Banks

The 12 **Federal Reserve Banks** serve as central banks, quasipublic banks, and bankers' banks.

Central Banks   Most nations have one central bank, for example, Britain's Bank of England or Germany's Bundesbank. The United States has, in effect, 12 "central" banks whose policies are coordinated by the Board of Governors. The 12 Federal Reserve Banks partly accommodate the geographical size and economic diversity of the United States and the nation's large number of commercial banks and thrifts. These central banks are also the result of a political compromise between proponents of centralization and those who distrust powerful financial institutions.

Figure 13-5 locates the 12 Federal Reserve Banks and indicates the district each serves. These central banks carry out the basic policy of the Board of Governors. The Federal Reserve Bank in New York City is the most important of the central banks since it carries out most of the Fed's open-market operations.

FIGURE 13-5 The 12 Federal Reserve Districts The Federal Reserve System divides the United States into 12 districts, each having one central bank and in some instances one or more branches of the central bank. Hawaii and Alaska are included in the twelfth district. *(Source: Federal Reserve Bulletin.)*

Quasipublic Banks The 12 Federal Reserve Banks are quasigovernmental banks, meaning that they are a blend of private ownership and public control. Each Federal Reserve Bank is owned by the private commercial banks in its district. (Commercial banks are required to purchase shares of stock in the Federal Reserve Bank in their district.) But a governmental body, the Board of Governors, sets the basic policies that the Federal Reserve Banks pursue. The owners of these central banks thus control neither the central bank officials nor their policies.

Despite their private ownership, the Federal Reserve Banks are essentially public institutions. Unlike private firms, they are not motivated by profit. The policies the central banks follow are designed by the Board of Governors to promote the well-being of the economy as a whole. Thus, the activities of the Federal Reserve Banks are frequently at odds with the profit motive.[4] Also, the Federal Reserve Banks do not compete with commercial banks. With rare exceptions, the Federal Reserve Banks do not deal with the public but, rather, deal with the government and the commercial banks and thrifts.

Bankers' Banks The Federal Reserve Banks are "bankers' banks." They perform essentially the same functions for banks and thrifts as those institutions perform for the public. Just as banks and thrifts accept the deposits of and make loans to the public, so the central banks accept the deposits of and make loans to banks and thrifts. But the Federal Reserve Banks have a third function which banks and thrifts do not perform: They issue currency. Congress has authorized the Federal Reserve Banks to put into circulation Federal Reserve Notes, which constitute the economy's paper money supply.

Commercial Banks and Thrifts

The workhorses of the U.S. banking system are its 9500 **commercial banks.** Roughly two-thirds are **state banks,** private banks chartered (authorized) by individual states to operate within those states. One-third are private banks chartered by the Federal government to operate nationally; they are **national**

banks. While some of the U.S. national banks are very large, none of them rank among the world's largest private banks (see Global Perspective 13-1).

The 14,000 thrift institutions are regulated by agencies separate and apart from the Board of Governors and the Federal Reserve Banks. For example, the operation of savings and loan associations is regulated and monitored by the Treasury Department's Office of Thrift Supervision. But the thrifts are subject to monetary control by the Federal Reserve System. In particular, like the banks, thrifts are required to keep a certain percentage of their checkable deposits as "reserves." In Figure 13-4 we use orange arrows to denote that the thrift institutions are partially subject to the

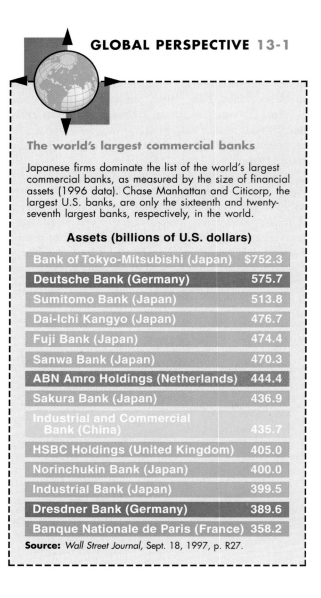

GLOBAL PERSPECTIVE 13-1

The world's largest commercial banks

Japanese firms dominate the list of the world's largest commercial banks, as measured by the size of financial assets (1996 data). Chase Manhattan and Citicorp, the largest U.S. banks, are only the sixteenth and twenty-seventh largest banks, respectively, in the world.

Assets (billions of U.S. dollars)

Bank of Tokyo-Mitsubishi (Japan)	$752.3
Deutsche Bank (Germany)	575.7
Sumitomo Bank (Japan)	513.8
Dai-Ichi Kangyo (Japan)	476.7
Fuji Bank (Japan)	474.4
Sanwa Bank (Japan)	470.3
ABN Amro Holdings (Netherlands)	444.4
Sakura Bank (Japan)	436.9
Industrial and Commercial Bank (China)	435.7
HSBC Holdings (United Kingdom)	405.0
Norinchukin Bank (Japan)	400.0
Industrial Bank (Japan)	399.5
Dresdner Bank (Germany)	389.6
Banque Nationale de Paris (France)	358.2

Source: *Wall Street Journal,* Sept. 18, 1997, p. R27.

---

[4]Although it is not their goal, the Federal Reserve Banks have actually operated profitably, largely as a result of Treasury debts held by them. Part of the profits are used to pay dividends to banks on their holdings of stock; the remaining profit is usually turned over to the U.S. Treasury.

control of the Board of Governors and the central banks. Decisions concerning monetary policy affect the thrifts along with the commercial banks.

Fed Functions and the Money Supply

The Fed performs several functions, some of which we have already identified:

1. *Issuing currency*   The Fed issues Federal Reserve Notes, the paper currency used in the U.S. monetary system. (The Federal Reserve Bank which issued a particular bill is named in the circle to the left on the face of the bill. The newly designed $50 and $100 bills, however, identify the bank only by its district number. "A1," for example, identifies the Boston bank, "B2" the New York bank, and so on.)

2. *Setting reserve requirements and holding reserves*   The Fed sets reserve requirements. The central banks accept as deposits from the banks and thrifts any portion of their mandated reserves not held as vault cash.

3. *Lending money to banks and thrifts*   At times, the Fed lends money to banks and thrifts, charging them an interest rate called the *discount rate*.

4. *Providing for check collection*   Another important function of the Fed is to provide the means for the collection of checks. If Sarah writes a check on her Salem bank or thrift to Sam, who deposits it in his San Diego bank or thrift, how does the San Diego bank collect the money represented by the check drawn against the Salem bank? Answer: The Fed handles it in 2 or 3 days by adjusting the reserves (deposits) of the two banks.

5. *Acting as fiscal agent*   The Fed acts as the fiscal agent (provider of financial services) for the Federal government. The government collects huge sums through taxation, spends equally large amounts, and sells and redeems bonds. The government uses the Fed's facilities in carrying out these activities.

6. *Supervising banks*   The Fed supervises the operation of banks. Periodic bank examinations access bank profitability, ascertain that banks perform in accordance with the myriad regulations to which they are subject, and uncover questionable practices or fraud.[5]

7. *Controlling the money supply*   Finally, and most important, the Fed has ultimate responsibility for regulating the supply of money, and this in turn enables it to affect interest rates. The major task of the Fed is to manage the money supply (and thus interest rates) on the basis of the needs of the economy. This involves making an amount of money available that is consistent with high and rising levels of output and employment and a relatively constant price level. While all the other functions are more or less routine or of a service nature, correctly managing the nation's money supply requires making basic but unique policy decisions. (These decisions are discussed in detail in Chapter 15.)

Federal Reserve Independence

The independence of the Fed is a matter of continuing controversy. Opponents of an independent Fed say that it is undemocratic to have a powerful economic agency whose members are not elected and thus not directly subject to the will of the people. They also point out that since the legislative and executive branches of government bear ultimate responsibility for maintaining economic stability and promoting economic growth, they should have available *all* the policy tools essential to the economy's health, including monetary policy. Voters tend to hold Congress and the president responsible for the consequences of Fed policies over which they have no control. Critics cite instances of the Fed using monetary policy to counter the effects of Congress' fiscal policy.

Defenders of Fed independence, including most economists, contend that the Fed must be protected from political pressures so that it can effectively control the money supply and maintain price stability. They point out that countries with less central bank independence, on average, have higher rates of inflation than countries with more central bank independence (see Global Perspective 13-2). It is often politically useful for Congress and the executive branch to enact inflationary fiscal policies, including tax cuts and special-interest spending. Citizens would likely pressure Congress to keep interest rates low, via expansions in the money supply, even though at times high interest rates are necessary to reduce aggregate

---

[5]The Fed is not alone in this task of supervision. The individual states supervise all banks that they charter. The Comptroller of the Currency supervises all national banks, and the Office of Thrift Supervision oversees all thrifts. Also, the Federal Deposit Insurance Corporation supervises all banks and thrifts whose deposits it insures.

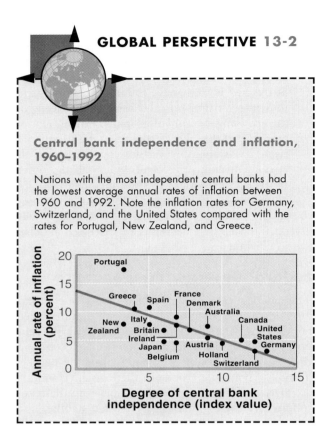

Central bank independence and inflation, 1960–1992

Nations with the most independent central banks had the lowest average annual rates of inflation between 1960 and 1992. Note the inflation rates for Germany, Switzerland, and the United States compared with the rates for Portugal, New Zealand, and Greece.

demand and thus to control inflation. Fed defenders argue that an independent monetary authority is needed to control the consequent inflation.

RECENT DEVELOPMENTS IN MONEY AND BANKING

The banking industry is undergoing a series of sweeping changes, spurred by competition from other financial institutions, globalization of banking, and advances in information technology.

The Relative Decline of Banks and Thrifts

Banks and thrifts are just two of several types of firms offering financial services. Table 13-2 identifies and briefly describes the major categories of firms within the U.S. *financial services industry* and lists examples of firms in each category. Although banks and thrifts remain the main institutions offering checkable deposits, their shares of *total* financial assets (value

of things owned) are declining. As shown in Figure 13-6, in 1980 banks and thrifts together held nearly 60 percent of financial assets in the United States. By 1996 that percentage had declined to 30 percent. The share held by thrifts decreased from 23 percent to 7 percent, largely as a result of the financial collapse of the numerous savings and loan associations in the late 1980s and early 1990s. The 37 percent share held by banks in 1980 declined to 24 percent by 1996.

Figure 13-6 reveals that pension funds, insurance companies, securities-related firms, and especially mutual funds have all expanded their shares of financial assets. Clearly, U.S. households and businesses are channeling relatively more saving away from banks and thrifts and toward these other financial institutions, mainly because these other institutions generally offer higher rates of return than do banks and thrifts. They are able to do so largely because they can participate more fully than banks and thrifts in national and international stock and bond markets.

Banks and thrifts have responded to the relative decline in traditional banking in several ways.

Expansion of Services In recent years, banks and thrifts have begun offering a variety of new services. For example, banks have increased their lending for commercial real estate projects such as housing developments, apartments, and office buildings. Banks and thrifts have developed new loan "products" such as home equity loans (loans based on the value of one's house) and low- or zero-down-payment mortgages. They also now offer a variety of interest-bearing accounts such as money market deposit accounts.

Banks and thrifts have made banking more convenient by opening up full-service branch banks in suburbs and "minibanks" in shopping malls and grocery stores. Supplementing these branches has been an explosion in the number of bank-owned automatic teller machines (ATMs) which allow customers to withdraw cash, deposit checks, move money between accounts, and make other banking transactions. They have also introduced "bank-by-telephone" and, more recently, "bank by Internet" services.

Mergers with Other Banks and Thrifts During the past two decades, many banks have purchased bankrupt savings and loans and have merged with other banks. Recent examples of large bank mergers include Chase Manhattan's merger with Chemical Bank and Wells Fargo's merger with First Interstate. Major savings and loans have also merged; for exam-

TABLE 13-2 Major U.S. Financial Institutions

Institution	Description	Examples
Commercial banks	State and national banks which provide checking and savings accounts, sell certificates of deposit, and make loans. The Federal Deposit Insurance Corporation (FDIC) insures checking and savings accounts up to $100,000.	Chase Manhattan, Citicorp, BankAmerica, J. P. Morgan, Wells Fargo
Thrifts	Savings and loan associations (S&Ls), mutual savings banks, and credit unions which offer checking and savings accounts and make loans. Historically, S&Ls made mortgage loans for houses while mutual savings banks and credit unions made small personal loans, such as automobile loans. Today, major thrifts offer the same range of banking services as commercial banks. The Federal Deposit Insurance Corporation insures checking and savings deposits up to $100,000.	Home Savings of America, Washington Mutual, Golden West Financial
Insurance companies	Firms which offer policies (contracts) through which individuals pay premiums to insure against some loss, say, disability or death. In some life insurance policies and annuities, the funds are invested for the client in stocks and bonds and paid back after a specified number of years. Thus, insurance sometimes has a saving or financial-investment element.	Prudential, New York Life, Travelers Group, Massachusetts Mutual
Mutual fund companies	Firms which pool deposits by customers to purchase stocks or bonds (or both). Customers thus own a part of a particular set of stocks or bonds, say, stocks in companies expected to grow rapidly (a growth fund) or bonds issued by state governments (a municipal bond fund).	Fidelity, Putnam, Dreyfus, Kemper
Pension funds	For-profit or nonprofit institutions which collect savings from workers (or from employers on their behalf) throughout their working years and then buy stocks and bonds with the proceeds and make monthly retirement payments.	Teachers Insurance and Annuity Association-College Retirement Equity Fund, Teamsters' Union
Securities-related firms	Firms which offer security advice and buy and sell stocks and bonds for clients. More generally known as *stock brokerage firms.*	Merrill-Lynch, Solomon, Leyman Brothers, Charles Schwab

ple, Washington Mutual recently acquired Great Western Financial. The purpose of such mergers is to create large regional or national banks or thrifts which can compete more effectively with the other participants in the financial services industry. Consolidation of traditional banking is expected to continue; there are 4500 fewer banks today than in 1990.

Push for Regulatory Reform In 1994 Congress ended Federal restrictions on banks' branching into

other states, and a 1996 reform partially ended the legal separation of the banking industry and the securities-related industry. Banks are now allowed to obtain up to one-fourth of their revenues from security transactions. This change set up a flurry of purchases of small security firms by banks. Banks have pressed for further latitude in engaging in security-related activities. They would like to offer stock accounts, much as mutual fund companies and security-related companies do now.

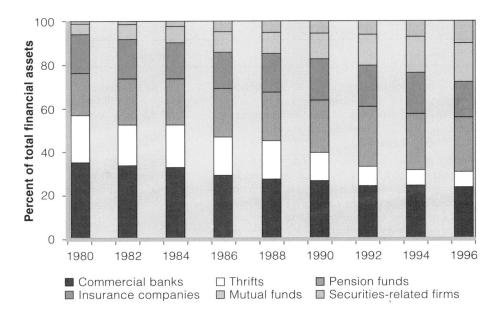

FIGURE 13-6 Financial assets held by major categories of U.S. financial services firms The combined share of total financial assets held in U.S. banks and thrifts has declined significantly since 1980. The shares of pension funds, insurance companies, mutual funds, and securities-related firms have increased. (*Source:* Federal Reserve Bank of Dallas; updated.)

Banks point out that less-regulated firms have invaded traditional banking, while banks have been prohibited from offering nonbanking products. For example, General Motors and AT&T now offer credit cards, and mutual fund companies now offer money market mutual funds, which pay relatively high interest and on which large checks ($500 or more) can be written. To counter such encroachments, banks want changes in the law so that they can own and operate companies in any line of business. With such reform, a bank could merge with, say, an insurance company or even a manufacturer of cash registers.

Critics of these reforms are concerned that increased participation by banks in nonbanking businesses could endanger the stability of the banking system. Losses in other lines of business during times of recession might cause the firms to fail, collapsing their banking operations along with them. Such bank failures might undermine confidence in the entire banking system and in the Fed's ability to maintain an adequate supply of money.

Globalization of Financial Markets

Another significant banking development is the increased integration of world financial markets. Major foreign financial institutions have operations in the United States, and U.S. financial institutions do business abroad. For example, VISA, MasterCard, and American Express offer worldwide credit card services. Moreover, U.S. mutual fund companies now offer a variety of international stock and bond funds. Globally, financial capital increasingly flows in search of the highest risk-adjusted returns. As a result, U.S. banks must increasingly compete with foreign banks for both deposits and loan customers.

Recent advances in computer and communications technology mean the trend toward international financial integration is likely to accelerate. Nevertheless, we must not overstate the extent of this globalization. Studies indicate that the bulk of investment in the major nations is still financed through domestic saving within each nation.

Electronic Money

Technological progress has also led to a new form of money: electronic cash and "smart cards." Although still in their infancies, these innovations potentially are of great significance to commercial banks, thrifts, and central banks.

Electronic money, dubbed **E-cash,** is simply an entry in an electronic file stored in a computer. The Internet and the widespread availability of personal computers have made it possible for individuals to use E-cash instead of checks or currency in making transactions. E-cash is deposited, or "loaded," into the account through Internet payments such as a paycheck,

The Global Greenback

A large amount of U.S. currency is circulating abroad.

Russians use them. So do Argentineans, Brazilians, Poles, Vietnamese, Chinese, and even Cubans. They are U.S. dollars. Like blue jeans, computer software, and movie videos, the dollar has become a major U.S. "export." Billions of dollars of U.S. currency currently are circulating overseas. Russians hold about $30 billion in U.S. cash; Argentineans, $5 to $7 billion. The Polish government estimates that $5 billion of U.S. dollars is circulating in Poland.

The currency leaves the United States when Americans buy imports, travel in other countries, or send dollars to relatives living abroad. The United States profits when the dollars stay in other countries. It costs the government about 4 cents to print a dollar. For someone abroad to obtain this new dollar, $1 worth of resources, goods, or services must be sold to Americans. These commodities are U.S. gains. The dollar goes abroad and, assuming it stays there, presents no claim on U.S. resources or goods or services. Americans in effect make 96 cents on the dollar (= $1 gain in resources, goods, or services *minus* the 4-cent printing cost). It's like American Express selling traveler's checks which never get cashed.

Black markets and other illegal activity undoubtedly fuel some of the demand for U.S. cash abroad. The dollar is king in covert trading in diamonds, weapons, and pirated software. Billions of cash dollars are involved in the narcotics trade. But the illegal use of dollars is only a small part of the story. The massive volume of dollars in other nations reflects a global search for monetary stability. On the basis of past experience, foreign citizens are confident the dollar's purchasing power will remain relatively steady.

Argentina has pegged its peso directly to the dollar, with the central bank issuing new pesos only when it has more dollars or gold on hand. The result has been a remarkable decline in inflation. In Russia and the newly independent countries of eastern Europe, the U.S. dollar has retained its buying power while that of domestic currencies has plummeted. As a result, many Russians hold their savings in dollars. In Brazil, where the inflation rate at times has been more than 1000 percent annually, people have long sought the stability of dollars. In the shopping districts of Beijing and Shanghai, Chinese consumers trade their domestic currency for dollars. In Bolivia half of all bank accounts are denominated in dollars. There is a thriving "dollar economy" in Vietnam, and even Cuba has partially legalized the use of U.S. dollars. The U.S. dollar is the official currency in Panama and Liberia.

There is little risk to the United States in satisfying the world's demand for dollars. If all the dollars came rushing back to the United States at once, the nation's money supply would surge, possibly causing demand-pull inflation. But there is not much chance of that happening. Overall, the global greenback is a positive economic force. It is a reliable medium of exchange, unit of account, and store of value which facilitates transactions that might not otherwise occur. Dollar holdings have helped buyers and sellers abroad overcome special monetary problems. The result has been increased output in those countries and thus greater output and income globally.

retirement benefit, or stock dividend. It is withdrawn, or "unloaded," from the account through Internet payments to others for a wide variety of goods and services.

In the future, account holders will be able to load sums from their E-cash accounts onto so-called *stored-value cards*. These **smart cards** are plastic cards containing computer chips which store information, including the amount the consumer has loaded. The amount of each purchase or other payment is then automatically deducted from the balance in the card's memory. Consumers will be able to transfer traditional money to their smart cards through their computers or telephones or at automatic teller machines. Thus, nearly all payments could be made with a personal computer or a smart card.

You can easily see why banks and thrifts would like to have the exclusive right to issue E-cash and smart cards; these innovations threaten to push banks out of the payment system. Any firm—a telephone company, a group of local merchants, or a hotel chain, for instance—could issue smart cards. Also, computer-related firms such as software producers could get into "banking" by developing and selling E-cash software programs. More likely, however, banks themselves will implement such software and set up E-cash and smart-card systems of their own since they know the banking business better than anyone else. Chase Manhattan, Citibank, VISA, and MasterCard have already teamed up to test a "first-generation" smart-card system in various parts of the country.

It is too early to predict the extent to which E-cash and smart cards will gain widespread public acceptance. If electronic money does catch on, however, it will present special problems for central banks.

Unlike currency, E-cash is "issued" by private firms rather than by government. To control the money supply, the central banks will need to find ways to control the total amount of E-cash, including that created through Internet loans.

QUICK REVIEW 13-4

■ The Federal Reserve System consists of the Board of Governors, 12 Federal Reserve Banks, commercial banks, and thrift institutions.

■ The 12 Federal Reserve Banks are publicly controlled central banks which deal with banks and thrifts rather than the public.

■ The Federal Reserve's major role is to regulate the supply of money in the economy.

■ Three recent developments in banking are the relative decline in traditional banking, the internationalization of banking, and the emergence of E-cash and smart cards.

CHAPTER SUMMARY

1. Anything that is accepted as **(a)** a medium of exchange, **(b)** a unit of monetary account, and **(c)** a store of value can be used as money.

2. The Federal Reserve System recognizes three "official" definitions of the money supply. *M*1 is currency and checkable deposits; *M*2 is *M*1 plus noncheckable savings deposits, money market deposit accounts, small (less than $100,000) time deposits, and money market mutual fund balances; and *M*3 is *M*2 plus large ($100,000 or more) time deposits. In our analysis we concentrate on *M*1 since its components are immediately spendable.

3. Money is the debts of government and depository institutions (commercial banks and thrift institutions) and has value because of the goods, services, and resources it will command in the market. Maintaining the purchasing power of money depends largely on the government's effectiveness in managing the money supply.

4. The total demand for money consists of the transactions and asset demands for money. The transactions demand varies directly with the nominal GDP; the asset demand varies inversely with the interest rate. The money market combines the total demand for money with the money supply to determine the equilibrium interest rate.

5. Disequilibria in the money market are corrected through changes in bond prices. As bond prices change,

interest rates move in the opposite direction. At the equilibrium interest rate, bond prices are stable and the amounts of money demanded and supplied are equal.

6. The U.S. banking system is composed of **(a)** the Board of Governors of the Federal Reserve System, **(b)** the 12 Federal Reserve Banks, and **(c)** some 9500 commercial banks and 14,000 thrift institutions. The Board of Governors is the basic policymaking body for the entire banking system. The directives of the Board are made effective through the 12 Federal Reserve Banks, which are simultaneously **(a)** central banks, **(b)** quasipublic banks, and **(c)** bankers' banks.

7. The major functions of the Fed are to **(a)** issue Federal Reserve Notes, **(b)** set reserve requirements and hold reserves deposited by banks and thrifts, **(c)** lend money to banks and thrifts, **(d)** provide for the rapid collection of checks, **(e)** act as the fiscal agent for the Federal government, **(f)** supervise the operations of the banks, and **(g)** regulate the supply of money in the best interest of the economy.

8. The Fed is essentially an independent institution, meaning that it is under the control of neither the president of the United States nor Congress. Opponents of an independent Fed say that monetary policy should be in the hands of elected officials (the president and Congress).

Defenders of Fed independence say that freedom from political pressure is critical to the Fed's role of providing the economy with an adequate, noninflationary supply of money.

9. Since the 1980s banks and thrifts have lost considerable market share to pension funds, insurance companies, mutual funds, and securities-related firms. Other significant banking developments include globalization of banking services and the emergence of electronic money, including smart cards.

TERMS AND CONCEPTS

medium of exchange
unit of account
store of value
M1, M2, M3
token money
intrinsic value
Federal Reserve Notes
checkable deposits
thrift (savings)
  institutions

savings and loan
  associations
mutual savings banks
credit unions
near-monies
noncheckable savings
  account
money market deposit
  account
time deposits

money market mutual
  fund
legal tender
fiat money
transactions demand
asset demand
total demand for money
money market
Federal Reserve System
Board of Governors

Federal Open Market
  Committee
Advisory Councils
Federal Reserve Banks
commercial banks
state banks
national banks
E-cash
smart cards

STUDY QUESTIONS

1. Describe how rapid inflation can undermine money's ability to perform each of its three basic functions.

2. What are the disadvantages of commodity money (for example, money made from precious metals)? What are the advantages of paper money and check money compared with commodity money?

3. Explain and evaluate the following statements:
   a. The invention of money is one of the great achievements of humankind, for without it the enrichment which comes from broadening trade would have been impossible.
   b. Money is whatever society says it is.
   c. In most economies of the world, the debts of government and commercial banks are used as money.
   d. People often say they would like to have more money, but what they usually mean is that they would like to have more goods and services.
   e. When the prices of everything go up, it is not because everything is worth more but because the currency is worth less.
   f. Any central bank can create money; the trick is to create enough of it, but not too much of it.

4. KEY QUESTION What are the components of the M1 money supply? What is the largest component? Why is the face value of a coin greater than its intrinsic value? Distinguish between M2 and M3.

What are near-monies? Of what significance are they? What arguments can you make for including noncheckable savings deposits in a definition of money?

5. What "backs" the money supply in the United States? What determines the value of money? Who is responsible for maintaining the value of money? Why is it important to be able to alter the money supply? What is meant by **(a)** "sound money" and **(b)** a "52-cent dollar"?

6. KEY QUESTION Suppose the price level and value of the dollar in year 1 are 1.0 and $1, respectively. If the price level rises to 1.25 in year 2, what is the new value of the dollar? If, instead, the price level falls to .50, what is the value of the dollar? What generalization can you draw from your answers?

7. KEY QUESTION What is the basic determinant of **(a)** the transactions demand and **(b)** the asset demand for money? Explain how these two demands might be combined graphically to determine total money demand. How is the equilibrium interest rate in the money market determined? How might **(a)** the expanded use of credit cards, **(b)** a shortening of worker pay periods, and **(c)** an increase in nominal GDP each independently affect the transactions demand for money and the equilibrium interest rate?

8. Suppose the following data characterize a hypothetical economy: money supply = $200 billion; quantity of money demanded for transactions = $150 billion; quantity of money demanded as an asset = $10 billion at 12 percent interest, increasing by $10 billion for each 2-percentage-point fall in the interest rate.
   a. What is the equilibrium interest rate? Explain.
   b. At the equilibrium interest rate, what are the quantity of money supplied, the total quantity of money demanded, the amount of money demanded for transactions, and the amount of money demanded as an asset?

9. Suppose a bond with no expiration date has a face value of $10,000 and annually pays a fixed amount of interest of $800. Compute and enter in the space provided below either the interest rate which the bond would yield to a bond buyer at each of the bond prices listed or the bond price at each of the interest yields shown. What generalization can be drawn from the completed table?

Bond price	Interest yield, %
$ 8,000	_____
_____	8.9
$10,000	_____
$11,000	_____
_____	6.2

10. Assume that the money market is initially in equilibrium and that the money supply is now increased. Explain the adjustments toward a new equilibrium interest rate. Will bond prices be higher or lower at the new equilibrium rate of interest? What effects would you expect the interest-rate change to have on the levels of output, employment, and prices? Answer the same questions for a decrease in the money supply.

11. How is the chair of the Federal Reserve System selected? Describe the relationship between the Board of Governors of the Federal Reserve System and the 12 Federal Reserve Banks. What is meant when economists say that the Federal Reserve Banks are central banks, quasipublic banks, and bankers' banks? What are the seven basic functions of the Federal Reserve System?

12. Following are two hypothetical ways that the Federal Reserve Board might be appointed. Would you favor either of these two methods over the present method? Why or why not?
   a. Upon taking office, the U.S. president appoints 7 people to the Federal Reserve Board, including a chair. Each appointee must be confirmed by a majority vote of the Senate, and each serves the same 4-year term as the president.
   b. Congress selects 7 members from its ranks (4 from the House of Representatives and 3 from the Senate) to serve at its pleasure as the Board of Governors of the Federal Reserve System.

13. What are the major categories of firms which make up the U.S. financial services industry? Which of these categories have experienced a declining share of financial assets since 1980? How have firms in these categories responded?

14. In what way are E-cash accounts and smart cards potentially related? Do you think E-cash and smart cards will dominate transactions sometime within the next 20 years?

15. (Last Word) Over the years, the Federal Reserve Banks have printed many billions of dollars more in currency than U.S. households, businesses, and financial institutions now hold. Where is this "missing" money? Why is it there?

16. WEB-BASED QUESTION   Board of Governors—Create Some Trading Cards The Federal Reserve Board http://www.bog.frb.fed.us/BIOS/ provides a detailed biography of the seven members of the Board of Governors. Create "Baseball Card"-types of descriptions and photos (use your Web browser to copy their photos) of the Board members (swapping with your classmates is optional). What is the composition of the Board with regard to age, gender, education, previous employment, and ethnic background? Who are the forthcoming "free agents" near the end of their terms?

17. WEB-BASED QUESTION   Everything You Wanted to Know About U.S. Currency but Were Afraid to Ask U.S. currency is made up of coins and paper money. Visit the Federal Reserve Bank of Atlanta http://www.frbatlanta.org/publica/brochure/fundfac/money.htm and the U.S. Treasury http://www.treas.gov/bep/index.html to answer the following questions. What is the largest denomination note currently in circulation? What has been the largest denomination note in circulation, and when was it last printed? The Federal Reserve Act requires that adequate backing be pledged for all Federal Reserve Notes in circulation. What is this backing? Who owns the notes, The Treasury or the Federal Reserve? What are some tips for spotting counterfeit currency? When was the last silver dollar minted? What have been the largest and smallest U.S. coin denominations since the Coinage Act of 1792?

CHAPTER FOURTEEN

How Banks
Create Money

If you visit Washington, D.C., you might enjoy touring the U.S. Bureau of Engraving and Printing. There, each day, more than $25 million of Federal Reserve Notes rolls off the printing presses in large sheets, which are then cut into individual bills and sent to the 12 Federal Reserve Banks for distribution.

Although the government printing presses create some of the nation's money, the bulk of the money in the U.S. economy is checkable deposits of commercial banks and thrifts, *not* currency. Who creates these checkable deposits? The answer is loan officers at commercial banks and thrifts. Although this may sound like something *60 Minutes* and a congressional committee should investigate, banking authorities are well aware that banks and thrifts create checking-deposit money. In fact, the Federal Reserve *relies* on these institutions to create a large part of the nation's money supply.

Because the bulk of all checkable deposits are "demand deposits" of commercial banks, this chapter explains how those banks can create demand-deposit money. Specifically, you will see how money can be created by (1) a *single* commercial bank which is part of a multibank system and (2) the commercial banking *system* as a whole. Keep in mind that thrift institutions also provide checkable deposits. Therefore, when we say "commercial bank," we also mean "thrift institution." And the more inclusive term "checkable deposits" can be substituted for "demand deposits."

THE BALANCE SHEET OF A COMMERCIAL BANK

An understanding of the basic items on a bank's balance sheet, and of how various transactions change these items, will provide the tools for analyzing the workings of the U.S. monetary system.

A **balance sheet** is a statement of assets and claims on assets which summarizes the financial position of a firm—in this case a commercial bank (*or* thrift)—at a specific point in time. Every balance sheet must balance, because every known *asset*, being something of economic value, will be claimed by someone. Can you think of an asset—something of monetary value—which no one claims? A balance sheet balances when the value of assets equals the amount of claims against those assets. The claims shown on a balance sheet are divided into two groups: the claims of the owners of the firm against the firm's assets, called *net worth*, and the claims of nonowners, called *liabilities*. Thus, a balance sheet balances because

Assets = liabilities + net worth

A balance-sheet approach to our study of the money-creating ability of commercial banks is valuable in two respects:

1. A bank's balance sheet provides a convenient point of reference from which we can introduce new terms and concepts in an orderly way.

2. The use of balance sheets allows us to quantify certain concepts and relationships which are difficult to comprehend if discussed in words alone.

PROLOGUE: THE GOLDSMITHS

Let's now see how a *fractional reserve system of banking* operates. The characteristics and working of such a system can be better understood by first considering a bit of economic history.

When early traders began to use gold in making transactions, they soon realized that it was both unsafe and inconvenient for consumers and merchants to carry gold and have it weighed and assessed for purity every time a transaction was negotiated. It therefore became commonplace by the sixteenth century to deposit one's gold with goldsmiths whose vaults or strongrooms could be used for a fee. Upon receiving a gold deposit, a goldsmith issued a receipt to the depositor. Soon goods were traded for the goldsmiths' receipts, and the receipts became the first kind of paper money.

At this point the goldsmiths—embryonic bankers—used a 100 percent reserve system; their circulating paper money receipts were fully backed by gold, which was "in reserve" in their vaults. But because of the public's acceptance of the goldsmiths' receipts as paper money, the goldsmiths became aware that the gold they stored was rarely redeemed. In fact, they found themselves in charge of enterprises where the amount of gold deposited with them in any week or month was likely to exceed the amount withdrawn.

Then some adroit goldsmith hit on the idea that paper money could be issued *in excess of* the amount of gold held. Goldsmiths would put these additional "receipts" redeemable in gold—their paper money—into circulation by making interest-earning loans to merchants, producers, and consumers. Borrowers were willing to accept loans in the form of gold receipts because the receipts were accepted as a medium of exchange.

This was the beginning of the **fractional reserve system** of banking, in which only a fraction of the money supply is backed by currency (here, gold) held in reserve in bank vaults. If, for example, our ingenious goldsmith made loans equal to the amount of gold stored, then the total value of paper money in circulation would be twice the value of the gold. Gold reserves would be 50 percent of outstanding paper money.

Fractional reserve banking—the system in the United States and most other countries today—has two significant characteristics:

1. *Money creation and reserves* Banks in such a system can *create money*. When a goldsmith made loans by giving borrowers paper money not fully backed by gold reserves, money was being created. The quantity of such money the goldsmith could create would depend on the amount of reserves deemed prudent to keep on hand. The smaller the amount of reserves thought necessary, the larger the amount of paper money the goldsmith could create. Although gold is no longer used to "back" the U.S. money supply, bank lending (money creation) today is constrained by the amount of currency reserves banks feel obligated, or are required by law, to keep.

2. *Bank panics and regulation* Banks which operate on the basis of fractional reserves are vulnerable to bank "panics" or "runs." A goldsmith who issued paper money equal to twice the value of gold reserves could not convert all that paper money into gold in the event all holders of that paper money appeared simultaneously demanding gold. In fact, many European and U.S. banks were once ruined by this unfortunate circumstance. However, a bank panic is highly unlikely *if* the banker's reserve and lending policies are prudent. Indeed, a basic reason why banking systems are highly regulated industries is to prevent bank runs. This is also the reason why the United States has in place a system of deposit insurance.

A SINGLE COMMERCIAL BANK

We need to explore how money can be created by a single bank which is part of a multibank banking system. Here are some questions we will consider: What items make up a commercial bank's balance sheet? How does a single commercial bank create money? If it can create money, can it destroy money too? What factors govern how a bank creates money?

Formation of a Commercial Bank

To answer these questions we must understand what is on a commercial bank's balance sheet and how certain transactions affect it. Let's begin with the organization of a local commercial bank.

Transaction 1: Creating a Bank Suppose farsighted citizens of the metropolis of Wahoo, Nebraska (yes, there is such a place), decide their town needs a new commercial bank to provide banking services for that growing community. Once these enterprising individuals secure a state or national charter for their bank, they turn to the task of selling, say, $250,000 worth of capital stock (equity shares) to buyers, both in and out of the community. These financing efforts meet with success and the Bank of Wahoo now exists—at least on paper. How does the Wahoo bank's balance statement appear at its birth?

The new owners of the bank have sold $250,000 worth of shares of stock in the bank—some to themselves, some to other people. As a result, the bank now has $250,000 in cash on hand and $250,000 worth of capital stock outstanding. The cash is an asset to the bank. Cash held by a bank is sometimes called **vault cash** or *till money*. The outstanding shares of stock constitute an equal amount of claims which the owners have against the bank's assets. The shares of stock are the net worth of the bank. The bank's balance sheet reads:

CREATING A BANK

BALANCE SHEET 1: WAHOO BANK

Assets		Liabilities and net worth	
Cash	$250,000	Capital stock	$250,000

Each item listed in a balance sheet such as this is called an *account*.

Transaction 2: Acquiring Property and Equipment The board of directors must now get the newborn bank off the drawing board and make it a reality. First, property and equipment must be acquired. Suppose the directors, confident of the suc-

cess of their venture, purchase a building for $220,000 and buy $20,000 worth of office equipment. This simple transaction changes the composition of the bank's assets. The bank now has $240,000 less in cash and $240,000 of new property assets. Using blue to denote those accounts affected by each transaction, we find that the bank's balance sheet at the end of transaction 2 appears as follows:

ACQUIRING PROPERTY AND EQUIPMENT

BALANCE SHEET 2: WAHOO BANK

Assets		Liabilities and net worth	
Cash	$ 10,000	Capital stock	$250,000
Property	240,000		

Note that the balance sheet still balances, as it must.

Transaction 3: Accepting Deposits Commercial banks have two basic functions: to accept deposits of money and to make loans. Now that the bank is operating, suppose that the citizens and businesses of Wahoo decide to deposit $100,000 in the Wahoo bank. What happens to the bank's balance sheet?

The bank receives cash, which we know is an asset to the bank. Suppose this money is placed in the bank as demand deposits (checking accounts), rather than time deposits or savings accounts. These newly created demand deposits constitute claims which depositors have against the assets of the Wahoo bank. Thus, the depositing of money in the bank creates a new liability account—demand deposits. The bank's balance sheet now looks like this:

ACCEPTING DEPOSITS

BALANCE SHEET 3: WAHOO BANK

Assets		Liabilities and net worth	
Cash	$110,000	Demand deposits	$100,000
Property	240,000	Capital stock	250,000

There has been no change in the economy's total supply of money, but a change has occurred in the composition of the money supply as a result of transaction 3. Bank money, or demand deposits, has *increased* by $100,000, and currency held by the public has *decreased* by $100,000. Currency held by a bank, you will recall, is *not* part of the economy's money supply.

It is apparent that a withdrawal of cash will reduce the bank's demand-deposit liabilities and its holdings of cash by the amount of the withdrawal. This, too, changes the composition, but not the total supply, of money in the economy.

Transaction 4: Depositing Reserves in a Federal Reserve Bank
All commercial banks and thrift institutions which provide checkable deposits must keep a *legal reserve* or **required reserves**. These required reserves are *an amount of funds equal to a specified percentage of the bank's own deposit liabilities. A member bank must keep these reserves on deposit with the Federal Reserve Bank in its district or as vault cash.* To simplify, we suppose the Bank of Wahoo keeps its required reserves *entirely* as deposits in the Federal Reserve Bank of its district. But remember that vault cash is counted as reserves and real-world banks keep a significant portion of their reserves in their vaults.

The "specified percentage" of its deposit liabilities which the commercial bank must keep as reserves is known as the **reserve ratio**—the ratio of the required reserves the commercial bank must keep to the bank's own outstanding deposit liabilities:

$$\text{Reserve ratio} = \frac{\text{commercial bank's required reserves}}{\text{commercial bank's demand-deposit liabilities}}$$

If the reserve ratio were $\frac{1}{10}$, or 10 percent, the Wahoo bank, having accepted $100,000 in deposits from the public, would have to keep $10,000 as reserves. If the ratio were $\frac{1}{5}$, or 20 percent, $20,000 of reserves would be required. If $\frac{1}{2}$, or 50 percent, $50,000 would be required.

The Fed has the authority to establish and vary the reserve ratio within limits legislated by Congress. The limits now prevailing are shown in Table 14-1. A 3 percent reserve is required on the first $49.3 million of checkable deposits held by an institution. A 10 percent reserve is required on an institution's checkable deposits over $49.3 million, although the Fed can vary this between 8 and 14 percent. Currently, no reserves are required against noncheckable nonpersonal (business) savings and time deposits; up to 9 percent *can* be required. Also, after consultation with appropriate congressional committees, the Fed may impose reserve requirements for 180 days in excess of those specified in Table 14-1.

To simplify our discussion suppose the reserve ratio for commercial banks is $\frac{1}{5}$, or 20 percent, and this requirement applies only to demand deposits.

TABLE 14-1   Reserve requirements (reserve ratios) for banks and thrift institutions

Type of deposit	Current requirement	Statutory limits
Checkable deposits		
$0–49.3 million	3%	3%
Over $49.3 million	10	8–14
Noncheckable nonpersonal savings and time deposits	0	0–9

Source: Federal Reserve. Data are for 1997.

Although it's higher than in reality, 20 percent is convenient for computations. And because we are concerned with checkable (spendable) demand deposits, we ignore reserves on noncheckable savings and time deposits. The main point is that reserve requirements are *fractional*, meaning they are less than 100 percent. This point is vital in our analysis of the lending ability of the banking system.

The Wahoo bank will just be meeting the required 20 percent ratio between its reserves in the Federal Reserve Bank and its own deposit liabilities by depositing $20,000 in the Federal Reserve Bank. We will use "reserves" to mean the funds commercial banks deposit in the Federal Reserve Banks, thereby distinguishing them from the public's *deposits* in commercial banks.

But suppose the Wahoo bank anticipates that its holdings of the public's demand deposits will grow in the future. Thus, instead of sending just the minimum amount, $20,000, it sends an extra $90,000, for a total of $110,000. In so doing, the bank will avoid the inconvenience of sending additional reserves to the Federal Reserve Bank each time its own demand-deposit liabilities increase. And, as you will see, it is on the basis of extra reserves that banks can lend and thereby earn interest income.

Actually, the bank would not deposit *all* its cash in the Federal Reserve Bank. However, because (1) banks as a rule hold vault cash only in the amount of $1\frac{1}{2}$ or 2 percent of their total assets, and (2) vault cash can be counted as reserves, we can assume all the bank's cash is deposited in the Federal Reserve Bank and therefore constitutes the commercial bank's total reserves. Then we do not need to bother adding two assets—"cash" and "deposits in the Federal Reserve Bank"—to determine "reserves."

After Wahoo bank deposits $110,000 of reserves at the Fed, its balance sheet becomes:

DEPOSITING RESERVES AT THE FED
BALANCE SHEET 4: WAHOO BANK

Assets		Liabilities and net worth	
Cash	$ 0	Demand	
Reserves	110,000	deposits	$100,000
Property	240,000	Capital stock	250,000

There are three things you should understand about this latest transaction.

1. Excess Reserves Some terminology: The amount by which the bank's **actual reserves** exceed its *required reserves* is the bank's **excess reserves:**

$$\frac{\text{Actual}}{\text{reserves}} - \frac{\text{required}}{\text{reserves}} = \frac{\text{excess}}{\text{reserves}}$$

In this case,

Actual reserves	$110,000
Required reserves	−20,000
Excess reserves	$90,000

The only reliable way of computing excess reserves is to multiply the bank's demand-deposit liabilities by the reserve ratio to obtain required reserves ($100,000 × 20 percent = $20,000) and then to subtract required reserves from the actual reserves listed on the asset side of the bank's balance sheet.

To make sure you understand this, you should compute the bank's excess reserves from balance sheet 4, assuming that the reserve ratio is (1) 10 percent, (2) $33\frac{1}{3}$ percent, and (3) 50 percent.

We will soon demonstrate that the ability of a commercial bank to make loans depends on the existence of excess reserves. So understanding this concept is crucial in seeing how the banking system creates money.

2. Control What is the rationale underlying the requirement that member banks deposit reserves in the Federal Reserve Bank of their district? You might think the basic purpose of reserves is to enhance the liquidity of a bank and protect commercial bank depositors from losses. Reserves would constitute a ready source of funds from which commercial banks can meet large and unexpected cash withdrawals by depositors.

But this reasoning breaks down under scrutiny. Although historically reserves were seen as a source of liquidity and therefore as protection for depositors, a bank's required reserves are not great enough to meet sudden, massive cash withdrawals. If the banker's nightmare should materialize—everyone with demand deposits appearing at once to demand these deposits in cash—the legal reserves held as vault cash or at the Federal Reserve Bank would be insufficient. The banker simply could not meet this "bank panic." Because reserves are fractional, demand deposits may be 10 to 20 times greater than a bank's required reserves.

Commercial bank deposits must be protected by other means. Periodic bank examinations are one way of promoting prudent commercial banking practices. And banking laws restrict banks as to the kinds of assets they may acquire; for example, banks are generally prohibited from buying common stocks. Furthermore, insurance funds administered by the Federal Deposit Insurance Corporation (FDIC) exist to insure individual deposits in banks and thrifts up to $100,000.

If it is not the purpose of reserves to provide for commercial bank liquidity, then what is their function? *Control* is the basic answer. Required reserves help the Fed influence the lending ability of commercial banks. Chapter 15 will examine how the Fed can take certain actions which either increase or decrease commercial bank reserves and affect the ability of banks to grant credit. The objective is to prevent banks from *over*extending or *under*extending bank credit. To the degree that these policies are successful in influencing the volume of commercial bank credit, the Fed can help the economy avoid business fluctuations. Another function of reserves is to facilitate the collection or "clearing" of checks. **(Key Question 2)**

3. Asset and Liability Transaction 4 brings up another accounting matter. Specifically, the reserves created in transaction 4 are an asset to the depositing commercial bank because they are a claim this bank has against the assets of another institution. But reserves are a liability to the Federal Reserve Bank because they are a claim against it. To the Wahoo bank the reserves are an asset; they are a claim this bank has against assets of another institution—the Federal Reserve Bank. To the Federal Reserve Bank these reserves are a liability, a claim which another institution—the Bank of Wahoo—has against it. The demand deposit you get by depositing money in a commercial bank is an asset to you and a liability to the bank. In the same way, *the reserves which a commercial bank establishes by depositing money in a bankers' bank are an asset to that bank and a liability to the Federal Reserve Bank.*

Transaction 5: Clearing a Check Drawn Against the Bank

Assume that Clem Bradshaw, a Wahoo farmer, deposited a substantial portion of the $100,000 in demand deposits which the Wahoo bank received in transaction 3. Suppose now that Clem buys $50,000 of farm machinery from the Ajax Farm Implement Company of Beaver Crossing, Nebraska. Bradshaw pays for this machinery by writing a $50,000 check, against his deposit in the Wahoo bank, to the Ajax company. We need to know (1) how this check is collected or cleared and (2) the effect the collection of the check has on the balance sheets of the banks involved in the transaction.

To learn this, we must consider the Wahoo bank (Bradshaw's bank), the Beaver Crossing bank (the Ajax Company's bank), and the Federal Reserve Bank of Kansas City. For simplicity, we deal only with changes which occur in the specific accounts affected by this transaction. We trace the transaction in three steps, keyed by letters to Figure 14-1.

a. Bradshaw gives his $50,000 check, drawn against the Wahoo bank, to the Ajax company. Ajax deposits the check in its account with the Beaver Crossing bank. The Beaver Crossing bank increases Ajax's demand deposits by $50,000 when the check is deposited. Ajax is now paid in full. Bradshaw is pleased with his new machinery.

b. Now the Beaver Crossing bank has Bradshaw's check. This check is simply a claim against the assets of the Wahoo bank. The Beaver Crossing bank will collect this claim by sending the check (along with checks drawn on other banks) to the Federal Reserve

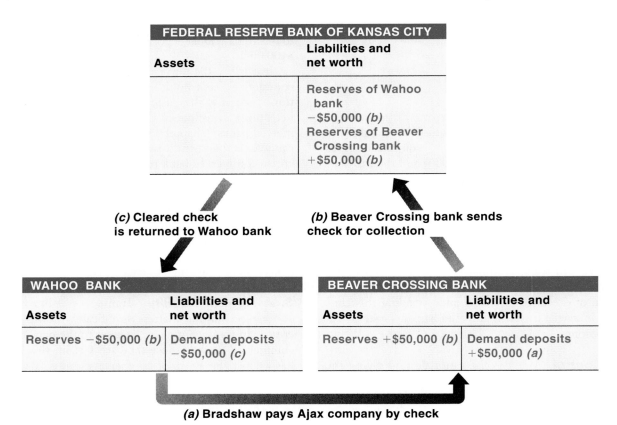

FIGURE 14-1 The collection of a check through a Federal Reserve Bank The bank against which a check is drawn and cleared (Wahoo bank) loses both reserves and deposits; the bank in which the check is deposited (Beaver Crossing bank) acquires reserves and deposits.

Bank of Kansas City. Here a clerk will *clear*, or collect, the check for the Beaver Crossing bank by *increasing* Beaver's reserve in the Federal Reserve Bank by $50,000 and *decreasing* Wahoo's reserve by a like amount. The check is collected merely by making bookkeeping notations to the effect that Wahoo's claim against the Federal Reserve Bank has been reduced by $50,000 and Beaver's claim increased by $50,000. Note these changes on the balance sheets in Figure 14-1.

c. Finally, the Federal Reserve Bank sends the cleared check back to the Wahoo bank, and for the first time the Wahoo bank discovers that one of its depositors has drawn a check for $50,000 against his demand deposit. Accordingly, the Wahoo bank reduces Bradshaw's demand deposit by $50,000 and notes that the collection of this check has caused a $50,000 decline in its reserves at the Federal Reserve Bank. Observe that the balance statements of all three banks balance. The Wahoo bank has reduced both its assets and liabilities by $50,000. The Beaver Crossing bank has $50,000 more in reserves and in demand deposits. Ownership of reserves at the Federal Reserve Bank has changed—Wahoo owning $50,000 less, Beaver owning $50,000 more—but total reserves stay the same.

Whenever a check is drawn against one bank and deposited in another bank, collection of that check will reduce both reserves and demand deposits of the bank on which the check is drawn. Conversely, if a bank receives a check drawn on another bank, the bank receiving the check will, in the process of collecting it, have its reserves and deposits *increased* by the amount of the check. In our example, the Wahoo bank loses $50,000 in both reserves and deposits to the Beaver Crossing bank. But there is no loss of reserves or deposits for the banking system as a whole. What one bank loses, another bank gains.

If we bring all the other assets and liabilities back into the picture, the Wahoo bank's balance sheet looks like this at the end of transaction 5:

CLEARING A CHECK

BALANCE SHEET 5: WAHOO BANK

Assets		Liabilities and net worth	
Reserves	$ 60,000	Demand deposits	$ 50,000
Property	240,000	Capital stock	250,000

You should verify that with a 20 percent reserve requirement, the bank's *excess* reserves now stand at $50,000.

Transaction 5 is reversible. If a check drawn against another bank is deposited in the Wahoo bank, the Wahoo bank will receive both reserves and deposits equal to the amount of the check when it is collected.

QUICK REVIEW 14-1

■ When a bank accepts deposits of cash, the composition of the money supply is changed but the total supply of money is not directly altered.

■ Commercial banks and thrifts are required to keep required reserves, equal to a specified percentage of their own deposit liabilities, as cash or on deposit with the Federal Reserve Bank of their district.

■ The amount by which a bank's actual reserves exceed its required reserves is called excess reserves.

■ A bank which has a check drawn and collected against it will lose to the recipient bank both reserves and deposits equal to the value of the check.

Money-Creating Transactions of a Commercial Bank

The next three transactions are crucial because they explain (1) how a commercial bank can literally create money by making loans, (2) how money is destroyed when loans are repaid, and (3) how banks create money by purchasing government bonds from the public.

Transaction 6: Granting a Loan In addition to accepting deposits, commercial banks grant loans to borrowers. What effect does lending by a commercial bank have on its balance sheet?

Suppose Grisley Meat Packing Company of Wahoo decides it is time to expand its facilities. Suppose, too, the company needs exactly $50,000—which just happens to be equal to the Wahoo bank's excess reserves—to finance this project.

Grisley goes to the Wahoo bank and requests a loan for this amount. The Wahoo bank knows the Grisley company's fine reputation and financial soundness and is convinced of its ability to repay the loan. So the loan is granted. In return, the president of Grisley hands a promissory note—a fancy IOU—to the Wahoo bank. Grisley wants the convenience and safety of paying its obligations by checks. So, instead of receiving a bushelbasket full of currency from the bank, Grisley gets a $50,000 increase in its demand-deposit account in the Wahoo bank.

The Wahoo bank has acquired an interest-earning asset (the promissory note which it files under "Loans") and has created demand deposits (a liability) to "pay" for this asset. Grisley has swapped an IOU for the right to draw an additional $50,000 worth of checks against its demand deposit in the Wahoo bank. Both parties are pleased.

At the moment the loan is completed, the Wahoo bank's position is shown by balance sheet 6a:

WHEN A LOAN IS NEGOTIATED
BALANCE SHEET 6a: WAHOO BANK

Assets		Liabilities and net worth	
Reserves	$ 60,000	Demand deposits	$100,000
Loans	50,000		
Property	240,000	Capital stock	250,000

All this looks simple enough. But a close examination of the Wahoo bank's balance statement will reveal a startling fact: *When a bank makes loans, it creates money.* The president of Grisley went to the bank with something which is *not* money—her IOU—and walked out with something that *is* money—a demand deposit.

Contrast transaction 6a with transaction 3, in which demand deposits were created but only by currency going out of circulation. There was a change in the *composition* of the money supply in that situation but no change in the total *supply* of money. But when banks lend, they create demand deposits which *are* money. By extending credit the Wahoo bank has "monetized" an IOU. Grisley and the Wahoo bank have created and then swapped claims. The claim created by Grisley and given to the bank is not money; an individual's IOU is not acceptable as a medium of exchange. But the claim created by the bank and given to Grisley is money; checks drawn against a demand deposit are acceptable as a medium of exchange.

The bulk of the money we use in our economy is created through the extension of credit by commercial banks. This checking account money may be thought of as "debts" of commercial banks and thrift institutions. Checks are bank "debts" in the sense that they are claims which banks and thrifts promise to pay "on demand."

But there are forces limiting the ability of a commercial bank to create demand deposits ("bank money") by lending. The Wahoo bank can expect the newly created demand deposit of $50,000 to be a very active account. Grisley would not borrow $50,000 at, say, 7, 10, or 12 percent interest for the sheer joy of knowing funds were available if needed.

Assume that Grisley awards a $50,000 building contract to the Quickbuck Construction Company of Omaha. Quickbuck, true to its name, completes the expansion job and is paid with a check for $50,000 drawn by Grisley against its demand deposit in the Wahoo bank. Quickbuck, with headquarters in Omaha, does *not* deposit this check in the Wahoo bank but instead deposits it in the Fourth National Bank of Omaha. Fourth National now has a $50,000 claim against the Wahoo bank. This check is collected in the manner described in transaction 5. As a result, the Wahoo bank *loses* both reserves and deposits equal to the amount of the check; Fourth National *acquires* $50,000 of reserves and deposits.

In summary, assuming a check is drawn by the borrower for the entire amount of the loan ($50,000) and given to a firm which deposits it in some other bank, the Wahoo bank's balance sheet will read as follows *after the check has been cleared against it*:

AFTER A CHECK IS DRAWN ON THE LOAN
BALANCE SHEET 6b: WAHOO BANK

Assets		Liabilities and net worth	
Reserves	$ 10,000	Demand deposits	$ 50,000
Loans	50,000		
Property	240,000	Capital stock	250,000

After the check has been collected, the Wahoo bank just meets the required reserve ratio of 20 percent (= $10,000 ÷ $50,000). The bank has *no excess reserves.* This poses a question: Could the Wahoo bank have lent more than $50,000—an amount greater than its excess reserves—and still have met the 20 percent reserve requirement if a check for the full amount of the loan were cleared against it? The answer is "no"; the bank is "fully loaned up."

Here is why: Suppose the Wahoo bank had loaned $55,000 to the Grisley company. Collection of the check against the Wahoo bank would have lowered its reserves to $5,000 (= $60,000 − $55,000), and deposits would once again stand at $50,000 (= $105,000 − $55,000). The ratio of actual reserves to deposits would then be $5,000/$50,000, or only 10 percent. The Wahoo bank could thus *not* have lent $55,000.

By experimenting with other amounts over $50,000, you will find that the maximum amount the Wahoo bank could lend at the outset of transaction 6 is $50,000. This amount is identical with the amount of excess reserves the bank had available when the loan was negotiated. *A single commercial bank in a multibank banking system can lend only an amount equal to its initial preloan excess reserves.* When it lends, the lending bank faces the likelihood that checks for the entire amount of the loan will be drawn and cleared against it. A lending bank can expect to lose to other banks reserves equal to the amount it lends.[1]

Transaction 7: Repaying a Loan If commercial banks create demand deposits—money—when they make loans, is money destroyed when loans are repaid? Yes. We see this by noting what happens when Grisley repays the $50,000 it borrowed.

To simplify, we (1) suppose the loan is repaid not in installments but in one lump sum 2 years after it is made and (2) ignore interest charges on the loan. Grisley simply writes a check for $50,000 against its demand deposit, which we assume was $50,000 before the Grisley loan was negotiated. As a result, the Wahoo bank's demand-deposit liabilities decline by $50,000; Grisley has given up $50,000 worth of its claim against the bank's assets. In turn, the bank will surrender Grisley's IOU, which it has been holding these many months. The bank and the company have reswapped claims. But the claim given up by Grisley is money; the claim it is repurchasing—its IOU—is not. The supply of money has therefore been reduced by $50,000; that amount of demand deposits has been destroyed, unaccompanied by an increase in the money supply elsewhere in the economy.

The Grisley company's IOU has been "demonetized," as shown in balance sheet 7. The Wahoo bank's demand deposits and loans have each returned to zero. The decline in demand deposits lowers the bank's required reserves to zero and gives it new excess reserves (= its reserves of $10,000); this provides the basis for new loans to be made. **(Key Questions 4 and 8)**

---

[1]Qualification: If some of the checks written on a loan are redeposited in the lending bank by their recipients, then that bank will be able to lend an amount somewhat greater than its initial excess reserves.

REPAYING A LOAN

BALANCE SHEET 7: WAHOO BANK

Assets		Liabilities and net worth	
Reserves	$ 10,000	Demand	
Loans	0	deposits	$ 0
Property	240,000	Capital stock	250,000

In the unlikely event Grisley repays the loan with cash, the money supply will still decline by $50,000. In this case, Grisley would repurchase its IOU by handing over $50,000 in cash to the bank. Loan balances decline in the asset column by $50,000 and cash increases by $50,000. Remember, we exclude currency held by banks from the money supply because to include such cash would be double counting; it is apparent that this constitutes a $50,000 reduction in the supply of money.

Transaction 8: Buying Government Securities
When a commercial bank buys government bonds from the public, the effect is substantially the same as lending. New money is created.

Assume that the Wahoo bank's balance sheet initially stands as it did at the end of transaction 5. Now suppose that, instead of making a $50,000 loan, the bank buys $50,000 of government securities from a securities dealer. The bank receives the interest-bearing bonds, which appear on its balance statement as the asset "Securities," and gives the dealer an increase in its demand-deposit account. The Wahoo bank's balance sheet appears as follows:

BUYING GOVERNMENT SECURITIES

BALANCE SHEET 8: WAHOO BANK

Assets		Liabilities and net worth	
Reserves	$ 60,000	Demand	
Securities	50,000	deposits	$100,000
Property	240,000	Capital stock	250,000

Demand deposits, that is, the supply of money, have been increased by $50,000, as in transaction 6. *Bond purchases from the public by commercial banks increase the supply of money in the same way as does lending to the public.* The bank accepts government bonds (which are not money) and gives the securities dealer an increase in its demand deposits (which are money).

Of course, when the securities dealer draws and clears a check for $50,000 against the Wahoo bank, the bank loses both reserves and deposits in that amount and then just meets the legal reserve requirement. Its balance sheet now reads precisely as in 6b except that "Securities" is substituted for "Loans" on the asset side.

Finally, the selling of government bonds to the public by a commercial bank—like the repayment of a loan—reduces the supply of money. The securities buyer pays by check, and both "Securities" and "Demand deposits" (the latter being money) decline by the amount of the sale.

Profits, Liquidity, and the Federal Funds Market

The asset items on a commercial bank's balance sheet reflect the banker's pursuit of two conflicting goals:

1. **Profit**   One goal is profit. Commercial banks, like any other business, seek profits, which is why the bank makes loans and buys securities—the two major earning assets of commercial banks.

2. **Liquidity**   The other goal is safety. For a bank, safety lies in liquidity, specifically such liquid assets as cash and excess reserves. A bank must be on guard for depositors' wanting to transform their demand deposits into cash. Similarly, it must guard against more checks clearing against it than are cleared in its favor, causing a net outflow of reserves. Bankers thus seek a balance between prudence and profit. The compromise is between assets that earn high returns and highly liquid assets.

An interesting way banks can partly reconcile the goals of profit and liquidity is to lend temporary excess reserves held at the Federal Reserve Banks to other commercial banks. Normal day-to-day flows of funds to banks rarely leave all banks with their exact levels of legally required reserves. Also, funds held at the Federal Reserve Banks are highly liquid, but they do not draw interest. Banks therefore lend these excess reserves to other banks on an overnight basis as a way to earn additional interest without sacrificing long-term liquidity. Banks which borrow in this *Federal funds market*—the market for immediately available reserve balances at the Federal Reserve—do so because they are temporarily short of required reserves. The interest rate paid on these overnight loans is called the **Federal funds rate.**

In Figure 14-1, we would show an overnight loan of reserves from the Beaver Crossing bank to the

Wahoo bank as a decrease in reserves at the Beaver Crossing bank and an increase in reserves at the Wahoo bank. Ownership of reserves at the Federal Reserve Bank of Kansas City would change, but total reserves would not be affected. Exercise: Determine what other changes would be required on the Wahoo and Beaver Crossing bank balance sheets as a result of the overnight loan.

QUICK REVIEW 14-2

■ Banks create money when they make loans; money vanishes when bank loans are repaid.

■ New money is created when banks buy government bonds from the public; money disappears when banks sell government bonds to the public.

■ Banks balance profitability and safety in determining their mix of earning assets and highly liquid assets.

■ Banks borrow and lend temporary excess reserves on an overnight basis in the Federal funds market; the interest rate on these loans is the Federal funds rate.

THE BANKING SYSTEM: MULTIPLE-DEPOSIT EXPANSION

Thus far we have seen that a single bank in a banking system can lend one dollar for each dollar of its excess reserves. The situation is different for all commercial banks as a group. We will find that *the commercial banking system can lend, that is, can create money, by a multiple of its excess reserves. This multiple lending is accomplished even though each bank in the system can only lend "dollar for dollar" with its excess reserves.*

Our immediate task is to uncover how these seemingly paradoxical results come about. To do this, we must keep our analysis uncluttered. Therefore, we will rely on three simplifying assumptions:

1. The reserve ratio for all commercial banks is 20 percent.

2. Initially all banks are exactly meeting this 20 percent reserve requirement. No excess reserves exist; all banks are "loaned up" (or "loaned out").

3. If any bank can increase its loans as a result of acquiring excess reserves, an amount equal to these excess reserves will be loaned to one borrower, who will write a check for the entire amount of the loan and give it to someone else, who will deposit the check in another bank. This third assumption means the worst thing possible happens

to every lending bank—a check for the entire amount of the loan is drawn and cleared against it in favor of another bank.

The Banking System's Lending Potential

Suppose a junkyard owner finds a $100 bill while dismantling a car which has been on the lot for years. He deposits the $100 in bank A, which adds the $100 to its reserves. We will record only *changes* in the balance sheets of the various commercial banks. The deposit changes bank A's balance sheet as shown by entries (a_1):

MULTIPLE-DEPOSIT EXPANSION PROCESS			
BALANCE SHEET: COMMERCIAL BANK A			
Assets		Liabilities and net worth	
Reserves	$+100 ($a_1$) − 80 ($a_3$)	Demand deposits	$+100 ($a_1$) + 80 ($a_2$) − 80 ($a_3$)
Loans	+ 80 (a_2)		

Recall from transaction 3 that this $100 deposit of currency does *not* alter the money supply. While $100 of demand-deposit money comes into being, it is offset by the $100 of currency no longer in the hands of the public (the junkyard owner). What *has* happened is that bank A has acquired *excess reserves* of $80. Of the newly acquired $100 in reserves, 20 percent, or $20, must be earmarked for the required reserves on the new $100 deposit and the remaining $80 is excess reserves. Remembering that a single commercial bank can lend only an amount equal to its excess reserves, we conclude that bank A can lend a maximum of $80. When a loan for this amount is made, bank A's loans increase by $80 and the borrower gets an $80 demand deposit. We add these figures—entries (a_2)—to bank A's balance sheet.

But now we use our third assumption: The borrower draws a check for $80—the entire amount of the loan—and gives it to someone who deposits it in another bank, bank B. As we saw in transaction 6, bank A *loses* both reserves and deposits equal to the amount of the loan, as indicated in entries (a_3). The net result of these transactions is that bank A's reserves now stand at +$20 (= $100 − $80), loans at +$80, and demand deposits at +$100 (= $100 + $80 − $80). When the dust has settled, bank A is just meeting the 20 percent reserve ratio.

Recalling transaction 5, we know that bank B *acquires* both the reserves and the deposits that bank A has lost. Bank B's balance sheet is changed as in entries (b_1):

MULTIPLE-DEPOSIT EXPANSION PROCESS			
BALANCE SHEET: COMMERCIAL BANK B			
Assets		Liabilities and net worth	
Reserves	$+80 ($b_1$) −64 ($b_3$)	Demand deposits	$+80 ($b_1$) +64 ($b_2$) −64 ($b_3$)
Loans	+64 (b_2)		

When the borrower's check is drawn and cleared, bank A *loses* $80 in reserves and deposits and bank B *gains* $80 in reserves and deposits. But 20 percent, or $16, of bank B's new reserves must be kept as required reserves against the new $80 in demand deposits. This means that bank B has $64 (= $80 − $16) in excess reserves. It can therefore lend $64 [entries ($b_2$)]. When the new borrower draws a check for the entire amount and deposits it in bank C, the reserves and deposits of bank B both fall by the $64 [entries ($b_3$)]. As a result of these transactions, bank B's reserves now stand at +$16 (= $80 − $64), loans at +$64, and demand deposits at +$80 (= $80 + $64 − $64). After all this, bank B is just meeting the 20 percent reserve requirement.

We are off and running again. Bank C acquires the $64 in reserves and deposits lost by bank B. Its balance sheet changes as in entries (c_1):

MULTIPLE-DEPOSIT EXPANSION PROCESS			
BALANCE SHEET: COMMERCIAL BANK C			
Assets		Liabilities and net worth	
Reserves	$+64.00 ($c_1$) −51.20 ($c_3$)	Demand deposits	$+64.00 ($c_1$) +51.20 ($c_2$) −51.20 ($c_3$)
Loans	+51.20 (c_2)		

Exactly 20 percent, or $12.80, of these new reserves will be required reserves, the remaining $51.20 being excess reserves. Hence, bank C can safely lend a maximum of $51.20. Suppose it does [entries (c_2)]. And suppose the borrower draws a check for the entire amount and gives it to someone who deposits it in another bank [entries (c_3)].

Bank D—the bank receiving the $51.20 in reserves and deposits—now notes these changes on its balance sheet [entries (d_1)]:

MULTIPLE-DEPOSIT EXPANSION PROCESS
BALANCE SHEET: COMMERCIAL BANK D

Assets		Liabilities and net worth	
Reserves	$+51.20 (d_1)	Demand	
	−40.96 (d_3)	deposits	$+51.20 (d_1)
Loans	+40.96 (d_2)		+40.96 (d_2)
			−40.96 (d_3)

It can now lend $40.96 [entries (d_2)]. The newest borrower draws a check for the full amount and deposits it in still another bank [entries (d_3)].

Now, if we wanted to be particularly obnoxious, we could go ahead with this procedure by bringing banks E, F, G, H, . . . , N into the picture. But, we suggest you work through the computations for banks E, F, and G to be sure you understand the procedure.

The entire analysis is summarized in Table 14-2. Data for banks E through N are supplied so that you may check your computations. Our conclusion is star-

tling: On the basis of only $80 in excess reserves (acquired by the banking system when someone deposited $100 of currency in bank A), the *entire commercial banking system* is able to lend $400, the sum of the amounts in column 4. The banking system can lend excess reserves by a multiple of 5 when the reserve ratio is 20 percent. Yet each single bank in the banking system is lending only an amount equal to its own excess reserves. How do we explain this? Why can the *banking system* lend by a multiple of its excess reserves, when *each individual bank* can only lend "dollar for dollar" with its excess reserves?

The answer is that *reserves lost by a single bank are not lost to the banking system as a whole.* The reserves lost by bank A are acquired by bank B. Those lost by B are gained by C. C loses to D, D to E, E to F, and so forth. Although reserves can be, and are, lost by *individual* banks in the banking system, there is no loss of reserves for the banking *system* as a whole.

An individual bank can safely lend only an amount equal to its excess reserves, but the commercial banking system can lend by a multiple of its excess reserves. This contrast, incidentally, is an illustration of why it is imperative that we keep the fallacy of composition (Chapter 1) firmly in mind. Commercial

TABLE 14-2   Expansion of the money supply by the commercial banking system

Bank	(1) Acquired reserves and deposits	(2) Required reserves (reserve ratio = .2)	(3) Excess reserves, (1) − (2)	(4) Amount bank can lend; new money created = (3)
Bank A	$100.00 (a_1)	$20.00	**$80.00**	$ 80.00 (a_2)
Bank B	80.00 (a_3, b_1)	16.00	64.00	64.00 (b_2)
Bank C	64.00 (b_3, c_1)	12.80	51.20	51.20 (c_2)
Bank D	51.20 (c_3, d_1)	10.24	40.96	40.96 (d_2)
Bank E	40.96	8.19	32.77	32.77
Bank F	32.77	6.55	26.22	26.22
Bank G	26.22	5.24	20.98	20.98
Bank H	20.98	4.20	16.78	16.78
Bank I	16.78	3.36	13.42	13.42
Bank J	13.42	2.68	10.74	10.74
Bank K	10.74	2.15	8.59	8.59
Bank L	8.59	1.72	6.87	6.87
Bank M	6.87	1.37	5.50	5.50
Bank N	5.50	1.10	4.40	4.40
Other banks	21.97	4.40	17.57	17.57
Total amount of money created (sum of the amounts in column 4)				**$400.00**

banks *as a group* can create money by lending in a manner much different from that of the *individual banks* in that group.

The Monetary Multiplier

The banking system magnifies any original excess reserves into a larger amount of newly created demand-deposit money. The *demand-deposit multiplier,* or **monetary multiplier,** is similar in concept to the spending-income multiplier in Chapter 10. That multiplier exists because the expenditures of one household are received as income by another; it magnifies a change in initial spending into a larger change in GDP. The spending-income multiplier is the reciprocal of the MPS (the leakage into saving which occurs at each round of spending).

In contrast, the monetary multiplier exists because the reserves and deposits lost by one bank are received by another bank. It magnifies excess reserves into a larger creation of demand-deposit money. The monetary multiplier m is the reciprocal of the required reserve ratio R (the leakage into required reserves which occurs at each step in the lending process). In short,

$$\text{Monetary multiplier} = \frac{1}{\text{required reserve ratio}}$$

or, using symbols,

$$m = \frac{1}{R}$$

In this formula, m represents the maximum amount of new demand-deposit money which can be created by a *single dollar* of excess reserves, given the value of R. By multiplying the excess reserves E by m, we can find the maximum amount of new demand-deposit money, D, which can be created by the banking system. That is,

$$\text{Maximum demand-deposit creation} = \text{excess reserves} \times \text{monetary multiplier}$$

or, more simply,

$$D = E \times m$$

In our example in Table 14-2, R is .20 so m is 5 (= 1/.20). Then

$$D = \$400 = \$80 \times 5$$

Higher reserve ratios mean lower monetary multipliers and therefore less creation of new deposit

money via loans; smaller reserve ratios mean higher monetary multipliers and thus more creation of new deposit money via loans. With a high reserve ratio, say, 50 percent, the monetary multiplier would be 2 (= 1/.5), and in our example the banking system could create only $160 (= $80 of excess reserves × 2) of new deposit money. With a low reserve ratio, say, 5 percent, the monetary multiplier would be 20 (= 1/.05), and the banking system could create $1600 (= $80 of excess reserves × 20) of new deposit money. Again you should note similarities with the spending-income multiplier, in which higher MPSs mean lower multipliers and lower MPSs mean higher multipliers. Also, like the spending-income multiplier, the monetary multiplier works in both directions. *The monetary multiplier applies to money destruction as well as to money creation.*

But keep in mind that, despite the similar rationales underlying the spending-income and monetary multipliers, the former has to do with changes in income and output and the latter with changes in the supply of money.

Figure 14-2 depicts the final outcome of our example of a multiple-deposit expansion of the money supply. The initial deposit of $100 of currency into

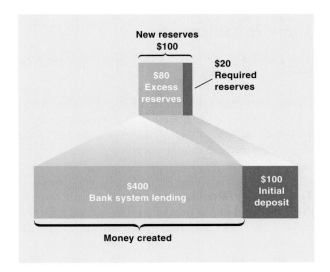

FIGURE 14-2 The outcome of the money expansion process A deposit of $100 of currency into a checking account creates an initial demand deposit of $100. If the reserve ratio is 20 percent, only $20 of reserves is legally required to support the $100 demand deposit. The $80 of excess reserves allows the banking system to create $400 of demand deposits through making loans. The $100 of reserves supports a total of $500 of money ($100 + $400).

the bank (lower right box) creates new reserves of an equal amount (upper box). With a 20 percent reserve ratio, however, only $20 of currency reserves is needed to "back up" this $100 demand deposit. The excess reserves of $80 permit the creation of $400 of new demand deposits via the making of loans, confirming a monetary multiplier of 5. The $100 of new reserves supports a total supply of money of $500, consisting of the $100 initial demand deposit plus $400 of demand deposits created through lending.

You might experiment with the following two brain teasers to test your understanding of multiple credit expansion by the banking system:

1. Rework the analysis in Table 14-2 (at least three or four steps of it) assuming the reserve ratio is 10 percent. What is the maximum amount of money the banking system can create upon acquiring $100 in new reserves and deposits? (The answer is not $800!)

2. Suppose a banking system is "loaned up" and faces a 20 percent reserve ratio. Explain how the banking system might have to *reduce* its outstanding loans by $400 when a $100 cash withdrawal from a demand-deposit account forces one bank to draw down its reserves by $100. **(Key Question 13)**

Some Modifications

There are complications which might modify the preciseness of our analysis.

Other Leakages Aside from the leakage of required reserves at each step of the lending process, two other leakages of money from commercial banks might dampen the money-creating potential of the banking system:

1. Currency Drains A borrower might request that part of his or her loan be paid in currency. Or the recipient of a check drawn by a borrower might ask the bank to redeem it partially or wholly in currency rather than add it to the recipient's account. If the person who borrowed the $80 from bank A in our illustration asked for $16 of it in cash and the remaining $64 as a demand deposit, bank B would later receive only $64 in new reserves (of which only $51.20 would be excess) rather than $80 (of which $64 was excess). This decline in excess reserves would reduce the lending potential of the banking system accordingly. In fact, if the first borrower had taken the en-

tire $80 in cash and if this currency remained in circulation, the multiple expansion process would have stopped then and there. But the convenience and safety of demand deposits make this unlikely.

2. Excess Reserves Our analysis of the commercial banking system's ability to expand the money supply by lending is based on the supposition that commercial banks are willing to meet precisely the legal reserve requirement. To the extent that bankers hold excess reserves, the overall credit expansion potential of the banking system will be reduced. For example, suppose bank A, upon receiving $100 in new cash, decided to add $25, rather than the legal minimum of $20, to its reserves. Then it would lend only $75, rather than $80, and the monetary multiplier would be diminished accordingly.[2] In fact, the amount of excess reserves which banks have held in recent years has been very minimal. The explanation is very simple: Excess reserves earn no interest income for a bank; loans and investments do. Hence, our assumption that a bank will lend an amount equal to its excess reserves is reasonable and generally accurate.

QUICK REVIEW 14-3

■ Whereas a single bank in a multibank system can safely lend (create money) by an amount equal to its excess reserves, the banking system can lend (create money) by a multiple of its excess reserves.

■ The monetary multiplier is the reciprocal of the required reserve ratio; it is the multiple by which the banking system can expand the money supply for each dollar of excess reserves.

■ Currency drains and a desire by banks to hold excess reserves may reduce the size of the monetary multiplier.

Need for Monetary Control

Our illustration of the banking system's ability to create money rests on the assumption that commercial banks are willing to create money by lending and that households and businesses are willing to borrow. In

---

[2]Specifically, in our $m = 1/R$ monetary multiplier, we now add to R, the required reserve ratio, the additional excess reserves which bankers choose to keep. For example, if banks want to hold additional excess reserves equal to 5 percent of any newly acquired demand deposits, then the denominator becomes .25 (equal to the .20 reserve ratio plus the .05 addition to excess reserves). The monetary multiplier is reduced from 5 to 1/.25, or 4.

The Bank Panics of 1930 to 1933

A series of bank panics in the early 1930s resulted in a multiple contraction of the money supply.

In the early months of the Great Depression, before there was deposit insurance, several financially weak banks became insolvent. As word spread that customers of these banks had lost their deposits, a general concern arose that something similar could happen at other banks. Depositors became frightened that their banks did not, in fact, still have all the money they had deposited. And, of course, in a fractional reserve banking system, that is precisely the reality. Acting on their fears, people en masse tried to withdraw currency—that is, "cash out" their accounts—from their banks. They wanted to get their money before it was all gone. This "run on the banks" caused many previously financially sound banks to declare bankruptcy. More than 9000 banks failed within 3 years.

The massive conversion of checkable deposits to currency during 1930 to 1933 reduced the nation's money supply. This might seem strange since a check written for "cash" reduces demand-deposit money and increases currency in the hands of the public by the same amount. So how does the money supply decline? Our discussion of the money-*creation* process provides the answer, but now the story becomes one of money *destruction*.

Suppose that people collectively cash out $10 billion from their checking accounts. As an immediate result, demand-deposit money declines by $10 billion, while currency held by the public increases by $10 billion. But here is the catch: Assuming a reserve ratio of 20 percent, the $10 billion of currency in the banks had been sup-

porting $50 billion of deposit money, the $10 billion of deposits plus $40 billion created through loans. The $10 billion withdrawal of currency forces banks to reduce loans (and thus demand-deposit money) by $40 billion to continue to meet their reserve requirement. In short, a $40 billion destruction of deposit money occurs. This is the scenario which occurred in the early years of the 1930s.

Accompanying this multiple contraction of demand deposits was the banks' "scramble for liquidity" to try to meet further withdrawals of currency. To obtain more currency, they sold many of their holdings of government securities to the public. You know from this chapter that a bank's sale of government securities to the public, like a reduction in loans, reduces the money supply. The public writes checks for the securities, reducing their demand deposits, and the bank uses the currency it obtains to meet the ongoing bank run. In short, the loss of reserves from the banking system, in conjunction with the scramble for security, reduced the amount of demand-deposit money by far more than the increase in currency in the hands of the public. Thus, the money supply collapsed.

In 1933, President Franklin Roosevelt ended the bank panics by declaring a "national bank holiday," which closed all national banks for 1 week and resulted in the federally insured deposit program. Meanwhile, the nation's money supply had plummeted by 25 percent, the largest such drop in U.S. history. This decline in the money supply contributed to the nation's worst and longest depression.

Today, a multiple contraction of the money supply on the 1930–1933 magnitude is unthinkable. FDIC insurance has kept individual bank failures from becoming general panics. Also, while the Fed stood idly by during the bank panics of 1930 to 1933, today it would take immediate and dramatic actions to maintain the banking system's reserves and the nation's money supply. These actions are the subject matter of Chapter 15.

reality the willingness of banks to lend on the basis of excess reserves varies cyclically, and therein lies the rationale for governmental control of the money supply to promote economic stability.

When prosperity reigns, banks will expand credit to the maximum of their ability. Loans are interest-earning assets, and in good economic times there is little fear of borrowers' defaulting. But, as you will find in Chapter 15, the money supply has an effect on aggregate demand. By lending and thereby creating money to the maximum of their ability during prosperity, commercial banks may contribute to excessive aggregate demand and therefore to inflation.

If recession appears on the economic horizon, bankers may hastily withdraw their invitations to borrow, seeking the safety of liquidity (excess reserves) even if it means sacrificing potential interest income. Bankers may fear large-scale withdrawal of deposits by a panicky public and simultaneously doubt the ability of borrowers to repay. It is not too surprising that during some years of the Great Depression of the 1930s, banks had excess reserves but lending was at a low ebb. The point is that during recession banks may decrease the money supply by cutting back on lending. This contraction of the money supply will restrain aggregate demand and intensify the recession. A rapid shrinkage of the money supply did indeed contribute to the Great Depression, as this chapter's Last Word indicates.

We thus conclude that profit-motivated bankers can be expected to vary the money supply in a way that reinforces cyclical fluctuations. For this reason the Federal Reserve System has at its disposal certain monetary tools to alter the money supply in a countercyclical, rather than procyclical, fashion. We turn to an analysis of these tools in Chapter 15.

CHAPTER SUMMARY

1. The operation of a commercial bank can be understood through its balance sheet, where assets equal liabilities plus net worth.

2. Modern banking systems are fractional reserve systems: only a fraction of deposits is backed by currency.

3. Commercial banks must keep required reserves on deposit in a Federal Reserve Bank or as vault cash. These required reserves are equal to a specified percentage of the commercial bank's demand-deposit liabilities. Excess reserves are equal to actual reserves minus required reserves.

4. Banks lose both reserves and demand deposits when checks are drawn against them.

5. Commercial banks create money—create demand deposits, or deposit money—when they make loans. The creation of checkable deposits by bank lending is the most important source of money in our economy. Money is destroyed when bank loans are repaid.

6. The ability of a single commercial bank to create money by lending depends on the size of its *excess* reserves. Generally speaking, a commercial bank can lend only an amount equal to the amount of its excess reserves. Money creation is thus limited because, in all likelihood, checks drawn by borrowers will be deposited in other banks, causing a loss of reserves and deposits to the lending bank equal to the amount it has loaned.

7. Rather than making loans, banks may decide to use excess reserves to buy bonds from the public. In doing so, banks merely credit the demand-deposit accounts of the bond sellers, thus creating demand-deposit money. Money vanishes when banks sell bonds to the public because bond buyers must draw down their demand-deposit balances to pay for the bonds.

8. Banks earn interest by making loans and purchasing bonds; they maintain liquidity by holding cash and excess reserves. Banks having temporary excess reserves often lend them overnight to banks which are short of required reserves. The interest rate paid on loans in this Federal funds market is called the Federal funds rate.

9. The commercial banking system as a whole can lend by a multiple of its excess reserves because the banking *system* cannot lose reserves, although individual banks can lose reserves to other banks in the system.

10. The multiple by which the banking system can lend on the basis of each dollar of excess reserves is the reciprocal of the reserve ratio. This multiple credit expansion process is reversible.

11. The fact that profit-seeking banks would alter the money supply in a procyclical direction underlies the need for the Federal Reserve System to control the money supply.

TERMS AND CONCEPTS

balance sheet	required reserves	actual reserves	Federal funds rate
fractional reserve system	reserve ratio	excess reserves	monetary multiplier
vault cash			

STUDY QUESTIONS

1. Why must a balance sheet always balance? What are the major assets and claims on a commercial bank's balance sheet?

2. KEY QUESTION Why are commercial banks required to have reserves? Explain why reserves are an asset to commercial banks but a liability to the Federal Reserve Banks. What are excess reserves? How do you calculate the amount of excess reserves held by a bank? What is the significance of excess reserves?

3. "Whenever currency is deposited in a commercial bank, cash goes out of circulation and, as a result, the supply of money is reduced." Do you agree? Explain why or why not.

4. KEY QUESTION "When a commercial bank makes loans, it creates money; when loans are repaid, money is destroyed." Explain.

5. Explain why a single commercial bank can safely lend only an amount equal to its excess reserves but the commercial banking system can lend by a multiple of its excess reserves. What is the monetary multiplier, and how does it relate to the reserve ratio?

6. Assume that Jones deposits $500 in currency into her demand-deposit account in First National Bank. A half-hour later Smith obtains a loan for $750 at this bank. By how much and in what direction has the money supply changed? Explain.

7. Suppose the National Bank of Commerce has excess reserves of $8000 and outstanding demand deposits of $150,000. If the reserve ratio is 20 percent, what is the size of the bank's actual reserves?

8. KEY QUESTION Suppose Continental Bank has the following simplified balance sheet and that the reserve ratio is 20 percent:

Assets				Liabilities and net worth			
		(1)	(2)			(1)	(2)
Reserves	$22,000	__	__	Demand			
Securities	38,000	__	__	deposits	$100,000	__	__
Loans	40,000	__	__				

  a. What is the maximum amount of new loans which this bank can make? Show in column 1 how the bank's balance sheet will appear after the bank has loaned this additional amount.
  b. By how much has the supply of money changed? Explain.

  c. How will the bank's balance sheet appear after checks drawn for the entire amount of the new loans have been cleared against the bank? Show the new balance sheet in column 2.
  d. Answer questions **(a)**, **(b)**, and **(c)** on the assumption that the reserve ratio is 15 percent.

9. Third National Bank has reserves of $20,000 and demand deposits of $100,000. The reserve ratio is 20 percent. Households deposit $5000 in currency into the bank which is added to reserves. How much excess reserves does the bank now have?

10. Suppose again that Third National Bank has reserves of $20,000 and demand deposits of $100,000. The reserve ratio is 20 percent. The bank now sells $5000 in securities to the Federal Reserve Bank in its district, receiving a $5000 increase in reserves in return. How much excess reserves does the bank now have? Why does your answer differ (yes, it does!) from the answer to question 9?

11. Suppose a bank discovers that its reserves will temporarily fall slightly short of those legally required. How might it remedy this situation through the Federal funds market? Now assume the bank finds that its reserves will be substantially and permanently deficient. What remedy is available to this bank? (Hint: Recall your answer to question 4.)

12. Suppose that Bob withdraws $100 of cash from his checking account at Security Bank and uses it to buy a camera from Joe, who deposits the $100 in his checking account in Serenity Bank. Assuming a reserve ratio of 10 percent and no initial excess reserves, determine the extent to which **(a)** Security Bank must reduce its loans and demand deposits because of the cash withdrawal and **(b)** Serenity Bank can safely increase its loans and demand deposits because of the cash deposit. Have the cash withdrawal and deposit changed the money supply?

13. KEY QUESTION Suppose the simplified consolidated balance sheet shown below is for the entire commercial banking system. All figures are in billions. The reserve ratio is 25 percent.

Assets			Liabilities and net worth		
		(1)			(1)
Reserves	$ 52	___	Demand		
Securities	48	___	deposits	$200	___
Loans	100	___			

a. How much excess reserves does the commercial banking system have? What is the maximum amount the banking system might lend? Show in column 1 how the consolidated balance sheet would look after this amount has been lent. What is the monetary multiplier?

b. Answer the questions in (a) assuming the reserve ratio is 20 percent. Explain the resulting difference in the lending ability of the commercial banking system.

14. What are banking "leakages"? How might they affect the money-creating potential of the banking system?

15. Explain why there is a need for the Federal Reserve System to control the money supply.

16. (Last Word) Explain how the bank panics of 1930 to 1933 produced a decline in the nation's money supply. Why are such panics highly unlikely today?

17. WEB-BASED QUESTION How's Your Own Bank Doing? The FDIC (Federal Deposit Insurance Corporation) http://192.147.69.47/drs/id20/ *Institution Directory (ID)* system provides demographic data and financial profiles for each FDIC-insured institution. The *ID* system can be used to identify and list FDIC-insured institutions and compare individual bank performance and condition ratios with statistics published in the *Quarterly Banking Profile* http://www.fdic.gov/databank/qbp/homepage.html. Look up your own bank's financial statement and see how it has performed over the past year in the following categories: net worth, total assets, total liabilities, short-term liabilities, net income, number of employees, and number of branches. Compare your bank's performance with the banking industry's performance found in the *Quarterly Banking Profile*.

18. WEB-BASED QUESTION Assets and Liabilities of All Commercial Banks in the United States The Federal Reserve http://www.bog.frb.fed.us/releases/h8/about.htm provides an aggregate balance sheet for commercial banks in the United States and for several subgroups of banks: domestically chartered, large domestic, small domestic, and foreign-related. Balance sheet detail is limited mainly to bank loans and investments; estimates of the major deposit and nondeposit liability terms are povided for each bank group. The release is published weekly. Check the current release and look at Loans and leases in bank credit. Rank the following components with regard to size: commercial and industrial, real estate, consumer, security, and other. Over the past 12 months, which has increased by the largest percentage? By absolute amounts? Has the net worth (assets less liabilities) of all commercial banks in the United States increased during the past year?

15

Monetary Policy

In Chapter 13 you saw that the supply of money and the demand for money determine the economy's equilibrium interest rate. In Chapter 14 you learned that the banking system can create deposit money, thus greatly affecting the supply of money. In this chapter you will see how the Fed can change the supply of money and thus change the equilibrium interest rate. You will also discover the reasons why the Fed might want to do so.

The Fed's variety of techniques for changing the supply of money, and thus interest rates, are reflected in headlines such as "Bank Reserve Requirement Lowered—First Change since 1983," "Fed Aggressively Selling Bonds," and "Fed Increases Discount Rate to 4 Percent." What stories are these and similar headlines telling?

In this chapter, we first discuss the objectives of *monetary policy* and the roles of participating institutions. Next, we look at the combined balance sheet of the Federal Reserve Banks; it is through these central banks that monetary policy is implemented. Third, we analyze in detail the techniques of monetary control, asking what the key instruments of monetary control are and how they work. Fourth, we examine the cause-and-effect chain of monetary policy and evaluate the effectiveness of monetary policy. We end the chapter with a brief recapitulation of mainstream macroeconomic theory and policy.

THE GOAL OF MONETARY POLICY

Recall from Chapter 13 that the Board of Governors of the Federal Reserve System (the "Fed") is responsible for supervising and controlling the operation of the U.S. banking system. (For the names of central banks in various nations, see Global Perspective 15-1.) This Board formulates basic policies which the banking system follows. Because the Board of Governors is a public body, its decisions are made in what it perceives to be the public interest. The 12 Federal Reserve Banks—the U.S. central banks—implement the policy decisions of the Board. As quasipublic banks, the Federal Reserve Banks are not guided by the profit motive but, rather, pursue measures the Board of Governors recommends.

However, to say that the Board follows policies which "promote the public interest" is not enough. We must pinpoint the goal of monetary policy. *The fundamental objective of* **monetary policy** *is to assist the economy in achieving a full-employment, noninflationary level of total output.* Monetary policy consists of altering the economy's money supply to stabilize aggregate output, employment, and the price level. It en-

tails increasing the money supply during a recession to stimulate spending and restricting it during inflation to constrain spending.

The Federal Reserve Board alters the amount of the nation's money supply by manipulating the size of excess reserves held by commercial banks. Excess reserves, you will recall, are critical to the money-creating ability of the banking system. Once you see how the Federal Reserve controls excess reserves and the money supply, we will explain how changes in the stock of money affect interest rates, aggregate demand, and the economy.

CONSOLIDATED BALANCE SHEET OF THE FEDERAL RESERVE BANKS

Because U.S. monetary policy is implemented by the Federal Reserve Banks, we need to consider the balance sheet of these banks. Some of the Fed's assets and liabilities differ from those found on the balance sheet of a commercial bank. Table 15-1 is a simplified consolidated balance sheet showing the pertinent assets and liabilities of the 12 Federal Reserve Banks as of September 30, 1997.

Assets

There are two Fed assets we need to consider.

Securities The securities shown in the table are government bonds which Federal Reserve Banks have purchased. These bonds consist largely of Treasury bills (short-term securities) and Treasury bonds (long-term securities) issued by the U.S. government to finance past and present budget deficits. These securities are part of the public debt—money borrowed and

TABLE 15-1 Twelve Federal Reserve Banks' consolidated balance sheet, September 30, 1997 (in millions)

Assets		Liabilities and net worth	
Securities	$424,518	Reserves of commercial banks	$ 21,791
Loans to commercial banks	313	Treasury deposits	7,692
All other assets	63,257	Federal Reserve Notes (outstanding)	433,581
		All other liabilities and net worth	25,024
Total	$488,088	Total	$488,088

Source: Federal Reserve Bulletin, December 1997.

owed by the Federal government. Some of the bills and bonds may have been purchased directly from the Treasury, but most are bought in the open market from commercial banks or the public. Although these bonds are an important source of income to the Federal Reserve Banks, they are not bought and sold purposely for income. Rather, they are bought and sold primarily to influence the size of commercial bank reserves and, therefore, the banks' ability to create money by lending.

Loans to Commercial Banks   For reasons we will discuss soon, commercial banks occasionally borrow from Federal Reserve Banks. The IOUs which commercial banks give to these "bankers' banks" in return for loans are listed as loans to commercial banks. From the Federal Reserve Banks' point of view, these IOUs are assets—they are claims against commercial banks which have borrowed from them. To commercial banks, these IOUs are liabilities. By borrowing in this way, commercial banks obtain increases in their reserves in exchange for IOUs.

Liabilities

On the liability side we find three items.

Reserves of Commercial Banks   You are familiar with this account. It is an asset from the viewpoint of member banks but a liability to Federal Reserve Banks.

Treasury Deposits   Just as businesses and private individuals find it convenient and desirable to pay their obligations by check, so does the United States Treasury. It keeps deposits in the Federal Reserve Banks and draws checks on them to pay its obligations. To the Treasury such deposits are assets; to the Federal Reserve Banks they are liabilities. The Treasury creates and replenishes these deposits by depositing tax receipts and money borrowed from the public or the banks through the sale of bonds.

Federal Reserve Notes Outstanding   The paper money supply in the United States consists of Federal Reserve Notes issued by the Federal Reserve Banks. When it is in circulation, this paper money constitutes claims against assets of Federal Reserve Banks and is thus treated by them as a liability. Just as your own IOU is neither an asset nor a liability to you when it is in your own possession, so Federal Reserve

Notes resting in the vaults of Federal Reserve Banks are neither an asset nor a liability. Only notes in circulation (outstanding) are liabilities to the bankers' banks. These notes come into circulation through commercial banks and are not part of the money supply until they are in the hands of the public.

TOOLS OF MONETARY POLICY

With this cursory look at the Federal Reserve Banks' balance sheet, we can now explore how the Board of Governors of the Federal Reserve System can influence the money-creating abilities of the commercial banking system. The Board can use three instruments of monetary control to influence commercial bank reserves:

1. Open-market operations
2. The reserve ratio
3. The discount rate

Open-Market Operations

Open-market operations are the most important means the Fed has to control the money supply. **Open-market operations** refers to the *buying and selling of government bonds (securities) by the Federal Reserve Banks in the open market*—that is, the buying of bonds from, or the selling of bonds to, commercial banks and the general public.

Buying Securities   Suppose the Board of Governors orders the Federal Reserve Banks to buy government bonds in the open market. The bonds can be purchased from commercial banks or the public. In both cases the overall effect is the same—commercial bank reserves are increased.

From Commercial Banks   When Federal Reserve Banks buy government bonds *from commercial banks,*

(a) Commercial banks give up part of their holdings of securities to the Federal Reserve Banks.

(b) The Federal Reserve Banks pay for these securities by increasing the reserves of commercial banks by the amount of the purchase.

A commercial bank may pay for a bond bought from a private individual by increasing the seller's demand deposit; similarly, the bankers' bank may pay for bonds bought from commercial banks by increasing the banks' reserves. The transaction would change the consolidated balance sheets of the commercial banks and the Federal Reserve Banks as shown below.

The upward arrow shows that securities have moved from the commercial banks to the Federal Reserve Banks. Therefore, we write "− Securities" (minus securities) in the asset column of the balance sheet of the commercial banks. For the same reason, we write " + Securities" in the asset column of the balance sheet of the Federal Reserve Banks.

The downward arrow indicates that the Federal Reserve Banks have provided reserves to the commercial banks. We therefore write " + Reserves" in the asset column of the balance sheet for the commercial banks. The plus sign in the liability column of the balance sheet of the Federal Reserve Banks indicates that commercial bank reserves have increased; they are a liability to the Federal Reserve Banks.

The important aspect of this transaction is that, when Federal Reserve Banks purchase securities from commercial banks, the reserves—and therefore the lending ability—of the commercial banks are increased.

From the Public If Federal Reserve Banks purchase securities *from the general public*, the effect on commercial bank reserves is much the same. Suppose the Grisley Meat Packing Company has negotiable government bonds which it sells in the open market to the Federal Reserve Banks. The transaction goes like this:

(a) Grisley gives up securities to the Federal Reserve Banks and gets in payment a check drawn by the Federal Reserve Banks on themselves.

(b) Grisley promptly deposits this check in its account with its Wahoo bank.

(c) The Wahoo bank collects this check against the Federal Reserve Banks by sending it to a Federal Reserve Bank for collection. As a result, the Wahoo bank receives an increase in its reserves.

Balance sheet changes are as follows:

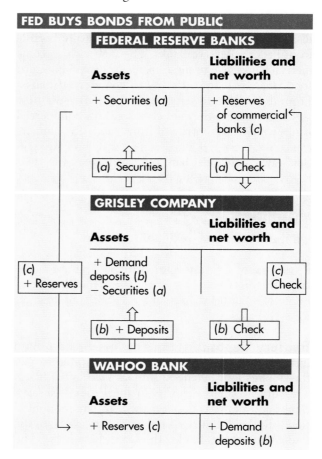

We need to understand two aspects of this transaction.

1. As with Federal Reserve purchases of securities directly from commercial banks, the reserves and lending ability of the commercial banking system have been increased. This is indicated by the " + Reserves," showing an increase in assets of the Wahoo bank.

2. The supply of money is directly increased by the central banks' purchase of government bonds (aside from any expansion of the money supply which may occur from the increase in commercial bank reserves). This direct increase in the money supply has taken the form of an increased amount of checking account money in the economy, as a result of Grisley's deposit; thus the "+ Demand deposits" in the Wahoo bank's balance sheet. Because these demand deposits are an asset as viewed by Grisley, demand deposits have increased (plus sign) on Grisley's balance sheet.

There is a slight difference between the Federal Reserve Banks' purchases of securities from the commercial banking system and those from the public. If we assume all commercial banks are "loaned up" initially, Federal Reserve bond purchases *from commercial banks* increase actual reserves and excess reserves of commercial banks by the entire amount of the bond purchases. As shown in the left panel in Figure 15-1, a $1000 bond purchase from a commercial bank increases both the actual and excess reserves of the commercial bank by $1000.

In contrast, Federal Reserve Bank purchases of bonds *from the public* increase actual reserves but also increase demand deposits. Thus, a $1000 bond pur-

chase from the public would increase demand deposits and hence the actual reserves of the "loaned up" banking system by $1000. But with a 20 percent reserve ratio applied to the demand deposit, the excess reserves of the banking system would only be $800.

However, in both transactions the result is the same: *When Federal Reserve Banks buy securities in the open market, commercial banks' reserves are increased.* When the banks lend out their excess reserves, the nation's money supply will rise. Observe in Figure 15-1 that a $1000 purchase of bonds by the Federal Reserve results in $5000 of additional money, regardless of whether the purchase was made from commercial banks or from the general public.

Selling Securities You should now suspect that Federal Reserve Bank sales of government bonds reduce commercial bank reserves. Let's see why.

To Commercial Banks Suppose the Federal Reserve Banks sell securities in the open market to *commercial banks:*

(a) Federal Reserve Banks give up securities which the commercial banks acquire.

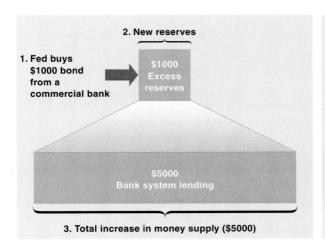
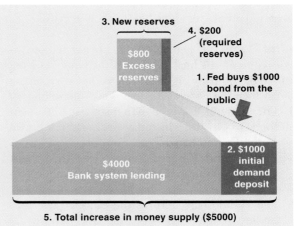

FIGURE 15-1 The Federal Reserve's purchase of bonds and the expansion of the money supply Assuming all banks are "loaned up" initially, a Federal Reserve purchase of a $1000 bond from either a commercial bank or the public can increase the money supply by $5000 when the reserve ratio is 20 percent. In the left panel of the diagram, the purchase of a $1000 bond from a commercial bank creates $1000 of excess reserves which support a $5000 expansion of demand deposits through loans. In the right panel, the purchase of a $1000 bond from the public creates a $1000 demand deposit but only $800 of excess reserves, because $200 of reserves is required to "back up" the $1000 new demand deposit. The commercial banks can therefore expand the money supply by only $4000 by making loans. This $4000 of checking account money *plus* the new demand deposit of $1000 equals $5000 of new money.

(b) Commercial banks pay for these securities by drawing checks against their deposits—that is, against their reserves—in Federal Reserve Banks. The Fed collects these checks by reducing the commercial banks' reserves accordingly.

The balance sheet changes appear as follows:

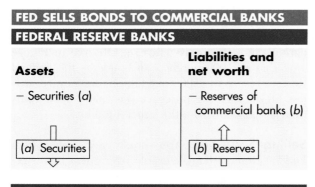

The reduction in commercial bank reserves is indicated by the minus signs before these entries.

To the Public   If Federal Reserve Banks sell securities *to the public*, the final outcome is the same. Let's put the Grisley company on the buying end of government bonds which the Federal Reserve Banks are selling:

(a) The Federal Reserve Bank sells government bonds to Grisley, which pays with a check drawn on the Wahoo bank.

(b) The Federal Reserve Banks clear this check against the Wahoo bank by reducing Wahoo's reserves.

(c) The Wahoo bank returns the canceled check to Grisley, reducing Grisley's demand deposit accordingly.

The balance sheets change as shown in the right text column.

Federal Reserve bond sales of $1000 to the commercial banking system reduce the system's actual and excess reserves by $1000. But a $1000 bond sale to the public reduces excess reserves by $800 because the public's demand-deposit money is also reduced by $1000 by the sale. Since the commercial banking system's outstanding demand deposits are reduced by $1000, banks need keep $200 less in reserves.

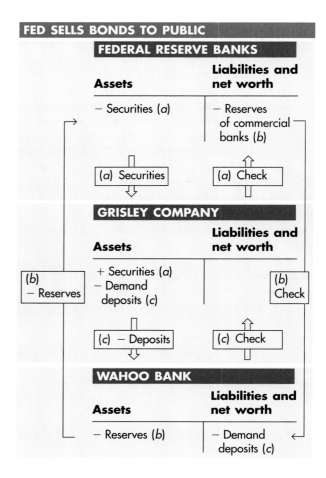

Whether the Fed sells bonds to the public or to commercial banks, the result is the same: *When Federal Reserve Banks sell securities in the open market, commercial bank reserves are reduced.* If all excess reserves are already lent out, this decline in commercial bank reserves produces a decline in the nation's money supply. In our example, a $1000 sale of government securities results in a $5000 decline in the money supply whether the sale is made to commercial banks or to the general public. You can verify this by reexamining Figure 15-1 and tracing the effects of a *sale* of a $1000 bond by the Fed either to commercial banks or to the public.

What makes commercial banks and the public willing to sell government securities to, or buy them from, Federal Reserve Banks? The answer lies in the price of bonds and their interest rates. We know from Chapter 13 that bond prices and interest rates are inversely related. When the Fed buys government bonds, the demand for them increases. Government bond prices rise and their interest rates decline. The higher bond prices and their lower interest rates prompt banks, securities firms, and individual holders of government bonds to sell them to the Federal Reserve Banks.

When the Fed sells government bonds, the additional supply of bonds in the bond market lowers bond prices and raises their interest rates, making government bonds attractive purchases for banks and the public.

The Reserve Ratio

The Fed's Board of Governors can also manipulate the **reserve ratio** to influence the ability of commercial banks to lend. The following example shows how: Suppose a commercial bank's balance sheet shows that reserves are $5000 and demand deposits $20,000. If the legal reserve ratio is 20 percent (row 2, Table 15-2), the bank's *required* reserves are $4000. Since *actual* reserves are $5000, the *excess* reserves of this bank are $1000. On the basis of $1000 of excess reserves, this single bank can lend $1000; however, the banking system as a whole can create a maximum of $5000 in new checking account money by lending (column 7).

Raising the Reserve Ratio Now, what if the Board of Governors raised the reserve ratio from 20 to 25 percent? (See row 3.) Required reserves would jump from $4000 to $5000, shrinking excess reserves from $1000 to zero. *Raising the reserve ratio increases the amount of required reserves banks must keep. Either banks lose excess reserves, diminishing their ability to create money*

by lending, or they find their reserves deficient and are forced to contract checkable deposits and therefore the money supply. In the example in Table 15-2, excess reserves are transformed into required reserves, and the money-creating potential of our *single bank* is reduced from $1000 to zero (column 6). Moreover, the *banking system's* money-creating capacity declines from $5000 to zero (column 7).

What if the Board of Governors increases the reserve requirement to 30 percent? (see row 4.) The commercial bank would face the prospect of failing to meet this requirement. To protect itself against such an eventuality, the bank would be forced to lower its demand deposits and at the same time increase its reserves. To reduce its demand deposits, the bank could let outstanding loans mature and be repaid without extending new credit. To increase reserves, the bank might sell some of its bonds, adding the proceeds to its reserves. Both actions would reduce the supply of money (if unclear on this, see Chapter 14, transactions 6 and 8).

Lowering the Reserve Ratio What would happen if the Board of Governors lowered the reserve ratio from the original 20 to 10 percent? (See row 1.) In this case, required reserves would decline from $4000 to $2000, and excess reserves would jump from $1000 to $3000. The single bank's lending (money-creating) ability would increase from $1000 to $3000 (column 6), and the banking system's money-creating potential would expand from $5000 to $30,000 (column 7). *Lowering the reserve ratio changes required reserves to excess reserves and enhances the ability of banks to create new money by lending.*

TABLE 15-2 The effects of changes in the reserve ratio on the lending ability of commercial banks

(1) Reserve ratio, %	(2) Demand deposits	(3) Actual reserves	(4) Required reserves	(5) Excess reserves, (3) – (4)	(6) Money-creating potential of single bank, = (5)	(7) Money-creating potential of banking system
(1) 10	$20,000	$5000	$2000	$ 3000	$ 3000	$30,000
(2) 20	20,000	5000	4000	1000	1000	5,000
(3) 25	20,000	5000	5000	0	0	0
(4) 30	20,000	5000	6000	– 1000	– 1000	– 3,333

From the examples in Table 15-2 we can see that a change in the reserve ratio affects the money-creating ability of the *banking system* in two ways:

1. It changes the amount of excess reserves.

2. It changes the size of the monetary multiplier.

For example, when the legal reserve ratio is raised from 10 to 20 percent, excess reserves are reduced from $3000 to $1000 and the demand-deposit multiplier is reduced from 10 to 5. The money-creating potential of the banking system declines from $30,000 (= $3000 × 10) to $5000 (= $1000 × 5).

Changing the reserve ratio is a powerful technique of monetary control, but it is used infrequently. The last such change was in 1992, when the Fed lowered the reserve ratio from 12 to 10 percent.

The Discount Rate

One of the functions of a central bank is to be a "lender of last resort." Occasionally, commercial banks have unexpected and immediate needs for additional funds. In such cases, each Federal Reserve Bank will make short-term loans to commercial banks in its district.

When a commercial bank borrows, it gives the Federal Reserve Bank a promissory note (IOU) drawn against itself and secured by acceptable collateral—typically U.S. government securities. Just as commercial banks charge interest on their loans, so too Federal Reserve Banks charge interest on loans they grant to commercial banks. The interest rate they charge is called the **discount rate.**

As a claim against the commercial bank, the borrowing bank's promissory note is an asset to the lending Federal Reserve Bank and appears on its balance sheet as "Loans to commercial banks." To the commercial bank the IOU is a liability, appearing as "Loans from the Federal Reserve Banks" on the commercial bank's balance sheet. [See entries (*a*) on the balance sheets in the right-hand column.]

In providing the loan, the Federal Reserve Bank *increases* the reserves of the borrowing commercial bank. Since no required reserves need be kept against loans from Federal Reserve Banks, *all* new reserves acquired by borrowing from Federal Reserve Banks are excess reserves. [These changes are reflected in entries (*b*) on the balance sheets.]

The main point is that *commercial bank borrowing from the Federal Reserve Banks increases the reserves of commercial banks, enhancing their ability to extend credit.*

COMMERCIAL BANK BORROWING FROM THE FED

FEDERAL RESERVE BANKS

Assets	Liabilities and net worth
+ Loans to commercial banks (*a*) ⇑ IOUs	+ Reserves of commercial banks (*b*) ⇓ + Reserves

COMMERCIAL BANKS

Assets	Liabilities and net worth
+ Reserves (*b*)	+ Loans from the Federal Reserve Banks (*a*)

The Fed's Board of Governors has the power to establish and change the discount rate at which commercial banks borrow from Federal Reserve Banks. From the commercial banks' point of view, the discount rate is a cost of acquiring reserves. When the discount rate is decreased, commercial banks are encouraged to obtain additional reserves by borrowing from Federal Reserve Banks. Commercial bank lending based on these new reserves then constitutes an increase in the money supply.

An increase in the discount rate discourages commercial banks from obtaining additional reserves through borrowing from the central banks. An increase in the discount rate therefore is used by the Fed to restrict the money supply. **(Key Question 2)**

Easy Money and Tight Money

Suppose the economy is faced with recession and unemployment. The Fed decides an increase in the supply of money is needed to stimulate aggregate demand so as to employ idle resources. To increase the supply of money, the Board of Governors must expand the excess reserves of commercial banks. What actions will bring this about?

1. *Buy securities*   The Board of Governors should order Federal Reserve Banks to buy securities in the open market. These bond purchases will be paid for by increases in commercial bank reserves.

2. *Reduce the reserve ratio*   The reserve ratio should be reduced, automatically changing required reserves into excess reserves and increasing the size of the monetary multiplier.

3. *Lower the discount rate* The discount rate should be lowered to induce commercial banks to add to their reserves by borrowing from Federal Reserve Banks.

This set of actions is called an **easy money policy.** Its purpose is to make bank loans cheaply and easily available to increase aggregate demand and employment.

Suppose, on the other hand, excessive spending is pushing the economy into an inflationary spiral. The Board of Governors should attempt to reduce aggregate demand by limiting or contracting the supply of money. The key to this goal lies in reducing the reserves of commercial banks. How is this done?

1. *Sell securities* Federal Reserve Banks should sell government bonds in the open market to reduce commercial bank reserves.

2. *Increase the reserve ratio* Increasing the reserve ratio will automatically strip commercial banks of excess reserves and decrease the monetary multiplier.

3. *Raise the discount rate* A boost in the discount rate will discourage commercial banks from building up their reserves through borrowing at Federal Reserve Banks.

This group of directives is called a **tight money policy.** The objective is to tighten the supply of money to reduce spending and control inflation.

Relative Importance

Of the three instruments of monetary control, open-market operations clearly are the most important.

The discount rate is less important for two interrelated reasons. First, the amount of commercial bank reserves obtained by borrowing from the central banks is typically very small. On average, only 2 or 3 percent of bank reserves are acquired this way. Indeed, open-market operations often lead commercial banks to borrow from Federal Reserve Banks. That is, if Fed sales of bonds to the public leave commercial banks temporarily short of reserves, commercial banks will be prompted to seek loans from the Federal Reserve Banks. Commercial bank borrowing from the Fed occurs largely *in response to open-market operations* and not so much in response to discount-rate changes.

Second, while changes in the reserve ratio and open-market operations are initiated by actions of the Fed, the discount rate depends on actions (borrowing) of commercial banks to be effective. For exam-

ple, if the Fed lowers the discount rate at a time when very few banks are inclined to borrow from Federal Reserve Banks, the lower rate will have little or no impact on bank reserves and the money supply.

Nevertheless, some economists say that a change in the discount rate has an "announcement effect"; it is a clear and explicit way for the Fed to communicate to the financial community and the general economy the intended direction of monetary policy. Other economists dismiss this claim, contending that changes in the discount rate are usually "passive"; the discount rate is changed mainly to keep it in line with other short-term interest rates, not to implement a policy change.

What about changes in reserve requirements? The Fed has used this instrument of monetary control only sparingly. Normally, it can accomplish its monetary goals through open-market operations, without resorting to changes in reserve requirements. The limited use of changes in the reserve ratio undoubtedly is related to the fact that reserves earn no interest. Raising or lowering reserve requirements can have substantial effects on bank profits.

But there are more positive reasons why open-market operations are the primary technique of monetary policy. This mechanism of monetary control has the advantage of flexibility—government securities can be purchased or sold in large or small amounts—and the impact on bank reserves is prompt. Yet, compared with reserve-requirement changes, open-market operations work subtly and less directly. Furthermore, there is no question about the ability of the Federal Reserve Banks to affect commercial bank reserves through bond sales and purchases. A glance at the consolidated balance sheet for the Federal Reserve Banks (Table 15-1) reveals very large holdings of government bonds ($425 billion), the sales of which could theoretically reduce commercial bank reserves from $22 billion to zero.

QUICK REVIEW 15-1

■ The objective of monetary policy is to help the economy achieve a full-employment, noninflationary level of domestic output.

■ The Fed has three main methods of monetary control, each of which works by changing the amount of excess reserves in the banking system:

a. Conducting open-market operations (the Fed's buying and selling of government bonds to the banks and the public)

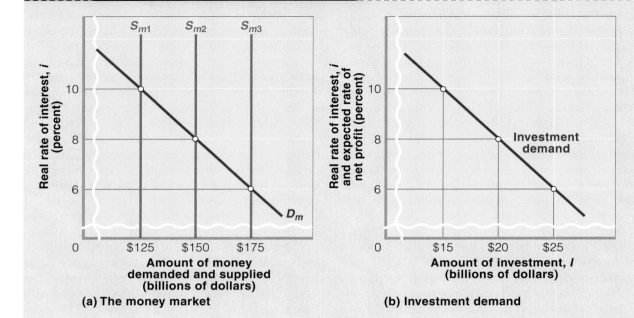

(a) The money market

(b) Investment demand

b. Changing the reserve ratio (the percentage of commercial bank deposit liabilities required as reserves)
c. Changing the discount rate (the interest rate the Federal Reserve Banks charge on loans to banks and thrifts)

■ Open-market operations are the Fed's most important monetary control mechanism.

MONETARY POLICY, REAL GDP, AND THE PRICE LEVEL

Thus far, we have explained only how the Fed can change the money supply. We next need to link up the

money supply, the interest rate, investment spending, and aggregate demand to see how monetary policy affects the economy. How does monetary policy work?

Cause-Effect Chain

The three diagrams in **Figure 15-2 (Key Graph)** will help you understand how monetary policy works toward achieving the goal of full employment and price stability.

Money Market Figure 15-2a represents the money market, in which the demand curve for money and

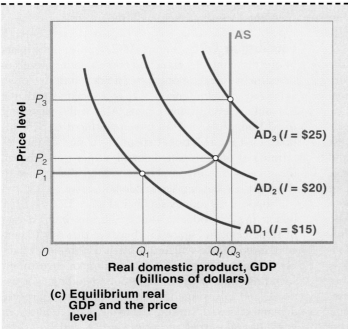

**(c) Equilibrium real
GDP and the price
level**

**FIGURE 15-2 Monetary policy and equilib-
rium GDP** An easy money policy which shifts the
money supply curve rightward from S_{m1} to S_{m2} lowers
the interest rate from 10 to 8 percent. As a result, investment spending increases from $15 billion to $20
billion, shifting the aggregate demand curve rightward
from AD_1 to AD_2. Real output rises from the recessionary level Q_1 to the full-employment level Q_f. A tight
money policy which shifts the money supply curve leftward from S_{m3} to S_{m2} increases the interest rate from 6
to 8 percent. Investment spending thus falls from $25
billion to $20 billion and the aggregate demand curve
shifts leftward from AD_3 to AD_2, curtailing inflation.

**3. The Federal Reserve could increase the
money supply from S_{m1} to S_{m2} by:**
 a. increasing the discount rate.
 b. reducing taxes.
 c. buying government securities in the open market.
 d. increasing the reserve requirement.

**4. If the spending-income multiplier is 4 in the
economy depicted, an increase in the
money supply from $125 billion to $150
billion will:**

 a. shift the aggregate demand curve rightward by
$20 billion.
 b. increase real GDP by $25 billion.
 c. increase real GDP by $100 billion.
 d. shift the aggregate demand curve leftward by $5
billion.

Answers: 1. d; 2. c; 3. c; 4. a

the supply curve of money are brought together. Recall from Chapter 13 that the total demand for money is made up of the transactions and asset demands. The transactions demand is directly related to the nominal GDP. The asset demand is inversely related to the interest rate. The interest rate is the opportunity cost of holding money as an asset; the higher the cost, the smaller the amount of money the public wants to hold. The total demand for money D_m is thus inversely related to the interest rate, as is indicated in Figure 15-2a. Also, recall that an increase in nominal GDP will shift D_m to the right, and a decline in nominal GDP will shift D_m to the left.

We complete our graphical portrayal of the money market by showing three potential money supply curves, S_{m1}, S_{m2}, and S_{m3}. In each case the money supply is shown as a vertical line representing some fixed amount of money determined by the Fed's Board of Governors. While monetary policy (specifically, the supply of money) helps determine the interest rate, the interest rate does *not* determine the location of the money supply curve.

The equilibrium interest rate is the rate at which the amounts of money demanded and supplied are equal. With money demand D_m in Figure 15-2a, if the supply of money is $125 billion ($S_{m1}$), the equilibrium interest rate is 10 percent. With a money supply of $150 ($S_{m2}$), the interest rate is 8 percent; with a money supply of $175 billion ($S_{m3}$), it is 6 percent.

You know from Chapter 10 that the real, not the nominal, rate of interest is critical for investment decisions. So here we assume Figure 15-2a portrays real interest rates.

Investment These 10, 8, and 6 percent real interest rates are carried rightward to the investment demand curve in Figure 15-2b. This curve shows the inverse relationship between the interest rate—the cost of borrowing to invest—and the amount of investment spending. At the 10 percent interest rate it will be profitable for the nation's businesses to invest $15 billion; at 8 percent, $20 billion; at 6 percent, $25 billion.

The investment component of total spending is more likely to be affected by changes in the interest rate than is the consumer spending component. Of course, consumer purchases of automobiles, which depend heavily on installment credit, are sensitive to interest rates. But overall the interest rate is *not* a very crucial factor in determining how households divide their disposable incomes between consumption and saving.

The impact of changing interest rates on investment spending is great because of the large cost and long-term nature of capital purchases. Capital equipment, factory buildings, and warehouses are tremendously expensive. In absolute terms, interest charges on funds borrowed for these purchases are considerable.

Similarly, the interest cost on a house purchased on a long-term contract will be very large: A $\frac{1}{2}$ percentage point change in the interest rate could amount to thousands of dollars on the total cost of a home.

Also, changes in the interest rate may affect investment spending by changing the relative attractiveness of purchases of capital equipment versus purchases of bonds. In purchasing capital goods, the interest rate is the *cost* of borrowing the funds to make the investment. In purchasing bonds, the interest rate is the *return* on the financial investment. If the interest rate increases, the cost of buying capital goods increases while the return on bonds increases. Businesses are then more inclined to use business saving to buy securities than to buy equipment. Conversely, a drop in the interest rate makes purchases of capital goods relatively more attractive than bond ownership.

In brief, the impact of changing interest rates is mainly on investment (and, through that, on aggregate demand, output, employment, and the price level). Moreover, as Figure 15-2b shows, investment spending varies inversely with the interest rate.

Equilibrium GDP Figure 15-2c shows the impact of our three interest rates and corresponding levels of investment spending on aggregate demand. As noted, aggregate demand curve AD_1 is associated with the $15 billion level of investment, AD_2 with investment of $20 billion, and AD_3 with investment of $25 billion. That is, investment spending is one of the determinants of aggregate demand. Other things equal, the greater this investment spending, the farther to the right lies the aggregate demand curve.

Suppose the money supply in Figure 15-2a is $125 billion ($S_{m1}$), producing an equilibrium interest rate of 10 percent. In Figure 15-2b we see that this 10 percent interest rate will bring forth $15 billion of investment spending. This $15 billion of investment spending joins with consumption spending, net exports, and government spending to yield aggregate demand curve AD_1 in Figure 15-2c. The equilibrium levels of real output and prices are Q_1 and P_1, as determined by the intersection of AD_1 and the aggregate supply curve AS.

To test your understanding of these relationships, you should explain why each of the other two levels of money supply in Figure 15-2a results in a different interest rate, level of investment, aggregate demand curve, and equilibrium real output and price level.

Effects of an Easy Money Policy

We have assumed the money supply is $125 billion ($S_{m1}$) in Figure 15-2a. Because the resulting real output Q_1 in Figure 15-2c is far below the full employment output, Q_f, the economy must be experiencing substantial unemployment. The Fed therefore should institute an *easy money policy*.

To increase the money supply, the Federal Reserve Banks will take some combination of the following actions: (1) Buy government securities from banks and the public in the open market, (2) lower the legal reserve ratio, and (3) lower the discount rate. The result will be an increase in excess reserves in the commercial banking system. Because excess reserves are the basis on which commercial banks and thrifts can earn profit by lending and thereby expand the money supply, the nation's money supply likely will rise. An increase in the money supply will lower the interest rate, increasing investment, aggregate demand, and equilibrium GDP.

For example, an increase in the money supply from $125 billion to $150 billion ($S_{m1}$ to S_{m2}) will reduce the interest rate from 10 to 8 percent, as indicated in Figure 15-2a, and increase investment from $15 billion to $20 billion, as shown in Figure 15-2b. This $5 billion increase in investment spending will shift the aggregate demand curve rightward by more than the increase in investment because of the multiplier effect. If the economy's MPC is .75, the multiplier will be 4, meaning that the $5 billion increase in investment will shift the AD curve rightward by $20 billion (= 4 × $5) at each price level. Specifically, aggregate demand will shift from AD_1 to AD_2 as shown in Figure 15-2c. This rightward shift in the aggregate demand curve will increase GDP from Q_1 to the desired full-employment GDP of Q_f.

Column 1 in Table 15-3 summarizes the chain of events associated with an easy money policy.

Effects of a Tight Money Policy

Now let's assume the money supply and interest rate are $175 billion ($S_{m3}$) in Figure 15-2a. This results in an interest rate of 6 percent, investment spending of $25 billion, and aggregate demand AD_3. As you can see in Figure 15-2c, we have depicted severe demand-pull inflation. Aggregate demand AD_3 is excessive relative to the economy's full-employment level of real output Q_f. To reign in spending, the Fed will institute a *tight money policy*.

The Federal Reserve Board will direct Federal Reserve Banks to undertake some combination of the following actions: (1) Sell government securities to banks and the public in the open market, (2) increase the legal reserve ratio, and (3) increase the discount rate. Banks then will discover their reserves are below those required. They therefore will need to reduce their demand deposits by refraining from issuing new loans as old loans are paid back. This will shrink the money supply and increase the interest rate. The higher interest rate will discourage investment, decreasing aggregate demand and restraining demand-pull inflation.

If the Fed reduces the money supply from $175 billion to $150 billion ($S_{m3}$ to S_{m2} in Figure 15-2a), the interest rate will increase from 6 to 8 percent and investment will decline from $25 billion to $20 billion (Figure 15-2b). This $5 billion decrease in investment, bolstered by the multiplier process, will shift the aggregate demand curve leftward from AD_3 to AD_2. For example, if the MPC is .75, the multiplier

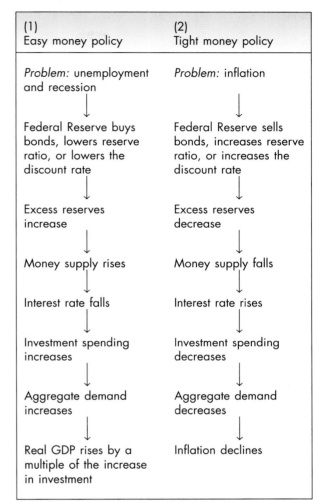

TABLE 15-3 **Monetary policies for recession and inflation**

(1) Easy money policy	(2) Tight money policy
Problem: unemployment and recession	*Problem:* inflation
↓	↓
Federal Reserve buys bonds, lowers reserve ratio, or lowers the discount rate	Federal Reserve sells bonds, increases reserve ratio, or increases the discount rate
↓	↓
Excess reserves increase	Excess reserves decrease
↓	↓
Money supply rises	Money supply falls
↓	↓
Interest rate falls	Interest rate rises
↓	↓
Investment spending increases	Investment spending decreases
↓	↓
Aggregate demand increases	Aggregate demand decreases
↓	↓
Real GDP rises by a multiple of the increase in investment	Inflation declines

will be 4 and the aggregate demand curve will shift leftward by $20 billion (= 4 × $5 billion of investment) at each price level. This leftward shift of the aggregate demand curve will eliminate the excessive spending and thus the demand-pull inflation. In the real world, of course, the goal will be to stop inflation—halt further increases in the price level—rather than to actually drive down the price level.

Column 2 in Table 15-3 summarizes the cause-effect chain of a tight money policy. **(Key Question 3)**

Refinements and Feedback

The components in Figure 15-2 let us (1) see some of the factors which determine the effectiveness of monetary policy and (2) note the existence of a "feed-back" or "circularity" problem which complicates monetary policy.

Policy Effectiveness

Figure 15-2 reveals the magnitudes by which an easy or tight money policy will change the interest rate, investment, and aggregate demand. These magnitudes are determined by the particular shapes of the money demand and investment demand curves. Pencil in other curves to see that *the steeper the* D_m *curve is, the larger the effect of any change in the money supply on the equilibrium rate of interest. Furthermore, any change in the interest rate will have a larger impact on investment—and hence on aggregate demand and GDP—the flatter the investment demand curve.* A specific change in money supply will be most effective when the demand curve for money is relatively steep and the investment demand curve is relatively flat.

A particular change in the quantity of money will be relatively ineffective when the money demand curve is flat and the investment demand curve is steep. In that case, neither the interest rate nor the level of investment will significantly change.

Feedback Effects

You may have sensed in Figure 15-2 a feedback problem which complicates monetary policy. The problem is this: By reading from Figure 15-2a to 15-2c we discover that the interest rate, working through the investment demand curve, is a determinant of the equilibrium GDP. Now we must recognize that causation also runs the other way. The level of GDP is a determinant of the equilibrium interest rate. This link comes about because the transactions component of the money demand curve is directly related to the level of nominal GDP.

How does this feedback from Figure 15-2c to 15-2a affect monetary policy? It means that the increase in the GDP which an easy money policy brings about will *increase* the demand for money, partially offsetting the interest-rate-reducing effect of the easy money policy. A tight money policy will reduce the nominal GDP. But this will *decrease* the demand for money and slow the interest-rate-increasing effect of the tight money policy. **(Key Question 4)**

Monetary Policy and Aggregate Supply

As is true of fiscal policy, the effect of a specific monetary policy depends on where the initial and subse-

quent equilibrium points are located on the aggregate supply curve. In Figure 15-2c, if the economy is initially at a leftward point in the horizontal range of AS, then an easy money policy which shifts the aggregate demand curve rightward from AD_1 to AD_2 will have a large impact on real GDP and have little or no impact on the price level.

But if the economy is already near, at, or beyond full employment, an increase in aggregate demand will have little or no effect on real output and employment. It will, however, substantially increase the price level. To see this, observe in Figure 15-2c that an increase in the aggregate demand curve from AD_2 to AD_3 would occur mainly in the vertical range of the aggregate supply curve. Needless to say, an easy money policy would be inappropriate when the economy is already achieving full employment. Figure 15-2c makes clear the reason why: It would be highly inflationary.

Similarly, a tight money policy is appropriate when the economy is fully employed and suffering demand-pull inflation but would be inappropriate when the economy is suffering substantial cyclical unemployment. In the latter case, the main impact of such a policy would be to reduce real output and worsen unemployment.

EFFECTIVENESS OF MONETARY POLICY

In this section we discuss some strengths and weaknesses of monetary policy as a stabilization tool and see how it has worked in the real world.

Strengths of Monetary Policy

Most economists regard monetary policy as an essential component of U.S. national stabilization policy, especially in view of the following features and evidence.

Speed and Flexibility

Compared with fiscal policy, monetary policy can be quickly altered. Recall that the application of fiscal policy may be delayed by congressional deliberations. In contrast, the Open Market Committee of the Federal Reserve System can buy or sell securities on a daily basis and thus affect the money supply and interest rates almost immediately.

Isolation from Political Pressure

Since members of the Fed's Board of Governors are appointed for 14-year terms, they are not often subject to lobbying and need not concern themselves with their popularity with voters. Thus the Board, more easily than Congress, can engage in politically unpopular policies which might be necessary for the long-term health of the economy. And, monetary policy itself is a more subtle and more politically conservative measure than fiscal policy. Changes in government spending directly affect the allocation of resources, and changes in taxes can have extensive political ramifications. By contrast, monetary policy works more subtly and therefore is more politically palatable.

Success During the 1980s and 1990s

The case for monetary policy has been greatly bolstered by its successful use during the 1980s and 1990s. A tight money policy helped bring the inflation rate down from 13.5 percent in 1980 to 3.2 percent 3 years later.

In the early 1990s, the Fed successfully used monetary policy to help move the economy out of the 1990–1991 recession. This success is noteworthy because the huge budget deficits of the 1980s and early 1990s had put fiscal policy "on the shelf." Congressional budgeting was mainly aimed at reducing the budget deficit, not at stimulating the economy. From a fiscal policy perspective, the tax hikes and government spending reductions during this period were mildly contractionary. But the Fed's easy money policy reduced interest rates on commercial loans from 10 percent in 1990 to 6 percent in 1993. Eventually, these low interest rates had their intended effects: Investment spending and interest-sensitive consumer spending rose rapidly, increasing the economy's real GDP.

The expansion of GDP which began in 1992 has continued, with the unemployment rate falling from 7.5 percent that year to less than 5 percent in 1997. To ensure against renewed inflation, in 1994 and 1995, and then again in early 1997, the Fed reduced reserves in the banking system to increase the interest rate and slow the growth of borrowing and spending. Thus far, the strategy has worked; inflation has been held in check throughout the expansion.

In view of Congress' focus on balancing the Federal budget and the Fed's recent policy successes in controlling inflation and promoting growth, for the time being *monetary policy has assumed the role of primary stabilization tool in the United States.*

Shortcomings and Problems

Despite its recent successes, monetary policy has certain limitations and it encounters real-world complications.

Less Control?

Some commentators suggest that changes in banking practices (some of which we discussed in Chapter 13) may reduce, or make less predictable, the Fed's control of the money supply. People can now move near-monies quickly from mutual funds and other financial investments to checking accounts, and vice versa. A particular monetary policy aimed at changing bank reserves might then be rendered less effective by movements of funds within the financial system. For example, people might respond to a tight money policy by quickly converting near-monies in their mutual fund accounts or other liquid financial investments to money in their checking accounts. Bank reserves would then not fall as intended by the Fed, the interest rate would not rise, and aggregate demand might not change. Also, banking and finance are increasingly global. Flows of funds to or from the United States might undermine or render inappropriate a particular domestic monetary policy. Finally, the prospects of E-cash and smart cards might complicate the measurement of money and make its issuance more difficult to control.

How legitimate are these concerns? These financial developments could make the Fed's task of monetary policy more difficult. But recent studies and Fed experience confirm that the traditional central bank tools of monetary policy remain effective in changing the money supply and interest rates.

Cyclical Asymmetry

If pursued vigorously, tight money can deplete commercial banking reserves to the point where banks are forced to reduce the volume of loans. This means a contraction of the money supply. But an easy money policy suffers from a "You can lead a horse to water, but you can't make it drink" problem. An easy money policy can ensure only that commercial banks have the excess reserves needed to make loans. It cannot guarantee that the banks will actually make the loans and thus that the supply of money will increase. If commercial banks, seeking liquidity, are unwilling to lend, the efforts of the Board of Governors will be to little avail. Similarly, the public can frustrate the intentions of the Fed by deciding not to borrow excess reserves. Additionally, the money the Fed injects into the system by buying bonds from the public could be used by the public to pay off existing loans.

In short, a potential *cyclical asymmetry* is at work. Monetary policy may be highly effective in slowing expansions and controlling inflation but largely ineffective in moving the economy from a recession or depression toward its full-employment output. This potential cyclical asymmetry, however, has *not* created major difficulties for monetary policy in recent eras. Since the Great Depression, higher excess reserves have generally translated into added lending and therefore into an increase in the money supply.

Changes in Velocity

Total expenditures may be regarded as the money supply *multiplied* by the **velocity of money**—the number of times per year the average dollar is spent on goods and services. If the money supply is $150 billion, total spending will be $600 billion if velocity is 4 but only $450 billion if velocity is 3.

Some economists feel that velocity changes in the opposite direction from the money supply, offsetting or frustrating policy-related changes in the money supply. During inflation, when the money supply is restrained by policy, velocity may increase. Conversely, when measures are taken to increase the money supply during recession, velocity may fall.

Velocity might behave this way because of the asset demand for money. An easy money policy, for example, means an increase in the supply of money relative to the demand for it and therefore a reduction in the interest rate (Figure 15-2a). But when the interest rate—the opportunity cost of holding money as an asset—is lower, the public will hold larger money balances. This means dollars will move from hand to hand—from households to businesses and back again—less rapidly. That is, the velocity of money will decline. A reverse sequence of events may cause a tight money policy to induce an increase in velocity.

The Investment Impact

Some economists doubt that monetary policy has as much impact on investment as Figure 15-2 implies. The combination of a relatively flat money demand curve and a relatively steep investment demand curve will mean that a particular change in the money supply will not cause a very large change in investment and, thus, not a large change in the equilibrium GDP.

Furthermore, the operation of monetary policy as portrayed in Figure 15-2 may be complicated, or temporarily offset, by unfavorable changes in the location of the investment demand curve. For example, a tight money policy designed to drive up interest rates may have little impact on investment spending if the investment demand curve in Figure 15-2b at the same time shifts to the right because of business optimism, technological progress, or expectations of higher future prices of capital. Monetary policy would have to raise interest rates extraordinarily high under these circumstances to be effective in reducing aggregate demand. Conversely, a severe recession may undermine business confidence, push the investment demand curve to the left, and frustrate an easy money policy.

Interest as Income

Monetary policy is based on the idea that expenditures on capital goods and interest-sensitive consumer goods are *inversely* related to interest rates. We must now acknowledge that businesses and households are also *recipients* of interest income. The size of such income and the spending which flows from it vary *directly* with the level of interest rates.

Suppose inflation is intensifying and the Fed raises interest rates to increase the cost of capital goods, housing, and automobiles. The complication is that higher interest rates on a wide range of financial instruments (for example, bonds, certificates of deposits, checking accounts) will increase the incomes and spending of the households and businesses that own them. Such added spending is obviously at odds with the Fed's effort to restrict aggregate demand. Here is an opposite example: In 1991 and 1992 the Fed repeatedly lowered interest rates to stimulate a sluggish economy. One possible reason this strategy took so long to become effective was that households that were receiving 8 or 10 percent on their bonds and CDs in the late 1980s received only 4 or 5 percent in the early 1990s. This diminished interest income undoubtedly lowered their spending.

The point is this: For those who pay interest as an *expense*, a rise in the interest rate reduces spending, while a decline in the interest rate increases spending. But for those who view interest as *income*, a rise in the interest rate increases spending, while a decline in the interest rate reduces spending. The change in spending by interest-income receivers *partly* offsets and weakens the change in spending by purchasers of capital goods, homes, and autos.

Recent Focus: The Federal Funds Rate

In the past few years, the Fed has communicated its changes in monetary policy by announcing changes in its targets for the *Federal funds rate.* (Recall that this rate is the interest rate which banks charge one another on overnight loans.) Statements by the Fed that it intends to increase the Federal funds rate suggest a "tighter" monetary policy is coming, while statements that it intends to reduce the Federal funds rate foretell an "easier" monetary policy. Interest rates, in general, rise and fall with the Federal funds rate. For example, in Figure 15-3 observe that changes in the **prime interest rate**—the interest rate banks charge their most creditworthy customers—generally track changes in the Federal funds rate.

The Fed does not *set* either the Federal funds rate or the prime rate; each is established by the interaction of lenders and borrowers. But because the Fed can change the supply of excess reserves in the banking system and then the money supply, it normally can obtain the market interest rates it desires. To increase the Federal funds interest rate, the Fed *sells* bonds in the open market. Such open-market operations reduce excess reserves in the banking system, lessening the excess reserves available for overnight loans in the Federal funds market. The decreased supply of excess reserves in that market increases the Federal funds interest rate. In addition, reduced excess reserves decrease the amount of bank lending and hence the amount of deposit money. We know that declines in the supply of money lead to increases in interest rates in general, including the prime interest rate.

In contrast, when the Fed wants to reduce the Federal funds rate, it *buys* bonds from banks and the public. As a result, the supply of reserves in the Federal funds market increases and the Federal funds rate declines. The money supply rises because the increased supply of excess reserves leads to greater lending and creation of deposit money. As a result, interest rates in general fall, including the prime interest rate. **(Key Question 5)**

QUICK REVIEW 15-2

■ The Fed is engaging in an easy money policy when it increases the money supply to reduce interest rates and increase investment spending and real GDP; it is engaging in a tight money policy when it reduces the money supply to increase interest rates and reduce investment spending and inflation.

■ The steeper the money demand curve and the flatter the investment demand curve, the larger the impact of a change in the money supply on the economy.

■ The main strengths of monetary policy are **(a)** speed and flexibility and **(b)** political acceptability; its main weaknesses are **(a)** potential reduced effectiveness during recession and **(b)** the possibility that changes in velocity will offset it.

■ The Fed communicates changes in monetary policy by announcing changes it targets for the federal funds interest rate.

■ In the past two decades, the Fed has quite successfully used alternate tight and loose money policies to stabilize the economy.

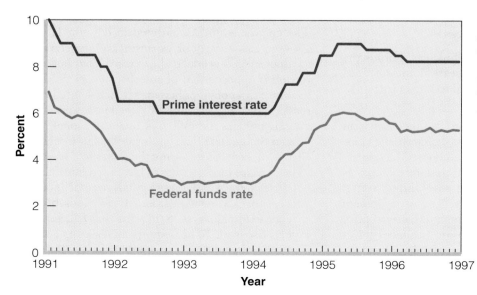

FIGURE 15-3 **The prime interest rate and the Federal funds rate in the United States, 1991–1997** Changes in the prime interest rate rise and fall with changes in the Federal funds rate.

For the Fed, Life Is a Metaphor

The popular press often describes the Federal Reserve Board and its chair (Alan Greenspan, 1987–present) in colorful terms.

The Federal Reserve Board leads a very dramatic life, or so it seems when one reads journalistic accounts of its activities. It loosens or tightens reins while riding herd on a rambunctious economy, goes to the rescue of an embattled dollar, tightens spigots on credit . . . you get the picture. For the Fed, life is a metaphor.

The Fed as Mechanic   The Fed sometimes must roll up its sleeves and adjust the economic machinery. The Fed spends a lot of time either tightening things, loosing things, or debating about whether to tighten or loosen.

Imagine a customer taking his car into Greenspan's Garage:

Normally calm, Skeezix Greenspan took one look at the car and started to sweat. This would be hard to fix—it was an economy car:

"What's the problem?" asked Greenspan.

"It's been running beautifully for over 6 years now," said the customer. "But recently it's been acting sluggish."

"These cars are tricky," said Greenspan.

"We can always loosen a few screws, as long as you don't mind the side effects."

"What side effects?" asked the customer.

"Nothing at first," said Greenspan. "We won't even know if the repairs have worked for at least a year. After that, either everything will be fine, or your car will accelerate wildly and go totally out of control."

"Just as long as it doesn't stall," said the customer. "I hate that."

The Fed as Warrior   The Fed must fight inflation. But can it wage a protracted war? There are only seven Fed governors, including Greenspan—not a big army:

Gen. Greenspan sat in the war room plotting strategy. You never knew where the enemy would strike next—producer prices, retail sales, factory payrolls, manufacturing inventories.

Suddenly, one of his staff officers burst into the room: "Straight from the Western European front, sir—the dollar is under attack by the major industrial nations."

Greenspan whirled around toward the big campaign map. "We've got to turn back this assault!" he said.

"Yes sir." The officer turned to go.

"Hold it!" Greenspan shouted. Suddenly, his mind reeled with conflicting data. A strong dollar was good for inflation, right? Yes, but it was bad for the trade deficit. Or was it the other way around? Attack? Retreat?

Monetary Policy and the International Economy

In Chapter 12 we noted that linkages among the economies of the world complicate domestic fiscal policy. These linkages also extend to monetary policy.

Net Export Effect   You saw in Chapter 12 that an expansionary U.S. fiscal policy (a budget deficit) increases the demand for money and boosts the domestic interest rate. The higher interest rate increases foreign financial investment in the United States, strengthening the demand for dollars in the foreign exchange market and boosting the international price of dollars. This dollar appreciation produces lower net exports and thus weakens the stimulus of the expansionary fiscal policy (review Figure 12-6d).

Will an easy money policy have a similar effect? The answer is no. As outlined in column 1, Table 15-4, an easy money or expansionary monetary policy does indeed produce a *net export effect*, but its direction is opposite that of an expansionary fiscal policy. An easy money policy in, say, the United States reduces the domestic interest rate. The lower interest rate discourages the inflow of financial capital to the United States. The demand for dollars in foreign exchange markets falls, causing the dollar to *depreciate* in value. It takes more dollars to buy, say, a Japanese yen or a French franc. All foreign goods become more expensive to U.S. residents, and U.S. goods become cheaper to foreigners. U.S. imports thus fall, and U.S. exports rise; so U.S. net exports increase. As a result, aggregate expenditures and equilibrium GDP expand in the United States.

Macroeconomic forces were closing in.

"Call out the Reserve!" he told the officer.

"Uh . . . we are the Reserve," the man answered.

The Fed as the Fall Guy Inflation isn't the only tough customer out there. The Fed must also withstand pressure from administration officials who are regularly described as "leaning heavily" on the Fed to ease up and relax. This always sounds vaguely threatening:

Alan Greenspan was walking down a deserted street late one night. Suddenly a couple of thugs wearing pin-stripes and wingtips cornered him in a dark alley.

"What do you want?" Greenspan asked.

"Just relax," said one.

"How can I relax?" asked Greenspan. "I'm in a dark alley talking to thugs."

"You know what we mean," said the other. "Ease up on the federal funds rate—or else."

"Or else what?" asked Greenspan.

"Don't make us spell it out. Let's just say that if anything unfortunate happens to the gross [domestic] product, I'm holding you personally responsible."

"Yeah," added the other. "A recession could get real painful."

The Fed as Cosmic Force The Fed may be a cosmic force. After all, it does satisfy the three major criteria—power, mystery, and a New York office. Some observers even believe the Fed can control the stock market, either by action, symbolic action, anticipated action, or non-action. But saner heads realize this is ridiculous—the market has always been controlled by sunspots.

I wish we could get rid of all these romantic ideas about the Federal Reserve. If you want to talk about the Fed, keep it simple. Just say the Fed is worried about the money. This is something we all can relate to.

Source: Paul Hellman, "Greenspan and the Feds: Captains Courageous," *Wall Street Journal*, Jan. 31, 1991, p. 18. Reprinted with permission of *The Wall Street Journal* © 1990 Dow Jones & Company, Inc. All rights reserved.

Conclusion: Unlike an expansionary fiscal policy which reduces net exports, an expansionary monetary policy increases net exports. *Exchange-rate changes which occur in response to interest-rate changes strengthen domestic monetary policy.* This conclusion holds equally for a tight money policy, which we know increases the domestic interest rate. To see how this happens, follow through the analysis in column 2, Table 15-4.

Macro Stability and the Trade Balance

Assume that, in addition to domestic macroeconomic stability, a widely held economic goal is that the United States should balance its exports and imports. That is, U.S. net exports should be zero. In simple terms, the United States wants to "pay its own way" in international trade by earning from its exports an amount of money sufficient to finance its imports.

Consider column 1 in Table 15-4 once again, but now suppose the United States initially has a very large balance-of-international-trade *deficit*, which means its imports substantially exceed its exports and so it is *not* paying its way in world trade. By following through the cause-effect chain in column 1, we find that an easy money policy lowers the international value of the dollar and thus U.S. exports increase and U.S. imports decline. This increase in net exports works to correct the assumed initial balance-of-trade deficit.

Conclusion: *The easy money policy which is appropriate for the alleviation of unemployment and sluggish growth is compatible with the goal of correcting a balance-of-trade deficit.* Similarly, if the initial problem was a U.S. trade surplus, a *tight* money policy would tend to resolve that surplus.

TABLE 15-4 **Monetary policy and the net export effect**

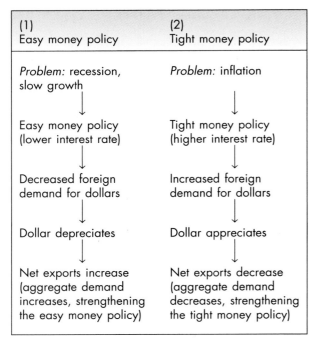

(1) Easy money policy	(2) Tight money policy
Problem: recession, slow growth	*Problem:* inflation
↓	↓
Easy money policy (lower interest rate)	Tight money policy (higher interest rate)
↓	↓
Decreased foreign demand for dollars	Increased foreign demand for dollars
↓	↓
Dollar depreciates	Dollar appreciates
↓	↓
Net exports increase (aggregate demand increases, strengthening the easy money policy)	Net exports decrease (aggregate demand decreases, strengthening the tight money policy)

Now consider column 2 in Table 15-4 and assume again that the United States has a large balance-of-trade deficit. In using a tight money policy to restrain inflation the Fed would cause net exports to decrease—U.S. exports would fall and imports would rise. This means a larger trade deficit.

Conclusion: *A tight money policy used to alleviate inflation conflicts with the goal of correcting a balance-of-trade deficit.* However, if the initial problem were a trade surplus, a tight money policy would help to resolve it.

Overall we find that an easy money policy alleviates a trade deficit and aggravates a trade surplus; a tight money policy alleviates a trade surplus and aggravates a trade deficit. The point is that certain combinations of circumstances create conflicts or trade-offs between the use of monetary policy to achieve domestic stability and the realization of a balance in the nation's international trade. **(Key Questions 6)**

THE "BIG PICTURE"

Figure 15-4 (Key Graph) on pages 326 and 327 brings together the analytical and policy aspects of macroeconomics discussed in this and the eight preceding chapters. This "big picture" shows how the many concepts and principles discussed relate to one another and how they constitute a coherent theory of the level of resource use in a market economy.

Study this diagram and you will see that the levels of output, employment, income, and prices all result from the interaction of aggregate supply and aggregate demand. In particular, note those items—shown in red—which constitute (or are strongly influenced by) public policy.

CHAPTER SUMMARY

1. Like fiscal policy, the goal of monetary policy is to assist the economy in achieving price stability, full employment, and economic growth.

2. In regard to monetary policy, the most important assets of the Federal Reserve Banks are securities and loans to commercial banks. The basic liabilities are the reserves of member banks, Treasury deposits, and Federal Reserve Notes.

3. The three instruments of monetary policy are **(a)** open-market operations, **(b)** the reserve ratio, and **(c)** the discount rate.

4. Monetary policy operates through a complex cause-effect chain: **(a)** Policy decisions affect commercial bank reserves; **(b)** changes in reserves affect the money supply; **(c)** changes in the money supply alter the interest rate;

(d) changes in the interest rate affect investment; **(e)** changes in investment affect aggregate demand; **(f)** changes in aggregate demand affect the equilibrium real GDP and the price level. Table 15-3 draws together all the basic notions relevant to the use of monetary policy.

5. The advantages of monetary policy include its flexibility and political acceptability. In the past two decades monetary policy has been used successfully both to reduce rapid inflation and to push the economy away from recession. Today, almost all economists view monetary policy as a significant stabilization tool.

6. Monetary policy has some limitations and potential problems: **(a)** Financial innovations and global considerations have made monetary policy more difficult to administer and its impact less certain. **(b)** Policy-instigated changes in the supply of money may be partially offset by changes in the velocity of money. **(c)** The impact of monetary policy will be lessened if the money demand curve is flat and the investment demand curve is steep. The investment demand curve may also shift, negating monetary policy. **(d)** Changes in interest rates resulting from monetary policy change the amount of interest income received by lenders, altering some people's spending in a way opposite to the intent of the monetary policy.

7. Recently, the Fed has communicated its changes in monetary policy via announcements concerning its targets for the Federal funds rate. When it deems it necessary, the Fed uses open-market operations to change this rate, which is the interest rate banks charge one another on overnight loans of excess reserves. Interest rates in general, including the prime interest rate, rise and fall with the Federal funds rate. The prime interest rate is the rate which banks charge to their most creditworthy loan customers.

8. The effect of an easy money policy on domestic GDP is strengthened by the increase in net exports which results from a lower domestic interest rate. Likewise, a tight money policy is strengthened by a decline in net exports. In some situations, there may be a tradeoff between the effect of monetary policy on the international value of a nation's currency (and thus on its trade balance) and the use of monetary policy to achieve domestic stability.

TERMS AND CONCEPTS

monetary policy	reserve ratio	easy money policy	velocity of money
open-market operations	discount rate	tight money policy	prime interest rate

STUDY QUESTIONS

1. Use commercial bank and Federal Reserve Bank balance sheets to demonstrate the impact of each of the following transactions on commercial bank reserves:
  a. Federal Reserve Banks purchase securities from private businesses and consumers.
  b. Commercial banks borrow from Federal Reserve Banks.
  c. The Fed reduces the reserve ratio.

2. KEY QUESTION In the table below and on page 328 you will find simplified consolidated balance sheets for the commercial banking system and the 12 Federal Reserve Banks. Use columns 1 through 3 to indicate how the balance sheets would read after each of transactions **a** to **c** is completed. Do not cumulate your answers; that is, analyze each transaction separately, starting in each case from the figures provided. All accounts are in billions of dollars.
  a. A decline in the discount rate prompts commercial banks to borrow an additional $1 billion from the Federal Reserve Banks. Show the new balance-sheet figures in column 1 of each table.
  b. The Federal Reserve Banks sell $3 billion in securities to members of the public, who pay for the bonds with checks. Show the new balance-sheet figures in column 2 of each table.

Consolidated balance sheet: all commercial banks

	(1)	(2)	(3)
Assets:			
Reserves ....$ 33	_____	_____	_____
Securities 60	_____	_____	_____
Loans.................................. 60	_____	_____	_____
Liabilities and net worth:			
Demand deposits..................$150	_____	_____	_____
Loans from the Federal Reserve Banks................... 3	_____	_____	_____

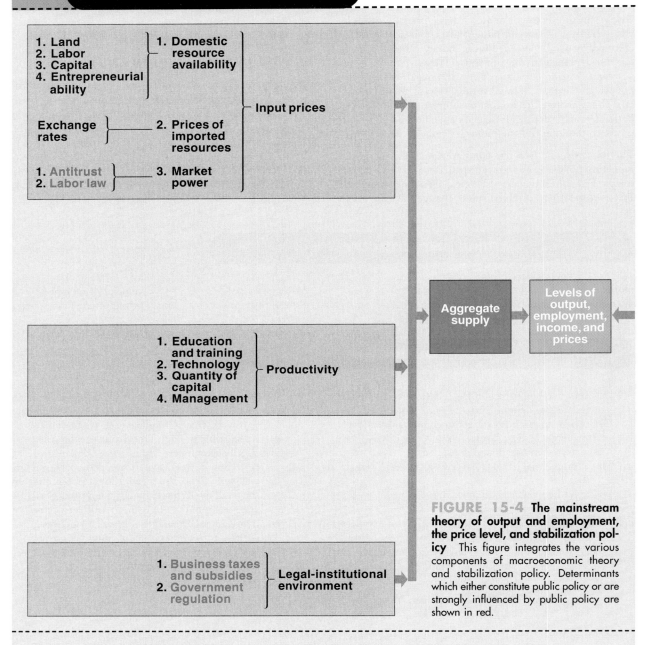

FIGURE 15-4 The mainstream theory of output and employment, the price level, and stabilization policy This figure integrates the various components of macroeconomic theory and stabilization policy. Determinants which either constitute public policy or are strongly influenced by public policy are shown in red.

QUICK QUIZ 15-4

1. All else equal, an increase in domestic resource availability will:
   a. increase input prices, reduce aggregate supply, and increase real output.
   b. raise labor productivity, reduce interest rates, and lower the international value of the dollar.
   c. increase net exports, increase investment, and reduce aggregate demand.
   d. reduce input prices, increase aggregate supply, and increase real output.

2. All else equal, an easy money policy during a recession will:
   a. lower the interest rate, increase investment, and reduce net exports.
   b. lower the interest rate, increase investment, and increase aggregate demand.
   c. increase the interest rate, increase investment, and reduce net exports.
   d. reduce productivity, aggregate supply, and real output.

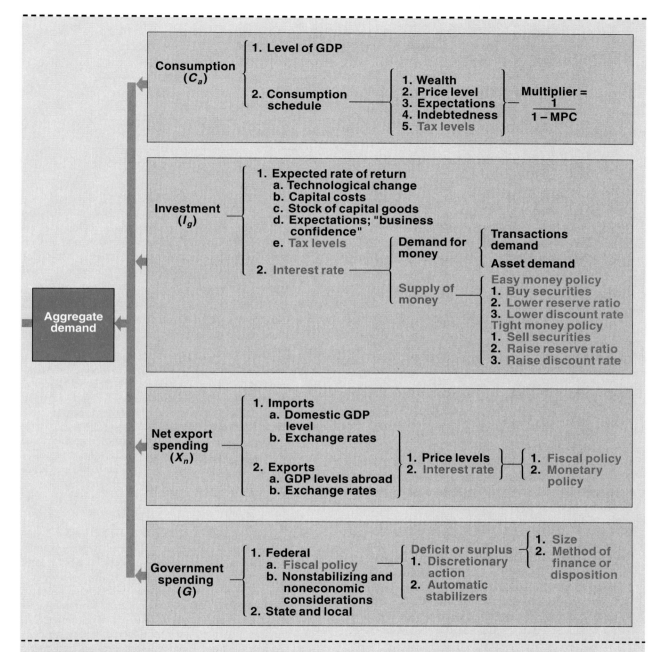

3. A personal income tax cut, combined with a reduction in corporate income and excise taxes, would:

   a. increase consumption, investment, aggregate demand, and aggregate supply.

   b. reduce productivity, raise input prices, and reduce aggregate supply.

   c. increase government spending, reduce net exports, and increase aggregate demand.

   d. increase the supply of money, reduce interest rates, increase investment, and expand real output.

4. An appreciation of the dollar would:

   a. reduce the price of imported resources, lower input prices, and increase aggregate supply.

   b. increase net exports and aggregate demand.

   c. increase aggregate supply and aggregate demand.

   d. reduce consumption, investment, net export spending, and government spending.

Answers: 1. d; 2. b; 3. a; 4. a

Consolidated balance sheet: the 12 Federal Reserve Banks

	(1)	(2)	(3)
Assets:			
Securities $60	_____	_____	_____
Loans to commercial banks............................. 3	_____	_____	_____
Liabilities and net worth:			
Reserves of commercial banks..............................$33	_____	_____	_____
Treasury deposits.................. 3	_____	_____	_____
Federal Reserve Notes 27	_____	_____	_____

    c. The Federal Reserve Banks buy $2 billion of securities from commercial banks. Show the new balance-sheet figures in column 3 of each table.

    d. Now review each of the above three transactions, asking yourself these three questions: (1) What change, if any, took place in the money supply as a direct and immediate result of each transaction? (2) What increase or decrease in the commercial banks' reserves took place in each transaction? (3) Assuming a reserve ratio of 20 percent, what change in the money-creating potential of the commercial banking system occurred as a result of each transaction?

3. KEY QUESTION Suppose you are a member of the Board of Governors of the Federal Reserve System. The economy is experiencing a sharp and prolonged inflationary trend. What changes in **(a)** the reserve ratio, **(b)** the discount rate, and **(c)** open-market operations would you recommend? Explain in each case how the change you advocate would affect commercial bank reserves, the money supply, interest rates, and aggregate demand.

4. KEY QUESTION What is the basic objective of monetary policy? State the cause-effect chain through which monetary policy is made effective. Using Figure 15-2 as a point of reference, discuss how **(a)** the shapes of the demand-for-money and investment demand curves and **(b)** the size of the MPC influence the effectiveness of monetary policy. How do feedback effects influence the effectiveness of monetary policy?

5. KEY QUESTION Distinguish between the Federal funds rate and the prime interest rate. In what way is the Federal funds rate a measure of the tightness or looseness of monetary policy? In 1994 the Fed used open-market operations to increase the Federal funds rate. What was the logic? What was the effect on the prime interest rate?

6. KEY QUESTION Suppose the Fed decides to engage in a tight money policy as a way to reduce demand-pull inflation. Use the aggregate demand–aggregate supply model to show what this policy is intended to accomplish in a closed economy. Now introduce the open economy and explain how changes in the international value of the dollar might affect the location of your aggregate demand curve.

7. (Last Word) How do each of the following metaphors apply to the Federal Reserve's role in the economy: Fed as a mechanic; Fed as a warrior; Fed as a fall guy?

8. WEB-BASED QUESTION **Principles of Monetary Policy** Each Federal Reserve District Bank has its own Web site. An index can be found at http://www.frbsf.org/system/otherdist/otherdist.html. Visit the San Francisco district bank http://www.frbsf.org/pubsindx.html to answer the following questions: How is the Fed structured to make monetary policy decisions? What are its goals? What tools does it use to implement its policies? How does monetary policy affect the U.S. economy? How does the Fed formulate strategies to reach its goals?

9. WEB-BASED QUESTION **The Federal Reserve Annual Report** The Federal Reserve Annual Report provides an extensive overview of the U.S. economy for the previous year. It discusses operations of the Board during the year; it also provides minutes of the Federal Open Market Committee, financial statements of the Board, developments in services provided by the Reserve Banks, priced-services financial statements, directories of Federal Reserve officials and advisory committees, statistical tables, and maps of the System's District and Branch boundaries. Visit the Reports to the Congress section at http://www.bog.frb.fed.us/ and retrieve the current annual report (in Adobe's PDF format only). Summarize the policy actions of the Board of Governors during the current period. In the Fed's opinion, how did the U.S. economy perform? What changes, if any, occurred on the Fed's balance sheet during this period?

4

Problems and
Controversies
in Macro-
economics

CHAPTER SIXTEEN

Extending the Analysis of Aggregate Supply

Macroeconomic theory and stabilization policy as represented in Figure 15-4 has dominated the thinking of most economists in market-oriented industrial economies since the early 1960s. In the United States, Democratic and Republican administrations alike have accepted these precepts, at least as evidenced by policy actions. Presently, the stabilization policies of nearly all the major industrial nations can be understood through Figure 15-4.

But it would be misleading to suggest there is agreement on all aspects of macroeconomic theory and policy. In particular, there has been new, controversial thinking about aggregate supply in the short run and the long run. The result has been renewed debates on whether the economy is "self-correcting" and the desirability and effectiveness of fiscal and monetary policy.

This chapter deals with this new analysis of aggregate supply along with related topics. First, we extend the AD-AS model, distinguishing between short-run and long-run aggregate supply. Second, we apply this extended AD-AS model to demand-pull inflation, cost-push inflation, and recession, gleaning new insights on each. Next, we examine the relationships between inflation and unemployment and look at how expectations can affect the economy. Finally, we state and evaluate the tenets of so-called supply-side economics.

In Chapter 17 we use some of the ideas developed here to examine several issues and disputes about macroeconomic theory and policy. In Chapter 18 we discuss the expansion of long-run aggregate supply over time, that is, economic growth. Finally, in Chapter 19 the facts and issues relating to Federal budget deficits and the public debt are examined.

SHORT-RUN AND LONG-RUN AGGREGATE SUPPLY

Up to this point we have assumed that the aggregate supply curve is stable (does not move) when the aggregate demand curve shifts posi-

tions. This assumption greatly simplifies our analysis and is realistic for most circumstances. An increase in aggregate demand in the upsloping portion of the aggregate supply curve, for example, can be expected to increase both the price level and real output. Nevertheless, the story becomes more complicated when long periods are considered. For instance, once workers fully recognize that the price level has increased, and thus that their real wages (their nominal wages divided by the price level) have declined, they will demand and obtain higher nominal wages to restore their real wages. This increase in nominal wages, other things equal, will shift the aggregate supply curve leftward. That is, nominal wages are one of the factors which determine the location of the aggregate supply curve itself (review Figure 11-6).

To analyze longer time periods, then, we need to extend the analysis of aggregate supply to account for changes in nominal wages *which are in response to changes in the price level.* That is, we need to distinguish between short-run and long-run aggregate supply.

Definitions: Short Run and Long Run

Exactly what are the *short run* and the *long run* as they specifically relate to macroeconomics?

The Short Run   For macroeconomists the short run is *a period in which nominal wages (and other input prices) remain fixed as the price level changes.* There are at least two reasons why nominal wages may remain constant for a time even though the price level has changed:

1. Workers may not immediately be aware of the extent to which inflation (or deflation) has changed their real wages, and thus they may not adjust their labor supply decisions and wage demands accordingly.

2. Many employees are hired under fixed-wage contracts. Unionized employees, for example, receive nominal wages spelled out in their collective bargaining agreements. Also, most managers and many professionals receive set salaries established in annual contracts. In these circumstances, nominal wages remain constant for the lives of the contracts, regardless of changes in the price level.

The upshot of these two factors is that price-level changes do not immediately give rise to changes in nominal wages. Instead, considerable amounts of time usually pass before these adjustments occur.

The Long Run   Once sufficient time has elapsed for contracts to expire and nominal wage adjustments to occur, the economy enters the long run—*a period in which nominal wages are fully responsive to changes in the price level.* With sufficient time, workers gain full information about price-level changes and thus determine how these changes have affected their real wages. For example, workers become aware that a price-level *increase* has reduced their real wages. If your *nominal* wage was $10 an hour when the price index was 100 (or, in decimals, 1.0), your *real* wage was also $10 (= $10 of nominal wage divided by 1.0). But when the price level has increased to, say, 120, your $10 real wage has declined to $8.33 (= $10/1.2). In such circumstances, you and other workers will demand and probably obtain increases in your nominal wages such that the purchasing power from an hour of work is restored. In our example, your nominal wage likely will rise from $10 to $12, returning your real wage to $10 (= $12/1.2).

Short-Run Aggregate Supply

With these definitions of short run and long run clearly in mind, we can extend Chapter 11's discussion of aggregate supply.

First, consider the **short-run aggregate supply curve** AS_1 in Figure 16-1a. (Our focus now is on the intermediate range of the AS curve of Chapter 11.) Curve AS_1 is constructed on three assumptions: (1) the initial price level is P_1, (2) nominal wages have been established on the *expectation that this specific price level will persist*, and (3) the price level is flexible both upward and downward. Observe from point a_1 that at price level P_1 the economy is operating at its full-employment output Q_f. This output is the real production forthcoming when the economy is operating at its natural rate of unemployment.

Now let's determine the short-run consequences of changes in the price level by first examining an *increase* in the price level from P_1 to P_2 in Figure 16-1a. The higher product prices associated with P_2 increase revenues to firms, and because the nominal wages they are paying are fixed, their profits rise. In response, firms collectively increase their output from Q_f to Q_2; the economy moves from a_1 to a_2 on curve AS_1. Observe that at Q_2 the economy is operating beyond its full-employment output. This is made possible by extending the work-hours of part-time and full-time workers, enticing new workers such as homemakers and retirees into the labor force, and hiring and training the structurally unemployed. Thus, the nation's unemployment rate declines below its natural rate.

How will producers respond when there is a *decrease* in the price level, say, from P_1 to P_3 in Figure

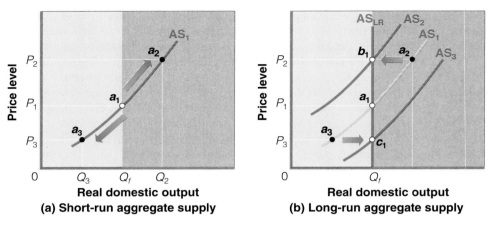

FIGURE 16-1 **Short-run and long-run aggregate supply** (a) In the short run, nominal wages are assumed to be fixed and based on price level P_1 and the expectation that it will continue. An increase in the price level from P_1 to P_2 increases profits and output, moving the economy from a_1 to a_2; a decrease in the price level from P_1 to P_3 reduces profits and real output, moving the economy from a_1 to a_3. The short-run aggregate supply curve therefore slopes upward. (b) In the long run, a price-level rise increases nominal wages and thus shifts the short-run aggregate supply curve leftward. Conversely, a decrease in the price level reduces nominal wages and shifts the short-run aggregate supply curve rightward. After such adjustments, the economy reaches equilibrium at points such as b_1 and c_1. Thus, the long-run aggregate supply curve is vertical.

16-1a? Firms then discover their revenues and profits have diminished or disappeared. After all, the prices they receive for their products have dropped while the nominal wages they pay workers have not. Under these circumstances, firms reduce their employment and production, and, as shown by the move from a_1 to a_3, real output falls to Q_3. The decline in real output is accompanied by increased unemployment; at output Q_3 the unemployment rate is greater than the natural rate of unemployment associated with output Q_f.

Long-Run Aggregate Supply

By definition, nominal wages in the long run are fully responsive to changes in the price level. What are the implications of this responsiveness for aggregate supply?

For the answer, look at Figure 16-1b, again assuming the economy is initially at point a_1 (P_1 and Q_f). Our previous discussion indicated that an *increase* in the price level from P_1 to P_2 will move the economy from point a_1 to a_2 along the short-run aggregate supply curve AS_1. In the long run, however, workers discover their real wages have declined *because* of

this increase in the price level. They demand and presumably obtain their previous level of real wages via hikes in their nominal wages. The short-run supply curve then shifts leftward from AS_1 to AS_2, which now reflects the higher price level P_2 *and the new expectation that* P_2, *not* P_1, *will continue.* The leftward shift in the short-run aggregate supply curve to AS_2 moves the economy from a_2 to b_1. Real output returns to its full-employment level Q_f, and the unemployment rate returns to its natural rate.

And what is the result of a decrease in the price level? *Assuming downward wage flexibility,* a decline in the price level from P_1 to P_3 in Figure 16-1b works in the opposite way from a price-level increase. The economy initially moves from point a_1 to a_3 on AS_1. Profits are squeezed or eliminated because prices have fallen and nominal wages have not. But this movement along AS_1 is the short-run response. With enough time, the lower price level P_3—which has *increased* the real wage—results in a decline in nominal wages such that the original real wage is restored. Sufficiently lower nominal wages shift the short-run aggregate supply curve rightward from AS_1 to AS_3. Real output returns to its full-employment level of Q_f at point c_1.

By tracing a line between the long-run equilibrium points b_1, a_1, and c_1, we obtain a **long-run aggregate supply curve.** Observe that it is vertical at the full-employment level of real GDP. After long-run adjustments in nominal wages, real output is Q_f, regardless of the specific price level. **(Key Question 3)**

Equilibrium in the Extended AD-AS Model

Figure 16-2 shows the long-run equilibrium in the AD-AS model, now extended to include the distinction between short-run and long-run aggregate supply. (Hereafter, we will refer to this model as the *extended AD-AS model*, with "extended" referring to inclusion of both the short-run and the long-run aggregate supply curves.) Equilibrium in the figure occurs at point *a*, where the nation's aggregate demand curve AD_1 intersects the vertical long-run aggregate supply curve AS_{LR}. Observe at point *a* that the aggregate demand curve also intersects the short-run aggregate supply curve AS_1. In long-run equilibrium, the economy's price level and real output are P_1 and Q_f.

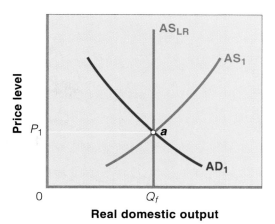

FIGURE 16-2 Equilibrium in the extended AD-AS model The equilibrium price level P_1 and level of real output Q_f occur at the intersection of the aggregate demand curve AD_1, the long-run aggregate supply curve AS_{LR}, and the short-run aggregate supply curve AS_1.

- -

QUICK REVIEW 16-1

■ The short-run aggregate supply curve has a positive slope because nominal wages remain constant as the price level changes.

■ The long-run aggregate supply curve is vertical because nominal wages eventually change by the same amount as changes in the price level.

■ The equilibrium GDP and price level occur at the intersection of the aggregate demand curve, the long-run aggregate supply curve, and the short-run aggregate supply curve.

APPLYING THE EXTENDED AD-AS MODEL

The extended AD-AS model helps us better understand the economy and the controversies occasionally swirling around macroeconomics. We will defer discussion of most of these controversies until the next chapter. For now, our intention is simply to apply the extended AD-AS model to three situations: demand-pull inflation, cost-push inflation, and recession.

Demand-Pull Inflation in the Extended AD-AS Model

Recall that *demand-pull inflation* occurs when an increase in aggregate demand pulls up the price level. We previously depicted this inflation by shifting an aggregate demand curve rightward along a stable aggregate supply curve (see Figure 11-8b and 11-8c).

In our more complex version of aggregate supply, however, an increase in the price level will eventually produce an increase in nominal wages and thus a leftward shift of the short-run aggregate supply curve. This is shown in Figure 16-3, where we initially suppose the price level is P_1 at the intersection of aggregate demand curve AD_1, short-run supply curve AS_1, and long-run aggregate supply curve AS_{LR}. Observe that at point *a* the economy is achieving its full-employment real output Q_f.

Now consider the effects of an increase in aggregate demand as represented by the rightward shift from AD_1 to AD_2. This shift can result from any one of a number of factors, including an increase in investment spending and a rise in net exports. Whatever its cause, the increase in aggregate demand boosts the price level from P_1 to P_2 and expands real output from Q_f to Q_2 at point *b*.

So far, none of this is new to you. But now the distinction between short-run and long-run aggregate

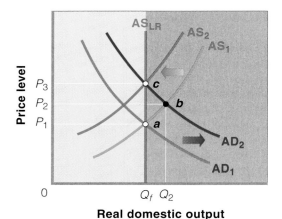

FIGURE 16-3 Demand-pull inflation in the extended AD-AS model An increase in aggregate demand from AD$_1$ to AD$_2$ drives up the price level and increases real output in the short run. But in the long run, nominal wages rise and the short-run aggregate supply curve shifts leftward, as from AS$_1$ to AS$_2$. Real output then returns to its prior level, and the price level rises even more. In this scenario, the economy moves from a to b and then eventually to c.

----

supply becomes important. Once workers have realized that their real wages have declined, and when their existing contracts have expired, nominal wages will rise. As they do, the short-run aggregate supply curve will ultimately shift leftward such that it intersects long-run aggregate supply at point c.[1] There, the economy has reestablished long-run equilibrium, with the price level and real output now P_3 and Q_f, respectively. Only at point c does the new aggregate demand curve AD$_2$ intersect both the short-run aggregate supply curve AS$_2$ and the long-run aggregate supply curve AS$_{LR}$.

In the short run, demand-pull inflation drives up the price level and increases real output; in the long run, only the price level rises. In the long run, the initial increase in aggregate demand has moved the economy *along* its vertical aggregate supply curve AS$_{LR}$.

----

[1]We say "ultimately" because the initial leftward shift in short-run aggregate supply will intersect the long-run aggregate supply curve AS$_{LR}$ at price level P_2 (review Figure 16-1b). But the intersection of AD$_2$ and this new short-run aggregate supply curve (not shown) will produce a price level above P_2. (You may want to pencil this in to make sure that you understand this point.) Again nominal wages will rise, shifting the short-run aggregate supply curve farther leftward. The process will continue until the economy moves to point c, where the short-run aggregate supply curve is AS$_2$, the price level is P_3, and real output is Q_f.

For a while, an economy can operate beyond its full-employment level of output. But the demand-pull inflation eventually causes adjustments of nominal wages which move the economy back to its full-employment output Q_f.

Cost-Push Inflation in the Extended AD-AS Model

Cost-push inflation arises from factors which increase the cost of production at each price level—that is, factors which shift the aggregate supply curve leftward—and therefore increase the price level. But in our previous analysis (Figure 11-11) we considered only short-run aggregate supply. We now want to examine cost-push inflation in its long-run context.

Analysis Look at Figure 16-4, in which we again assume the economy is initially operating at price level P_1 and output level Q_f(point a). Suppose that international oil producers get together and boost the price of oil by, say, 50 percent. What is the effect on the short-run aggregate supply curve of a major oil-consuming economy? The answer is that the hike in the oil price increases the per-unit production cost of producing and transporting goods and services. This

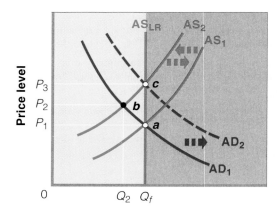

FIGURE 16-4 Cost-push inflation in the extended AD-AS model Cost-push inflation occurs when the short-run aggregate supply curve shifts leftward, as from AS$_1$ to AS$_2$. If government counters the decline in real output by increasing aggregate demand to the broken line, the price level rises even more. That is, the economy moves in steps from a to b to c. In contrast, if government allows a recession to occur, nominal wages eventually fall and the aggregate supply curve shifts back rightward to its original location. The economy moves from a to b and then eventually back to a.

----

shifts the short-run aggregate supply curve to the left, as from AS_1 to AS_2. The price level rises from P_1 to P_2, as seen by comparing points *a* and *b*. In this case, the increase in the price of a key resource—namely, oil—shifts the short-run aggregate supply curve to the left. This shift is not a *response* to a price-level increase, as it was in our previous discussions of demand-pull inflation; it is the initiating *cause* of the price-level increase.

Policy Dilemma Cost-push inflation creates a dilemma for policymakers. Without expansionary stabilization policy, aggregate demand in Figure 16-4 remains at AD_1—the curve does not shift—and real output declines from Q_f to Q_2. Government can counter this recession and the attendant rise in unemployment by using fiscal policy and monetary policy to increase aggregate demand to AD_2. But there is a potential policy trap here: An increase in aggregate demand to AD_2 will further increase inflation by increasing the price level from P_2 to P_3 (a move from point *b* to *c*).

Also, the P_2 to P_3 increase in the price level is not likely to be the end of the story because wage earners eventually respond to their decline in real wages by seeking and presumably receiving increases in nominal wages. The higher nominal wages cause another increase in per-unit production costs, which in turn shifts the short-run aggregate supply curve to a position to the left of AS_2. This (not shown) leftward shift of the aggregate supply curve is in *response* to the higher price level P_3, which was caused by the policy-created rightward shift of aggregate demand to AD_2. The new leftward shift of short-run aggregate supply will regenerate recession. In brief, government will have to increase aggregate demand once again to restore the Q_f level of real output. But if it does so, the scenario may simply repeat itself.

Suppose government recognizes this policy trap and decides *not* to increase aggregate demand from AD_1 to AD_2 (so you can now disregard the dashed AD_2 curve). Instead, it implicitly decides to allow a cost-push-created recession to run its course. How will that happen? Widespread layoffs, plant shutdowns, and business failures eventually occur. At some point the demands for oil, labor, and other inputs fall such that oil prices and nominal wages decline. When that happens, the initial leftward shift of the short-run aggregate supply curve is undone. In time the recession will shift the short-run aggregate supply curve rightward from AS_2 to AS_1. The price level will re-

turn to P_1, and the full-employment level of output will be restored at Q_f (point *a* on the long-run aggregate supply curve AS_{LR}).

This analysis yields two generalizations:

1. If government attempts to maintain full employment when there is cost-push inflation, an inflationary spiral may occur.

2. If government takes a hands-off approach to cost-push inflation, a recession will occur. Although the recession eventually may undo the initial rise in per-unit production costs, the economy in the meantime will experience high unemployment and a loss of real output.

Recession and the Extended AD-AS Model

By far the most controversial application of the extended AD-AS model is to recession (or depression). This controversy will be looked at in some detail in Chapter 17; here we simply want to present the model and identify the key point of contention.

Suppose in Figure 16-5 that aggregate demand initially is AD_1 and that short-run and long-run aggregate supply curves are AS_1 and AS_{LR}, respectively. Therefore, as shown by point *a*, the price level is P_1

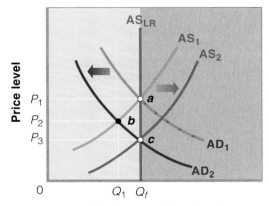

FIGURE 16-5 Recession in the extended AD-AS model
A recession occurs when aggregate demand shifts leftward, as from AD_1 to AD_2. If prices and wages are downwardly flexible, the price level falls from P_1 to P_2. This decline in the price level reduces nominal wages, which in turn eventually shift the aggregate supply curve from AS_1 to AS_2. The price level declines to P_3, and output increases back to Q_f. The economy moves from *a* to *b* and then eventually to *c*.

----

and output is Q_f. Now suppose that investment spending dramatically declines, reducing aggregate demand to AD$_2$. Real output declines from Q_f to Q_1, meaning a recession has occurred. But if we make the controversial assumption that prices and wages are flexible downward, the price level falls from P_1 to P_2. This lower price level increases *real* wages for people still working since each dollar of nominal wage has greater purchasing power. Eventually, nominal wages themselves fall to restore the previous real wage; when this happens, the short-run aggregate supply curve shifts rightward from AS$_1$ to AS$_2$. The recession ends—without expansionary fiscal or monetary policy—since real output expands from Q_1 (point b) back to Q_f (point c). The economy is again located on its long-run aggregate supply curve AS$_{LR}$, but now at lower price level P_3.

There is much disagreement about this theoretical scenario. The key point of dispute is how long it would take in the real world for the necessary price and wage adjustments to occur to achieve the indicated outcome. For now, suffice it to say that most economists believe that *if* such adjustments are forthcoming, they will occur only after the economy has experienced a long-lasting recession with its accompanying high unemployment and great loss of output. **(Key Question 4)**

QUICK REVIEW 16-2

■ In the short run, demand-pull inflation increases both the price level and real output; in the long run, nominal wages rise, the short-run aggregate supply curve shifts to the left, and only the price level increases.

■ Cost-push inflation creates a policy dilemma for government: If it engages in an expansionary policy to increase output, an inflationary spiral may occur; if it does nothing, a recession will occur.

■ In the short run, a decline in aggregate demand reduces real output (creates a recession); in the long run, prices and nominal wages presumably fall, the short-run aggregate supply curve shifts to the right, and real output returns to its full-employment level.

THE PHILLIPS CURVE

Cost-push inflation and the macroeconomic distinction between the short run and the long run shed light on a relationship called the **Phillips Curve,**

named after A. W. Phillips, who developed the idea in Great Britain.

The Basic Idea

To convey the concept of the Phillips Curve, let's look at the short-run aggregate supply curve in Figure 16-6 and perform a simple mental experiment. Suppose that in a specific period aggregate demand expands from AD$_0$ to AD$_2$. This shift could result from a change in any one of the determinants of aggregate demand. Businesses may decide to buy more investment goods, or government may decide to increase its expenditures. Whatever the cause of the increase in aggregate demand, in the short run the price level rises from P_0 to P_2 and real output expands from Q_0 to Q_2. We know that this increase in real output is accompanied by a decrease in the unemployment rate.

Now let's compare what would have happened if the increase in aggregate demand had been larger, say, from AD$_0$ to AD$_3$. The new equilibrium tells us that the amount of inflation and the growth of real output would both have been greater (and that the unemployment rate would have been lower). Similarly, suppose aggregate demand in our specific year had increased only modestly, from AD$_0$ to AD$_1$. Compared with our shift from AD$_0$ to AD$_2$, the amount of infla-

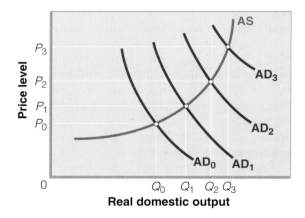

FIGURE 16-6 The effect of changes in aggregate demand on real output and the price level Comparing the effects of various possible increases in aggregate demand yields the conclusion that the larger the increase in aggregate demand, the higher the rate of inflation and the greater the increase in real output. Because real output and the unemployment rate are inversely related, we can generalize that, given short-run aggregate supply, high rates of inflation should be accompanied by low rates of unemployment.

----

tion and the growth of real output would have been smaller (and the unemployment rate higher).

The generalization from this mental experiment is this: Assuming a constant short-run aggregate supply curve, high rates of inflation are accompanied by low rates of unemployment, and low rates of inflation are accompanied by high rates of unemployment. Figure 16-7a generalizes how the expected relationship should look.

Do the facts fit the theory? Empirical work by economists in the late 1950s and 1960s verified this inverse relationship for various countries, including Great Britain and the United States. As we have noted, it came to be known as the Phillips Curve. Figure 16-7b shows the relationship between the unemployment rate and the rate of inflation in the United States for 1961–1969.

Tradeoffs

On the basis of the kind of evidence shown in Figure 16-7b, economists came to believe that a stable, predictable tradeoff existed between unemployment and inflation. Moreover, national economic policy was built on this supposed tradeoff. According to this thinking, it was impossible to achieve "full employment without inflation": Manipulation of aggregate demand through fiscal and monetary measures would simply move the economy along the Phillips Curve. An expansionary fiscal and monetary policy which boosts aggregate demand and lowers the unemployment rate would simultaneously cause a higher rate of inflation. A restrictive fiscal and monetary policy could be used to reduce the rate of inflation, but only at the cost of a higher unemployment rate and more forgone production. Society had to choose between incompatible goals of price stability and full employment; it had to decide where to *locate* on its Phillips Curve.

Stagflation: A Shifting Phillips Curve?

The stable Phillips Curve of the 1960s gave way to great instability of the curve in the 1970s and 1980s. Events during those years were clearly at odds with the notion of a stable inflation-unemployment tradeoff. Figure 16-8 enlarges Figure 16-7b by adding data for 1970 through 1997. The obvious inverse relationship of 1961–1969 has now become obscure and highly questionable.

Note in Figure 16-8 that in many years of the 1970s the economy experienced increasing inflation *and* rising unemployment—in a word, **stagflation**—a

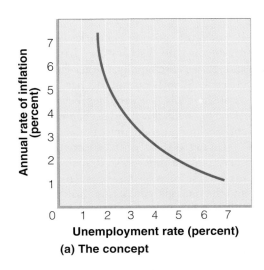

(a) The concept

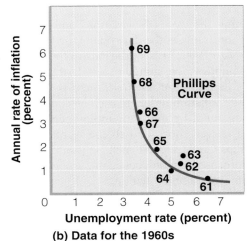

(b) Data for the 1960s

FIGURE 16-7 The Phillips Curve: concept and empirical data (a) The Phillips Curve purports to show a stable relationship between the rate of inflation and the unemployment rate. Because this relationship is inverse, there is presumably a tradeoff between unemployment and inflation. (b) Data points for the 1960s seemed to confirm the Phillips Curve concept. (*Note:* Inflation rates are on a December-to-December basis, and unemployment rates are for all workers, including members of the armed forces.)

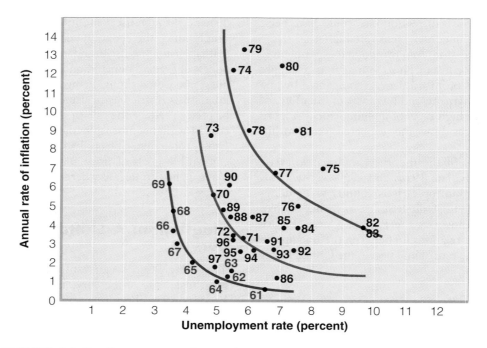

FIGURE 16-8 Inflation rates and unemployment rates, 1961–1997 Data points for 1961 to 1997 suggest no clear relationship between unemployment rates and rates of inflation. This raises questions as to the stability or existence of the Phillips Curve. Some economists think the curve shifted to the right in the 1970s and early 1980s, as shown, and then collapsed back inward during the later 1980s. (*Note:* Inflation rates are on a December-to-December basis and unemployment rates are for all workers, including members of the armed forces.)

term combining the words "stagnation" and "inflation." Trace, for example, the data points for 1972 to 1974 and 1977 to 1980. At best, the data in the figure suggest the Phillips Curve shifted to less desirable positions where each level of unemployment is accompanied by more inflation or where each level of inflation is accompanied by more unemployment. The downsloping curves above and to the right of the original Phillips Curve suggest such rightward shifts. At worst, the data imply *no* dependable tradeoff between unemployment and inflation.

Adverse Aggregate Supply Shocks

What caused the stagflation of the 1970s and early 1980s? One answer is that a series of adverse **aggregate supply shocks** occurred. Such shocks are rapid and significant increases in resource costs, which jolt an economy's short-run aggregate supply curve leftward. The most significant of these supply shocks was a quadrupling of oil prices by the Organization of

Petroleum Exporting Countries (OPEC). The cost of producing and distributing virtually every product and service rose rapidly. (Other factors working to increase U.S. costs during this period included agricultural shortfalls, a greatly depreciated dollar, catch-up of wages held down by earlier wage-price controls, and declining productivity.)

Leftward shifts of the short-run aggregate supply curve make a difference. Remember that we derived the inverse relationship between the rate of inflation and the unemployment rate shown in Figure 16-7a by shifting the aggregate demand curve along a *stable* short-run aggregate supply curve in Figure 16-6. But review the cost-push inflation model shown in Figure 16-4. There, a leftward shift of the short-run aggregate supply curve causes the price level to rise and the level of output to fall (unemployment to rise). This, say most economists, is what happened in two periods in the 1970s. The U.S. unemployment rate shot up from 4.8 percent in 1973 to 8.3 percent in 1975, contributing to a $42 billion decline in real GDP. In the same period, the U.S. price level rose by 21 percent. The stagflation scenario recurred in 1978, when OPEC increased oil prices by more than 100 percent. The U.S. price level increased by 26 percent over the 1978–1980 period, while unemployment increased from 6.0 to 7.5 percent.

The "Great Stagflation" of the 1970s made it clear that the Phillips Curve did not represent a stable inflation-unemployment relationship. Declines in short-run aggregate supply were at work, which explain those occasions when the inflation rate and the unemployment rate increased simultaneously. To most economists, the experience of the 1970s and early 1980s suggests that the Phillips Curve was shifting to the right and confronting the economy with higher rates of inflation and unemployment.

Stagflation's Demise

Another look at Figure 16-8 reveals a generally inward movement of the inflation-unemployment points between 1982 and 1989. By 1989 the lingering effects of the early period had subsided. One precursor to this favorable trend was the deep recession of 1981 to 1982, largely caused by a tight money policy aimed at reducing double-digit inflation. The recession upped the unemployment rate to 9.5 percent in 1982. With so many workers unemployed, those who were working accepted smaller increases in their nominal wages—or in some cases wage reductions—to preserve their jobs. Firms, in turn, restrained their price increases to try to retain their relative shares of a greatly diminished market.

Other factors were also at work. Foreign competition throughout this period held down wage and price hikes in several basic industries such as automobile and steel. Deregulation of the airline and trucking industries also resulted in wage reductions or so-called wage givebacks. A significant decline in OPEC's monopoly power produced a stunning fall in the price of oil and its derivative products, such as gasoline.

All these factors combined to reduce per-unit production costs and to shift the short-run aggregate supply curve rightward (as from AS_2 to AS_1 in Figure 16-4). Employment and output expanded and the unemployment rate fell from 9.5 percent in 1983 to 5.2 percent in 1989. Figure 16-8 reveals that the inflation-unemployment points for recent years are closer to the points associated with the Phillips Curve of the 1960s than to the points in the late 1970s and early 1980s. The points for 1996 and 1997, in fact, are

very close to points on the 1960s curve. (The low U.S. level of the so-called *misery index*, shown in Global Perspective 16-1, is also relevant to this later period.)

NATURAL-RATE HYPOTHESIS

The standard explanation for the scattering of inflation rate–unemployment points to the right of the 1960s Phillips Curve is that a series of supply shocks shifted the short-run aggregate supply curve leftward, moving the Phillips Curve rightward and upward as in Figure 16-8. The inward movement of inflation rate–unemployment points in the 1980s was caused by rightward shifts of short-run aggregate supply curves. In this view, there is still a tradeoff between

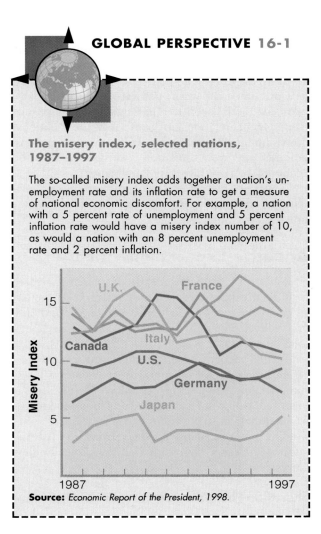

GLOBAL PERSPECTIVE 16-1

The misery index, selected nations, 1987–1997

The so-called misery index adds together a nation's unemployment rate and its inflation rate to get a measure of national economic discomfort. For example, a nation with a 5 percent rate of unemployment and 5 percent inflation rate would have a misery index number of 10, as would a nation with an 8 percent unemployment rate and 2 percent inflation.

Source: *Economic Report of the President, 1998.*

the inflation rate and the unemployment rate, but changes in short-run aggregate supply may alter the menu of inflation and unemployment choices—that is, shift the Phillips Curve itself—during abnormal periods.

A second explanation of simultaneously higher rates of unemployment and inflation, the **natural-rate hypothesis,** questions the very existence of an inverse relationship between the rate of inflation and the rate of unemployment. This view is that the economy is generally stable at its natural rate of unemployment (or full-employment rate of output). We know from Chapter 8 that the natural rate of unemployment is the rate of unemployment existing when cyclical unemployment is zero; it is the full-employment rate of unemployment.

According to the natural-rate hypothesis, the incorrect assumption of a stable Phillips Curve resulted in misguided attempts by government to push the unemployment rate below the economy's natural rate. The end result was accelerating inflation. The natural-rate hypothesis has its empirical roots in Figure 16-8, where you can argue that a vertical line located at a presumed 6 percent natural rate of unemployment for the full period represents the inflation-unemployment "relationship" better than the traditional downsloping Phillips Curve. In the natural-rate hypothesis, any rate of inflation is compatible with the economy's natural rate of unemployment.

There are two variations of this natural-rate perspective: the adaptive expectations theory and the rational expectations theory.

Adaptive Expectations Theory

The **adaptive expectations theory** assumes people form their expectations of future inflation on the basis of previous and present rates of inflation and only gradually change their expectations as experience unfolds.

In this theory, there is a short-run tradeoff between inflation and unemployment but not a long-run tradeoff. Any attempt to reduce the unemployment rate below the natural rate sets in motion forces which destabilize the Phillips Curve and shift it rightward. Thus, the adaptive expectations view distinguishes between a "short-run" and "long-run" Phillips Curve.

Short-Run Phillips Curve Consider Phillips Curve PC_1 in Figure 16-9. Suppose the economy initially is

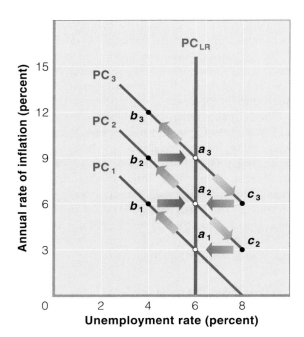

FIGURE 16-9 The adaptive expectations theory Expansionary monetary policy and fiscal policy may temporarily boost profits, output, and employment (as from a_1 to b_1). But nominal wages will soon rise, reducing profits and thereby negating the short-run stimulus to production and employment (the economy moves from b_1 to a_2). Consequently, there is no tradeoff between the rates of inflation and unemployment in the long run; that is, the long-run Phillips Curve is vertical.

experiencing a 3 percent rate of inflation and a 6 percent natural rate of unemployment. In the adaptive expectations theory, such short-term curves as PC_1, PC_2, and PC_3 (drawn as straight lines for simplicity) exist because the actual rate of inflation is not always the same as the expected rate.

Establishing an additional point on Phillips Curve PC_1 will clarify this for you. We begin at a_1, where we assume nominal wages are set on the assumption that the 3 percent rate of inflation will continue. But suppose government mistakenly judges the full-employment unemployment rate to be 4 percent instead of 6 percent. This misjudgment might occur because the economy achieved a 4 percent rate of unemployment in some earlier, inflationary period. To achieve the targeted 4 percent rate of unemployment, government undertakes expansionary fiscal and monetary policies.

The increase in aggregate demand which results causes the rate of inflation to rise to 6 percent. With a specific level of nominal wages set on the expectation that the 3 percent rate of inflation will continue, the higher product prices raise business profits. Firms respond to these expanded profits by hiring more workers and increasing output. In the short run, the economy moves to b_1, which, in contrast to a_1, involves a lower rate of unemployment (4 percent) and higher rate of inflation (6 percent). The movement from a_1 to b_1 is consistent both with an upsloping aggregate supply curve and with our previous interpretation of the Phillips Curve. Presumably, the economy has accepted some additional inflation as the "cost" of achieving a reduced level of unemployment. But the natural-rate theory interprets the movement from a_1 to b_1 differently. In this view, it is simply a manifestation of the following principle: *When the actual rate of inflation is higher than expected, profits temporarily rise and the unemployment rate temporarily falls.*

Long-Run Vertical Phillips Curve

Point b_1 is not a stable equilibrium position in this theory. Workers will recognize their nominal wages have not increased as fast as inflation and will therefore obtain nominal wage increases to restore their lost purchasing power. But as nominal wages rise to restore the level of real wages which existed at a_1, business profits will fall to their earlier level. The reduction in profits means the original motivation to employ more workers and increase output has disappeared.

Unemployment then returns to its natural level at point a_2. Note, however, that the economy now faces a higher actual *and* expected rate of inflation—6 percent rather than 3 percent. The higher level of aggregate demand that originally moved the economy from a_1 to b_1 still exists, so the inflation it created still persists.

In view of the higher 6 percent expected rate of inflation, the short-run Phillips Curve shifts upward from PC$_1$ to PC$_2$ in Figure 16-9. An "along-the-Phillips-Curve" kind of movement from a_1 to b_1 on PC$_1$ is merely a short-run or transient occurrence. In the long run, after nominal wages catch up with price-level increases, unemployment returns to the natural rate at a_2, and there is a new short-run Phillips Curve PC$_2$ at the higher expected rate of inflation.

The process may now be repeated. Government may reason that certain extraneous events like oil price increases have frustrated its expansionary policies, and it will try again. Fiscal policy and monetary policy are then used to increase aggregate demand, and the scenario repeats. Prices rise momentarily ahead of nominal wages, profits expand, and employ-

ment and output increase (as implied by the move from a_2 to b_2). But, in time, nominal wages increase so as to restore real wages. Profits then fall to their original level, pushing employment back to the normal rate at a_3. Government's "reward" for forcing the actual rate of unemployment below the natural rate is the perverse one of a still higher (9 percent) rate of inflation.

If we conceive of a_1b_1, a_2b_2, and a_3b_3 as a series of short-run Phillips Curves, the adaptive expectations theory says that government attempts to move the economy along the short-run Phillips curve (a_1 to b_1 on PC$_1$) *cause* the curve to shift to a less favorable position (PC$_2$, then PC$_3$, and so on). A stable Phillips Curve with the dependable series of unemployment rate–inflation rate tradeoffs does not exist in the long run.

The vertical line through a_1, a_2, and a_3 shows the *long-run relationship* between unemployment and inflation. Any rate of inflation is consistent with the 6 percent natural rate of unemployment. So society ought to choose a low rate of inflation rather than a high one.

Disinflation

We can also employ the adaptive expectations theory to explain **disinflation**—reductions in the rate of inflation. Suppose that in Figure 16-9 the economy is at a_3, where the inflation rate is 9 percent. Next assume that a decline in aggregate demand such as that occurring in the 1981–1982 recession reduces inflation below the 9 percent expected rate, say, to 6 percent. Business profits fall because product prices are rising less rapidly than wages. The nominal wage increases, remember, were set on the assumption that the 9 percent rate of inflation would continue. In response to the profit decline, firms reduce their employment and consequently the unemployment rate rises. The economy temporarily slides downward from point a_3 to c_3 along the short-run Phillips Curve PC$_3$. In the natural-rate theory, *when the actual rate of inflation is lower than the expected rate, profits temporarily fall and the unemployment rate temporarily rises.*

Firms and workers eventually adjust their expectations to the new 6 percent rate of inflation, and thus newly negotiated wage increases decline. Profits are restored, employment rises, and the unemployment rate returns to its natural rate of 6 percent at a_2. Because the expected rate of inflation is now 6 percent, the short-run Phillips Curve PC$_3$ shifts leftward to PC$_2$.

If aggregate demand falls farther, the scenario will continue. Inflation declines from 6 percent to, say, 3 percent, moving the economy from a_2 to c_2 along PC$_2$. The lower-than-expected rate of inflation (lower prices) squeezes profits and reduces employment. But, in the long run, firms respond to the lower profits by reducing their nominal wage increases. Profits are restored and unemployment returns to its natural rate at a_1 as the short-run Phillips Curve moves from PC$_2$ to PC$_1$. Once again, the long-run Phillips Curve is vertical at the natural rate of unemployment.

Rational Expectations Theory

The adaptive expectations theory assumes that increases in nominal wages lag behind increases in the price level because the increases in the price level are not anticipated. This lag gives rise to *temporary* increases in profits which *temporarily* stimulate employment.

The **rational expectations theory** is the second version of the natural-rate hypothesis. It contends that businesses, consumers, and workers understand how government policies will affect the economy and *anticipate* the impacts in their own decision making.

Suppose, when government undertakes expansionary policies, workers anticipate that the result will be higher inflation and thus a decline in their real wages. They thus immediately incorporate this expected inflation into their nominal wage demands. If workers correctly and fully anticipate the amount of inflation and adjust their current nominal wage demands accordingly, then even the temporary increases in profit, output, and employment will *not* occur. Instead of the temporary decline in unemployment from a_1 to b_1 in Figure 16-9, the movement is directly from a_1 to a_2. Fully anticipated inflation by labor means that the price level and nominal wages rise simultaneously and by the same percent. Inflation, fully anticipated in the nominal wage demands of workers, therefore generates a vertical "Phillips Curve" through a_1, a_2, and a_3.

The policy implication is this: Fiscal and monetary policy designed to push unemployment below its natural rate will quickly (if not instantaneously) increase the rate of inflation, not reduce unemployment. Note that the adaptive and rational expectations theories are consistent with the conservative philosophy that government's attempts to do good deeds typically fail, and at a considerable cost to soci-

ety. In this instance the "cost" is accelerating inflation. **(Key Question 6)**

Changing Interpretations

Interpretations of the Phillips Curve have changed dramatically over the past three decades. The original idea of a stable tradeoff between inflation and unemployment has given way to the adaptive expectations view that while there is a short-run tradeoff, there is no such tradeoff in the long run. The much more controversial rational expectations theory stresses that macroeconomic policy is completely ineffective when its outcomes are fully anticipated by workers and other participants in the economy. Not even a short-run tradeoff between inflation and unemployment exists. This conclusion is clearly contrary to the idea of the original Phillips Curve.

Which perspective is correct? Does an inverse relationship exist between the inflation rate and unemployment rate as the original Phillips Curve implies? Or is there no long-run tradeoff as the natural-rate theory contends? Perhaps the safest answer is that most economists accept the idea of a short-run tradeoff—where the short-run may last several years—while now recognizing that in the long run such a tradeoff is much less likely. Also, most economists agree that adverse aggregate supply shocks, such as those of the 1970s, can cause periods of rising unemployment rates and rising inflation, particularly when government undertakes policies to limit the rise in the unemployment rate. That is, most economists contend that the episodes of stagflation during the 1970s and early 1980s were *not* exclusively the results of misguided government stabilization policies, as some natural-rate theorists suggest.

QUICK REVIEW 16-3

■ The original Phillips Curve for the 1960s showed an apparent stable, inverse relationship between annual inflation rates and unemployment rates over a period of years.

■ Stagflation occurred from 1973 to 1975 and 1978 to 1980, producing Phillips Curve data points above and to the right of the Phillips Curve for the 1960s.

■ The central cause of the stagflation in the 1970s and early 1980s was a series of large increases in oil prices which reduced short-run aggregate supply.

■ In the natural-rate theory, the economy automatically gravitates to its natural rate of unemployment; therefore, the Phillips Curve is vertical at that rate in the long run.

SUPPLY-SIDE ECONOMICS

Our final aggregate supply topic is **supply-side economics.** "Supply-siders" contend that changes in aggregate supply must be recognized as active forces in determining the levels of both inflation and unemployment. Economic disturbances can be generated on the supply side, as well as on the demand side, of the economy. Moreover, certain government policies allegedly have reduced the growth of aggregate supply over time. By reversing these policies, say the supply-siders, the U.S. economy can achieve low levels of unemployment without producing rapid inflation.

Tax-Transfer Disincentives

Supply-side economists argue that the spectacular growth of the U.S. tax-transfer system has negatively affected incentives to work, invest, innovate, and assume entrepreneurial risks. The tax-transfer system allegedly has eroded the economy's productivity, and this decline in efficiency has slowed the expansion of long-run aggregate supply. The argument is that high taxes reduce the after-tax rewards of workers and producers, making work, innovation, investing, and risk bearing less financially attractive. According to supply-side economists, *marginal tax rates* are most relevant to decisions to undertake *additional* work and *additional* saving and investing.

Taxes and Incentives to Work Supply-siders believe that how long and how hard individuals work depends on how much additional *after-tax* earnings they derive from work. To induce more work—to increase aggregate inputs of labor—government should reduce marginal tax rates on earned incomes. Lower marginal tax rates make work more attractive by increasing the opportunity cost of leisure. Thus, individuals choose to substitute work for leisure. This increase in productive effort can occur in many ways: by increasing the number of hours worked per day or week, by encouraging workers to postpone retirement, by inducing more people to enter the labor force, by making people willing to work harder, and by discouraging long periods of unemployment.

Transfer Disincentives Supply-side economists also believe the existence of a wide variety of public transfer programs has eroded incentives to work. Unemployment compensation and welfare programs have made job loss less of an economic crisis for some people. The fear of being unemployed, and therefore the need to be a disciplined, productive worker, is simply less acute than it once was. Many transfer programs are structured to discourage work. Our social security program and welfare system encourage recipients *not* to be productive by imposing a "tax" in the form of a loss of transfer benefits on those who work. Only very recently have work requirements and time limits been introduced into the program providing aid to families with dependent children.

Incentives to Save and Invest The rewards for saving and investing have also been reduced by high marginal tax rates. Assume you save $1000 at 10 percent, so you earn $100 interest per year. If your marginal tax rate is 40 percent, your after-tax-interest earnings will be $60 and the after-tax interest rate you receive is only 6 percent. While you might be willing to save (forgo current consumption) for a 10 percent return on your saving, you might prefer to consume when the return is only 6 percent.

Saving, remember, is the prerequisite of investment. Thus supply-side economists recommend lower marginal tax rates on saving. They also call for lower taxes on investment income to ensure there are ready investment outlets for the economy's enhanced pool of saving. A critical determinant of investment spending is the expected *after-tax* return of that spending.

To summarize: Lower marginal tax rates encourage saving and investing. Workers therefore find themselves equipped with more and technologically superior machinery and equipment. Labor productivity rises, and this expands aggregate supply, which in turn keeps unemployment rates and inflation low.

Laffer Curve

In the supply-side view, reductions in marginal tax rates increase the nation's aggregate supply. Moreover, according to supply-side economist Arthur Laffer, lower tax *rates* are compatible with constant or even enlarged tax *revenues.* Thus, supply-side tax cuts need not produce federal budget deficits.

This idea is based on the **Laffer Curve,** which, as shown in Figure 16-10, depicts the relationship between tax rates and tax revenues. As tax rates increase from 0 to 100 percent, tax revenues increase from zero to some maximum level (at *m*) and then decline to zero. Tax revenues decline beyond some point because higher tax rates discourage economic activity,

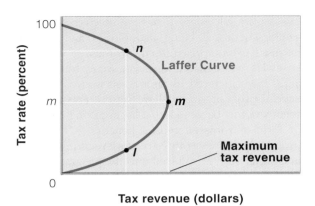

FIGURE 16-10 The Laffer Curve The Laffer Curve suggests that up to point *m* higher tax rates will result in larger tax revenues. But still higher tax rates will adversely affect incentives to work and produce, reducing the size of the tax base (output and income) to the extent that tax revenues will decline. It follows that if tax rates are above *m*, reductions in tax rates may produce increases in tax revenues.

- -

diminishing the tax base (domestic output and income). This is easiest to see at the extreme, where tax rates are 100 percent. Tax revenues here are, in theory, reduced to zero because the 100 percent confiscatory tax rate has halted production. A 100 percent tax rate applied to a tax base of zero yields no revenue.

In the early 1980s Laffer suggested that the United States was at a point such as *n* on the curve in Figure 16-10. There, tax rates are so high that production is discouraged to the extent that tax revenues are below the maximum at *m*. If the economy is at *n*, then lower tax rates are quite compatible with constant tax revenues. Lowering tax rates moves the economy from point *n* to point *l*, and government brings in the same total amount of tax revenue as before. Laffer's reasoning is that lower tax rates stimulate incentives to work, save and invest, innovate, and accept business risks, thus triggering an expansion of real output and income. This enlarged tax base sustains tax revenues even though tax rates are lowered. Indeed, between *n* and *m* lower tax rates result in increased tax revenue.

Supply-side economists think tax rates can be lowered without producing budget deficits for two additional reasons:

1. Less tax evasion Tax avoidance (which is legal) and tax evasion (which is not) decline when taxes are reduced. High marginal tax rates prompt taxpayers to avoid taxes through various tax shelters, such as buying municipal bonds on which inter-

est earned is tax-free. They also encourage some taxpayers to conceal income from the Internal Revenue Service. Lower tax rates reduce the inclination to engage in tax avoidance and tax evasion.

2. Reduced transfers The stimulus to production and employment which a tax cut provides reduces government transfer payments. For example, having more job opportunities reduces transfer payments and decreases a budget deficit. **(Key Question 8)**

Criticisms of the Laffer Curve

The Laffer Curve and its supply-side implications have been subject to severe criticism.

Taxes, Incentives, and Time A fundamental criticism has to do with the sensitivity of economic incentives to changes in tax rates. Skeptics say there is ample empirical evidence showing that the impact of a tax cut on incentives is small, of uncertain direction, and relatively slow to emerge. For example, with respect to work incentives, studies indicate that decreases in tax rates lead some people to work more but others to work less. Those who work more are enticed by the higher after-tax pay; they substitute work for leisure because the opportunity cost of leisure has increased. Those who work less do so because the higher after-tax pay increases their ability to "buy leisure." They can meet their after-tax income goals by working fewer hours.

Inflation Most economists think that the demand-side effects of a tax cut exceed the supply-side effects. Thus, tax cuts undertaken when the economy is at or near its full-employment level of output may produce increases in aggregate demand which overwhelm any increase in aggregate supply. Demand-pull inflation is the likely result.

Position on the Curve Skeptics say the Laffer Curve is merely a logical proposition, asserting that there must be some level of tax rates between 0 and 100 percent at which tax revenues will be at their maximum. Economists of all persuasions can agree with this. But the issue of where a particular economy is located on its Laffer Curve is an empirical question. If we assume—as Laffer did in the early 1980s—that we are at point *n* in Figure 16-10, then tax cuts will increase tax revenues. But critics say that the economy's location on the Laffer Curve is undocumented and unknown. If the economy is at any point below *m* on the curve, then tax *reductions* will reduce tax revenues and create budget deficits. And, in fact, the sizable *increases* in marginal tax rates imposed by the federal government in 1993 have generated large increases in tax revenue.

Overregulation

Supply-siders also claim that government's regulatory involvement in the economy has adversely affected productivity and long-run aggregate supply. Two points should be noted here:

1. "Industrial regulation"—government regulation of specific industries such as transportation or communications—frequently provides regulated firms with a legal monopoly or cartel. Government regulation protects such firms from competition, the result being that these firms are less efficient and incur higher costs of production.

2. The "social regulation" of industry has increased substantially in the past decades. New government regulations have been imposed on industry in response to problems of pollution, product safety, worker health and safety, and equal access to job opportunities. Supply-side economists point out that social regulation has greatly increased the costs of doing business.

The overall impact of both types of regulation is that costs and prices are higher and economic growth is slower.

Reaganomics

The elements of supply-side economics just discussed provided the intellectual underpinnings of the economic policies of the Reagan administration (1981–1988). Along with a substantial reduction in government regulation, personal and corporate income tax rates were cut sharply, the latter by about 25 percent over 3 years. In 1986, the marginal tax rate on wealthy taxpayers fell from 50 to 28 percent. (Today, the top rate is 39.6 percent.)

The real world is an imperfect laboratory for judging the success of a vast socioeconomic experiment such as **Reaganomics.** For one thing, Congress did not accept all the expenditure reductions which the Reagan administration requested in its program. Even so, the Reagan years did in fact witness significant declines in inflation and interest rates, a record-long

peacetime economic expansion, and eventual attainment of full employment. These years were also characterized by a resurgence of the spirit of entrepreneurialism. Nevertheless, it is fair to say that, as such, supply-side economics largely failed to increase aggregate supply more rapidly than its historical pace. There is little evidence that this program had any significant positive impacts on saving and investment or incentive to work. The saving rate, in fact, trended downward throughout the 1980s. Productivity growth surged in 1983 and 1984, as it usually does during recovery from recession, but was disappointingly low in the rest of the 1980s. Most economists attribute the post-1982 economic recovery to the demand-side expansionary effects of the Reagan tax cuts and not to the use of tax cuts as a pro-growth, supply-side measure.

The large tax cuts, together with rising levels of government expenditures, particularly for national defense, created record-high U.S. budget deficits. The prediction of the Laffer Curve that tax cuts would enhance tax revenues beyond those associated with normal economic expansions simply did not bear fruit. The large deficits may have increased interest rates and crowded out some unknown amount of private investment. To cope with the large deficits, the Bush administration increased the top marginal tax rate from 28 to 31 percent. But huge deficits persisted, and in 1993 the Clinton administration again raised tax rates, pushing the top marginal tax rate to 39.6 percent.

In summary, the evidence casts considerable doubt on the key supply-side proposition that tax cuts can directly and significantly shift the U.S. long-run aggregate supply curve rightward.

QUICK REVIEW 16-4

■ Supply-side economists say that the U.S. tax-transfer system reduces work effort, saving and investing, innovation, and risk bearing.

■ The Laffer Curve suggests that when tax rates are higher than optimal from a revenue standpoint, reductions in tax rates can expand real output and income (the tax base) and simultaneously increase tax revenue.

■ The supply-side policies of the Reagan administration (1981–1988) did not increase aggregate supply more rapidly than otherwise would have been expected for this 8-year period.

Price and Wage Controls

If inflation is a problem for a society, why not simply outlaw inflationary price and wage increases? That is, why not enact price and wage controls?

During inflationary times, it is natural for people to look for culprits. Who exactly is causing prices and wages to rise and how can government alter their actions? Casual observation leads many to conclude that firms are the *cause* of rising prices and unions are the *cause* of rising wages. After all, firms and unions are the ones directly announcing price increases and negotiating wage increases.

If firms and unions are viewed as the causes of inflation, then one solution is to limit price and wage increases by law so that inflation would be held to, say, 2 percent annually. Such kinds of *price and wage controls* have a long history. For example, the Roman emperor Diocletian attempted them in 301. So did the Mongol, Kublai Khan, in the thirteenth century; the city leaders of Antwerp in 1584; the Continental Congress in America in 1775; U.S. president Richard Nixon in 1971; and several South American countries in the 1980s. In each case, inflation eventually won and controls lost. The reasons why are as follows:

1. Controls for Symptoms, Not Causes In most circumstances, increases in prices and wages are the *symptoms,* not the underlying *cause,* of inflation. Inflation is caused by excessive growth of the money supply, excessive investment spending, inappropriate fiscal policy, or oil price "shocks." Wage and price controls leave the root cause of inflation untreated.

2. Circumvention and Compliance Problems Wage and price controls have the force of law; therefore, government can use fines and imprisonment to coerce labor and management to obey them. Nevertheless, enforcement and compliance problems can be severe. Because the controls produce below-equilibrium prices and wages, they also produce shortages of products and workers. *Black markets*—illegal markets in which prices and wages exceed legal maximums—become common. Buyers willing to pay more than the controlled price seek out sellers willing to sell the product for more than the controlled price. Thus, price increases show up "off the books."

Businesses and workers also respond in other ways to circumvent controls. For example, firms can reduce product quality instead of raising product price. If the price of a candy bar is frozen at 60 cents, reducing its size by one-half can effectively double its price. Workers can sidestep wage controls by moving to newly created job classifications that firms set up to circumvent the wage controls. The firm, in a sense, converts *illegal* wage increases into *legal* promotions.

CHAPTER SUMMARY

1. In macroeconomics, the short run is a period in which nominal wages are fixed; they do not change in response to changes in the price level. In contrast, the long run is a period in which nominal wages are fully responsive to changes in the price level.

2. The short-run aggregate supply curve is upsloping. Because nominal wages are fixed, increases in the price level (prices received by firms) increase profits and real output. Conversely, decreases in the price level reduce profits and real output. However, the long-run aggregate supply curve is vertical. With sufficient time for adjustment, nominal wages rise and fall with the price level, moving the economy along a vertical aggregate supply curve at the economy's full-employment output.

3. In the short run, demand-pull inflation increases the price level and real output. Once nominal wages have increased, the temporary increase in real output is reversed.

4. In the short run, cost-push inflation increases the price level *and* reduces real output. Unless government expands aggregate demand, nominal wages eventually will decline under conditions of recession and the short-run aggregate supply curve will shift back to its initial location. Prices and real output will eventually return to their original levels.

5. If prices and wages are flexible downward, a decline in aggregate demand will reduce output *and* the price level. The decline in the price level will eventually reduce nom-

3. Inability to Maintain Long-Term Public Support The same public that called for wage and price controls often turns against them once it realizes their impacts. Wage and price controls interfere with accepted, well-established rights and expectations. They interfere with the right of workers to freely bargain for wages with employers through union representation. They interfere with the right of firms to freely set prices and adjust them rapidly to changing supply and demand circumstances. And the shortages they create do not fit with consumer expectations of products being available in shops and stores. As a result, the public often quickly tires of wage and price controls.

4. Allocative Inefficiency and Rationing Where effective, wage and price controls prohibit the market system from making necessary price and wage adjustments. If the demand for one product, say, retirement housing, should rise sharply (independent of inflation), its price could not rise to signal society's wish for more of this output and therefore more resources to produce it. The same problem occurs in the labor market. A large increase in the demand for, say, software designers could not produce the salary increase needed to attract workers from other occupations. Nor would there be proper incentives for college students to take up this field of study.

Also, price controls strip the market mechanism of the rationing function—its ability to equate quantity demanded and quantity supplied. Which buyers are to obtain the product when there are shortages? The product can be rationed on a first-come, first-served basis or by favoritism. But both are highly arbitrary and inequitable; those first in line or those able to cultivate a friendship with the seller get as much of the product as they want, while others get none at all. Government may therefore decide to impartially ration the product to all consumers by issuing ration coupons to prospective buyers on a fair basis. But this means adding another costly government bureaucracy to that already required to police compliance with the controls.

In view of the distortions caused by price and wage controls and their overall poor results, most contemporary economists reject this approach to trying to reduce inflation.

---

inal wages and shift the short-run aggregate supply curve rightward. Full-employment output will thus be restored.

6. Assuming a stable upsloping aggregate supply curve, rightward shifts of the aggregate demand curve of various sizes yields the generalization that high rates of inflation are associated with low rates of unemployment, and vice versa. This inverse relationship is known as the Phillips Curve, and empirical data for the 1960s seemed to be consistent with it.

7. In the 1970s and early 1980s the Phillips Curve apparently shifted rightward, reflecting stagflation—simultaneously rising inflation rates and unemployment rates. The standard interpretation is that the stagflation mainly resulted from huge oil price increases which caused large leftward shifts in the short-run aggregate supply curve (so-called supply shocks). The Phillips Curve shifted inward toward its original position in the 1980s. By 1989 stagflation had subsided.

8. The adaptive expectations version of the natural-rate hypothesis says that while there is a short-run tradeoff between inflation and unemployment, there is no such long-run tradeoff. Workers will adapt their expectations to new inflation realities, and when they do, the unemployment rate will return to the natural rate. The long-run Phillips Curve is therefore vertical at the natural rate, meaning that higher rates of inflation do not "buy" the economy less unemployment.

9. The rational expectations version of the natural-rate hypothesis contends that workers will anticipate the inflationary effects of monetary policy and fiscal policy and will build these expectations into their wage demands. As a result, not even a short-run Phillips Curve will exist; the economy will simply move along its vertical long-run Phillips Curve when the government undertakes expansionary policies.

10. Supply-side economists trace slow economic growth to expansion of government and, specifically, to the negative effects of the tax-transfer system on incentives. They say that excessive government regulation of business has

contributed to slow growth. The Laffer Curve relates tax rates to levels of tax revenue and suggests that, under some circumstances, cuts in tax rates can expand the tax base (output and income) and increase tax revenues. Massive tax cuts undertaken by the Reagan administration failed to increase aggregate supply more rapidly than would have been expected without the cuts.

TERMS AND CONCEPTS

short-run aggregate
  supply curve
long-run aggregate
  supply curve
Phillips Curve

stagflation
aggregate supply shocks
natural-rate hypothesis
adaptive expectations
  theory

disinflation
rational expectations
  theory
supply-side economics

Laffer Curve
Reaganomics

STUDY QUESTIONS

1. Distinguish between the short run and the long run as they relate to macroeconomics.

2. Which of the following statements are true? Which are false? Explain the false statements.
   a. Short-run aggregate supply curves reflect an inverse relationship between the price level and the level of real output.
   b. The long-run aggregate supply curve assumes that nominal wages are fixed.
   c. In the long run, an increase in the price level will result in an increase in nominal wages.

3. KEY QUESTION Suppose the full-employment level of real output (*Q*) for a hypothetical economy is $250 and the price level (*P*) initially is 100. Use the short-run aggregate supply schedules below to answer the questions which follow:

AS (P_{100})		AS (P_{125})		AS (P_{75})	
P	Q	P	Q	P	Q
125	280	125	250	125	310
100	250	100	220	100	280
75	220	75	190	75	250

   a. What will be the level of real output in the *short run* if the price level unexpectedly rises from 100 to 125 because of an increase in aggregate demand? What if the price level falls unexpectedly

from 100 to 75 because of a decrease in aggregate demand? Explain each situation, using numbers from the table.
   b. What will be the level of real output in the *long run* when the price level rises from 100 to 125? When it falls from 100 to 75? Explain each situation.
   c. Show the circumstances described in parts **a** and **b** on graph paper, and derive the long-run aggregate supply curve.

4. KEY QUESTION Use graphical analysis to show how each of the following would affect the economy first in the short run and then in the long run. Assume that the United States is initially operating at its full-employment level of output, that prices and wages are eventually flexible both upward and downward, and that there is no counteracting fiscal or monetary policy.
   a. Because of a war abroad, the oil supply to the United States is disrupted, sending oil prices rocketing upward.
   b. Construction spending on new homes rises dramatically, greatly increasing total U.S. investment spending.
   c. Economic recession occurs abroad, significantly reducing foreign purchases of U.S. exports.

5. Assume that a particular short-run aggregate supply curve exists for an economy and that the curve is relevant for several years. Use the AD-AS analysis to show graphically why higher rates of inflation over this period would be associated with lower rates of unemployment, and vice versa. What is this inverse relationship called?

6. KEY QUESTION Distinguish between adaptive expectations and rational expectations. Why are adaptive expectations consistent with a short-run Phillips Curve while rational expectations are not? Explain why both types of expectations result in a vertical long-run Phillips Curve.

7. Explain: "If expectations are rational and fully correct, the unemployment rate will never diverge from the natural rate."

8. KEY QUESTION What are the two broad tenets of supply-side economics? What is the Laffer Curve, and how does it relate to one of these tenets?

9. Why might one person work more, earn more, and pay more income tax when his or her tax rate is cut, while another person will work less, earn less, and pay less income tax under the same circumstance?

10. (Last Word) Relate this statement to price and wage controls: "Controlling prices to halt inflation is like breaking a thermometer to control the heat."

11. WEB-BASED QUESTION Phillips Curve— **Do Real Data Confirm?** The Phillips Curve purports to show a stable relationship between the rate of inflation and the unemployment rate. Plot the data points between inflation and unemployment over the past decade to the present in the following manner. For inflation data, first use the Consumer Price Index—All Urban Consumers, then the Producer Price Index—All Commodities. For unemployment data, first use Unemployment Rate— Civilian Labor Force, then use data from your population group (e.g., Unemployment Rate—Civilian Labor Force 20 Years and Over, Male). Do any of your data point plots seem to confirm the Phillips Curve concept? Retrieve unemployment data from the Bureau of Labor Statistics http://stats.bls.gov/ cpshome.htm and select Most Requested Series. For inflation data, go to http://stats.bls.gov/cpihome.htm and select Most Requested Series.

12. WEB-BASED QUESTION The Laffer Curve— **Does It Really Exist?** The Laffer Curve suggests that beyond some point higher tax rates will result in lower tax revenues. Over the past 60 years the marginal income tax rates have varied widely, with the top rate exceeding 90 percent in the early 1940s and falling to under 30 percent in the 1980s. This would imply that personal income taxes as a percentage of gross domestic output would also vary widely. Visit the U.S. Commerce Department http://www.doc.gov/ and search for 1998 Budget Historical Table (or the latest year instead of 1998) for the document titled Tax Receipts by Source as a Percentage of GDP. At present, individual income taxes are what percentage of GDP? How has the percentage varied over the past 60 years? Does this support the Laffer Curve?

17

Disputes in Macro Theory and Policy

One of the great traditions in scholarship is the challenging of mainstream thinking. Many such challenges to the "conventional wisdom" fail; either the new theories are not logical or they do not conform to facts. At the opposite extreme, some new theories gain full support and replace the existing theories. More often, the new ideas modify the existing body of mainstream thinking, which thereafter is improved or extended. This certainly is true in economics.

As any academic discipline evolves, it draws criticism and disagreement. In this chapter we examine some of the major disputes in macro theory and policy. We initially provide historical background by contrasting classical and Keynesian macroeconomic theories. Then we turn to contemporary disagreements on three interrelated questions: (1) What causes instability in the economy? (2) Is the economy self-correcting? (3) Should government adhere to *rules* or use *discretion* in setting economic policy? Finally, we summarize the alternative perspectives discussed in this chapter and the previous chapter.

SOME HISTORY: CLASSICS AND KEYNES

Classical economics, which dominated economic thought in the 1800s, suggested that full employment is the norm in a market economy and that a *laissez-faire* ("let it be") policy by government is best. In contrast, Keynes contended in the 1930s that laissez-faire capitalism is subject to recurring recessions or depressions with widespread unemployment. In the Keynesian view, active government stabilization policy is required to avoid the waste of idle resources.

Because the classical and Keynesian views of the macroeconomic world provide great insight on modern debates, it is worthwhile to compare their basic forms through modern aggregate demand and aggregate supply analysis.

Classical View

In the classical view, the aggregate supply curve is vertical and exclusively determines the level of real output. The downsloping aggregate demand curve is stable and solely establishes the price level.

Vertical Aggregate Supply Curve In the classical perspective, the aggregate supply curve is a vertical line as shown in Figure 17-1a. This line is located at the full-employment level of real output, which in this designation is also the full-capacity real output. According to the classical economists, the economy will operate at its full-employment level of output, Q_f, because of (1) Say's law (Chapter 9) and (2) responsive, flexible prices and wages.

We stress that classical economists believed that Q_f does *not* change in response to changes in the price level. Observe that as the price level falls from P_1 to P_2 in Figure 17-1a, real output remains anchored at Q_f.

But this stability of output might seem at odds with Chapter 3's upsloping supply curves for individual products. There we found that lower prices would make production less profitable and cause producers to offer *less* output and employ *fewer* workers. The classical response to this view is that input costs would fall along with product prices to leave *real* profits and output unchanged.

Consider a one-firm economy in which the firm's owner must receive a *real* profit of $20 to produce the full-employment output of 100 units. You know from Chapter 8 that what ultimately counts is the *real* reward one receives and not the level of prices. Assume

the owner's only input (aside from personal entrepreneurial talent) is 10 units of labor hired at $8 per worker for a total wage cost of $80 (= 10 × $8). Also suppose the 100 units of output sell for $1 per unit, so total revenue is $100 (= 100 × $1). This firm's *nominal* profit is $20 (= $100 − $80), and, using the $1 price to designate the base price index of 100 percent, its *real* profit is also $20 (= $20 ÷ 1.00). Well and good; full employment is achieved. But suppose the price level declines by one-half. Would our producer still earn the $20 of real profits needed to support production of a 100-unit full-employment output?

The classical answer is "yes." Now that product price is only 50¢, total revenue will be only $50 (= 100 × 50¢). But the cost of 10 units of labor will be reduced to $40 (= 10 × $4) because the wage rate will be halved. Although *nominal* profits fall to $10 (= $50 − $40), *real* profits remain at $20. By dividing money profits of $10 by the new price index (expressed as a decimal), we obtain *real* profits of $20 (= $10 ÷ .50).

With perfectly flexible wages there would be no change in the real rewards and therefore in the production behavior of businesses. With perfect wage flexibility, a change in the price level will not cause the economy to stray from full employment.

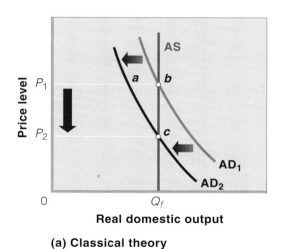

(a) Classical theory

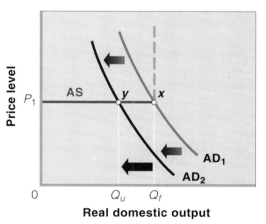

(b) Keynesian theory

FIGURE 17-1 Classical and Keynesian views of the macroeconomy (a) In classical theory, aggregate supply determines the full-employment level of real output, while aggregate demand establishes the price level. Aggregate demand normally is stable, but if it should decline, say, from AD₁ to AD₂, the price level will quickly fall from P_1 to P_2 to eliminate the temporary excess supply of *ab* and to restore full employment at *c*. (b) The Keynesian view is that aggregate demand is unstable and that prices and wages are downwardly inflexible. An AD₁ to AD₂ decline in aggregate demand has no effect on the price level. Instead, the economy moves from point *x* to *y* and real output falls to Q_u, where it can remain indefinitely.

Stable Aggregate Demand Classical economists theorize that money underlies aggregate demand. The amount of real output which can be purchased depends on (1) the quantity of money households and businesses possess and (2) the purchasing power of that money as determined by the price level. The purchasing power of the dollar refers to the real quantity of goods and services a dollar will buy. Thus, as we move down the vertical axis of Figure 17-1a, the price level is falling. This means that the purchasing power of each dollar is rising. If the price level declined by one-half, a particular quantity of money would now purchase a real output twice as large. With a fixed money supply, the price level and real output are inversely related.

And what of the *location* of the aggregate demand curve? According to the classical economists, aggregate demand will be stable as long as the nation's monetary authorities maintain a constant supply of money. With a fixed aggregate supply of output, increases in the supply of money will shift the aggregate demand curve rightward and spark demand-pull inflation. Reductions in the supply of money will shift the curve leftward and trigger deflation. The key to price-level stability, then, is to control the nation's money supply to prevent unwarranted shifts in aggregate demand.

A final observation: Even if there are declines in the money supply and therefore in aggregate demand, the economy depicted in Figure 17-1a will *not* experience unemployment. Admittedly, the immediate effect of a decline in aggregate demand from AD_1 to AD_2 is an excess supply of output since the aggregate output of goods and services exceeds aggregate spending by the amount ab. But, with the presumed downward flexibility of product and resource prices, this excess supply will reduce product prices along with workers' wages and the prices of other inputs. As a result, the price level will quickly decline from P_1 to P_2 until the amounts of output demanded and supplied are brought once again into equilibrium, this time at c. While the price level has fallen from P_1 to P_2, real output remains at the full-employment level.

Keynesian View

The core of crude, or extreme, **Keynesianism** is that product prices and wages are downwardly inflexible over very long time periods. The result is graphically represented as a horizontal aggregate supply curve. Also, aggregate demand is subject to periodic changes

caused by changes in the determinants of aggregate demand.

Horizontal Aggregate Supply Curve (to Full-Employment Output) The presumed downward inflexibility of prices and wages translates to a horizontal aggregate supply curve as shown in Figure 17-1b. Here, a decline in real output from Q_f to Q_u will have no impact on the price level. Conversely, an increase in real output from Q_u to Q_f will also leave the price level unchanged. The aggregate supply curve therefore extends from zero real output rightward to point x, where real output is at its full-employment level, Q_f. Once full employment is reached, the aggregate supply curve is vertical. This is shown by the dashed line extending upward from the horizontal aggregate supply curve at x.

Unstable Aggregate Demand Keynesian economists view aggregate demand as unstable from one period to the next, even without changes in the money supply. In particular, the investment component of aggregate demand fluctuates, altering the location of the aggregate demand curve. Suppose aggregate demand in Figure 17-1b declines from AD_1 to AD_2. The sole impact is on output and employment. Real output falls from Q_f to Q_u, while the price level is unchanged at P_1. Moreover, Keynesians believe that unless there is a fortuitous offsetting increase in aggregate demand, real output may remain at Q_u, which is below the full-employment level Q_f. Active government policies to increase aggregate demand are essential to move the economy from point y to point x. Otherwise, the economy will suffer the wastes of recession and depression. **(Key Question 1)**

QUICK REVIEW 17-1

In classical macroeconomics:
■ The aggregate supply curve is vertical at the full-employment level of real output.

■ The aggregate demand curve is stable as long as the money supply is constant.

In Keynesian macroeconomics:
■ The aggregate supply curve is horizontal up to the full-employment level of output; then it becomes vertical.

■ The aggregate demand curve is unstable largely because of the volatility of investment spending; such shifts cause either recession or demand-pull inflation.

WHAT CAUSES MACRO INSTABILITY?

You are aware from previous chapters that the capitalist economies have, in fact, experienced considerable instability during this century. The United States, for example, has experienced the Great Depression, numerous recessions, and periods of inflation. Contemporary economists have different perspectives on why this instability occurs.

Mainstream View

The mainstream view is Keynesian-based. It holds that instability in the economy arises from two sources: (1) significant changes in investment spending which change aggregate demand, and, occasionally, (2) adverse aggregate supply shocks which change aggregate supply. These factors are not new to you, so let's just briefly review them here.

Changes in Investment Spending   Mainstream macroeconomics focuses on aggregate spending and its components. Recall that the basic equation underlying aggregate expenditures is

$$C_a + I_g + X_n + G = \text{GDP}$$

That is, the aggregate amount of after-tax consumption, gross investment, net exports, and government spending determines the total amount of the goods and services produced and sold. In equilibrium, $C_a + I_g + X_n + G$ (aggregate expenditures) is equal to GDP (real output). A decrease in the price level increases equilibrium GDP and thus allows us to trace out a downsloping aggregate demand curve for the economy. Any change in one of the spending components in the aggregate expenditures equation shifts the aggregate demand curve. This, in turn, changes equilibrium real output, the price level, or both.

Investment spending, in particular, is subject to wide "booms" and "busts." Significant increases in investment spending get multiplied into even greater increases in aggregate demand and thus can produce demand-pull inflation. In contrast, major declines in investment spending get multiplied into even greater decreases in aggregate demand and thus can cause recessions.

Adverse Aggregate Supply Shocks   In the mainstream view, the second source of macroeconomic instability arises on the supply side. Occasionally, such external events as wars or artificial supply restrictions boost prices of key imported resources and significantly raise per-unit production costs. The result is a sizable decline in a nation's aggregate supply, which destabilizes the economy by simultaneously causing cost-push inflation *and* recession.

Monetarist View

Classical economics has emerged in several modern forms. One is **monetarism,** which (1) focuses on the money supply, (2) holds that markets are highly competitive, and (3) says that a competitive market system gives the economy a high degree of macroeconomic stability. Like classical economics, monetarism argues that the price and wage flexibility provided by competitive markets would cause fluctuations in aggregate demand to alter product and resource prices rather than output and employment. Thus the market system would provide substantial macroeconomic stability *were it not for government interference in the economy.*

The problem, as monetarists see it, is that government has promoted downward wage inflexibility through the minimum-wage law, pro-union legislation, guaranteed prices for some farm products, pro-business monopoly legislation, and so forth. The free-market system could provide macroeconomic stability, but, despite good intentions, government interference has undermined this capability. Moreover, monetarists say that government has contributed to the economy's business cycles through its clumsy and mistaken attempts to achieve greater stability through monetary policies.

Equation of Exchange   The fundamental equation of monetarism is the **equation of exchange:**

$$MV = PQ$$

where M is the supply of money; V is the **velocity** of money, that is, *the number of times per year the average dollar is spent on final goods and services;* P is the price level or, more specifically, the average price at which each unit of physical output is sold; and Q is the physical volume of all goods and services produced.

The label "equation of exchange" is easily understood. The left side, MV, represents the total amount *spent* by purchasers of output, while the right side, PQ, represents the total amount *received* by sellers of that output. The nation's money supply (M) multiplied by the number of times it is spent each year (V) *must* equal the nation's nominal GDP ($= P \times Q$).

The dollar value of total spending has to equal the dollar value of total output.

Stable Velocity   Monetarists say that velocity, V, in the equation of exchange is stable. As used here, "stable" is not synonymous with "constant." Monetarists are aware that velocity is higher today than it was several decades ago. Shorter pay periods, greater use of credit cards, and faster means of making payments enable people to hold less money and turn it over more rapidly than was possible in earlier times. These factors have enabled people to reduce their holdings of cash and checkbook money relative to the size of the nation's nominal GDP.

When monetarists say velocity is stable they mean that the factors altering velocity change gradually and predictably. Changes in velocity from one year to the next can be easily anticipated. Moreover, velocity does not change in response to changes in the money supply itself. In this view, people have a stable desire to hold money relative to holding other financial assets, holding real assets, and buying current output. The factors which determine the amount of money the public wants to hold depend mainly on the level of nominal GDP.

Example: Suppose that when the level of nominal GDP is $400 billion, the public desires $100 billion of money to purchase this output. That means V is 4 (= $400 billion of nominal GDP/$100 billion of money). If we further assume that the actual supply of money is $100 billion, the economy is in equilibrium with respect to money; the *actual* amount of money supplied equals the *desired* amount the public wants to hold.

If velocity is stable, the equation of exchange suggests there is a predictable relationship between the money supply and nominal GDP (= PQ). An increase in the money supply of, say, $10 billion upsets equilibrium in our example since the public finds itself holding more money or liquidity than it wants. That is, the actual amount of money held ($110 billion) exceeds the amount of holdings desired ($100 billion). The reaction of the public (households and businesses) is to restore its desired balance of money relative to other items, such as stocks and bonds, factories and equipment, houses and automobiles, and clothing and toys. But the spending of money by individual households and businesses leaves more cash in others' checkable deposits or billfolds. Those other households and firms also try to "spend down" their excess cash balances, but, overall, *the $110 billion supply of money cannot be spent down.*

Instead, the collective attempt to reduce cash balances increases aggregate demand, boosting the *nominal* GDP. Because velocity in our example is 4—that is, the typical dollar is spent four times per year—nominal GDP rises from $400 to $440 billion. At that higher nominal GDP, the money supply of $110 billion equals the amount of money desired ($440 billion/4 = $110 billion), and equilibrium is reestablished.

The $10 billion increase in the money supply thus eventually increases nominal GDP by $40 billion. Spending on goods, services, and assets expands until nominal GDP has gone up enough to restore the original 4-to-1 equilibrium relationship between nominal GDP and the money supply.

Note that the relationship GDP/M defines V. A stable relationship between nominal GDP and M means a stable V. And a change in M causes a proportionate change in nominal GDP. Thus, changes in the money supply allegedly have a predictable effect on nominal GDP (= $P \times Q$). An increase in M increases P or Q, or some combination of both; a decrease in M reduces P or Q, or some combination of both. **(Key Question 4)**

Monetary Causes of Instability   *Monetarists say that inappropriate monetary policy is the single most important cause of macroeconomic instability.* An increase in the money supply directly increases aggregate demand. Under conditions of full employment, this increase in aggregate demand increases the price level. For a time, higher prices cause firms to increase their real output, and the rate of unemployment falls below its natural rate. But once nominal wages rise to reflect the higher prices and thus to restore real wages, real output moves back to its full-employment level and the unemployment rate returns to its natural rate. The inappropriate increase in the money supply leads to inflation, together with instability of real output and employment.

Conversely, a decrease in the money supply reduces aggregate demand. Real output temporarily falls, and the unemployment rate rises above its natural rate. Eventually, nominal wages fall and real output returns to its full-employment level. The inappropriate decline in the money supply leads to deflation, together with instability of real GDP and employment.

The contrast between mainstream macroeconomics and monetarism on the causes of instability thus comes into sharp focus. Mainstream economists view instability of investment as the main cause of the economy's instability. They see monetary policy as a stabilizing factor. Changes in the money supply raise or lower interest rates as needed, smooth out swings in investment, and thus reduce macroeconomic instability. In contrast, monetarists view changes in the money supply as the main cause of the instability in the economy. For example, they say that the Great Depression largely occurred because the Fed allowed the money supply to fall by nearly 40 percent in that period. According to Milton Friedman, a prominent monetarist:

> And [the money supply] fell not because there were no willing borrowers—not because the horse would not drink. It fell because the Federal Reserve System forced or permitted a sharp reduction in the [money supply], because it failed to exercise the responsibilities assigned to it in the Federal Reserve Act to provide liquidity to the banking system. The Great Contraction is tragic testimony to the power of monetary policy—not as Keynes and so many of his contemporaries believed, evidence of its impotence.[1]

Real-Business-Cycle View

A third modern view of the cause of macroeconomic instability is that business cycles are caused by *real* factors affecting aggregate supply rather than by *monetary*, or spending, factors causing fluctuations in aggregate demand. In the **real-business-cycle theory**, business fluctuations result from significant changes in technology and resource availability. Those changes affect productivity and thus the long-run growth trend of aggregate supply.

An example focusing on recession will clarify this thinking. Suppose productivity (output per worker) sharply declines because of a large increase in oil prices, which makes it prohibitively expensive to operate certain types of machinery. This decline in productivity implies a reduction in the economy's ability to produce real output. The result would be a decrease in the economy's long-run aggregate supply curve, as represented by the leftward shift from AS_{LR1} to AS_{LR2} in Figure 17-2.

As real output falls from Q_1 to Q_2, the public does not need as much money to buy the reduced volume of goods and services. So the demand for money falls. Moreover, the slowdown in business activity lessens

business borrowing from banks, reducing checkable deposits. Thus, the supply of money also falls. In this controversial scenario, changes in the supply of money respond to changes in the demand for money. The decline in the money supply then reduces aggregate demand, as from AD_1 to AD_2 in Figure 17-2. The overall outcome is a decline in real output from Q_1 to Q_2, with no change in the price level.

Conversely, a large increase in aggregate supply (not shown) caused by, say, major new innovations in the production process would shift the long-run aggregate supply curve rightward. Real output would increase, and money demand and money supply would both increase. Aggregate demand would shift rightward by an amount equal to the rightward shift of long-run aggregate supply. Real output would increase, without driving up the price level.

Conclusion: In the real-business-cycle theory, macro instability arises on the aggregate supply side of the economy, not on the aggregate demand side as mainstream economists and monetarists generally say.

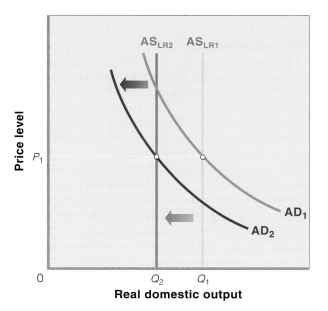

FIGURE 17-2 The real-business-cycle theory In the real-business-cycle theory, a decline in resource availability shifts the nation's long-run aggregate supply curve to the left from AS_{LR1} to AS_{LR2}. The decline in real output from Q_1 to Q_2, in turn, reduces money demand (less is needed) and money supply (fewer loans are taken out) such that aggregate demand shifts leftward from AD_1 to AD_2. The result is a recession in which the price level remains constant.

---

[1]Milton Friedman, *The Optimum Quantity of Money and Other Essays* (Chicago: Aldine, 1969), p. 97.

Coordination Failures

A fourth and final modern view of macroeconomic instability relates to so-called **coordination failures.** Such failures occur *when people do not reach a mutually beneficial equilibrium because they lack some way to jointly coordinate their actions.*

Noneconomic Example

Consider first a noneconomic example. Suppose you learn of an impending volleyball party at a nearby lake, but it looks like it might rain. If you expect others to be there, you will decide to go. If you expect that others will not attend, you will decide to stay home. There are several possible equilibrium outcomes, depending on the mix of people's expectations. Let's consider just two. If each person assumes all others will be at the party, all will go. The party and volleyball game will occur and presumably everyone will have a good time. But if each person assumes that everyone else will stay home, each person will stay home and there will be no party. When the volleyball party does *not* take place, *even though all would be better off if it did happen,* a coordination failure has occurred.

Macroeconomic Example

Now let's apply this idea to macroeconomic instability, specifically recession. Suppose individual firms and households expect other firms and consumers to cut back their investment and consumption spending. As a result, each firm and household will anticipate a reduction of aggregate demand. Firms therefore will cut back their own investment spending since they will anticipate future excess production capacity. Households will also reduce their own spending (increase their saving) because they anticipate reduced work-hours, possible layoffs, and falling income. Aggregate demand will indeed decline and the economy will experience a recession *due to a self-fulfilling prophecy.* Moreover, the economy will *stay* at a below-full-employment level of output because, once there, producers and households have no individual incentive to increase spending. If *all* producers and households would agree to simultaneously increase their investment and consumption spending, then aggregate demand would rise, and real output and real income would expand. Each producer and consumer would be better off. However, this outcome does not occur because there is no mechanism for firms and households to agree on such a joint spending increase.

In this case, the economy is stuck in an *unemployment equilibrium* because of a coordination failure. With a different set of expectations, a coordination failure might leave the economy in an *inflation equilibrium.* In this view, there are a number of such potential equilibrium positions in the economy, some good and some bad, depending on people's mix of expectations. Macroeconomic instability, then, reflects the movement of the economy from one such equilibrium position to another as expectations change.

> ### QUICK REVIEW 17-2
>
> ■ Mainstream economists say that macroeconomic instability usually stems from swings in investment spending and, occasionally, from adverse aggregate supply shocks.
>
> ■ Monetarists view the economy through the equation of exchange ($MV = PQ$). If velocity V is stable, changes in the money supply M directly lead to changes in nominal GDP ($= P \times Q$). For monetarists, changes in M via inappropriate monetary policy are the single most important cause of macroeconomic instability.
>
> ■ In the real-business-cycle theory, significant changes in "real" factors such as technology, resource availability, and productivity change the economy's long-run aggregate supply, causing macroeconomic instability.
>
> ■ Macroeconomic instability can result from coordination failures—less-than-optimal equilibrium positions which occur because businesses and households lack some way to jointly coordinate their actions.

DOES THE ECONOMY "SELF-CORRECT"?

Just as there are disputes over the causes of macroeconomic instability, there are debates on whether or not the economy corrects itself when instability does occur. Also, economists disagree as to the length of time it will take for any such self-correction to happen.

New Classical View of Self-Correction

Monetarist and rational expectations economists (Chapter 16) take the view of **new classical economics,** which is that when the economy occasionally diverges from its full-employment output, internal mechanisms within the economy automatically move it back to that output. This perspective is associated with the adaptive and rational expectations theories (the natural-rate theories) discussed in Chapter 16.

Graphical Analysis

Figure 17-3a is useful for relating the new classical analysis to the issue of self-correction. Specifically, an increase in aggregate demand, say, from AD_1 to AD_2, moves the economy upward along its short-run aggregate supply curve AS_1 from a to b. The price level rises and real output increases. In the long run, however, nominal wages rise to restore real wages. Per-unit production costs then increase, and the short-run aggregate supply curve shifts leftward, eventually from AS_1 to AS_2. The economy moves from b to c and real output returns to its full-employment level, Q_1. This level of output is dictated by the economy's vertical long-run aggregate supply curve, here AS_{LR}.

Conversely, a decrease in aggregate demand from AD_1 to AD_3 in Figure 17-3b first moves the economy downward along its short-run aggregate supply curve AS_1 from point a to d. The price level *and* the level of real output fall. But in the long run, nominal wages decline such that real wages fall to their previous levels. When that happens, per-unit production costs decline and the short-run aggregate supply curve shifts to the right, eventually from AS_1 to AS_3. The economy moves back to e, where it again achieves its full-

employment level, Q_1. As in Figure 17-3a, the economy in Figure 17-3b has automatically self-corrected to its full-employment output and natural rate of unemployment.

Speed of Adjustment

There is some disagreement among new classical economists on how long it will take for self-correction to occur. Monetarists usually hold the *adaptive expectations* view that people form their expectations on present realities and only gradually change their expectations as experience unfolds. This means that the shifts in the short-run aggregate supply curves shown in Figure 17-3 may not occur for 2 or 3 years, or even longer. Other new classical economists, however, accept the *rational expectations* assumption that workers *anticipate* some future outcomes before they occur. When price-level changes are fully anticipated, adjustments of nominal wages are very quick, or even instantaneous. Let's see why.

Although several new theories incorporate rational expectations, including Keynesian ones, our interest here is the new classical version of the rational expectations theory (hereafter, RET). RET is based on two assumptions:

1. People behave rationally, gathering and intelligently processing information to form expecta-

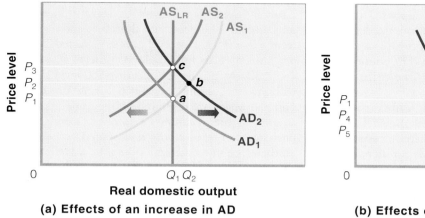

(a) Effects of an increase in AD

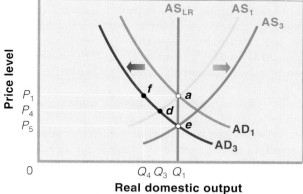

(b) Effects of a decrease in AD

FIGURE 17-3 **New classical view of self-correction** (a) An unanticipated increase in aggregate demand from AD_1 to AD_2 first moves the economy from a to b. The economy then self-corrects to c. An anticipated increase in aggregate demand moves the economy directly from a to c. (b) An unanticipated decrease in aggregate demand from AD_1 to AD_3 moves the economy from a to d. The economy then self-corrects to e. An anticipated decrease in aggregate demand moves the economy directly from a to e. (Mainstream economists, however, say that if the price level remains at P_1, the economy will move from a to f, and even if the price level falls to P_2, the economy may remain at d because of downward wage inflexibility.)

tions about things which are economically important to them. These expectations are adjusted quickly as new developments affecting future economic outcomes occur. Where there is adequate information, people's beliefs about future economic outcomes *accurately reflect the likelihood that those outcomes will occur.* For example, if it is clear that some policy will cause inflation, people will recognize that fact and adjust their economic behavior in anticipation of inflation.

2. Like classical economists, RET economists assume that all product and resource markets are highly competitive and that prices and wages are flexible both upward and downward. RET goes further, assuming that new information is quickly (in some cases instantaneously) taken into account in the demand and supply curves of such markets. The upshot is that equilibrium prices and quantities adjust rapidly to unforeseen events, say, technological change or aggregate supply shocks. They adjust instantaneously to events with known outcomes, for example, changes in fiscal or monetary policy.

Unanticipated Price-Level Changes

The implication of RET is not only that the economy is self-correcting but that self-correction occurs quickly. In this thinking, *unanticipated* changes in the price level—so called **price-level surprises**—do cause temporary changes in real output. Suppose, for example, an unanticipated increase in foreign demand for U.S. goods increases U.S. aggregate demand from AD_1 to AD_2 in Figure 17-3a. The immediate result is an unexpected increase in the price level from P_1 to P_2.

But now an interesting question arises. If wages and prices are flexible as assumed in RET, why doesn't the higher price level immediately cause nominal wages to rise, such that there is no increase in real output at all? Why does the economy temporarily move from point *a* to *b* along AS_1? In RET, firms increase output from Q_1 to Q_2 because of *misperceptions* about rising prices of their own products relative to prices of other products (and to prices of labor). They mistakenly think the higher prices of their own products have resulted from increased demand for those products relative to the demands for other products. Expecting higher profits, they increase their own production. But in fact *all* prices, including the price of labor (nominal wages), are rising because of the general increase in aggregate demand. Once firms

see that *all* prices and wages are rising, they decrease their production to previous levels.

In terms of Figure 17-3a, the increase in nominal wages shifts the short-run aggregate supply curve leftward, ultimately from AS_1 to AS_2, and the economy moves from *b* to *c*. Thus, the increase in real output caused by the *price-level surprise* corrects itself.

The same analysis applies in reverse for an *unanticipated* price-level decrease. In the economy represented by Figure 17-3b, firms misperceive that the prices for their own products are falling due to decreases in the demands for those products relative to other products. They respond to anticipated profit declines by cutting production. As a result of their collective actions, real output in the economy falls. But seeing that *all* prices and wages are dropping, firms increase their output to prior levels. The short-run aggregate supply curve in Figure 17-3b shifts rightward from AS_1 to AS_3, and the economy "self-corrects" by moving from *d* to *e*.

Fully Anticipated Price-Level Changes

In RET, fully *anticipated* price-level changes do *not* change real output, even for short periods. In Figure 17-3a, again consider the increase in aggregate demand from AD_1 to AD_2. Businesses immediately recognize that the higher prices being paid for their products are part of the inflation they had anticipated. They understand that the same forces which are causing the inflation result in higher nominal wages, leaving their profits unchanged. The economy therefore moves *directly* from *a* to *c*. The price level rises as expected, and output remains at its full-employment level Q_1.

Similarly, a fully *anticipated* price-level decrease will leave real output unchanged. Firms conclude that nominal wages are declining by the same percentage amount as the declining price level, leaving profits unchanged. The economy represented by Figure 17-3b therefore moves *directly* from *a* to *e*. Deflation occurs, but the economy continues to produce its full-employment output Q_1. The anticipated decline in aggregate demand causes no change in real output.

Mainstream View of Self-Correction

Almost all economists acknowledge that new classical economists have made significant contributions to the theory of aggregate supply. In fact, mainstream economists have incorporated some aspects of RET into their own more detailed models. However, most economists strongly disagree with RET on the question of *downward* price and wage flexibility. While the stock market, foreign exchange market, and certain commodity markets experience day-to-day or minute-to-minute price changes, including price declines, this is not true in many product markets and in most labor markets. There is ample evidence, say mainstream economists, that *many prices and wages are inflexible downward for long periods.* As a result, it may take years for the economy to move from recession back to full-employment output, unless it gets help from fiscal and monetary policy.

Graphical Analysis

To understand this mainstream view, again examine Figure 17-3b. Suppose aggregate demand declines from AD_1 to AD_3 because of a significant decline in investment spending. If the price level remains at P_1, the economy will *not* move from *a* to *d* to *e*, as suggested by RET. Instead, the economy will move from *a* to *f*, as if it were moving along a *horizontal aggregate supply curve* between these two points. Real output will decline from its full-employment level, Q_1, to the recessionary level, Q_4.

But let's assume that surpluses in product markets eventually cause the price level to fall to P_4. Will this lead to the decline in nominal wages needed to shift aggregate supply from AS_1 to AS_2, as suggested by new classical economists? "Highly unlikely" say mainstream economists. Even more so than prices, nominal wages tend to be inflexible downward. If nominal wages do not decline in response to the decline in the price level, then the short-run aggregate supply curve will not shift rightward. The self-correction mechanism assumed by RET and new classical economists will break down. Instead, the economy will remain at *d*, experiencing less-than-full-employment output and a high rate of unemployment.

Downward Wage Inflexibility

In Chapter 11 we listed and discussed several reasons firms may not be able to, or may not want to, reduce nominal wages. Firms *may not be able to* cut wages because of wage contracts and the legal minimum wage. And firms *may not want to* reduce wages if they fear potential problems with morale, effort, and efficiency. Businesses also may not want to cut wages if doing so will mean losing skilled workers to other firms— workers in whom the current firms have heavy training investments.

While contracts are thought to be the main cause of wage rigidity, so-called *efficiency wages* and *insider-*

outsider relationships may also play a role. Let's explore these aspects of **new Keynesian economics.**

Efficiency Wage Theory

Recall from Chapter 11 that an **efficiency wage** is one which minimizes the firm's labor cost per unit of output. Normally, we would think that the market wage is the efficiency wage since it is the lowest wage at which a firm can obtain a particular type of labor. But where the cost of supervising workers is high, or where worker turnover is great, firms may discover that paying a wage which is higher than the market wage will lower their wage cost per unit of output. Example: Suppose a firm's workers, on average, produce 8 units of output at a $9 market wage but 10 units of output at a $10 above-market wage. The efficiency wage is $10, not the $9 market wage. At the $10 wage, the per-unit cost of output is only $1 (= $10 wage/10 units of output), compared with $1.12 (= $9 wage/8 units of output) at the $9 wage.

How can a higher wage result in greater efficiency?

1. *Greater work effort* The above-market wage, in effect, raises the cost to workers of losing their jobs because of poor performance. Because workers have a strong incentive to retain their relatively high-paying jobs, they are more apt to provide greater work effort. Looked at differently, workers are more reluctant to *shirk* (neglect or avoid work) because the higher wage makes job loss more costly to them. Consequently, the above-market wage can be the efficient wage; it can enhance worker productivity so much that the higher wage more than pays for itself.

2. *Lower supervision costs* With less worker incentive to shirk, the firm needs fewer supervisory personnel to monitor work performance. This, too, can lower the firm's overall wage cost per unit of output.

3. *Reduced job turnover* The above-market pay discourages workers from voluntarily leaving their jobs. The lower job turnover reduces the firm's cost of hiring and training workers. It also gives the firm a more experienced, more productive workforce.

The key implication for macroeconomic instability is that efficiency wages add to downward wage inflexibility. Firms paying efficiency wages will be reluctant to cut wages when aggregate demand declines since such cuts may encourage shirking, require more supervisory personnel, and increase turnover. In other words, wage cuts that reduce productivity and raise per-unit labor costs are self-defeating.

Insider-Outsider Relationships   Other new Keynesian economists theorize that downward wage inflexibility may relate to relationships between "insiders" and "outsiders." *Insiders* are workers who retain employment even during recession. *Outsiders* are workers laid off from a particular firm and other unemployed workers who would like to work at that firm.

When recession produces layoffs and widespread unemployment, we might expect outsiders to offer to work for less than the current wage rate, in effect, bidding down wage rates. We might also expect firms to accept such wage offers to reduce their costs. But, according to the **insider-outsider theory,** outsiders may not be able to underbid existing wages because employers may view the cost of hiring them to be prohibitive. Employers might conclude that insiders would view this underbidding as undermining years of efforts to increase wages or, worse, as "stealing" jobs. Insiders therefore may refuse to cooperate with the new workers who have undercut their pay. Where teamwork is critical for production, such lack of cooperation will reduce overall productivity and thereby lower the firms' profits.

Even if firms were willing to employ outsiders at less than the present wage, these unemployed workers might not choose to work for less than the existing wage. To do so would risk harassment from the insiders whose pay they have undercut. Thus, outsiders may remain unemployed, relying on past saving, unemployment compensation, and other social programs to makes ends meet.

As in the efficiency wage theory, the insider-outsider theory implies that wages will be inflexible downward when aggregate demand declines. Self-correction may *eventually* occur, but not nearly as rapidly as the new classical economists contend. **(Key Question 7)**

QUICK REVIEW 17-3

■ New classical economists believe that the economy "self-corrects" when unanticipated events divert it from its full-employment level of real output.

■ In RET unanticipated price-level changes cause changes in real output in the short run but not in the long run.

■ According to RET, market participants immediately change their actions in response to anticipated price-level changes such that no change in real output occurs.

■ Mainstream economists believe that downward price and wage inflexibility means that the economy can get mired in recession for long periods.

■ Sources of downward wage inflexibility include contracts, efficiency wages, and insider-outsider relationships.

RULES OR DISCRETION?

The different views on the causes of instability and the speed of self-correction lead to vigorous debate on macro policy. Should government adhere to *policy rules* which prohibit it from causing instability in an economy that otherwise is stable? Or should it use *discretionary fiscal and monetary policy*, when needed, to stabilize a sometimes unstable economy?

In Support of Policy Rules

Monetarists and other new classical economists believe policy rules would reduce instability in the economy. The rules would prevent government from trying to "manage" aggregate demand. In this view, such management is misguided and thus likely to *cause* more instability than it cures.

Monetary Rule   Since inappropriate monetary policy is the major source of macroeconomic instability, say monetarists, then enactment of a **monetary rule** would make sense. Such a rule would direct the Fed to expand the money supply each year at the same annual rate as the typical growth of the economy's production capacity. The Fed's sole monetary role would then be to use its tools (open-market operations, discount-rate changes, and changes in reserve requirements) to ensure that the nation's money supply grows steadily by, say, 3 to 5 percent a year. According to Milton Friedman,

> Such a rule . . . would eliminate . . . the major cause of instability in the economy—the capricious and unpredictable impact of countercyclical monetary policy. As long as the money supply grows at a constant rate each year, be it 3, 4, or 5 percent, any decline into recession will be temporary. The liquidity provided by a constantly growing money supply will cause aggregate demand to expand. Similarly, if the supply of money does not rise at a more than average rate, any

inflationary increase in spending will burn itself out for lack of fuel.[2]

Figure 17-4 helps illustrate the rationale for a monetary rule. Suppose the economy represented there is operating at its full-employment real output, Q_1. Also suppose the nation's long-run aggregate supply curve shifts rightward, as from AS_{LR1} to AS_{LR2}, each year, depicting the average annual potential increase in real output. You know from earlier chapters that these annual increases in "potential GDP" result from added resources, improved resources, and improved technology.

Monetarists argue that a monetary rule would tie increases in the money supply to the typical rightward shift of long-run aggregate supply. In view of the direct link between changes in the money supply and aggregate demand, this would ensure that the AD curve will shift rightward, as from AD_1 to AD_2, each year. As a result, real GDP would rise from Q_1 to Q_2 and the price level would remain constant at P_1. A monetary rule, then, would promote steady growth of real output along with price stability.

---

[2]As quoted in Lawrence S. Ritter and William L. Silber, *Money*, 5th ed. (New York: Basic Books, 1984), pp. 141–142.

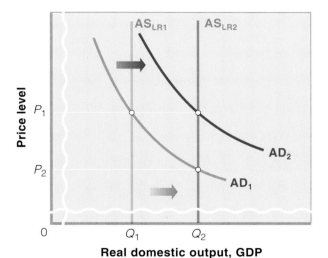

FIGURE 17-4 Rationale for a monetary rule A monetary rule which fixed the annual increase in the money supply to the increase in potential GDP would shift aggregate demand rightward, as from AD_1 to AD_2, at the same pace as the shift in long-run aggregate supply, here AS_{LR1} to AS_{LR2}. Thus the economy would experience growth without inflation or deflation.

Generally, RET economists also support a monetary rule. They conclude that an easy or tight money policy will alter the rate of inflation but not real output. Suppose, for example, the Fed implements an easy money policy to reduce interest rates, expand investment spending, and boost real GDP. On the basis of past experience and economic knowledge, the public anticipates that this policy is inflationary and takes self-protective actions. Workers press for higher nominal wages; firms increase their product prices; and lenders raise their nominal interest rates on loans.

All these responses are designed to prevent inflation from having adverse effects on the real incomes of workers, businesses, and lenders. But collectively this behavior immediately raises wage and price levels. So the increase in aggregate demand brought about by the easy money policy is completely dissipated in higher prices and wages. Real output and employment do not expand.

In this view, the combination of rational expectations and instantaneous market adjustments dooms monetary policy to ineffectiveness. If monetary policy produces only inflation (or deflation), say the RET economists, then it makes sense to limit the Fed's discretion. Specifically, Congress ought to enact a monetary rule consistent with achieving zero or low inflation at all times.

Balanced Budget Monetarists and new classical economists question the effectiveness of fiscal policy. At the extreme, a few of these economists favor a constitutional amendment to require the Federal government to balance its budget annually. Others simply suggest that government be "passive" in its fiscal policy, not *intentionally* creating budget deficits or surpluses. Deficits and surpluses caused by recession or inflationary expansion will eventually correct themselves as the economy self-corrects to its full-employment output.

Monetarists particularly oppose expansionary fiscal policy. They believe that the deficit spending accompanying such a policy has a strong tendency to crowd out private investment. Suppose government runs a budget deficit by printing and selling U.S. securities, which means borrowing from the public. Through this borrowing, government competes with private businesses for funds. The added government borrowing increases the demand for money, which then raises the interest rate and crowds out a substantial amount of private investment that would otherwise have been profitable. The net effect of a

Profit Sharing: Making Wages Flexible

Are there any ways that downward wage flexibility can be increased so that declines in aggregate demand do not have such a negative effect on output and employment?

Our comparison of mainstream and new classical views on the macroeconomy suggests that if wages are inflexible downward, output and employment will decline when aggregate demand falls. Most economists recognize that labor contracts, among other considerations, make wages inflexible downward, at least in the short run. The declines in labor demand accompanying recessions therefore primarily affect real output and employment. This problem has led some economists to propose profit sharing as a way to increase the flexibility of wage rates. The idea is to make labor markets operate more like the new classical model, with its vertical aggregate supply curve, by creating greater employment stability.

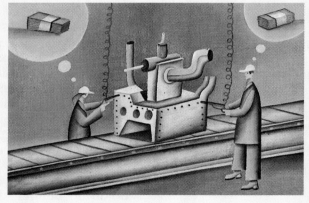

The essence of these profit-sharing proposals is to tie some portion of wages directly to the firm's profitability, making profit-sharing payments a part of workers' pay. Instead of paying workers a guaranteed wage rate of, say, $10 per hour, workers might be guaranteed $5 per hour (the base wage) and additional compensation equal to some predetermined percentage of the firm's profits (the profit-share wage). Total compensation (base wage + profit-share wage) may exceed or fall short of $10 per hour, depending on the firm's economic fortunes.

How would such a plan affect employment? Initially assume workers are receiving $10 per hour—$5 as a guaranteed wage and another $5 as profit-sharing compensation. Now suppose a recession occurs and the employer's sales and profits plummet. The $5 of profit-sharing income will fall and might decline to zero, so the actual wages paid by the firm fall from $10 to $5 an hour. With the new, depressed demand for labor, the firm would clearly choose to employ more workers under this wage system than the standard system. Hourly wages will have automatically fallen from $10 to $5.

There are a number of criticisms of such profit-sharing wage plans. The plans might jeopardize the wage uniformity and wage gains achieved by organized labor. A further criticism is that employers might respond to the low base wage by adopting production techniques which use relatively more labor and less capital. Because the amount of capital equipment per worker is critical to productivity and economic growth, this pay scheme might impair the long-run expansion of real GDP. At the pragmatic level, critics point out that wage plans linked to profits eliminate the present certainty which workers have as to whether their employers have properly fulfilled the labor contract. With profit sharing, employers might use accounting and other techniques to hide profits and therefore evade paying share wages.

Finally, there is the fundamental question of whether workers will accept more jobs and greater employment stability in exchange for a reduced hourly wage guarantee and higher variability of earnings. But it should be noted that in the past decade a growing number of union and nonunion contracts have contained profit-sharing arrangements. Although a full-blown profit-sharing economy seems improbable, limited profit sharing appears to be spreading.

budget deficit on aggregate demand therefore is unpredictable and, at best, modest.

If a deficit was financed through printing new money instead of borrowing, the crowding out could be avoided and the deficit would be followed by expansion of real GDP. The monetarists point out, however, that such an expansion would *not* be the result of the deficit per se but, rather, of the expansion of the money supply. Moreover, this expansion of real output would be only temporary. A boost in nominal wages would soon follow the inflation, returning real output to its previous level.

RET economists reject discretionary fiscal policy for the same reason they reject active monetary policy: they do not think it works. Business and labor will immediately adjust their behavior in anticipation of the price-level effects of a change in fiscal policy. The economy will move directly to the anticipated new price level. Like monetary policy, say the RET theorists, fiscal policy can move the economy along its vertical long-run aggregate supply curve. But because its effects on inflation are fully anticipated, fiscal policy cannot alter real GDP even in the short run. The best course of action for government is to balance its budget.

In Defense of Discretionary Stabilization Policy

Mainstream economists oppose a monetary rule and a balanced-budget requirement. They believe that monetary policy and fiscal policy are important tools for achieving and maintaining full employment, price stability, and economic growth.

Discretionary Monetary Policy

In supporting discretionary monetary policy, mainstream economists argue that the rationale for a monetary rule is flawed. While there is indeed a close relationship between the money supply and nominal GDP over long periods, in shorter periods this relationship breaks down. The reason is that the velocity of money has proved to be more variable and unpredictable than monetarists contend. Arguing that velocity is variable both cyclically and over time, mainstream economists contend that a constant annual rate of increase in the money supply need not eliminate fluctuations in aggregate demand. In terms of the equation of exchange, a steady rise of M does not guarantee a steady expansion of aggregate demand because V—the rate at which money is spent—can change.

Again reconsider Figure 17-4, in which we demonstrated the monetary rule. During the period in question, optimistic business expectations might create a boom in investment spending and thus shift the aggregate demand curve to some location to the right of AD_2. (You may want to pencil in a new AD curve, labeling it AD_3.) The price level would then rise above P_1; that is, demand-pull inflation would occur. In this case, the monetary rule will not accomplish its goal of maintaining price stability. Mainstream economists say that the Fed can use a tight money policy to reduce the excessive investment spending and thereby

hold the rightward shift of aggregate demand to AD_2, thus avoiding inflation.

Similarly, suppose that investment instead declines because of pessimistic business expectations. Aggregate demand will then increase by some amount less than the increase from AD_1 to AD_2 in Figure 17-4. Again, the monetary rule fails the stability test: the price level sinks below P_1 (deflation occurs). Or if the price level is inflexible downward at P_1, the economy does not achieve its full-employment output (unemployment rises). An easy money policy can help avoid either outcome.

Mainstream economists quip that the trouble with the monetary rule is that it tells the policymaker: "Don't do something, just stand there."

Discretionary Fiscal Policy

Mainstream economists support the use of fiscal policy to keep recessions from deepening or to keep mild inflation from becoming severe inflation. They recognize the possibility of crowding out but do not think it is a serious problem when business borrowing is depressed, as is usually the case in recession. Because politicians can abuse fiscal policy, most economists feel that it should be held in reserve for situations where monetary policy appears to be ineffective or working too slowly.

As indicated earlier, mainstream economists oppose requirements to balance the budget annually. Tax revenues fall sharply during recessions and rise briskly during periods of demand-pull inflation. Therefore, a law or constitutional amendment mandating an annually balanced budget would require government to *increase* tax rates and *reduce* government spending during recession and *reduce* tax rates and *increase* government spending during economic booms. The first set of actions would worsen recession, and the second set would fuel inflation. (You may want to review Figure 12-6.)

Increased Macro Stability

Finally, mainstream economists point out that, as shown in Figure 17-5, the U.S. economy has been about one-third more stable since 1946 than in earlier periods. It is not a coincidence, they say, that use of discretionary fiscal and monetary policy characterized the latter period but not the former. These policies have helped tame the business cycle. Moreover, mainstream economists point out several specific policy successes in the past two decades:

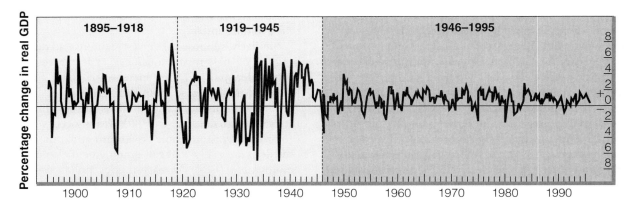

FIGURE 17-5 **American real GDP, percentage change on previous quarter (3 months), 1895–1995** Since 1946, quarterly changes in real GDP have been about one-third less volatile than those in the 1895–1918 period and 1919–1945 period. Mainstream macroeconomists attribute at least part of this increased stability to use of fiscal and monetary policy. [*Source:* Victor Zarnowitz, *Business Cycles* (Chicago: University of Chicago Press, 1995, pp. 80–81). Truncated and updated.]

1. A tight money policy dropped inflation from 13.5 percent in 1980 to 3.2 percent in 1983.

2. An expansionary fiscal policy reduced the unemployment rate from 9.7 percent in 1982 to 5.5 percent in 1988.

3. An easy money policy helped the economy recover from the 1990–1991 recession.

4. Judicious tightening of monetary policy in the mid-1990s helped the economy remain on a noninflationary, full-employment growth path. (**Key Question 13**)

SUMMARY OF ALTERNATIVE VIEWS

Here and in Chapter 16 we presented the central ideas and policy implications of a number of macroeconomic theories. In Table 17-1 we summarize four of them: mainstream macroeconomics, monetarism, rational expectations theory, and supply-side economics. You will observe that we broadly defined new classical economics to include both monetarism and the rational expectations theory since both adhere to the natural-rate hypothesis that the economy tends automatically to achieve equilibrium at its full-employment output. Also note that "mainstream macroeconomics" remains based on Keynesian ideas.

These different perspectives have forced mainstream economists to rethink some of their fundamental principles. And as is true of many debates, much compromise and revision of positions have occurred. Although considerable disagreement remains, mainstream macro economists agree with monetarists that "money matters" and that excessive growth of the money supply is the major cause of long-lasting, rapid inflation. They also agree with RET proponents and theorists of coordination failures that expectations are important. If government can create expectations of price stability, full employment, and economic growth, households and firms will tend to act in ways to make that happen. Finally, mainstream economists concur with supply-side economists and real-business-cycle theorists that government needs to focus on policies to increase economic growth. In short, thanks to ongoing challenges to the conventional wisdom, macroeconomics continues to evolve.

CHAPTER SUMMARY

1. In classical economics the aggregate supply curve is vertical and establishes the level of real output, while the aggregate demand curve is generally stable and establishes the price level. In this view the economy is highly stable.

Issue	Mainstream macroeconomics (Keynesian based)	New classical economics (natural-rate hypothesis)		Supply-side economics
		Monetarism	Rational expectations	
View of the private economy	Potentially unstable	Stable in long run at natural rate of unemployment	Stable in long run at natural rate of unemployment	May stagnate without proper work, saving, and investment incentives
Cause of the observed instability of the private economy	Investment plans unequal to saving plans (changes in AD); AS shocks	Inappropriate monetary policy	Unanticipated AD and AS shocks in the short run	Changes in AS
Appropriate macro policies	Active fiscal and monetary policy	Monetary rule	Monetary rule	Policies to increase AS
How changes in the money supply affect the economy	By changing the interest rate, which changes investment and real GDP	By directly changing AD, which changes GDP	No effect on output because price-level changes are anticipated	By influencing investment and thus AS
View of the velocity of money	Unstable	Stable	No consensus	No consensus
How fiscal policy affects the economy	Changes AD and GDP via the multiplier process	No effect unless money supply changes	No effect on output because price-level changes are anticipated	Affects GDP and price level via changes in AS
View of cost-push inflation	Possible (wage-push, AS shock)	Impossible in the long run in the absence of excessive money supply growth	Impossible in the long run in the absence of excessive money supply growth	Possible (tax-transfer disincentives, higher costs due to regulation)

2. In Keynesian economics the aggregate supply curve is horizontal at less-than-full-employment levels of real output, while the aggregate demand curve is inherently unstable. In this view the economy is highly unstable.

3. The mainstream view is that macro instability is caused by volatility of investment spending which shifts the aggregate demand curve. If aggregate demand increases too rapidly, demand-pull inflation can occur; if aggregate demand decreases, recession can occur. Occasionally, adverse supply shocks also cause instability.

4. Monetarism focuses on the equation of exchange: $MV = PQ$. Because velocity is thought to be stable, changes in M create changes in nominal GDP (= PQ). Monetarists believe that the most significant cause of macroeconomic instability has been inappropriate monetary policy. Too rapid increases in M cause inflation; in-

sufficient growth of M causes recession. In this view, a major cause of the Great Depression was inappropriate monetary policy which allowed the money supply to decline by nearly 40 percent.

5. Real-business-cycle theory views changes in resource availability and technology (real factors), which alter productivity, as the main causes of macroeconomic instability. In this theory, shifts in the economy's long-run aggregate supply curve change real output. In turn, money demand and money supply change, shifting the aggregate demand curve in the same direction as the initial change in long-run aggregate supply. Real output thus can change without a change in the price level.

6. A coordination failure is said to occur when people do not reach a mutually beneficial equilibrium because they lack some way to jointly coordinate their actions to achieve it. Depending on people's expectations, the economy can come to rest at a good equilibrium (noninflationary full-employment output) or bad equilibriums (less-than-full-employment output or demand-pull inflation). These bad equilibriums are coordination failures.

7. The rational expectations theory (RET) rests on two assumptions: (1) With sufficient information, people's beliefs about future economic outcomes accurately reflect the likelihood that those outcomes will occur; and (2) markets are highly competitive, meaning that prices and wages are flexible both upward and downward.

8. New classical economists (monetarists and rational expectations theorists) see the economy as automatically correcting itself when disturbed from its full-employment level of real output. In RET, unanticipated changes in aggregate demand change the price level, which in the short run leads firms to change output. But once the firms realize that all prices are changing (including nominal wages) as part of general inflation or deflation, they change their output to the previous level. Anticipated changes in aggregate demand produce only changes in the price level, not changes in real output.

9. Mainstream economists reject the new classical view that all prices and wages are flexible downward. Nominal wages, in particular, are inflexible downward because of several factors including labor contracts, efficiency wages, and insider-outsider relationships. This means that declines in aggregate demand decrease real output, not simply wages and prices.

10. Monetarist and RET economists recommend a monetary rule in which the money supply is increased at a rate equal to the long-run growth of potential GDP. They also support maintaining a "neutral" fiscal policy, as opposed to using discretionary fiscal policy to create budget deficits or budget surpluses. A few monetarists and RET economists favor a constitutional amendment that would require the Federal government to balance its budget annually.

11. Mainstream economists oppose a monetary rule and a balanced-budget requirement, vigorously defending discretionary monetary and fiscal policy. They say that theory and evidence suggest that these policies are helpful in achieving full employment, price stability, and economic growth.

TERMS AND CONCEPTS

classical economics	velocity	new classical economics	efficiency wage
Keynesianism	real-business-cycle	price-level surprises	insider-outsider theory
monetarism	theory	new Keynesian	monetary rule
equation of exchange	coordination failures	economics	

STUDY QUESTIONS

1. KEY QUESTION Use the aggregate demand–aggregate supply model to compare the "old" classical and Keynesian interpretations of **(a)** the aggregate supply curve and **(b)** the stability of the aggregate demand curve. Which of these interpretations seems most consistent with the realities of the Great Depression?

2. What is the usual cause of macroeconomic instability, according to mainstream economists? What role does the spending-income multiplier play in creating instability? How might adverse aggregate supply factors cause instability, according to mainstream economists?

3. State and explain the basic equation of monetarism. What is the major cause of macroeconomic instability, as viewed by monetarists?

4. KEY QUESTION Suppose that the money supply and the nominal GDP for a hypothetical economy are $96 billion and $336 billion, respectively. What is the velocity of money? How will households and businesses react if the central bank reduces the money supply by $20 billion? By how much will nominal GDP have to fall to restore equilibrium, according to the monetarist perspective?

5. Briefly describe the difference between a so-called real business cycle and a more traditional "spending" business cycle.

6. Andrew and Craig were walking directly toward each other in a congested store aisle. Andrew moved to his left to avoid Craig, and at the same time Craig moved to his right to avoid Andrew. They bumped into each other. What concept does this example illustrate? How does this idea relate to macroeconomic instability?

7. KEY QUESTION Use an AD-AS graph to demonstrate and explain the price-level and real-output outcome of an anticipated decline in aggregate demand, as viewed by RET economists. (Assume that the economy initially is operating at its full-employment level of output.) Then, demonstrate and explain on the same graph the outcome, as viewed by mainstream economists.

8. What is an efficiency wage? How might payment of an above-market wage reduce shirking by employees and reduce worker turnover? How might efficiency wages contribute to downward wage inflexibility, at least for a time, when aggregate demand declines?

9. How might relationships between so-called insiders and outsiders contribute to downward wage inflexibility?

10. Use the equation of exchange to explain the rationale for a monetary rule. Why does the rule run into trouble if V unexpectedly falls because of, say, a drop in investment spending by businesses?

11. Answer questions **(a)** and **(b)** on the basis of the following information for a hypothetical economy in year 1: money supply = $400 billion; long-term annual growth of potential GDP = 3 percent; velocity = 4. Assume that the banking system initially has no excess reserves and the reserve requirement is 10 percent. Also assume that velocity is constant and the economy initially is operating at its full-employment real output.
    a. What is the level of nominal GDP in year 1?
    b. Suppose the Fed adheres to a monetary rule through open-market operations. What amount of U.S. securities will it have to sell to, or buy from, banks or the public between years 1 and 2 to meet its monetary rule?

12. Explain the difference between "active" discretionary fiscal policy advocated by mainstream economists and "passive" fiscal policy advocated by new classical economists. Explain: "The problem with a balanced-budget amendment is that it would, in a sense, require active fiscal policy—but in the *wrong* direction—as the economy slides into recession."

13. KEY QUESTION Place MON, RET, or MAIN besides statements which most closely reflect monetarist, rational expectations, or mainstream views, respectively.
    a. Anticipated changes in aggregate demand affect only the price level; they have no effect on real output.

b. Downward wage inflexibility means that declines in aggregate demand can cause long-lasting recession.
c. Changes in the money supply M increase PQ; at first only Q rises because nominal wages are fixed, but once workers adapt their expectations to new realities, P rises and Q returns to its former level.
d. Fiscal and monetary policy smooth out the business cycle.
e. The Fed should increase the money supply at a fixed annual rate.

14. You have just been elected president of the United States, and the present chair of the Federal Reserve Board has resigned. You need to appoint a new person to this position, as well as a person to chair your Council of Economic Advisers. Using Table 17-1 and your knowledge of macroeconomics, identify the perspectives on macro theory and policy you would want your appointees to hold. Remember, the economic health of the entire nation—and your chances for reelection—may depend on these selections.

15. (Last Word) How would profit sharing by labor increase downward "wage" flexibility? Why is greater downward wage flexibility desirable?

16. WEB-BASED QUESTION The Equation of Exchange—What Is the Current Velocity of Money? The fundamental equation of monetarism is the equation of exchange: $MV = PQ = GDP$. The velocity of money, V, can be found by dividing GDP by M, the money supply. Calculate the velocity of money for the past few years. Which GDP data should be used: real or nominal GDP? Why? How stable is V during this time? Is V increasing or decreasing? Get GDP data from the NIPA Data section at the Bureau of Economic Analysis http://www.bea.doc.gov/bea/glance.htm. Money supply data can be found at the Federal Reserve http://www.bog.frb.fed.us/releases/h6/about.htm under Money Stock, Liquid Assets, and Debt Measures—Historical Data.

17. WEB-BASED QUESTION American Real GDP—Is It Really More Stable Than Other Countries'? Since 1946, quarterly changes in American real GDP have been less volatile than in earlier decades. How does recent U.S. GDP volitility compare to other countries? Would you expect it to be more or less stable? Why or why not? Is there a pattern (e.g., is lower volatility associated with higher GDP countries)? Would the comparison be valid if nominal GDP data was used rather than real GDP data? Visit the Quarterly Growth Rates in GDP at Constant Prices section at the OECD http://www.oecd.org/std/nahome.htm.

18

Economic Growth

Despite periods of macroeconomic instability, the capitalist countries have experienced impressive economic growth during this century. In the United States, real output has increased 15-fold since 1900, while population has only tripled. This means that five times more goods and services are available to the average U.S. resident than were available in 1900. Moreover, today's goods and services are of much higher quality than those of 1900. This expansion and improvement of output has created greater material abundance, lifted the standard of living, and eased the unlimited-wants–scarce-resources problem.

But the U.S. growth story is not totally upbeat. Since 1970 U.S. economic growth has slowed considerably relative to that in earlier periods and other nations. Twenty-one advanced industrial nations, not to mention many developing nations, grew more rapidly than the United States over the past three decades.

We begin our analysis of economic growth by clearly defining it. Next, we show how economic growth can be depicted within our graphical models. Then, we examine the long-term growth record of the United States, paying particular attention to the contributing factors. Since productivity is one of these factors, we examine the post-1970 slowdown of productivity growth in the United States. Next, we explore whether the United States is achieving a "new economy," which might deliver a stronger future rate of growth. Finally, we ask what government can do, if anything, to boost the rate of economic growth.

GROWTH ECONOMICS

The subset of economics called *growth economics* examines the factors which expand an economy's production capacity over time. It also analyzes public policies designed to increase economic growth.

Two Definitions

Economic growth is defined and measured in two ways:

1. An increase in real GDP occurring over some time period

2. An increase in real GDP *per capita* occurring over some time period

In measuring military potential or political preeminence, the first definition is more relevant. The second definition, however, is superior for comparing living standards. While China's GDP is $744 billion compared with Denmark's $155 billion, Denmark's GDP per capita is $29,890 compared with only $620 in China.

In either definition, economic growth is calculated as an annual percentage rate of growth. For example, if real GDP was $200 billion in some country last year and $210 billion this year, the rate of growth would be 5 percent {= [($210 − $200)/$200] × 100}.

Growth as a Goal

Growth is a widely held economic goal. The expansion of total output relative to population means rising real wages and incomes and thus higher standards of living. *An economy experiencing economic growth is better able to meet people's wants and resolve socioeconomic problems.* Rising real wages and incomes provide new opportunities to individuals and families—a vacation trip, a home computer, higher education—*without* sacrificing other opportunities and enjoyments. A growing economy can take on new programs to alleviate poverty and clean up the environment *without* impairing existing levels of consumption, investment, and public goods production.

In short, *growth lessens the burden of scarcity.* A growing economy, unlike a static economy, can consume more today while increasing its capacity to produce more in the future. By easing the burden of scarcity—by relaxing society's production constraints—economic growth allows a nation to attain economic goals more fully and to undertake new endeavors which require goods and services.

Arithmetic of Growth

Why do economists make such a big deal about small changes in the rate of growth? Because it really matters! For the United States, with a current real GDP of about $8000 billion, the difference between a 3 percent and a 4 percent rate of growth is about $80 billion of output per year. For a very poor country, a 0.5-percentage-point change in the growth rate may mean the difference between starvation and mere hunger.

When viewed over many years, an apparently small difference in the rate of growth becomes highly significant because of compounding. Suppose Alta and Zorn have identical GDPs, but Alta grows at a 4 percent yearly rate, while Zorn grows at 2 percent. Based on the rule of 70, Alta's GDP would double in about 18 years (= 70/4); Zorn's would double in 35 years (= 70/2).

Some economists argue that growth is more important to a nation's future than is economic stability. Eliminating a gap between actual GDP and potential GDP might increase the national income by, say, 3 percent on a one-time basis. In contrast, a 3 percent annual growth rate will increase the national income by more than 6 percent in 2 years, more than 9 percent in 3 years, and so on.

INGREDIENTS OF GROWTH

There are six ingredients in the growth of any economy. They can be grouped as supply, demand, and efficiency factors.

Supply Factors

Four ingredients of growth relate to the physical ability of the economy to expand. They are (1) increases in the quantity and quality of natural resources, (2) increases in the quantity and quality of human resources, (3) increases in the supply (or stock) of capital goods, and (4) improvements in technology. These **supply factors**—physical and technical agents of greater production—permit an economy to increase its real output.

Demand Factor

The fifth ingredient of economic growth is the **demand factor.** To realize its growing production potential, a nation must fully employ its expanding supplies of resources. This requires a growing level of aggregate demand.

Efficiency Factor

The sixth ingredient of economic growth is the **efficiency factor.** To reach its production potential, a nation must achieve not only full employment but also economic efficiency. The country must use its existing and added resources in the least costly way (*productive efficiency*) in producing the specific mix of goods and services that maximizes society's well-being (*allocative efficiency*). The ability to expand production, together with the full use of available resources, are *not* sufficient for achieving maximum possible growth. Also required is the efficient use of those resources.

The supply, demand, and efficiency factors in growth are related. Unemployment caused by insufficient aggregate demand (the demand factor) can retard the rate of new capital accumulation (a supply factor) and slow expenditures on research (also a supply factor). Conversely, low spending on innovation and investment (supply factors) can cause insufficient aggregate demand (the demand factor) and unemployment. Widespread inefficiency in the use of resources (the efficiency factor) may translate into higher costs of goods and services and thus lower profits. This may slow the accumulation of capital (a supply factor).

GRAPHICAL ANALYSIS

We can place the six factors underlying economic growth in proper perspective through Chapter 2's production possibilities curves and Chapter 16's extended AD-AS analysis.

Growth and Production Possibilities

Recall that a curve such as *AB* in Figure 18-1 is a production possibilities curve. It indicates the various *maximum* combinations of products the economy can produce with its fixed quantity and quality of natural, human, and capital resources and its stock of technological knowledge. An improvement in any of the supply factors will push the production possibilities curve outward, as from *AB* to *CD*.

But the demand and efficiency factors remind us the economy need not attain its maximum production potential. The curve may shift outward but leave the economy behind at some level of operation such as *a* on *AB*. Because *a* is inside the new production possibilities curve *CD*, the economy has not achieved its growth potential. This enhanced production potential will not be realized unless (1) aggregate demand increases sufficiently to sustain full employment, and (2) the additional resources are employed efficiently such that they make the maximum possible dollar contribution to output.

An increase in aggregate demand is needed to move the economy from *a* to a point on *CD*. And to realize the greatest increase in the monetary value of its output—its greatest real GDP growth—this loca-

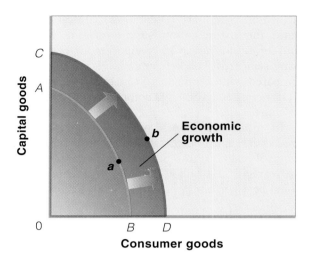

FIGURE 18-1 Economic growth and the production possibilities curve Economic growth is made possible by the four supply factors which shift the production possibilities curve outward, as from *AB* to *CD*. Economic growth is realized when the demand factor and efficiency factor move the economy from point *a* to *b*.

- -

tion on *CD* must be optimal. You know from Chapter 2 that this "best allocation" is determined by expanding production of each good until its marginal benefit equals its marginal cost. Here, we assume this optimal combination of capital and consumer goods is *b*.

Example: The net increase in the labor force of the United States is roughly 1.5 million workers per year. This increment raises the production capacity of the economy. But obtaining the extra output these added workers can produce presumes they can find jobs. It also presumes these jobs are in firms and industries where their talents are fully and optimally used. Society does not want new labor-force entrants to be unemployed. Nor does it want pediatricians working as plumbers or workers producing goods which have higher marginal costs than marginal benefits. **(Key Question 2)**

Labor and Productivity Although demand and efficiency considerations are important, discussions of growth focus primarily on the supply side. Figure 18-2 provides a framework for discussing the supply factors in growth. It indicates two fundamental ways society can increase its real output and income: (1) by increasing its inputs of resources, and (2) by increasing the productivity of those inputs. Let's focus on inputs of labor. We can say that *a nation's real GDP in any year depends on the input of labor (measured in worker-*

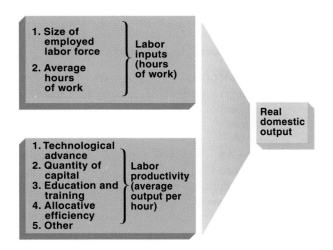

FIGURE 18-2 **The supply determinants of real output** Real GDP is usefully viewed as the product of the quantity of labor inputs multiplied by labor productivity.

----

hours) multiplied by **labor productivity** *(measured as real output per worker per hour).*

Total output = worker-hours × labor productivity

Illustration: Assume an economy has 10 workers, each working 2000 hours per year (50 weeks at 40 hours per week). The total input of worker-hours therefore is 20,000 hours. If productivity—average real output per worker-hour—is $5, then total output or real GDP will be $100,000 (= 20,000 × $5).

What determines the number of hours worked each year? And what determines labor productivity? Figure 18-2 provides some answers. The hours of labor input depend on the size of the employed labor force and the length of the average workweek. Labor-force size depends on the size of the working-age population and the **labor-force participation rate**—*the percentage of the working-age population actually in the labor force.* The average workweek is governed by legal and institutional considerations and by collective bargaining.

Productivity is determined by technological progress, the quantity of capital goods available to workers, the quality of labor itself, and the efficiency with which inputs are allocated, combined, and managed. Productivity rises when the health, training, education, and motivation of workers are improved; when workers have more and better machinery and natural resources with which to work; when production is better organized and managed; and when labor is reallocated from less efficient industries to more efficient industries.

Extended AD-AS Model

We can also view economic growth through the extended AD-AS model developed in Chapter 16.

Suppose an economy's aggregate demand curve, long-run aggregate supply curve, and short-run aggregate supply curve are AD_1 AS_{LR1}, and AS_1, as shown in Figure 18-3. The equilibrium price level

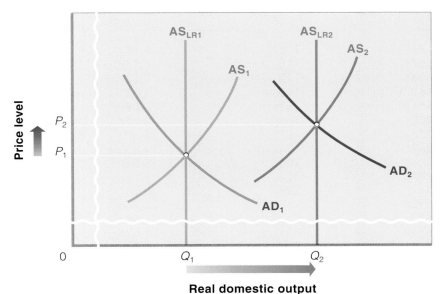

FIGURE 18-3 **Economic growth in the extended AD-AS model** Long-run and short-run aggregate supply have increased over time, as from AS_{LR1} to AS_{LR2} and AS_1 to AS_2. Simultaneously, aggregate demand has shifted rightward, as from AD_1 to AD_2. The outcome of these combined shifts has been economic growth, shown as the increase in real output from Q_1 to Q_2, accompanied by inflation, shown as the rise in the price level from P_1 to P_2.

----

and level of real output are P_1 and Q_1. At price level P_1, the short-run aggregate supply is AS_1; it slopes upward because, in the short run, changes in the price level change the level of real output. However, in the long run, nominal wages change in the same direction and by the same percentage as the price level. Real output then returns to its prior level, making the long-run aggregate supply curve vertical at the economy's full-employment level of output, here Q_1. As with the location of the production possibilities curve, real supply factors—the quantity and quality of resources and technology—determine the full-employment level of real output. Price-level changes do not shift a nation's production possibilities curve; neither do they shift the nation's long-run aggregate supply curve.

Increase in Short- and Long-Run Aggregate Supply Let's now assume that changes in the supply factors shift the long-run aggregate supply curve rightward from AS_{LR1} to AS_{LR2}. This means the production possibilities curve in Figure 18-2 has moved outward. The economy's *potential* output has increased.

Increase in Aggregate Demand Assuming downward price and wage inflexibility, the economy can *realize* its greater production potential only through an increase in aggregate demand. In Figure 18-3, suppose that increases in consumption, investment, gov-

ernment, and net export spending shift the aggregate demand curve from AD_1 to AD_2. Also suppose the economy continues to use its resources efficiently.

Economic Outcomes The increases of aggregate supply and aggregate demand in our figure have increased real output from Q_1 to Q_2 and boosted the price level from P_1 to P_2. At the higher price level P_2, the economy confronts a new short-run aggregate supply curve AS_2. The result of the dynamics described in Figure 18-3 is economic growth, accompanied by mild inflation. These outcomes are consistent with the actual secular trend of real GDP and the price level in the United States. (You can confirm this by examining items 18 and 21 on the inside covers of this book.) **(Key Question 3)**

GROWTH IN THE UNITED STATES

Table 18-1 is an overview of economic growth in the United States over past decades. Column 2 reveals strong growth as measured by increases in real GDP. Specifically, *real GDP has increased sixfold since 1940.* But the U.S. population has also increased. Nevertheless, in column 4 we find that *real GDP per capita has increased by threefold since 1940.*

TABLE 18-1 **Real GDP and per capita GDP, 1929–1997**

(1) Year	(2) GDP, billions of 1992 dollars	(3) Population, millions	(4) Per capita GDP, 1992 dollars (2) ÷ (3)
1929	$ 791	122	$ 6,484
1933	577	126	4,579
1940	941	132	7,129
1945	1627	140	11,621
1950	1611	152	10,599
1955	2001	166	12,054
1960	2263	181	12,503
1965	2881	194	14,851
1970	3398	205	16,576
1975	3874	214	18,103
1980	4615	228	20,241
1985	5324	239	22,276
1990	6136	250	24,544
1995	6742	263	25,635
1997	7191	268	26,832

Source: Economic Report of the President, 1998; U.S. Department of Commerce.

What has been the *rate* of U.S. growth? Observe in Global Perspective 18-1 that *real GDP* has grown at an annual rate of 3.1 percent since 1948. Not shown, *real GDP per capita* has increased nearly 2 percent annually since then. However, we must qualify these raw numbers in four ways:

1. *Improved products and services* The numbers in Table 18-1 and Global Perspective 18-1 do not fully account for improvements in products and services; they thus understate the growth of economic well-being. Purely quantitative data do not accurately compare an era of iceboxes and LPs with an era of refrigerators and CDs.

2. *Added leisure* The increases in real GDP and per capita GDP identified in Table 18-1 were accomplished despite large increases in leisure. The standard workweek, once 50 hours, is now about 40 hours. Again the raw growth numbers understate the gain in economic well-being.

3. *Environmental effects* In contrast, these measures of growth do not account for any adverse

effects growth may have had on the environment and the quality of life. If growth debases the physical environment and creates a stressful work environment, the bare growth numbers will overstate the gains from growth.

4. *International comparisons* Over the past half-century, the growth record of the United States is less impressive than that of many other nations. Observe in Global Perspective 18-1 that Japan's growth rate averaged more than twice that of the United States during this period. In recent years, however, the growth rates in Japan and Germany have slowed. Also, in recent decades countries with smaller GDPs per capita have tended to grow more rapidly than countries with already high GDPs per capita.

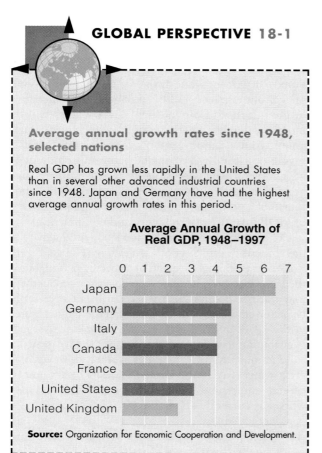

GLOBAL PERSPECTIVE 18-1

Average annual growth rates since 1948, selected nations

Real GDP has grown less rapidly in the United States than in several other advanced industrial countries since 1948. Japan and Germany have had the highest average annual growth rates in this period.

Average Annual Growth of Real GDP, 1948–1997

Source: Organization for Economic Cooperation and Development.

ACCOUNTING FOR GROWTH

Table 18-2 provides estimates of the relative importance of the factors contributing to U.S. economic growth. The categories and data are based on the work of Edward Denison, who estimated what percentage of annual U.S. growth between 1929 and 1982 was accounted for by each factor listed in the table. We have projected Denison's estimates to the present, making only slight adjustments to his numbers on the basis of post-1982 trends.

Inputs versus Productivity

The most evident conclusion from Table 18-2 is that productivity growth has been the most important force underlying the growth of U.S. real output and

TABLE 18-2   The sources of growth in U.S. real national income, 1929–1997

Sources of growth		Percentage of total growth
1. Increase in quantity of labor		33
2. Increase in labor productivity		67
3. Technological advance	28	
4. Quantity of capital	20	
5. Education and training	12	
6. Economies of scale	8	
7. Improved resource allocation	8	
8. Legal-human environment and other	−9	
		100

Source: Edward F. Denison, *Trends in American Economic Growth, 1929–1982* (Washington: Brookings Institution, 1985), p. 30; *Economic Report of the President,* various years; authors' estimates.

income. Increases in the quantity of labor (item 1) account for only about one-third of the increase in real output since 1929; two-thirds is attributable to rising labor productivity (item 2).

Quantity of Labor

The U.S. population and labor force have both expanded significantly. Since 1929 total population grew from 122 to 268 million and the labor force increased from 49 to 136 million workers. Reductions in the length of the workweek reduced the growth of labor inputs before World War II, but the workweek has declined little since then. Falling birthrates in the past 30 years have slowed the growth of the native population, but increased immigration has partly offset this slowdown. Of most significance, however, has been a surge of participation of women in the labor force. Largely because of this trend, the U.S. labor force has grown by about 2 million workers per year during the past 25 years.

Technological Advance

Technological advance (item 3 in Table 18-2) is a critical engine of growth, accounting for 28 percent of the increase in real output since 1929.

Technological advance includes not merely new production techniques but also new managerial methods and new forms of business organization. Generally, it is linked with *the discovery of new knowl-*

edge, which permits firms to combine a specific amount of resources in new ways to achieve a greater output.

Technological advance and capital formation (investment) are closely related; technological advance often, but not always, requires investment in new machinery and equipment. The purchase of new computers not only means more computers but quicker, more powerful computers embodying new technology. In contrast, modern crop-rotation practices and contour plowing are ideas which contribute to expanded output, although they do not necessarily use new kinds of, or increased amounts of, capital equipment.

Technological advance has been both rapid and profound. Gas and diesel engines, conveyor belts, and assembly lines are significant developments of the past. More recently, technology has produced automation and the push-button factory. Bigger, faster, and more fuel-efficient commercial aircraft, integrated microcircuits, computers, xerography, containerized shipping, and the Internet—not to mention biotechnology, lasers, and superconductivity—are technological achievements which were in the realm of fantasy only a generation or two ago.

Quantity of Capital

Some 20 percent—one-fifth—of the annual growth of real output since 1929 is attributable to increases in the quantity of capital (item 4). A worker will be more productive when equipped with more capital goods. And a nation acquires more capital through saving and the investment in plant and equipment which saving makes possible. A recent estimate suggests that total output will increase by about one-fourth of a percentage point for each extra percentage of GDP invested in machinery and equipment.

The critical consideration for labor productivity is the amount of capital goods *per worker.* The aggregate stock of capital might expand in a specific period, but if the labor force also increases rapidly, labor productivity may not rise because each worker will not necessarily be better-equipped. This happened in the United States in the 1970s and 1980s when the labor force surged, contributing to a slowing of U.S. productivity growth.

The quantity of capital per worker, however, has greatly increased in the United States. The amount of capital equipment (machinery and buildings) per worker is currently about $90,000.

Two addenda:

1. The United States has been saving and investing a smaller percentage of its GDP in recent years than have most other industrially advanced nations. This helps explain the lower growth rate in the United States. Lower levels of investment as a percentage of GDP are associated with lower growth rates of real GDP per capita (review Global Perspective 2-1).

2. Investment is not only private but also public. Some observers contend that U.S. **infrastructure**—highways and bridges, public transit systems, wastewater treatment facilities, municipal water systems, airports, and so on—faces growing problems of deterioration, technological obsolescence, and insufficient capacity to serve future growth.

Also, public capital (infrastructure) and private capital are complementary. Investments in new highways promote private investment in new factories and retail establishments along their routes. Industrial parks which are developed by local governments in turn attract manufacturing firms. Some economists view the slowdown in the development of U.S. infrastructure as a significant source of reduced private investment.

Education and Training

Ben Franklin once said: "He that hath a trade hath an estate." He meant that education and training improve a worker's productivity and result in higher earnings. Like investment in physical capital, investment in human capital is an important means of increasing labor productivity. As shown in Table 18-2, an estimated 12 percent of the growth of U.S. real output since 1929 is attributable to such improvements in the quality of labor (item 5).

Perhaps the simplest measure of labor quality is the level of educational attainment. Figure 18-4 reflects educational gains in the past several decades. Currently 82 percent of the U.S. population, aged 25 or more, has at least a high school education; 22 percent has a college education or more. It is clear from Figure 18-4 that education has become accessible to more people in the United States.

But there are concerns about the quality of U.S. education. Scores on standardized college admissions tests have declined relative to scores of a few decades ago. Furthermore, U.S. students in science and mathematics do not do as well as students in many other industrialized nations (see Global Perspective 18-2). Japanese children have a longer school day and attend school 240 days per year compared with 180 in the United States. Also, we have been producing fewer

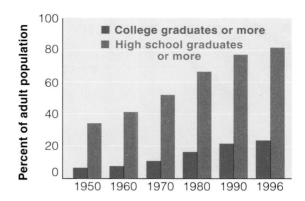

FIGURE 18-4 Changes in the educational attainment of the U.S. adult population The percentage of the U.S. adult population, aged 25 or more, completing high school and college has been rising in recent decades (*Source: Statistical Abstract of the United States, 1997,* p. 159.)

engineers and scientists, a problem which may trace back to inadequate training in math and science in elementary and high schools. And it is argued that on-the-job training (apprenticeship programs) in Japan and Germany—nations with high rates of productivity growth—are more available and superior to those in the United States.

Resource Allocation and Scale Economies

Table 18-2 also tells us that U.S. labor productivity has increased because of economies of scale (item 6) and improved resource allocation (item 7).

Economies of Scale Economies of scale are production advantages deriving from increased market and firm size. A large corporation often can select more efficient production techniques than can a small-scale firm. A large manufacturer of autos can use elaborate assembly lines with computerization and robotics, while smaller producers must settle for less advanced technologies. Markets have increased in scope over time and firms have increased in size, allowing more efficient production methods to be used. Accordingly, U.S. labor productivity has increased and economic growth has occurred.

Improved Resource Allocation Improved resource allocation means that workers over time have reallocated themselves from low-productivity em-

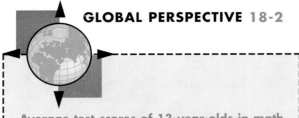

GLOBAL PERSPECTIVE 18-2

Average test scores of 13-year-olds in math and science, top 10 countries and the United States

The test performance of U.S. 13-year-olds did not rank favorably with that of 13-year-olds in several other nations in the Third International Math and Science Study (1997).

Mathematics

Rank		Score
1	Singapore	643
2	South Korea	607
3	Japan	605
4	Hong Kong	588
5	Belgium	565
6	Czech Republic	564
7	Slovakia	547
8	Switzerland	545
9	Netherlands	541
10	Slovenia	541
28	United States	500

Science

Rank		Score
1	Singapore	607
2	Czech Republic	574
3	Japan	571
4	South Korea	565
5	Bulgaria	565
6	Netherlands	560
7	Slovenia	560
8	Austria	558
9	Hungary	554
10	England	552
17	United States	534

ployment to high-productivity employment. Historically, much labor has shifted from agriculture, where labor productivity is low, to manufacturing, where it is quite high. More recently, labor has shifted away from some manufacturing industries to even higher-productivity industries such as computer software, business consulting, and pharmaceuticals. As a result of such shifts, the average productivity of U.S. workers in the aggregate has increased.

Also, labor market discrimination has historically denied women and minorities access to high-productivity jobs. The decline of such discrimination over time has shifted these groups from low-productivity jobs to higher-productivity jobs, increasing overall labor productivity and raising real GDP.

Tariffs, import quotas, and other barriers to international trade often keep resources in relatively unproductive employments. The long-run movement toward liberalized international trade has therefore improved the allocation of resources and expanded real output in the United States.

Detriments to Growth

Some developments *detract* from the growth of real output and income. The entry for the legal and human environment (item 8) in Table 18-2 aggregates these detriments to productivity growth. Since 1929 there have been several changes in the regulation of industry, environmental pollution, and worker health and safety which have negatively affected growth. The expansion of government regulation in such areas as pollution control, worker health and safety, and access for the disabled has diverted investment spending away from growth-increasing capital goods and toward expenditures for cleaner air and water, greater worker protection, and improved access for disabled workers and consumers.

A firm required to spend $1 million on a new scrubber to meet government standards for air pollution or to make its stores accessible to the disabled will not have that $1 million to spend on machinery and equipment which would expand real output. The diversion of resources to deal with dishonesty and crime, the effects of work stoppages because of labor disputes, and the impact of bad weather on agricultural output are also factors which impede economic growth.

It should be noted that while worker safety, clean air and water, equal access for the disabled, and the overall quality of life may come at the expense of economic growth, the reverse is also true. Economic growth does not automatically enhance society's welfare. Growth of real output may involve opportunity costs of other things (a clean environment, a fair society) we value more highly. *Productivity measures output per hour of work*, not *overall well-being per hour of work*. Increases in real GDP are not necessarily matched with equal increases in well-being. Thus, society may rationally decide to "trade off" some economic growth to achieve other desirable ends. **(Key Question 5)**

Other Contributing Factors

There are other difficult-to-quantify characteristics which affect an economy's growth rate. For example, large and varied supplies of natural resources in the United States have been an important contributor to its economic growth. The United States enjoys an abundance of fertile soil, desirable climatic and weather conditions, large quantities of most mineral resources, and generous sources of power. With the possible exceptions of Russia and Canada, the United States has a larger variety and greater quantity of natural resources than any other nation.

While an abundant natural resource base is helpful to growth, a meager resource base does not doom a nation to slow growth. Although Japan's natural resources are severely constrained, its post-World War II growth has been remarkable. In contrast, some of the lower-income countries of Africa and South America have substantial amounts of natural resources but have grown slowly.

There are additional unmeasurable factors affecting a nation's growth rate. In particular, the overall social-cultural-political environment of the United States generally has promoted economic growth. Several factors contribute to this favorable environment:

1. Unlike the case in many other nations, there are virtually no social or moral taboos on production and material progress in the United States. The nation's social philosophy has embraced material advance as an attainable and desirable economic goal. The inventor, the innovator, and the business executive are accorded high degrees of prestige and respect in U.S. society.

2. Americans have traditionally possessed positive attitudes toward work and risk taking; the United States has benefited from a willing labor force and an ample supply of entrepreneurs.

3. The market system has many personal and corporate incentives encouraging growth; the U.S. economy rewards actions which increase output.

4. The U.S. economy is founded on a stable political system characterized by democratic principles, internal order, the right of property ownership, the legal status of enterprise, and the enforcement of contracts. Recent studies show that politically open societies grow much more rapidly on average than those where freedom is limited.

Although difficult to quantify, these "other characteristics" have provided an excellent foundation for U.S. economic growth and stability.

Macroeconomic Instability and Growth

The information in Table 18-2 reflects the actual growth experience of the United States, not the growth which would have occurred if the economy had achieved its potential output year after year. Without macroeconomic instability, the annual growth rate in the United States would have been about 0.2 to 0.3 percentage point higher than the 2.9 percent rate actually occurring since 1929.

The Great Depression of the 1930s, in particular, was a serious blow to the long-run growth record of the United States. Between 1929 and 1933 real output (measured in 1992 prices) declined from $791 billion to $577 billion. In 1938, U.S. real GDP was at about the same level as in 1929. More recently, the back-to-back recessions of 1980 to 1982 cost the economy more than $600 billion in lost real output.

But that is only part of the picture. Recession and unemployment can have harmful "carryover" effects on the growth rate in subsequent years of full employment through negative effects on other growth factors. Recession and unemployment may depress investment and capital accumulation. Moreover, firms may cut back on research and development efforts during recession, so technological advance diminishes; union resistance to technological change may stiffen; skills of idle workers deteriorate; and so forth. While it is difficult to quantify the effect of these considerations on the growth rate, they undoubtedly are important.

THE PRODUCTIVITY SLOWDOWN

In the 1970s—and to a lesser degree in the 1980s and early 1990s—the United States experienced a much-publicized productivity slowdown. This has led to concern among some Americans that the nation is in relative economic decline. Table 18-3 portrays the course of U.S. labor productivity in the post-World War II period. Observe in column 2 that for about two decades following World War II (1948–1966) labor productivity increased at a vigorous average annual rate of 3.2 percent, only to decline sharply in the 1966–1973 period. This was followed by a dismal performance in the years 1973 to 1981 and a modest resurgence of productivity growth since 1981. Although labor productivity growth has been slowing worldwide, U.S. productivity growth has been slower than that in most other major industrialized nations. The United States still enjoys the highest absolute level of output per worker, but its productivity advantage is diminishing.

Significance

The U.S. productivity slowdown has many implications.

Standard of Living Productivity growth is the basic source of improvements in real wage rates and the standard of living. Over long periods, real income per worker-hour can increase only at the same rate as real output per worker-hour. More output per hour means more real income to distribute for each hour worked. The simplest case is of Robinson Crusoe on his deserted island. The number of fish he can catch or coconuts he can pick per hour *is* his real income or wage per hour.

TABLE 18-3 Growth of labor productivity and real per capita GDP, 1948–1997

(1) Period	(2) Annual productivity growth rate, %	(3) Annual real per capita GDP growth rate, %
1948–1966	3.2	2.2
1966–1973	2.0	2.0
1973–1981	0.7	1.1
1981–1990	1.3	1.8
1990–1997	1.2	1.3

Source: Economic Report of the President, 1988, p. 67. End points of calculations are cyclical peaks, except for 1997. Updated.

We observe in column 3 in Table 18-3 that the broadest measure of living standards—the growth of real per capita GDP—followed the path of labor productivity. Living levels thus measured grew by only 1.1 percent per year during the severe 1973–1981 productivity stagnation compared with 2.2 percent in the 1948–1966 postwar decades.

The slowdown in productivity is also reflected in Figure 18-5, which tracks the median real income of U.S. families since 1947. Median family income increased substantially in real terms from 1947 to 1973. But it fell during the 1980s and is not a whole lot higher today than it was in 1973.

Inflation Productivity increases offset increases in nominal wage rates, partly or fully lessening cost-push inflationary pressures. Other things equal, a decline in the rate of productivity growth contributes to rising unit labor costs and a higher rate of inflation. Many economists believe that productivity stagnation contributed to the unusually high inflation rates of the 1970s.

World Markets Other things equal, the slow rate of productivity growth in the United States compared with its major international trading partners increases relative prices of U.S. goods in world markets. The result is a decline in U.S. competitiveness and a loss of international markets for U.S. producers.

Causes of the Slowdown

There is no consensus among experts as to why U.S. productivity growth has slowed and fallen behind the

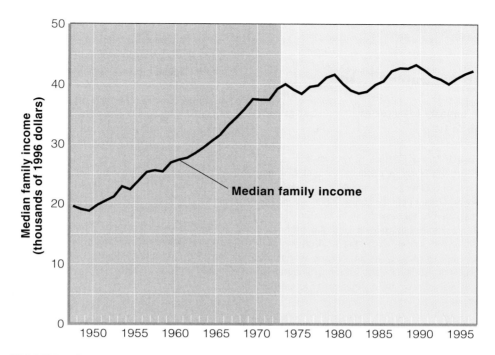

FIGURE 18-5 **Median income of U.S. families, 1947–1996**   After World War II the median real income of U.S. families grew rapidly until the early 1970s. Since 1973 real family income has stagnated. (*Source:* Bureau of the Census.)

rates of Japan and western Europe. Because so many factors affect productivity, there may be no simple explanation. Nevertheless, let's survey some of the possible causes.

Labor Quality   One possibility is that slower improvements in labor quality may have dampened productivity growth. Three factors may have been at work.

1. Decline in Experience Level   The experience level of the labor force may have declined. The large number of baby-boom workers who entered the labor force had little experience and training and were therefore less productive. The labor-force participation of women increased significantly over the past two decades. But many were married women with little or no prior labor-force experience who therefore had low productivity.

2. Less Able Workers   The declining test scores of students on standardized examinations during the past few decades may indicate a decline in worker ca-

pabilities. If so, this decline may have contributed to the productivity slowdown.

3. Slowing of Rise in Educational Attainment   The historical rise in the average level of educational attainment of the labor force has been slowing in recent years. The median number of years of school completed by the adult population was 12.1 in 1970 and increased to only 12.8 by 1996.

Technological Progress   Technological advance—usually reflected in improvements in the quality of capital goods and the efficiency with which inputs are combined—may also have faltered. Technological progress is fueled by expenditures for formal research and development (R&D) programs. In the United States, R&D spending declined as a percentage of GDP from a peak of 3 percent in the mid-1960s to about 1 percent by the late 1970s, before rising again in the 1980s.

However, some economists discount the R&D decline in explaining the productivity slowdown. They say R&D *spending* alone tells us little about R&D *ac-*

Is Growth Desirable?

Economists usually take for granted that growth is desirable. Is It?

The Antigrowth View Critics of growth say industrialization and growth result in pollution, global warming, ozone depletion, and other environmental problems. These adverse spillover costs occur because inputs in the production process reenter the environment as some form of waste. The more rapid our growth and the higher our standard of living, the more waste the environment must absorb—or attempt to absorb. In an already wealthy society, further growth usually means satisfying increasingly trivial wants at the cost of mounting threats to our ecological system.

Critics of growth also argue there is little compelling evidence that economic growth has solved sociological problems such as poverty, homelessness, and discrimination. Consider poverty. In the antigrowth view, American poverty is a problem of distribution, not production. The requisite for solving the problem is commitment and political courage to redistribute wealth and income, not further increases in output.

Antigrowth sentiment also says that while growth may permit us to "make a better living," it does not give us

"the good life." We may be producing more and enjoying it less. Growth means assembly-line jobs, worker burnout, and alienated employees who have little or no control over decisions affecting their lives. The changing technology at the core of growth poses new anxieties and new sources of insecurity for workers. Both high-level and low-level workers face the prospect of having their hard-earned skills and experience rendered obsolete by an onrushing technology. High-growth economies are high-stress economies, which may impair our physical and mental health.

In Defense of Growth The primary defense of growth is that it is the path to greater material abundance and rising living standards. Rising output and incomes allow us to buy:

more education, recreation, and travel, more medical care, closer communications, more skilled personal and professional services, and better-designed as well as more numerous products. It also means more art, music, and poetry, theater, and drama. It can even mean more time and resources devoted to spiritual growth and human development.*

Growth also enables us to improve the nation's infrastructure, enhance the care of the sick and elderly, provide greater access for the disabled, and provide more police

complishments. There is clear evidence of continuing technological advance during the past two decades.

Investment Other things equal, the greater the percentage of a nation's GDP devoted to investment goods, the larger its productivity gains. A worker using a bulldozer can move more earth per hour than the same worker using a hand shovel. An engineer using a computer can complete a design task more rapidly than is possible with pencil and paper.

The United States has been investing a smaller percentage of its GDP than it did in earlier periods. Several factors may have contributed to the weak growth of investment:

1. Low Saving Rate The United States has had a low saving rate which, coupled with strong private and public demands for credit, has resulted in high real interest rates relative to historical standards. High real interest rates discourage investment spending.

2. Import Competition Growing import competition may have made some U.S. producers reluctant to invest in new capital equipment. They may have shifted more investment overseas toward nations with low-wage workers.

3. Regulation The expansion of government regulations in the areas of pollution control, worker health and safety, and access for the disabled diverted some investment spending away from output-increasing capital goods. This investment spending surely increased total utility to society but did not directly increase output itself. The composition of investment may have shifted toward uses which do not increase productivity.

4. Reduced Infrastructure Spending Reduced spending on the economy's infrastructure may have slowed productivity growth. We have noted that these public capital goods are complementary to private

and fire protection. Economic growth may be the only realistic way to reduce poverty, since there is little political support for greater redistribution of income. The way to improve the economic position of the poor is to increase household incomes through higher productivity and economic growth. Also, a no-growth policy among industrial nations might severely limit growth in poor nations. Foreign investment and development assistance in these nations would fall, keeping the world's poor in poverty longer.

Economic growth has not made labor more unpleasant or hazardous, as critics suggest. New machinery is usually less taxing and less dangerous than the machinery it replaces. Air-conditioned workplaces are more pleasant than steamy workshops. Furthermore, why would an end to economic growth reduce materialism or alienation? The loudest protests against materialism are heard in those nations and groups who now enjoy the highest levels of material abundance! The high standard of living which growth provides has increased our leisure and given us more time for reflection and self-fulfillment.

Does growth threaten the environment? The connection between growth and environment is tenuous, say growth proponents. Increases in economic growth need not mean increases in pollution. Pollution is not so much a by-product of growth as it is a "problem of the commons." Much of the environment—streams, lakes, oceans, and the air—is treated as "common property," with no restrictions on its use. The commons have become our dumping grounds; we have overused and debased them. Environmental pollution is a case of spillover or external costs, and correcting this problem involves regulatory legislation or specific taxes ("effluent charges") to remedy misuse of the environment.

There *are* serious pollution problems. But limiting growth is the wrong solution. Growth has allowed economies to reduce pollution, be more sensitive to environmental considerations, set aside wilderness, and clean up hazardous waste, while still enabling rising household incomes.

*Alice M. Rivlin, *Reviving the American Dream* (Washington: Brookings Institution, 1992), p. 36.

---

capital goods. Data show that between 1950 and 1970 the public capital stock of infrastructure grew at a 4.1 percent annual rate and labor productivity growth was 2.0 percent per year. During 1971 to 1985, however, the yearly increase in the infrastructure fell to 1.6 percent and the annual productivity increase dropped to 0.8 percent. A slowing of spending on public investment goods may have contributed to diminishing private investments and to declines in productivity growth.

Energy Prices
Perhaps the prime suspect in the productivity slowdown was the large increases in oil prices occurring from 1973 to 1975 and 1978 to 1980. Productivity growth diminished sharply after the quadrupling of oil prices between 1973 and 1975. Also, the impact of rocketing energy prices was worldwide, as was the productivity slowdown.

The *direct* impact of higher oil prices was an increase in the cost of operating capital equipment, which in effect raised the "price" of capital relative to labor. Producers were therefore more inclined to use less-productive labor-intensive techniques.

The *indirect* macroeconomic effects of rising energy prices may have had even more to do with reducing productivity growth. The two episodes of soaring energy prices produced stagflation—simultaneous inflation and rising unemployment. Government's restrictive macroeconomic policies to control inflation worsened and prolonged the periods of recession and slow economic growth. Recessions diminish productivity—output per worker—since output normally declines more rapidly than employment. The long periods of underuse of production capacity in many industries probably contributed to the productivity slowdown.

Dismal Growth of Service Productivity
Finally, it is important to note that the slowdown in U.S. productivity growth has been greater in the service sec-

tor than in the manufacturing (goods-producing) sector. Since 1973 productivity in manufacturing has increased by about 2.75 percent annually compared with 3.4 percent between 1960 and 1972. But productivity in the service sector has increased by only 0.7 percent annually since 1973, compared with 2.7 percent between 1960 and 1972. This slow growth of service-sector productivity has been a drag on the overall productivity rate.

There are several possible reasons for the slower productivity growth in services:

1. It may be more difficult for service companies to increase their productivity by substituting capital for workers. How do you substitute machinery for a barber, dentist, cook, day-care worker, or retail clerk?

2. The competitive pressures to increase productivity may be weaker in services. Customers may be more loyal to service providers than to brands of manufactured products. Moreover, the U.S. service sector has been relatively immune from stiff foreign competition.

3. As they become wealthier, consumers usually demand higher-quality services, which often require more, not fewer, service workers. Service firms may need to employ more retail clerks, security personnel, pizza deliverers, maintenance workers, or stock market analysts to stay competitive.

Some economists contend that the slow growth of productivity in services is at least partly illusory. Unlike the case in manufacturing, there are no "product quantities" to count in determining service productivity. Many increases in productivity show up as improvements in services, and such improvements are not always reflected in higher product prices (and thus greater output). Because present measurement methods do not adequately "pick up" increases in service productivity, say some economists, the overall increase of U.S. productivity growth is greatly understated.

A "NEW ECONOMY"?

Since 1981 there has been a modest improvement in productivity growth. Observe in Table 18-3 that the 0.7 percent annual productivity growth for 1973 to 1981 improved to a 1.3 percent annual increase between 1981 and 1990. The recession of 1990 to 1991 halted this upward trend, but productivity growth

eventually picked up during the recovery and averaged 1.2 percent over the 1990–1997 period. In 1996 productivity growth was 2.0 percent; in 1997 it was 1.9 percent. In 1997 real GDP grew by a healthy 3.4 percent. Moreover, the unemployment rate and inflation rates were both low (4.9 percent and 2.3 percent, respectively), with no signs of rising inflation.

Is the United States experiencing a resurgence of productivity growth? Is it, as a few economists claim, establishing a "new economy," based on innovations in computers and communications, coupled with global capitalism? Can it now grow at a 3 to 4 percent annual rate, rather than the previous 2 to 2.5 percent annual rate, without igniting inflation?

Indeed, many of the factors which were depressing productivity growth have eased or been reversed. Energy prices are stable, and the stagflation problem has been overcome. Research and development spending has generally increased as a percentage of GDP. Innovations in computers, telecommunications, genetic engineering, and medicine are providing a stimulus to productivity. Also, real interest rates are now low, promoting purchases of new plant and equipment. Downsizing of workforces has boosted productivity in many firms. Wages of college graduates have risen relative to wages of high school graduates, and this wage premium is attracting more students to universities. The inexperienced baby boomers who flooded labor markets in previous decades are now more mature, more experienced, and thus more productive workers. International markets are opening up, expanding U.S. exports. Meanwhile, global competition is spreading, holding down the U.S. rate of inflation.

Nevertheless, whether these factors will produce a long period of high U.S. productivity and real GDP growth remains to be seen; 1 or 2 years does not constitute a trend. The current higher rates of productivity and real GDP growth *are* consistent with that possibility. Unfortunately, they are also consistent with the possibility that the United States is simply experiencing a rapid short-run economic expansion fueled by high levels of investment and consumption spending. Such "booms" raise productivity by increasing real output faster than employment (labor inputs), but they are unsustainable over longer periods. History tells us that demand-pull inflation, restrictive government stabilization policy, and economic recession often follow short-run surges in productivity and GDP growth. Hence, only time will tell whether the very recent increases in productivity are permanent or transitory. The jury is still out on the notion of a "new economy." **(Key Question 8)**

GROWTH POLICIES

If we accept the view that economic growth is desirable and sustainable, then a question arises as to what public policies might stimulate growth. Several policies either are in use or have been suggested. They fit within two broad categories: demand-side policies and supply-side policies.

Demand-Side Policies

Low growth is often the consequence of inadequate aggregate demand and the GDP gap to which it gives rise. The purpose of demand-side policies is to eliminate or reduce the severity of recessions through discretionary fiscal and monetary policies. The idea is to use these tools to ensure that aggregate demand increases at an appropriate, noninflationary pace. Adequate aggregate demand not only keeps present resources fully employed, it also creates an incentive for firms to expand their operations.

In particular, monetary policy which provides low real interest rates helps promote high levels of investment spending. This spending not only sustains full employment of existing resources but also expands capital resources and thus the economy's production capacity. Government can achieve low real interest rates through a combination of a relatively easy money policy and a fiscal policy which eliminates budget deficits. Recall that the government borrowing required for financing large budget deficits drives up real interest rates, particularly when the economy is near or at full employment.

Supply-Side Policies

These policies emphasize factors which directly increase the potential output of the economy over time. Regarding Figure 18-3, the goal is to shift the economy's long-run aggregate supply curve rightward. Policies fitting this category include *education and training policies* designed to increase the nation's stock of human capital. Recent examples are (1) programs which provide retraining for workers who lose jobs because of international trade, and (2) tuition tax credits designed to increase college enrollment.

Other programs fitting the supply-side category include *tax policies* designed to increase saving, investment, and R&D. An example is tax deductions for those who save money in a special retirement account. Some economists favor a national consumption tax as a full or partial replacement for the personal income tax. The idea is to make consumption more expensive and thereby encourage saving. Similarly, some economists propose eliminating the corporate income tax or allowing more generous tax credits for investment and research spending. Such spending often "pays off" in rightward shifts of the nation's long-run aggregate supply curve.

Government might also promote growth via other pro-growth initiatives. Specifically, it might redirect some of its current expenditures away from transfer payments and toward expansion of public infrastructure and funding of research, basic education, and skill training. It might promote growth by further deregulating industries where sufficient competition exists to ensure improved efficiency. And it might negotiate further international trade agreements, which increase specialization, boost output, and expand trade.

While the litany of potential growth-enhancing policies is long and involved, most economists agree that it is not easy to increase a nation's growth rate through public policy. Nevertheless, they also agree there is ample international evidence to suggest that government policies *can make a difference;* they can affect an economy's long-term growth rate for better or worse.

QUICK REVIEW 18-3

■ Economists have cited the following reasons for the U.S. slowdown in productivity over the past 25 years: **(a)** declines in labor quality, **(b)** a slowing of technological progress, **(c)** decreasing investment spending as a percentage of GDP, **(d)** high energy prices during the 1970s and early 1980s, and **(e)** lagging growth of service productivity.

■ Some observers see the recent upsurge in productivity as evidence of a "new economy" that can achieve higher rates of GDP growth than those in the past two decades. This new economy is based on innovation in computers and communications coupled with the globalization of capitalism.

■ Skeptics of the new-economy view say that it is far too early to tell whether the recent upsurge of productivity growth is transient or permanent.

CHAPTER SUMMARY

1. Economic growth may be defined as either **(a)** an expanding real output or **(b)** an expanding per capita real output. Growth lessens the burden of scarcity and provides increases in real output which can be used to resolve socioeconomic problems.

2. The supply factors in economic growth are **(a)** the quantity and quality of a nation's natural resources, **(b)** the quantity and quality of its human resources, **(c)** its stock of capital facilities, and **(d)** its technology. Two other factors—a sufficient level of aggregate demand and economic efficiency—are essential for the economy to realize its growth potential.

3. Economic growth is shown graphically as an outward shift of a nation's production possibilities curve or as a rightward shift of its aggregate supply curve.

4. The post-World War II growth rate of real GDP for the United States has been slightly more than 3 percent annually; real GDP per capita has grown at about a 2 percent annual rate.

5. U.S. real GDP has grown, partly because of increased inputs of labor and primarily because of increases in the productivity of labor. Technological progress, increases in the quantity of capital per worker, improvements in the quality of labor, economies of scale, and an improved allocation of labor are among the more important factors which increase labor productivity.

6. The rate of productivity growth declined sharply in the 1970s, causing a slowdown in the rise of U.S. living

standards and contributing to inflation. Although productivity growth has increased somewhat in the 1980s and 1990s, it remains substantially below the rates attained in the two decades after World War II.

7. Suspected causes of the decline in productivity growth include decreases in labor quality, slowing of technological progress, declining investment spending as a percentage of GDP, higher energy prices, and dismal growth in service productivity.

8. Many of the trends that are thought to have slowed productivity growth in the 1970s and 1980s have slowed or reversed themselves. Also, the U.S. economy has recently had a surge of innovation in computers and communications. This technological progress, coupled with the opening of global markets, has led a few economists to speak of a "new economy" characterized by high growth of productivity and real GDP.

9. Skeptics of the new-economy notion urge a wait-and-see approach. They point out that surges in productivity and real GDP growth are common during vigorous economic expansions but are not necessarily permanent.

10. Government can promote economic growth through demand-side policies (fiscal policy, monetary policy) which ensure that present production capacity is fully used and that the capital stock enlarges. It can also promote growth through supply-side policies (education and training policies, tax policies, and other pro-growth initiatives) which directly increase the economy's potential output over time.

TERMS AND CONCEPTS

economic growth
supply factors
demand factor

efficiency factor
labor productivity

labor-force participation
rate

infrastructure

STUDY QUESTIONS

1. Why is economic growth important? Explain why the difference between a 2.5 percent and a 3.0 percent annual growth rate might be of great significance over many years.

2. KEY QUESTION What are the major causes of economic growth? "There are both a demand side

and a supply side to economic growth." Explain. Illustrate the operation of both sets of factors in terms of the production possibilities curve.

3. KEY QUESTION Suppose an economy's real GDP is $30,000 in year 1 and $31,200 in year 2. What is the growth rate of its real GDP? Assume that population was 100 in year 1 and 102 in year 2. What is the growth rate of GDP per capita? Between 1959 and 1996 the U.S. price level rose by about 285 percent while its real output increased by about 212 percent. Use the aggregate demand-aggregate supply model to show these outcomes graphically.

4. Briefly describe the growth record of the United States. Compare the rates of growth in real GDP and real GDP per capita, explaining any differences. How does the U.S. growth rate compare to the rates of Japan and Germany since World War II? To what extent might growth rates understate or overstate economic well-being?

5. KEY QUESTION To what extent have increases in U.S. real GDP been the result of more labor inputs? Of increasing labor productivity? Discuss the factors which contribute to productivity growth in order of their quantitative importance.

6. Using examples, explain how changes in the allocation of labor can affect labor productivity.

7. How do you explain the close correlation between changes in the rate of productivity growth and changes in real wage rates? Discuss the relationship between productivity growth and inflation.

8. KEY QUESTION Account for the slowdown in the U.S. rate of productivity growth. What are the consequences of this slowdown? "Most of the factors which contributed to poor productivity growth in the 1970s are now behind us and are unlikely to recur in the near future." Do you agree?

9. "If we want economic growth in a free society, we may have to accept a measure of instability." Evaluate. The philosopher Alfred North Whitehead once remarked that "the art of progress is to preserve order amid change and to preserve change amid order." What did he mean? Is this contention relevant for economic growth? What implications might this have for public policy? Explain.

10. True or false? If false, explain why.
   a. Technological advance, which thus far has played only a small role in U.S. economic growth, is destined to play a more important role in the future.
   b. Nations lacking political freedom on average have faster growth rates than democratic nations.
   c. Many public capital goods are complementary to private capital goods.
   d. The rate of productivity growth in the manufacturing sector severely lags such advances in the service sector.

11. Suppose you are the chair of the Council of Economic Advisers and have been asked to prepare a set of proposals for increasing the productivity of U.S. workers as a way to raise the rate of economic growth. What would you put on your list? What impediments do you see in accomplishing your policies?

12. Evaluate: "Major innovations in computer and communication technologies in the United States, together with the globalization of markets, is creating a 'new economy' capable of achieving much faster rates of productivity and real GDP growth than those in the 1970s and 1980s."

13. Productivity often rises during economic expansions and falls during economic recessions. Can you think of reasons why? Briefly explain. (Hint: Remember that the level of productivity involves both levels of output and levels of labor input.)

14. (Last Word) Do you think economic growth is desirable? Explain your position on this issue.

15. WEB-BASED QUESTION **Current GDP Growth Rates and Per Capita Incomes—Is There a Relationship?** The OECD (Organization for Economic Cooperation and Development) http://www.oecd.org/std/nahome.htm provides both quarterly growth rates of real gross domestic product (GDP) for OECD member countries and an annual comparison of levels of GDP per capita based on exchange rates and purchasing power parities (PPPs). Which countries have the highest and lowest current GDP growth rates? Which have the highest and lowest per capita incomes? Does there seem to be a relationship? In your comparison, does it matter if you use per capita income based on exchange rates or PPPs? Which is more reliable?

16. WEB-BASED QUESTION **Increased Productivity Through Technology—Find Examples of Innovations in Computers and Communications** Recent innovations in computers and communications technologies are increasing productivity. Lucent Technologies (formerly Bell Labs) http://www.lucent.com/ideas2/ideas.html provides a timeline of innovations over the past 70 years. During this period, which increased the fastest: technological "home runs" (e.g., the transitor in 1947) or technological "singles" (e.g., free space optical switching in 1990)? Which innovation do you think has increased productivity the most? What are some current innovations which could increase productivity and in what way?

19

Budget Deficits and the Public Debt

The United States has amassed $5.4 trillion of public debt. How large is $5.4 trillion? We can put it into perspective this way: "One *million* seconds have ticked by in the past 12 days. One *billion* seconds took more than 31 years to elapse. One *trillion* seconds ago, it was around 30,000 BC—the Ice Age—and much of America was buried by glaciers."[1] So a debt of $5.4 trillion is a huge amount! It took more than 200 years for the public debt to reach $1 trillion. Then in only 15 years—1982 to 1997—it reached the $5.4 trillion mark. These are stunning numbers. Should we be concerned about them?

In this chapter we examine the Federal budget deficits and the rising public debt resulting from these deficits. We first present relevant definitions and then compare different budget philosophies. Next, we explore the quantitative dimensions of the public debt. How large is the debt relative to American GDP? We then consider the alleged "problems" associated with the public debt, explaining why some are bogus while others are real. Next, we look at the budget deficits during the past two decades and explain why these deficits may have negatively affected U.S. investment and international trade. Finally, we examine recent laws and proposals to eliminate budget deficits and point out that the budget deficit is quickly nearing zero.

DEFICITS AND DEBT: DEFINITIONS

A *budget deficit* is the amount by which government expenditures exceed its revenues in a particular year. For example, in 1997 the Federal government spent $1601 billion while its revenues were $1579 billion, resulting in a $22 billion deficit.

The national or **public debt** is the total accumulation of the Federal government's total deficits and surpluses which have occurred

through time. At the end of 1997 the public debt was about $5.4 trillion.

The term "public debt" as ordinarily used does *not* include the entire public sector; in particular, state and local finance is omitted. While the Federal government has been incurring large deficits, state and local governments in the aggregate have been realizing

[1]Marcia Stepanek, "The National Debt: Red Ink Rising," *Seattle Post-Intelligencer* (Hearst Newspapers), Apr. 13, 1994, p. 1.

surpluses. For example, in 1997 all state and local governments combined had a budgetary surplus in excess of $105 billion.[2]

BUDGET PHILOSOPHIES

Is it good or bad to incur deficits and let the public debt grow? Should the budget be balanced annually, if necessary by constitutional amendment? You saw in Chapter 12 that countercyclical fiscal policy should move the Federal budget toward a deficit during recession and toward a surplus during inflation. This means discretionary fiscal policy is unlikely to result in a balanced budget in any particular year. Is this a matter of concern?

Let's approach this question by examining the economic implications of several contrasting budget philosophies.

Annually Balanced Budget

Until the Great Depression of the 1930s, the **annually balanced budget** was viewed as the desirable goal of public finance. On examination, however, it becomes clear that an annually balanced budget is not compatible with government fiscal activity as a countercyclical, stabilizing force. Worse yet, an annually balanced budget intensifies the business cycle.

Illustration: Suppose the economy encounters an onset of unemployment and falling incomes. As Figure 12-3 shows, in such circumstances tax receipts automatically decline. To balance its budget, government must either (1) increase tax rates, (2) reduce government expenditures, or (3) do both. All these policies are contractionary; each further dampens, rather than expands, aggregate demand.

Similarly, an annually balanced budget will intensify inflation. Again, Figure 12-3 tells us that as nominal incomes rise during the course of inflation, tax collections automatically increase. To avoid the impending surplus, government must either (1) cut tax rates, (2) increase government expenditures, or (3) do both. But any of these policies adds to inflationary pressures.

An annually balanced budget is not economically neutral; the pursuit of such a policy is pro-cyclical, not coun-

tercyclical. Despite this problem, there is considerable support for a constitutional amendment requiring an annually balanced budget.

More recently, some economists have advocated an annually balanced budget not because of a fear of deficits and a mounting public debt but because they feel an annually balanced budget is essential in constraining an undesirable expansion of the public sector. Budget deficits, they argue, are a manifestation of political irresponsibility. Deficits allow politicians to give the public the benefits of government programs while *currently* avoiding raising taxes to pay for them.

These economists believe government has a tendency to grow larger than it should because there is less popular opposition to this growth when it is financed by deficits rather than taxes. Wasteful governmental expenditures are likely to creep into the Federal budget when deficit financing is readily available. Some conservative economists and politicians want a constitutional amendment to force a balanced budget to slow government growth. They view deficits as a symptom of a more fundamental problem—government encroachment on the private sector.

Cyclically Balanced Budget

The idea of a **cyclically balanced budget** is that government exerts a countercyclical influence and at the same time balances its budget. However, the budget would not be balanced annually—there is nothing sacred about 12 months as an accounting period—but, rather, over the course of the business cycle.

The rationale is simple, plausible, and appealing. To offset recession, government should lower taxes and increase spending, purposely incurring a deficit. During the ensuing inflationary upswing, taxes would be raised and government spending slashed. The resulting surplus could be used to retire the Federal debt incurred in financing the recession. Government fiscal operations would therefore exert a positive countercyclical force, and the government could still balance its budget—not annually, but over a period of years.

The problem with this budget philosophy is that the upswings and downswings of the business cycle may not be of equal magnitude and duration. The goal of stabilization may therefore conflict with balancing the budget over the cycle. A long and severe slump followed by a modest and short period of prosperity would mean a large deficit during the slump, little or no surplus during prosperity, and a cyclical deficit in the budget.

---

[2]This figure includes the states' pension funds. Exclusion of these funds greatly reduces the size of this collective surplus.

Functional Finance

With **functional finance,** a balanced budget—annually or cyclically—is secondary. The primary purpose of Federal finance is to provide for noninflationary full employment—to balance the economy, not the budget. If this objective causes either persistent surpluses or a large and growing public debt, so be it. In this philosophy, the problems of government deficits or surpluses are minor compared with the undesirable alternatives of prolonged recession or persistent inflation. The Federal budget is first and foremost an instrument for achieving and maintaining macroeconomic stability. How best to finance government spending—through taxation or borrowing—depends on existing economic conditions. Government should not hesitate to incur any deficits and surpluses required to achieve macroeconomic stability and growth.

To those who express concern about the large Federal debt which might result from the pursuit of functional finance, advocates of this budget philosophy offer three arguments:

1. The U.S. tax system is such that tax revenues automatically increase as the economy expands.

Assuming constant government expenditures, a deficit successful in increasing GDP will be partially self-liquidating.

2. Because of its taxing powers and the ability to create money, the government has a remarkable capacity to finance deficits.

3. A large Federal debt is less burdensome than most people think. **(Key Question 1)**

THE PUBLIC DEBT: FACTS AND FIGURES

Because modern fiscal policy endorses unbalanced budgets to stabilize the economy, its application may lead to a growing public debt. Let's consider the public debt—its causes, characteristics, and size—and its burdens and benefits.

The public debt, as column 2 in Table 19-1 shows, has grown considerably in nominal terms since 1929. (Not shown, it has also increased rapidly in real terms.) As we have noted, the public debt is the accumulation of all past deficits, minus surpluses, of the Federal budget.

TABLE 19-1   Quantitative significance of the public debt: the public debt and interest payments in relation to GDP, select years, 1929–1997

(1) Year	(2) Public debt, billions*	(3) Gross domestic product, billions*	(4) Interest payments, billions*	(5) Public debt as percentage of GDP, (2) ÷ (3)	(6) Interest payments as percentage of GDP, (4) ÷ (3)	(7) Per capita public debt*
1929	$ 16.9	$ 103.8	$ 0.7	16%	0.7%	$ 134
1940	50.7	100.2	0.9	51	0.9	384
1946	271.0	222.6	4.1	122	1.8	1917
1950	256.9	294.6	4.8	87	1.6	1667
1955	274.4	415.1	4.9	66	1.2	1654
1960	290.5	526.6	6.9	55	1.3	1610
1965	322.3	719.1	8.6	45	1.2	1659
1970	380.9	1035.6	14.4	37	1.4	1858
1975	541.9	1630.6	23.2	33	1.4	2507
1980	909.1	2784.2	52.5	33	1.9	3992
1985	1817.5	4180.7	129.5	43	3.1	7622
1990	3206.6	5743.8	184.2	56	3.2	12,829
1995	4921.0	7265.4	232.2	68	3.2	18,708
1997	5369.7	8083.4	244.0	66	3.0	20,044

*In current dollars

Source: Economic Report of the President, 1998; U.S. Department of Commerce.

Causes

Why has the U.S. public debt increased historically? What has caused the nation to incur these large and persistent deficits? The answer is fourfold: wars, recessions, tax cuts, and lack of political will.

Wars Some of the public debt has resulted from the deficit financing of wars. The public debt increased substantially during World War I and grew more than fivefold during World War II.

Consider World War II and the options it posed. The task was to reallocate a substantial portion of the economy's resources from civilian to war goods production. Government expenditures for armaments and military personnel soared. There were three financing options: increase taxes, print the needed money, or use deficit financing. Government feared that tax financing would require tax rates so high they would diminish incentives to work. The national interest required attracting more people into the labor force and encouraging those already participating to work longer hours. Very high tax rates were felt to interfere with these goals. Printing and spending additional money would be inflationary. Thus, much of World War II was financed by selling bonds to the public, thereby draining off spendable income and freeing resources from civilian production so they would be available for defense industries.

Recessions Another cause of the public debt is recessions and, more specifically, the built-in stability characterizing the U.S. fiscal system. In periods when the national income declines, tax collections automatically fall and deficits arise. Thus the public debt rose during the Great Depression of the 1930s and, more recently, during the recessions of 1974 to 1975, 1980 to 1982, and 1990 to 1991.

Tax Cuts A third consideration has accounted for much of the large deficits since 1981. The Economic Recovery Tax Act of 1981 provided for substantial cuts in both individual and corporate income taxes. The Reagan administration and Congress did *not* make offsetting reductions in government outlays. Therefore, a *structural deficit* was built into the Federal budget in the sense that the budget would not balance even if the economy were operating at full employment. Unfortunately, the economy was not at full employment during the early 1980s. The 1981 tax cuts combined with the severe 1980–1982 recessions to

generate rapidly rising annual deficits which were $128 billion in 1982 and accelerated to $221 billion by 1986. Although annual budget deficits declined between 1986 and 1989, they remained historically high even though the economy reached full employment. Due partly to the earlier tax-rate cuts, tax revenues were not high enough to cover rising Federal spending. Annual deficits, and thus the public debt, again rose between 1991 and 1993 as the economy experienced recession and the Federal government incurred massive expenses in bailing out failed savings and loan associations.

Lack of Political Will Without being too cynical, we might also assert that deficits and a growing public debt are the result of lack of political will and determination. Spending often gains votes; tax increases precipitate political disfavor. While opposition to deficits is expressed by politicians and their constituencies, *specific* proposals to cut spending programs or raise taxes typically encounter more opposition than support.

Particularly difficult to cut are **entitlement programs,** the subject of this chapter's Last Word. These programs, such as social security, Medicaid (health care for the poor), Medicare (health care for those on social security), and veterans' benefits, "entitle" or guarantee particular levels of transfer payments to all who fit the programs' criteria. Total spending on these programs automatically rises along with the number of qualifying individuals and has rocketed in recent years, contributing to budget deficits and the rising public debt. Cutting these benefits produces severe political opposition. For example, older Americans may favor smaller budget deficits as long as funds for social security and Medicare are not reduced.

Similarly, new taxes or tax increases to reduce budget deficits may be acceptable in the abstract but are far less popular when specific tax changes are proposed. The popular view of taxation seems to be "Don't tax me, don't tax thee, tax the person behind the tree." But there are not enough taxpayers "behind the tree" to raise the amounts of new revenue needed to close the budget deficit.

The Clinton administration's struggle to pass a deficit-reduction package in 1993 is an example of political difficulties of reducing spending and increasing taxes. The specific package of spending cuts and tax increases passed the Senate by only a single vote, even though nearly all senators agreed that deficit reduction was a worthy goal. (With the package in place, the annual deficit shrank from $255 billion in 1993 to $22 billion in 1997. Based on present economic projections, the Federal budget will achieve a surplus in 1999).

Quantitative Aspects

In 1997 the U.S. debt reached $5400 billion—or 5.4 trillion. That amount is more than twice what the debt was just 10 years earlier. But *we must not fear large, seemingly incomprehensible numbers.* You will see why when we put the size of the U.S. public debt into better perspective.

Debt and GDP A bald statement of the absolute size of the debt ignores that the wealth and productive ability of the U.S. economy is also vast. A wealthy nation can incur and carry a large public debt more easily than a poor nation, which is why it is more meaningful to measure the public debt *in relation to* the economy's GDP, as shown in column 5 in Table 19-1. Instead of the 20-fold increase in the debt between 1950 and 1997 shown in column 2, observe that the relative size of the debt was considerably less in 1997 than in 1950. However, our data *do* show that the relative size of the debt has doubled since 1980. Also, column 7 indicates that, on a per capita basis, the nominal debt has increased more or less steadily through time.

International Comparisons As shown in Global Perspective 19-1, public debts of many other industrial nations are greater than those in the United States as a percentage of GDP. On this basis, for example, public debt in 1997 was larger in Italy, Canada, Japan, Sweden, and Germany than in the United States.

Interest Charges Many economists conclude that the primary burden of the debt is the annual interest charge accruing as a result. The absolute size of these interest payments is shown in column 4 in Table 19-1. Interest payments have increased sharply beginning in the 1970s. This reflects not only increases in the debt but also periods of very high interest rates. Interest on the debt is now the fourth-largest item of expenditures in the Federal budget (see Figure 5-7). Interest charges as a percentage of the GDP are shown in column 6 in Table 19-1. Interest payments as a proportion of GDP have increased significantly in recent years. This ratio reflects the level of taxation (the

average tax rate) required to service the public debt. In 1997 the Federal government had to collect taxes equal to 3.0 percent of GDP to pay interest on its debt.

Ownership Figure 19-1 shows that slightly less than two-thirds of the total public debt is held outside the Federal government by state and local governments, banks and other financial institutions, and private parties. The remaining debt is held by Federal agencies and the Federal Reserve. Foreign individuals and institutions hold about 23 percent of the total debt. This statistic is significant because, as you will see shortly, there are different implications of internally and externally held debt.

GLOBAL PERSPECTIVE 19-1

Public debt: international comparisons

Although the United States has the world's largest public debt, a number of other nations have larger debts as a percentage of their GDPs.

Public Sector Debt as Percentage of GDP, 1997

Belgium
Italy
Canada
Japan
Sweden
Holland
Spain
Denmark
Germany
France
United States
Britain
Finland
Australia

Source: Organization for Economic Cooperation and Development.

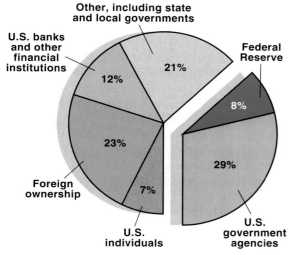

Debt held outside the Federal government and Federal Reserve (63%)

Debt held by the Federal government and Federal Reserve (37%)

Other, including state and local governments

U.S. banks and other financial institutions

Federal Reserve

12%

21%

8%

23%

29%

7%

Foreign ownership

U.S. individuals

U.S. government agencies

Total debt: $5.4 trillion

FIGURE 19-1 Ownership of the public debt Less than two-thirds of the public debt is held outside the Federal government; more than one-third is held internally by Federal agencies and the Federal Reserve System. Twenty-three percent of the public debt is foreign-owned.

Accounting and Inflation The data on budget deficits and public debt may not be as straightforward as they appear. Governmental accounting procedures may not reflect government's actual financial position. Private firms have a separate *capital budget* because, in contrast to current expenses on labor and raw materials, expenditures for capital equipment represent tangible money-making assets. In calculating its budget deficit, the Federal government treats expenditures for highways, harbors, and public buildings the same as it does welfare payments. But, in fact, the former outlays are investments in physical assets. Federal budget deficits in the 1980s and 1990s would have been smaller had the Federal government employed a capital budget which included depreciation costs.

Also, inflation works to benefit debtors. A rising price level reduces the real value or purchasing power of the dollars paid back by borrowers. Taking this "inflationary tax" into account further reduces the sizes of budget deficits and public debt.

The point is there are different ways of measuring the public debt and government's overall financial po-

sition. Some of these alternative measures differ greatly from the data presented in Table 19-1.

ECONOMIC IMPLICATIONS: FALSE ISSUES

How does the public debt and its growth affect the economy? Can a rising public debt bankrupt the nation? Does the debt place a burden on our children and grandchildren?

Fortunately, these are false or bogus issues. The debt is not about to bankrupt the government or the nation. Nor, except under certain specific circumstances explored later, does the debt place a burden on future generations.

Going Bankrupt?

Can a large public debt bankrupt the Federal government, leaving it unable to meet its financial obligations? No, for the following three reasons.

1. Refinancing There is no reason why the public debt needs to be reduced, much less eliminated. As portions of the debt come due each month, government does not cut expenditures or raise taxes to provide funds to *retire* the maturing bonds. Rather, the government *refinances* the debt; it sells new bonds and uses the proceeds to pay off holders of the maturing bonds.

2. Taxation Government has the constitutional authority to levy and collect taxes. A tax increase is a government option for gaining sufficient revenue to pay interest and principal on the public debt. Financially distressed private households and corporations *cannot* raise revenue via taxes; governments *can*. Private households and corporations *can* go bankrupt; the Federal government *cannot*.

3. Creating Money   Bankruptcy is also difficult to imagine because the Federal government (via the "Fed") can print money to pay both the principal and the interest on the debt. A government bond obligates the government to redeem that bond for some specific amount of money on its maturity date. Government can use the proceeds from the sale of other bonds *or* it can borrow newly created money from the Fed to retire the maturing bonds. The creation of new money to pay interest on debt or to retire debt *may* be inflationary. But it is difficult to conceive of governmental bankruptcy when government has the power to create new money by running the printing presses.

Shifting Burdens

Does the public debt impose a burden on future generations? Recall that per capita public debt in 1997 was $20,044. Did each child born in 1997 enter the world to be handed a $20,044 bill from Uncle Sam? Not really!

We first must ask to whom the United States owes the public debt. The answer is that it owes a substantial portion of it to itself. About 77 percent of U.S. government bonds are owned and held by citizens and institutions—banks, businesses, insurance companies, governmental agencies, and trust funds—within the United States. Thus *the public debt is also a public credit*. While the public debt is a liability to Americans (as taxpayers), *most* of the same debt is simultaneously an asset to Americans (as holders of Treasury bills, Treasury notes, Treasury bonds, and U.S. savings bonds).

To retire the public debt would call for a gigantic transfer payment from Americans to Americans. Taxpayers would pay higher taxes, and government would pay out those tax revenues to the same taxpaying individuals in the aggregate in redeeming the U.S. securities they hold. Although a redistribution of income would result from this huge financial transfer, it need not entail any immediate decline in the economy's aggregate wealth or standard of living. Repayment of an internally held public debt entails no leakage of purchasing power from the economy as

a whole. New babies who on the average inherit the $20,044-per-person public debt obligation are also bequeathed that same amount of government securities.

We noted earlier that the public debt increased sharply during World War II. Was some of the economic burden of World War II shifted to future generations by the decision to finance military purchases through the sale of government bonds? No. Recalling the production possibilities curve, we realize that the economic cost of World War II was the civilian goods society had to forgo in shifting scarce resources to war goods production. Regardless of whether society financed this reallocation through higher taxes or borrowing, the real economic burden of the war would have been the same. The burden of the war was borne almost entirely by those who lived during the war; they were the ones who did without a multitude of consumer goods to permit the United States to arm itself and its allies.

Also, wartime production may slow the growth of a nation's stock of capital as resources are shifted from production of capital goods to production of war goods. As a result, future generations inherit a smaller stock of capital goods. This occurred in the United States during World War II. But, again, this shifting of costs is independent of how a war is financed.

> ### QUICK REVIEW 19-2
> ■ There is no danger of the Federal government's going bankrupt because it need only refinance (not retire) the public debt and can raise revenues, if needed, through higher taxes or printing money.
> ■ Usually, the public debt is not a means of shifting economic burdens to future generations.

IMPLICATIONS AND ISSUES

We must be careful not to leave the impression that the public debt is of no concern to economists. The large debt *does* pose some real potential problems, although economists attach varying importance to them.

Income Distribution

The distribution of government security ownership is uneven. Some people own much more than their $20,044 per capita share of government securities; others, less or none at all. Although our knowledge of the ownership of the public debt by income class is limited, we presume that ownership is concentrated among wealthier groups. Because the tax system is only mildly progressive, payment of interest on the public debt probably increases income inequality. Income is transferred from people who, on average, have lower incomes to the higher-income bondholders. If greater income equality is one of our social goals, then this redistributive effect is clearly undesirable.

Incentives

Table 19-1 indicates that the present public debt necessitates annual interest payments of $244 billion. With no increase in the size of the debt, this annual interest charge must be paid out of tax revenues. These added taxes may dampen incentives to bear risk, to innovate, to invest, and to work. In this indirect way, a large public debt can impair economic growth. As noted earlier, the ratio of interest payments to GDP indicates the level of taxation needed to pay interest on the debt. Thus, many economists are concerned that this ratio is roughly twice as high as it was two decades earlier (column 6, Table 19-1).

External Debt

External debt—U.S. debt held by citizens and institutions of foreign countries—*is a burden.* This part of the public debt is *not* "owed to ourselves," and in real terms the payment of interest and principal requires transferring some of U.S. real output to other nations. Foreign ownership of the public debt is higher today than in earlier periods. In 1960 only 5 percent of the debt was foreign-owned; today foreign ownership is 23 percent. The assertion that "we owe the debt to ourselves" and the implication that the debt should thus be of little concern is less accurate than it was four decades ago. **(Key Question 3)**

Curb on Fiscal Policy

A large and growing public debt makes it politically difficult to use fiscal policy during a recession. For example, in 1991 and 1992 the Fed substantially reduced interest rates to stimulate a sluggish economy. But this easy money policy was slow to expand output and reduce unemployment. Had the public debt not been at a historic high and increasing due to the aforementioned structural deficit, it would have been politically feasible to reduce taxes or increase govern-

ment spending to generate the stimulus of a deficit. But the growing "debt problem" ruled out this stimulus on political grounds. In general, a large and growing public debt creates political impediments to the use of antirecessionary fiscal policy.

Crowding Out and the Stock of Capital

There is a potentially more serious problem. One way the public debt can transfer a real economic burden to future generations is by causing future generations to inherit a smaller stock of capital goods: a smaller "national factory." This possibility involves the *crowding-out effect*, the idea that deficit financing will increase interest rates and reduce private investment spending. If this happens, future generations would inherit an economy with a smaller production capacity and, other things equal, the standard of living would be lower than otherwise.

Suppose the economy is operating at its full-employment level of output and the Federal budget is initially in balance. Then assume that for some reason government increases its spending. The impact of this increase in government spending will fall on those living when it occurs. Think of a nation's production possibilities curve with "government goods" on one axis and "private goods" on the other. In a full-employment economy an increase in government spending will move the economy *along* the curve toward the government goods axis, meaning fewer private goods.

But private goods may be consumer or investment goods. If the increased government goods are provided at the expense of *consumer goods*, then the present generation bears the entire burden as a lower current standard of living. The current investment level is *not* affected, and therefore neither is the size of the national factory inherited by future generations. But if the increase in government goods means a reduction in production of *capital goods*, then the present generation's level of consumption (standard of living) will be unimpaired. But in the future our children and grandchildren will inherit a smaller stock of capital goods and will have lower income levels than otherwise.

Two Scenarios   Let's sketch the two scenarios yielding these different results.

First Scenario   Suppose the presumed increase in government spending is financed by an increase in taxation, say, personal income taxes. We know that most income is consumed. Therefore, consumer spending falls by almost as much as the increase in taxes. Here, the burden of the increase in government spending falls primarily on today's generation; it has fewer consumer goods.

Second Scenario   Assume the increase in government spending is financed by increasing the public debt, meaning government enters the money market and competes with private borrowers for funds. With the supply of money fixed, this increase in money demand will increase the interest rate—the "price" paid for the use of money.

In Figure 19-2 the curve I_{d1} reproduces the investment demand curve in Figure 9-5. (Ignore curve I_{d2} for now.) The investment demand curve is downsloping, indicating investment spending varies inversely with the interest rate. Here, government deficit financing drives up the interest rate, reducing private investment. If government borrowing in-

creases the interest rate from 6 to 10 percent, investment spending would fall from \$25 to \$15 billion. That is, \$10 billion of private investment would be crowded out.

Conclusion: An assumed increase in public goods production is more likely to come at the expense of private investment goods when financed by deficits. In comparison with the tax-financing scenario, the future generation inherits a smaller national factory and therefore has a lower standard of living with deficit financing.

Two Qualifications   But there are two loose ends to our discussion which might mitigate or even eliminate the size of the economic burden shifted to future generations.

1. Public Investment   Our discussion has neglected the character of the increase in government spending. Just as private goods may involve consumption or investment, so it is with public goods. If the increase in government spending consists of consumption-type outlays—purchases of recreational equipment for prisons or provision of limousines for government officials—then our second scenario's conclusion that the debt increase has shifted a burden to future generations is correct. But what if the government spending is investment-type outlays, for example, for construction of highways, harbors, and flood-control projects? Similarly, what if they are "human capital" investments in education, job training, and health?

Like private expenditures on machinery and equipment, **public investments** increase the economy's future production capacity. The capital stock of future generations need not be diminished; rather, its composition is changed so there is more public capital and less private capital.

2. Unemployment   The other qualification relates to our assumption that the initial increase in government expenditures occurs when the economy is at full employment. Again the production possibilities curve reminds us that *if* the economy is at less than full employment or, graphically, at a point inside the production possibilities curve, then an increase in government expenditures can move the economy *to* the curve without any sacrifice of either current consumption or private capital accumulation. If unemployment exists initially, deficit spending by government need *not* mean a burden for future generations in the form of a smaller national factory.

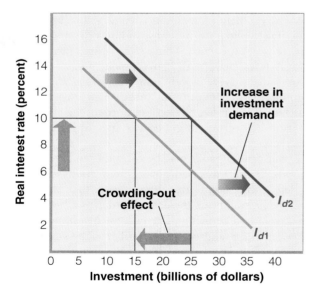

FIGURE 19-2 The investment demand curve and the crowding-out effect   The crowding-out effect suggests that with a fixed investment demand curve (I_{d1}), an increase in the interest rate caused by a government deficit will reduce private investment spending and decrease the size of the "national factory" inherited by future generations. In this case an increase in the interest rate from 6 to 10 percent crowds out \$10 billion of private investment. However, if the economy is initially in a recession, the government deficit may improve profit expectations of businesses and shift the investment demand curve rightward as from I_{d1} to I_{d2}. This shift may offset the crowding-out effect wholly or in part.

Look at Figure 19-2 again. If deficit financing increases the interest rate from 6 to 10 percent, a crowding-out effect of $10 billion will occur. But suppose the increase in government spending stimulates a recession economy via the multiplier effect, improving profit expectations and shifting private investment demand rightward to I_{d2}. Then, investment spending remains at $25 billion despite the higher 10 percent interest rate. Of course, the increase in investment demand might be smaller or larger than that in Figure 19-2. In the former case, the crowding-out effect would not be fully offset; in the latter, it would be more than offset. The point? An increase in investment demand may counter the crowding-out effect. **(Key Question 7)**

RECENT FEDERAL DEFICITS

Federal deficits and the growing public debt have been in the economic spotlight in the last two decades.

Large Size

As Figure 19-3 makes clear, the absolute size of annual Federal deficits increased enormously in the 1980s and 1990s. The average annual deficit for the 1970s was approximately $35 billion. In the 1980s annual deficits averaged five times that amount. Consequently, the public debt tripled during the same time (Table 19-1).

The Federal deficit jumped to $269 billion in 1991 and $290 billion in 1992, mainly because of the 1990–1991 recession and a weak recovery, which slowed the inflow of tax revenues. Government's expensive bailout of the savings and loan associations also contributed to the huge deficits in these years. The deficits then began to fall in 1993 and 1994 as the economy's expansion quickened and the Clinton administration's efforts to reduce the deficit took hold. By 1997 the deficit had dropped to $22 billion.

Understatement? The most recent annual budget deficits shown in Figure 19-3 may be understated. Over the past few years government has raised more money from social security taxes than it has paid out as benefits to current retirees. The purpose of this surplus is to prepare for the future time when "baby boomers" retire. Some economists argue that these revenues should be excluded when calculating present deficits because they represent future government obligations on a dollar-for-dollar basis. In this view

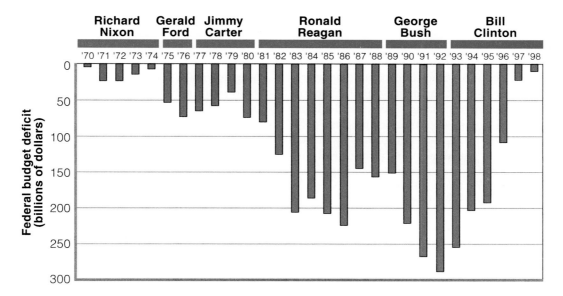

FIGURE 19-3 Annual Federal budget deficits, fiscal years 1970–1998 (in billions of dollars) Compared with the 1970s, annual budget deficits (here in nominal terms) ballooned in the 1980s and 1990s. (*Source: Economic Report of the President, 1998.* Fiscal years are 12-month periods ending September 30 of each year, rather than December 31 as in calendar years. The amount for 1998 is an estimate.)

the social security surplus should not be considered as an offset to *current* government spending. When we exclude the social security surplus from the deficit figures, recent budget deficits rise by $60 to $80 billion annually.

Rising Interest Costs   Column 4 in Table 19-1 indicates that interest payments on the public debt have increased about 17-fold since 1970. Interest payments were $244 billion in 1997, an amount greater than the entire deficit in many previous years! Because interest payments are part of government expenditures, the debt feeds on itself through interest charges. Interest payments on the debt are the only component of government spending which Congress cannot cut. The spiraling of such payments therefore complicates the problem of controlling government spending and the size of future deficits.

Inappropriate Policy   Some large U.S. annual deficits have occurred in an economy operating at or near full employment. Historically, deficits—particularly sizable ones—have been associated with wartime finance and recessions. While the 1980–1982 and 1990–1991 recessions contributed to huge deficits, it is clear that a major part of the deficits reflect the 1981 tax cuts and rising government spending. In terms of Figure 12-3, the 1981 tax cuts shifted the tax line downward. Meanwhile, mainly due to increased entitlement spending, the government spending line shifted upward. Thus, even at a full-employment level of output (GDP$_2$) sizable structural deficits remained.

Large deficits during times of economic prosperity raise the concern of fueling demand-pull inflation. To counteract potentially rising prices, the Federal Reserve is forced to employ a tighter monetary policy. Along with the strong demand for money in the private sector, the tight money policy raises real interest rates and reduces investment spending. The greatest potential for budget deficits to produce a crowding-out effect occurs when the economy is at or near full employment.

Balance-of-Trade Problems   Large budget deficits make it difficult for the nation to achieve a balance in its international trade. As you will see, large annual budget deficits promote imports and stifle exports. Also, budget deficits are thought to be a main cause of two related phenomena: (1) the nation's status as the "world's leading debtor nation" and (2) the so-called selling of the United States to foreign investors.

BUDGET DEFICITS AND TRADE DEFICITS

Many economists see cause-effect between Federal budget deficits and balance-of-trade deficits. Figure 19-4 is a guide to understanding their thinking.

Higher Interest Rates

Beginning with boxes 1 and 2, we note again that in financing its deficits, government must enter the money market to compete with the private sector for funds. We know this drives up real interest rates. High real interest rates have two important effects. First, as shown in box 3, they discourage private investment spending; this is the crowding-out effect. When the economy is close to full employment, the crowding-out effect is likely to be large. Therefore, although willing to admit that the short-run impact of deficits is expansionary, some economists express concern that the long-run effect of structural deficits is to retard the economy's growth rate. They envision deficits being used to finance entitlement programs and consumption-type government goods at the expense of investment in modernized factories and equipment. Deficits, it is contended, push the economy onto a slower long-run growth path.

Dollar Appreciation

The second effect, shown by box 4, is that high real interest rates on both U.S. government and private securities make financial investment in the United States more attractive for foreigners. While the resulting inflow of foreign funds helps finance both the deficit and private investment, box 5 reminds us that this inflow represents an increase in the U.S. external debt. Paying interest on and retiring debts to the rest of the world means a reduction in future real output available to the U.S. domestic economy.

Box 6 indicates that, to purchase high-yielding U.S. securities, foreigners must first buy U.S. dollars with their own currencies. This increases the worldwide demand for dollars and increases the international price or exchange value of the dollar. To illustrate: Suppose that before the United States incurred large deficits, the dollar ($) and the French franc (F) exchanged in the market at a rate of $1 = F10. But now the financing of large U.S. deficits increases real interest rates in the United States, increasing the demand for dollars with which to buy U.S. securities.

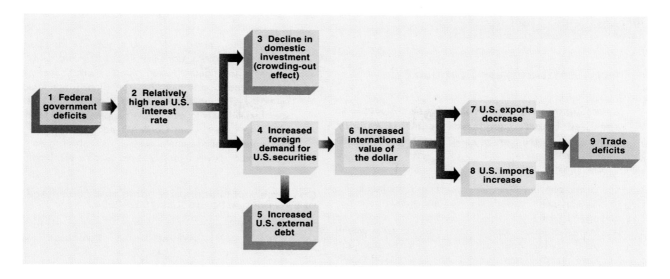

FIGURE 19-4 **Budget deficits and trade deficits** Large U.S. budget deficits can have a variety of effects. They can raise domestic interest rates, resulting in both a crowding out of private investment and an increase in the demand for U.S. securities. The latter increases the U.S. external debt and the demand for dollars. The strong demand for dollars causes the dollar to appreciate, making U.S. exports more expensive to foreigners and imports less costly to Americans. As U.S. exports fall and imports rise, a trade deficit arises.

Suppose this raises the price of the dollar to, say, $1 = F11.

Trade Deficits

This appreciation of the dollar will eventually depress U.S. exports (box 7) and increase U.S. imports (box 8), leading to an "unfavorable" balance of trade. Let's see how this comes about. We know that exchange rates link the price levels of the world's nations. When the value of the dollar increases—when dollars become more expensive to foreigners—all U.S. goods become more expensive to foreign buyers.

In our example the increase in the value of the dollar from $1 = F10 to $1 = F11 increases prices of all U.S. goods by 10 percent to the French. The U.S. product that formerly cost 10 francs now costs 11 francs. The French will react to this by buying fewer U.S. goods; U.S. exports will fall. Conversely, at the higher exchange rate Americans get 11 rather than 10 francs for a dollar, so French goods are cheaper to people in the United States. They therefore buy more French goods; U.S. imports rise. Bringing these together, U.S. net exports (exports *minus* imports) fall and a trade deficit emerges (box 9).

Related Effects

There are three complications here.

1. The inflow of foreign funds does augment domestic funds and helps keep U.S. real interest rates from rising as much as they would otherwise. The inflow of foreign funds to the United States diminishes the size of the crowding-out effect. In contrast, domestic saving and investment will be smaller in foreign nations transferring funds to the United States.

2. Deficit-caused high real interest rates in the United States impose an increased burden on heavily indebted developing countries such as Mexico and Brazil. Their dollar-denominated debts to U.S. banks, in effect, go up since the dollar appreciation that results means they need a greater amount of their own currencies to pay interest and principal on their debts. Also, any refinancing of their debts with U.S. banks means higher real interest rates.

3. A trade deficit means a nation is not exporting enough to pay for its imports. The difference can be paid for either by borrowing from abroad or by selling assets. The United States has been doing both. It has become the world's leading debtor nation and has sold off assets such as factories, shopping centers, and

"The Entitlements Problem"

Spending on programs which "entitle" people to specified transfer payments is rising rapidly, absorbing a greater part of total government spending

The accompanying figure divides Federal spending into three components and shows spending trends as a percentage of GDP.

1. *Interest spending* consists of Federal interest payments on the public debt. Since 1980 interest payments have increased from 1.9 to 3.0 percent of GDP, mainly because of the enormous growth of the public debt.

2. *Discretionary spending* involves programs controlled by annual appropriations bills. Congress can decide how much it wants to spend on these programs each year; it has full "discretion" over the amounts spent. This component of Federal expenditures includes spending on defense, transportation, law enforcement, and government operations. Observe that discretionary spending shrank from 13.5 percent of GDP in 1962 to about 7 percent in 1998.

3. *Mandatory spending*—or "entitlement spending"— comprises benefits paid out in programs such as so-

cial security, Medicare, Medicaid, veterans' compensation and pensions, agricultural subsidies, aid to families with dependent children, Supplementary Security Income, and food stamps. This spending is mandated by past legislation which directs Congress to pay out specified benefits to all eligible recipients. Entitlement spending grows when Congress adds new transfer programs or raises benefit levels in existing programs. It also expands when more people become eligible for

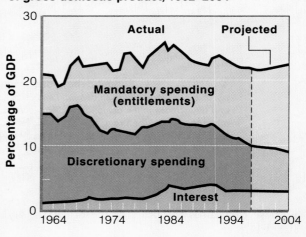

Components of Federal spending as a percentage of gross domestic product, 1962–2004

farms to foreign investors. To repay these debts and repurchase these assets, the United States would have to export more in the future than it imports. That is, it would have to consume and invest less than it produces. **(Key Question 8)**

■ Federal budget deficits are linked to U.S. trade deficits as follows: Budget deficits increase domestic interest rates; the dollar appreciates; U.S. exports fall, and U.S. imports rise; and a trade deficit emerges.

QUICK REVIEW 19-3

■ The borrowing and interest payments associated with the public debt **(a)** increase income inequality, **(b)** require higher taxes which dampen incentives, **(c)** curb the use of antirecessionary fiscal policy, and **(d)** impede the growth of the nation's capital stock through crowding out of private investment.

■ The Federal deficits of the past two decades have caused great concern because of **(a)** their enormous size, **(b)** the possibility of their understatement, **(c)** the rising total interest costs associated with them, and **(d)** their inappropriateness in the years when the economy was near, or at, full employment.

Policy Responses

Concern about large budget deficits and an expanding public debt has spawned several major policy responses.

Deficit-Reduction Legislation   By 1992 it became clear that previous legislative efforts to reduce the budget deficit—including an increase in the top marginal tax rate on personal income from 28 to 31 percent—would still leave annual budget deficits of $175 to $225 billion. Spurred by the Clinton administration, in 1993 Congress passed the Deficit

the benefits. Entitlement spending doubled between 1962 and 1998, rising from 6 to 13 percent of GDP.

It is clear from the diagram that rapidly rising Federal entitlements and interest payments are squeezing discretionary spending. Entitlements and interest are projected to consume *all* Federal tax revenues by 2015, leaving the Federal government with no money for education, children's programs, highways, national defense, or anything else.

Solutions proposed to avoid this startling scenario include:

1. Increasing tax rates
2. Eliminating some entitlement programs
3. Reducing benefit levels in some or all entitlement programs
4. Denying wealthier citizens social security and Medicare benefits
5. Reducing health care benefits under Medicare
6. Fully taxing entitlement benefits as if they were ordinary income

None of these possibilities is politically popular. *About half of all U.S. families receive benefits from one or more of the 11 largest entitlement programs.* A mid-1990s poll found that 61 percent of the public favored cutting government entitlement programs to curb the deficit. But when asked if they favored cuts in programs such as social security, Medicare, and farm subsidies, 66 percent said "no."

Social security and Medicare are the largest Federal entitlement programs. Social security is currently sound, collecting more revenues from 124 million workers than it pays to 44 million beneficiaries. But this self-financing will end in 2029 because of growing social security payments to the massive baby-boom generation. Spending for Medicare—the fastest growing entitlement program—will rise even more when the baby boomers retire.

Policymakers have begun to confront this issue. For example, Congress recently ended the entitlement aspect of the aid to families with dependent children program. There is little doubt the question of what to do about entitlements will continue to be the subject of intense discussion over the next several years.

Reduction Act, designed to increase tax revenues by $250 billion over the following 5 years and to reduce Federal spending by the same amount.

Specifically, this legislation (1) increased the top marginal tax rate on personal income from 31 to 39.6 percent, (2) raised the corporate income tax from 34 to 35 percent, and (3) added 4.3 cents per gallon to the Federal excise tax on gasoline. The largest spending "cut" resulted from holding all *discretionary spending*—the spending not mandated by law—to 1993 nominal levels. Normally, this spending would have increased at least as fast as inflation. Aided by strong economic growth, the Deficit Reduction Act reduced the deficit to $22 billion by 1997.

In 1996 Congress and the president agreed to a tax and spending package which included selected tax reductions but also increased some tax rates and reduced several types of government spending. Under this law, the deficit is designed to fall to zero by 2002, if the economy avoids recession. Recent estimates indicate that budget balance may occur as early as 1998. This outcome would be historic; not since 1969 has the Federal government balanced its budget.

Line-Item Veto In 1995 Congress gave the president the authority to veto individual spending items (called *line items*) in legislation passed by Congress. A typical appropriations bill merges hundreds of programs and projects into a single piece of legislation. The **line-item veto** will allow the president to cull from such legislation those projects whose benefits go to relatively few in a particular state, at a far greater expense to the nation's taxpayers. As a hypothetical example, the president could veto a specific provision to spend, say, $30 million for a monument in Chicago in honor of a local politician. Thus, the line-item veto—and perhaps even the threat of its use—might reduce government spending and help the Federal government balance its budget.

In 1996 President Clinton used the line-item veto for the first time. This use has enabled critics to challenge the constitutionality of the line-item veto in the courts, and the outcome of that challenge is still pending. Critics say that the line-item veto gives too much power to the president—power that the Constitution allegedly reserves for Congress. They also point out that this power could be abused for political purposes. For example, the president could veto a home-state project of a political "enemy" in Congress, leaving untouched a home-state project of a political "friend."

Proposed Constitutional Amendment The most extreme proposal is that a constitutional amendment should be passed which mandates that Congress balance the budget each year. Proponents of this proposed **balanced-budget amendment** assume that future Congresses will find it difficult to act "responsibly" because government spending enhances and tax increases diminish a politician's popular support. Political rhetoric and recent deficit reductions aside, Federal deficits allegedly will continue to occur until a constitutional amendment requires an annually balanced budget.

Thus far, the proposed amendment has not passed Congress. Critics have successfully pointed out that a strict requirement to balance the budget annually would force government to increase tax rates or reduce government spending during recession. As previously noted, such actions would worsen a recession (review Figure 12-6).

Positive Role of Debt

Having completed this survey of imagined and real problems of deficits and the public debt, we conclude our discussion on a more positive note. Debt, both public and private, plays a positive role in a prosperous and growing economy. As national income increases, saving also rises. For the economy to continue to grow, this saving must be obtained and spent. The process by which saving is transferred to spenders is *debt creation*. Ideally, consumers and firms borrow and spend this growing saving. And, in fact, this usually is the case; the total private debt in the United States is about $11 trillion.

But, at times, consumers and firms are unwilling to borrow and thereby increase private debt sufficiently fast to absorb the growing volume of saving. When that happens, it is appropriate for government to expand its debt in order to absorb the remainder. Otherwise, the economy might falter from full employment and not realize its growth potential.

CHAPTER SUMMARY

1. A budget deficit is the excess of government expenditures over its receipts; the public debt is the total accumulation of its deficits and surpluses over time.

2. Budget philosophies include the annually balanced budget, the cyclically balanced budget, and functional finance. The basic problem with an annually balanced budget is that it is pro-cyclical rather than countercyclical. Similarly, it may be difficult to balance the budget over the course of the business cycle if upswings and downswings are not of roughly comparable magnitude. Functional finance is the view that the primary purpose of Federal finance is to stabilize the economy, and problems associated with consequent deficits or surpluses are of secondary importance.

3. Historically, growth of the public debt has been caused by the deficit financing of wars and by recessions. The large structural deficits of the 1980s and most of the 1990s primarily resulted from tax-rate reductions, accompanied by increases in entitlement spending.

4. The U.S. public debt (1997) is $5.4 trillion, or $20,044 per person. The public holds about two-thirds of this debt, while the other one-third is held by government agencies and the Federal Reserve System. In the 1980s and early 1990s, the public debt and its associated interest expense increased sharply as percentages of GDP. Only very recently have these percentages declined.

5. The contention that a large public debt may bankrupt the government is false because **(a)** the debt need only be refinanced rather than refunded and **(b)** the Federal government has the power to levy taxes and create money.

6. The crowding-out effect aside, the public debt is not a vehicle for shifting economic burdens to future generations.

7. More substantive problems associated with public debt include the following: **(a)** Payment of interest on the debt may increase income inequality. **(b)** Interest payments on the debt require higher taxes, which may impair incentives. **(c)** A large and growing public debt creates political impediments to the use of antirecessionary fiscal policy. **(d)** Paying interest or principal on the portion of the debt held by foreigners means a transfer of real output abroad. **(e)** Government borrowing to refinance or pay interest on the debt may increase interest rates and crowd out private investment spending.

8. The large Federal budget deficits of the 1980s and early 1990s increased real interest rates in the United States, and this then **(a)** crowded out private investment and **(b)** increased the foreign demand for U.S. securities. Increased demand for U.S. securities in turn caused the dollar to appreciate, reducing U.S. exports and increasing U.S. imports. Thus the large budget deficits contributed to U.S. trade deficits.

9. The large deficits and expanding public debt of the 1980s and early 1990s produced several policy responses. Legislation in 1993 cut expenditures and raised tax rates on personal income, corporate profit, and gasoline. In 1996, Congress gave the president the authority to veto specific spending items ("line items") from larger spending bills. Also in 1996, Congress passed a tax-spending package projected to reduce the budget deficit to zero by 2002 or earlier. The large deficits also created a call for a constitutional amendment which would require the Federal government to balance its budget annually.

TERMS AND CONCEPTS

public debt
annually balanced budget
cyclically balanced
 budget

functional finance
entitlement programs
external debt
public investments

line-item veto
balanced-budget
 amendment

STUDY QUESTIONS

1. KEY QUESTION Assess the potential for using fiscal policy as a stabilization tool under **(a)** an annually balanced budget, **(b)** a cyclically balanced budget, and **(c)** functional finance.

2. What have been the major sources of the public debt historically? Why were deficits so large in the 1980s? Why did the deficit rise sharply in 1991 and 1992?

3. KEY QUESTION Discuss the two ways of measuring the size of the public debt. How does an internally held public debt differ from an externally held public debt? What would be the effects of retiring an internally held public debt? An externally held public debt? Distinguish between refinancing and retiring the debt.

4. Explain or evaluate each of the following statements:
  a. A public debt is like a debt of the left hand to the right hand.
  b. The least likely problem arising from a large public debt is that the Federal government will go bankrupt.
  c. The basic cause of the growing Federal debt is a lack of political courage.

  d. The social security reserves are not being reserved. They are being spent, masking the real deficit.

5. Is the crowding-out effect likely to be larger during recession or when the economy is near or at full employment? Explain.

6. Some economists argue that the quantitative importance of the public debt can best be measured by interest payments on the debt as a percentage of the GDP. Explain why.

7. KEY QUESTION Is the $5.4 trillion public debt a burden to future generations? If so, in what sense? Why might deficit financing be more likely to reduce the future size of the U.S. "national factory" than would financing government expenditures through taxes?

8. KEY QUESTION Trace the cause-and-effect chain through which large deficits might affect domestic real interest rates, domestic investment, the international value of the dollar, and U.S. international trade. Comment: "There is too little recognition that the deterioration of the United States' position in world trade is more the result of our own policies than the harm wrought by foreigners."

9. Explain how a significant decline in the nation's budget deficit would be expected to affect **(a)** the size of the U.S. trade deficit, **(b)** the total debt Americans owe to foreigners, and **(c)** foreign purchases of U.S. assets such as factories and farms.

10. What major legislative actions has Congress taken since 1993 to reduce the size of the Federal deficit? Why has this process been so politically painful to Congress? Have the actions succeeded?

11. Do you favor a constitutional amendment which would require the Federal government to balance its budget each year? Why or why not? Relate your answer to the "rules versus discretion debate" discussed in Chapter 17.

12. Explain: "Congressional knowledge that the president *has* the line-item veto, more than such vetoes themselves, may reign in some government spending."

13. (Last Word) What does the term "entitlement programs" mean? Cite several examples of such programs. Why have entitlement programs grown so rapidly? What are the implications for future generations if this growth continues?

14. WEB-BASED QUESTION The Debt—To the Penny Go to the Web site of the Department of Treasury–Bureau of the Public Debt http://www.publicdebt.treas.gov/opd/opdpenny.htm and find the amount of the public debt, to the penny, as of the latest date. How does it compare to the debt of 10 years ago? What has been the trend over the past 12 months? For general information, visit http://www.publicdebt.treas.gov/opd/opd.htm.

15. WEB-BASED QUESTION Frequently Asked Questions About the Public Debt Visit the U.S. Treasury's Public Debt Frequently Asked Questions (FAQ) site http://www.publicdebt.treas.gov/opd/opdfaq.htm and answer the following questions. Why does the public debt sometimes go down? Why does the public debt change only once a day? As of today, who owns the public debt?

5

International Economics and the World Economy

20

International Trade

The WTO, trade deficits, dumping. Exchange rates, the EU, the G-7 nations. The IMF, official reserves, currency interventions. Capital flight, brain drains, the ruble. This is the language of international economics, and people across the globe are speaking it in newspapers, corporate offices, retail outlets, and union halls.

This chapter builds on Chapter 6, providing deeper analysis of international trade and protectionism. We begin by reviewing key facts about world trade, and then we look more closely at how international specialization based on comparative advantage can mutually benefit the participating nations. After using supply and demand analysis to examine equilibrium prices and quantities of imports and exports, we examine the economic impact of trade barriers such as tariffs and import quotas and evaluate the arguments for protectionism. Finally, we discuss the costs of protectionism and look at continuing controversies in international trade.

Subsequent chapters discuss other international topics. Chapter 21 examines exchange rates and the balance of payments; Chapter 22 looks at the special problems of developing economies, and Chapter 23 focuses on two economies—Russia and China—which are making transitions from central planning to capitalism.

FACTS OF INTERNATIONAL TRADE

In Chapter 6 we developed a number of facts about international trade. Let's briefly review those facts and add a few others.

1. Exports of goods and services make up about 12 percent of total U.S. output. This percentage is far lower than in many other nations. Examples: Netherlands, 56 percent; Canada, 38 percent; New Zealand, 30 percent; the United Kingdom, 30 percent.

2. The United States leads the world in the volume of exports and imports. Currently, it provides about one-eighth of the world's exports, down from one-third in 1947. Germany, Japan, Britain, and France follow in the list of top five merchandise exporters by volume.

3. Since 1965, U.S. exports and imports have increased in volume and more than doubled as a percentage of GDP.

4. In 1996 the United States had a $191 billion trade deficit—meaning that imports of goods exceeded exports of goods by

this amount. But in that year U.S. exports of services exceeded its imports of services by $80 billion. Thus, the combined goods and services deficit was $111 billion.

5. The U.S.'s principal commodity exports are computers, chemicals, semiconductors, consumer durables, and aircraft. Its main imports are petroleum, automobiles, computers, and clothing.

6. Like other advanced industrial nations, the United States imports some of the same categories of goods that it exports. Examples: automobiles, computers, chemicals, semiconductors, and telecommunications equipment.

7. The bulk of U.S. export and import trade is with other industrially advanced nations, specifically Canada, nations of western Europe, and Japan.

8. Improved transportation and communications technologies, declines in tariffs, and peaceful relations among major industrial nations have all helped expand world trade since World War II.

9. Although trade is still dominated by the United States, Japan, and western European nations (Global Perspective 20-1), several new "players" have greatly increased their roles. Collectively, Hong Kong, Singapore, South Korea, and Taiwan have expanded their share of world trade from 3 percent in 1972 to nearly 10 percent today. China has emerged as a new international trader, and the collapse of communism has led eastern European nations and Russia to look globally for new trade partners.

10. International trade (and finance) link economies. Through trade, changes in economic conditions in one spot on the globe can quickly affect other places. Example: In early 1998, economists scaled back forecasts for economic growth in the United States and Europe because of economic problems in the southeast Asian countries of Japan, South Korea, Indonesia, Malaysia, and the Philippines. Reduced purchases of U.S. and European imports mean lower U.S. and European exports and thus slower U.S. and European output growth.

11. International trade is often at the center of international policy. Examples: the North American Free Trade Agreement (NAFTA), the conclusion of negotiations on the General Agreement on Tariffs and Trade (GATT), and U.S.-Japan negotiations on reducing U.S. deficits with Japan.

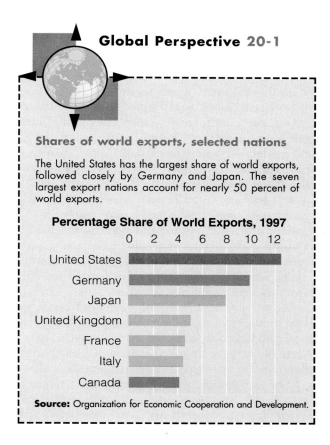

Global Perspective 20-1

Shares of world exports, selected nations

The United States has the largest share of world exports, followed closely by Germany and Japan. The seven largest export nations account for nearly 50 percent of world exports.

Percentage Share of World Exports, 1997

Source: Organization for Economic Cooperation and Development.

With these facts in mind, let's now look closer at the economics of international trade.

THE ECONOMIC BASIS FOR TRADE

In Chapter 6 we found that international trade allows nations to specialize, increase the productivity of their resources, and obtain more goods and services. Sovereign nations, like individuals and regions of a nation, can gain by specializing in products they can produce with greatest relative efficiency and by trading for goods they cannot produce as efficiently. This rationale for trade is correct, but a more detailed understanding is needed. The more complete answer to the question "Why do nations trade?" hinges on two facts:

1. The distribution of economic resources—natural, human, and capital goods—among nations is uneven; nations vary in their endowments of economic resources.

2. Efficient production of various goods requires different technologies or combinations of resources.

The character and interaction of these two facts can be readily illustrated. Japan, for example, has a large, well-educated labor force; skilled labor is abundant and therefore inexpensive. Japan can produce efficiently (at low cost) a variety of goods whose design and production require much skilled labor: Cameras, transistor radios, and video recorders are examples of such **labor-intensive goods.**

In contrast, Australia has vast amounts of land compared with its human and capital resources and can inexpensively produce goods requiring much land; it produces such **land-intensive goods** as wheat, wool, and meat. Brazil has the soil, tropical climate, rainfall, and lots of unskilled labor needed for efficient, low-cost production of coffee.

Industrially advanced economies with relatively large amounts of capital can produce inexpensively those goods whose production requires much capital. Automobiles, agricultural equipment, machinery, and chemicals are such **capital-intensive goods.**

The distribution of both resources and technology among nations, however, is not forever fixed. When the distribution changes, the relative efficiency with which nations produce goods also changes. For example, in the past few decades South Korea has upgraded the quality of its labor force and has greatly expanded its stock of capital. Although South Korea was primarily an exporter of agricultural products and raw materials a half-century ago, it now exports large

quantities of manufactured goods. Similarly, the new technologies which gave us synthetic fibers and synthetic rubber drastically altered the resource mix needed to produce these goods and changed the relative efficiency of nations in manufacturing them.

As national economies evolve, the size and quality of their labor forces may change, the volume and composition of their capital stocks may shift, new technologies will develop, and even the quality of land and quantity of natural resources may be altered. As these changes occur, the relative efficiency with which a nation can produce specific goods will also change.

COMPARATIVE ADVANTAGE: GRAPHICAL ANALYSIS

Implicit in what we just discussed is the principle of comparative advantage, described in Chapter 6. Let's again look at that idea, now using graphical analysis.

Two Isolated Nations

Suppose the world economy is composed of just two nations: the United States and Brazil. Each nation can produce both wheat and coffee, but at differing levels of economic efficiency. Suppose U.S. and Brazilian domestic production possibilities curves for coffee and wheat are as shown in Figure 20-1a and b. Two characteristics of these production possibilities curves should be noted:

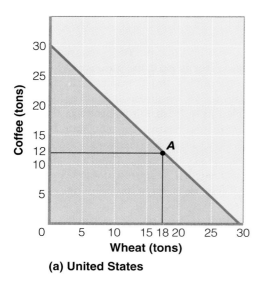

(a) United States

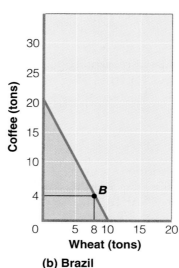

(b) Brazil

FIGURE 20-1 Production possibilities for the United States and Brazil The two production possibilities curves show the combinations of coffee and wheat which (a) the United States and (b) Brazil can produce domestically. The curves for both countries are straight lines because we are assuming constant opportunity costs. The different cost ratios, 1 coffee ≡ 1 wheat for the United States, and 2 coffee ≡ 1 wheat for Brazil, are reflected in the different slopes of the two lines.

----

1. *Constant costs* The "curves" are drawn as straight lines, in contrast to the concave-from-the-origin production possibilities frontiers introduced in Chapter 2. This means that the law of increasing opportunity costs has been replaced with the assumption of constant costs. This simplifies our discussion but does not impair the validity of our analysis and conclusions. We later will consider the effects of the more realistic increasing costs.

2. *Different costs* The production possibilities curves of the United States and Brazil are different, reflecting different resource mixes and differing levels of technological progress. Specifically, the curves tell us that the opportunity costs of producing wheat and coffee differ between the two nations.

United States In Figure 20-1a, with full employment, the United States will operate on its production possibilities curve. On that curve, it can increase its output of wheat 30 tons by forgoing 30 tons of coffee output. This means that the slope of the production possibilities curve is -1 ($= -30$ coffee/$+30$ wheat), implying that 1 ton of coffee must be sacrificed for each extra 1 ton of wheat. In the United States the domestic exchange ratio or **cost ratio** for the two products is 1 ton of coffee for 1 ton wheat, or $1C \equiv 1W$. The United States can "exchange" a ton of coffee for a ton of wheat. Our constant-cost assumption means that this exchange or opportunity cost equation prevails for all possible moves from one point to another along the U.S. production possibilities curve.

Brazil Brazil's production possibilities curve in Figure 20-1b represents a different full-employment opportunity cost ratio. In Brazil, 20 tons of coffee must be given up to get 10 tons of wheat. The slope of the production possibilities curve is -2 ($= -20$ coffee/$+10$ wheat). This means that in Brazil the cost ratio for the two goods is 2 tons of coffee for 1 ton of wheat, or $2C \equiv 1W$.

Self-Sufficiency Output Mix If the United States and Brazil are isolated and are to be self-sufficient, then each country must choose some output mix on its production possibilities curve. Assume point *A* in Figure 20-1a is the optimal output mix in the United States; that is, the combination of 18 tons of wheat and 12 tons of coffee equates the marginal benefit and marginal cost of both goods. Suppose Brazil's optimal product mix is 8 tons of wheat and 4 tons of coffee, indicated by point *B* in Figure 20-1b. These choices are also reflected in column 1, Table 20-1.

Specializing According to Comparative Advantage

With these different cost ratios, determining the products in which the United States and Brazil should specialize is as follows: The **principle of comparative advantage** says that *total output will be greatest when each good is produced by that nation which has the lowest domestic opportunity cost for that good.* In our two-nation illustration, the United States has the lower domestic opportunity cost for wheat; the United States need only forgo 1 ton of coffee to produce 1 ton of wheat,

TABLE 20-1   International specialization according to comparative advantage and the gains from trade
(in tons)

Country	(1) Outputs before special- ization	(2) Outputs after special- ization	(3) Amounts exported (−) and imported (+)	(4) Outputs available after trade	(5) = (4) − (1) Gains from special- ization and trade
United States	18 wheat 12 coffee	30 wheat 0 coffee	−10 wheat +15 coffee	20 wheat 15 coffee	2 wheat 3 coffee
Brazil	8 wheat 4 coffee	0 wheat 20 coffee	+10 wheat −15 coffee	10 wheat 5 coffee	2 wheat 1 coffee

whereas Brazil must forgo 2 tons of coffee for 1 ton of wheat. *The United States has a comparative (cost) advantage in wheat and should specialize in wheat production.* The "world" (the United States and Brazil) clearly is *not* economizing in the use of its resources if a specific product (wheat) is produced by a high-cost producer (Brazil) when it could have been produced by a low-cost producer (the United States). To have Brazil produce wheat would mean that the world economy would have to give up more coffee than is necessary to obtain a ton of wheat.

Brazil has the lower domestic opportunity cost for coffee; it must sacrifice only $\frac{1}{2}$ ton of wheat in producing 1 ton of coffee, while the United States must forgo 1 ton of wheat in producing a ton of coffee. *Brazil has a comparative advantage in coffee and should specialize in coffee production.* Again, the world would *not* be employing its resources economically if coffee were produced by a high-cost producer (the United States) rather than a low-cost producer (Brazil). If the United States produced coffee, the world would be giving up more wheat than necessary to obtain each ton of coffee. *Economizing—using fixed quantities of scarce resources to obtain the greatest total output—requires that any particular good be produced by that nation having the lowest domestic opportunity cost, or the comparative advantage for that good.* The United States should produce wheat and Brazil, coffee.

In column 2 of Table 20-1 we verify that specialized production in accordance with the principle of comparative advantage allows the world to get more output from its fixed amount of resources. By specializing completely in wheat, the United States can produce 30 tons of wheat and no coffee. Brazil, by specializing completely in coffee, can produce 20 tons of coffee and no wheat. The world ends up with more wheat—30 tons compared with 26 (= 18 + 8)—*and* more coffee—20 tons compared with 16 (= 12 + 4)—than when there is self-sufficiency or unspecialized production.

Terms of Trade

But consumers of each nation want *both* wheat and coffee. They can have both if the two nations trade or exchange the two products. But what will be the **terms of trade?** That is, at what exchange ratio will the United States and Brazil trade wheat and coffee?

Because $1W \equiv 1C$ in the United States, the United States must get *more than* 1 ton of coffee for each ton of wheat exported or it will not benefit from export-

ing wheat in exchange for Brazilian coffee. The United States must get a better "price" (more coffee) for its wheat in the world market than it can get domestically, or there is no gain from trade and it will not occur.

Similarly, because $1W \equiv 2C$ in Brazil, Brazil must get 1 ton of wheat by exporting some amount *less than* 2 tons of coffee. Brazil must be able to pay a lower "price" for wheat in the world market than it must pay domestically, or it will not want to trade. The international exchange ratio or *terms of trade* must lie somewhere between

$1W \equiv 1C$ (United States' cost conditions)

and

$1W \equiv 2C$ (Brazil's cost conditions)

But where between these limits will the world exchange ratio fall? The United States will prefer a rate close to $1W \equiv 2C$, say, $1W \equiv 1\frac{3}{4}C$. The United States wants to get much coffee for each ton of wheat it exports. Similarly, Brazil wants a rate near $1W \equiv 1C$, say, $1W \equiv 1\frac{1}{4}C$. Brazil wants to export as little coffee as possible for each ton of wheat it receives in exchange. The exchange ratio or terms of trade determines how the gains from international specialization and trade are divided between the two nations.

The final exchange ratio depends on world supply and demand for the two products. If overall world demand for coffee is weak relative to its supply and the demand for wheat is strong relative to its supply, the price of coffee will be lower and the price of wheat higher. The exchange ratio will settle nearer the $1W \equiv 2C$ figure the United States prefers. Under the opposite world supply and demand conditions, the ratio will settle nearer the $1W \equiv 1C$ level favorable to Brazil. (We discuss equilibrium world prices later in this chapter.)

Gains from Trade

Suppose the international terms of trade are $1W \equiv 1\frac{1}{2}C$. The possibility of trading on these terms permits each nation to supplement its domestic production possibilities line with a **trading possibilities line.** This can be seen in **Figure 20-2 (Key Graph).** Just as a production possibilities curve shows the amounts of these products a full-employment economy can obtain by shifting resources from one to the other, a trading possibilities line shows the amounts of two products a nation can obtain by specializing in one product and trading for the other. The trading

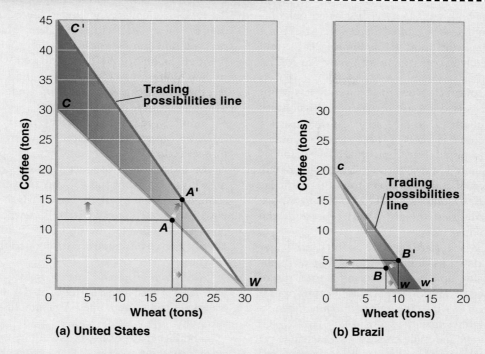

FIGURE 20-2 Trading possibility lines and the gains from trade As a result of specialization and trade, the United States and Brazil both can have higher levels of output than those attainable on their domestic production possibilities curves. (a) The United States can move from point A on its domestic production possibilities curve to, say, A' on its trading possibilities line. (b) Brazil can move from B to B'.

QUICK QUIZ 20-2

1. The production possiblities curves in graphs (a) and (b) imply:
   a. increasing domestic opportunity costs.
   b. decreasing domestic opportunity costs.
   c. constant domestic opportunity costs.
   d. first decreasing, then increasing, domestic opportunity costs.

2. Before specialization, the domestic opportunity cost of producing 1 unit of wheat is:
   a. 1 unit of coffee in both the United States and Brazil.
   b. 1 unit of coffee in the United States and 2 units of coffee in Brazil.
   c. 2 units of coffee in the United States and 1 unit of coffee in Brazil.
   d. 1 unit of coffee in the United States and 1/2 unit of coffee in Brazil.

3. After specialization and trade, the world output of wheat and coffee is:
   a. 20 tons of wheat and 20 tons of coffee.
   b. 45 tons of wheat and 15 tons of coffee.
   c. 30 tons of wheat and 20 tons of coffee.
   d. 10 tons of wheat and 30 tons of coffee.

4. After specialization and international trade:
   a. the United States can obtain units of coffee at less cost than before trade.
   b. Brazil can obtain more than 20 tons of coffee, if it so chooses.
   c. the United States no longer has a comparative advantage in producing wheat.
   d. Brazil can benefit by prohibiting coffee imports from the United States.

Answers: 1. c; 2. b; 3. c; 4. a

possibilities lines in Figure 20-2 are drawn on the assumption that both nations specialize based on comparative advantage—the United States specializes completely in wheat (at point W in Figure 20-2a) and Brazil completely in coffee (at point c in Figure 20-2b).

Improved Options   Now, the United States is not constrained by its domestic production possibilities line, which requires it to give up 1 ton of wheat for every ton of coffee it wants as it moves up its domestic production possibilities line from, say, point W. Instead, the United States, through trade with Brazil, can get $1\frac{1}{2}$ tons of coffee for every ton of wheat it exports to Brazil, so long as Brazil has coffee to export. Trading possibilities line WC' thus represents the $1W \equiv 1\frac{1}{2}C$ trading ratio.

Similarly, Brazil, starting at, say, point c, no longer has to move down its domestic production possibilities curve, giving up 2 tons of coffee for each ton of wheat it wants. It can now export just $1\frac{1}{2}$ tons of coffee for each ton of wheat it wants by moving down its trading possibilities line cw'.

Specialization and trade create a new exchange ratio between wheat and coffee, reflected in each nation's trading possibilities line. This exchange ratio is superior for both nations to the unspecialized self-sufficiency exchange ratio embodied in their production possibilities curves. By specializing in wheat and trading for Brazil's coffee, the United States can obtain *more than* 1 ton of coffee for 1 ton of wheat. By specializing in coffee and trading for U.S. wheat, Brazil can get 1 ton of wheat for *less than* 2 tons of coffee.

Added Output   By specializing based on comparative advantage and trading for those goods produced in the other nation with greater domestic efficiency, the United States and Brazil can realize combinations of wheat and coffee beyond their production possibilities boundaries. *Specialization according to comparative advantage results in a more efficient allocation of world resources, and larger outputs of both products are therefore available to both nations.*

Suppose that at the $1W \equiv 1\frac{1}{2}C$ terms of trade, the United States exports 10 tons of wheat to Brazil and in return Brazil exports 15 tons of coffee to the United States. How do the new quantities of wheat and coffee available to the two nations compare with the optimal product mixes that existed before specialization and trade? Point A in Figure 20-2a reminds us that the United States chose 18 tons of wheat and 12 tons of coffee originally. But, by producing 30 tons of

wheat and no coffee, and by trading 10 tons of wheat for 15 tons of coffee, the United States can obtain 20 tons of wheat and 15 tons of coffee. This new, superior combination of wheat and coffee is indicated by point A' in Figure 20-2a. Compared with the non-trading figures of 18 tons of wheat and 12 tons of coffee, the United States' **gains from trade** are 2 tons of wheat and 3 tons of coffee.

Similarly, recall that Brazil's optimal product mix was 4 tons of coffee and 8 tons of wheat (point B) before specialization and trade. Now, by specializing in coffee and trading—producing 20 tons of coffee and no wheat and exporting 15 tons of its coffee in exchange for 10 tons of American wheat—Brazil can have 5 tons of coffee and 10 tons of wheat. This new position is indicated by point B' in Figure 20-2b. Brazil's gains from trade are 1 ton of coffee and 2 tons of wheat.

As a result of specialization and trade, both countries have more of both products. Table 20-1 summarizes the transactions and outcomes. You should study it very carefully.

The fact that points A' and B' are economic positions superior to A and B is extremely important. Recall from Chapter 2 that a nation can expand its production possibilities boundary by (1) expanding the quantity and improving the quality of its resources or (2) realizing technological progress. We have now explained another way—international trade—for a nation to circumvent the output constraint imposed by its production possibilities curve. The effects of international specialization and trade are the equivalent of having more and better resources or discovering improved production techniques.

Trade with Increasing Costs

To explain the basic principles underlying international trade, we simplified our analysis in several ways. For example, we limited discussion to two products and two nations. But multiproduct/multinational analysis yields the same conclusions. We also assumed constant opportunity costs (linear) production possibilities curves, which is a more substantive simplification. Let's consider the effect of allowing increasing opportunity costs (concave-from-the-origin production possibilities curves) to enter the picture.

Suppose that the United States and Brazil initially are at positions on their concave production possibilities curves where their domestic cost ratios are $1W \equiv 1C$ and $1W \equiv 2C$, as they were in our constant-cost analysis. As before, comparative advantage indicates that the United States should specialize in wheat and Brazil in coffee. But now, as the United States begins to expand wheat production, its $1W \equiv 1C$ cost ratio will *fall*; it will have to sacrifice *more than* 1 ton of coffee to get 1 additional ton of wheat. Resources are no longer perfectly shiftable between alternative uses, as the constant-cost assumption implied. Resources less and less suitable to wheat production must be allocated to the U.S. wheat industry in expanding wheat output, and this means increasing costs—the sacrifice of larger and larger amounts of coffee for each additional ton of wheat.

Similarly, Brazil, starting from its $1W \equiv 2C$ cost ratio position, expands coffee production. But as it does, it will find that its $1W \equiv 2C$ cost ratio begins to *rise*. Sacrificing a ton of wheat will free resources which are only capable of producing something *less than* 2 tons of coffee because these transferred resources are less suitable to coffee production.

As the U.S. cost ratio falls from $1W \equiv 1C$ and the Brazilian ratio rises from $1W \equiv 2C$, a point will be reached where the cost ratios are equal in the two nations, perhaps at $1W \equiv 1\frac{3}{4}C$. At this point the underlying basis for further specialization and trade—differing cost ratios—has disappeared, and further specialization is therefore uneconomical. And most importantly, this point of equal cost ratios may be reached while the United States is still producing some coffee along with its wheat and Brazil is producing some wheat along with its coffee. *The primary effect of increasing opportunity costs is to make specialization less than complete.* For this reason we often find domestically produced products competing directly against identical or similar imported products within a particular economy. **(Key Question 4)**

The Case for Free Trade

The case for free trade reduces to one potent argument: *Through free trade based on the principle of comparative advantage, the world economy can achieve a more efficient allocation of resources and a higher level of material well-being than without free trade.* The resource mixes and technological knowledge of the world's nations are all somewhat different. Therefore, each nation can produce particular commodities at different real costs. Each nation should produce goods for which its domestic opportunity costs are lower than the domestic opportunity costs of other nations and exchange these goods for products for which its do-

mestic opportunity costs are high relative to those of other nations. If each nation does this, the world can realize the advantages of geographic and human specialization. The world—and each free-trading nation—can obtain a larger real income from the fixed supplies of resources available to it. Protection—barriers to free trade—lessens or eliminates gains from specialization. If nations cannot freely trade, they must shift resources from efficient (low-cost) to inefficient (high-cost) uses to satisfy their diverse wants.

One side benefit of free trade is that it promotes competition and deters monopoly. The increased competition from foreign firms forces domestic firms to find and use the lowest-cost production techniques. It also compels them to be innovative with respect to both product quality and production methods, thereby contributing to economic growth. And free trade gives consumers a wider range of product choices. The reasons to favor free trade are the same reasons which endorse competition.

A second side-benefit of free trade is that it links national interest and breaks down national animosities. Confronted with political disagreements, trading partners tend to negotiate rather than make war.

QUICK REVIEW 20-1

■ International trade is increasingly important to the United States and other nations of the world; the percentage of total output traded has increased since World War II.

■ International trade enables nations to specialize, enhance the productivity of their resources, and obtain a greater output.

■ Comparative advantage means total world output will be greatest when each good is produced by that nation having the lowest domestic opportunity cost.

■ Specialization is less than complete among nations because opportunity costs normally rise as any particular nation produces more of a particular good.

SUPPLY AND DEMAND ANALYSIS OF EXPORTS AND IMPORTS

Supply and demand analysis helps us see how equilibrium prices and quantities of exports and imports are determined. The amount of a good or service a nation will export or import depends on differences between the equilibrium world price and the domestic price. The equilibrium **world price** is determined by interaction of *world* supply and demand; it is the price at which the quantities supplied and demanded are equal globally. The equilibrium **domestic price** is determined by *domestic* supply and demand; it is the price which would prevail in a closed economy—one having no international trade. It is the price at which domestic quantity supplied and demanded are equal.

Because of comparative advantages and disadvantages, no-trade domestic prices *may* or *may not* equal world equilibrium prices. When economies are opened for international trade, differences between world and domestic prices motivate exports or imports. To see how, let's now look at the international effects of such price differences in a simple two-nation world.

Supply and Demand in the United States

Suppose the world consists of just the United States and Canada, each producing aluminum. There are no trade barriers such as tariffs and quotas. Also, to keep things simple, let's ignore international transportation costs.

Figure 20-3a shows the domestic supply curve S_d and domestic demand curve D_d for aluminum in the United States. The intersection of S_d and D_d determines the equilibrium domestic price of $1 per pound and the equilibrium domestic quantity of 100 million pounds. Domestic suppliers produce 100 million pounds and sell them all at $1, meaning that there are no domestic surpluses or shortages of aluminum.

But what if the U.S. economy is opened to trade and the *world price* of aluminum is above or below this $1 domestic price?

United States Export Supply   If the world aluminum price exceeds $1, U.S. firms will produce more than 100 million pounds and export the excess domestic output to the rest of the world (Canada). First, consider a world price of $1.25. We see from the supply curve S_d that U.S. aluminum firms will produce 125 million pounds of aluminum at that price. The demand curve D_d tells us the United States will purchase only 75 million pounds at $1.25. A domestic surplus of 50 million pounds of aluminum will result. U.S. producers will export these 50 million pounds at the $1.25 world price.

What if the world price is $1.50? The supply curve shows that U.S. firms will produce 150 million pounds of aluminum, while the demand curve tells us that U.S. consumers will buy only 50 million pounds. The domestic surplus of 100 million pounds will be exported.

Toward the top of Figure 20-3b we plot the domestic surpluses—the U.S. exports—occurring at world prices above the $1 domestic equilibrium price. When the world and domestic prices are equal (= $1), the quantity of exports supplied is zero (point *a*). There is *no* surplus of domestic output to export. But when the world price is $1.25, U.S. firms export 50 million pounds of surplus aluminum (point *b*). At a $1.50 world price, the domestic surplus of 100 million pounds is exported (point *c*).

The U.S. **export supply curve,** found by connecting points *a*, *b*, and *c*, shows the amount of aluminum U.S. producers will export at each world price above $1. This curve *slopes upward*, indicating a direct or positive relationship between the world price and the amount of U.S. exports. *As world prices rise relative to domestic prices, U.S. exports increase.*

United States Import Demand   If the world price is below the domestic $1 price, the United States will end up importing aluminum. Consider a $.75 world price. The supply curve in Figure 20-3a reveals that at that price U.S. firms will produce only 75 million pounds of aluminum. But the demand curve shows that the United States wants to buy 125 million pounds at that price. The result is a domestic shortage of 50 million pounds. To satisfy this shortage, 50 million pounds of aluminum will be imported into the United States.

At an even lower $.50 world price, U.S. producers will supply only 50 million pounds. Because U.S. consumers want to buy 150 million pounds at that price, there is a domestic shortage of 100 million pounds. Imports will flow to the United States to make up the difference. That is, at a $.50 world price U.S. firms will supply 50 million pounds and foreign firms will supply 100 million pounds.

In Figure 20-3b we plot the U.S. **import demand curve** from these data. This *downsloping curve* shows the amounts of aluminum which will be imported at world prices below the $1 U.S. domestic price. The relationship between world prices and imported amounts is inverse or negative. At a world price of $1, domestic output will satisfy U.S. demand; imports will

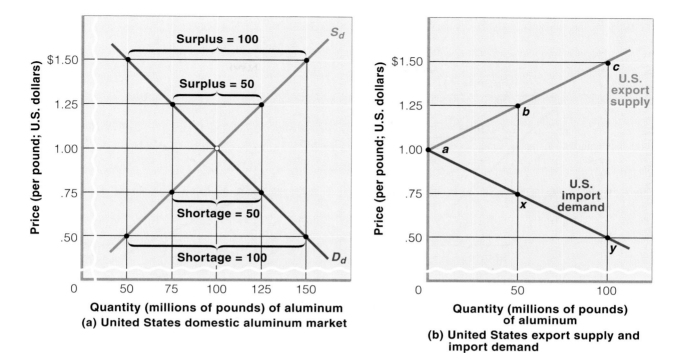

FIGURE 20-3 **United States' export supply and import demand** (a) Domestic supply S_d and demand D_d set the domestic equilibrium price of aluminum at $1 per pound. At world prices above $1 there are domestic surpluses of aluminum. At prices below $1 there are domestic shortages. (b) Surpluses are exported (top curve), and shortages are met by importing aluminum (lower curve). The export supply curve shows the direct relationship between world prices and U.S. exports; the import supply curve portrays the inverse relationship between world prices and U.S. imports.

----

be zero (point *a*). But at $.75 the United States will import 50 million pounds of aluminum (point *x*); at $.50, they will import 100 million pounds (point *y*). Connecting points *a*, *x*, and *y* yields the *downsloping* U.S. import demand curve. *It reveals that as world prices fall relative to U.S. domestic prices, U.S. imports increase.*

Supply and Demand in Canada

We repeat our analysis in Figure 20-4, this time for Canada. (We have converted Canadian dollar prices to U.S. dollar prices via the exchange rate.) Note that the domestic supply curve S_d and demand curve D_d for aluminum in Canada yield a domestic price of $.75, which is $.25 lower than the $1 U.S. domestic price.

The analysis proceeds exactly as for the United States. If the world price is $.75, Canadians will neither export nor import aluminum (which gives us

point *q* in Figure 20-4b). At world prices above $.75, Canadian firms will produce more aluminum than Canadian consumers will buy. The surplus will be exported. At a $1 world price, Figure 20-4a tells us that Canada will have and export a domestic surplus of 50 million pounds (yielding point *r*). At $1.25, it will have and export a domestic surplus of 100 million pounds (point *s*). Connecting these points yields the upsloping Canadian *export supply curve*, which reflects the domestic surpluses (and hence exports) occurring when the world price exceeds the $.75 Canadian domestic price.

Domestic shortages occur in Canada at world prices below $.75. At a $.50 world price, Figure 20-4a shows that Canadian consumers want to buy 125 million pounds of aluminum but Canadian firms will produce only 75 million pounds. The shortage will bring 50 million pounds of imports to Canada (point *t* in Figure 20-4b). The Canadian *import demand curve*

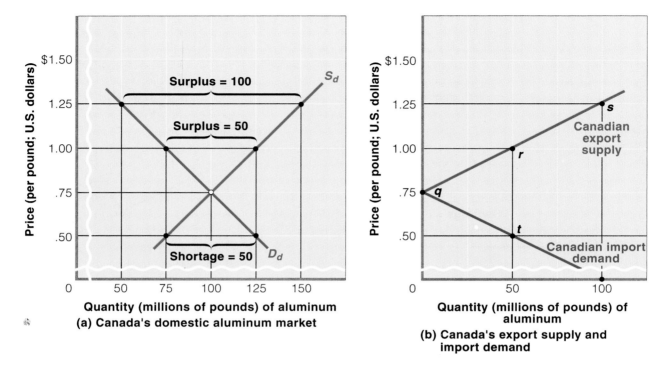

FIGURE 20-4 **Canadian export supply and import demand** (a) At world prices above the $.75 domestic price, production in Canada exceeds domestic consumption. At world prices below $.75, domestic shortages occur. (b) Surpluses result in exports, and shortages result in imports. The Canadian export supply curve and import demand curve depict the relationships between world prices and exports or imports.

-----

in that figure shows Canadian imports which will occur at all world aluminum prices below the $.75 Canadian domestic price.

Equilibrium World Price, Exports, and Imports

We now have the tools to determine the equilibrium world price of aluminum and the equilibrium world levels of exports and imports. Figure 20-5 combines the U.S. export supply curve and import demand curve in Figure 20-3b and the Canadian export supply curve and import demand curve in Figure 20-4b. The two U.S. curves proceed rightward from the $1 U.S. domestic price; the two Canadian curves proceed rightward from the $.75 Canadian domestic price. *International equilibrium occurs in this two-nation model where one nation's import demand curve intersects another nation's export supply curve.* In this case the U.S. import demand curve intersects Canada's export supply curve at *e*. There, the world price of aluminum is

$.88. The Canadian export supply curve indicates that Canada will export 25 million pounds of aluminum at this price. Also at this price the United States will import 25 million pounds from Canada, indicated by the U.S. import demand curve. The $.88 world price equates the quantity of imports demanded and the quantity of exports supplied (25 million pounds). Thus there will be world trade of 25 million pounds of aluminum at $.88 per pound.

Note that after trade, the single $.88 world price will prevail in both Canada and the United States. *Only one price for a standardized commodity can persist in a highly competitive world market.* With trade, all consumers can buy a pound of aluminum for $.88, and all producers can sell it for that price. This world price means that Canadians will pay more for aluminum with trade ($.88) than without it ($.75). The increased Canadian output caused by trade raises Canadian per-unit production costs and therefore raises the price of aluminum in Canada. The United States, however, pays less for aluminum with trade ($.88) than without

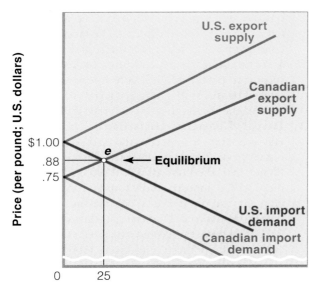

Quantity (millions of pounds) of aluminum

FIGURE 20-5 Equilibrium world price and quantity of exports and imports In a two-nation world, the equilibrium world price (= $.88) is determined by the intersection of one nation's export supply curve and the other nation's import demand curve. This intersection also decides the equilibrium volume of exports and imports. Here, Canada exports 25 million pounds of aluminum to the United States.

- -

it ($1). The U.S. gain comes from Canada's comparative cost advantage in producing aluminum.

Why would Canada willingly send 50 million pounds of its aluminum output to the United States for U.S. consumption? After all, producing this output uses up scarce Canadian resources and drives up the price of aluminum for Canadians. Canadians are willing to export aluminum to the United States because Canadians gain the means—the U.S. dollars—to import other goods, say, computer software, from the United States. Canadian exports enable Canadians to acquire imports that have greater value to Canadians than the exported aluminum. Canadian exports to the United States finance Canadian imports from the United States. **(Key Question 6)**

TRADE BARRIERS

No matter how compelling the case for free trade, barriers to free trade *do* exist. Let's examine Chapter 6's list of trade impediments more closely.

1. **Tariffs** are excise taxes on imported goods; they may be imposed to obtain revenue or to protect domestic firms.

   A **revenue tariff** is usually applied to a product not produced domestically, for example, tin, coffee, or bananas in the case of the United States. Rates on revenue tariffs are modest; their purpose is to provide the Federal government with revenues.

   A **protective tariff** is designed to shield domestic producers from foreign competition. Although protective tariffs are usually not high enough to stop the importation of foreign goods, they put foreign producers at a competitive disadvantage in selling in domestic markets.

2. An **import quota** specifies the maximum amount of a commodity which may be imported in any period. Import quotas can more effectively retard international commerce than tariffs. A product might be imported in large quantities despite high tariffs; low import quotas completely prohibit imports once quotas are filled.

3. A **nontariff barrier** (NTB) is a licensing requirement, unreasonable standards pertaining to product quality and safety, or unnecessary bureaucratic red tape which is used to restrict imports. Japan and the European countries frequently require their domestic importers of foreign goods to obtain licenses. By restricting the issuance of licenses, imports can be restricted. Great Britain uses this barrier to bar importation of coal.

4. A **voluntary export restriction** (VER) is a trade barrier by which foreign firms "voluntarily" limit the amount of their exports to a particular country. VERs, which have the effect of import quotas, are agreed to by exporters in the hope of avoiding more stringent trade barriers. Japanese auto manufacturers agreed to a VER on exports to the United States under the threat of higher U.S. tariffs or the imposition of low import quotas.

Later in this chapter we will consider the specific arguments and appeals which are made to justify protection.

Economic Impact of Tariffs

Once again we turn to supply and demand analysis—now to examine the economic effects of protective tariffs. Curves D_d and S_d in Figure 20-6 show

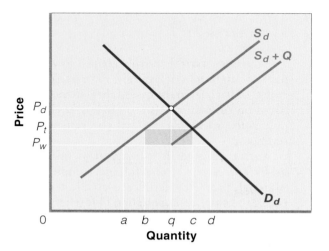

FIGURE 20-6 The economic effects of a protective tariff or an import quota   A tariff that increases the price of a good from P_w to P_t will reduce domestic consumption from d to c. Domestic producers will be able to sell more output (b rather than a) at a higher price (P_t rather than P_w). Foreign exporters are injured because they sell less output (bc rather than ad). The orange area indicates the amount of tariff paid by domestic consumers. An import quota of bc units has the same effect as the tariff, with one exception: The amount represented by the orange area will go to foreign producers rather than to the domestic government.

---

domestic demand and supply for a product in which a nation, say, the United States, has a comparative *dis*advantage, for example, video cassette recorders (VCRs). (Disregard curve $S_d + Q$ for now.) Without world trade, the domestic price and output would be P_d and q, respectively.

Assume now that the domestic economy is opened to world trade and that the Japanese, who have a comparative advantage in VCRs, begin to sell their recorders in the United States. We assume that with free trade the domestic price cannot differ from the world price, which here is P_w. At P_w domestic consumption is d and domestic production is a. The horizontal distance between the domestic supply and demand curves at P_w represents imports of ad. Thus far, our analysis is similar to the analysis of world prices in Figure 20-3.

Direct Effects   Suppose now that the United States imposes a tariff on each imported VCR. The tariff raises the price of imported VCRs from P_w to P_t and has four effects:

1. **Decline in consumption**   Consumption of video recorders in the United States declines from d to

c as the higher price moves buyers up and to the left along their demand curve. The tariff prompts consumers to buy fewer recorders; they reallocate a portion of their expenditures to less desired substitute products. U.S. consumers are clearly injured by the tariff since they pay P_wP_t more for each of the c units they buy at price P_t.

2. **Increased domestic production**   U.S. producers—who are *not* subject to the tariff—receive the higher price P_t per unit. Because this new price is higher than the pretariff world price P_w, the domestic VCR industry moves up and to the right along its supply curve S_d, increasing domestic output from a to b. Domestic producers thus enjoy both a higher price and expanded sales, which explains why domestic producers lobby for protective tariffs. But from a social point of view, the greater domestic production from a to b means the tariff permits domestic producers of recorders to bid resources away from other, more efficient, U.S. industries.

3. **Decline in imports**   Japanese producers are hurt. Although the sales price of each recorder is higher by P_wP_t, that amount accrues to the U.S. government, not to Japanese producers. The after-tariff world price, and thus the per-unit revenue to Japanese producers, remains at P_w, while the volume of U.S. imports (Japanese exports) falls from ad to bc.

4. **Tariff revenue**   The orange rectangle represents the amount of revenue which the tariff yields. Total revenue from the tariff is determined by multiplying the tariff, P_wP_t per unit, by the number of recorders imported, bc. This tariff revenue is a transfer of income from consumers to government and does *not* represent any net change in the nation's economic well-being. The result is that government gains this portion of what consumers lose by paying more for VCRs.

Indirect Effect   Tariffs have a subtle effect beyond what our supply and demand diagram can show. Because Japan sells fewer VCRs in the United States, it earns fewer dollars and so must buy fewer U.S. exports. U.S. export industries—industries in which the United States has a comparative advantage—must then cut production and release resources. These are highly efficient industries, as we know from their comparative advantage and ability to sell goods in world markets.

Tariffs directly promote the expansion of inefficient industries which do not have a comparative advantage; they

also indirectly cause the contraction of relatively efficient industries which do have a comparative advantage. This means tariffs cause resources to be shifted in the wrong direction—and that is not surprising. We know that specialization and world trade lead to more efficient use of world resources and greater world output. But protective tariffs reduce world trade. Therefore, tariffs also reduce efficiency and the world's real output.

Economic Impact of Quotas

We noted previously that an import quota is a legal limit placed on the amount of some product which can be imported each year. Quotas have the same economic impact as a tariff, with one big difference: While tariffs generate revenue for the domestic government, a quota transfers that revenue to foreign producers.

Suppose in Figure 20-6 that, instead of imposing a tariff, the United States prohibits any Japanese imports of VCRs in excess of bc units. In other words, an import quota of bc recorders is imposed on Japan. We deliberately chose the size of this quota to be the same amount as imports would be under a $P_w P_t$ tariff so that we are comparing "equivalent" situations. As a consequence of the quota, the supply of recorders is $S_d + Q$ in the United States. This supply consists of the domestic supply plus the fixed amount bc (= Q) which importers will provide at each domestic price. The supply curve $S_d + Q$ does not extend below price P_w because Japanese producers would not export recorders to the United States at any price *below P_w;* instead they would sell them to other countries at the world market price of P_w.

Most of the economic results are the same as with a tariff. VCR prices are higher (P_t instead of P_w) because imports have been reduced from *ad* to *bc*. Domestic consumption of VCRs is down from *d* to *c*. U.S. producers enjoy both a higher price (P_t rather than P_w) and increased sales (*b* rather than *a*).

The difference is that the price increase of $P_w P_t$ paid by U.S. consumers on imports of *bc*—the orange area—no longer goes to the United States Treasury as tariff (tax) revenue but flows to those Japanese firms which have acquired the rights to sell VCRs in the United States. For consumers in the United States, a tariff produces a better economic outcome than a quota, other things being the same. A tariff generates government revenue which can be used to cut other taxes or to finance public goods and services which benefit the United States. In contrast, the higher price created by quotas results in additional revenue for foreign producers. **(Key Question 7)**

THE CASE FOR PROTECTION: A CRITICAL REVIEW

Despite the logic of specialization and trade, there are still protectionists in some union halls, corporate boardrooms, and the halls of Congress. What arguments do protectionists make to justify trade barriers? How valid are these arguments?

Military Self-Sufficiency Argument

The argument here is not economic but political-military: Protective tariffs are needed to preserve or strengthen industries which produce the materials essential for national defense. In an uncertain world, the political-military objectives (self-sufficiency) sometimes must take precedence over economic goals (efficiency in the use of world resources.)

Unfortunately, it is difficult to measure and compare the benefit of increased national security against the cost of economic inefficiency when protective tariffs are imposed. The economist can only point out that there are economic costs when a nation levies tariffs to increase military self-sufficiency.

All people in the United States would agree that it is not a good idea to import missile guidance systems from Iraq, yet the self-sufficiency argument is open to serious abuse. Nearly every industry can claim that it makes direct or indirect contributions to national security and hence deserves protection from imports.

Are there not better ways than tariffs to provide needed strength in strategic industries? When it is achieved through tariffs, this self-sufficiency increases the domestic prices of the products of the protected industry. Thus only those consumers who buy the industry's products shoulder the cost of greater military security. A direct subsidy to strategic industries, financed out of general tax revenues, would distribute these costs more equitably.

Increased Domestic Employment Argument

Arguing for a tariff to "save U.S. jobs" becomes fashionable as an economy encounters a recession. In an economy which engages in international trade, exports involve spending on domestic output and imports reflect spending to obtain part of another nation's output. So, in this argument, reducing imports will divert spending on another nation's output to spending on domestic output. Thus domestic output and employment will rise. But this argument has several shortcomings:

1. *Job creation from imports* While imports may eliminate some U.S. jobs, they create others. Imports may have eliminated the jobs of some U.S. steel and textile workers in recent years, but other workers have gained jobs unloading ships and selling imported cars and imported electronic equipment. Import restrictions alter the composition of employment, but they may have little or no effect on the volume of employment.

2. *Fallacy of composition* All nations cannot simultaneously succeed in restricting imports while maintaining their exports; what is true for *one* nation is not true for *all* nations. The exports of one nation must be the imports of another nation. To the extent that one country is able to expand its economy through an excess of exports over imports, the resulting excess of imports over exports worsens another economy's unemployment problem. It is no wonder that tariffs and import quotas meant to achieve domestic full employment are called "beggar my neighbor" policies: They achieve short-run domestic goals by making trading partners poorer.

3. *Possibility of retaliation* Nations adversely affected by tariffs and quotas are likely to retaliate, causing a "trade-barrier war" which will choke off trade and make all nations worse off. The *Smoot-Hawley Tariff Act of 1930*, which imposed the highest tariffs ever enacted in the United States, backfired miserably. Rather than increasing U.S. output, this tariff act only led to retaliatory restrictions by affected nations. This trade war caused a further contraction of international trade and lowered the income and employment levels of all nations. As stated by a U.S. international trade expert:

> A trade war in which countries restrict each other's exports in pursuit of some illusory advantage is not much like a real war. On the one hand, nobody gets killed. On the other, unlike real wars, it is almost impossible for anyone to win, since the main losers when a country imposes barriers to trade are not foreign exporters but domestic residents. In effect, a trade war is a conflict in which each country uses most of its ammunition to shoot itself in the foot.[1]

4. *Long-run feedbacks* In the long run, forcing an excess of exports over imports cannot exceed in raising domestic employment. It is through U.S. imports that foreign nations earn dollars for buying U.S. exports. In the long run a nation must import to export. The long-run impact of tariffs is not to increase domestic employment but at best to reallocate workers away from export industries and to protected domestic industries. This shift implies a less efficient allocation of resources.

Diversification for Stability Argument

Highly specialized economies such as Saudi Arabia's (based on oil) and Cuba's (based on sugar) are very dependent on international markets for their incomes. In these economies, wars, international political developments, recessions abroad, and random fluctuations in world supply and demand for one or two particular goods can cause deep declines in export revenues and therefore in domestic income. Tariff and quota protection are allegedly needed in such nations to enable greater industrial diversification. That way, these economies will not be so dependent on exporting one or two products to obtain the other goods they need. Such goods will be available domestically, thereby providing greater domestic stability.

There is some truth in this diversification for stability argument. There are also two serious shortcomings:

1. The argument has little or no relevance to the United States and other advanced economies.

2. The economic costs of diversification may be great; for example, one-crop economies may be highly inefficient at manufacturing.

Infant Industry Argument

The infant industry argument contends that protective tariffs are needed to allow new domestic industries to establish themselves. Temporarily shielding young domestic firms from the severe competition of more mature and more efficient foreign firms will give infant industries a chance to develop and become efficient producers.

This argument for protection rests on an alleged exception to the case for free trade. The exception is that young industries have not had, and if they face mature foreign competition will never have, the chance to make the long-run adjustments needed for larger

---

[1]Paul Krugman, *Peddling Prosperity* (New York: W. W. Norton, 1994), p. 287.

scale and greater efficiency in production. In this view, tariff protection for such infant industries will correct a misallocation of world resources perpetuated by historically different levels of economic development between domestic and foreign industries.

Counterarguments There are some logical problems with this infant industry argument:

1. In the developing nations it is difficult to determine which industries are the infants that are capable of achieving economic maturity and therefore deserving protection.
2. Protective tariffs may persist even after industrial maturity has been realized.
3. Most economists feel that if infant industries are to be subsidized, there are better means than tariffs for doing it. Direct subsidies, for example, have the advantage of making explicit which industries are being aided and to what degree.

Strategic Trade Policy In recent years the infant industry argument has taken a modified form in advanced economies. Now proponents contend that government should use trade barriers to reduce the risk of investing in product development by domestic firms, particularly where advanced technology is involved. Firms protected from foreign competition can grow more rapidly and achieve greater economies of scale than unprotected foreign competitors. The protected firms can eventually dominate world markets because of their lower costs. Supposedly, dominance of world markets will enable the domestic firms to return high profits to the home nation. These profits will exceed the domestic sacrifices caused by trade barriers. Also, advances in high-technology industries are deemed beneficial because the advances achieved in one domestic industry often can be transferred to other domestic industries.

Japan and South Korea, in particular, have been accused of using this form of **strategic trade policy.** The problem with this strategy and therefore this argument for tariffs is that the nations put at a disadvantage by strategic trade policies tend to retaliate with tariffs of their own. The outcome may be higher tariffs worldwide, reductions of world trade, and the loss of potential gains from technological advances.

Protection Against Dumping Argument

This argument contends that tariffs are needed to protect domestic firms from "dumping" by foreign producers. **Dumping** is the selling of excess goods in a foreign market at a price below cost. Economists cite two plausible reasons for this behavior:

1. Firms may use dumping abroad to drive out domestic competitors there, thus obtaining monopoly power and monopoly prices and profits for the importing firm. The long-term economic profits resulting from this strategy may more than offset the earlier losses that accompany the below-cost sales.
2. Dumping may be a form of *price discrimination,* which is charging different prices to different customers even though costs are the same. The foreign seller may find it can maximize its profit by charging a high price in its monopolized domestic market while unloading its surplus output at a lower price in the United States. The surplus output may be needed so the firm can obtain the overall per-unit cost saving associated with large-scale production. The higher profit in the home market more than makes up for the losses incurred on sales abroad.

Because dumping is a legitimate concern, many nations prohibit it. For example, where dumping is shown to injure U.S. firms, the Federal government imposes tariffs called "antidumping duties" on the specific goods. But there are relatively few documented cases of dumping each year, and those few cases do *not* justify widespread, permanent tariffs.

In fact, foreign producers argue that the United States uses dumping allegations and antidumping duties to restrict legitimate trade. Some foreign firms clearly can produce certain goods at substantially less per-unit cost than U.S. competitors. So, what may seem to be dumping actually is comparative advantage at work. If antidumping laws are abused, they can increase the price of imports and restrict competition in the U.S. market. This reduced competition can allow U.S. firms to raise prices at consumers' expense. And even where true dumping does occur, U.S. consumers gain from the lower-priced product, at least in the short run, much as they gain from a price war among U.S. producers.

Cheap Foreign Labor Argument

The cheap foreign labor argument says that domestic firms and workers must be shielded from the ruinous competition of countries where wages are low. If protection is not provided, cheap imports will flood U.S. markets and the prices of U.S. goods—along with the wages of U.S. workers—will be pulled down. That is, the domestic living standards in the United States will be reduced.

This argument can be rebutted at several levels. The logic of the argument suggests that it is *not* mutually beneficial for rich and poor persons to trade with one another. However, that is not the case. A low-income farm worker may pick lettuce or tomatoes for a rich landowner, and both may benefit from the transaction. And U.S. consumers gain when they buy a Taiwanese-made pocket radio for $12 as opposed to a similar U.S.-made radio selling for $20.

Also, recall that gains from trade are based on comparative advantage, not on absolute advantage. Looking back at Figure 20-1, suppose the United States and Brazil have labor forces of exactly the same size. Noting the positions of the production possibilities curves, we observe that U.S. labor can produce more of *either* good. Thus, it is more productive. Because of this greater productivity, we can expect wages and living standards to be higher for U.S. labor. Brazil's less productive labor will receive lower wages.

The cheap foreign labor argument suggests that, to maintain our standard of living, the United States should not trade with low-wage Brazil. Suppose it does not. Will wages and living standards rise in the United States as a result? No. To obtain coffee the United States will have to reallocate a portion of its labor from its efficient wheat industry to its inefficient coffee industry. As a result, the average productivity of U.S. labor will fall, as will real wages and living standards. The labor forces of *both* countries will have diminished standards of living because without specialization and trade they will have less output available to them. Compare column 4 with column 1 in Table 20-1 or points *A'* and *B'* with *A* and *B* in Figure 20-2 to confirm this point.

A Summing Up

These many arguments for protection are not weighty. Under proper conditions, the infant-industry argument stands as a valid exception, justifiable on economic grounds. And on political-military grounds, the self-sufficiency argument can be used to validate some protection. But both arguments are open to severe overuse, and both neglect other ways of promoting industrial development and military self-sufficiency. Most other arguments are emotional appeals—half-truths and fallacies. These arguments

see only the immediate and direct consequences of protective tariffs. They ignore the fact that in the long run a nation must import to export.

There is also compelling historical evidence suggesting that free trade has led to prosperity and growth and that protectionism has had the opposite effects. Here are several examples:

1. The U.S. Constitution forbids individual states from levying tariffs, and that makes the United States a huge free-trade area. Economic historians cite this as a positive factor in the economic development of the United States.

2. Great Britain's shift toward freer international trade in the mid-nineteenth century was instrumental in its industrialization and growth at that time.

3. The creation of the Common Market in Europe after World War II eliminated tariffs among member nations. Economists agree that creation of this free-trade area, now the European Union, was a major ingredient in western European prosperity.

4. The trend toward tariff reduction since the mid-1930s stimulated post-World War II expansion of the world economy.

5. The high tariffs imposed by the Smoot-Hawley Act of 1930 and the retaliation which it engendered worsened the Great Depression of the 1930s.

6. Studies of developing countries strongly suggest that those which have relied on import restrictions to protect their domestic industries have had slow growth compared to those pursuing more open economic policies (see Global Perspective 20-2).

QUICK REVIEW 20-2

■ A nation will export a particular product if the world price exceeds the domestic price; it will import the product if the world price is less than the domestic price.

■ In a two-country model, equilibrium world prices and equilibrium quantities of exports and imports occur where one nation's export supply curve intersects the other nation's import demand curve.

■ Trade barriers include tariffs, import quotas, nontariff barriers, and voluntary export restrictions.

■ A tariff on a product increases price, reduces consumption, increases domestic production, reduces imports, and generates tariff revenue for government; an import quota does the same, except a quota generates revenue for

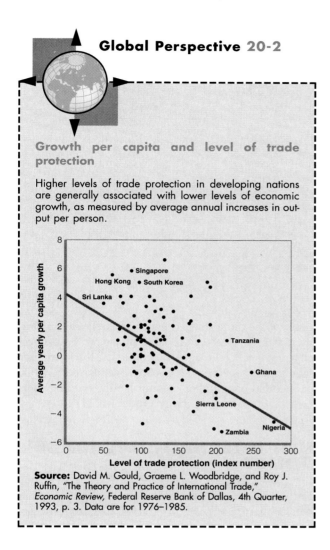

Source: David M. Gould, Graeme L. Woodbridge, and Roy J. Ruffin, "The Theory and Practice of International Trade," *Economic Review*, Federal Reserve Bank of Dallas, 4th Quarter, 1993, p. 3. Data are for 1976–1985.

foreign producers rather than for the government imposing the quota.

■ Most arguments for trade protection are special-interest pleas which, if followed, would create gains for protected industries and their workers at the expense of greater losses for the economy.

COSTS OF PROTECTION

In spite of the weakness of most arguments for trade protection, the United States and most other countries continue to impose some protective measures. (These tariffs and quotas, however, are falling under terms of the recent world trade agreements.) How costly are trade protections to the United States?

Cost to Society

Figure 20-6 shows that tariffs and quotas impose costs on domestic consumers but provide gains to domestic producers, and in the case of tariffs, revenue to the Federal government. The consumer cost of trade restrictions can be calculated by determining the effect they have on the prices of protected goods. Protection raises the price of a product in three ways:

1. The price of the imported product goes up.
2. The higher price of imports causes some consumers to shift their purchases to higher-priced domestically produced goods.
3. The prices of domestically produced goods rise because import competition has declined.

Recent studies indicate that costs to consumers of protected products substantially exceed gains to producers and government.[2] There is a sizable net cost or efficiency loss to society from trade protection. Most recently the United States International Trade Commission (USITC)—the agency which hears unfair trade complaints—estimated that U.S. trade barriers resulted in a net cost to the United States of more than $15 billion annually in the mid-1990s.

Furthermore, net losses from trade barriers are greater than the losses reported in most studies. Tariffs and quotas produce many costly, difficult-to-quantify secondary effects. For example, import restraints on steel in the 1980s drove up the price of steel to all U.S. buyers of steel, including the U.S. automobile industry. Therefore, U.S. automakers had higher costs than otherwise and were less competitive in world markets.

Finally, industries employ large amounts of economic resources to influence Congress to pass and retain protectionist laws. Because these rent-seeking efforts divert resources away from more socially desirable purposes, trade restrictions also impose that cost on society.

Conclusion: The gains which U.S. trade barriers create for protected industries and their workers come at the expense of much greater losses for the entire economy. The result is economic inefficiency.

Column 1 in Table 20-2 lists the U.S. industries with the highest net costs due to trade protection; column 2 lists those net costs. Column 3 shows the

---

[2]United States International Trade Commision, *The Economic Effects of Significant U.S. Import Restraints: First Biannual Investigation*, December, 1995; Gary C. Hufbauer and Kimberly A. Elliot, *Measuring the Costs of Protectionism in the United States* (Washington: Institute for International Economics, 1994), pp. 8–9.

TABLE 20-2   The net costs of trade protection, eight industries

(1) Industry	(2) Annual loss to economy from barriers	(3) Net employment loss if barrier removed	(4) Annual cost per job saved
Textile and apparel	$ 10.04 billion	55,000	$ 182,545
Maritime transport	2.79 billion	2,450	1,138,775
Dairy	1.01 billion	2,083	484,878
Motor vehicles	710.00 million	3,400	208,824
Sugar	661.00 million	1,694	390,200
Meat	185.00 million	100	1,850,000
Steel mills	162.00 million	1,265	128,063
Nonrubber footwear	147.00 million	1,316	111,702

Source: Compiled from United States International Trade Commission data released in December 1995. Data are for 1993.

number of U.S. jobs which would be lost if the trade barriers were eliminated. Column 4 reveals how much the trade barriers cost per U.S. job they save (column 2 divided by column 3). Two items stand out in the table:

1. Trade restrictions in the textile and apparel industries are especially costly to the United States. The Federal government has imposed import quotas on more than 3000 kinds of textile products. [These quotas eventually will be replaced with tariffs under the terms of the General Agreement on Tariffs and Trade (Chapter 6).]

2. The cost of saving jobs through trade protection is enormous. Because annual wages per job in these industries are only a fraction of the amounts in column 4, protectionism to save jobs is hardly a bargain. Moreover, it is clear from historical experience that eliminating trade barriers does not cause a *net* loss of jobs in the United States; it simply redistributes employment, and it may even increase it.

Impact on Income Distribution

Also, import restrictions affect low-income families proportionately more than high-income families. Because tariffs and quotas act much like sales or excise taxes, these trade restrictions are highly regressive. That is, the "overcharge" associated with trade protection falls *as a percentage of income* as income increases. For example, a family with an annual income of $10,000 may pay an overcharge of $100 per year be-

cause of the trade restrictions on apparel, while a family with an income of $100,000 may pay a $500 overcharge. As a percentage of income, the lower-income family pays 1 percent (= $100 of overcharge/$10,000 of income); the higher-income family, only 0.5 percent ($500/$100,000). **(Key Question 11)**

U.S. INTERNATIONAL TRADE POLICY

In the past decade U.S. international trade policy has been a mixture of generalized trade liberalization, aggressive export promotion, and bilateral negotiations on specific trade disputes.

Generalized Trade Liberalization

In Chapter 6 we discussed two recent regional and global agreements to reduce trade barriers.

North American Free Trade Agreement   This accord, which took effect in 1994, eliminates tariffs and other trade barriers among Canada, Mexico, and the United States over a 15-year period. When fully implemented, the North American Free Trade Agreement (NAFTA) will constitute the largest geographical free-trade zone in the world.

General Agreement on Tariffs and Trade   In 1994 more than 120 of the world's nations successfully completed negotiation of the Uruguay Round of the General Agreement on Tariffs and Trade (GATT). GATT provisions to be implemented between 1995 and 2005 include:

1. Reduction of tariffs worldwide
2. Liberalization of rules which have impeded trade in services
3. Reduction of agricultural subsidies which have distorted the global pattern of trade in agricultural goods
4. New protections for intellectual property (copyrights, patents, trademarks)
5. Phasing out quotas on textiles and apparel, replacing them with gradually declining tariffs
6. Establishment of the **World Trade Organization** to oversee the provisions of the agreement and to resolve any disputes under the new rules

When completed in 2005, GATT will boost the world's GDP by an estimated $6 trillion, or 8 percent.

Aggressive Export Promotion

The Federal government recently began aggressively promoting U.S. exports in a number of ways. Undoubtedly, the reason is that such exports generally support high-paying jobs and increases in exports are needed to end U.S. trade deficits. Perhaps, too, the popular myth that the global marketplace is a battleground for economic supremacy played a role. But trade is not like war, or like a World Cup match, in which one nation wins and the other loses. Every nation is both seller *and* buyer in the world market. Gains from trade come from the increased consumable output shared by the trading countries. Exports are *not* the end goal of international trade; they simply enable a country to pay for imports—goods which would cost the nation more to produce at home.

Here are five recent examples of export promotion policy at work:

1. Direct government advocacy of export interests of U.S. producers. High U.S. government officials have hawked U.S. goods throughout the world. Example: President Clinton and other administration officials directly lobbied King Fahd of Saudi Arabia to buy commercial aircraft from America's Boeing rather than from Europe's Airbus.
2. Relaxation of **export controls.** In the past, national security and foreign policy objectives restricted the exporting of certain high-technology products such as computers and advanced communications equipment. Many of these controls have now been ended.

3. Increased government funding of America's Export-Import Bank. This government-funded "bank" provides interest-rate subsidies to foreign firms which buy U.S. exports on credit. The result is a lower total price (product price + interest on loan) and therefore increased exports.
4. Renewed emphasis on *industrial policy* designed to aid exporting firms or industries. This involves the payment of government subsidies to specific high-technology industries for the development of products which bolster exports. The government payments are actually **export subsidies** which reduce development or production costs. Thus the payments tend to lower the price of exported goods and increase their sales in world markets.

   Example: In 1994 the Clinton administration initiated a $1 billion plan to help industry compete with Japan in developing advanced flat-panel computer screens. The administration justified this massive subsidy as necessary for national defense. But this action had as much to do with competing with Japan in a burgeoning world export market as with ensuring national defense.
5. Threats or actual uses of *retaliatory tariffs* to force other nations to reduce their trade barriers with the United States. Such retaliation has resulted in negotiations which have given some U.S. firms freer access to foreign markets. Since 1989 the United States has used retaliatory tariffs to address specific trade issues with Japan, Brazil, India, South Korea, Taiwan, France, and other nations. For example, in 1992 the United States tripled the import duty on French white wine to spur France to reduce its barriers against U.S. soybean exports.

Bilateral Negotiations

Bilateral trade negotiations, discussions between two countries rather than among many, are another facet of U.S. international trade policy. Such negotiations have occurred directly between the United States and China, Japan, South Korea, and Canada. Usually these negotiations have focused on specific trade restrictions or on alleged dumping of specific goods. But negotiations with China and Japan have dealt with broader trade issues.

Continuing Renewal of China's Most-Favored-Nation Status (MFN) The United States continues to renew (annually) China's **most-favored-**

Petition of the Candlemakers, 1845

French economist Frédéric Bastiat (1801–1850) devastated the proponents of protectionism by satirically extending their reasoning to its logical and absurd conclusions.

Petition of the Manufacturers of Candles, Waxlights, Lamps, Candlesticks, Street Lamps, Snuffers, Extinguishers, and of the Producers of Oil Tallow, Rosin, Alcohol, and, Generally, of Everything Connected with Lighting.

TO MESSIEURS THE MEMBERS OF THE CHAMBER OF DEPUTIES.

Gentlemen—You are on the right road. You reject abstract theories, and have little consideration for cheapness and plenty. Your chief care is the interest of the producer. You desire to emancipate him from external competition, and reserve the *national market* for *national industry.*

We are about to offer you an admirable opportunity of applying your—what shall we call it? your theory? No; nothing is more deceptive than theory; your doctrine? your system? your principle? but you dislike doctrines, you abhor systems, and as for principles, you deny that there are any in social economy: we shall say, then, your practice, your practice without theory and without principle.

We are suffering from the intolerable competition of a foreign rival, placed, it would seem, in a condition so far superior to ours for the production of light, that he absolutely *inundates* our *national market* with it at a price fabulously reduced. The moment he shows himself, our trade leaves us—all consumers apply to him; and a branch of native industry, having countless ramifications, is all at once rendered completely stagnant. This rival . . . is no other than the Sun.

What we pray for is, that it may please you to pass a law ordering the shutting up of all windows, skylights, dormerwindows, outside and inside shutters, curtains, blinds, bull's-eyes; in a word, of all openings, holes, chinks, clefts, and fissures, by or through which the light of the sun has been in use to enter houses, to the prejudice of the meritorious manufacturers with which we flatter ourselves we have accommodated our country,—a country which, in gratitude, ought not to abandon us now to a strife so unequal.

If you shut up as much as possible all access to natural light, and create a demand for artificial light, which of our French manufacturers will not be encouraged by it?

If more tallow is consumed, then there must be more oxen and sheep; and, consequently, we shall behold the multiplication of artificial meadows, meat, wool, hides, and, above all, manure, which is the basis and foundation of all agricultural wealth.

The same remark applies to navigation. Thousands of vessels will proceed to the whale fishery; and, in a short time, we shall possess a navy capable of maintaining the honor of France, and gratifying the patriotic aspirations of your petitioners, the undersigned candlemakers and others.

Only have the goodness to reflect, Gentlemen, and you will be convinced that there is, perhaps, no Frenchman, from the wealthy coalmaster to the humblest vender of lucifer matches, whose lot will not be ameliorated by the success of this our petition.

Source: Frédéric Bastiat, *Economic Sophisms* (Edinburgh: Oliver and Boyd, Tweeddale Court, 1873), pp. 49–53, abridged.

nation status, first conferred in 1980. The MFN status applies to most U.S. trading partners and means that imports from China face the lowest U.S. tariffs. Also, this status means that any reductions in tariffs which the United States negotiates with other nations will also apply to Chinese imports to the United States. These low U.S. tariffs are important to China because the United States buys about $60 billion worth of such Chinese-made goods as toys, shoes, and clothes each year.

Renewal of MFN status for China is controversial for two reasons. First, China has had a poor record on "human rights"; its government has been dictatorial and repressive. Some critics of China's MFN status see it as supporting the current government in China. Second, the United States has a $44 billion trade deficit with China. Removal of MFN status, say these critics, would send notice to China that it needs to increase its access to U.S. goods.

Thus far, U.S. presidents and Congress have concluded that the benefits of renewing MFN status for China outweigh the costs. Proponents of MFN status have successfully argued that U.S. international trade with China is consistent with the U.S. goal of improved Chinese human rights. International trade opens China to the outside world and exposes it to the personal and social benefits of economic freedom. Greater freedom in one sphere may whet the appetite for freedom in other spheres. Also, international trade expands the political influence of leaders in China's business sector. These business leaders are more reform-minded than the older political leadership and, in general, lack commitment to communist ideology—an ideology which supports dictatorship and political repression.

Despite the renewal of China's MFN status, trade relations between the United States and China remain fragile. Example: In 1995 the United States temporarily invoked high tariffs against selected Chinese imports in retaliation for China's unwillingness to crack down on massive, unauthorized reproduction and sale of U.S.-made software, videos, and recordings. Although the situation was resolved with a negotiated agreement, trade discussions between China and the United States continue over issues such as China's trade barriers and its desire to join the World Trade Organization.

Negotiations with Japan Much recent U.S. bilateral negotiation has centered on the United States' annual $50 billion trade deficit with Japan. Specific goods for which there are large deficits are automobiles and parts, computers and office machines, elec-

trical machinery and appliances, television sets and radios, and photo and optical gear.

The United States and Japan have held numerous, sometimes testy, negotiations on this deficit problem. The initial U.S. position was that Japan needed to set numerical targets for increasing imports from the United States. The Japanese retorted that it vehemently opposed "managed trade" of this sort. The trade balance between two nations should be determined by market forces, say the Japanese. U.S. negotiators counter that the deficit is not totally a "market" deficit. Japan's widespread system of nontariff trade barriers impedes the working of the global market, contributing heavily to Japan's trade surplus. Also, the Japanese system of *keiretsu*—large groups of interlocked Japanese firms which buy and sell exclusively from one another—denies U.S. firms access to Japanese markets. U.S. negotiators have pointed out that even products such as cellular phones, which U.S. firms produce in high quality and at low cost, have not made inroads in Japan. And while U.S. firms hold about 45 percent of the global market for large-scale construction projects, their share in Japan is less than 1 percent.

The Japanese have pointed out that the average Japanese spends more on U.S. imports than the average person in the United States spends on Japanese imports. (The U.S. trade deficit results from the far greater number of U.S. citizens.) Japan also points to its large annual *deficit* in *services* (as opposed to goods) with the United States. No one in the United States views that U.S. *surplus* as a problem, say the Japanese.

While new trade agreements between the United States and Japan have been reached, the two nations will not end their trade imbalance soon. Elimination of *all* tariffs and nontariff trade barriers in Japan would increase U.S. exports to Japan by only an estimated $9 billion to $18 billion annually, while the current deficit is $50 billion.

CHAPTER SUMMARY

1. The United States is the world's largest international trader in terms of volume. Since 1965 U.S. exports and imports have more than doubled as a percentage of GDP. Other major trading nations are Germany, Japan, the western European nations, and the newly industrialized Asian tigers (Hong Kong, Singapore, South Korea, and Taiwan).

2. World trade is based on two considerations: the uneven distribution of economic resources among nations

and the fact that efficient production of various goods requires particular techniques or combinations of resources.

3. Mutually advantageous specialization and trade are possible between any two nations if they have different domestic opportunity-cost ratios for any two products. By specializing based on comparative advantage, nations can obtain larger real incomes with fixed amounts of resources. The terms of trade determine how this increase in world output is shared by the trading nations. Increasing (rather than constant) opportunity costs limit specialization and trade.

4. A nation's export supply curve shows the quantities of a product it will export at world prices which exceed the domestic price—the price in a closed, no-international-trade economy. Its import demand curve reveals the quantities of a product it will import at world prices below the domestic price. In a two-nation model, the equilibrium world price and the equilibrium quantities of exports and imports occur where one nation's export supply curve intersects the other nation's import demand curve.

5. Trade barriers take the form of protective tariffs, quotas, nontariff barriers, and "voluntary" export restrictions. Supply and demand analysis reveals that protective tariffs and quotas increase the prices and reduce the quantities demanded of affected goods. Sales by foreign exporters diminish; domestic producers, however, gain higher prices and enlarged sales. Tariffs and quotas promote a less efficient allocation of domestic and world resources.

6. The strongest arguments for protection are the infant-industry and military self-sufficiency arguments. Most other arguments for protection are half-truths, emotional appeals, or fallacies which emphasize the immediate effects of trade barriers while ignoring long-run consequences. Numerous historical examples suggest that free trade promotes economic growth; protectionism does not.

7. Protectionism costs U.S. consumers substantial amounts annually. The cost to consumers for each job saved is far greater than the average salary paid. Consumer losses from trade restrictions greatly exceed producer and government gains, creating an efficiency loss to society.

8. Recent U.S. international trade policy entails: **(a)** general liberalization of trade through NAFTA and GATT; **(b)** aggressive export promotion by government, and **(c)** bilateral negotiations over specific trade disputes, including the problem of the large U.S. trade deficits with Japan and China.

TERMS AND CONCEPTS

labor-intensive goods
land-intensive goods
capital-intensive goods
cost ratio
principle of comparative
   advantage
terms of trade

trading possibilities line
gains from trade
world price
domestic price
export supply curve
import demand curve
tariffs

revenue tariff
protective tariff
import quota
nontariff barrier
voluntary export
   restriction
strategic trade policy

dumping
World Trade
   Organization
export controls
export subsidies
most-favored-nation
   status

STUDY QUESTIONS

1. Quantitatively, how important is international trade to the United States relative to other nations?

2. Distinguish among land-, labor-, and capital-intensive commodities, citing one nontextbook example of each. What role do these distinctions play in explaining international trade?

3. Suppose nation A can produce 80 units of X by using all its resources to produce X and 60 units of Y by devoting all its resources to Y. Comparable figures for nation B are 60 units of X and 60 units of Y. Assuming constant costs, in which product should each nation specialize? Why? What are the limits of the terms of trade?

4. KEY QUESTION Here are hypothetical production possibilities tables for New Zealand and Spain.

New Zealand's production possibilities table
(millions of bushels)

Product	Production alternatives			
	A	B	C	D
Apples	0	20	40	60
Plums	15	10	5	0

Spain's production possibilities table (millions of bushels)

	Production alternatives			
Product	R	S	T	U
Apples	0	20	40	60
Plums	60	40	20	0

Plot the production possibilities data for each of the two countries separately. Referring to your graphs, determine:

a. Each country's cost ratio of producing plums and apples.

b. Which nation should specialize in which product.

c. The trading possibilities lines for each nation if the actual terms of trade are 1 plum for 2 apples. (Plot these lines on your graph.)

d. Suppose the optimum product mixes before specialization and trade were alternative B in New Zealand and alternative S in Spain. What are the gains from specialization and trade?

5. "The United States can produce X more efficiently than can Great Britain. Yet we import X from Great Britain." Explain.

6. KEY QUESTION Refer to Figure 3-5. Assume the graph depicts the United States' domestic market for corn. How many bushels of corn, if any, will the United States export or import at a world price of $1, $2, $3, $4, and $5? Use this information to construct the U.S. export supply curve and import demand curve for corn. Suppose the only other corn-producing nation is France, where the domestic price is $4. Which country will export corn; which will import it?

7. KEY QUESTION Draw a domestic supply and demand diagram for a product in which the United States does not have a comparative advantage. What impact do foreign imports have on domestic price and quantity? On your diagram show a protective tariff which eliminates approximately one-fourth the assumed imports. What are the price-quantity effects of this tariff on **(a)** domestic consumers, **(b)** domestic producers, and **(c)** foreign exporters? How would the effects of a quota which creates the same amount of imports differ?

8. "The most valid arguments for tariff protection are also the most easily abused." What are these particular arguments? Why are they susceptible to abuse? Evaluate the use of artificial trade barriers, such as tariffs and import quotas, as a means of achieving and maintaining full employment.

9. Evaluate the following statements:

a. Protective tariffs limit both the imports and the exports of the nation levying tariffs.

b. The extensive application of protective tariffs destroys the ability of the international market system to allocate resources efficiently.

c. Unemployment can often be reduced through tariff protection, but by the same token inefficiency typically increases.

d. Foreign firms which "dump" their products onto the U.S. market are in effect giving gifts to the country's citizens.

e. In view of the rapidity with which technological advance is dispersed around the world, free trade will inevitably yield structural maladjustments, unemployment, and balance of payments problems for industrially advanced nations.

f. Free trade can improve the composition and efficiency of domestic output. Only the Volkswagen forced Detroit to make a compact car, and only foreign success with the oxygen process forced American steel firms to modernize.

g. In the long run foreign trade is neutral with respect to total employment.

10. Between 1981–1985 the Japanese agreed to a voluntary export restriction which reduced U.S. imports of Japanese automobiles by about 10 percent. What would you expect the short-run effects of these restrictions to be on the U.S. and Japanese automobile industries? If this restriction were permanent, what would be its long-run effects in the two nations on **(a)** the allocation of resources, **(b)** the volume of employment, **(c)** the price level, and **(d)** the standard of living?

11. KEY QUESTION What are the costs and the benefits of protectionist policies? Which are larger?

12. What are NAFTA and GATT, and how do they relate to international trade? What policies has the U.S. government recently used to promote U.S. exports? What factors make it difficult for U.S. firms to sell their goods in Japan? What actions do you think the United States should take to reduce U.S. trade deficits with Japan and China?

13. (Last Word) What point is Bastiat trying to make with his petition of the candlemakers?

14. WEB-BASED QUESTION Multilateral Trade Liberalization—GATT and WTO GATT (General Agreement on Tariffs and Trade) was founded in 1947 to reduce world trade barriers on a multilateral basis. GATT partners have to grant one another the lowest tariffs they grant any of the other nations which have most-favored-nation status. GATT was subsumed by the World Trade Organization (WTO) http://www.wto.org/ on Jan. 1, 1995. Review how the WTO is trying to reduce trade barriers in two disparate industries: information technology and textiles; visit http://www.wto.org/wto/goods/goods.htm. What types of trade barriers are present in each industry? What timetable has been set for barrier reductions? Why is it more difficult to negotiate trade barrier reductions in textiles rather than information technology?

15. WEB-BASED QUESTION **The Economic Basis for Trade—Japan and the United States**   The United States and Japan are major traders with each other. Both nations are industrially advanced and

ranked 1 and 2, respectively, in gross domestic product. A comparison of their economic fundamentals can be found at JETRO (Japan External Trade Organization) http://www.jetro.go.jp/FACTS/UA-HANDBOOK/1.html. JETRO is a nonprofit, Japanese-government-related organization whose main activity is trade-related public relations. At http://www.jetro.go.jp/FACTS/UA-HANDBOOK/index.html, look at the statistics on United States and Japan. Can the principle of comparative advantage be applied to actual United States-Japan trade? How can two industrially advanced nations export capital-intensive goods to each other? Does this violate the principle of comparative advantage?

21

Exchange Rates, The Balance of Payments, and Trade Deficits

If you take a U.S. dollar to the bank and ask to exchange it for U.S. currency, you will get a puzzled look. If you persist, you may get a dollar's worth of change: One U.S. dollar can buy exactly one U.S. dollar. But on January 8, 1998, for example, one U.S. dollar could buy 210,035 Turkish lira, 1.58 Australian dollars, .62 British pounds, 1.43 Canadian dollars, 6.09 French francs, 1.82 German marks, 132.72 Japanese yen, or 8.03 Swedish krona. What explains this seemingly haphazard array of exchange rates?

In Chapter 20 we examined comparative advantage as the underlying economic basis of world trade and discussed the effects of barriers to free trade. Here we first introduce the monetary or financial aspects of international trade: How are currencies of different nations exchanged when import and export transactions occur? Next, we analyze and interpret the international balance of payments: What is meant by a "favorable" or "unfavorable" balance of payments? Then we look at the two "pure" types of exchange-rate systems—flexible and fixed—which could be used to determine the worth of one currency in terms of another. After that, we examine the systems of exchange rates which major trading nations have actually used. Finally, we discuss the causes and consequences of the large trade deficits the United States has encountered during the past several years.

FINANCING INTERNATIONAL TRADE

One factor which makes international trade different from domestic trade is the involvement of different national currencies. When a U.S. firm exports goods to a South Korean firm, the U.S. exporter wants to be paid in dollars. But South Korean importers deal in won; they must exchange their won for dollars to enable the U.S. export transaction to occur.

This problem is resolved in foreign exchange markets in which dollars can purchase South Korean wons, British pounds, Japanese yen, German marks, or any other currency, and vice versa. Sponsored by major banks in New York, London, Zurich, Tokyo, and elsewhere, foreign exchange markets facilitate exports and imports.

U.S. Export Transaction

Suppose a U.S. exporter agrees to sell $30,000 of computers to a British firm. Assume also that the rate of exchange—the rate at which pounds can be exchanged for, or converted into, dollars, and vice versa—is $2 for £1. This means the British importer must pay the equivalent of £15,000 to the U.S. exporter. Let's track what occurs in terms of the simple bank balance sheets in Figure 21-1. (A *balance sheet* is a statement showing a firm's *assets* and its *liabilities plus net worth;* the latter are claims on the assets by creditors and owners, respectively. Assets must always equal liabilities plus net worth because every asset of a firm is claimed by someone; those assets not claimed by creditors are claimed by owners.)

a. To pay for the computers, the British buyer draws a check for £15,000 on its checking account in a London bank. In Figure 21-1, this transaction (a) is shown by the −£15,000 checking account entry on the right side of the London bank's balance sheet.

b. The British firm sends this £15,000 check to the U.S. exporter. But the U.S. exporting firm must pay its bills in dollars, not pounds. Thus the exporter sells the £15,000 check on the London bank to its bank in, say, New York City, which is a dealer in foreign exchange. The bank adds $30,000 to the U.S. firm's checking account (b) for the £15,000 check. Note the new checking account entry of +$30,000 in the New York bank.

c. The New York bank deposits the £15,000 in a correspondent London bank for future sale. Thus,

+£15,000 of deposits (c) appear in the liabilities column for the London bank. To simplify, we assume that the correspondent bank in London is the same bank from which the British importer obtained the £15,000 draft. This +£15,000 ($30,000) is an asset (c) as viewed by the New York bank, and it appears as such on that bank's balance sheet.

Note this important point: *U.S. exports create a foreign demand for dollars, and the fulfillment of this demand increases the supply of foreign currencies (pounds in this case) owned by U.S. banks and available to U.S. buyers.*

U.S. Import Transaction

Why would the New York bank be willing to buy pounds for dollars? As just indicated, the New York bank is a dealer in foreign exchange; it is in the business of buying (for a fee) and selling (also for a fee) one currency for another.

Let's now examine how the New York bank would sell pounds for dollars in financing a U.S. import (British export) transaction. Suppose a U.S. retail firm wants to import £15,000 of compact disks produced in Britain by a hot new rock group. Again, bank balance sheets, as shown in Figure 21-2, track what happens [as coded by (a), (b), and (c)].

a. Because the British exporting firm wants to be paid in pounds rather than dollars, the U.S. importer must exchange dollars for pounds, which it does by going to the New York bank and purchasing £15,000 for $30,000. (Perhaps the U.S.

LONDON BANK: Balance sheet 1	
Assets	**Liabilities and net worth**
	(a) Checking account of British importer: −£15,000
	(c) Deposit of New York bank: +£15,000

NEW YORK BANK: Balance sheet 1	
Assets	**Liabilities and net worth**
(c) Deposit in London bank: +£15,000 ($30,000)	(b) Checking account of U.S. exporter: +$30,000

FIGURE 21-1 Financing a U.S. export transaction In transaction (a), a British importer writes a check for £15,000 on its London bank account and uses it to pay for a U.S. import. In transaction (b), the U.S. exporter sells the £15,000 British check to its New York bank at the $1 = £2 exchange rate and deposits $30,000 in its New York checking account. In transaction (c), the New York bank deposits the £15,000 British check in its corresponding London bank for future use.

LONDON BANK: Balance sheet 2	
Assets	Liabilities and net worth
	(b) Demand deposit of British exporter: +£15,000
	(a) Deposit of New York bank: −£15,000

NEW YORK BANK: Balance sheet 2	
Assets	Liabilities and net worth
(a) Deposit in London bank: −£15,000 ($30,000)	(a) Checking account of U.S. importer: −$30,000

FIGURE 21-2 Financing a U.S. import transaction In transaction (a), a U.S. importer purchases £15,000 at the $1 = £2 exchange rate by writing a check for $30,000 on its New York bank. This reduces the importer's New York checking account by $30,000 and reduces the New York bank's £15,000 deposit in its corresponding London bank. In transaction (b), the £15,000 payment goes to the British exporter, who deposits it in its checking account in its London bank.

----

importer purchases the same £15,000 which the New York bank acquired from the U.S. exporter.) In Figure 21-2, this purchase reduces the U.S. importer's checking account in the New York bank by $30,000, and the New York bank gives up its £15,000 deposit in the London bank.

b. The U.S. importer sends its newly purchased check for £15,000 to the British firm, which deposits it in the London bank; there, it is recorded as a +£15,000 deposit in the London bank.

Here you see that *U.S. imports create a domestic demand for foreign currencies (pounds, in this case), and the fulfillment of this demand reduces the supplies of foreign currencies held by U.S. banks and available for U.S. consumers.*

The combined export and import transactions bring one more point into focus. United States exports (the computers) make available, or "earn," a supply of foreign currencies for U.S. banks, and U.S. imports (the compact disks) create a demand for these currencies. In a broad sense, any nation's exports finance or "pay for" its imports. Exports provide the foreign currencies needed to pay for imports.

Postscript: Although our examples are confined to exporting and importing goods, demand for and supplies of pounds also arise from transactions involving services and the payment of interest and dividends on foreign investments. The United States demands pounds not only to buy imports but also to buy insurance and transportation services from the British, to vacation in London, to pay dividends and interest on British investments in the United States, and to make new financial and real investments in Britain. **(Key Question 2)**

THE BALANCE OF PAYMENTS

A nation's **balance of payments** is the sum of all transactions which take place between its residents and the residents of all foreign nations. These transactions include merchandise exports and imports, imports of goods and services, tourist expenditures, interest and dividends received or paid abroad, and purchases and sales of financial or real assets abroad. *The balance of payments statement shows all the payments a nation receives from foreign countries and all the payments it makes to them.* Table 21-1 is a simplified balance of payments statement for the United States in 1996. Let's take a close look at this accounting statement to see what it reveals about U.S. international trade and finance. To help our explanation, we divide the single balance of payments account into three components: the current account, the capital account, and the official reserves account.

Current Account

The top portion of Table 21-1 summarizes U.S. trade in currently produced goods and services and is called the **current account.** Items 1 and 2 show U.S. exports and imports of goods (merchandise) in 1996. U.S. exports have a *plus* (+) sign because they are a *credit;* they earn and make available foreign exchange in the United States. As you saw in the previous section, any export-type transaction which obligates foreigners to make "inpayments" to the United States generates supplies of foreign currencies in the U.S. banks.

TABLE 21-1   **The U.S. balance of payments, 1996 (in billions)**

Current account		
(1) U.S. goods exports...	$ +612	
(2) U.S. goods imports...	−803	
(3) *Balance of trade*		$−191
(4) U.S. exports of services	+237	
(5) U.S. imports of services	−157	
(6) *Balance on goods and services*		−111
(7) Net investment income.......................................	+3	
(8) Net transfers	−40	
(9) **Balance on current account**		−148
Capital account		
(10) Foreign purchases of assets in the United States ..	+517*	
(11) U.S. purchases of assets abroad	−376*	
(12) **Balance on capital account**		+141
Official reserves account		
(13) **Official reserves**		+7
		$ 0

*Includes one-half of a $37 billion statistical discrepancy which shows up in the balance of payments account.
Source: Survey of Current Business, September 1997.

U.S. imports have a *minus* (−) sign because they are a *debit;* they reduce the stock of foreign currencies in the United States. Our earlier discussion of trade financing indicated that U.S. imports obligate the United States to make "outpayments" to the rest of the world which reduce available supplies of foreign currencies held by U.S. banks.

Trade Balance   Items 1 and 2 in Table 21-1 reveal that in 1996 U.S. goods exports of $612 billion did not earn enough foreign currencies to finance U.S. goods imports of $803 billion. A country's goods balance of trade, or simply, its **trade balance,** is the difference between its exports and imports of goods. If exports exceed imports, the result is a trade surplus or "favorable balance of trade." If imports exceed exports, there is a trade deficit or "unfavorable balance of trade." We note in item 3 that in 1996 the United States incurred a trade deficit (of goods) of $191 billion. (Global Perspective 21-1 shows U.S. trade deficits and surpluses for selected nations or groups of nations.)

Balance on Goods and Services   Item 4 reveals that the United States not only exports goods, such as airplanes and computer software, but also services, such as insurance, consulting, travel, and brokerage

services, to residents of foreign nations. These service "exports" totaled $237 billion in 1996 and are a credit (thus the + sign). Item 5 indicates that the United States "imports" similar services from foreigners; these service imports were $157 billion in 1996 and are a debit (thus the − sign).

The **balance on goods and services,** shown as item 6, is the difference between U.S. exports of goods and services (items 1 and 4) and U.S. imports of goods and services (items 2 and 5). In 1996, U.S. imports of goods and services exceeded U.S. exports of goods and services by $111 billion.

Balance on Current Account   Item 7, *net investment income,* represents the excess of interest and dividend payments people abroad have paid the United States for the services of exported U.S. capital over what the United States paid in interest and dividends for the use of foreign capital invested in the United States. It shows that in 1996 U.S. net investment income was $3 billion worth of foreign currencies.

Item 8 shows net transfers, both public and private, between the United States and the rest of the world. Included here is foreign aid, pensions paid to citizens living abroad, and remittances by immigrants to relatives abroad. These $40 billion of transfers are net U.S. outpayments which decrease available supplies of for-

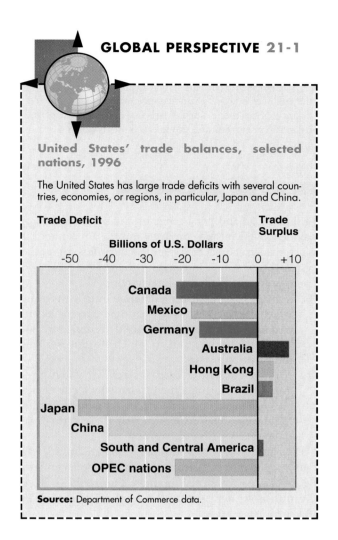

GLOBAL PERSPECTIVE 21-1

United States' trade balances, selected nations, 1996

The United States has large trade deficits with several countries, economies, or regions, in particular, Japan and China.

Source: Department of Commerce data.

eign exchange. They are, in a sense, the exporting of good will and the importing of "thank-you notes."

By adding all transactions in the current account, we obtain the **balance on current account** shown in item 9. In 1996 the United States had a current account deficit of $148 billion. This means that the U.S. current account transactions (items 2, 5, and 8) created a greater outpayment of foreign currencies from the United States than an inpayment of foreign currencies to the United States.

Capital Account

The second account within the overall balance of trade account is the **capital account,** which summarizes the flows of payments (money "capital") from the purchase or sale of real or financial assets. For ex-

ample, a foreign firm may buy a *real* asset, say, an office tower in the United States, or a financial asset, for instance, a U.S. government bond. Both kinds of transactions involve the "export" of the ownership of U.S. assets from the United States in return for inpayments of foreign currency (money "capital" inflows). As indicated in line 10, these "exports" of ownership of assets are designated *foreign purchases of assets in the United States.* They have a + sign because, like exports of U.S. goods and services, they represent an inpayment of foreign currencies.

Conversely, a U.S. firm may buy, say, a hotel chain (real asset) in a foreign country or common stock (financial asset) of a foreign firm. Both transactions involve "imports" of the ownership of real or financial assets to the United States and are paid for by outpayments (money "capital" outflows). These "imports" are designated *U.S. purchases of assets abroad* and, as shown in line 12, have a − sign; like U.S. imports of goods and services, they represent an outpayment of foreign currencies from the United States.

Items 10 and 11 combined yield a **balance on capital account** of +$141 billion in 1996 (line 12). In 1996 the United States "exported" $517 billion of ownership of its real and financial assets and "imported" $376 billion. This capital account *surplus* brought in $141 billion of foreign currencies to the United States.

Official Reserves Account

The third account in the overall balance of payments is the official reserves account. The central banks of nations hold quantities of foreign currencies called **official reserves.** These reserves can be drawn on to make up any net deficit in the combined current and capital accounts (much as you would draw on your savings to pay for a special purchase.) In 1996 the United States had a $7 billion deficit in the combined current and capital accounts (line 9 minus line 12). Balance in the U.S. international payments required the U.S. government to deplete its official reserves of foreign currencies by $7 billion (item 13). The + sign indicates that this drawdown of reserves is a credit— the inpayment from official reserves which was needed to balance the overall balance of payments account.

In some years, the current and capital accounts balances may be positive, meaning that the United States earned more foreign currencies than it needed. The surplus would create an outpayment, not to other countries, but to the stock of official reserves. As such, item 13 would have a − sign since it is a debit.

The three components of the balance of payments—the current account, the capital account, and the official reserves account—must together equal zero. Every unit of foreign exchange used (as reflected in a *minus* outpayment or debit transaction) must have a source (a *plus* inpayment or credit transaction).

Payments Deficits and Surpluses

Although the balance of payments *must always sum to zero*, economists and political officials speak of **balance of payment deficits and surpluses;** they are referring to imbalances between the current and capital accounts (line 9 minus line 12) which cause a drawing down or building up of foreign currencies. *A drawing down of official reserves (to create a positive official reserves entry in Table 21-1) measures a nation's balance of payments deficit; a building up of official reserves (which is shown as a negative official reserves entry) measures its balance of payments surplus.*

A balance of payments deficit is not necessarily bad, nor is a balance of payments surplus necessarily good. Both simply are realities. However, any nation's official reserves are limited. Persistent payments deficits, which must be financed by drawing down those reserves, would ultimately deplete the reserves. That nation would have to make policies to correct its balance of payments. These policies might require painful macroeconomic adjustments, trade barriers and similar restrictions, or a major depreciation of its currency. For this reason, nations seek to achieve payments balance, at least over several-year periods.

It is clear from Table 21-1 that in 1996 the United States had a large current account deficit, a large capital account surplus, and a relatively small payments deficit. Large current account deficits have been the pattern for the United States for several years. We need to examine the causes and consequences of trade deficits, but we will defer that discussion until later in this chapter. **(Key Question 3)**

QUICK REVIEW 21-1

■ U.S. exports create a foreign demand for dollars, and fulfillment of that demand increases the domestic supply of foreign currencies; U.S. imports create a domestic demand for foreign currencies, and fulfillment of that demand reduces the supplies of foreign currency held by U.S. banks.

■ The current account balance is a nation's exports of goods and services less its imports of goods and services plus its net investment income and net transfers.

■ The capital account balance is a nation's sale of real and financial assets to people living abroad less its purchases of real and financial assets from foreigners.

■ A balance of payments deficit occurs when the sum of the balances on current and capital accounts is negative; a balance of payments surplus arises when the sum of the balances on current and capital accounts is positive.

FLEXIBLE EXCHANGE RATES

Both the size and persistence of a nation's balance of payments deficits and surpluses and the adjustments it must make to correct these imbalances depend on the system of exchange rates being used. There are two "pure" types of exchange-rate systems:

1. A **flexible** or **floating exchange-rate system** by which the rates at which national currencies are exchanged for one another are determined by demand and supply and in which no government intervention occurs

2. A **fixed exchange-rate system** by which governments determine the rates at which currencies are exchanged and make necessary adjustments in their economies to ensure that these rates continue.

We being by looking at flexible exchange rates. Let's examine the rate, or price, at which U.S. dollars might be exchanged for British pounds. **Figure 21-3 (Key Graph)** shows demand D_1 and supply S_1 of pounds in the currency market.

The *demand for pounds curve* is downsloping because, if pounds become less expensive to the United States, then all British goods and services will be cheaper to the United States. That is, at lower dollar prices for pounds, the United States can get more pounds and therefore more British goods and services per dollar. To buy these cheaper British goods, U.S. consumers will increase the quantity of pounds they demand.

The *supply of pounds curve* is upsloping because, as the dollar price of pounds rises (that is, the pound price of dollars falls), the British will purchase more U.S. goods. When the British buy more U.S. goods, they supply a greater quantity of pounds to the foreign exchange market. In other words, they must exchange pounds for dollars to purchase U.S. goods.

The intersection of the supply curve and demand curve will determine the dollar price of pounds. Here, that price (exchange rate) is $2 for £1.

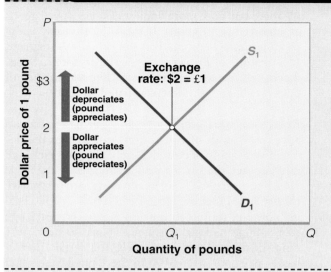

FIGURE 21-3 The market for foreign currency (pounds) The intersection of the demand for pounds D_1 and the supply of pounds S_1 determines the equilibrium dollar price of pounds, here, $2. That means that the exchange rate is $2 = £1. The upward green arrow is a reminder that a higher dollar price of pounds (say, $3 = £1) means that the dollar has depreciated (pound has appreciated). The downward green arrow tells us that a lower dollar price of pounds (say, $1 = £1) means that the dollar has appreciated (pound has depreciated). Such changes in equilibrium exchange rates would result from shifts of the supply and demand curves.

QUICK QUIZ 21-3

1. Which of the following is a true statement?
  a. The quantity of pounds demanded falls when the dollar appreciates.
  b. The quantity of pounds supplied declines as the dollar price of pounds rises.
  c. At the equilibrium exchange rate, the pound price of $1 is 1/2 pound.
  d. The dollar would appreciate if the demand for pounds increased.

2. At the price of $2 for 1 pound in this figure:
  a. the dollar-pound exchange rate is unstable.
  b. the quantity of pounds supplied equals the quantity demanded.
  c. the dollar price of 1 pound equals the pound price of $1.
  d. U.S. merchandise exports to Britain must equal U.S. merchandise imports from Britain.

3. All else equal, a leftward shift of the demand curve in this figure:
  a. would depreciate the dollar.

  b. creates a shortage of pounds at the previous price of $2 for 1 pound.
  c. might be caused by a major recession in the United States.
  d. might be caused by a significant rise of real interest rates in Britain.

4. All else equal, a rightward shift of the supply curve in this figure would:
  a. depreciate the dollar and might be caused by a significant rise of real interest rates in Britain.
  b. depreciate the dollar and might be caused by a significant fall of real interest rates in Britain.
  c. appreciate the dollar and might be caused by a significant rise of real interest rates in the United States.
  d. appreciate the dollar and might be caused by a significant fall of interest rates in the United States.

Answers: 1. c; 2. b; 3. c; 4. c.

Depreciation and Appreciation

An exchange rate determined by market forces can, and often does, change daily, just as do stock and bond prices. When the dollar price of pounds increases, for example, from $2 for £1 to $3 for £1, the value of the dollar has depreciated relative to the pound. When a nation's currency depreciates, it takes more units of that nation's currency (dollars) to buy a single unit of some foreign currency (a pound).

When the dollar price of pounds decreases, say, from $2 for £1 to $1 for £1, the dollar has appreciated relative to the pound. When a nation's currency appreciates, it takes fewer units of that nation's currency (dollars) to buy a single unit of some foreign currency (pounds).

In our United States-Britain illustrations, depreciation of the dollar means an appreciation of the pound, and vice versa. A change in the exchange rate from $2 = £1 to $3 = £1 means that it takes more dollars to buy £1; the dollar has depreciated. But it now takes fewer pounds to buy $1. At the initial rate it took £½ to buy $1; at the new rate it takes only £⅓ to buy $1. The pound has appreciated relative to the dollar. If the dollar depreciates relative to the pound, the pound appreciates relative to the dollar. If the dollar appreciates relative to the pound, the pound depreciates relative to the dollar.

Determinants of Exchange Rates

So what factors would cause a nation's currency to appreciate or depreciate in the market for foreign exchange? Here are three generalizations:

1. If the demand for a nation's currency increases (all else equal), that currency will appreciate; if the demand declines, that currency will depreciate.
2. If the supply of a nation's currency increases, that currency will depreciate; if the supply decreases, that currency will appreciate.
3. If a nation's currency appreciates, some foreign currency depreciates relative to it.

With these generalizations in mind, let's examine the determinants of exchange rates, which are the factors that change either the demand for or supply of a nation's currency.

Changes in Tastes
Any change in consumer tastes or preferences for the products of a foreign country may alter the demand for that nation's currency and change its exchange rate. If technological advances in U.S. cell phones make them more attractive to British consumers and businesses, then the British will supply more pounds in the exchange market in order to purchase more U.S. cell phones. The supply-of-pounds curve will shift rightward, the pound will depreciate, and the dollar will appreciate.

In contrast, if British woolen apparel becomes more fashionable in the United States, the U.S. demand for pounds will increase, the pound will appreciate, and the dollar will depreciate.

Relative Income Changes
If the growth of a nation's income is more rapid than that of other countries', its currency is likely to depreciate. Here's why. A country's imports vary directly with its level of in-

come. As total income rises in the United States, people there buy both more domestically produced goods *and* more foreign goods. If the U.S. economy is expanding rapidly and the British economy is stagnant, U.S. imports of British goods, and therefore U.S. demands for pounds, will increase. The dollar price of pounds will rise, so the dollar will depreciate.

Relative Price-Level Changes
Changes in the relative price levels of two nations can change the demand and supply of currencies and alter the exchange rate between the two nations' currencies.

At the extreme, the **purchasing power parity theory** holds that exchange rates *equate* the purchasing power of various currencies. That is, the exchange rates among national currencies adjust to match the ratios of the nations' price levels: If a certain market basket of goods costs $100 in the United States and £50 in Great Britain, the exchange rate will be $2 = £1. In this theory, a dollar spent on goods sold in Britain, Japan, Turkey, and other nations will have equal purchasing power.

In practice, however, exchange rates depart from purchasing power parity, even over long periods. Nevertheless, changes in relative price levels are a determinant of exchange rates. If, for example, the domestic price level rises rapidly in the United States and remains constant in Great Britain, U.S. consumers will seek out low-priced British goods, increasing the demand for pounds. The British will purchase fewer U.S. goods, reducing the supply of pounds. This combination of demand and supply changes will cause the pound to appreciate and the dollar to depreciate.

Relative Interest Rates
Changes in relative interest rates between two countries can alter their exchange rate. Suppose that real interest rates rise in the United States but stay constant in Great Britain. British citizens will then find the United States an attractive place in which to make financial investments. To undertake these investments, they will have to supply pounds in the foreign exchange market to obtain dollars. The increase in the supply of pounds results in depreciation of the pound and appreciation of the dollar.

Speculation
Currency speculators are people who buy and sell currencies with an eye toward reselling or repurchasing them at a profit. Suppose speculators expect the U.S. economy to (1) grow more rapidly

than the British economy and (2) experience a more rapid rise in its price level than Britain. These expectations translate to an anticipation that the pound will appreciate and the dollar will depreciate. Speculators who are holding dollars will therefore try to convert them into pounds. This effort will increase the demand for pounds and cause the dollar price of pounds to rise (that is, the dollar to depreciate). A self-fulfilling prophecy occurs: The pound appreciates and the dollar depreciates because speculators act on the belief that these changes will in fact take place. In this way, speculation can cause changes in exchange rates. (We deal with currency speculation in more detail in this chapter's Last Word.)

Table 21-2 has more illustrations of the determinants of exchange rates; we urge you to give the table a good look.

Flexible Rates and the Balance of Payments

Proponents argue that flexible exchange rates have an important feature: *They automatically adjust to eventually eliminate balance of payment deficits or surpluses.* We can explain this concept with S_1 and D_1 in Figure 21-4; they are the supply and demand curves for pounds from Figure 21-3. The equilibrium exchange rate of $2 = £1 means there is no balance of payments

TABLE 21-2   Determinants of exchange rates: factors which change the demand for or supply of a particular currency and thus alter the exchange rate

Determinant	Examples
Change in tastes	Japanese autos decline in popularity in the United States (Japanese yen depreciates; U.S. dollar appreciates)
	German tourists flock to the United States (U.S. dollar appreciates; German mark depreciates)
Change in relative incomes	England encounters a recession, reducing its imports, while U.S. real output and real income surge, increasing U.S. imports (British pound appreciates; U.S. dollar depreciates)
Change in relative prices	Germany experiences a 3% inflation rate compared to Canada's 10% rate (German mark appreciates; Canadian dollar depreciates)
Change in relative real interest rates	The Federal Reserve drives up interest rates in the United States, while the Bank of England takes no such action (U.S. dollar appreciates; British pound depreciates)
Speculation	Currency traders believe France will have much more rapid inflation than Sweden (French franc depreciates; Swedish krona appreciates)
	Currency traders think German interest rates will plummet relative to U.S. rates (German mark depreciates; U.S. dollar appreciates)

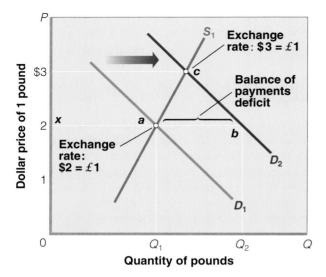

FIGURE 21-4 Adjustments under flexible exchange rates and fixed exchange rates Under flexible exchange rates, a shift in the demand for pounds from D_1 to D_2, other things equal, would cause a U.S. balance of payments deficit *ab*; it would be corrected by a change in the exchange rate from $2 = £1 to $3 = £1. Under fixed exchange rates, the United States would cover the shortage of pounds *ab* by using international monetary reserves, restricting trade, implementing exchange controls, or enacting a contractionary stabilization policy.

----

deficit or surplus between the United States and Britain. At the $2 = £1 exchange rate, the quantity of pounds demanded by U.S. consumers to import British goods, buy British transportation and insurance services, and pay interest and dividends on British investments in the United States equals the amount of pounds supplied by the British in buying U.S. exports, purchasing services from the United States, and making interest and dividend payments on U.S. investments in Britain. The United States would have no need to either draw down or build up its official reserves to balance its payments.

Suppose tastes change and U.S. consumers buy more British automobiles; the U.S. price level increases relative to Britain's; or interest rates fall in the United States compared to those in Britain. Any or all of these changes will cause the U.S. demand for British pounds to increase from D_1 to, say, D_2 in Figure 21-4.

If the exchange rate remains at the initial $2 = £1, a U.S. balance of payments deficit will be created in the amount of *ab*. That is, at the $2 = £1 rate, U.S. consumers will demand the quantity of pounds represented by point *b*, but Britain will supply the amount

represented by *a*; there will be a shortage of pounds. However, because this is a competitive market, the shortage will alter the exchange rate (the dollar price of pounds) from $2 = £1 to, say, $3 = £1; that is, the dollar will depreciate.

At this point we need to reemphasize that the exchange rate links all domestic (U.S.) prices with all foreign (British) prices. The dollar price of a foreign good is found by multiplying the foreign price by the exchange rate (in dollars per unit of the foreign currency). At an exchange rate of $2 = £1, a British automobile priced at £9000 will cost a U.S. consumer $18,000 (= 9000 × $2).

A change in the exchange rate alters the prices of all British goods to U.S. consumers and all U.S. goods to British buyers. The shift in the exchange rate (here from $2 = £1 to $3 = £1) changes the relative attractiveness of U.S. imports and exports and restores equilibrium in the U.S. (and British) balance of payments. From the U.S. point of view, as the dollar price of pounds changes from $2 to $3, the British auto priced at £9000, which formerly cost a U.S. consumer $18,000, now costs $27,000 (= 9000 × $3). Other British goods will also cost U.S. consumers more, and U.S. imports of British goods will decline. A movement from point *b* toward point *c* in Figure 21-4 graphically illustrates this concept.

From Britain's standpoint, the exchange rate (the pound price of dollars) has fallen (from £½ to £⅓ for $1). The international value of the pound has appreciated. The British previously got only $2 for £1; now they get $3 for £1. U.S. goods are therefore cheaper to the British, and U.S. exports to Britain will rise. In Figure 21-4, this is shown by a movement from point *a* toward point *c*.

The two adjustments—a decrease in U.S. imports from Britain and an increase in U.S. exports to Britain—are just what are needed to correct the U.S. balance of payments deficit. These changes end when, at point *c*, the quantities of British pounds demanded and supplied are equal. **(Key Questions 6 and 10)**

Disadvantages of Flexible Exchange Rates

Even though flexible exchange rates automatically work to eliminate payment imbalances, they may cause several significant problems.

Uncertainty and Diminished Trade The risks and uncertainties associated with flexible exchange rates may discourage the flow of trade. Suppose a U.S. automobile dealer contracts to purchase 10 British cars for £90,000. At the current exchange rate of, say, $2 for £1, the U.S. importer expects to pay $180,000 for these automobiles. But if in the 3-month delivery period the rate of exchange shifts to $3 for £1, the £90,000 payment contracted by the U.S. importer will now be $270,000.

This increase in the dollar price of pounds may thus turn the U.S. importer's anticipated profit into substantial losses. Aware of the possibility of an adverse change in the exchange rate, the U.S. importer may not be willing to assume the risks involved. The U.S. firm may confine its operations to domestic automobiles, with the result that international trade in this item does not occur.

The same thing can happen with investments. Assume that, when the exchange rate is $3 to £1, a U.S. firm invests $30,000 (or £10,000) in a British enterprise. It estimates a return of 10 percent; that is, it anticipates annual earnings of $3000 or £1000. Suppose these expectations prove correct in that the British firm earns £1000 in the first year on the £10,000 investment. But suppose that during the year, the value of the dollar appreciates to $2 = £1. The absolute return is now only $2000 (rather than $3000), and the rate of return falls from the anticipated 10 percent to only $6\frac{2}{3}$ percent (= $2000/$30,000). Investment is risky anyway. The added risk of changing exchange rates may persuade the U.S. investor to not venture overseas.[1]

Terms of Trade Changes

A nation's terms of trade will be worsened by a decline in the international value of its currency. For example, an increase in the dollar price of pounds will mean that the United States must export more goods and services to finance a specific level of imports from Britain.

Instability

Flexible exchange rates may have destabilizing effects on the domestic economy because wide fluctuations stimulate and then depress industries producing exported goods. If the U.S. economy is operating at full employment and its currency depreciates as in our illustration, the results will be inflationary, for two reasons. (1) Foreign demand for U.S. goods may increase, increasing total spending and pulling up U.S. prices. Also, the prices of all U.S. imports will increase. (2) Conversely, appreciation of the dollar will lower U.S. exports and increase imports, possibly causing unemployment.

Flexible or floating exchange rates may also complicate the use of domestic stabilization policies in seeking full employment and price stability. This is especially true for nations whose exports and imports are large relative to their total domestic output.

FIXED EXCHANGE RATES

To circumvent the disadvantages of flexible exchange rates, at times nations have fixed or "pegged" their exchange rates. For our analysis of fixed exchange rates, we assume the United States and Britain agree to maintain a $2 = £1 exchange rate.

The problem is that such a governmental agreement cannot keep from changing the demand for and supply of pounds. With the rate fixed, a shift in demand or supply will put pressure on the exchange rate system, and government must intervene if the exchange rate is to be maintained.

In Figure 21-4, suppose the U.S. demand for pounds increases from D_1 to D_2 and a U.S. payment deficit *ab* arises. This means that the U.S. government is committed to an exchange rate ($2 = £1) which is below the new equilibrium rate ($3 = £1). How can the United States prevent the shortage of pounds from driving the exchange rate up to the new equilibrium level? The answer is to alter market demand or market supply or alter both so that they will intersect at the $2 = £1 rate of exchange. There are several ways to do this.

Use of Reserves

One way to maintain a pegged exchange rate is to manipulate the market through the use of official reserves. By selling part of its reserves of pounds, the U.S. government could increase the supply of pounds, shifting supply curve S_1 to the right so that it intersects D_2 at *b* in Figure 21-4 and thereby maintains the exchange rate at $2 = £1.

How do official reserves originate? Perhaps in the past the opposite market conditions prevailed, so there was a surplus, rather than a shortage, of pounds. The U.S. government would have acquired that surplus.

---

[1]You will see in this chapter's Last Word, however, that a trader can circumvent part of the risk of unfavorable exchange rate fluctuations by "hedging" in the "futures market" or "forward market" for foreign exchange.

That is, at some earlier time the U.S. government may have spent dollars to buy surplus pounds which were threatening to reduce the $2 = £1 exchange rate to, say, $1 = £1. That condition would have built up the U.S. official reserves of pounds.

Nations have also used gold as "international money" to obtain official reserves. In our example, the U.S. government could sell some of the gold it owns to Britain for pounds. The pounds acquired could then be sold for dollars, as above, to shift the supply of pounds to the right so as to maintain the $2 = £1 exchange rate.

It is critical that the amount of reserves and gold be enough to accomplish the required increase in the supply of pounds. This is not a problem if deficits and surpluses occur more or less randomly and are about the same size. That is, last year's balance of payments surplus with Britain will increase the U.S. reserve of pounds, and that reserve can be used to "finance" this year's deficit. But if the United States encounters persistent and sizable deficits for an extended period, its reserves can become exhausted, forcing the United States to abandon fixed exchange rates. Or, at the least, a nation whose reserves are inadequate must use less appealing options to maintain exchange rates. Let's consider some of these options.

Trade Policies

To maintain fixed exchange rates, a nation can try to control the flow of trade and finance directly. The United States could try to maintain the $2 = £1 exchange rate in the face of a shortage of pounds by discouraging imports (thereby reducing the demand for pounds) and encouraging exports (thus increasing the supply of pounds). Imports can be reduced with new tariffs or import quotas; special taxes can be levied on the interest and dividends U.S. financial investors receive from foreign investments. Also, the U.S. government could subsidize certain U.S. exports to increase the supply of pounds.

The fundamental problem is that these policies reduce the volume of world trade and change its makeup from what is economically desirable. When we impose tariffs, quotas, and the like, we lose some of the economic benefits of a free flow of world trade. This loss should not be underestimated: Trade barriers by one nation lead to retaliatory responses from other nations, multiplying the loss.

Exchange Controls and Rationing

Another option is exchange controls and rationing. Under exchange controls, the U.S. government could handle the problem of a pound shortage by requiring that all pounds obtained by U.S. exporters be sold to the Federal government. Then the government would allocate or ration this short supply of pounds (represented by *xa* in Figure 21-4) among various U.S. importers, who actually demand the quantity *xb*. The effect of this policy is to restrict the value of U.S. imports to the amount of foreign exchange earned by U.S. exports. Assuming balance in the capital account, there is then no balance of payments deficit. U.S. demand for British imports with the value *ab* would simply not be fulfilled.

There are major objections to exchange controls:

1. *Distorted trade*   Like tariffs, quotas, and export subsidies (trade controls), exchange controls distort the pattern of international trade away from that suggested by comparative advantage.
2. *Favoritism*   The process of rationing scarce foreign exchange can lead to government favoritism toward selected importers (big contributors to reelection campaigns, for example).
3. *Restricted choice*   Controls limit freedom of consumer choice. The U.S. consumers who prefer Volkswagens may have to buy Chevrolets. The business opportunities for some U.S. importers may be impaired because government limits imports.
4. *Black markets*   There are likely to be enforcement problems. U.S. importers might want foreign exchange badly enough to pay more than the $2 = £1 official rate, setting the stage for black-market dealings between importers and illegal sellers of foreign exchange.

Domestic Macroeconomic Adjustments

A final way to maintain a stable exchange rate is to use domestic stabilization policies (monetary policy and fiscal policy) to eliminate the shortage of foreign currency. Tax hikes, reductions in government spending, and a high-interest-rate policy would reduce total spending in the U.S. economy and thus domestic income. Because imports vary directly with domestic income, demand for British goods, and therefore for pounds, would be restrained.

If these "contractionary" policies reduce the domestic price level relative to Britain's, U.S. buyers of consumer and capital goods would divert their demands from British goods to U.S. goods, also reducing the demand for pounds. Moreover, the high-interest-rate policy would lift U.S. interest rates relative to those in Britain.

Lower prices on U.S. goods and higher U.S. interest rates would increase British imports of U.S. goods and increase British financial investment in the United States. Both developments would increase the supply of pounds. The combination of a decrease in the demand for and an increase in the supply of pounds would reduce or eliminate the original U.S. balance of payments deficit. In Figure 21-4 the new supply and demand curves would intersect at some new equilibrium point on line *ab*, where the exchange rate remains at $2 = £1.

This way to maintain pegged exchange rates is hardly appealing. The "price" of exchange-rate stability for the United States would be falling output, employment, and price levels—in other words, a recession. Eliminating a balance of payments deficit and realizing domestic stability are both important national economic goals, but to sacrifice stability for payments balance is to let the tail wag the dog.

QUICK REVIEW 21-2

■ In a system in which exchange rates are flexible (meaning that they are free to float), the rates are determined by the demand for and supply of individual national currencies in the foreign exchange market.

■ Determinants of flexible exchange rates—factors which shift currency supply and demand curves—include changes in **(a)** tastes, **(b)** relative national incomes, **(c)** relative price levels, **(d)** real interest rates, and **(e)** speculation.

■ Under a system of fixed exchange rates, nations set their exchange rates and then maintain them by buying or selling reserves of currencies, establishing trade barriers, employing exchange controls, or incurring inflation or recession.

INTERNATIONAL EXCHANGE-RATE SYSTEMS

In recent times the world's nations have used three different exchange rate systems: a fixed rate system, a modified fixed rate system, and a modified flexible rate system.

The Gold Standard: Fixed Exchange Rates

Between 1879 and 1934 the major nations of the world adhered to a fixed-rate system called the **gold standard.** In this system, each nation must:

1. Define its currency in terms of a quantity of gold
2. Maintain a fixed relationship between its stock of gold and its money supply
3. Allow gold to be freely exported and imported

If each nation defines its currency in terms of gold, the various national currencies will have fixed relationships to one another. For example, if the United States defines $1 as worth 25 grains of gold, and Britain defines its pounds as worth 50 grains of gold, then a British pound is worth 2×25 grains, or $2. This exchange rate would be fixed; it would not change in response to changes in currency demand and supply.

Gold Flows   If we ignore the costs of packing, insuring, and shipping gold between countries, under the gold standard the rate of exchange would not vary from this $2 = £1 rate. No one in the United States would pay more than $2 = £1 because 50 grains of gold could always be bought for $2 in the United States and sold for £1 in Britain. Nor would the British pay more than £1 for $2. Why should they when they could buy 50 grains of gold in Britain for £1 and sell it in the United States for $2?

Under the gold standard, the potential free flow of gold between nations would result in exchange rates which are fixed.

Domestic Macroeconomic Adjustments   When the demand for, or supply of, currencies changes, the gold standard requires domestic macroeconomic adjustments for the fixed exchange rate to be maintained. To see why, suppose that U.S. tastes change such that U.S. consumers want to buy more British goods. The demand for pounds increases such that there is a shortage of pounds in the United States (recall Figure 21-4), implying a U.S. balance of payments deficit.

What will happen? Remember that the rules of the gold standard prohibit the exchange rate from moving from the fixed $2 = £1 rate; the rate cannot move to, say, a new equilibrium at $3 = £1 to correct the imbalance. Instead, gold will flow from the United States to Britain to remove the payments imbalance.

But recall that the gold standard required participants to maintain a fixed relationship between their domestic money supplies and their quantities of gold. The flow of gold from the United States to Britain will require a reduction of the money supply in the United States. Other things equal, this will reduce total spending in the United States and thereby lower U.S. real domestic output, employment, income, and perhaps, prices. Also, the decline in the money supply will boost U.S. interest rates.

The opposite will occur in Britain. The inflow of gold will increase the money supply, which will increase total spending in Britain. Domestic output, employment, income, and perhaps, prices will rise. The British interest rate will fall.

Declining U.S. incomes and prices will reduce U.S. demand for British goods and therefore reduce the U.S. demand for pounds. Lower interest rates in Britain will make it less attractive for U.S. investors to make financial investments there, also lessening the demand for pounds. For all these reasons, the demand for pounds in the United States will decline. In Britain, higher incomes, prices, and interest rates will make U.S. imports and U.S. financial investments more attractive. In buying these imports and making these financial investments, British citizens will supply more pounds in the exchange market.

In short, domestic macroeconomic adjustments in the United States and Britain, triggered by the international flow of gold, will produce new demand and supply conditions for pounds such that the $2 = £1 exchange rate is maintained. After all the adjustments are made, the United States will not have a payments deficit, and Britain will not have a payments surplus.

The gold standard thus has the advantage of stable exchange rates and automatic correction of balance of payments deficits and surpluses. However, its critical drawback is that nations must accept domestic adjustments in such distasteful forms as unemployment and falling incomes, on the one hand, or inflation, on the other hand. Under this system, a nation's money supply is altered by changes in supply and demand in currency markets. Under the gold standard, nations cannot set their own money supply in their own national interest. If the United States, for example, was experiencing declining output and incomes, the loss of gold under the gold system would reduce the U.S. money supply, which might cause higher interest rates, lower borrowing and spending, and cause further declines in output and income.

Demise of the Gold Standard   The worldwide depression in the 1930s led to the collapse of the gold standard. As domestic outputs and employment fell worldwide, the restoration of prosperity became the primary goal of afflicted nations. These nations enacted protectionist measures to reduce imports. The idea was to expand consumption of domestically produced goods and get their economies moving again. To make their exports less expensive abroad, many nations redefined their currencies at lower levels in terms of gold. For example, a country previously defining the value of its currency at 1 unit = 25 ounces of gold might redefine it as 1 unit = 10 ounces of gold. Such redefining is an example of **devaluation**— a deliberate action by government to reduce the international value of its currency. A series of such devaluations in the 1930s meant that exchange rates were no longer fixed; a major tenet of the gold standard was violated, and the system broke down.

The Bretton Woods System

The Great Depression and World War II left world trade and the world monetary system in shambles. To lay the groundwork for a new international monetary system, an international conference of nations was held at Bretton Woods, New Hampshire, in 1944. The conference produced a commitment to a modified fixed exchange-rate system called an *adjustable-peg system*, or, simply, the **Bretton Woods system.** The new system sought to capture the advantages of the old gold standard (fixed exchange rate) while avoiding its disadvantages (painful domestic macroeconomic adjustments).

Furthermore, the conference created the **International Monetary Fund** (IMF) to make the new exchange-rate system feasible and workable. The new international monetary system managed through the IMF prevailed with modifications until 1971. (The IMF still plays a basic role in international finance; in recent years it has performed a major role in providing loans to developing countries and to economies making transitions to capitalism.)

IMF and Pegged Exchange Rates   How did the adjustable-peg system of exchange rates work? First, as with the gold standard, each IMF member had to define its currency in terms of gold (or dollars), thus establishing rates of exchange between its currency and the currencies of all other members. In addition, each nation was obligated to keep its exchange rate stable with respect to every other currency. To do so, nations would have to use their official currency reserves to intervene in foreign exchange markets.

Assume again that the U.S. dollar and the British pound were "pegged" to each other at $2 = £1. Now again suppose that the demand for pounds temporarily increases so that a shortage of pounds occurs in the United States (the United States has a balance of payments deficit). How can the United States keep its pledge to maintain a $2 = £1 exchange rate when the new equilibrium rate is, say, $3 = £1? The United States can supply additional pounds to the exchange market, increasing the supply of pounds such that the equilibrium exchange rate falls back to $2 = £1.

Under the Bretton Woods system there were three main sources of the needed pounds:

1. *Official reserves* The United States might currently possess pounds in its official reserves, as the result of past actions against the opposite exchange-market condition (payments surplus).
2. *Gold sales* The U.S. government might sell some of its gold to Britain for pounds. The proceeds would then be offered in the exchange market to augment the supply of pounds.
3. *IMF borrowing* The needed pounds might be borrowed from the IMF. Nations participating in the Bretton Woods system were required to make contributions to the IMF based on the size of their national income, population, and volume of trade. If necessary, the United States could borrow pounds on a short-term basis from the IMF by supplying its own currency as collateral.

Fundamental Imbalances: Adjusting the Peg

The Bretton Woods system recognized that from time to time a nation may be confronted with persistent and sizable balance of payments problems which cannot be corrected through the means listed above. In these cases, the nation would eventually run out of official reserves and be unable to maintain its fixed exchange-rate system. The Bretton Woods remedy was correction by devaluation, that is, by an "orderly" reduction of the nation's pegged exchange rate. Also, the IMF allowed each member nation to alter the value of its currency by 10 percent, on its own, to correct a so-called fundamental (persistent and continuing) balance of payments deficit. Larger exchange-rate changes required the permission of the Fund's

board of directors. By requiring approval of significant rate changes, the Fund guarded against arbitrary and competitive currency devaluations by nations seeking only to boost output in their own countries at the expense of other countries. In our example, devaluation of the dollar would increase U.S. exports and lower U.S. imports, correcting its persistent payments deficit.

Demise of the Bretton Woods System Under this adjustable-peg system, gold and the dollar came to be accepted as international reserves. The acceptability of gold as an international medium of exchange derived from its earlier use under the gold standard. The dollar became accepted as international money because the United States had accumulated large quantities of gold, and between 1934 and 1971 it maintained a policy of buying gold from, and selling gold to, foreign governments at a fixed price of $35 per ounce. The dollar was convertible into gold on demand; thus the dollar came to be regarded as a substitute for gold, or "as good as gold." And, since the discovery of new gold was limited, the growing volume of dollars helped provide a medium of exchange for the expanding world trade.

But a major problem arose. The United States experienced persistent payments deficits throughout the 1950s and 1960s. These deficits were financed in part by U.S. gold reserves, but mostly by payment of U.S. dollars. As the amount of dollars held by foreigners soared and the U.S. gold reserves dwindled, other nations began to question whether the dollar was really "as good as gold." The U.S. ability to continue to convert dollars into gold at $35 per ounce became increasingly doubtful, as did the role of dollars as international monetary reserves. Thus the dilemma was: To maintain the dollar as a reserve medium, the U.S. payment deficit had to be eliminated. But elimination of the payments deficit would remove the source of additional dollar reserves and thus limit the growth of international trade and finance.

The problem came to a head in 1971 when the United States ended its 37-year-old policy of exchanging gold for dollars at $35 per ounce. It severed the link between gold and the international value of the dollar, thereby "floating" the dollar and letting its value be determined by market forces. The floating of the dollar in effect withdrew U.S. support from the Bretton Woods system of fixed exchange rates and sounded the system's death knell.

The Current System: The Managed Float

The current international exchange-rate system (1971–present) is an "almost" flexible system called **managed floating exchange rates.** Exchange rates among major currencies are free to float to their equilibrium market levels, but nations occasionally intervene in the foreign exchange market to stabilize or alter market exchange rates.

Normally, the major trading nations allow their exchange rates to float up or down to equilibrium levels based on supply and demand in the foreign exchange market. They recognize that changing economic conditions among nations require continuing changes in equilibrium exchange rates to avoid persistent payments deficits or surpluses. They rely on freely operating foreign exchange markets to accomplish the necessary adjustments. The result has been considerably more volatile exchange rates than during the Bretton Woods era (see Global Perspective 21-2).

But nations also recognize that some trends in the movement of equilibrium exchange rates may be at odds with national or international objectives. On occasion, nations therefore intervene in the foreign exchange market by buying or selling large amounts of specific currencies. This way, they can "manage" or stabilize exchange rates by influencing currency demand and supply.

For example, in 1987 the Group of Seven industrial nations (G-7 nations)—the United States, Germany, Japan, Britain, France, Italy, and Canada—

GLOBAL PERSPECTIVE 21-2

Changes in exchange rates relative to the dollar

The floating exchange rate system (managed float) introduced in 1971 has produced far more volatile exchange rates than those produced during the earlier Bretton Woods era. (Here, changes in the index show changes in each nation's dollar exchange rate relative to the dollar exchange rate which existed in 1948.)

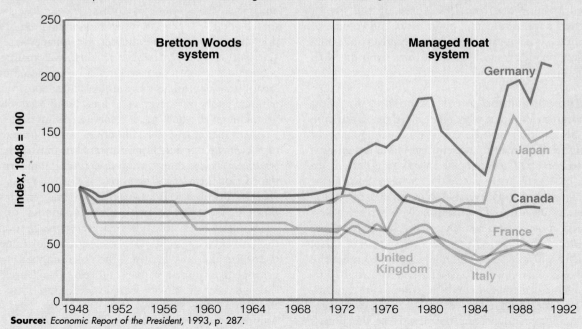

Source: *Economic Report of the President,* 1993, p. 287.

agreed to stabilize the values of the dollar. During the previous 2 years the dollar had declined rapidly because of large U.S. trade deficits. Although the U.S. trade deficits remained sizable, the G-7 nations concluded that further dollar depreciation might disrupt economic growth in member nations (other than the United States). The G-7 nations therefore purchased large amounts of dollars to boost the dollar's value. Since 1987 the G-7 nations (now G-8 with the addition of Russia) have periodically intervened in foreign exchange markets to stabilize currency values.

The current exchange-rate system is thus an "almost" flexible exchange-rate system. The "almost" mainly refers to the periodic currency interventions by governments; it also refers to the fact that the actual system is more complicated than described. While the major currencies—dollars, marks, pounds, yen, and the like—fluctuate in response to changing supply and demand, some of the European nations have tried to peg their currencies to one another. Also, many developing nations peg their currencies to the dollar and allow their currencies to fluctuate with it against other currencies. Finally, some nations peg the value of their currencies to a "basket" or group of other currencies.

How well has the managed float worked? It has both proponents and critics.

In Support of the Managed Float
Proponents argue that the managed float system has functioned well—far better than anticipated. Skeptics had predicted that fluctuating exchange rates would reduce world trade and finance. But in real terms world trade under the managed float has grown at about the same rate as during the 1960s under the Bretton Woods system of the fixed exchange rates. Moreover, as supporters are quick to point out, the currency crises in Mexico and Southeast Asia in the last half of the 1990s were not the result of the floating exchange-rate system itself. Rather, the abrupt currency devaluations and depreciations resulted from internal problems in those nations, in conjunction with the nations' tendency to peg their currencies to the dollar or to a basket of currencies. In some cases, flexible exchange rates would have made these adjustments far more gradual.

Proponents also point out that the managed float has weathered severe economic turbulence which might have caused a fixed-rate system to break down. Such events as extraordinary oil price increases in 1973–1974 and again in 1981–1983, inflationary recessions in several nations in the mid-1970s, major national recessions in the early 1980s, and large U.S.

budget deficits in the 1980s and the first half of the 1990s all caused substantial imbalances in international trade and finance. Flexible rates allowed the system to adjust to these developments, whereas the same events would have put unbearable pressures on a fixed-rate system.

Concerns with the Managed Float
There is still much sentiment in favor of greater exchange-rate stability. Those favoring stable exchange rates see problems with the current system. They argue that exchange rates have been excessively volatile under the managed float; this volatility threatens the continued expansion of international investment and trade. Moreover, some volatility has occurred even when underlying economic and financial conditions have been relatively stable, suggesting that speculation is playing too large a role in determining exchange rates. Perhaps more importantly, assert the critics, the managed float has not eliminated trade imbalances, as flexible rates are supposed to do. Thus, the United States has run persistent trade deficits for many years, while Germany and Japan have had persistent surpluses. Changes in exchange rates between dollars, marks, and yen have not yet corrected these imbalances, as is supposed to be the case under flexible exchange rates.

Skeptics say the managed float is basically a "non-system"; the guidelines concerning what each nation may or may not do with its exchange rates are not specific enough to keep the system working in the long run. Nations inevitably will be tempted to intervene in the foreign exchange market, not merely to smooth out short-term fluctuations in exchange rates but to prop up their currency if it is chronically weak or to manipulate the exchange rate to achieve domestic stabilization goals.

Flexible exchange rates have not worked perfectly, but they have not failed miserably. Thus far they have *survived*, and no doubt *eased*, several major shocks to the international trading system. Meanwhile, the "managed" part of the float has given nations some sense of control over their collective economic destinies. On balance, most economists favor continuation of the present system of "almost" flexible exchange rates.

by tying their stocks of money to gold, and by allowing gold to flow between nations when balance of payments deficits and surpluses occurred.

■ The Bretton Woods exchange-rate system (1944–1971) fixed or pegged short-run exchange rates but permitted orderly long-run adjustments of the pegs.

■ The managed floating system of exchange rates (1971–present) relies on foreign exchange markets to establish equilibrium exchange rates. The system also permits nations to buy and sell foreign currency to stabilize short-term changes in exchange rates or to correct exchange-rate imbalances which are negatively affecting the world economy.

RECENT U.S. TRADE DEFICITS

Figure 21-5 reveals that U.S. trade and current account deficits in the 1990s have been large and persistent. For example, the goods trade deficit for 1997 was $199 billion. That year, the goods and services deficit was $114 billion, and the current account deficit was $166 billion.

Causes of the Trade Deficit

There are several reasons for these persistent trade deficits. First, since 1992 the U.S. economy has grown more rapidly than the economies of several major trading nations. This growth of income has boosted U.S. purchases of foreign goods (U.S. imports). In contrast, Japan, some European nations, and Canada have suffered recession or slow income growth during this period. Thus, their purchases of U.S. goods (U.S. exports) have not kept pace with the rise of U.S. imports. Persistent U.S. trade imbalances with Japan are particularly noteworthy.

Second, until recently the United States had large annual Federal budget deficits. These deficits required the Federal government to compete with the private sector for financing, which bid up real interest rates. The high real interest rates increased the foreign demand for dollars. The resulting high international value of the dollar made U.S. exports more expensive to foreigners and U.S. imports cheaper to consumers.

Finally, a declining saving rate in the United States has contributed to U.S. trade deficits. The saving rate (saving/total income) in the United States has declined at the same time the investment rate (investment/total income) has remained stable or even

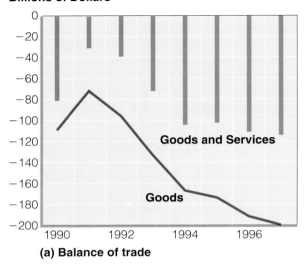

(a) Balance of trade

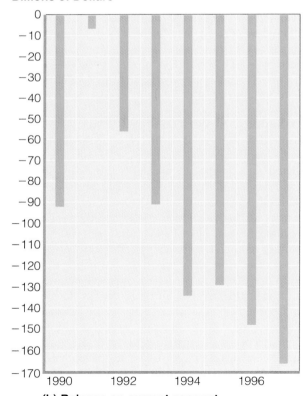

(b) Balance on current account

FIGURE 21-5 Recent U.S. Trade Deficits U.S. trade deficits in (a) "goods" and "goods and services" and (b) the current account recently have been very large. (*Source:* U.S. Department of Commerce.)

increased. The gap has been met through foreign purchases of U.S. real and financial assets, creating a large capital account surplus. Because foreigners are financing more of U.S. investment, U.S. citizens are able to save less and consume more, including consumption of imported goods. That is, the capital account surplus may partly cause the trade deficit, not simply result from it.

Implications of U.S. Trade Deficits

Are large trade deficits something that should concern the United States? There is disagreement on this issue, but most economists see both benefits and costs to trade deficits.

Increased Current Consumption   At the time a trade or current account deficit is occurring, U.S. consumers benefit. A trade deficit means that the United States is receiving more goods and services as imports from abroad than it is sending out as exports. Taken alone, a trade deficit allows the United States to consume outside its production possibilities curve; a trade deficit augments the domestic standard of living. But as we will see next, there is a catch: The gain in present consumption comes at the expense of reduced future consumption.

Increased U.S. Indebtedness   A trade deficit is considered "unfavorable" because it must be financed by borrowing from the rest of the world, selling off assets, or dipping into foreign currency reserves. Recall that current account deficits are financed primarily by net inpayments of foreign currencies to the United States. When U.S. exports are insufficient to finance U.S. imports, the United States increases both its debt to people abroad and the value of foreign claims against assets in the United States. Financing of the U.S. trade deficit has resulted in a larger foreign accumulation of claims against U.S. financial and real assets than the U.S. claim against foreign assets. Today, the United States is the world's largest debtor nation. In 1996, foreigners owned $831 billion more of U.S. assets (corporations, land, stocks, bonds, loan notes) than the United States owned in foreign assets.

Just one implication is that the United States no longer has its once-large net inflow of dividend and interest payments (item 7 in Table 21-1) to help offset its trade deficits in its goods and services trade. That amount, as high as $30 billion in the early 1980s, is now approaching zero. Another implication is that if the United States wants to *regain* ownership of these domestic assets, at some future time it will have to export more than it imports. At that time, domestic consumption will be lower because the United States will need to send more of its output abroad than it receives as imports. Therefore, the current consumption gains delivered by U.S. trade deficits mean permanent debt, permanent foreign ownership, or large sacrifices of future consumption.

CHAPTER SUMMARY

1. U.S. exports create a foreign demand for dollars and make a supply of foreign exchange available to the United States. Conversely, U.S. imports create a demand for foreign exchange and make a supply of dollars available to foreigners. Generally, a nation's exports earn the foreign currencies needed to pay for its imports.

2. The balance of payments records all international trade and financial transactions taking place between a given nation and the rest of the world. The trade balance compares exports and imports of goods. The balance on goods and services compares exports and imports of both goods and services. The current account balance includes not only goods and services transactions but also net investment income and net transfers.

3. A deficit in the current account may be offset by a surplus in the capital account. Conversely, a surplus in the current account may be offset by a deficit in the capital account. A balance of payments deficit occurs when the sum of the current and capital accounts is negative. Such a deficit is financed with official reserves. A balance of payments surplus occurs when the sum of the current and capital accounts is positive. A payments surplus results in an increase in official reserves. The desirability of a balance of payments deficit or surplus depends on its size and its persistence.

4. Flexible or floating exchange rates between international currencies are determined by the demand for and supply of those currencies. Under floating rates a currency

Speculation in Currency Markets

Are speculators a negative or a positive influence in currency markets and international trade?

Most people buy foreign currency to facilitate the purchase of goods or services from another country. A U.S. importer buys Japanese yen to purchase Japanese autos. A Hong Kong financial investor purchases Australian dollars to invest in the Australian stock market. But there is another group of participants in the currency market—speculators—that buys and sells foreign currencies in the hope of reselling or rebuying them later at a profit.

1. Contributing to Exchange-Rate Fluctuations Speculators were much in the news in late 1997 and 1998 when they were widely accused of driving down the values of the South Korean won, Thailand baht, Malaysian ringgit, and Indonesian rupiah. The value of these currencies fell by as much as 50 percent within 1 month, and speculators undoubtedly contributed to the swiftness of these declines. The expectation of currency depreciation (or appreciation) can be self-fulfilling. If speculators, for example, expect the Indonesian rupiah to be devalued or to depreciate, they quickly sell rupiah and buy currencies which will increase in relative value. The sharp increase in the supply of rupiah indeed reduces its value; this reduction then may trigger further selling of rupiah in expectation of further declines in its value.

But changed economic realities, not speculation, are normally the *underlying* causes of changes in currency values. That was largely the case with the Southeast Asian countries in which actual and threatened bankruptcies in the financial and manufacturing sectors undermined confidence in the strength of the currencies. Anticipating the eventual declines in currency values, speculators simply hastened that decline. That is, the declines in value probably would have occurred with or without speculators.

Moreover, on a day-to-day basis, speculation clearly has positive effects in foreign exchange markets.

2. Smoothing Out Short-Term Fluctuations in Currency Prices When temporarily weak demand or strong supply reduces a currency's value, speculators quickly buy the currency, adding to its demand and strengthening its value. When temporary strong demand or weak supply increases a currency's value, speculators sell the currency. This selling increases the supply of the currency and reduces its value. In this way speculators smooth out supply and demand, and thus exchange rates, over short time periods. This day-to-day exchange-rate stabilization aids international trade.

3. Absorbing Risk Speculators also absorb risk which others do not want to bear. Because of potential adverse changes in exchange rates, international transactions are riskier than domestic transactions. Suppose AnyTime, a hypothetical retailer, signs a contract with a German manufacturer to buy 10,000 German clocks to be delivered in 3 months. The stipulated price is 75 marks per clock,

will depreciate or appreciate as a result of changes in tastes, relative income changes, relative price changes, relative changes in real interest rates, and speculation.

5. The maintenance of fixed exchange rates requires adequate reserves to accommodate periodic payments deficits. If reserves are inadequate, nations must invoke protectionist trade policies, engage in exchange controls, or endure undesirable domestic macroeconomic adjustments.

6. The gold standard, a fixed rate system, provided exchange-rate stability until its disintegration during the 1930s. Under this system, gold flows between nations precipitated sometimes painful changes in price, income, and employment levels in bringing about international equilibrium.

7. Under the Bretton Woods system, exchange rates were pegged to one another and were stable. Participating

nations were obligated to maintain these rates by using stabilization funds, gold, or loans from the IMF. Persistent or "fundamental" payments deficits could be resolved by IMF-sanctioned currency devaluations.

8. Since 1971 the world's major nations have used a system of managed floating exchange rates. Rates are generally set by market forces, although governments intervene with varying frequency to alter their exchange rates.

9. The United States has experienced large trade deficits in the 1990s. Causes include: **(a)** faster growth of U.S. income than in some European nations, Canada, and Japan, resulting in expanding U.S. imports; **(b)** until recently, large U.S. budget deficits, resulting in high real interest rates, a strong dollar, and expanding U.S. imports; and **(c)** a declining U.S. saving rate which has produced a large capital account surplus and freed U.S. income for spending on imports.

which in dollars is $50 per clock at the present exchange rate of $1 = 1.5 marks. AnyTime's total bill for the 10,000 clocks will be $500,000 (= 750,000 marks).

But if the German mark were to appreciate, say, to $1 = 1 mark, the dollar price per clock would rise from $50 to $75 and AnyTime would owe $750,000 for the clocks (= 750,000 marks). AnyTime may reduce the risk of such an unfavorable exchange-rate fluctuation by *hedging* in the *futures market*. Hedging is an action by a buyer or seller to protect against a change in future prices. The futures market is a market in which currencies are bought and sold at prices fixed now, for delivery at a specified date in the future.

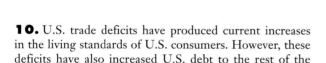

AnyTime can purchase the needed 750,000 marks at the current $1 = 1.5 marks exchange rate, but with delivery in 3 months when the German clocks are delivered. And here is where speculators come in. For a price determined in the futures market, they agree to deliver the 750,000 marks to AnyTime in 3 months at the $1 = 1.5 marks exchange rate, regardless of the exchange rate then. The speculators need not own marks when the agreement is made. If the German mark *depreciates* to, say, $1 = 2 marks in this period, the speculators profit. They can

buy the 750,000 marks stipulated in the contract for $375,000, pocketing the difference between that amount and the $500,000 AnyTime has agreed to pay for the 750,000 marks. If the German mark *appreciates*, the speculators, but not AnyTime, suffer a loss.

The amount AnyTime must pay for this "exchange-rate insurance" will depend on how the market views the likelihood of the mark depreciating, appreciating, or staying constant over the 3-month period. As in all competitive markets, supply and demand determines the price of the futures contract.

The futures market thus eliminates much of the exchange-rate risk associated with buying foreign goods for future delivery. Without it, AnyTime might have decided against importing German clocks. But the futures market and currency speculators greatly increase the likelihood that the transaction will occur. Operating through the futures market, speculation promotes international trade.

In short, although speculators in currency markets occasionally contribute to swings in exchange rates, on a day-to-day basis they play a positive role in currency markets.

10. U.S. trade deficits have produced current increases in the living standards of U.S. consumers. However, these deficits have also increased U.S. debt to the rest of the world and have resulted in greater foreign ownership of assets in the United States.

TERMS AND CONCEPTS

balance of payments
current account
trade balance
balance on goods and
   services
balance on current
   account

capital account
balance on capital account
official reserves
balance of payments
   deficits and surpluses
flexible or floating
   exchange-rate system

fixed exchange-rate
   system
purchasing power parity
   theory
gold standard
devaluation

Bretton Woods system
International Monetary
   Fund
managed floating
   exchange rates

1. Explain how a U.S. automobile importer might finance a shipment of Toyotas from Japan. Demonstrate how a U.S. export of machinery to Italy might be financed. Explain: "U.S. exports earn supplies of foreign currencies that Americans can use to finance imports."

2. KEY QUESTION Indicate whether each of the following creates a demand for, or a supply of, French francs in foreign exchange markets:
   a. A U.S. importer purchases a shipload of Bordeaux wine.
   b. A French automobile firm decides to build an assembly plant in Los Angeles.
   c. A U.S. college student decides to spend a year studying at the Sorbonne.
   d. A French manufacturer ships machinery from one French port to another on a Liberian freighter.
   e. The U.S. economy grows faster than the French economy.
   f. A U.S. government bond held by a French citizen matures and the loan amount is paid back to that person.
   g. It is widely believed that the international value of the franc will fall in the near future.

3. KEY QUESTION Alpha's balance of payments data for 1998 are shown below. All figures are in billions of dollars. What are **(a)** the balance of trade, **(b)** the balance on goods and services, **(c)** the balance on current account, and **(d)** the balance on capital account? Does Alpha have a balance of payments deficit or surplus? Explain.

Goods exports	+$40	Net transfers	+$10
Goods imports	− 30	Foreign purchases	
Service exports	+ 15	of assets in the	
Service imports	− 10	United States	+ 10
Net investment income	− 5	U.S. purchases of	
		assets abroad	− 40
		Official reserves	+ 10

4. "A rise in the dollar price of yen necessarily means a fall in the yen price of dollars." Do you agree? Illustrate and elaborate: "The critical thing about exchange rates is that they provide a direct link between the prices of goods and services produced in all trading nations of the world." Explain the purchasing power parity theory of exchange rates.

5. The Swedish auto company Saab imports car components from Germany and exports autos to the United States. In 1990 the dollar depreciated, and the German mark appreciated, relative to the Swedish krona. Speculate as to how this hurt Saab—twice.

6. KEY QUESTION Explain why the U.S. demand for Mexican pesos is downsloping and the supply of pesos to Americans is upsloping. Assuming a system of flexible exchange rates between Mexico and the United States, indicate whether each of the following would cause the Mexican peso to appreciate or depreciate:
   a. The United States unilaterally reduces tariffs on Mexican products.
   b. Mexico encounters severe inflation.
   c. Deteriorating political relations reduce American tourism in Mexico.
   d. The U.S. economy moves into a severe recession.
   e. The United States engages in a high-interest-rate monetary policy.
   f. Mexican products become more fashionable to U.S. consumers.
   g. The Mexican government encourages U.S. firms to invest in Mexican oil fields.
   h. The rate of productivity growth in the United States diminishes sharply.

7. Explain why you agree or disagree with the following statements:
   a. "A country which grows faster than its major trading partners can expect the international value of its currency to depreciate."
   b. "A nation whose interest rate is rising more rapidly than in other nations can expect the international value of its currency to appreciate."
   c. "A country's currency will appreciate if its inflation rate is less than that of the rest of the world."

8. "Exports pay for imports. Yet in 1996 the rest of the world exported about $111 billion more worth of goods and services to the United States than were imported from the United States." Resolve the apparent inconsistency of these two statements.

9. KEY QUESTION Diagram a market in which the equilibrium dollar price of one unit of fictitious currency Zee is $5 (the exchange rate is $5 = Z1). Then show on your diagram a decline in the demand for Zee.
   a. Referring to your diagram, discuss the adjustment options the United States would have in maintaining the exchange rate at $5 = Z1 under a fixed exchange-rate system.

b. How would the U.S. balance of payments surplus which is created (by the decline in demand) get resolved under a system of flexible exchange rates?

10. Compare and contrast the Bretton Woods system of exchange rates with that of the gold standard. What caused the demise of the gold standard? What caused the demise of the Bretton Woods system?

11. Describe what is meant by the term "managed float." Did the managed float system precede or follow the adjustable-peg system? Explain.

12. What have been the major causes of the large U.S. trade deficits since 1992? What are the major benefits and costs associated with trade deficits? Explain: "A trade deficit means that a nation is receiving more goods and services from abroad than it is sending abroad." How can that be called "unfavorable"?

13. (Last Word) Suppose Winter Sports—a French retailer of snowboards—wants to order 5000 snowboards made in the United States. The price per board is $200, the present exchange rate is 6 francs = $1, and payment is due in dollars when the boards are delivered in 3 months. Use a numerical example to explain why exchange-rate risk might make the French retailer hesitant to place the order. How might speculators absorb some of Winter Sports' risk?

14. WEB-BASED QUESTION U.S. International Trade in Goods and Services—Latest Figures The U.S. Census http://www.census.gov/indicator/www/ustrade.html provides the latest data on U.S. trade in goods and services. Over the past year, has the trade balance in goods and services improved (that is, yielded a smaller deficit or larger surplus) or deteriorated? The major U.S. trade strength is in which category: goods or services? The largest increases in exports were in what products? The largest increases in imports were in what products?

15. WEB-BASED QUESTION The Yen/Dollar Exchange Rate and Trade Deficits The Japanese yen/U.S.$ exchange rate is determined by market forces and changes frequently. A key determinant of exchange rates is a trade deficit or a trade surplus. Other things equal, if the United States has a trade deficit with Japan, the dollar should depreciate relative to the yen. The Federal Reserve Board of Governors http://www.bog.frb.fed.us/releases (Foreign Exchange Rates—Historical Data) provides yen/dollar exchange rates for the last decade. Trade data can be found at http://www.census.gov/indicator/www/ustrade.html under Exports, Imports, and Balance of Goods by Selected Countries. Select a time period, and compare the U.S. trade deficit with Japan with the yen/dollar exchange rate during that period. Do the data support the theory? What other factors might be influencing the yen/dollar rate?

22

The Economics of Developing Countries

It is difficult for those of us in the United States, where per capita (per person) GDP in 1997 was $27,571, to grasp the fact that some two-thirds of the world's population lives at, or perilously close to, the subsistence level. Hunger, squalor, and disease are common in many nations of the world. More than 1 billion people—about 20 percent of the world population—live on incomes of less than $2 per day.

Here we first identify the *developing countries* and discuss their characteristics. Then we discuss why these countries have such low standards of living: What obstacles have impeded their growth? Next, we examine the potentials and pitfalls of government's role in economic development. We also examine private money flows from the *advanced industrial countries* to the developing countries and assess the debt problem the developing countries face. Finally, we distill a list of possible policies which might help developing countries increase their growth rates.

THE RICH AND THE POOR

Just as there is considerable income inequality among individual families within a nation, so too is there great income inequality among the family of nations. Table 22-1 shows the remarkable degree of income differences in the world. The richest 20 percent of the world's population receive almost 83 percent of the world's income; the poorest 20 percent obtain less than 1.5 percent. The poorest 60 percent get less than 6 percent of the world's income.

Figure 22-1 helps us sort out the rich and poor by grouping high-income, middle-income, and low-income nations.

1. *Industrially advanced countries* The 26 high-income nations, shown in yellow, are known as the **industrially advanced countries (IACs);** they include the United States, Japan, Canada, Australia, New Zealand, and most of the nations of western Europe. These nations have well-developed market economies based on large stocks of capital goods, advanced production technologies, and well-educated workers. In 1995 these economies had a per capita output (or income) of $24,930.

2. *Developing countries* The remaining nations of the world, located mainly in Africa, Asia, and Latin America, are called **developing countries (DVCs).** These 107 nations have relatively low levels of industrialization. In general, literacy rates are low, unemployment is high, population growth

TABLE 22-1   **Global income disparity**

World population	Percentage of world income
Richest 20%	82.7
Second 20%	11.7
Third 20%	2.3
Fourth 20%	1.9
Poorest 20%	1.4

Source: United Nations Development Program, *Human Development Report 1992* (New York: Oxford University Press, 1992), p. 36.

is rapid, and exports consist largely of agricultural produce (such as cocoa, bananas, sugar, raw cotton) and raw materials (such as copper, iron ore, natural rubber). Capital equipment is minimal, production technologies are relatively simple, and labor productivity is very low. About three-fourths of the world's population live in these nations, all of which have widespread poverty.

Figure 22-1 breaks down these developing nations into *middle-income* and *low-income countries.* The first group of 58 middle-income DVCs (shown in purple) had an average per capita output of $2390 in 1995. Per capita output for this diverse group ranged from $766 to $9385. The other group is made up of 49 low-income DVCs (shown in red) with per capita outputs of $765 or less in 1995 and averaging only $430 that year. India, China, and the sub-Saharan nations of Africa dominate this group.

Several comparisons will bring global income differences into sharper focus.

1. In 1995, U.S. total output was approximately $6.9 trillion; the combined GDPs of the 107 DVCs in that year was only $5.5 trillion.

2. The United States, with only 5 percent of the world's population, produces one-fourth of the world's output.

3. The annual sales of the world's largest corporations exceed the GDPs of many of the DVCs. General Motors' annual world revenues are greater than the GDPs of all but 22 nations.

4. Per capita GDP in the United States is 337 times greater than in Mozambique, the world's poorest nation.

Growth, Decline, and Income Gaps

Two other things concerning Figure 22-1 should be noted. First, the various nations have demonstrated considerable differences in ability to improve their circumstances over time. On the one hand, DVCs such as China, Malaysia, Chile, and Thailand achieved high annual growth rates in their GDPs in recent decades. Consequently, their real output per capita rose several fold. Several previous DVCs such as South Korea, Singapore, and Hong Kong (now part of China) have achieved IAC-status. In contrast, many DVCs, such as those in sub-Saharan Africa, have experienced declining GDPs per capita during the past decade.

Second, the *absolute income gap* between rich and poor nations has been widening. To understand this point, suppose the per capita incomes of the advanced and developing countries were growing at about 2 percent per year. Because the income base in the advanced countries is initially much higher, the absolute income gap grows. If per capita income is $400 a year in a DVC, a 2 percent growth rate means an $8 increase in income. Where per capita income is $20,000 per year in an IAC, the same 2 percent growth rate translates into a $400 increase in income. Thus, the absolute income gap will have increased from $19,600 (= $20,000 − $400) to $19,992 (= $20,400 − $408). The DVCs must grow faster than the IACs to narrow the gap. **(Key Question 3)**

Implications

Mere statistics conceal the human implications of the extreme poverty characterizing so much of our planet:

. . . let us examine a typical "extended" family in rural Asia. The Asian household is likely to comprise ten or more people, including parents, five to seven children, two grandparents, and some aunts and uncles. They have a combined annual income, both in money and in "kind" (i.e., they consume a share of the food they grow), of from $250 to $300. Together they live in a poorly constructed one-room house as tenant farmers on a large agricultural estate owned by an absentee landlord who lives in the nearby city. The father, mother, uncle, and the older children must work all day on the land. None of the adults can read or write; of the five school-age children, only one attends school regularly; and he cannot expect to proceed beyond three or four years of primary education. There is only one meal a day; it rarely changes and it is rarely sufficient to alleviate the childrens' constant hunger pains. The house has no electricity, sanitation, or fresh water supply. There is much sickness, but qualified doctors and medical practitioners are far away in the cities attending to the needs of wealthier families. The work is

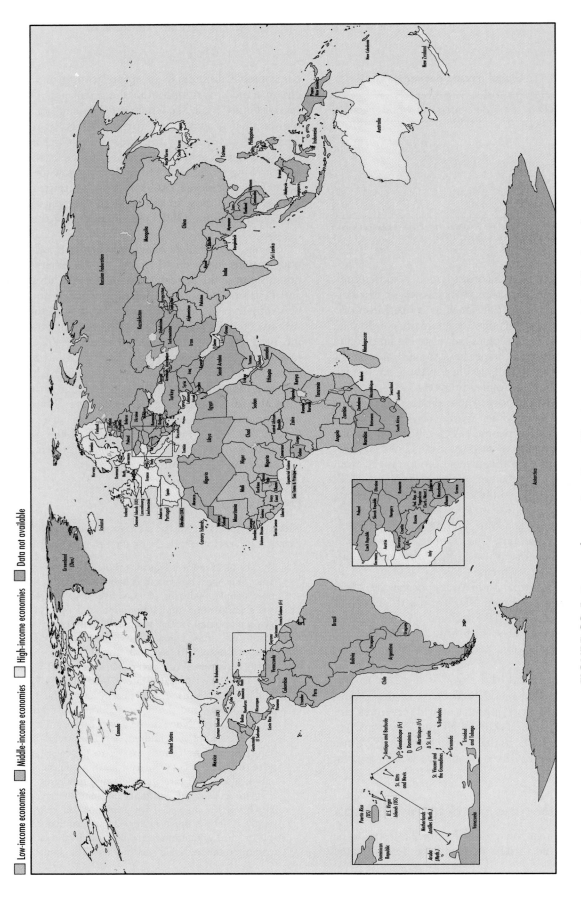

FIGURE 22-1 Groups of economies The world's nations are grouped into industrially advanced countries (IACs) and developing countries (DVCs). The IACs (shown in yellow) are high-income countries. The DVCs are middle-income and low-income countries (shown respectively in purple and in red.) (*Source:* World Bank data.)

Low-income economies
Middle-income economies
High-income economies
Data not available

hard, the sun is hot and aspirations for a better life are constantly being snuffed out. In this part of the world the only relief from the daily struggle for physical survival lies in the spiritual traditions of the people.[1]

In Table 22-2 we contrast various socioeconomic indicators for selected DVCs with those for the United States and Japan. You will see that these data confirm the major points stressed in the quotation from Todaro.

OBSTACLES TO ECONOMIC DEVELOPMENT

The paths of economic development (economic growth) are essentially the same for developing countries as for the industrially advanced economies.

1. The DVCs must use their existing supplies of resources more efficiently. This means they must eliminate unemployment and underemployment and also combine labor and capital resources efficiently to achieve lowest-cost production. The DVCs must also direct their scarce resources such that they achieve allocative efficiency.

---

[1]Michael P. Todaro, *Economic Development in the Third World*, 5th ed. (New York: Longman, 1994), p. 4.

2. The DVCs must expand their available supplies of resources. Through greater supplies of raw materials, capital equipment, and productive labor, together with improved technological knowledge, a DVC can push its production possibilities curve outward.

All DVCs are aware of these two paths. Why then have some nations successfully traveled these paths while others have lagged far behind? The difference is in the physical, human, and socioeconomic environments of the various nations.

Natural Resources

There is no simple generalization as to the role of natural resources in the economic development of DVCs because the distribution of natural resources among them is very uneven. Some DVCs have valuable deposits of bauxite, tin, copper, tungsten, nitrates, and petroleum and have been able to use their natural resource endowments to achieve rapid growth and a significant redistribution of income from the rich to the poor nations. The Organization of Petroleum Exporting Countries (OPEC) is a standard example. In other instances, natural resources are owned or controlled by the multinational corporations of industrially advanced countries, with the economic benefits from these resources largely diverted

TABLE 22-2   Selected socioeconomic indicators of development

Country	(1) Per capita output, 1995	(2) Life expectancy at birth, 1995	(3) Infant mortality per 1000 live births, 1995	(4) Adult illiteracy rate, percent, 1995	(5) Percent of labor force in agriculture, 1990	(6) Per capita energy consumption, 1994*
Japan	$39,640	80 years	4	under 5	11	3,856
United States	26,980	77	8	under 5	3	7,819
Brazil	3,640	67	44	17	23	718
Mauritania	460	51	96	—	55	103
China	620	69	34	19	74	664
India	340	62	68	48	64	248
Bangladesh	240	58	79	62	64	64
Ethiopia	100	49	112	65	80	22
Mozambique	80	47	113	60	83	40

*Kilograms of oil equivalent.
Source: World Development Report, 1997.

abroad. Furthermore, world markets for many of the farm products and raw materials which the DVCs export are subject to large price fluctuations that contribute to instability in their economies.

Other DVCs lack mineral deposits, have little arable land, and have few sources of power. Also, most of the poor countries are in Central and South America, Africa, the Indian subcontinent, and Southeast Asia, where tropical climates prevail. The hot, humid climate hinders productive labor; human, crop, and livestock diseases are widespread; and weed and insect infestations plague agriculture.

A weak resource base can be a serious obstacle to growth. Real capital can be accumulated and the quality of the labor force improved through education and training. But it is difficult to augment the natural resource base. It may be unrealistic for many of the DVCs to envision an economic destiny comparable with that of, say, the United States and Canada. But we must be careful in generalizing: Switzerland and Japan, for example, have achieved high levels of living *despite* restrictive natural resource bases.

Human Resources

Three statements describe many of the DVCs circumstances with respect to human resources:

1. They are overpopulated.
2. Unemployment and underemployment are widespread.
3. Labor productivity is low.

Overpopulation Many of the DVCs with the most meager natural and capital resources have the largest populations to support. Table 22-3 shows the high population densities and population growth rates of a few selected nations compared with those of the United States and the world.

Most important for the long run is the contrast in growth rates. The middle- and low-income DVCs in Figure 22-1 currently are experiencing a 1.6 percent annual increase in population compared with a 0.7 percent annual rate for IACs. Since such a large percentage of the world's present population already resides in DVCs, this percentage difference in population growth rates is highly significant: 9 out of every 10 people added to the world population during the next 15 years will live in developing nations. (See Global Perspective 22-1.)

Population statistics help explain why the per capita income gap between the DVCs and IACs has

TABLE 22-3 **Population statistics for selected countries**

Country	Population per square mile, 1996	Annual rate of population increase, 1990–1995
United States	75	1.0%
Pakistan	430	2.9
Bangladesh	2380	1.6
Venezuela	65	2.3
India	829	1.8
China	336	1.1
Kenya	128	2.7
Philippines	647	2.2
World	**114**	**1.5%**

Sources: Statistical Abstract of the United States, 1996; World Development Report, 1997.

widened. In some of the poorest DVCs, rapid population growth actually presses on the food supply so much that per capita food consumption falls to or below the biological subsistence level. In the worst instances, only malnutrition and disease, and the high death rate they cause keep incomes near subsistence.

It would seem at first glance that, since

$$\frac{\text{Standard}}{\text{of living}} = \frac{\text{consumer goods (food) production}}{\text{population}}$$

the standard of living could be raised by boosting consumer goods—particularly food—production. But the problem is more complex because any increase in consumer goods production which initially raises the standard of living may induce a population increase. This increase, if sufficiently large, will dissipate the improvement in living standards, and subsistence living levels will again prevail.

But why might population growth in DVCs accompany increases in output? First, the nation's *death* or *mortality rate* will decline with initial increases in production. This decline is the result of (1) a higher level of per capita food consumption and (2) the basic medical and sanitation programs which accompany the initial phases of economic development.

Second, the *birthrate* will remain high or may increase, particularly as medical and sanitation programs cut infant mortality. The cliché that "the rich get richer and the poor get children" is uncomfortably accurate for many of the poorest DVCs. An in-

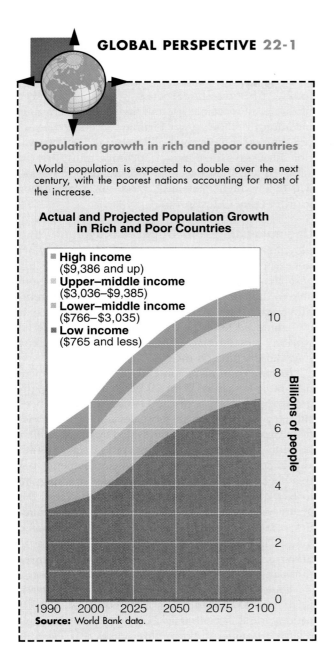

GLOBAL PERSPECTIVE 22-1

Population growth in rich and poor countries

World population is expected to double over the next century, with the poorest nations accounting for most of the increase.

Actual and Projected Population Growth in Rich and Poor Countries

- High income ($9,386 and up)
- Upper–middle income ($3,036–$9,385)
- Lower–middle income ($766–$3,035)
- Low income ($765 and less)

Billions of people

1990 2000 2025 2050 2075 2100

Source: World Bank data.

reasons why population expansion is often an obstacle to development.

Saving and Investment Large families reduce the capacity of households to save, restricting the economy's ability to accumulate capital.

Productivity As population grows, more investment is required to maintain the amount of real capital per person. If investment fails to keep pace, each worker will have fewer tools and equipment, reducing worker productivity (output per worker). Declining productivity implies stagnating or declining per capita incomes.

Resource Overuse Because most developing countries are heavily dependent on agriculture, rapid population growth may result in overuse of limited natural resources such as land. The much-publicized African famines are partially the result of past overgrazing and overplanting of land caused by the pressing need to feed a growing population. (This chapter's Last Word is relevant.)

Urban Problems Rapid population growth in the cities of the DVCs, accompanied by unprecedented flows of rural migrants, are generating massive urban problems. Substandard housing in impoverished slums, poor public services, congestion, pollution, and crime are all problems worsened by rapid population growth. The resolution or lessening of these difficulties necessitates a diversion of resources from growth-oriented uses.

Most authorities advocate birth control as the most effective means for breaking out of this dilemma. And breakthroughs in contraceptive technology in recent decades have made this solution increasingly relevant. But obstacles to population control are great. Low literacy rates make it difficult to disseminate information about contraceptive devices. In peasant agriculture, large families are a major source of labor. Adults may regard having many children as a kind of informal social security system: The more children, the greater the probability of having a relative to care for you during old age. Finally, many nations which stand to gain the most through birth control are often the least willing, for religious and sociocultural reasons, to embrace contraception programs. Population growth in Latin America, for example, is among the most rapid in the world.

China—with about one-fifth of the world's population—adopted a harsh "one-child" program in 1980.

crease in the per capita standard of living may lead to a population upsurge which will cease only when the standard of living has again been reduced to the level of bare subsistence.

In addition to the fact that rapid population growth can convert an expanding GDP into a stagnant or slow-growing GDP per capita, there are four other

The government advocated late marriages and one child per family. Couples having more than one child are fined or lose various social benefits. Even though the rate of population growth has diminished under this program, China's population continues to expand at about 100 million per decade. India, the world's second most populous nation, had a 242 million or 35 percent population increase in the 1980–1995 period. With a total population of 929 million, India has 16 percent of the world's population but less than 2.5 percent of its land mass.

Qualifications But our focus on population growth as a major cause of low incomes needs to be qualified in several ways.

As with natural resources, the relationship between population and economic growth is less clear than one might expect. A high population density and rapid population growth do not necessarily mean poverty. China and India have immense populations and are poor, but Japan and Hong Kong are densely populated and wealthy.

Also, population growth rates for the DVCs as a group have declined somewhat in recent decades. In the 1960s the annual population growth rate was about 2.0 percent; for the 1990s, it looks like it will be about 1.4 percent. Experts predict that this percentage will fall to about 1.2 percent by 2010.

Finally, there is a view contrary to the traditional one that reducing population growth is the key to increasing GDP per capita in developing countries. The **demographic transition view** holds that rising income first must be achieved; only then will slower population growth follow. This view observes there are both marginal benefits and marginal costs of having another child. In DVCs the marginal benefits are relatively large because the extra child becomes an extra worker who can help support the family. Extra children can provide financial support and security for their parents in their old age, so people in poor countries have high birthrates. But in wealthy IACs the marginal cost of children is much greater than in the DVCs. Care of children may require that one of the parents sacrifice high earnings, or there may be the need to purchase expensive childcare. Also, children require extended and expensive education for the highly skilled jobs characteristic of the IAC economies. Finally, the wealth of the IACs results in "social safety nets" which protect adults from the insecurity associated with old age and the inability to work. In this view, people in the IACs recognize that

high birthrates are not in the family's short-term or long-term interest, so they choose to have fewer children.

Note the differences in causation the two views imply. The traditional view says that reduced birthrates must come first and then higher per capita income will follow; lower birthrates are the cause of per capita income growth. The demographic transition view says that higher incomes must first be achieved and then lower rates of population growth will follow; higher incomes cause slower population growth. **(Key Question 6)**

Unemployment and Underemployment Employment-related data for many DVCs either are nonexistent or highly unreliable. But observation suggests that *unemployment* is high; many people are unable to find jobs. There is also significant **underemployment,** which means that a large number of people are employed fewer hours per week than they want, work at jobs unrelated to their training, or spend much of the time on their jobs unproductively.

Many economists contend that unemployment may be as much as 15 to 20 percent in the rapidly growing urban areas of the DVCs. There has been substantial migration in most developing countries from rural to urban areas, motivated by the *expectation* of finding jobs with higher wage rates than are available in agricultural and other rural employments. But this huge migration reduces the chance of a migrant in fact obtaining a job. Migration to the cities has greatly exceeded the growth of urban job opportunities, resulting in very high urban unemployment rates. Thus, rapid rural-urban migration has given rise to urban unemployment rates which are two or three times as great as rural rates.

Underemployment is widespread and characteristic of most DVCs. In many of the poorer developing nations, rural agricultural labor may be so abundant relative to capital and natural resources that a significant percentage of this labor contributes little or nothing to agricultural output. Similarly, many DVC workers are self-employed as proprietors of small shops, in handicrafts, or as street vendors. A lack of demand means that small shop owners or vendors spend idle time in the shop or on the street. While they are not without jobs, these people are underemployed.

Low Labor Productivity Labor productivity tends to be low in DVCs. As we will see, the developing nations have found it difficult to invest in *physical capi-*

tal. As a result, their workers are underequipped with machinery and tools and hence are relatively unproductive. Keep in mind that rapid population growth tends to reduce the amount of physical capital available per worker, which decreases labor productivity and real incomes.

In addition, most poor countries have not been able to invest sufficiently in their *human capital* (see Table 22-2, columns 3 and 4); that is, expenditures on health and education have been meager. Low levels of literacy, malnutrition, lack of proper medical care, and insufficient educational facilities all contribute to populations which are ill-equipped for industrialization and economic expansion. Attitudes may also play a role: In some countries, hard work is associated with slavery, servitude, and inferiority, so people try to avoid it.

Particularly vital is the absence of a vigorous entrepreneurial class willing to bear risks, accumulate capital, and provide the organizational requisites essential to economic growth. Closely related is the lack of labor trained to handle the routine supervisory functions basic to any program of development. Ironically, the higher education systems of some DVCs are oriented toward the humanities and offer little work in business, engineering, and the sciences. Some DVCs are characterized by an authoritarian view of human relations—often fostered by repressive governments—which generates an environment hostile to independent thinking, taking initiatives, and assuming economic risks. Authoritarianism discourages experimentation and change—the essence of entrepreneurship.

An additional irony is that, while migration from the DVCs has modestly offset rapid population growth, it has also deprived some DVCs of highly productive workers. Often the best-trained and most highly motivated workers—physicians, engineers, teachers, and nurses—leave the DVCs to seek their fortunes in the IACs. This so-called **brain drain** contributes to the deterioration in the overall skill level and productivity of the labor force.

Capital Accumulation

An important focal point of economic development is the accumulation of capital goods, for several reasons:

1. All DVCs suffer from shortages of capital goods such as factories, machinery and equipment, and public utilities. Better-equipped labor forces would greatly enhance their productivity and help boost the per capita standard of living. There is a close relationship between output per worker (labor productivity) and real income per worker. A nation must produce more goods and services per worker to enjoy more goods and services per worker as income. One way of increasing labor productivity is to provide each worker with more tools and equipment. Indeed, studies for the DVCs confirm a positive relationship between investment and the growth of GDP. On the average, a 1 percentage point increase in the ratio of investment to GDP raises the overall growth rate by about one-tenth of 1 percentage point. Thus an increase in the investment-to-GDP ratio from 10 to 15 percent would increase the growth of real GDP by one-half of 1 percentage point.[2]

2. Increasing the stock of capital goods is crucial because of the very limited possibility of increasing the supply of arable land. If there is little likelihood of increasing agricultural output by increasing the supply of land, an alternative is to use more and better capital equipment with the available agricultural workforce.

3. Once initiated, the process of capital accumulation *may* be cumulative. If capital accumulation can increase output faster than population grows, a margin of saving may arise which permits further capital formation. In a sense, capital accumulation can feed on itself.

Let's first consider the prospects for developing nations to accumulate capital domestically. Then we will examine the possibility of foreign funds flowing into them to support expansion of capital.

Domestic Capital Formation

A developing nation, as does any nation, accumulates capital through saving and investing. A nation must save (refrain from consumption) to release resources from production of consumer goods. Investment spending must then absorb these released resources in the production of capital goods. But impediments to saving and investing are much greater in a low-income nation than in an advanced economy.

Savings Potential Consider first the savings side of the picture. The situation here is mixed and varies

_____

[2] International Monetary Fund, *World Economic Outlook* (Washington, 1988), p. 76.

greatly between countries. Some of the very poor countries, such as Ethiopia, Bangladesh, Uganda, Haiti, and Madagascar, save only 2 to 5 percent of their GDPs. The people are simply too poor to save a significant portion of their incomes. Interestingly, however, other developing countries save as large a percentage of their domestic outputs as do advanced industrial countries. In 1995 India and China saved 22 and 42 percent of their domestic outputs, respectively, compared to 29 percent for Japan, 23 percent for Germany, and 15 percent for the United States. The problem is that the domestic outputs of the DVCs are so low that even when saving rates are comparable to advanced nations, the total absolute volume of saving is not large.

Capital Flight Some of the developing countries have suffered **capital flight,** the transfer of private DVC savings to accounts held in the IACs. (In this usage, "capital" is simply "money," "money capital," or "financial capital.") Many wealthy citizens of DVCs have used their savings to invest in the more economically advanced nations, allowing them to avoid the high investment risks at home, such as loss of saving or real capital from government expropriation, abrupt changes in taxation, potential hyperinflation, or high volatility of exchange rates. If a DVC's political climate is unsettled, savers may shift their funds overseas to a "safe haven" in fear that a new government might confiscate their wealth. Likewise, rapid or skyrocketing inflation in a DVC would have similar detrimental effects. The transfer of saving overseas may also be a means of evading high domestic taxes on interest income or capital gains. Finally, money capital may flow to the IACs, where there are higher interest rates or a greater variety of investment opportunities.

Whatever the motivation, the amount of capital flight from some nations is significant. This outflow of money capital offsets a considerable portion of the IACs' lending and giving of money capital to the developing nations.

Investment Obstacles There are as many obstacles on the investment side of capital formation in DVCs as on the saving side. These investment obstacles involve a lack of investors and a lack of incentives to invest.

In some developing nations, the major obstacle to investment is the lack of entrepreneurs who are willing to assume the risks associated with investment.

This is a special case of the qualitative limitations of the labor force previously discussed.

But the incentive to invest may be weak even if substantial saving and a large number of willing entrepreneurs are present. Several factors may combine in a DVC to reduce investment incentives. In our discussion of capital flight we mentioned such factors as political instability and higher rates of inflation. Similarly, very low incomes in a DVC result in a limited domestic market, meaning a lack of buying power and thus weak demand for all but agricultural goods. This factor is crucial because the chances of successfully competing with mature industries in the IACs in the international market are slim. Then, too, lack of trained administrative personnel may be a factor in retarding DVC investment.

Finally, many DVCs simply do not have an adequate **infrastructure** (stock of public capital goods), which is necessary for achieving adequate returns on private investment. Poor roads and bridges, inadequate railways, little gas and electricity production, poor communications, unsatisfactory housing, and meager educational and public health facilities create an inhospitable environment for private investment. Much of any new private investment would have to be for the infrastructure needed by all firms. Rarely can firms provide such infrastructure themselves and still earn a positive return on their overall investment.

For all these reasons, investment incentives in many DVCs are lacking. It is significant that for multinational firms, about four-fifths of their overseas investments goes to IACs.

How then can developing nations build up the infrastructure necessary to attract investment? The higher-income DVCs may be able to accomplish this through taxation and public spending. But there is little income to tax in the poorest DVCs. Nevertheless, with leadership and a willingness to cooperate, a poor DVC can accumulate capital by transferring surplus agricultural labor to the improvement of the infrastructure. If each agricultural village allocated its surplus labor to the construction of irrigation canals, wells, schools, sanitary facilities, and roads, significant amounts of capital might be accumulated at no significant sacrifice of consumer goods production. Such investment simply bypasses the problems inherent in the financial aspects of the capital accumulation process. It does not require consumers to save portions of their money income, nor does it presume the presence of an entrepreneurial class anxious to invest. When leadership and cooperative spirit are present, this "in-kind" investment is a promising avenue for accumulation of basic capital goods. **(Key Question 7)**

Technological Advance

Technological advance and capital formation are frequently part of the same process. Yet there are advantages in treating technological advance and capital formation as separate processes.

The rudimentary state of technology in the DVCs leaves them far from the frontiers of technological advance. But there is an enormous body of technological knowledge accumulated by the advanced nations which developing countries *might* adopt and apply without expensive research. Crop rotation and contour plowing require no additional capital equipment and may contribute significantly to productivity. By raising grain storage bins a few inches aboveground, a large amount of grain spoilage can be avoided. Such changes may sound trivial to people of advanced nations. However, resulting gains in productivity can mean the difference between subsistence and starvation in some poverty-ridden nations.

In most instances application of either existing or new technological knowledge involves new and different capital goods. But, within limits, this capital can be obtained without an increase in the rate of capital formation. If the annual flow of replacement investment is rechanneled from technologically inferior to technologically superior capital equipment, productivity can be increased out of a constant level of investment spending. Actually, some technological advances may be **capital-saving technology** rather than **capital-using technology.** A new fertilizer, better adapted to a nation's topography and climate, might be cheaper than one currently employed. A seemingly high-priced metal plow which will last 10 years may be cheaper in the long run than an inexpensive but technologically inferior wooden plow which requires annual replacement.

To what extent have DVCs transferred and effectively used available IAC technological knowledge? The picture is mixed. There is no doubt that such technological borrowing has been instrumental in the rapid growth of such Pacific Rim countries as Japan, South Korea, Taiwan, and Singapore. Similarly, the OPEC nations benefitted greatly from IAC knowledge of oil exploration, production, and refining. Recently Russia, the nations of eastern Europe, and China have been using western technology to hasten their conversions to market-based economies.

At the same time, we must be realistic about the transferability of advanced technologies to the poorest developing countries. In industrially advanced nations technologies are usually predicated on relatively scarce, highly skilled labor and relatively abundant capital. Such technologies tend to be capital-using or, alternatively stated, labor-saving. In contrast, developing economies require technologies appropriate to *their* resource endowments—abundant unskilled labor and very limited quantities of capital goods. Labor-using and capital-saving technologies are appropriate to DVCs. But much of the highly advanced technology of advanced nations is inappropriate in the developing countries; they must develop their own technologies. Recall, too, that many DVCs still have "traditional economies" and are not highly receptive to change. This is particularly true in peasant agriculture, which dominates the economies of most poorer DVCs. A potential technological advance which fails can mean hunger and malnutrition; therefore, there is a strong tendency to retain traditional production techniques.

Sociocultural and Institutional Factors

Economic considerations alone do not explain why an economy does or does not grow. Substantial social and institutional readjustments are usually an integral part of the growth process. Economic development means not only changes in a nation's physical environment (new transportation and communications facilities, new schools, new housing, new plants and equipment) but also changes in the way people think, behave, and associate with one another. Emancipation from custom and tradition is frequently a prerequisite of economic development. A critical but intangible ingredient in economic development is **the will to develop.** Economic growth may hinge on what individuals within DVCs want for themselves and their children. Do they want more material abundance? If so, do they want it badly enough to make the necessary changes in their institutions and old ways of doing things?

Sociocultural Obstacles Sociocultural impediments to growth are numerous and varied:

1. Some of the very low income countries have failed to achieve the preconditions for a national economic unit. Tribal and ethnic allegiances take precedence over national identity. Warring tribes confine all economic activity to within the tribe, eliminating any possibility for production-increasing specialization and trade. The desperate economic circumstances in Somalia, Sudan, Liberia, Zaire, and other sub-Saharan nations of Africa are due in no small measure to martial and political conflicts among rival clans.

2. The existence of a formal or informal caste system causes labor to be allocated to occupations on the basis of status or tradition rather than on the basis of skill or merit. The result is a misallocation of human resources.

3. Religious beliefs and observances may seriously restrict the length of the workday and divert resources which might have been used for investment to ceremonial uses. Some religious and philosophical beliefs are dominated by the fatalistic **capricious universe view,** that is, the notion that there is little or no correlation between an individual's activities and endeavors and the outcomes or experiences which that person encounters.

> If the universe is deemed capricious, the individual will learn to expect little or no correlation between actions and results. This will result in a fatalistic attitude . . . .
>
>   These attitudes impinge on all activities including saving, investment, long-range perspective, supply of effort, and family planning. If a higher standard of living and amassing of wealth is treated as the result of providence rather than springing from hard work and saving, there is little rationale for saving, hard work, innovations, and enterprise.[3]

Other attitudes and cultural factors may impede economic activity and growth: emphasis on the performance of duties rather than the exertion of individual initiative; the focus on group rather than individual achievement; the notion of a preordained and unalterable universe; the belief in reincarnation, which reduces the importance of one's present life.

Institutional Obstacles   Political corruption and bribery are common in many DVCs. School systems and public service agencies are often ineptly administered and their functioning impaired by petty politics. Tax systems are frequently arbitrary, unjust, cumbersome, and detrimental to incentives to work and invest. Political decisions are often motivated by a desire to enhance the nation's international prestige rather than to foster development.

---

[3]Inder P. Nijhawan, "Socio-Political Institutions, Cultural Values, and Attitudes: Their Impact on Indian Economic Development," in J. S. Uppal (ed.), *India's Economic Problems* (New Delhi: Tata McGraw-Hill Publishing Company, Ltd., 1975), p. 33.

Because of the predominance of farming in DVCs, the problem of achieving an optimal institutional environment in agriculture is a vital consideration in any growth program. Specifically, the institutional problem of **land reform** demands attention in many DVCs. But needed reform may vary tremendously between specific nations. In some DVCs the problem is excessive concentration of land ownership in the hands of a few wealthy families. This situation is demoralizing for tenants, weakening their incentive to produce, and typically does not promote capital improvements. At the other extreme is the absurd arrangement whereby each family owns and farms a minute fragment of land far too small for the application of modern agricultural technology. An important complication to the problem of land reform is that political considerations sometimes push reform in that direction which is least defensible on economic grounds. For many nations, land reform may well be the most acute institutional problem to be resolved in initiating the process of economic development.

Examples: Land reform in South Korea undermined the political control of the landed aristocracy and made way for the development of strong commercial and industrial middle classes, all to the benefit of the country's economic development. In contrast, the prolonged dominance of the landed aristocracy in the Philippines has allegedly helped stifle the development of that economy.

QUICK REVIEW 22-1

■ About three-fourths of the world's population lives in the DVCs of Africa, Asia, and Latin America.

■ Natural resource scarcities and inhospitable climates restrict economic growth in many DVCs.

■ Most of the poorest DVCs are characterized by overpopulation, high unemployment rates, underemployment, and low labor productivity.

■ Low saving rates, capital flight, weak infrastructures, and lack of investors impair capital accumulation in many DVCs.

■ Sociocultural and institutional factors are often serious impediments to growth in DVCs.

THE VICIOUS CIRCLE

Many of the characteristics of DVCs just described are simultaneously *causes* and *consequences* of their poverty. These countries are caught in a **vicious cir-**

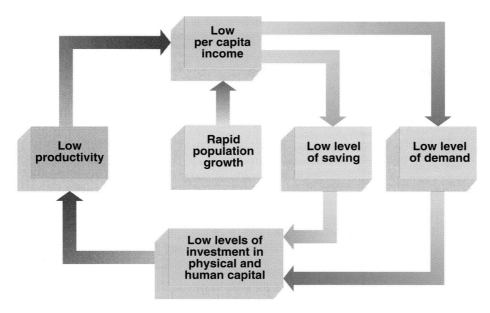

FIGURE 22-2 The vicious circle of poverty Low per capita incomes make it difficult for poor nations to save and invest, a condition which perpetuates low productivity and low incomes. Furthermore, rapid population growth may quickly absorb increases in per capita real income and thereby may negate the possibility of breaking out of the poverty circle.

----

cle of poverty. They *stay* poor because they *are* poor! Consider Figure 22-2. The fundamental feature of a DVC is low per capita income. Being poor, a family has little ability or incentive to save. Furthermore, low incomes means low levels of product demand. Thus, there are few available resources, on the one hand, and no strong incentives, on the other hand, for investment in physical or human capital, which means that labor productivity is low. And, since output per person is real income per person, it follows that per capita income is low.

Many economists think that the key to breaking out of this vicious circle is to increase the rate of capital accumulation, to achieve a level of investment of, say, 10 percent of the national income. But Figure 22-2 reminds us that rapid population growth may partially or entirely undo the potentially beneficial effects of this higher rate of capital accumulation. Suppose that initially a DVC is realizing no growth in its real GDP. But now it somehow manages to increase its saving and investment to 10 percent of its GDP. As a result, its real GDP begins to grow at, say 2.5 percent per year. With a stable population, real GDP per capita will also grow at 2.5 percent per year. If this growth persists, the standard of living will *double* in about 28 years. But what if population grows at the middle east and northern Africa rate of 2.5 percent per year? Then real income per person is unchanged and the vicious circle persists.

More optimistically, *if* population can be kept constant or constrained to some growth rate significantly below 2.5 percent, then real income per person will rise. This implies the possibility of still further enlargement in the flows of saving and investment, continued advances in productivity, and the continued growth of per capita real income. If a process of self-sustaining expansion of income, saving, investment, and productivity can be achieved, the self-perpetuating vicious circle of poverty can be transformed into a self-regenerating, beneficent circle of economic progress. The challenge is to make effective those policies and strategies which will accomplish this transition. **(Key Question 13)**

ROLE OF GOVERNMENT

Economists do not agree on the appropriate role of government in fostering DVC growth.

A Positive Role

One view is that, at least during initial stages of development, government should play a major role because of the character of the obstacles facing DVCs.

Law and Order Some of the poorest countries are plagued by banditry and intertribal warfare which divert both attention and resources from the task of development. A strong and stable national government is needed to establish domestic law and order and to achieve peace and unity. Research demonstrates that political instability (as measured by the number of revolutions and coups per decade) is associated with slow growth.

Lack of Entrepreneurship   The lack of a sizable and vigorous entrepreneurial class, ready and willing to accumulate capital and initiate production, indicates that in some DVCs, private enterprise is not capable of spearheading the growth process. Government may initially have to take the lead.

Infrastructure   Many obstacles to economic growth relate to an inadequate infrastructure. Sanitation and basic medical programs, education, irrigation and soil conservation projects, and construction of highways and transportation-communication facilities are all essentially nonmarketable goods and services yielding widespread spillover benefits. Government is the sole institution in a position to provide these public goods and services in required quantities.

Forced Saving and Investment   Government action may also be required to break through the saving-investment dilemma which impedes capital formation in DVCs.

It may be that only governmental fiscal action can provide a solution by forcing the economy to accumulate capital. There are two alternatives. One is to force the economy to save by increasing taxes. These tax revenues can then be channeled into priority investment projects. However, problems of honestly and efficiently administering the tax system and achieving a high degree of compliance with tax laws can be great.

The other alternative is to force the economy to save through inflation. Government can finance capital accumulation by creating and spending new money or by selling bonds to banks and spending the proceeds. The resulting inflation is the equivalent of an arbitrary tax on the economy.

There are serious arguments against public sector saving through inflation. First, inflation often distorts the composition of investment away from productive facilities to such items as luxury housing, precious metals and jewels, or foreign securities, which provide a better hedge against rising prices. Also, significant inflation may reduce voluntary private saving as potential savers become less willing to accumulate depreciating money or securities payable in money of declining value. Inflation also often induces capital flight. Internationally, inflation may boost the nation's imports and retard its flow of exports, creating balance of payments difficulties.

Social-Institutional Problems   Government is in the key position to deal effectively with the social-institutional obstacles to growth. Controlling population growth and land reform are problems which call for the broad approach only government can provide. And government is in a position to nurture the will to develop, to change a philosophy of "Heaven and faith will determine the course of events" to one of "God helps those who help themselves."

Public Sector Problems

But serious problems and disadvantages may exist with a governmentally directed development program. If entrepreneurial talent is lacking in the private sector, can we expect quality leaders in the ranks of government? Is there not a real danger that government bureaucracy will impede, not stimulate, much-needed social and economic change? And what of the tendency of some political leaders to favor spectacular "showpiece" projects at the expense of less showy but more productive programs? Might not political objectives take precedence over the economic goals of a governmentally directed development program?

Development experts are less enthusiastic about the role of government in the growth process than they were 30 years ago. Government maladministration and corruption are common in many DVCs. Government officials often line their own pockets with foreign aid funds. Similarly, political leaders frequently confer monopoly privileges on relatives, friends, and political supporters. A political leader may grant exclusive rights to relatives or friends to produce, import, or export certain products. These monopoly privileges lead to higher domestic prices for the relevant products and diminish the DVC's ability to compete in world markets. Similarly, managers of state-owned enterprises are often appointed on the basis of cronyism rather than competence. Many DVC governments, particularly in Africa, have created "marketing boards" as the sole purchaser of agricultural products from local farmers. The boards buy farm products at artificially low prices and sell the output at higher world prices; the "profit" ends up in the pockets of government officials. In recent years the perception of government has shifted from that of catalyst and promoter of growth to that of a potential impediment to development.

A Mixed Bag

It is possible to muster causal evidence on both sides of this question. Positive government contributions to development are evident in Japan, South Korea, and Taiwan. In comparison, Mobutu's Zaire, Somoza's Nicaragua, Marcos' Philippines, and Haiti under the Duvaliers are recognized examples of corrupt and inept governments which functioned as impediments to economic progress. Certainly the revolutionary transformations of the former Soviet Union and other eastern European nations away from communism and toward market-oriented economies make clear that central planning is no longer recognized as an effective mechanism for development. Many DVCs are belatedly recognizing that capitalism, with its focus on individual economic incentives and on competition, is the surest, most sustainable, avenue to economic growth.

ROLE OF ADVANCED NATIONS

How can industrially advanced nations help developing countries in their quest for growth? To what degree have IACs pursued these avenues of assistance?

Generally, developing nations can benefit from (1) an expanding volume of trade with advanced nations, (2) foreign aid in the form of grants and loans from governments of advanced nations, and (3) flows of private capital from the more affluent nations.

Expanding Trade

Some authorities maintain that the simplest and most effective way the United States and other industrially advanced nations can aid developing nations is by lowering international trade barriers. Such actions enable DVCs to expand their national incomes through increased trade.

Although there is some truth in this view, lowered trade barriers are not a panacea. Some poor nations do need only large foreign markets for their raw materials to achieve growth. But the problem for many poor nations is not one of obtaining markets to use existing production capacity or to sell relatively abundant raw materials but the more fundamental problem of getting the capital and technical assistance needed to produce something for export.

Moreover, close trade ties with advanced nations have some disadvantages. Dependence on import de-

mand from the IACs leaves DVCs vulnerable to temporary declines in the IACs' production. By reducing the demand for resources, recessions in the IACs can have disastrous consequences for the prices of raw materials and the export earnings of the DVCs. For example, during the recession in the IACs in the early 1990s, the world price of zinc fell from $.82 per pound to $.46 per pound and the world price of tin fell from $5.20 per pound to $3.50 per pound. Because mineral exports are a major source of DVC income, stability and growth in IACs are important to economic progress in the developing nations.

Foreign Aid: Public Loans and Grants

Foreign capital—both public and private—can supplement an emerging country's saving and investment and play a crucial role in breaking the circle of poverty.

As previously noted, many DVCs are lacking in the infrastructure prerequisites for attracting either domestic or foreign private capital. Foreign public aid which increases infrastructure can thus enhance the flow of private capital to the DVCs.

Direct Aid The United States and other IACs have assisted DVCs directly through a variety of programs and through participating in international institutions designed to stimulate economic development. Over the past decade, U.S. aid to the DVCs in the forms of both loans and grants averaged $10–$14 billion per year. The bulk of this aid is administered by the U.S. Agency for International Development (USAID). Some aid, however, is in the form of grants of surplus food under the Food for Peace program. Other advanced nations also have substantial foreign aid programs. In recent years foreign aid from all IACs has been about $60 billion per year.

The IACs' aid programs merit several additional comments. First, aid is typically distributed on the basis of political and military rather than economic considerations. Israel, Turkey, Egypt, and Greece are major recipients of U.S. aid at the expense of Asian, Latin American, and African nations with much lower standards of living. Second, aid from the IACs amounts to only about one-third of 1 percent of the IAC's collective GDPs (see Global Perspective 22-2). Finally, the shift of Russia and eastern Europe toward more democratic, market-oriented systems has made these nations "new players" as foreign aid recipients. The DVCs worry that IAC aid which formerly flowed

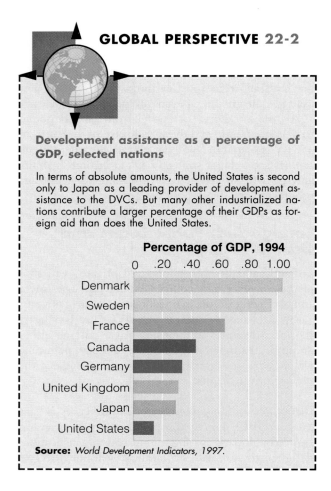

GLOBAL PERSPECTIVE 22-2

Development assistance as a percentage of GDP, selected nations

In terms of absolute amounts, the United States is second only to Japan as a leading provider of development assistance to the DVCs. But many other industrialized nations contribute a larger percentage of their GDPs as foreign aid than does the United States.

Percentage of GDP, 1994

0   .20   .40   .60   .80   1.00

Denmark
Sweden
France
Canada
Germany
United Kingdom
Japan
United States

Source: *World Development Indicators, 1997.*

2. Because many World Bank loans have been for basic development projects—dams, irrigation projects, health and sanitation programs, communications and transportation facilities—the Bank's activities help provide the infrastructure needed to encourage flows of private capital.

3. The Bank has provided technical assistance to the LDCs by helping them discover what avenues of growth seem appropriate for their economic development.

The World Bank affiliates function in areas where the World Bank has been weak. The *International Finance Corporation (IFC)* has the primary function of investing in *private* enterprises in the DVCs. The *International Development Association (IDA)* makes "soft loans" (which may not be self-liquidating) to the poorest DVCs on more liberal terms than does the World Bank.

Foreign Harm?   However, foreign aid to the DVCs has been subject to several criticisms:

Dependency and Incentives   A basic criticism is that, like domestic welfare programs, foreign aid may generate dependency rather than self-sustaining growth. It is argued that transfers of wealth from the IACs allow the DVCs to avoid the painful economic decisions, the institutional and cultural changes, and the alterations in attitudes regarding thrift, industry, hard work, and self-reliance which are needed for growth. Critics say that, after some five decades of foreign aid, the DVCs' demand for foreign aid has increased; if aid programs had been successful in promoting sustainable growth, demand should have fallen.

Bureaucracy and Centralized Government
IAC aid is given, not directly to the residents and businesses of the LDCs, but to their governments. The consequence is that aid typically generates massive, relatively unproductive government bureaucracies and centralizes government power over the economy. The stagnation and collapse of the Soviet Union and eastern Europe is evidence that market-oriented economies are much more conducive to growth and development than are centrally planned economies. Furthermore, not only does the bureaucratization of the DVCs divert valuable human resources from the private to the public sector, it shifts the nation's focus from the *production* of output and income to its *redistribution.*

to Latin America, Asia, and Africa is now redirected to, say, Poland, Hungary, and Russia. Similarly, there is the prospect of a substantially larger aid flow to the Middle East if the PLO-Israeli peace accord is durable.

The World Bank Group   The United States is a participant in the **World Bank,** whose major objective is helping DVCs achieve growth. [The World Bank was established in 1945, along with the International Monetary Fund (IMF).] Supported by nearly 180 member nations, the World Bank not only lends out of its capital funds, it also (1) sells bonds and lends the proceeds and (2) guarantees and insures private loans.

Several characteristics of the World Bank are noteworthy:

1. The World Bank is a "last resort" lending agency; its loans are limited to economic projects for which private funds are not readily available.

Corruption and Misuse Critics also allege that foreign aid is ineffectively used. Corruption is rampant in many DVCs, and some estimates suggest 10 to 20 percent of aid is diverted to government officials. Some of the wealthiest individuals in the world are rulers of DVCs. Foreign aid may create an ironic and perverse incentive for DVCs leaders to keep their populations poor so they continue to qualify for aid.

Also, IAC-based aid consultants and multinational corporations are major beneficiaries of aid programs. Some economists contend that as much as one-fourth or more of each year's aid is spent on expert consultants. Furthermore, because IAC corporations carry out most aid projects, they are major beneficiaries of, and lobbyists for, foreign aid.

The Decline of Foreign Aid
Foreign aid to developing countries is on the decline. In 1990 IACs provided $58 billion of foreign aid; by 1996 that aid had dropped to $40 billion. The criticisms of foreign aid just discussed are undoubtedly one reason for this decline. Another reason is the end of the Cold War, in which the United States and the former Soviet Union vied for the political and military allegiance of developing nations. Nations such as Cuba, Ethiopia, and North Korea which adhered to communist principles received substantial foreign aid from the Soviet Union. The United States, in turn, lavished foreign aid on developing nations such as Egypt, Mexico, Thailand, Turkey, and Chile, which tended to support U.S. policies. But with the disintegration of the former Soviet Union, the political-military rationale for foreign aid lost much of its force.

Private Capital Flows

The DVCs have also received substantial flows of *private* capital from the IACs. These private investors are corporations, commercial banks, and, more recently, financial investment companies. General Motors or Chrysler might finance construction of plants in Mexico or Brazil to assemble autos or produce auto parts. Citicorp or Bank of America might make loans to private firms operating in Argentina or China or directly to the governments of Thailand and Malaysia. And the financial investment companies Fidelity or Putnam might purchase stock of promising Hungarian and Chilean firms as part of their "emerging markets" mutual funds, which then could be purchased by individual investors in the IACs.

The DVCs' Debt Crisis of the 1980s
Private capital flows to the DVCs averaged $28 billion annually in the 1970s and increased throughout the period. Then in the 1980s several DVCs experienced a major *debt crisis:* They could not pay back their loans. This crisis was precipitated by a combination of factors:
1. Soaring prices of imported oil caused growing current account deficits in the DVCs, which financed these deficits largely through foreign borrowing.
2. In the early 1980s, a tight U.S. money policy (to control rapid inflation) had two detrimental effects on the DVCs. First, national income in the United States fell, causing a decline in U.S. imports from the DVCs. This decline sharply reduced DVC export earnings—earnings needed to pay interest and principal on their debts. Second, the high interest rates in the United States greatly increased the interest expense to the DVCs in refinancing loans from U.S. banks.
3. An appreciating dollar meant that DVCs had to pay more for their imports of U.S. goods. And because much DVC debt is denominated in dollars, it also meant that DVCs had to export a larger amount of their output to acquire each dollar needed to pay interest and principal on their debts.
4. Because of political corruption and economic mismanagement, DVC investment of loan funds was frequently unproductive. Returns on such investments were not sufficient to cover interest and principal payments, thereby generating loan defaults.

Actual defaults or near-defaults on existing loans in Mexico and several other DVCs brought an end to most of the flow of new and private foreign capital to the DVCs. A period of "muddling through" followed, in which creditor nations in cooperation with the International Monetary Fund tried to cope with the crisis on a nation-by-nation basis. The debts of many DVCs were rescheduled (stretched out over a longer period) to reduce the burden of annual interest and principal payments. And in some cases, commercial banks in the IACs had to "write off" much DVC debt as uncollectible, and thus as losses.

Reform and Revival in the 1990s
Although private capital flows to the DVCs virtually ceased in the 1980s, they have increased briskly in the 1990s. Specifically, they jumped from $50 billion in 1990 to

$250 billion in 1996. The major reason is that, as part of the debt renegotiations, heavily indebted DVCs agreed to reform their economies to promote growth and avert future debt crises. At the macro level, DVCs have made greater efforts to reduce budget deficits and control inflation. At the micro level, some governments have privatized state-owned businesses and deregulated industry. Some DVCs have reduced tariffs and adjusted unrealistically fixed exchange rates. In general, the DVCs have reduced the economic role of government and increased the role of free markets. These reforms have made the DVCs more attractive to foreign lenders.

The makeup of the revived private capital flows to the DVCs, however, is now different than before the debt crisis. First, private IAC firms and individuals, rather than commercial banks, are the primary lenders. Second, a greater proportion of the flows is now **direct foreign investment** in DVCs, rather than loans to DVC governments. Such direct investment includes the building of new factories by multinational firms in DVCs and the purchases of DVC firms (or parts of them). Whereas once DVCs viewed direct foreign investment as "exploitation," many of them now seek out direct foreign investment as a way to expand their capital stock and improve their citizen's job opportunities and wages. These wages are often very low by IAC standards but high by DVC standards. Another potential advantage of directly investing in DVCs is that management skills and technological knowledge often accompany such capital flows.

Two words of caution: The revived flow of capital is highly selective. Recently, most of the flow has been directed toward China, Mexico, Southeast Asian nations, and eastern European nations. Relatively little IAC capital is flowing toward extremely impoverished DVCs such as those in Africa.

Also, it is still premature to say that the DVC debt crisis has been totally resolved. Some developing nations still face staggering debt burdens, and there is no assurance that some combination of circumstances will not bring about future defaults. The DVC debt problem has been alleviated, not solved. For example, in 1995 the United States, other G-7 nations, and the IMF found it necessary to provide a $50 billion package of loan guarantees to offset the collapse of the Mexican peso. The immediate cause of the peso's dramatic fall was an expansion of Mexican debt in excess of export earnings. More recently, in late 1997 and early 1998 the currencies of Thailand, Malaysia, South

Korea, and Indonesia suddenly nose-dived in international value. Because most of these nations' debts are dollar-denominated, the depreciation of their currencies increased their expense of making interest and principal payments on their loans from the IACs. As in the earlier Mexican situation, the IMF coordinated multibillion dollar "financial rescue efforts" to help these countries cope with their domestic economic difficulties and to meet their financial obligations.

QUICK REVIEW 22-2

■ Governments of the DVCs may encourage growth by (a) providing law and order, (b) taking the lead in establishing enterprises, (c) improving the infrastructure, (d) forcing higher levels of saving and investing, and (e) resolving social-institutional problems.

■ The IACs can assist the DVCs through expanded trade, foreign aid, and private capital flows.

■ Many DVCs have large external debts which have become an additional obstacle to growth.

■ A decline in foreign aid to DVCs and an increase in private capital flows (particularly direct investment) have characterized the 1990s.

WHERE FROM HERE?

The developing nations face daunting tasks. There simply are no magic methods for quick economic development. Nevertheless, our discussion provided, or at least implied, several policies that DVCs and IACs might undertake to increase economic growth in the developing nations. We end this chapter by briefly summarizing these policies.

DVC Policies for Promoting Growth

Economists suggest that developing nations have several ways of enhancing their economic growth:

1. *Establishing the rule of law* Clearly defined and enforced property rights bolster economic growth by ensuring that individuals receive and retain the fruits of their labor. The rule of law also encourages direct foreign investments by firms from the IACs since legal protections reduce investment risk. Government itself must live by the law. The presence of government corruption in a sense sanctions criminality throughout the entire economic system. Such criminality undermines the growth of output because it diverts scarce resources toward activities which "transfer" income from others and away from activities which actually produce goods and services.

2. ***Opening economies to international trade*** Studies indicate that, other things equal, open economies grow as much as 1.2 percentage points per year faster than closed economies.

3. ***Controlling population growth*** Slower population growth converts increases in real output and income to increases in real output and income *per capita*. Fewer children reduce family consumption and enable family saving; smaller families also free up time for women to participate in the labor market.

4. ***Encouraging foreign direct investment*** DVCs which welcome and encourage direct foreign investment have had greater growth rates than nations which view such investment suspiciously and thus place severe obstacles in its way.

5. ***Building human capital*** Programs which increase basic literacy, education, and labor-market skills help enhance economic growth. Higher education loans and grants should contain strong incentives for recipients to remain in the home country (or return to the home country) after receiving their degrees.

6. ***Making peace with neighbors*** Countries at war or fear of war with neighboring nations divert scarce resources to armaments, rather than to, say, private capital or public infrastructure. Peace among neighboring nations can eventually lead to economic cooperation and integration, broadened markets, and enhanced growth.

7. ***Establishing independent central banks*** Hyperinflation is not conducive to economic investment and growth. DVCs can keep inflation in check by establishing independent central banks which maintain proper control over the nations' money supplies. Studies indicate that DVCs which control inflation have higher growth rates than those which do not.

8. ***Establishing realistic exchange-rate policies*** Exchange rates fixed at unrealistic levels invite balance of payments problems and speculative currency trading. Often, such trading forces a nation into abrupt revaluation of its currency, which shocks its economy. More flexible exchange rates enable more gradual adjustments and thus less susceptibility to major currency shocks and the domestic disruption they can cause.

9. ***Privatizing state industries*** Many DVCs could benefit by converting state enterprises into private firms. State enterprises often are inefficient; for example, they may be more concerned with appeasing labor unions than using modern technology and delivering goods and services at minimum per-unit cost. Also, relative to private firms, state enterprises are poor "incubators" for the development of profit-focused, entrepreneurial persons who may leave the firm to set up their own businesses.

IAC Policies for Fostering DVC Growth

What can the IACs do to improve living conditions and promote growth in the developing nations? While there is no consensus view, development economists offer a variety of suggestions, some of which we have already discussed:

1. ***Directing foreign aid to the poorest DVCs*** Much of the foreign aid from the IACs is strongly influenced by political and military considerations. Consequently, DVCs do not receive aid based on their economic needs or degree of destitution. Only one-fourth of foreign aid goes to those 10 countries whose population constitutes 70 percent of the world's poorest people. The most affluent 40 percent of the DVC population receives over twice as much aid as the poorest 40 percent. Many economists argue that the IACs should shift foreign aid away from the middle-income developing countries and toward the poorest group of DVCs.

2. ***Reducing tariffs and import quotas*** Trade barriers in the IACs are often highest for labor-intensive manufactured goods such as textiles, clothing, footwear, and processed agricultural products. These are precisely the types of goods in which DVCs have a comparative advantage. Also, many tariffs increase with the degree of product processing; for example, tariffs on chocolates are higher than on cocoa. This effectively denies the DVCs the opportunity to develop processing industries. One estimate suggests that trade barriers reduce the DVCs' gross domestic products by 3 percent, causing an annual loss of $75 billion in income. Thus, reducing such tariffs could greatly benefit the DVCs.

3. ***Providing debt relief to DVCs*** Development economists argue that, to the extent possible, the

Famine in Africa

The roots of Africa's persistent famines include both natural and human causes.

The early 1990s famine in Somalia—documented by shocking photos of fly-tormented, emaciated children with bloated bellies—is not uncommon in sub-Saharan Africa. Before U.S. armed forces and U.N. aid arrived in Somalia in late 1992, severe famine had caused an estimated 2000 deaths each day; 1 out of 4 Somali children under the age of 5—about 300,000—are believed to have died. Similarly, despite an outpouring of aid from the rich nations, the 1983–1984 Ethiopian famine caused 1 million deaths. A number of other African nations—including Ethiopia, Sudan, Angola, Liberia, Zaire, Mozambique, and Malawi—are persistently threatened by famine. Estimates put 5 to 20 million Africans at risk. This tragedy is ironic because most African countries were self-sufficient in food at the time they became independent nations; they are now heavily dependent on imported foodstuffs for survival.

The immediate cause of this catastrophe is drought. But the ultimate causes of Africa's declining ability to feed itself are more complex, an interplay of natural and human conditions. Lack of rainfall, chronic civil strife, rapid population growth, widespread soil erosion, and counterproductive public policies, all contribute to Africa's famines.

1. Civil Strife Regional rebellions and prolonged civil wars have devastated some African nations. Both Ethiopia and Sudan, for example, have been plagued by decades of civil strife. Not only do these conflicts divert precious resources from civilian uses, they also greatly complicate the ability of wealthy nations to provide famine and developmental aid. In the 1983–1984 famine the Ethiopian government denied food aid to areas occupied by rebel forces. Donated food is frequently diverted to the army and denied to starving civilians. During Ethiopia's 1973–1974 famine, Haile Selassie sold much of the donated food on world markets to enrich his regime! In Somalia, factional feuding destroyed most institutions—schools, factories, and government ministries—and reduced the country to anarchy. Armed gangs stole water pumps, tractors, and livestock from farms and looted ports of donated foodstuffs.

2. Population Growth In Africa population is growing more rapidly than is food production. Population is increasing about 3 percent per year while food output is growing only 2 percent per year. This grim arithmetic suggests declining living standards, hunger, and malnutrition. The World Bank reports that during the 1980s per capita incomes of the sub-Saharan nations fell to about three-quarters of the level reached by the end of the 1970s.

3. Ecological Degradation But apart from the simple numbers involved, population growth has contributed to the ecological degradation of Africa. With population pressures and the increasing need for food, marginal land has been deforested and put into crop production. In many

IACs should help the DVCs by stretching out payments of their debts. The present DVC debt is so large that it is a severe roadblock to DVC growth.

4. *Allowing in temporary workers while discouraging brain drains* Economists recognize that the IACs could help the DVCs by accepting more temporary workers from the DVCs. Temporary migration is not only an outlet for surplus DVC labor but also a source of income in the form of migrant remittance to their families in the home country. Also, IACs could discourage "brain drains" from the DVCs, in which the brightest and best-educated workers in the DVCs are recruited to the IACs. As you might imagine, these proposals have more support in the DVCs than in the IACs.

5. *Discouraging arms sales to the DVCs* Finally, the IACs should discourage sale of military equipment to the DVCs. Such purchases by the DVCs divert public expenditures from infrastructure and education.

cases trees which have served as a barrier to the encroachment of the desert have been cut for fuel, allowing the fragile topsoil to be blown away by desert winds. The scarcity of wood which has accompanied deforestation has forced the use of animal dung for fuel, thereby denying its traditional use as fertilizer. Furthermore, traditional fallow periods have been shortened, resulting in overplanting and overgrazing and a wearing out of the soil. Deforestation and land overuse have reduced the capacity of the land to absorb moisture, diminishing its productivity and its ability to resist drought. Some authorities feel that the diminished ability of the land to absorb water reduces the amount of moisture which evaporates into the clouds to return ultimately as rainfall. All this is complicated by the fact that there are few facilities for crop storage. Even when crops are good, it is difficult to accumulate a surplus for future lean years. A large percentage of domestic farm output in some parts of Africa is lost to rats, insects, and spoilage.

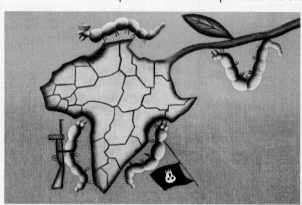

4. Public Policies and Debt Ill-advised public policies have contributed to Africa's famines. First, African governments generally have neglected investment in agriculture in favor of industrial development and military strength. It is estimated that African governments on the average spend four times as much on armaments as they do on agriculture. Second, many African governments have followed the policy of establishing the prices of agricultural commodities at low levels to provide cheap food for growing urban populations. This low-price policy has diminished farmers' incentives to increase productivity. While foreign aid has helped ease the effects of Africa's food-population problems, most experts reject aid as a long-term solution. Experience suggests that aid in the form of food can provide only temporary relief and may undermine the realization of long-run local self-sufficiency. Foreign food aid, it is contended, treats symptoms, not causes.

All this is made more complex by the fact that the sub-Saharan nations are burdened with large and growing external debts. The IMF reports that the aggregate debt of these nations rose from $84 billion in 1980 to $226 billion in 1995. As a condition of further aid, these nations have had to invoke austerity programs which have contributed to declines in their per capita incomes. One tragic consequence is that many of these nations have cut back on social service programs for children.

CHAPTER SUMMARY

1. The majority of the world's nations are developing countries (low- and middle-income nations) as opposed to high-income industrially advanced countries. While some DVCs have been realizing rapid growth rates in recent years, other have experienced little or no growth.

2. Initial scarcities of natural resources and the limited possibility of increasing existing supplies may limit a nation's ability to develop.

3. The large and rapidly growing populations in many DVCs contributes to low per capita incomes. Increases in per capita incomes frequently induce greater population growth, again reducing per capita incomes to near subsistence levels. The "demographic transition view," however, suggests that rising living standards must precede declining birthrates.

4. Most DVCs suffer from unemployment and underemployment. Labor productivity is low because of insufficient investment in physical and human capital.

5. In many DVCs, formidable obstacles impede both the saving and investment aspects of capital formation. In some of the poorest DVCs, the savings potential is very low. Many savers in DVCs transfer their funds to the IACs rather than invest domestically. The lack of a vigorous entrepreneurial class and the weakness of investment incentives also impede capital accumulation.

6. Appropriate social and institutional changes and, in particular, the presence of "the will to develop" are essential ingredients in economic development.

7. The vicious circle of poverty brings together many of the obstacles to growth, saying in effect that "poor countries stay poor because of their poverty." Low incomes inhibit saving and accumulation of physical and human capital, making it difficult to increase productivity and incomes. Rapid population growth can offset otherwise promising attempts to break the vicious circle.

8. The nature of the obstacles to growth—the absence of an entrepreneurial class, the dearth of infrastructure, the saving-investment dilemma, and the presence of social-institutional obstacles to growth—suggests a major role for government in initiating growth. However, the corruption and maladministration which are quite common to the public sectors of many DVCs suggest that government may not be very effective in instigating growth.

9. Advanced nations can assist in DVC development by reducing IAC trade barriers and by providing both public and private capital. Critics of foreign aid say that it **(a)** creates DVC dependency, **(b)** contributes to the growth of bureaucracies and centralized economic control, and **(c)** is ineffective because of corruption and mismanagement.

10. Rising energy prices, declining export prices, depreciation of the dollar, the unproductive use of borrowed funds, and concern about DVCs' creditworthiness combined to create a DVC debt crisis in the 1980s. External debt problems of many DVCs remain serious and hinder growth.

11. Economists suggest that DVCs can make future progress by establishing the rule of law, opening their economies to international trade, controlling population growth, encouraging foreign direct investment, building human capital, making peace with neighbors, establishing independent central banks, establishing realistic exchange rates, and privatizing state industries. The IACs can help in this process by directing foreign aid to the neediest nations, reducing tariffs and import quotas, providing debt relief, allowing more low-skilled immigration, and discouraging arms sales to the DVCs.

TERMS AND CONCEPTS

industrially advanced countries (IACs)	underemployment	capital-saving technology	land reform
developing countries (DVCs)	brain drain	capital-using technology	vicious circle of poverty
demographic transition view	capital flight	the will to develop	World Bank
	infrastructure	capricious universe view	direct foreign investment

STUDY QUESTIONS

1. What are the characteristics of a developing nation? List the two basic avenues of economic growth available to such a nation. State and explain obstacles that DVCs face in breaking the poverty barrier. Use the "vicious circle of poverty" concept to outline steps a DVC might take to initiate economic development.

2. Explain how the absolute per capita income gap between rich and poor nations might increase, even though per capita income (or output) is growing faster in DVCs than in IACs.

3. KEY QUESTION Assume a DVC and an IAC presently have real per capita outputs of $500 and $5000, respectively. If both nations have a 3 percent increase in their real per capita outputs, by how much will the per capita output gap change?

4. Discuss and evaluate:
   a. "The path to economic development has been clearly blazed by American capitalism. It is only for the DVCs to follow this trail."
   b. "The problem with the DVCs is that income is too equally distributed. Economic inequality promotes saving, and saving is prerequisite of investment. Therefore, greater inequality in the income distribution of the DVCs would be a spur to capital accumulation and growth."

c. "The core of economic development involves changing human beings more than it does altering a nation's physical environment."

d. "The U.S. 'foreign aid' program is a sham. In reality it represents neocolonialism—a means by which the DVCs can be nominally free in a political sense but remain totally subservient in an economic sense."

e. "The biggest obstacle facing poor nations in their quest for development is the lack of capital goods."

5. Studies indicate that, in general, landlocked countries tend to have lower per capita income levels than surrounding nations which are bordered by oceans and seas. Why do you think this is the case? Use Global Perspective 22-1 to identify a major exception to this generalization.

6. KEY QUESTION Contrast the "demographic transition view" of population growth with the traditional view that slower population growth is a prerequisite for rising living standards in the DVCs.

7. KEY QUESTION Because real capital is supposed to earn a higher return where it is scarce, how do you explain the fact that most international investment flows to the IACs (where capital is relatively abundant) rather than to the DVCs (where capital is very scarce)?

8. Do you think that the nature of the problems the DVCs face require governmentally directed as opposed to a private-enterprise-directed development process? Explain why or why not.

9. How did the DVC debt crisis of the 1980s come about? How did it get resolved?

10. What have been the trends relating to government-provided foreign aid versus private capital flows to the DVCs in the 1990s? Why do you think these trends are occurring?

11. What types of products do the DVCs typically export? How do these exports relate to the law of comparative advantage?

12. Do you think that IACs such as the United States should open their doors wider to immigration of low-skilled DVC workers to help the DVCs develop? Do you think that it is appropriate for students from DVC nations to stay in IAC nations to work and build careers?

13. KEY QUESTION Use Figure 22-2 (changing the box labels as necessary) to explain rapid economic growth in a country such as South Korea or Chile. What factors other than those contained in the figure might contribute to that growth?

14. (Last Word) Explain how civil wars, population growth, and public policy decisions have contributed to periodic famines in Africa.

15. WEB-BASED QUESTION Group of 77—Promoting the Developing World The Group of 77 (G-77) http://www.g77.org/ was established in 1964 by 77 developing countries. The Group of 77 promotes the collective economic interests of the developing world. What are the group's current developmental activities? What are the highlights in the latest *Group of 77 Journal* http://www.g77.org/Journal/message.htm?

16. WEB-BASED QUESTION The World Bank Group—What's Hot in Development Economics The major objective of the World Bank Group http://www.worldbank.org/ is to assist developing countries in achieving economic growth. What are three legs of the World Bank's development stool? What are the five agencies which make up the World Bank Group? Which one is the most influential? Go to the Development Economics section of the Topics in Development area and read the current research findings in What's Hot in Development Economics? What are the problems or opportunities, and what is the World Bank doing about them?

23

Transition Economies: Russia and China

Two of the most profound economic events of the past two decades are the collapse of communism in the Soviet Union and the rapid emergence of the market system in China. Russia (which emerged from the breakup of the Soviet Union) and China are perhaps the world's most significant developing economies: together they constitute 20 percent of the world's surface area and 24 percent of the world's population. (Global Perspective 23-1 compares salient facts about China, Russia, and the United States.)

In this final chapter, first we briefly look at the Marxian (communist) ideology which gave rise to the command economies. Then we examine the institutions and techniques of central planning common to both the Soviet Union and prereform China. Next, we discuss the coordination and incentive problems that central planning created. Finally, our attention turns to Russia and China's transitions to market economies.

IDEOLOGY AND INSTITUTIONS

To understand the command economies of the Soviet Union (prior to its collapse) and China (prior to market reforms), we must look back at the Marxian ideology which gave rise to central planning. Russia and China each have a unique history, but both nations established command economies following communist revolutions based on the ideas of Karl Marx. These revolutions established the Communist Party as the dominant force in political and economic life. The Russian revolution of 1917 resulted in a communist dictatorship under Vladimir Lenin and, later, Joseph Stalin and others. The Chinese revolution of 1947 led to a communist dictatorship under Mao Zedong. At the heart of the communist ideology was belief in state (or communal) ownership of capital and land.

The Communist Party in the Soviet Union and China viewed itself as the representative of the *proletariat* (the working class) and the *peasantry*. Based on Marxist-Leninist and Marxist-Maoist doctrines, the communists envisioned their systems as the inevitable successor to capitalism, a system they believed was plagued by internal contradictions resulting from the private ownership of capital and land. To communists, the market system was chaotic, unstable, and inequitable. Markets bred infla-

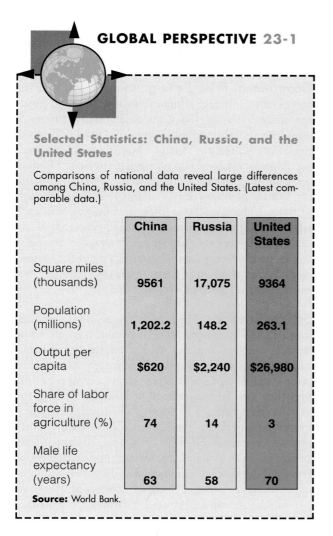

GLOBAL PERSPECTIVE 23-1

Selected Statistics: China, Russia, and the United States

Comparisons of national data reveal large differences among China, Russia, and the United States. (Latest comparable data.)

	China	Russia	United States
Square miles (thousands)	9561	17,075	9364
Population (millions)	1,202.2	148.2	263.1
Output per capita	$620	$2,240	$26,980
Share of labor force in agriculture (%)	74	14	3
Male life expectancy (years)	63	58	70

Source: World Bank.

lack bargaining power because capitalists can dismiss labor agitators and replace them from the large "reserve army of the unemployed." Capitalists exploit workers by paying them a wage far below the value of workers' production. That is, capitalists can and will expropriate the remaining fruits of workers' labor as profit, or what Marx termed **surplus value.** While all value comes from labor, in the capitalist system labor does not receive all value. In the communist planned economic system, the state as an agency of the working class would extract surplus value and distribute it in large part through subsidies for public or quasipublic goods (for example, education, transportation, health care, and housing).

The function of communism was to overthrow capitalism and replace it with a classless society void of human exploitation. The Communist Party viewed itself as the vanguard of the working class and peasantry, and its actions were held to be in keeping with the goals of those groups. In reality, the Communist Party was a strong, one-party dictatorship which often pursued the interests of it party members.

STATE OWNERSHIP AND CENTRAL PLANNING

Two major institutional characteristics of the prereform and precollapse economies of Russia and China were (1) state (government) ownership of property resources and (2) authoritarian central planning.

State Ownership **State ownership** meant that the Soviet and Chinese governments owned all land, natural resources, transportation facilities, communication networks, the banking system, and virtually all industry. Most retail and wholesale enterprises and most urban housing were also government owned. Many farms were state-owned; most, however, were government collective farms, essentially cooperatives to which the state assigned land.

Central Economic Planning **Central economic planning** meant that the two nations had centralized "command" economies functioning according to a detailed economic plan. Both economies were government-directed rather than market-directed. Choices that are made through the market in the United States and other market economies were made by bureaucratic decisions in the Soviet Union and China. Through the central 5-year or 7-year plan

tion, unemployment, discrimination, and an unfair distribution of income. In contrast, the communists viewed central planning of the economy as a way to rationally organize the economy's resources, meet basic human needs, achieve macroeconomic stability, provide greater equality, and end exploitation of labor by capitalists.

Marxists believed in a **labor theory of value,** which is the idea that the value of any good is determined solely by the amount of labor required for its production. Because of the capitalist institution of private property, Marxists argue, capitalists own the machinery and equipment necessary for production in an industrial society. The working class owns no such capital goods and therefore is dependent on capitalists for employment and its livelihood. Workers

(and its many subsets), the governments attempted to coordinate all economic activities of the economy as if they were parts of a large enterprise directed from their central headquarters.

Planning Goals and Techniques

Although central planning was far more complete in the Soviet Union than in China, each nation relied on direction from the central government. Several generalizations describe the functioning of central planning in both countries.

Industrialization (and Rural Development in China)

The former Soviet Union was dedicated to the task of rapid industrialization, economic growth, and military strength. These goals were achieved through extensive investment in heavy industry (such as steel, chemicals, and machine tools) and the allocation to the military of a large percentage of domestic output. In China, emphasis was also on rural development; for example, small-scale industries were scattered throughout the rural areas. But in both countries, the plans greatly neglected consumer goods industries and the distribution and service sectors.

Resource Overcommitment

In their efforts to increase total output (GDP), both the Soviet Union and China often overcommitted their economy's available resources. As a result, not every planning target could be achieved. In particular, the production of consumer goods suffered since planning priorities emphasized heavy industry, rural development, and the military.

Resource Mobilization

Both the Soviet Union and China initially achieved industrialization and economic growth through the mobilization of labor, capital, and raw materials. In the early years of planning there was substantial surplus labor in agriculture, which the central plans reallocated to industrial production. Similarly, both China and the Soviet Union induced or coerced a larger proportion of the population into the labor force. These countries achieved growth mainly by adding inputs rather than by using fixed amounts of inputs more productively. In the 1930s and again in the early post-World War II era, this strategy produced higher growth rates than those in the United States and other industrialized nations.

Allocation by Directives

Central planners directed the allocation of inputs among industries and firms, thereby determining the composition of output. Planning directives were substituted for the market system as an allocative mechanism.

Government Price Setting

Government, not the forces of supply and demand, set resource and product prices. Planners seldom changed the prices of consumer goods, and as a matter of social policy, the prices of "necessities" such as housing and food were set at low levels. Rents on housing in the Soviet Union, for example, averaged only 3 percent of income and did not change between 1928 and 1992. Government also determined resource prices and the prices of each firm's output. Such prices were used primarily as accounting devices to gauge a firm's progress in meeting its production goals. The emphases of the various 5- or 7-year plans were on the quantity of output, not on the cost or price of output.

Self-Sufficiency

The Soviet Union and China each viewed itself as a single socialist nation, surrounded by hostile capitalist countries. Moreover, neither communist country trusted the other. They each maintained a strong military presence along their common border, and they vied for supremacy of influence among the developing countries. Because of the hostility they perceived around them, the central plan in each country stressed economic self-sufficiency. Each country greatly restricted trade with western nations, and neither country established easy convertibility between their respective currencies and those of other countries. The Soviet Union and China traded largely among other communist nations such as East Germany, Poland, Hungary, Cuba, North Korea, and Vietnam.

Passive Macroeconomic Policies

Both the Soviet and prereform Chinese economies were quantity-directed systems in which money and prices played only a limited role in resource allocation. Monetary policy (changes in the money supply and interest rates) and fiscal policy (changes in government spending and taxes) were passive rather than active. Historically, unemployment—but not underemployment—was quite low, partly the result of ambitious planning targets and the various admonitions and "educational" campaigns to promote work. But low unemployment perhaps had more to do with overstaffing (managers could not fire redundant workers) and a lack of interest in cost-minimization (gross output was the overriding objective). It also had to do with the massive, highly labor-intensive, public works projects which both nations used to build infrastructure and glorify the socialist state.

Both countries primarily used direct government price setting as the primary device to control the price level. By simply not allowing prices to go up, both nations repressed any inflationary pressures. These price controls, however, created rising shortages of consumer goods.

PROBLEMS WITH CENTRAL PLANNING

Central planning was fraught with difficulties which ultimately led to the collapse of the Soviet economy and to the market reforms in China.

The Coordination Problem

As you have learned, the market system is a powerful organizing force which coordinates millions of individual decisions by consumers, resource suppliers, and businesses. In so doing, it promotes the efficient use of scarce resources. It is not easy to substitute central planning as a coordinating mechanism; such planning produces a significant **coordination problem.**

Example: Suppose that an enterprise in Moscow or Beijing is producing men's shoes. Planners must establish a realistic production target for that enterprise and then make available all the necessary inputs—labor, electric power, leather, rubber, thread, nails, appropriate machinery, transportation—for the production and delivery of that product. When the product is not as simple a one as shoes but a more complex one such as farm tractors, the planners' allocation problem are greatly compounded.

Because the outputs of many industries are inputs to other industries, the failure of any single industry to fulfill its output target will cause a chain reaction of adverse repercussions. If iron mines, for want of machinery or labor or transportation, do not supply the steel industry with the required inputs of iron ore, the steel mills will be unable to fulfill the input needs of the many industries dependent on steel. These steel-using industries (such as automobile, tractor, and transportation) will be unable to fulfill their planned production goals. Eventually the bottleneck chain reaction spreads to all firms using steel components as inputs.

The problem of centrally coordinating economic activity becomes more difficult as the economy grows.

Early planning under Stalin in the late 1930s and 1940s and Mao in China in the 1950s resembled the highly focused planning of capitalist nations in directing resources to the effort to fight World War II. The Communist Party established a few key production goals and directed resources toward fulfilling those goals regardless of costs or consumer welfare. But the past success of such "campaign planning" in the Soviet Union and China resulted in increasing complexity. Products and production processes became more sophisticated, and the number of industries for which to plan increased. Planning techniques which worked for a simple economy became inadequate and inefficient as these economies grew. Bottlenecks and production stoppages occurred with alarming regularity.

A lack of adequate success indicators adds to the coordination problem in central planning. Market economies have a single, comprehensive success indicator: profit. Profit or loss measures each firm's success or failure. Profit depends on consumer demand, production efficiency, and product quality. In contrast, the major success indicator of the Soviet and prereform China economies was a quantitative production target assigned by the central planners. Production costs, product quality, and product mix become secondary considerations. Managers and workers often sacrificed product quality since they were awarded bonuses for meeting quantitative, not qualitative, targets. If meeting production goals meant sloppy assembly work, so be it.

In fact, it is difficult at best for planners to assign quantitative production targets without unintentionally producing ridiculous distortions in output. If the production target for an enterprise manufacturing nails is specified in terms of weight (tons of nails), the producer will tend to produce all large nails. But if its target is a quantity (thousands of nails), it will be motivated to use available inputs to produce all small nails. The problem is that the economy needs *both* large and small nails.

The Incentive Problem

In the capitalist system, profits and losses not only signal success and failure, they also act as incentives for firms to increase or decrease production. If there is a product shortage, its price and profitability increase and producers are motivated to expand production. Conversely, a product surplus means falling prices and profits and a reduction in output. Improved product quality and better production techniques are sought because of their profitability. Improved job skills and greater work effort by labor mean higher money incomes which can be translated into a higher standard of living.

These actions and adjustments do not occur under central planning; there is an **incentive problem.** Central planners determined the output mix of the Soviet Union and the prereform China. When they misjudged how many automobiles, furniture, underwear, and chickens were wanted at the government-determined prices, there were persistent shortages and surpluses of those products. But since the managers who oversaw the production of these goods were rewarded for meeting their assigned production goals, they had no incentive to adjust production in response to product shortages or surpluses. And they did not have changes in prices and profitability to signal that more or less of certain products was desired. Thus, in the Soviet Union and China many products were unavailable or in short supply while other overproduced goods sat for months and years in warehouses.

The centrally planned system also lacked entrepreneurship. In market systems, the large potential monetary rewards to innovators is a stimulus to technological advancement. Moreover, firms which improve their products or production processes profit, while those which do not eventually suffer losses. Communist central planning does not allow the profit motive and does not reward innovation and enterprise.

The route for getting ahead in the centrally planned economies of the Soviet Union and China was by movement up the political hierarchy of the Communist Party. Moving up the hierarchy meant better housing, better access to health care, and the right to shop in special stores. Meeting planning targets and skillfully maneuvering through the minefields of party politics measured success in "business." But a definition of success based solely on political savvy is not conducive to technological advance, which is often disruptive to existing products, production methods, and organizational structures.

Indeed, in both the Soviet Union and prereform China, innovation was often resisted. Enterprises were essentially government-owned monopolies. As a result, there was no private gain to managers or workers for improving product quality or developing more efficient production techniques. Enterprise managers and workers actually resisted government-imposed innovations because higher and sometimes unrealistic production targets usually accompanied them.

Innovation also lagged because of a lack of competition. There were no new startup firms, driven by the profit motive, to introduce better products, superior managerial techniques, or more efficient production methods. Similarly, the goal of economic self-sufficiency isolated Soviet and Chinese enterprises from import competition. Over an extended period, enterprises produced the same products with the same techniques, even as both the products and techniques became increasingly obsolete by world standards.

Finally, individual workers lacked motivation to work hard because there were few material incentives. Because of the low priority assigned to consumer goods in the production plans, only a limited array of inferior products and services was available to consumers. While hard work might result in promotions and bonuses, the increase in money income did not translate into a proportionate increase in real income. Why work hard for additional money if there is nothing to buy with the money you earn? As a Soviet worker once lamented to a western journalist: "The government pretends to pay us and we pretend to work."

QUICK REVIEW 23-1

■ Marxian ideology is based on the labor theory of value and views capitalism as a system which expropriates surplus value from workers.

■ The main features of the former Soviet economy and the prereform Chinese economy were state ownership of property resources and central economic planning.

■ Central plans in the Soviet Union and China were characterized by (a) an emphasis on rapid industrialization, rural development (in China), and military power; (b) resource overcommitment; (c) growth through the use of more inputs rather than greater efficiency; (d) resource allocation by government directives rather than markets; (e) government price determination; (f) an emphasis on economic self-sufficiency; and (g) passive monetary and fiscal policies.

■ Two major problems of central planning are the (a) difficulty of coordinating inputs and outputs and (b) problem of fostering incentives, including those which cause technological advance.

COLLAPSE OF THE SOVIET ECONOMY

The general problems of central planning contributed to market reform in China and the collapse of the Soviet economy. Let's consider Russia first, then China.

In 1991, the Soviet Union broke into several newly independent states, the largest of which is the Russian Republic. The immediate reason for the collapse was political: a clumsy, failed attempt of old-line communists to wrest control of the government. (The failed military coupe led to the ascendancy of Boris Yeltsin in Russia and independence of the former republics of the Soviet Union). But behind the collapse of the Soviet Union were a number of economic problems, some stemming directly from the failures of central planning.

Declining Growth

Soviet economic growth in the 1950s and 1960s (at least as measured by questionable Soviet statistics) was quite impressive: The economy grew at roughly a 5 to 6 percent annual rate. But growth fell to 2 to 3 percent annually in the 1970s and declined to less than 2 percent in the mid-1980s. In the last year or two before the system broke down, real output was falling sharply.

Poor Product Quality

Further evidence of failure was the poor quality of Soviet goods. In such vital manufacturing sectors as computers and machine tools, Soviet technology lagged some 7 to 12 years behind the United States, Japan, and Germany.

It lagged even more in consumer goods, which were of notoriously poor quality and limited assortment. Durable goods such as automobiles, large household appliances, and consumer electronics were primitive by U.S. standards. Also, widespread shortages of basic goods, interminable shopper lines, black markets, and corruption in product distribution characterized the consumer sector.

Lack of Consumer Goods

Not only were consumer goods of poor quality, they were also in short supply. In the early decades of Soviet Communism, the government established a "social contract" with its citizens to the effect that, by enduring the consumer sacrifices associated with rapid industrialization and growth, the population would be rewarded with consumer abundance in the future. The failure of the system to meet such expectations contributed to frustration and deteriorating morale among consumers and workers. The rewards of past sacrifices simply never materialized.

Large Military Burden

Large Soviet military expenditures of 15 to 20 percent of domestic output, compared to 6 percent in the United States, absorbed great quantities of resources which otherwise would have been available for the development and production of consumer and capital goods. The government's policy during the Cold War era was to channel superior management and the best scientists and engineers to defense and space research, which adversely affected technological progress and the quality (and thus productivity) of capital in the civilian sector.

Agricultural Drag

By standards of the market economies, agriculture in the Soviet Union was a monument to inefficiency and a drag on economic growth. This sector used about 30 percent of the labor force and roughly one-fourth of annual investment. Furthermore, output per worker was only 10 to 25 percent of the U.S. level. The low productivity of Soviet agriculture was attributable to many factors: relative scarcity of good land, erratic weather patterns and growing seasons, serious errors in planning and administration, and perhaps most important, a lack of an effective incentive system.

Once a major exporter of grain and other agricultural products, the Soviet Union became one the world's largest importers of farm goods. This reliance on imports seriously drained the foreign currency reserves which the leadership might otherwise have used to import western capital goods and technology.

THE RUSSIAN TRANSITION TO A MARKET SYSTEM

The former Soviet republics, and particularly Russia, have committed themselves to making the transition to a market economy. There has been dramatic reform in the Russian economy since 1992, when Boris Yeltsin replaced Mikhail Gorbachev as Russia's leader.

Privatization

Private property rights have been established to encourage entrepreneurship. Much of the existing government property—housing, factories, machinery, equipment, and farmland—has been *privatized*, meaning transferred to private owners. Many new firms have formed and developed. Since 1992 more than two-thirds of former state-owned enterprises have been privatized: 90 percent of small companies are now privately owned, and 80 percent of service-sector companies are private.

The privatization process involved two phases. In the first phase, the government gave vouchers, each with a designated monetary value, to 40 million Russian citizens. Recipients could then pool these vouchers to purchase enterprises. The second phase, begun in 1994, allowed state enterprises to be purchased for cash. This enabled foreign investors to buy Russian enterprises and provided much-needed direct investment from abroad to those enterprises.

Land reform, on the other hand, has progressed more slowly. Although Boris Yeltsin decreed in 1996 that Russian peasants could buy and sell land, it will take many years to develop a functional market for farmland. Farmers, who have worked for decades on collective farms, in general fear the uncertainties and potential problems which might accompany privatization and free markets.

Price Reform

Unlike competitive market prices, the prices the Soviet government established bore no relationship to the economic value of either products or resources. In a competitive market system, the price of a product equals (at the margin) the value which consumers place on that good (the marginal benefit) and the value of the resources used in its production (the marginal cost). When free markets achieve this equality for all goods and services, the economy's scarce resources are being used efficiently to satisfy consumer wants.

But in the Soviet economy, government fixed both input and output prices and in many instances did not change those prices for many years. Because input prices did not measure the relative scarcities of resources, it was impossible for a firm to minimize real production costs. With fixed prices, it is impossible to produce a unit of a particular product in such a way as to minimize the sacrifice of alternative goods.

Example: High energy prices have caused firms in market economies to reduce energy use per unit of output. But the government underpriced such energy in the former Soviet Union (the world's largest producer of energy), so its industries used two or three times as much energy per unit of output as leading industrial countries.

Historically, not only was energy priced far below its true price, so too were many basic consumer goods. The Soviet rationale for these low prices was to ensure that everyone could afford such goods. As Figure 23-1 shows, this pricing policy helps explain the chronic product shortages and long lines which had frustrated Soviet consumers. The perfectly inelastic supply curve S_1 reflects the fixed output of, say, shoes which the central plan provided. The demand curve D_1 slope downward as it would in a market economy. In view of S_1, the equilibrium price would be P_a. But in an effort to make shoes accessible to those with lower incomes, the government fixed the price at P_f.

The result was that not everyone who wanted shoes at P_f could obtain them. At P_f the quantity demanded Q_f was substantially greater than the quantity supplied Q_a, so there was a shortage of shoes and other consumer goods priced below their market equilibrium. This explains the long lines of consumers and the empty shelves the rest of the world saw in television news clips. It also explains the black markets in which goods were sold at much higher prices than those fixed by government.

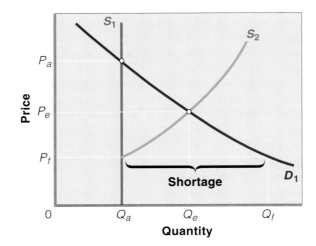

FIGURE 23-1 The effects of centrally planned prices
Central planners in the Soviet Union established below-equilibrium prices such as P_f on many basic consumer goods to allow low-income persons to buy them. But in fact, at such low prices quantity demanded (here Q_f) exceeded quantity supplied (set by planners at Q_a). This shortage meant that many consumers could not obtain such goods. The removal of government price setting at first increased price from P_f to P_a. But with privatization in Russia, the higher price stimulated greater output along supply curve S_2. Price therefore settled at P_e while output jumped from Q_a to Q_e.

The task, then, was to remove these price controls. In January 1992, the government decontrolled about 90 percent of all prices. The international value of the ruble (the Russian currency) also was decontrolled, that is, allowed to float to the value determined by demand and supply. As a result, domestic prices immediately surged and the international value of the Russian ruble sank.

The decontrol of prices, however, did have several positive effects. In terms of Figure 23-1, the decontrol at first raised prices rapidly, here from P_f to P_a. There simply was no mechanism for firms to expand the amount of output for sale in response to the price increases. But with privatization, the higher prices signaled profit opportunities to enterprises and thus a positive supply response. The relevant supply curve then took on its more familiar upward slope as in S_2, and equilibrium output increased from Q_a to Q_e. Equilibrium price moved downward from P_a to P_e. More generally, prices began to more closely reflect the marginal cost to the Russian economy of producing goods, which helped reallocate resources to where they were best suited to meet consumer wants.

Promotion of Competition

As we have seen, the industrial sector of the former Soviet Union consisted of large state-owned enterprises. Single firm "industries" produced about 30 to 40 percent of total industrial output. When several enterprises produced a product, the planning process coordinated their actions to create a cartel. In short, most production took place under monopoly or near-monopoly conditions.

Russian reformers realize that an efficient market economy requires the dismantling of these public monopolies and the creation of antitrust laws to sustain competition. But only limited "demonopolization" has accompanied privatization thus far. Private monopolies rather than public monopolies now reign in several industries. Joint ventures between Russia and foreign companies are one avenue for increasing competition, and Russian legislation has recently opened the door for foreign firms to invest directly in Russia. **(Key Question 5)**

Joining the World Economy

The Soviet economy was largely isolated from the world economy for 75 years. A key step in the transition to a market economy is to open the economy to international trade and finance. Russia has had some success in this endeavor; for example, it has made the ruble a fully convertible currency. This means that the ruble is acceptable in exchange for other currencies. The plunging value of the ruble (from 90 rubles = $1 in 1992 to 5800 rubles = $1 in 1997) was obviously detrimental to Russia's world trade. But recently the international value of the ruble has stabilized, which has helped Russia increase its volume of international trade and finance.

Price-Level Stabilization

The transition to free markets brought with it hyperinflation. The decontrol of prices in January 1992 tripled and quadrupled prices almost overnight. Also, Russian households had stored huge amounts of currency and deposits at saving banks during years of waiting for scarce consumer goods to become more abundant. This so-called "ruble overhang" helped fuel inflation once prices were decontrolled and privatization began to deliver consumer goods to the marketplace.

But the most important source of inflation was the large government deficits financed by increases in the money supply. The deficits in turn had many roots. Privatization of state enterprises caused the government to lose those profits, an important source of revenue. The uncertainties inherent in the transition led to general disorder and widespread tax evasion. To ease enterprise losses incurred during the transition, the government extended massive subsidy credits (financed by printing new money) to both industry and agriculture. Finally, the government also increased pensions and welfare benefits by printing money.

Russia's economic reforms, however, have created an independent central bank which has implemented an anti-inflationary monetary policy that has paid off in a swift decline in the rate of inflation. As shown in column 3 in Table 23-1, inflation declined from 1353 percent in 1992 to 14 percent in 1997. This decline has increased investor confidence in the stability of the Russian government and has been a major factor in the stabilization of the international value of the ruble. **(Key Question 6)**

Major Problems

Along with the successes and difficulties we just noted, the Russian transition to the market system has encountered two other significant problems:

TABLE 23-1   Real GDP growth and inflation in Russia, 1991–1997

(1) Year	(2) Growth of real GDP (percent)	(3) Rate of inflation (percent)
1991	−13	93
1992	−19	1353
1993	−12	896
1994	−15	302
1995	− 4	190
1996	− 6	22
1997	+ 1	14

Source: International Monetary Fund and Russian authorities.

Falling Output and Living Standards Thus far, the transition to capitalism in Russia has not paid off in rising real output and an improved standard of living for the great majority of Russians. Real output began to fall in the 1980s, but its decline accelerated during the reforms. Column 2 in Table 23-1 documents recent declines. Note, however, that the fall in real GDP bottomed out in 1992 at 19 percent. Declines of real output of this magnitude resemble those associated with the Great Depression in the United States.

Causes of these declines include the (1) rapid inflation, which created an uncertain environment for borrowing and investing, (2) unraveling of Russia's international trade relationships with former communist-bloc nations of eastern Europe, (3) bankruptcy and closing of many former state-owned enterprises which could not survive in a market environment, and (4) massive reallocation of resources required by the reforms and the major reduction in government spending on the military.

Because real output equals real income, declining real output has meant declines in Russian living standards. Farmers, government employees, and pensioners have been hard hit, and many workers have had to accept deep real wage cuts to keep their jobs. Some workers are owed large amounts of "back pay" because of the inability of their employers to make wage payments. At least 30,000 scientists have left Russia to work in other nations.

Russian authorities, however, believe that the decline in real output has reached an end. Real output increased by 1 percent in 1997 and is expected to rise by about that same amount in 1998.

Inequality and Social Costs Economic inequality has increased during the transition. While many people have become impoverished, a wealthy class of "new Russians" has emerged. Many of these people have gained their wealth through entrepreneurship. Others have prospered as executives, managers, and scientists in the newly privatized industries. Still others, however, have enriched themselves via corruption and illegal activities. The major disruptions, swift changes, and lack of regulatory oversight which accompanied the transition have created major opportunities for organized crime to expand and flourish.

Considerable friction between gainers and losers, the growth of organized crime, and "crony capitalism" fuels public doubts as to the desirability of a market economy. Greater economic freedom has also brought greater economic insecurity; medical and educational services have deteriorated, and school enrollments have declined. Alcoholism, historically high in Russia, has increased sharply, and life expectancy of Russian men declined from 65 in 1988 to 57 in 1997.

Future Prospects

A remaining concern about the transition to markets in Russia is the weakness of government in enforcing its laws, including the collection of taxes owed by enterprises and political subdivisions. Widespread tax evasion results in declining tax revenues, enlarged budget deficits, and the potential for financial instability. Declining tax revenues further weaken the government's ability to enforce tax laws, so a kind of vicious circle could continue until another political and economic collapse results. Declining tax revenues also cripple the central government's ability to perform other basic functions, such as maintaining law and order, providing regulatory oversight of banks and security markets, and providing a social safety net for its citizens. Pessimists point out that a government borrowing crisis, coupled with, say, a collapse of the Russia banking system, might plunge Russia into another depression. That could lead to the abandonment of capitalistic reforms and even an end to democracy.

The more likely scenario, however, is that Russia will eventually succeed in creating a vibrant market economy. The most severe economic dislocations in the form of inflation and a declining real output seem to have ended. Economists who closely monitor the progress of Russia believe that its transition from central planning to markets might span another decade or so but that the market reforms are now largely irreversible and that another economic collapse is highly unlikely. In this view, although Russia is still far from being an advanced market economy, the nation is on a path to achieving one of the truly amazing economic transitions in world history.

QUICK REVIEW 23-2

■ The former Soviet economy collapsed under pressure of declining economic growth, poor product quality, a lack of consumer goods, a large military burden, and agricultural inefficiency.

■ Russia has committed itself to becoming a capitalistic market economy. Ingredients in its transition from central planning to markets include **(a)** creating private property and property rights, **(b)** removing domestic price controls, **(c)** promoting competition, **(d)** opening the economy to international trade and finance, **(e)** ending inflation.

■ Russia's transition to markets has been accompanied by declining output and living standards, increasing income inequality, and social costs such as corruption, organized crime, increasing alcoholism, and reduced life expectancy.

■ Although Russia still faces difficult economic times, it has made substantial progress in its move from communism to capitalism.

MARKET REFORMS IN CHINA

China has taken a different path than Russia in its transition to a market economy. Russia pursued a "shock therapy" approach to reform in 1992, attempting to achieve "irreversibility" of its reforms through a rapid and radical transformation to private property and free markets. China's market reforms began far earlier—in 1978—in a piecemeal, experimental, and gradual manner. In 1992 Russia concluded that its political apparatus, the Communist Party in particular, was an obstacle to economic reform; political reform or democratization preceded economic reform. China, in contrast, has sought economic reform under the strong direction of its Communist Party. China's view is that the upsetting of the political system would generate endless debate, competition for power, and ultimate stagnation and failure for its economic reforms. Unlike Russia, China feels that communist dictatorship and markets are compatible. China has protected the existence and development of its state-owned enterprises while simultaneously encouraging the creation of competing private enterprises.

Although China's GDP per capita is only $620 compared to Russia's $2240, China has instituted its market reforms without suffering the economic depression which confronted Russia. In fact, China has achieved a 9 percent annual growth of real output over the past two decades (as compared to typical growth rates of 2 to 5 percent for most advanced economies).

Market reforms in China began in 1978 under the leadership of Deng Xiaoping, the successor to Mao Zedong. Deng did not share Mao's utopian vision of an eventual communist economy in which people would work for the glory of the community and monetary incentives would play only a minor role. Instead, Deng recognized that the profit incentives of a market economy could increase China's living standard. But he also realized that only a gradual transition to such an economy could preserve the Communist Party's political control over China. Many Chinese critics of Deng derisively called him "a capitalist roader," implying that he was setting China on the road toward capitalism. In retrospect, they were at least partly right.

Agricultural and Rural Reform

Market reform in China began in agriculture in 1978, at which time nearly 70 percent of the Chinese labor force was rural. The key elements of the 1978–1984 reforms were the leasing of land to individual farmers ("decollectivization") and the establishment of a *two-track price system*. For the first time, individual farmers were allowed to lease government-owned land (for 15-year periods). Under the dual price system, farmers had to sell a prescribed amount of farm output to the government at a set price but could sell any surplus in markets at market-determined prices. Farmers were eventually allowed to sell increasing portions of their output at market-determined prices rather than at lower government-determined prices. In 1978 farmers sold only 8 percent of their commodities in competitive markets, but by 1990 that share had increased to 80 percent.

Decollectivization and price reform greatly strengthened production incentives and swiftly moved the Chinese economy toward market-based agriculture. Responding to the profit motive, individual farmers boosted their productivity by substituting tools for labor, shifting crops toward more valuable commodities, and farming previously untilled land. Agricultural output in China rose dramatically throughout the

1980s. Equally important, the greater productivity in agriculture released labor resources to a growing number of privately owned rural manufacturing firms called **township and village enterprises.**

Reform of Urban Industries

The success of reforms in agriculture led the central government to extend the reforms to the **state-owned enterprises** (SOEs) in urban areas. These enterprises were granted more authority to determine the quantity and variety of their outputs, to make their own employment decisions, and to retain much of their profits. (Previously, they had to send the bulk of their profits to the central government.) The government also extended the two-track system of prices to nonagricultural products. SOEs were allowed to buy increasing portions of their inputs at market prices rather than at government-set prices. They were also allowed to sell increasing portions of their outputs at market prices as opposed to being forced to sell output to the government at fixed prices. The share of output sold at market prices rather than at government-set prices rose from 12 percent in 1980 to 66 percent in 1987.

Furthermore, the Chinese government encouraged the formation of nonstate enterprises called **urban collectives**—enterprises owned jointly by managers and their workforces. Like town and village enterprises, these nonstate firms were *not* subject to the directives of the central plan, so they were far more capable than SOEs of gauging and meeting consumer wants. The urban collectives experienced explosive growth of output and employment, some of it at the expense of SOEs. Also, the competition among these nonstate enterprises and the SOEs spurred productivity advance and innovation in many of the SOEs.

Special Economic Zones

In 1980 China created **special economic zones** (SEZs) open to foreign investment, private ownership, and international trade. Located in coastal regions, these special zones attracted increasing amounts of foreign capital (particularly from Hong Kong). They also significantly increased Chinese exports. As the successes of the SEZs became apparent, China increased their number and scope. The SEZs in China's southern provinces, in particular, became booming enclaves of "near-capitalism." The success of the SEZs relative to other regions in China eventually undercut support for central planning.

Development of Supporting Institutions

The reforms in China also included the building of institutions to facilitate the market system and its macroeconomic control. Specific examples: First, the Chinese government established the Bank of China as the central bank and gave it the power to regulate the banking system and control the money supply to avoid inflation. Second, China replaced the system of "profit transfers" from state enterprises to the central government with an *enterprise tax system*. Third, it established a so-called "swap market" in which Chinese enterprises could trade foreign currency as needed to conduct international business. Finally, it developed a stock market for the exchange of the shares of newly created stockholder-owned corporations.

Transformation of the SOEs

In the 1990s Chinese reform turned to making state-owned enterprises more "corporate-like." The idea was to replace Communist Party operatives with professional managers who were independent of the central government. The government also redirected the goals of such enterprises away from social objectives (providing employment, housing, health care, and day care) and toward economic objectives (producing high-quality goods which people desire). This partial *"corporatization"* of state-enterprises, however, exposed the inefficiencies of the SOEs. In the competitive rather than state-directed environment, many SOEs found that they were producing the wrong goods, in the wrong amounts, using the wrong combinations of inputs. In short, thousands of SOEs simply were inefficient and unprofitable.

After Deng's death in the mid-1990s, leadership of China passed to Jiang Zemin. In 1997 Jiang and the Communist Party called for consolidation of the major SOEs into 1000 large enterprises. These SOEs will issue stock and become shareholder-owned corporations. The idea is to make the firms' management responsive to the shareholders. The government, however, will hold the controlling share of stock ownership in these 1000 corporations. All the other 300,000 state-owned enterprises will be sold to private individuals (or groups) or, if they have no value, will be allowed to go bankrupt.

OUTCOMES AND PROSPECTS

Economic reform in China has achieved impressive results, but is still incomplete.

Positive Outcomes of Reform

China's economic growth rate in the past two decades is among the highest recorded for any country during any period of world history; it has averaged nearly 9 percent annually since the beginning of reforms in 1978. That means that real output and real income have quadrupled in less than two decades. About 40 percent of this growth has resulted from increased capital. Expanded output and income has boosted domestic saving and investment. The expansion of capital goods has in turn further increased productivity, output, and income. The rising income has attracted more direct foreign investment. (Growth rates for recent years are shown in column 2, Table 23-2.)

A rapid expansion of China's international trade has accompanied the expansion of real output. Chinese exports rose from $5 billion in 1978 to more than $160 billion in 1996. These exports have provided the foreign currency needed to import consumer goods and capital goods. Imports of capital goods from industrially advanced countries have brought with them the highly advanced technology which is embodied within, for example, factory design, industrial machinery, office equipment, and telecommunications systems.

During the period of reform, China's real GDP and real income have grown much more rapidly than

TABLE 23-2 **Real GDP growth and inflation in China, 1991–1997**

(1) Year	(2) Growth of real GDP (percent)	(3) Rate of inflation (percent)
1991	9	3
1992	14	5
1993	13	12
1994	12	22
1995	10	15
1996	9	5
1997	9	2

Source: International Monetary Fund and Chinese authorities.

China's population. Per capita income has increased at a very high annual rate of 8 percent since 1980. This is noteworthy because China's population has expanded by 14 million a year (despite a policy which encourages "one-child" per family). Per capita income in China is now $620 annually based on exchange rates. But since the prices of many basic items in China are still low, Chinese per capita purchasing power is estimated to be nearly $3000.

The growth of per capita income in China has resulted from increased use of capital, improved technology, and shifts of labor away from lower-productivity toward higher-productivity uses. One such shift of employment has been from agriculture toward rural and urban manufacturing. Another such shift has been from state-owned enterprises toward private firms. Both shifts have raised the productivity of Chinese workers. And because these employment shifts have been gradual, they have not produced widespread unemployment. Currently, China's unemployment rate is about 7 percent, although there is substantial underemployment in many regions.

Problems

China still faces some significant economic problems in its transition to the market system.

Incomplete Property Rights After the initial surges in the 1980s, productivity growth in agriculture has stagnated. A possible reason may be that property rights are incomplete. The Communist Party has opposed privatization of farmland, fearing a reversion to the wealthy landlord system it fought to abolish. Instead, the government policy has been to lease land for 15-year periods. But without ownership rights, many farmers are reluctant to invest in farm equipment and capital improvements on the land. The return on such investment is dependent on the assurance of having land to farm. Thus, further capital investment in Chinese agriculture may be dependent on the right to buy and sell land.

Macroeconomic Instability At times investment booms in China have resulted in too much spending relative to production capacity. The result has been occasional periods of 15 to 25 percent annual rates of inflation. (See column 3 in Table 23-2 for recent Chinese inflation rates.) China is confronting this problem by giving its central bank more power so that when appropriate the bank can damp down

I Think Everything Will Be OK.

A Russian baked-goods company is successfully making the difficult transition to capitalism.

MOSCOW (AP)—In Soviet times, a movie might have had a heroine much like Lyudmila Korilkova. She would be dressed in a white smock, her dark hair tufting out from behind a scarf, the tools of industrial production in her hands.

"I love my job very much," she would say. "Otherwise, I would not have stayed here for 40 years." Actually, Korilkova—in the smock and scarf, a pastry bag in her hand—said those words just the other day. More amazing still, she seemed to mean them. Maybe it had something to do with the fact that on January 1, her factory doubled her salary.

In today's Russian economy, Korilkova is a lucky woman. She works for a baked-goods company, Bolshevik, which has weathered the transition to a market economy and under new French management appears poised on the brink of success. Last year, Bolshevik's production increased for the first time in eight years. The improvement was modest—3 percent—but it comes close to mirroring national statistics that suggest the worst years of Russia's economic transition may be in the past.

You can see this at a company like Bolshevik, which has betrayed its name and wholeheartedly joined the capitalist mainstream. Siou and Company, as it was originally called, was founded by a French couple in Moscow in 1855. By the late 19th century, it was the biggest cookie baker in Russia. It acquired its current name in 1924, when it was nationalized by the new Bolshevik (communist) government. Even now, a statue of Bolshevik leader Vladimir Lenin stands watch over the courtyard of the landmark brick factory. By the late 1980s, Bolshevik was turning out 78,000 tons of cookies, cakes and other baked goods a year, as dictated by central planners. Quality was poor, factory workers now say, and production methods archaic.

In 1992, after the collapse of the Soviet Union, Bolshevik was privatized. In 1994, the French yogurt-maker Groupe Danone bought a 59 percent stake. In 1996, with sales slumping 14 percent a year, Danone brought in a Franco-Russian manager, Jacques Ioffe, to turn things around. A former physicist from St. Petersburg, Ioffe emigrated to France in 1977, went to business school and wound up managing a publishing company in Paris. Fluent in Russian, French and English, he had the credentials Danone was looking for.

investment spending by raising interest rates. Nevertheless, the financial and monetary control systems in China are still weak and inadequate. One potential problem is that many unprofitable SOEs owe colossal sums of money on loans made by the Chinese state-owned banks (a recent estimate is $96 billion). Because most of these loans are not collectable, there is a danger that China will need to bail out the banks to keep them in operation. If China (through its central bank) simply prints additional money to accomplish this bailout, renewed inflation could result.

Integration into the Global Economy   China still has much work to do to fully integrate its economy into the world's system of international finance and trade. For example, China is not a member of the World Trade Organization, the successor to GATT, and it still has very high tariffs on many imported goods and restrictions on foreign ownership. In addi-

tion, China's record of protecting intellectual property rights such as copyrights, trademarks, and patents is very poor. Unauthorized copying of computer software, movie videos, and compact disks has been a major source of trade friction between China and the United States.

Geographically Uneven Development   Finally, there is great regional unevenness in China's economic development. This fact is even more apparent now that the former British colony of Hong Kong is part of China. Hong Kong is a wealthy capitalist economy with per capita income of about $22,000. The standard of living is also relatively high in China's southern provinces and China's coastal cities, although not nearly as high as in Hong Kong. In fact, people living in these special economic zones have been the major beneficiaries of China's rapid growth. In contrast, the majority of people living elsewhere in China

"Danone said, 'Look, we've got a big company, we don't know what to do with it, we don't understand what they're saying,'" Ioffe recalled during an interview in his office, which is decorated with photos of Paris and little French and Russian flags. The biggest problem he found at Bolshevik was one of mentality. The Russian managers, while well meaning, simply couldn't grasp the idea of a market economy. There was no sales department, no marketing department, and the idea of basing production plans on sales was still foreign.

Today, all that is changing. The new marketing department recently unveiled its first billboard, just outside the factory gates. Television commercials will follow in June. And while Bolshevik now produces only half as much as it did a decade ago, it is producing what the market wants. Ioffe has set a goal of 20 percent growth for 1998. "Before, the quality lacked," said Svetlana Gritskova, who has worked at Bolshevik for 20 years and is in charge of assembling cakes for special orders. Now, she said, quality is much better. Plus, "our production is more versatile."

A few yards away, Korilkova decorated cakes, squeezing pink icing out of a pastry bag to form delicate flowers. Although her methods rely on classic—and simple—French tools, she pointed approvingly to modern mixers and refrigerators nearby. "We've become better technically equipped," she said. "Before, the state showed little concern for equipment to make our lives easier." Nor did it do what her current bosses have done: raise her monthly salary from $250 to $500. Others may fret, but Korilkova is now optimistic about the future of Russia.

"Yes," she said. "I think everything will be OK."

Source: "Russia's Economy May Be Past Worst," Associated Press, January 25, 1998. Printed by permission of the Associated Press.

have very low incomes. Despite its tremendous growth since 1978, China's per person income level, on average, suggests that it continues to be a relatively low-income developing country. **(Key Question 8)**

QUICK REVIEW 23-3

■ Market reform began earlier in China (1978) than in Russia (1992) and involves gradualism rather than "shock therapy."

■ Key elements of China's economic reform are decollectivization of agriculture, establishment of township and village enterprises, price reform, establishment of privately owned urban enterprises, creation of special economic zones, development of support and control institutions, and "corporatization" of state-owned enterprises.

■ Since the beginning of market reform in 1978, China's real output and per capita income have grown at average annual rates of 9 percent and 8 percent, respectively.

■ China's economy still faces problems of incomplete property rights, periodic inflation, lack of full integration with the world economy, and great unevenness in regional development.

CONCLUSION

Clearly, Russia and China have taken different paths in their transitions to market systems. It may seem that China's path of dictatorship and gradualism is superior economically (political realities aside) to Russia's path of democracy and swift transformation to capitalism. While Russia has suffered years of declining output and income, China has experienced very high rates of economic growth. But we must not be too hasty in reaching this conclusion. The disorder arising from Russia's abrupt transition to democracy and capitalism may be behind it, placing Russia in a stronger position than China to succeed in the future. The present "forced order" in China via the Communist Party may or may not last. History suggests that *economic* freedom usually creates demands for *political* freedom: free speech, freedom of peaceful assembly, freedom to organize political parties, free elections, and so on. Are China's communist leaders

willing and able to design a gradual path toward political freedom? Or is China's period of disorder still to come? We have no answers for these questions. We simply note, in the words of a well-known sage: "the times they are a-changin."[1]

---

[1]Bob Dylan song lyrics from *The Times They Are A-Changin'* (1963).

CHAPTER SUMMARY

1. The labor theory of value is a central principle of Marxian ideology. Capitalists, as property owners, allegedly expropriate most of labor's value as profits, or surplus value. The supposed solution was for the workers and peasants to take control of all production processes through their representative: the Communist Party.

2. Virtually complete state ownership of property resources, collective farming, and central planning were the major features of the Soviet economy and the prereform Chinese economy.

3. Characteristics of Soviet and Chinese central planning included **(a)** emphasis on industrialization, rural development (in China), and military strength; **(b)** overcommitment of resources through the central plans; **(c)** allocation of resources by bureaucracy rather than market decisions; **(d)** government price setting; **(e)** economic self-sufficiency; and **(f)** passive macroeconomic policies.

4. Central planners in the Soviet Union and China faced a coordination problem, which was the difficulty of achieving internal consistency in plans to avoid bottlenecks and the chain reaction of production failures which they cause. The more complex their economies became, the greater became the problem of coordinating inputs and outputs.

5. Central planners also faced a difficult incentive problem. Without private property, entrepreneurship, and availability of consumer goods, it proved difficult if not impossible to achieve efficiency, promote innovation, and induce hard work.

6. Along with the difficulties of central planning, the collapse of the Soviet economy resulted from a diminishing growth rate, limited and shoddy consumer goods, a large military burden, and stagnation of agriculture.

7. The key elements of the Russian transition to capitalism were privatizing firms, establishing market-based prices, promoting greater competition, liberalizing international trade and finance, and ending rapid inflation. Russia's transition to capitalism has not been easy. Output and income have declined, income inequality has increased, and social problems such as crime and alcoholism have worsened. Nevertheless, Russia has succeeded in making its reforms largely irreversible, and its output and income are now expected to rise.

8. Market reform in China has differed from reform in Russia in several ways: **(a)** it began earlier than in Russia (1978 compared to 1992); **(b)** it was not precipitated by collapse of the political system, as was true in Russia; **(c)** it has used a gradual approach, not "shock therapy"; **(d)** it has been directed by the Communist Party, not by anticommunist reformers; and **(e)** it only recently has begun the process of privatizing state-owned enterprises, whereas Russia has privatized most of its industry.

9. China's market reforms began with leasing of farmland and allowing farmers to sell increasing amounts of their output at market-determined rather than state-determined prices. Subsequent reforms included the establishment of township and village enterprises and urban collectives (both are types of private enterprises) and the setting up of special enterprise zones open to international trade and direct foreign investment. More recently, China's reforms have involved development of support and control institutions for the market system and the corporatization of state-owned enterprises, in some cases via issuance of stock.

10. China's reforms have generated two decades of rapid economic growth, with real GDP rising by 9 percent annually and per capita income rising by 8 percent annually. Nevertheless, this growth has been very uneven geographically and at times has been accompanied by rapid inflation. To continue its success, China may have to end prohibitions against ownership of land, integrate its economy more fully with the international system of trade and finance, and privatize state industries.

TERMS AND CONCEPTS

labor theory of value
surplus value
state ownership

central economic
 planning
coordination problem

incentive problem
township and village
 enterprises

state-owned enterprises
urban collectives
special economic zones

STUDY QUESTIONS

1. Compare the economic ideology of the former Soviet Union and prereform China with that of the capitalist economies as to the **(a)** source and role of profits, **(b)** ownership of capital, and **(c)** best method of allocating resources.

2. What does the term "central economic planning" mean? Describe the coordination problem which central planners in the Soviet Union and prereform China faced. Explain how a planning failure can cause a chain reaction of additional failures.

3. Why were new product introductions and the use of new methods of production so uncommon in the Soviet Union and prereform China compared to such capitalist economies as the United States?

4. What factors contributed to the collapse of the Soviet economy?

5. KEY QUESTION Use a supply and demand diagram to explain why persistent shortages of many consumer goods occurred under central planning in the Soviet Union and in prereform China. Why were black markets common in each country?

6. KEY QUESTION What are the major components of economic reform in Russia? What is meant when these reforms are described as "shock therapy"? How successful has Russia been thus far in its reforms?

7. In what general respects have Chinese economic reforms differed from those of Russia? Do you believe that these differences account for China's higher growth rate? Why?

8. KEY QUESTION Relate each of the following items to the success of market reform in China: **(a)** leasing farm land, **(b)** price reform, **(c)** private rural and urban enterprises, **(d)** special economic zones, and **(e)** corporatization of state-owned enterprises.

9. What progress has China achieved in its transition to a market economy? What problems remain?

10. Do you think that China's economic reforms will eventually result in the demise of the Communist Party in China? Explain your answer.

11. "Paradoxically, Russia's disorder may provide a firmer base for future growth than China's order." Do you agree or disagree? Explain.

12. (Last Word) Why was "marketing" a foreign concept to managers such as those of the baked-goods enterprise discussed in this chapter's Last Word? Why do you think the quality of the baked goods produced in this enterprise has increased?

13. WEB-BASED QUESTION **Russia's Transition to a Market Economy—Today's Business Headlines** Russia Today http://www.russiatoday. com/rtoday/business/business.html provides weekday business headlines about Russia. Review the Russian business headlines for the past 2 weeks. Identify which are related to its transition to a market economy (e.g., increased company profit) and which are nontransition-related (e.g., cold weather depletes heating-oil stocks). What portion of the transition-related headlines are reporting difficulties? What portion are describing success stories?

14. WEB-BASED QUESTION **China and Hong Kong—Beyond 1997** On July 1, 1997, Hong Kong, the world's fourth-largest trading entity, entered a new phase of its existence as Asia's business hub. After a 14-year transition period, its status changed from that of a Dependent Territory of Britain to that of a Special Administration Region of China. How is Hong Kong's capitalist system supposed to survive the control of China's Communist Party? Visit the Hong Kong 1997 Web Site http://www.hk1997. china.com/ and the South China Morning Post http://scmp.com/ for your answers.

GLOSSARY

Note: Terms in *italic* type are defined separately in this glossary.

A

Ability-to-pay principle The idea that those who have greater income (or wealth) should pay a greater proportion of it as taxes than those who have less income (or wealth).

Abstraction Elimination of irrelevant and noneconomic facts to obtain an *economic principle*.

Actual budget A listing of amounts spent by the *Federal government* (to purchase goods and services and for *transfer payments*) and the amounts of tax revenue collected by it in any (fiscal) year.

Actual deficit The size of the Federal government's *budget deficit* actually recorded in any particular year.

Actual investment The amount which *firms* do invest; equal to *planned investment* plus *unplanned investment*.

Actual reserves The funds which a bank has on deposit at the *Federal Reserve Bank* of its district (plus its *vault cash*).

Adaptive expectations theory The idea that people determine their expectations about future events (for example, inflation) on the basis of past and present events (rates of inflation) and only change their expectations as events unfold.

Adjustable pegs The device used in the *Bretton Woods system* to alter *exchange rates* in an orderly way to eliminate persistent payments deficits and surpluses. Each nation defined its monetary unit in terms of (pegged it to) gold or the dollar, kept the *rate of exchange* for its money stable in the short run, and adjusted its rate in the long run when faced with international payments disequilibrium.

Aggregate demand A schedule or curve which shows the total quantity of goods and services demanded (purchased) at different *price levels*.

Aggregate demand–aggregate supply model The macroeconomic model which uses *aggregate demand* and *aggregate supply* to determine and explain the *price level* and the real *domestic output*.

Aggregate expenditures The total amount spent for final goods and services in the economy.

Aggregate expenditures–domestic output approach Determination of the *equilibrium gross domestic product* by finding the real GDP at which aggregate expenditures equal *domestic output*.

Aggregate expenditures schedule A schedule or curve showing the total amount spent for final goods and services at different levels of GDP.

Aggregate supply A schedule or curve showing the total quantity of goods and services supplied (produced) at different *price levels*.

Aggregation Combining individual units or data into one unit or number. For example, all prices of individual goods and services are combined into a *price level*, or all units of output are aggregated into *real gross domestic product*.

Allocative efficiency The apportionment of resources among firms and industries to obtain the production of the products most wanted by society (consumers); the output of each product at which its *marginal cost* and *price* or *marginal benefit* are equal.

Annually balanced budget A budget in which government expenditures and tax collections are equal each year.

Anticipated inflation Increases in the price level (*inflation*) which occur at the expected rate.

Antitrust laws Legislation (including the *Sherman Act* and *Clayton Act*) which prohibit anticompetitive business activities such as *price fixing*, bid rigging, monopolization, and *tying contracts*.

Applied economics (See *Policy economics*.)

Appreciation (of the dollar) An increase in the value of the dollar relative to the currency of another nation so that a dollar buys a larger amount of the foreign currency and thus of foreign goods.

"Asian tigers" The newly industrialized and rapidly growing economies of Hong Kong, Singapore, South Korea, and Taiwan.

Asset Anything of monetary value owned by a firm or individual.

Asset demand for money The amount of *money* people want to hold as a *store of value*; this amount varies inversely with the *rate of interest*.

Authoritarian capitalism An economic system in which property resources are privately owned and government extensively directs and controls the economy.

Average product   The total output produced per unit of a *resource* employed (*total product* divided by the quantity of that employed resource).

Average propensity to consume   Fraction (or percentage) of *disposable income* which households plan to spend for consumer goods and services; *consumption* divided by *disposable income*.

Average propensity to save   Fraction (or percentage) of *disposable income* which households save; *saving* divided by *disposable income*.

Average tax rate   Total tax paid divided by total (taxable) income, as a percentage.

B

Balanced-budget amendment   Proposed constitutional amendment that would require Congress to balance the Federal budget annually.

Balanced-budget multiplier   The extent to which an equal change in government spending and taxes changes *equilibrium gross domestic product*; always has a value of 1 since it is equal to the amount of the equal changes in *G* and *T*.

Balance of payments   (See *International balance of payments*.)

Balance of payments deficit   The amount by which the sum of the *balance on current account* and the *balance on the capital account* is negative in a year.

Balance of payments surplus   The amount by which the sum of the *balance on current account* and the *balance on the capital account* is positive in a year.

Balance on current account   The exports of goods and services of a nation less its imports of goods and services plus its *net investment income* and *net transfers* in a year.

Balance on goods and services   The exports of goods and services of a nation less its imports of goods and services in a year.

Balance on the capital account   The *capital inflows* of a nation less its *capital outflows*.

Balance sheet   A statement of the *assets*, *liabilities*, and *net worth* of a firm or individual at some given time.

Bank deposits   The deposits which individuals or firms have at banks (or thrifts) or which banks have at the *Federal Reserve Banks*.

Bankers' bank   A bank which accepts the deposits of and makes loans to *depository institutions*; in the United States, a *Federal Reserve Bank*.

Bank reserves   The deposits of commercial banks and thrifts at *Federal Reserve Banks* plus bank and thrift *vault cash*.

Barter   The exchange of one good or service for another good or service.

Base year   The year with which other years are compared when an index is constructed, for example, the base year for a *price index*.

Benefit-cost analysis   Comparing the *marginal benefits* of a government project or program with the *marginal costs* to decide whether or not to employ resources in that project or program and to what extent.

Board of Governors   The 7-member group which supervises and controls the money and banking system of the United States; the Board of Governors of the Federal Reserve System; the Federal Reserve Board.

Bond   A financial device through which a borrower (a firm or government) is obligated to pay the principle and interest on a loan at a specific date in the future.

Brain drain   The emigration of highly educated, highly skilled workers from a country.

Break-even income   The level of *disposable income* at which *households* plan to consume (spend) all their income and to save none of it; also denotes that level of earned income at which subsidy payments become zero in an income transfer program.

Bretton Woods system   The international monetary system developed after World War II in which *adjustable pegs* were employed, the *International Monetary Fund* helped to stabilize foreign exchange rates, and gold and the dollar were used as *international monetary reserves*.

Budget deficit   The amount by which the expenditures of the Federal government exceed its revenues in any year.

Budget surplus   The amount by which the revenues of the Federal government exceed its expenditures in any year.

Built-in stabilizer   A mechanism which increases government's budget deficit (or reduces its surplus) during a recession and increases government's budget surplus (or reduces its deficit) during inflation without any action by policymakers; the tax system is one such mechanism.

Business cycle   Recurring increases and decreases in the level of economic activity over periods of years. Consists of peak, *recession*, trough, and recovery phases.

Business firm   (See *Firm*.)

C

Capital   Human-made resources (buildings, machinery, and equipment) used to produce goods and services; goods which do not directly satisfy human wants; also called capital goods.

Capital account   The section of a nation's *international balance of payments* statement in which the foreign purchases of assets in the United States (producing money *capital inflows*) and U.S. purchases of assets abroad (producing money *capital outflows* of that nation) are recorded.

Capital account deficit   A negative *balance on the capital account*.

Capital account surplus   A positive *balance on the capital account*.

Capital flight   The transfer of savings from developing countries to industrially advanced countries to avoid government expropriation, taxation, and high rates of inflation or to realize better investment opportunities.

Capital gain The gain realized when securities or properties are sold for a price greater than the price paid for them.

Capital goods (See *Capital.*)

Capital inflow The expenditures made by the residents of foreign nations to purchase real and financial capital from the residents of a nation.

Capital-intensive commodity A product which requires a relatively large amount of *capital* to produce.

Capitalism (See *Pure capitalism.*)

Capital outflow The expenditures made by the residents of a nation to purchase real and financial capital from the residents of foreign nations.

Capital-saving technological advance An improvement in *technology* which permits a greater quantity of a product to be produced with a specific amount of *capital* (or permits the same amount of the product to be produced with a smaller amount of capital).

Capital stock The total available *capital* in a nation.

Capital-using technological advance An improvement in *technology* which requires the use of a greater amount of *capital* to produce a specific quantity of a product.

Causation A relationship in which the occurrence of one or more events brings about another event.

CEA (See *Council of Economic Advisers.*)

Central bank A bank whose chief function is the control of the nation's *money supply*; in the United States, the *Federal Reserve System.*

Central economic planning Government determination of the objectives of the economy and how resources will be directed to attain those objectives.

Ceteris paribus assumption (See *"Other things equal" assumption.*)

Change in demand A change in the *quantity demanded* of a good or service at every price; a shift of the *demand curve* to the left or right.

Change in supply A change in the *quantity supplied* of a good or service at every price; a shift of the *supply curve* to the left or right.

Checkable deposit Any deposit in a *commercial bank* or *thrift institution* against which a check may be written; includes *demand deposits.*

Checking account A *checkable deposit* in a *commercial bank* or *thrift institution.*

Check clearing The process by which funds are transferred from the checking accounts of the writers of checks to the checking accounts of the recipients of the checks.

Circular flow model The flow of resources from *households* to *firms* and of products from firms to households. These flows are accompanied by reverse flows of money from firms to households and from households to firms.

Classical economics The macroeconomic generalizations accepted by most economists before the 1930s which led to the conclusion that a capitalistic economy was self-regulating and therefore would usually employ its resources fully.

Closed economy An economy which neither exports nor imports goods and services.

Coincidence of wants A situation in which the good or service which one trader desires to obtain is the same as that which another trader desires to give up, and an item which the second trader wishes to acquire is the same as that which the first trader desires to surrender.

COLA (See *Cost-of-living adjustment.*)

Command economy An economic system (method of organization) in which property resources are publicly owned and government uses *central economic planning* to direct and coordinate economic activities.

Commercial bank A firm which engages in the business of banking (accepts deposits, offers checking accounts, and makes loans).

Commercial banking system All *commercial banks* and *thrift institutions* as a group.

Communism (See *Command economy.*)

Comparative advantage A lower relative or comparative cost than another producer.

Competing goods (See *Substitute goods.*)

Competition The presence in a market of a large number of independent buyers and sellers competing with one another and the freedom of buyers and sellers to enter and leave the market.

Complementary goods Products and services which are used together; when the price of one falls the demand for the other increases (and conversely).

Complex multiplier The *multiplier* which exists when changes in the *gross domestic product* change *net taxes* and *imports*, as well as *saving.*

Conglomerate combination A group of *plants* owned by a single *firm* and engaged at one or more stages in the production of different products (of products that do not compete with each other).

Consumer goods Products and services which satisfy human wants directly.

Consumer price index (CPI) An index which measures the prices of a fixed "market basket" of some 300 goods and services bought by a "typical" consumer.

Consumer sovereignty Determination by consumers of the types and quantities of goods and services which will be produced with the scarce resources of the economy; consumer direction of production through dollar votes.

Consumption of fixed capital Estimate of the amount of *capital* worn out or used up (consumed) in producing the *gross domestic product*; also called *depreciation.*

Consumption schedule A schedule showing the amounts *households* plan to spend for *consumer goods* at different levels of *disposable income.*

Contractionary fiscal policy A decrease in *government expenditures* for goods and services, an increase in *net taxes*, or some combination of the two, for the purpose of decreasing *aggregate demand* and thus controlling inflation.

Coordination failure A situation in which people do not reach a mutually beneficial outcome because they lack some way to jointly coordinate their actions; a possible cause of macroeconomic instability.

Corporate income tax A tax levied on the net income (profit) of corporations.

Corporation A legal entity ("person") chartered by a state or the Federal government which is distinct and separate from the individuals who own it.

Correlation A systematic and dependable association between two sets of data (two kinds of events); does not itself indicate causation.

Cost-of-living adjustment (COLA) An automatic increase in the incomes (wages) of workers when inflation occurs; guaranteed by a collective bargaining contract between firms and workers.

Cost-push inflation Increases in the price level (inflation) resulting from an increase in resource costs (for example, higher wage rates and raw material prices) and hence in *per-unit production costs;* inflation caused by reductions in *aggregate supply.*

Cost ratio An equality showing the number of units of two products which can be produced with the same resources; the cost ratio 1 corn ≡ 3 olives shows that the resources required to produce 3 units of olives must be shifted to corn production to produce 1 unit of corn.

Council of Economic Advisers A group of three persons that advises and assists the President of the United States on economic matters (including the preparation of the annual *Economic Report of the President*).

Credit An accounting item which increases the value of an asset (such as the foreign money owned by the residents of a nation).

Credit union An association of persons who have a common tie (such as being employees of the same firm or members of the same labor union) which sells shares to (accepts deposits from) its members and makes loans to them.

Crowding model of occupational discrimination A model of labor markets suggesting that *occupational discrimination* has kept many women and minorities out of high-paying occupations and forced them into a limited number of low-paying occupations.

Crowding-out effect A rise in interest rates and a resulting decrease in *planned investment* caused by the Federal government's increased borrowing in the money market.

Currency Coins and paper money.

Currency appreciation (See *Exchange rate appreciation.*)

Currency depreciation (See *Exchange rate depreciation.*)

Current account The section in a nation's *international balance of payments* which records its exports and imports of goods and services, its *net investment income*, and its *net transfers.*

Customary economy (See *Traditional economy.*)

Cyclical deficit A Federal *budget deficit* which is caused by a recession and the consequent decline in tax revenues.

Cyclical unemployment A type of *unemployment* caused by insufficient total spending (or by insufficient *aggregate demand*).

Cyclically balanced budget The equality of *government expenditures* and *net tax collections* over the course of a *business cycle;* deficits incurred during periods of recession are offset by surpluses obtained during periods of prosperity (inflation).

D

Debit An accounting item which decreases the value of an asset (such as the foreign money owned by the residents of a nation).

Deduction Reasoning from assumptions to conclusions; a method of reasoning which first develops a hypothesis (an assumption) and then tests the hypothesis with economic facts.

Deflating Finding the *real gross domestic product* by decreasing the dollar value of the GDP for a year in which prices were higher than in the *base year.*

Deflation A decline in the economy's *price level.*

Demand A schedule showing the amounts of a good or service buyers (or a buyer) wish to purchase at various prices during some time period.

Demand curve A curve illustrating *demand.*

Demand deposit A deposit in a *commercial bank* or *thrift* against which checks may be written; a *checkable deposit.*

Demand-deposit multiplier (See *Monetary multiplier.*)

Demand factor (in growth) The increase in the level of *aggregate demand* which brings about the *economic growth* made possible by an increase in the production potential of the economy.

Demand management The use of *fiscal policy* and *monetary policy* to increase or decrease *aggregate demand.*

Demand-pull inflation Increases in the price level (inflation) resulting from an excess of demand over output at the existing price level, caused by an increase in *aggregate demand.*

Dependent variable A variable which changes as a consequence of a change in some other (independent) variable; the "effect" or outcome.

Depository institutions Firms which accept the deposits of *money* of the public (businesses and persons); *commercial banks, savings and loan associations, mutual savings banks,* and *credit unions.*

Depreciation (See *Consumption of fixed capital.*)

Depreciation (of the dollar) A decrease in the value of the dollar relative to another currency so that a dollar buys a smaller amount of the foreign currency and therefore of foreign goods.

Derived demand The demand for a resource which depends on the demand for the products it can be used to produce.

Determinants of aggregate demand Factors such as consumption spending, *investment*, government spending, and *net exports* which, if they change, shift the *aggregate demand curve*.

Determinants of aggregate supply Factors such as input prices, *productivity*, and the legal-institutional environment which, if they change, shift the *aggregate supply curve*.

Determinants of demand Factors other than its price which determine the quantities demanded of a good or service.

Determinants of supply Factors other than its price which determine the quantities supplied of a good or service.

Devaluation A decrease in the governmentally defined value of a currency.

Developing countries Many countries of Africa, Asia, and Latin America which are characterized by a lack of capital goods, use of nonadvanced technologies, low literacy rates, high unemployment, rapid population growth, and labor forces heavily committed to agriculture.

Direct foreign investment The building of new factories (or the purchase of existing capital) in a particular nation by corporations of other nations.

Direct relationship The relationship between two variables which change in the same direction, for example, product price and quantity supplied.

Discount rate The interest rate which the *Federal Reserve Banks* charge on the loans they make to *commercial banks* and *thrift institutions*.

Discouraged workers Employees who have left the *labor force* because they have been unable to find employment.

Discrimination According individuals or groups inferior treatment in hiring, occupational access, education and training, promotion, wage rates, or working conditions, even though they have the same abilities, education and skills, and work experience as other workers.

Discretionary fiscal policy Deliberate changes in taxes (tax rates) and government spending by Congress to promote full-employment, price stability, and economic growth.

Diseconomies of scale Increase in the *average total cost* of producing a product as the *firm* expands the size of its *plant* (its output) in the *long run*.

Disinflation A reduction in the rate of *inflation*.

Disposable income *Personal income* less personal taxes; income available for *personal consumption expenditures* and *personal saving*.

Dissaving Spending for consumer goods and services in excess of *disposable income*; the amount by which *personal consumption expenditures* exceed disposable income.

Dividends Payments by a corporation of all or part of its profit to its stockholders (the corporate owners).

Division of labor Dividing the work required to produce a product into a number of different tasks which are performed by different workers; *specialization* of workers.

Dollar votes The "votes" which consumers and entrepreneurs cast for the production of consumer and capital goods, respectively, when they purchase them in product and resource markets.

Domestic capital formation Addition to a nation's stock of *capital* by saving and investing part of its own domestic output.

Domestic output *Gross* (or net) *domestic product*; the total output of *final goods and services* produced in the economy.

Domestic price The price of a good or service within a country, determined by domestic demand and supply.

Double taxation The taxation of both corporate net income (profits) and the *dividends* paid from this net income when they become the personal income of households.

Dumping The sale of products below cost in a foreign country or below the prices charged at home.

Durable good A consumer good with an expected life (use) of 3 or more years.

Dynamic efficiency The development over time of less costly production techniques, improved products, and new products; technological progress.

E

E-cash Electronic money; an entry (usable as money) stored in a computer or a stored-value card ("smart card").

Earnings The money income received by a worker; equal to the *wage* (rate) multiplied by the amount of time worked.

Easy money policy Federal Reserve System actions to increase the *money supply* to lower interest rates and expand *real GDP*.

Economic analysis Deriving *economic principles* from relevant economic facts.

Economic cost A payment which must be made to obtain and retain the services of a *resource*; the income a firm must provide to a resource supplier to attract the resource away from an alternative use; equal to the quantity of other products which cannot be produced when resources are instead used to make a particular product.

Economic efficiency Obtaining the socially optimal amounts of goods and services using minimum necessary resources; entails both *productive efficiency* and *allocative efficiency*.

Economic growth (1) An outward shift in the *production possibilities curve* which results from an increase in resource quantity or quality or an improvement in *technology*; (2) an increase either in real output (*gross domestic product*) or in real output per capita.

Economic integration Cooperation among and the complete or partial unification of the economies of different nations; the elimination of barriers to trade among these nations; the bringing together of the markets in each of the separate economies to form one large (a common) market.

Economic law   (See *Economic principle*.)

Economic model   A simplified picture of economic reality; an abstract generalization.

Economic perspective   A viewpoint which envisions individuals and institutions making rational decisions by comparing the marginal benefits and marginal costs associated with their actions.

Economic policy   A course of action intended to correct or avoid a problem.

Economic principle   A widely accepted generalization about the economic behavior of individuals and institutions.

Economic profit   The *total revenue* of a firm less all its *economic costs;* also called "pure profit" and "above normal profit."

Economic regulation   (See *Industrial regulation*.)

Economic rent   The price paid for the use of land and other natural resources, the supply of which is fixed (*perfectly inelastic*).

Economic resources   The *land, labor, capital,* and *entrepreneurial ability* which are used in the production of goods and services; productive agents; factors of production.

Economics   The social science dealing with the use of scarce resources to obtain the maximum satisfaction of society's virtually unlimited material wants.

Economic theory   Deriving *economic principles* from relevant economic facts; an *economic principle*.

Economic system   A particular set of institutional arrangements and a coordinating mechanism for solving the economizing problem; a method of organizing an economy; of which the *market economy, command economy,* and *traditional economy* are three general types.

Economies of scale   Reductions in the *average total cost* of producing a product as the firm expands the size of plant (its output) in the *long run*; the economies of mass production.

Economizing problem   The choices necessitated because society's material wants for goods and services are unlimited but the *resources* available to satisfy these wants are limited (scarce).

Efficiency factors (in growth)   The capacity of an economy to combine resources effectively to achieve growth of real output which the *supply factors* (of growth) make possible.

Efficient allocation of resources   That allocation of the resources of an economy among the production of different products which leads to the maximum satisfaction of the wants of consumers; producing the socially optimal mix of output with society's scarce resources.

Employment Act of 1946   Federal legislation that committed the Federal government to the maintenance of economic stability (a high level of employment, a stable price level, and economic growth); established the *Council of Economic Advisers* and the *Joint Economic Committee*; and re-

quired an annual economic report of the President to Congress.

Employment rate   The percentage of the *labor force* employed at any time.

Entrepreneurial ability   The human resources which combine the other resources to produce a product, make nonroutine decisions, innovate, and bear risks.

Equation of exchange $MV = PQ$, in which M is the supply of money, V is the *velocity of money, P* is the *price level,* and Q is the physical volume of *final goods and services* produced.

Equilibrium real domestic output   The *gross domestic product* at which the total quantity of final goods and services purchased (*aggregate expenditures*) is equal to the total quantity of final goods and services produced (the real domestic output); the real domestic output at which the *aggregate demand curve* intersects the *aggregate supply curve*.

Equilibrium price   The *price* in a competitive market at which the *quantity demanded* and the *quantity supplied* are equal; where there is neither a *shortage* nor a *surplus*; and where there is no tendency for price to rise or fall.

Equilibrium price level   The price level at which the *aggregate demand curve* intersects the *aggregate supply curve*.

Equilibrium quantity   (1) The quantity demanded and supplied at the equilibrium price in a competitive market; (2) the profit-maximizing output of a firm.

European Union (EU)   An association of European nations initiated in 1958 which has eliminated tariffs and import quotas that existed among them, established common tariffs for goods imported from outside the member nations, allowed the free movement of labor and capital among them, and created other common economic policies.

Excess reserves   The amount by which a bank or thrift's *actual reserves* exceed its *required reserves;* actual reserves minus required reserves.

Exchange control   (See *Foreign exchange control*.)

Exchange rate   The *rate of exchange* of one nation's currency for another nation's currency.

Exchange-rate appreciation   An increase in the value of a nation's currency in foreign exchange markets; an increase in the *rate of exchange* for foreign currencies.

Exchange-rate depreciation   A decrease in the value of a nation's currency in foreign exchange markets; a decrease in the *rate of exchange* for foreign currencies.

Exchange-rate determinant   Any factor other than the *rate of exchange* which determines a currency's demand and supply in the *foreign exchange market*.

Excise tax   A tax levied on the production of a specific product or on the quantity of the product purchased.

Exclusion principle   The ability to exclude those who do not pay for a product from receiving its benefits.

Exhaustive expenditure   An expenditure by government resulting directly in the employment of *economic resources* and in the absorption by government of the goods and services those resources produce; a *government purchase*.

Expanding industry An industry whose firms earn *economic profits* and which experience an increase in output as new firms enter the industry.

Expansionary fiscal policy An increase in *government expenditures* for goods and services, a decrease in *net taxes*, or some combination of the two for the purpose of increasing *aggregate demand* and expanding real output.

Expectations The anticipations of consumers, firms, and others about future economic conditions.

Expected rate of return The increase in profit a firm anticipates it will obtain by purchasing capital (or engaging in research and development), expressed as a percentage of the total cost of the investment (or R&D) activity.

Expenditures approach The method which adds all expenditures made for *final goods and services* to measure the *gross domestic product.*

Expenditures-output approach (See *Aggregate expenditures-domestic output approach.*)

Export controls The limitation or prohibition of the export of certain products on the basis of foreign policy or national security objectives.

Export-Import Bank A Federal institution which provides interest-rate subsidies to foreign borrowers who buy U.S. exports on credit.

Exports Goods and services produced in a nation and sold to customers in other nations.

Export subsidies Government payments to domestic producers to enable them to reduce the *price* of a good or service to foreign buyers.

Export supply curve An upsloping curve showing the amount of a product domestic firms will export at each *world price* above the *domestic price.*

Export transactions A sale of a good or service which increases the amount of foreign currency flowing to the citizens, firms, and governments of a nation.

External benefit (See *Spillover benefit.*)

External cost (See *Spillover cost.*)

External debt Private or public debt owed to foreign citizens, firms, and institutions.

Externality (See *Spillover.*)

F

Face value The dollar or cents value stamped on a U.S. coin.

Factors of production *Economic resources: land, capital, labor,* and *entrepreneurial ability.*

Fallacy of composition Incorrectly reasoning that what is true for the individual (or part) is necessarily true for the group (or whole).

Fallacy of limited decisions The false notion that there are a limited number of economic decisions to be made so that, if government makes more decisions, there will be fewer private decisions to render.

FDIC (See *Federal Deposit Insurance Corporation.*)

Federal Advisory Committee The group of 12 commercial bankers that advises the Board of Governors on banking policy.

Federal Deposit Insurance Corporation (FDIC) The Federally chartered corporation which insures the deposit liabilities of *commercial banks* and *thrift institutions.*

Federal funds rate The interest rate banks and other depository institutions charge one another on overnight loans made out of their *excess reserves.*

Federal government The government of the United States, as distinct from the state and local governments.

Federal Open Market Committee (FOMC) The 12-member group that determines the purchase-and-sale policies of the *Federal Reserve Banks* in the market for U.S. government securities.

Federal Reserve Banks The 12 banks chartered by the U.S. government to control the *money supply* and perform other functions. (See *Central bank, Quasipublic bank,* and *Banker's bank.*)

Federal Reserve Notes Paper money issued by the *Federal Reserve Banks.*

Feedback effects (of monetary policy) The effects that a change in the money supply will have (because it affects the interest rate, planned investment, and the equilibrium GDP) on the demand for money, which is itself directly related to the GDP.

Fiat money Anything which is *money* because government has decreed it to be money.

Final goods and services Goods and services which have been purchased for final use and not for resale or further processing or manufacturing.

Financial capital (See *Money capital.*)

Firm An organization which employs resources to produce a good or service for profit and owns and operates one or more *plants.*

Fiscal federalism The system of transfers (grants) by which the Federal government shares its revenues with state and local governments.

Fiscal policy Changes in government spending and tax collections designed to achieve a full-employment and non-inflationary domestic output; also called *discretionary fiscal policy.*

Five fundamental economic questions The 5 questions which every economy must answer: how much to produce, what to produce, how to produce it, how to divide the total output, and how to ensure economic flexibility.

Fixed exchange rate A *rate of exchange* which is set in some way and hence prevented from rising or falling with changes in currency supply and demand.

Flexible exchange rate A *rate of exchange* determined by the international demand for and supply of a nation's money; a rate free to rise or fall (to float).

Floating exchange rate   (See *Flexible exchange rate.*)

Foreign competition   (See *Import competition.*)

Foreign exchange control   The control a government may exercise over the quantity of foreign currency demanded by its citizens and firms and over the *rates of exchange* in order to limit its *outpayments* to its *inpayments* (to eliminate a *payments deficit*).

Foreign exchange market   A market in which the money (currency) of one nation can be used to purchase (can be exchanged for) the money of another nation.

Foreign exchange rate   (See *Rate of exchange.*)

Foreign purchase effect   The inverse relationship between the *net exports* of an economy and its price level relative to foreign price levels.

45-degree line   A line along which the value of *GDP* (measured horizontally) is equal to the value of *aggregate expenditures* (measured vertically).

Fractional reserve   A *reserve ratio* that is less than 100 percent of the deposit liabilities of a *commercial bank* or *thrift institution*.

Freedom of choice   The freedom of owners of property resources to employ or dispose of them as they see fit, of workers to enter any line of work for which they are qualified, and of consumers to spend their incomes in a manner which they think is appropriate.

Freedom of enterprise   The freedom of *firms* to obtain economic resources, to use these resources to produce products of the firm's own choosing, and to sell their products in markets of their choice.

Free-rider problem   The inability of potential providers of an economically desirable but indivisible good or service to obtain payment from those who benefit because the *exclusion principle* is not applicable.

Free trade   The absence of artificial (government-imposed) barriers to trade among individuals and firms in different nations.

Frictional unemployment   A type of unemployment caused by workers voluntarily changing jobs and by temporary layoffs; unemployed workers between jobs.

Full employment   (1) Use of all available resources to produce want-satisfying goods and services. (2) The situation when the *unemployment rate* is equal to the *full-employment unemployment rate* and there is *frictional* and *structural* but no *cyclical unemployment* (and the *real output* of the economy equals its *potential real output*).

Full-employment budget   A comparison of the government expenditures and tax collections which would occur if the economy operated at *full employment* throughout the year.

Full-employment unemployment rate   The *unemployment rate* at which there is no *cyclical unemployment* of the *labor force*; equal to about 5.5 percent in the United States because some *frictional* and *structural unemployment* are unavoidable.

Full production   Employment of available resources so that the maximum amount of (or total value of) goods and services is produced; occurs when both *productive efficiency* and *allocative efficiency* are realized.

Functional distribution of income   The manner in which *national income* is divided among the functions performed to earn it (or the kinds of resources provided to earn it); the division of national income into wages and salaries, proprietors' income, corporate profits, interest, and rent.

Functional finance   The use of *fiscal policy* to achieve a noninflationary full employment *gross domestic product* without regard to the effect on the *public debt*.

G

G-7 Nations   A group of seven major industrial nations (the United States, Japan, Germany, United Kingdom, France, Italy, and Canada) whose leaders meet regularly to discuss common economic problems and try to coordinate economic policies. (Recently has also included Russia, making it unofficially the G-8.)

Gains from trade   The extra output which trading partners obtain through specialization of production and exchange of goods and services.

GDP   (See *Gross domestic product.*)

GDP deflator   The *price index* found by dividing *nominal GDP* by *real GDP*; a price index used to adjust money (or nominal) GDP to real GDP.

GDP gap   The amount by which actual *gross domestic product* falls below *potential gross domestic product*.

General Agreement on Tariffs and Trade (GATT)   The international agreement reached in 1947 in which 23 nations agreed to give equal and nondiscriminatory treatment to the other nations, to reduce tariff rates by multinational negotiations, and to eliminate *import quotas*. Now includes most nations and has become the *World Trade Organization*.

Generalization   Statement of the nature of the relation between two or more sets of facts.

Gold standard   A historical system of fixed exchange rates in which nations defined their currency in terms of gold, maintained a fixed relationship between their stock of gold and their money supplies, and allowed gold to be freely exported and imported.

Government purchases   Disbursements of money by government for which government receives a currently produced good or service in return; the expenditures of all governments in the economy for *final goods and services*.

Government transfer payment   The disbursement of money (or goods and services) by government for which government receives no currently produced good or service in return.

Gross domestic product (GDP)   The total market value of all *final goods and services* produced annually within the boundaries of the United States, whether by U.S. or foreign-supplied resources.

Gross private domestic investment Expenditures for newly produced *capital goods* (such as machinery, equipment, tools, and buildings) and for additions to inventories.

Guiding function of prices The ability of price changes to bring about changes in the quantities of products and resources demanded and supplied.

H

Horizontal axis The "left-right" or "west-east" axis on a graph or grid.

Horizontal combination A group of *plants* in the same stage of production which are owned by a single *firm*.

Horizontal range The horizontal segment of the *aggregate-supply curve* along which the price level is constant as real domestic output changes.

Household An economic unit (of one or more persons) which provides the economy with resources and uses the income received to purchase goods and services that satisfy material wants.

Human capital The accumulation of prior investments in education, training, health, and other factors which increase productivity.

Hyperinflation A very rapid rise in the price level.

Hypothesis A tentative, untested economic principle.

I

IMF (See *International Monetary Fund.*)

Import competition The competition which domestic firms encounter from the products and services of foreign producers.

Import demand curve A downsloping curve showing the amount of a product which an economy will import at each *world price* below the *domestic price.*

Import quota A limit imposed by a nation on the quantity (or total value) of a good which may be imported during some period of time.

Imports Spending by individuals, *firms,* and governments for goods and services produced in foreign nations.

Import transaction The purchase of a good or service which decreases the amount of foreign money held by citizens, firms, and governments of a nation.

Income approach The method that adds all the income generated by the production of *final goods and services* to measure the *gross domestic product.*

Income effect A change in the price of a product changes a consumer's *real income* (*purchasing power*) and thus the quantity of the product purchased.

Income inequality The unequal distribution of an economy's total income among persons or families.

Income-maintenance system Government programs designed to eliminate poverty and reduce inequality in the distribution of income.

Increase in demand An increase in the *quantity demanded* of a good or service at every price; a shift of the *demand curve* to the right.

Increase in supply An increase in the *quantity supplied* of a good or service at every price; a shift of the *supply curve* to the right.

Independent goods Products or services for which there is no relationship between the price of one and the demand for the other; when the price of one rises or falls, the demand for the other remains constant.

Independent variable The variable causing a change in some other (dependent) variable.

Indirect business taxes Such taxes as *sales, excise,* and business *property taxes,* license fees, and *tariffs* which firms treat as costs of producing a product and pass on (in whole or in part) to buyers by charging higher prices.

Individual demand The demand schedule or *demand curve* of a single buyer.

Individual supply The supply schedule or *supply curve* of a single seller.

Induction A method of reasoning which proceeds from facts to *generalization.*

Industrially advanced countries High-income countries such as the United States, Canada, Japan, and the nations of western Europe which have highly developed *market economies* based on large stocks of technologically advanced capital goods and skilled labor forces.

Industrial policy Any policy by which government takes a direct and active role in promoting specific firms or industries for purposes of expanding their output and achieving economic growth; called "technology policy" when its goal is to promote *technological advance.*

Industry A group of (one or more) *firms* which produces identical or similar products.

Inferior good A good or service whose consumption declines as income rises (and conversely), price remaining constant.

Inflating Determining *real gross domestic product* by increasing the dollar value of the *nominal gross domestic product* produced in a year in which prices are lower than in a *base year.*

Inflation A rise in the general level of prices in an economy.

Inflation premium The component of the *nominal interest rate* which reflects anticipated inflation.

Inflationary expectations The belief of workers, firms, and consumers that substantial inflation will occur in the future.

Inflationary gap The amount by which the *aggregate expenditures schedule* must shift downward to decrease the *nominal GDP* to its full-employment noninflationary level.

Infrastructure The capital goods usually provided by the *public sector* for the use of its citizens and firms (for example, highways, bridges, transit systems, wastewater treatment facilities, municipal water systems, and airports).

Injection An addition of spending to the income-expenditure stream: *investment, government purchases,* and *net exports.*

In-kind investment (See *Nonfinancial investment.*)

Innovation The first commercially successful introduction of a new product, the use of a new method of production, or the creation of a new form of business organization.

Inpayments The receipts of its own or foreign money which individuals, firms, and governments of one nation obtain from the sale of goods and services abroad, or as investment income, *remittances,* and *capitals inflows* from abroad.

Insider-outsider theory The hypothesis that nominal wages are inflexible downward because firms are aware that workers ("insiders") who retain employment during recession may refuse to work cooperatively with previously unemployed workers ("outsiders") who offer to work for less than the current wage.

Interest The payment made for the use of money (of borrowed funds).

Interest income Payments of income to those who supply the economy with *capital.*

Interest rate The annual rate at which interest is paid; a percentage of the borrowed amount.

Interest-rate effect The tendency for increases in the *price level* to increase the demand for money, raise interest rates, and, as a result, reduce total spending in the economy (and the reverse for price level decreases).

Intermediate goods Products which are purchased for resale or further processing or manufacturing.

Intermediate range The upsloping segment of the *aggregate supply curve* lying between the *horizontal range* and the *vertical range.*

Internally held public debt *Public debt* owed to citizens, firms, and institutions of the same nation issuing the debt.

International balance of payments A summary of all the transactions which took place between the individuals, firms, and government unit of one nation and those in all other nations during a year.

International balance of payments deficit (See *Balance of payments deficit.*)

International balance of payments surplus (See *Balance of payments surplus.*)

International Bank for Reconstruction and Development (See *World Bank.*)

International gold standard (See *Gold standard.*)

International Monetary Fund (IMF) The international association of nations which was formed after World War II to make loans of foreign monies to nations with temporary *payments deficits* and, until the early 1970s, to administer the *adjustable pegs;* it now mainly makes loans to nations facing possible defaults on private and government loans.

International monetary reserves The foreign currencies and such assets as gold a nation may use to settle a *payments deficit.*

International value of the dollar The price which must be paid in foreign currency (money) to obtain one U.S. dollar.

Intrinsic value The market value of the metal within a coin.

Inventories Goods which have been produced but are still unsold.

Inverse relationship The relationship between two variables which change in opposite directions, for example, product price and quantity demanded.

Investment Spending for the production and accumulation of *capital* and additions to inventories.

Investment goods Same as *capital.*

Investment schedule A curve or schedule which shows the amounts firms plan to invest at various possible values of *real gross domestic product.*

Investment-demand curve A curve which shows the amount of *investment* demanded by an economy at a series of *real interest rates.*

Investment in human capital (See *Human-capital investment.*)

Invisible hand The tendency of firms and resource suppliers seeking to further their own self-interests in competitive markets to also promote the interest of society as a whole.

J

Joint Economic Committee (JEC) Committee of Senators and Representatives which investigates economic problems of national interest.

K

Keynesian economics The macroeconomic generalizations which lead to the conclusion that a capitalistic economy is characterized by macroeconomic instability and that *fiscal policy* and *monetary policy* can be used to promote *full employment, price-level stability,* and *economic growth.*

Keynesianism The philosophical, ideological, and analytical views pertaining to *Keynesian economics.*

L

Labor The physical and mental talents and efforts of people which are used to produce goods and services.

Labor force Persons 16 years of age and older who are not in institutions and who are employed or are unemployed (and seeking work).

Labor force participation rate The percentage of the working-age population which is actually in the *labor force.*

Labor-intensive commodity A product requiring a relatively large amount of *labor* to produce.

Labor productivity Total output divided by the quantity of labor employed to produce it; the *average product* of labor or output per worker per hour.

Labor theory of value The Marxian idea that the economic value of any commodity is determined solely by the amount of labor required to produce it.

Labor union A group of workers organized to advance the interests of the group (to increase wages, shorten the hours worked, improve working conditions, and so on.).

Laffer curve A curve showing the relationship between tax rates and the tax revenues of government and on which there is a tax rate (between 0 and 100 percent) where tax revenues are a maximum.

Laissez faire capitalism (See *Pure capitalism.*)

Land Natural resources ("free gifts of nature") used to produce goods and services.

Land-intensive commodity A product requiring a relatively large amount of land to produce.

Law of demand The principle that, other things equal, an increase in a product's price will reduce the quantity of it demanded; and conversely for a decrease in price.

Law of increasing opportunity costs As the production of a good increases, the *opportunity cost* of producing an additional unit rises.

Law of supply The principle that, other things equal, an increase in the price of a product will increase the quantity of it supplied; and conversely for a price decrease.

Leakage (1) A withdrawal of potential spending from the income-expenditures stream via *saving*, tax payments, or *imports*. (2) A withdrawal which reduces the lending potential of the banking system.

Leakages-injections approach Determination of the equilibrium *gross domestic product* by finding the real GDP at which *leakages* are equal to *injections*.

Least-cost combination of resources The quantity of each resource a firm must employ in order to produce a particular output at the lowest total cost; the combination at which the ratio of the *marginal product* of a resource to its *marginal resource cost* (to its *price* if the resource is employed in a competitive market) is the same for the last dollar spent on each resource employed.

Legal reserves The minimum amount a *depository institution* must keep on deposit with the *Federal Reserve Bank* in its district, or in *vault cash*.

Legal tender Anything which government says must be accepted in payment of a debt.

Lending potential of an individual commercial bank The amount by which a single bank can safely increase the *money supply* by making new loans to (or buying securities from) the public; equal to the bank's excess reserves.

Lending potential of the banking system The amount by which the banking system can increase the money supply by making new loans to (or buying securities from) the pub-

lic; equal to the *excess reserves* of the banking system multiplied by the *monetary multiplier.*

Liability A debt with a monetary value; an amount owed by a firm or an individual.

Limited liability Restriction of the maximum loss to a predetermined amount for the owners (stockholders) of a *corporation;* the maximum loss is the amount they paid for their shares of stock.

Limited-liability company An unincorporated business whose owners are protected by *limited liability.*

Line-item veto The presidential power to delete specific expenditure items from spending legislation passed by Congress.

Liquidity *Money* or things which can be quickly and easily converted into money with little or no loss of purchasing power.

Long run (1) In *microeconomics*, a period of time long enough to enable producers of a product to change the quantities of all the resources they employ; period in which all resources and costs are variable and no resources or costs are fixed. (2) In *macroeconomics*, a period sufficiently long for *nominal wages* and other input prices to change in response to a change in the nation's *price level.*

Long-run aggregate supply curve The *aggregate supply curve* associated with a time period in which input prices (especially *nominal wages*) are fully responsive to changes in the *price level.*

Lump-sum tax A tax which is a constant amount (the tax revenue of government is the same) at all levels of GDP.

M

M1 The most narrowly defined *money supply;* the *currency* and *checkable deposits* not owned by the *Federal government*, *Federal Reserve Banks*, or *depository institutions.*

M2 A more broadly defined money supply; equal to *M1* plus *noncheckable savings deposits, money market deposit accounts,* small *time deposits* (deposits of less than $100,000), and individual *money market mutual fund balances.*

M3 Very broadly defined *money supply;* equal to *M2* plus large *time deposits* (deposits of $100,000 or more).

Macroeconomics The part of economics concerned with the economy as a whole; with such major aggregates as the household, business, and governmental sectors; and with measures of the total economy.

Managed floating exchange rate An *exchange rate* which is allowed to change (float) as a result of changes in currency supply and demand but at times is altered (managed) by governments via their buying and selling of particular currencies.

Marginal analysis The comparison of marginal ("extra" or "additional") benefits and marginal costs, usually for decision making.

Marginal benefit The extra (additional) benefit of consuming one more unit of some good or service; the change in total benefit when one more unit is consumed.

Marginal cost   The extra (additional) cost of producing one more unit of output; equal to the change in *total cost* divided by the change in output (and in the short run to the change in total *variable cost* divided by the change in output).

Marginal propensity to consume   The fraction of any change in *disposable income* spent for *consumer goods*; equal to the change in consumption divided by the change in disposable income.

Marginal propensity to save   The fraction of any change in *disposable income* which households save; equal to the change in *saving* divided by the change in disposable income.

Marginal tax rate   The tax rate paid on each additional dollar of income.

Marginal utility   The extra *utility* a consumer obtains from the consumption of one additional unit of a good or service; equal to the change in total utility divided by the change in the quantity consumed.

Market   Any institution or mechanism which brings together buyers (demanders) and sellers (suppliers) of a particular good or service.

Market demand   (See *Total demand.*)

Market economy   An economy in which only the private decisions of consumers, resource suppliers, and firms determine how resources are allocated; the market system.

Market failure   The failure of a market to bring about the allocation of resources which best satisfies the wants of society. In particular, the over- or underallocation of resources to the production of a particular good or service because of *spillovers* or informational problems and because markets fail to provide desired *public goods.*

Market socialism   An *economic system* (method of organization) in which property resources are publicly owned *and* markets and prices are used to direct and coordinate economic activities.

Market system   All the product and resource markets of a *market economy* and the relationships among them; a method which allows the prices determined in these markets to allocate the economy's scarce resources and to communicate and coordinate the decisions made by consumers, firms, and resource suppliers.

Medium of exchange   Items sellers generally accept and buyers generally use to pay for a good or service; *money*; a convenient means of exchanging goods and services without engaging in *barter.*

Microeconomics   The part of economics concerned with such individual units as *industries, firms,* and *households;* and with individual markets, particular prices, and specific goods and services.

Minimum wage   The lowest *wage* employers may legally pay for an hour of work.

Mixed capitalism   An economy in which both government and private decisions determine how resources are allocated.

Monetarism   The macroeconomic view that the main cause of changes in aggregate output and the price level are fluctuations in the *money supply;* advocates of a *monetary rule.*

Monetary multiplier   The multiple of its *excess reserves* by which the banking system can expand *demand deposits* and thus the *money supply* by making new loans (or buying securities); and equal to 1 divided by the *required reserve ratio.*

Monetary policy   A central bank's changing of the *money supply* to influence interest rates and assist the economy in achieving a full-employment, noninflationary level of total output.

Monetary rule   The rule suggested by *monetarism;* the *money supply* should be expanded each year at the same annual rate as the potential rate of growth of the *real gross domestic product;* the supply of money should be increased steadily from 3 to 5 percent per year.

Money   Any item which generally is acceptable to sellers in exchange for goods and services.

Money capital   Money available to purchase *capital.*

Money income   (See *Nominal income.*)

Money interest rate   The *nominal interest rate;* the interest rate which includes an *inflationary premium* (if any).

Money market   The market in which the demand for and the supply of money determine the *interest rate* (or the level of interest rates) in the economy.

Money market deposit account (MMDA)   Interest-earning accounts at *banks* and *thrift institutions,* which pool the funds of depositors to buy various short-term securities.

Money market mutual funds (MMMF)   Interest-bearing accounts offered by investment companies, which pool depositors' funds for the purchase of short-term securities; depositors may write checks in minimum amounts or more against their accounts.

Money supply   Narrowly defined *M*1; more broadly defined, *M*2 and *M*3.

Money wage   (See *Nominal wage.*)

Money wage rate   (See *Nominal wage.*)

Monopoly   A market structure in which the number of sellers is so small that each seller is able to influence the total supply and the price of the good or service. (Also see *Pure monopoly.*)

Most-favored-nation (MFN) status   An agreement by the United States to allow some other nation's *exports* into the United States at the lowest tariff level levied by the United States, then or at any later time.

Multinational corporation   A firm which owns production facilities in other countries and produces and sells its product abroad.

Multiple counting   Wrongly including the value of *intermediate goods* in the *gross domestic product;* counting the same good or service more than once.

Multiplier   The ratio of a change in the *equilibrium GDP* to the change in *investment* or in any other component of *aggregate expenditures* or *aggregate demand;* the number by which a change in any component of aggregate expenditures or aggregate demand must be multiplied to find the resulting change in the equilibrium GDP.

Multiplier effect The effect on equilibrium GDP of a change in *aggregate expenditures* or *aggregate demand* (caused by a change in the *consumption schedule, investment, government expenditures,* or *net exports*).

Mutual savings bank A firm without stockholders which accepts deposits primarily from small individual savers and lends primarily to individuals to finance the purchases of autos and residences.

Mutually exclusive goals Two or more goals which conflict and cannot be achieved simultaneously.

N

National bank A *commercial bank* authorized to operate by the U.S. government.

National income Total income earned by resource suppliers for their contributions to *gross national product;* equal to the gross domestic product minus *nonincome charges,* minus *net foreign factor income.*

National income accounting The techniques used to measure the overall production of the economy and other related variables for the nation as a whole.

Natural monopoly An industry in which *economies of scale* are so great the product can be produced by one firm at a lower average total cost than if the product were produced by more than one firm.

Natural rate hypothesis The idea that the economy is stable in the long run at the *natural rate of unemployment;* views the long-run *Phillips Curve* as vertical at the *natural rate of unemployment.*

Natural rate of unemployment The *full-employment unemployment rate;* the unemployment rate occurring when there is no *cyclical unemployment* and the economy is achieving its *potential output;* the unemployment rate at which actual inflation equals expected inflation.

Near-money Financial assets, the most important of which are *noncheckable savings accounts, time deposits,* and U.S. short-term securities and savings bonds, which are not a medium of exchange but can be readily converted into money.

Negative relationship (See *Inverse relationship.*)

Net domestic product *Gross domestic product* less the part of the year's output which is needed to replace the *capital goods* worn out in producing the output; the nation's total output available for consumption or additions to the *capital stock.*

Net export effect The idea that the impact of a change in *monetary policy* or *fiscal policy* will be strengthened or weakened by the consequent change in *net exports;* the change in net exports occurs because of changes in real interest rates, which affect exchange rates.

Net exports *Exports* minus *imports.*

Net foreign factor income Payments by a nation of resource income to the rest of the world minus receipts of resource income from the rest of the world.

Net investment income The interest and dividend income received by the residents of a nation from residents of other nations less the interest and dividend payments made by the residents of that nation to the residents of other nations.

Net private domestic investment *Gross private domestic investment* less *consumption of fixed capital;* the addition to the nation's stock of *capital* during a year.

Net taxes The taxes collected by government less *government transfer payments.*

Net transfers The personal and government transfer payments made by one nation to residents of foreign nations, less the personal and government transfer payments received from residents of foreign nations.

Net worth The total *assets* less the total *liabilities* of a firm or an individual; the claims of the owners of a firm against its total assets.

New classical economics The theory that, although unanticipated price level changes may create macroeconomic instability in the short run, the economy is stable at the full-employment level of domestic output in the long run because prices and wages adjust automatically to correct movements away from the full employment, noninflationary output.

Nominal gross domestic product (GDP) The *GDP* measured in terms of the price level at the time of measurement (unadjusted for *inflation*).

Nominal income The number of dollars received by an individual or group for its resources during some period of time.

Nominal interest rate The interest rate expressed in terms of annual amounts currently charged for interest and not adjusted for inflation.

Nominal wage The amount of money received by a worker per unit of time (hour, day, etc.); money wage.

Noncheckable savings account A *savings account* against which a check can *not* be written.

Nondiscretionary fiscal policy (See *Built-in stabilizer*).

Nondurable good A *consumer good* with an expected life (use) of less than 3 years.

Nonexhaustive expenditure An expenditure by government which does not result directly in the employment of economic resources or the production of goods and services; see *Government transfer payment.*

Nonfinancial investment An investment which does not require *households* to save a part of their money incomes; but which uses surplus (unproductive) labor to build *capital goods.*

Nonincome charges *Consumption of fixed capital* and *indirect business taxes;* amounts subtracted from *GDP* (along with *net foreign factor income*) in determining *national income.*

Nonincome determinants of consumption and saving All influences on *consumption* and *saving* other than the level of *GDP.*

Noninterest determinants of investment All influences on the level of investment spending other than the *interest rate.*

Noninvestment transaction An expenditure for stocks, bonds, or second-hand *capital goods.*

Nonmarket transactions   The production of goods and services excluded in the measurement of the *gross domestic product* because they are not bought and sold.

Nonproduction transaction   The purchase and sale of any item which is not a currently produced good or service.

Nontariff barriers   All barriers other than *protective tariffs* which nations erect to impede international trade: include *import quotas*, licensing requirements, unreasonable product-quality standards, and unnecessary red tape in customs procedures.

Normal good   A good or service whose consumption increases when income increases and falls when income decreases, price remaining constant.

Normal profit   The payment made by a firm to obtain and retain *entrepreneurial ability*; the minimum income which entrepreneurial ability must receive to induce it to perform entrepreneurial functions for a firm.

Normative economics   That part of economics involving value judgments about what the economy should be like; concerned with identifying economic goals and promoting them via public policies.

North American Free Trade Agreement (NAFTA)   A 1993 agreement establishing, over a 15-year period, a free trade zone composed of Canada, Mexico, and the United States.

O

Official reserves   Foreign currencies owned by the central bank of a nation.

Okun's Law   The generalization that any one percentage point rise in the *unemployment rate* above the *full-employment unemployment rate* will increase the GDP gap by 2 percent of the *potential output* (GDP) of the economy.

OPEC   An acronym for the *Organization of Petroleum Exporting Countries.*

Open economy   An economy which exports and imports goods and services.

Open-market operations   The buying and selling of U.S. government securities by the *Federal Reserve Banks* for purposes of carrying out *monetary policy.*

Opportunity cost   The amount of other products which must be forgone or sacrificed to produce a unit of a product.

Organization of Petroleum Exporting Nations (OPEC)   The cartel formed in 1970 by 13 oil-producing countries to control the price and quantity of crude oil exported by its members, and which accounts for a large proportion of the world's export of oil.

Other things equal assumption   The assumption that factors other than those being considered are held constant.

Outpayments   The expenditures of its own or foreign currency which the individuals, firms, and governments of one nation make to purchase goods and services, for *remittances*, as investment income, and *capital outflows* abroad.

P

Paper money   Pieces of paper used as a *medium of exchange*; in the United States, *Federal Reserve Notes.*

Partnership   An unincorporated firm owned and operated by two or more persons.

Patent   An exclusive right to inventors to produce and sell a new product or machine for a set period of time.

Payments deficit   (See *Balance of payments deficit.*)

Payments surplus   (See *Balance of payments surplus.*)

Payroll tax   A tax levied on employers of labor equal to a percentage of all or part of the wages and salaries paid by them; and on employees equal to a percentage of all or part of the wages and salaries received by them.

Per capita GDP   *Gross domestic product* (GDP) per person; the average GDP of a population.

Per capita income   A nation's total income per person; the average income of a population.

Personal consumption expenditures   The expenditures of *households* for *durable* and *nondurable consumer goods* and services.

Personal distribution of income   The manner in which the economy's *personal* or *disposable income* is divided among different income classes or different households.

Personal income   The earned and unearned income available to resource suppliers and others before the payment of *personal taxes.*

Personal income tax   A tax levied on the *taxable income* of individuals, households, and unincorporated firms.

Personal saving   The *personal income* of households less *personal taxes* and *personal consumption expenditures*; *disposable income* not spent for *consumer goods.*

Per-unit production cost   The average production cost of a particular level of output; total input cost divided by units of output.

Phillips Curve   A curve showing the relationship between the *unemployment rate* (on the horizontal axis) and the annual rate of increase in the *price level* (on the vertical axis).

Planned economy   An economy in which government determines how resources are allocated.

Planned investment   The amount which *firms* plan or intend to invest.

Plant   A physical establishment which performs one or more functions in the production, fabrication, and distribution of goods and services.

Policy economics   The formulation of courses of action to bring about desired economic outcomes or to prevent undesired occurrences.

Political business cycle   The alleged tendency of Congress to destabilize the economy by reducing taxes and increasing government expenditures before elections and to raise taxes and lower expenditures after elections.

Positive economics   The analysis of facts or data to establish scientific generalizations about economic behavior.

Positive relationship   Direct relationship between two variables.

***Post hoc, ergo propter hoc* fallacy**   Incorrectly reasoning that when one event precedes another the first event must have caused the second event.

Potential output   The real output (*GDP*) an economy can produce when it fully employs its available resources.

Premature inflation   A type of inflation which sometimes occurs before the economy has reached *full employment*.

Price   The amount of money needed to buy a particular good, service, or resource.

Price index   An index number which shows how the weighted average price of a "market basket" of goods changes through time.

Price leadership   An informal method which firms in an *oligopoly* may employ to set the price of their product: one firm (the leader) is the first to announce a change in price, and the other firms (the followers) soon announce identical or similar changes.

Price level   The weighted average of the prices of all the final goods and services produced in an economy.

Price-level surprises   Unanticipated changes in the price level.

Price-level stability   A steadiness of the price level from one period to the next; zero or low annual inflation; also called "price stability."

Price-wage flexibility   Changes in the *prices* of products and in the *wages* paid to workers; the ability of prices and wages to rise or fall.

Price war   Successive and continued decreases in the prices charged by the firms in an oligopolistic industry; each firm lowers its price below rivals' prices, hoping to increase its sales and revenues at its rivals expense.

Prime interest rate   The *interest rate* banks charge their most creditworthy borrowers, for example, large corporations with excellent financing credentials.

Principal-agent problem   A conflict of interest which occurs when agents (workers or managers) pursue their own objectives to the detriment of the principals' (stockholders) goals.

Private good   A good or service which is subject to the *exclusion principle* and which is provided by privately owned firms to consumers who are willing to pay for it.

Private property   The right of private persons and firms to obtain, own, control, employ, dispose of, and bequeath *land*, *capital*, and other property.

Private sector   The *households* and business *firms* of the economy.

Production possibilities curve   A curve showing the different combinations of two goods or services that can be produced in a *full-employment, full-production* economy in which the available supplies of resources and technology are fixed.

Productive efficiency   The production of a good in the least costly way; occurs when production takes place at the output at which *average total cost* is a minimum and at which *marginal product* per dollar's worth of input is the same for all inputs.

Productivity   A measure of average output or real output per unit of input. For example, the productivity of labor may be found by dividing real output by hours of work.

Productivity slowdown   The decline in the rate at which *labor productivity* in the United States has increased in recent decades.

Product market   A market in which products are sold by *firms* and bought by *households*.

Profit   The return to the resource *entrepreneurial ability* (see *Normal profit*); *total revenue* minus *total cost* (see *Economic profit*).

Profit sharing plan   A compensation device through which workers receive part of their pay in the form of a share of their employer's profit (if any).

Progressive tax   A tax whose *average tax rate* increases as the taxpayer's income increases and decreases as the taxpayer's income decreases.

Property tax   A tax on the value of property (*capital*, *land*, stocks and bonds, and other *assets*) owned by *firms* and *households*.

Proportional tax   A tax whose *average tax rate* remains constant as the taxpayer's income increases or decreases.

Proprietor's income   The net income of the owners of unincorporated firms (proprietorships and partnerships).

Protective tariff   A *tariff* designed to shield domestic producers of a good or service from the competition of foreign producers.

Public debt   The total amount owed by the Federal government to the owners of government securities; equal to the sum of past government *budget deficits* less government *budget surpluses*.

Public finance   The branch of economics which analyzes government revenues and expenditures.

Public good   A good or service which is indivisible and to which the *exclusion principle* does not apply; a good or service with these characteristics provided by government.

Public sector   The part of the economy which contains all government entities; government.

Purchasing power   The amount of goods and services which a monetary unit of income can buy.

Purchasing power parity   The idea that exchange rates between nations equate the purchasing power of various currencies; exchange rates between any two nations adjust to reflect the price-level differences between the countries.

Pure capitalism   An economic system in which property resources are privately owned and markets and prices are used to direct and coordinate economic activities.

Pure rate of interest   An essentially risk-free, long-term interest rate which is free of the influence of market imperfections.

Q

Quantity demanded The amount of a good or service buyers (or a buyer) desire to purchase at a particular price during some period.

Quantity supplied The amount of a good or service producers (or a producer) offer to sell at a particular price during some period.

Quasipublic bank A bank which is privately owned but governmentally (publicly) controlled; each of the U.S. *Federal Reserve Banks*.

Quasipublic good A good or service to which the *exclusion principle* could apply but which has such a large *spillover benefit* that government sponsors its production to prevent an underallocation of resources.

R

R&D Research and development activities undertaken to bring about *technological progress*.

Ratchet effect The tendency for the *price level* to rise when *aggregate demand* increases but not fall when aggregate demand declines.

Rate of exchange The price paid in one's own money to acquire one unit of a foreign currency; the rate at which the money of one nation is exchanged for the money of another nation.

Rate of return The gain in net revenue divided by the cost of an investment or a *R&D* expenditure; expressed as a percentage.

Rational expectations theory The hypothesis that firms and households expect monetary and fiscal policies to have certain effects on the economy and (in pursuit of their own self-interests) take actions which make those policies ineffective.

Rationing function of prices The ability of market forces in a competitive market to equalize *quantity demanded* and *quantity supplied* and to eliminate shortages and surpluses via changes in prices.

Real-balances effect The tendency for increases in the price level to lower the real value (or purchasing power) of financial assets with fixed money value and, as a result, to reduce total spending; and conversely for decreases in the price level; also called the *wealth effect*.

Real business cycle theory A theory that *business cycles* result from changes in technology and resource availability, which affect *productivity* and thus increase or decrease *long-run aggregate supply*.

Real capital (See *Capital*.)

Real gross domestic product (GDP) *Gross domestic product* adjusted for inflation; gross domestic product in a year divided by the *GDP deflator* for that year, expressed as a decimal.

Real GDP (See *Real gross domestic product*.)

Real income The amount of goods and services which can be purchased with *nominal income* during some period of time; nominal income adjusted for inflation.

Real interest rate The interest rate expressed in dollars of constant value (adjusted for *inflation*); and equal to the *nominal interest rate* less the expected rate of inflation.

Real wage The amount of goods and services a worker can purchase with his or her *nominal wage*; the purchasing power of the nominal wage.

Recession A period of declining real GDP, accompanied by lower real income and higher unemployment.

Recessionary gap The amount by which the *aggregate expenditures schedule* must shift upward to increase the *real GDP* to its full-employment, noninflationary level.

Reciprocal Trade Agreements Act A 1934 Federal law which gave the President the authority to negotiate up to 50 percent lower tariffs with foreign nations that agreed to reduce their tariffs on U.S. goods (and which incorporated the *most-favored-nation clause*).

Refinancing the public debt Paying owners of maturing government securities with money obtained by selling new securities or with new securities.

Regressive tax A tax whose *average tax rate* decreases as the taxpayer's income increases, and increases as the taxpayer's income decreases.

Required reserves The funds which banks and thrifts must deposit with the *Federal Reserve Bank* (or hold as *vault cash*) to meet the legal *reserve requirement*; a fixed percentage of the bank or thrift's checkable deposits.

Reserve requirement The specified minimum percentage of its checkable deposits which a bank or thrift must keep on deposit at the Federal Reserve Bank in its district, or in *vault cash*.

Resource market A market in which *households* sell and *firms* buy resources or the services of resources.

Retiring the public debt Reducing the size of the *public debt* by paying money to owners of maturing U.S. government securities.

Revaluation An increase in the governmentally defined value of its currency relative to other nations' currencies.

Revenue tariff A *tariff* designed to produce income for the Federal government.

Roundabout production The construction and use of *capital* to aid in the production of *consumer goods*.

Rule of 70 A method for determining the number of years it will take for some measure to double, given its annual percentage increase. Example: To determine the number of years it will take for the *price level* to double; divide 70 by the annual rate of *inflation*.

S

Sales tax A tax levied on the cost (at retail) of a broad group of products.

Saving Disposable income not spent for consumer goods; equal to *disposable income* minus *personal consumption expenditures*.

Savings deposit An interest-bearing deposit which normally can be withdrawn by the depositor at any time.

Savings and Loan association (S&L) A firm which accepts deposits primarily from small individual savers and lends primarily to individuals to finance purchases such as autos and homes; now nearly indistinguishable from a *commercial bank.*

Saving schedule A schedule which shows the amounts *households* plan to save (plan not to spend for *consumer goods*), at different levels of *disposable income.*

Savings institution A *thrift institution.*

Say's law The largely discredited macroeconomic generalization that the production of goods and service (supply) creates an equal *demand* for these goods and service.

Scarce resources The limited quantities of *land, capital, labor,* and *entrepreneurial ability* which are never sufficient to satisfy the virtually unlimited material wants of humans.

Seasonal variations Increases and decreases in the level of economic activity within a single year, caused by a change in the season.

Secular trend Long-term tendency; change in some variable over a very long period of years.

Self-interest That which each firm, property owner, worker, and consumer believes is best for itself and seeks to obtain.

Seniority The length of time a worker has been employed absolutely or relative to other workers; may be used to determine which workers will be laid off when there is insufficient work for them all, and who will be rehired when more work becomes available.

Separation of ownership and control The fact that different groups of people own a *corporation* (the stockholders) and manage it (the directors and officers).

Service An (intangible) act or use for which a consumer, firm, or government is willing to pay.

Shirking Actions by workers to increase their *utility* or well-being by neglecting or evading work.

Shortage The amount by which the *quantity demanded* of a product exceeds the *quantity supplied* at a particular (below-equilibrium) price.

Short run (1) In *microeconomics,* a period of time in which producers are able to change the quantity of some but not all of the resources they employ; a period in which some resources (usually plant) are fixed and some are variable. (2) In *macroeconomics,* a period in which nominal wages and other input prices do not change in response to a change in the price level.

Short-run aggregate supply curve An aggregate supply curve relevant to a time period in which input prices (particularly *nominal wages*) do not change in response to changes in the *price level.*

Simple multiplier The *multiplier* in an economy in which government collects no *net taxes,* there are no *imports,* and

investment is independent of the level of income; equal to 1 divided by the *marginal propensity to save.*

Slope of a line The ratio of the vertical change (the rise or fall) to the horizontal change (the run) between any two points on a line. The slope of an upward sloping line is positive, reflecting a direct relationship between two variables; the slope of a downward sloping line is negative, reflecting an inverse relationship between two variables.

Smoot-Hawley Tariff Act Legislation passed in 1930 which established very high tariffs. Its objective was to reduce imports and stimulate the domestic economy, but it only resulted in retaliatory tariffs by other nations.

Social accounting (*See National income accounting.*)

Sole proprietorship An unincorporated *firm* owned and operated by one person.

Special economic zones Regions of China open to foreign investment, private ownership, and relatively free international trade.

Specialization The use of the resources of an individual, a firm, a region, or a nation to produce one or a few goods and services.

Speculation The activity of buying or selling with the motive of later reselling or rebuying for profit.

Spillover A benefit or cost from production or consumption, accruing without compensation to nonbuyers and nonsellers of the product (see *Spillover benefit; Spillover costs*).

Spillover benefit A benefit obtained without compensation by third parties from the production or consumption of sellers or buyers. Example: A beekeeper benefits when a neighboring farmer plants clover.

Spillover cost A cost imposed without compensation on third parties by the production or consumption of sellers or buyers. Example: A manufacturer dumps toxic chemicals into a river, killing the fish sport fishers seek.

Stagflation Inflation accompanied by stagnation in the rate of growth of output and an increase in unemployment in the economy; simultaneous increases in the *price level* and the *unemployment rate.*

State bank A *commercial bank* authorized by a state government to engage in the business of banking.

State-owned enterprises Businesses which are owned by government; the major types of enterprises in Russia and China before their transitions to the market system.

Stock (corporate) An ownership share in a corporation.

Store of value An *asset* set aside for future use; one of the three functions of *money.*

Strategic trade policy The use of trade barriers to reduce the risk inherent in product development by domestic firms, particularly that involving advanced technology.

Structural deficit The extent to which the Federal government's expenditures exceed its tax revenues when the economy is at full employment (or the extent to which its current expenditures exceed the projected tax revenues which would accrue if the economy were at full employment); also known as a full-employment budget deficit.

Structural unemployment   Unemployment of workers whose skills are not demanded by employers, they lack sufficient skill to obtain employment, or they cannot easily move to locations where jobs are available.

Subsidy   A payment of funds (or goods and services) by a government, firm, or household for which it receives no good or service in return; when made by a government, it is a *government transfer payment.*

Substitute goods   Products or services which can be used in place of each other. When the price of one falls the demand for the other falls, and conversely with an increase of price.

Substitution effect   (1) A change in the price of a *consumer good* changes the relative expensiveness of that good and hence changes the consumer's willingness to buy it rather than other goods. (2) The effect of a change in the price of a *resource* on the quantity of the resource employed by a firm, assuming no change in its output.

Superior good   (See *Normal good.*)

Supply   A schedule showing the amounts of a good or service sellers (or a seller) will offer at various prices during some period.

Supply curve   A curve illustrating *supply.*

Supply factor (in growth)   An increase in the availability of a resource, an improvement in its quality, or an expansion of technological knowledge which makes it possible for an economy to produce a greater output of goods and services.

Supply shock   An event which increases production costs, decreases *aggregate supply*, reduces *real GDP*, and increases *unemployment.*

Supply-side economics   A view of macroeconomics which emphasizes the role of costs and *aggregate supply* in explaining *inflation, unemployment*, and *economic growth.*

Surplus   The amount by which the *quantity supplied* of a product exceeds the *quantity demanded* at a specific (above-equilibrium) price.

Surplus value   A Marxian term; the amount by which the value of a worker's daily output exceeds the worker's daily wage; workers' output appropriated by capitalists as profit.

T

Tariff   A tax imposed by a nation on an imported good.

Tax   An involuntary payment of money (or goods and services) to a government by a *household* or *firm* for which the household or firm receives no good or service directly in return.

Tax incidence   The person or group who ends up paying a tax.

Technology   The body of knowledge and techniques which can be used to produce goods and services from *economic resources.*

Technological advance   New and better goods and services and new and better ways of producing or distributing them.

Terms of trade   The rate at which units of one product can be exchanged for units of another product; the price of a good or service; the amount of one good or service which must be given up to obtain one unit of another good or service.

Thrift institution   A *savings and loan association, mutual savings bank*, or *credit union.*

Tight money policy   *Federal Reserve System* actions which contract, or restrict, the growth of the nation's *money supply* for the purpose of reducing or eliminating inflation.

Till money   (See *Vault cash.*)

Time deposit   An interest-earning deposit in a *commercial bank* or *thrift institution* which the depositor can withdraw without penalty after the end of a specified period.

Token money   Coins having a *face value* greater than their *intrinsic value.*

Total demand   The demand schedule or the *demand curve* of all buyers of a good or service; also called market demand.

Total demand for money   The sum of the *transactions demand for money* and the *asset demand for money.*

Total product   The total output of a particular good or service produced by a firm (or a group of firms or the entire economy).

Total revenue   The total number of dollars received by a firm (or firms) from the sale of a product; equal to the total expenditures for the product produced by the firm (or firms); equal to the quantity sold (demanded) multiplied by the price at which it is sold.

Total-revenue test   A test to determine elasticity of *demand* between any two prices: Demand is elastic if *total revenue* moves in the opposite direction as price; it is inelastic when it moves in the same direction as price; and it is of unitary elasticity when it does not change when price changes.

Total spending   The total amount buyers of goods and services spend or plan to spend; also called *aggregate expenditures.*

Total supply   The supply schedule or the supply curve of all sellers of a good or service; also called market supply.

Township and village enterprises   Privately owned rural manufacturing firms in China.

Trade balance   The export of goods (or goods and services) of a nation less its imports of goods (or goods and services).

Trade bloc   A group of nations which lowers or abolishes trade barriers among members. Examples include the *European Union* and the nations of the *North American Free Trade Agreement.*

Trade controls   *Tariffs, export subsidies, import quotas*, and other means a nation may use to reduce *imports* and expand *exports.*

Trade deficit   The amount by which a nation's *imports* of goods (or goods and services) exceed its *exports* of goods (or goods and services).

Tradeoffs   The sacrifice of some or all of one economic goal, good, or service to achieve some other goal, good, or service.

Trade surplus   The amount by which a nation's exports of goods (or goods and services) exceed its imports of goods (or goods and services).

Trading possibilities line   A line which shows the different combinations of two products an economy is able to obtain (consume) when it specializes in the production of one product and trades (exports) it to obtain the other product.

Traditional economy   An economic system in which traditions and customs determine how the economy will use its scarce resources.

Transactions demand for money   The amount of money people want to hold for use as a *medium of exchange* (to make payments), and which varies directly with the *nominal GDP.*

Transfer payment   A payment of *money* (or goods and services) by a government to a *household* or *firm* for which the payer receives no good or service directly in return.

U

Unanticipated inflation   Increases in the price level (*inflation*) at a rate greater than expected.

Underemployment   (1) Failure to produce the maximum amount of goods and services which can be produced from the resources employed; failure to achieve *full production.* (2) A situation in which workers are employed in positions requiring less than the amount of education and skill than they have.

Undistributed corporate profits   After-tax corporate profits not distributed as dividends to stockholders; corporate or business saving; also called retained earnings.

Unemployment   Failure to use all available *economic resources* to produce goods and services; failure of the economy to fully employ its *labor force.*

Unemployment compensation   (See *Unemployment insurance.*)

Unemployment insurance   The social insurance program which in the United States is financed by state *payroll taxes* on employers and makes income available to workers who become unemployed and are unable to find jobs.

Unemployment rate   The percentage of the *labor force* unemployed at any time.

Unit labor cost   Labor costs per unit of output; total labor cost divided by total output; also equal to the *nominal wage rate* divided by the *average product* of labor.

Unit of account   A standard unit in which prices can be stated and the value of goods and services can be compared; one of the three functions of *money.*

Unlimited liability   Absence of any limits on the maximum amount which an individual (usually a business owner) may become legally required to pay.

Unlimited wants   The insatiable desire of consumers for goods and services which will give them satisfaction or *utility.*

Unplanned investment   Actual investment less *planned investment;* increases or decreases in the *inventories* of firms resulting from production greater than sales.

Urban collectives   Chinese enterprises jointly owned by their managers and their workforces, located in urban areas.

Uruguay Round   The eighth and most recent round of trade negotiations under *GATT* (now the *World Trade Organization*).

Utility   The want-satisfying power of a good or service; the satisfaction or pleasure a consumer obtains from the consumption of a good or service (or from the consumption of a collection of goods and services).

V

Value added   The value of the product sold by a *firm* less the value of the products (materials) purchased and used by the firm to produce the product.

Value judgment   Opinion of what is desirable or undesirable; belief regarding what ought or ought not to be (regarding what is right or just and wrong or unjust).

Value of money   The quantity of goods and services for which a unit of money (a dollar) can be exchanged; the purchasing power of a unit of money; the reciprocal of the *price level.*

Vault cash   The *currency* a bank has in its vault and cash drawers.

Velocity   The number of times per year the average dollar in the *money supply* is spent for *final goods and services;* nominal GDP divided by the money supply.

Vertical axis   The "up-down" or "north-south" axis on a graph or grid.

Vertical combination   A group of *plants* engaged in different stages of the production of a final product and owned by a single *firm.*

Vertical intercept   The point at which a line meets the vertical axis of a graph.

Vertical range   The vertical segment of the aggregate supply curve along which the economy is at full capacity.

Vicious circle of poverty   A problem common in some developing countries in which their low per capita incomes are an obstacle to realizing the levels of saving and investment requisite to acceptable rates of economic growth.

Voluntary export restrictions   Voluntary limitations by countries or firms of their exports to a particular foreign nation to avoid enactment of formal trade barriers by that nation.

W

Wage   The price paid for the use or services of *labor* per unit of time (per hour, per day, and so on).

Wage rate   (See *Wage.*)

Wealth effect   (See *Real balances effect.*)

"Will to develop"   Wanting economic growth strongly enough to change from old to new ways of doing things.

World Bank   A bank which lends (and guarantees loans) to developing nations to help them increase their *capital stock* and thus achieve *economic growth;* formally, the International Bank for Reconstruction and Development.

World price   The international market price of a good or service, determined by world demand and supply.

World Trade Organization   An organization established in 1994 to replace *GATT* to oversee the provisions of the *Uruguay round* and resolve any disputes stemming therefrom.

INDEX

Note: Page numbers followed by *n.* refer to footnotes.

Ability, entrepreneurial, **24**
Abstractions, **8**
Account, money as unit of, **265**
Acquisition costs, investment demand curve and, **184**
Actual budget, full-employment budget versus, **249–251**
Actual investment, planned investment versus, **193–195**
  attainment of equilibrium and, **193–195**
  disequilibrium and inventories and, **193**
Actual reserves, **291**
Adaptive expectations theory, **340–342**
Administrative lag, **253**
Advisory Councils of Federal Reserve System, **277**
Africa:
  economies of, **462**
  famine in, **34, 470–471**
"After this, therefore because of this" fallacy, **11**
Age, unemployment rates and, **156–157**
Aggregate(s), **9**
Aggregate demand, **221–227**
  aggregate demand curve and, **221–223**
    classical perspective on, **352**
    derivation of, **223**
    foreign purchases effect and, **223**
    interest-rate effect and, **222–223**
    Keynesian perspective on, **352**
    wealth effect and, **222**
  aggregate demand shocks originating from abroad and, domestic fiscal policy and, **256**
  determinants of, **223–227**
  in Europe, unemployment and, **238**
  shifts in, **227, 234**
  (*See also* Extended AD-AS model)
Aggregate expenditures-domestic output approach, **188–190**
  graphical analysis of, **190**
  tabular analysis of, **188–190**
Aggregate expenditures model, **172–196, 199–218**
  aggregate demand curve derivation from, **223**
  aggregate demand shifts and, **227**
  assumptions of, **174**
  classical economics and Say's law and, **172–173**
  consumption and saving and, **174–181**
    average and marginal propensities and, **178–179**
    consumption schedule and, **175–176**
    income-consumption and income-saving relationships and, **175**
    nonincome determinants of, **179–180**
    saving schedule and, **176**
    shifts and stability and, **180–181**
  equilibrium GDP and, **183–193**
  Great Depression and, **173**
  historical applications of, **213–217**
    to Great Depression, **214–217**
    to Vietnam War, **217**
  investment and, **181–188**

  expected rate of return and, **181**
  instability of, **186–188**
  investment demand curve and, **182–185**
  investment schedule and, **185–186**
  planned versus actual, **193–195**
  real interest rate and, **181–182**
Keynes and Keynesian economics and, **173–174**
multiplier effect and (*see* Multipliers)
public sector in, **207–213**
  assumptions of, **207**
  balanced-budget multiplier and, **212–213**
  government purchases and, **207–209**
  taxation and, **209–212**
tools of, **174**
Aggregate supply, **227–233, 330–348**
  aggregate supply curve and, **228–229**
    classical perspective on, **351**
    horizontal range of, **228–229**
    intermediate range of, **229**
    Keynesian perspective on, **352**
    vertical range of, **229**
  determinants of, **229–233**
  fiscal policy and, **255–256**
  long-run, **331–333**
  monetary policy and, **318**
  shifts in, **237, 239**
  short-run, **330–332**
  supply shocks and instability and, **353**
  Phillips Curve and, **338–339**
  (*See also* Extended AD-AS model)
Agriculture, in China, reform of, **483–484**
Airbus Consortium, **423**
Alaska, national parks and monuments in, **33–34**
Allocations approach to GDP, **127, 132–134**
Allocative efficiency, **25, 369–370**
  production possibilities curve and, **28–29**
American Express, **282**
Angola:
  famine in, **470**
  inflation in, **161**
Annually balanced budget, **387**
Anticipated inflation, **164, 165–166**
Antimonopoly laws, **85**
APC (average propensity to consume), **178**
  global perspective on, **178**
APEC (Asian-Pacific Economic Cooperation), **117**
Appreciation of currencies, **111–112, 435–436**
  of dollar, budget deficits and trade deficits and, **396–397**
APS (average propensity to save), **178**
Asia, trade of, **105**
Asian-Pacific Economic Cooperation (APEC), **117**
Asian tigers, **105**
Asset(s):
  of banks, **287–288**
  of Federal Reserve Banks, **306–307**
Asset demand for money, **272–274**

ATMs (automated teller machines), **280**
AT&T, **117, 282**
Authoritarian capitalism, **35**
Automated teller machines (ATMs), **280**
Automatic stabilizers (*see* Built-in stabilizers)
Average propensity to consume (APC), **178**
  global perspective on, **178**
Average propensity to save (APS), **178**
Average tax rate, **94**
Axes, in graphs, **15**

Baby boom, change in demand and, **46**
Balanced-budget amendment, **400**
Balanced-budget multiplier, **212–213**
Balanced-budget requirement, **251–253**
Balance of payments, **431–434**
  capital account and, **433**
  current account and, **431–433**
  deficits and surpluses in, **434**
  flexible exchange rates and, **437–438**
  official reserves account and, **433–434**
Balance of trade, public debt and, **396**
Balance on capital account, **433**
Balance on current account, **432–433**
Balance on goods and services, **432**
Balance sheets:
  of commercial banks, **287–288**
  consolidated, of Federal Reserve Banks, **306–307**
Bank(s):
  ATMs and, **280**
  central, **277**
    global perspective on, **306**
    inflation and, global perspective on, **280**
    [*See also* Federal Reserve System (Fed)]
  commercial (*see* Commercial banks; Money creation)
  decline of, **280–282**
  Federal Reserve, **276–280**
  loans to, **279**
  regulation of, **288**
BankAmerica, **281**
Bank panics, **288**
  during 1930s, **301**
Bankruptcy, public debt and, **391–392**
Barriers to trade (*see* Tariffs; Trade barriers)
Barter, **66**
Bastiat, Frédéric, **424**
Bayer Chemicals, **104**
"Beggar thy neighbor" policies, **418**
Bethlehem Steel, **80**
Biases, **10–11**
Bilateral trade negotiations, **423–425**
Birthrate, declining, employment of women and, **39**
Black markets, exchange controls and rationing and, **440**
BLS (Bureau of Labor Statistics), **155**
BMW, **117**
Board of Governors, **276–277, 322–323**
Boeing, **100, 117, 423**
Bolshevik Bakery, **486–487**
Bonds, **82–83, 96–97**

Borrowing:
  to finance deficits, **247**
  inflation and, **165**
  [*See also* Debt; Loan(s); Public debt]
Boulding, Kenneth E., **7**
Brain drain, **459**
Brazil, trade of, **423**
Break-even income, **176**
Bretton Woods system, **442–443, 444**
  demise of, **443**
Britain:
  trade of, **104**
  unemployment in, **238**
British Petroleum, **104**
Buchwald, Art, **118–119, 216**
Budget deficits, **244, 395–400**
  cyclical, **250**
  global perspective on, **252**
  legislation to reduce, **398–399**
  size of, **395–396**
  structural, **250, 389**
  trade deficits and, **396–400**
    dollar appreciation and, **396–397**
    interest rates and, **396**
    policy responses and, **398–400**
    positive role of debt and, **400**
Budget surplus, **246**
Built-in stabilizers, **248–253**
  actual versus full-employment budget and, **249–251**
  economic importance of, **248–249**
  proposed balanced-budget requirement and, **251–253**
  tax progressivity and, **249**
Bulgaria, inflation in, **161**
Bureaucracy, foreign aid and, **466**
Bureau of Labor Statistics (BLS), **155**
Burger King, **100**
Business cycle, **149–152**
  causes of, **150**
  impact of, **151**
  noncyclical fluctuations and, **150–151**
  phases of, **149–150**
  political, **254**
  real-business-cycle theory and, **355**
  (*See also* Great Depression)
Business debt, Great Depression and, **215**
Business sector, **80–84**
  importance of economics for, **4–5**
  legal forms of business and, **81–84**
  (*See also* Corporations; Firms)
Business taxes, **94**
  aggregate demand and, **226**
  aggregate supply and, **232**
  indirect, in GDP, **133**
  investment demand curve and, **184**
Buyers; number of:
  change in demand and, **46**
  competition and, **63**

Canada, trade of, **102, 116–117, 405, 422**
  supply and demand analysis of imports and exports and, **413–414**
Canterbery, E. Ray, **194n.**

Capacity:
  excess:
    aggregate demand and, **226**
    Great Depression and, **215**
  net investment and, **129–131**
Capital, **23–24**
  accumulation of:
    economic development and, **459–461**
    in market system, **73**
  availability of, aggregate supply and, **231**
  fixed, consumption of, **133–134**
  private, flows of, economic development and, **467–468**
  quantity of, economic growth and, **374–375**
  real, **24**
Capital account, **433**
Capital flight, **460**
Capital goods, **26**
  consumer goods versus, **23**
  stock of, investment demand curve and, **184–185**
  use of, under capitalism, **64–65**
Capital-intensive goods, **406**
Capitalism:
  authoritarian, **35**
  pure, **34–35, 61–75**
Capital-saving technology, **461**
Capital stock, public debt and, **393–395**
Capital-using technology, **461**
Capricious universe view, **462**
Cash, vault, **289**
Causation, correlation versus, **11–13**
Causation fallacies, **11–13**
CEA (Council of Economic Advisers), **204, 244**
Central banks, **277**
  Federal Reserve System (Fed), **276–280**
  global perspective on, **306**
  inflation and, global perspective on, **280**
Central economic planning, **475–477**
Centralized government, foreign aid and, **466**
Centrally planned economies, **35, 474–479**
  coordination problem and, **477**
  economic planning and, **475–477**
  ideology and institutions of, **474–475**
  incentive problem and, **477–478**
  Soviet, collapse of, **478–479**
  state ownership and, **475**
Ceteris paribus assumption, **8**
  graphs and, **17**
Chain-type annual-weights price index, **140–141**
Change in demand, **45–47**
  market equilibrium and, **53–56**
Change in quantity demanded, **47–48**
Change in quantity supplied, **51**
Change in supply, **49–51**
  market equilibrium and, **53–56**
Charles Schwab, **281**
Chase Manhattan, **280, 281, 284**
Cheap foreign labor argument for protection, **419–420**
Checkable deposits, **266–267**
Check clearing, **292–293**
Check collection, **279**
Chemical Bank, **280**
Chile:
  economic growth of, **453**
  foreign aid to, **467**
  trade of, **117**

China:
  central economic planning in (*see* Centrally planned economies)
  economic development of, **486–487**
  economic growth of, **453, 461**
  economy of, **35, 475**
  market reforms in, **483–487**
    agricultural and rural, **483–484**
    development of supporting institutions and, **484**
    positive outcomes of, **485**
    problems with, **485–487**
    special economic zones and, **484**
    state-owned enterprise transformation and, **484**
    of urban industries, **484**
  population policy of, **457–458**
  trade of, **105**
    most-favored-nation status and, **423–425**
Choice:
  freedom of, under capitalism, **62**
  production possibilities table and, **26**
  restriction of, exchange controls and rationing and, **440**
  scarcity and, **4**
Chrysler Corporation, **117**
Circular flow model, **35–36**
  GDP and, **136**
  with government, **89–91**
  with international trade, **105–107**
  limitations of, **36**
  resource and product markets in, **36**
Citibank, **284**
Citicorp, **281**
Citizenship, economics for, **5**
Classical economics, **172–173, 350–352**
Clinton administration:
  deficit-reduction legislation under, **398–399**
  line-item veto use in, **400**
  public debt under, **389–390**
  trade policy under, **423**
Coca-Cola, **47, 117**
Coin(s), **265–266**
  (*See also* Currencies)
Coincidence of wants, **66**
COLA (cost-of-living adjustment) clauses, **165**
Command economies (*see* Centrally planned economies)
Commercial banks, **266, 278–279, 281**
  balance sheets of, **287–288**
  buying of securities from, **307–308**
  formation of, **289–293**
  global perspective on, **278**
  loans to, as Federal Reserve Bank assets, **307**
  money creation by, **287–302**
  reserves of, as Federal Reserve Bank liabilities, **307**
  selling of securities to, **309–310**
Common Market, **116**
Communications, rapid growth of international trade and, **104**
Communist Party, **474–488, 483**
  (*See also* Centrally planned economies)
Comparative advantage, **109, 406–411**
  case for free trade and, **411**
  gains from trade and, **408–410**
  with increasing costs, **410–411**

specialization according to, **407–408**
terms of trade and, **408**
Compensation of employees [*see* Income; Wage(s)]
Competition:
under capitalism, **63**
international, U.S. firms and, **117–119**
promotion of, in Russian Republic, **481**
Competitive market system, **67–73**
accommodation of change and, **71–73**
determination of what is to be produced and, **68–69**
distribution of total output and, **70–71**
Five Fundamental Questions and, **67**
foreign exchange market as, **110**
"invisible hand" and, **73–74**
organization of production and, **69–70**
Complementary goods, **47**
Complex multiplier, **204**
Composition, fallacy of, **11**
domestic employment argument for protection and, **418**
Conglomerate combination, **80**
Consumer(s), importance of economics for, **5**
(*See also* Consumption; Household sector)
Consumer Advisory Council, **277**
Consumer goods, **26**
capital goods versus, **23**
durable and nondurable, **128**
Consumer price index (CPI), **141**
base period for, **160**
inflation overstatement by, **143**
Consumer sovereignty, **68**
Consumption:
aggregate demand and, **224–226**
aggregate expenditures model, **174–181**
average propensity to consume and, **178**
global perspective on, **178**
consumption schedule and, **175–176**
shifts in, **180–181**
decline in, tariffs and, **416**
of fixed capital, **133–134**
near-monies and, **268**
personal, **79**
rise in, U.S. trade deficits and, **447**
Contractionary fiscal policy, **246–247**
decreased government spending and, **246, 247**
increased taxes and, **246–247**
Control, separation from ownership, in corporations, **83**
Coordination failures, **356**
Coordination problem, **477**
Corporations, **82–84**
finance of, **96–97**
income taxes of, **94**
large, **84**
multinational, **104**
profits of, in GDP, **133**
"Corporatization," of state-owned enterprises, **484**
Correlation, causation versus, **11–13**
Corruption, foreign aid and, **467**
Cost(s):
acquisition, investment demand curve and, **184**
comparative, specialization and, **108–109**

economic (opportunity):
determination of what is to be produced and, **68**
increasing, law of, **27–28**
of unemployment, **156–158**
increasing, trade with, **410–411**
maintenance, investment demand curve and, **184**
marginal, **4–5**
menu, downward price-level inflexibility and, **237**
noneconomic, of unemployment, **158–159**
operating, investment demand curve and, **184**
of production, **163**
of protection, **421–422**
income distribution and, **422**
to society, **421–422**
societal, of government trade intervention, **114**
Cost-of-living adjustment (COLA) clauses, **165**
Cost-push inflation, **163, 237**
in extended AD-AS model, **334–335**
output and unemployment and, **167**
Cost ratio, **407**
Council of Economic Advisers (CEA), **204, 244**
CPI (consumer price index), **141**
base period for, **160**
inflation overstatement by, **143**
Credit, price of [*see* Interest rate(s)]
Credit cards, **268, 282**
Creditors, inflation and, **165**
Credit unions, **267**
Crowding-out effect, **254–255**
public debt and, **393**
Cuba:
economy of, **35**
foreign aid to, **467**
trade of, **105**
Currencies:
depreciation and appreciation of, **111–112, 435–436**
dollar:
appreciation of, budget deficits and trade deficits and, **396–397**
circulation abroad, **283**
value of, prices and, **270–271**
issuance of, **279**
in *M*1, **265–266**
(*See also* Exchange rates)
Current account, **431–433**
Cyclical deficit, **250**
Cyclically balanced budget, **387**
Cyclical unemployment, **153**
Czechoslovakia, trade of, **105**

Debt:
business, Great Depression and, **215**
creation of, **400**
household:
aggregate demand and, **225**
consumption and saving and, **180**
international crisis of, **467**
money as, **269**
public, **388–395**
relief from, to promote economic development, **469–470**
retirement of, to dispose of surpluses, **247**
[*See also* Borrowing; Loan(s)]

Debtors, inflation and, **165**
Declining industries, losses and, **68–69**
"Decollectivization," **483–484**
Deduction, **7**
Defense, as argument for protection, **417**
Deficient-demand unemployment, **153**
Deficit(s):
in balance of payments, **434**
budget, **244, 395–400**
definition of, **386**
financing of, **247**
trade, **102, 446–447**
causes of, **446–447**
implications of, **447**
Deficit Reduction Act (1993), **398–399**
Definitions of economic terms, **11**
Deflation, **161, 166**
Demand, **43–48**
aggregate (*see* Aggregate demand; Extended AD-AS model)
change in, **45–47**
market equilibrium and, **53–56**
change in quantity demanded and, **47–48**
demand curve and, **44**
for investment, **182–185**
demand schedule and, **43**
derived, **68**
determinants of, **45**
economic growth and, **369**
for exports and imports, **411–415**
in Canada, **413–414**
equilibrium world price and, **414–415**
in United States, **412–413**
individual and market, **44–45**
law of, **43–44**
market equilibrium and, **52–58**
for money, **272–274**
Demand-deposit multiplier, multiple-deposit expansion and, **299–300**
Demand-pull inflation, **161–162**
in extended AD-AS model, **333–334**
output and, **167**
Demand shifters (*see* Determinants of demand)
Demand-side growth policies, **383**
Demographic transition view of population, **458**
Deng Xiaoping, **483, 484**
Dependency, foreign aid and, **466**
Dependent variables, **15–17**
Deposits:
checkable, **266–267**
time, **267**
Treasury, as Federal Reserve Bank liabilities, **307**
Depreciation:
of capital equipment, in GDP, **133–134**
of currencies, **111–112, 435–436**
Depressions, **130–131, 173**
Derived demand, **68**
Determinants of aggregate demand, **223–227**
Determinants of aggregate supply, **229–233**
Determinants of demand, **45**
Determinants of supply, **49**
Developing countries (DVCs), **452–472**
classification of, **453**
economic development of, **455–471**
famine in Africa and, **470–471**
growth, decline, and income gaps and, **453**
implications of poverty and, **453, 455**

policies for promoting growth, **468–469**
vicious circle of poverty faced by,
462–463
Diminishing marginal utility, **43**
Direct foreign investment, **468**
Directing function of prices, **71–72**
Direct relationships, **15–16**
Discount rate, **312**
Discouraged workers, **155–156**
Discretionary fiscal policy, **244–248, 363**
Discretionary monetary policy, **363**
Discretionary spending, **300**
Discrimination, in employment, production possibilities curve and, **33**
Disequilibrium:
expenditures-output approach and, **189–190**
planned versus actual investment and, **193**
Disinflation, **341–342**
Disposable income (DI), **135–136**
Distribution:
in market system, **70–71**
of output, GDP and, **142**
Diversification for stability argument for protection, **418**
Division of labor, under capitalism, **65**
Divorce rate, employment of women and, **39**
Dollar:
appreciation of, budget deficits and trade deficits and, **396–397**
circulation abroad, **283**
value of, prices and, **270–271**
Dollar votes, **68, 72**
Domestic investment, private
gross, in GDP, **128–131**
net, **129**
Domestic prices, **412**
Double taxation, of corporations, **83**
Dow Chemical, **117**
Dreyfus, **281**
Dumping, protection against, as argument for protection, **419**
Durable goods, **79**
business cycle and, **151**
consumer goods, **128**
DVCs (Developing countries), **452–472**

Earnings approach to GDP, **127, 132–134**
Eastern Europe
economic development of, **465**
economic growth of, **461**
foreign aid to, **465–466**
trade of, **105**
East Germany, trade of, **105**
Easy money policy, **312–313**
real GDP and price level and, **316–317**
E-cash, **282–284**
Economic analysis, **6–8**
Economic collapse, hyperinflation and, **168**
Economic costs:
determination of what is to be produced and, **68**
increasing, law of, **27–28**
of unemployment, **156–158**
Economic development, **455–471**
advanced nations' role in, **465–468**
expanding trade and, **465**
foreign aid and, **465–467**
private capital flows and, **467–468**

future of, **468–470**
developing nations' policies for promoting growth and, **468–469**
industrially advanced nations' policies for promoting growth and, **469–470**
global perspective on assistance for, **466**
government role in, **463–465**
positive, **463–464**
problems with, **464**
obstacles to, **455–462**
capital accumulation, **459–461**
human resources, **456–459**
natural resources, **455–456**
sociocultural and institutional factors, **461–462**
technological advance, **461**
Economic efficiency, in market economy, **70**
Economic goals, **9**
Economic growth, **368–384, 453**
accounting for, **373–378**
detriments to growth and, **376–377**
education and training and, **375**
inputs versus productivity and, **373–374**
macroeconomic instability and, **377**
quantity of capital and, **374–375**
quantity of labor and, **374**
resource allocation and scale economies and, **375–376**
technological advance and, **374**
arithmetic of, **369**
definitions of, **368–369**
demand factor and, **369**
demand-side policies and, **383**
desirability of, **380–381**
efficiency factor and, **369–370**
extended AD-AS model and, **371–372**
global perspective on, **33, 34, 373**
as goal, **369**
net investment and, **129–131**
production possibilities and, **30–32, 370–371**
productivity slowdown and, **378–382**
causes of, **378–382**
significance of, **378**
turnaround of, **382–383**
supply factors and, **369**
supply-side policies and, **383**
in United States, **372–373**
Economic perspective, **4–5**
pitfalls in applying, **10–11**
Economic planning, central, **475–477**
Economic principles, **7**
Economic profit, determination of what is to be produced and, **68**
Economic Recovery Tax Act (1981), public debt and, **389**
Economic Report of the President, **5**
Economic resources, **23**
scarcity of, **23–24**
Economics, **3**
empirical, **7**
methods of, **6–9**
normative, **10**
positive, **10**
reasons to study, **5–6**
theoretical, **6–8**
Economic systems, **34–35**
Economic well-being, GDP and, **141–144**
Economies, underground, GDP and, **142, 144**

Economies of scale, economic growth and, **375**
Economizing problem, **22–39**
circular flow model and, **35–36**
economic systems and, **34–35**
scarce resources and, **23–24**
unlimited wants and, **22–23**
(*See also* Production possibilities curve)
Edgeworth, F. Y., **172n.**
Education:
economic growth and, **375**
unemployment rates and, **158**
Education policies, economic growth and, **383**
Efficiency:
allocative, **25, 369–370**
production possibilities curve and, **28–29**
economic, in market economy, **70**
economic growth and, **369–370**
of market system, **73–74**
productive, **25, 369**
unemployment and, **29–30**
Efficiency wages, **359–360**
downward price-level inflexibility and, **236–237**
Efficiency wage theory, **359–360**
Egypt, foreign aid to, **465, 467**
Electronic money, **282–284**
Elf Aquitaine, **104**
Elliot, Kimberly A., **421n.**
Empirical economics, **7**
Employees (*see* Labor; Workers)
Employment:
discrimination in, production possibilities curve and, **33**
domestic, as argument for protection, **417–418**
full, **24–25, 153–154**
by government, global perspective on, **89**
part-time, **155**
of women, production possibilities curve and, **38–39**
(*See also* Unemployment)
Employment Act (1946), **243–244**
Energy prices:
aggregate supply shock and, **338, 339**
Organization of Petroleum Exporting Countries (OPEC), **102, 231, 237, 338, 339, 461**
productivity slowdown and, **381**
Enterprise, freedom of, under capitalism, **62**
Enterprise tax system, in China, **484**
Entrepreneurship:
ability and, **24**
availability of, aggregate supply and, **231**
lack of, economic development and, **464**
Environment, GDP and, **142**
Equations:
of exchange, **353–354**
of linear relationships, **18–19**
Equilibrium, **232–239**
market, **52–58**
Equilibrium GDP:
in aggregate expenditures model, **188–193**
graphical analysis of, **190**
tabular analysis of, **188–190**
attainment of, planned versus actual investment and, **193–195**
full-employment GDP versus, **213**

government purchases and, **207–209**
leakages-injections approach, **190–193**
monetary policy, real GDP, and price level
and, **316**
multipliers, **216**
net exports and, **204–207**
aggregate expenditures and, **204**
economic linkages and, **206–207**
net export schedule and, **204–205**
real, **234**
taxation and, **209–212**
Equilibrium imports and exports, **414–415**
Equilibrium price, **52–53**
world price, **414–415**
Equilibrium price level, **234**
Equilibrium quantity, **52–53**
Equilibrium real domestic output, **234**
Estonia, trade of, **105**
Ethiopia:
famine in, **470**
foreign aid to, **467**
Europe (see Eastern Europe; Western Europe)
European Union (EU), **116**
Excess capacity:
aggregate demand and, **226**
Great Depression and, **215**
Excess reserves, **291**
Exchange:
equation of, **353–354**
money as medium of, **65–67, 265**
Exchange controls, **440**
Exchange rates, **110, 434–446**
aggregate demand and, **227**
equilibrium GDP and, **207**
fixed, **434, 439–441**
domestic macroeconomic adjustments and,
440–441
exchange controls and rationing and, **440**
gold standard and, **441–442**
trade policies and, **440**
use of reserves and, **439–440**
flexible (floating), **434–439**
balance of payments and, **437–438**
depreciation and appreciation and,
435–436
determinants of, **436–437**
disadvantages of, **438–439**
managed, **444–445**
global perspective on, **110, 444**
international systems of, **441–446**
Bretton Woods system and, **442–443**
gold standard and, **441–442**
managed float, **444–445**
pegged, **442–443**
speculation and, **436–437, 448–449**
Excise taxes, **94**
Exclusion principle, **87**
Expanding industries, profits and, **68**
Expansionary fiscal policy, **244–246**
increased government spending and, **244–246**
tax reductions and, **245–246**
Expectations:
adaptive expectations theory and, **340–342**
change in demand and, **47**
change in supply and, **50–51**
of consumers, aggregate demand and, **225**
consumption and saving and, **179–180**
investment demand curve and, **185**

rational expectations theory and, **342**
for returns on investment:
aggregate demand and, **226**
investment and, **181**
variability of, instability of investment and,
188
Expenditures:
consumer (see Consumption)
discretionary, **300**
government spending, **91**
for infrastructure, economic growth and,
380–381
for investment:
aggregate demand and, **226**
instability and, **353**
Expenditures approach to GDP, **127, 128–132**
Export(s):
equilibrium, **414–415**
global perspective on, **105, 405**
net [see Net export(s)]
U.S. promotion of, **423**
(See also International trade)
Export controls, **423**
Export-Import Bank, **423**
Export subsidies, **113, 423**
Export supply curve, **412, 413**
Extended AD-AS model:
cost-push inflation in, **334–335**
demand-pull inflation in, **333–334**
economic growth and, **371–372**
equilibrium in, **333**
recession and, **335–336**
External debt, **393**
Externalities, **86–87**
benefits of, **86–87**
costs of, **86**

Factors of production, **23–24**
prices of, aggregate supply and, **230–232**
productivity versus, economic growth and,
373–374
[See also Capital; Labor; Land; Resource(s)]
Fahd, King of Saudi Arabia, **423**
Fallacies:
causation, **11–13**
of composition, **11**
domestic employment argument for protection and, **418**
Famine, in Africa, **34, 470–471**
Farming, in China, reform of, **483–484**
Fast-food industry:
dollar votes in, **68**
lines at restaurants and, **12**
Favoritism, exchange controls and rationing and,
440
FDIC (Federal Deposit Insurance Corporation),
291, 301
Federal Advisory Council, **277**
Federal budget:
actual versus full-employment, **249–251**
balanced:
annually, **387**
balanced-budget multiplier and, **212–213**
balanced-budget requirement and, **251–253**
cyclically, **387**
policy rules and, **361–363**
deficits in, **244, 395–400**
functional finance and, **388**

Federal Deposit Insurance Corporation (FDIC),
291, 301
Federal funds market, **296**
Federal funds rate, **296**
monetary policy and, **320–321**
Federal Open Market Committee (FOMC), **277**
Federal Reserve Notes, **266**
outstanding, as Federal Reserve Bank liabilities, **307**
Federal Reserve System (Fed), **276–280**
Advisory Councils of, **277**
Board of Governors of, **276–277**
commercial banks and thrifts and, **278–279**
Federal Open Market Committee of, **277**
Federal Reserve Banks of, **277–278**
functions of, **279**
historical background of, **276**
independence of, **279–280**
monetary policy and, **305–325**
Feedback effects, monetary policy and, **318**
Females:
employment of, production possibilities curve
and, **38–39**
unemployment rates and, **158**
Fiat, **104**
Fiat money, **269**
Fidelity, **281**
Final goods, **125**
Finance:
of corporations, **96–97**
of deficits, **247**
functional, **388**
of government, **91–96**
[See also Government spending; Tax(es);
Transfers]
Financial markets, globalization of, **282**
Financial services industry, **280**
Financial transactions, exclusion from GDP,
126–127
Firms, **80**
mergers of banks and thrifts and, **280–281**
(See also Corporations)
First Interstate, **280**
Fiscal federalism, **95–96**
Fiscal policy, **243–260**
aggregate supply and inflation and, **255–256**
crowding-out effect and, **254–255**
discretionary, **244–248, 363**
contractionary, **246–247**
expansionary, **244–246**
financing of deficits and disposing of surpluses and, **247**
options for, **247–248**
legislation and, **243–244**
nondiscretionary, **248–253**
in open economy, **256–257**
political problems with, **253–254**
public debt and, **393**
supply-side, **257–258**
timing problems with, **253**
Five Fundamental Questions, **67**
Fixed exchange rates (see Exchange rates)
Fixed nominal income, inflation and, **164–165**
Fixed-weight price indexes, **141**
Flexible (floating) exchange rates (see Exchange
rates)
Fluctuations (see Business cycle; Great
Depression)

FOMC (Federal Open Market Committee), **277**
Foot Locker, **80**
Ford Motor, **104, 117**
Foreign aid, **469**
   expansion of, **465–467**
Foreign exchange market, **110–112**
   depreciation and appreciation of currencies
      and, **111–112**
   speculation in, **436–437, 448–449**
   (*See also* Exchange rates)
Foreign factor income, net, in GDP, **134**
Foreign purchases effect, **223**
45 degree line, **190**
Fractional reserve system of banking, **288**
France:
   trade of, **104, 423**
   unemployment in, **238**
Franklin, Ben, **375**
Freedom:
   of choice, under capitalism, **62**
   of enterprise, under capitalism, **62**
   market restraints on, **68**
   in market system, **74**
Free-rider problem, **88**
Free trade, case for, **411**
Frictional unemployment, **152**
Friedman, Milton, **355, 360–361**
Full employment, **24–25, 153–154**
Full-employment budget, actual budget versus,
   249–251
Full-employment GDP, equilibrium GDP ver-
   sus, **213**
Full employment unemployment rate, **153**
Full production, **25**
Functional distribution of income, **77–78**
Functional finance, **388**
Future generations, public debt as burden on,
   392

Gains from trade, **109–110, 408–410**
   misunderstanding of, government trade inter-
      ventions and, **113**
Gates, Bill, **231**
GATT (General Agreement on Tariffs and
   Trade), **115–116, 405, 422–423**
   change in demand and, **46**
GDP gap, **156**
GDP price index, **140–141**
   gross domestic product (GDP), **125, 134,
      136–144**
Gender:
   employment and, production possibilities
      curve and, **38–39**
   unemployment rates and, **158**
General Agreement on Tariffs and Trade
   (GATT), **115–116, 405, 422–423**
   change in demand and, **46**
Generalizations, **7–8**
General Motors (GM), **81, 84, 104, 117, 282**
*The General Theory of Employment, Interest, and
   Money* (Keynes), **173, 194**
Geographic specialization, under capitalism, **65**
Germany:
   inflation in, **168, 271**
   Nazi, economy of, **35**
   on-the-job training in, **375**
   trade of, **104**
   unemployment in, **238**

Globalization, of financial markets, **282**
Global perspective:
   average propensity to consume, **178**
   budget deficits, **252**
   central banks, **306**
      independence and inflation and, **280**
   changes in industrial production during
      1929–1930 and 1937–1938, **215**
   commercial banks, **278**
   development assistance, **466**
   economic growth, **373**
   exchange rates, **110, 444**
   exports, **105, 405**
   GDP, **132**
   government employment, **89**
   gross investment expenditures, **185**
   Index of Economic Freedom, **62**
   inflation, **161**
   investment and economic growth, **33**
   math test scores, **376**
   misery index, **339**
   net exports, **206**
   population growth, **457**
   public debt, **390**
   tax revenue as percentage of domestic output,
      92
   trade balances, **433**
   trade protection, **421**
   underground economy, **144**
   unemployment rates, **159n.**
GM (General Motors), **81, 84, 104, 117,
   282**
G-7 (Group of Seven) nations, **444–445**
Golden West Financial, **281**
Goldsmiths, **288**
Gold standard, **441–442**
   demise of, **442**
Goods:
   balance of payments on, **432**
   capital (*see* Capital; Capital goods)
   capital-intensive, **406**
   complementary, **47**
   consumer, **26**
      capital goods versus, **23**
      durable and nondurable, **128**
   durability of, instability of investment and,
      186–187
   durable, **79**
      business cycle and, **151**
   final, **125**
   independent, **47**
   inferior, **47**
   intermediate, **125**
   investment (capital) (*see* Capital; Capital
      goods)
   labor-intensive, **406**
   land-intensive, **406**
   nondurable, **79**
      business cycle and, **151**
   normal, **47**
   public, **86–88**
      resource allocation to, **88**
   quasipublic, **88**
   related, prices of, **47**
   stock of, investment demand curve and,
      184–185
   substitute, **47**
Gorbachev, Mikhail, **479**

Government, **84–96**
   centralized, foreign aid and, **466**
   in circular flow model, **89–91**
   economic functions of, **84**
   employment by, global perspective on, **89**
   finance of, **91–96**
      federal, **92–94**
      state and local, **94–96, 253**
      [*See also* Budget deficits; Federal budget;
         Government spending; Tax(es); Transfers]
   income redistribution and, **85–86**
   intervention in international trade, **112–114**
      reasons for, **113–114**
      societal costs of, **114**
      types of, **112–113**
      (*See also* Tariffs; Trade barriers)
   legal and social framework provided by,
      84–85
   monopoly control by, **85**
   ownership by:
      in centrally planned economies, **475**
      of monopolies, **85**
   price setting by, in centrally planned
      economies, **476**
   regulation by (*see* Regulation)
   resource reallocation by, **86–88**
   role in economic development, **463–465**
      positive, **463–464**
      problems with, **464**
   role under capitalism, **64**
   stabilization function of, **88–89**
   trade interventions of, **112–114**
      reasons for, **113–114**
      societal costs of, **114**
      types of, **112–113**
Government securities, buying, **295–296**
Government spending, **91**
   aggregate demand and, **226**
   decreased, contractionary fiscal policy and,
      246, 247
   discretionary, **300**
   equilibrium GDP and, **207–209**
   federal, **92**
   in GDP, **131**
   increased, expansionary fiscal policy and,
      244–246
Graham, Frank G., **271n.**
Grants, economic development and, **465–467**
Graphs, **8, 15–19**
   axes in, **15**
   construction of, **15**
   dependent and independent variables in,
      15–17
   direct and inverse relationships in, **15–16**
   equation of linear relationship and, **18–19**
   other things equal assumption and, **17**
   slope of lines in, **17–18**
   slope of nonlinear curves in, **19**
   vertical intercept in, **18**
Great Britain:
   trade of, **104**
   unemployment in, **238**
Great Depression, **130–131, 173**
   aggregate supply during, **231**
   bank panics during, **301**
   and business debt, **215**
   deflation during, **161**
   economic growth and, **377**

recessionary gap concept and, **214–217**
social and political change brought by, **159**
Greece, foreign aid to, **465**
Greenspan, Alan, **322–323**
Gritskova, Svetlana, **487**
Gross domestic product (GDP), **125–134, 136–144**
   avoidance of multiple counting in, **125–126**
   economic well-being and, **141–142, 144**
   equation for, **132**
   equilibrium (*see* Equilibrium GDP)
   exclusion of nonproduction transactions in, **126–127**
   expansion in 1990s, monetary policy and, **319**
   expenditures (output) approach to, **127, 128–132**
   full-employment, equilibrium GDP versus, **213**
   global perspective on, **132**
   income approach to, **127, 132–134**
   nominal versus real, **136, 138–141**
      adjustment process in one-good economy and, **138–140**
      in real-world, **140–141**
   public debt and, **390**
   Russian, fall in, **482**
Gross investment expenditures, global perspective on, **185**
Gross private domestic investment, in GDP, **128–131**
Groupe Danone, **486–487**
Group of Seven (G-7) nations, **444–445**
Growth economics (*see* Economic growth)
Growth policies, **383**
Guiding function of prices, **71–72**
Gulf War, destruction from, **34**

Haiti, economic development of, **465**
Health care, in federal budget, **92**
Hewlett-Packard, **117**
Home Savings of America, **281**
Honda, **47, 117**
Hong Kong:
   economic growth of, **453**
   trade of, **105, 405**
Horizontal axis, **15**
Horizontal combination, **80**
Horizontal range of aggregate supply curve, **228–229**
Household sector, **77–80**
   debt of:
      aggregate demand and, **225**
      consumption and saving and, **180**
   functional distribution of income and, **77–78**
   personal consumption expenditures and, **79**
   personal distribution of income and, **78**
   personal saving and, **79**
   personal taxes and, **78–80**
   [*See also* Consumer(s)]
Hufbauer, Gary C., **421***n.*
Human resources, **23, 24**
   economic development and, **456–459**
   income from, **24**
Hungary:
   inflation in, **168**
   trade of, **105**

Hyperinflation, **167–168**
Hypotheses, **7**
Hyundai, **117**

IACs (Industrially advanced nations), **452**
IBM, **104**
IDA (International Development Association), **466**
Identities, **127**
IFC (International Finance Corporation), **466**
IMF (International Monetary Fund), **442–443**
Import:
   decline in, tariffs and, **416**
   equilibrium, **414–415**
   job creation from, **418**
   (*See also* International trade)
Import demand curve, **412–414**
Import quotas, **113, 415**
   reducing to promote economic development, **469**
Impounding, to dispose of surpluses, **247**
Incentive(s):
   foreign aid and, **466**
   of market system, **72–74**
   public debt and, **393**
Incentive problem, **477–478**
Income:
   absolute income gap between rich and poor nations and, **453**
   break-even, **176**
   change in demand and, **46–47**
   consumption related to, **175**
   disposable, **135–136**
   exchange rates and, **436**
   functional distribution of, **77–78**
   in GDP, **132**
   interest, **24**
      monetary policy and, **320**
   national, **133, 135**
      abroad, aggregate demand and, **226–227**
   nominal and real, **164**
   personal, **135**
      distribution of, **78**
   proprietors,' **77**
      in GDP, **133**
   rental, **24**
   saving related to, **175**
   taxable, **92**
   [*See also* Wage(s)]
Income approach to GDP, **127, 132–134**
Income distribution:
   of personal income, **78**
   public debt and, **392–393**
   trade protection and, **422**
   (*See also* Income redistribution)
Income effect, **44**
Income inequality:
   redistribution and, **85–86**
   Russian, **482**
Income redistribution, **85–86**
   by government, **85–86**
   by inflation, **164–167**
   output effects of, **167–168**
      cost-push inflation and unemployment and, **167**
      demand-pull inflation stimulus and, **167**
      hyperinflation and breakdown and, **167–168**

Income taxes:
   corporate, **94**
   personal, **92–94**
Increased domestic employment argument for protection, **417–418**
Independent goods, **47**
Independent variables, **15–17**
Index of Economic Freedom, global perspective on, **62**
India, trade of, **423**
Indirect business taxes, in GDP, **133**
Individual(s), importance of economics for, **4**
Individual demand, **44**
Indonesia:
   currency fall in, **468**
   trade of, **105, 405**
Induction, **7**
Industrialization in centrally planned economies, **476**
Industrially advanced nations (IACs), **452**
   policies for promoting growth, **469–470**
   role in economic development, **465–468**
      expanding trade and, **465**
      foreign aid and, **465–467**
      private capital flows and, **467–468**
Industrial policy, trade policy and, **423**
Industries, **80–81**
   declining, losses and, **68–69**
   expanding, profits and, **68**
   infant industry argument for protection and, **418–419**
Inefficiency (*see* Efficiency)
Infant industry argument for protection, **418–419**
Inferior goods, **47**
Infinite slope, **18**
Inflation, **159–168**
   acceptability of money and, **271**
   anticipated, **164, 165–166**
   central banks and, global perspective on, **280**
   complexities of, **163**
   cost-push (supply-side), **163, 237**
      in extended AD-AS model, **334–335**
      output and unemployment and, **167**
   CPI overstatement of, **143**
   demand-pull, **161–162**
      in extended AD-AS model, **333–334**
      output and, **167**
   fiscal policy and, **255–256**
   global perspective on, **161**
   historical record of, **161**
   income redistribution by, **164–167**
      anticipated inflation and, **165–166**
      debtors and creditors and, **165**
      fixed-nominal income receivers and, **164–165**
      nominal and real income and, **164**
      savers and, **165**
   Laffer Curve and, **344**
   meaning of, **159–160**
   measurement of, **160**
   premature, **162**
   productivity slowdown and, **378**
   public debt and, **391**
   reductions in, **341–342**
   stabilization and, **89**
   supply-shock, **163**

unanticipated, **164**
wage-push, **163**
(*See also* Price level)
Inflationary gap, **213**
Vietnam War and, **217**
Inflation premium, **166**
Infrastructure, **375**
economic development and, **460, 464**
spending on, economic growth and, **380–381**
Injections, **191–193**
Innovation:
by entrepreneurs, **24**
irregularity of, instability of investment and, **187**
(*See also* Technological advance)
Inputs [*see* Capital; Factors of production; Labor; Land; Resource(s)]
Insatiable wants, **22–23**
Insider-outsider theory, **360**
Instability, **353–356**
in China, **485–486**
coordination failures and, **356**
economic growth and, **377**
flexible exchange rates and, **439**
mainstream view of, **353**
monetarist view of, **353–355**
real-business-cycle view of, **355**
(*See also* Stabilization; Stability)
Institutional factors, economic development and, **461, 462**
Insurance companies, **281**
Intel Corporation, **117**
Interest charges:
on public debt, **92, 396**
public debt and, **390**
Interest income, **24**
in GDP, **132**
monetary policy and, **320**
Interest rate(s):
aggregate demand and, **226**
budget deficits and trade deficits and, **396**
discount rate, **312**
exchange rates and, **436**
Federal funds, **296**
nominal, **166**
prime, **321**
real, **166**
investment and, **181–182**
Interest-rate effect, **222–223**
Intermediate goods, **125**
Intermediate range of aggregate supply curve, **229**
International competition, U.S. firms and, **117–119**
International debt crisis, **467**
International Development Association (IDA), **466**
International Finance Corporation (IFC), **466**
International Monetary Fund (IMF), **442–443**
International trade, **101–120, 404–426**
balance of payments and, **431–434**
balance of trade and, public debt and, **396**
barriers to (*see* Tariffs; Trade barriers)
in circular flow, **105–107**
comparative advantage and, **109, 406–411**
competition in, economic growth and, **380**
diminished, flexible exchange rates and, **438–439**

economic basis for, **405–406**
expansion of, economic development and, **465**
exports and [*see* Export(s); Net export(s)]
finance of, **429–431**
(*See also* Exchange rates)
foreign exchange market and, **110–112, 436–437, 448–449**
gains from, **109–110**
government intervention in, **112–114**
reasons for, **113–114**
societal costs of, **114**
types of, **112–113**
(*See also* Tariffs; Trade barriers)
imports and, **414–418**
multilateral trade agreements and free-trade zones and, **114–117**
participants in, **104–105**
production possibilities curve and, **32**
productivity slowdown and, **378**
rapid growth of, **104**
specialization and comparative advantage and, **107–110**
supply and demand analysis of, **411–415**
in Canada, **413–414**
equilibrium world price, exports, and imports and, **414–415**
in United States, **412–413**
terms of trade and, **109**
volume and pattern of, **101–104**
(*See also* Trade; United States)
Intrinsic value, of money, **265**
Inventories:
planned versus actual investment and, **193**
private domestic investment and, **128–129**
Inverse relationships, **16**
Investment:
aggregate expenditures model, **172–196, 199–218**
domestic, private:
gross, in GDP, **128–131**
net, **129**
economic development and, **457, 460–461, 464**
global perspective on, **33**
gross versus net, **129**
incentives for, supply-side economics and, **343**
monetary policy and, **320**
real GDP and price level and, **316**
productivity slowdown and, **380–381**
supply-side fiscal policy and, **257**
(*See also* Capital; Capital goods)
Investment demand curve, **182–185**
shifts in, **184–185**
Investment goods (*see* Capital; Capital goods)
Investment schedule, **185–186**
Investment spending:
aggregate demand and, **226**
instability and, **353**
"Invisible hand," **73–74**
Ioffe, Jacques, **486–487**
Iraq, Gulf War and, **34**
Israel, foreign aid to, **465**
Italy, trade of, **104**

J. P. Morgan, **281**
Japan:
economic development of, **465**
economic growth of, **34, 461**

economy of, **35**
inflation in, **168**
on-the-job training in, **375**
trade of, **102, 104, 405, 423**
trade policy and, **419**
U.S. negotiation and, **425**
JC Penney, **80**
JEC (Joint Economic Committee), **244**
Jiang Zemin, **484**
Job creation, from imports, **418**
Joint Economic Committee (JEC), **244**

Keiretsu, **425**
Kemper, **281**
Keynes, John Maynard, **5, 173, 194**
Keynesian economics, **173–174, 352**
Korea (*see* North Korea; South Korea)
Korilkova, Lyudmila, **486**
Krugman, Paul, **418***n.*
Kuwait, Gulf War and, **34**

Labor, **24**
availability of, aggregate supply and, **231**
cheap foreign labor argument for protection, **419–420**
division of, under capitalism, **65**
quality of, productivity slowdown and, **379**
supply of, economic growth and, **374**
(*See also* Workers)
Labor force, **154**
Labor-force participation rate, **371**
Labor-intensive goods, **406**
Labor market, compensation and [*see* Income; Wage(s)]
Labor market discrimination, production possibilities curve and, **33**
Labor theory of value, **475**
Laffer Curve, **343–345**
criticisms of, **344–345**
Laissez-faire capitalism (*see* Pure capitalism)
Laissez-faire economics, **350**
Land, **23**
availability of, aggregate supply and, **230–231**
controversies over use of, production possibilities curve and, **33–34**
national parks and monuments and, **33–34**
Land-intensive goods, **406**
Land reform, **462**
Law(s), economic, **7**
(*See also* Legislation)
Law and order, economic development and, **463–464**
Law of demand, **43–44**
Law of increasing opportunity cost, **27–28**
Law of supply, **49**
Leading indicators, **258–259**
Leakages, **190–193**
Leakages-injections approach, **190–193**
graphical analysis of, **192–193**
tabular analysis of, **192**
Legal-institutional environment, aggregate supply and, **232–233**
Legal tender, **269–270**
Legislation:
antimonopoly, **85**
to correct spillover costs, **86**
deficit-reduction, **398–400**
with stabilizing effect, **243–244**

Leisure:
  GDP and, 142
  Laffer Curve and, 344
Lenin, Vladimir, 474, 486
Leyman Brothers, 281
Liabilities:
  of banks, 288
  of Federal Reserve Banks, 307
Liability:
  limited, of corporations, 83
  unlimited, of sole proprietorships, 82
Liberia:
  economy of, 462
  famine in, 470
Limited liability, of corporations, 83
Limited-liability companies (LLCs), 83–84
Linear relationships, 15
  equations of, 18–19
Line-item veto, 399–400
Liquidity, federal funds market and, 296
Living standard:
  productivity slowdown and, 378
  Russian, fall in, 482
LLCs (limited-liability companies), 83–84
Loaded terminology, 11
Loan(s):
  banking system's lending potential and,
    297–299
  to commercial banks, as Federal Reserve Bank
    assets, 307
  economic development and, 465–467
  granting of, 293–295
  repayment of, 295
  (See also Borrowing; Debt; Public debt)
Local government, finance of, 94–96
  fiscal policy and, 253
Logging industry, environmentalists and, 33
Losses, declining industries and, 68–69
Lotteries, 96

McDonald's, 68, 117
Macroeconomics, 9–10
  gross domestic product (GDP), 125–134,
    136–144
  measurement and, 124–125
  overview of, 324, 326–327
Mainstream macroeconomics, 365
  on instability, 353
  on self-correction, 358–360
    efficiency wage theory and, 359–360
    insider-outsider relationships and, 360
    wage inflexibility and, 359
Maintenance costs, investment demand curve
  and, 184
Malawi, famine in, 470
Malaysia:
  economic growth of, 453
  trade of, 105, 405
Males:
  unemployment rates and, 158
  wages of, 39
Managed floating exchange rates,
  444–445
Mao Zedong, 474, 477, 483
Marginal analysis, 4–5
  slope of straight line and, 18
Marginal benefit (MB), 4–5
Marginal cost (MC), 4–5

Marginal propensity to consume (MPC),
  178–179
  multiplier and, 203
  as slope, 179
Marginal propensity to save (MPS), 178–179
  multiplier and, 202–203
  as slope, 179
Marginal tax rates, 93, 343
Marginal utility, diminishing, 43
Market(s), 34, 42
  black, exchange controls and rationing and,
    440
  capitalist (see Competitive market system)
  product, in circular flow model, 36
  resource, in circular flow model, 36
Market-clearing price, 52–53
  world price, 414–415
Market demand, 45
Market entry, competition and, 63
Market equilibrium, 52–58
  changes in, 234–239
    multiplier with price-level changes and,
      234–236
    ratchet effect and, 236–237
    shifting of aggregate demand and, 234
    shifting of aggregate supply and, 237,
      239
  changes in supply and demand and, 53–56
  equilibrium price and quantity and, 52–53
  in extended AD-AS model, 333
  other things equal assumption and, 57
  in pink salmon market, 57–58
  rationing function of prices and, 53
  shortages and, 52
  surpluses and, 52
Market exit, competition and, 63
Market failure (see Externalities; Public goods
  and services)
Market intervention, 86
Market power, aggregate supply and,
  231–232
Market socialism, 35
Market systems, 34
Marshall, Alfred, 172n.
Marx, Karl, 5, 474
Massachusetts Mutual, 281
MasterCard, 282, 284
Math test scores, global perspective on, 376
MB (marginal benefit), 4–5
MC (marginal cost), 4–5
Measurement units, slope of straight line and,
  17–18
Medium of exchange, money as, 65–67, 265
Men:
  unemployment rates and, 158
  wages of, 39
Menu costs, downward price-level inflexibility
  and, 237
Mercosur, 117
Mergers, of banks and thrifts, 280–281
Merrill-Lynch, 281
Mexico:
  foreign aid to, 467
  peso's collapse in, 468
  trade of, 116–117, 405, 422
MFN (most-favored-nation) clauses, 114–115
MFN (most-favored-nation) status, of China,
  423–425

Microeconomics, 10
Microsoft, 117
Military self-sufficiency argument for protection,
  417
Mill, John Stuart, 5, 172n.
Minimum wage, downward price-level inflexibil-
  ity and, 237
Misery index, global perspective on, 339
Misuse of foreign aid, 467
Mitsubishi, 104
Mitsui, 104
Mixed economic systems, 35
MMDAs (money market deposit accounts), 267
MMMFs (money market mutual funds), 267
M1 money definition, 265–267
M2 money definition, 267
M3 money definition, 267–268
Models, 7
Monetarism, 353–355, 365
Monetary multiplier, multiple-deposit expansion
  and, 299–300
Monetary policy, 305–325
  consolidated balance sheet of Federal Reserve
    Banks and, 306–307
  discretionary, 363
  Federal funds rate and, 320–321
  goal of, 305–306
  international economy and, 322–324
  near-monies and, 268
  real GDP and price level and, 314–318
    aggregate supply and, 318
    cause-effect chain and, 314–316
    easy money policy and, 316–317
    refinements and feedback and, 317–318
    tight money policy and, 317
  shortcomings and problems of, 319–320
  strengths of, 318–319
  tools of, 307–314
    discount rate, 312
    easy money and tight money, 312–313
    open-market operations, 307–311
    relative importance of, 313
    reserve ratio, 311–312
Monetary rules, 360–361
Money:
  as debt, 269
  demand for, 272–274
    asset, 272–274
    total, 274
    transactions, 272
  easy versus tight, 312–313
    real GDP and price level and, 316–317
  electronic, 282–284
  fiat, 269
  functions of, 264–265
  as medium of exchange, 65–67
  prices and, 270–271
  supply of, 265–269
    control of, 279
    credit cards in, 268
    during Great Depression, 217
    M1 in, 265–267
    M2 in, 267
    M3 in, 267–268
    near-monies in, 268
    need for control of, 300–302
    shortage of, 274–275
    surplus of, 275

till, **289**
token, **265**
uses of, under capitalism, **65–67**
value of, **269–270**
    acceptability and, **269**
    legal tender and, **269–270**
    relative scarcity and, **270**
    stabilization of, **271–272**
velocity of, **353–354**
Money creation, **287–302**
    bank balance sheet and, **287–288**
    goldsmiths and, **288**
    multiple-deposit expansion and, **296–302**
        banking system's lending potential and, **297–299**
        monetary multiplier and, **299–300**
        need for monetary control and, **300–302**
    public debt and, **392**
    by single commercial bank, **288–296**
        formation of bank and, **289–293**
        money-creating transactions and, **293–296**
        profits, liquidity, and federal funds market and, **296**
Money market:
    monetary policy, real GDP, and price level and, **314–316**
    shortage of money and, **274–275**
    surplus of money and, **275**
Money market deposit accounts (MMDAs), **267**
Money market mutual funds (MMMFs), **267**
Monopolies, **85**
    government control of, **85**
    government ownership of, **85**
    natural, **85**
Monopoly power, **85**
    business cycle and, **151**
Monsanto, **117**
Monuments, **33–34**
Morgan, Theodore, **168***n*.
Most-favored-nation (MFN) clauses, **114–115**
Most-favored-nation (MFN) status, of China, **423–425**
Mozambique, famine in, **470**
MPC (marginal propensity to consume), **178–179**
    multiplier and, **203**
    as slope, **179**
MPS (marginal propensity to save), **178–179**
    multiplier and, **202–203**
    as slope, **179**
Multinational corporations, **104**
Multiple counting, avoidance of, **125–126**
Multiple-deposit expansion, **296–302**
    banking system's lending potential and, **297–299**
    monetary multiplier and, **299–300**
    need for monetary control and, **300–302**
Multipliers, **216**
    balanced-budget, **212–213**
    complex, **204**
    monetary (demand-deposit), multiple-deposit expansion and, **299–300**
    with price-level changes, **234–236**
    simple, **201–204**
        generalizing, **203–204**
        marginal propensities and, **202–203**

rationale for, **201–202**
    significance of, **203**
Mutual fund companies, **281**
Mutual savings banks, **267**

NAFTA (North American Free Trade Agreement), **116–117, 405, 422**
    change in demand and, **46**
National banks, **278**
National defense, in federal budget, **92**
National income (NI), **133, 135**
    abroad, aggregate demand and, **226–227**
National income accounting, **124–125**
National parks, **33–34**
Natural monopolies, **85**
Natural-rate hypothesis, **339–342**
    adaptive expectations theory and, **340–342**
    changing interpretations of, **342**
    rational expectations theory and, **342**
Natural rate of unemployment, **153–154**
    in Europe, **238**
Natural resources, economic development and, **455–456**
NDP (net domestic product), **134–135**
Near-monies, **267, 268**
Negative slope, **17**
Nestlé, **104**
Net domestic product (NDP), **134–135**
Net export(s):
    aggregate demand and, **226–227**
    equilibrium GDP and, **204–207**
        aggregate expenditures and, **204**
        economic linkages and, **206–207**
        net export schedule and, **204–205**
    in GDP, **131**
    global perspective on, **206**
Net export effect:
    domestic fiscal policy and, **256**
    of monetary policy, **322–323**
Net export schedule, **204–205**
Net foreign factor income, in GDP, **134**
Net investment, economic growth and, **129–131**
Net private domestic investment, **129**
Net worth of banks, **288**
New classical economics, **356–358**
    anticipated and unanticipated price-level changes and, **358**
    speed of adjustment and, **357–358**
New money to finance deficits, **247**
New York Life, **281**
NI (national income), **133, 135**
    abroad, aggregate demand and, **226–227**
Nicaragua, economic development of, **465**
Nijhawan, Inder P., **462***n*.
Nike, **47**
Nissan, **117**
Nominal GDP, **136, 138–141**
    adjustment process in one-good economy and, **138–140**
    in real world, **140–141**
Nominal income, **164**
    fixed, inflation and, **164–165**
Nominal interest rate, **166**
Noncheckable savings accounts, **267**
Nondiscretionary fiscal policy (*see* Built-in stabilizers)

Nondurable goods, **79**
    business cycle and, **151**
    consumer goods, **128**
Nonlinear curves, slope of, **19**
Nonmarket transactions, GDP and, **141**
Nontariff barriers (NTBs), **113, 415**
Normal goods, **47**
Normal profit, **68**
Normative economics, **10**
North American Free Trade Agreement (NAFTA), **116–117, 405, 422**
    change in demand and, **46**
North Korea:
    economy of, **35**
    foreign aid to, **467**
    trade of, **105**
NTBs (nontariff barriers), **113, 415**

Occupation, unemployment rates and, **156**
Office of Thrift Supervision, **278**
Official reserves account, **433–434**
Oil:
    foreign, U.S. dependence on, **102**
    OPEC (Organization of Petroleum Exporting Countries), **102, 231, 237, 338, 339, 461**
Okun, Arthur M., **156**
Okun's law, **156**
OPEC (Organization of Petroleum Exporting Countries), **102, 231, 237, 338, 339, 461**
Open Market Committee, **318**
Open-market operations, **277, 307–311**
    buying of securities, **307–309**
    selling of securities, **309–311**
Operating costs, investment demand curve and, **184**
Operational lag, **253**
Opportunity costs:
    determination of what is to be produced and, **68**
    increasing, law of, **27–28**
    of unemployment, **156–158**
Organization of Petroleum Exporting Countries (OPEC), **102, 231, 237, 338, 339, 461**
    aggregate supply and, **237, 338, 339**
    economic growth of member nations of, **461**
    market power of, **231**
"Other things equal" assumption, **8**
    graphs and, **17**
Output:
    per capita, GDP and, **142**
    composition of, GDP and, **142**
    distribution of:
        GDP and, **142**
        in market system, **70–71**
    potential, **153**
    [*See also* Equilibrium GDP; Gross domestic product (GDP)]
Output approach to GDP, **127, 128–132**
Overallocation of resources (*see* Allocative efficiency)
Overpopulation, economic development and, **456–457**
Ownership:
    government:
        in centrally planned economies, **475**
        of monopolies, **85**

of public debt, 390
state, 475

Pacific Northwest, logging industry in, 33
Paper money, 265–266
Partnerships, 82
Part-time employment, 155
Payroll taxes, 94
Peace, rapid growth of international trade and, 104
Peaks, 149
Pegged exchange rates, 442–443
Pension funds, 281
Pensions and income security in federal budget, 92
PepsiCo, 47
Per capita output, GDP and, 142
Personal consumption expenditures, 79
    in GDP, 128
Personal distribution of income, 78
Personal income (PI), 135
Personal income taxes, 92–94
Personal savings, 79
Personal taxes, 78–79
Per-unit production costs, 163
Philippines:
    economic development of, 465
    trade of, 405
Phillips, A. W., 336
Phillips Curve, 336–342
    adverse aggregate supply shocks and, 338–339
    natural-rate hypothesis and, 339–342
        adaptive expectations theory and, 340–342
        changing interpretations of, 342
        rational expectations theory and, 342
    stagflation and, 337–339
    tradeoffs and, 337
PI (personal income), 135
Pigou, A. C., 172n.
Pink flamingos, dollar votes and, 72
Pink salmon market, equilibrium in, 57–58
Planned investment, actual investment versus, 193–195
    attainment of equilibrium and, 193–195
    disequilibrium and inventories and, 193
Plants, 80
Poland, trade of, 105
Policy economics, 8–9
Policy rules, 360–363
    balanced budget and, 362–363
    monetary, 360–361
Political business cycle, 254
Politics:
    of fiscal policy, 253–254
    government trade interventions and, 113–114
    isolation of monetary policy from, 319
    lack of political will and, public debt and, 389–390
Population growth:
    economic development and, 456–458
    global perspective on, 457
Positive economics, 10
Positive slope, 17
Post hoc fallacy, 11
Potential output, 153
Poverty, in developing countries, 462–463, 468–469

Preferences:
    change in demand and, 45–46
    exchange rates and, 436
Premature inflation, 162
Price(s):
    under capitalism, 64
    of credit [see Interest rate(s)]
    domestic, 412
    equilibrium, 52–53
        world price, 414–415
    foreign exchange market and, 111
    government setting of, in centrally planned economies, 476
    guiding function of, 71–72
    money and, 270–271
    of other goods, change in supply and, 50
    rationing function of, 53
    reform of, in Russian Republic, 480–481
    of resources, 49–50
    of stock, macroeconomy and, 169
    world, 412
        equilibrium, 414–415
    [See also Energy prices; Organization of Petroleum Exporting Countries (OPEC)]
Price controls, 346–347
Price discrimination, 419
Price indexes, 138–139
    consumer price index, 141
        base period for, 160
        inflation overstatement by, 143
    fixed-weight, 141
    GDP (chain-type annual-weights price index), 140–141
Price level:
    anticipated and unanticipated changes in, new classical view of, 358
    changes in, multiplier with, 234–236
    equilibrium, 234
    exchange rates and, 436
    monetary policy and real GDP, 314–318
    stabilization of, in Russian Republic, 481
    (See also Inflation)
Price-level surprises, 358
Price wars, fear of, downward price-level inflexibility and, 237
Prime interest rate, 321
Principal-agent problem, 83
Principle(s), 7
Principle of comparative advantage, 407–408
Private domestic investment
    gross, in GDP, 128–131
    net, 129
Private property, under capitalism, 61–62
Private sector [see Business sector; Consumer(s); Household sector]
Privatization, in Russian Republic, 479–480
Procter & Gamble, 117
Production:
    determination of what is to be produced and, 68–69
    domestic, increase in, tariffs and, 416
    factors of (see Capital; Factors of production; Labor; Land)
    full, 25
    during 1929–1930 and 1937–1938, global perspective on, 215
    organization in market economy, 69–70

roundabout, 65
    wartime, production possibilities curve and, 33
Production capacity:
    excess:
        aggregate demand and, 226
        Great Depression and, 215
    net investment and, 129–131
Production costs, per-unit, 163
Production possibilities curve, 26–34
    allocative efficiency and, 28–29
    applications of, 33–34
    economic growth and, 370–371
    employment of women and, 38–39
    in growing economies, 30–32
    international trade and, 32
    law of increasing opportunity cost and, 27–28
    unemployment and productive inefficiency and, 29–30
Production possibilities table, 25–26
    need for choice and, 26
Productive efficiency, 25, 369
    unemployment and, 29–30
Productivity
    aggregate supply and, 232
    economic development and, 457, 458–459
    inputs versus, economic growth and, 373–374
    of labor, 370–371
Productivity slowdown, 378–382
    causes of, 378–382
    significance of, 378
    turnaround of, 382–383
Product markets, in circular flow model, 36
Product quality, GDP and, 142
Profit(s), 24
    corporate, in GDP, 133
    economic (pure), determination of what is to be produced and, 68
    expanding industries and, 68
    federal funds market and, 296
    normal, 68
    variability of, instability of investment and, 187–188
Profit sharing, 362
Progressive taxes, 92, 249
Property resources, 23–24
Property rights:
    under capitalism, 61–62
    incomplete, in China, 485
Property taxes, 95
Proportional taxes, 249
Proprietors' income, 77
    in GDP, 133
Prosperity, abroad, equilibrium GDP and, 206
Protection against dumping argument for protection, 419
Protectionism (see Tariffs; Trade barriers)
Protective tariffs, 113, 415
Prudential, 281
Public:
    buying of securities from, 308–309
    selling of securities to, 310–311
Public debt, 386, 388–395
    causes of, 389–390
    crowding out and stock of capital and, 393–395
    definition of, 386

entitlement programs and, **398–399**
external debt and, **393**
false issues concerning, **391–392**
fiscal policy and, **393**
global perspective on, **390**
incentives in, **393**
income distribution and, **392–393**
increased, U.S. trade deficits and, **447**
positive role of, **400**
quantitative aspects of, **390–391**
Public goods and services, **86–88**
resource allocation to, **88**
Public investments, public debt and, **394**
Purchases (*see* Consumption; Expenditures;
Government spending)
Purchasing power parity theory, **436**
Pure capitalism, **34–35, 61–75**
competition under, **63**
freedom of enterprise and choice under,
62
limited government under, **64**
markets and prices under, **64**
market system of (*see* Competitive market
system)
money uses under, **65–67**
private property under, **61–62**
self-interest and, **63**
specialization under, **65**
use of technology and capital goods under,
64–65
Pure Food and Drug Act (1906), **84–85**
Pure profit, determination of what is to be produced and, **68**
Putnam, **281**

Quantity, equilibrium, **52–53**
Quantity demanded, change in, **47–48**
Quasipublic goods, **88**
Quotas, import, **113, 415**
economic impact of, **417**

Race:
employment discrimination and, **33**
unemployment rates and, **157–158**
Ratchet effect, **236–237**
Rate of return, expected, investment and,
181
Rational behavior, **4**
Rational expectations theory, **342, 365**
policy rules and, **361, 363**
Rationing:
fixed exchange rates and, **440**
as function of prices, **53**
RCA, **100**
R&D (research and development), productivity
slowdown and, **379–380**
Reagan administration:
public debt under, **389**
supply-side economics of, **345**
Reaganomics, **345**
Real-business-cycle theory, **355**
Real capital, **24**
Real GDP, **136, 138–141**
adjustment process in one-good economy and,
138–140
equilibrium, **234**
expenditures-output approach and, **188**
leading indicators and, **258–259**

monetary policy and price level and,
314–318
in real world, **140–141**
Real income, **164**
Real interest rate, **166**
investment and, **181–182**
Recession(s), **149**
extended AD-AS model and, **335–336**
of 1990-1991, monetary policy and, **319**
public debt and, **389**
Recessionary gap, **213**
Great Depression and, **214–217**
Reciprocal Trade Agreements Act (1934),
114–116
Recognition lag, **253**
Recoveries, **149**
Reebok, **47**
Refinancing of public debt, **391**
Regressive taxes, **249**
Regulation:
aggregate supply and, **232**
of banks, **288**
reform of, **281–282**
economic growth and, **380**
excessive, Laffer Curve and, **345**
of monopolies, **85**
Rental income, **24**
in GDP, **132**
Republic Steel, **80**
Required reserves, **290**
Research and development (R&D), productivity
slowdown and, **379–380**
Reserve(s), **288, 290–293**
actual, **291**
excess, **291**
fixed exchange rates and, **439–440**
required, **290**
Reserve ratio, **290, 311–312**
Residential construction, Great Depression and,
215
Resource(s):
availability of, aggregate supply and,
230–231
human, **23, 24**
mobilization of, in centrally planned
economies, **476**
natural, economic development and,
455–456
overuse of:
in centrally planned economies, **476**
economic development and, **457**
prices of, change in supply and,
49–50
property, **23–24**
underemployment of, **25**
(*See also* Capital; Factors of production;
Labor; Land)
Resource allocation:
in centrally planned economies, **476**
economic growth and, **375–376**
government reallocation of resources and,
86–88
(*See also* Efficiency)
Resource market in circular flow model, **36**
Resource supply, increase in, production possibilities curve and, **30**
Retaliatory tariffs, **423**
Reuss, Henry R, **159***n*.

Revenue:
from tariffs, **416**
tax, **92**
Revenue tariffs, **415**
Ricardo, David, **5, 108, 172***n*.
Risk:
entrepreneurial risk taking and, **24**
supply-side fiscal policy and, **258**
Ritter, Lawrence S., **361***n*.
Rivlin, Alice M., **381***n*.
Roosevelt, Franklin, **301**
Roundabout production, **65**
Royal Dutch Shell, **104**
Rule of **70, 160**
Rural development, in centrally planned
economies, **476**
Rural reform, in China, **483–484**
Russian Republic, **478–483, 486–487**
economic growth of, **461**
economy of, **475**
foreign aid to, **465**
future prospects for, **482–483**
major problems in, **481–482**
price-level stabilization in, **481**
price reform in, **480–481**
privatization in, **479–480**
promotion of competition in, **481**
trade of, **105**
in world economy, **481**

Sales taxes, **94**
Salmon market, equilibrium in, **57–58**
Savers, inflation and, **165**
Saving:
aggregate expenditures model and, **172–196,
199–218**
average propensity to save and, **178**
economic development and, **457, 459–460,
464**
economic growth and, **380**
incentives for, supply-side economics and,
343
near-monies and, **268**
personal, **79**
supply-side fiscal policy and, **257**
Savings and loan institutions, **267**
Saving schedule, **176**
shifts in, **180–181**
Savings institutions, **267**
Say, J. B., **173**
Say's law, **173**
Scale economies, economic growth and,
375
Scalping tickets, **56**
Scarcity:
choice and, **4**
of economic resources, **23–24**
S corporations, **83, 84**
Search unemployment, **152**
Secondhand sales, exclusion from GDP, **127**
Secular trends, **150–151**
Securities:
buying and selling of, by Federal Reserve
Banks, **307–311**
as Federal Reserve Bank assets, **306–307**
transaction exclusion from GDP and, **127**
Securities-related firms, **281**
Security, saving for, **79**

Self-correction, 356–360
mainstream view of, 358–360
efficiency wage theory and, 359–360
insider-outsider relationships and, 360
wage inflexibility and, 359
new classical view of, 356–358
anticipated and unanticipated price-level
changes and, 358
speed of adjustment and, 357–358
Self-interest under capitalism, 63
Self-sufficiency in centrally planned economies, 476
Sellers, number of:
change in supply and, 51
competition and, 63
single (see Monopolies)
Services, 79
balance of payments on, 432
consumer expenditures for, in GDP, 128
productivity slowdown and, 381–382
public, 86–88
resource allocation to, 88
SEZs (special economic zones), in China, 484
Shock(s):
demand, originating from abroad, domestic
fiscal policy and, 256
originating from abroad, domestic fiscal policy
and, 256
supply:
inflation and, 163
instability and, 353
Phillips Curve and, 338–339
Shortages:
market equilibrium and, 52
of money, market response to, 274–275
Siemens, 104
Silber, William L., 361*n*.
Simple multiplier (see Multipliers)
Singapore:
economic growth of, 453, 461
trade of, 105, 405
Siou and Company, 486
Slope:
of nonlinear curve, 19
of straight line, 17–18
Smart cards, 283
Smith, Adam, 5, 73, 107
Smoot-Hawley Tariff Act (1930), 114, 418
Socialism market, 35
(See also Centrally planned economies)
Sociocultural factors, economic development
and, 461–462
SOEs (state-owned enterprises), reform of, 484
Sole proprietorships, 81–82
Solomon, 281
Somalia:
economy of, 462
famine in, 470
South Korea:
currency fall in, 468
economic development of, 465
economic growth of, 453, 461
trade of, 105, 405, 423
trade policy and, 419
Southwest, national parks and monuments in, 33–34

Soviet Union, former
central economic planning in (see Centrally
planned economies)
economic development of, 465
economy of, 35
production of, during World War II, 33
trade of, 105
Special economic zones (SEZs), in China, 484
Specialization, 107–110
under capitalism, 65
comparative advantage and, 407–408
comparative costs and, 108–109
diversification for stability argument for protection and, 418
gains from specialization and trade and, 109–110
production possibilities curve and, 32
terms of trade and, 109
Specific taxes, 86
Speculation:
exchange rates and, 436–437, 448–449
saving for, 79
Spending (see Consumption; Expenditures;
Government spending)
Spillover(s):
benefits of, 86–87
costs of, 86
Spillover benefits, 86–87
Spillover costs, 86
Stability:
of consumption and saving schedules, 181
increased, 363–364
of investment, 186–188
durability and, 186–187
irregularity of innovation and, 187
variability of expectations and, 188
variability of profits and, 187–188
monetary policy and, 323–324
near-monies and, 268
(See also Instability)
Stabilization, 88–89
built-in stabilizers and, 248–253
of money's value, 271–272
of price level, in Russian Republic, 481
Stagflation, 337–339
Stalin, Joseph, 474, 477
Standard of living:
productivity slowdown and, 378
Russian, fall in, 482
State banks, 278
State government, finance of, 94–96
fiscal policy and, 253
State-owned enterprises (SOEs), reform of, 484
State ownership, 475
Stepanek, Marcia, 386*n*.
Stock(s), 82–83, 96–97
prices of, macroeconomy and, 169
Stock market crash, Great Depression and, 215–216
Stock of goods, investment demand curve and, 184–185
Stored-value cards, 283
Store of value, money as, 265
Straight lines, slope of, 17–18
Strategic trade policy, 419
Structural deficits, 389
Structural unemployment, 152–153

Subsidies:
aggregate supply and, 232
change in supply and, 50
to correct for spillover benefits, 87
export, 113, 423
Substitute goods, 47
Substitution effect, 44
Sudan:
economy of, 462
famine in, 470
Superior goods, 47
Supply, 48–51
change in, 49–51
market equilibrium and, 53–56
change in quantity supplied and, 51
determinants of, 49
economic growth and, 369
of exports and imports, 411–415
in Canada, 413–414
equilibrium world price and, 414–415
in United States, 412–413
law of, 49
market equilibrium and, 52–58
of money, 217, 265–269
supply curve and, 49
supply schedule and, 48
Supply-shock inflation, 163
Supply-side economics, 343–345, 365
Laffer Curve and, 343–345
overregulation and, 345
Reaganomics and, 345
tax-transfer disincentives and, 343
Supply-side fiscal policy, 257–258
Supply-side growth policies, 383
Supply-side inflation, 163, 237
in extended AD-AS model, 334–335
output and unemployment and, 167
Surpluses:
in balance of payments, 434
budget, 246
disposing of, 247
market equilibrium and, 52
of money, market response to, 275
trade, 102
Surplus value, 475
"Swap market," in China, 484
Sweden, economy of, 35

Taiwan:
economic development of, 465
economic growth of, 461
trade of, 105, 423
Tangent lines, 19
Tariffs, 113
decline in, rapid growth of international trade
and, 104
economic impact of, 415–417
equilibrium GDP and, 206–207
reducing to promote economic development, 469
retaliation for, 418
retaliatory, 423
revenue from, 416
types of, 415
Taste(s) (see Preferences)

Tax(es):
  aggregate demand and, **226**
  business, **94**
    aggregate demand and, **226**
    aggregate supply and, **232**
    indirect, in GDP, **133**
    investment demand curve and, **184**
  change in supply and, **50**
  to correct spillover costs, **86**
  cuts in, public debt and, **389**
  enterprise tax system in China and, **484**
  excise, **94**
  income:
    corporate, **94**
    personal, **92–94**
  increased, contractionary fiscal policy and, **246–247**
  Laffer Curve and, **344**
  payroll, **94**
  personal, **78–79**
  progressive, **92**
  property, **95**
  reductions in, expansionary fiscal policy and, **245–246**
  sales, **94**
  supply-side economics and, **343**
  tax revenue as percentage of domestic output and, global perspective on, **92**
Taxable income, **92**
Taxation:
  consumption and saving and, **180**
  double, of corporations, **83**
  equilibrium GDP and, **209–212**
  income redistribution and, **86**
  public debt and, **391–392**
Tax Freedom Day, **92**
Tax policies, economic growth and, **383**
Tax rates:
  average, **94**
  marginal, **93, 343**
Teachers Insurance and Annuity Association, **281**
Teamsters' Union, **281**
Technological advance:
  aggregate demand and, **226**
  change in supply and, **50**
  economic development and, **461**
  economic growth and, **374**
  investment demand curve and, **184**
  in market system, **72–73**
  production possibilities curve and, **30–31, 34**
  productivity slowdown and, **379–380**
  rapid growth of international trade and, **104**
Technology, use of, under capitalism, **64–65**
Terms of trade, **109, 408**
  flexible exchange rates and, **439**
Thailand:
  currency fall in, **468**
  economic growth of, **453**
  foreign aid to, **467**
Theoretical economics:
  abstractions and, **8**
  generalizations and, **7–8**
  graphs and, **8**
  "other things equal" assumption and, **8**
  terminology of, **7**
Theories, **7**
Thompson, Carolyn, **72n.**
3M Corporation, **117**

Thrift institutions, **266–267, 281**
  decline of, **280–282**
  loans to, **279**
Thrift Institutions Advisory Council, **277**
Ticket scalping, **56**
Tight money policy, **312–313**
  real GDP and price level and, **317**
Till money, **289**
Time deposits, **267**
Timing, of fiscal policy, **253**
Todaro, Michael P., **455n.**
Token money, **265**
Total demand for money, **274**
Township and village enterprises, **484**
Toyota, **47, 117**
Toys "Я" Us, **80**
Trace blocs, **116–117**
  hostile, **117**
Trade, international (see International trade)
Trade balance, **432**
  global perspective on, **433**
  monetary policy and, **323–324**
  public debt and, **396**
Trade barriers, **415–422**
  arguments for, **417–421**
  Bastiat's position on, **424**
  costs of, **421–422**
    income distribution and, **422**
    to society, **421–422**
  economic impact of, **415–417**
  global perspective on, **421**
  (See also Tariffs)
Trade deficits, **102, 446–447**
  budget deficits, **396–400**
  causes of, **446–447**
  implications of, **447**
Trade interventions, **112–114**
  reasons for, **113–114**
  societal costs of, **114**
  types of, **112–113**
  (See also Tariffs; Trade barriers)
Tradeoffs, **9**
  Phillips Curve and, **337**
Trade policy, **422–425**
  aggressive export promotion, **423**
  bilateral negotiations, **423–425**
  fixed exchange rates and, **440**
  generalized trade liberalization, **422–423**
  strategic, **419**
Trade surpluses, **102**
Trade wars, **114**
Trading possibilities line, **408**
Traditional economies, **35**
Training:
  downward price-level inflexibility and, **237**
  economic growth and, **375**
Training policies, economic growth and, **383**
Transactions demand for money, **272**
Transfers, **85, 91, 92**
  exclusion from GDP, **126–127**
  supply-side economics and, **343**
Transportation, rapid growth of international trade and, **104**
Travelers Group, **281**
Treasury deposits, as Federal Reserve Bank liabilities, **307**
Troughs, **149**

Turkey:
  foreign aid to, **467**
  inflation in, **161**
Turkmenistan, inflation in, **161**
Turner, Ted, **231**
Two-track price system, establishment in China, **483–484**

Ukraine, trade of, **105**
Unanticipated inflation, **164**
Uncertainty, flexible exchange rates and, **438–439**
Underallocation of resources (see Allocative efficiency)
Underemployment of resources, **25**
  labor, economic development and, **458**
Underground economy:
  GDP and, **142, 144**
  global perspective on, **144**
Undistributed corporate profits, **133**
Unemployment, **152–159**
  cyclical (deficient-demand), **153**
  duration of, **158**
  economic cost of, **156–158**
  economic development and, **458**
  in Europe, **238**
  frictional (search, wait), **152**
  full employment and, **153–154**
  measurement of, **154–156**
  productive inefficiency and, **29–30**
  public debt and, **394–395**
  stabilization and, **89**
  structural, **152–153**
Unemployment rate, **154–155**
  full employment, **153**
  global perspective on, **159**
  natural, **153–154**
  in Europe, **238**
Unilever, **104**
United States:
  budget:
    actual versus full-employment, **250–252**
    proposed balanced-budget requirement in, **251–253**
  economic growth of, **34, 372–373**
    instability and, **377**
  economy of, **35, 475**
  fiscal policy in (see Built-in stabilizers; Fiscal policy)
  foreign aid provided by, **465–467**
  functional distribution of income in, **77–78**
  Great Depression in, **130–131, 173**
  gross domestic product of (GDP), **125–134, 136–144**
  Gulf War and, **34**
  inflation in, **161**
  productivity slowdown in, **378–382**
    causes of, **378–382**
    significance of, **378**
    turnaround of, **382–383**
  public debt of, **386, 388–395**
  stagflation in, **337–339**
  supply and demand analysis of imports and exports of, **412–413**
  Tax Freedom Day in, **92**
  trade deficits of, **446–447**
    causes of, **446–447**
    implications of, **447**

trade of, **104, 117–119, 405, 422**
  with Canada, **102**
  European Union and, **116**
  export transactions and, **430**
  import transactions and, **430–431**
  international competition and, **117–119**
  with Japan, **102**
  linkages and, **104**
  NAFTA and, **46, 116–117, 405, 422**
  patterns of, **102–103**
  U.S. dependence on world economy and, **102**
  volume of, **102**
 trade policy of, **422–425**
  aggressive export promotion, **423**
  bilateral negotiations, **423–425**
  generalized trade liberalization, **422–423**
 wartime production of, **33**
U.S. Agency for International Development (USAID), **465**
United States International Trade Commission (USITC), **421**
Unit of account, money as, **265**
Unlimited liability, of sole proprietorships, **82**
Unlimited wants, **22–23**
Urban collectives, **484**
Urban problems, economic development and, **457–458**
Uruguay Round, **115–116**
USAID (U.S. Agency for International Development), **465**
USITC (United States International Trade Commission), **421**
USX, **80**
Utility, **22**
 marginal, **43**

Value:
 of dollar, prices and, **270–271**
 intrinsic, of money, **265**
 labor theory of, **475**
 of money, **265**
 money as store of, **265**
 surplus, **475**
Value added, **126**
Variable(s), independent and dependent, **15–17**

Vault cash, **289**
Velocity of money, **353–354**
 monetary policy and, **320**
Venezuela, inflation in, **161**
VERs (voluntary export restrictions), **415**
Vertical axis, **15**
Vertical combination, **80**
Vertical intercept, **18**
Vertical range of aggregate supply curve, **229**
Vicious circle of poverty, **462–463**
Vietnam War:
 inflationary gap and, **217**
 production during, **33**
VISA, **282, 284**
Voluntary export restrictions (VERs), **415**

Wage(s), **24**
 efficiency, **359–360**
  downward price-level inflexibility and, **236–237**
 flexibility of, **362**
 inflexibility of, self-correction and, **359**
 minimum, downward price-level inflexibility and, **237**
 of women, **38**
 (See also Income)
Wage contracts, downward price-level inflexibility and, **236**
Wage controls, **346–347**
Wage-price inflationary spiral, **167–168**
Wage-push inflation, **163**
Wait unemployment, **152**
Wal-Mart, **80**
Wants:
 coincidence of, **66**
 unlimited, **22–23**
War(s):
 military:
  destruction from, **34**
  public debt and, **389**
  trade, **114**
Warner-Lambert Company, **80**
Wartime production, production possibilities curve and, **33**
Washington Mutual, **281**
Wealth:
 aggregate demand and, **224–225**
 consumption and saving and, **179**

Wealth effect, **222**
The Wealth of Nations (Smith), **73, 107**
Wells Fargo, **280, 281**
Western Europe:
 trade of, **104**
 unemployment in, **238**
Williams, Raburn M., **168n.**
Will to develop, **461**
Women:
 employment of, production possibilities curve and, **38–39**
 unemployment rates and, **158**
 wages of, **38**
Workers:
 discouraged, **155–156**
 training investment in, downward price-level inflexibility and, **237**
 [See also Income; Labor; Wage(s)]
Work incentives:
 Laffer Curve and, **344**
 supply-side economics and, **343**
 fiscal policy and, **257–258**
World Bank, **466**
World economy
 China in, **486**
 Russian Republic in, **481**
World price, **412**
 equilibrium, **414–415**
World trade [see Export(s); Import(s); International trade; Net export(s); Trade]
World Trade Organization (WTO), **116, 423**
World War II:
 inflation and, **168**
 production during, **33**
 public debt and, **389**
WTO (World Trade Organization), **116, 423**

Yeltsin, Boris, **479, 480**

Zaire:
 economic development of, **465**
 economy of, **462**
 famine in, **470**
Zero slope, **18**

National income and related statistics for selected years, 1974–1997

National income statistics in rows 1–17 are in billions of current dollars. Details may not add to totals because of rounding.

			1974	1975	1976	1977	1978	1979	1980	1981	1982	1983
THE SUM OF	1	Personal consumption expenditures	931.2	1,029.1	1,148.8	1,277.1	1,428.8	1,593.5	1,760.4	1,941.3	2,076.8	2,283.4
	2	Gross private domestic investment	245.6	225.4	286.6	356.6	430.8	480.9	465.9	556.2	501.1	547.1
	3	Government purchases	323.2	362.6	385.9	416.9	457.9	507.1	572.8	633.4	684.8	735.7
	4	Net exports	−3.1	13.6	−2.3	−23.7	−26.1	−24.0	−14.9	−15.0	−20.5	−51.7
EQUALS	5	Gross domestic product	1,496.9	1,630.6	1,819.0	2,026.9	2,291.4	2,557.5	2,784.2	3,115.9	3,242.1	3,514.5
LESS	6	Consumption of fixed capital	162.5	188.7	206.0	228.6	258.3	296.7	339.4	388.5	424.3	445.3
EQUALS	7	Net domestic product	1,334.4	1,441.9	1,613.0	1,798.3	2,033.1	2,260.8	2,444.8	2,727.4	2,817.8	3,069.2
LESS	8	Net foreign factor income earned in the U.S.	−15.7	−13.3	−17.2	−20.7	−22.1	−32.9	−35.3	−34.7	−31.1	−32.0
LESS	9	Indirect business taxes	135.2	149.3	170.8	181.0	192.9	215.2	235.6	260.7	248.1	307.9
EQUALS	10	National income	1,214.9	1,305.9	1,459.4	1,638.0	1,862.3	2,078.5	2,244.5	2,501.4	2,600.8	2,793.3
LESS	11	Social security contributions	111.7	121.1	137.7	155.4	177.0	204.2	225.0	261.6	280.6	301.9
	12	Corporate income taxes	51.8	50.9	64.2	73.0	83.5	88.0	84.8	81.1	63.1	77.2
	13	Undistributed corporate profits	60.6	59.4	73.7	89.6	108.6	121.3	97.3	79.1	43.8	54.8
PLUS	14	Transfer payments	225.1	244.5	275.6	296.1	332.7	390.8	455.6	488.9	513.9	541.4
EQUALS	15	Personal income	1,215.9	1,319.0	1,459.4	1,616.1	1,825.9	2,055.8	2,293.0	2,568.5	2,727.2	2,900.8
LESS	16	Personal taxes	159.1	156.4	182.3	210.0	240.1	280.2	312.4	360.2	371.4	369.3
EQUALS	17	Disposable income	1,056.8	1,162.6	1,277.1	1,406.1	1,585.8	1,775.7	1,980.5	2,208.3	2,355.8	2,531.5

RELATED STATISTICS

		1974	1975	1976	1977	1978	1979	1980	1981	1982	1983
18	Real gross domestic product (in billions of 1992 dollars)	3,891.2	3,873.9	4,082.9	4,273.6	4,503.0	4,630.6	4,615.0	4,720.7	4,620.3	4,803.7
19	Percent change in real GDP	−0.6	−0.4	5.4	4.7	5.4	2.8	−0.3	2.3	−2.1	4.0
20	Real disposable income per capita (in 1992 dollars)	13,344	13,444	13,837	14,142	14,715	14,951	14,867	15,064	15,053	15,332
21	Consumer price index (1982–84 = 100)	49.3	53.8	56.9	60.6	65.2	72.6	82.4	90.9	96.5	99.6
22	Rate of inflation (%)	11.0	9.1	5.8	6.5	7.6	11.3	13.5	10.3	6.2	3.2
23	Index of industrial production (1992 = 100)	69.6	63.4	69.3	74.9	79.3	82.0	79.7	81.0	76.7	79.5
24	Supply of money, M1 (in billions of dollars)	274.2	287.4	306.3	331.2	358.4	382.9	408.9	436.8	474.6	521.2
25	Prime interest rate (%)	10.81	7.86	6.84	6.83	9.06	12.67	15.27	18.87	14.86	10.79
26	Population (in millions)	213.9	216.0	218.0	220.2	222.6	255.1	227.7	230.0	232.3	234.3
27	Civilian labor force (in millions)	91.9	93.8	96.2	99.0	102.3	105.0	106.9	108.7	110.2	111.6
28	Unemployment (in millions)	5.2	7.9	7.4	7.0	6.2	6.1	7.6	8.3	10.7	10.7
29	Unemployment rate as % of civilian labor force	5.6	8.5	7.7	7.1	6.1	5.8	7.1	7.6	9.7	9.6
30	Index of productivity (1992 = 100)	77.1	79.8	82.5	83.9	84.9	84.5	84.2	85.7	85.3	88.0
31	Annual change in productivity (%)	−1.7	3.5	3.4	1.7	1.1	−0.4	−0.3	1.8	−0.5	3.2
32	Trade balance on current account (in billions of dollars)	2.0	18.1	4.3	−14.3	−15.1	−0.2	2.3	5.0	−11.4	−44.0
33	Public debt (in billions of dollars)	483.9	541.9	629.0	706.4	776.6	828.9	909.1	994.8	1,137.3	1,371.2

†Preliminary data

1984	1985	1986	1987	1988	1989	1990	1991	1992	1993	1994	1995	1996	1997†
2,492.3	2,704.8	2,892.7	3,094.5	3,349.7	3,594.8	3,839.3	3,975.1	4,219.8	4,459.2	4,717.0	4,957.7	5,207.6	5,488.6
715.6	715.1	722.5	747.2	773.9	829.2	799.7	736.2	790.4	876.2	1,007.9	1,038.2	1,116.5	1,237.6
796.6	875.0	938.5	992.8	1,032.0	1,095.1	1,176.1	1,225.9	1,263.8	1,283.4	1,313.0	1,355.5	1,406.7	1,453.9
−102.0	−114.2	−131.5	−142.1	−106.1	−80.4	−71.3	−20.5	−29.5	−60.7	−90.9	−86.0	−94.8	−96.7
3,902.4	4,180.7	4,422.2	4,692.3	5,049.6	5,438.7	5,743.8	5,916.7	6,244.4	6,558.1	6,947.0	7,265.4	7,636.0	8,083.4
461.5	486.6	517.9	545.8	582.2	625.4	651.5	679.9	713.5	727.9	777.5	796.8	830.1	868.0
3,440.9	3,694.1	3,904.3	4,146.5	4,467.4	4,813.3	5,092.3	5,236.8	5,530.9	5,860.2	6,169.5	6,468.5	6,805.9	7,215.4
−31.1	−20.4	−12.9	−8.9	−13.0	−14.2	−21.1	−15.7	−11.1	−18.7	−8.2	−5.3	−1.7	−21.0
307.6	331.1	366.9	324.6	335.1	430.2	461.3	490.9	551.6	612.1	587.0	561.5	553.1	545.0
3,164.4	3,383.4	3,550.3	3,813.0	4,145.3	4,397.3	4,652.1	4,761.6	4,990.4	5,266.8	5,590.7	5,912.3	6,254.5	6,650.0
345.5	375.9	402.0	423.3	462.8	491.2	518.5	543.5	571.4	596.0	630.5	659.1	692.0	732.0
94.0	96.5	106.5	127.1	137.0	141.3	140.5	133.4	143.0	165.2	186.6	213.2	229.0	319.0
66.9	40.6	58.0	59.5	100.5	67.9	79.4	77.7	93.9	104.5	132.3	145.0	142.8	149.0
557.2	579.4	674.6	685.6	739.6	804.1	890.5	974.6	1,095.1	1,118.1	1,150.5	1,255.8	1,304.5	1,424.4
3,215.3	3,449.8	3,658.4	3,888.7	4,184.6	4,501.0	4,804.2	4,981.6	5,277.2	5,519.2	5,791.8	6,150.8	6,495.2	6,874.4
395.5	437.7	459.9	514.2	532.0	594.9	624.8	624.8	650.5	690.0	739.1	795.1	886.9	987.9
2,819.8	3,012.1	3,198.5	3,374.6	3,652.6	3,906.1	4,179.4	4,356.8	4,626.7	4,829.2	5,052.7	5,355.7	5,608.3	5,886.6
1984	1985	1986	1987	1988	1989	1990	1991	1992	1993	1994	1995	1996	1997+
5,140.1	5,323.5	5,487.7	5,649.5	5,865.2	6,062.0	6,136.3	6,079.4	6,244.4	6,389.6	6,610.7	6,742.1	6,928.4	7,191.4
7.0	3.6	3.1	2.9	3.8	3.4	1.2	−0.9	2.7	2.3	3.5	2.0	2.8	3.8
16,309	16,654	17,039	17,164	17,678	17,854	17,996	17,809	18,113	18,221	18,431	18,861	19,116	19,497
103.9	107.6	109.6	113.6	118.3	124.0	130.7	136.2	140.3	144.5	148.2	152.4	156.9	160.5
4.3	3.6	1.9	3.6	4.1	4.8	5.4	4.2	3.0	3.0	2.6	2.8	3.0	2.3
86.6	88.0	89.0	93.2	97.4	99.1	98.9	97.0	100.0	103.6	109.2	114.5	118.5	124.5
552.2	619.9	724.4	749.7	787.0	794.2	825.8	897.3	1,025.0	1,129.8	1,150.7	1,129.0	1,081.1	1,068.7
12.04	9.93	8.33	8.21	9.32	10.87	10.01	8.46	6.25	6.00	7.15	8.83	8.27	8.44
236.4	238.5	240.7	242.9	245.1	247.3	250.0	252.7	255.4	258.1	260.6	263.0	265.5	267.9
113.5	115.5	117.8	119.9	121.7	123.9	125.8	126.3	128.1	129.2	131.1	132.3	133.9	136.3
8.5	8.3	8.2	7.4	6.7	6.5	7.0	8.6	9.6	8.9	8.0	7.4	7.2	6.7
7.5	7.2	7.0	6.2	5.5	5.3	5.6	6.8	7.5	6.9	6.1	5.6	5.4	4.9
90.2	91.7	94.0	94.0	94.6	95.4	96.1	96.7	100.0	100.2	100.6	100.5	102.6	104.5
2.5	1.6	2.6	−0.1	0.6	0.8	0.7	0.7	3.4	0.2	0.4	0.0	2.0	1.9
−99.0	−124.0	−153.2	−168.1	−128.2	−104.2	−91.9	−5.7	−56.4	−90.8	−133.5	−129.1	−148.2	−166.4
1,564.7	1,817.5	2,120.6	2,346.1	2,601.3	2,868.0	3,206.6	3,598.5	4,002.1	4,351.4	4,643.7	4,921.0	5,181.9	5,369.7

Source: *Survey of Current Business, Federal Reserve Bulletin, Economic Report of the President, Economic Indicators.*